The Framers' Coup

"Michael Klarman has written the best single-volume analysis of the flaws in the Articles of Confederation that led to the Constitutional Convention, the debate in that Convention, the ratification of the proposed Constitution, and the drafting and adoption of the Bill of Rights. With great insight, Klarman explains the complexities of America's postwar economic, political, and constitutional struggles, showing how a people who fought a long war for their rights could then approve a democracy-limiting Constitution that greatly restricted those rights. Klarman commands the documentary sources like no other historian. His page-turning narrative is equal to the epic story he unveils. Every serious scholar of the period must read this masterful work."

—**John Kaminski**, Director, Center for the Study of the American Constitution, University of Wisconsin-Madison

"*The Framers' Coup* is the first comprehensive account of the entire struggle for the United States Constitution, from the inception of the amalgamating impulse in the early 1780s all the way through to the ratification of the Bill of Rights in 1791. A lot of us who write books about the Constitution are about to see our royalties trail off, because Michael Klarman, in a brisk narrative, deftly summarizes all the major interpretations in developing his own provocative and persuasive take. I for one will take my lumps, because this book is a beaut."

—**Woody Holton**, Bancroft Prize winner and author of *Unruly Americans and the Origins of the Constitution*

"At last, we have a definitive account of the entire Framing period. Klarman has brought to the task the narrative skill and situation sense of a historian, the attention to detail and language of a lawyer, and the wisdom and insight of the great scholar that he is."

—**Louis Michael Seidman**, Carmack Waterhouse Professor of Constitutional Law, Georgetown University Law Center

"The fullest explanation of the origins of the Constitution that we are ever likely to get in a single volume. Klarman ably shows how an interest-ridden Constitutional Convention that was fearful of democracy nevertheless created a document that transcended those interests and became the basis for a democracy that has survived for over two centuries."

—**Gordon S. Wood**, Pulitzer Prize-winning author of *The Radicalism of the American Revolution*

"This remarkable book tells a gripping story of how the Constitution, often lauded as principled and visionary, was the work of intensely political individuals who were preoccupied with the issues of their day but were still able to accomplish something the nation needed. If you are interested in the Constitution and you do not read this book, you are making a big mistake."

—**David A. Strauss**, Gerald Ratner Distinguished Service Professor of Law, University of Chicago Law School

"In this thoroughly researched volume, Michael Klarman gives us a book that has strangely gone unwritten: a comprehensive account of the adoption of the Constitution, from the reform initiatives of the 1780s through the ratification of the first amendments in 1791. Anyone who wants to understand the origins and character of the American constitutional project will need to wrestle with Klarman's incisive and balanced judgments."

—**Jack Rakove**, Pulitzer Prize-winning author of *Original Meanings*

The Framers' Coup

The Making of the United States Constitution

MICHAEL J. KLARMAN

OXFORD
UNIVERSITY PRESS

Oxford University Press is a department of the University of Oxford. It furthers
the University's objective of excellence in research, scholarship, and education
by publishing worldwide. Oxford is a registered trade mark of Oxford University
Press in the UK and certain other countries.

Published in the United States of America by Oxford University Press
198 Madison Avenue, New York, NY 10016, United States of America.

CIP data is on file at the Library of Congress
ISBN 978–0–19–994203–9

1 3 5 7 9 8 6 4 2

Printed by Sheridan Books, Inc., United States of America

To my brother, Seth,
with admiration, gratitude, and love

CONTENTS

PREFACE AND ACKNOWLEDGMENTS

This started out as a very different book. In the summer of 2011, I submitted a proposal to Dave McBride, my editor at Oxford University Press, to write a book for that press's Inalienable Rights series on the topic of the Founding—that is, the background, drafting, and ratification of the US Constitution (and the Bill of Rights, which was added to the Constitution a few years later). I had already written a book on the topic of race in American history for that series, and I thought a volume on the Founding might be a useful addition to it. Books in that series are supposed to be roughly fifty thousand words. This book is a great deal longer than that (though much of the heft is in the endnotes).

I am a law professor who teaches and writes mostly about how Supreme Court interpretations of the Constitution over the course of American history have been influenced by—and, in turn, themselves influence—the social and political context within which the justices operate. For the last twenty-five years, I have also taught the course "American Constitutional History from the Founding to the Civil War," which begins with about three weeks devoted to the background, drafting, and ratification of the Constitution. Consequently, I have long been an avid consumer of scholarship on the Founding. When, in 2011, the students on the *Harvard Law Review* asked me to write a review of Pauline Maier's outstanding book, *Ratification*, the idea for this book was born.

What happened next is that I made the mistake of getting interested in the primary source materials of the Founding—correspondence, newspaper essays, pamphlets, legislative and convention debates—which I had never previously explored in any systematic way. With assistance in gathering materials from a generous and expert law librarian, as well as from many talented and energetic Harvard Law School students, I have spent most of the last four years immersed in the primary materials of the Founding era.

I conceive of this book as making three principal contributions to the rich and voluminous existing scholarship on the origins of the US Constitution.

First and foremost, nobody has previously attempted to write a comprehensive account of the Founding. Many books—some of them quite wonderful—have been written on the various pieces of the Founding story: the flaws in the Articles of Confederation that seemed to cry out for redress, the conflicts over fiscal and monetary policy in the states in the mid-1780s that contributed mightily to the making of the Constitution, the Philadelphia convention that produced the Constitution, the contrasting ideas and interests of the Federalists and Antifederalists (i.e., those who, respectively, supported and opposed the Constitution), the campaign for ratification of the Constitution, and, finally, the enactment of the Bill of Rights. Yet it seemed to me that the absence of a single volume telling the entire story of the Founding between two covers was a gap that might be usefully filled.

Second, I have tried to tell this story, to the greatest extent possible, in the words of the participants. Doing so helps us to understand them as political actors engaged in a controversial enterprise rather than as the mythical Founding Fathers we have long been taught to revere. If nothing else, allowing the principal figures in these events to speak for themselves ought to better enable readers to make up their own minds as to how to interpret the making of the Constitution.

Finally, this book advances a view of the Founding that differs somewhat from those previously offered. Plainly, no single motive or explanatory variable can account for the making of the Constitution. However, experts will recognize that I have been especially drawn to the view, long advanced by others, that the Constitution was a conservative counterrevolution against what leading American statesmen regarded as the irresponsible economic measures enacted by a majority of state legislatures in the mid-1780s, which they diagnosed as a symptom of excessive democracy.

Along that dimension, I hope to provide more complete answers than have previously been given to two questions raised by this interpretation of the Founding. First, why were the delegates to the Philadelphia convention inclined and able to write a constitution that was very different from the one most Americans expected and wanted them to write? Second, how were the Federalists able to convince the nation, in the course of a reasonably democratic (at least for the era) ratifying process, to approve a document that was severely constraining of popular influence on government, especially when contrasted with the state constitutions of the period? These were extraordinary accomplishments—whether or not one regards them as legitimate or desirable—and I hope to shed additional light on how the Framers were able to bring them about.

I could not have written this book in such a relatively short time—a little under four years—without a great deal of help. One of the luxuries of teaching at Harvard Law School is the ability to obtain research assistance from members of our marvelously talented student body. My research assistants located and copied materials for me, and they checked my writing against the sources on which I relied to ensure accuracy. By performing these tasks, they enabled me to spend more time reading, thinking, organizing, and writing.

The following students all helped me with this project: Sam Callahan, Yaira Dubin, Louis Fisher, Caitlin Halpern, Chen-Chen Jiang, Jeremy Kreisberg, Rebecca Matte, Daniel Nessim, Kevin Neylan, Sean Ouellette, Susan Pelletier, Sylvanus Polky, Albert Rivero, Ari Ruben, Andres Salinas, Eden Schiffmann, and Marisa Schnaith. I would be remiss not to single out for special thanks another, smaller group of student research assistants, all of whom spent, I would estimate, hundreds of hours working on this project: Maya Brodziak, Cole Carter, Sean Driscoll, Katie Flanagan, Afroditi Giovanopoulou, Sean Mirski, and Laura Myron. I am immensely grateful to all these talented, hard-working, conscientious, and good-natured young people for their substantial contributions to this book.

My (nonstudent) assistants—first, Kimberly O'Hagan, and then for the past eighteen months, Mindy Eakin—have also made it possible for me to research this book far more extensively than I could have done without their help. I would estimate that, together, they have transcribed as many as two thousand pages of notes I dictated on primary and secondary sources that I have read. They have done so with what appears to be effortless efficiency— as well as great accuracy and unfailing good grace. Mindy has also collected for me hundreds of articles and books, and she arranged the illustrations for this volume pretty much single-handedly. I owe both Kimberly and Mindy an enormous debt of gratitude for their help.

Mindy Kent, one of the librarians at Harvard Law School, has also collected scores of journal articles and many hundreds of letters from the Founding era, without once complaining of the ridiculous burdens I have imposed upon her. Juliet Frey, a professional editor, helped polish my prose with a deft touch and, with her good humor, actually made the editing process fun.

I presented versions of what I consider the core argument of the book—that the Constitution was, in an important sense, a "coup" against public opinion— at two faculty workshops and various student events at Harvard Law School, at the public law colloquium run by Martha Minow and Dick Fallon at Harvard, at a workshop for federal judges organized by John Manning at Harvard Law School, at a Constitution Day lecture at Johns Hopkins University (at the kind invitation of Joel Grossman), and as a McCorkle Lecture at the University of Virginia School of Law (where I had the good fortune to teach for twenty years before relocating in 2008 to Cambridge, which has the advantage of being much closer to Fenway Park). I received many helpful comments from participants/audiences on these occasions, including, specifically, Larry Lessig, Jim Patterson, Sai Prakash, and Matt Stephenson.

One of the most gratifying aspects of writing this book has been receiving feedback on the manuscript from many generous readers. A number of friends, colleagues, and scholars read all or significant portions of the manuscript and gave me many useful suggestions for improvement: Jonathan Gienapp, Ken Hoge, Daryl Levinson, John Manning, Martha Minow, Matt Rowen, Andrew Schroeder, and Mike Seidman. Three historians whose scholarship I have long admired and whose work has greatly influenced my own thinking about the Founding—Max Edling, Jack Rakove, and Gordon Wood—also read all or most of the manuscript and gave me many pages of extremely helpful comments.

I must single out for special thanks another handful of readers whose contributions to this project were even more substantial. Woody Holton, whose book *Unruly Americans* has greatly influenced my perspective on the Constitution, not only gave me several pages of helpful general comments but also did a considerable amount of line editing of the entire manuscript. Michael Coenen and Marco Basile—a former mentee and a former student, respectively—each gave me more than twenty pages of the sort of detailed, incisive comments that are invaluable for improving a manuscript in its late stages of preparation.

My two largest debts are to Rich Leffler and John Kaminski. Both of them have, for decades, served as editors of the *Documentary History of the Ratification of the Constitution* (an absolutely extraordinary resource, without which this book would have been inconceivable). On many aspects of the story recounted here, they may well know as much as any two people alive. Rich read chapters 1 through 4; John read the entire manuscript (and portions of chapter 6, on ratification, more than once). Bringing their extraordinary knowledge of the era to bear, they caught countless errors, spotted logical contradictions, directed me to additional sources (primary and secondary), and improved both my prose and my method of citation. Since I have never met either of them in person, I can only describe their efforts—each must have spent many dozens of hours on the manuscript—as extraordinary acts of collegial generosity. To my mind, they represent what is best about the scholarly enterprise.

Finally, I thank Martha Minow, Dean of Harvard Law School, for financial and moral support. I also thank, perhaps more unusually, the Boston Red Sox for floundering miserably in 2015, which enabled me to work harder on finishing the book (though perhaps this was only reimbursement for the time away from the project caused by their improbable World Championship run in 2013). I thank my spouse, Lisa Landsverk, for her willingness to tolerate my utter and complete obsession with this project. And I thank my brother, Seth, to whom this book is dedicated, for a lifetime's worth of love and support.

Michael Klarman
Sanibel Island, Florida
January 2016

Introduction

As the Constitutional Convention came to a close on September 17, 1787, Benjamin Franklin offered two observations on its proceedings. First, he noted that "when you assemble a number of men to have the advantage of their joint wisdom, you inevitably assemble with those men, all their prejudices, their passions, their errors of opinion, their local interests, and their selfish views." Second, Franklin thought that, in light of this inevitability, it was astonishing "to find this system [the Constitution] approaching so near to perfection as it does."[1]*

Over the course of the ensuing 225 years, Americans have tended to embrace the second part of Franklin's observation (the astonishing near perfection of the Constitution) and to neglect the first part (the inherent passions, prejudices, and errors of the Framers). Americans came to revere the Constitution and the men who wrote it, often regarding them as divinely inspired. In 1928, the great civil liberties lawyer Louis Marshall described the Constitution as "our holy of holies, an instrument of sacred import. It has been the guiding principle of the freest Government on earth. Let no unhallowed hand be laid upon it."[2]

This tendency toward worship of the Constitution and the Framers began early. Just months after the Philadelphia convention ended, James Madison observed that "[i]t is impossible for the man of pious reflection not to perceive in it [the Constitution] a finger of that Almighty hand which has been so frequently and signally extended to our relief in the critical stages of the revolution." Given the extraordinary diversity of opinions expressed at the Constitutional Convention and the difficulty of adjusting competing considerations in the Constitution, Madison told Thomas Jefferson that one could

---

* For the convenience of readers, I have modernized spelling, capitalization, and punctuation in quotations, while attentive to the need not to alter the speaker's meaning. I have also expanded abbreviations in a similar manner.

hardly "consider the degree of concord which ultimately prevailed as less than a miracle."[3]

During the national debate over whether to ratify the Constitution, supporters ("Federalists") regularly made similar observations. One Federalist opined that "[t]he unexpected harmony of the federal convention ... must be attributed to the special influence of Heaven," while another noted that "Heaven smiled on their deliberations and inspired their councils with a spirit of conciliation." Dr. Benjamin Rush, a leading Pennsylvania Federalist, told his state's ratifying convention that "the hand of God was employed in this work, as that God had divided the Red Sea to give a passage to the children of Israel." After the requisite number of states had ratified the Constitution, Rush declared that it was "as much the work of a divine providence as any of the miracles recorded in the Old and New Testament were the effects of a divine power." Ratification of the Constitution left little doubt, in Rush's mind, "of heaven having favored the federal side of the question."[4]

Invocations of divine inspiration for the Constitution by supporters of ratification were, at least in part, a conscious political strategy to maximize the chances of winning. At the convention itself, Madison had explained, "The respectability of this convention will give weight to their [the delegates'] recommendation of it." During the ratifying contest in Virginia, he told Governor Edmund Randolph, "Had the Constitution been framed and recommended by an obscure individual, instead of a body possessing public respect and confidence, there can not be a doubt that although it would have stood in the identical words, it would have commanded little attention from most who now admire its wisdom." In the days immediately following the Philadelphia convention, as Alexander Hamilton mulled the prospects of ratification, he similarly observed that one important Federalist advantage was the influence of those who framed the Constitution—and especially that of George Washington.[5]

Federalists played this advantage—the extraordinary public reputations of many of the delegates to the Philadelphia convention—to the hilt. Indeed, even while the convention was still completing its work in Philadelphia, one advocate for a more powerful national government observed that "[s]uch a body of enlightened and honest men perhaps never before met for political purposes in any country upon the face of the earth." Such men were "entitled to the universal confidence of the people of America." A man such as Washington, wrote another essayist of similar political predispositions, "surely will never stoop to tarnish the luster of his former actions by having an agency in any thing capable of reflecting dishonor on himself or his countrymen." The nation could "[r]est assured" that "worthies" such as Washington and Franklin "have the good of America at heart."[6]

Once the Philadelphia convention had actually unveiled the Constitution, Federalists repeatedly invoked the wisdom and virtue of the convention's delegates as an argument for ratification. For example, an essay supporting ratification in Pennsylvania urged readers to "[b]ear witness with what solicitude the great council of America, headed by a *Franklin* and a *Washington*, the fathers of their country, have deliberated upon the dearest interests of men, and labored to frame a system of laws and constitutions that shall perpetuate the blessings of that independence, which you obtained by your swords!" It was "the duty of all honest, well-disposed men," one New York Federalist wrote, "to cultivate and diffuse . . . a spirit of submission to the counsels of this great patriot band." When some opponents of ratification ("Antifederalists") charged that the Constitution had been a premeditated scheme to enslave the people, one Virginia Federalist responded by urging his countrymen to remember that included among the convention delegates were "a Washington, whose hair has become grey and eyes dim in watching over your safety," and a Franklin, "whose philosophical and political abilities have procured him the admiration of the world." Was it really possible that such men "could conspire to enslave their country?"[7]*

For their part, opponents of ratification worried that the people were "too apt to yield an implicit assent to the opinions of those characters whose abilities are held in the highest esteem, and to those in whose integrity and patriotism they can confide." Was it fair or reasonable to treat people "as infidels in politics," a New York Antifederalist wondered, simply for refusing to give the Constitution "their approbation, until they should have had an opportunity of examining it?" William Findley, a leading Pennsylvania Antifederalist, protested that the Federalists ought to be "addressing our reason with solid arguments" rather than "address[ing] our implicit faith so much with great names." Responding to the argument that "an implicit confidence should be placed in the convention," leading Massachusetts Antifederalist Elbridge Gerry, who had also been an important dissenting delegate at the Philadelphia convention, noted that "however respectable the members may be who signed the

---

* Direct criticism of Washington was simply out of bounds, and Antifederalists were usually careful not to step over that line. When they did, however, the Federalists pounced: "Can human nature sink so low as to be guilty of such base ingratitude to a man to whom America owes her independence and liberties?" Only an "unprincipled monster would insinuate a thing so vile" as that a man such as Washington "who, for eight years, . . . fought and struggled to obtain and secure to you freedom and independence, should now be engaged in a design to subvert your liberties and reduce you to a state of servitude."

For the references supporting this footnote—and an explanation of where to find the references supporting subsequent footnotes—see the endnote whose call number immediately follows the call for this footnote in the text.

Constitution, it must be admitted that a free people are the proper guardians of their rights and liberties—that the greatest men may err—and that their errors are sometimes of the greatest magnitude."[8]

Much as at the Founding, throughout American history political actors have invoked the wisdom and virtue of the Framers as arguments against constitutional change, and they have attacked their political opponents as "impious." The Constitution has been analogized to "the Ark of the Covenant." Independence Hall in Philadelphia, the "hallowed ground of its birthplace," has been portrayed as "the holiest spot of American earth," and visitors to it have been described as "pilgrims" and as "worshippers before a shrine."[9]

Meanwhile, others have denigrated this tendency toward Constitution worship as "fetishism." Jefferson described and criticized this impulse to attribute to the past "a wisdom more than human" and to treat "constitutions with sanctimonious reverence and deem them like the ark of the covenant, too sacred to be touched."[10]

Madison's principal reason for deifying the Founders was his belief that the people could not be trusted to intelligently rule themselves. Citizens must be taught through habit and tradition to obey constituted governmental authority, and reverence for the Founders served that purpose. Without it, the people might too frequently change their constitution, which would "in a great measure, deprive the government of that veneration which time bestows on everything, and without which perhaps the wisest and freest governments would not possess the requisite stability." Experiments in the system of government were "of too ticklish a nature to be unnecessarily multiplied." It was dangerous to "disturb the public tranquility by interesting too strongly the public passions."[11]

Later historical actors have similarly deified the Founders for the purpose of blocking proposed changes to the Constitution or its traditional interpretation. In 1865, opponents of the Thirteenth Amendment, emphasizing the hallowed nature of the Constitution, which had not been altered in more than sixty years, argued that amending it to bar slavery would itself be unconstitutional. One of those opponents, Senator Lazarus Powell of Kentucky, described how the Founders had "stood around the baptismal font and proclaimed the birth of the Constitution." In the late 1890s, as the Supreme Court came under attack for invalidating the progressive income tax and upholding the labor injunction, the Court's defenders portrayed the Constitution as the nation's "greatest jewel . . . created by our fathers in a moment of Divine inspiration." After World War I, self-proclaimed patriots pressured Congress into establishing Constitution Day and putting the Constitution on display at the Library of Congress. For them, Constitution worship was a defense against communism, atheism, and other alien political ideologies. In 1937, the year of the Constitution's sesquicentennial, opponents of President Franklin Roosevelt's Court-Packing Plan, such as the American Liberty League, worshiped at the "Shrine of the Constitution."[12]

Constitution worship, however, is no substitute for actual knowledge of how the Constitution came into being. As the leading historian of this practice has observed, "[I]dolatry has too often served as a convenient cover for ignorance."[13]

In this book, I try to tell the story of the Constitution's origins in a way that demythifies it. The men who wrote the Constitution were extremely impressive, but they were not demigods; they had interests, prejudices, and moral blind spots. They could not foresee the future, and they made mistakes.

As we shall see, the Articles of Confederation—the system for governing the United States that preceded the Constitution—suffered from a variety of flaws. Most important, under the Articles, Congress lacked the power to levy taxes, to regulate interstate or foreign commerce, and even to enforce national treaties against recalcitrant states. Chapter 1 examines these flaws in the Articles and considers why efforts to redress them prior to the Constitutional Convention of 1787 proved unavailing. Several amendments to the Articles *were* proposed, but particular states had interests that led them to block the proposals, which in turn inspired resentment and spawned retaliatory actions by other states. This chapter also considers how a dispute over Secretary for Foreign Affairs John Jay's negotiations with Spain involving Americans' claim to navigation rights on the Mississippi River created deep sectional divisions that seemed to threaten the survival of the union and indeed led some statesmen to fear civil war.

Yet the Constitution was not simply a response to certain widely perceived defects in the Articles of Confederation. To a considerable degree, it was also a response to economic conflicts that had developed in the states in the mid-1780s. Chapter 2 examines how, in the midst of a severe postwar economic recession, a majority of states enacted measures for tax and debt relief, which were reviled by most of the nation's political and economic elite and soured them on political arrangements that they deemed overly responsive to public opinion. In one of the states where popular demands for relief legislation were defeated—Massachusetts—debtors and taxpayers arose in insurrection and closed the civil courts in an effort to prevent mass foreclosures and extort tax relief from the legislature. Many prominent statesmen were horrified by Shays's Rebellion, which they saw as a broadscale assault on government and perhaps even on private property.

To the extent that the Constitution was designed in part to block legislation for tax and debt relief, it represented a victory for one party in a debate that genuinely had two sides—which was less true with regard to the aspects of the Constitution that redressed flaws in the Articles of Confederation, where a powerful consensus existed for remedial measures. Shays's Rebellion also had a profound impact on the Philadelphia convention and its handiwork. A constitution written in the years before Shays's Rebellion and the enactment of populist relief legislation by many states probably would have looked very different from the one drafted in Philadelphia.

In the 1780s, several unsuccessful efforts had been made to reform the Articles incrementally. How was the decision made to pursue more radical reform through an open-ended constitutional convention, which the Articles did not authorize? With the aid of hindsight, many of the steps leading to the Philadelphia convention seem fortuitous. What might have happened had no such convention taken place in 1787? Many statesmen observed that the Confederation Congress was on the brink of collapse and the union on the edge of dissolution. They predicted that the demise of the Confederation probably would lead to civil war and might induce Americans to lose their faith in republican government. Were such statements simply rhetoric designed to frighten people into supporting drastic constitutional reform, or were they plausible predictions of what might have happened had the Constitution not been drafted and ratified when it was?

Chapter 3 examines the constitutional convention that assembled in Philadelphia in May 1787, including how its agenda got set and how the principal issues it addressed got resolved. As we shall see, from the outset the convention was beset by deep conflict. Delegates disagreed about ideas (such as the nature of political representation and the ideal structure of an executive branch), but they also had conflicting interests (such as over the relative power that small and large states should exercise within the national legislature). While the delegates mostly argued over issues in terms of political principles, often their ostensibly principled arguments simply served as rationalizations for the interests being advanced.

For weeks, the delegates struggled over the convention's most intractable issue: how to apportion representation in the national government in a manner that was acceptable to both large and small states. This chapter examines the arguments that informed that debate, the extent to which the convention nearly dissolved over it, and the compromise that eventually resolved the issue.

In the end, the Philadelphia convention designed a constitution that dramatically expanded the powers of the national government while insulating it far more from popular political influence than most Americans at the time would have anticipated or desired. That is why the battle over ratification was so closely fought. Chapter 3 also investigates why the convention proved so unrepresentative of public opinion in the nation: What were the circumstances and decisions that created the conditions enabling the delegates to write the constitution they did?

As delegates from large states and small states battled over how to apportion representation in Congress, Madison observed more than once that the real conflict of interest among the states at the convention was a function of their differing degrees of dependence on slave labor. Chapter 4 examines the role that debate over slavery played in Philadelphia. Although there was probably never a serious possibility that the convention would take significant steps toward the abolition of slavery, delegates from slave states and from (mostly) free states found plenty to disagree about at the convention. In the several compromises over slavery that enabled the Framers to agree upon a constitution, did northerners make the best possible bargains, or were they unduly intimidated by the southern delegations' repeated threats to walk out of the convention if their slavery-related demands were not satisfied?

In the contest over ratification of the Constitution, some northern Federalists argued that the Constitution put slavery on the road to extinction. By contrast, many of their southern allies argued that the Constitution was a strongly proslavery document. Which of these claims was nearer to the truth?

Slavery, of course, was not the only issue—or even one of the principal ones—in the ratifying contest. Chapter 5 examines the debate over ratification more broadly: What arguments did Antifederalists make in opposition to ratification, and how did Federalists respond? In defending particular constitutional provisions, how closely did Federalists' arguments during the ratifying contest track those made by the Framers at the Philadelphia convention?

Arguments made against ratification did not, of course, necessarily reflect the underlying interests motivating the opposition. Some reasons for opposing the Constitution were widely seen as more legitimate than others. Moreover, those who had decided to oppose ratification had an incentive to make whatever arguments seemed most likely to convince swing voters and ratifying convention delegates to reject the Constitution.

In addition to considering the arguments made against the Constitution, chapter 5 investigates the factors that actually seem to have influenced positions on ratification. Although Federalists and Antifederalists sometimes simply held different ideas about government, interests having to do with class, occupation, and the size and circumstances of one's state and region— East versus West, North versus South, and urban versus rural—seem to have proved more important in determining votes on ratification.

The Framers had written a constitution that vastly expanded the powers of the federal government and constrained populist influence upon it. How did Federalists manage to convince Americans, through a reasonably democratic process, to approve a constitution that seemed to contravene their preferences in many ways and that significantly curbed democracy at the national level?

Chapter 6 examines the process of ratification, which in some ways was not entirely a fair fight. Federalists enjoyed certain advantages, some of which were the result of luck but others of which they had helped to construct. For example, in some states, malapportionment of ratifying conventions worked to the Federalists' advantage. In nearly all states, the press was overwhelmingly on the Federalists' side of the debate, and the economic and educational elite also generally favored ratification. One of the Federalists' most important advantages was Article VII of the Constitution, which eliminated the requirement from the Articles of Confederation that constitutional change be unanimously approved by the states and stipulated instead that the acquiescence of nine states would suffice to put the Constitution into operation (although those states could bind only themselves). Only by changing the existing ground rules—and getting their opponents to acquiesce in the new ones—were the Federalists able to give themselves a fighting chance in the ratifying contest. Yet, in the end, they probably still would not have won without some important strategic blunders by their adversaries.

Chapter 6 also describes the ratifying contest as it unfolded state by state, noting the importance of momentum shifts, tactical choices made by the two sides, and the contingency of the outcome, which was very much in doubt for most of the contest. Although the issue of whether the Constitution would be ratified was one of the most important in the nation's history, the contest over ratification was, perhaps to a surprising degree, fought largely with the weapons of ordinary politics. Both sides questioned their opponents' motives and attacked their characters, appealed to the material interests of voters, employed dirty tricks, and made back-room deals when necessary.

Throughout the ratifying contest, Antifederalists made arguments—many of them quite persuasive—for ratification conditional upon antecedent amendments, and for a second constitutional convention that would consider amendments proposed by the state ratifying conventions. Federalists adamantly resisted both conditional ratification and a second convention, offering both legal and practical political arguments for their position. But those arguments did not fully capture the reasons the Federalists were so averse to such proposals. In the end, most Americans probably would have preferred a constitution lying somewhere on the spectrum between the obviously defective Articles of Confederation and the vastly more nationalist and democracy-constraining Constitution. Yet the Federalists managed to deny them any intermediate options.

The original Constitution contains no bill of rights—a striking omission from the perspective of most Americans, then and now. Chapter 7 examines how a bill of rights came into existence. In this part of the Founding story, as elsewhere, Madison played an enormously important role. How did he evolve from an opponent of all amendments to the Constitution, during the ratifying contest, to the great champion of the Bill of Rights? And how did Madison convince the first Congress to adopt constitutional amendments when most Federalists had little enthusiasm for the entire project of amendments and most Antifederalists had little interest in the particular amendments that Madison proposed?

Throughout the ratifying contest, Antifederalists raised challenges to the legitimacy of the Constitution: Congress had exceeded its authority by endorsing the Philadelphia convention; the convention had ignored its limiting instructions; and the Articles required that amendments be approved unanimously by state legislatures, yet the Constitution stipulated that it would become operational once ratifying conventions in nine states had approved it. These were substantial irregularities in the process of constitutional change, yet, once the new national government had commenced operations, Antifederalists quickly abandoned their legitimacy challenges.

Chapter 8, the concluding chapter, considers why Antifederalists may have chosen to do so. One possibility is that the nation quickly prospered under the Constitution—and perhaps *because of* the Constitution. Another possibility is that former Antifederalists quickly discovered that, even while limited to operating within the Constitution's bounds, they could still make essentially the same political arguments they had made in opposing its ratification. Indeed, for much of the period from 1800 to the Civil War, the Antifederalists' ideological and political descendants seemed largely to control the Constitution's interpretation, both within the political branches of the national government and in the Supreme Court (at least after the demise of Chief Justice John Marshall and his Federalist/Whig compatriot justices in the early to mid-1830s). Even though Antifederalists lost the contest over the Constitution's ratification, they seem largely to have won the battle over its interpretation—at least until after the Civil War.

Chapter 8 also examines how some important constitutional provisions proved sufficiently malleable to accommodate the powerful democratizing forces of the Jacksonian era without any formal constitutional amendment. However, other constitutional provisions had been written too precisely to accommodate change through interpretation, and they also proved resistant to formal amendment, given the formidable barriers to such change posed by Article V of the Constitution. How ought one to think about such provisions continuing to bind Americans today despite their inconsistency with modern democratic norms? More generally, how should one feel about a modern democratic society's being governed by a constitution that was written 225 years ago by people possessed of very different assumptions, concerns, and values?

This is one of the most important questions confronting modern constitutional theory. Although history alone cannot provide the answer, understanding how the Constitution actually came into being is an important step in the right direction. That is the story this book seeks to tell.

1

Flaws in the Articles of Confederation

By 1786–87, the government of the newly independent United States seemed, in the eyes of many leading citizens, to be disintegrating. The nation was default-ing on its debts, foreign and domestic. States had largely ceased fulfilling their financial obligations to Congress, which under the Articles of Confederation could only requisition funds from the states and had no power to coerce com-pliance. Proposals to supply Congress with independent revenue-raising authority—such as the power to levy import duties—had failed to secure the ratification of every state, as required for amendments under the Articles. An effort by Congress in October 1786 to borrow half a million dollars from pri-vate subscribers to finance an emergency expansion of the army to suppress an insurrection of tax resisters and debtors in backcountry Massachusetts had proved a complete failure, as states declined to pledge their tax support for repayment. Foreign nations and foreign bankers, too, were growing weary of lending money to the US government. Powerless to raise additional revenue, Congress might not have been able to put an army in the field, even to protect the nation in the event of a foreign invasion. Congress had no response when Spain closed the Mississippi River to American navigation in 1784, or when Algerian pirates attacked American ships in the Mediterranean Sea in 1785, kidnapping American citizens and holding them for ransom.[1]

In addition to lacking basic revenue-raising capacity, the Confederation Congress had no authority to regulate foreign commerce. After the Revolutionary War, when Great Britain sought to exclude American ships from the Atlantic carrying trade, and several European nations sought to exclude certain American goods from European markets and from European colonies in the western hemisphere, Congress was powerless to respond with retalia-tory trade restrictions. Because Congress also lacked the authority to compel states to abide by their own nation's treaty obligations, the British continued to hold forts along the northwestern frontier of the United States—forts they had agreed to evacuate under the Treaty of Paris that ended the Revolutionary War. In the mid-1780s, American states were beginning to impose discriminatory trade restrictions upon one another, and Congress, which lacked the power to regulate even interstate commerce, was helpless to intervene. In 1786, stark regional conflict erupted in Congress when Secretary for Foreign Affairs John Jay attempted to barter away American claims to free navigation of the Mississippi River, which southerners considered vital, in exchange for a favorable commercial treaty with Spain, which northerners desired. Many Americans began to speak openly of splitting the nation into separate confederacies.[2]

Early in 1787, James Madison, a young but already prominent statesman from Virginia, observed that "[o]ur situation is becoming every day more and more critical." Persons of reflection "unanimously agree that the existing Confederacy is tottering to its foundation." The present system of governance "neither has nor deserves advocates." Madison continued: "No money is paid into the public treasury; no respect is paid to the federal authority. Not a single state complies with the [congressional] requisitions, several pass them over in silence, and some positively reject them." Madison concluded, "It is not possible that a government can last long under these circumstances." Americans were "losing all confidence in our political system."[3]

Other leading statesmen were reaching similar conclusions. Governor Edmund Randolph of Virginia told George Washington that the "nerves of government seem unstrung, both in energy and money," and he expressed "alarm at the storms which threaten the United States." William Grayson, another Virginia political leader, told Madison that many congressional delegates had concluded "that the present Confederation is utterly inefficient, and that if it remains much longer in its present state of imbecility we shall be one of the most contemptible nations on the face of the earth." Grayson reported to William Short, who was serving as Thomas Jefferson's private secretary in Paris, that "American affairs in general wear the worst aspect you can possibly conceive: the people discontented, the public treasury without money (and laws in several of the states but faintly executed) and the states either refusing or not complying with the requisition of Congress."[4*]

---

* Grayson was born in 1736 in Prince William County, Virginia. He entered the College of Philadelphia (later, the University of Pennsylvania) in 1758, then studied in Great Britain, probably at the University of Edinburgh, before receiving his legal training at Inner Temple in London.

Returning home in the mid-1760s, Grayson took up the practice of law and became actively involved in the movement for American independence. In 1766, he attended the Westmoreland County meeting that pledged resistance to execution of the Stamp Act, denying Parliament's authority to tax the colonies. In 1774, Grayson served on the Prince William County Committee of Safety, and in 1775 he was a delegate to the extralegal convention that moved the colony closer to independence.

How had the United States arrived at such a state of crisis just years after the nation's unlikely founding in a successful war for independence against Great Britain? In part, it was flaws in the Articles of Confederation that were responsible for the crisis, which in turn paved the way for the Constitution.

Lack of a Taxing Power

The colonies that jointly declared their independence from Great Britain in 1776 had deep differences among themselves—ethnic, religious, and economic. Before the mid-1760s, the idea of centrally coordinating resistance to burdensome British trade measures would have struck most American colonists as bizarre. A self-conscious sense of nationalism among Americans arose only as a result of organizing their shared opposition to British policies.[5]

Since its formation in 1774, the Continental Congress had exercised significant political, economic, and military powers. It had created an army, issued currency, and negotiated treaties with foreign nations. The Articles of Confederation, not approved by Congress and sent to the states for ratification until 1777, formalized Congress's powers by designing a system of government to enable the thirteen states to coordinate their war efforts. Because the Articles were drafted during wartime, they conferred mostly military powers

In 1776, Grayson was appointed a colonel in the state militia and then quickly became a Continental Army officer and one of General Washington's aides-de-camp. From 1776 to 1779, he served as a regimental commander in several of the principal battles of the Revolutionary War. Afterwards, he served two years on Congress's Board of War, which oversaw logistics for the army.

In the mid-1780s, Grayson represented Prince William County in the Virginia House of Delegates for two years and also served as one of the state's delegates to Congress from 1785 to 1787. There, he played a significant role in passing the Northwest Ordinance of 1787.

When the Philadelphia convention sent the constitution it had drafted to Congress in September 1787, congressional delegate Grayson criticized it and supported a proposal to amend it. Afterwards, he became one of the most prominent Antifederalists in Virginia. With his breadth of learning and formidable oratorical skills, Grayson, as we shall see, was one of the leading voices opposing ratification at the Virginia ratifying convention. Although his service in Congress had convinced him that the federal government needed additional powers, Grayson believed that the Constitution lacked adequate safeguards to secure a southern minority from economic and political domination by a northern majority. He insisted that other states would acquiesce if Virginia demanded the enactment of suitable amendments before ratifying the Constitution.

In 1789, an Antifederalist-dominated Virginia legislature chose Grayson as one of the state's first US senators. In that capacity, he sought, without success, to convince the Senate to approve constitutional amendments that were considerably more far-reaching than the ones James Madison had maneuvered through the House of Representatives. After just one year of service in the Senate, Grayson died of a gout attack. In his will, he emancipated his slaves.

on Congress—such as raising an army, appointing a commander-in-chief, authorizing privateers against foreign shipping, and negotiating treaties with foreign nations.[6]

Because of the exigencies of war, the Articles did not spawn the same sort of great public debate that the Constitution would in 1787–88. Yet, despite the widely perceived imperative for quick approval, three small states—Delaware, New Jersey, and Maryland—resisted ratification for years. According to Madison's subsequent account, one of New Jersey's main objections was that the Articles provided no remedy for its "peculiar situation" as a state with "no convenient ports for foreign commerce," which left it like "a cask tapped at both ends," situated between Philadelphia and New York City and "subject to be[ing] taxed by . . . neighbors, through whose ports [its] commerce was carried on."[7]

For many of the states, the Articles were deficient because they did not include a provision—which an early draft had contained—authorizing Congress to force states such as Virginia to cede to the union their claims to vast, unsold western lands. The states lacking western-land claims—about half of the states—took the position that those lands, which the entire nation bore the burden of securing in the war against Great Britain, should be held in common and used to defray the costs of a war fought for the benefit of all (rather than benefiting only the taxpayers of the states that had claims to such lands). Madison later observed that these western lands, vast in extent and growing in value, were "the occasion of much discussion and heart-burning and proved the most obstinate of the impediments to an earlier consummation of the [Articles]." Indeed, resolution of the states' western-land claims would remain one of the most time-consuming and divisive of the Confederation Congress's* preoccupations during its decade of existence. Maryland, the last holdout state, did not acquiesce to the Articles until January 1781—nearly three and a half years after they had been submitted to the states.[8]

The Articles were more a treaty among independent states than a framework for a new national government. In 1776, few Americans would have thought that the thirteen states had formed a single nation; most people still thought of their state as their country. Indeed, the Articles expressly provided that "[e]ach state retains its sovereignty, freedom and independence." Moreover, despite desultory resistance from large-state delegates, Congress had approved an article guaranteeing every state equal voting power in Congress—an arrangement that connoted a confederation rather than a nation.[9]

---

* Once the Articles had been approved by the last of the thirteen states, the Continental Congress became the Confederation Congress.

Under the Articles, Congress lacked some of the basic powers of a sovereign government: It could neither impose taxes nor enact statutes. Congress's powers, which mainly pertained to issues of war and external relations, were more akin to those of the British Crown than of Parliament. Reacting against what they perceived as the tyranny of the British government, most Americans had been loath to invest Congress with expansive powers. As Madison later wrote Washington, "Nothing but the peculiarity of our circumstances could ever have produced those sacrifices of sovereignty"—minimal as they were—"on which the federal government now rests." Alexander Hamilton agreed, noting that resistance to British encroachments had been "the great object of all our public and private institutions. The zeal for liberty became predominant and excessive. In forming our Confederation, this passion alone seemed to actuate us, and we appear to have had no other view than to secure ourselves from despotism."[10]

Indeed, after the Revolutionary War ended in 1783, many Americans saw little if any need for Congress, and they certainly were not inclined to augment its powers. Gouverneur Morris, who was the deputy to the Confederation's superintendent of finance, Robert Morris (no relation), had feared as much.*

---

* Gouverneur Morris was born in 1752 to a privileged background on his family's manor near New York City. He entered King's College (later, Columbia University) at the age of twelve and served in New York's Provincial Congress at the age of twenty-three. Morris also participated in the drafting of New York's constitution of 1777 (he advocated the abolition of slavery in the state) and represented his state in the Continental Congress, where he was a strong nationalist. For three and a half years, beginning in 1781, he was assistant superintendent of finance under Robert Morris.

Afterwards, Morris remained in Philadelphia and was appointed in 1787 by the Assembly to serve as a delegate to the Philadelphia convention. There, as we shall see, Morris was one of the three or four most important participants, and he made more speeches than any other delegate. In a sketch of fellow delegates, William Pierce described Morris as "one of those geniuses in whom every species of talents combine to render him conspicuous and flourishing in public debate.... No man has more wit—nor can any one engage the attention more than Mr. Morris." However, Pierce also noted that, despite "all these powers, he [Morris] is fickle and inconstant—never pursuing one train of thinking."

At the convention, Morris advocated both a powerful national government and mechanisms to reduce popular influence upon it. He favored a strong Senate, an executive with lifetime tenure, proportional representation in both houses of Congress, and limits on the potential political clout of newly admitted western states. As a member of the convention's Committee of Style, Morris was given primary responsibility for putting the Constitution into its final form. Several decades later, Madison wrote that "the finish given to the style and arrangement of the Constitution fairly belongs to the pen of Mr. Morris."

In 1792, President Washington appointed Morris minister plenipotentiary to France—a controversial appointment in light of the facts that Morris was "a man of ... known monarchical principles" (in the words of George Mason) and that France was in the midst of a revolution against its king. Beginning in 1800, Morris briefly served as one of New York's US senators. In that capacity, he was an ardent Federalist and vigorously criticized the Jefferson administration's

In 1782, he urged against negotiating a quick peace treaty with Great Britain because a vigorous government was necessary to the nation's continuing to make "rapid and constant progress towards strength and greatness," and a premature cessation of the war would stymie the conviction that was becoming "daily sensible" that Congress was too weak. His boss, Robert Morris, agreed. Speaking as "a patriot," he opined that a rapidly negotiated peace was not in the nation's interest because "a continuance of the war is necessary until our confederation is more strongly knit, until a sense of the obligations to support it shall be more generally diffused amongst all ranks of American citizens, [and] until we shall acquire the habit of paying taxes (the means we possess already)." Once the war was over, Hamilton confirmed that, even though "[e]very day proves the inefficacy of the present confederation, yet the common danger being removed, we are receding instead of advancing in a disposition to amend its defects."[11]

Over the course of the 1780s, American political leaders increasingly recognized deficits in Congress's power as serious flaws in the Articles that required remediation. The most glaring omission was the lack of independent revenue-raising authority. Fighting a war in opposition to the British Parliament's efforts to tax the colonies, Americans were naturally reluctant to delegate taxing authority to the Confederation Congress—another distant government in an era of relatively primitive communication and transportation. This generation of Americans generally embraced the maxim that "the power which holds the purse-strings absolutely [will] rule." A government possessed of coercive taxing authority could, for example, finance a standing army to oppress the people in their liberties. Thus, the Articles conferred upon Congress only the authority to requisition money from the states. Congress had neither the power to coerce states into fulfilling their quotas nor the authority to tax individuals.[12]

---

early challenge to the authority of the federal judiciary. During the War of 1812, Morris endorsed the Hartford Convention and advocated the secession of New York and New England from the United States.

Morris's critics highlighted his haughty manner and his loose morals. Washington explained to Morris that opponents of his appointment as minister to France had denounced his "mode of expression [as] imperious, contemptuous and disgusting to those who might happen to differ from [his] opinion." Another contemporary observed, "[T]he world in general allows greater credit for his abilities than his integrity."

Morris was tall, handsome, and self-confident. Chancellor James Kent of New York later described him as "very commanding" in appearance, with a "noble head" and a "majestic mien." Morris also had a reputation as what one historian has called a "consummate philanderer." When Morris had to have his leg amputated at the knee after a carriage accident in 1780, John Jay wrote to Robert Morris, "Gouverneur's leg has been a tax on my heart. I am almost tempted to wish he had lost something else."

Indeed, Congress initially had sought to finance the Revolutionary War by printing money rather than requisitioning contributions from the states. By contrast, the British government usually financed wars through loans. Yet foreign nations would not lend money to the United States until its prospects for winning the war improved. Raising money from domestic creditors also proved difficult given the dearth of hard currency in the country. Banks that might lend money to the government did not exist in the mid-1770s. Congress was initially reluctant to try to raise money by asking the states to levy taxes, given both the scarcity of hard currency and the depth of Americans' opposition to paying taxes—the very stance that had helped ignite the war.[13]

So instead Congress printed paper money, which would retain its value only if holders were convinced that Congress possessed the will and capacity eventually to raise the revenue necessary to redeem it. Congress pledged the faith of the thirteen states to redeeming the paper. Each state was responsible for withdrawing a certain quota from circulation.[14]

As war expenses burgeoned, Congress emitted increasing amounts of paper, which eventually the economy could not absorb without rapid depreciation. Newly established state governments, which were already imposing high taxes to finance the war, were disinclined to enact the additional taxes that would have been necessary to do their part to retire the paper money from circulation. Further, the war impeded the ability of states to derive revenue from import and export duties—ordinarily an important source of income for many of the states.[15]

By 1779, Continental currency was trading at just 5 percent of its face value. A desperate Congress recommended price controls and called on states to enact laws to confiscate goods useful to the army. In 1780, Congress was so strapped for money that it asked the states to assume responsibility for providing supplies to their own citizens serving in the Continental Army.[16]

As congressional paper quickly depreciated in value, Congress turned to requisitioning funds and supplies from the states. The Articles of Confederation provided for apportioning requisitions among the states based on land values, but in the absence of a reliable land census, which could not possibly have been conducted during the war, Congress had to rely on guesswork. The first requisition came late in 1777, with others quickly to follow, as Congress desperately sought to stem the depreciation of its currency. Congress also tried to raise money from private investors by issuing loan certificates, which were also used to pay suppliers. But this alternative form of paper also depreciated in value, as Congress was unable to pay the interest it had promised on the certificates.[17]

By turning from printing money to requisitioning funds from the states, Madison noted, "Congress has undergone a total change from what it originally was." He wrote Jefferson, "Whilst they [congressional delegates] exercised the indefinite power of emitting money on the credit of their constituents, they had the whole wealth and resources of the continent within their command, and could go on with their affairs independently and as they pleased. Since the resolution passed for shutting the press [March 18, 1780], this power has been entirely given up and they are now as dependent on the states as the King of England is on the Parliament." Madison warned that "[u]nless the [state] legislatures are sufficiently attentive to this change of circumstances and act in conformity to it, every thing must necessarily go wrong or rather must come to a total stop."[18]

As Madison feared, congressional requisitions upon the states proved problematic from the start. In the spring of 1780, Washington complained, "One state will comply with a requisition of Congress; another neglects to do it; a third executes it by halves; and all differ either in the manner, the matter, or so much in point of time that we are always working up hill." Around the same time, Madison observed that "[o]ur great danger at present arises from the dilatory proceedings of the states and the real difficulty of drawing forth those resources which the new system is to operate upon." Madison believed that even the "most capable" states were guilty of "shameful deficiency" in complying with requisitions. Yet even states that sought in good faith to raise their share of congressional requisitions failed either to levy sufficiently high taxes or to vigorously enforce collection of those they did impose. State governments were concerned about provoking popular resistance if they pushed too hard to raise additional tax revenue from constituents who were long accustomed to being lightly taxed under British rule and were already paying much higher taxes than they were accustomed to in order to finance the war.[19]

Under the Articles of Confederation, Congress had no power to coerce states that were delinquent in paying their requisitions. In the absence of any mechanism for coercion, the requisition system suffered from a massive collective-action problem. States worried that even if they exerted themselves to satisfy their congressional requisitions, other states might not do the same. States that promptly complied with their requisitions naturally resented those that did not. As early as 1783, Madison had concluded that revenue laws must "operate at the same time through all the states, and [be] exempt from the control of each." Otherwise, "the mutual jealousies which begin already to appear among them will assuredly defraud both our foreign and domestic creditors of their just claims." As Madison later observed, "If some states contribute their quotas and others do not, justice is violated; the violation of justice is the ground of disputes among states as well as among individuals. . . . Those who furnish most will complain of those who furnish least."[20]*

---

* Indeed, a report by the Confederation's Board of Treasury in March 1788 revealed huge variation in the percentages of their requisitions paid by the states between 1781 and 1787,

Moreover, because much of the money that Congress requisitic
states was allocated to paying interest to domestic creditors, even st...
had been relatively faithful about paying their requisitions could easily ratio-
nalize diverting their contributions to pay their own citizens who held federal
debt, rather than sending the money to Congress, which might use it for other
purposes. In 1782, both New Jersey and Pennsylvania threatened to do this,
the former on the grounds that such action was required by "common justice"
to its soldiers in the Continental Army who had not been paid in some time.[21]

A congressional committee responded that such action would be "not only
a breach of the federal system but of the faith pledged to the public creditors."
Moreover, such an example was likely to be "followed by other states and extended to other instances," with the result being that "our bond of union would
be dissolved." In 1786, a congressional delegation consisting of Rufus King of
Massachusetts and James Monroe of Virginia pleaded with the Pennsylvania
Assembly to end this practice, which King later recalled had "increased the financial embarrassment of Congress, and, if followed, would have put an end to
all the contributions from the other states." Yet Pennsylvania refused to relent,
and New York decided to follow its example.[22]

Superintendent of Finance Robert Morris sought to pressure the states
into meeting their requisitions by instructing federal tax receivers to publish the amounts of state deficiencies in local newspapers, which might embarrass states into explaining their delinquencies. Yet his repeated messages
urging state legislatures and executives to pay their requisitions were, he told
Washington, "like preaching to the dead." In 1785, Massachusetts congressional delegate Nathan Dane lamented that "a mere recommendatory power only
in Congress to the states is inadequate to the important purposes of calling
forth resources of the people to discharge the expense of war and peace, the
foreign and domestic engagements entered into by Congress." He concluded
that "so long as the supplying of the continental treasury shall depend on the
interests and pleasures of the several states, there is no certainty of their doing
it." In 1786, Washington observed, "[R]equisitions are a perfect nullity where
thirteen sovereign, independent, disunited states are in the habit of discussing
and refusing compliance with them at their option. Requisitions are actually
little better than a jest and a by-word throughout the land."[23]

In the end, congressional requisitions proved an abysmal failure. Congress
made six requisitions on the states between October 1781 and August 1786,
and the overall rate of compliance was about 37 percent. Moreover, compliance rates declined precipitously over time. During the war, states had felt

---

ranging from a high of 67 percent by New York and 57 percent by Pennsylvania to a low of 3 percent by North Carolina and 0 percent by Georgia.

greater urgency in meeting their requisitions because, as Gouverneur Morris observed, people were convinced "of the necessity of obedience to common counsels for general purposes." However, states that had dutifully imposed taxes to satisfy federal requisitions in the early 1780s had largely given up on doing so by the middle of the decade. South Carolina, which in 1783 had allocated 52 percent of its annual revenue to satisfying federal requisitions, reduced that percentage to 28 in 1784, and then made no provision at all for Congress between 1785 and 1787. Massachusetts, which had imposed a hard-currency tax in 1781 earmarked for Congress and collected $200,000 of the $300,000 allocated, took no action in response to Congress's requisition of October 1786.[24]

By the spring of 1787, states had paid two-thirds of the congressional requisition of October 1781, 20 percent of the September 1785 requisition, and only 2 percent of that of August 1786. The requisition system seemed to be defunct. Early in 1787, Madison told his father that "payments to the federal treasury are ceasing everywhere, and the minds of people are losing all confidence in our political system." Later that year, he told Jefferson, who was serving as American minister to France, that the fiscal situation was so bad that "[i]t may well be doubted whether the present government can be kept alive through the ensuing year." At year's end, Madison reported that "[t]he treasury board seems to be in despair of maintaining the shadow of government much longer," while North Carolina's congressional delegation declared that "we are at the eve of a bankruptcy and of a total dissolution of government."[25]

The dearth of federal revenue was leading to national humiliation. In the summer of 1786, Secretary for Foreign Affairs John Jay told Congress that because the nation was "destitute of funds, and without public credit, either at home or abroad," it could not credibly threaten Spain with war over its denial of American navigation rights on the Mississippi River. In 1787, Virginia congressional delegate Edward Carrington reported to Governor Randolph that "[t]he reduced state of our treasury" had forced Congress to abandon its plan to raise troops to help suppress Shays's Rebellion in Massachusetts—discussed in chapter 2—and had left Congress without the means to pay troops stationed on the Ohio River, to whom Congress was already "considerably in arrears." Madison told Jefferson that disbanding the handful of troops on the frontier would "probably bring on an Indian war, and make an impression to our disadvantage on the British garrisons within our limits." A New Hampshire congressional delegate, Nicholas Gilman, wrote that without a more "efficient national government," the United States would "become contemptible even in the eyes of savages themselves." Moreover, unable to pay even the interest on the foreign debt, Congress, according to North Carolina's delegates, was "reduced to the dreadful alternative of borrowing principal to pay interest." Yet, "[t]he deception cannot be much longer kept up," and pretty soon "[o]ur friends must give us up and we shall become a laughingstock to our enemies."[26]

By 1787, most American statesmen would have agreed with the observation of Edmund Pendleton, chancellor of Virginia, who told Madison that Congress must have "independent, coercive power" to levy taxes to pay the public debt and provide for the annual expenses of civil government because a system of requisitions dependent "upon the various sentiments and whims of thirteen different assemblies has proved as unproductive in practice as it is futile in reason." Even as much of a skeptic regarding expansive congressional power as Richard Henry Lee, a former president of Congress from Virginia, now conceded that the states had been "so unpardonably remiss in furnishing their federal quotas as to make [an] impost necessary, for a term of time." Washington wrote Madison, "[M]y opinion of public virtue is so far changed that I have my doubts whether any system without the means of coercion in the sovereign will enforce obedience to the ordinances of a general government, without which, everything else fails."[27]

Lack of a Commerce Power

In addition to lacking the power of taxation, the Confederation Congress was not authorized to regulate foreign or interstate commerce. Indeed, Article IX expressly forbade Congress from making treaties that interfered with the power of a state to prohibit the importation or exportation of any category of goods. In the 1780s, Congress's inability to regulate commerce proved exceedingly inconvenient.

After the Revolutionary War ended, European nations discriminated against American commerce. Most important, even before the Treaty of Paris had been approved in the fall of 1783, Great Britain barred American ships from ports in the British West Indies, sought to exclude Americans from the lucrative transatlantic carrying trade (meaning that British ships came to American ports to carry American goods to Great Britain), and barred certain American-produced goods (such as fish and whale oil) from the British Empire. France and Spain soon followed suit with various restrictions on American ships and goods, especially with regard to their colonies in the West Indies. Noting that these forms of trade had been "great sources of wealth and convenience to the United States" before the war, a congressional committee called such measures "most pernicious to the interests of America." In addition, "the great nursery for seamen will be in a good degree lost" if the transatlantic carrying trade were to be "engrossed by Europeans."[28]

In 1785, Madison reported that British shippers were using their monopoly of the carrying trade to perpetrate "the most visible and shameful frauds" on Virginia tobacco growers, costing them as much as 50 percent of the value of their crop. One Boston lawyer estimated that the British were collecting $300,000 in "freight and charges" for every million dollars of tobacco exported from southern states and about half of the value of every shipment of timber exported from New England. He lamented that these freight fees were "money which belongs to the New England states because we can furnish the ships as well as, and much better than, the British." From Madison's perspective, "[a]nother unhappy effect of a continuance of the present anarchy of our commerce" was an unfavorable balance of trade, which "by draining us of our metals, furnishes pretexts for the pernicious substitution of paper money, for indulgences to debtors, [and] for postponements of taxes." Virginia congressional delegate James Monroe told Jefferson that the commerce of the nation was "daily declining" as a result of such discriminatory trade restrictions.[29]

Expressing concern that other nations might soon copy the British model—which they did—the Confederation Congress announced its wish and duty to respond "with similar and adequate restrictions on [British] commerce," if only the Articles could be amended to empower it to do so. Without such authority, the United States could "never command reciprocal advantages in trade, and without such reciprocity our foreign commerce must decline and eventually be annihilated." Washington declared that Great Britain was waging "a war of imposts" against the United States, "professedly upon a belief that we [the American states] never could unite in opposition to it." Until proving otherwise, Americans would be left standing "in a ridiculous point of view in the eyes of the nations of the earth." Rufus King reported that letters from American emissaries in Britain—especially John Adams, the American minister in London—were "most explicit that nothing is to be expected from the disposition of the court of London," which asked, "why should we form a commercial treaty, when we at present pocket all the advantages of the American commerce without a treaty?" Writing from Paris, Jefferson told Madison that granting Congress power over foreign trade "would produce a total revolution in their [Europeans'] opinion of us, and respect for us," which was critically important because "insult and war are the consequences of a want of respectability in the national character."[30]

States tried to respond on their own to British trade discrimination. For example, in 1785, New York imposed double duties and Rhode Island triple duties on all goods imported in British vessels. Such duties protected budding American manufacturers while simultaneously retaliating against British trade discrimination. In addition, beginning with Maryland in 1783, several states imposed discriminatory tonnage duties on British vessels docking in their ports.[31]

Yet, as Madison observed to Monroe, states acting in their separate capacities could never regulate trade effectively, any more than "they could separately carry on war." In a letter to Jefferson, Madison called it "little short of madness" for Virginia to bar British imports or to impose enormous duties on them without the concurrence of other states. Such measures "must prove vain and abortive," a congressional committee observed in 1785, because states would "avail themselves of this circumstance to turn it to their particular advantage." As Virginia congressional delegate Edward Carrington explained, states would enact such laws with "surreptitious views against each other, which must eventually destroy a source of revenue that might be immensely valuable to the whole union, and every effort prohibitory of foreign articles will also be vain."[32]

This is precisely what happened. When northern states with excellent ports (Massachusetts, Rhode Island, New York, and Pennsylvania) enacted duties on British trade, their neighbors (Connecticut, New Jersey, and Delaware) responded by establishing free ports. Naturally enough, in 1785 New York countered by decreeing that its steep import duties would also apply to goods produced and manufactured outside the United States that were imported into New York from surrounding states, unless it could be proved to the collector's satisfaction that the goods were not brought into America by British vessels.[33]

Observing such actions, Carrington noted that experience had demonstrated "the impossibility of managing the trade of America by state arrangements, and [the] necessity of vesting the federal head with full authority over that and every interest of the like general nature." Madison wrote Jefferson, "The necessity of harmony in the commercial regulations of the states has been rendered every day more apparent [as] . . . local efforts to counteract the policy of Great Britain, instead of succeeding, have in every instance recoiled more or less on the states which ventured on the trial." Madison worried that Great Britain and the rest of the world would be confirmed "in the belief that we are not to be respected, nor apprehended as a nation in matters of commerce." Indeed, by 1786, Britain was planning to bypass Congress entirely and send consuls to individual states to negotiate separate trade agreements.[34]

Under the Articles, Congress was powerless to regulate commerce between the states as well as with foreign nations. Thus, when several states began discriminating against the trade of their neighbors in the 1780s, Congress had no remedy available. In 1785, Monroe told Jefferson that fully to accomplish their objectives, states were finding it necessary to apply their laws regulating foreign trade to other states as well, which was producing "very mischievous effects." Several states imposed greater tonnage fees on vessels owned by citizens of other states that entered their ports than on those owned by their own citizens. In addition, beginning with Virginia in the early 1780s, some states subjected imported goods produced in other states to the same duties as those originating in other nations. For example, some southern states imposed the same duties on fish coming from New England as on fish imported from Canada. Madison concluded that such interstate trade discrimination, "though not [expressly] contrary to the federal [A]rticles, is certainly adverse to the spirit of the union, and tends to beget retaliating regulations, not less expensive and vexatious in themselves, than they are destructive of the general harmony."[35]

Indeed, when New York imposed port fees and tonnage duties on vessels coming from Connecticut and New Jersey, those states retaliated. New Jersey taxed the lighthouse that New York had erected at Sandy Hook, and some Connecticut merchants agreed to suspend all commercial dealings with New York for a year. Nathaniel Gorham, a Massachusetts congressional delegate, observed that it was only "the restraining hand of Congress (weak as it is) that prevents New Jersey and Connecticut from entering the lists very seriously with New York and bloodshed would very quickly be the consequence." Similarly, Governor Randolph of Virginia warned of the "jealousy, rivalship, and hatred" that were developing between trade rivals Virginia and Maryland as they retaliated against one another's commerce. Madison reported that Connecticut was imposing heavier duties on imports from Massachusetts than on those from Great Britain.[36]

Failed Efforts at Amendment

Contemporary statesmen were fully cognizant of the inconveniences caused by the absence of congressional power to levy taxes and to regulate foreign and domestic commerce. In 1781, New York congressional delegate James Duane wrote Washington, "The day is at length arrived when dangers and distresses have opened the eyes of the people and they perceive the want of a common head to draw forth in some just proportion the resources of the several branches of the federal union." Duane thought that people were coming to appreciate that state legislatures, "however reluctantly, must resign a portion of their authority to the national representative." Two years later, New York congressional delegate Alexander Hamilton wrote to Governor George Clinton: "Every day proves more and more the insufficiency of the Confederation. The proselytes to this opinion are increasing fast." In June 1783, General Washington, in his last official address to the nation as commander-in-chief, declared that the states must either "give such a tone to the federal government as will enable it to answer the ends of its institution" or else "relax the powers of the union, annihilate the cement of the Confederation and expose us to become the sport of European politics, which may play one state against another."[37]

Yet, augmenting Congress's powers under the Articles was difficult for two reasons. First, Article II authorized Congress to exercise only *expressly* delegated powers. In 1781, a congressional committee that included Madison was tasked with proposing a new article to confer upon Congress "full and explicit powers for effectually carrying into execution in the several states all acts or resolutions passed agreeably to the Articles of Confederation." The committee declared that, although Congress possessed a general and implied power to enforce the Articles against states refusing to abide by them, it was "most consonant to the spirit of a free Constitution that ... all exercise of power should be explicitly and precisely warranted." Because congressional exercise of implied powers was disfavored, to increase Congress's powers required an amendment to the Articles. (Indeed, as we shall see, this committee proposed a formal amendment to authorize Congress to use force to compel states to "fulfill their federal engagements.")[38]

Second, the Articles provided that amendments, once approved by Congress, required the unanimous consent of the thirteen state legislatures. Yet, as Hamilton noted in 1783, "The road to popularity in each state is to inspire jealousies of the power of Congress, though nothing can be more apparent than that [Congress has] no power." Moreover, because states had at least partially conflicting interests on virtually every imaginable issue, unanimous consent to proposed amendments would be extremely difficult to obtain. By 1787, Charles Pinckney, a congressional delegate from South Carolina, had concluded that "the depressed situation of the union is undoubtedly owing" to this "absurd" requirement of unanimous consent for amendments.[39]

During the 1780s, Congress proposed several amendments to expand its powers, but none of them secured the unanimous consent of the states that was required for ratification. In 1781, as the Revolutionary War continued to rage, Congress proposed an "indispensably necessary" amendment to empower it to levy a 5 percent duty on foreign imports.* The revenue therefrom was earmarked to pay interest and principal on the federal government's war-related debt. To minimize what Madison called "republican jealousy" toward the measure, the amendment provided that this grant of power to Congress would lapse once the debt was paid off. A broader proposal to grant Congress exclusive power to tax imports for any purpose it deemed sufficient could not even pass Congress.[40]

---

* Import duties became a practicable form of revenue only after France entered the war, and its navy weakened the British blockade on American ports.

In the 1780s, import duties were widely seen as "the most easy and equitable mode of raising a revenue." They were consumption taxes and thus, in a sense, voluntary. They were partially invisible to those who paid them because the tax blended with the price of the good. They were easy to collect—at a port in one fell swoop rather than at people's homes, one at a time. They also were usually imposed on luxury items—"[a]rticles which are generally consumed by the rich and affluent." Thus, they were progressive in their incidence relative to land or poll (head) taxes, which hit "the industrious farmer and mechanic" with equal force.[41]

Superintendent of Finance Robert Morris thought that the nation's future depended on enactment of the impost amendment: "We cannot be called a nation, nor do we deserve to be ranked amongst the nations of the earth, until we do justice to those who have served and trusted us. A public debt supported by public revenue will prove the strongest cement to keep our confederacy together." In addition, "in order that we may have pretension to credit in future," the United States must "do justice to those who have served and trusted us." Hamilton agreed that it would be "shocking and indeed an eternal reproach to this country, if we begin the peaceable enjoyment of our independence by a violation of all the principles of honesty and true policy." An additional benefit of a reliably funded public debt, as Morris and Hamilton noted, would be the creation of a medium that would circulate at face value and facilitate the payment of taxes—a significant attraction at a time of scarce hard currency.[42]

By the summer of 1782, all of the states required for ratification but one had approved the impost amendment.* However, tiny Rhode Island, with one-sixtieth of the nation's population, rejected the amendment, thus putting "a negative upon the collected wisdom of the continent." According to Madison and Hamilton, Rhode Island opposed the amendment because its own import duties had enabled it to fund part of its government expenses by taxing the portion of Connecticut's commerce that was imported through Providence and Newport.[43]

One of Rhode Island's congressional delegates, David Howell, offered a different explanation for his state's opposition to the impost amendment: Because Rhode Island had suffered the greatest maritime losses of any state during the war—Newport had 150 ships at sea in 1774, but only 3 in 1782—it was entitled to capitalize on its commercial advantages as a form of compensation.

---

* While the Articles required that amendments be approved by all thirteen states, Congress had determined that ratification of the impost amendment would be effective without the endorsement of those states unable to assemble their legislatures because of the war—i.e., Georgia and South Carolina, which were occupied by British troops when the amendment was proposed. However, South Carolina did manage to ratify in October 1782.

Rhode Islanders thought this especially justified while states such as Virginia were unjustly holding onto their claims to western lands, which—from Rhode Island's perspective—should have been ceded to Congress, which could then have sold the lands to pay off the federal government's debt.[44]

In addition, Howell argued that because Rhode Island had little manufacturing of its own, the state was unusually dependent on imports, which meant that its taxpayers would supply a disproportionate share of the federal government's funding under a congressional impost. Rhode Islanders also objected to the indefinite duration of the impost power (i.e., until the federal debt was retired, with no limits placed on Congress's ability to continue contracting debts) and to the use of federal officials to collect it—a "derogat[ion] from the sovereignty and independence of the state," from Rhode Island's perspective. As Rhode Island's congressional delegates told their governor, "The object of a seven-years war has been to preserve the liberties of this country, and not to assume, into our own [i.e., Congress's] hands, the power of governing tyranically."[45]

Whatever the true explanation, when Congress pressed Rhode Island, which had been stalling, for its answer in the autumn of 1782, the state legislature unanimously rejected the impost amendment.* Soon thereafter, Virginia rescinded its previous ratification, which some state legislators explained had been given only "amidst the alarms of war," when the legislature had been driven out of Richmond by the British army.[46]

Congress could not afford to drop the matter, however, because by the end of 1782, disgruntled army officers stationed at Newburgh, New York, were sending a deputation to petition Congress for their back pay and pensions and to hint at the use of force, if necessary, to secure their demands. One North Carolina congressional delegate, Abner Nash, reported that "[a] deputation from the northern army is now before Congress stating their distress and prophesying what will be the probable consequence if practicing any longer on the patience of the soldiery." A Connecticut congressional delegate, Eliphalet Dyer, who opposed the officers' pension claims, noted that they had "thrown out many indecent threats" and, "at the point of a bayonet, threaten not to disband even if peace is established, but to make themselves a complete compensation by force of arms."[47]

At least some nationalists within the government—most notably, congressional delegate Hamilton, and Superintendent of Finance Robert Morris and his deputy Gouverneur Morris—were not averse to encouraging the officers

---

* In 1790, Vice President John Adams observed that Rhode Island's rejection of the impost amendment "seems to have been the instrument which Providence thought fit to use for the great purpose of establishing the . . . Constitution."

to threaten mutiny unless their demands were satisfied, in order to pressure Congress into supporting an impost amendment and other revenue-raising measures. Virginia congressional delegate Arthur Lee, an opponent of the nationalists, observed that "[t]he terror of a mutinying army is played off with considerable efficacy" in an effort "to obtain permanent taxes and the appointment of [revenue] collectors by Congress."[48]*

While the officers' deputation was still in Philadelphia, Gouverneur Morris wrote to General Henry Knox, who headed the committee of army officers that had drafted the petition to Congress. Morris told Knox that the army should connect itself "with the public creditors of every kind, both foreign and domestic, and unremittingly urge the grant of general permanent funds." He warned, "The same principle of convenience which will lead them to take care of the army and leave other creditors unnoticed will operate effectually against the army when it is disbanded after a peace. During the war they find you useful and after a peace they will wish to get rid of you and then they will see you starve rather than pay a six penny tax." Hugh Williamson, a congressional delegate from North Carolina, similarly declared that he "did not wish the army to disband until proper provision should be made for [it]; that if force should be necessary to excite justice, the sooner force were applied the better."[49]

Even Knox, who did not wish to sully "the reputation of the American Army, as one of the most immaculate things upon earth," admitted that "there is a point beyond which there is no sufferance." Only a timely and deft intervention by General Washington averted the possible mutiny.[50]

Meanwhile, Congress debated proposals for a new impost amendment and for empowering Congress to lay other taxes as well, such as taxes on land and polls and an excise tax on liquor. Robert Morris had strongly recommended such measures in his Report on Public Credit the previous year. But in early 1783, Congress had difficulty reaching any consensus—for several reasons.[51]

---

* Expressing anxiety to "avert the consequences which would result from their [the soldiers'] disappointment" over not being paid, John Francis Mercer, a Virginia congressional delegate, supported a proposal to allocate entirely to the pay of soldiers the proceeds of a proposed amendment authorizing Congress to lay import duties. However, nationalists in Congress, such as Hamilton and James Wilson of Pennsylvania, strongly opposed this proposal, which they knew would diminish the incentive of other federal creditors to lobby state legislatures to approve the amendment. Hamilton told Washington that states whose civilian citizens owned a large share of the federal debt would not support an impost amendment if the proceeds were dedicated to paying only soldiers: "It is in vain to tell men who have parted with a large part of their property on the public faith that the services of the army are entitled to a preference." The nationalists believed that enacting an impost amendment would require the joint lobbying efforts of all federal creditors.

Figure 1.1 Robert Morris (on the right) and Gouverneur Morris, the superintendent of finance and his deputy, respectively. (Courtesy of the Pennsylvania Academy of the Fine Arts, Philadelphia. Bequest of Richard Ashhurst)

First, at least some delegates preferred that Congress remain, in the words of Richard Henry Lee of Virginia, more "a rope of sand than a rod of iron." To grant the power of the purse to a body that already possessed the power of the sword was "pregnant with dangerous consequences to the liberties of the confederated states." Second, according to Madison, even though most congressional delegates were "convinced of the necessity of a continental revenue for an honorable discharge of the continental engagements and for making future provision for the war," they feared their constituents would revolt at the "enormous" sums required—perhaps as much as $3 million annually.[52]

Third, states had obviously conflicting interests over which sorts of taxes should be imposed. For example, with regard to a land tax, New Englanders favored a flat rate based on acreage rather than an assessment based on the value of land because most farmland in that region had been improved; southerners preferred the opposite. Proposals for a poll tax raised the inevitable question of whether slaves would be counted. As Virginia congressional delegate Joseph Jones reported to Washington, "[D]ifficulties apparently insurmountable presented themselves in almost every stage of the business, owing to the different circumstances of the several states." One additional advantage of the impost was that nobody knew precisely where its incidence would fall—that is, which states' citizens would pay the most of it. Moreover, all proposals to raise revenue from taxes reignited resentment among delegates from the states without claims to western lands, who argued that the revenue to be raised from selling those lands should belong to the nation.[53]

In the end, lack of consensus within Congress disabled it from going further in 1783 than simply requesting again that the states enact an impost amendment—this time authorizing Congress to impose specified import duties on particular items, and a flat 5 percent rate on all others, for the sole purpose of discharging interest and principal "on the debts contracted on the faith of the United States for supporting the war." To make the proposal more palatable to the states, this proposed amendment limited the authorization to twenty-five years and provided that officials appointed by the states (though removable only by Congress) would collect the revenue. Congress simultaneously recommended that the states establish—also for a term limited to twenty-five years and to be collected by state officials—"substantial and effectual revenues of such nature as they may judge most convenient" for supplying their respective proportions of an additional $1.5 million annually to be used to discharge the federal debt.[54]

Deeming the 1783 proposals badly deficient, the ultranationalist Hamilton voted against them as likely to "fail in the execution" even if ratified by the states (although he urged New York's governor to support ratification). Hamilton declared there was "a moral certainty" that the public debt would not be "fairly extinguished" before the twenty-five-year authorization had expired, and states whose citizens owned only a small share of the federal debt probably would appoint as collectors the people least likely to vigorously raise the revenue, thus throwing an unfair burden on "those states which are governed by most liberal principles." By this time, Robert Morris had grown so desperate that he would have preferred that Congress issue an ultimatum to the states, announcing that because of its obligation to pay the federal debt, it would simply assert the power to collect taxes within any state that had failed to pay its quota.[55]

Once again, twelve states ratified the impost amendment—with far fewer approving Congress's recommendation for supplemental funding, which was supposed to be indivisible from the impost amendment—though in Massachusetts and Virginia, considerable opposition had to be overcome. Even formerly recalcitrant Rhode Island approved the amendment. This time, New York was the holdout.[56]

In 1780, when New York City was still occupied by British troops and the war was going badly, the New York legislature had instructed its congressional delegates and its commissioners to a convention of northern states meeting in Hartford, Connecticut, that Congress should "exercise every power which [it] may deem necessary for an effectual prosecution of the war" (including using the army to collect requisitions from delinquent states). In 1781, the New York legislature had quickly ratified the first impost amendment, and the following year it had called for a national convention to amend the Articles to empower Congress to levy an impost.[57]

Yet with the end of the war in 1783, New Yorkers' military rationale for a strong federal government empowered to levy impost duties evaporated. By the mid-1780s, New Yorkers were making ideological arguments against granting Congress independent revenue-raising authority. Combining the sword with the purse, especially in a government responsible for such a broad geographic area, would be certain to "sacrifice our liberties." Congress already was vested with greater power than most confederation governments in history had been. To grant it independent taxing authority as well, these New Yorkers argued, would inevitably raise "a mighty continental legislat[ure]" that would eventually "merge and swallow up the legislatures of the particular states." That the impost was the least onerous of taxes actually constituted an argument against its enactment because its "imperceptible operation will render it more easy to be continued and made perpetual." Finally, New Yorkers objected to Congress's having sent deputations to legislatures in Virginia and Rhode Island to influence deliberations on the first impost amendment, which they thought resembled the king's trying to influence proceedings in the House of Commons.[58]

Yet the true basis of New Yorkers' opposition to the second impost amendment was probably more self-interested: New York had enacted its own import duties in 1784, which generated substantial revenue as transatlantic trade picked up following the war. In the mid-1780s, New York's impost generated enough revenue to fund one-third to one-half of the state's annual operating expenses. Such revenue enabled the legislature to keep real estate taxes low, which helped New York to avoid the rural discontent that plagued many other states around this time, while simultaneously making higher per capita contributions to Congress than any other state.[59]

Not surprisingly, New Yorkers were reluctant to approve a federal impost that would inevitably interfere with or entirely displace their own. One New Yorker observed that the revenue derived from the port of New York City was "a privilege Providence hath endowed us with"—not something that should be surrendered to Congress. Monroe told Madison that, in addition, New York legislators who owned large amounts of federal securities intended for the state to assume that debt and reasoned that "[t]he more extensive the funds of the state, and the more fully they exclude the citizens of other states and foreigners from such provision, the better of course for the[m]."[60]

New Yorkers also had grievances against Congress that may have contributed to the legislature's refusal to unconditionally ratify the second impost amendment. They blamed Congress for not pressuring the British, in accordance with their treaty obligations, to relinquish the western forts, which New Yorkers felt had "robbed them of the fur trade," at a cost of at least tens of thousands of dollars per year. In addition, many New Yorkers resented Congress for largely siding with Vermonters since 1777, when they had declared themselves an independent state on land claimed by New York. Whatever the true explanation, the New York legislature resisted ratifying the second impost amendment, leading Washington to observe that it was "somewhat singular" that New York, previously "foremost in all federal measures," had now turned "her face against them in almost every instance."[61]

New York sought to leverage its holdout position—as the only state not to have ratified the amendment—to extract concessions from Congress. In 1786, rather than flatly rejecting the amendment, the New York legislature approved it on the conditions that New York retain removal authority over the customs officers collecting the duties and that Congress accept the state's paper money in lieu of the hard currency collected. Madison regarded New York's proposal as a compliance "more . . . in appearance than reality." Congress balked at these conditions, and New York governor George Clinton twice refused Congress's request to call a special legislative session to reconsider them. The impost amendment went unratified.[62]

Citizens of New Jersey and Connecticut were outraged by New York's refusal to ratify the impost amendment. Half of the foreign goods imported into those states came through the port of New York City. As a leading New Jersey statesman complained, "New York and Pennsylvania can raise their quota of specie [gold and silver] by state imposts, to which our citizens by trading with them will contribute as much as theirs in proportion to their numbers, and after will have the full quota of this state to pay besides. This is a burden too unequal and grievous for this state to submit to."[63]

With New York declining to unconditionally approve the impost amendment, the New Jersey legislature resolved no longer to honor congressional requisitions until the impost had been ratified or states had repealed their own import duties. The legislature declared that it was unfair for New Jersey to have to resort to direct taxes when all "cool and considerate men [agree] that an impost was the only practicable means of procuring money to pay the interest of our foreign debt, and that it is the most easy and equitable mode of raising a revenue," yet "neither the justice [n]or magnanimity of some of the states will suffer it to be done in th[is] way."[64]

Many congressional delegates were reported to be "a good deal alarmed" by New Jersey's action, which was a direct challenge to Congress's rapidly fading authority. Although conceding that the state had just grounds for feeling aggrieved by New York, Nathaniel Gorham believed that New Jersey's refusal to pay its congressional requisitions was unjustified, and he predicted that such an action would "work the end of all federal government." John Beatty, a former congressional delegate from New Jersey, called the legislature's action "mortifying" and "extremely reprehensible," and he warned that it would tend "to the dissolving of a union already too feebly united." Beatty thought that New Jersey should have asked Congress for an abatement of its quota on account of its "unfavorable local situation in point of trade" before "attempt[ing] to redress ourselves at the expense of the union at large." Madison likewise called New Jersey's action "certainly a rash one," which would "furnish fresh pretexts to unwilling states for withholding their contributions."[65]

Congress immediately dispatched a delegation of three congressmen to New Jersey to try to convince the legislature of "the fatal consequences that must inevitably result to the said state, as well as to the rest of the union, from [its] refusal to comply with the requisition." The delegation warned the legislature that its actions would constitute "a breach of the confederation," that small states such as New Jersey had the most to lose from disunion, and that a new confederation might reject the principle of equal state representation in its legislature. The proper course of action, the delegation explained, was for New Jersey's congressmen to propose that Congress call a general convention to revise the Articles.[66]

While the New Jersey legislature eventually rescinded its resolution rejecting the congressional requisition, it never attempted to collect the taxes necessary to pay the state's quota. The impost amendment was never ratified, despite Congress's pleas to the states that nothing else could "rescue us from bankruptcy, or preserve the union of the several states from dissolution."[67]

Another proposed amendment to vest Congress with certain powers over commerce met a similar fate. In 1783, a congressional committee, responding to reports that Great Britain and France were contemplating discriminatory trade restrictions against the United States, deemed it "of the highest importance" that "a general power be somewhere lodged" to respond in kind. Two years later, Charles Thomson, the secretary of Congress, reported that "[t]he conduct of our late enemy since the peace has done a great deal towards preparing the minds of the people" to grant Congress the power to regulate foreign commerce. Only such a power could relieve the nation "from the embarrassed and humiliating state under which we now labor."[68]

Thus, in 1784, Congress approved an amendment to invest it, for a term of fifteen years, with certain powers to regulate foreign trade. Specifically, the proposal would have empowered Congress to prohibit the importation or exportation of goods shipped in vessels owned or navigated by citizens of nations that had not concluded commercial treaties with the United States. In addition, Congress would have been empowered to bar foreign subjects trading in America from importing goods produced in any country but their own, unless so authorized by treaty. These powers would have enabled Congress to press other nations for reciprocal trade agreements.[69]

In 1785, a congressional committee proposed an even broader commerce amendment, which was enthusiastically supported by northern merchants. Under this proposal, Congress would gain the power "of regulating the trade of the states as well with foreign nations as with each other and of laying such imposts and duties upon imports and exports as may be necessary for the purpose." Monroe, who served on the committee making the proposal, called it an "absolute investment of the United States with the control of commerce." He told Jefferson the amendment would empower Congress to enact "[t]he measures necessary to obtain the carrying trade [and] to encourage domestic [manufactures] by a tax on foreign industry."[70]

Various provisos were added to the 1785 amendment to allay the concerns of southern delegates and of those delegates who, as Monroe described their objections, considered it "dangerous to concentrate power since it might be turned to mischievous purposes." Under the committee's proposal, US citizens were never to be subjected to higher duties and imposts than those imposed on subjects of foreign powers. In addition, the legislative power of the states would "not be restrained from prohibiting the importation or exportation of any species of goods or commodities whatsoever," and "all such duties as may be imposed [by Congress] shall be collected under the authority and accrue to the use of the state in which the same shall be payable." Finally, a supermajority of nine state delegations would have been necessary for all exercises of this congressional commerce power—a mechanism that would enable the South, a regional minority, to veto commercial regulations that it feared would disadvantage it.[71]

Notwithstanding the provisos that were intended to ease suspicions, Congress delayed taking up the committee report because, as Monroe told Jefferson, "The importance of the subject and the deep and radical change it will create in the bond of the union, together with the conviction that something must be done, seems to create an aversion or rather a fear of acting on it." Congress eventually twice debated the committee proposal but never approved it because of the strong opposition manifested toward it.[72]

Meanwhile, the states were considering Congress's 1784 proposal to invest itself with a limited power to regulate foreign commerce. While all the states eventually approved this proposal, they did so with so many different qualifications—especially as to the effective date from which the fifteen-year grant of power would run—that Congress could not consider the amendment to have been unanimously ratified. In general, the largest obstacle to ratification of any grant of commercial power to Congress was resistance from southern states, which feared that such power would be used to their disadvantage.[73]

In the 1780s, the southern economy was dominated by the export of agricultural staples—mostly tobacco, indigo, and rice (not cotton until the 1790s). Southerners imported almost all of their manufactured items and luxury consumer goods. Lacking a merchant marine, the South depended almost entirely on others to ship both its imports and its exports. Although southern planters stood to benefit if Congress could use a commerce power to pry open foreign markets for their agricultural exports, they worried that Congress would use the power to enact "navigation acts" designed to protect the northern carrying trade from foreign competition—laws that would raise the cost of southern shipping. To a somewhat lesser extent, southerners were also concerned that Congress would use the commerce power to enact tariffs to protect northern manufacturers from the competition of foreign imports—laws that would raise the cost of southern imports.[74]

Thus, for example, Virginia chancellor Edmund Pendleton told Madison that while he agreed that Congress needed additional power, he was wary of granting it the authority to regulate commerce. Pendleton explained that Virginians, possessed of "a valuable staple to export" (tobacco) and few manufacturing establishments to furnish farm implements and consumer necessities, naturally favored free trade, which would enable them to secure the highest prices for their crops and the lowest prices for their imports. By contrast, the northern manufacturing states favored import duties to enable them to raise the price of the goods they sold. Moreover, the relatively greater number of northern states must "at least awak[en] caution" with regard to how Congress would exercise a power to regulate commerce.[75]

Pendleton's fellow Virginian Richard Henry Lee, who was president of Congress at this point, had a similar perspective.* Lee conceded that Congress might use the power to regulate commerce to pressure the British to be "reasonable by a very careful and considerate restraining of their trade in all cases where we shall not injure ourselves more than them by the restraint." Yet

---

* Richard Henry Lee was born in 1732 in Westmoreland County, Virginia, to a family of politically and socially prominent planters. Lee himself was elected to the Virginia House of Burgesses in 1758. In the 1760s, he was an early advocate of resistance to British measures such as the Stamp Act and an architect of Virginia's policy of boycotting British imports. In the 1770s, he helped establish colonial committees of correspondence and rallied resistance in Virginia to

he also worried that "giving Congress a power to legislate over the trade of
the union would be dangerous in the extreme to the five southern or staple
states, whose want [i.e., lack] of ships and seamen would expose their freightage and their produce to a most pernicious and destructive monopoly." The
eight northern states "would be stimulated by extensive interest to shut close
the door of monopoly" and put both the purchasing price of the South's produce and the fees for carrying it at their mercy.* Moreover, "the progress of
intrigues in Congress" demonstrated "[w]hat little difficulty there would be
in drawing over one of the five [southern states] to join the eight interested
states," thus satisfying the requisite supermajority for commercial legislation.
As inconvenient as British trade discrimination was, "it demands most careful
circumspection that the remedy be not worse than the disease." Lee concluded
that Congress did not need the power to regulate commerce because "a well
digested system of restraint being properly laid before the states by Congress
would be universally adopted by the different assemblies," as it would be "most
evidently the interest of all to do so."[76]

Parliament's so-called Intolerable Acts, which, in response to the Boston Tea Party, closed the
port of Boston and dismantled the Massachusetts system of government.

In 1774, the Virginia legislature appointed Lee as one of the state's delegates to the First
Continental Congress. Known as a great orator, Lee was an influential figure in the drive for
American independence. Among other things, he endorsed the Suffolk Resolves, which urged defiance of the Intolerable Acts, called for a boycott of trade with Great Britain, and encouraged the
colonies to raise militia for defense. In May 1776, Lee and John Adams secured a congressional
resolution advising the colonies to form their own state governments. The following month, Lee,
acting on instructions from a Virginia convention, made a motion for a congressional declaration
of independence. Lee served in Congress for several years during the war and in 1784 was elected
its president.

In 1787, Lee, pleading ill health, declined his appointment to represent Virginia at the
Constitutional Convention. The following year, he offered the same reason for declining to stand
for election as a delegate to the Virginia ratifying convention. However, as we shall see, Lee
nonetheless emerged as one of the most prominent and influential Antifederalists in the country.
First, he sought to amend the Constitution in Congress, where it was sent immediately after the
Philadelphia convention. Failing in that effort, Lee then tried, through his correspondence, to
organize opposition throughout the country, and he may have been the author of one of the most
widely read and admired Antifederalist tracts, Letters to the Republican, authored by "Federal
Farmer." While Lee praised many features of the Constitution, he insisted on the need for
amendments prior to ratification and especially urged the importance of securing a bill of rights.

In 1788, the Virginia legislature appointed Lee as one of Virginia's first US senators, rejecting Madison in the process. As a senator, Lee criticized as inadequate the constitutional amendments Madison maneuvered through the House of Representatives, which became the Bill of
Rights. In 1792, Lee resigned from the Senate and returned to Virginia, where he died in 1794.

* Most contemporaries spoke of eight northern states and five southern states, with the
boundary being the northern border of Maryland. However, occasionally, Delaware would be put
in the southern camp, which meant that there were six southern states and seven northern ones.
Because the eight-to-five division was more frequently used, I will adhere to that convention.

Not all southerners felt as Pendleton and Lee did about the commerce power. Washington thought it "so self-evident" that Congress ought to have this power that he was "at a loss to discover wherein lies the weight of the objection." Nor did Madison have any doubt that Congress required a plenary power to regulate trade. While free trade might be preferable in the abstract, the United States could not remain a "passive victim" of British trade discrimination, and the states were powerless to respond effectively on their own. Moreover, Madison did not believe that southerners had much to fear from such a power. The supermajority requirement for any commercial legislation was an important safeguard because "a case can scarcely be imagined in which it would be the interest of any two-thirds of the states to oppress the remaining one-third."[77]

Perhaps more important, Madison believed that "the commercial interests of the states . . . meet in more points than they differ." Every state, north and south, ought to have been keenly interested in reopening the West Indies trade. Moreover, given Britain's current domination of the South's carrying trade, Madison could not understand why southerners would object to transferring that trade to their northern brethren from "those who have not yet entitled themselves to the name of friends."[78]

Yet Madison predicted that his arguments would not be "relished in the public councils" of Virginia, where minds were "unaccustomed to consider the interests of the state as they are interwoven with those of the Confederacy, much less as they may be affected by foreign politics." Only the fact that the power requested by Congress was "to be exerted against Great Britain and the proposition will consequently be seconded by the animosities which still prevail in a strong degree against her" gave Madison any hope that Virginia might acquiesce to the proposed amendment.[79]

Madison was right to have been pessimistic about the Virginia legislature's reaction to the proposal. When it was debated there, he found the opponents to be "bitter and illiberal against Congress and the northern states, beyond example." One legislator even expressed the view, according to Madison, that Virginia should prefer "to encourage the British than the eastern* marine." In the end, supporters of the amendment concluded that the best they could secure from the Virginia legislature was worse than nothing, so they dropped the proposal and substituted a resolution calling for a general convention of

---

* Contemporary usage often referred to the New England states as "eastern," whereas today we would be more inclined to call them "northern" or "northeastern." I will stick with the modern convention but will not change quotations from the contemporary sources, except where not doing so might cause confusion (and, of course, I will indicate with brackets when I have made changes from the original).

state commissioners to consider and recommend a federal plan for regulating commerce—what became the Annapolis convention, as we shall see in chapter 2.[80]

The failure of the commerce amendment was gravely disturbing to Virginia nationalists. Monroe, who was at least a seminationalist on this issue, told Madison that he had "always considered the regulation of trade in the hands of the United States as necessary to preserve the union. Without it, it will infallibly tumble to pieces." Remedying defects in the federal system was crucial, Madison told Monroe, "not only because such amendments will make it better answer the purpose for which it was instituted, but because I apprehend danger to its very existence from a continuance of defects which expose a part if not the whole of the empire to severe distress." Madison told Jefferson that he dreaded the consequences if the minority of southern states deprived the majority of northern states "of a regular remedy for their distresses by the want of a federal spirit." Such a development might create "the strongest motives to some irregular experiments," as the suffering part of the union could not "long respect a government which is too feeble to protect their interest." Indeed, Madison wondered if the British did not discriminate against American trade "as much from the hope of effecting a breach in our confederacy as of monopolizing our trade."[81]

Madison had good reason to be worried, as some northerners were indeed growing exasperated with southern intransigence on the commerce amendment. Great Britain's discriminatory trade restrictions hit northerners—shippers, shipbuilders, and fishermen—the hardest. Rufus King,* a congressional delegate from Massachusetts, wrote to John Adams in London, "Our commerce is almost ruined because jealousies of an unwarrantable nature

---

* King was born near Portland, Maine, in 1755, the son of a prosperous lawyer-merchant, who became a Loyalist during the Revolutionary War. After graduating from Harvard in 1777, King studied law under Theophilus Parsons (who later served as chief justice of the Supreme Judicial Court of Massachusetts) in Newburyport. In 1778, he volunteered for militia service, but saw only limited battlefield action.

In the mid-1780s, King served in the Massachusetts House of Representatives and then in the Confederation Congress, where he helped to draft the ordinance that organized the Northwest Territory and forbade slavery there. While in Congress, King also, as we shall see, supported Secretary for Foreign Affairs John Jay's efforts to barter American claims to free navigation of the Mississippi River in exchange for a commercial treaty with Spain. A fellow delegate described King as exercising "unrivaled influence" in Congress as a result of his outstanding oratorical skills.

King initially opposed the call for the Constitutional Convention in 1786, though he later changed his mind and was appointed to the Massachusetts delegation. At the convention, King was an important voice in support of a strong national government and a powerful executive. According to the description of fellow convention delegate William Pierce, King was "much

have been disseminated through the more southern states." He told Adams of the "bitter regret" that "the false commercial reasonings and ill-founded policy" of the southern states were causing in the North. In a letter to wealthy Boston merchant Jonathan Jackson, King wondered "[h]ow long the most valuable and important interest of the states will continue to be sacrificed to these unfounded jealousies."[82]

King explained that even if the British were right to believe that "the southern and [northern] states cannot agree in any system of commerce which will oppose to Great Britain commercial disadvantages similar to those which she imposes on our commerce and navigation," the eight northern states *could* agree. They had "common objects, are under similar embarrassments, [and] would vest adequate powers in Congress to regulate external and internal commerce." If the southern states continued to "decline to vest similar powers in Congress or to agree in some uniform system," then the northern states would form "a sub-confederation" to remedy "their present embarrassment."[83]

In the end, the commerce amendment failed, as did every other proposed alteration of the Articles. Even when a strong consensus for reform existed, at least one state had interests militating against it. In 1786, King observed that "the imaginary interests of the states are so opposite that without the danger of some evil that will affect each member of the confederacy, a reasonable

distinguished for his eloquence and great parliamentary talents" and "ranked among the luminaries of the present age." King later supported ratification of the Constitution as a delegate to the Massachusetts ratifying convention.

In 1789, King moved to New York City, three years after marrying the daughter of a wealthy New York merchant. The New York legislature quickly appointed him one of the state's original US senators. That same year, contemporaries referred to King as "a man of genius" and "the most eloquent man in the United States." As a senator, King strongly supported the economic policies of Secretary of the Treasury Alexander Hamilton, and he was appointed one of the directors of the first Bank of the United States. After staunchly defending the controversial treaty that John Jay negotiated with Great Britain in 1795, King, with Hamilton's strong endorsement, was appointed the following year by President Washington as minister plenipotentiary to Great Britain, a post he held until 1803.

Returning to the United States, King was the Federalist Party's candidate for vice president in both 1804 and 1808. (The Federalist ticket was badly defeated both times.) Appointed again to the US Senate in 1812, King led the opposition to the Madison administration's conduct of the War of 1812, though he refused to participate in the secessionist Hartford Convention. In 1816, King was the presidential candidate of the dying Federalist Party, winning the electoral votes of just three states. Appointed yet again to the Senate in 1820, King strongly opposed the admission of Missouri to the union as a slave state. He remained in the Senate until 1825, then served one more year as minister to Great Britain, before returning to New York, where he died in 1827. All told, King served his state and nation for more than thirty years as a politician and diplomat, rising to the highest ranks in one of the two parties that dominated politics in the early decades of the republic.

Figure 1.2 Rufus King (in 1818), who represented Massachusetts in the Philadelphia convention and supported ratification of the Constitution at the Massachusetts ratifying convention. (Courtesy of Independence National Historical Park)

hope cannot be indulged of a reform." Madison lamented to Jefferson that all efforts to reform the federal system were "frustrated by the selfishness or perverseness of some part or other of their [congressional delegates'] constituents." The problem would only grow worse in the future, Madison told Washington: "[T]he difficulty now found in obtaining a unanimous concurrence of the states in any measure whatever," deriving from "caprice, jealousy, and diversity of opinions," would "increase with every increase of [the] number [of states] and perhaps in a greater ratio, as the ultramontane states may either have or suppose they have a less similitude of interests to the Atlantic states than these have to one another."[84]

In 1786, a congressional committee proposed discarding the unanimity requirement and stipulating that the concurrence of eleven states would suffice to change the Articles with regard to congressional proposals for "any new systems of revenue" or "new regulations in the finances of the United States," for a limited term not exceeding fifteen years, but Congress never approved this amendment. In 1787, the Philadelphia convention would address this problem by eliminating the unanimity requirement—both for ratification of the Constitution and for subsequent amendments to it.[85]

Other Flaws in the Articles

The lack of congressional power to levy taxes and the inability to regulate commerce were the most glaring deficiencies of the Articles, but they were not the only ones. Chief among other flaws were the requirement of unanimity for amendments and the supermajority requirement for Congress to exercise its most important enumerated powers—meaning that the approval of delegations from nine states, rather than a simple majority of seven, was necessary before Congress could, for example, declare war, enter into treaties, appropriate funds, or borrow money.[86]

Securing the assent of nine state delegations to any measure proved difficult at a time when Congress frequently lacked even a simple operating quorum, which required the presence of at least two delegates apiece from seven states. In the summer of 1785, William Grayson of Virginia reported that "the states have been so irregularly represented that it has been impracticable to act upon any matter of consequence," and several months later he observed that Congress was "in a kind of political torpor" because of the small number of state delegations in attendance. Nathaniel Gorham of Massachusetts complained of "the great inattention and negligence of the states with regard to their representation," which prevented Congress from attending to "matters in which the welfare of the union is deeply interested." In the summer of 1786, Secretary for Foreign Affairs John Jay complained to Jefferson that, for lack of a quorum, he "often experiences unseasonable delays and successive obstacles in obtaining the decision and sentiments of Congress, even on points which require dispatch."[87]

Grayson diagnosed the problem: State delegations would "come forward and be very assiduous till they have carried some state job and then decamp with precipitation, leaving the public business to shift for itself." In addition, congressional delegates often were absent from Congress because their salaries did not adequately cover their living expenses, much less compensate them for the inconvenience caused to their personal lives from being absent from home for months at a time. In an era of relatively primitive transportation, simply getting to New York City or Philadelphia (or wherever Congress happened to be sitting at the moment) could be onerous. Service in state legislatures, which unlike Congress were not in virtually continuous session, required much less personal sacrifice because of the lesser distances to be traveled.[88]

Thus, in 1779, Virginia delegate William Fleming told Governor Thomas Jefferson that he did not wish to be reappointed to another term in Congress because "besides my own loss of time, and the long separation from my family, my expenses are so enormous that I find my fortune quite insufficient to support them," notwithstanding his frugal living habits. Fleming warned that if the state legislature did not better support its congressional delegates, it would "shortly find that none of those of small fortunes will be able to continue here long enough to make themselves acquainted with the business they come to transact." Two years later, another Virginia delegate, Theodorick Bland, complained that the legislature had failed to pay his salary, his private credit was exhausted, and he could feed neither himself nor his horses, which he had been forced to offer for sale. He wrote Jefferson, "The anxiety I feel in this situation (new, to me) is insupportable especially as it in some degree incapacitates me from turning my thoughts with that application I would wish to do to those important concerns which I would wish to engross my whole attention."[89]

Not only did Congress have trouble mustering a simple quorum, but the Articles' supermajority requirement for the exercise of important congressional powers disabled action in the face of a large and durable minority voting bloc. As Hamilton noted in 1783, such a supermajority requirement tended "to subject the sense of the majority to that of the minority, by putting it in the power of a small combination to retard and even to frustrate the most necessary measures and to oblige the greater number, in cases which require speedy determinations, as happens in the most interesting concerns of the community, to come into the views of the smaller." In the 1780s, the requirement that nine state delegations concur in order for Congress to act on most important issues meant that the five southern states could effectively block measures favored by the eight northern states.[90]

Even when the Confederation Congress was able to act, the method of delegate selection employed by the Articles ensured that they would take a parochial—rather than a nationalist—approach. Congressional delegates were chosen in a manner specified by state legislatures—in practice, this generally meant legislative appointment—for one-year terms, during which time they were subject to legislative recall. They were also beholden to their state legislatures for their salaries. As Madison complained to Jefferson, "[T]he spirit of those who compose Congress is rather that of advocates for the respective interest of their constituents" than "of impartial judges."[91]

It seems extraordinary that so many Americans would be deeply suspicious of expanding the powers of a Congress whose members were this dependent upon state legislatures. In 1784, when a congressional committee recommended that Congress be empowered to regulate commerce, it expressed doubt "that a free people would be jealous of [i.e., anxious about] men whom they choose from year to year to consult and guard their interest." In 1785, Washington wrote, "[I]t is one of the most extraordinary things in nature that we should confederate for national purposes, and yet be afraid to give the rulers . . .—who are the creatures of our own making, appointed for a limited and short duration, who are amenable for every action, recallable at any moment, and subject to all the evils they may be instrumental in producing— sufficient powers to order and direct the affairs of [the] nation." The following year, he told John Jay, "To be fearful of vesting Congress, constituted as that body is, with ample authorities for national purposes, appears to me the very climax of popular absurdity and madness." Washington feared that rather than abusing their powers, such congressional representatives would exercise their authority "very timidly and inefficaciously for fear of losing their popularity and future election."[92]

Not only were congressional delegates limited to annual terms, but to avoid the possibility of their becoming entrenched in office, the Articles limited service to three years within any six-year period. Thus, even the most gifted congressional delegates, such as Madison, were periodically rotated out of office. Critics of the Articles denounced this "custom of turning men out of power or office as soon as they are qualified for it." Government was "a science, and can never be perfected in America until we encourage men to devote not only three years, but their whole lives to it." Some of the most talented individuals would refuse to serve under such conditions.[93*]

The Articles were flawed in yet another fundamental way. Even when Congress could assemble the requisite quorum or supermajority to act on an issue upon which the Articles explicitly granted it authority, Congress had no effective means of imposing its will upon the states. As Madison wrote later, the Articles manifested "a mistaken confidence . . . [in] the justice, the good faith, the honor, [and] the sound policy of the several legislative assemblies." It had become clear that "a unanimous and punctual obedience of 13 independent bodies to the acts of the federal government ought not be calculated on."[94]

For example, the Articles expressly authorized Congress to enter into treaties with foreign nations. One provision in the Treaty of Paris, which ended the Revolutionary War with Great Britain, declared that "creditors on either side shall meet with no lawful impediment to the recovery of the full value

---

* Madison also worried that, in practice, mandatory rotation was producing "a change in the federal councils not favorable to those catholic arrangements on which the harmony and stability of the union must greatly depend." He also observed that "experience constantly teaches that new members of a public body do not feel the necessary respect or responsibility for the acts of their predecessors, and that a change of members and of circumstances often proves fatal to consistency and stability of public measures."

in sterling money of all bona fide debts heretofore contracted." Other provisions in the treaty obliged Congress to "earnestly recommend" that the states provide restitution for property confiscated from British subjects or American Loyalists (American citizens who remained loyal to Great Britain during the war) and forbade future confiscations and prosecutions for actions taken during the war.[95]

Yet words on a piece of paper were insufficient to deter state legislatures from pursuing policies that were popular among constituents. On Congress's recommendation, many states during the war had enacted legislation confiscating Loyalists' land, which netted some of them—New York especially—millions of dollars. Little political support existed for undoing such confiscations. Nor, after a long and bitter war, were most Americans eager to repay prewar debts to British creditors. Indeed, George Mason reported that many Virginians seemed to have regarded the whole point of the war as being to escape paying debts owed to British merchants. Several states passed laws temporarily barring recovery of such debts, allowing recovery only in installments, authorizing repayment in kind rather than in cash, and precluding recovery of interest on debts that had gone unpaid during the lengthy war. In at least one state, public opinion was so hostile to repayment of such debts that lawyers were intimidated from filing suits for recovery.[96]

As Madison later explained, for states to behave this way was hardly surprising. Congressional measures necessarily bore unequally on different states, which were understandably partial to the interests of their own citizens. "Courtiers of popularity," according to Madison, exaggerated the inequalities that existed and suspected others that did not. In addition, states would be reluctant to perform burdensome federal obligations if they suspected that other states might refuse to comply. Thus, Madison reported to Monroe that when the subject of paying prewar British debts came up in the Virginia legislature, "no pains were spared to disparage the treaty by insinuations against Congress, the eastern states, and the negotiators of the treaty, particularly John Adams." Grayson worried that even if Virginia acknowledged its obligations under the treaty, other states might refuse to do so, which would leave Great Britain free to ignore those treaty commitments that Virginians were most interested in seeing enforced.[97]

In theory, the Articles may have been binding on the states. Article XIII provided that "[e]very state shall abide by the determinations of the United States in Congress assembled, on all questions which by this Confederation are submitted to them. And the Articles of this Confederation shall be inviolably observed by every state." Jay thought this language clearly obligated states to comply with congressional treaties, the meaning of which would be finally determined by state courts, not state legislatures. Grayson agreed, telling Madison that once the Treaty of Paris had been ratified, it automatically became the law of every state and thus would bind a Virginia court to cease enforcing the state's law prohibiting lawsuits to recover prewar debts.[98]

However, not everyone agreed that the Articles and treaties enacted under the Articles were legally binding upon the states. Grayson himself acknowledged doubts as to whether under the law of nations, separate state sovereignties could be legally bound by undertakings of their federal governments. Yet more important than the theoretical question of federal supremacy was the matter of practical enforcement. As Washington informed Jay, "If you tell the legislatures they have violated the treaty of peace, and invaded the prerogatives of the confederacy, they will laugh in your face."[99]

Concretely, the issue might arise in the following way: A British creditor would sue on a prewar debt. Because the Articles did not provide for federal courts of general jurisdiction—only admiralty courts and appellate prize courts—such a suit necessarily would be brought in state court. A state judge—under no oath to obey the Articles, dependent for his salary and tenure in office upon the state legislature, and possibly sympathetic to the state policy that he was being asked to subordinate to federal law—would then decide whether a state law barring recovery of prewar debts violated the federal treaty. Moreover, the Articles authorized no appeal from the state court's judgment to a federal tribunal. Finally, even if state judges did not prove to be biased in favor of state interests in cases of potential conflict with federal law, thirteen state judiciaries might resolve ambiguities in federal law in conflicting ways, thus creating a serious uniformity problem.[100]

In 1786, Jay investigated the allegation that states had violated the Treaty of Paris. He told Washington that although it was possible "to deceive ourselves and others by fallacious, though plausible, palliations and excuses," it would be "better fairly to confess and correct errors." Jay's report to Congress confirmed the accuracy of British charges that the treaty provisions requiring the repayment of prewar debts and forbidding future confiscations of Loyalist property had been violated. Jay urged Congress to pass a resolution calling upon the states to repeal all laws repugnant to the treaty, and early in 1787, Congress did so.[101]

Yet Jay doubted that such a resolution would be effective, given that "[s]ome of the states have gone so far in their deviations from the treaty that . . . they will not easily be persuaded to tread back their steps, especially as the recommendations of Congress, like most of the recommendations, are seldom efficient when opposed by interest." Grayson agreed that Congress's resolution would "create great uneasiness in most of the states"—and especially in Virginia, where "so many people will be affected" if prewar debts to British creditors had to be paid.[102]

American violations of the treaty not only were an embarrassment to the national honor but also offered the British what Washington called a "well grounded ... pretext for their [own] palpable infractions" of the treaty. In 1783, the British had violated the treaty provision in which they promised not to carry away American-owned slaves in their possession when their military forces departed from the United States. In the following years, the British continued to violate their treaty commitment to evacuate the forts they held along the northwestern frontier of the United States.[103]

In 1786, when American minister John Adams demanded evacuation of the forts, the British demurred, observing that several states were violating the treaty provision on repayment of prewar debts. According to Adams's report to Congress, the British government had told him that "[i]t would ... be the height of folly as well as injustice to suppose one party alone obliged to a strict observance of the public faith, while the other might remain free to deviate from its own engagements, as often as convenience might render such deviation necessary." The British would carry "into real and complete effect" their treaty obligations once the United States "shall manifest a real determination" to do the same.[104]

Jay's investigation into American treaty violations concluded that the British charges were just: Americans had violated the treaty first, and the British were therefore justified in refusing to fulfill their treaty obligations. Jay told Adams that "there has not been a single day since it [the treaty] took effect, on which it has not been violated in America, by one or other of the states." Madison agreed that the United States' claims upon Britain for enforcement of the treaty were greatly weakened by its own violations, which "were not only most numerous and important but were of earliest date."[105]

In 1781, Congress had appointed a committee to propose a remedy for the Articles' omission of any mechanism for enforcing federal supremacy. That committee, which included Madison, was charged with preparing a plan to invest Congress with "full and explicit powers for effectually carrying into execution in the several states all acts or resolutions passed agreeably to the Articles of Confederation." Without such powers, Madison told Jefferson, "the whole confederacy may be insulted and the most salutary measures frustrated by the most inconsiderable state in the union." The committee opted in favor of coercion: The Articles should be amended to empower Congress "to employ the force of the United States as well by sea as by land to compel such state or states to fulfill their federal engagements."[106]

Specifically, the proposed amendment would have authorized Congress to seize the vessels and merchandise of states—and their citizens—that were in default on their federal obligations and to prohibit trade between such states and other states, the citizens of other states, and foreign nations. As Madison later explained to Jefferson, it was "a fortunate circumstance for the United States that the use of coercion, or such provision as would render the use of it unnecessary, might be made at little expense and perfect safety, [as a] single frigate under the orders of Congress could make it the interest of any one of the Atlantic states to pay its just quota." The committee had offered its recommendation in the context of states' failing to fulfill their requisitions to Congress, but the same principle could have applied to states' reneging on their treaty obligations.[107]

Congress rejected the committee's proposal. Even during the war, when the congressional need to secure compliance from recalcitrant states was most urgent, physical coercion was widely considered to be too drastic a remedy.[108]

The other obvious mechanism for enforcing federal supremacy would have been a system of federal courts. In 1786, a congressional committee proposed the establishment of a federal court vested with appellate jurisdiction over state court decisions interpreting, among other things, federal treaties. Such a court could ensure a uniform interpretation of federal law and perhaps avoid the bias in favor of state law that state judges were likely to manifest in cases involving a conflict between state and federal interests. While the committee recommendation did not go beyond an appeals court, an even more effective mechanism for enforcing federal supremacy—as the delegates at the Constitutional Convention would recognize—would include the establishment of federal trial courts that could protect federal interests from being undermined by biased fact-finders.[109]

Yet in the absence of some such mechanism for enforcing federal supremacy, foreign nations had little incentive to enter into treaties with the United States, where such pacts might be interpreted to mean something different in every state and not be meaningfully enforceable in any of them. In 1785, Washington wondered, who would "enter into commercial treaties" with a nation that lacked "means of carrying them into effect?" In 1788, Massachusetts congressional delegate George Thatcher observed that experience under the Articles had "exhibited to all Europe too evident marks of incompetency for any national purposes to induce foreign powers to trust to treaties made under them."[110]

Even had the Articles established federal courts of general jurisdiction, there would have been nobody to enforce the judgments of such courts, as the Articles did not provide for any federal executive. Executive as well as legislative power at the federal level was vested in the Confederation Congress. The absence of an executive department, which could provide the federal government with energy, dispatch, and responsibility, was another of the Articles' major flaws.[111]

As early as 1780, Hamilton had concluded that one "defect in our system is want [i.e., lack] of method and energy in the administration," which was partly due to "the want of a proper executive." Congress had "kept the power too much into [its] own hands and meddled too much with details of every sort," whereas "Congress is properly a deliberative corps and it forgets itself when it attempts to play the executive." The following year, Hamilton told Superintendent of Finance Robert Morris that the proper management of the nation's affairs required "administration by single men" rather than by Congress as a whole or even by administrative boards. He predicted that an executive ministry composed of men of ability and honesty "would speedily restore the credit of government abroad and at home."[112]

By 1786–87, Jay was regularly observing that "the constitution of our federal government is fundamentally wrong." The three "great departments of sovereignty"—legislative, executive, and judicial—must be "forever separated." An executive department was essential because a deliberative body as large as the Confederation Congress could not act with sufficient secrecy or speed, both of which were especially critical in the field of foreign affairs. Washington agreed that a properly designed federal government must have an executive department separate from the legislature.[113]

Sectional Conflict

By 1786, Congress was destitute of funds and had proved powerless to respond either to other nations' trade discrimination or to the states' widespread defiance of federal treaties. Yet the nation's political leaders had grown equally alarmed by the development of sectional antagonisms so severe as to jeopardize the union's very survival. The divergent interests of the northern and southern states dated back to before independence and had made the creation of "two grand republics" in the mid-1770s a distinct possibility. During the Revolutionary War, commonality of interest had temporarily subdued intersectional tensions. Yet regional conflict erupted again after the war—most dramatically over the question of how the United States should respond to Spain's refusal to recognize American navigation rights on the Mississippi River below the nation's southern border (which itself was contested between Spain and the United States).[114]

Southerners had long been committed to keeping the Mississippi River open to American navigation. In 1763, the Peace of Paris, which ended the French and Indian War, stipulated free navigation of the river for subjects of Great Britain and France. Soon thereafter, France turned over Louisiana to Spain, and under international law, treaty rights remained intact despite the change of sovereignty. However, Spain regarded Americans' western settlements as a threat to its possessions in the western hemisphere—and especially to New Orleans.[115]

During the Revolutionary War, when the South was being overrun by British armies and was desperate for foreign assistance, Spain had pressured Congress into relinquishing American claims to navigation rights on the Mississippi River in exchange for Spain's recognition of American independence. Nonetheless, in 1781, Spain had reopened the river to American navigation for the duration of the war. In 1783, the treaty of peace between Great Britain and the United States provided that "[t]he navigation of the river Mississippi, from its sources to the ocean, shall forever remain free and open to the subjects of Great Britain, and the citizens of the United States," but the peace treaty between Great Britain and Spain failed to make any mention of the issue.[116]

After the war, Americans in great numbers poured across the Appalachian Mountains. Rufus King of Massachusetts referred to westerners' "yearly making almost incredible accessions of strength." The population of Kentucky, which was still part of Virginia, grew from twelve thousand in 1783 to seventy thousand by 1790. In the words of one westerner, these migrants sought to escape "a barren country loaded with taxes and impoverished with debts" for "the most luxurious and fertile soil in the world." After settling for only a few years—"and that in the midst of an inveterate enemy, and most of the first adventurers fallen a prey to the savages"—"the quantities of produce . . . are immense." According to this report, three times the quantity of corn and tobacco could be raised on a western acre than on one east of the mountains—and with less cultivation.[117]

The governor of Louisiana reported to his superiors in Madrid that Americans were a "vast and restless population," "hostile to all subjection," and consumed by "unmeasured ambition." In 1784, increasingly concerned Spanish officials tried to slow Americans' westward migration by terminating their access to the region's most convenient commercial outlet, the Mississippi River. Spain claimed the right to control navigation of the river by virtue of controlling the territory on both banks, but Americans disputed Spanish control of territory on the eastern bank. By early 1785, Spain was regularly seizing American vessels that were engaging in "illicit" trade on the river.[118]

With a clash between the two nations seeming increasingly likely, Spain dispatched a minister, Don Diego de Gardoqui, to the United States for the purpose of securing congressional recognition of Spain's exclusive control over the Mississippi River. Gardoqui was also instructed to settle boundary disputes between the United States and Spain, which disagreed about how much of the territory between the Mississippi River and the Appalachian Mountains belonged to each nation. Gardoqui was authorized to offer a commercial treaty as an

Figure 1.3 Don Diego de Gardoqui, the Spanish minister to the United States. (Palace of the Governors, New Mexico History Museum)

inducement to the United States—for example, committing Spain to purchase American fish and timber—but was instructed to stand firm on the boundary dispute and navigation rights on the Mississippi. A French diplomat with knowledge of Spanish intentions reported that Spain considered it "of infinite importance . . . not to encourage establishments on the Mississippi which might one day become neighbors so much the more dangerous for the Spanish possessions." Even in "their present weakness," the western settlers "were already conceiving vast schemes for the conquest of the western bank of the river."[119]

Congress appointed Jay to negotiate with Gardoqui.* It initially gave him very restrictive instructions—requiring Jay to communicate with Congress

---

* Jay was one of the giants of the Founding generation. Born in 1745 into a prosperous and prominent family, he entered King's College in 1764 and became a member of the New York bar after graduation. As a New York delegate to the First and Second Continental Congresses, Jay was a relatively late convert to the movement for independence, though he did draft Congress's *Address to the People of Great Britain*, which rejected Parliament's right to tax the colonists without their consent.

after receiving any "propositions" from Gardoqui. But after Jay protested at these "exceedingly embarrassing" restrictions, Congress relented and substituted specific limitations on just two subjects of the negotiations: Jay was "particularly to stipulate the right of the United States to [its] territorial bounds, and the free navigation of the Mississippi from the source to the ocean as established in [its] treaties with Great Britain."[120]

In 1777, Jay helped draft New York's first constitution and was elected chief justice of the state supreme court. After the New York legislature in 1778 reappointed him as a delegate to Congress, Jay was quickly elected president of that body. In 1779, Congress sent him to Spain to negotiate financial assistance and recognition of American independence, but the Spanish mostly resisted his overtures. From there, Jay went to Paris, where he negotiated—along with Benjamin Franklin and John Adams—the treaty ending the Revolutionary War. Jay's contributions were critical to securing an advantageous treaty, and he received a hero's welcome upon his return to the United States in 1784. Congress promptly appointed him secretary for foreign affairs, a position he held throughout the remainder of the Confederation.

While Jay neither supported the call for the Philadelphia convention nor attended it, he was, as we shall see, a prominent voice in support of the Constitution during the ratification struggle in New York. Jay wrote five numbers of *The Federalist*—his contributions were limited by illness—and he played a critical mediating role at the New York ratifying convention, ultimately securing an unconditional ratification of the Constitution despite the fact that Antifederalist delegates outnumbered Federalists there by more than two to one.

Afterwards, Jay turned down Washington's offer to become the first secretary of state, instead accepting the position of first Chief Justice of the United States. Although the Supreme Court handled few cases in its early years, Jay's opinions bolstered the authority of the national government. He also provided unofficial advice to President Washington, including authoring the first draft of the 1793 Neutrality Proclamation. Ironically, Jay then declined, in his official capacity as chief justice, to adjudicate the proclamation's constitutionality on the grounds that the Court lacked power to issue advisory opinions.

In 1792, while continuing to serve on the Supreme Court, Jay ran for governor of New York, winning a majority at the polls only to see his victory snatched away by a partisan electoral commission. In 1794, President Washington appointed Jay (still serving as chief justice) as special envoy to Great Britain to negotiate over several contentious issues—including, most prominently from the American perspective, the impressment of American sailors into the British navy and violations of American neutrality rights. Jeffersonian critics of the Washington administration deemed the treaty Jay negotiated so lopsided in favor of British interests that Jay's effigy was burned across the nation. But a war was averted.

Jay left the Court in 1795 when he was elected governor of New York. He served two terms and in 1799 signed into law an act for the gradual emancipation of the state's slaves. Jay, who in 1785 became the first president of the New York Manumission Society, had been pushing the legislature to emancipate slaves for more than two decades.

In 1800, Jay rejected President John Adams's offer to reappoint him as chief justice. Jay pleaded ill health as well as the federal judiciary's lack of "the energy, weight, and dignity which are essential to its affording due support to the national government." Jay's refusal to accept the position opened the door to the appointment of John Marshall, who became the most important chief justice in American history and laid the groundwork for the Court's eventually assuming the stature it commands today. When Jay's second gubernatorial term ended in 1801, he retired to an estate in Bedford, New York, where he lived until his death in 1829.

Figure 1.4 John Jay, who supported ratification of the Constitution at the New York ratifying convention and then became the first Chief Justice of the United States. (Photography © New-York Historical Society)

Americans had long divided along regional lines over the importance of navigation rights on the Mississippi River. For the tens of thousands of Americans who by the mid-1780s had already crossed the Appalachian Mountains into the region that would later become the states of Kentucky and Tennessee, access to the Mississippi River was vital to their ability to export their agricultural products to world markets and, consequently, to the value of their land.

Thus, as early as 1783, George Mason* had warned that westerners were "extremely uneasy, lest the free navigation of the River Mississippi to the sea should not be secured to them upon a treaty of peace [with Great Britain]."

---

* Mason was born in 1725 in what is today Fairfax County, Virginia, the eldest son of a wealthy planter. His father drowned in a boat accident when Mason was only nine, and he was raised by his uncle, John Mercer, one of Virginia's leading lawyers.

Throughout his life, Mason preferred to be home at Gunston Hall, a Georgian mansion overlooking the Potomac River that he built in the 1750s, rather than away engaged in public service.

They regarded river access as "a natural right," which within a few years they would be "strong enough to enforce." Madison similarly referred to "the right of those who live on the waters of the Mississippi to use it as the high road given by nature to the sea." Westerners insisted they had the same right to navigate the Mississippi that easterners had to use the Potomac River or the James River—a right that derived "from nature, from the principles of the revolution, and from the treaty with Great Britain." Indeed, many westerners were prepared to go to war with Spain over the issue. George Muter, a Kentucky judge

He once referred to himself as "content with the blessings of a private station" without regard for "the smiles and frowns of the great." Mason's large family and chronic ill health also conspired to keep him mostly at home. Other than a brief tenure in the Virginia House of Burgesses from 1758 to 1761, Mason's public service prior to the Revolution consisted entirely of a local sort.

However, in 1769, Mason drafted the terms of a nonimportation association designed to force British merchants to support the American colonists in their demand for a repeal of the Townsend duties—taxes imposed by Parliament on paper, paint, lead, glass, and tea imported into the colonies—and his proposal was adopted by an extralegal session of the Burgesses. Then, in 1774, Mason composed the Fairfax County resolutions condemning the Intolerable Acts and calling for a Continental Congress.

Mason twice declined appointments to the Continental Congress, but in 1776, he accepted the call of Fairfax County voters to serve in the Virginia convention that ultimately endorsed independence. In that same convention, Mason became the principal draftsman of both the Virginia Declaration of Rights and the state's first constitution.

Mason also accepted the legislature's call, in 1787, to represent Virginia at the Constitutional Convention. His four-month sojourn to Philadelphia was the first time in his life he ventured outside of Virginia for more than a few days. Having never been to a major city before, Mason complained to his son of the "etiquette and nonsense so fashionable." (Ironically, Mason, a wealthy planter who lived in an elegant mansion and owned hundreds of slaves, urged at the Philadelphia convention that Congress be granted power to enact sumptuary laws to restrict conspicuous consumption.)

As we shall see, Mason was one of the most active and significant participants at the Philadelphia convention. William Pierce, in his sketches of convention delegates, described Mason as "a gentleman of remarkable strong powers . . . able and convincing in debate, steady and firm in his principles, and undoubtedly one of the best politicians in America."

Although, earlier in the 1780s, Mason had opposed efforts to expand the powers of the Confederation Congress, at the Philadelphia convention he initially supported Madison's plan to abrogate rather than reform the Articles and to create a powerful national government. However, over the course of the proceedings, Mason became disaffected with the scheme that was emerging, and toward the end of the convention, he announced he "would sooner chop off his right hand than put it to the Constitution as it now stands." Departing Philadelphia in an ill humor, Mason became one of the nation's most prominent opponents of ratification, insisting that amendments were necessary before the Constitution was ratified and supporting the call for a second national convention to consider amendments.

In 1790, Mason declined appointment to the US Senate, and two years later he died at Gunston Hall. Jefferson later described him as "a man of the first order of wisdom among those who acted on the theater of the Revolution, of expansive mind, profound judgment, [and] cogent in argument."

and political leader, told Madison that he had "not met with one man [in the West], who would be willing to give the navigation up, for ever so short a time, on any terms whatever."[121]

Most of these western settlers came from southern states. In 1785, one southerner observed that "the emigrations from the southern states to the waters of the Mississippi are incredible." Thus, these westerners were not, as Madison noted, "a foreign people" but rather "a bone of our bones, and flesh of our flesh." Moreover, these regions still belonged to Virginia and North Carolina in the mid-1780s, and thus those states tended to represent the interest of westerners in Congress. Of at least equal importance, many southerners hoped that westward expansion ultimately would lead to the creation of several western states, which would increase the South's weight within the union. Yet if the Mississippi River were closed, Monroe warned, "we separate those people—I mean all those westward of the mountains—from the federal government and perhaps throw them into the hands eventually of a foreign power."[122]

To be sure, not all southerners felt this way about the issue of Mississippi River access. For years, Washington had believed that improving navigation on the Potomac and James Rivers through canals was a better way of securing westerners a convenient route to the sea. Washington feared that opening navigation on the Mississippi River would strengthen westerners' connections with the Spanish, whereas improving Virginia's rivers running from west to east would bolster westerners' ties to their American brethren. Moreover, once the western territory had become so populous "as really to need it [Mississippi River access], there is no power that can deprive them [westerners] of the use." Washington saw no reason to prematurely press a matter "which is disagreeable to others and may be attended with embarrassing consequences if it is our interest to let it sleep."[123]

One of Virginia's congressional delegates, Henry Lee III (also known as Light-Horse Harry Lee, and the father of Confederate general Robert E. Lee), went even further than Washington. Lee was "very solicitous to form a treaty with Spain for commercial purposes," as "no [other] nation in Europe can give us conditions so advantageous to our trade." Lee thought it worthwhile to "agree to the occlusion of the Mississippi" to secure "the benefits of a free liberal system of trade with Spain," especially because the "occlusion cannot exist longer than the infancy of the western emigrants." A commercial treaty was "highly important" to the northern states, and there were "no prospects" of securing it without "yielding the navigation of the Mississippi."[124]

Still another Virginian, Richard Henry Lee, thought the benefits of opening the Mississippi River to American navigation were "chimerical," and he worried that one of its consequences would be to "depopulate and ruin the old states." In any event, the object was "unattainable for many years, and probably never without war, not only with Spain but most likely with the Bourbon alliance [i.e., France as well]." Why risk "discarding the friendship for the enmity of a powerful monarch," especially when several million dollars a year in codfish, not to mention flour and other American articles of production that Spain was offering to buy, were at stake? Such considerations, to Lee's mind, "greatly outweigh" any concerns about possibly driving the Kentuckians into the arms of the British.[125]

Northerners were not entirely of one mind either on the issue of Mississippi River access. Some northerners agreed with most southerners that the United States should insist upon free navigation of the Mississippi River. Those northerners involved in the western fur trade and speculation in western lands favored keeping the Mississippi River open, as did the many northerners who preferred that Congress raise revenue to pay the federal debt by selling its western lands rather than imposing taxes on commerce. Thus, northern states had approved Jay's instruction not to bargain away the American claim of access rights to the Mississippi. In March 1785, the Massachusetts legislature had instructed its congressional delegates "to proceed immediately to the important business of securing to the states the free navigation of the River Mississippi."[126]

Yet northerners generally were less vitally concerned about the Mississippi issue than southerners because relatively little settlement thus far had taken place in the territory north of the Ohio River. Indeed, many northerners affirmatively opposed rapid development of the American West. Rufus King deemed "every emigrant to that [the western] country from the Atlantic states as forever lost to the confederacy." According to King, "Nature has severed the two countries [East and West] by a vast and extensive chain of mountains, interest and convenience will keep them separate, and the feeble policy of our disjointed government will not be able to unite them." For that reason, "the United States would [n]ever receive a penny of revenue from the inhabitants who may settle the western territory should there be an uninterrupted use of the Mississippi at this time by the citizens of the United States." Moreover, "[t]he states situated on the Atlantic are not sufficiently populous, and losing our men is losing our greatest source of wealth."[127]

Other northerners worried that western expansion would soon translate into additional southern states, which might eventually enable the South to outvote the North in Congress. Thus, Grayson of Virginia reported that some northerners were "apprehensive of the consequences which may result from the new states taking their positions in the Confederacy."[128]

In addition, anger among northerners over the southern states' resistance to granting commercial powers to Congress disinclined many of them to support southern demands for Mississippi River access. Northerners were far more interested in securing a commercial treaty with Spain, which might enable them to enjoy some of the benefits that southern resistance to expanding Congress's power over commerce was preventing them from obtaining through legislation. Spanish markets for northern goods might replace British markets, which had been shut after the war. As one Virginia congressional representative observed, "The eastern states consider a commercial connection with Spain as the only remedy for the distresses which oppress their citizens, most of which, they say, flow from the decay of their commerce." A commercial treaty with Spain might be "the only effectual mode to revive the trade of their country."[129]

In his negotiations with Jay in New York City, Gardoqui adamantly rejected the American claim to navigation rights on the Mississippi, but he indicated his willingness to reach a commercial agreement, the terms of which he and Jay discussed in some detail. When Madison learned of these developments, he concluded that Gardoqui's motive had been "to work a total separation of interest and affection between the western and eastern settlements and to foment the jealousy between the eastern and southern states" with the motive of checking western settlements and thus promoting the security of Spanish possessions in North America.[130]

In May 1786, Jay told Congress that "certain difficulties" had arisen in his negotiations with Gardoqui, and he suggested the appointment of a committee "with power to instruct and direct me on every point and subject relative to the proposed treaty with Spain." Monroe, who was named to that committee, told Madison and Governor Patrick Henry of Virginia that Jay's objective, although not explicitly acknowledged, was to be relieved of his restrictive instructions regarding the Mississippi River and the contested boundaries.[131]

Southerners, who had previously regarded Jay as a friend, now accused him of manipulating Congress to his own ends. Monroe told Jefferson that "Jay has managed this negotiation dishonestly" and that he was engaged in "an intrigue" with "the most illiberal" Massachusetts congressional delegation to evade his instructions. Monroe wrote Henry, "This is one of the most extraordinary transactions I have ever known, a minister negotiating expressly for the purpose of defeating the object of his instructions, and by a long train of intrigue and management seducing the representatives of the states to concur in it."[132]

Madison likewise denounced Jay's "shortsighted [and] dishonorable policy" and expressed "amazement that a thought should be entertained of surrendering the Mississippi and of guaranteeing the possessions of Spain in America." Even in the South's most desperate moments during the Revolutionary War, Madison had strenuously resisted efforts to trade American navigation rights on the Mississippi River for a Spanish alliance. Now, in 1786, Madison believed that Jay was simply undertaking "a voluntary barter in time of profound peace of the rights of one part of the empire to the interests of another part." This was no different, in Madison's mind, from Virginia's suggesting that the fishery rights of Massachusetts be relinquished to Great Britain in exchange for a higher price for Virginia tobacco. Timothy Bloodworth, a North Carolina congressional delegate, similarly complained that the southern states were being asked to "pay the purchase by giving up the Mississippi" for a treaty that would secure commercial advantages to northern states in the sale of fish and whale oil while alienating westerners and depreciating their land values.[133]

In August, Congress summoned Jay to appear before it, and he enumerated the advantages of a commercial treaty with Spain. Geopolitically, Spain was close to France, an important American ally, and to alienate Spain might be to anger France. Likewise, Great Britain, which "remembers that we were once her subjects and loves us not," would rejoice to find the United States at odds with Spain. Consummating the treaty that Gardoqui offered might also induce Spain to use its influence with the Barbary powers to help open up the Mediterranean Sea to American commerce. Spain was courting America's friendship, Jay explained, at a time when other nations were "showing us no extraordinary marks of respect."[134]

Commercially, Jay argued, a treaty with Spain would greatly advantage the United States because, in the trade between the two nations, Spain imported more than it exported and thus would have to settle its accounts in specie. Spain was willing to extend "perfect reciprocity" with regard to all commercial regulations, meaning that American goods and manufactures (with the exception of tobacco) could be imported into any part of Spain—in American or Spanish vessels—as if they were Spanish products. The Spanish king also agreed to purchase from the United States in hard currency the masts and timbers for his royal navy. A letter from Gardoqui that Jay transmitted to Congress emphasized that Spain annually consumed codfish from Newfoundland worth $4 or $5 million. A commercial treaty between Spain and the United States could replace that British cod with New England cod (of a higher quality), which would mean the employment of thousands of American seamen.[135]

In exchange for a commercial treaty, Spain insisted that the United States relinquish its claims to navigation rights on the Mississippi River below the southern border of the United States for twenty-five or thirty years. In his congressional testimony, Jay explained that he had always been—and remained still—opposed to abandoning such rights, but that Gardoqui had declared that the Spanish king would not relent on this issue. When Jay had tried to persuade him that the reality of burgeoning western settlements would one day force Spain to make such concessions, Gardoqui responded that the "time alluded to was far distant and that treaties were not to provide for contingencies so remote and future."[136]

Jay also explained to Congress that for the United States to forbear from use of the Mississippi River for a generation until it had become "more really and truly a nation than it at present is" would represent no great sacrifice of American interests. Destitute of funds and deeply divided along regional lines, the United States was in no position to fight a war with Spain over this issue. Given that reality, Jay asked, why not stipulate to forbear from use of the river, and in exchange receive the valuable consideration of a commercial treaty? Furthermore, given how little American commercial traffic currently existed on the Mississippi, navigation rights were "not at present important, nor will they probably become . . . so in less than twenty-five or thirty years." Finally, Jay warned that Spain would probably be "mortified" if the United States declined to make the proposed commercial treaty, which would likely lead to a war that the nation was ill-prepared to fight.[137]

Westerners were outraged when they discovered what Jay was proposing. One prominent Kentuckian told Madison:

> [T]he minds of all the western people are agitated on account of the proposed cession of the Mississippi navigation to Spain. Every person talks of it with indignation and reprobates it as a measure of the greatest injustice and despotism, declaring that if it takes place, they will look upon themselves [as] relieved from all federal obligations and fully at liberty to exact alliances and connections wherever they find them and that the British officers at Detroit have already been tampering with them.[138]

Another westerner wrote to an eastern friend that "[p]olitics, which a few months ago were scarcely thought of, are now sounded aloud in this part of the world and discussed by almost every person." Jay's proposal to forgo the exercise of American navigation rights on the Mississippi River had "given this western country a universal shock and struck its inhabitants with an amazement. Our foundation is affected. . . . To sell us and make us vassals to the merciless Spaniards is a grievance not to be borne." If in control of the river, the Spanish would "take our produce at any price they please." Westerners were determined, if necessary, "to drive the Spaniards from their settlements at the mouth of the Mississippi. In case we are not countenanced and succored by the United States (if we need it) our allegiance will be thrown off, and some other power [i.e., Great Britain] applied to." John Brown, a Virginia congressional delegate from the region of Kentucky, told Jefferson that "the ill-advised attempt to cede the navigation of that river has laid the foundation for the dismemberment of the American empire by destroying the confidence of the people in the western country in the justice of the union and by inducing them to despair of obtaining possession of that right by means of any other exertions than their own."[139]

Many of Virginia's political leaders were distressed by these developments. Madison told Jefferson that it would not "be an unnatural consequence if they [westerners] consider themselves as absolved from every federal tie [by Jay's proposal] and court some protection for their betrayed rights"—perhaps from the British, who would be eager "to seize an opportunity of embroiling our affairs." Jefferson agreed that "the act which abandons the navigation of the Mississippi is an act of separation between the eastern and western country." While he did not doubt the "honest intentions" of Jay and his northern allies, Jefferson thought they must have been unaware of the character of western settlers, "who, right or wrong, will suppose their interests sacrificed on this occasion to the contrary interests of that part of the confederacy in possession of present power." Even Washington, who was less opposed than most Virginians to a temporary relinquishing of American navigation rights on the Mississippi, worried about the effect that this might "have on the minds of the western settlers," who might "be influenced by the demagogues of the country to acts of extravagance and desperation under a popular declamation that their interests are sacrificed."[140]

Many southern leaders worried that yielding claims to the Mississippi River would not only alienate westerners from the union but also entrench the North's political advantage in Congress. Monroe told Governor Patrick Henry that the object of northerners in ceding the Mississippi was to break up "the settlements on the western waters, prevent any in future, and thereby to keep the states southward as they are now." Even if western settlement were to continue, it would "be on such principles as to make it the interest of the people to separate from the confederacy, so as effectually to exclude any new state from it." By "throw[ing] the weight of the population eastward and keep[ing] it there," northerners also hoped to "appreciate the vacant lands of New York and Massachusetts."[141]

North Carolina congressional delegate Timothy Bloodworth agreed that "the policy of the eastern states is . . . to prevent emigration." It was "well known that the balance of power [in Congress] is now in the eastern states," Bloodworth wrote, and their present conduct indicated that they were "determined to keep it in that direction."[142]

Indeed, the French chargé d'affaires reported to his foreign minister that "the true motive" of the South's "vigorous opposition" to relinquishing the claim to navigation rights on the Mississippi River was "to be found in the great preponderance of the northern states" and southerners' eagerness "to incline the balance toward their side." Southerners "neglect no opportunity of increasing the population and importance of the western territory, and of drawing thither by degrees the inhabitants of New England, whose ungrateful soil only too much favors emigration." Rhode Island especially had "already suffered considerably from the new establishments of Ohio, and a great number of families daily leave their homes to seek lands more fertile and a less rigorous climate." This emigration "doubly enfeebles New England, since on the one hand it deprives her of industrious citizens, and on the other it adds to the population of the southern states." Once these regions "gradually form themselves into separate governments, they will have their representation in Congress, and will augment greatly the mass of the southern states."[143]

Wishing to protect the interests of their western constituents and to secure the South's future power within the union, southern state legislators instructed their congressional delegates to oppose "in the most decided terms" any effort by Congress to barter away American rights to the free use of the Mississippi as likely to provoke "the just resentments and reproaches of our western brethren whose essential rights and interests would be thereby sacrificed and sold." Thus, according to Monroe's subsequent account, southern delegates to Congress "warmly opposed" Jay's effort to secure reinstruction.[144]

Congressional representatives Grayson of Virginia and Charles Pinckney of South Carolina gave lengthy speeches accusing Jay of seeking to sell out the interests of westerners and southerners for the benefit of northerners, while questioning how valuable those benefits really would be. The commercial treaty Jay negotiated provided that neither country would impose duties on goods imported from the other above those ordinarily paid by its own citizens on imported goods, yet this was of limited benefit to American exporters because Spain ordinarily imposed much higher duties on imports than did American states. In addition, the treaty explicitly excepted tobacco—the great staple crop of several southern states—which Spain secured from its own colonies in the western hemisphere. The principal items that Spain was likely to import from the United States under the treaty—fish and timber, both northern products—were already permitted into Spain without protective tariffs because they were not produced in Spanish colonies. Because wheat and rice were always in demand in Europe, they did not require the aid of a treaty. Thus, according to these southern congressional delegates, the proposed treaty neither secured trade with Spain that would not occur in its absence nor opened up Spain's valuable possessions in the western hemisphere to American trade. The southern delegates also deprecated the notions that Spain would be of much assistance to the United States in dealing with Algerian pirates or that Spain would go to war if its demands with regard to the Mississippi were resisted. Even if Spain were willing to go to war with the United States, France was unlikely to support it.[145]

While the ostensible benefits of the treaty were small, the costs were said to be enormous. To relinquish American claims to navigation rights on the Mississippi would "check, perhaps destroy, the spirit of emigration" and thus depreciate the value of unsold western lands, which were a critical fund for retiring the federal debt. Closing the Mississippi would both "separate the interest of the western inhabitants from that of the rest of the union and render them hostile to it" and "destroy the hopes of the principal men in the southern states in establishing the future fortunes of their families." When southerners saw "their deepest interests sacrificed and given up to obtain a trivial commercial advantage for their brethren in the East," their allegiance to the union would also be jeopardized. If nothing else, a Spanish treaty formed "upon principles calculated to promote the interests of one part of the union at the expense of others" would give the party seeing itself as injured "great reason" to urge "the impropriety of vesting that body [Congress] with farther powers, which has so recently abused those [it] already possess[es]."[146]

By contrast, most northern statesmen were elated over the proposed commercial treaty, which they believed would open Spanish markets to northern fish, flour, timber, and other products. Rufus King, who served on the committee charged with responding to Jay's request for reinstruction, told Elbridge Gerry, a fellow Massachusetts political leader, that the proposed treaty would "be of vast importance to the Atlantic states." Given that Great Britain was New England's "rival in the fisheries" and that "France does not wish us prosperity in this branch of commerce," a treaty with Spain securing a European market for New England fish was extremely desirable. King also worried about "embarrass[ing] ourselves in the attempts of imprudent men to navigate the Mississippi" below the southern border of the United States, which might "embroil ourselves with Spain."[147]

In Congress, King and Pennsylvania delegate Arthur St. Clair, who had been a major general in the Revolutionary Army, defended Jay's proposed commercial treaty as vital to the relief of the distressed northern economy. Because of the North's "ungrateful soil," its only valuable staple was what it could "draw from the sea," and Spain was the most promising market for that, which made Jay's proposed treaty "of the utmost consequence to the [northern] states." They also argued that expanding the northern fisheries would encourage shipbuilding and the carrying trade and thus increase the number of seamen, which ultimately would be a source of greater national security. The northern delegates denied that the treaty was vulnerable to the objection that "the immediate benefits will be reaped by one part of the union." Gains secured by one region through foreign commerce would be "quickly communicated to the rest by internal intercourse" and thus ultimately would "redound to the advantage of the whole union."[148]

By contrast, the concession offered to Spain in Jay's proposed treaty—"to forbear the use of that which we could not at present enjoy"—"was of no great consequence," according to the northern congressional delegates. Simply by virtue of controlling the mouth of the river at New Orleans, Spain would exclude American navigation "until we were able to assert our right by arms." Moreover, rejecting Gardoqui's terms would "buoy up . . . the hopes" of westerners, who would probably "force a passage" and thus precipitate a war before the United States was prepared to fight it. In such an event, France would probably side with Spain, and no other maritime power of Europe would ally with the United States because they "looked upon us with a jealous eye and, though they wished us to be independent, they never wished us to be powerful." Furthermore, a war with Spain over the Mississippi River would endanger the Confederation because northerners would not be "willing to incur the expense and danger of a war brought upon them as they will think unnecessarily and prematurely" when their own commercial interests were being "neglected if not sacrificed."[149]

The northern delegates also argued that forbearing to use the river for a generation would enable Americans to strengthen the union in the meantime and arrange the nation's affairs so as to be prepared to forcefully assert its rights at the end of that period. Indeed, for Spain to enter into a treaty in which Americans agreed for a limited time not to exercise a particular right would imply that Spain "yields her exclusive claim and confirms our right." Finally, the United States was already "too thin of inhabitants," lacking "hands sufficient for the cultivation of our lands, much less for manufacturers of the most necessary kind." Therefore, western migration "in our present situation is hurtful," and settlement of the western territory should be curtailed.[150]

With Congress divided along sectional lines, a delegate from the middle of the country, John Cleves Symmes of New Jersey, proposed a compromise: The United States would relinquish its right to navigate the Mississippi River but only for twelve years. Yet southerners adamantly opposed that suggestion, which was also said to be unacceptable to Spain, and it was quickly abandoned.[151]

The Articles of Confederation expressly provided that treaties required the approval of nine state delegations. Believing that, as Monroe later explained, "[t]he instruction is the foundation of the treaty—for, if it is formed agreeably thereto, good faith requires that it be ratified"—southern delegates insisted that any reinstruction of Jay required the same supermajority support. Nine states had approved Jay's initial instructions, and nine states should be required to alter them.[152]

Virginia's congressional delegates introduced a motion declaring that "the establishment of a precedent enabling seven states to alter the instructions of a minister on the subject of treaties to which the assent of nine was in the first place necessary would be productive of the most serious danger, in destroying the guard which the confederation has wisely provided on this important subject." In letters to his governor, North Carolina delegate Timothy Bloodworth went even further. If this "precedent dangerous to the liberties of the southern states" were established, whereby "seven states can barter any part of the privileges of the different states, for any advantage whatsoever," then "the confederated compact is no more than a rope of sand" and "dissolution of the union must take place."[153]

Yet efforts by southern delegates to bar the reinstruction of Jay by less than a supermajority vote were consistently defeated by tallies of seven northern delegations to five southern ones (Delaware being absent). After what Monroe later called a "tedious and lengthy discussion" of the issue, Congress voted in late August 1786 by the same seven-to-five margin to remove the stipulation in Jay's instructions that had barred him from relinquishing American claims to navigation rights on the Mississippi River.[154]

A couple of days later, northern state delegations forced a change in Congress's procedural rules that prevented Jay's instructions from being subsequently altered if fewer than twelve state delegations were present—a change that Madison later called "the offspring of the intemperance which characterized the epoch of its birth." By the same regional division, Congress also voted to leave in place the injunction of secrecy that barred delegates from informing their state legislatures of the status of negotiations between the United States and Spain. Congressional debates on the Mississippi issue had been so acrimonious that they blocked progress on any other issues. Congress's regional divide had become a yawning chasm.[155]

These congressional proceedings left Jay in a "very embarrassing" situation, according to a shrewd analysis by the French chargé d'affaires, Louis Guillaume Otto. Jay clearly could not conclude a treaty abandoning navigation rights on the Mississippi River "without encountering bitter reproaches from the five southern states, who loudly accuse him of having by all sorts of intrigues directed the actions of the northern delegates, in order not to suffer the negotiation to slip from his hand." Yet neither could Jay "refuse to execute the orders of a party of which he is himself the most zealous partisan, without losing his popularity and influence." Whatever Jay did, "it is to be feared that this discussion will cause a great coolness between the two parties and may be the germ of a future separation of the southern states."[156]

Believing that Jay had "risked his reputation" upon completing the treaty and had engaged his northern allies "too firmly in the business to have a possibility of their forsaking him," Monroe was convinced that northerners would "risk the preservation of the confederacy" rather than back down. Indeed, Monroe believed that northern delegates were already holding meetings outside of Congress—he claimed even to have been present at one of them—"upon the subject of a dismemberment of the states east of the Hudson from the union and the erection of them into a separate government." Although he still hoped that disunion might be avoided, Monroe told Governor Patrick Henry that they must "contemplate it as an event which may possibly happen and for which we should be guarded." In the event of disunion, Monroe considered it critical that Pennsylvania and perhaps New Jersey be included in the southern confederation to avoid "too much strength" in the northern one. If necessary, Virginia should employ force to prevent Pennsylvania from combining with the northern states. Monroe's Virginian colleague Henry Lee also voiced alarm that "gentlemen talk so lightly of a separation and dissolution of the Confederation."[157]

The Virginians were not being paranoid: Southern resistance to commercial reform and to Jay's proposed treaty with Spain was indeed leading some northerners to question the value of the union. Theodore Sedgwick, a Massachusetts congressional delegate, wrote privately that "[i]t well becomes [i.e., behooves] the eastern and middle states, who are in interest one, seriously to consider what advantages result to them from their connection with the southern states. They can give us nothing as an equivalent for the protection which they derive from us but a participation in their commerce. This they deny to us." Sedgwick concluded that "[e]ven the appearance of a union cannot in the way we are long be preserved. It becomes us seriously to contemplate a substitute; for if we do not control events we shall be miserably controlled by them."[158]

In a shroud of secrecy, Jay continued to negotiate with Gardoqui under his new instructions. Madison complained to Randolph that "[t]he negotiations with Spain are carried on, if they go on at all, entirely behind the curtain" and that Jay had total discretion over how to proceed and what information to communicate to Congress. Many southerners feared the worst. In December 1786, Virginia congressional delegate Edward Carrington, while acknowledging that he had no solid evidence, predicted to Madison that Jay would consummate the treaty with Spain and then hope that the southern states would be too timid to block its ratification in Congress. Congressional delegate Bloodworth reported to the North Carolina legislature that there was "reason to fear the treaty is now on foot, if not completed."[159]

Yet, in fact, Jay was not impervious to the outcry raised by southerners and westerners against his reinstruction. In October, Monroe told Madison that he was "inclined to suspect" that when Jay was shown Congress's journal, which revealed the depth of southern hostility to his reinstruction, this probably "made a different impression on him" than had "the narrative of its contents" conveyed to him previously "by those in his party in the late transaction." Southern congressional delegations also plied Congress—and the secretary for foreign affairs—with information to demonstrate the extent of western discontent at the supposed surrender of the Mississippi. Jay later admitted that he had been "much embarrassed by the ferment excited in the western country by the rumored intention to cede the Mississippi." In December, he told Jefferson of his regret that "[m]ischief has been very incautiously dropped where it should never have entered that the interests of the Atlantic and western parts of the United States are distinct" and that "the western people have reason to be jealous of the northern."[160]

By February 1787, Madison was telling Jefferson that Jay had "not ventured to proceed in his project and I suppose will not now do it." In March, Madison had a private interview with Gardoqui. According to Madison's account, although the Spanish minister "would not listen to the idea of a right to the navigation of Mississippi by the United States" and warned that "Spain would make us feel the vulnerable side of our commerce by abridging it in her ports," Gardoqui confided that he had not conferred with Jay since October, did not expect to do so again, and would soon be leaving America. After his conversation with Gardoqui, Madison told Jefferson that Jay's negotiations were "arrested."[161]

In April, Congress called upon Jay to report on his negotiations. Jay announced that he had drawn up several drafts of a treaty provision implicitly suggesting that the United States claimed a right to navigate the Mississippi to the sea but explicitly forbearing from exercise of that right. Jay also described increasing confrontations between Americans and the Spanish on the river and warned Congress that no reputable middle ground existed between a commercial treaty and war. Yet Jay also admitted that "a treaty disagreeable to one half of the nation had better not be made, for it would be violated." At this point, southern delegates proposed moving the negotiations to Europe, where they anticipated that Jefferson, the minister to France, would do a better job than Jay of protecting southern interests. Soon thereafter, Madison reported that "[i]t was considered on the whole that the project of shutting the Mississippi was at an end—a point deemed of great importance in reference to the approaching convention [in Philadelphia] for introducing a change in the federal government and to the objection to an increase of its powers foreseen from the jealousy which had been excited by that project."[162]

Jay never did conclude a treaty with Gardoqui. By early 1788, Kentuckian John Brown had concluded that "little is to be feared from the project for ceding the navigation of the Mississippi to Spain." He reported that "almost a total change of sentiment upon that subject has taken place," partly because sales of western lands had turned "many inhabitants of the eastern states of great influence and powerful connections . . . [into] adventurers in that country."[163]

Later that year, Congress resolved that free navigation of the Mississippi River was "a clear and essential right of the United States" and that the subject of Jay's negotiations with Spain should be referred to the new federal government created by the Constitution, which would assume office early in 1789. Madison told Randolph that this resolution was "well calculated to appease the discontents of our western brethren," and he told Jefferson that Congress had been "brought into the true policy which is demanded by the situation of the western country." Hugh Williamson, one of North Carolina's congressional delegates, observed that "no power remains in the hands of any minister" to make a treaty bartering American navigation rights on the Mississippi River. Northern delegates, according to Williamson, were now "perfectly convinced that the measure would not be prudent nor practicable," given the sudden and extraordinary "increase of settlers in the western country."[164]

In fact, the South never had been in serious danger of having a disadvantageous treaty forced upon it. Even though Congress had reinstructed Jay by a vote of seven to five, the Articles clearly required a supermajority of nine states for the ratification of a treaty, and no more than seven states had signified a willingness to relinquish American navigation rights on the Mississippi River. Moreover, after lobbying by the Virginians, the New Jersey legislature had quickly changed its position on the Spanish negotiations, declaring that closing the Mississippi River would reduce the value of the western lands held by Congress that could be sold to pay off the national debt, and instructing its congressional delegation to insist on retaining American navigation rights to the river. Pennsylvania was also a soft vote for the northern position on the Spanish negotiations because its western settlements near the Ohio River gave it a strong interest in keeping the Mississippi open. Monroe had predicted all along that should Pennsylvania and New Jersey desert the northern states on the Mississippi issue, "this intrigue is at an end."[165]

Yet while the South's interests may never have been genuinely at risk, the imbroglio over Jay's Spanish negotiations did serious damage to the causes of intersectional unity and, relatedly, of remedying flaws in the Articles by bolstering the powers of the federal government. In August 1786, Madison told Jefferson that ever since he had left Congress in 1783—and rejoined the Virginia House of Delegates in 1784—he had "been inculcating on our assembly a confidence in the equal attention of Congress to the rights and interests of every part of the republic and on the western members in particular, the necessity of making the union respectable by new powers to Congress if they wished Congress to negotiate with effect for the Mississippi." He asked Jefferson to "figure to yourself the effect" of Jay's proposed reinstruction regarding Mississippi River navigation rights "on the assembly of Virginia, already jealous of northern policy, and which will be composed of about thirty members from the western waters." Furthermore, Madison noted, there were others in Virginia "who, though indifferent to the Mississippi, will zealously play off the disgust of its friends against federal measures." Westerners would "consider themselves as sold [out] by their Atlantic brethren." Even if nine states would never approve of Jay's proposed treaty, "an unsuccessful attempt by six or seven . . . will be fatal, I fear, to an augmentation of the federal authority, if not to the little now existing."[166]

Virginia congressional delegate Henry Lee had shared Madison's concern about "the Mississippi business," which he considered "full of difficulty." Although, as we have seen, Lee actually agreed with most northerners on how to balance the benefits of a commercial treaty with Spain against the costs of abandoning the American claim to navigation rights on the Mississippi River, he nonetheless concluded that "[i]n the debilitated condition of the federal government, it is unwise to risk the offense of any part of the empire, unless to effect great good." In a letter written to Washington while Congress was deliberating on Jay's reinstruction, Lee wrote, "In every state the amplification of the powers of the union has too many enemies," and agreeing to a treaty conferring advantages "not so great to the whole as to a part" would enable "popular declaimers" to thwart "the great object [of] bracing the federal government." Thus, Lee told Congress that regardless of the advantages to be derived from a commercial treaty with Spain, preserving the union trumped all other considerations. Bolstering the union, in turn, required that "the powers of Congress should be enlarged," which would never happen due to southern and western resistance if Congress approved Jay's proposed reinstruction.[167]

Two months after Congress debated the Spanish negotiations, Madison confirmed to Washington that the influence of the Mississippi issue "on the federal spirit is not less than was apprehended." Western members of the Virginia House of Delegates had presented it with resolutions expressing themselves "greatly alarmed" by Jay's "unconstitutional and dangerous" proposal to abandon navigation rights on the Mississippi River. Not only would such a policy provoke "the just resentments and reproaches of our western brethren, whose essential rights and interests would be thereby sacrificed and sold," but it also would destroy "that confidence in the wisdom, justice and liberality of the federal councils which is so necessary at this crisis, to a proper enlargement of their authority."[168]

Madison told his father that the issue "excited much heat" in the Virginia legislature, where even those members who did not come from the western districts tended to sympathize with their interests. Although Madison was confident that northern efforts to relinquish access to the Mississippi River would

Figure 1.5 Virginia congressional delegate Henry Lee III (also known as Light-Horse Harry Lee), who was a decorated cavalry officer during the Revolutionary War, supported ratification of the Constitution at the Virginia ratifying convention, and later became governor of Virginia and represented that state in Congress. (National Portrait Gallery, Smithsonian Institution/Art Resource, NY)

ultimately be frustrated, he feared that they already had produced effects that would be "a great bar to an amendment of the Confederacy, which I consider as essential to its continuance." Many of Virginia's "most federal leading men," Madison wrote Washington, were "extremely soured with what has already passed," and he feared that "unless the project of Congress can be reversed, the hopes of carrying this state into a proper federal system will be demolished." Washington agreed, telling Secretary at War Henry Knox that Virginia showed "a prompt disposition to support and give energy to the federal system," but only "if the unlucky stirring of the dispute respecting the navigation of the Mississippi does not become a leaven that will ferment and sour the mind of it." Madison managed to get the westerners' resolutions watered down in the House of Delegates, though he still described those that passed as "very pointed."[169]

The Mississippi imbroglio seemed to corroborate the suspicion of many southern statesmen that—through either treaties or legislation enacted under a broad power to regulate commerce—a northern majority in Congress would betray the South's economic interests. Thus, for example, in the fall of 1786, Chancellor Edmund Pendleton of Virginia told Madison that while he agreed that Congress's powers should be expanded, he could not "suppress my fears of giving that of regulating commerce," especially in light of "the project for bartering away the navigation of the Mississippi." At the Constitutional Convention in 1787, according to one participant's subsequent recollection, southerners insisted on a supermajority requirement for Senate ratification of treaties because "the navigation of the Mississippi, after what had already happened in Congress, was not to be risked in the hands of a mere majority." More immediately, in the summer of 1786, one of North Carolina's congressional delegates reported that the "unhappy dispute" over Jay's reinstruction had put "out of view" a congressional committee's proposal for numerous amendments to the Articles, including ones granting Congress plenary power over foreign and interstate commerce and establishing a federal court to hear appeals from states in cases involving questions of foreign relations and congressional commercial regulations.[170]

Yet Madison remained able to put an optimistic spin on the Mississippi episode. The lesson he chose to draw was that a more powerful national government, invested with the powers to regulate foreign commerce and to raise sufficient revenue to support a respectable military, could have simultaneously redressed commercial suffering in New England and pressured Spain into opening the Mississippi River to American navigation. Likewise, talk of the union's possibly fragmenting into separate confederacies seemed only to incline Madison more urgently to seek what he called a "radical" overhaul of the Articles of Confederation. Early in 1787, he told Pendleton that dismemberment of the union would be such a great evil that he hoped "the danger of it will rouse all the real friends to the Revolution to exert themselves in favor of such an organization of the Confederacy as will perpetuate the union and redeem the honor of the republican name."[171]

By 1787, most politically prominent Americans agreed that the Articles of Confederation were flawed and in need of amendment. Experience had proved that the requisition system was inadequate and that Congress required some independent revenue-raising authority. Congress also needed to be able to respond to foreign nations' trade discrimination and to enforce national treaty obligations upon the states. Moreover, something had to be done to curtail the ability of states with superior ports—especially New York—to extract tax revenue from surrounding states through their own import duties, which was causing great dissatisfaction and inciting retaliation from their neighbors.

Newspapers were filled with calls for a more powerful federal government. In September 1786, a South Carolina newspaper, reporting intelligence from

New York City, wrote that the nation was "hourly falling into disgrace and this solely for want of those powers required by Congress to levy the impost and to regulate the trade of the states." The article concluded that "[a]s well may ye expect to behold a huge camel shooting through the eye of a needle, as America happy or safe without a federal government." An essay published in Boston around the same time similarly concluded that Congress needed both additional powers and the ability to execute its measures without depending on state cooperation. Washington wrote Jay that things could not "go on in the same train forever," and that it was "the very climax of popular absurdity and madness" to distrust Congress with the powers required to accomplish national purposes. Jay agreed, telling Jefferson that the federal government "(if it may be called a government) is so inadequate to its objects that essential alterations or essential evils must take place."[172]

The real question in 1787 was not whether the Articles should be amended but how radical the changes ought to be. Opponents of major constitutional reform had two significant advantages on their side. First, the experience of Americans within the British Empire had made them deeply distrustful of a powerful central government. William Grayson observed that "the more slack [in] the government, the better the people like it," and he doubted that Americans were "ripe for any great innovations" that would require "the people to pay money or part with power." As Tobias Lear, Washington's private secretary, observed, "[I]n a country as free as this, [the people] must feel very severely before they are fully convinced of the necessity of being governed." Congressional delegate Stephen Mix Mitchell doubted that "those indomitable spirits, who have stood forth in the foremost ranks in this revolution, will ever give up so much of their natural or acquired liberty as is absolutely necessary in order to form a strong and efficient federal government." Only after the Revolutionary generation had passed from the scene, Mitchell believed, could something "easily and efficaciously be done in and for our new republic."[173]

Second, the Articles of Confederation required the unanimous consent of state legislatures for amendments. Experience had shown that securing such unanimity was virtually impossible.[174]

A few bold nationalists such as Hamilton had favored radical reform of the Articles almost from their inception. As early as 1780 and 1781, Hamilton suggested in private correspondence that a constitutional convention be called to reform the "futile and senseless confederation" by investing Congress with "complete sovereignty in all but the mere municipal law of each state." In 1782, the New York legislature approved resolutions probably authored by Hamilton recommending such a convention to Congress. Hamilton confessed to Robert Morris that he doubted other states would concur in the recommendation, but without such a convention, Hamilton feared the states would never "be brought to cooperate in any reasonable or effectual plan. Urge reforms, or exertions, and the answer constantly is, What avails it for one state to make them without the concert of the others?" Indeed, Hamilton opposed the incrementalism of the 1781 and 1783 impost amendments because he saw it as fundamentally inadequate to the needs of the federal government.[175]

In 1786, Grayson voiced a similar opinion, worrying that "a partial reformation will be fatal" because "[i]f particular states gain their own particular objects, it will place other grievances perhaps of equal importance at a greater distance." Grayson preferred that matters "remain as they are than not to probe them to the bottom," and he was not convinced that the nation had yet "arrived at such a crisis as to ensure success to a reformation on proper principles." If it were possible to wait until all matters could be simultaneously considered, however, "one object will facilitate the passage of another, and by a general compromise perhaps a good government may be procured."[176]

Hamilton was a brilliant visionary. Most Americans would require additional time to be persuaded that the Articles required radical reform so soon after their enactment. At a time when Congress could not even convince all the states simultaneously to authorize it to impose a simple impost duty, a fundamental restructuring of the federal government was not in the cards. In 1785, Massachusetts's congressional delegates resisted as "premature" their legislature's instruction to recommend that Congress call a constitutional convention. Upon inquiry, they had discovered that prevailing opinion in Congress, which was then considering specific proposals for commercial reform, provided "no cause to expect" approval of a convention. As late as 1786, Madison told Monroe that because public opinion probably was not yet ripe for a sweeping reform of the Articles, the effort to secure incremental change at the Annapolis convention—discussed in chapter 2—should be allowed to proceed.[177]

To have prematurely attempted a fundamental restructuring of the federal government might have ignited Americans' visceral fears of a conspiracy afoot to interfere with individual liberties. In 1785, the secretary of Congress, Charles Thomson, wrote that for Congress to seek too rapid an expansion of its powers "would only tend to awaken jealousy and might enable designing men to divert the people from what a concurrence of circumstances seems to be preparing them to grant." In advocating an amendment to empower Congress to regulate trade and raise revenue through an impost, Thomson explained that by expanding Congress's powers one at a time, "the minds of the people will be better disposed for granting other necessary powers, and the federal government will without any convulsion be gradually improved as circumstances require, until it attain[s] some degree of perfection."[178]

The congressional delegates of Massachusetts had a different concern when, in 1785, they resisted complying with their legislature's instruction to call for a constitutional convention. Noting that all of the states currently had republican governments, they warned that "plans have been artfully laid and vigorously pursued, which had they been successful ... would inevitably have changed our republican governments into baleful aristocracies." A call for a convention at that moment would "produce throughout the union an exertion of the friends of an aristocracy to send members who would promote a change of government."[179]*

By 1787, a decade's worth of failed efforts at securing incremental reform within the framework of the Articles had convinced many political leaders of the need to pursue more fundamental change—and through other avenues. Congress was broke, yet the states had twice rejected a minimalist proposal to vest it with power to lay import duties. Congress plainly needed the power to respond to other nations' trade discrimination, yet proposals for commercial reform had failed. The imbroglio over American navigation rights on the Mississippi River had sown deep sectional discord within the union. Finally, as we shall see in the next chapter, a rebellion by protestors seeking tax and debt relief that shut down civil courts in several Massachusetts counties in 1786–87 had convinced many Americans that constitutional reform was imperative.[180]

---

* Although their specific concerns were left unstated, the Massachusetts delegates may have worried that southerners, due to their deep commitments to slavery, would never support the sort of democratic and relatively efficacious governments that had developed in northern states. On the eve of independence, John Adams had told his wife that the southern "gentry are very rich, and the common people very poor," and that "[t]his inequality of property gives an aristocratical turn to all their proceedings." In 1782, a Rhode Island congressional delegate, David Howell, observed that "as you go southward, government verges towards aristocracy" and "the common people have less and less to do in government." He bragged, "In New England alone have we pure and unmixed democracy."

2

Economic Turmoil in the States and the Road to Philadelphia

In the mid-1780s, in the midst of a severe economic depression, the Massachusetts legislature, rather than providing the sort of tax and debt relief that a majority of other state legislatures had enacted in response to populist political pressure, cracked down on tax enforcement. In the fall of 1786, thousands of protestors in central Massachusetts responded by shutting down the civil courts to prevent farm foreclosures due to tax delinquencies and indebtedness—a protest that became known to history as Shays's Rebellion.

Many of the nation's political leaders were appalled by both Shays's Rebellion and the economic relief measures that had enabled other states to avoid similar uprisings. Secretary at War Henry Knox, who was appointed by the Confederation Congress to investigate the rebellion, reported that the protestors were "determined to annihilate all debts public and private" and that "anarchy with its horrid train of miseries seems ready to overwhelm this region marked by nature for happiness." Virginia congressional delegate Henry Lee went even further, informing George Washington that "the malcontents" had as "their object together with the abolition of debts, the division of property, and re-union with Great Britain." Lee reported from New York City, where the Confederation Congress was sitting, that "we are all in dire apprehension that a beginning of anarchy with all its calamities has approached and have no means to stop the dreadful work."[1]

Such reports, which were hugely exaggerated, elicited an anguished response from Washington, who declared himself "mortified beyond expression." The accounts he had heard of the commotions in Massachusetts were "equally to be lamented and deprecated," as they "exhibit a melancholy proof of what our transatlantic foe has predicted . . .—that mankind left to themselves are unfit for their own government." Despair over the situation led Washington to write Madison that "no morn ever dawned more favorable than ours did—and no day was ever more clouded than the present!" Washington told his former aide-de-camp David Humphreys that Americans were rendering themselves "ridiculous and contemptible in the eyes of all Europe."[2]

Many members of the American political elite drew the lesson from Shays's Rebellion that, as Henry Lee put it, "[w]eak and feeble governments are not adequate to resist such high handed offenses." Washington expressed alarm to Madison: "Without some alteration in our political creed, the superstructure we have been seven years raising at the expense of much blood and treasure must fall. We are fast verging to anarchy and confusion!" Shays's Rebellion, together with the tax and debt relief measures enacted in most states during the mid-1780s, played a critical role in both the calling of the Constitutional Convention and the drafting of the Constitution itself.[3]

Paper Money and Debtor Relief Legislation

In chapter 1, we saw that the Constitution was in part a response to flaws in the Articles of Confederation—yet it was even more a reaction to the economic relief measures enacted by most states in the mid-1780s. As Madison later reported, interferences by states with "the security of private rights and the steady dispensation of justice" were the "evils which had more perhaps than anything else produced [the Philadelphia] convention." Republican liberty could not, Madison opined, "long exist under the abuses of it practiced in some of the states."[4]

Two months before the Continental Congress in July 1776 declared American independence from Great Britain, it urged the colonies to draft their own constitutions, which most of them did. The imperative of rallying ordinary Americans in support of the revolutionary cause ensured that these constitutions featured many of the following democratic features (though none of them contained all): annual elections, reduced property qualifications for voting and officeholding, secret ballots, popular election of local officials, open legislative sessions, mandatory rotation in office, and weak executives.[5]*

From the outset, some political leaders feared that these constitutions were too democratic, rendering the governments overly dependent upon the people and providing insufficient protection for property rights. In 1776, Charles Carroll of Maryland predicted that the separation from Great Britain would ruin America, not so much because of the "calamities of war" as because of the bad governments it would produce in the states: "[T]hey will be simple

---

* As the French chargé d'affaires later observed, "In those stormy times it was necessary to agree that all power ought to emanate only from the people; that everything was subject to [their] supreme will, and that the magistrates were only [their] servants."

democracies, of all governments the worst, and will end as all other democracies have, in despotism." Robert R. Livingston, one of the drafters of the
Declaration of Independence and soon to become New York's first chancellor, warned of the danger of creating new governments at a time when people
had such "absurd ideas" on the subject, such as direct popular election of government officials. Carter Braxton, a Virginia political leader and signer of the
Declaration of Independence, worried that these state constitutions would
be "fraught with all the tumult and riot incident to simple democracy." In the
mid-1780s, some of the worst fears of these political leaders were realized.[6]

The United States endured a severe economic depression in the wake of the
Revolutionary War—described by many historians as the worst economic climate suffered by the nation until the Great Depression of the 1930s. The war
had damaged a great deal of productive land, especially in the South and the
mid-Atlantic states. Many thousands of slaves, encouraged by the British, had
liberated themselves from southern plantations in the turmoil of war, wiping
out vast amounts of southern "wealth" in the process. Moreover, as the supply
needs of the British and Continental armies disappeared, slackening demand
in the economy led to declining prices and falling farm values.[7]

In addition, while many Americans had envisioned the opening of vast new
economic opportunities once political independence ended British monopolization of their trade, in fact the immediate effect on the American economy of
the rescission of trading privileges within the British Empire was devastating.
The British quickly shut Americans out of the lucrative carrying trade with the
British West Indies and barred the importation into Great Britain of American
goods that could be obtained from British colonies. British shippers were forbidden to buy ships in America, where one-third of British merchant vessels
had been purchased before the war. In an increasingly interconnected economy, international trade fluctuations affected huge numbers of Americans. Per
capita gross national product plummeted nearly 50 percent in the fifteen years
after Americans declared their independence.[8]

In addition, hard currency grew even scarcer than usual as gold and silver
("specie") were shipped overseas to finance a growing trade deficit with Europe
and especially Great Britain, which flooded American markets with goods offered on easy credit after the war. The amount of specie in circulation in the
United States in the early 1780s may have been as little as 20 percent of what it
had been before the war. In 1782, Hamilton told Robert Morris of "an extreme
and universal scarcity of money" in New York. Once rumors began to circulate
of paper money being issued by the states, people became even more inclined
to hoard their gold and silver or send it to Europe for safekeeping.[9]

Amid a depressed economy, most states imposed substantial tax increases
to fund their war debt and to satisfy congressional requisitions—which were

themselves designed primarily to service the nation's own enormous war debt. The $3 million congressional requisition of 1785, which states had to levy additional taxes to supply, seems to have been the straw that broke the camel's back. The taxes imposed by states in the early to mid-1780s were severalfold higher than those Americans had been accustomed to paying as subjects of the British Empire. Holders of government securities—state and federal—provided vigorous political support for raising taxes and then rigorously collecting them.[10]

Because the American economy was much less diversified than Great Britain's, fewer sources of potential tax revenue existed. Only a few states conducted enough foreign trade through their ports to derive significant revenue from import duties. Manufacturing was scarce, which eliminated excise taxes on manufactured goods as a fruitful source of revenue, and states lacking western lands could not raise revenue from that source. Thus, most states had little choice but to impose both poll taxes (taxes on people) and land taxes; these were regressive in that they bore more heavily on the poor, and were a hardship for farmers, who had little wealth that could be readily converted into money.[11]

Furthermore, states generally required that these new taxes be paid in specie. This requirement was imposed because Congress would accept nothing but specie in payment of state requisitions, since its foreign creditors required repayment of loans in gold and silver. In 1785, Abraham Clark proclaimed that it would be "vain and fruitless" for New Jersey to try to raise in specie the sum required to satisfy the recent congressional requisition; only "trading states" such as New York and Pennsylvania could "raise their quota of specie by state imposts."[12]

Given the scarcity of specie and the falling prices of land and farm produce, large numbers of farmers could not pay the increased taxes. When governments cracked down on enforcement, tens of thousands lost their farms. In the 1780s, 60 to 70 percent of taxpaying farmers in some particularly stricken Pennsylvania counties saw their property foreclosed upon. Yet distress sales yielded little at a time when currency was in short supply and hard times were widespread. In 1787, one of Madison's correspondents reported that distress sales were yielding much lower returns than before the war because of "the extreme scarcity of hard money." In one Virginia county, protestors discussed entering into an "association" and collectively refusing to bid on property sold at execution. Many farmers ended up in debtors' prison—as much as 10 percent of the population in one Pennsylvania county in the 1780s. Other landholders simply pulled up stakes and moved west, seeking to escape their debts, avoid debtors' prison, and gain a new financial start in life.[13]

Seeking political remedies for their woes, financially strapped farmers petitioned state legislatures for fiscal, monetary, and debt relief, and the legislatures were highly responsive. Because landownership was much more widely distributed in the United States than in Europe, the brunt of the newly imposed taxes was broadly felt. Moreover, American states offered the least fettered access to suffrage of any jurisdictions in the world. Although voter qualifications varied among the states, by the 1780s at least 60 percent—and perhaps as much as 90 percent—of the adult, white male population was enfranchised. Furthermore, state constitutions established much shorter terms in office for legislators than existed in Great Britain—mostly one-year terms, at least in the lower house of state legislatures, as compared with seven-year terms for Members of Parliament. Shorter terms meant greater political accountability, increasing the inclination of state legislators to respond favorably to popular pressure for economic relief.[14]

The most widely sought form of relief was state issuance of paper money, which would facilitate trade by increasing the circulating medium and enable the payment of debts and taxes—at least to the extent that states agreed to accept tax payments in paper currency. Between the end of the war and 1785, most states had resisted pressure to issue paper currency, but in the following two years seven states capitulated to the demands of harried constituents. Opponents of paper money were denounced as "flint-hearted misers" who were "lying in wait to buy our lands [at auction] for less than a quarter of their real value." Legislative opponents were reported to have been burned in effigy. In June 1786, representatives in the lower house of the Delaware legislature announced that they were "deeply impressed with the distresses of their constituents and anxious to give them relief." Unable to "devise any plan so likely to answer the desired purpose," they approved both the issue of £21,000 in bills of credit and a suspension on foreclosure executions until the bills had been put into circulation.[15]

With several states capitulating to constituent pressure for monetary relief, other states found it increasingly difficult to resist following that path. When the Delaware Assembly agreed to issue paper money, it acknowledged that the upper house of the legislature had recently rejected a similar measure, yet it insisted on trying again in view of popular distress and the information that "several of the neighboring states have emitted paper money." In addition to the seven states that began issuing paper money, there were four other states where proponents only narrowly failed to secure that form of relief, primarily because of opposition from upper legislative houses or executive councils.[16]

In some of the states that issued paper money, legislatures had been taken over by the relief faction. For example, in Rhode Island in 1786, legislators had run for office on a platform promising "to relieve the distressed." In other states, legislators had decided to make tactical concessions to head off populist revolts. As Madison explained with regard to a relief measure—a tax relief measure, not a paper money law—passed by the Virginia legislature in 1786, "This indulgence to the people as it is called and considered, was so warmly wished for out of doors, and so strenuously pressed within that it could not be rejected, without danger of exciting some worse project of a popular cast."[17]

In six of the seven states issuing paper money, at least some of the paper was in the form of long-term loan certificates—twelve years was the norm—offered in fairly small denominations. Borrowers had to pay interest on the loans—usually 6 percent—which were backed by a security interest in land, the value of which was required to be two or three times that of the loan. During the colonial era, such land-bank loans had increased the money supply without causing inflation and had gained widespread popularity, even among creditor merchants who appreciated the need for paper money in a cash-poor economy. When the Delaware House voted in 1786 to issue bills of credit, it noted the "happy effects" of such paper currency before the Revolution, when the paper had traded equally with gold and silver. However, the Delaware Council, while conceding that in an earlier time a "happy concurrence of circumstances gave an advantageous credit to our paper currency," observed that circumstances had changed and defeated the measure. To many opponents of paper money, the drastic depreciation of continental and state currencies during the war was seen as a conclusive argument.[18]

In some states, part of the issuance also took the form of bills of credit given out as interest payments to state creditors. Indeed, in Pennsylvania, New York, and New Jersey, legislatures might not have enacted paper money laws without the supportive lobbying efforts of public creditors. In Pennsylvania, one-third of the paper issuance in 1785 went to the loan office, and two-thirds was designated to pay the interest on state securities. In New York, the state senate rejected a land-bank bill in 1785, but the following year the legislature approved twice as large a paper emission when it was expanded to include bills of credit for public securities holders, who received one-fourth of the total issued. Georgia issued bills of credit as emergency financing for its escalating war against Creek Indians. Several of the seven states issuing paper money made it legal tender for debts (meaning creditors were legally obliged to accept it), including tax obligations owed to the government. Sometimes, the paper was made legal tender only in case of a lawsuit—which had the effect of a stay law (i.e., suspending but not repudiating a debt obligation). In New Jersey, refusal to accept the paper as payment for a debt had the effect of suspending the debt for twelve years, by which point the statute of limitations on suing for repayment would have expired. In Rhode Island, refusal to accept the paper would extinguish the debt entirely.[19]

In 1781, no less an authority than Hamilton had insisted that paper money was essential in a specie-starved economy and that without it, "a great part of the transactions of traffic must be carried on by barter—a mode inconvenient, partial, confined, destructive both of commerce and industry." Those who rejected all paper money because of the drastic depreciation of the continental currency during the war were, according to Hamilton, "not making proper distinctions." Paper money could be "substantial [and] durable" if there were funds to back it up and if it united "the interest and influence of the monied men in its establishment and preservation."[20]

The value of the paper issued in the mid-1780s fluctuated dramatically from state to state, depending in large part on whether the local business community supported it and whether the legislature seemed committed to raising the taxes eventually needed to retire it from circulation. The paper held its value against specie best in New York, where, in the summer of 1786, it was reported to be "pass[ing] universally equal with gold and silver," probably because the local chamber of commerce had declared its willingness to support the measure so long as the legislature did not make the paper legal tender. Similarly, paper held its value in South Carolina, where, according to the Dutch minister plenipotentiary to the United States, the planters "in the most solemn manner, bound themselves together to uphold the credit of the paper money of their state, to receive it at par with gold and silver and to make no discount for payments in hard money." The paper also did reasonably well in Pennsylvania and New Jersey. In the summer of 1786, Madison reported to Jefferson that Pennsylvania, which had taken "the lead in this folly"—Madison did not approve of paper money, as we shall see—had limited the amount to a "not considerable" sum, established good "funds for sinking it," and declined to make it legal tender for debts. As a result, the paper had depreciated by only 10 to 12 percent.[21]

By contrast, the paper depreciated significantly in Georgia and North Carolina—perhaps by 25 to 30 percent in the latter by the summer of 1786. A year later, Madison reported that Pennsylvania's paper, which had been circulating at a relatively small discount, had suddenly stagnated when "a combination of a few people with whom the country people deal on market days" decided no longer to accept it. Only a "timely interposition of some influential characters prevented a riot" by prevailing upon the paper's opponents to announce their willingness to accept it, which "stifled the popular rage and got the paper into circulation again."[22]

Rhode Island's £100,000 paper issue proved by far the weakest and most controversial of any state. Although the law made the paper legal tender, many merchants and more affluent farmers were reluctant to accept it. In response, the legislature quickly enacted serious penalties for refusing to accept the paper on terms equal with specie: a £100 fine for a first offense and disfranchisement for a second. Refusing to be intimidated, the leading merchants of

Providence and Newport simply closed shop rather than accept the paper. In the summer of 1786, one traveler reported that those cities "make a most doleful appearance, half the shops being shut, and little or no business of any kind brought to pass."[23]

In a letter to the editor, a "gentleman from Providence" described what happened next: The merchants' boycott of the paper enraged the "lower class of people in Newport to such a degree that they proceeded in a riotous manner" to distribute among themselves all the corn and flour they could "violently lay their hands on." After "a great disturbance" in which "clubs and fists were liberally made use of for ten or fifteen minutes," the rioters were quelled. Yet country farmers were reported to be determined to "starv[e] out" the city merchants to force them to "swallow the paper money." Madison told Jefferson that Rhode Island was "in a sort of convulsion." The value of its paper money quickly declined to about 20 percent of face value and a couple of years later was reported to be trading at less than 10 percent.[24]

Refusing to back down before the merchants, the Rhode Island legislature enacted even more punitive enforcement mechanisms. Creditors who refused to accept the paper money as legal tender were to be tried within three days of an informant's pressing charges in special court proceedings without juries or the right to appeal a conviction. When a state court suggested this law was probably unconstitutional—without actually striking it down, because the court ruled that it lacked jurisdiction in the case—the legislature threatened the judges with impeachment. The legislature also began to redeem the state's debt in paper money, forcing public creditors to accept it at face value despite its dramatic depreciation. Finally, while the legislature was willing to force out-of-state creditors to accept Rhode Island paper money tendered by the state's debtors, it passed a law to protect Rhode Island creditors from being forced to accept the same paper when tendered by out-of-state debtors—a stance that naturally provoked retaliatory action by surrounding states.[25]

State legislative responses to populist pressure for relief did not end with paper money. Several states deferred tax obligations. Virginia permitted them to be paid in produce—tobacco—instead of money. Some states also enacted more lenient tax collection procedures. For example, Pennsylvania passed a law requiring tax collectors, before seizing the property of someone who was delinquent in the payment of taxes, to submit the target's name to a justice of the peace—a popularly elected official likely to be swayed by local public opinion—who would then determine whether the seizure was justified.[26]

Other states went even further in their relief measures, enacting laws to ameliorate private debt obligations, which—amid rampant deflation—had become relatively more expensive to repay. Tax crackdowns and rumors that paper money was about to be issued increased the urgency of private debt adjustment because private creditors would sue to recover debts in order to satisfy their tax obligations, and all creditors had incentives to force the repayment of debts before the issuance of paper money of unreliable value could reduce the value of those debts.[27]

To preempt such actions by creditors, some states enacted stay laws, which enabled debtors to defer repayment of private debts for a certain period of time, and laws allowing debts to be paid in installments. Other states authorized repayment of private debts in kind rather than in cash. South Carolina allowed debtors to tender real property in lieu of money to pay debts and provided for that property to be appraised by the debtors' neighbors, forbade auction sales that failed to realize three-quarters of the appraised value, and barred imprisonment of those whose auctioned property failed to cover an unpaid debt.[28]

From the perspective of debtor farmers, tax and debt relief measures were not dishonest attempts to escape the obligation of lawful debts but rather eminently reasonable efforts to ameliorate an economic depression by easing an oppressive tax burden, loosening the money supply, and preventing massive farm foreclosures. Thus, in the South Carolina backcountry, 189 farmers signed a petition explaining that "[t]he ravages of the enemy [in the] late war" had "greatly reduced" their ability to pay hard-money taxes, and pleading with the legislature to issue paper currency and make taxes payable in kind. A South Carolina newspaper essayist declared, "Let a medium be circulated through the state, and the backcountry will pay its taxes and debts with as much alacrity as those parts of the state where specie can be had." A Rhode Island newspaper defended the relief measures adopted by its state legislature: "Many irreproachable characters, who are perfectly clear of debt likewise . . . are persuaded that without any increase of medium the middling and lower class of mankind must be ruined by gaols [jails] and sheriffs' vendues [public auctions]." Abraham Clark, a leader of the paper money faction in the New Jersey Assembly, defended a republican government's right to "help the feeble against the mighty."[29]

Relief measures were especially appropriate, proponents argued, because the beneficiaries of the heavy state taxes being levied were primarily speculators who were purchasing government debt at a fraction of par during stringent economic times. One Pennsylvanian wondered why "should we make crafty speculators, who have neither had the credit of their country, the welfare of their fellow citizens, nor even their own honor in view, the most wealthy men in the state." It would be "unjust and cruel" for these "trading people" to "acquire fortunes with an unheard of degree of rapidity," funded by taxes on the very same people who had sold their certificates for a pittance. Another Pennsylvania farmer thought the people of the state would never agree "to pay such an enormous perpetual tax purely to enrich a few men who had bought up the certificates for a mere song."[30]

Those Revolutionary War veterans who had been paid their salaries in government notes that they later sold to speculators were especially aggrieved by higher taxes that were imposed to enrich those speculators. An "Old Soldier" complained in a Massachusetts newspaper that war veterans had been forced by economic exigencies to sell their paper at 10 to 15 percent of face value, yet now they were being taxed to pay off the notes at a much higher value for the benefit of "the man who has sauntered at home during the war, enjoying the smiles of fortune, wallowing in affluence, and fattening in the sunshine of ease and prosperity." Raising a very different objection, other relief seekers protested paying taxes that were partially allocated to funding the pensions of Continental Army officers—pensions that they believed had been extracted through a threatened mutiny against their government.[31]

As much as 90 percent of government securities ultimately fell into the hands of speculators, who had the financial resources to be patient in holding onto them and the political clout necessary to pressure governments to redeem them at face value. By 1785, federal securities were trading at roughly one-eighth of their face value, which meant that speculators would enjoy an enormous profit if the paper was redeemed at par, as they were demanding. State securities were trading at similar values. Because interest was paid on the face value of the paper, speculators earned extraordinary rates of return on their investments. For example, when Virginia paid 6 percent annual interest on military certificates that had traded at one-fifth of face value, speculators earned an annual return of 30 percent. Many relief seekers did not demand that their governments entirely repudiate public obligations but only that, when redeeming the debt, they discriminate between the original holders and the speculators who had purchased at a fraction of par.[32]

Not only was government debt increasingly owned by speculators rather than the original holders, but it also was being concentrated in fewer and fewer hands. In 1786, a Rhode Island legislative committee observed that just sixteen people held nearly half of the largest category of state securities. In Massachusetts, thirty-five people held nearly 40 percent of the state's debt. In 1789, a Pennsylvania newspaper declared that of the £111,000 that the state had annually raised from taxpayers and paid to securities holders, £70,000 had gone to just twelve investors. Some relief seekers warned that enriching so few people at the expense of so many would exacerbate economic inequalities and ultimately destroy the political equality required for republican government to succeed.[33]

While opponents of tax and debt relief criticized legislatures for capitulating to populist pressure, supporters of relief attacked legislatures for being insufficiently responsive to constituent demands and overly stingy in the relief provided. Thus, for example, even in the states that issued paper money, relief seekers generally wanted more of it than they got. Moreover, in several of the issuing states, paper money was not made legal tender, meaning that creditors were under no pressure to accept it at face value.[34]

More prosperous Americans tended to have a vastly different perspective on relief legislation than that of most debtor farmers. From the vantage point of the economic elite, public creditors had a sacred right to be repaid what the government had borrowed from them. Americans had gone to war with Great Britain because taking their property through taxation without their consent was "a most manifest display of arbitrary power, pregnant with vassalage and ruin." Yet those who had lent the government money and provided services during the war on the promise of repayment with interest were now essentially having their property appropriated without their consent. It was "exceedingly criminal for a government to treat its best friends and supporters in this manner." In response to the argument that speculators had bought up government debt at discounted rates and thus did not deserve payment at face value, relief opponents argued that investors were entitled to returns on their investment and noted the practical difficulty of distinguishing among classes of public creditors.[35]

Despite the fact that postwar tax rates were high, commodity prices were low, and money was scarce, opponents of relief argued, in the words of John Jay, that the people "are far more unwilling than unable to pay taxes," and that "the treasury is empty though the country abounds in resources." Edward Rutledge of South Carolina lamented that "it will be many years before our people will be convinced of the necessity of paying taxes."[36]

From the perspective of more affluent Americans, people's failure to pay taxes was primarily attributable to their indolence and licentiousness. Governor William Livingston of New Jersey, writing as a "Primitive Whig," complained that Americans who had promised to stand by Congress and General Washington with their lives and fortunes in opposing British tyranny were "now grumbling about paying the taxes, which that opposition, all brilliant in its progress, and victorious in its conclusion, indispensably occasioned." He complained of the "lazy, lounging, lubberly" fellows who sat around drinking, "working perhaps but two days in the week and receiving for that work double the wages [they] earn and spending the rest of [their] time in squandering those . . . non-earnings in riot and debauch," yet then dared to complain "when the collector calls for his tax of the hardness of the times." The farmer who protested that he could not pay taxes was "a man whose three daughters are under the discipline of a French dancing master when they ought every one of them to be at the spinning wheel," and while they should be "dressed in decent homespun, as were their frugal grandmothers, now carry half of their father's crop upon their backs."[37]

The well-to-do held a similar perspective on paper money laws and debtor relief legislation, opining that these measures simply enabled "idle spendthrifts [and] dissipating drones of the community" to live "upon the sweat of their neighbors' brows." Because private debt "almost universally arises from idleness and extravagance," Richard Henry Lee of Virginia argued, the remedy lay in "industry and economy," not relief legislation. The Maryland senate blamed debtors' predicaments on "the exorbitant importation of foreign luxuries, ruinous and gambling contracts, and the extravagance and dissipation of money." Rejecting a paper money bill that had passed the lower house, the Delaware Council explained that debtors' distress "very rarely" flowed from "inevitable misfortune" and much more frequently from "men's living beyond their income or speculating indiscreetly upon their neighbor's property." According to one newspaper writer, paper money was not the solution when specie had been wasted on "gewgaws and trifles."[38]

To the prosperous, relief legislation both symbolized and contributed to the depravity of the people. The "greatest evil" of paper money, according to an article in the *Pennsylvania Gazette*, was that it "destroys the morals of our citizens, creates extravagance, produces endless disputes and frauds, multiplies lawsuits, promotes art and chicanery in business, and thereby prepares us for aristocracy and slavery." According to Virginia congressional delegate William Grayson, relief measures were "violently opposed by the upright and respectable part of the community," and he referred to one particular paper money bill as "one of the most iniquitous things" he had ever seen. One letter writer from New Jersey opined that such laws were "expressly calculated . . . to the utter abolition of both public and private integrity" and would be more honestly entitled "acts conducing to the encouragement of villainy." Massachusetts political leader Theodore Sedgwick saw paper money as a battle between "men of talents and of integrity," who were "firmly determined to support public justice and private faith," and "the dregs and the scum of mankind."[39]

From the perspective of the well-to-do, paper money laws with a legal tender requirement not only undermined public integrity but also violated natural rights to property. Grayson wrote Madison that to issue paper money, which was bound to depreciate, for the purpose of enabling debtors to repay their debts on easier terms was "cheating." He also thought it was obviously unconstitutional because it was "an attack upon property, the security of which is made a fundamental [right] in every state." Grayson concluded, "The ancients were surely men of more candor than we are. They contended openly for an abolition of debts in so many words, while we strive as hard for the same thing under the decent and specious pretense of a circulating medium."[40]

Government also had a sacred obligation, according to these people, to enforce the sanctity of private contracts. Farmers in distressed circumstances were perhaps "the objects of private compassion but they are not the subjects of public legislation." Government acted unconstitutionally when it "devises expedients for succoring a few at the expense of thousands" whose property was thereby rendered "precarious and insecure."[41]

More affluent Americans also made consequentialist arguments against relief legislation. One newspaper contributor opined that "the present fashionable wretched expedient of emitting paper money without solid funds for its redemption" would have "ruinous consequences." Opponents of paper money argued that it inevitably lost its value, citing the disastrous depreciation of continental and state currency during the war and ignoring the more favorable experiences with the paper issued by colonial land banks.[42]

Upper-class Americans defended specie taxes even at a time of scarce hard currency. Robert Morris argued that requiring the payment of taxes in specie inspired industry and thrift, thus countering the natural human disposition to "indolence and profusion." By contrast, paper money, like alcohol, simply fostered dependency and indulgence. One of Washington's correspondents warned that if the Virginia legislature postponed tax collections, then "the people, from being unaccustomed to a regular payment of taxes, may at length refuse to pay any." Madison told Jefferson that deferring taxes simply encouraged people to spend their money on luxury items imported from Europe, which compounded the problem of scarce specie, led to price deflation, and thus made paying future taxes even more difficult.[43]

Opponents of paper money argued that it diverted the investment of capital from more useful enterprises into speculation. Paper money also was said to deter private loans or at least to result in exorbitant interest rates as creditors sought to protect themselves against the possibility that they would be forced to accept it by a tender law. In 1787, the Virginia legislature approved a resolution sponsored by George Mason, which declared that "the present scarcity of circulating money has been, in a great measure, caused by the general fear and apprehension of paper currency, inducing men to lock up their gold and silver or remit it to Europe, and prefer receiving a very low interest for it there, to the risk of lending or letting it out here." A "Primitive Whig" asked why anyone should send his hard money "into this breathing cheating world, as long as any legislature lends weapons to the borrower to defend himself against the honest repayment of the loan." Opponents also argued that paper money encouraged delay in the payment of taxes and debts in the hope that its depreciation would enable payment on easier terms, and inhibited interstate commerce because out-of-state merchants had difficulty ascertaining the true value of paper money issued by states other than their own.[44]

Madison held precisely the negative view of relief legislation just described, which is important given his critical role in creating the Constitution. In the Virginia legislature, Madison coauthored a resolution opposing paper money as "unjust, impolitic, destructive of public and private confidence, and of that virtue which is the basis of republican governments." He told Jefferson that "[n]othing but evil springs from this imaginary money," which he called a "fictitious" medium unknown to natural law. Experiments in paper money were "morally certain" to fail because "depreciation is inevitable." Another of paper money's "numerous ills" was that it produced "the same warfare and retaliation among the states as were produced by the state regulations of commerce," as states sought to protect their creditors from being victimized by other states' paper money.[45]

Madison's correspondence in 1786 and 1787 constantly referred to the "appetite for" and the "itch for" paper money and debtor relief legislation. He always described such measures in derogatory terms—"not consonant to the proper principles of legislation" and an "epidemic malady." When in 1786 Madison uncharacteristically voted in favor of a bill to accept tobacco in lieu of specie in the payment of taxes, he justified his vote to Washington as "a prudential compliance with the clamors within doors and without, and as a probable means of obviating more hurtful experiments"—that is, the "greater evil" of paper money.[46]

To most well-to-do Americans, the tax and debtor relief legislation of the mid-1780s represented a "revolution" in government. They diagnosed the problem as one of excess democracy. State governments had proved too responsive to the public will—to the derogation of property rights.[47]

As early as 1782, Hamilton had told Robert Morris that "the general disease which infects all our constitutions [is] an excess of popularity. . . . The inquiry constantly is what will please, not what will benefit the people. In such a government there can be nothing but temporary expedient, fickleness and folly." In 1786, Grayson wrote Madison, "Montesquieu was not wrong when he said the democratical might be as tyrannical as the despotic; for where is there a greater act of despotism than that of issuing paper to depreciate for the purpose of paying debts on easy terms?" Madison likewise deprecated "the unruly temper of the people," which had led to "unwise and wicked proceedings" in many states.[48]

Richard Henry Lee now concluded that a departure "from simple democracy" was "indispensably necessary." Lee's cousin Charles Lee wrote Washington that unless state legislatures could be reconstructed to make them "more powerful and independent of the people, the public debts and even private debts will in my opinion be extinguished by [them]." Reflecting on the state relief measures of the 1780s, Grayson concluded that, "however excellent democratical governments may be in some respects, the payment of money and the preservation of the public faith are not among their good qualifications."[49]

The solution, according to one Boston writer, was for rulers to be made "more firm and independent." As Hamilton put it, state governments needed to be supplied with an "order that has a will of its own," so that they would be willing to use coercive measures, if necessary, to collect taxes and enforce the repayment of debts. Washington told Jay, "We have, probably, had too good an opinion of human nature." Experience taught "that men will not adopt and carry into execution measures best calculated for their own good without the intervention of a coercive power." Perhaps for the first time, some leading statesmen began to consider whether Congress ought to be empowered not only to raise taxes and regulate commerce but also to block populist economic policies in the states.[50]

Rhode Island's extremist monetary policy seems to have played an especially important role in rallying elite opinion in support of a national solution to the perceived problem of state relief legislation. Newspaper contributors and prominent statesmen denounced Rhode Island's government for its "villainy, rascality, oppression, cruelty and devilishness." A Massachusetts resident wrote that "the other states will justly consider [Rhode Island] as cheats—traitors to the nation, public robbers, and armed plunderers of their neighbors." A Connecticut critic denounced Rhode Island's paper money law as "the most extraordinary that ever disgraced the annals of democratical tyranny." Only "the depravity of human nature . . . can sanctify such palpable fraud and dishonesty by a solemn act of legislation."[51]

Critics began frequently to refer to the state as "Rogue Island" and "Fool Island." Early in 1787, the *Providence Gazette* reported that a bill introduced in the Rhode Island legislature would discharge all existing debts and provide for an equal distribution of property within the state. The article was probably a spoof—the bill was said to be entitled "An Act for the More Equal Distribution of Political Happiness"—but it was widely reprinted throughout the country as if it were serious. Rhode Island's reputation was not improved when its governor refused a request from the governor of Massachusetts to issue a proclamation noting that a reward was being offered for the capture of fugitives from Shays's Rebellion—discussed momentarily—who had fled to surrounding states. Even Rhode Island's delegate to Congress admitted this failure to cooperate was "unneighborly."[52]

Observing that "Rhode Island has not many more strides to make to complete her disgrace and ruin," James Manning, one of that state's congressional delegates, noted that "[t]he flagrant violations of the public faith solemnly plighted in the late emissions of paper money on the conditions on which it is emitted" were deemed in Congress "as the completion of our ruin as a nation" and demonstrated the need for "a speedy reform in the policy of the states." One month before the Constitutional Convention met in Philadelphia, one southerner sent a message to Rhode Islanders that was reprinted in newspapers across the nation. Observing that "matters have come to such an alarming crisis that the confederation must take notice of you," he expressed the hope that the Philadelphia convention would take measures "to reduce you to order and good government, or strike your state out of the union and annex you to others; for as your legislature now conducts [itself, it] is dangerous to the community at large."[53]

Shays's Rebellion

With good reason, state legislators feared violent repercussions if they did not provide the tax and debt relief that the people demanded. In Pennsylvania in 1783 and New Hampshire in 1786, angry protestors surrounded statehouses to force the enactment of relief measures. David Humphreys told Washington that in New Hampshire only the intervention of the state militia had suppressed a "very considerable insurrection without the effusion of blood." In the summer of 1785, tax collectors in several backcountry districts in South Carolina met armed resistance. Altogether, during the 1780s, scores of western counties across half a dozen states endured debtor and taxpayer revolts that temporarily closed courts.[54]

In Massachusetts, one of the states in which the legislature refused to issue paper money or otherwise provide significant tax or debt relief, popular discontent resulting from widespread farm foreclosures erupted into a full-scale rebellion. The Massachusetts constitution of 1780, which was drafted (largely by John Adams) several years after most other states had written their constitutions, was one of the least populist in the nation, reflecting conservative desires to restrain direct popular influence on government. The constitution raised property qualifications for voting and officeholding and apportioned the lower house of the legislature to the advantage of eastern mercantile towns. It also empowered the governor, unlike the chief executives of every other state, to veto legislation.[55]

Probably in part because of its conservative constitution, Massachusetts was the only state in the 1780s that sought both to fund its public debt at face value and to retire it quickly, which translated into an onerous tax burden on its citizens. In 1785, voters elected James Bowdoin governor, and his administration increased the rigor of tax enforcement, demanding immediate payment—including arrears—and threatening to hold county sheriffs personally liable if they did not quickly settle outstanding accounts.[56]

To service and retire the state's debt, as well as to satisfy the congressional requisition of 1785, the Massachusetts legislature imposed new taxes in 1786, including levies on property and polls. Several of the new taxes required payment in specie, which was scarce. The taxes proved especially burdensome to farmers in the counties of central and western Massachusetts, where people were poorer and hard currency difficult to obtain.[57]

As John Adams later explained to Thomas Jefferson, "The Massachusetts Assembly had, in its zeal to get the better of [its] debt, laid on a tax, rather heavier than the people could bear." Farmers protested to the legislature that taxes could not be paid "without a greater quantity of circulating cash" and complained that, in the prevailing economic climate, auction sales of forfeited property would realize only a small fraction of fair value. One petition noted that "some of our persons are seized for taxes, some children are destitute of milk and other necessaries of life by the driving of the collectors." Another petition warned that without relief half of the county's residents would be

Figure 2.1 Governor James Bowdoin, who was a revolutionary leader in Massachusetts, was elected president of the convention that wrote the state's 1780 constitution and later supported ratification of the Constitution at the Massachusetts ratifying convention. (Courtesy of Independence National Historical Park)

bankrupted and hordes of farmers simply would leave the state. Petitioners called for reducing interest payments on the state's funded debt, cutting the salaries of public officials, relocating the state capital from Boston, and creating a paper-money land bank, which could lend money to farmers based on the value of their land. One petition urged the suspension of debt suits and tax collection for nine months, "[c]onsidering the calamitous circumstances into which unhappy debtors are involved."[58]

The Massachusetts legislature rejected all pleas for relief. Ignoring the high tax rates maintained to pay the war debt, the eastern commercial elite, which dominated the government, blamed farmers for squandering their money in taverns and on European imports. According to the future lexicographer Noah Webster, it was "fact, demonstrated by correct calculation, that the common people in this country drink rum and tea sufficient every year to pay the interest of the public debts—articles of luxury which so far from doing them any good, injure their morals, impair [their] health and shorten their lives." For the government to grant relief would simply encourage indulgence and luxury. Benjamin Lincoln, who led the army that eventually suppressed the rebellion, explained to Washington that Massachusetts farmers had been "diverted from their usual industry and economy, [and a] luxuriant mode of living crept into vogue." Then, instead of "the indolent and improvident" repudiating their "idleness and sloth," they complained "of the weight of public taxes, of the insupportable debt of the union, of the scarcity of money, and of the cruelty of suffering the private creditors to call for their just dues."[59]

Many towns in central Massachusetts protested the legislature's refusal to grant relief by withdrawing their representatives. Beginning late in the summer of 1786, tax collectors in some central Massachusetts counties encountered armed resistance, and newspapers reported "alarming insurrections in different counties to prevent the sitting of their courts of justice." The Dutch minister plenipotentiary to the United States reported that "[i]n the state of Massachusetts, which has always distinguished itself by the wisdom of its measures, the fire of discord begins . . . to kindle; and the people have even assembled in a tumultuous manner and forcibly hindered the sitting of their court." The episode known to history as Shays's Rebellion had begun.[60]

The rebels consisted of several thousand residents of five Massachusetts counties. While their forcible resistance focused primarily on tax collection, it extended to the payment of private debts. Between August 1786 and February 1787, armed protestors forced courts in those five counties to adjourn without doing their business. Kinship and community ties played an important role in determining who participated in the rebellion. Many of the rebels fell within the top 20 percent of local taxpayers; indebtedness was not correlated with poverty. Many participants were Revolutionary War veterans and political

Figure 2.2 Benjamin Lincoln, who was a major general in the Continental Army, served as the Confederation's first secretary at war and later voted to ratify the Constitution at the Massachusetts ratifying convention. (Courtesy of Independence National Historical Park)

leaders in their communities. Their protest reflected not just their specific grievances with high taxes and unmanageable debt but also a more general resentment toward an eastern elite that they felt was determined to impose aristocratic rule upon them—for example, by retaining property restrictions on suffrage, which most western towns simply disregarded.[61]

The Massachusetts legislature responded to the rebellion with a mixed message. On the one hand, it tried to pacify the rebels by offering some relief to taxpayers and debtors. On the other hand, it passed a harsh Riot Act and delegated broad power to the governor to suspend the writ of habeas corpus.[62]

Protestors responded by organizing military units to defend themselves and their farms. The climax of the rebellion came late in January 1787, when Captain Daniel Shays, a thirty-nine-year-old farmer and Revolutionary War veteran, led a group of protestors on a march to the federal arsenal in Springfield in search of weapons and ammunition. Four insurgents were killed when a better equipped army blocked their way. Because local militia units from the affected counties had refused to respond to Governor Bowdoin's call to arms, and because Massachusetts was too financially strapped to borrow the money, private subscribers had had to raise the $20,000 necessary to finance the military force deployed to suppress the insurrection. Significantly, at least half of these financial backers were holders of government securities who had an immediate stake in suppressing the rebellion and enforcing tax collection.[63]

The rebellion's denouement came in February when several thousand of the privately financed troops surrounded and subdued Shays's men. About 150 of the rebels were taken prisoner, and the remainder dispersed, some taking refuge in Vermont or Canada. The rebellion was now reported to be "on the point of being extinguished."[64]

When the rebellion ended, the government, in response to demands of eastern merchants, initially took a hard line against the insurgents, including enacting legislation to disfranchise them and bar them from holding public office for three years. In addition, thousands of insurgents confessed to wrongdoing, hundreds were indicted on charges including treason and sedition, and many received harsh sentences, including the death penalty. However, as we shall see, this initially severe response to the rebellion was ultimately tempered.[65]

Shays's Rebellion played a critical role in the creation of the Constitution. The events in Massachusetts were, according to one of Madison's correspondents, "truly deplorable" and "distressing indeed." Upon hearing the first reports of Shays's Rebellion, a Virginia congressional delegate wrote, "The period seems to be fast approaching when the people of these United States must determine to establish a permanent capable government or submit to the horrors of anarchy and licentiousness," as "[w]eak and feeble governments are not adequate to resist such high handed offenses." A Pennsylvania congressional delegate found Shays's Rebellion especially distressing because he "feared that insurgency and rebellion may pervade more states than Massachusetts."[66]*

Because of the federal arsenal at Springfield, Congress had a direct interest in Shays's Rebellion and had dispatched Secretary at War Henry Knox to Massachusetts to investigate it. In October 1786, Knox had issued an alarming report, noting "great numbers of people in Massachusetts and the neighboring states who avow the principle of annihilating all debts public and private." Such persons probably would "combin[e] themselves into an armed body for

---

* To be sure, not all American political leaders were horrified by Shays's Rebellion. John Adams, who was in London at the time, told Jefferson, who was in Paris, not to "be alarmed at the late turbulence in New England," which he blamed on the Massachusetts legislature's excessive zeal to collect taxes. Jefferson, too, had a famously measured reaction to Shays's Rebellion, telling Abigail Adams that "I like a little rebellion now and then," as the "spirit of resistance to government is so valuable on certain occasions that I wish it to be always kept alive."

the purpose of executing their designs." Knox urged Congress to send troops
to assist the state militia in guarding the military stores in Springfield, and
he warned that "unless the present commotions are checked with a strong
hand, . . . an armed tyranny may be established on the ruins of the present
constitutions."[67]

Viewing the "commotions now existing in Massachusetts . . . as the most
important subject that ever came before that respectable assembly"—in the
words of Massachusetts congressional delegate Rufus King—Congress decided quickly and unanimously to send assistance. Thirteen hundred forty
troops were to be raised—to supplement the seven hundred already in federal
service—under the guise, as Knox explained to Washington, of "averting the
evils on the frontiers," where Indians were "giving indisputable evidence of
their hostile dispositions." Yet the real purpose of the troops was to "strengthen
the principle of government," as Congress had been "fully impressed with the
importance [of] supporting her [Massachusetts] with great exertions."[68]

In letters to Washington, Knox elaborated on his view of Shays's Rebellion.
The laws of Massachusetts had been "arrested and trampled underfoot." While
burdensome taxes "are the ostensible cause of the commotions, . . . that they
are the real cause is as far remote from truth as light from darkness." Knox insisted that the insurgents had paid only very little in taxes and denied that they
were "in a considerable degree oppressed by that government." The real causes
of the insurgency were weak government and the rebels' view that American
property, which had been protected from British confiscation by joint exertions, had become the common property of all. According to Knox, the insurgents had three goals. First, they would "annihilate their courts of justice,
that is private debts." Second, they would abolish the public debt. Third, they
sought "to have a division of property by means of the darling object of most of
the states: paper money."[69]

Knox also told Washington that the insurgents constituted as much as
20 percent of the population in several populous Massachusetts counties.
He estimated their numbers at twelve to fifteen thousand "desperate and unprincipled men," a mob composed "chiefly of the young and active part of the
community." Even worse, there were many of "similar sentiments" in Rhode
Island, Connecticut, and New Hampshire.[70]

Virginia congressional delegate Henry Lee, who served on the committee
tasked with formulating policy in response to Knox's reports, transmitted the
former general's findings to his Virginia friends Washington and Madison,
supplemented by his own embellishments. Lee told Washington that "the
malcontents" in Massachusetts were "a majority of the people" and that they
had as their object abolishing all debts, dividing up property, and reuniting
with Great Britain. He also reported that "the same temper prevails more or

less" in all of New England and would "certainly break forth whenever the op-
portune moment may arrive." In his report to Madison, Lee added a warning
of "extensive national calamity [as t]he contagion will spread and may reach
Virginia."[71]*

Crediting Knox's information as far more reliable than "those vague and
contradictory reports which are handed to us in newspapers," Washington expressed horror at the news of Shays's Rebellion. He lamented the "inconsistency
and perfidiousness" that the insurrection revealed in man's character: How
could the rebels be "unsheathing the sword to overturn" the constitutions
which "but the other day we were shedding our blood to obtain?" Washington
was certain that the British would not remain "an unconcerned spectator of
the present insurrections," but rather would seize the opportunity "to foment
the spirit of turbulence within the bowels of the United States, with a view
of distracting our governments and promoting divisions." He also worried
that the rebellion might spread, as "[c]ommotions of this sort, like snowballs,
gather strength as they roll, if there is no opposition in the way to divide and
crumble them."[72]

Madison, too, believed such reports of "ominous events" and "great commotions," and he shared Washington's grave concern. The insurgents, who
Madison believed had "become formidable to the government" and might
indeed be "as numerous as the friends of government," were probably "secretly stimulated by British influence." Echoing the reports of Lee and Knox,
Madison told his father that while the rebels "profess to aim only at a reform of
their constitution and of certain abuses in the public administration," in fact
"an abolition of debts public and private, and a new division of property are
strongly suspected to be in contemplation." Madison considered it "not improbable that civil blood may be shed" and was "somewhat uncertain whether
the government or its adversaries will be victorious."[73]

Shays's Rebellion also distressed other leading statesmen who would soon
become prominent supporters of constitutional reform at the federal level.
John Jay, for example, informed Jefferson of the "spirit of licentiousness [that]
has infected Massachusetts, which appears more formidable than some at
first apprehended." Jay, too, disbelieved the rebels' professed objectives and

* In the spring of 1787, one of Madison's correspondents reported that in some of Virginia's
tidewater counties "they talk boldly of following the example of the insurgents in Massachusetts
and preventing the courts proceeding to business." Such an insurrection in Virginia could be
even more dangerous, Washington's private secretary explained, because "three-quarters of the
people have nothing to lose." Indeed, in the summer of 1787, Madison wrote Jefferson that in
several Virginia counties, tax protestors had "wilfully burnt . . . the prisons and courthouses and
clerks' offices," and in one of them "the course of justice has been mutinously stopped."

insisted that they had far-reaching clandestine motives: "a rage for property and little regard to the means of acquiring it, together with a desire of equality in all things." Combining such objectives with "the influence of ambitious adventurers," there was no limit to the "injustice and evil" they might do.[74]

When Jefferson first learned of Shays's Rebellion, he expressed concern to Madison that the conclusion many people would draw from it was that "nature has formed man insusceptible of any other government but that of force"— a conclusion that Jefferson thought "not founded in truth, nor experience." Jefferson was right to be worried about how the insurrection would influence the political thinking of elite statesmen. Henry Lee opined that "the impotency of government" had proved to be "an encouragement to . . . the licentious" and concluded that weak governments were inadequate to suppressing "schemes portending the dissolution of order and good government." Washington declared that what the country needed was a government "by which our lives, liberties, and properties will be secured." If the insurgents had genuine grievances, they should be redressed. If not, then the force of the government should be employed against them. If that force proved inadequate, then "all will be convinced that the superstructure is bad, or wants support." Reflecting on Shays's Rebellion in a letter to Jefferson, Jay wrote, "As the knaves and fools of this world are forever in alliance, it is easy to perceive how much vigor and wisdom a government from its construction and administration should possess, in order to repress the evils which naturally flow from such copious sources of injustice and evil."[75]

In New England especially, elite opinion was profoundly influenced by Shays's Rebellion, which seemed to demonstrate the impotence of existing state governments. Knox wrote Washington, "The commotions of Massachusetts have wrought prodigious changes in the minds of men in that state respecting the powers of government. Everybody says they must be strengthened and that unless this shall be effected, there is no security for liberty or property." Boston merchant Stephen Higginson told Knox that "[t]he present moment is very favorable to the forming [of] further and necessary arrangements for increasing the dignity and energy of government" and that "so very favorable an opening shall not be lost."[76]

Massachusetts legislator Christopher Gore wrote to Rufus King that "our government is [too] weak and languid and inefficient" to protect the "personal liberty and property of the subject." Theodore Sedgwick told King, "Every man of observation is convinced that the end of government security [cannot] be attained by the exercise of principles founded on democratic equality." King announced that Shays's Rebellion had taught him that "the great body of the people are without virtue and are not governed by any internal restraints of conscience," and thus he was reconsidering his prior advocacy of "government free as air," which had been based on the mistaken belief that his "countrymen were virtuous, enlightened, and governed by a sense of right and wrong." In a letter to Elbridge Gerry, King actually seemed to celebrate the insurrection, observing that he could "already mark good consequences in the opinions which it authorizes relative to our vigor and spirit."[77]

Shays's Rebellion not only influenced the views of New England statesmen with regard to state government but also convinced many of them that a more powerful national government was necessary. Knox reported to Washington that "men of reflection and principle" believed that the nation had arrived "at that point of time in which we are forced to see our national humiliation," and therefore were "determined to endeavor to establish a government which shall have the power to protect them in their lawful pursuits and which will be efficient in all cases of internal commotions or foreign invasions." Without such a powerful national government, the nation faced "the horror of faction and civil war without a prospect of its termination."[78]

In November 1786, as the rebellion was gathering strength, Stephen Higginson told Knox that he had never seen "so great [a] change in the public mind, on any occasion, as has lately appeared in this state [Massachusetts] as to the expediency of increasing the powers of Congress, not merely as to commercial objects, but generally." He thought that the lamentable weakness of the Massachusetts legislature would "tend much to prepare the public mind for transferring power from the individual governments to the federal" and predicted that, within several months, "we shall here be prepared for anything that is wise and fitting." The following summer, looking back on the rebellion, Samuel Breck, a Boston merchant and speculator in government securities, told Knox that "[t]he danger to which this commonwealth has been exposed . . . will show the necessity of parting with a greater share of our privileges to secure the remainder than we have been willing to do at any former period," and he endorsed a stronger national government that would "reduce the powers of each state to that of our [Massachusetts's] counties."[79]

Shays's Rebellion was disturbing enough to the nation's propertied elite, but what happened next in Massachusetts must have been even more distressing. The relief seekers now sought, as one of their critics observed, to win "the same objects by legislation, which their more manly brethren last winter would have procured by arms"—and the newly elected state legislature gave them much of what they wanted.[80]

The progression toward what many regarded as legislative softness had been underway even before the first blood was spilled in Shays's Rebellion. In the fall of 1786, the Bowdoin administration had relaxed the rigor of its tax enforcement machinery, permitting farmers to pay some back taxes in produce and postponing for several months the date by which sheriffs were obliged to transmit tax collections to the state treasury. The legislature also enacted a stay law that suspended for eight months the requirement that private debts be paid in specie, instead permitting debtors to repay creditors in land or personal property to be appraised by community referees.[81]

Many political leaders throughout the nation criticized such lenient actions. In a letter to Monroe, Grayson disparaged the legislature as "fearful of taking any vigorous steps against the insurgents." In missives to Washington, Knox condemned the legislature's "temporizing expedients," which only led the insurgents to "despise" the government's "impotency" and "proceed in the execution of their designs." Knox declared that "lenient measures instead of correcting, rather inflame the disorders," and he insisted that had coercion been used earlier, "the rebellion would not have arisen to its present height."[82]

In April 1787, less than two months after Shays's Rebellion had been suppressed on the battlefield, legislative elections and a gubernatorial contest were underway in Massachusetts. An incredulous Madison reported to Washington, "We understand that the discontents in Massachusetts which lately produced an appeal to the sword are now producing a trial of strength in the field of electioneering." Madison told Pendleton that if the insurgents could "muster sufficient numbers, their wicked measures are to be sheltered under the forms of the constitution."[83]

John Hancock, whose "acknowledged merits" Madison thought were "not a little tainted by a dishonorable obsequiousness to popular follies," sought to recapture the governorship. Governor Bowdoin's supporters warned that "[t]he insurgents, whose measures have been utterly defeated, when they threatened you by arms, now build their hopes upon their influence in the present election," and they urged voters to re-elect the officeholders who had suppressed the rebellion. Bowdoin's supporters also charged that Hancock had made a deal with the paper money faction and warned that if Hancock won the election, "[t]he same spirit of insurrection, which now reigns in some parts of the country, will be transferred to the seaports, and universal anarchy [will] prevail." Madison, too, assumed that a Hancock victory would mean that paper money would be "the engine to be played off against creditors both public and private."[84]

In the gubernatorial election, Hancock won 75 percent of the vote. Amid unprecedented voter turnout, 71 percent of the seats in the Massachusetts House of Representatives changed hands, and many of the newly elected representatives were insurgents or their sympathizers. Madison told Monroe that the Massachusetts election had "shifted the legislative power into the hands of the discontented party, and it is much feared that a grievous abuse of it will characterize the new administration." Governor Hancock promptly pardoned most of the insurgents, including Daniel Shays, who had fled to Vermont but returned after the pardon. Moreover, the new legislature dramatically cut taxes and eased the stringency of tax collection (though it continued to resist issuing paper money). In June, legislators repealed the law punishing insurgents with disfranchisement and exclusion from office.[85]

Much of the nation's political elite was appalled by this turn of events. Washington's private secretary, Tobias Lear, asked Benjamin Lincoln, "What frenzy can have seized upon the people of your state [Massachusetts] to induce them to aim at an establishment of those principles by law, which, but a few days ago, they were opposing by arms?" Lear feared that unless "some measures are pointed out and adopted to give security to property," the nation was verging "fast towards a point which may . . . involve us in a civil war with all its terrible consequences." In a similar vein, Jay expressed consternation to Jefferson that "the spirit" of Shays's Rebellion had "operated powerfully in the late election. The governor, whose conduct was upright and received the approbation of the legislature, is turned out, and Mr. Hancock is elected. Many respectable characters in both houses are displaced, and men of other principles and views elected."[86]

In the end, the principal difference between Massachusetts and most other states was that tax and debt relief came later to the commonwealth. Because the Massachusetts constitution established a government somewhat more insulated from direct populist pressure than that of most states, officeholders were initially able to resist popular demands for relief. Eventually, though, the relief demands boiled over into open rebellion and the insurgents—though defeated on the battlefield—realized many of their objectives at the ballot box.[87]

In other states, legislators averted rebellions by capitulating to populist demands for relief. For example, as early as 1783, an organized political campaign by relief seekers in Connecticut had produced legislative turnover of 60 percent, followed by the enactment of tax relief. Four years later, the Connecticut legislature simply refused to pay Congress's latest requisition rather than risk something similar to Shays's Rebellion. Grayson reported that "Connecticut would have been in the situation of Massachusetts" had the legislature raised taxes to satisfy the requisition, and he declared that no Connecticut man could "be elected to the office of a constable if he was to declare that he meant to pay a copper towards the domestic debt." Hamilton observed that the Connecticut government "had entirely given way to the people, and had in fact suspended many of its ordinary functions in order to prevent those turbulent scenes which had appeared elsewhere."[88]

Grayson believed that a similar situation prevailed in other states as well. He predicted that if New Hampshire attempted to tax its citizens to pay the domestic debt, "500 Shays would arise in a fortnight." Indeed, Grayson was convinced that "a considerable party in every state" opposed "payment of the domestic debt," and even though that faction had "showed itself openly only in Massachusetts," the "pressure of taxation" would draw it forth elsewhere as well.[89]

By the time Shays's Rebellion had been suppressed, not a single state government was pressing its citizens for tax payments in specie. Even the states with the least populist constitutions—New York and Massachusetts—had capitulated to populist demands for tax and debt relief.[90]

By 1787, many leading statesmen were concluding that only a more powerful national government could check the populist politics of the states. If even Massachusetts could not resist demands for relief legislation, then perhaps reforming state governments would not be a sufficient solution to the crisis sweeping the nation.[91]

Madison declared that Shays's Rebellion "furnish[es] new proofs of the necessity of such a vigor in the general government as will be able to restore health to any diseased part of the federal body." Similarly, Henry Lee predicted that if the "officers of the nation" were not invested with "that power which is indispensably necessary to chastise evil and reward virtue," the time was "fast approaching" when the American people would have to "submit to the horrors of anarchy and licentiousness." Washington thought that only "a liberal and energetic constitution" empowering Congress to check the state governments could provide adequate security to life, liberty, and property.[92]

The moment was thus ripe and immediate action was required. Early in 1787, King told Gerry, "Events are hurrying us to a crisis. Prudent and sagacious men should be ready to seize the most favorable circumstances to establish a more perfect and vigorous government." Richard Henry Lee reported that "the minds of men have been so hurt by the injustice, folly and wickedness of the state legislatures and state executives that people in general seem ready for anything."[93]

Indeed, absent an adequate solution to the problem of state governments succumbing to populist political pressure, it was becoming clear that some people might grow so desperate for order and security that they would repudiate republican government and turn instead to monarchy. Critics of republican government had always depicted it as too weak to adequately protect property rights. In the mid-1780s, many leading American political figures concluded that such predictions were being vindicated.[94]

Responding to Shays's Rebellion, a Massachusetts legislator stated, "I cannot give up the idea that monarchy in our present situation is to become absolutely necessary to save the states from sinking into the lowest abyss of misery." A Providence conservative, reacting to the radical monetary policies of the Rhode Island legislature, declared, "I pray the Lord soon to raise up some good monarch or even an Oliver Cromwell to establish a government, which shall be stable and put our national credit [on firm footing] and secure the lives and property of the people." A Connecticut man who had once been "as strong a republican as any man in America" now declared that "a republic is almost the last kind of government I should choose." Observing that "some of the late laws of Rhode Island are greater stretches of tyranny than have been tolerated in the despotic governments of Europe, and life and property are less secure in Massachusetts, than in the Turkish dominions," he insisted that he "should infinitely prefer a limited monarchy, for [he] would sooner be subject to the caprice of one man than to the ignorance of a multitude."[95]

National leaders such as Jay, Washington, and Madison took seriously such expressions of growing disaffection with republican government. Even before Shays's Rebellion, Jay had told Washington of his fear

> that the better kind of people (by which I mean people who are orderly and industrious, who are content with their situations, and not uneasy in their circumstances) will be led by the insecurity of property, the loss of confidence in their rulers, and the want of public faith and rectitude, to consider the charms of liberty as imaginary and delusive. A state of uncertainty and fluctuation must disgust and alarm such men, and prepare their minds for almost any change that may promise them quiet and security.[96]

As Shays's Rebellion was unfolding, Jay confessed to Jefferson his worries as to "the sentiments which such a state of things is calculated to infuse into the minds of the rational and well intended." For such people, "the charms of liberty will daily fade, and in seeking for peace and security, they will too naturally turn towards systems in direct opposition to those which oppress and disquiet them." If the "very unpleasant situation" continued for long, "tyranny may raise its head, or the more sober part of the people may even think of a king."[97]

In a letter to Jay, Washington agreed that persons disgusted with the weakness of a Confederation Congress that could neither raise funds nor enforce treaties "will have their minds prepared for any revolution whatever." Washington reflected that people were "apt to run from one extreme into another. . . . What astonishing changes a few years are capable of producing!" He reported, "I am told that even respectable characters speak of a monarchical form of government without horror."[98]

Madison also took such sentiments seriously. In February 1787, he told Edmund Randolph, "Many individuals of weight, particularly in the eastern district [i.e., New England], are suspected of leaning towards monarchy." Writing to Pendleton, Madison observed, "The late turbulent scenes in

Massachusetts and infamous ones in Rhode Island have done inexpressible injury to the republican character in that part of the United States, and a propensity towards monarchy is said to have been produced by it in some leading minds."[99]

Yet Madison also believed in the possibility, as he told Washington, of "rendering the republican form competent to its purposes." Doing so might induce those who "lean towards a monarchical government" to "abandon an unattainable object." A properly designed republican government at the federal level, Madison believed, could both redress flaws in the Articles, such as Congress's inability to raise revenue or regulate commerce, and remedy the problem of populist politics in the states. Through mechanisms such as lengthy terms in office, indirect elections, and large constituencies, a new constitution could render the federal government less responsive to populist pressures than the state governments had proved to be. If empowered with a veto over state legislation, that federal government also might be able to curtail the abuses of populist democracy in the states.[100]

Yet Madison and his political allies appreciated that they must act quickly and decisively, before many well-to-do Americans had grown irremediably disillusioned with republican government. As Madison later told his colleagues at the Philadelphia convention, if they did not improve the republican form of government and left people to judge of it by the "operations of the defective systems under which they now live, it is much to be feared the time is not distant when, in universal disgust, they will renounce the blessing which they have purchased at so dear a rate, and be ready for any change that may be proposed to them."[101]

The Annapolis Convention

The Constitutional Convention came about in a haphazard, almost fortuitous fashion. By the end of 1785, after the apparent failure of several proposed amendments to expand Congress's power, many advocates of reform had concluded that effective change must originate with some source other than Congress. Monroe declared that Congress's proposals to expand its own power were "received with such suspicion by the states that their success, however proper they may be, is always to be doubted." Perhaps a separate body, "assembled under the particular direction of the states for a temporary purpose, in whom the lust for power cannot be supposed to exist," would be more successful. Washington was also "strongly inclined to believe that it [Congress] would not be found the most efficacious channel" for recommending changes to the Articles.[102]

Moreover, by 1786, congressional delegates were no longer able to achieve consensus on which amendments to propose. Even before the Mississippi River issue had greatly exacerbated sectional tensions, Grayson reported to Madison that congressional delegates would "never be able to agree on the proper amendments even among themselves" because New Englanders "mean nothing more than to carry the commercial point," and they would support no amendments of interest to other regions.[103]

In the summer of 1786, a congressional committee proposed several amendments to the Articles. Among other things, Congress would be empowered—subject to a supermajority requirement—to regulate foreign and interstate commerce and to penalize states failing to meet their requisitions for funds and soldiers, and even to collect such requisitions itself. In addition, the number of states required to ratify amendments changing the system of federal revenue would be reduced from thirteen to eleven, and federal courts would be created to hear appeals from the state courts in cases adjudicating the meaning of treaties and federal regulations involving trade and revenue. Because the committee issued its recommendations amid rising sectional tension over the Mississippi River issue, its proposals were tabled—never to be reconsidered.[104]

Madison, however, had already decided to pursue a different approach. Rotated out of office as a congressional delegate in 1783, as required by the Articles, Madison had been elected to the Virginia House of Delegates. Late in 1785, observing that the states' efforts to counteract British trade discrimination had "recoiled more or less on the states which ventured on the trial" and that "[t]he necessity of harmony in the commercial regulations of the states has been rendered every day more apparent," Madison tried to convince the Virginia legislature to approve a resolution calling on the state's congressional delegates to propose a general congressional power to regulate trade. To ensure that Congress would be granted "such direct power only as would not alarm," Madison's proposal specified that the exercise of this power would require a two-thirds majority in Congress and that the money collected from any duties Congress imposed would belong to the states in which they accrued. Madison hoped that if Virginia, a southern state, approved such a resolution, it would help to conciliate the North over the commercial issue.[105]

Yet Madison was disappointed by the reaction of the Virginia House of Delegates to his proposal, which he attributed to the delegates' deep hostility toward northern interests. When the House voted to limit the duration of the proposed commerce power to thirteen years, Madison reported that this "so far destroyed its value in the judgment of its friends that they chose rather to do nothing than to adopt it in that form." Madison explained to Washington that to grant a temporary commercial power to Congress in "the hope of renewal" was "visionary," because "caprice, jealousy, and diversity of opinions" would make it "impossible to revive" the grant once it expired. Perhaps he shared Monroe's concern that Congress would be reluctant to take "decisive measures" under a temporary grant of power for fear of "prevent[ing] its renewal" and that foreign nations would "avoid those stipulations in our favor which may hereafter furnish arguments for its renewal." Whatever his precise reasoning, Madison concluded that it would be "better to trust to further experience and even distress for an adequate remedy than to try a temporary measure which may stand in the way of a permanent one."[106]

In place of a watered-down version of Madison's proposal, those delegates favorable to granting commercial powers to Congress suggested a conference of "politico-commercial commissioners" from all of the states "for the purpose of digesting and reporting the requisite augmentation of the power of Congress over trade." Madison, who was not very enthusiastic about the idea of such a conference, told Washington that this proposal would "have fewer enemies" and would seem "naturally to grow out of the proposed appointment of commissioners for Virginia and Maryland, concerted at Mount Vernon for keeping up harmony in the commercial regulations of the two states." On the last day of its session ending in January 1786, the Virginia legislature approved a call for a convention of the states "to consider how far a uniform system in their commercial regulations may be necessary to their common interest and their permanent harmony" and to propose an appropriate amendment to the Articles to be considered by Congress and the states. Madison was appointed as a commissioner.[107]

This was not the first proposal that had been made for a convention of the states. As we have seen, as early as 1780, Hamilton had mentioned such an idea in private correspondence (and he was not the first to do so), and in 1782, the New York legislature had called for such a convention. Others had sporadically made similar proposals in the years since.[108]

Indeed, early in 1786, responding to Congress's financial woes, Charles Pinckney of South Carolina made a motion that Congress call a convention to alter the Articles to invest Congress with greater powers.* Grayson told Madison that "some serious thought" was being given in Congress to Pinckney's motion

---

* Charles Pinckney was born in 1757 in Charleston, South Carolina, the son of a prominent lawyer-planter. Elected to the state's House of Representatives in 1779 at the age of twenty-two, Pinckney became a junior officer in a Charleston militia regiment during the Revolutionary War and saw action in battles in Savannah and Charleston in 1779 and 1780. When Charleston surrendered to the British, Pinckney became a prisoner of war.

In the 1780s, Pinckney served several terms in the Confederation Congress, where, as we have seen, he opposed Secretary for Foreign Affairs John Jay's efforts to barter American claims to navigation rights on the Mississippi River for a commercial treaty with Spain, and he served on a congressional delegation appointed in 1786 to remonstrate with the New Jersey legislature

because the present confederation was "utterly inefficient, and that if it remains much longer in its present state of imbecility we shall be one of the most contemptible nations on the face of the earth." Although Grayson had not made up his mind whether to endorse such a convention, he confided to Madison (borrowing the words of Shakespeare's Hamlet) that he was "doubtful whether it is not better to bear those ills we have than fly to others that we know not of."[109]

Meanwhile, the Virginia commissioners appointed by the legislature proposed Annapolis as the venue for the commercial convention it had called and early September 1786 as its date. Randolph explained to Madison that Annapolis was chosen because it was "most central and farther removed from the suspicion, which Philadelphia or New York might have excited, of congressional or mercantile influence."[110]

over its threat not to pay its congressional requisitions until New York unconditionally ratified the impost amendment. Pinckney was one of the most prominent advocates within Congress for constitutional reform, and in the summer of 1786, he chaired a committee that proposed several amendments to expand Congress's powers.

At the Constitutional Convention, as we shall see, Pinckney was a frequent contributor to debates, and he submitted his own plan for constitutional reform, though it never became the focus of extended discussion. (Decades later, Madison was incensed at Pinckney's postconvention claims, based on this plan, to have been the principal draftsman of the Constitution. Both Madison and Washington considered Pinckney a shameless self-promoter.) In Philadelphia, Pinckney advocated a strong national government with an unqualified veto over state legislation. He also favored constitutional mechanisms for minimizing popular influence on the national government, such as indirect elections and very high property qualifications for office. Together with the other South Carolina delegates at the Philadelphia convention, Pinckney was a powerful advocate for the interests of slave owners, insisting that slaves ought to count equally with free persons in apportioning representation in Congress and demanding constitutional protection for the foreign slave trade.

Pinckney strongly supported ratification of the Constitution in the South Carolina legislature and in the state's ratifying convention. Beginning in 1789, he served four nonconsecutive terms as governor of South Carolina, leaving office for the last time in 1808. During the Washington administration, Pinckney unsuccessfully sought diplomatic posts in Europe. Eventually, however, he broke with the Federalist Party, was appointed to the US Senate as a Jeffersonian Democratic-Republican in 1798, and campaigned for the Jefferson-Burr ticket in 1800, despite the fact that his cousin Charles Cotesworth Pinckney was the Federalist vice presidential candidate.

In 1801, President Jefferson appointed Pinckney minister to Spain, where, in 1803, he was instrumental in obtaining Spanish acquiescence to the treaty by which the United States purchased the Louisiana Territory from Emperor Napoleon of France (though Pinckney failed in his efforts to secure a Spanish cession of Florida to the United States). Four years after purportedly retiring from politics in 1814, Pinckney was elected to Congress, where he participated in the debates over northern efforts to condition Missouri's admission to the union on its abolishing slavery. In these debates, Pinckney, as one of the few surviving members of the Constitutional Convention, enjoyed a privileged status when it came to expounding on the Framers' "original understanding" of Congress's powers regarding slavery. After serving a single term in the House, Pinckney returned to Charleston, where he died in 1824.

Figure 2.3 Charles Pinckney, who played a prominent role in the Philadelphia convention and was a strong supporter of ratification at the South Carolina ratifying convention. (Library of Congress)

The idea of the Annapolis convention appealed to Madison because, as he told Monroe, efforts to expand congressional powers "through the medium of Congress have miscarried." Madison defended the limited agenda of the convention on the grounds that the Virginia legislature "would have revolted . . . against a plenipotentiary commission to their deputies." Thus, the option "lay between doing what was done and doing nothing." Moreover, while Madison was "not in general an advocate for temporizing or partial remedies," he thought that, on this occasion, "push[ing] too far may hazard everything." The nation's situation might become "desperate" if "the present paroxysm of our affairs be totally neglected."[111]

Grayson, by contrast, worried that if supporters of commercial reform got what they wanted in Annapolis, they might lose interest in further amendments to the Articles. He told Madison, "The state of Virginia having gone thus far, it is [a] matter of great doubt with me whether she had not better go farther and propose to the other states to augment the powers of the delegates so as to comprehend all the grievances of the union."[112]

The stakes of the Annapolis convention rose in February 1786, when the New Jersey legislature resolved not to comply with further congressional requisitions until New York unconditionally ratified the second impost amendment. At this point, Madison told Jefferson that if the Annapolis convention "should come to nothing, it will I fear confirm Great Britain and all the world in the belief that we are not to be respected, nor apprehended as a nation in matters of commerce."[113]

Madison was in fact pessimistic about the prospects of the coming convention. Given the disastrous position in which Congress's inability to regulate commerce had left American trade, Madison thought that the calling of the Annapolis convention should have commanded universal assent among the states, yet he predicted to Jefferson that this view "assuredly will not be taken by all even of those whose intentions are good." Indeed, he "almost despair[ed] of success" when he considered "that the states must first agree to the proposition for sending deputies, that these must agree in a plan to be sent back to the states, and that these again must agree unanimously in a ratification of it." Still, something had to be attempted, and in his view this was "the best that could possibly be carried through the legislature here [in Virginia]."[114]

Madison also told Jefferson that delaying the project of constitutional reform might prove fatal, for two reasons. First, "foreign machinations" within some state governments were increasingly likely to become a problem. Second, "the probability of an early increase" in the number of states—as Vermont had been petitioning for statehood since 1777 and Kentucky was now preparing to separate from Virginia—would render the unanimity required for amendments even more difficult to secure, especially as new western states might "bring sentiment[s] and interests less congenial with those of the Atlantic states." Even if the Annapolis experiment were to fail and "nothing can be done" concerning commerce, Madison told Monroe, "such a piece of knowledge will be worth the trouble and expense of obtaining it."[115]

The month before the Annapolis convention met, Madison told Jefferson, "Many gentlemen both within and without Congress wish to make this meeting subservient to a plenipotentiary convention for amending the Confederation." Although Madison confessed that his "wishes are in favor of such an event," the crisis over Jay's negotiations with Spain had led him to temper any expectations of proceeding "beyond a commercial reform." "To speak the truth," Madison acknowledged, "I almost despair even of this." He worried that southerners who felt betrayed by northerners' efforts to have Congress reinstruct Jay would resist any attempts to increase Congress's powers.[116]

Many northern statesmen had similarly low expectations for the Annapolis convention. Rufus King of Massachusetts doubted that the convention would go more than "a little way in effecting those measures essentially necessary for the prosperity and safety of the states." King was dubious of a conference to discuss commercial reform that originated with Virginians, who he thought did not really believe in the necessity of "a commercial system common to all the states." Although King believed that merchants throughout the nation were "of one mind," he suspected that a majority of southern planters were opposed to granting the federal government the power to regulate commerce, "the only plan which can insure the prosperity and honor of the confederacy."[117]

Another Massachusetts political leader, Theodore Sedgwick, likewise doubted that any "reasonable expectations of advantage can be formed from the commercial [Annapolis] convention." Sedgwick had "decisive evidence" that the Virginia legislators who proposed the convention had acted "with an intention of defeating the enlargement of the powers of Congress." He believed that if Congress were not to be authorized to regulate commerce, then northern and mid-Atlantic states should begin seriously to calculate the value of the union. In a letter to Caleb Strong, Jr., a Massachusetts legislator and later a delegate to the Constitutional Convention, Sedgwick wrote, "Should their [the southern states'] conduct continue the same, and I think there is not any prospect of an alteration, an attempt to perpetuate our connection with them, which at last too will be found ineffectual, will sacrifice everything to a mere chimera." Instead, "the limits of the confederacy" should be restricted to what was "natural and reasonable," and "a real and an efficient government" could be established therein.[118]

Probably aware of such sentiments, Monroe worried that the New England states would not even attend the Annapolis convention, and he tried to convince the chief executive of New Hampshire that the meeting would be "the source of infinite blessings to this country." Monroe told Madison that New Englanders had to be assured that the convention would lead to broad commercial reform or else their "intrigues" for splitting the union into separate confederacies would accelerate. He concluded that Annapolis represented "a most important era in our affairs."[119]

A month before the scheduled date of the Annapolis convention, half of the states had yet to appoint commissioners. Observing that there must be "no risk of [the convention's] being rendered contemptible," a Delaware commissioner worried, "[H]ow ridiculous will all this parade appear?" In the end, only nine states appointed commissioners to the convention. According to Madison, Connecticut had not objected in principle, but the convention had been "rendered obnoxious by some internal conventions which embarrassed the legislative authority." The South Carolina legislature, after approving the proposed amendment expanding Congress's commercial powers for fifteen years, apparently considered the Annapolis convention superfluous and did not appoint commissioners.[120]

Explaining Maryland's failure to appoint commissioners to Annapolis, Daniel Carroll told Madison that the Maryland senate had vetoed the appointment for fear that the convention, even if proposed by the Virginia legislature "with the best intentions," would "have a tendency to weaken the authority of Congress, on which the union, and consequently the liberty and safety of all the states, depend." Carroll noted that "sound policy, if not the spirit of the confederation, dictates that all matters of a general tendency should be in the representative body of the whole or under its authority." In addition, a convention of the states to discuss trade might "retard" ratification of the impost amendment, because "reluctant states are very willing to lay hold of anything which will procrastinate that measure." It is also possible, although Carroll did not mention it, that a commercial faction in Baltimore that supported a joint project with Delaware and Pennsylvania to develop the Susquehanna River as a western trade route may have been suspicious of a convention initiated by Virginians, who naturally would prefer development of the Potomac River instead.[121]

Had the Annapolis convention been well attended, Madison probably would have adhered to his strategy to propose only a specific amendment limited to trade regulation. Had that amendment then been ratified by the states, an important precedent for incremental reform would have been established. In May 1786, when Congress was considering calling for a general convention even though the Annapolis convention was scheduled for September, Madison had cautioned Monroe that he thought it "best on the whole to suspend measures for a more thorough cure of our federal system till the partial experiment shall have been made." Then, "[i]f the spirit of the conventioners should be friendly to the union, and their proceedings are well conducted, their return into the councils of their respective states will greatly facilitate any subsequent measures which may be set on foot by Congress, or by any of the states."[122]

Of the nine states slated to attend, however, delegations from only five— Virginia, Delaware, Pennsylvania, New Jersey, and New York—had appeared in Annapolis within a week of the appointed date. Ironically, not a single New England state was represented—although three of the four had appointed delegations—at a convention that had been called to address a topic of special concern to that region, commercial regulation.[123]

The commissioners who had made it to Annapolis agreed to wait several days for the possible arrival of additional state delegations. When no more had appeared by September 14, those who were present decided to terminate the convention.[124]

The Annapolis commissioners issued no substantive recommendations, reporting that they did not think it "advisable to proceed on the business of their mission, under the circumstance of so partial and defective a representation."

Yet to do nothing at all would have been to highlight the direness of the situation, especially amid the dangerously rising sectional tensions over the Mississippi issue.[125]

Making the best of a bad situation, Madison, Hamilton, and the other commissioners present announced "their earnest and unanimous wish that speedy measures may be taken to effect a general meeting of the states in a future convention, for the same and such other purposes as the situation of public affairs may be found to require." Specifically, they noted that the defects of the Articles of Confederation might "be found greater and more numerous" than the omission of congressional power to regulate commerce, and they recommended that deputies to a future convention be given broader instructions. Calling the situation "delicate and critical," they recommended that a convention be called to meet in Philadelphia on the second Monday in May 1787, "to devise such further provisions as shall appear to them necessary to render the constitution of the federal government adequate to the exigencies of the union." The proposals of the Philadelphia convention would be submitted to Congress and, assuming it approved them, would then require the ratification of "the legislatures of every state" in order to become operational.[126]

Other commissioners had been on their way to Annapolis when the meeting adjourned, and those in attendance had not waited very long—in this era of primitive transportation and communication—for a quorum to materialize. For those reasons, the decision to end the proceedings prematurely later fueled suspicion among critics of the Constitution that Annapolis had always been conceived as a first step toward something bigger.[127]*

Whether or not that was the case, St. George Tucker, one of Virginia's commissioners to the Annapolis convention, conceded that the delegates had

---

* Louis Guillaume Otto, the French chargé d'affaires, who was an unusually astute observer of the American political scene, independently embraced this conspiratorial account. In his view, "[f]or a very long time," gentlemen of wealth, talent, and education had felt "the necessity of imparting to the federal government more energy and vigor." These men, "[t]he majority of them being merchants," wished "to establish the credit of the United States in Europe on a solid foundation by the exact payment of debts, and to grant to Congress powers extensive enough to compel the people to contribute for this purpose." Moreover, as creditors, they were "interested in strengthening the government, and watching over the execution of the laws," and "almost all of them dread the efforts of the people to despoil them of their possessions."

However, these "gentlemen" faced an insuperable obstacle in convincing the people to relinquish the "absolute freedom" to which they had become accustomed: "The people are not ignorant that the natural consequence of an increase of power in the government would be a regular collection of taxes, a strict administration of justice, extraordinary duties on imports, rigorous executions against debtors—in short, a marked preponderance of rich men." Thus, these "gentlemen" had tried in "vain, by pamphlets and other publications to spread notions of justice and integrity, and to deprive the people of a freedom which they have so misused." "[A]ll minds would

"certainly exceeded our powers" in calling for a second convention. Yet given the "unfavorable" circumstances, they had judged it "expedient, if possible, to prevent our enemies from receiving the same impression of the disjointed councils of the states as we ourselves felt." Discovering that "they had not power to do that which was entrusted to them, it was better to do something extraneous than to let it be discovered that the plan of the convention had altogether miscarried." Tucker conceded, however, that "the veil under which this concealment is made may be too thin to beguile even a common observer." Rufus King, for one, was not fooled; he told John Adams that the Annapolis convention had "terminated without credit or prospect of having done much good."[128]

To the Philadelphia Convention

The report of the Annapolis commissioners was formally addressed only to the states "they have the honor to represent," yet "motives of respect" led them to transmit copies to Congress and to the executives of the other states as well. St. George Tucker urged Monroe, as one of Virginia's congressional delegates, to

have been revolted" had they "propos[ed] a new organization of the federal government." Yet "circumstances ruinous to the commerce of America have happily arisen to furnish the reformers with a pretext for introducing innovations."

These men "represented to the people that the American name had become opprobrious among all the nations of Europe; that the flag of the United States was everywhere exposed to insults and annoyance; [and that] the husbandman, no longer able to export his produce freely, would soon be reduced to extreme want." They told the people that "it was high time to retaliate . . . but that strong measures could be taken only with the consent of the thirteen states, and that Congress, not having the necessary powers, it was essential to form a general assembly instructed to present to Congress the plan for its adoption, and to point out the means of carrying it into execution."

"The people, generally discontented with the obstacles in the way of commerce, and scarcely suspecting the secret motives of their opponents, ardently embraced this measure, and appointed commissioners, who were to assemble at Annapolis." Yet "[t]he authors of this proposition had no hope, nor even desire, to see the success of this assembly of commissioners, which was only intended to prepare a question much more important than that of commerce. The measures were so well taken that . . . no more than five states were represented at Annapolis, and the commissioners from the northern states tarried several days at New York, in order to retard their arrival."

The delegates who did turn up then "separated under the pretext that they were not in sufficient numbers to enter on business." But they also issued a report that employs "an infinity of circumlocutions and ambiguous phrases to show to their constituents the impossibility of taking into consideration a general plan of commerce . . . without at the same time touching upon other objects closely connected with the prosperity and national importance of the United States." Because of "the obscurity of this document," "the people will penetrate [it] with difficulty, but . . . the strong and enlightened citizens will not fail to turn [it] to account."

try to secure Congress's approbation for the Philadelphia convention. Tucker argued that by conveying "a sense of the expediency, not to say necessity, of the proposed plan," Congress's approval might "induce them [the states] unanimously to adopt it." King thought it uncertain whether enough states would appoint delegates to the convention for it to have any prospect of success. Why would states that had just bypassed a convention in Annapolis agree to attend one in Philadelphia?[129]

The initial public responses to the call for a convention in Philadelphia were not promising.* In the fall of 1786, King and Nathan Dane, two of Massachusetts's congressional delegates, argued against the proposal in the Massachusetts House of Representatives. King maintained that Congress—not a constitutional convention—was "the proper body to propose alterations" to the Articles, which were the act of the people and no part of which "could be altered but by consent of Congress and confirmation of the several legislatures." He also warned that if a convention met and issued recommendations, and Congress did not concur, "the most fatal consequences might follow."[130]

Dane declared that the report from the Annapolis convention had used "very general and indefinite expressions." He thought it unclear whether the Annapolis commissioners had contemplated that the Philadelphia convention would propose only a few changes to the current system to give the federal government "more strength and energy" or instead would devise a new system grounded on different principles. Dane doubted whether the public mind was prepared for the latter alternative, and he warned that "the first principles of government should be touched with care and attention." He also warned that several states would consider such a convention "highly inexpedient" and others would deem it "unconstitutional." Finally, Dane questioned the need for such a convention, given his view that the impost amendment proposed by Congress in 1783 and the commerce amendment proposed in 1784 were close to securing the unanimous ratification of the states.[131]

After King and Dane had spoken, the Massachusetts legislature declined to endorse the Philadelphia convention and then adjourned; it was not scheduled to reconvene before the date set for the convention. Around the same time, the Connecticut legislature likewise declined to take action on the report of the Annapolis convention.[132]

Madison worried that the call for a national convention would not be well received in Virginia because it came during the Mississippi River imbroglio. He regretted that "the season at which" Jay's request for reinstruction on his

---

* In November, Otto observed that the states, other than Virginia, "are little disposed to introduce a new system of confederation, and Congress appears to wish to reserve to itself the right of proposing the changes necessary to consolidate the union."

negotiations with Spain had "been brought forward in Congress was of all possible ones the most ill chosen." He hoped that the Virginia House of Delegates would take up the call for the Philadelphia convention before the Mississippi issue had had a chance "to ferment."[133]

It turned out that Madison had been needlessly concerned. The proposed Philadelphia convention was, he reported to Jefferson, "well received" in Richmond, and the Virginia House of Delegates unanimously endorsed it. Madison believed that this action marked "the revolution of sentiment which the experience of one year has effected in this country." The Confederation was so obviously defective that even "the most obstinate adversaries to a reform" in the Virginia legislature had approved the convention.[134]

When the Virginia legislature endorsed the convention, it also approved a list of prominent Virginians to represent the state in Philadelphia. The purpose of the delegate selections, according to Madison, was to "give this subject a very solemn dress and all the weight which could be derived from a single state." The legislature's "earnestness on this point," he told Washington, was marked by "the liberty which is used of placing your name at the head of them [the delegates]," which would constitute "an invitation to the most select characters from every part of the Confederacy." Washington's participation would confer important legitimacy on the convention, which under the terms of the Articles was an extralegal gathering. Hamilton later explained that one of the advantages of holding a convention was that the country could "avail [itself] of the weight and abilities of men who could not have been induced to accept an appointment to Congress"—men such as Washington.[135]

Washington, of course, had long been an enthusiastic proponent of expanding Congress's powers. During the war, he had warned that unless Congress was vested with sufficient powers by the states or "assumes them as a matter of right, . . . our cause is lost." Soon after the war ended, he wrote, "[U]nless adequate powers are given to Congress for the general purposes of the federal union, we shall soon moulder in dust, and become contemptible in the eyes of Europe, if we are not made the sport of their politics." In 1785, Washington had endorsed the proposed amendment to confer commercial powers on Congress, declaring that "[w]e are either a united people under one head, and for federal purposes, or we are thirteen independent sovereignties, eternally counteracting each other."[136]

Yet Washington's strong support for constitutional reform did not guarantee that he would participate in the Philadelphia convention. Indeed, his initial response to the invitation was to reject it, telling Madison that he had "bid a public adieu to the public walks of life." Conceding that a "sense of . . . obligation" might have compelled him to accept the Virginia legislature's request that he serve on an occasion "so interesting to the well-being of the Confederacy,"

Washington insisted that it was "out of my power to do this with any degree of consistency." The difficulty was that Washington had been re-elected president of the Society of the Cincinnati—an organization of Revolutionary War officers formed in 1783, which had proved controversial because of its hereditary membership. The Society's triennial meeting was scheduled to take place in Philadelphia early in May 1787. Washington had already announced that he would not attend the Society's convention, and so he "could not appear at the same time and place on any other occasion without giving offense to a very respectable and deserving part of the community."[137]

Other considerations also counseled against Washington's attendance. Part of his extraordinary reputation was based upon his renunciation of public office after the Revolutionary War, when he possibly could have become a dictator had he wished to do so. In 1783, in his last official address to the nation as commander-in-chief, Washington had indicated an intention "to pass the remainder of life in a state of undisturbed repose." Now, he worried about doing anything "inconsistent with my public declaration delivered in a solemn manner at an interesting era of my life never more to intermeddle in public matters."[138]

Perhaps most important, Washington's reputation was such that he had little to gain by attending the convention—and potentially much to lose. In December 1786, Washington told his former aide David Humphreys that if the convention failed, then the "deputies would return home chagrined at their ill success and disappointment. This would be a disagreeable predicament for any of them to be in, but more particularly so for a person in my situation. If no further application is made to me, of course I do not attend."[139]

Appreciating that Washington's attendance might be critical to the convention's success, Madison and Randolph pressed him to change his mind. Madison flattered Washington: It had been "the opinion of every judicious friend whom I consulted that your name could not be spared" from the Virginia delegation. Madison hoped that "the peculiarity of the mission and its acknowledged preeminence over every other public object may possibly reconcile your undertaking it." Randolph played on Washington's natural desire to preserve what he had helped to create, noting that the "one ray of hope" for avoiding "dissolution" of the union, which he knew would be "to you a source of the deepest mortification," was for "those who began, carried on, and consummated the revolution [to] rescue America from the impending ruin."[140]

Madison and Randolph succeeded in persuading Washington at least not to shut the door absolutely on his attendance. In December, Washington told Madison that it was "not for me to predict" what might happen between then and May that might "remove the difficulties which at present labor in my mind against the acceptance of this honor which has lately been conferred on me by the Assembly." Encouraged, Madison urged Washington not to finally reject his appointment to the convention "in case the gathering clouds should become so dark and menacing as to supersede every consideration but that of our national existence or safety."[141]

Washington then turned to his friends and former military aides Henry Knox and David Humphreys for their advice on the matter. Among other things, he asked if they knew the reason that the New England states had failed to attend the Annapolis convention. Apparently, Washington was seeking insight into whether those states would be likely to send delegations to Philadelphia.[142]

Knox, who favored the convention, offered Washington mixed advice. While he did not know why the New England states had failed to send delegations to Annapolis, Knox was confident that if Washington announced his intention to participate in the Philadelphia convention, that alone would be sufficient to induce those states to send delegates. Yet he also thought that if Washington was once again to "exert your utmost talents to promote the happiness of your country," the "solemn occasion" should "be of an unequivocal nature in which the enlightened and virtuous citizens should generally concur." However, Knox acknowledged, there were "different sentiments" on the Philadelphia convention. Some objected to it as "an irregular assembly, unauthorized by the Confederation, which points out the mode by which any alterations shall be made." Such persons were "of opinion that Congress ought to take up the defects of the present system, point them out to the respective legislatures, and recommend certain alterations."[143]

On the other hand, according to Knox, other people felt that "the recommendations of Congress are attended with so little effect that any alterations by that means seem to be a hopeless business." Opinions such as this would seem to favor the convention route, the legitimacy of which Knox thought could be defended. Although a convention was "not the regular mode pointed out by the confederation," the current system was "so very defective" that it might "reasonably be doubted whether the constitutional mode of amendment would be adequate to our critical situation," in which case a convention might be "the best expedient that could be devised."[144]

Yet Knox recognized that some people were worried the Philadelphia convention might simply "devise some expedients to brace up the present defective confederation so as just to keep us together, while it would prevent those exertions for a national character which are essential to our happiness." If so, the convention might have "the bad effect of assisting us to creep on in our present miserable condition, without a hope of a generous constitution." Given such varying opinions, Knox concluded that it might be very difficult to bring people "to concur in any effective government," and this made him reluctant to suggest that Washington attend the convention.[145]

Figure 2.4 Secretary at War Henry Knox, who was the Continental Army's chief artillery officer during the Revolutionary War and a close adviser to General Washington, investigated Shays's Rebellion for Congress and later served as the first secretary of war under the Constitution. (Courtesy of Independence National Historical Park)

Humphreys offered less equivocal advice: Washington should not attend the convention. Humphreys expressed some concern about the "diversity of sentiment respecting the legality and expediency of such a meeting." He also worried that some of the New England states might not appoint delegations, which would leave the convention "but partial in point of representation." But his greatest concern was that even if all thirteen states sent delegations and the convention was unanimous in its proposals, "the states will not all comply with the recommendations [because t]hey have a mortal reluctance to divest themselves of the smallest attribute of independent, separate sovereignty." Since Washington's "particular and private reasons against attending"—including his pledge not to engage again with public affairs and his desire not to offend the Cincinnati—were "clearly sufficient to convince any reasonable man of the propriety and consistency of your conduct," Humphreys concluded that Washington's course of action was clear.[146]

While Washington was deliberating on whether to attend, it was still unclear whether any convention would take place at all. Observing that "the public mind is fluctuating," Jay remarked in January 1787 that "it is not clear that all the states will join in that measure [the Philadelphia convention]." Indeed, while Virginia and New Jersey had approved the convention in November 1786 and Pennsylvania in December, the New England states and New York were proving much more resistant, and this was alarming news for nationalists. If this second effort to call a convention proved abortive because of inadequate state representation, Washington believed it would "be considered as an unequivocal proof that the states are not likely to agree in any general measure which is to pervade the union, and consequently, that there is an end put to federal government."[147]

In January 1787, King reported that several New York leaders opposed the convention, "not alone because it is unauthorized but from an opinion that the result will prove inefficacious." New York governor George Clinton had twice refused Congress's request in 1786 to summon the state legislature into special session to reconsider its position on the 1783 impost amendment. When the legislature at its regular session early in 1787 refused by a large majority to alter its earlier conditional approval of the amendment (which Congress had already rejected as insufficient), Madison noted that this action did "not augur well" for the state's sending a delegation to Philadelphia. He told Washington that dominant political interests in New York apparently had concluded that they "might be incommoded by the control of an efficient federal government."[148]

As late as February, King would not even "venture a conjecture" as to whether his home state of Massachusetts would send a delegation to Philadelphia. He told Gerry that "the thing is so problematical" that he was "at some loss" as to what ought to be done. King had no "expectation that much good will flow from it [the convention]." Yet apparently fearful that the mid-Atlantic states would fall under southern influence at the convention without the watchful eye of New England, he was still inclined to send a delegation "from an idea of prudence, or for the purpose of watching."[149]

Madison believed that Massachusetts, "though hitherto not well inclined," would ultimately decide to attend, but he was more concerned about Connecticut, which was "habitually disinclined to abridge her state prerogatives" and had "a great aversion to conventions." As to Rhode Island, Madison thought it could "be relied on for nothing that is good" (though he believed that ultimately "[o]n all great points she must sooner or later bend to Massachusetts and Connecticut"). Around the same time, Knox told Washington that he feared Massachusetts would be the only New England state to appoint delegates.[150]

Congress was slow to endorse the convention as well. Although the Annapolis convention had bypassed Congress and appealed to the states directly to call a convention, a congressional endorsement might ameliorate the tinge of illegitimacy associated with the Philadelphia convention. When King first learned of the call for the convention, he told John Adams that he did not think Congress would "interfere in such a manner as to patronize the project" and that he was "fully convinced . . . that Congress can do all a convention can, and certainly with more safety to original principles." Monroe's initial conversations with congressional delegates convinced him that "the eastern states will not grant an unlimited commission [to a convention], but would accede to it if its objects were defined." Indeed, in October 1786, when Monroe had proposed that the Annapolis report be referred to a congressional committee, the New England states did object. The referral was made over their objection, but the end of the congressional session prevented further action until the next session of Congress was able to assemble a quorum to meet.[151]

Edward Carrington, one of Virginia's congressional delegates, warned Madison that when Congress assembled again, the Massachusetts delegation would try to block Congress's endorsement of the Philadelphia convention. The delegates' rationale, Carrington explained, was that the Articles provided a clear mode of amendment, which did not involve a convention. In addition, a convention would further "derogate from the dignity and weight of that body [Congress]." Carrington conceded that this would be a "wise" argument if the nation actually enjoyed "an efficient" government. But "[t]he truth is, we have not a government to wield and correct, but must pursue the most certain means for obtaining one."[152]

The culmination of Shays's Rebellion apparently convinced most of the holdout state legislatures and Congress to endorse the convention. State governments had been revealed to be a "ridiculous farce," and the argument for bolstering the national government now seemed more compelling. Leading political figures in Massachusetts, who just two years earlier had warned that charters of government should not be lightly altered and that a constitutional convention might foist a "baleful aristocrac[y]" on the nation, were convinced by Shays's Rebellion to support the Philadelphia convention. Grayson wrote Monroe, "The Massachusetts delegation have been much more friendly I have understood since the late insurrection in their state. They look upon the federal assistance as a matter of the greatest importance."[153]

The next session of Congress, which had been scheduled to begin early in November 1786, did not achieve a steady quorum until February 1787. At that point, it appointed a grand committee to resume consideration of the Annapolis convention's report. Madison, who had returned to Congress for the first time since he was rotated out of office in 1783, reported to Washington that Congress was "much divided" on the question of whether its "taking an interest in the measure [calling the convention] would impede or promote it." Madison recorded two principal arguments in opposition to Congress's intervention: First, "lending its sanction to an extraconstitutional mode of proceeding" would "tend to weaken the federal authority." Second, "the interposition of Congress would be considered by the jealous [i.e., suspicious] as betraying an ambitious wish to get power into [its] hands by any plan whatever that might present itself."[154]

One of the principal arguments in favor of Congress's approving the convention, Madison reported, was that "some of the backward states have scruples against acceding to it without some constitutional sanction," which Congress's endorsement might supply. Around the same time, Knox similarly observed that Congress's approval would "take away the objections against the legality of the proposed convention and meet the ideas of the eastern states."[155]

After what Madison described as "considerable difficulty," the grand committee decided by the margin of a single vote that the Annapolis commissioners had been right "as to the inefficiency of the federal government and the necessity of devising such farther provisions as shall render the same adequate to the exigencies of the union." Accordingly, the committee urged that Congress "strongly recommend to the different legislatures to send forward delegates" to the Philadelphia convention.[156]

Around this time, congressional delegates from Massachusetts received information leading them to suppose that their legislature would agree to send delegates to the proposed convention "in case Congress should give [its] sanction to it." The New York legislature now instructed its congressional delegation to move that Congress recommend to the states the appointment of delegates to a convention—to be held at an unspecified location on an unspecified date—"for the purpose of revising the Articles of Confederation . . . to render them adequate to the preservation and support of the union." This resolution made no reference to the report of the Annapolis convention.[157]

In Congress, New York's delegates moved to postpone consideration of the grand committee's report in favor of endorsing the Philadelphia convention in order to take up instead the mysterious proposal of their own legislature. Madison reported, "There was reason to believe, however, from the language of the instruction from New York that her object was to obtain a new convention, under the sanction of Congress, rather than to accede to the one on foot or perhaps by dividing the plans of the states in their appointments to frustrate all of them." Because New York's resolution had passed by only a single vote in the state senate and because the New York Assembly had just refused by a large majority to unconditionally ratify the 1783 impost amendment, Madison concluded there was "room to suspect" that New York's disposition was still not "very federal."[158]

On February 21, Congress narrowly rejected New York's proposal. Then, Massachusetts delegates, who according to one report opposed the Philadelphia convention but were concerned that a resolution approving it "would be carried without them," urged an alternative resolution. Congress would endorse the Philadelphia convention, as "the most probable mean[s] of establishing in these states a firm national government," but limit its agenda to "the sole and express purpose of revising the Articles of Confederation." The convention, according to this resolution, was to report to Congress and the state legislatures "such alterations and provisions therein [the Articles] as shall when agreed to in Congress and confirmed by the states render the federal constitution adequate to the exigencies of government and the preservation of the union."[159]

All of the nine state delegations present, except that of Connecticut, then endorsed this proposal. Some of the delegates, according to Pennsylvanian William Irvine, did not agree with the limiting instructions for the convention but concluded that it was better to compromise and thus "keep up the smallest appearance of opposition to public view."[160]

Madison reported, "It appeared from the debates and still more from the conversations among the members that many of them considered this resolution [approving the Philadelphia convention] as a deadly blow to the existing confederation." Some of the delegates approved of this as a "harbinger of a better confederation," while others did not. Everyone "agreed that the federal government in its existing shape was inefficient and could not last long."[161]

By quieting some concerns about the legality and propriety of the convention, Congress's endorsement probably influenced additional states to appoint delegations; only seven had done so before Congress's action. Madison told Washington that one of the Massachusetts congressional delegates had informed him that the state would "certainly accede and appoint deputies if Congress declares [its] approbation of the measure." (In fact, Massachusetts did not wait for Congress's approval to appoint a delegation.) Madison said that he had "similar information" from Connecticut (though he also noted that congressional acquiescence would be seen by some people in that state as "interference"). In March, Knox wrote Washington that Congress's approval "has had good effects" and that "[i]t is now highly probable that the convention will be general[ly attended]." In April, Carrington confirmed that some states had hesitated to support the convention while it had been "unauthorized by Congress," but that Congress's endorsement had "remove[d] every possible difficulty."[162]

While Congress's approval had increased the likelihood of the convention's taking place, it had not immediately convinced Washington that he should participate. In early February, Washington had informed Knox "in confidence" that he was not planning to attend despite the persistent lobbying of "some of the principal characters of [the state]." In March, Randolph told Madison that he had "assayed every means to prevail on" Washington to join the Virginia delegation, but he "fear[ed] ineffectually."[163]

That month, Washington again solicited the advice of Knox and Humphreys. Although still troubled by the indelicacy of his appearing at the Philadelphia convention after having declined the invitation of the Society of the Cincinnati to attend its meeting in that same city, Washington was now concerned that his failure to attend might be "considered as a dereliction to republicanism—nay more, whether other motives may not (however injuriously) be ascribed to me for not exerting myself on this occasion in support of it."* Therefore, he wished his former aides to inform him of the "public expectation" regarding his attendance.[164]

Humphreys continued to strongly discourage Washington from participating in the convention: "The probability, which existed when I wrote before, that nothing general or effectual would be done by the convention amounts now almost to a certainty." The Rhode Island Assembly had decided not to appoint a delegation, and the Connecticut legislature, "under the influence of a few such miserable, narrow minded and, I may say, wicked politicians," probably would follow suit. Even if Connecticut's lawmakers decided to appoint a delegation, its mission probably would be "to impede any salutary measures that might be proposed." Moreover, two of the three delegates appointed by New York would be "directly anti-federal." Given such developments, there was little chance that unanimity would prevail in Philadelphia.[165]

Noting that he had heard speculation from many people about the convention, Humphreys told Washington that few of them had expressed "any sanguine expectations concerning the successful issue of the meeting," and none had thought that Washington ought to participate. Humphreys reassured

---

* Washington's allusion is vague; the closest he came to clarifying was in a letter to Madison later that month. There, Washington began with the premise that "a thorough reform of the present system is indispensable." He hoped that reform would "be essayed in a full convention." But if after that attempt, "more powers and more decision is not found in the existing form [of government]"—that is, republicanism—"then, and not till then, in my opinion, can it [a change in the form of government] be attempted without involving all the evils of civil discord." Apparently, Washington had not ruled out the possibility that, at some point, the United States would have to give up on republicanism. Should that happen, as his letter to Knox makes clear, Washington did not want it to be said that he had been derelict in the cause of republicanism, and he worried that his not attending the Philadelphia convention could be so construed.

Washington that neither supporters nor opponents of major constitutional reform would regard his failure to attend "as a dereliction of republicanism." Opponents of reform, said Humphreys, deemed the convention "rather intended to subvert than support republicanism, and will readily excuse your non-attendance." Supporters of reform thought that for Washington "to come forward at present" would possibly be "injurious to the national interests."[166]

Knox offered nearly diametrically opposite advice. He reasoned that Washington's "satisfaction or chagrin" over the decision to attend—as well as that of his friends—would turn "entirely on the result of the convention." This was partly because, "however reluctantly," Washington would inevitably "be constrained to accept of the president's chair," and thus "the proceedings of the convention will more immediately be appropriated to you than to any other person." Were the convention to propose only a "patchwork to the present defective confederation, your reputation would in a degree suffer." Yet if the convention proposed "an energetic and judicious system . . . , it would be a circumstance highly honorable to your fame, in the judgment of the present and future ages, and doubly entitle you to the glorious republican epithet—The Father of Your Country."[167]

Knox also reported that placing Washington's name at the head of the list of the Virginia delegation "has had already great influence to induce the states to come into the measure," and he was impressed with the roster of delegates appointed by other states. Moreover, Washington's presence "would more than any other circumstance induce a compliance to the propositions of the convention." Thus, Knox concluded, "the balance of my opinion preponderates greatly in favor of your attendance." As to Washington's concern about having already declined the invitation of the Cincinnati, Knox proposed that Washington come to Philadelphia a week before the start of the convention, which would "cheer the hearts of your old military friends . . . , rivet their affections, and entirely remove your embarrassment in this respect of attending the convention."[168]

One month later, in April, Knox even more forcefully urged Washington to attend. A broad representation of the states now appeared likely, and "the delegates will have ample powers to point out radical cures for the present political evils." Knox reported a "general wish" that Washington attend because his presence was "conceived to be highly important to the success of the propositions of the convention." He told Washington, "The mass of the people feel the inconveniences of the present government and ardently wish for such alterations as would remedy them." Changes could come only through agreement or force, and the convention, if attended "by a proper weight of wisdom and character," appeared to be "the only mean[s] to effect the alterations peaceably." Were Washington to decline to attend, "slander and malice might suggest that force would be the most agreeable mode of reform to you." Not even Washington's "purity of character" and "exalted" past service would "entirely shield [you] from the shafts of calumny." Finally, "the unbounded confidence the people have of your tried patriotism and wisdom would exceedingly facilitate the adoption of any important alterations that might be proposed by a convention of which you were a member . . . and president."[169]

Knox's last missive proved unnecessary. On March 28, Washington had written to Governor Randolph to announce that, "as my friends, with a degree of solicitude which is unusual, seem to wish my attendance on this occasion [the Philadelphia convention], I have come to a resolution to go if my health will permit." (Washington was suffering from "a rheumatic complaint" that made it difficult to raise his arm as high as his head.) He explained to Lafayette, "The pressure of the public voice was so loud, I could not resist the call to a convention . . . which is to determine whether we are to have a government of respectability."[170]*

About the same time that Washington decided to attend, Madison reported to his father that all states except Connecticut, Maryland, and Rhode Island had appointed delegations to Philadelphia. Moreover, it was "not doubted" that Connecticut would eventually appoint delegates, and the Maryland legislature had "already resolved on the expediency of the measure." Only Rhode Island seemed determined not to participate. Madison complained to Randolph, "Nothing can exceed the wickedness and folly which continue to reign there [in Rhode Island]. All sense of character as well as of right is obliterated. Paper money is still their idol, though it is debased to 8 for 1."[171]

Indeed, the lower house of the Rhode Island legislature had already voted in March by a majority of greater than twenty not to send a delegation to Philadelphia, despite Congress's endorsement of the convention and the urging of some governors and Rhode Island's own congressional delegation that the state be represented. A Massachusetts newspaper declared that the absence of Rhode Island was "a circumstance far more joyous than grievous" because any deputation from that state would have reflected the views

---

* Indeed, in the end, Washington not only attended the convention but was present at every day's proceedings. His presence undoubtedly helped to legitimize the convention and the Constitution it produced in the minds of many Americans. Before the convention had even finished its work, Monroe told Jefferson that "the signature of his [Washington's] name to whatever act shall be the result of [its] deliberations will secure its passage through the union." Soon after the convention ended, Gouverneur Morris, who played an important role in its deliberations, declared that having Washington's name on the Constitution had "been of infinite service." Had Washington "not attended the convention, and the same paper had been handed out to the world, it would have met with a colder reception, with fewer and weaker advocates, and with more and more strenuous opponents."

of its current administration, and this would have been the "cause of much mortification to the illustrious characters who now compose that assembly [i.e., the Philadelphia convention]." Francis Dana, who was appointed by the Massachusetts legislature to represent the state in Philadelphia but was unable to attend due to illness, wrote joyfully that Rhode Island's failure to appoint a delegation would "give grounds to strike it out of the union, and divide [its] territory between [its] neighbors."[172]*

In late April, Madison was still having doubts whether Connecticut would send a delegation, based on "unpropitious" state elections and a "numerous and persevering" antifederal party in the state. Yet he told Pendleton that the absence of one or two states would not "materially affect" the convention's deliberations. To Jefferson, he reported that "[t]he prospect of a full and respectable convention grows stronger every day," especially now that Washington seemed likely to attend. Indeed, in May, at its regularly scheduled spring session, the Connecticut legislature finally appointed a delegation to represent the state in Philadelphia.[173]

Although Madison had grown increasingly confident "that a meeting will take place, and that it will be a pretty full one," the likely outcome of the convention remained "inscrutable" to him. Washington had his own doubts as to whether anything good would come from the convention. Several months earlier, referring to Shays's Rebellion, he had told Humphreys that candor obliged him "to confess that as we could not remain quiet more than three or four years (in time of peace) under the constitutions of our own choice, which it was believed, in many instances were formed with deliberation and wisdom, I see little prospect either of our agreeing upon any other or that we should remain long satisfied under it if we could." Yet Washington wished "to see any thing and every thing essayed to prevent the effusion of blood and to avert the humiliating and contemptible figure we are about to make in the annals of mankind."[174]

Just one month before the convention was set to assemble, Washington told Randolph that although he had decided to attend, "I very much fear that all the states will not appear in convention, and that some of them will come fettered so as to impede rather than accelerate the great ends of their calling."

---

* Several Rhode Island merchants and tradesmen later wrote apologetically to the Philadelphia convention, noting "their regret" that their state was not represented there and seeking to "prevent any impressions unfavorable to the commercial interest of this state." During the convention, James Mitchell Varnum, one of Rhode Island's congressional delegates, wrote to Washington to assure him that "the measures of our present legislature do not exhibit the real character of the state" and that "all the worthy citizens of this state . . . place their fullest confidence in the wisdom and moderation of the national council [i.e., the Philadelphia convention] and indulge the warmest hopes of being favorably considered in their deliberations."

Washington was alluding to the limiting instructions that some states had issued to their delegates—not to go beyond revising the Articles and, in the case of Delaware, not to depart from the provision of the Articles guaranteeing each state an equal vote in Congress. Madison, too, had been distressed when he learned of such limiting instructions.[175]

Many other political leaders were similarly dubious as to the convention's prospects for success. Grayson predicted that despite the "great expectations" people had for the convention, "the whole will terminate in nothing." Either delegates would not agree on proposed solutions or, if they did, the states would reject their proposals. The nation's "distresses are not sufficiently great to produce decisive alterations," Grayson observed.[176]

Grayson's congressional colleague, James Mitchell Varnum, who had been one of the earliest advocates in Congress for a national convention, similarly predicted that the Philadelphia assemblage would accomplish very little. The delegates would probably "investigate the defects of our present national government and point out the means of removing them." But the states would then "greatly differ in their ideas upon the subject and their increasing animosities will precipitate the period of anarchy and confusion."[177]

Rufus King wrote, "What the convention may do at Philadelphia is very doubtful. . . . [M]y fears are by no means inferior to my hopes on this subject." Washington's private secretary, Tobias Lear, told General Benjamin Lincoln, "Much, indeed everything, depends upon the doings of the convention, though I fear every good which is expected will not come out of it. The reins of government are extremely relaxed throughout the union." Lear doubted that the people would "submit to a regular, permanent and energetic government" without more episodes such as Shays's Rebellion.[178]

Madison, who had done so much to bring about the convention and to persuade Washington to attend, was having second thoughts as the date set for it to begin drew near. In mid-April, he told Randolph that Washington's participation was "flattering," but that he almost wished Washington's attendance could be postponed "until some judgment can be formed of the result of the meeting. It ought not to be wished by any of his friends that he should participate in any abortive undertaking."[179]

Indeed, Madison had serious concerns that the enterprise might prove "abortive." He explained to Pendleton, "The necessity of gaining the concurrence of the convention in some system that will answer the purpose, the subsequent approbation of Congress, and the final sanction of the states, presents a series of chances, which would inspire despair in any case where the alternative was less formidable." Madison expressed even greater pessimism to his father: Given "[t]he probable diversity of opinions and prejudices, and of supposed or real interests among the states," he thought "no very sanguine expectations can well be indulged." The only basis for hope, Madison observed, was that "[t]he existing embarrassments and mortal diseases of the Confederacy" would produce "a spirit of concession on all sides" and enable the delegates to avoid the alternative, which was "general chaos or at least partition of the union."[180]

3

The Constitutional Convention

During the first week of the Philadelphia convention, Virginia delegate George Mason wrote to his son, "The eyes of the United States are turned upon this assembly, and their expectations [are] raised to a very anxious degree." About the same time, James Monroe wrote to James Madison, "We all look with great anxiety to the result of the convention at Philadelphia. Indeed it seems to be the sole point on which all future movements will turn."[1]

The stakes were widely perceived to be enormous. As the convention began, Henry Knox told George Washington, "I have no hope of a free government but from the convention. If that fails us, we shall find ourselves afloat on an ocean of uncertainty." Washington told Thomas Jefferson that the federal government was "at an end, and, unless a remedy is soon applied, anarchy and confusion will inevitably ensue." Monroe wrote Jefferson, "The affairs of the federal government are, I believe, in the utmost confusion. The convention is an expedient that will produce a decisive effect. It will either recover us from our present embarrassments or complete our ruin."[2]

One reason the stakes were so high was that, as Randolph told the delegates assembled in Philadelphia, the nation was "on the eve of [civil] war, which is only prevented by the hopes of this convention." Tobias Lear declared that unless "some measures are pointed out and adopted to give security to property," then "a civil war with all its terrible consequences" was the likely result. Charles Pinckney of South Carolina agreed that "should the convention dissolve without coming to some determination," and the people consequently lost all hope "of providing by a well-formed government for the[ir] protection and happiness," then "[t]hey might possibly turn their attention to effecting that by force which had been in vain constitutionally attempted."[3]

Even if civil war was not in the offing, at least a dissolution of the union into separate confederacies seemed likely. Madison worried that if the convention failed, thus proving that the union could not "be organized efficiently," then "the partition of the empire into rival and hostile confederacies will ensue." In February 1787, one Boston newspaper, wondering how long the citizens of

Massachusetts were expected to endure the obstruction of commercial reform that earned the United States the "contempt of Europe," urged New England states to form a separate confederacy and "leave the rest of the continent to pursue their own imbecile and disjointed plans." One of Rhode Island's congressional delegates, James Mitchell Varnum, confirmed that some New Englanders had become "warm espousers of separate confederacies."[4]

Yet dissolution of the union into separate confederacies was not the worst fear of Madison and other political leaders. If the convention failed to improve the organization of the union "on republican principles," Madison told Randolph, then "innovations of a much more objectionable form may be obtruded"—that is, monarchy.[5]

Thus, Madison told the delegates gathered in Philadelphia that they "would decide forever the fate of republican government." So did Hamilton, who explained that if the convention did not manage to give republican government "due stability and wisdom, it would be disgraced and lost among ourselves, disgraced and lost to mankind forever." John Jay, who was not at the convention, agreed that if the "cause of liberty" could not survive in American soil, "little pains will be taken to cultivate it in any other," which is why Gouverneur Morris told the delegates that "the whole human race will be affected by the proceedings of this convention."[6]

Yet, despite the enormous stakes, just weeks into its deliberations the convention seemed destined for failure. An impasse between delegations from large and small states over how to apportion representation in the national legislature had led to threats of a walkout. On June 30, Mason reported that disagreement over "fundamental principles" rendered it "very doubtful" that "any sound and effectual system can be established." A few days later, Hamilton left the convention, telling Washington that he was "seriously and deeply distressed" by the tenor of the proceedings and fearful that "we shall let slip the golden opportunity of rescuing the American empire from disunion, anarchy and misery." A week later, Washington reported to Hamilton that "narrow minded" delegates "under the influence of local views" had put the proceedings, "if possible, in a worse train than ever." Washington concluded, "I almost despair of seeing a favorable issue to the proceedings of the convention, and do therefore repent having had any agency in the business."[7]

Madison's Agenda

In 1787, Virginia was by far the most populous state—its population (counting slaves) was 60 percent larger than that of the second most populous state, Pennsylvania—and it sent the most illustrious delegation to Philadelphia (though Pennsylvania's was not far behind). The Virginians would make the most important contributions to the convention, largely because of the doings of one man—James Madison. Madison was not the most distinguished participant in the Constitutional Convention—far from it—but he was largely responsible for devising the so-called Virginia Plan, which became the starting point for the convention's deliberations.[8]

Madison had been preparing for the convention even before he could be confident that it would take place. In February 1787, he told Washington that he hoped that a convention, if it happened, would pursue "a thorough reform of the existing system." In reply, Washington agreed that a convention should "adopt no temporizing expedient, but probe the defects of the Constitution to the bottom and provide radical cures, whether they are agreed to or not."[9]

By April, Madison had decided to go full bore. He wrote Randolph, "In truth my ideas of a reform strike so deeply at the old Confederation, and lead to such a systematic change, that they scarcely admit of the expedient" of allowing the states to partially adopt the convention's proposals (as Randolph

Figure 3.1 James Madison, who later became the fifth president of the United States, and, more than any other single individual, was the driving force behind the Constitution and the Bill of Rights. (Courtesy of Independence National Historical Park)

had suggested). Pleased to discover that Washington shared his preference for wholesale reform, Madison replied, "Temporizing applications will dishonor the councils which propose them and may foment the internal malignity of the disease, at the same time that they produce an ostensible palliation of it. Radical attempts, although unsuccessful, will at least justify the authors of them."[10]

As noted in chapter 2, a few months before the convention, Rufus King had emphasized the importance of "prudent and sagacious" men seizing the moment to establish a more perfect government. Madison, it turned out, was just such a man. He understood the significance of taking the initiative and devising a plan that could become the convention's initial agenda. In the early months of 1787, Madison drafted a document explicating the "vices" of the Articles of Confederation and of the state governments, and proposing possible remedies. His advance preparation led one of the delegates to the Philadelphia convention to describe Madison as "the best informed man" there.[11]

Some of the flaws in the Articles, as we have seen, were obvious to virtually everyone. For example, Congress plainly needed a power of compulsory taxation. At least since 1780, Madison had recognized "the distress of public credit" resulting from the states' delinquencies in meeting their requisitions, and he had served on congressional committees that proposed replacing the flawed requisition system with a federal impost and even granting Congress the power to use force against states that shirked their financial obligations to the union. In addition, Madison had worked for years to persuade southerners that Congress must have the power to regulate foreign and interstate commerce in order to respond effectively to foreign trade discrimination and to prevent trade wars from developing between the states. In addition to stressing the need to remedy these glaring deficits in Congress's power, Madison identified a broader problem of "want [i.e., lack] of concert in matters where common interest requires it"—such as in laws regarding the naturalization of citizens and the protection of intellectual property.[12]

Madison wanted not only to extend the sphere of Congress's authority but also to prevent states from interfering with its prerogatives. Although he included, as examples of this problem, states' negotiating separate treaties with each other and with Indian tribes (in direct violation of the Articles), his central concern was states' violating federal treaties and the law of nations, which he believed had happened constantly under the Articles. Madison also objected to states' interfering with each other's rights, especially through discriminatory trade restrictions. Although such practices were not explicitly barred by the Articles, Madison believed that they violated the spirit of the Articles and had already incited retaliation.[13]

Solving such problems required an effective mechanism for enforcing federal supremacy. Under the Articles, the federal system had a "want of sanction . . . and of coercion," yet "[a] sanction is essential to the idea of law." Thus, the Articles were really "nothing more than a treaty of amity of commerce and of alliance between so many independent and sovereign states." The problem was that "[e]very general act of the union must necessarily bear unequally hard on some particular member or members," and states naturally were partial to their own interests. In addition, "[c]ourtiers of popularity will naturally exaggerate the inequality where it exists, and even suspect it where it has no existence." Finally, "a distrust of the voluntary compliance of each other may prevent the compliance of any." Experience had shown that the Articles' drafters had manifested "a mistaken confidence [in] the justice, the good faith, the honor, the sound policy, of the several legislative assemblies." Only legal sanctions could ensure the "unanimous and punctual obedience of 13 independent bodies."[14]

Of course, one possible legal sanction is force, and Madison told Washington that "the right of coercion should be expressly declared." Yet he acknowledged that "the difficulty and awkwardness of operating by force on the collective will of a state render it particularly desirable that the necessity of it might be precluded." A milder method of enforcing federal supremacy would be the creation of a federal judiciary, and Madison wanted national supremacy extended "to the judiciary departments." If the only judges applying and expounding upon federal law were state judges, who were dependent on state legislatures for their appointment and bound by their oaths of loyalty to the states, then "the intention of the law and the interests of the nation may be defeated by the obsequiousness of the tribunals to the policy or prejudices of the states." At a minimum, Madison thought that "the oaths of the [state] judges should include a fidelity to the general as well as local constitution, and that an appeal should lie to some national tribunals in all cases to which foreigners or inhabitants of other states may be parties."[15]

Another major innovation Madison had in mind was abolishing the rule of equal state suffrage in Congress established by the Articles. Under the new governmental scheme that he envisioned, Congress would be empowered to act directly upon individuals, not only upon states. To reflect that shift, Madison thought that the "principle of representation" in Congress ought to change. While equality of state suffrage in Congress may never have been "just" to the larger states, at least it had been "safe" for them, "as the liberty they exercise of rejecting or executing the acts of Congress is uncontrollable by the nominal sovereignty of Congress." In other words, so long as the implementation of congressional measures depended in practice on state assistance, "the equality of votes does not destroy the inequality of importance and influence in the states." Yet in a new system, with "such an augmentation of the federal power as will render it efficient without the intervention of the [state] legislatures, a vote in the general councils from Delaware would be of equal value with one from Massachusetts or Virginia," and this was indefensible. Representation in the national legislature, Madison believed, ought to be apportioned according to population.[16]

Madison understood the radicalism of this proposal, yet he believed that the change in the principle of representation was not only just but also practicable, because "[a] majority of the states conceive that they will be gainers by it." The northern states would be reconciled to the change "by the actual superiority of their populousness" at the present moment, and "the southern by their expected superiority" in the future. The change in the formula for representation was essential, Madison explained, because with "[t]his principle established, the repugnance of the large states to part with power will in a great degree subside." Thus, representation apportioned according to population was, for Madison, partly in the service of a larger objective: expanding the powers of the federal government. Once the large states had acquiesced to the change, he believed, the smaller states would have no choice but to "yield to the predominant will."[17]

Perhaps the most original aspect of Madison's exploration of the Articles' vices was the emphasis placed on the deficiencies in *state* legislation of the Confederation period. In addition to a general concern with the "multiplicity" and "mutability" of state laws, which had become a "nuisance," Madison specifically objected to the "injustice" of state legislation, which was "a defect still more alarming." Here, Madison referred explicitly to the paper money and debtor relief laws of the mid-1780s, which he had previously called "unjust, impolitic, [and] destructive of public and private confidence."[18]

Madison blamed such unjust state laws partly on legislators, who were driven by "ambition" and by "personal interest" rather than by concerns for "the public good." Yet he also believed that a "more fatal if not more frequent cause" of such legislation was "the people themselves." The underlying problem, Madison thought, was the division of all societies "into different interests and factions, as they happen to be creditors or debtors—rich or poor—husbandmen, merchants or manufacturers—members of different religious sects."[19]

To Madison, "[t]he great desideratum in government" was how to "render it sufficiently neutral between the different interests and factions, to control one part of the society from invading the rights of another, and at the same time sufficiently controlled itself, from setting up an interest adverse to that of the whole society." While an absolute monarch perhaps could be trusted to be "sufficiently neutral towards his subjects," he would also "frequently sacrifice their happiness to his ambition or his avarice." By contrast, in a republican government, where the majority "ultimately gives the law," nothing restrained that majority "from unjust violations of the rights and interests of the minority, or of individuals." As Madison had told Monroe in the context of the Mississippi River imbroglio, if "the interest of the majority is the political standard of right and wrong," then "the majority in every community can despoil and enslave the minority of individuals."[20]

Madison thought that the best solution to this problem of majority tyranny was "an enlargement of the sphere" of government—that is, expanding the jurisdiction of the federal government relative to that of the states. Such a shift in power would "lessen the insecurity of private rights," not because of any reduction in the majority's impulse to interfere with those rights but rather "because a common interest or passion is less apt to be felt and the requisite combinations less easy to be formed by a great than by a small number." A larger geographic community almost inevitably would feature "a greater variety of interests, of pursuits, [and] of passions." Moreover, "common sentiment will have less opportunity of communication and concert" over a broader geographic area.[21]

In addition, through careful design, the federal government could be further insulated from the pressures of a majority faction. The rules for electing officeholders—such as the frequency of elections, whether the people participated directly or only indirectly, and the size of constituencies—could be designed to "extract from the mass of the society the purest and noblest characters which it contains." On the eve of the convention, Madison wrote Washington, "There has not been any moment since the peace at which the representatives of the union would have given an assent to paper money or any other measure of a kindred nature." The Philadelphia convention would have an opportunity to devise a federal government constituted in such a fashion that it would be even less vulnerable to populist pressure for relief measures.[22]

As Madison developed the idea that the federal government could be trusted more than the states to do justice between factions—a notion that he later admitted to Jefferson was "in contradiction to the concurrent opinions of theoretical writers"—he also mulled over possible mechanisms by which that government could block unjust state legislation. In the spring of 1787, he shared his tentative ideas with Jefferson, Washington, and Randolph.[23]

Madison had concluded that it was "essential" that the federal legislature be armed with "a negative in all cases whatsoever on the legislative acts of the states, as the King of Great Britain heretofore had [over colonial legislation]." A federal veto power would enable Congress "not only to guard the national rights and interests against invasion, but also to restrain the states from thwarting and molesting each other." Further, it would enable Congress to control "the internal vicissitudes of state policy, and the aggressions of interested majorities on the rights of minorities and of individuals"—such as through "paper money and other unrighteous measures." Simply forbidding certain state legislation "on paper" would be insufficient because such limits would be "easily and continually baffled by the legislative sovereignties of the states."[24]

At the Philadelphia convention, Madison repeatedly defended this broad conception of the federal government's proper sphere of authority. When some of his colleagues articulated a narrower set of objects for the federal government, Madison disagreed with them and reiterated "the necessity of providing more effectually for the security of private rights and the steady dispensation of justice." He insisted it was state interferences with such rights—he was thinking specifically of measures for paper money and debtor relief—which had "more perhaps than anything else produced this convention." Madison doubted that "republican liberty could long exist under the abuses of it practiced in some of the states." Enlarging the sphere of government and empowering the federal government to veto state legislation were "the only defense against the inconveniences of democracy consistent with the democratic form of government."[25]

Other convention delegates shared these views, but Madison appears to have been the only one to develop them systematically. In a letter to Randolph written before the convention, Madison stated, "I hold it for a fundamental point that an individual independence of the states is utterly irreconcilable with the idea of an aggregate sovereignty." Yet Madison acknowledged that simply consolidating the states into an undifferentiated nation would be both "unattainable" and "inexpedient." The convention must seek a middle ground, "which will at once support a due supremacy of the national authority, and leave in force the local authorities so far as they can be subordinately useful."[26]

The Virginia Plan

Madison arrived in Philadelphia more than a week before the convention was scheduled to begin on May 14. He had urged at least Randolph among his fellow Virginians to come to Philadelphia early, even if this proved inconvenient to his travel plans, so that the Virginia delegates could take the lead by preparing "some materials for the work of the convention." Most of the convention's delegates were slow to arrive—a dilatoriness that Washington noted was beginning "to sour the temper of the punctual members who do not like to idle away their time," though the delay afforded Madison additional time to build support for the dramatic reforms he contemplated. Mason reported to his son from Philadelphia before the convention had assembled a quorum that the Virginia delegates were conferring among themselves two or three hours a day. Randolph later stated that before he arrived in Philadelphia, he had believed that the Confederation "was not so eminently defective as it had been supposed," but his early conversations with other delegates convinced him that the Articles were "destitute of every energy which a constitution of the United States ought to possess."[27]

The early-arriving Virginians also coordinated with the Pennsylvania delegates, none of whom had to travel far to get to the convention because they were all from Philadelphia (which was a source of complaint among western Pennsylvanians). The Pennsylvania delegation included eminent statesmen—most notably, Benjamin Franklin, Robert Morris, and Gouverneur Morris—who proved sympathetic to Madison's objectives. Beginning at a dinner at Franklin's house, the delegations of these two largest states discussed a plan for what Mason described as "a total alteration of the present federal system." As the convention began, Madison reported that he was pleasantly surprised to discover that, "[i]n general, the members seem to accord in viewing our situation as peculiarly critical and in being averse to temporizing expedients."[28]

The convention achieved its quorum of seven state delegations on May 25. Over the course of its proceedings, fifty-five delegates participated, though not all at the same time. The delegates were, in general, an extraordinarily talented bunch. Franklin reportedly called the convention "the most august and respectable assembly he ever was in in his life." Madison agreed that the convention contained "in several instances the most respectable characters in the United States and in general may be said to be the best contribution of talents the states could make for the occasion."[29]

Twelve states eventually sent delegates. Rhode Island refused to do so, which suited Madison fine: "If her deputies should bring with them the complexion of the state, their company will not add much to our pleasure or to the progress of the business." New Hampshire's delegation did not arrive until late July, and Madison had not expected them to attend at all, "the state treasury being empty it is said, and a substitution of private resources being inconvenient or impracticable."[30]

The delegates were uncertain how long their business would detain them. As the convention began, Mason told his son that it might last beyond July. Randolph arranged to bring his family to Philadelphia, as he was expecting "a very long sojournment here." A couple of weeks into the convention, North Carolina's delegates reported that several of their colleagues had sent for their wives, as "a summer's campaign" seemed likely. In fact, the convention ended up sitting for nearly four months, from May 25 to September 17, with the delegates generally meeting six days a week, though not on Sundays.[31]

The convention began with the delegates' electing Washington as president and William Jackson (who was not a delegate) as secretary to keep the official minutes.* Then, they appointed a committee to propose rules to govern the convention's proceedings. The most pertinent rules agreed upon provided that a quorum would consist of seven delegations, that voting would be by

---

* We know a great deal about what was said and done at the Philadelphia convention, especially given that there was no stenographer present, unlike at some of the state ratifying conventions that followed. In addition to the official record maintained by Jackson, Madison kept detailed notes, and he was present every day of the proceedings. About ten other delegates also took at least some notes that have survived, though many of these delegates recorded speeches only sporadically, and some of them did not attend major portions of the convention. For example, Robert Yates, whose notes are almost as detailed as Madison's—though not particularly reliable, given that they were posthumously edited for political purposes before being published—left Philadelphia on July 10 and did not return.

While we know a lot about the convention's proceedings, it is important to emphasize the qualified nature of our knowledge. It has been estimated that even Madison's fairly detailed notes could not have captured even 10 percent of the words that were spoken at the convention. He did not record verbatim accounts of speeches—it would have been impossible for him to do so even had he wished to—but instead summarized them, often imposing his own thought structure upon them in the process. Madison also had a tendency, as compared with many of the other note takers, of draining the emotion from delegates' speeches. Moreover, Madison's notes, unsurprisingly, are less detailed on topics that did not greatly interest him (such as the nature of the federal courts' jurisdiction). His note taking also flagged at the end of lengthy speeches, and he sometimes minimized the contributions of delegates who seemed to annoy him (especially Charles Pinckney of South Carolina). Beginning in August, Madison's notes generally become much less detailed.

In addition, Madison could not possibly speak and take notes at the same time, so his record of his own speeches may or may not accurately reflect what he actually said. Judging from a comparison of his notes with those taken by other delegates, Madison tended to revise his own speeches to make himself appear less dogmatic. He also—again, unsurprisingly—was not the most accurate reporter of other delegates' speeches that criticized his ideas.

Furthermore, Madison repeatedly revised his notes—both during and after the convention. Once or twice a week during the convention, he transcribed his shorthand notes of the days' proceedings into something more formal. His notes tend to be more detailed for the days immediately preceding such transcriptions, and, inevitably, his transcriptions were distorted by his knowledge of what had transpired in the days since a particular speech was given. For example, if Madison knew that a particular proposal had gone nowhere in the days after it was made, he was less likely to give it much attention in his notes.

After August 21, Madison ended this practice of transcribing his shorthand notes altogether, as he was consumed by illness and committee work in the final weeks of the convention. Only in 1789–90 did Madison transcribe his shorthand notes from those final weeks, and by that point in time, he had trouble deciphering his own handwriting and recalling details of the proceedings.

Madison also subsequently revised his notes of the convention—both in 1789–90, perhaps for the benefit of Thomas Jefferson, who was returning from France to join the Washington administration, and again in the 1790s and after his retirement from the presidency in 1817, when the changes were mostly made for political reasons. The nationalism and skepticism of popular participation in government that Madison evinced in 1787 had become extremely inconvenient

delegation with each state's delegation counting equally, and that decisions would be made by a majority vote of those delegations present. In addition, the convention rejected a rule proposed by the committee that would have empowered a single delegate to demand a roll-call vote on any motion. The delegates apparently agreed with George Mason that "such a record of the opinions of members would be an obstacle to a change of [mind]" and that, if the official journal of the convention should become public, a record of roll-call votes would "furnish handles to the adversaries of the result of the meeting." The delegates also agreed that, provided a day's notice was given, any matter already decided upon by the convention could be reconsidered.[32]

Finally, the delegates agreed to close the doors of their meeting place, the Pennsylvania statehouse (now known as Independence Hall), to the public and to take a pledge of secrecy—that "nothing spoken in the house be printed or otherwise published or communicated without leave." That pledge was, for the most part, scrupulously observed.[33]

Jefferson was unhappy when he learned of the secrecy rule, telling Adams that he was "sorry they [the delegates] began their deliberations by so abominable a precedent as that of tying up the tongues of their members." Although conceding "the innocence of their intentions," Jefferson nonetheless thought they had manifested "ignorance of the value of public discussions."[34]

By contrast, in a letter to his son, Mason defended the secrecy rule as "a proper precaution to prevent mistakes and misrepresentation until the business shall have been completed, when the whole may have a very different complexion from that in which the several crude and indigested parts might in their first shape appear if submitted to the public eye." Madison likewise defended this "prudent" rule on the grounds that it would "effectually secure the requisite freedom of discussion" and also would "save both the convention and the community from a thousand erroneous and perhaps mischievous reports."[35]

Many years later, Madison strongly defended the secrecy rule as critical to the convention's success. Delegates had expressed opinions that "were so various and at first so crude that it was necessary they should be long debated." An "accommodating spirit" had been essential to achieving "any uniform system

---

for him politically as he and Jefferson founded a states' rights, pro-democratic political party in the 1790s, and as Jacksonian democracy swept the nation in the early decades of the nineteenth century. As Madison revised some of his convention speeches on these subsequent occasions, he excised some of the most inconvenient passages. He may also have added some disapproving comments about slavery to remarks he ostensibly made at the convention in late August. It is impossible to know how much Madison's speeches, as recorded in his own notes, were altered by these subsequent emendations.

In sum, while we have a fairly detailed record of what transpired at the Philadelphia convention, it is important to be aware of the limits on what we can know.

of opinion." Had the delegates "committed themselves publicly at first, they would have afterwards supposed consistency required them to maintain their ground" even if they had changed their initial views.[36]

With the ground rules established, Edmund Randolph,* as the governor of the state that had set in motion the events leading to the convention, introduced the scheme for which Madison was largely responsible. Quickly denoted

---

* Randolph was born in 1753 in Williamsburg, Virginia, into one of the state's most prominent families of lawyer-statesmen. After attending the College of William and Mary, he read law in his father's office.

In 1775, Randolph's Loyalist parents departed for England, while he stayed behind and joined the Revolutionary cause. Partly on the recommendation of Virginia planter-merchant Benjamin Harrison (the father and great-grandfather of future American presidents), who considered Randolph "one of the cleverest young men in America" but worried that he might be penalized for the political choice made by his parents, George Washington hired Randolph as an aide-de-camp. However, the sudden death of Randolph's uncle, Peyton Randolph, who was serving as president of the Continental Congress, forced Randolph to leave the army to accompany his uncle's body home and to settle his affairs.

In 1776, Randolph was the youngest delegate to the Virginia convention that wrote the state's constitution. He became the state's first attorney general and also was twice appointed as a delegate to the Continental Congress, where he began a lifelong friendship with his fellow Virginia delegate James Madison. In 1786, the Virginia legislature elected Randolph governor, and he also served as one of the state's commissioners to the Annapolis convention. Contemporary character sketches portrayed Randolph as "one of the most distinguished men in America by his talents and his influence" and as "a young gentleman in whom unite all the accomplishments of the scholar and the statesman."

Although Randolph introduced the Virginia Plan at the start of the Philadelphia convention, he was, as we shall see, one of only three delegates present who refused to sign the Constitution at the end of the convention. In late 1787, during the ratifying contest in Virginia, Randolph published a letter accounting for his actions in Philadelphia. In addition to noting his principal objections to the Constitution, Randolph's letter explained that, while he favored amendments to be enacted prior to Virginia's ratification, he would support unconditional ratification if insisting on antecedent amendments might jeopardize the union. Then, at Virginia's ratifying convention in June 1788, Randolph came out in support of ratification on the grounds that it was too late in the process—eight other states had ratified by this point—for Virginia to insist on antecedent amendments. Antifederalists were outraged by what they considered Randolph's inconstancy, and Patrick Henry fiercely attacked him at the Virginia convention. Several years later, reflecting a similar perspective, Jefferson described Randolph as "the poorest chameleon I ever saw, having no color of his own, and reflecting that nearest him."

In 1789, Washington appointed Randolph the nation's first attorney general, and he became a close adviser to the president, drafting many of his speeches. When, in 1793, Jefferson resigned as secretary of state, Randolph replaced him. In that capacity, he opposed the appointment of John Jay in 1794 as special envoy to Great Britain, and he opposed ratification of the controversial treaty that Jay negotiated. In 1795, Washington forced Randolph out of the cabinet, believing the account contained in captured communiqués from the French minister to the United States that suggested Randolph had revealed sensitive information. (Modern scholarship exonerates Randolph of any wrongdoing.) Randolph then published two "vindications" of his conduct, which suggested a British plot to remove him from office and did little to restore his reputation.

Figure 3.2 Governor Edmund Randolph of Virginia, who later provided critical support to Federalists at the Virginia ratifying convention and then became the nation's first attorney general during the Washington administration. (Library of Congress)

the "Virginia Plan," its resolutions became the convention's first substantive business and would remain its focal point for its duration.[37]

As Randolph explained to the convention, the Virginia Plan was a response to the deficiencies of the Articles of Confederation. He conspicuously avoided disparaging the abilities of the Articles' authors—"wise and great men," who perhaps could not have done better given "the jealousy of the states with regard to their sovereignty." Unable to predict the future, Randolph explained, the Articles' drafters could not have foreseen the inefficiency of the requisition system, Congress's inability to pay foreign debts, commercial discord among the states, Shays's Rebellion, state violations of federal treaty obligations, and "the havoc of paper money."[38]

After leaving the cabinet, Randolph returned to his law practice in Richmond. In 1807, he helped defend Aaron Burr against a treason prosecution in the federal circuit court in Richmond. Randolph died in 1813.

Yet Randolph insisted that the Articles had proved badly flawed, in ways that he proceeded to itemize. The nation was not safe from foreign invasion, as Congress had no independent authority to raise troops, state militias were inadequate for defense, and enlistments required money, which Congress did not have. Congress had no power to prevent state infractions of federal treaties or the law of nations, which meant "that particular states might by their conduct provoke war without control." Congress had the power neither to "check the quarrels between states" nor to suppress rebellions within them. Congress could not "counteract . . . the commercial regulations of other nations," nor impose "a productive impost." The Articles were not even supreme over state constitutions because they had been ratified only by state legislatures, not by the people. Finally, Randolph warned of "the prospect of anarchy from the laxity of government everywhere."[39]

Observing that the remedy for such deficiencies must lie within "the republican principle," Randolph then introduced the resolutions of the Virginia Plan. The first resolution disingenuously stated that the Articles ought to be "corrected and enlarged" to better accomplish their objects—"common defense, security of liberty, and general welfare." The remainder of the resolutions then essentially repudiated the Articles.[40]

The Virginia Plan provided that the national legislature, unlike the Confederation Congress, would consist of two branches. Representation in the legislature would "be proportioned to the quotas of contribution, or to the number of free inhabitants, as the one or the other rule may seem best in different cases." Thus, although the scheme for apportioning representation was left somewhat murky, the Virginia Plan clearly abrogated the Articles' provision for equal state voting power in Congress.[41]

Members of the first branch of the legislature would be elected by the people of the states for terms of unspecified length with mandatory rotation in office required after an unspecified number of terms. Representatives also would be subject to recall during their term of office. Members of the second branch were to be elected by the lower house from a "proper number" nominated by the state legislatures. The Plan did not stipulate a particular length of term for members of the second branch but provided only that they should "hold their offices for a term sufficient to ensure their independency."[42]

The national legislature would be vested with the legislative authority enjoyed by the Confederation Congress. In addition, it would have the power "to legislate in all cases to which the separate states are incompetent, or in which the harmony of the United States may be interrupted by the exercise of individual legislation." The national legislature would also be empowered "to negative all laws passed by the several states, contravening in the opinion of the national legislature the articles of union" (a narrower veto than Madison

had favored in his correspondence). Finally, Congress would have the power
"to call forth the force of the union against any member of the union failing to
fulfill its duty under the articles thereof."[43]

The Virginia Plan also called for a national executive to be chosen by the national legislature for a single term of unspecified length. The executive would
possess "a general authority to execute the national laws" and also "enjoy the
executive rights vested in Congress by the Confederation" (such as the powers
to make war and enter into treaties). The executive, together with "a convenient
number" of federal judges, would constitute a "council of revision" empowered
to veto any act of the national legislature, including its "negatives" (vetoes) of
state legislation. A veto by the council of revision could be overridden by the
votes of an unspecified number of members of both legislative branches.[44]

The Plan also called for a national judiciary "to consist of one or more supreme tribunals and of [an indeterminate number of] inferior tribunals to be
chosen by the national legislature to hold their offices during good behavior"
and to enjoy fixed salaries not to be increased or diminished during their terms
in office. The jurisdiction of the federal courts would extend to piracies and
felonies on the high seas, enemy captures, cases in which foreigners or citizens of multiple states "may be interested," cases involving the collection of the
national revenue, questions involving "the national peace and harmony," and
impeachments of national officers.[45]

In addition, the Plan called for provision to be made for the admission of
new states "lawfully arising within the limits of the United States" (which the
Articles had not explicitly provided for). The United States would guarantee a
republican government to all states. Provision would be made for amendments
when deemed necessary, without requiring the assent of Congress. State legislative, executive, and judicial officers would be bound by oath to support the
"articles of union" (i.e., the Constitution). Finally, amendments to the Articles
of Confederation proposed by the convention would be submitted for consideration, after Congress approved them, to assemblies called by the state legislatures and whose members were to be chosen by the people.[46]

The Virginia Plan was a stunning departure from the Articles. Although the
Plan misleadingly claimed that it simply "corrected and enlarged" the Articles
to better accomplish their objects, in fact it amounted to a thoroughgoing repudiation of the status quo. Congress would receive the power to legislate in
all cases where national uniformity or collective-action barriers to effective
state regulation required it—a grant of authority broad enough to include
levying taxes and regulating commerce. Under the Articles, nothing like a national veto upon state legislation existed—or even had been publicly proposed
as a reform. With regard to representation in the federal government, the foun-
dational commitment of the Articles—equality of state voting power—was

eliminated by the Virginia Plan. Moreover, while under the Articles state legislatures selected congressional delegates, who were the principal federal officeholders, the Virginia Plan contemplated only minimal state involvement in constituting the branches of the national government: The people would pick the lower house of the legislature, the lower house would select the upper house (from candidates nominated by state legislatures), and the legislature would choose the executive. The Virginia Plan also created both a federal executive and a general system of federal courts—neither of which existed under the Articles.[47]

The day after introducing the Virginia Plan, Randolph, prompted by Gouverneur Morris of Pennsylvania, moved to replace the disingenuous first resolution, which claimed that the Plan merely corrected and enlarged the Articles, with three other resolutions. Taken together, these resolutions directly acknowledged the inadequacy of a "merely federal" government and proposed replacing it with a "national" government that was "supreme." Morris explained that while a federal government was "a mere compact resting on the good faith of the parties," a national government was one that had "a complete and compulsive operation."[48]

Some delegates immediately raised legitimacy objections. Congress had approved a convention "for the sole and express purpose of revising the Articles," and two states had bound their delegations with a similar restriction. Charles Cotesworth Pinckney of South Carolina warned that if the delegates now declared that a merely federal union could not accomplish the important objects enumerated by the Articles, then they were effectively "declaring that the convention does not act under the authority of the recommendation of Congress," and this would mean that "their business was at an end." Elbridge Gerry* of Massachusetts agreed: His state's delegation was expressly limited

---

* Gerry was born in 1744 in Marblehead, Massachusetts. His father, who had emigrated from England, was a successful ship captain and merchant, who became wealthy supplying dried codfish to the West Indies and southern Europe. Gerry graduated from Harvard in 1765, returned home, and entered his father's business.

In the first half of the 1770s, Gerry was involved in local politics, serving on Marblehead committees to enforce the policy of boycotting British imports and to collect and distribute relief donations when the Coercive Acts shut down the port of Boston. He also represented his town in the colonial legislature and in the extralegal Massachusetts provincial congress and helped gather supplies for the militia units that were forming in anticipation of armed conflict with Great Britain.

In 1776, Gerry was appointed to represent Massachusetts in the Continental Congress, where he was an early and vigorous advocate of independence. His congressional colleague John Adams called him "a man of immense worth" and declared, "If every man here was a Gerry, the liberties of America would be safe against the gates of earth and hell." In Congress, where Gerry was an influential member for most of the decade from 1776 to 1785, he focused on matters of supply and

to proceeding along the lines recommended by Congress. He thought it "questionable not only whether this convention can propose a government totally different [but also] whether Congress itself would have a right to pass such a resolution as that before the house [i.e., the convention]."[49]

Over the following weeks, other delegates raised similar concerns about exceeding their limiting instructions. For example, John Lansing, Jr., of

finance, including the collection of military supplies in Europe, where he had business contacts that he put to good use. Gerry also developed a reputation in Congress as a fierce opponent of a peacetime military establishment.

In 1785, Gerry retired to private life, married, and relocated from Marblehead to Cambridge, Massachusetts, where he bought an elegant Georgian mansion that had belonged to the colony's last royal lieutenant governor before being confiscated by the state during the Revolutionary War. (Today, it is known as Elmwood and is the official residence of the president of Harvard University.) However, Shays's Rebellion, which to Gerry demonstrated the anarchic tendencies of democracy, induced him to re-enter politics and accept an appointment to the Massachusetts delegation to the Philadelphia convention.

There, as we shall see, Gerry was a frequent participant in debates, although his fellow delegate William Pierce described him as a "hesitating and laborious speaker." Gerry offered some of the convention's most strident criticisms of democracy, opposing popular election of the president and even of the House of Representatives. Unlike many of his fellow delegates, however, Gerry balanced his fear of democracy with an equally strong suspicion of elites, such as the Society of the Cincinnati, that he worried might aspire to establish an aristocracy or monarchy. Reflecting this concern, Gerry strongly supported annual elections of House members, an explicit enumeration of Congress's powers, and strict limits on a peacetime standing army. He also chaired the committee that proposed the critical compromise between large and small states over apportionment of representation in the national legislature, without which the convention would probably have failed. At the end of the proceedings, Gerry was one of three delegates—along with Mason and Randolph—who refused to sign the Constitution.

Soon after the convention, Gerry wrote a letter enumerating his objections to ratification, which was widely circulated and quickly became one of the Antifederalists' canonical critiques of the Constitution. In the ratifying contest, he was a frequent target of Federalist barbs, including the charge that he had sought to secure at the convention a constitutional provision guaranteeing the redemption at face value of continental currency, of which Gerry was said to have purchased a huge quantity.

In 1788, after being defeated in the Massachusetts gubernatorial contest, Gerry was elected to the first US House of Representatives, where he pressed for stronger constitutional amendments than Madison, who had assumed firm control of the amendments project, was inclined to support. Serving in the House from 1789 to 1793, Gerry proved a strong supporter of Secretary of the Treasury Alexander Hamilton's financial policies.

In 1797, President John Adams, a longtime friend and admirer, appointed Gerry to a diplomatic mission to France, which became known to history as the XYZ Affair and nearly resulted in a war. In 1800, Gerry, concerned by the Federalists' military buildup in preparation for war with France, finally jettisoned his aversion to party labels, joined the Jeffersonian Democratic-Republican Party, and ran for governor of Massachusetts. He lost this and a subsequent contest but was finally elected governor in 1810. After losing his re-election bid in the spring of 1812, Gerry, a strong supporter of the war that broke out with Great Britain that summer, was awarded the vice presidential slot on his party's national ticket in the election that fall. Running with the incumbent president, James Madison, Gerry was elected vice president and served until his death in 1814.

Figure 3.3 Elbridge Gerry of Massachusetts, who played a prominent role at the Philadelphia convention but refused to sign the Constitution and then became one of the nation's leading Antifederalists. (Courtesy of Independence National Historical Park)

New York opposed the Virginia Plan because he was "decidedly of opinion that the power of the convention was restrained to amendments of a federal nature and having for their basis the confederacy in being." William Paterson of New Jersey similarly observed that "the people of America were sharp sighted and not to be deceived" and would accuse the delegates of "usurpation" if they exceeded their charge. The delegates' commissions "give a complexion to the business," Paterson argued, and they had been sent there "as the deputies of 13 independent, sovereign states, for federal purposes" and not to "consolidate their sovereignty and form one nation."[50]

Randolph responded to such charges of illegitimacy: "When the salvation of the Republic was at stake, it would be treason to our trust not to propose what we found necessary." According to Madison's notes, Randolph "painted in strong colors the imbecility of the existing confederacy and the danger of delaying a substantial reform." He declared that this was one of those occasions "of a peculiar nature where the ordinary cautions must be dispensed with."[51]

Hamilton endorsed Randolph's position: "[W]e owed it to our country to do on this emergency whatever we should deem essential to its happiness. The states sent us here to provide for the exigencies of the union. To propose any plan not adequate to these exigencies, merely because it was not clearly within our powers, would be to sacrifice the means to the end." In any event, Hamilton argued, the delegates' instructions, which were to pursue "a good government," authorized them to depart from the terms of the Confederation. James Wilson of Pennsylvania offered a slightly different justification for pursuing the recommendations of the Virginia Plan, despite Congress's limiting instructions: "With regard to the power of the convention, he conceived himself authorized to conclude nothing, but to be at liberty to propose anything."[52]

Many other delegates made similar statements. A majority of them were clearly not deterred by the legitimacy objection. When the convention took its first vote on whether a national—as opposed to a merely federal—government ought to be established, six of the seven delegations casting a ballot opted to repudiate the Articles. Those delegates committed to working within the Articles were so clearly in the minority* that Lansing told his brother they had "no prospect of succeeding" and that he was contemplating "whether it would not be proper for him to leave" (which he soon did).[53]

Expanding the Powers of
the National Government

After the convention, Madison reported to Jefferson that the delegates had "generally agreed that the objects of the union could not be secured by any system founded on the principle of a confederation of sovereign states." In accepting the Virginia Plan—and the clarifying resolutions offered the day after the Plan's introduction—as the starting point for their deliberations, the delegates evinced a strikingly nationalist perspective.[54]

Yet there were delegates in Philadelphia who attacked the Virginia Plan, defended the idea of state sovereignty, and insisted that the Articles should be amended rather than scrapped. Oliver Ellsworth of Connecticut asked why, simply "because we have found defects in the confederation, must we therefore pull down the whole fabric, foundation and all, in order to erect a new building totally different from it without retaining any of its materials?" Domestic happiness, Ellsworth insisted, "depends as much on the existence of my state

---

* The conclusion to this chapter considers why the opponents of the nationalizing Virginia Plan were such a distinct minority at the Philadelphia convention.

government, as a new-born infant depends upon its mother for nourishment." Paterson warned that the people were not ready for "a national government as contradistinguished from a federal one," and "[a] confederacy supposes sovereignty in the members composing it." John Dickinson of Delaware, who had played a prominent role in drafting the Articles of Confederation, insisted that he "had no idea of abolishing the state governments as some gentlemen seemed inclined to do." "The happiness of this country," he opined, "required considerable powers to be left in the hands of the states."[55]

Some delegates specifically objected to the Virginia Plan's broad grant of power to Congress "to legislate in all cases to which the separate states are incompetent or in which the harmony of the United States may be interrupted by the exercise of individual legislation." Protesting the vagueness of this language, two South Carolinians demanded "an exact enumeration" of Congress's powers. Denying that he had ever intended to grant "indefinite powers" to Congress, Randolph explained that delegates should first agree upon general principles and defer consideration of the details until later discussion.

Figure 3.4 John Dickinson of Delaware, who was one of the leading propagandists, political thinkers, and statesmen of the Revolutionary generation. (Courtesy of Independence National Historical Park)

Unpersuaded, Roger Sherman* of Connecticut, who proved to be one of the nationalists' main adversaries at the convention, insisted that "the objects of the union" were few—mostly limited to foreign relations and settling internal disputes—and they ought to be specifically defined.[56]

In response, James Wilson† protested that "it would be impossible to enumerate the powers which the federal legislature ought to have." Madison declared that although he had come to the convention with "a strong bias in favor of an enumeration and definition" of Congress's powers, his "doubts concerning [the] practicability" of such an enumeration "had become stronger" since

---

* Sherman was sixty-six years old in 1787, the second-oldest member of the convention. Originally a shoemaker, he eventually held as many different state and federal offices as virtually anyone in the nation, and he had served on the congressional committees that drafted both the Declaration of Independence and the Articles of Confederation. While, under the Confederation, Sherman had supported empowering Congress to regulate trade and collect an impost, he was as committed to protecting state prerogatives as any delegate at the Philadelphia convention. As we shall see, Sherman played a large role in crafting the compromises that ultimately enabled the convention to succeed. Ironically, he was there only because another delegate appointed by the Connecticut legislature had declined to attend.

† Wilson was born in Scotland in 1742 and educated for the Presbyterian ministry at St. Andrews, where he studied Scottish Enlightenment thinkers, including David Hume and Adam Smith. Wilson immigrated to the United States in the mid-1760s, studied law with John Dickinson, and became a tutor at the College of Philadelphia (later, the University of Pennsylvania). In 1774, he rose to political prominence as a result of an influential pamphlet he published denying American political subservience to Parliament (while pledging loyalty to the king). Wilson was a Pennsylvania delegate to the Second Continental Congress in 1775 and, although he initially resisted the movement toward independence, ultimately signed the Declaration of Independence. In the 1780s, he supported reform of Pennsylvania's radically democratic constitution, and he served several terms as a delegate to the Confederation Congress, where he supported the Bank of North America and favored the expansion of congressional power.

At the Philadelphia convention, Wilson proved to be one of the three or four most important delegates. According to William Pierce's sketch, "Wilson ranks among the foremost in legal and political knowledge." Government was his "peculiar study, all the political institutions of the world he knows in detail." While no delegate was "more clear, copious and comprehensive," Wilson was, according to Pierce, "no great orator. He draws the attention not by his eloquence, but by the force of his reasoning." As we shall see, Wilson was one of the strongest proponents of national power in Philadelphia; he also made notable contributions to the design of a powerful executive branch and was an ardent supporter of the proposed federal veto. More than any of his colleagues, Wilson favored direct popular participation in the election of senators and the president.

After the convention, as we shall also see, Wilson played the preeminent role in advocating ratification of the Constitution in Pennsylvania. After ratification, he became one of the original six justices on the US Supreme Court, as well as one of the nation's first law professors, at the College of Philadelphia. However, Wilson had a long history of what John Adams called "ardent speculations" in land, which eventually proved his undoing. In 1797, while still a Supreme Court justice, he spent time in debtors' prison in Philadelphia. After his son paid the debt to secure his release, Wilson fled to North Carolina, "absconding from his creditors," as one of his Supreme

the convention began. Indeed, later in the proceedings, he insisted that drawing a line between the powers of Congress and the states was so difficult that
it probably "cannot be done."* Hamilton likewise denied that any "boundary
could be drawn between the national and state legislatures." Because states
would simply exploit any enumerated limits to "gradually subvert" the national
government, it was necessary to vest Congress with "indefinite authority."
Early in the convention, the state delegations unanimously agreed (with one
delegation divided) to the Virginia Plan's definition of congressional power,
though many delegates clearly expected that a committee of detail would later
liquidate the Plan's broad formula into specific grants of power.[57]

Much later in the convention, disaffected by Virginia's significant defeat
on the issue of how to apportion the upper house of the national legislature,
Randolph himself insisted that the Virginia Plan's broad language regarding
congressional power must be translated into specific enumerated powers.
When the Committee of Detail[†] submitted its first draft of the Constitution
on August 6—Randolph wrote the first draft of the committee's report—it did
precisely this. Not even the most nationalist delegates objected.[58]

With regard to those specific enumerated powers, the delegates easily
agreed to remedy the omissions that had proved to be glaring deficiencies in the
Articles. By 1787, the vast majority of American statesmen had concluded that
the system of congressional requisitions was a disaster and that Congress must
be granted independent revenue-raising authority. As Hamilton explained at
the convention, the problem with requisitions was that states would "grant or
not grant as they approve or disapprove of [Congress's object]," and "[t]he de-
linquency of one will invite and countenance it in others." Moreover, taxing

---

Court colleagues wrote. Wilson died there of a stroke in 1798. One contemporary observed,
"What a miserable termination to such distinguished abilities, and what a dark cloud overcast
the last days of a life that had once been marked with uncommon lustre."

* Much later in life, Madison insisted that he had never intended the broad "descriptive
phrases" of the Virginia Plan "to be left in their indefinite extent to legislative discretion" and
that he had always expected the convention ultimately to narrow and define Congress's powers.
Madison was misremembering.

† For the first two months of the convention, the delegates met as a "committee of the whole,"
debating and revising the resolutions of the Virginia Plan. On July 23, they appointed a "committee of detail" to convert the resolutions that had been approved into a first draft of the
Constitution. Five delegates were appointed to the committee: Randolph, Wilson, Ellsworth,
John Rutledge of South Carolina, and Nathaniel Gorham of Massachusetts. The convention then
adjourned from July 26 through August 6, so the committee could do its work. This work proved
considerably more substantive than simply collating what the delegates had agreed to up to that
date, and the convention would spend the rest of August debating the committee's report. As we
shall see in chapter 4, the committee's proposals with regard to issues relating to slavery were
especially controversial.

individuals was a great deal easier than forcing states to fulfill their quotas of requisitions. Individuals who failed to pay their taxes could be imprisoned, while against recalcitrant states, the ultimate remedy was war.[59]

Indeed, nearly three weeks before Hamilton's denunciation of the requisition system, Mason had explained—"very cogently," according to Madison— the difficulties inherent in coercing states. This had led Madison quickly to agree to abandon the Virginia Plan's provision empowering the federal government to "call forth the force of the union" against a delinquent state.* Madison conceded that "the more he reflected on the use of force, the more he doubted the practicability, the justice, and the efficacy of it when applied to people collectively and not individually." To use force "against a state would look more like a declaration of war than an infliction of punishment, and would probably be considered by the party attacked as a dissolution of all previous compacts by which it might be bound."[60]

Hamilton agreed that a system of forcible coercion was "utopian." How could a state as large and powerful as Virginia be coerced? The assistance of foreign powers would be required, but to invoke such assistance would "dissolve the union and destroy your freedom." The consensus among delegates for empowering Congress to levy taxes—rather than simply requisition funds— which would obviate the need for a power to coerce states, was so strong that little discussion was devoted to the subject.[61]

The delegates not only preferred a taxing power to a system of requisitions but also rejected the idea of qualifying that power by duration or by the kind or amount of the taxes to be raised (though they did, as we shall see in chapter 4, impose certain other limits on the taxing power that bore mainly on issues relating to slavery). Some delegates did propose such qualifications. Mason suggested limiting the duration of taxes because a "perpetual revenue . . . must of necessity subvert the liberty of any country." Sherman proposed limiting Congress to the "power of levying taxes on trade" while withholding "the power of direct taxation." Luther Martin of Maryland suggested that Congress be permitted to supplement indirect taxes with direct taxes—such as land and poll taxes—only in "cases of absolute necessity," and even then only if a state had first failed to satisfy its quota of a congressional requisition. Such proposals to limit the taxing power elicited no significant support. Instead, the delegates conferred upon Congress a vastly expanded power of taxation— broader than anyone had publicly proposed during the Confederation era, and

---

* In 1860, President James Buchanan invoked the Philadelphia convention's repudiation of the Virginia Plan's provision authorizing the use of force against a recalcitrant state to justify his conclusion that the national government lacked the power to coerce seceding states to remain in the union.

so far-reaching that it would elicit powerful resistance during the contest over ratification.[62]

Effective national governments need to be able to extract from the citizenry not only taxes but also manpower for military service. The Articles limited Congress to requisitioning troops from the states in the same way that it requisitioned funds (although the apportionment of troops was based on white population while the apportionment of funds was supposed to be based on land values). Delegates to the Philadelphia convention overwhelmingly agreed that Congress must have unlimited authority to raise armies and navies. Expressing "a scanty faith in militia," Charles Cotesworth Pinckney, who had been a Continental Army officer during the war and seen significant battlefield action, noted that "[t]he United States had been making an experiment without . . . a real military force," and the consequence had been "rapid approaches towards anarchy" (alluding to Shays's Rebellion). Reflecting on the convention from the distance of a quarter-century, Gouverneur Morris would recall that "[t]hose who, during the revolutionary storm, had confidential acquaintance with the conduct of affairs, knew well that to rely on militia was to lean on a broken reed."[63]

Elbridge Gerry, who as a congressional delegate had strongly opposed maintaining a standing army after the end of the Revolutionary War, objected that "an army is dangerous in time of peace." Predicting "great opposition to the plan" if it allowed a peacetime army of "an indefinite number," Gerry proposed a limit of two or three thousand troops. Sherman agreed that reasonable restrictions should be imposed on the size and duration of a peacetime army.[64]

Dismissing such objections, the convention imposed neither numerical nor other limits on Congress's power to raise an army, even in peacetime. As Hamilton explained, under the Articles, Congress plainly could "raise no troops nor equip vessels before war is actually declared. [It] cannot therefore take any preparatory measure before an enemy is at your door. How unwise and inadequate [its] powers!" Jonathan Dayton of New Jersey agreed that preparations for war needed to be made in time of peace, and John Langdon of New Hampshire argued that the people's representatives could safely be entrusted with an unqualified power to raise an army. As a small concession to dissenters such as Gerry, the convention agreed that no congressional appropriations for the military should extend beyond two years. But the delegates refused even symbolically to discountenance standing armies, rejecting a provision proposed by Mason to explain that the purpose of authorizing congressional control over state militias was to better secure "the liberties of the people . . . against the danger of standing armies in time of peace."[65]

In addition to granting Congress an unqualified power to raise armies and navies, the convention authorized Congress to call state militias into federal service in time of invasion or insurrection. Mason, who disfavored standing armies, pointed out that conferring broad authority upon Congress to regulate the militias might obviate the need for peacetime armies. Charles Cotesworth Pinckney argued that state militias would have little value when called into federal service unless Congress had the authority to impose uniformity in their arms and training.[66]

However, those delegates most solicitous of state power objected that the states "would pine away to nothing" if Congress exercised plenary power over their militias. Sherman noted that "the states might want their militia for defense against invasions and insurrections, and for enforcing obedience to their laws." Ellsworth proposed that Congress's power to impose uniformity in the arms and training of militias be limited to occasions when they had been called into actual federal service or states had neglected to regulate their own militias. Dickinson warned that "the states never would nor ought to give up all authority over the militia," and he proposed that Congress be limited to training one-quarter of the militia at a time.[67]

Madison strongly objected to such proposed restrictions: The regulation of the militia must belong to the authority charged with the public defense— Congress—and could not be divided between two distinct authorities. If states were to trust the federal government with power over "the public treasure," Madison wondered, why should they not "grant it the direction of the public force?"[68]

The convention ultimately delegated the militia issue to a committee, which proposed a compromise: Congress would organize, arm, and discipline the militia, but the states would appoint officers and provide training according to the discipline prescribed by Congress. Gerry objected that this proposal would make "the states drill sergeants," and he warned that Massachusetts citizens would consider awarding control of the state militia to Congress "as a system of despotism." Martin agreed.[69]

Madison responded that states already neglected effective discipline of their militias—Randolph attributed this to their "court[ing] popularity too much to enforce a proper discipline"—and Madison predicted they would grow even more lax as consolidation of the nation rendered states less dependent on their militias for self-defense. Randolph argued that so long as states controlled the appointment of officers, Congress could be trusted with control over the militia. The convention then overwhelmingly approved the committee's proposal. Although the delegates rejected Madison's effort to limit states to the appointment of only lower-ranking militia officers, they imposed no restrictions on the duration of congressional call-ups of the militia into federal service or on Congress's ability to deploy a militia outside its home state without the state legislature's consent.[70]

Most of the convention delegates also thought that the Articles' failure to confer upon Congress the power to regulate commerce was a serious flaw. Without fear of retaliation, foreign nations had discriminated against American goods and shipping. Left to themselves, states had been powerless to coordinate effective responses. In addition, states had begun discriminating against one another's trade, thus undermining one of the principal benefits of a common economic union. When states with desirable ports had imposed their own import duties on foreign goods, neighboring states that bore a heavy share of the incidence of such taxes without deriving any of the benefits were keen to retaliate. Indeed, much later in life, Madison recalled that the grant of power to Congress to regulate interstate commerce "grew out of the abuse of the power by the importing states in taxing the non-importing, and was intended as a negative and preventive provision against injustice among the states themselves, rather than as a power to be used for the positive purposes of the general government."[71]

Thus, none of the delegates objected to a prohibition on states' laying import duties without Congress's consent. Madison would have preferred to make that prohibition absolute to guard against the possibility that those states wishing to impose their own import duties would form a majority in Congress to permit them to do so. Yet he was outvoted.[72]

However, efforts to confer upon Congress a general power to regulate foreign and interstate commerce met with the same southern resistance as had similar proposals under the Articles. As Charles Cotesworth Pinckney explained at the convention, "the true interest" of southern states, which were primarily exporters of agricultural staples and importers of manufactured goods, was "to have no regulation of commerce." Southerners feared that Congress would use the power to regulate commerce to impose protective tariffs to benefit northern manufacturers, and to enact navigation laws to benefit northern shippers. Mason observed that the South was likely to be a minority in both houses of Congress, and he asked, "Is it to be expected that they [southerners] will deliver themselves bound hand and foot to the eastern states?" Maryland's delegates similarly resisted granting Congress power to control "the dearest interests of trade."[73]

George Clymer of Pennsylvania responded that "[t]he northern and middle states will be ruined if not enabled to defend themselves against foreign regulations." Gouverneur Morris defended navigation acts on the grounds that shipping was the "most precarious kind of property and stood in need of public patronage." Awarding preferences to American ships would quickly "multiply them, till they can carry the southern produce cheaper than it is now carried." In addition, "[a] navy was essential to security, particularly of the southern states," and the only way to secure one, Morris said, was "by a navigation act encouraging American bottoms [i.e., ships] and seamen." Madison, who was atypical among southern political leaders in believing that Congress must be empowered to regulate commerce, agreed that the disadvantage to the South from a "temporary rise of freight [rates]" would be outweighed by a long-term "increase of southern as well as northern shipping" and the "removal of the existing and injurious retaliations among the states on each other."[74]

Charles Pinckney of South Carolina (cousin of Charles Cotesworth Pinckney) argued that to secure southerners against abuse of the commerce power, the consent of two-thirds of both houses of Congress should be required for the enactment of commercial legislation. Roger Sherman of Connecticut objected that requiring a supermajority for legislation "was always embarrassing, as had been experienced in cases requiring the votes of nine states in Congress." But Hugh Williamson of North Carolina denied that any desirable measures had been defeated in the Confederation Congress by the supermajority requirement and insisted that "the southern people were apprehensive on this subject and would be pleased with the precaution."[75]

In the end, some southern delegates were induced to drop their insistence on a supermajority requirement for commercial legislation by concessions that were made by some northern delegates on issues involving slavery—a topic to be pursued in the next chapter. This deal enabled the convention by a slender margin to approve empowering Congress, by simple majority vote, to regulate foreign and interstate commerce. Madison believed that the Constitution's grant of the commerce power to Congress automatically would preempt states from enacting laws interfering with foreign or interstate commerce, even in the absence of congressional regulation. He declared himself "more and more convinced that the regulation of commerce was in its nature indivisible and ought to be wholly under one authority." But Sherman thought this went too far: "[T]here is no danger to be apprehended from a concurrent jurisdiction," since Congress's power to regulate trade was "supreme" and it could therefore pass laws to preempt any state interference. The convention did not expressly resolve this question of whether Congress's control over commerce should be "exclusive" and, as such, would automatically preempt state commercial regulations. The Supreme Court would struggle mightily with this issue during the antebellum era.[76]

In addition to approving broad congressional authority to tax, raise armies and navies, co-opt state militias, and regulate foreign and interstate commerce, convention delegates agreed that the national legislature ought not to be limited to expressly delegated powers, as the Confederation Congress had been under the Articles. When the Committee of Detail enumerated Congress's specific powers, it authorized Congress, in addition, to exercise those powers that were "necessary and proper" to executing the enumerated ones. Though the Necessary and Proper Clause would generate intense criticism during the struggle over ratification of the Constitution, the convention approved it without discussion.[77]

In sum, the Philadelphia convention displayed a striking degree of consensus on substantially expanding Congress's powers. Even the small-state delegations, which (as we shall see in a moment) nearly brought the convention to a halt over the Virginia Plan's proposal to end equal state representation in Congress, generally proved to be enthusiastic nationalists once their states had been guaranteed an equal vote in the upper house of the national legislature. The small-state delegates were primarily concerned with preserving their states' influence within Congress, not with limiting the scope of Congress's authority.[78]

Declaring himself "astonished" and "alarmed" at the proposal to destroy the equality of state voting power in Congress, David Brearley, chief justice of the relatively small state of New Jersey, insisted that he had "come to the convention with a view of being as useful as he could in giving energy and stability to the federal government." Dickinson, representing the even smaller state of Delaware, accurately informed Madison that the small states would prove "friends to a good national government" once given what they wanted in terms of congressional representation. After being assured of his state's equal representation in the upper house of the national legislature (which the Committee of Detail, in early August, officially named "the Senate"), Dickinson's Delaware colleague George Read announced his hope that "the objects of the general government would be much more numerous than seemed to be expected by some gentlemen, and that they would become more and more so." As former president Madison explained to future president Martin Van Buren in 1828, "[t]he threatening contest, in the Convention of 1787, did not, as you supposed, turn on the degree of power to be granted to the federal government: but on the rule by which the states should be represented and vote in the government. . . . The contests and compromises turning on the grants of power, though very important in some instances, were knots of a less 'Gordian' character."[79]

The behavior of New Jersey's delegation at the convention confirmed that once small-state delegates had been assuaged with regard to their states' relative influence within Congress, they were as likely to support a powerful national government as were large-state nationalists such as Madison, Wilson, and Morris. The New Jersey delegation gave its name to the plan that was introduced in mid-June as the primary alternative to the Virginia Plan. Its proponents—mostly delegates from Connecticut, New York, New Jersey, and Delaware—described it as a "purely federal" plan, which purported to "revise" and "correct" the Articles rather than repudiate them (though even the New Jersey Plan would have granted Congress plenary power to regulate interstate and foreign commerce and considerable taxing authority). The principal distinguishing features of the New Jersey Plan were equal state representation in a unicameral federal legislature and the preservation of the notion from the Confederation that Congress acted upon states rather than individuals.[80]

Yet, in fact, New Jersey had been one of the most nationalist states during the Confederation (when, of course, it had possessed an equal vote in Congress). New Jersey had strongly supported the impost amendments—at least in part to protect itself from New York's import duties, the incidence of which bore heavily on New Jersey residents. New Jersey also had been the first state to support granting Congress the power to regulate foreign trade. Its delegation to the Annapolis convention was the only one that had been instructed to pursue a broader agenda than simple commercial reform, including "other important matters" that "might be necessary to the common interest and permanent harmony of the several states." New Jersey had been the first state to appoint a delegation to the Philadelphia convention.[81]

The New Jersey Plan was, in fact, mostly a bargaining ploy by small-state delegations to extract equal state representation in at least one house of the national legislature. During debates over that plan, Charles Pinckney had predicted, "Give New Jersey an equal vote, and she will dismiss her scruples, and concur in the national system." Pinckney was right: Once the small states had secured equality in the Senate, New Jersey's delegates proved as staunchly nationalist as any delegation in Philadelphia. As the great nineteenth-century historian George Bancroft wrote, "From the day when every doubt of the right of the smaller states to an equal vote in the Senate was quieted, they—so I received it from the lips of Madison, and so it appears from the records—exceeded all others in zeal for granting powers to the general government. . . . Paterson of New Jersey was for the rest of his life a federalist of federalists."[82]

Southern delegations also proved mostly to be enthusiastic supporters of a powerful national government, so long as they could ensure that their states' power within that government reflected the South's large slave population and that the Constitution provided certain safeguards for slavery. The radical states' rights sentiment that would characterize southern politics in the decades before the Civil War was entirely absent from the southern delegations in Philadelphia. As we shall see, convention delegates almost universally assumed that future demographic shifts would benefit the South and the Southwest, and the southern delegates were comfortable expanding the power of a federal government that they assumed their states would soon control.[83]

Establishing the Supremacy of the National Government

Despite the strikingly nationalist bent of the convention, the delegates rejected some aspects of the Virginia Plan as too destructive of state prerogatives. Most notably, Madison could not, in the end, convince his colleagues to support the most novel aspect of the scheme—the proposed federal power to veto state legislation.

As we have seen, the Virginia Plan provided that the federal legislature would be empowered "to negative all laws passed by the several states, contravening in the opinion of the national legislature the articles of union." To Madison, this veto power was essential both to protecting federal prerogatives such as treaties from state interference and to securing justice within the states.[84]

Madison told the convention that states had a propensity "to pursue their particular interests in opposition to the general interest." For example, under the Articles of Confederation, states had violated federal treaties, which risked embroiling the nation in a foreign war, and had entered into treaties with one another without congressional consent, in direct violation of the Articles. This "same tendency of the parts to encroach on the authority of the whole" would "continue to disturb the system, unless effectually controlled. Nothing short of a negative on their laws will control it." Moreover, only a federal veto could remedy the "dreadful class of evils" perpetrated by state legislatures in the 1780s: the multiplicity, mutability, and injustice of laws—including, most notably, debtor relief legislation and the issuance of paper money.[85]

To be sure, even in the absence of a federal veto power, Congress could still preempt, through legislation, state laws that were inconsistent with federal objectives, and federal courts might be able to invalidate such laws if directly contrary to the federal Constitution or a federal statute. (The extent to which the Framers were contemplating judicial review is discussed later.) Yet state laws might "accomplish their injurious objects" before the federal authorities could overrule them. Further, Madison doubted that state judges could be trusted to invalidate such measures, as they were too dependent on their legislatures to be true "guardians of the national authority and interests." In any event, clever state legislators would figure out how to evade explicit constitutional limitations that were entrusted to the courts to enforce. The federal veto, which Madison analogized to the British Privy Council's authority to block colonial legislation, would be "the most mild and certain means of preserving the harmony of the system." It could "stifle in the birth" every state measure "tending to discord or encroachment." Without a federal veto, "the only remedy would lie in an appeal to coercion"—which would be impractical.[86]

Most of Madison's nationalist allies at the convention also supported the notion of a federal veto. Indeed, Wilson, noting that the federal government needed "[t]he power of self defense," called the veto "the key-stone wanted [i.e., needed] to complete the wide arch of government we are raising." Hamilton proposed a slightly different scheme for blocking state legislation that was "contrary to the Constitution or laws of the United States": The national government should be empowered to appoint state governors, who would be afforded a veto over state legislation. Before the convention, Jay had similarly proposed that the national government be granted the power to remove state officials from office. In its first week of deliberations, the convention unanimously endorsed the principle of the federal veto as stated in the Virginia Plan.[87]

About one week after that vote, Charles Pinckney proposed expanding the veto to enable Congress to block *all* state laws that Congress "should judge to be improper," not just those violating the Constitution. Pinckney argued that "such a universality of the power was indispensably necessary to render it effectual." If the veto power were limited to state laws on particular subjects, state legislatures would figure out ways of circumventing the limits and obstructing federal measures that were disagreeable to them. Without an unlimited veto power, "it would be impossible to defend the national prerogatives, however extensive they might be on paper." Pinckney concluded, "This universal negative was in fact the cornerstone of an efficient national government."[88]

Madison, who had favored an unlimited federal veto in his preconvention correspondence, seconded Pinckney's motion, arguing that "an indefinite power to negative legislative acts of the states was absolutely necessary to a perfect system." Wilson agreed that it would be "impracticable" to define the occasions upon which a federal veto would be appropriate. The convention must inevitably repose discretion somewhere, and Wilson thought it could be "most safely lodged on the side of the national government." However, by a vote of seven delegations to three (with one delegation divided), the convention rejected Pinckney's proposal to expand the federal veto.[89]

Indeed, in the end, Madison was unable to convince his colleagues to embrace any form of the federal veto, despite their early agreement to it in principle. Delegates raised a number of objections—theoretical, practical, and strategic.[90]

In terms of theoretical objections, Sherman thought that "the cases in which the negative ought to be exercised might be defined." Williamson opposed conferring "a power that might restrain the states from regulating their internal police." Gerry objected that the veto might "extend to the regulations of the militia, a matter on which the existence of a state might depend," and he opposed granting the federal government a power that could be used to "enslave the states." Jefferson, who was in Paris, had raised a similar objection when Madison had first broached the idea of the federal veto with him: "Prima facie I do not like it," Jefferson declared. "It fails in an essential character that the hole and the patch should be commensurate. But this proposes to mend a small hole by covering the whole garment." Not more than one out of every hundred state laws, Jefferson protested, "concern[s] the confederacy."[91]

Opponents of the veto wondered why such a "terrible" measure was even necessary. Gouverneur Morris, in a departure from his usual support for nationalist initiatives, argued that "[a] law that ought to be negatived will be set aside in the judiciary department." Even if "that security should fail," so long as "sufficient legislative authority" were conferred upon Congress, it could simply repeal state laws inconsistent with its own, thus obviating the need for a preemptive veto power.[92]

The small-state delegations also strongly objected to the proposed veto. The convention first discussed the issue at a time when it appeared that small states might be denied equal voting power in both houses of the federal legislature. Thus, Gunning Bedford worried that Delaware, which under a system of representation apportioned according to population might enjoy only one-ninetieth of the representation in Congress, would find its laws being constantly vetoed, especially if it were involved in "a rivalry in commerce or manufacture" with larger states. By contrast, Bedford protested, Virginia and Pennsylvania—which would jointly share one-third of the congressional representatives under such an apportionment scheme—would rarely, if ever, see their laws blocked.[93]

When the convention voted on Pinckney's proposal to make the federal veto unlimited in scope, the only support came from the three largest states,* which would seem to confirm that many delegates thought the issue implicated the conflicting interests of large and small states. Yet when nationalists sought approval of the more limited version of the veto after the adoption of the compromise that guaranteed the small states equal voting power in the Senate, which should have removed any objections to the veto based on small-state concerns of domination, the convention nonetheless rejected it by the same margin of seven states to three.[94]

Pierce Butler raised a different theoretical objection to the veto: It would "cut off all hope of equal justice to the distant states," by which he probably meant Georgia and his own state of South Carolina. Butler may have had an unstated concern in mind as well: How could southerners entrust the national government with authority to veto state legislation that might implicate the institution of slavery?[95]

Several delegates also raised objections of a practical nature to the proposed veto. Mason wondered if every state law, no matter how local its concerns, would have to be reviewed by Congress: "Is no road nor bridge to be established

---

* Virginia, Pennsylvania, and Massachusetts were almost universally regarded as the three largest states, although the 1790 census revealed that North Carolina actually had a larger population (slaves included) than Massachusetts. Despite this, I will adhere to the convention of referring to the first three as "the large states."

without the sanction of the general legislature?" If so, then Congress would have to be in perpetual session "to receive and revise the states' laws." Bedford asked, "Are the laws of the states to be suspended in the most urgent cases until they can be sent seven or eight hundred miles?" Lansing wondered if a representative from Georgia would have the knowledge required to judge wisely of the expediency of a law enacted in New Hampshire.[96]

Madison proffered practical solutions to these practical problems: The concern of "urgent necessity" could be met by "some emanation of the power from the national government into each state so far as to give a temporary assent at least." The concern about Congress's having to be in perpetual session to exercise the veto might be addressed by lodging the power solely in the Senate, so that "the more numerous and expensive branch [i.e., the House] therefore might not be obliged to sit constantly."[97]

Finally, some delegates raised strategic objections to the veto: Granting such a power to Congress would jeopardize ratification of the constitution they were drafting. John Rutledge of South Carolina declared, "If nothing else, this [the veto] alone would damn and ought to damn the Constitution. Will any state ever agree to be bound hand and foot in this manner?" Gerry agreed that "[s]uch an idea as this," which nobody had heretofore publicly proposed, would "never be acceded to."[98]

Because Madison regarded the veto as "essential to the efficacy and security of the general government" and to his goal of empowering it to block state relief measures, he refused to drop the matter even after repeated defeats. Increasingly exasperated by Madison's persistence, other delegates protested that he was wasting their time. Not even efforts by nationalists to modulate the proposal by requiring a two-thirds majority in both houses of Congress to exercise the veto could convince enough delegates to support it. Madison was despondent over his defeat on this issue.[99]

Although the convention rejected the federal veto, delegates appreciated the importance of establishing some mechanism for enforcing federal supremacy. As Madison explained much later to future president John Tyler, "The necessity of some constitutional and effective provision guarding the Constitution and laws of the union against violations of them by the laws of the states was felt and taken for granted by all, from the commencement to the conclusion of the work performed by the convention." At a minimum, states could not be permitted freely to violate the terms of federal treaties, as they had done under the Articles. As Madison explained at the convention, the tendency of states to such violations had "been manifested in sundry instances," and "if not prevented, must involve us in the calamities of foreign wars."[100]

Immediately after the convention took one of its votes rejecting the veto, Luther Martin introduced what would become the Supremacy Clause of the

Constitution. The New Jersey Plan, which had not included a federal veto of state legislation, instead had explicitly declared that federal laws and treaties were to be "the supreme law of the respective states." In addition to this theoretical statement of federal supremacy, the New Jersey Plan provided a practical method of enforcement: "[T]he judiciary of the several states shall be bound thereby [i.e., by the declaration of federal supremacy] in their decisions, anything in the respective laws of the individual states to the contrary notwithstanding."[101]

The similarly worded version of the Supremacy Clause proposed by Martin was the convention's substitute for the rejected federal veto, and it passed unanimously. The Committee of Detail then added that state constitutions— not just state statutes—would be subordinate to federal law. Finally, toward the end of the convention, the clause was amended to include the federal Constitution—not just federal statutes and treaties—as part of "the supreme law."[102]

In providing that state judges would be bound by federal law, notwithstanding anything in state law to the contrary, the Supremacy Clause seemed plainly to contemplate some form of judicial review (i.e., judicial invalidation of legislation) at least by *state* judges in the context of interpreting *federal* law. What could it mean for state judges to be "bound" by federal law, notwithstanding anything in state law to the contrary, other than that they must invalidate state laws that contravened federal law (including the federal Constitution)?[103]

That judges could invalidate legislation was a fairly radical concept in 1787. In Great Britain, Parliament was supreme—at least it had been for the last century—and courts had no authority to invalidate its laws. American political leaders of the Revolutionary era generally exalted legislative supremacy and tended to regard courts with suspicion because judges had been seen mainly as agents of the Crown before the Revolution. But the well-to-do's faith in legislatures had been shaken by the capitulation of state assemblies to populist pressure for tax and debt relief in the mid-1780s.[104]

Some of the first rudimentary rumblings regarding judicial review came in the context of newspaper articles pondering whether legislatures were truly omnipotent when, rather than protecting lives and property, they passed "laws directly contrary to the nature" of their trust—such as debtor relief and paper money legislation. Early in 1786, William Grayson mused to Madison that if, indeed, a law contrary to a constitution could be invalidated, then "surely paper money with a tender annexed to it is void," for it was "an attack upon property," which was deemed a fundamental right in every state. When a Rhode Island court threatened to invalidate the state's punitive tender law of 1786, which deprived defendants of their rights to jury trial and appeal, judicial review began to seem a very attractive concept to many members of the political and economic elite.[105]

The Rhode Island court's pronouncement, together with a few cases from other states in which courts either invalidated laws under state constitutions or threatened to do so, had planted the seeds of judicial review by 1787. Nearly all the convention delegates would have known of such decisions, one of which was being reported in the newspapers even as they gathered in Philadelphia. Indeed, at least two explicit references were made to these decisions at the convention. Yet the delegates also would have known how intensely controversial such judicial assertions of the authority to invalidate legislation had been. The Rhode Island legislature had threatened to impeach the judges who dared to think they could invalidate the will of the sovereign people, as manifested through their legislature. Thus, although the delegates knew of a budding practice of judicial review in the states, it was not sufficiently well established for them simply to have taken it for granted in the Constitution.[106]

Although the topic of judicial review was explicitly discussed on several occasions at the Philadelphia convention, it never received the sort of sustained attention that was devoted to many other issues, such as the proposed federal veto of state laws or the executive veto of congressional legislation. When delegates mentioned judicial review, it was usually in one of two contexts. First, as we have just seen, some delegates opposed the federal veto on the grounds that a state law in violation of the federal Constitution would be invalidated by judges (and thus there was no reason to vest Congress with power to veto it).[107]

The second context in which judicial review was discussed was the Virginia Plan's proposal for a "council of revision" to be invested with the authority to examine and possibly veto every act of the national legislature (including its vetoes of state legislation). This council of revision would consist of the federal executive, together with "a convenient number" of federal judges. Some delegates criticized the inclusion of judges on the grounds, as Gerry explained, that they would "have a sufficient check against encroachments on their own department by their exposition of the laws, which involved a power of deciding on their constitutionality." Martin agreed that including judges in the council of revision would be "a dangerous innovation" because it would give them "a double negative," as the constitutionality of laws "will come before the judges in their proper official character."[108]

Over the course of the convention, eight delegates—including very prominent ones, such as Madison, Wilson, and Gouverneur Morris—stated that judges would have the authority under the Constitution to invalidate legislation. For example, Morris said that he could not agree that the judiciary "should be bound to say that a direct violation of the Constitution was law," and Madison insisted that a constitutional ban on ex post facto laws would "oblige the judges to declare such interferences null and void." By contrast, just two delegates expressly rejected the idea of judicial review. John Francis Mercer of Maryland, who attended the convention only very briefly, "disapproved of the doctrine that the judges as expositors of the Constitution should have authority to declare a law void." Rather, in his view, "laws ought to be well and cautiously made, and then to be uncontrollable." Dickinson declared that he was "strongly impressed" with Mercer's remark and agreed that "no such power ought to exist."[109]

Because judicial review was never a focal point of their discussions and because most of the delegates probably had given the matter little thought, the convention failed to explicitly provide for judicial review either of federal legislation or by federal courts. The Supremacy Clause, which is the Constitution's only express authorization of judicial review, speaks only of *state* judges invalidating *state* laws that violate the Constitution or other federal law.

The Supremacy Clause is only a procedural mechanism for enforcing federal supremacy. The substantive standards against which judges were to measure state laws to determine if federal supremacy had been violated would come from other provisions in the Constitution, as well as from federal treaties and statutes. Although most convention delegates had opposed Madison's proposed federal veto, they overwhelmingly agreed with the veto's primary object: to block state laws issuing paper money and providing relief to debtors. Thus, for example, while Gerry opposed an unqualified federal veto, he declared that he "had no objection to authoriz[ing] a negative to paper money and similar measures."[110]

To accomplish this goal, the Committee of Detail drafted a provision that ultimately became Article I, Section 10, of the Constitution, which provides: "No state shall . . . coin money; emit bills of credit; make any thing but gold and silver coin a tender in payment of debts; [or] pass any . . . law impairing the obligation of contracts. . . ." This provision would have barred most of the state relief measures of the 1780s—paper money emissions (including in the form of state land-bank loans), tender laws, and retrospective debtor relief measures, such as stay laws and installment laws. Under the Supremacy Clause, state judges—and, by implication, perhaps federal judges as well—would be enjoined to invalidate such state legislation.[111]

Most of the delegates regarded Article I, Section 10, as a critical component of their handiwork.* The Committee of Detail report would have permitted states, so long as Congress consented, to issue bills of credit or make

---

* The Framers' enthusiasm for this provision is somewhat ironic, given American protests against Great Britain's prohibition of colonial issues of paper money in the decades leading up to the Revolutionary War.

something other than specie a legal tender. Nathaniel Gorham defended the committee's proposal on the grounds that "an absolute prohibition of paper money would rouse the most desperate opposition" to the Constitution. But Sherman insisted, in reply, that "this is a favorable crisis for crushing paper money." If Congress were authorized to allow state emissions, then "the friends of paper money would make every exertion to get into the legislature in order to license it." The delegates then voted overwhelmingly in favor of the absolute prohibition.[112]

The provisions in Article I, Section 10, were uncontroversial at the convention. Most of them were approved without any serious debate. Even a fervent defender of state prerogatives such as Sherman had no qualms about barring states from issuing paper money. None of the three delegates who were present at the end of the convention but refused to sign the Constitution—Gerry, Mason, and Randolph—disagreed with the Constitution's ban on states' issuing paper money and enacting retrospective debtor relief laws.[113]

The delegates' loathing of paper money was starkly revealed in a debate on a provision reported by the Committee of Detail that would have authorized Congress—in contrast to the states—to emit bills of credit (in addition to its power of borrowing money). Morris, who moved to delete this provision, warned that the "[m]onied interest will oppose the plan of government if paper emissions be not prohibited."* Mason objected to Morris's motion, but he first took advantage of the occasion to reiterate his "mortal hatred to paper money." Yet because he "could not foresee all emergencies, he was unwilling to tie the hands of the legislature. . . . [T]he late war could not have been carried on, had such a prohibition existed." Mercer raised another objection to Morris's proposal: "It was impolitic also to excite the opposition of all those who were friends to paper money. The people of property would be sure to be on the side of the plan, and it was impolitic to purchase their further attachment with the loss of the opposite class of citizens."[114]

But the supporters of the motion proceeded to heap abuse on paper money. Oliver Ellsworth declared that this was "a favorable moment to shut and bar the door against paper money. The mischiefs of the various experiments which had been made were now fresh in the public mind and had excited the disgust of all the respectable part of America. By withholding the power from the new government, more friends of influence would be gained to it than by almost anything else." Wilson concurred: Barring Congress from emitting

* In 1783, Hamilton had proposed that Congress be deprived of the power to issue bills of credit—a power that "in its nature is pregnant with abuses and liable to be made the engine of imposition and fraud, holding out temptations equally pernicious to the integrity of government and to the morals of the people."

paper money would "have a most salutary influence on the credit of the United States. . . . This expedient [paper money] can never succeed whilst its mischiefs are remembered. And as long as it can be resorted to, it will be a bar to other resources." Butler declared himself "urgent for disarming the government of such a power." George Read "thought the words [authorizing Congress to emit bills of credit], if not struck out, would be as alarming as the mark of the Beast in Revelations." John Langdon stated that he would "rather reject the whole plan" than retain this language. The delegates then voted overwhelmingly to strike this provision.[115]*

Although a majority of states had issued paper money and enacted debtor relief laws in the mid-1780s, proponents of such measures were largely absent from the Philadelphia convention. At one point, Mercer did refer to himself as "a friend to paper money," yet almost all of his colleagues were enemies to it. Indeed, many of the delegates had played prominent roles in their state legislatures resisting what they called that "iniquitous system." For example, in 1786, Delaware had only narrowly resisted a paper money emission, yet none of its five delegates in Philadelphia had supported that measure, and Read had played a prominent role in defeating it. In the Virginia legislature, Madison and Mason had cosponsored a resolution denouncing the injustice of paper money.[116]

To deal with the related problem of debtors and tax protestors who tried to shut down courts rather than persuade legislatures to grant relief, the delegates authorized Congress to suppress insurrections, to suspend the writ of habeas corpus in cases of rebellion, and to guarantee to every state a republican form of government. In 1786, the Confederation Congress had voted to raise an army to suppress Shays's Rebellion, though the troops never took the field. Because the Articles authorized Congress to fight Indians but not to suppress domestic insurrections, Congress had used the pretext that the troops were needed to defend the western frontier against hostile Indians. At the convention, Randolph complained that "Congress was intended to be a body to preserve peace among the states," yet during Shays's Rebellion, "it was found [Congress was] not authorized to use the troops of the confederation to quell it."[117]

To be sure, some delegates thought that states should suppress their own rebellions, and others noted the difficulty of the federal government's having to determine which of two contending factions within a state should be

---

* Congress did not issue paper money until the Civil War. After the war, the Supreme Court first invalidated the Legal Tender Act, which made that paper money legal tender for debts, then narrowly reversed itself after President Ulysses S. Grant quickly appointed two new justices to the Court.

considered to be its legitimate government. Yet most delegates thought it "essential" that Congress have the power to suppress rebellions such as the recent one by debtors and tax protestors in Massachusetts. The possibility of slave insurrections may have been another reason to grant Congress this power, though none of the delegates said so.[118]

The delegates disagreed about whether Congress should be empowered to suppress a rebellion within a state without the state's consent. The Committee of Detail report had authorized Congress to intervene against rebellions within a state only on the application of the state's legislature. But several nationalist delegates supported a motion by Charles Pinckney to strike that qualification. Morris objected that it was "very strange" to "first form a strong man to protect us, and at the same time wish to tie his hands behind him." Congress could be trusted, Morris argued, "with such a power to preserve the public tranquility." Langdon observed that the mere prospect of federal military intervention would "have a salutary effect in preventing insurrections."[119]

However, those delegates more protective of state prerogatives strongly objected to Pinckney's motion. Gerry declared that he "was against letting loose the Myrmidons of the United States on a state without its own consent," and Martin agreed that to do so would be "dangerous and unnecessary." Gerry even ventured the opinion that "more blood would have been spilt" during Shays's Rebellion had Congress "intermeddled."[120]

By an evenly divided vote, the delegates failed to strike the requirement of state consent for congressional intervention. However, in response to concerns that it might not be possible to convene the legislature of a state when the violence requiring congressional intervention erupted, the convention provided that application to Congress could be made in such cases by the state executive.[121]

As we have seen, the convention rejected one possible mechanism for enforcing federal supremacy—the federal veto—and unanimously embraced another: the Supremacy Clause. To ensure the practical enforcement—as opposed to the merely theoretical proclamation—of federal supremacy, the delegates also created a federal supreme court and authorized Congress to create inferior federal courts as well. The Articles of Confederation had provided for no federal courts of general jurisdiction.

Although the Supremacy Clause bound state judges to elevate federal law—the Constitution, federal treaties, and federal statutes—over state law (including state constitutions) in cases of conflict, it could not guarantee they would actually do so. As Randolph observed at the convention, state courts could not "be trusted with the administration of the national laws. The objects of jurisdiction are such as will often place the general and local policy at variance." Specifically, as Madison had explained before the convention, state judges, dependent on state legislatures for their tenure in office and salaries, might feel pressure to side with state interests, as inscribed in state law, when they conflicted with federal law. Moreover, even state judges endeavoring in good faith to do their duty under the Supremacy Clause might be unconsciously tempted to favor the laws of their states, toward which they might feel a natural sympathy, over those of the federal government. Finally, even if state judges manifested no bias in favor of state law in cases of conflict with federal law, the unavoidable ambiguities of language could lead judges in different states to interpret federal law differently.[122]

In a letter to Madison in which he criticized the proposed federal veto, Jefferson explained in concrete terms what was at stake in such instances of state-federal conflict, and he suggested a mechanism—other than the veto— for safeguarding federal interests. In Jefferson's hypothetical, a British creditor sues on a prewar debt in a Virginia court. The debtor invokes as a defense a state law barring such suits from state court. The creditor replies by invoking a federal treaty "as controlling the state law." Yet Jefferson worried that the state judges would be "weak enough to decide according to the views of their legislature." Should that happen, "[a]n appeal to a federal court sets all to rights."[123]

Virtually all the delegates at the Philadelphia convention agreed with Jefferson's reasoning: There must be a federal tribunal with jurisdiction to review state court decisions interpreting federal law. Even the New Jersey Plan contained such a provision. A federal supreme court vested with such jurisdiction could both ensure a uniform interpretation of federal law and block blatant state attempts to defy federal authority.[124]

However, some delegates strongly opposed the Virginia Plan provision creating federal *trial* courts (in addition to one or more "supreme tribunals"), which they thought would usurp much of the jurisdiction exercised by state courts. The New Jersey Plan did not contemplate lower federal courts, though some small-state delegates became more supportive of such tribunals once the small states had secured equal voting power in the Senate. Thus, early in the convention's proceedings, Sherman objected to lower federal courts because of "the supposed expensiveness of having a new set of courts, when the existing state courts would answer the same purpose." Later, he changed his position.[125]

The South Carolinians were the staunchest opponents of creating lower federal courts. Rutledge declared that state tribunals "ought to be left in all cases to decide in the first instance" because a right of appeal to the Supreme Court would be "sufficient to secure the national rights and uniformity of judgments." Mandating federal trial courts not only would be "an unnecessary encroachment on the jurisdiction of the states" but also would create "unnecessary obstacles" to ratification of the Constitution. Butler agreed that "[t]he people will not bear such innovations. The states will revolt at such encroachments." He thought that the convention should "follow the example of Solon, who gave the Athenians not the best government he could devise, but the best they would receive." Martin supported the South Carolinians: Lower federal courts, by interfering with the jurisdiction of state tribunals, would "create jealousies and oppositions." When Mason later decided that he could not sign the Constitution, one of his stated objections was that the federal judiciary was constructed so as "to absorb and destroy the judiciaries of the several states."[126]

By contrast, Madison and his nationalist allies believed that federal trial courts were necessary because "an appeal would not in many cases be a remedy." Madison asked, "What was to be done after improper verdicts in state tribunals obtained under the biased directions of a dependent judge or the local prejudices of an undirected jury?" If state trial judges and juries were hostile to—or unconscionably prejudiced against—federal interests, they could subvert federal law through biased evidentiary rulings or findings of fact. Such decisions might prove difficult to reverse in an appeal to the US Supreme Court.[127]

It was essential, Madison declared, that there be "[a]n effective judiciary establishment commensurate to the legislative authority." A government lacking a proper judiciary (and executive) "would be the mere trunk of a body without arms or legs to act or move." Gorham agreed that federal trial courts were "essential to render the authority of the national legislature effectual," and he observed that states had not complained about federal trial tribunals vested with jurisdiction over piracies that had been established under the Articles. Addressing financial concerns, Rufus King argued that "the establishment of inferior tribunals would cost infinitely less than the appeals that would be prevented by them."[128]

Just over one week into the convention, the nationalists narrowly lost this battle over whether the Constitution would create lower federal courts. Rather than admitting defeat, they immediately regrouped and argued that at least Congress ought to have discretion to create such courts, even if the Constitution did not mandate them (as it did a supreme court). That proposal easily carried the day, and the Constitution authorizes but does not require Congress to create "tribunals inferior to the Supreme Court." In 1789, the first Congress similarly split the difference between nationalists and those more protective of state sovereignty by establishing lower federal courts but not bestowing upon them all of the jurisdiction authorized by the Constitution.[129]

The jurisdiction vested by the Constitution in the federal judiciary reflects the delegates' understanding of which sorts of cases state tribunals could not be trusted fairly to adjudicate. In mid-June, the delegates agreed to the broad outlines of that jurisdiction, approving a resolution "that the jurisdiction of the national judiciary shall extend to cases which respect the collection of the national revenue, impeachments of any national officers, and questions which involve the national peace and harmony." The delegates were especially determined to ensure that foreigners would have access to tribunals that would fairly adjudicate their rights under federal treaties, and that federal rather than state courts would adjudicate cases involving the federal government's collection of its revenue. The convention delegated to the Committee of Detail the task of spelling out the specific jurisdictional provisions that ultimately appeared in Article III of the Constitution and then devoted very little time or attention to debating the committee's jurisdictional proposals.[130]

The jurisdiction of the federal courts would obviously extend to admiralty cases and to suits involving prize ships, which even the Articles (though authorizing no federal courts of *general* jurisdiction) had allocated, respectively, to federal trial courts and federal appellate tribunals. Such cases were especially likely to involve foreign litigants, which meant that national interests were directly affected. More generally, cases in which foreign nationals and foreign nations were parties implicated foreign affairs, which came within the purview of the federal government and thus properly belonged in its tribunals.[131]

The delegates also allocated to federal courts jurisdiction over cases "arising under" federal law, which would enable them to ensure a uniform interpretation of federal law and to protect it from state subversion. Under this jurisdictional provision, states could no longer effectively nullify federal treaties through their courts' interpretations, as they had done to the Treaty of Paris. Such "arising under" jurisdiction would also enable federal courts to control the interpretation of federal revenue laws—a vital means of self-protection for any government.[132]

In a move that would prove more controversial during the ratifying contest, the delegates also extended federal court jurisdiction to many traditional state-law issues, such as tort claims and contract disputes, when the parties to the litigation were citizens of different states. In such cases, a federal court presumably would be a more neutral arbiter than a state tribunal located in a state in which only one of the parties was a citizen.[133]

The convention also had to decide how federal judges would be appointed and what their term of office would be. In the American colonies, judges held their offices at the Crown's pleasure, and one of the grievances expressed by Americans in the Declaration of Independence was that the king had "made judges dependent on his will alone, for the tenure of their offices, and the amount and payment of their salaries."[134]

The delegates in Philadelphia easily agreed that federal judges should enjoy tenure "during good behavior," rather than serving a fixed term of years. However, late in the convention, Dickinson suggested that federal judges

ought to be removable "on address"—that is, "by the executive on the application by the Senate and House of Representatives." Sherman defended this
proposal as similar to the British practice, but most of the delegates agreed
with Morris that "it was fundamentally wrong to subject judges to so arbitrary
an authority." Rutledge, who was a judge in South Carolina, thought it an "insuperable objection" to this proposal that federal judges would be the arbiters
of disputes between states and the United States. Wilson agreed that "[t]he
judges would be in a bad situation if made to depend on every gust of faction
which might prevail in the two branches of our government." Randolph opposed the proposal as "weakening too much the independence of the judges."
The delegates overwhelmingly defeated Dickinson's motion.[135]

To further safeguard the independence of federal judges, the convention
unanimously agreed that Congress should be barred from diminishing their
salaries during their terms in office. For the same reason, Madison would
have preferred that Congress be forbidden from *increasing* federal judges'
salaries during their time in office. However, most of the delegates thought
that a salary increase might be warranted during a federal judge's potentially
lengthy tenure in office (during good behavior), and they rejected Madison's
proposal. In this regard, they specifically differentiated the nation's executive,
who would serve a much shorter term in office and thus ought to have his independence from Congress secured by a constitutional prohibition on increases
as well as decreases of his salary.[136]

The federal judiciary—vested with tenure during good behavior; removable
from office only through conviction on an impeachment for treason, bribery, or
other "high crimes and misdemeanors" by a two-thirds vote in the Senate; and
protected against salary diminution—was far more independent of popular
and legislative influence than were state judiciaries of the era. In several states,
judges were appointed only to a fixed term of years, and in a couple of states,
they were subject to annual reappointment. Thus, for example, none of the
Rhode Island judges who had dared to question the constitutionality of the
stringent enforcement mechanisms in the state legislature's 1786 paper money
scheme were reappointed by the legislature the following year. Moreover, in
some states, the judges could be removed by "address" of the legislature, which
was entirely at that body's discretion, requiring no allegation of wrongdoing.
Finally, few state constitutions protected the salaries of judges from diminution while in office.[137]

Although the delegates to the Philadelphia convention agreed that federal judges should be independent, they disagreed about who should appoint
them—the national legislature, the Senate, or the executive. This was part of
a larger disagreement over the federal appointment power, which is discussed
later in this chapter.[138]

With regard to one final issue involving the federal judiciary, the convention provided for jury trials in federal criminal cases but made no mention of them in civil cases. Several delegates objected to this omission. For example, Gerry thought that juries were necessary to guard against corrupt judges, and he warned that the Constitution authorized "a Star Chamber as to civil cases." But other delegates argued that it would be difficult to specify in the Constitution the criteria that distinguished those civil cases in which jury trials were traditionally required from those, such as equity cases, in which they were not. (Courts of equity handled lawsuits in which plaintiffs sought remedies other than money damages, such as an injunction.) Moreover, those delegates opposing the inclusion of constitutional protection for jury trials in civil cases argued that Congress could be trusted to provide by statute for jury trials in the appropriate cases.[139]

The National Legislature

Although Madison's defeat on the proposed federal veto was his most bitter loss at the convention, it was not his only one. On two issues involving the upper house of the national legislature—how to apportion representation among the states and how to select its members—Madison also suffered major defeats.

The Virginia Plan provided for a bicameral national legislature—to which only Benjamin Franklin, the convention's oldest delegate, objected. Franklin was fond of the unicameral legislature established by the Pennsylvania constitution of 1776, which he had helped to write. Committed democrats in Pennsylvania had not wished to "balance" the people's will with an upper legislative house. Only one other state, Georgia, had emulated this feature of the Pennsylvania constitution, and few of the delegates in Philadelphia admired it. Thus, the convention quickly and easily (perhaps even unanimously) agreed to a bicameral Congress.[140]

About three weeks into the convention, small-state delegates proposed the New Jersey Plan, which would have preserved the unicameral nature of Congress. William Paterson defended unicameralism at the federal level, where "legislative objects are few and simple." Wilson objected, noting the "danger of a legislative despotism," which could be restrained only by dividing the legislature "within itself, into distinct and independent branches." As we have seen, the New Jersey Plan, with its unicameral Congress, was mainly a bid by small-state delegations to preserve the principle of equal state representation in at least one branch of the national legislature, not an embrace of unicameralism on its merits. Replacing the unicameral Confederation

Congress with a bicameral legislature was one of the easier decisions made in Philadelphia.[141]

The delegates disagreed a bit more over the Virginia Plan's proposal that the people directly elect their representatives in the lower house of the national legislature. To Madison, it was "essential to every plan of free government" that one branch of it be popularly elected because there must be some "sympathy between them [the people] and their rulers." Although conceding that he "was an advocate for the policy of refining the popular appointments by successive filtrations," Madison declared that it would be pushing that principle too far to apply it to the lower house of the national legislature as well as to the upper house, the executive, and the judiciary. In addition, only direct popular election of representatives would put Congress on a par with state legislatures in terms of their authority to claim to speak for the people. If nothing else, as Jefferson later pointed out to Madison, because Congress was vested with the power of taxation, the lower house must be popularly elected to preserve "inviolate the fundamental principle that the people are not to be taxed but by representatives chosen immediately by themselves."[142]

The proposal for direct popular election of members of the lower house elicited some of the most vigorous denunciations of democracy heard at the convention. Invoking Shays's Rebellion, Gerry opposed direct election of representatives on the grounds that the people were "the dupes of pretended patriots" and were "daily misled into the most baneful measures and opinions by the false reports circulated by designing men." Sherman preferred that state legislatures choose members of the lower house because he considered the people unqualified to do so. Moreover, the selection of congressional representatives by state legislatures would, Sherman said, "preserve harmony between the national and state governments." Charles Cotesworth Pinckney defended state legislative selection of members of the House on the grounds that a majority of his state's citizens had been "notoriously for paper money as a legal tender," while the state legislature, from "some sense of character," had refused to comply with that demand.[143]

Yet most of the delegates agreed with Madison that the people must have some direct role in electing the federal legislature. A well-established maxim of government, often explicitly quoted in state constitutions of the era, held that all power was vested in and derived from the people. Mason insisted that government had a duty "to attend to the rights of every class of the people." Conceding that "we had been too democratic," now he was "afraid we should incautiously run into the opposite extreme." However inconvenient the democratic principle might prove to be in practice, "it must actuate one part of the government. It is the only security for the rights of the people." Wilson called popular election of the House "the cornerstone" of the entire system.[144]

Although several delegates defended popular election of the House primarily in terms of principle, pragmatic calculations may have been at least equally important. First, as Wilson explained, providing for the people to elect their congressional representatives would be critical to rallying public support for the Constitution, without which it would be impossible to create the much stronger national government that many of the delegates desired. He favored "raising the federal pyramid to a considerable altitude, and for that reason wished to give it as broad a basis as possible. No government could long subsist without the confidence of the people."[145]

Second, if congressional representatives were not to be chosen by the people, then they probably would be selected by state legislatures. Yet Madison thought the convention should avoid giving "too great an agency [to] the state governments in [constituting] the general one." King worried that state legislatures "would constantly choose men subservient to their [the legislatures'] own views as contrasted to the general interest," and Wilson agreed that state legislatures would be influenced in their choice of congressional representatives "by an official sentiment opposed to the general government." Wilson blamed state officeholders, not the people, for opposing federal measures under the Articles. Mason went so far as to argue that state legislatures had issued paper money when the people were against it, and that those legislatures would probably "send to the national legislature patrons of such projects if the choice depended on them." By substantial margins, the convention approved popular election of House members, defeating repeated efforts by Charles Cotesworth Pinckney to substitute state legislative selection.[146]

Despite their embrace of direct popular election of the House, the delegates sought ways to neutralize populist influence upon national representatives. State constitutions of the 1770s had greatly increased the number of legislative representatives on the theory that the resulting smaller constituencies per legislator would ensure better representation of the people's will and closer scrutiny of legislative self-dealing. Rejecting that approach, Madison observed at the convention that elections of representatives might "safely be made by the people if you enlarge the sphere of election." If the people had made bad choices in electing representatives, Madison believed, "it will generally be found to have happened in small districts." Larger districts would favor the election of large property holders—because they commanded wider spheres of influence through patronage networks—who could be relied upon not to support legislative action that threatened property rights.[147]

Other delegates stated similar views. Wilson observed, "There is no danger of improper elections if made by large districts. Bad elections proceed from the smallness of the districts which give an opportunity to bad men to intrigue themselves into office." Invoking with approval the example of the Virginia senate, John Francis Mercer, who had lived most of his life in Virginia before recently relocating to Maryland, explained how that body's larger geographic districts had made it easier for town dwellers, who were less likely to support policies such as debtor relief, to "unite their votes in favor of one favorite, and by that means always prevail over the people of the country, who being dispersed will scatter their votes among a variety of candidates."[148]

The convention eventually approved an initial Congress of only sixty-five members (assuming all thirteen states approved the Constitution and joined the union), which was much smaller than almost all of the lower houses of state legislatures, while Congress represented a vastly larger number of constituents. One congressman would represent much more than ten times the number of constituents as the average state legislator.[149]

Even Madison, despite his preference for large districts that diluted populist influence, thought that the number of congressmen in the first House should be doubled. He warned that too small a House "would not possess enough of the confidence of the people and would be too sparsely taken from the people to bring with them all the local information which would be frequently wanted." Madison also argued that the additional expense of a larger body, which some delegates had invoked as an argument for keeping the House small, was "too inconsiderable to be regarded." Supporting Madison, Gerry added that a larger House would have the advantage of being harder to corrupt. Yet Madison's motion to double the size of the first House was overwhelmingly defeated.[150]

Near the close of the convention, Hugh Williamson of North Carolina twice suggested that the delegates reconsider increasing the size of the House, and Madison seconded Williamson's initial proposal. Hamilton, who had left the convention but then returned in order to be present for its conclusion, strongly endorsed the proposed change. As "a friend to a vigorous government," he considered it "essential that the popular branch of it should be on a broad foundation." At the very least, Hamilton worried that a House of only sixty-five would "warrant a jealousy in the people for their liberties." Yet the convention narrowly rejected Williamson's proposal both times he made it. When Mason explained his unwillingness to sign the Constitution at the end of the convention, he listed among his grievances the fact that the House offered "not the substance but the shadow only of representation." This would be one of the Antifederalists' principal criticisms of the Constitution.[151]

However, on the last day of the convention, the delegates agreed to a proposal made by Gorham and forcefully endorsed by Washington—his only substantive contribution to the convention's proceedings—that would authorize a larger House in the near future. In August, the delegates had agreed that the ratio for apportioning representatives to constituents after a national census had been taken should not *exceed* one for every forty thousand persons. On September 17, Gorham suggested reducing the minimum size of each House district to thirty thousand. Supporting the motion, Washington explained, "The smallness of the proportion of representatives had been considered by many members of the convention an insufficient security for the rights and interests of the people." He also argued that making the change would enhance the prospects of ratification. The delegates then unanimously agreed to Gorham's proposal, which authorized—but did not require—future Congresses to increase the size of the House. Notwithstanding the change, the convention had approved what most Americans would regard as a very small lower house of the national legislature.[152]

In addition to creating a small House with very large constituencies, the Constitution reposed in Congress the authority to revise state regulations of the "times, places, and manner" of congressional elections. At the convention, Madison defended vesting such a power in Congress on the grounds that states would "sometimes fail or refuse to consult the common interest at the expense of their local convenience or prejudices." Significantly, this revisionary power was understood to authorize a congressional mandate that states select their representatives "at large" rather than in districts. In other words, Congress could require that each member of a state's House delegation represent—and be elected by—the entirety of the state's electorate.[153]

At-large elections would be yet another means—and a more subtle one—of limiting local populist influence on congressional representatives. Statewide elections for congressmen would dilute the power of ordinary citizens, who would have a harder time coordinating their political efforts across large geographic areas. As Pennsylvania delegate George Clymer later observed, at-large elections would produce "a good and respectable representation"—that is, representatives unlikely to support tax and debtor relief legislation. Madison later told Jefferson that at-large elections would "confine the choice to characters of general notoriety and so far be favorable to merit." Indeed, Federalists would go so far as to claim that conducting House elections in single-member districts was "contrary to the true spirit of the Constitution, which aims at being as national as possible in the choice of representatives."[154]

The independence of congressional representatives from populist influence would inevitably be a function not only of how they were selected but also of how long they served in office—a point on which the Virginia Plan had taken no position. All convention delegates agreed that House members should serve shorter terms than other federal officeholders. In the 1780s, members of the lower house of two state legislatures—Connecticut and Rhode Island— served six-month terms. In ten other states, members of lower houses served annual terms, and in South Carolina they were elected biennially. Such short tenures in office partly reflected the reaction of Revolutionary-era Americans

Figure 3.5 Nathaniel Gorham, a Charlestown merchant, who represented Massachusetts in the Confederation Congress, served as chairman of the Committee of the Whole at the Philadelphia convention, and supported ratification at his state's ratifying convention. (Museum of Fine Arts, Boston)

against the seven-year terms served by members of the British House of Commons.[155]

At the Philadelphia convention, many delegates—both nationalists and antinationalists—supported annual elections for the House. Sherman declared, "Frequent elections are necessary to preserve the good behavior of rulers." Representatives "ought to return home and mix with the people. By remaining at the seat of government, they would acquire the habits of the place, which might differ from those of their constituents." Wilson observed that annual elections were "most familiar and pleasing to the people" and were best for "an effectual representation of the people at large." Agreeing that "[t]he people were attached to [the] frequency of elections," Randolph declared that he would prefer annual elections as well, were it not for "the inconvenience which would result from them to the representatives of the extreme parts of the empire."[156]

For years, New Englanders had suspected that the southern gentry would seize upon the occasion of a national convention to foist a more "aristocratic" government upon them. Thus, unsurprisingly, Gerry of Massachusetts now insisted, "The people of New England will never give up the point of annual elections." They knew that in the early eighteenth century, members of the British Parliament had extended their terms in office from three years to seven, and would consider any departure from annual elections "as the prelude to a like usurpation." Annual elections, Gerry declared, were "the only defense of the people against tyranny," and he opposed longer terms for House members as much as he would "a hereditary executive."[157]

However, other delegates preferred longer terms for congressional representatives. Daniel of St. Thomas Jenifer, a Maryland delegate, proposed three-year terms on the grounds that too great a frequency in elections "rendered the people indifferent to them and made the best men unwilling to engage in so precarious a service." Deeming instability to be one of the "great vices of our republics," Madison enthusiastically supported the proposal. Annual terms would be "almost consumed in preparing for and traveling to and from the seat of national business," and a longer term would "be necessary, in a government so extensive, for members to form any knowledge of the various interests of the states to which they do not belong." Hamilton defended three-year terms for House members on the grounds that the checks the convention was developing "in the other branches of government would be but feeble and would need every auxiliary principle that could be interwoven."[158]

In response to Gerry's argument that the people would resist any departure from annual elections, Madison objected that "if the opinions of the people were to be our guide, it would be difficult to say what course we ought to take." No convention delegate "could say what the opinions of his constituents were at this time; much less could he say what they would think if possessed of the information and lights possessed by the members here; and still less what would be their way of thinking 6 or 12 months hence." Instead, the delegates must simply consider "what was right and necessary in itself for the attainment of a proper government." A good plan would "recommend itself," and the "respectability of this convention" would further enhance the prospects of its proposals being approved.[159]

Unpersuaded, Gerry continued to insist "that it was necessary to consider what the people would approve." He objected that, according to Madison's reasoning, if "we supposed a limited monarchy the best form in itself, we ought to recommend it, though the genius of the people was decidedly adverse to it."[160]

About two weeks into the convention, the delegates voted by seven states to four in favor of triennial elections for the House. About ten days later, as a compromise measure, they reduced the term of congressmen to two years.[161]

On a series of additional issues, the convention also embraced positions that increased the independence of congressional representatives from state and popular influence. Under the Articles of Confederation, state legislatures had the power to "recall" their congressional delegates for any reason whatsoever during their one-year term in office. Both the Virginia Plan and (implicitly) the New Jersey Plan had continued the practice of recall for congressional representatives. Yet, in the end, the delegates, apparently agreeing with Hamilton's view that congressional representatives subject to recall would "come with the prejudices of their states rather than the good of the union" as their guiding light, voted unanimously to deny state legislatures such a power.[162]

The Virginia Plan had also rendered congressional representatives ineligible for re-election for an unspecified period of time after their term in office (of unspecified length) had expired. The Pennsylvania constitution of 1776 deemed such mandatory rotation in office essential to preventing "an inconvenient aristocracy of entrenched officials." In 1785, the Massachusetts legislature declared that "[t]he world cannot but admire that prudence and wisdom which by providing for a rotation of members in Congress fixed one important barrier against corruption." Indeed, the Massachusetts legislature had initially instructed its delegates to the Philadelphia convention not to agree to any departure from the Articles' mandate of rotation in office (before excising that instruction on the grounds that the state should offer an unqualified endorsement of the convention). Despite such precedents, the delegates in Philadelphia unanimously voted to reject mandatory rotation in office for congressional representatives.[163]

Many contemporary republicans also believed that popular sovereignty included a right of the people to "instruct" their representatives, and several state constitutions of the era explicitly provided for such a right. For example, New Hampshire's constitution of 1784 declared that the people have a right "to assemble" and "give instructions to their representatives." Indeed, more than one state legislature had "instructed" its delegation to the Philadelphia convention. Yet the delegates omitted such a right from the Constitution. Because instruction, recall, and mandatory rotation in office—all mechanisms for limiting the independence of representatives—were *omissions* from the Constitution, casual observers might have failed to notice such departures from the status quo.[164]

The relative independence of congressional representatives would also depend, in part, on who paid their salaries. Under the Articles of Confederation, state legislatures paid—not always very faithfully—the salaries of their congressional delegates. Those delegates to the Philadelphia convention who were most supportive of state influence within the federal government argued that congressional representatives ought to be paid from state treasuries. Opposing congressional payment of representatives' salaries, Ellsworth noted that reasonable compensation might vary across states, given different standards of living. Defending the same position, Williamson argued that eastern states ought not to have to subsidize representatives from future western states, which would probably contribute less to the federal treasury and whose representatives "would be employed in thwarting their [the easterners'] measures and interests."[165]

Nationalist delegates—including Madison, Wilson, and King—insisted that the federal government should pay the salaries of congressional representatives. According to Madison's notes, Hamilton "strenuously" opposed making national representatives dependent on state legislative payment of their salaries: "Those who pay are the masters of those who are paid." Randolph agreed that if states paid the salaries of congressional representatives, then "a dependence would be created that would vitiate the whole system." Mason warned that if state legislatures selected senators—as the convention had provisionally decided they would—and also determined the pay of congressmen, then "both houses will be made the instruments of the politics of the states." Gorham worried that thrifty state legislatures would cut congressional salaries in "such a manner as to keep out of offices men most capable of executing the functions of them." Morris argued that leaving states to pay the salaries of congressmen would be unjust to distant states, whose members would incur greater expenses.[166]

In response to this nationalist onslaught, Ellsworth warned that the state legislatures, which would inevitably play an important role in the ratifying process, would look askance at the argument that the convention delegates had given "the general government such powers because we could not trust you." Yet, in June, the convention narrowly defeated his proposal for state legislative payment of congressmen's salaries. Later, much to the surprise of many delegates, the Committee of Detail nonetheless reported a provision making state legislatures responsible for the salaries of members of both houses of Congress. Having experienced a nationalist conversion once small states were guaranteed equal representation in the Senate, Ellsworth objected to the committee's proposal on the grounds that it rendered the House too dependent on state legislatures, and the delegates rejected it.[167]

Even after the delegates had agreed that congressional salaries should be paid from the national treasury, the question remained whether Congress or the Constitution itself should set those salaries. Wilson opposed fixing congressional compensation in the Constitution because circumstances would inevitably change. Gorham worried that if the Constitution were to set congressional pay, the convention "could not venture to make it [the pay] as liberal as it ought to be without exciting an enmity against the whole plan." Gorham and Jacob Broom of Delaware argued that if state legislators could be trusted to set their own salaries, then so could congressional representatives.[168]

While Gorham worried that for the Constitution to fix a generous salary for congressmen would rally opposition to ratification, King was concerned that for the Constitution to leave congressional salaries to Congress's discretion "would excite greater opposition" than would specifying "any sum that would be actually necessary or proper." Ellsworth agreed that delegating Congress discretion "for that purpose would produce strong, though perhaps not insuperable objections." Madison argued that the Constitution should fix congressional pay because representatives were too self-interested to determine their own compensation: "It would be indecent to put their hands into the public purse for the sake of their own pockets." Sherman agreed that congressmen should not set their own salaries, though for the opposite reason—that they would fix wages too low rather than too high, thus disabling all but the wealthy from serving. He suggested that the Constitution fix a moderate salary to be paid from the US Treasury, which states would then be free to supplement as they saw fit. In the end, the convention voted in favor of Congress's setting congressional salaries, rather than their being established by the Constitution.[169]

In addition to all the mechanisms just discussed for limiting state and populist influence on congressional representatives, the delegates also considered adding to the Constitution a requirement of property qualifications for voting in congressional elections and for holding federal office generally. As to the former, such suffrage qualifications would prevent those most likely to have redistributive motives from participating in congressional elections. As to the latter, property qualifications for officeholding would ensure that the federal government would be administered by those persons—Hamilton called them "the rich and well born"—most inclined to resist populist influence upon their policymaking. Most elite statesmen of the era agreed that government should be staffed by people like themselves, who were affluent enough to possess the leisure time for public service and the financial independence to resist bribery and interest group influence.[170]

The egalitarian ideology of the Revolutionary War and the political imperative of raising soldiers to fight it had inspired the drafters of state constitutions in the mid-1770s to relax suffrage restrictions. Yet those constitutions nonetheless retained some property qualifications for voting, and most of the delegates at the Philadelphia convention favored such requirements for federal elections.[171]

Warning that "[t]he ignorant and the dependent can be as little trusted with the public interest" as small children, Morris argued that participation in congressional elections should be limited to those satisfying a certain real-property requirement. Without such a suffrage restriction, Morris warned, as the country came to "abound with mechanics and manufacturers who will receive their bread from their employers," voters could no longer be counted upon to be "the secure and faithful guardians of liberty." Dickinson agreed that limiting the vote to holders of real property was a "necessary defense against the dangerous influence of those multitudes without property and without principle, with which our country like all others will in time abound." Madison, too, thought that freeholders "would be the safest depositories of republican liberty" in the future, when "a great majority of the people will not only be without landed, but any other sort of, property" and thus would become "the tools of opulence and ambition."[172]

Franklin was the aberrational delegate who opposed property qualifications on the merits. He argued that the convention "should not depress the virtue and public spirit of our common people, of which they displayed a great deal during the war." Franklin expressed his "dislike of everything that tended to debase the spirit of the common people," and he reminded his colleagues that "[s]ome of the greatest rogues he was ever acquainted with were the richest rogues."[173]

Many other delegates objected to the Constitution's specifying property qualifications for voting in congressional elections, not because they objected in principle but because, as Ellsworth explained, "[t]he states are the best judges of the circumstances and temper of their own people." Wilson argued it would be "difficult to form any uniform rule of qualifications for all the states." Gorham observed that cities such as Philadelphia, New York, and Boston already permitted merchants and mechanics who could not satisfy a freehold requirement to vote and had endured no inconvenience from doing so. Mason noted that eight or nine states had already expanded the suffrage beyond freeholders, and that people who currently voted in state elections but would be excluded from participating in congressional contests if the Constitution imposed significant property qualifications would oppose ratification. Ellsworth agreed: "The people will not readily subscribe to the national Constitution if it should subject them to be disfranchised."[174]

For these practical reasons—the difficulty of devising uniform property qualifications for the entire nation and the inadvisability of disfranchising people who already voted—rather than for any principled opposition, the delegates overwhelmingly rejected specifying in the Constitution property qualifications for voting in congressional elections. Instead, they provided that the suffrage qualifications for such elections would be the same as those imposed by states in the elections for the larger house of their legislatures. The delegates assumed that states would continue to impose property qualifications, which would then automatically apply in federal elections as well.[175]

Convention delegates were even more supportive of property qualifications for federal officeholders. To be sure, a few delegates, including Morris and Dickinson, thought that imposing property qualifications for voters would

obviate the need to impose them for officeholders. Yet others agreed with
Gerry that, if "property be one object of government, provisions for securing
it cannot be improper." Mason proposed that the Constitution require federal
legislators—and his motion was soon amended to include members of the federal executive and judiciary as well—to own a certain amount of landed property and that it disqualify those with public indebtedness. He explained that
such debtors had often secured seats in state legislatures "in order to promote
laws that might shelter their delinquencies, and that this evil had crept into
Congress."[176]

Although most of the delegates favored property qualifications for federal officeholders, they encountered difficulties in figuring out which ones
to impose. Dickinson preferred to leave the issue to Congress's discretion, as
it would be impossible to make a complete list of appropriate qualifications,
"and a partial one would by implication tie up the hands of the legislature from
supplying the omissions." He also objected to inserting into a republican constitution "a veneration for wealth." King warned of "great danger in requiring
landed property as a qualification [for holding federal office] since it would
exclude the monied interest, whose aids may be essential in particular emergencies to the public safety."[177]

Madison agreed with King and proposed that the convention strike out the
word "landed" from Mason's motion to impose property qualifications for federal officeholding. He explained that many landholders were more indebted
than their land was worth, and the "unjust laws of the states" were more attributable to "this class of men than any others." Indeed, "[i]t had often happened
that men who had acquired landed property on credit got into the legislatures
with a view of promoting an unjust protection against their creditors." Thus,
Madison concluded that a small landed-property qualification "would be no
security," and a large one "would exclude the proper representatives of those
classes of citizens who were not landholders." In other words, Madison believed that commercial, financial, and manufacturing interests, despite their
probable inability to satisfy a substantial landed-property qualification, ought
to be eligible to hold federal office.[178]

Apparently agreeing with Madison, the delegates voted by ten states to one
to strike out the word "landed" from the proposed property qualification for
federal officeholding. Then they voted by eight states to three in favor of the
Constitution's imposing such (nonlanded) property qualifications—not only
for congressmen and senators but also for the federal judiciary and executive.[179]

Yet instead of setting property qualifications for federal office in the
Constitution as the delegates had wished, the Committee of Detail entrusted
the matter to Congress. Rutledge, who had chaired the committee, explained
that it "had reported no qualifications because they [the committee members]

could not agree on any among themselves, being embarrassed by the danger on one side of displeasing the people by making them high and on the other of rendering them nugatory by making them low." Ellsworth, who had also served on the committee, now offered two arguments for leaving property qualifications for federal officeholding to Congress's discretion rather than fixing them in the Constitution. First, "[t]he different circumstances of different parts of the United States" rendered uniform qualifications impractical: "Make them so high as to be useful in the southern states, and they will be inapplicable to the eastern states. Suit them to the latter, and they will serve no purpose in the former." Second, "the probable difference between the present and future circumstances" of the country made it likely that qualifications "accommodated to the existing state of things" would "be very inconvenient in some future state."[180]

Madison objected that delegating the task of setting property qualifications for federal officeholders to Congress would vest "an improper and dangerous power in the legislature." The qualifications for voting and officeholding were "fundamental articles in a republican government and ought to be fixed by the Constitution" to prevent legislatures from subverting them. Charles Pinckney objected that if the task of setting property qualifications were referred to Congress, then the first set of representatives elected would not have been subjected to those requirements. While professing opposition to "an undue aristocratic influence in the Constitution," Pinckney nonetheless thought it essential that national officeholders "be possessed of competent property to make them independent and respectable." He proposed that the Constitution fix the property requirements and suggested $100,000 for the president and half that for federal judges and members of Congress—thresholds that 99 percent of the population could not have satisfied.[181]

When Morris suggested broadening Congress's power to enable it to impose any qualifications whatsoever for federal office—not just property qualifications—Williamson expressed concern that a majority of lawyer legislators might limit officeholding to fellow attorneys. Rutledge suggested as an alternative that the Constitution specify that the officeholding qualifications for congressional representatives from a particular state be the same as those for that state's legislature. Yet when Wilson proposed abandoning qualifications for federal officeholding altogether on the grounds that Congress probably never would be able to devise a uniform rule for the entire nation and that specifying a congressional power to impose property qualifications implicitly would exclude the power to set other qualifications, a majority of the delegates agreed. Thus, even though most of the delegates strongly supported property qualifications for federal officeholding, the Constitution they drafted neither imposes any nor expressly authorizes Congress to do so.[182]

Apportioning Representation in
the National Legislature

Figuring out how to structure the upper house of the national legislature proved far more vexing to the convention than designing the lower house. Indeed, apportioning representation among the states in the Senate proved to be the most contentious issue in Philadelphia, initially creating an impasse that threatened to prematurely terminate the convention. As Madison later explained to Jefferson, this issue created "more embarrassment and a greater alarm for the issue of the convention than all the rest put together."[183]

As we have seen, the Virginia Plan proposed apportioning representation in both houses of the national legislature according "to the quotas of contribution, or to the number of free inhabitants, as the one or the other rule may seem best in different cases." In other words, the principle of equal state representation in Congress, which had been fundamental to the Articles of Confederation, was to be replaced with representation apportioned according to either population or tax contributions, or some combination of the two.[184]

For Madison, a population-based apportionment of representation in Congress seems to have been important partly because he believed that once it had been agreed to, "many of the objections now urged in the leading states against renunciations of power will vanish." In other words, Madison expected the larger states to become more nationalistic if they were guaranteed greater influence within the national government. He believed that the main reason Virginia had objected to proposed amendments to the Articles that would expand Congress's powers was that its population advantage was not reflected in a federal legislature where each state had an equal vote. In addition, equal state representation in the federal legislature connoted a confederation rather than a nation, and Madison wished to obliterate the Confederation. For both of these reasons, a population-based apportionment of congressional representation was, for Madison, mainly a means to his nationalist ends. Yet such an apportionment also appealed to him and most of the large-state delegates as a matter of simple justice.[185]

Shortly before the convention began, Madison had predicted that a majority of state delegations in Philadelphia would approve population-based representation in Congress. States that were already large—most notably, Virginia, Pennsylvania, and Massachusetts—would favor it based on their current population advantage, while the underpopulated southern states of Georgia and South Carolina would support it because they anticipated that their populations would increase dramatically in the near future. (North Carolina, already fairly populous, would support it for both reasons.) This assumption that southern states would soon experience large population gains was pervasive at the time. The territory comprising the southern states was four times that of the northern states. In addition, land in the North, which had been settled earlier, was largely occupied—excluding the vast Northwest Territory, which was only sparsely inhabited by white settlers—while the South still contained vast stretches of unoccupied land.[186]

In a preliminary discussion of the Virginia Plan's formula for apportioning representation in the national legislature, some northern delegates objected to the idea of apportionment based on "quotas of contribution." King pointed out that the states' financial contributions to the national government would constantly be changing, which would make it difficult to apportion representation on that basis. However, his real concern may have been that northerners, who on average were less wealthy than southerners, would fare better under an apportionment scheme based on population than under one based on tax contributions. As an alternative, Hamilton suggested the other half of the Virginia Plan's formula—apportionment based on "free inhabitants." Yet other northerners, such as Morris, objected to a purely population-based apportionment on the grounds that property was "the main object of society" and thus "it ought to be one measure of the influence due to those who were to be affected by the government."[187]

Agreeing that "property was certainly the principal object of society" and understanding that apportionment based on population might mean undercounting or not counting at all their slaves, most southern delegates strongly preferred an apportionment based on wealth or "quotas of contribution." Yet southern resistance to a population based apportionment of Congress would disappear if an accommodation could be reached about counting their slaves—a topic explored at length in chapter 4.[188]

Hoping to secure an early convention vote rejecting the principle of equal state representation in the federal legislature, Madison proposed deferring the question of whether the apportionment of Congress should be based on population, tax contributions, or some combination thereof. Instead, he wished the delegates simply to agree provisionally that "the equality of suffrage established by the Articles of Confederation" should be rejected. Yet Madison's goal was frustrated when George Read from the tiny state of Delaware objected.[189]

In the months prior to the convention, Read had written two letters to his Delaware colleague John Dickinson warning that the small-state delegates must "keep a strict watch upon the movements and propositions from the larger states, who will probably combine to swallow up the smaller ones by addition, division, or impoverishment." Read believed that Delaware "would at once become a cypher in the union" if deprived of an equal vote in Congress, and he had learned from newspaper reports and private conversations that the relative "voice of the states" in Congress was likely to be a topic at the convention. Read worried that "the argument or oratory of the smaller state commissioners will avail little" at a convention in which the interest of the states in securing majority control of the federal government would be so great. Read told Dickinson that he trusted nothing to the "candor, generosity or ideas of public justice" of the larger states, and thus advised that "every guard that can be devised for this state's protection against future encroachment should be preserved or made."[190]

Now, in response to Madison's resolution rejecting equal state representation in Congress, Read moved to postpone the issue on the grounds that the Delaware delegates, who were under instruction not to approve any such change from the Articles, would have to "retire" from the convention if the resolution were approved. Indeed, Read had cleverly ensured—"as a prudent measure on the part of our state"—that the Delaware legislature inserted such a restriction into its delegates' instructions to save them from "disagreeable argumentation" at the convention.[191]

As the debate over apportionment of representation in Congress unfolded, Madison and his nationalist allies insisted that anything other than a population-based apportionment would be "confessedly unjust." The minority ought not to be able, Madison argued, to "negative the will of the majority" or to "extort measures by making them a condition of [the minority's] assent to other necessary measures." Moreover, to give a legislature that was not apportioned according to population the power to directly tax individuals would be to "subject the system to the reproaches and evils which have resulted from the vicious representation in Great Britain"—the so-called rotten boroughs, in which mere handfuls of voters elected members of Parliament. Tiny Delaware, which at the time had fewer than 60,000 residents, ought not to have equal representation with massive Virginia, which had about 750,000.[192]

Madison also explained to the convention, as he had to his friends beforehand, that while equal state representation in Congress had also been unjust in principle under the Articles, at least it had been bearable then because "the acts of Congress depended so much for their efficacy on the cooperation of the states," which enabled the large states to have "a weight both within and without Congress nearly in proportion to their extent and importance." However, under the Constitution, congressional measures "would take effect without the intervention of the state legislatures," and thus a vote from a small state ought not to have "the same efficacy and importance as a vote from a large one."[193]

Other large-state delegates also insisted upon the unfairness of equal state representation in Congress. Hamilton declared that this practice would "shock too much the ideas of justice and every human feeling," and he insisted that "[i]t was not in human nature that Virginia and the large states should consent to it, or if they did, that they should long abide by it." Wilson argued that "as all authority was derived from the people, equal numbers of people ought to have an equal number of representatives and different numbers of people different numbers of representatives." The large states had approved the Articles in spite of their departure from this fundamental principle of justice, Wilson explained, only because "in the hour of danger" (the Revolutionary War) they had been willing to make "a sacrifice of their interest to the lesser states." Now, however, "the time has come when justice will be done to their claims." Morris likewise objected to the small states' treating as a "sacred compact" a concession they had extracted under the pressure of wartime exigencies.[194]

In addition, Madison noted that the injustice of equal state representation in Congress would only be compounded over time. As western states were added to the union on a footing of equality, "a more objectionable minority than ever" would exercise control over the federal government. Why should the delegates admit a principle that "must infuse mortality into a constitution which we wished to last forever?" Wilson similarly warned, "A vice in the representation, like an error in the first concoction, must be followed by disease, convulsions, and finally death itself."[195]

The large-state delegates also responded to their adversaries' argument that any injustice suffered by the large states as a result of equal state representation in one house of Congress would be minimal because that house could only block legislation, not enact it on its own. In reply, Wilson observed that bad governments were of two sorts: those that did too little and those that did too much. The United States suffered "under the weakness and inefficiency of its government." Equal state representation in the Senate would "leave the United States fettered precisely as heretofore." Madison added two additional arguments on this score. The small states could use their disproportionate power in an equally apportioned Senate to "extort measures [from the House] repugnant to the wishes and interest of the majority." In addition, the convention would probably allocate to the Senate "some great powers in which [the House] could not participate." Thus, the small states would, in fact, be able to "impose measures adverse" to the majority's interest even without the House's concurrence.[196]

In support of their justice-centered arguments, the large-state delegates contended that defenders of equal state representation in the national legislature were making a metaphysical mistake. Wilson asked, "Can we forget for whom we are forming a government? Is it for *men*, or for the imaginary beings called states? . . . We talk of states, till we forget what they are composed of." Hamilton similarly argued that it was "the rights of the people composing" the states, not the "artificial beings resulting from the composition," which deserved representation.[197]

Madison agreed that "too much stress was laid on the rank of the states as political societies." States forming a nation that could levy taxes and raise troops from the citizenry were more analogous to counties within a state, which were not generally afforded equal representation in a state legislature, than they were to sovereign nations forming a treaty on a footing of equality. Conceding that states might deserve equal representation in Congress if the national government were "to act on the states as such," Madison declared that he could not think of "a single instance in which the general government was not to operate on the people individually."[198]

Even to the extent that states had sovereign interests deserving of protection, large-state delegates questioned whether the states, large or small, had anything genuinely to fear from the federal government that the convention was designing. Wilson noted that state legislatures would select US senators—a decision the convention had already made, as we shall see—while the federal government enjoyed no "reciprocal opportunity" to defend itself by electing a branch of state governments. Madison wondered why the federal government would have any incentive to usurp the authority of state governments upon which it would have to depend in governing a vast continent.[199]

Even if the federal government dared to encroach on state prerogatives, Wilson noted, state legislatures would raise a general alarm in response. It was the federal government that "would be in perpetual danger of encroachment from the state governments," rather than the other way around. Madison confirmed that the history of all confederacies revealed a tendency "to anarchy [rather] than to tyranny."[200]

Large-state delegates also addressed the concern voiced by their opponents that a population-based apportionment of congressional representation would render small states vulnerable to oppression by a coalition of large states. Madison conceded that if there was "real danger" of such a combination, he would be willing to give the smaller states "defensive weapons," but he insisted that no such danger existed. Madison explained that the three largest states— Virginia, Pennsylvania, and Massachusetts—had little in common in regard to "manners" or religion, and their economies were "as dissimilar as any three other states." In Massachusetts, the staple was fish; in Pennsylvania, wheat and flour; and in Virginia, tobacco. So "[w]here is the probability of a combination?" Madison asked. The comparable size of the populations of the large states was not a circumstance to be feared by the small states, but rather one that would make "rivalships . . . more frequent than coalitions."[201]

Hamilton agreed that "there could not be any ground for combination among the states whose influence was most dreaded," given the geographic distance separating the large states from one another and "all the peculiarities which distinguish the[ir] interests." He insisted, "The only considerable distinction of interests lay between the carrying and non-carrying states, which divides instead of uniting the largest states." Although the small states spoke of the importance of being protected from domination, Hamilton declared, the apportionment dispute was really just "a contest for power." On at least one occasion, a small-state delegate, Gunning Bedford of Delaware, seemed almost to admit as much: The small states were not going to "act from pure disinterestedness." The rotten boroughs of Great Britain "held fast their constitutional rights . . . and are we to act with greater purity than the rest of mankind?"[202]

Hugh Williamson, who represented North Carolina—already a populous state and expecting soon to become even more so—went even further in denouncing what he saw as the small states' power grab. The objective of the small states, he explained, was to secure majority control of the national government, which would enable them to burden larger states with an undue proportion of the taxes required to support that government. The large states' vulnerability to oppressive taxation in an equally apportioned national legislature would soon be exacerbated by the admission into the union of low-population and relatively poor western states, which "would consequently be tempted to combine for the purpose of laying burdens on commerce and consumption, which would fall with greatest weight on the old states." Franklin confirmed that the large states feared "their money will be in danger" if the small states received equal voting power in Congress.[203]

Finally, large-state delegates warned that if their small-state counterparts insisted on equal state representation in the national legislature, the convention might fail, which could mean the end of the Confederation. Ought the small states not to consider the "consequences of suffering the Confederation to go to pieces?" Madison wondered. "If the large states possessed the avarice and ambition with which they were charged," he observed, then the small states would suffer the most from the absence of a strong national government to protect them. Worse yet, Madison hypothesized, a failure to unite on just terms would exacerbate external dangers that might transform the states "into vigorous and high toned governments" with "too much energy," which would not only leave the small states vulnerable to the large but might prove "fatal to the internal liberty of all." Indeed, "[t]he same causes which have rendered the old world the theater of incessant wars, and have banished liberty from the face of it, would soon produce the same effects here."[204]

Morris painted an even more lurid picture of the consequences of the small states' failing to accept equitable apportionment principles: "This country must be united. If persuasion does not unite it, the sword will." In such an

event, "[t]he stronger party will then make traitors of the weaker, and the gal-
lows and halter will finish the work of the sword."[205]

Small-state delegates offered a variety of responses to these arguments
for population-based apportionment of representation in both houses of
Congress. As we have seen, William Paterson of New Jersey questioned the
legitimacy of the convention's even considering a departure from the provision of the Articles guaranteeing equal state representation in Congress. The
convention had been charged with amending the Articles and had "no power
to go beyond the federal scheme." Even if the convention had such power,
Paterson insisted, "the people are not ripe for any other [scheme]," and the delegates "must follow the people; the people will not follow us." Moreover, Roger
Sherman of Connecticut wondered, why should the large states object now to
the principle of equal state representation in Congress when they had accepted
it under the Confederation? His fellow Connecticut delegate Oliver Ellsworth
asked, "[W]as it meant to pay no regard to this antecedent plighted faith?"[206]

Small-state delegates also denied that justice required population-based
apportionment of representation in the national legislature. While the large-
state delegates might have convinced themselves that they had "right on their
side," Bedford told them that "interest had blinded their eyes," and he ridiculed their "endeavor to amuse us with the purity of their principles and the
rectitude of their intentions." Luther Martin of Maryland declared that "an
equal vote in each state was essential to the federal idea, and was founded in
justice and freedom." The states had been put "in a state of nature towards each
other" by virtue of their separation from Great Britain, and in such circumstances, "[s]tates, like individuals, were . . . equally sovereign and free." The
states had then "entered into the Confederation on the footing of equality,"
and "they met now to amend it on the same footing." Although acknowledging
that governments derived their just powers from the people, Paterson denied
that the Confederation had rendered state distinctions obsolete: "When independent societies confederate for mutual defense, they do so in their collective
capacity; and then each state for those purposes must be considered as one of
the contracting parties." Paterson saw "no more reason that a great individual
state contributing much should have more votes than a small one contributing
little than that a rich individual citizen should have more votes than an indi-
gent one."[207]

Because the states were "so many political societies" and the federal government was to be formed for the states "in their political capacity as well as for
the individuals composing them," William Samuel Johnson of Connecticut*

---

* Born in 1727, Johnson, although he served in the Stamp Act Congress in 1765, was an opponent of independence and was arrested at one point on suspicion of communicating with the

Figure 3.6 William Paterson, who had served as New Jersey's attorney general and later became one of that state's original US senators, helped draft the 1789 Judiciary Act and then was appointed by President Washington to the US Supreme Court. (Collection of the Supreme Court of the United States)

argued that the states ought to be "armed with some power of self-defense." Sherman similarly observed that equal state representation in at least one house of the national legislature was "not so much . . . a security for the small states as for the state governments, which could not be preserved unless they were represented and had a negative in the general government."[208]

Martin argued that the large-state delegates were inconsistent in their treatment of state sovereignty. When the issue was whether small states deserved equal representation in at least one house of the national legislature, large-state delegates such as Pennsylvania's James Wilson treated the states as mere "phantoms, ideal beings." Yet when the issue was whether large states could be carved up against their will, suddenly "political societies were of a sacred

enemy. At the Philadelphia convention, he served as chairman of the Committee of Style, which put the finishing touches on the Constitution. From 1787 to 1800, he served as president of King's College (later, Columbia University).

nature." (The Constitution does, in fact, require the consent of a state's legis-lature before that state, in whole or in part, can be formed into a new state to be admitted into the union.) Paterson conceded that the elimination of state distinctions would justify population-based apportionment of representation in Congress, yet he observed that the large states did not appear eager to share their superior "stock of land" with the small states.[209]

More fundamentally, small-state delegates insisted that their states would be utterly dominated in Congress by the three largest states if both houses were apportioned according to population. Such a representation scheme, according to Paterson, would strike "at the existence of the lesser states." Bedford noted that population-based representation would entitle Delaware to just one-ninetieth of the representatives in the House, while Pennsylvania and Virginia together would receive one-third. He accused the large states of seeking "a system in which they would have an enormous and monstrous influ-ence" and would be able to "crush the small ones whenever they stand in the way of their ambitions or interested views." Paterson objected that New Jersey would "be swallowed up" by population-based apportionment and thus would "never confederate" on such a plan. Martin called congressional representa-tion apportioned according to population "a system of slavery for ten states," in which the three largest states would control nearly half the votes in Congress and could do as they pleased, barring "a miraculous union of the other ten."[210]

Moreover, small-state delegates dismissed the argument that their states had nothing to fear from large-state alliances in Congress. At a minimum, as Ellsworth observed, "three or four states can more easily combine than nine or ten states." In addition, he noted that the large states might agree to monopo-lize among themselves appointments to important federal offices or support a commercial treaty allowing only three or four free ports within the United States and then allocating those among themselves.[211]

Indeed, voting patterns at the convention itself dispelled the notion that large states had no common interests in opposition to those of the small ones. For example, on the Virginia Plan's proposal to empower the national govern-ment to veto state laws, the three largest states had voted in favor and the seven smaller ones against.[212]

In addition, small states and large states had clashed repeatedly in Congress during the early to mid-1780s over the issue of states' ceding their western land claims to the union—an issue that defined their very sizes. In those de-bates, small-state congressional delegates had argued that large states should transfer their claims to western lands to Congress, which could then sell the land to private parties and use the revenue to pay off the war debt. By contrast, congressional delegates from large states such as Virginia and Massachusetts had insisted that Congress commit itself "against the dismemberment of any state without the previous approbation of the state about to be dismembered."

Virginia's congressional delegates reported that small states that "wish for every facility to lessen the larger ones" opposed Congress's providing any such guarantee to the large states. In 1784, a delegate from the populous state of North Carolina had complained that "[t]he little states can't lose sight of that object; their size when compared to the larger ones appears so trifling, that it creates in them a degree of envy." Two years earlier, Madison had written that the small states opposed Virginia's western land claims both from "a lucrative desire of sharing in the vacant territory as a fund of revenue" and out of "the envy and jealousy naturally excited by superior resources and importance."[213]

The issue of western lands had not disappeared by the time of the convention, as Georgia and North Carolina had yet to cede theirs to Congress—much to the annoyance of those states that had already done so. Just months before the convention, George Read of Delaware had complained of Congress's policy on western lands, which he thought sacrificed "the just claims of the smaller and bounded states to a proportional share therein, for the purpose of discharging the national debt incurred during the war." Read reiterated that objection at the convention. When large-state delegates denied any commonality of interest among their states, Martin observed that they had a shared interest in securing constitutional protection against the union's seizing their western lands without their consent. When Wilson, from the large state of Pennsylvania, objected to a provision that would have allowed, in his words, a state "to be torn asunder without its own consent," the delegations divided along roughly the same lines as they did on the question of population-based apportionment of representation in the national legislature—thus suggesting that large and small states did indeed have conflicting interests on this issue.[214]

Finally, small-state delegates observed that if the large states really had no interests in common with each other and in opposition to those of the small states, then "there could be no danger" in providing all states with an equal vote in Congress. Yet if large states did have systematically different interests from the small states, then inequality of suffrage "would be dangerous to the smaller states."[215]

Two weeks into the convention, the delegates voted by seven states to three (with one delegation divided)—only eleven states were represented until New Hampshire's delegation arrived in Philadelphia in late July—to apportion representation in the lower house of the national legislature "according to some equitable ratio of representation" rather than the Articles' rule of equal state representation. The same day, the delegates voted by six states to five in favor of apportioning the second branch of the national legislature according to the same rule as the first, after defeating by the same margin a motion to give each state one vote in the upper house. Just as Madison had predicted before the convention, a coalition of the three largest states (Virginia, Pennsylvania, and

Massachusetts) and the three southernmost states, which were expecting soon to become large (Georgia, South Carolina, and North Carolina), voted in favor of population-based apportionment of representation. As Bedford explained, although Georgia was "a small state at present"—the third smallest in terms of population—"she is actuated by the prospect of soon becoming a great one."[216]

Convention delegates overwhelmingly shared the assumption that the population advantage would soon shift toward the South and the West.* Morris observed, "It has been said that North Carolina, South Carolina, and Georgia [alone] will in a little time have a majority of the people of America." Mason opined that the southern and western populations would predominate within only "a few years." Of course, this assumption about future demographic trends ultimately proved completely wrong, as the North's population advantage quickly grew in the decades after 1787, mainly because European immigrants generally preferred not to locate in the South, where they would have to live in a slave society and compete with slave labor.[217]

Despite being outvoted on initial tallies, the small-state delegations remained insistent upon securing equal state representation in at least one house of Congress, and they threatened to abandon the convention—and, if necessary, the union—rather than relinquish their position. The same day the initial votes were taken, Sherman announced that "[t]he smaller states would never agree to the plan on any other principle (than an equality of suffrage in this [the upper] branch)." His Connecticut colleague Ellsworth similarly warned that "if there was no compromise on this issue, then our meeting would . . . be in vain." The small states "would risk every consequence rather than part with so dear a right." Delaware's John Dickinson told Madison that the small states "would sooner submit to a foreign power, than submit to be deprived of an equality of suffrage in both branches of the legislature." Paterson declared that New Jersey would "rather submit to a monarch, to a despot, than to such a fate."[218]

---

* Debate on two other issues at the convention confirms this widespread contemporaneous assumption regarding demographic trends. First, expecting future population trends to favor their states, southern delegates demanded that Congress be required to take a periodic census and to reapportion congressional representation based on its results. They strongly opposed leaving such a census and readjustment to the discretion of what they expected would be, initially, a northern-dominated Congress. Second, on the question of whether newly admitted western states—which, from the perspective of 1787, seemed likely to be populated mostly by southerners—would be admitted to the union on equal terms with the original thirteen states, it was mostly northern delegates such as Gouverneur Morris who favored limiting the congressional representation of new states. By contrast, most southern delegates agreed with Mason that new states should be "subjected to no degrading discriminations."

Large-state delegates dug in their heels as well. Rufus King declared that Massachusetts "would never be prevailed on to yield on an equality of votes." If the small states were "fixed and unalterable" in their demand for equal representation in the Senate, King insisted, "there could not be less obstinacy on the other side." Wilson stated that he hoped the small states would "not abandon a country to which they were bound by such strong and endearing ties." However, "[i]f the minority of the people of America refuse to coalesce with the majority on just and proper principles [and] a separation must take place, it could never happen on better grounds." Wilson warned that "[i]f the small states will not confederate on this plan"—an "equitable" ratio of representation in both houses of Congress—"Pennsylvania and, he presumed, some other states would not confederate on any other."[219]

The issue of how to apportion representation in Congress dominated the convention for well over a month and began to color its deliberations on other issues. Gerry later recalled that the dispute had become "so serious as to threaten a dissolution of the convention." Similarly, Madison, much later in life, reported that the "[g]reat zeal and pertinacity" demonstrated by both the large and the small states over the representation issue had produced a situation that was "not only distressing but seriously alarming."[220]

Late in June, small-state delegates suggested that the convention appeal to New Hampshire's chief executive to immediately send that state's delegation, already appointed by the legislature, to Philadelphia. In his convention notes, Madison recorded that "it was well understood that the object was to add New Hampshire to the number of states opposed to the doctrine of proportional representation, which it was presumed from her relative size she must be adverse to." Large-state delegates questioned the propriety of such a missive: New Hampshire's political leaders knew about the convention and were free to send a delegation if they wished. And why not write a similar letter to Rhode Island? Wilson objected that such a communication would be inconsistent with the convention's confidentiality rules, and the proposal was defeated.[221]

The low point in the convention's proceedings may have been a speech by Gunning Bedford, whom delegate William Pierce described in his character sketches of the other delegates as "warm and impetuous in his temper and precipitate in his judgment." Observing that the large-state delegations had been voting based on their "interest" and "ambition," Bedford accused them of "evidently seeking to aggrandize themselves at the expense of the small [states]." Staring directly at them, he declared, "*I do not, gentlemen, trust you.*" If the large states refused to compromise and the Confederation dissolved as a result, Bedford threatened, then "the small [states] will find some foreign ally of more honor and good faith, who will take them by the hand and do them justice."[222]

King immediately upbraided Bedford for his "vehemence unprecedented," which had culminated in his threat to "court the protection of some foreign hand." King was "grieved that such a thought had entered into his [Bedford's] heart." Randolph also criticized "the warm [i.e., heated] and rash language of Mr. Bedford." A few days later, Bedford apologized for the "warmth" of expression that was "natural and sometimes necessary" among lawyers, and he backtracked from his statement, insisting that he had been misunderstood and that he "did not mean that the small states would court the aid and interposition of foreign powers." Yet Bedford continued to warn ominously that "no man can foresee to what extremities the small states may be driven by oppression," and he denounced threats by large-state delegates that "the sword is to unite."[223]

Franklin appealed for calm. Earlier, he had reminded his colleagues that they had been sent there "to consult, not to contend with each other," and he had warned that "declarations of a fixed opinion and of determined resolution never to change it neither enlighten nor convince us." Franklin had also observed that "[p]ositiveness and warmth on one side naturally beget their like on the other and tend to create and augment discord and division in a great concern."[224]

Now, with the convention at risk of dissolving, Franklin tried a different tack, wondering why the delegates had not theretofore thought of "humbly applying to the Father of lights to illuminate our understandings." Accordingly, he introduced a motion to require that, henceforth, the delegates engage in daily prayers "imploring the assistance of Heaven." In response, Hamilton and several other delegates warned, according to Madison's summary of their remarks, that while such a measure might have been appropriate at the convention's outset, to undertake it now might "lead the public to believe that the embarrassments and dissensions within the convention" had occasioned it. Evincing an unusual degree of consensus, the delegates overwhelmingly agreed that prayers were unnecessary, though out of respect to Franklin they permitted the motion to die without a formal rejection.[225]

Although tensions were high, hints of a possible compromise had been in the air for some time. Just one week into the convention, Dickinson had predicted that the issue of representation in Congress "must probably end in mutual concession," which would give each side its favored method of apportionment in one house of Congress. On June 11, Sherman had proposed what became known as the Connecticut Compromise,* named for its principal sponsors: Representation

---

* Although I will adhere to the traditional nomenclature by calling this resolution of the representation issue the "Connecticut Compromise," it bears emphasis that the compromise represented a major victory for the small states, as measured against the baseline of what a majority of delegations had initially approved—that is, representation apportioned according to population in both houses.

BENJAMIN
FRANKLIN.

Figure 3.7 Benjamin Franklin—author, inventor, statesman, and diplomat—who was a close second to Washington in the esteem of his fellow Americans. (Courtesy National Gallery of Art, Washington)

in the House would be apportioned according to population, while in the Senate each state would have an equal voice. Such an approach would combine the federal and national principles—the idea of states as "political societies" and as "districts of people," as described by Johnson of Connecticut. Sherman defended the notion that all national measures should require the concurrence of a majority of the states and a majority of the people. Although the Connecticut delegates repeatedly advanced this compromise, it took a month of anguished deliberations after they had first proposed it before the convention would agree to it.[226]

When two of Georgia's delegates who had voted consistently for population-based apportionment in both houses of Congress left Philadelphia in early July (to attend Congress, which was sitting in New York), the large states lost their slender majority on the issue. The convention now divided five states to five, with Georgia's remaining two delegates divided, on whether the states should be equally represented in the Senate.[227]

With Franklin urging both sides to "part with some of their demands in order that they may join in some accommodating proposition" and some large-state delegates dropping hints of their willingness to compromise, Charles Cotesworth Pinckney suggested the appointment of a grand committee, consisting of one delegate from each state, to work out a solution. Sherman supported the motion: "It seems we have got to a point that we cannot move one way or the other." He was certain that nobody "meant that we should break up without doing something," and a committee was "most likely to hit on some expedient." Likewise pleading for compromise, North Carolina's Hugh Williamson warned that "if we do not concede on both sides, our business must soon be at an end." A committee might be able to pursue a compromise "with more coolness." While Martin professed no objection to the appointment of a committee, he made clear that he thought there was nothing to compromise: "You must give each state an equal suffrage [in the Senate] or our business is at an end." Randolph went along with the appointment of a committee, though he held "no great hopes that any good will arise from it"—a viewpoint also stated by Lansing.[228]

Figure 3.8 Roger Sherman of Connecticut, one of the oldest delegates, a prominent figure in both state and national politics, and a molder of critical compromises at the Philadelphia convention. (Yale University Art Gallery)

Wilson and Madison strongly opposed appointment of the committee, which they feared would reach a compromise that violated principles of justice by departing from population-based apportionment. Yet the convention nonetheless voted to appoint the committee by nine states to two; even Madison's Virginia colleagues deserted him on this issue. The method of selecting the committee and its eventual composition virtually ensured that the small-state delegates would get what they wanted. By the rules of the convention, committees were chosen by a ballot of all state delegations present. In this case, the delegates chosen from the large states—such as Gerry and Mason—were those who had already evinced the greatest inclination to compromise, while those selected from the small states—such as Yates, Paterson, and Martin— were among those who had been most vociferous in demanding equal state representation in the Senate.[229]

The committee selected Gerry as its chair. When he presented its report to the convention, he explained that although members had held "different opinions," they had quickly agreed on the compromise proposed by the Connecticut delegates, "merely in order that some ground of accommodation might be proposed." According to the committee's recommendation, each state would receive one representative in the House for every forty thousand inhabitants, with any state lacking that number of residents nonetheless receiving one representative. Each state would receive an equal vote in the Senate. As a sop to the large states, which were relinquishing their commitment to population-based apportionment of the Senate—an arrangement that the convention had tentatively approved more than once—the committee proposed that bills for raising revenue or appropriating money must originate in the House and would not be subject to amendment in the Senate.[230]

The convention had earlier considered and rejected a proposal for such an "origination clause." Its principal proponent, Gerry, had argued that the House "was more immediately the representatives of the people, and it was a maxim that the people ought to hold the purse strings." In Great Britain, only the House of Commons could introduce money bills, and Gerry emphasized that the convention, even though "dislik[ing] the British government for the oppressive measures" imposed on American colonists, should "not be so far prejudiced as to make our [constitution] in everything opposite to theirs."[231]

However, during this earlier debate, other delegates had opposed restricting the power of the Senate in this way. Butler denied any analogy between the House of Lords and the Senate and warned that if "the Senate should be degraded by any such discriminations, the best men would be apt to decline serving in it in favor of the other branch." Madison agreed that "[t]he Senate would be the representatives of the people as well as the first branch." He also thought the proposed restriction was likely to prove inefficacious, as senators "would easily prevail on some member of the [House] to originate the bill they wished to be passed." Madison argued that senators "would be generally a more capable set of men," and thus "it would be wrong to disable them from any preparation of [this most important] business." Observing that the South Carolina constitution contained such an origination clause, Charles Cotesworth Pinckney reported that it had "been a source of pernicious disputes between the two branches." The convention then had rejected Gerry's proposal by a vote of seven states to three.[232]

However, as an inducement to the large-state delegates to accept the Connecticut Compromise, Gerry's committee had reintroduced an origination clause. As Gerry later explained the rationale, the committee had thought it "highly unreasonable and unjust" that a small state, which might contribute only 1/65th of any federal tax, should nevertheless have an equal right with a large state, which might contribute as much as 10/65ths of the same tax, "to take money from the pocket of the latter, more especially as it was intended that the powers of the new legislature should extend to internal taxation." Furthermore, Gerry stated, the right of spending money should be in proportion to the ability to raise it, and "the larger states would not have the least security for their property if they had not the due command of their own purses."[233]

However, other large-state delegates denigrated the concession of an origination clause as, in Madison's words, "nothing more than a nominal privilege." Madison thought that the powers to regulate trade and make treaties were more important than the power to raise money, yet the House was to receive no favoritism on those issues. Wilson agreed that this concession was "a trifle light as air." If both branches retained the power to block legislation, what difference did it make which originated a bill? Charles Cotesworth Pinckney proclaimed it astonishing that anyone could regard this origination clause as a genuine concession.[234]

By contrast, Gerry insisted that an origination clause was "of great consequence," and he called it "the cornerstone of the accommodation." For the Constitution to declare that the Senate did not possess "the confidence of the people in money matters" would reduce that branch's "weight and influence," which he considered desirable. Mason, who had also served on the committee that designed the compromise, defended the clause on the grounds that only the House consisted of "the immediate representatives of the people." By a narrow margin, the convention approved this origination clause, though the delegates later watered it down to cover only revenue-raising bills—excising appropriations bills from the clause—and to permit the Senate to amend such bills initiated by the House.[235]

On the Connecticut Compromise as a whole, Madison expressed firm opposition. It would be "in vain to purchase concord in the convention on terms which would perpetuate discord among their constituents." The convention should not "depart from justice in order to conciliate the smaller states and the minority of the people of the United States." Madison wanted to call the bluff of the small-state delegates: "He was not apprehensive that the people of the small states would obstinately refuse to accede to a government founded on just principles and promising them substantial protection." Specifically, he did not think that "Delaware would brave the consequences of seeking her fortunes apart from the other states," nor would it "pursue the rash policy of courting foreign support" (as suggested by Bedford). Similarly, Madison declared that he did not believe that "the people of New Jersey, notwithstanding the decided tone of the gentleman from that state [Paterson], would choose rather to stand on their own legs, and bid defiance to events, than to acquiesce under an establishment founded on principles the justice of which they could not dispute and absolutely necessary to redeem them from the exactions levied on them by the commerce of the neighboring states."[236]

Several other delegates who also supported population-based apportionment backed Madison. Butler of South Carolina agreed that the Connecticut Compromise was "evidently unjust," and Wilson insisted that "firmness was sometimes a duty of higher obligation" than conciliation. Morris denied that the small states would dissolve the union if they lost on this issue: "[T]he ties of interest, of kindred and of common habits which connect them with the other states will be too strong to be easily broken."[237]

By contrast, small-state delegates staunchly defended the compromise as "necessary" and "reasonable," and Paterson insisted that the small states would remain in the union on no other terms. Indeed—and this was of crucial importance—some delegates supporting population-based apportionment had concluded that a concession to the small states on representation in the Senate was inescapable. For example, Gerry, although he still had "material objections" to the compromise he had helped to formulate, stated that "if we do not come to some agreement among ourselves, some foreign sword will probably do the work for us." Mason agreed that an accommodation was necessary, observing that he "would bury his bones in this city rather than expose his country to the consequences of a dissolution of the convention without anything being done." Although he continued to defend the principle of population-based apportionment of representation in both houses of Congress, Mason "supposed that some points must be yielded for the sake of accommodation."[238]

The delegations from Virginia, Pennsylvania, and South Carolina continued to resist equal state representation in the Senate. But North Carolina had abandoned the large-state coalition, and the delegations from Georgia and

Massachusetts were now evenly divided on the issue, leaving the small states with a victory margin of six to three.[239]

Delegates from states that were either large or planned soon to become so proposed various intermediate solutions that would preserve an advantage for their states in the Senate, albeit short of what a straightforward population-based apportionment would afford them. Charles Pinckney, who had earlier suggested dividing the states into three different-sized "classes," which would be allocated different numbers of senators, now proposed a sliding scale by which the smallest states would get a single senator and the largest state, Virginia, would receive five. Wilson seconded the proposal, which Madison supported as a reasonable compromise. Yet Gerry, recognizing that the small-state delegates tasted victory and would not compromise further, declared that Pinckney's proposal had "no hope of success," and it was indeed rejected.[240]

Franklin proposed a different compromise: All states would have an equal vote in the Senate on issues affecting state sovereignty, a state's authority over its own citizens, and the appointment of federal government officials. But with regard to fixing federal officeholders' salaries, and raising and appropriating money more generally, voting power in Congress would be allocated proportionately to the states' relative contributions to the federal treasury. Randolph suggested yet another compromise: Both branches of the federal legislature would be apportioned according to population, but the executive would be selected through a system of equal state voting, which would afford the small states an effective check on Congress.[241]

King continued to insist that Massachusetts "would never be prevailed on to yield to an equality of votes [in the Senate]," but his fellow Massachusetts delegate Caleb Strong observed that the convention had appointed a committee and now had no choice but to accept the compromise that committee had proposed. According to Strong, everyone agreed that "Congress is nearly at an end. If no accommodation takes place [at the convention], the union itself must soon be dissolved." The small states had made a "considerable concession" in the origination clause, and they "might naturally expect some concession on the other side." Strong declared that he felt compelled to support the Connecticut Compromise.[242]

Thus, in the end, the small-state delegates got their way. On July 16, by the narrow margin of five states to four, with one delegation divided,* the convention approved the Connecticut Compromise, resolving an impasse that had threatened to prematurely terminate the proceedings. Later, on the

---

* This vote understates the amount of support for the small-state position within the union, as the three states not then represented at the convention—New Hampshire, New York, and Rhode Island—would presumably have voted for the compromise.

penultimate day of the convention's proceedings, in response to what Madison described as "the circulating murmurs of the small states," the delegates decided without debate or opposition to make unamendable, without the consent of every state, the provision guaranteeing equal state representation in the Senate.[243]

The small-state delegates had won a crucial victory partly because they were more united and intensely committed on the issue of apportioning the Senate than were the large-state delegates; this made their walkout threats sufficiently credible that they had to be taken seriously. As Madison noted after the compromise had passed, the "inflexibility" of the smaller states was so apparent, and the opinions of the large-state delegates "differed so much as to the importance" of the issue, that the small-state delegates had correctly calculated they could have their way. When Randolph proposed a temporary adjournment after the compromise had passed, so that the large-state delegations could take stock and "the small states might also deliberate on the means of conciliation," Rutledge declared, in response, that he saw no reason to adjourn because "he could see no chance of a compromise," given how fixed the small states were in their views.[244]

The small-state delegations won on this issue for another reason as well, one that had advantaged them from the outset. The Connecticut Compromise was endorsed by a committee on which each state represented at the convention had one member. That equal allocation of power on the committee constituted a rejection, as Wilson pointed out, of the very principle of population-based apportionment for which the large-state delegations were contending. That committee, in turn, had been appointed by a convention that was organized on the principle of equal state representation. This inescapably had the effect of biasing the outcome (although, to be sure, the vote to appoint the committee was approved by the hefty margin of nine states to two). As Wilson observed, the delegates at the convention who favored equal state representation in the Senate represented states that contained only about one-quarter of the American population.[245]

In the informal gatherings among delegates in the week before the convention achieved a quorum, some of the Pennsylvania delegates had proposed that "the large states should unite in firmly refusing to the small states an equal vote [at the convention] as unreasonable and as enabling the small states to negative every good system of government, which must in the nature of things, be founded on a violation of that equality." But the Virginians, according to Madison's notes, "conceiving that such an attempt might beget fatal altercations between the large and small states, and that it would be easier to prevail on the latter, in the course of the deliberations, to give up their equality for the sake of an effective government, than on taking the field of discussion to disarm themselves of the right and thereby throw themselves on the mercy of the large states, discountenanced and stifled the project." Thus, the convention rules provided that each state delegation would have an equal vote. Madison had been confident that if the delegations from a majority of states represented at the convention—he was thinking, as we have seen, of those states that were currently populous combined with those that were expecting to become so—coalesced behind population-based apportionment of congressional representation, then "the fewer and smaller states must finally bend to them." Events proved him wrong.[246]

The story extended back even further. As Williamson observed late in the convention, the reason the small states had been able to secure equality in the Senate was that they already enjoyed equal representation in Congress under the Articles. Changing the status quo regarding allocations of power in politics can be difficult because beneficiaries of the status quo both derive resources from it with which to resist change and often become convinced of its justice—and thus will feel justified in fighting to preserve it.[247]

In turn, the reason that small states enjoyed equal voting power under the Articles was that they had extracted it as a condition of their participation when the colonies first joined forces politically to secure their independence from Great Britain. On the first day of the First Continental Congress in 1774, a delegate from Rhode Island, the smallest state, argued for equal state representation. Patrick Henry, representing the largest state of Virginia, replied that apportionment in Congress should be based on population, wealth, or some combination thereof. In 1775, Delaware's delegates to the Second Continental Congress were instructed by their legislature to urge "decently but firmly" the state's right "to an equal voice in Congress." The large states had threatened not to confederate unless their weight in Congress was proportionate to their population, while small states had conditioned their participation in Congress on receiving an equal voice in its decision-making. The small states had won these early contests, and they emerged victorious once again when the Articles of Confederation were drafted in 1776–77. Gerry recounted this history at the Philadelphia convention, as recorded by Madison: "The injustice of allowing each state an equal vote was long insisted on. He voted for it, but it was against his judgment, and under the strain of public danger, and the obstinacy of the lesser states."[248]

Although the large states had yielded on this issue when Congress was created, they continued to resent equal state representation under the Articles. In 1782, Madison reported that large states had opposed the admission of Vermont as an independent state to the union partly on the grounds that "so unimportant a state" ought not to have "an equal vote in deciding on peace and all the other grand interests of the union now depending." Yet despite all the resentment large states had built up over the apportionment issue for more than a decade, they lost again on that issue at the Philadelphia convention.[249]

The Connecticut Compromise was generally perceived as a loss not only for large-state nationalists such as Madison and Wilson but also for the South. As we have seen, the southern states' delegations in Philadelphia had supported a population-based apportionment of Congress on the assumption that it would benefit them, either because they were already large, as was Virginia, or because they believed they were destined quickly to become so, as with Georgia. As the Connecticut Compromise was about to pass, Madison reiterated that, under a population-based apportionment of Congress, the North would enjoy only a temporary advantage because the South's share of the population was increasing every day. One of the strongest objections to equal state representation in the Senate, he observed, was the "perpetuity it would give to the preponderance of the northern [states] against the southern."[250]

The overlap between the two divides—of North and South, and of small states and large states—was especially troublesome, Madison observed, because it was "pretty well understood that the real difference of interests lay not between the large and small but between the northern and southern states." In the context of a divisive debate over how slaves would count for purposes of apportioning representation in the House—discussed in chapter 4—Morris confirmed Madison's observation. If southerners continued to insist on their slaves counting substantially in apportioning the House, Morris warned, then he would have to abandon his support for population-based apportionment of the Senate—support that one might have taken for granted from a delegate representing the large state of Pennsylvania. Instead, Morris said, he might have to vote for the "[v]icious principle of equality in the second branch in order to provide some defense for the northern states. . . ."[251]

Once the Connecticut Compromise, enacted as it was over mostly southern resistance, ensured that southern states would remain a minority in the Senate for the near future, southerners immediately conjured thoughts of how the Confederation Congress, over their united opposition and by a strictly regional vote of seven to five, had reinstructed Secretary for Foreign Affairs John Jay in his negotiations with Spain regarding navigation rights on the Mississippi River. Around the time that southern delegates realized they probably would lose the apportionment battle in the Senate, they began to insist that Congress be required to reapportion the House according to a periodic census and that (western) states newly admitted to the union not suffer discrimination in the allocation of voting power within the House—both of which were efforts to protect southern interests in light of predicted demographic patterns.[252]

Prior to approval of the Connecticut Compromise, Virginia delegates Mason and Randolph had consistently taken nationalist positions. After the compromise, however, they expressed fear that Virginia—and the South more generally—would be forever dominated in the Senate by the more numerous small states of the North. Thus, the day the Connecticut Compromise passed, Randolph exclaimed that it "had embarrassed the business extremely" because earlier convention votes to grant extensive powers to the federal government had been "founded on the supposition that a proportional representation was to prevail in both branches of the legislature." It was at this point, as noted earlier, that Randolph called for an adjournment of the convention to consider "the steps proper to be taken in the present solemn crisis of the business."[253]

The Virginians were not the only southerners distressed by the approval of the Connecticut Compromise. The day after it passed, Morris warned that if the convention turned to a consideration of the scope of the national government's powers immediately after the vote on apportioning the Senate, delegates would not consider "in the abstract . . . the powers necessary to be vested in the general government," but instead would be influenced by considerations of how much clout their states would have in national councils. Indeed, he was right: Immediately after the compromise was adopted, South Carolina delegates demanded an enumeration of the national government's powers in place of the vague formula of the Virginia Plan—empowering Congress to legislate in cases where "the separate states are incompetent" or where "the harmony of the United States" was critical—that previously had been provisionally agreed upon.[254]

Madison shared the concern of his fellow southerners on this point. He had already warned, just prior to the approval of the Connecticut Compromise, that "it would be impossible to say what powers could be safely and properly vested in the [federal] government before it was known in what manner the states were to be represented in it." Without a "just representation," Madison warned, "every effectual prerogative would be withdrawn or withheld." After the adoption of the Connecticut Compromise, he spoke out in favor of shifting to the executive branch some powers that had been provisionally assigned to the Senate.[255]

For example, the Virginia Plan had proposed that the national legislature have the power to appoint federal judges. When early in the proceedings some delegates objected to such appointments being made by so large a body, Madison suggested instead appointment by the Senate, which was "numerous enough to be confided in, [yet] not so numerous as to be governed by the motives of the other branch"—motives that included "intrigue and partiality."[256]

After the Connecticut Compromise, however, Madison took a different view of the matter. Observing that when the issue had been previously considered, "the second branch was very differently constituted . . . and was now to be composed of equal votes from all the states," he warned that allocating

the power to appoint federal judges to the Senate would "throw the appointments entirely into the hands of the northern states, [and] a perpetual ground
of jealousy and discontent would be furnished to the southern states." Noting
that the executive "would in general be more capable and likely to select fit
characters than the legislature," Madison now proposed that the executive be
empowered to appoint judges, subject to a veto by two-thirds of the Senate.
Later, when the Committee of Detail awarded the Senate the sole power to
make treaties, Madison objected on the grounds "that the Senate represented
the states alone." He preferred that the treaty-making power be divided between the Senate and the president.[257]

Of course, the small-state delegates, who had won an enormous victory in
the Connecticut Compromise, shifted their preferences in precisely the opposite way: They now favored expanding the Senate's power. Thus, Sherman, who
had first proposed the Connecticut Compromise, came to favor the Senate's
appointment of judges and even proposed making the executive's pardon
power contingent upon the Senate's approval.[258]

Other Features of the Senate

Other aspects of the Senate had proved less problematic for the convention
than the monumental issue of its apportionment. Chief among these other
issues was the method of appointing senators.

Although most of the delegates seemed to assume a strong practical linkage
between the method of selecting senators and the formula for apportioning
representation in the Senate, there is, in fact, no logical connection between
the two. For example, to empower state legislatures to choose senators would
have no bearing upon the separate issue of whether the Senate should be apportioned according to population or equally among the states. Yet even Madison
worried that empowering state legislatures to appoint senators would under-
cut the "proportional representation to which they [the large-state delegates]
were attached as a fundamental principle of just government." On the question
of how senators should be selected, Madison, who strongly opposed having
state legislatures make the choice, believed that he confronted a coalition of
small-state delegates (who cared about the issue only to the extent that it bore
on the more fundamental question of how to apportion the Senate) and some
large-state delegates who were "most anxious to secure the importance of the
state governments."[259]

The Virginia Plan had provided that the lower house would choose members of the upper house from among candidates nominated by state legislatures. Yet that proposal encountered considerable opposition from the

outset, as several delegates objected that state legislatures ought to choose senators (not just nominate candidates for the Senate). On a vote taken on just the third day of the convention's substantive deliberations, the delegates rejected this provision in the Virginia Plan by seven states to three, leading Madison to note "a chasm left in this part of the plan." This was the only major provision in the Virginia Plan that the convention flatly rejected from the outset.[260]

Fervently nationalist delegates such as Wilson wanted the people to elect the Senate as well as the House, not only because they believed this mode of selection would further the cause of population-based apportionment of representation in both houses but also because they worried that the likeliest alternative was selection of senators by state legislatures. Wilson noted that the convention was trying "to establish a national government," but if one branch were chosen by the people and the other by state legislatures, then "dissensions will naturally arise between them." Allowing state legislatures to choose senators would also "introduce and cherish local interests and local prejudices," whereas Wilson wanted states to have no influence "[w]ith respect to the province and objects of the general government." Madison, who bore at least some responsibility for the Virginia Plan's proposal that senators be selected by the House, agreed that state legislative selection of senators would render them "absolutely dependent" on the states.[261]

However, two weeks into the convention, when the delegates first conducted an extended debate on the issue, most of them rallied behind a proposal that state legislatures select senators. Sherman argued that this method of selection would keep the states "interested in supporting the national government" and also maintain "a due harmony between the two governments." Just "as the people ought to have the election of one of the branches of the legislature," Sherman observed, "the legislature of each state ought to have the election of the second branch, in order to preserve the state sovereignty." Mason similarly contended that state legislatures "ought to have some means of defending themselves against encroachments of the national government." Dickinson added the argument that state legislatures were more likely than the people to select "the most distinguished characters" for the Senate. Ellsworth agreed that state legislatures were "more competent" to produce a senate characterized by "wisdom and firmness."[262]

Gerry defended state legislative selection of senators on the different grounds that popular election of both houses of Congress would "leave no security" for commercial interests, as the people were "chiefly composed of the landed interest." Without "some check in favor of the commercial interest," Gerry contended, "oppression will take place." Madison countered that "[t]he great evils complained of were that the state legislatures run into schemes of paper money." How would empowering state legislatures to select senators check "a like propensity in the national legislature" rather than "promote it"? Gerry replied that "[t]he people are for paper money when the legislatures are against it," and he reiterated that "the commercial and monied interests would be more secure in the hands of the state legislatures than of the people at large."[263]

In the end, the delegates overwhelmingly favored state legislative selection of senators. Some of them seem genuinely to have believed that this mode of selection made the most sense. Specifically, for those small-state delegates committed to preserving core aspects of the confederation, preserving some "agency" for the states in selecting the federal government was "indispensable," as Dickinson observed. Accusing Wilson of wishing "to extinguish" the states—a charge that Wilson firmly denied—Dickinson objected that abolishing states "would degrade the councils of our country, would be impracticable, would be ruinous."[264]

For other delegates, however, considerations of political expediency rather than genuine policy preferences probably motivated their support for this method of selecting senators. State legislatures would inevitably play a major role in determining whether the constitution drafted in Philadelphia was ratified, and they would be unlikely to approve a system that denied them any direct influence upon the national government. Such expediential considerations probably explain the lopsided votes approving state legislative selection of senators, which were ten to zero and, later, nine to two, with only the largest states, Virginia and Pennsylvania, voting against. On many other issues as well, the delegates proved attentive to the consideration of whether states would ratify what the convention was proposing.[265]

The convention also had to determine the size of the Senate. Dickinson, who wanted a powerful second branch, thought that it could consist of as many as two hundred members, because "enlarging their numbers" would "increase their consequence and weight." Madison thought that Dickinson's reasoning was precisely backward: Weight and consequence were a function of having fewer members. Mason worried that, in addition, a large senate would be very expensive.[266]

The question of the size of the Senate intersected with that of its apportionment. William Davie of North Carolina expressed concern that if every state were guaranteed at least one senator and representation was apportioned according to population, then the Senate would have to consist of at least ninety members (because Delaware was estimated to have one-ninetieth of the nation's population). Wilson agreed that the Senate should not be that large, but he thought that Davie's concern could be addressed with a compromise by which each state would receive one senator for every hundred thousand inhabitants, while the small states would be guaranteed one senator even if their populations did not meet that threshold.[267]

After the Connecticut Compromise had approved equal state representation in the Senate, the convention overwhelmingly rejected a proposal of three senators per state, ultimately deciding upon two instead. Luther Martin of Maryland argued that the senators from each state should cast a single joint vote, which he said was consistent with the idea that they represented the interests of their state. Yet the delegates overwhelmingly decided instead that each state's senators would cast their votes independently.[268]

Some of the delegates most committed to preserving state prerogatives argued that state legislatures should pay senators' salaries, and the Committee of Detail agreed. Martin argued that because the Senate was to represent the states, its members should be paid by state legislatures. Butler observed that as the Senate was "the aristocratic part of our government"—a notion that is discussed later in this chapter—its members "must be controlled by the states, or they will be too independent." He also worried that senators would "be so long out of their respective states that they will lose sight of their constituents unless dependent on them for their support."[269]

However, other delegates worried that state legislative payment of senators' salaries would create too much dependency. Madison warned against senators' becoming "the mere agents and advocates of state interests and views, instead of being the impartial umpires and guardians of justice and general good." Madison declared that if House members were to serve only two years and the salaries of senators were to depend upon state legislatures that were mostly subject to annual elections, then he "could not see any chance for that stability in the general government, the want of which was a principal evil in the state governments." He also observed that under the Articles, "the public business had been frequently delayed" by states' failing to adequately compensate their congressional delegates. Most of the delegates in Philadelphia concurred with these sentiments, and the convention overwhelmingly rejected the proposal to have state legislatures pay senators' salaries.[270]

One of the most interesting and revealing debates at the convention concerned the length of senators' terms. In the states, upper houses of legislatures had longer (and often staggered) terms of office, larger constituencies, and higher property qualifications for voting and officeholding than did the lower houses. These design features had made the upper houses more resistant to pressure for debt and tax relief than the more populist lower houses. In half the states that resisted paper money in the mid-1780s, the lower house had approved the issuance but the upper house had killed it. Even in those states that did issue paper money, the upper houses frequently had delayed the emission, reduced the amount, or both.[271]

The delegates in Philadelphia mostly agreed with Randolph, who had explained when introducing the Virginia Plan that "[o]ur chief danger arises from the democratic parts of our constitutions" and that none of the state charters had "provided sufficient checks against the democracy." Later in the convention, Randolph argued that "[t]he democratic licentiousness of the state legislatures proved the necessity of a firm Senate." Morris agreed that the object of the second branch was "to check the precipitation, changeableness and excesses of the first branch." Specifically, the Senate would limit "the propensity in the first branch to legislate too much—to run into projects of paper money and similar expedients."[272]

Madison, too, believed that the Senate must be constructed in such a way as to give the government "that stability which was everywhere called for, and which the enemies of the republican form alleged to be inconsistent with its nature." Concretely, Madison explained that as the American population grew, those who "labor under all the hardships of life, and secretly sigh for a more equal distribution of its blessings," would become the majority. Power would "slide into the hands" of such people unless the convention established a body within the government "sufficiently respectable for its wisdom and virtue" to tilt the scales in favor of "the preponderance of justice." The Senate, in short, was needed "as a check on the democracy. It cannot therefore be made too strong."[273]

Madison argued that only "a considerable duration" in the term of office would enable the Senate to perform such a function. He had in mind Maryland's senators, who were indirectly elected and enjoyed the longest terms in office of any upper house members in the country—five years. In the summer of 1786, Madison had told Jefferson that the clamor for paper money was "universal" in Maryland, and only the state senate had "hitherto been a bar to [it]."[274]

The Virginia Plan had not specified the term of office for senators, providing only that it be "sufficient to ensure their independency." When the delegates first turned to the issue, Richard Dobbs Spaight of North Carolina suggested seven-year terms. A few delegates said that was too long. William Pierce of Georgia warned that seven years would raise an alarm because "[g]reat mischiefs had arisen in England" as a result of seven-year parliamentary terms, and he proposed three years instead. Charles Cotesworth Pinckney suggested four-year terms, expressing concern that anything longer "would fix them [senators] at the seat of government," where they "would acquire an interest . . . , perhaps transfer their property, and lose sight of the states they represent." Sherman also favored a term shorter than seven years, observing that "[f]requent elections are necessary to preserve the good behavior of rulers." Gerry argued that Senate terms longer than four or five years would jeopardize ratification.[275]

Yet most of the delegates favored longer terms than that. Randolph supported Spaight's proposal for seven-year terms on the grounds that the Maryland senate, with its five-year terms, "had been scarcely able to stem the popular torrent." Two weeks into the convention, the delegates overwhelmingly approved seven-year terms in office for senators.[276]

Stunningly, from a modern perspective, many delegates preferred even lengthier terms in office in the Senate, an institution they expected would function as a bastion of privilege. Madison declared that the Senate "ought to come from, and represent, the wealth of the nation." Dickinson wanted the Senate to consist of those "distinguished for their rank in life and their weight of property, and bearing as strong a likeness to the British House of Lords as possible." Butler agreed that the Senate was "the aristocratic part of our government." Charles Cotesworth Pinckney argued that because the Senate was "meant to represent the wealth of the country," its members should be paid no salary, and thus only the wealthy would be able to afford to serve.[277]

As he often did, Hamilton took the most extreme position of all on this issue. The House of Lords was "a most noble institution," which was able to check the oppression of the few by the many. It was to the absence of such a check that "we owe our paper money, installment laws, etc." Hamilton argued that "[n]othing but a permanent body can check the imprudence of democracy"; senators serving limited terms in office, no matter how long, would not "have firmness enough to answer the purpose." He also doubted that even terms as long as seven years "would induce the sacrifices of private affairs which an acceptance of public trust would require so as to ensure the services of the best citizens." Finally, Hamilton insisted that providing senators with tenure during good behavior would be consistent with republicanism, which required only that "all the magistrates are appointed and vacancies are filled by the people or a process of election originating with the people."[278]

Agreeing with Hamilton, Morris lamented that "[a]ll the guards contrived by America have not restrained the senatorial branches of the legislatures from a servile complaisance to the democratic." The Senate ought to display "the aristocratic spirit," and senators ought to possess "great personal property." A dependent second branch would be worse than none at all; "[t]o make it independent, it should be for life." To be useful, laws required permanency, and to "avoid a change of measures" required "avoiding a change of men." Only such stability would encourage people to lend money and enter into contracts. "A Senate for life" would also be "a noble bait"—encouraging state "demagogues" who might otherwise be inclined to oppose ratification of the Constitution to support it in the hope of securing a senate seat for themselves.[279]

Much later in life, Madison described Morris's speech in favor of lifetime tenure for senators as "very extravagant" and indicative of "his usual fondness for saying things and advancing doctrines that no one else would." Yet Charles Pinckney, George Read, and Robert Morris all endorsed lifetime tenure for senators as well (so did John Jay, who was not a convention delegate). Madison agreed that for the Senate to serve its purpose, its members must have "permanency and stability," although he thought that nine-year terms would be sufficient. Wilson also defended nine-year terms, although on the slightly different grounds that the Senate must be "made respectable in the eyes of foreign nations," because it would be involved in treaty making. Despite such sentiments, the convention eventually agreed on six-year terms (which would be easier to stagger than seven-year terms). However, the delegates overwhelmingly rejected mandatory rotation in office for the Senate, which in practice opened the door to much longer terms.[280]

Staggering the terms of senators was deemed to be another mechanism for frustrating populist political impulses. In 1786, Madison had worried that even the Maryland senate might capitulate to the demand for paper money, given the universal clamor for it and the unlucky fact that the state constitution provided that "the whole body" was "to be chosen at once." At the convention, Randolph argued that staggering the terms of senators would be "favorable to the wisdom and stability" of the body. The delegates agreed and provided that one-third of the Senate's seats would be contested every two years.[281]

The convention also decided to bestow distinctive powers upon the Senate. The Committee of Detail awarded the Senate sole power to make treaties and appoint ambassadors and Supreme Court justices, and the Constitution as it was finally approved gives the Senate the power to try the impeachments of federal officers. However, the convention ultimately decided to divide the powers of appointment and treaty making between the president and the Senate. We shall consider in a moment the convention's deliberations over the appointment power. With regard to treaty making, some delegates—especially from the large state of Pennsylvania—wanted to include the House, given that treaties would have the force of law. Yet most delegates apparently concluded that the House would be too large to preserve the secrecy required in treaty negotiations, and they overwhelmingly agreed to limit participation in treaty making to the president and the Senate.[282]

While a thoroughgoing majoritarian such as Wilson objected to a supermajority requirement for treaty making, the imbroglio over Jay's negotiations with Spain regarding navigation rights on the Mississippi River ensured that most southern delegates would insist on a supermajority requirement for Senate ratification of treaties, just as the Articles had imposed such a requirement on the Confederation Congress. North Carolina's Hugh Williamson, for one, defended such a requirement on the grounds that the Connecticut Compromise had opened up the possibility that a majority of the Senate need not represent a majority of the American people. Some New England delegates similarly supported a supermajority requirement owing to concerns that a treaty could be made that would relinquish their claim to the Newfoundland fisheries, which were vital to the region's economy. By an overwhelming margin, the convention approved a requirement that two-thirds of those senators present concur in the ratification of treaties. Rutledge and Gerry wished to make the supermajority requirement even more stringent by requiring that treaties be ratified by two-thirds of all senators, rather than simply two-thirds of those present, but the convention rejected their proposal.[283]

Madison, however, wished to eliminate the supermajority requirement for treaties of peace, which he thought ought to be easier to make. Alternatively, the requirement of presidential concurrence could be eliminated for such treaties, as Madison worried that the president "would necessarily derive so much power and importance from a state of war that he might be tempted, if authorized, to impede a treaty of peace." Butler agreed that such a safeguard was "a necessary security against ambitious and corrupt presidents." Wilson added the concern that if a two-thirds majority were necessary to make peace, then "the minority may perpetuate war." However, Gerry responded that Madison's concern was backward: Treaties of peace put at risk the nation's "dearest interests"— especially those of "the extremities of the continent," such as fisheries and territory—and thus should require an even greater supermajority to enact.[284]

After rejecting Madison's motion that peace treaties not require the president's concurrence, the delegates initially approved Madison's other proposal that a simple majority of the Senate suffice to ratify such treaties. But they quickly reconsidered that second vote. Gerry expressed concern that a simple majority requirement for certain treaties would make the Senate more vulnerable to foreign influence. Moreover, he objected to placing "the essential rights of the union in the hands" of a simple majority of senators, who might collectively represent as little as one-fifth of the nation's population. Williamson shared this concern that as few as eight senators—who would constitute a majority of a bare quorum—might have "the power to decide the conditions of peace."[285]

On the other hand, defending Madison's proposal, Morris argued that a supermajority requirement for making peace might render Congress too reluctant to declare war in the first place—even "on account of the fisheries or the Mississippi, the two great objects of the union." In addition, if a majority of senators wished for peace but were not allowed to make it, they might try to effectuate their purpose in "a more disagreeable way, such as vetoing the supplies for war." However, the delegates ultimately rejected Madison's effort to exempt treaties of peace from the two-thirds supermajority requirement for Senate ratification of treaties.[286]

The Executive Branch

The design of the executive branch also generated great controversy at the convention. Many issues had to be resolved. Should the executive (who was not formally named the "president" until the Committee of Detail report in early August) be unitary or plural? If unitary, should there nonetheless be a council to constrain the executive? What should the tenure in office be, and should the executive be eligible for multiple terms? How should the executive be selected and removed from office? What powers should the executive possess?

Because these issues intersected with one another, even figuring out how to discuss them sensibly proved difficult. Naturally, one's view of the proper powers of the executive both influenced and was influenced by the mode of selection and the determination of whether the executive was to be unitary or plural. Discussing all these issues simultaneously was obviously impossible, but which should be resolved first? As a result of this quandary, the delegates' debates on designing the executive branch were, as Madison later reported to Jefferson, "tedious and reiterated."[287]

The Articles of Confederation had provided for no executive as such but only for "a committee of the states," consisting of one congressional delegate per state, to act for the government when Congress was in recess. But this committee barely met and never transacted any important business. All the delegates in Philadelphia agreed that the federal government required a genuine executive branch.[288]

Revolutionary-era Americans were generally suspicious of executive power, which connoted to them royal governors' vetoing the laws of colonial assemblies or dissolving them entirely. The first three grievances listed in the Declaration of Independence had been directed at abuses of the veto power by the king. The controversial financial policies of Robert Morris as superintendent of finance in the early 1780s, not to mention the abortive effort of Secretary for Foreign Affairs John Jay to barter away American navigation rights on the Mississippi in exchange for a commercial treaty with Spain, would not have improved the view that many Americans held of executive power.[289]

In response to perceived abuses of executive power by the king and his royal governors, state constitutions of the Revolutionary era generally provided for eviscerated executive branches, which were made largely subordinate to state legislatures. In most states, legislatures selected the governor, who was limited to an annual term of office and was subject to mandatory rotation after a specified number of terms. Most governors had no power to veto legislation, and most either were denied the power to appoint judges and other government officers or else were forced to share that power with the legislature.* Finally, nearly all state constitutions—even those of New York and Massachusetts, which provided for the most powerful executives—bound governors to act only in conjunction with executive councils, whose members were appointed by the legislature or elected by the people. Thus, the immediate backdrop against which the delegates in Philadelphia were designing the executive branch—state constitutions—was one of emasculated executives.[290]

Most of the delegates to the Philadelphia convention were determined to change this state of affairs. The willingness of state legislatures in the mid-1780s to enact tax and debt relief legislation proved the need for strong executives who could resist populist political pressure. As Madison explained at the convention, "Experience had proved a tendency in our governments to throw all power into the legislative vortex." The state executives were "in general little more than cyphers, the legislatures omnipotent." If the convention could not devise "some expedient" consistent with republicanism to restrain "the instability and encroachments" of the legislature, "a revolution of some kind or other" would ensue. Gouverneur Morris agreed that "the way to keep out monarchical government was to establish such a republican government as would make the people happy and prevent a desire of change." One great object of the executive, Morris noted, must be "to control the legislature."[291]

Madison, who as we have seen was the driving force on many issues at the convention, had given relatively little thought to the matter of the national executive. A month before the convention, he confessed to Washington that he had "scarcely ventured as yet to form my own opinion either of the manner in which it [the executive branch] ought to be constituted or of the authorities with which it ought to be clothed." Because the delegates had little to draw upon from state constitutions or the Articles of Confederation in constructing a more powerful executive, they had to rely more on their imaginations.[292]

The Virginia Plan provided for a national executive to be chosen by the national legislature for an unspecified term of years, without eligibility for re-election. The executive would possess "a general authority to execute the national laws," as well as "the executive rights vested in Congress by the Confederation." In conjunction with "a convenient number" of federal judges, the executive would also have the power to veto laws passed by Congress, subject to override. The Virginia Plan took no position on whether the executive should be unitary or plural.[293]

---

* Critics of executive power deemed the power over appointments especially dangerous because it had, in their minds, enabled the Crown to corrupt Members of Parliament with the enticement of appointments to lucrative government offices.

The relative thinness of the Virginia Plan with regard to the executive branch left the delegates with a great deal to flesh out in their deliberations. The vast majority of them believed that the Articles' failure to create an executive was a major flaw and that a powerful executive was necessary to supply energy to any government. Charles Pinckney spoke for many when he supported the creation of a "vigorous executive." Morris explained that, especially in a country with such an extensive geographic scope, it was essential to create "an executive with sufficient vigor to pervade every part of it." Wilson agreed that the enormous size of the country seemed "to require the vigor of monarchy," although he cautioned that the nation's "manners are against a king and are purely republican." Sherman was the principal opponent of this view, insisting that the executive was "nothing more than an institution for carrying the will of the legislature into effect."[294]

In their first extended discussion of the issue, one week into the convention, the delegates confronted the important question elided by the Virginia Plan: Should the executive be unitary or plural? Wilson, who more than anyone in Philadelphia influenced the design of the presidency, argued vigorously for a unitary executive, which would give the "most energy, dispatch and responsibility to the office." Wilson warned that "if divided, the responsibility of the executive is destroyed." He also noted that not a single state constitution provided for multiple governors. Rutledge agreed that a unitary executive would "feel the greatest responsibility and administer the public affairs best." Indeed, Charles Pinckney deemed the arguments in favor of unitariness so "obvious and conclusive" that he assumed "no member would oppose."[295]

Yet Pinckney's assumption was wrong, for Randolph objected, according to Madison's notes, "with great earnestness." He opposed a unitary executive as "the fetus of monarchy" and protested against taking "the British government as our prototype." The American people, he warned, would never repose the necessary confidence in a single magistrate. Williamson similarly worried that a unitary executive would become "an elective king," who would first seek to entrench himself in office for life and then "lay a train for the succession of his children." Williamson said that it was "pretty certain . . . that we should at some time or other have a king, but he wished no precaution to be omitted that might postpone the event as long as possible."[296]

Other delegates raised similar concerns. Dickinson objected that some of his colleagues seemed to be envisioning an executive of a sort "not consistent with a republic." The United States could not have the same sort of executive as Great Britain because the weight of the executive there arose "from the attachments which the Crown draws to itself and not merely from the force of its prerogatives." Although Dickinson confessed his belief that a limited monarchy was "one of the best governments in the world," he considered it out of

the question in America: "The spirit of the times—the state of our affairs—
forbade the experiment, if it were desirable." Objecting both to a single executive and to the proposal for vesting that executive with substantial power
over appointments—discussed later in this chapter—Mason warned that the
convention was trending too far toward creating an elective monarchy, which
the "genius of the people" would never accept. However, if the executive were
made plural, as the New Jersey Plan would soon propose, then Mason believed
that greater power could be safely entrusted to it.[297]

Some of those delegates favoring a plural executive suggested that it consist
of three men to be chosen from different regions of the country, as was the
Confederation's Board of Treasury, which had replaced the superintendent of
finance after Robert Morris's resignation from that position. Defending such a
scheme, Randolph noted that a unitary executive would probably be selected
from near the center of the country, which would place remote states at a disadvantage. Mason argued that a three-person executive would have "a more

Figure 3.9 James Wilson of Pennsylvania, one of the most important contributors
to the convention's work, one of the leading craftsmen of Federalist arguments in the
contest over ratification of the Constitution, and one of the original justices of the US
Supreme Court. (Collection of the Supreme Court of the United States)

perfect and extensive knowledge of the real interests of this great union" and thus would "quiet the minds of the people and convince them that there will be proper attention paid to their respective concerns." Williamson declared that in light of the "essential difference of interests between the northern and southern states, particularly in the carrying trade," it would be dangerous to have a unitary executive, who would have to be chosen from one region or the other.[298]

In response to such proposals, Wilson observed that three equal members of the federal executive would produce "nothing but uncontrolled, continued and violent animosities." They would "contend among themselves till one becomes the master of his colleagues." Wilson argued that "unity in the executive, instead of being the fetus of monarchy, would be the best safeguard against tyranny." He cautioned that some of his colleagues were too preoccupied with the British model, which was irrelevant to America, where "the manners are so republican." Butler agreed that the members of a plural executive would be in a "constant struggle for local advantages," resulting in "[d]elays, divisions, and dissensions." Especially with regard to military matters, he said, a plural executive would be "mischievous."[299]

After twice postponing a vote, the convention, still in its first week of substantive deliberations, agreed by seven states to three to create a unitary executive. However, even a unitary executive could be constrained by requiring him to secure the consent of an executive council before acting. Conceding Wilson's point that no state constitution provided for multiple governors, Sherman noted that every state constitution established an executive council to constrain the governor's actions. Observing that "[e]ven in Great Britain, the King has a council," Sherman insisted that only such a restraint could render the presidency "acceptable to the people."[300]

Mason believed that a council could ensure that the executive would have "safe and proper information and advice," and he warned that to reject such a council would be to embark upon "an experiment on which the most despotic governments had never ventured." Franklin thought "a council would not only be a check on a bad president but be a relief to a good one." Gerry likewise favored an executive council "in order to give weight [to] and inspire confidence" in the executive. Ellsworth proposed an executive council consisting of the chief justice, the president of the Senate, and the heads of major executive ministries. Mason favored a council composed of six members, with two being selected from each section of the country. The appointments would be made by votes of the state delegations in the House, and the councilors would enjoy the same tenure in office as senators.[301]

On the other side of the debate, Charles Pinckney argued that while the executive should be able to call for advice as he pleased, he should not be restrained by a council. An able council might "thwart him," while he could "shelter himself under the sanction" of a weak one. Wilson also opposed the creation of an executive council, which he thought would serve more often "to cover than prevent malpractices."[302]

In the end, the convention rejected an executive council by a vote of eight states to three. In its place, the delegates approved the creation of an executive cabinet, which the president could choose to consult for advice, though he was not obliged to do so. The convention's decision to omit an executive council to restrain the president—"a thing unknown in any safe and regular government," according to Mason—was one of the Virginian's principal reasons for subsequently refusing to sign the Constitution.[303]

Another vital question was which powers should be granted to this unitary executive. Without dissent, the convention agreed that the executive should have the power to execute national laws. Of the possible additional powers to bestow upon the executive, the veto garnered the most attention from the delegates. The constitutions of only two states, Massachusetts and New Hampshire, conferred a veto power upon an executive acting alone, while New York's governor was part of a "council of revision"—also consisting of the chancellor and state supreme court justices—that was empowered to veto legislation.[304]

Despite such thin precedent for an executive veto, only a couple of delegates disagreed with the concept, which had been embraced in the Virginia Plan. Among those who did object, Sherman declared himself "against enabling one man to stop the will of the whole," while Gunning Bedford of Delaware thought "it would be sufficient to mark out in the Constitution the boundaries to the legislative authority" without empowering the executive with a veto. The New Jersey Plan also contemplated no executive veto.[305]

However, most of the delegates strongly supported such a veto power, which they hoped would be used to check Congress if it attempted to usurp the powers of the other branches or proved too responsive to populist political pressures, as the delegates believed state legislatures had in the 1780s. Wilson warned of Congress's "swallowing up all the other powers" and emphasized the need to give "sufficient self-defensive power" to the executive. Morris agreed that liberty was "in greater danger from legislative usurpations than from any other source." Notwithstanding constitutional safeguards, Mason worried that Congress "would so much resemble [the legislatures] of the individual states that it must be expected frequently to pass unjust and pernicious laws." John Francis Mercer of Maryland agreed that an executive veto was essential for checking "legislative usurpation and oppression."[306]

Specifically, the executive's veto would be a safeguard against paper money and debtor relief laws, should they ever pass Congress. Madison told the convention that the executive veto would act "as an additional check against a pursuit of those unwise and unjust measures which constituted so great a portion of our calamities." Morris canvassed the subject at some length. According to Madison's notes, Morris "dwelt on the importance of public credit and the difficulty of supporting it without some strong barrier against the instability of legislative assemblies. . . . He recited the history of paper emissions and the perseverance of the legislative assemblies in repeating them, with all the distressing effects of such measures before their eyes." Only a strong executive veto power could check "this ruinous expedient."[307]

Although the delegates overwhelmingly approved the concept of an executive veto, two aspects of it generated considerable disagreement among them. First, should the executive exercise the veto power alone, or as part of a council of revision (a distinct entity from an executive council)? Second, how absolute should the executive veto be?[308]

The Virginia Plan, modeled in this regard after the New York constitution, had proposed that a "convenient number" of the federal judiciary would join the executive in a council of revision that would be empowered to veto congressional legislation (as opposed to the executive alone exercising the veto power). As Madison explained at the convention, including judges in a council of revision would give them "an additional opportunity of defending [themselves] against legislative encroachments." Moreover, combining the executive with the judiciary would "inspir[e] additional confidence and firmness in exerting the revisionary power."[309]

Madison argued that in a republican system of government the executive would be especially in need of support in exercising the veto power. In a republic, no individual citizen enjoyed "settled pre-eminence in the eyes of the rest." Moreover, the executive, unlike a king, had no "permanent stake in the public interest which would place him out of the reach of foreign corruption." Thus, associating the judges with the executive in a council of revision "would both double the advantage and diminish the danger." Madison also believed that judges would offer valuable assistance in "preserving a consistency, conciseness, perspicuity and technical propriety in the laws." Ellsworth agreed that the aid of judges would "give more wisdom and firmness to the executive," and he observed that judges would have "competent information" to offer upon legislation that implicated the law of nations.[310]

Morris strongly supported including judges in the council of revision. Constraints upon the legislature were obviously required, and he doubted that an executive serving a limited term and subject to impeachment—and who, for much of the convention, was slated to be selected by Congress—"would be a very effectual check." As compared with the British king, "[t]he interest of our executive is so inconsiderable and so transitory, and his means of defending it

so feeble, that there is the justest ground to fear his want of firmness in resisting encroachments." Indeed, Morris worried that even adding "the auxiliary
firmness and weight of the judiciary would not supply the deficiency."[311]

As we have seen, some delegates objected to including judges in the council
of revision on the grounds that they would already exercise a functional veto
over legislation through the power of judicial review and ought not to enjoy
what Luther Martin of Maryland called "a double negative." Acknowledging
"weight to this observation," Wilson nonetheless noted that "[l]aws may be
unjust, may be unwise, may be dangerous, may be destructive; and yet not
be so unconstitutional as to justify the judges in refusing to give them effect."
Mason agreed that courts would strike down only legislation that plainly contravened the Constitution, whereas the council of revision could veto laws on
the broader grounds that they were "unjust, oppressive, or pernicious."[312]

Other delegates raised additional objections to including judges in a council of revision. Rufus King declared that for the same reason he preferred a
unitary executive—responsibility—he preferred a unitary veto. Others objected to giving judges a voice on public policy, as opposed to legal interpretation. For example, Nathaniel Gorham of Massachusetts noted that judges
were "not to be presumed to possess any peculiar knowledge of the mere
policy of public measures." Gerry similarly objected to "making statesmen
of the judges." Charles Pinckney worried about involving judges in partisan
dealings, and Sherman likewise "disapproved of judges meddling in politics
and parties." Caleb Strong of Massachusetts warned that judges who had
played a role in the enactment of legislation would probably be biased in its
interpretation.[313]

Those opposing the inclusion of judges in a council of revision also argued,
more generally, that associating judges with the executive in such a council violated the concept of the separation of powers, properly understood. Madison
countered that a paper separation of powers between the legislature, executive, and judiciary would be worthless. In order to "guarantee the provisions
on paper," there must be a "balance of powers and interests."[314]

Madison and Wilson relentlessly pressed for a council of revision including
judges rather than a veto wielded solely by the unitary executive—to the point
that other delegates expressed displeasure at the convention's being forced
to revisit the issue. Over the course of several votes, however, at no point did
more than three state delegations support their position.[315]

Although they rejected giving federal judges a share of the power to veto
congressional legislation, the delegates easily agreed upon a purely executive veto. That still left the question, however, of whether the veto should be
absolute or qualified. Several delegates, including Wilson, Hamilton, and
Morris, thought that the president's veto power should be absolute—that is,

not subject to override by Congress. Wilson, in particular, sought to dissuade his colleagues from their "prejudices against the executive"—prejudices that he said resulted from drawing erroneous lessons from Americans' experience with King George III. Wilson argued that while an absolute veto would rarely have to be exercised, its very existence would have a salutary influence upon Congress. He also warned of "tempestuous moments in which animosities may run high between the executive and legislative branches," when the president would need to be able to defend himself.[316]

For most of the delegates, however, an absolute veto would repose too much power in the executive. Gerry saw no need for so great an executive control over the legislature, given that "the best men in the community would be comprised in the two branches of it." Franklin warned that an absolute veto would enable the executive to extort money from Congress, as the royal governor of Pennsylvania had done to the colonial legislature. Butler declared that the executive power was "in a constant course of increase" and that "a Cromwell" might "arise in this country" just as easily as in any other. He said that he would not have supported a unitary executive earlier in the convention had he "entertained an idea that a complete negative on the laws was to be given him." Mason agreed that a unitary executive vested with an absolute veto too nearly resembled an elective monarchy.[317]

Even Madison thought that an absolute veto "would certainly be obnoxious to the temper of this country," and he suggested instead that "a proper proportion of each branch" be authorized to override an executive veto, as proposed in the Virginia Plan. One week into the proceedings, the convention unanimously rejected an absolute executive veto and agreed that Congress could override a veto by two-thirds votes in both houses. Proponents of a strong executive, such as Hamilton and Morris, who worried about "[t]he excess rather than the deficiency of laws," subsequently persuaded the convention to change that fraction to three-fourths. But those delegates who were concerned about "putting a dangerous power in the hands of a few senators headed by the president" ultimately persuaded the convention to switch back to a two-thirds requirement for overriding presidential vetoes.[318]

The convention's other major dispute over the appropriate powers to vest in the executive involved what role, if any, he would play in appointing national government officers—judges, ambassadors, and others. Madison later called the appointment power, of all the functions of republican government, "the most difficult to guard against abuse." Under most state constitutions of the era, executives were denied the appointment power—a reaction against "the venality and abuses" of that power by royal governors and the British king, who had used the inducement of appointment to executive office to bend Parliament to his will.[319]

As Madison reported to Jefferson after the convention, the delegates held a wide range of views on the appointment power. Some favored the president's appointing all federal government officers; some supported his appointing only certain officers; some preferred that the president be denied any share of the appointment power; and some endorsed a division of the appointment power between the president and the Senate. Moreover, some delegates' views on this issue shifted over the course of the convention—mostly because the Connecticut Compromise altered expectations as to whether small or large states would dominate the Senate.[320]

Proponents of a strong executive argued for broad or even exclusive executive authority over appointments. Wilson declared that experience had revealed "the impropriety of such appointments by numerous [i.e., large] bodies," which always resulted in "intrigue, partiality and concealment." A principal reason for establishing a unitary executive, Wilson argued, was that government officers should be appointed by a single responsible person. Randolph agreed that appointments made by legislatures "generally resulted from cabal, from personal regard, or some other consideration than a title derived from the proper qualifications," and he touted "the responsibility of the executive as security for fit appointments." Morris argued that the president was likely to be better informed about the character of appointees, because the nature of his job would require "intercourse with every part of the United States." Moreover, a president who could be trusted with control of the army surely could be trusted with the appointment power. Morris also argued that if the Senate were to try impeachments, including those of judges—as the convention had provisionally decided—then it should not have the power to appoint judges (which would include filling judicial vacancies that arose when the Senate convicted judges on an impeachment, thus removing them from office).[321]

Yet other delegates strongly objected to granting "so great a power to any single person." Rutledge worried that the convention was "leaning too much towards monarchy" as it contemplated a unitary executive vested with broad powers to veto legislation and make appointments to federal office. Mason expressed concern about granting the appointment power to an executive serving a lengthy term in office, who would be likely to "insensibly form local and personal attachments" at the seat of the national government, which would deprive persons of equal merit who resided elsewhere of an equal chance of promotion. He also pointed out that if federal judges were to try impeachments of the executive—a possibility that at least some delegates were considering—then the president surely ought not to have control over their appointment.[322]

Most of those delegates who opposed conferring the appointment power on the president favored bestowing it upon the Senate. Early in the convention, Madison argued that senators were "sufficiently stable and independent to follow their deliberate judgments" in making appointments. Charles Pinckney noted that the president could not possibly have personal knowledge of as many qualified candidates for appointment as the Senate would, and Sherman added that the Senate collectively would have greater wisdom than the president. Sherman also favored the Senate's making appointments on the grounds that federal government positions "ought to be diffused [geographically], which would be more likely to be attended to by the second branch than by the executive."[323]

The Virginia Plan said nothing generally about the appointment power but did provide that the national legislature would appoint national judges. In the first week of the convention, the delegates agreed to a proposal by Madison to empower the president "to appoint to offices in cases not otherwise provided for" in the Constitution. A few days later, in a debate over how federal judges would be selected, the convention voted by nine states to two to reject the Virginia Plan proposal to make the national legislature the appointing body, but the delegates did not choose an alternative, leaving the issue to what Madison called "maturer reflection." One week later, they agreed to vest the power of appointing federal judges in the Senate.[324]

As we have seen, however, after the Connecticut Compromise awarded small (mostly northern) states an equal vote in the Senate, Madison lost his enthusiasm for vesting the appointment power exclusively in that body. Now he argued that Senate appointment of judges would be unfair because a minority of the people—which could constitute a majority of the states—might be able to control appointments. Madison also warned that vesting the appointment power solely in the Senate would unfairly advantage the northern states.[325]

Madison argued instead for an appointment mechanism—first suggested by Gorham of Massachusetts and partially modeled on his state's constitution—that combined the executive with the Senate, which would ensure that both the people and the states played a role. Moreover, such a mechanism "would unite the advantage of responsibility in the executive with the security afforded in the second branch against any incautious or corrupt nomination." Madison initially and tentatively suggested that the concurrence of only one-third of the Senate be required to confirm presidential nominees. Mason objected that this arrangement would essentially amount to presidential appointment. Others suggested reversing Madison's proposal, so that the Senate would make the nomination and the president have the power to veto it. Wilson continued to hold out against any involvement whatsoever of the Senate in the appointment process: "Good laws are of no effect without a good executive, and there can be no good executive without a responsible appointment of officers to execute. Responsibility is in a manner destroyed by such an agency of the Senate."[326]

After their victory in the Connecticut Compromise, small-state delegates such as Luther Martin of Maryland were, unsurprisingly, "strenuous for an appointment by the second branch." Several days after that compromise passed, the convention voted by six states to three—the largest states dissenting—to reaffirm its earlier decision in favor of Senate appointment of judges. Accordingly, the Committee of Detail report in early August awarded the power of appointing Supreme Court judges—and ambassadors—to the Senate. The president would appoint only commissioned military officers and those federal officeholders whose appointments were not otherwise provided for in the Constitution.[327]

Later in the convention, however, a different committee that proved more favorable to the interests of the large states proposed that the president, "with the advice and consent of the Senate," be empowered to appoint ambassadors, other public ministers, Supreme Court judges, and all other federal officers whose appointments were not otherwise provided for in the Constitution. With minor changes, this was the arrangement that the convention ultimately approved.[328]

To guard against abuses of the appointment power, the delegates considered limitations upon the eligibility of members of Congress for appointment to other federal offices. The delegates easily agreed to bar members of Congress from simultaneously holding other federal offices. But they disagreed about whether this ineligibility should apply—and, if so, for how long—to members of Congress who vacated their legislative offices.[329]

The convention initially agreed to make members of Congress ineligible for appointment to other federal offices for one year after the expiration of the term for which they had been elected. Invoking examples of men who had run for seats in the British House of Commons with the purpose only of securing lucrative executive offices for themselves, Butler defended this ineligibility provision as a necessary "precaution against intrigue." Mason agreed that the convention must carefully guard against "corruption" of the appointment power, and he called the ineligibility provision "the corner-stone on which our liberties depend." Without such a restriction, Mason warned, Congress would "multiply offices in order to fill them," and the United States would end up with "ambassadors to every petty state in Europe—the little republic of St. Marino not excepted."[330]

However, other delegates warned that imposing such restrictions on the eligibility of members of Congress for appointment to federal office would, in King's words, "discourage merit." Hamilton argued that in order to interest men in public service, it was necessary to appeal to their "passions," not simply to motives of "pure patriotism." Morris went even further, noting the dangers of denying the wealthy an inducement to participate in government in a manner consistent with "the pursuit of honor and profit." Barring their way by law would simply induce them to "proceed in some left-handed way." Deferring to such arguments, the convention eventually dropped the one-year restriction.[331]

Madison wanted to further narrow this ineligibility provision to cover only federal offices created during the tenure of the member of Congress to be appointed—and also to existing offices for which the salaries had been increased during the member's tenure. He warned that the "impulse to the legislative service" was "too feeble" without the lure of appointment to executive office. Unduly restricting eligibility for such appointments would discourage the best men from serving in the national legislature; in Virginia, Madison said, an eligibility restriction had resulted in "too great success to unfit characters." The problem might be even worse at the national level, he observed, where the sacrifices required for legislative service would be greater. Wilson agreed that the convention "ought not to shut the door of promotion against the great characters in the public councils."[332]

Mason strongly opposed Madison's efforts to dilute the ineligibility provision: "[I]f we do not provide against corruption, our government will soon be at an end." Gerry, too, warned that by narrowing the disqualification, the convention risked destroying the distinction between the branches "by admitting the legislators to share in the executive or to be too much influenced by the executive in looking up to him for offices." In the end, however, the convention endorsed Madison's proposal to limit the ineligibility clause to offices created—or for which the salaries had been increased—during the term for which the appointee had been elected to Congress.[333]

As we have just seen, the convention discussed at length the president's powers to veto laws and to make appointments to federal office; it also easily agreed that the president would "carry into execution the national laws." The Committee of Detail proposed conferring several additional powers on the executive that had not been discussed by the delegates: providing information regarding the state of the union, recommending laws to Congress, receiving ambassadors, serving as commander-in-chief of the armed forces, calling Congress into special session on extraordinary occasions, and granting pardons (although not as a bar to impeachment). Toward the end of the convention, a different committee added to the executive's powers that of making treaties, with the advice and consent of the Senate.[334]

One traditional executive power that most delegates did not wish the president to exercise was that over war and peace. The Virginia Plan provided that the federal executive, among other things, would "enjoy the executive rights vested in Congress by the Confederation," and the Articles explicitly conferred upon Congress "the sole and exclusive right and power of determining on peace and war." When the delegates first debated the powers of the executive, Charles Pinckney, while insisting that he favored a "vigorous executive," warned against granting the power to determine upon peace and war, which would convert the executive into "a monarchy." In a much later debate, Gerry agreed, stating that he had "never expected to hear in a republic a motion to empower the executive alone to declare war." Even Wilson, one of the strongest proponents of executive power at the convention, agreed that the power over war and peace, even though it had been traditionally treated as a prerogative of the Crown, should be vested in Congress, not the president.[335]

Still, when the convention debated Congress's power to "make war," several delegates objected that legislative proceedings were too slow for effective war making. Madison suggested that they substitute the power to "declare" war for the power to "make" it, which would implicitly leave to the executive "the power to repel sudden attacks" (as well as the power, as commander-in-chief, to determine how to fight a war declared by Congress). The convention approved that change by a margin of seven states to two.[336]

How the powerful unitary executive the convention was designing should be selected was a matter of great concern. Wilson called it "in truth the most difficult of all on which we have had to decide," and he noted how "greatly divided" the convention was on the subject. Part of the complication was that the method of selection could not reasonably be disassociated from the questions of how long the executive's tenure in office would be and whether he would be eligible for multiple terms.[337]

The Virginia Plan, modeled in this regard upon a majority of state constitutions, proposed that the federal executive be selected by the federal legislature and that he be ineligible for re-election. Barring re-election would liberate the executive from dependency on whichever institution was responsible for electing him; a lengthy term of office would have much the same effect. Thus, for example, Mason favored an executive term of at least seven years and a bar on re-election, which would obviate the "temptation on the side of the executive to intrigue with the legislature for a reappointment." In addition, Mason considered it "the very palladium of civil liberty" that the great officers of state, including the executive, should "at fixed periods return to that mass from which they were at first taken, in order that they may feel and respect those rights and interests which are again to be personally valuable to them." Both Randolph and Rutledge likewise emphasized that ineligibility for re-election would foster the executive's independence from Congress (which they wanted to be the institution to appoint him). Wilson detected a consensus among the delegates that if Congress were to select the executive, then he must be made ineligible for re-election. In the first week of deliberations, the convention easily agreed that the executive would be selected by Congress for a seven-year term, without eligibility for re-election.[338]

However, some delegates continued to raise objections to this scheme for selecting the executive. Making the executive ineligible for re-election, Morris warned, would tend "to destroy the great motive to good behavior, the hope of being rewarded by a reappointment." Imposing such a restriction on the executive might be dangerous because, by shutting "the civil road to glory, . . . he may be compelled to seek it by the sword." In addition, Morris argued that barring re-eligibility would tempt the executive "to make the most of the short space of time allotted him to accumulate wealth and provide for his friends." Ineligibility for re-election would also deny the country an experienced executive and might make the executive less tenacious about preserving the prerogatives of his office from congressional encroachment. Finally, Ellsworth added the argument that "the most eminent characters" might not seek the office "if they foresee a necessary degradation at a fixed period."[339]

Madison, who had initially favored congressional selection of the executive, later identified "insuperable objections" to that approach. If it was "essential to the preservation of liberty" that the great powers of government be independently exercised by three different branches, then it made little sense to render the executive dependent on Congress for his selection. Moreover, the executive would enforce and interpret laws just like the judiciary, which everyone seemed to agree ought to be independent of the legislature. Even if the executive's ineligibility for re-election ameliorated concerns about his dependence on the legislature that had selected him, this method of selection would still "agitate and divide the legislature so much that the public interest would materially suffer by it." Madison also warned that "[m]inisters of foreign powers" would seek to influence Congress's choice of an executive.[340]

Butler largely agreed with Madison, noting that the two great evils to be avoided in selecting the executive were "cabal at home and influence from abroad," and he thought that averting either would be difficult if Congress chose the executive. Morris, too, worried that legislative selection of the executive would pose a "danger of intrigue and faction," and he insisted on the "indispensable necessity of making the executive independent of the legislature." By contrast, Sherman favored congressional selection precisely because he wanted the executive to be "absolutely dependent" on Congress. An executive independent of the legislature was, in his view, the "very essence of tyranny."[341]

One way to solve the problem of executive dependence on the legislature would be to vest the power of selecting the executive in the people—either directly or indirectly through the filter of electors. Invoking the Massachusetts and New York constitutions to confirm its feasibility, Wilson strongly advocated popular participation in the selection of the executive, which would "produce more confidence among the people in the first magistrate than an election by the national legislature." Morris agreed, arguing that the people would never fail "to prefer some man of distinguished character or services"—a man "of continental reputation." Madison also agreed that, all things considered, election by the people would be "the fittest" method of selecting the executive.[342]

Making the executive dependent upon the people for election seemed to some delegates to cultivate the right sort of dependency, but others raised three objections to popular election. First, most of the delegates did not trust the people with such an important task. Gerry called election of the executive by the people "radically vicious" because of their "ignorance," and he warned that popular election, in practice, would simply throw the choice into the hands of a well-organized cabal, such as the Order of the Cincinnati. Charles Pinckney agreed that selection by the people would devolve into "a few active and designing men" choosing the executive. Mason declared that "it would be as unnatural to refer the choice of a proper character for chief magistrate to the people, as it would be to refer a trial of colors to a blind man." The vast expanse of the country rendered "it impossible that the people can have the requisite capacity to judge of the respective pretensions of the candidates."[343]

Second, as Sherman explained, because the people would "never be sufficiently informed" about candidates from other states, they would "generally vote for some man in their own state," which would mean that "the largest state will have the best chance for the appointment." Even Madison agreed that one valid argument against popular election of the executive was that the people would be disposed "to prefer a citizen of their own state" and thus the smaller states would be disadvantaged. Hugh Williamson of North Carolina considered this the principal objection to direct popular election of the executive.[344]

Third, as Madison noted, direct popular election of the executive would pose a "serious" difficulty for southerners because their slaves would count for nothing in this method of selection, thus significantly diminishing southern influence upon the selection of the executive. However, declaring that "local considerations" such as this "must give way to the general interest," Madison announced that, as a southerner, he "was willing to make the sacrifice." Yet few other southern delegates were prepared to do so. For these three reasons, the proposal for direct popular election of the executive, which Wilson had described from the outset as "chimerical," was rejected by an overwhelming margin of nine states to one.[345]

Several delegates proposed an alternative means of solving the dependency problem—namely, giving the executive tenure during good behavior, thus liberating him from any dependence on the appointing institution. Insisting that no good executive "could be established on republican principles," Hamilton argued that the British king was the only sound model for the American executive and that an executive vested with lifetime tenure or at least tenure during good behavior would provide needed "stability and permanency" to the federal government. Expressing "great pleasure" at such a proposal, Morris declared that "[t]his was the way to get a good government." As long as the executive enjoyed tenure during good behavior, Morris professed not to care how he was elected.[346]

Mason, however, objected that an executive tenured for good behavior was "a softer name only for an executive for life," which was an "easy step" toward a hereditary monarch. Sherman agreed that this proposal was "by no means safe or admissible." Even Madison thought it was going too far.[347]

Yet, surprisingly, at one point in the convention, four state delegations voted in favor of executive tenure during good behavior. However, Madison's notes—which, on this point, he may have revised years later, rendering them possibly unreliable—indicate that this vote probably overstated the amount of genuine support for such an alternative. Madison wrote that the principal purpose of those delegates endorsing tenure during good behavior for the executive was "to alarm those attached to a dependence of the executive on the legislature," so that they would support an appointing institution other than Congress. According to Madison, only three or four *delegates*—not *delegations*—actually supported an executive serving during good behavior.[348]

Whether or not Madison was right, many delegates were plainly prepared to endorse extremely long terms in office for the executive. (Some proponents of long terms may have been genuinely seeking to ameliorate the dependency problem and thus render congressional selection more palatable, while others may have been seeking to frighten supporters of congressional selection into abandoning their position.) Martin proposed an executive term of eleven years, Williamson ten or twelve, and Gerry fifteen or twenty. By contrast, other delegates favored a much shorter term of three or four years, with eligibility for re-election. As already noted, in the first week of the convention, the delegates approved a seven-year term for the executive with a bar on re-election, but in mid-July they endorsed six-year terms with eligibility for re-election. Such a lengthy term would make the executive "firm" and induce "the best men" to undertake such service.[349]

The convention debated incessantly the issue of how to choose the executive. To break the impasse, some delegates proposed alternative selection mechanisms. Gerry, who thought that congressional selection was "radically and incurably wrong," suggested on several occasions that the executive be appointed by either state legislatures or governors. But nationalists strongly opposed such proposals. Randolph objected that a "national executive thus chosen will not be likely to defend with becoming vigilance and firmness the

national rights against state encroachments." Observing that state legislatures "had betrayed a strong propensity to a variety of pernicious measures,"
Madison worried that a federal executive appointed by state legislators or executives would not be able to check Congress if it became "infected with a
similar propensity."[350]

Delegates favoring congressional selection of the executive proposed
mechanisms to ameliorate the formidable dependency objection. Ellsworth
suggested that Congress generally choose the executive, but that when one
of the candidates for that office was the incumbent, the selection should be
made instead by electors chosen by state legislatures. Such a method would
enable a "deserving magistrate" to be re-elected without creating dependency
on Congress. Charles Pinckney suggested that Congress choose the executive
but that eligibility for service be restricted to no more than six years in every
twelve. Mason endorsed this proposal as fostering executive independence
while retaining the advantages of possible future service. Morris, however,
objected that mandatory rotation in office would not avoid the problems of
"intrigue and dependence."[351]

With Gerry noting that "[w]e seem to be entirely at a loss on this head," the
delegates were so desperate for a solution that Wilson proposed, as a method
of executive selection, choosing by lot a small number of national legislators
to serve as electors to choose the executive. Wilson admitted that this was not
"a digested idea and might be liable to strong objections," but Morris declared
that "[i]t would be better that chance should decide than intrigue." On numerous occasions, the delegates, after much debate, simply reaffirmed their original choice that Congress select the president for a term of seven years without
eligibility for re-election.[352]

Under this assumption that Congress would select the executive, delegates
from small states and large states naturally disagreed about whether the two
houses should vote separately or by joint ballot. Small-state delegates opposed
a joint ballot, which would result in their equal voting power in the Senate
being swamped by the large states' advantage in the much more numerous
House. Observing that "[t]he argument that the small states should not put
their hands into the pockets of the large ones did not apply" when selecting
the president, David Brearley of New Jersey argued for a separate ballot. In
response, large-state delegates noted the abstract problem that separate ballots
invited conflict and standoffs between the branches and also argued that their
population advantage ought to count for something in selecting the president.
The convention then voted by seven states to four in favor of Congress's selecting the president by joint ballot.[353]

Late in the convention, a grand committee appointed to tackle various unresolved issues endorsed a proposal first made by Wilson, which the

convention had already rejected on multiple occasions: The president would be chosen by special electors, whose appointment would be made according to a method specified by state legislatures. Because the body of electors would have no perpetual life, it would have no particular interests to defend. A president selected in this fashion would not be dependent upon the institution selecting him.[354]

Moreover, the electors would presumably be prominent people of superior knowledge and independence. This is what inclined the delegates to consider entrusting them with a task as important as choosing the president (although dissenting delegates denied that "first characters" or "the most respectable citizens" would be interested in holding a transitory position such as that of presidential elector). The report of the Committee on Unfinished Parts also specified that electors would cast ballots in their home states in order to preclude, in Morris's words, "the great evil of cabal." Requiring that electors in the different states meet simultaneously throughout the country made it "impossible to corrupt them." Moreover, the use of electors in place of direct popular election obviated the problem of slaves counting for nothing, which would have been disqualifying from the southerners' perspective. The electoral college system was ingenious, though Caleb Strong objected that it would "make the government too complex."[355]

The issue of how to apportion presidential electors naturally provoked disagreement between delegations from large and small states. When the issue was discussed earlier in the convention, at a time when the delegates were considering an electoral college system for choosing the president, small-state delegates had favored a relatively flat distribution, in which the small states received one elector and no large state more than three. Unsurprisingly, large-state delegates had thought their states deserved even greater influence in choosing the president. Connecticut delegate Ellsworth objected to giving large states extra clout in the electoral college, which he said their citizens would probably use simply to prefer candidates from their own states.[356]

The grand committee's report proposed a compromise on the apportionment of the electoral college: Each state's number of presidential electors would equal its number of congressional representatives plus its two senators. Small states would fare better than if the apportionment had been based strictly upon population, yet large states still derived a substantial advantage from their greater populations, as reflected in their number of congressional representatives. Thus, for example, Virginia would outnumber Delaware by ten to one in the first House but only by twelve to three in the first electoral college. Because the number of electors depended partly on a state's number of congressional representatives, the power of southern states in the electoral college would reflect their slave populations (because five slaves were counted the same as three free persons for purposes of apportioning the House of Representatives, as we shall see in chapter 4).[357]

In addition, the committee proposed that no candidate could be elected president without securing the votes of a majority of the electors appointed. If no candidate received such a majority, then the Senate would choose the president from among the top five vote getters. Convention delegates mostly assumed that presidential candidates would rarely win outright majorities in the electoral college—at least once Washington had ceased to be a candidate. The vast geographic scope of the country, combined with the relatively primitive state of transportation and communication, would prevent presidential candidates from becoming widely known or coordinating their campaigns across states—especially in the absence of national political parties, which the delegates did not assume would exist. Thus, Charles Pinckney protested that the electors would "not have sufficient knowledge of the fittest men and will be swayed by an attachment to the eminent men of their respective states," and Mason predicted that "nineteen times in twenty the president would be chosen by the Senate."[358]

Morris explained that the reason the committee had chosen the Senate as the institution to select the president when the electoral college vote failed to produce a majority was to ensure that the president would owe his appointment to fewer people. But the choice of the Senate was also clearly a sop to the small states, whose influence would be much greater in the Senate than in the House. In essence, the Senate, in which small states would exercise equal clout, would choose the president from among the candidates "nominated" by the electoral college, in which the large states would exercise greater influence.[359]

Accordingly, some large-state delegates objected to the committee's proposal and suggested eliminating the requirement that a presidential candidate receive the votes of a majority of the electors in order to be elected. Yet small-state delegates naturally resisted a proposal that would have ordinarily allowed the electors from just a few of the large states to pick the president by themselves, and it was easily defeated. The convention then also rejected a motion by Madison to substitute "one-third" for "a majority" as the requirement for the candidate winning the most votes in the electoral college to be elected president.[360]

As just noted, according to the committee's proposal, the Senate's choice would be made from among the top five vote getters in the electoral college. The number five was a compromise between the preference of a large-state delegate such as Mason, who suggested limiting the list to three, and that of a small-state delegate such as Sherman, who would have preferred expanding it to seven or even thirteen candidates. Madison expressed concern that if the president were to be chosen from a list as long as even five vote getters, "the attention of the electors would be turned too much to making candidates instead of giving their votes in order to [make] a definitive choice."[361]

Several delegates objected to the Senate's being made the de facto selector of the president on the grounds that, under the committee proposal, the Senate and the executive were also now slated to jointly exercise the powers of appointment and treaty making. For example, Wilson protested that if the Senate were to make the ultimate choice of the president, he "will not be the man of the people as he ought to be, but the minion of the Senate." Mason warned that "if a coalition should be established between these two branches, they will be able to subvert the Constitution." Williamson objected that referring the appointment of the president to the Senate "lays a certain foundation for corruption and aristocracy"—a view with which Randolph concurred.[362]

In addition, because the committee report had also assigned the Senate the responsibility of trying impeachments of the president—as discussed momentarily—some delegates expressed concerns about giving the Senate such a large potential role in selecting the president. Wilson warned that if the Senate chose the president, had the power to remove him through the trial of an impeachment, and shared with him authority over appointments and treaty making, then powers that ought to be distributed among different branches were being "combined and blended in the Senate." Moreover, after the Connecticut Compromise, large-state delegates were of course generally opposed to any expansion of the powers of the Senate.[363]

Thus, Wilson and other large-state delegates proposed that "the legislature" rather than just the Senate choose the president from among the top vote getters when no candidate received the votes of a majority of the appointed electors. Sherman suggested that the House—rather than the Senate alone or both houses of Congress together—should choose the president in such situations. Because Sherman proposed that the House, when selecting the president, vote by delegation rather than as individual representatives, small-state influence would be preserved, while "the aristocratic influence of the Senate" would be eliminated. The convention then overwhelmingly approved the substitution of the House for the Senate. Madison later explained that, in addition to other considerations, the House was thought safer "on account of the greater number of its members," which would "present greater obstacles to corruption than the Senate with its paucity of members."[364]

Lastly on the issue of selecting the president, the Committee on Unfinished Parts provided that each elector would cast two votes for president, one of which had to be for a candidate from a state other than the elector's. (Before the Twelfth Amendment was enacted in 1804, the electors' two votes were not designated specifically for "president" and "vice president"; they simply cast two ballots, and the person receiving the highest number of votes from the electors, once the president had been chosen, became the vice president.) The delegates assumed that requiring electors to cast one vote for a candidate not from their home state would enhance the chances of small-state candidates making the top-five list, because electors from large states would be reluctant to cast their second ballots for candidates from other large states for fear of inadvertently putting one of them over the top.[365]

Observing that the committee had created the office of vice president "only for the sake of a valuable mode of election which required two to be chosen at the same time," Williamson objected that "such an officer as the vice president was not wanted." However, to ensure that the vice president would not "be without employment," as Sherman explained, the committee had proposed that he be made ex officio president of the Senate. Because of "the close intimacy that must subsist between the president and vice president," Gerry warned that putting the vice president in charge of the Senate was no different from placing the president in charge, which would "destroy the independence of the legislature." Mason agreed that the convention should not excessively intermingle the legislative and executive departments.[366]

In response to this, Morris, observing that no "heir apparent . . . ever loved his father," denied that the president and vice president were likely to see eye to eye on most issues. Moreover, noting that the president of the Senate was likely to become the temporary successor of a president displaced from office regardless of whether or not he was denominated the vice president, Morris wondered what difference his title would make. The convention then voted in favor of the vice president's serving as ex officio president of the Senate.[367]

Having at last chosen a mode of appointment that would make the president independent of Congress, the convention could now consider on its own merits whether he should be eligible for re-election. The Committee on Unfinished Parts eliminated the bar on the president's re-election, which in turn led it to shorten the term in office to four years—which was still longer than the term authorized in state constitutions for governors, who exercised far less substantial powers than would the president. Although some delegates continued to prefer a longer term of six or seven years without eligibility for re-election, the convention endorsed the committee's proposal.[368]

In addition to making the president eligible for re-election, the convention omitted any provision for his mandatory rotation in office, which a majority of state constitutions imposed upon governors on the principle, as stated in the Maryland constitution of 1776, that "a long continuance in the first executive departments of power or trust is dangerous to liberty." Earlier in the convention, Franklin had argued strongly for mandatory rotation in the executive office, denying that "returning to the mass of the people was degrading

[to] the magistrate" and insisting that "[i]n free governments, the rulers are the servants and the people their superiors and sovereigns." Yet the convention placed no barrier to presidents being re-elected for the rest of their lives.[369]

The degree of presidential independence would be a function not only of the mechanism for appointment but also of that for removal: Which institution would have responsibility for removing an unfit president from office, and what should the standard for removal be? Most of the delegates agreed with Mason that "some mode of displacing an unfit magistrate is . . . indispensable." While the Virginia Plan made no specific reference to removing a president from office, it did propose generally that the national judiciary be granted jurisdiction over "impeachments of any national officers," without specifying a substantive standard for impeachment. In the first week of the convention, Dickinson proposed that the president be removable—without any specific allegation of malfeasance being required—by Congress, acting in response to a request from a majority of state legislatures. Similarly, the New Jersey Plan provided that the executive would be removable by Congress on application by a majority of state executives.[370]

Unsurprisingly, Sherman, who viewed the executive as simply the instrument of the legislature, argued that Congress should be able to remove the president "at pleasure." By contrast, Mason "opposed decidedly" making the executive "the mere creature of the legislature." Nationalists such as Madison and Wilson opposed authorizing the states to play a role in removing presidents whose administrations might simply have become unpopular without their having engaged in any malfeasance. They also objected to small states' exercising the same influence in that removal process as large ones.[371]

The convention overwhelmingly rejected Dickinson's proposal for removal of the president by congressional "address" and instead approved removal through "impeachment and conviction* of malpractice or neglect of duty." When the delegates later returned to the issue, some advocates of a strong executive argued against making the president impeachable at all. Concerned that providing for impeachment would "render the executive dependent on those who are to impeach," Morris preferred that the president be given a short term in office, rather than that he be made impeachable. Making his ministers impeachable, Morris argued, would be sufficient security against bad executive behavior. Charles Pinckney likewise worried that the legislature would hold impeachment over the president's head and "effectually destroy his independence," thus practically nullifying his authority to veto legislation. Rufus

---

* An impeachment is roughly the equivalent of a grand jury indictment. Conviction on the impeachment is what removes an official from public office (and, in some systems, results in the imposition of additional penalties).

King argued that while impeachment was necessary for federal judges, who would enjoy tenure during good behavior, no "intermediate trial by impeachment" was necessary for a president who would hold only a limited term in office and thus would be "tried for his behavior by his electors, who would continue or discontinue him in trust according to the manner in which he had discharged it."[372]

However, most of the delegates—even those favoring a very strong executive, such as Wilson—believed that the president ought to be impeachable. William Davie of North Carolina declared that impeachment was "essential security for the good behavior of the executive." Mason and Randolph considered it crucial that nobody—not even the president—be deemed above the law. Franklin warned that if the president could not be impeached, then there would be "recourse . . . to assassination." Madison thought it indispensable that some provision be made for removing a president based on "incapacity, negligence or perfidy." Limiting the president's term in office was not sufficient, as he might lose capacity, pervert his administration, or betray his trust to foreign powers. For a unitary executive to become incapacitated or corrupt, Madison warned, could be "fatal to the republic" without some provision for his removal from office.[373]

After this debate, the convention voted by eight states to two to make the president impeachable. However, the delegates encountered greater difficulty in figuring out which institution should be responsible for trying impeachments and what the substantive standard for impeachment should be. Empowering the two houses of Congress to impeach and remove a president from office would reduce the president's ability to exercise a powerful check upon Congress. Noting the desirability of "excluding as much as possible the influence of the legislature from the business," Randolph proposed empowering a tribunal composed of state judges to try impeachments against the president. The Committee of Detail proposed that the House be given the power to impeach the president and the US Supreme Court the power to try the impeachment and thus determine whether he should be removed from office.[374]

In early September, the Committee on Unfinished Parts, which designed the electoral college system for selecting the president, designated the Senate rather than the Supreme Court as the adjudicator of impeachments. With Congress denied direct control over the selection of the president, empowering the House to impeach him and the Senate to remove him from office seemed less problematic.[375]

However, Madison, who had grown disillusioned with the Senate as a result of the Connecticut Compromise, argued that making the president removable by the Senate would render him "improperly dependent." Madison preferred that the power to try an impeachment of the president be restored to the Supreme Court. Charles Pinckney, who shared Madison's concern about presidential dependency, warned that the two houses of Congress might conspire against the president if he vetoed "a favorite law."[376]

In response to Madison's proposal, Morris objected that the Supreme Court was an improper body to try impeachments of the president. Because the number of justices was likely to be small, they might too easily be "warped or corrupted." He also denied that senators, while under oath, were likely to find a president guilty of crimes that he had not committed. Sherman, who as a small-state delegate may have had an ulterior motive for preferring the Senate, noted the impropriety of justices appointed by a president trying his impeachment. The convention then overwhelmingly rejected Madison's motion to shift the power of trying impeachments of the president from the Senate back to the Supreme Court. Only the delegations of the two largest states, Virginia and Pennsylvania, voted in favor of this motion.[377]

The substantive standard for impeachment arguably mattered as much as the institution responsible for applying it. Although the convention had agreed early on upon a standard of "malpractice or neglect of duty" for impeachment, some delegates worried that such a low threshold for impeachment would render the president too dependent upon the institutions exercising the powers to impeach and remove him from office. Thus, the Committee of Detail substituted a more onerous standard of "treason, bribery, or corruption." Because the president would possess neither a hereditary nor a life interest in the office, even Morris, who favored a very strong executive, conceded that the president might prove susceptible to being bribed to betray his trust.[378]

After the Committee of Unfinished Parts narrowed the grounds for impeachment to just treason and bribery, Mason objected that a president could commit many "great and dangerous offenses," including subversion of the Constitution, that still would not qualify as grounds for removal under that restrictive standard. Thus, he proposed adding "maladministration" to the list of impeachable offenses. When Madison objected that "[s]o vague a term will be equivalent to a tenure during pleasure of the Senate," Mason agreed to substitute "other high crimes and misdemeanors against the State" as a supplement to treason and bribery. The convention approved the change, though Mason's substituted language was vague enough to elicit profound political disagreement during the impeachment trials of Presidents Andrew Johnson in 1868 and Bill Clinton in 1999.[379]

In sum, the Philadelphia convention created an extraordinarily powerful executive, especially given that just a decade earlier Americans had felt so aggrieved by the abuses of the British king that they eviscerated state executives in the constitutions they wrote during the Revolution. Unlike most state governors, the president would have a veto power and the predominant share of the appointment power. He would also be commander-in-chief of the armed forces and have the powers to negotiate treaties and pardon criminals. Through his State of the Union address and his duty to recommend to Congress such measures as he judged necessary and expedient, the president would participate in the formation of national policy.[380]

Moreover, the president vested with such powers would be a unitary executive and, unlike state governors, he could act without the constraint of an executive council. He would have a longer term in office than any of the state executives, and unlike most of them, he would not be subject to mandatory rotation in office. Had the delegates not been faced with "the genius of the people" as a constraint on ratification, many of them would have supported tenure during good behavior for the president and empowering him with an absolute veto (rather than one subject to congressional override). As Pierce Butler explained after the convention, the delegates probably would not have created such a powerful and independent executive "had not many of the members cast their eyes towards General Washington as president and shaped their ideas of the powers to be given to a president by their opinions of his virtue."[381]

Interpreting the Convention

The convention finished its work on September 17, 1787. At this point, Franklin called upon each of the forty-one delegates present* who still had objections to the Constitution to "doubt a little his own infallibility" and agree to "put his name to this instrument" in order "to make manifest our unanimity." Professing high regard for Randolph, who two days earlier had made it clear he was unlikely to sign, Franklin urged him to join the majority to "prevent the great mischief which the refusal of his name might produce." Hamilton seconded the importance of unanimity: "A few characters of consequence, by opposing or even refusing to sign the Constitution, might do infinite mischief by kindling the latent sparks which lurk under an enthusiasm in favor of the convention which may soon subside."[382]

Other delegates joined these appeals for unanimity. Morris emphasized that despite his own objections, he considered the Constitution "the best that was to be attained," and he would "take it with all its faults." Likewise confessing that he opposed "many parts" of the system, James McHenry of Maryland, who had been a surgeon in the Continental Army and then an assistant secretary to

---

* Of those forty-one delegates present, three refused to sign the Constitution. Dickinson was ill and had asked Read to sign for him, which is why there are thirty-nine signatures on the document.

General Washington, explained that he would sign because "I distrust my own judgment, especially as it is opposite to the opinion of a majority of gentlemen whose abilities and patriotism are of the first cast," and because alterations could be obtained through the amendment process. To ameliorate the concerns of those still harboring doubts, the convention agreed to offer individual delegates the alternative of simply signing a letter announcing that the state *delegations* were unanimous in approving the Constitution. That option would have enabled dissenting delegates to soothe their consciences while preserving some veneer of unanimity—at the cost of disingenuousness.[383]

Despite such entreaties, though, three delegates—Gerry, Mason, and Randolph—remained solid in their opposition. Acknowledging the gravity of his decision not to sign the Constitution, Randolph insisted that it was "dictated by his conscience." He also emphasized that his refusal to sign did not mean that he would actively oppose ratification—only that he was keeping "himself free to be governed by his duty as it should be prescribed by his future judgment." Insisting that signing the proposed letter would not be meaningfully different from signing the Constitution, these three dissenting delegates declined to embrace the compromise solution that had been offered to them.[384]

Mason and Randolph were Virginians who felt that their state had been unjustly treated in both the Connecticut Compromise and the deal made between the states of the Deep South and New England involving the foreign slave trade and Congress's power to regulate commerce (to be discussed in chapter 4). Gerry, from Massachusetts, feared that the convention had veered too far in the direction of aristocracy. Critics would deride him as a "Grumbletonian" who objected to everything in the Constitution that he himself had not proposed. All three of the dissenters would play prominent roles in the ratifying contest—discussed in chapter 6—and we shall consider their more detailed objections to the Constitution there.[385]

Despite the three dissenters, the convention had achieved nearly unanimous support for a constitution that was especially striking in two ways. First, it dramatically expanded the power of the federal government. Second, it shielded that government in a variety of ways from much of the populist political pressure that state governments had proved susceptible to in the mid-1780s.

The extent to which the convention centralized power in the hands of the federal government was extraordinary, given the baseline against which the delegates were operating. Under the Articles of Confederation, Congress could not impose any taxes, regulate foreign or interstate commerce, or enforce federal supremacy even in spheres that plainly lay within its delegated powers.

Although the most-nationalist delegates did not win on every issue at the convention—far from it—the Constitution in its nationalism is a stark

Figure 3.10 Signing of the Constitution, by Howard Chandler Christy. (Architect of
the Capitol)

contrast with the Articles. The Constitution bestows upon Congress virtually unlimited powers to tax, raise armies and navies, and regulate commerce. Without opposition, the convention explicitly granted Congress
implied powers through the Necessary and Proper Clause. The Supremacy
Clause and a federal court system—the Constitution mandates a supreme
court and authorizes Congress to create lower federal courts—provided,
respectively, a theoretical statement of federal supremacy and a practical
mechanism for enforcing it. Article I, Section 10, bars states from enacting
the sort of paper money and debtor relief legislation that had proliferated in
the mid-1780s.

Even with regard to an issue on which the nationalists ostensibly lost—the
method of choosing senators—they were able to design institutional features
that significantly ameliorated the scope of their defeat. Thus, while state legislatures would pick senators, they were denied the power to recall them during
their lengthy terms in office, to instruct them, or to pay their salaries. On other
issues, the convention preserved some influence for the states while nonetheless empowering the federal government to trump state choices. States would
initially set the times, places, and manner of congressional elections, but their
decisions were subject to congressional override. States would train and select
officers for their militias, but their militias would be subject to the discipline
imposed by Congress and to Congress's unfettered power to call them into
federal service. In sum, the nationalizing features of the Constitution were

such that ratification would prove difficult in a nation where most citizens continued to regard their states as their countries.[386]

Had the delegates not been forced to make concessions to political realities, the document they drafted in Philadelphia might have been even more nationalist. At the convention, delegates repeatedly observed that the Constitution they were designing must be tailored to what the nation would ratify. As Gerry explained, "[I]t was necessary to consider what the people would approve." Madison agreed that they must not pursue what was "unattainable."[387]

In his famous speech of June 18, Hamilton had told the convention that two sovereignties could not coexist within the same geographic limits. History revealed that "all federal governments are weak and distracted," Hamilton explained, and he doubted that the federal government they were creating could "long exist when opposed by such a weighty rival" as the state governments. Hamilton concluded that the convention "must establish a general and national government, completely sovereign, and annihilate the state distinctions and state operations." However, because he did not wish "to shock the public opinion" by proposing an abolition of the state governments, Hamilton suggested instead that the Constitution empower the federal government to appoint state governors, who would be vested with the authority to veto all state legislation in order to prevent conflicts with federal law.[388]

Other delegates also evinced a preference for abolishing the states if doing so had been politically feasible. Read thought that to achieve a "good general government," the states "must be done away" with and united "into one great society." Butler agreed with Read about "abolishing the state legislatures and becoming one nation instead of a confederation of republics," provided that the South's slaves counted sufficiently in apportioning representation in the national legislature. While King "doubted much the practicability of annihilating the states," he agreed "that much of their power ought to be taken from them." Dickinson expressed alarm that "some gentlemen" seemed inclined to abolish the state governments.[389]

Although Madison expressed no desire to abolish the states, he denied that they "possessed the essential rights of sovereignty," and he insisted that they "ought to be placed under the control of the general government—at least as much as they formerly were under the King and British Parliament." As we have seen, a fundamental feature of Madison's constitutional design was empowering Congress to veto state legislation. Charles Pinckney, who wanted to expand the limited federal veto proposed in the Virginia Plan to cover *all* state laws, agreed that the states long ago had abandoned their sovereignty, and he thought that they should retain no more power than that over "mere local legislation." Gouverneur Morris wanted to create a secretary of domestic affairs, whose jurisdiction would include matters of police, the state of agriculture and manufacturing, the building of roads and improving of navigation, and the facilitating of communications within the nation. Madison proposed that Congress be empowered to grant charters of incorporation and to establish a national university, and Pinckney wanted to grant Congress the power to subsidize the promotion of agriculture, trade, and manufacturing. All these proposals would have entailed a vast expansion of Congress's power, relative to what it was under the Articles.[390]

Even the three delegates who refused to sign the Constitution had been strongly nationalist—at least on certain issues—during much of the convention. Randolph, of course, had introduced the extremely nationalist Virginia Plan. Mason, according to Madison's postconvention account, had supported in principle the federal veto and even the idea of the national government's appointing state governors. Although Gerry did not support the veto, he eagerly embraced the ban on state debtor relief laws and emissions of paper money contained in Article I, Section 10. While the views of convention delegates fell along a spectrum, their overall predilection was stunningly nationalist when compared with the views of most ordinary Americans in 1787 (which is one reason that ratification was such a closely contested affair, as we shall see in chapter 6).[391]*

* Much later in life, Madison strenuously denied that more than two or three members of the Philadelphia convention had favored an "unlimited government founded on a consolidation of the states"—and even those had done so more "theoretically than practically." When notes of the convention taken by New York delegate Robert Yates were published—in 1808 and in 1821—and they portrayed both the convention and Madison in a strongly nationalist light, Madison disparaged the accuracy of Yates's account.

According to Madison, Yates's record consisted of "crude and broken notes" that were warped "to an unfavorable understanding of what was said in opposition to the prejudices felt." Those prejudices were "the strongest feelings of dissatisfaction against the contemplated change in the federal system," which would deprive New York of its ability to extract tax revenue from its neighbors through an impost. Moreover, Madison noted, Yates had been present for only about the first third of the convention (he left Philadelphia on July 10), during which time discussions "were of a more loose and general cast" and "before the rough materials were reduced to the size and shape proper for the contemplated edifice." On numerous occasions, according to Madison, Yates's notes had "totally mistaken what was said by me, or given it in scraps, which, taken without the developments or qualifications accompanying them, had an import essentially different from what was intended."

While Yates's notes had, in fact, been doctored for political reasons when published, it is also true that Madison's own recollections had been warped by political events and imperatives in his postconvention career. In the 1790s, Madison broke with Hamilton over issues such as the national bank, the national government's assumption of the states' war debts, and Hamilton's proposal that the national government subsidize manufacturing through bounties. As Madison and Jefferson came to lead a states' rights party that developed in opposition to the nationalist policies of the administrations of Washington and Adams, Madison's former nationalism proved extremely inconvenient. Then, in the late 1820s and early 1830s, radical states' righters used

The convention's predominant bent was not only nationalist but also strikingly antidemocratic—even by the standards of the time. Supporters of directly accountable republican government had long warned of efforts afoot to limit the people's influence upon government. As we have seen, in 1785, Massachusetts's congressional delegates had opposed a constitutional convention because of concerns that "plans have been artfully laid and vigorously pursued" to change "our republican governments into baleful aristocracies." In 1786, Boston merchant Stephen Higginson had warned that "esteemed great aristocrats," such as Madison and Hamilton, were intending the Annapolis convention to restructure the Confederation, not simply to grant it commercial powers. While the Philadelphia convention was underway, Richard Henry Lee expressed concern that while a departure "from simple democracy" was "indispensably necessary," "the minds of men have been so hurt by the injustice, folly, and wickedness of the state legislatures and state executives that people in general seem ready for anything." Lee hoped "that this tendency to extreme[s] will be so controlled as to secure fully and completely the democratic influence acting within just bounds." As the convention unfolded, Gerry objected that those supporting "a plan of vigorous government" were "pushing the experiment too far," and he warned that "[o]thers of a more democratic cast will oppose it with equal determination."[392]

To be sure, delegates to the Philadelphia convention understood that the legitimacy of the new government they were creating could not, in the words of James Wilson, "long subsist without the confidence of the people." They also appreciated the practical reality that if the people too strenuously opposed the Constitution, then popularly elected ratifying conventions would not approve it.[393]

Yates's account of Madison's supposed nationalism at the Philadelphia convention to discredit Madison's public opposition to their political platform—which included, most notably, a defense of South Carolina's right to nullify the federal tariff and possibly secede from the union.

To bolster his credibility in denying the constitutionality of nullification and secession, Madison deemed it imperative to minimize the extent of his former nationalism. Thus, his late-in-life characterizations of his political thought at the time of the Philadelphia convention and his denials of the convention's nationalist bent must be taken with a substantial grain of salt. For example, Madison's efforts in the early 1830s to downplay his support at the convention for a federal veto of state legislation are plainly unconvincing.

By contrast, historian Lance Banning argues strenuously that Madison was largely consistent throughout his career in the extent of his nationalism. He denies that Madison had ever advocated a very broad range of powers for the national government. Rather, on Banning's view, Madison was determined to ensure that the national government could effectively enforce its will against the states across only a fairly narrow range of powers. Banning also insists that Madison was educated out of whatever broadly nationalist views he might have held—both by the debates in Philadelphia and by the contest over ratification.

Yet the republican form of government can encompass a great deal of varia-tion, and the convention delegates mostly agreed that ordinary people ought to play little role in administering the new federal government. As Hamilton urged at the convention, "[W]e ought to go as far in order to attain stability and permanency as republican principles will admit." A critical objective of the Framers' enterprise was creating a national government that could check the populist impulses of the states, and in this sense, their nationalism and their antidemocratic aspirations were linked. Even the most conservative state constitutions had proved insufficient barriers against democracy. Randolph told the convention that the country's "chief danger arises from the democratic parts of our [state] constitutions," and even Gerry agreed that "[t]he evils we experience flow from the excess of democracy." In response, the delegates wished to create a federal government that would be as detached as possible from public opinion, without forfeiting the label of "republican."[394]

Behind the closed doors of the Philadelphia convention, the delegates outdid one another in the contempt they expressed for democracy. Gerry called democracy "the worst . . . of all political evils." Sherman declared that the people "should have as little to do as may be about the government. They want [i.e., lack] information and are constantly liable to be misled." Hamilton observed that "[t]he voice of the people has been said to be the voice of God; and however generally this maxim has been quoted and believed, it is not true in fact. The people are turbulent and changing; they seldom judge or determine right." On the question of whether public opinion should guide the delegates in designing particular provisions of the Constitution, Madison denigrated the fickleness of the public mind and Randolph declared it "neither incumbent on nor honorable for the convention to sacrifice right and justice" to "popu-lar prejudices." Virtually all the delegates—nationalists and defenders of state sovereignty, representatives of large states and small states, southerners and northerners—could agree upon the proposition that ordinary citizens ought not to have too great a role in governmental affairs.[395]

The delegates' disdain for popular influence on government was manifest in numerous choices they made in designing the Constitution. Because they favored what Madison called a "policy of refining the popular appointments by successive filtrations," they provided for indirect election of presidents and senators. Even with regard to the House, the configuration of which was partly a concession to the political reality of popular participation in ratification of the Constitution, the delegates designed features to increase its detachment from popular opinion. A small House with vast constituencies would loosen connections between representatives and the people. Moreover, the conven-tion gave Congress the power to revise state regulations of the times, places, and manner of federal elections, which could be used to require that House members be selected "at large," thereby further increasing the size of congress-men's constituencies. By omitting to provide for instruction, recall, or man-datory rotation in office, the convention made congressional representatives even more independent of popular opinion.[396]

To further reduce the people's influence on the federal government, the del-egates established terms in office for senators and presidents that were longer than any existing under state constitutions, which often limited even gover-nors and members of the upper houses of the legislatures to annual terms. US senators would serve six-year terms, which would enable them, as Randolph explained, "to provide a cure for the evils under which the United States la-bored," which were to be found "in the turbulence and follies of democracy." Presidents, who it was expected would use their veto power to check Congress if it ever succumbed to populist influence, served four-year terms and were eligible for re-election as long as they lived.[397]

The structure of representation established by the federal Constitution was a significant departure from that existing under most state constitu-tions, which featured annual elections, small constituencies, mandatory rotation in office, and (often) instruction of representatives. In addition to the specific ways in which federal representation was designed to constrain direct democracy, the existence at the federal level of different branches of government with different powers, different constituencies, and different time horizons would make it very difficult to translate populist impulses into federal law.[398]

Again, one might wonder how much more constraining of popular influ-ence the convention would have made the Constitution had it not been for the constraints imposed by the need for ratification. Many delegates plainly would have preferred much longer terms for federal officeholders. Hamilton doubted that even seven-year terms (which the convention at one point had provision-ally agreed upon) would give senators "adequate firmness . . . considering the amazing violence and turbulence of the democratic spirit." On multiple occa-sions, the convention had agreed on a seven-year term for the president. More than a few delegates would have preferred that senators and presidents enjoy tenure during good behavior.[399]

The delegates were disdainful of democracy for a very concrete reason: The populist politics of the mid-1780s, refracted through the relatively democratic state constitutions drafted in the mid-1770s, had pressured most state legisla-tures to issue paper money and enact tax and debt relief legislation, which most elite statesmen abhorred. As Gerry explained to the convention, he "had been taught by experience the danger of the leveling spirit." Most of the delegates agreed, as Butler put it, that "the great object of government" was to protect property, and that the states were doing a lousy job of it.[400]

References to the paper money emissions and debtor relief laws of the mid-1780s cropped up repeatedly as the convention delegates debated a wide variety of issues. Opponents of state legislative selection of senators argued that state legislatures, as the entities responsible for the reviled economic relief measures, hardly could be entrusted with such an important task. The delegates conceived of the Senate generally as an institution to block any populist economic measures that might emanate from the House. They regarded the presidential veto, judicial review, and the proposed federal power to veto state laws as, in significant measure, further checks on such legislation. When the delegates rejected the federal veto, they substituted Article I, Section 10, which explicitly forbids such measures. Unlike some of the other provisions in that section of the Constitution, the bans on state emissions of paper money and the making of anything but gold or silver as legal tender in payment of debts were rendered absolute, rather than subject to Congress's approval. The convention delegates passed up few opportunities to reiterate what Mason called their "mortal hatred to paper money" and to ensure that the Constitution would squelch it.[401]

As we shall see in chapter 6, the nationalist and democracy-constraining features of the Constitution made it extremely controversial with the American people, thus resulting in a closely fought ratifying contest. Why was the convention so much more nationalist and antidemocratic than the country as a whole? Why, in the words of one leading critic of the Constitution, "Federal Farmer," were "the democratic and aristocratic parts of the community" so disproportionately represented in Philadelphia?[402]

First, the process by which delegates were selected to represent their states in Philadelphia probably ensured that nationalist and antipopulist views would be overrepresented. In every state but South Carolina—where the governor performed the task—state legislatures chose the delegates to represent their states at the convention. As Rutledge stated in Philadelphia, "[i]f this convention had been chosen by the people in districts," very different "characters would have been preferred."[403]

State legislatures were apt to choose prominent citizens to represent their states at a national convention, and these citizens in turn were likely to hold relatively nationalist and antipopulist views. Forty-two of the fifty-five delegates who attended at least some portion of the Philadelphia convention had served in the Continental Congress—a nationalizing experience. Thirty had performed military service during the Revolutionary War, and of these no fewer than five had served as aides-de-camp to General Washington. Such military service had a profoundly nationalizing effect, first because it inclined men to think in terms of allegiance to a nation rather than a state, but also because many Revolutionary War veterans deeply resented the states for obstructing the war effort by failing to fulfill their requisitions for troops and money.[404]

Even those delegates who had served neither in the Continental Army nor in the Continental Congress were likely to be the sort of elite statesmen who disapproved of the populist economic relief measures enacted by most states in the mid-1780s. The delegates to the Philadelphia convention were an exceptionally well-educated and relatively affluent group. Most had attended college—no fewer than nine at the College of New Jersey (later renamed Princeton)—at a time when few Americans had done so. More than half of the delegates had trained as lawyers. Fourteen were merchants, and ten were involved in banking and finance. Nearly all of them owned substantial amounts of land, and many were extremely wealthy.[405]

Among Americans fitting this socioeconomic profile in the 1780s, the vast majority deeply disapproved of state tax and debt relief legislation and supported the expansion of federal government power to suppress it in the future. Less than a week into the convention, Mason told his son that "judging from casual conversations with gentlemen from the different states, I [am] very apprehensive that, soured and disgusted with the unexpected evils we had experienced from the democratic principles of our governments, we should be apt to run into the opposite extreme, and in endeavoring to steer too far from Scylla, we might be drawn into the vortex of Charybdis, of which I still think there is some danger."[406]

The political composition of one state's delegation—Pennsylvania's—was _____ _____ __ _ conscious legislative design than an unintended consequence of simply choosing delegates from among the state's most prominent citizens. According to the later account given by critics of the Constitution, the state legislature, acting under the influence of members from Philadelphia, decided not to pay the state's delegates to the Constitutional Convention, which would ensure that only men from Philadelphia or its environs could afford to attend. Such delegates—described by a leading critic as "those men who are esteemed aristocratical"—were strongly predisposed to support a nationalist and antipopulist constitution.[407]

After the convention, Madison told Jefferson that in light of the diversity of opinions expressed in Philadelphia, "it is impossible to consider the degree of concord which ultimately prevailed as less than a miracle." Washington made the same point to Lafayette: It was "little short of a miracle that the delegates from so many different states . . . should unite in forming a system of national government so little liable to well-founded objections."[408]

Yet considering the common characteristics of the delegates in Philadelphia—their wealth, education, occupations, and national military and governmental service—it does not seem surprising that they would share certain political views that might not be representative of those held by

Americans at large. From the convention's outset, Mason was impressed that there was "greater unanimity and less opposition" to the general plan proposed by the Virginia delegates than might have been expected. Madison likewise noted that "[i]n general the members seem to accord in viewing our situation as peculiarly critical and in being adverse to temporizing expedients."[409]

Generally like-minded delegates may have influenced the views of those less predisposed to a nationalist and antipopulist perspective. Randolph later explained that when he left for Philadelphia, he was not convinced that the Articles were as "eminently defective as it had been supposed," but his conversations with other delegates soon persuaded him that the Articles were "destitute of every energy which a constitution of the United States ought to possess."[410]

Second, the nationalist and antipopulist bent of the convention was a function not only of the process for selecting delegates but also of who chose not to participate. For a couple of different sorts of reasons, many of those who might have resisted the dominant tendencies of the convention opted not to attend. Some people probably wished to avoid legitimizing an enterprise with which they disagreed and, indeed, may have considered illegal. Some of the Connecticut legislators who represented towns that would later oppose ratification of the Constitution had resisted their state's even sending delegates to Philadelphia because they worried that participating in the convention would implicitly obligate them to support its handiwork.[411]

As we have seen, the Rhode Island legislature did not even appoint delegates to Philadelphia because the dominant paper money faction in the state suspected—rightly so, as it turned out—that the convention would propose limiting state legislatures' ability to issue paper money and enact debtor relief laws. As Madison colorfully explained to his father, Rhode Island legislators, "[b]eing conscious of the wickedness of the measures they are pursuing, . . . are afraid of everything that may become a control on them." A Massachusetts newspaper observed that had Rhode Island sent delegates to the convention, they would have been "birds of a feather" with the state's current administration. In other words, such delegates probably would have resisted the convention's strong inclinations to suppress state relief measures and to insulate the federal government from populist political influence.[412]

Declining to participate in an enterprise for fear of legitimizing it is always a risky strategy because it disables one from influencing the outcome. Acknowledging that a strict adherence to the Articles might justify a state's not attending the Philadelphia convention, Rhode Island's congressional delegates nonetheless had warned—to no avail—that in light of the convention's "momentous" objects, "common safety" demanded that the state appoint delegates. As Nathan Dane, a Massachusetts congressional delegate who initially opposed the Constitution, later explained to Melancton Smith, a leading

Antifederalist in New York, "When measures of any sort become necessary in a community, it is generally wise to take a part in them, and to bring them as near to our opinions as we can in the first instance."[413]

Another reason that some people who might have resisted the dominant tendencies of the convention chose not to participate was the lack of transparency in the convention's agenda. Most Americans probably expected the Philadelphia convention to propose relatively uncontroversial reforms—empowering Congress to raise revenue independently of state requisitions, to regulate foreign and interstate commerce, and to ensure the supremacy of federal treaties. As Gunning Bedford observed at the convention, the delegates had been sent there to empower the national government to collect an impost and to regulate trade. "Why then, when we are met, must entire, distinct, and new grounds be taken, and a government of which the people had no idea be instituted?" The Antifederalist "Federal Farmer" later noted that the convention had been appointed for the sole and express purpose of revising the Articles, and probably "not one man in ten thousand in the United States . . . had an idea that the old ship was to be destroyed." William Findley, a prominent opponent of ratification in Pennsylvania, explained that he probably would have supported the Constitution "had the federal convention given such powers only as we had ground to expect, or as Congress ever expressed a wish to enjoy."[414]

Madison and his like-minded colleagues had not publicized their hope and intention that the Philadelphia convention would thoroughly repudiate the Articles, vastly expand the powers of the national government, make it more resistant to populist influence, and explicitly constrain the redistributive tendencies of the more populist state governments. As Paterson objected at the convention, the idea of a national government—as distinct from a federal one—had "never entered into the mind of any of [their constituents]." An opponent of the Constitution in Massachusetts later noted that not a single state legislature "had the most distant idea when they first appointed members for a convention, entirely commercial, or when they afterwards authorized them to consider on some amendments of the federal union, that they would without any warrant from their constituents presume on so bold and daring a stride as ultimately to destroy the state governments and offer a consolidated system." At the convention, Gerry objected to Madison's proposed federal veto on the grounds that such a thing had "never been suggested or conceived among the people. No speculative projector, and there are enough of that character among us, in politics as well as in other things, has in any pamphlet or newspaper thrown out the idea."[415]

Had the nationalist and antipopulist agenda of Madison and his principal supporters been known in advance, their states' legislatures might not have appointed them as delegates, some states might have refused entirely to appoint delegates or might have severely constrained them with limiting instructions, and Congress might not have endorsed the enterprise. Just prior to the convention, Washington had warned Madison that "if the delegates come to it [the convention] under fetters, the salutary ends proposed will in my opinion be greatly embarrassed and retarded, if not altogether defeated." Lansing was almost certainly right when he declared that "New York would never have concurred in sending deputies to the convention, if she had supposed the deliberations were to turn on a consolidation of the states and a national government." Gerry, too, observed that had he known what would happen in Philadelphia, nothing could "have induced me to come here." Had a few states—discovering and disapproving of Madison's nationalist and antipopulist agenda—joined Rhode Island in declining to participate in the convention, its recommendations to the nation would have carried little weight.[416]

As it happens, several people who were not of a like mind with Madison— and not just Lansing and Gerry—*had* been appointed delegates by their states but had declined the appointment. Perhaps some of them agreed with William Grayson that despite the "great expectations" people had for the convention, "the whole will terminate in nothing." Others might not have been terribly interested in participating in a project to mildly expand the national government's power and did not fathom that a far more ambitious agenda was afoot— one of which they would not have approved. Had that agenda—as laid out in the Virginia Plan—been widely publicized in advance, perhaps some of these people would have been more inclined to attend the convention in order to resist its implementation. One cannot know for sure, but several of these individuals did play major roles in mobilizing opposition to the nationalist and antipopulist constitution that the convention had produced.[417]

Patrick Henry was the most prominent among those who turned down appointment to the Philadelphia convention and later played leading roles in mobilizing opposition to ratification of the Constitution. Henry had received the second most votes—trailing only Washington—when the Virginia legislature balloted members on the appointment of delegates to the convention. Henry's motives for declining his appointment are impossible to know with certainty. The well-known story that he "smelt a rat" is probably apocryphal, and Henry in all likelihood had other reasons for declining to attend.[418]

Randolph told Madison that he had "assayed every means to prevail on him [Henry] to go thither. But he is peremptory in refusing, as being distressed in his private circumstances." Madison believed that the imbroglio over Jay's negotiations with Spain involving American navigation rights on the Mississippi River had caused Henry to cease to be "the champion of the federal cause." He told Jefferson the "intended sacrifice of the Mississippi" had so disgusted Henry that he had declined his appointment to the Philadelphia convention to keep "himself free to combat or espouse the result of it according to the result of the Mississippi business." Madison also feared there was "good reason to believe" that Henry was "hostile to the object of the convention" and favored "either a partition or total dissolution of the confederacy." Yet, despite Madison's concerns about Henry's "ominous" decision not to attend the convention, Henry's presence in Philadelphia probably would have proved a major impediment to Madison and his nationalizing project.[419]

Richard Henry Lee, who would prove to be one of the nation's leading opponents of the Constitution's ratification, also declined his appointment to the convention for reasons that are impossible to verify. He explained to Governor Randolph that his health would not permit him to travel to Philadelphia in time for the convention, though he also expressed "a disposition to repose with confidence" in the "many gentlemen of good hearts and sound heads appointed to the convention." Later, Lee explained that his participation would have been incompatible with his service in the Confederation Congress, which would probably be called upon to review any proposals made by the convention before transmitting them to the states for ratification.[420]

Samuel Chase, a leader of the paper money faction in the Maryland legislature, also declined an appointment to the convention—possibly to remain in Annapolis to lead the campaign for a paper money emission, which was vital to the recovery of his personal financial health, given the debt he had incurred as a result of speculating in confiscated Loyalist estates. Two prominent supporters of tax and debt relief in Georgia and New Jersey—George Walton and Abraham Clark, respectively—also turned down appointments to the convention, though for reasons apparently unrelated to their substantive policy views. Willie Jones, later one of the leading Antifederalists in North Carolina, likewise declined an appointment to the Philadelphia convention, stating that the timing made it impossible for him to attend.[421]*

Whatever reasons they may have had for declining appointments, the absence of these individuals from Philadelphia plainly enhanced the convention's nationalist and antipopulist tendencies. As Dane reported to Smith during the ratifying contest, "certain individuals who were appointed to that convention, missed it exceedingly in not attending it." Had they participated, they might have "engrafted many of the principles and checks they now contend for into the system." A leading Pennsylvania critic of the Constitution agreed that the

---

* Erastus Wolcott turned down his appointment by the Connecticut legislature on the grounds that smallpox was present in Philadelphia, he had never had the disease, and did not wish "to hazard his life without the most pressing necessity." Roger Sherman was appointed in Wolcott's place. Sherman's fellow Connecticut delegate, Oliver Ellsworth, did indeed catch smallpox in Philadelphia—though he survived it.

absence of eight or nine "good republican characters" who had been appointed delegates was "a most unfortunate event to the United States." Had they gone to Philadelphia, "the result of the convention would not have had that strong tendency to aristocracy now discernible in every part of the plan."[422]

None of this is to say that there were no hints of what might happen in Philadelphia. In January 1787, King urged Gerry that if Massachusetts did send delegates to the convention, "for God sake be careful who are the men. The times are becoming critical. A movement of this nature ought to be carefully observed by every member of the community." In March, the Massachusetts senate voted to instruct the state's delegation to the convention—only later to rescind the instruction—not to agree to any changes to the section of the Articles providing that congressional delegates were subject to annual elections, recall, and mandatory rotation in office. In April, Grayson reported that those delegates appointed to the convention who were in New York City "conversed freely" on their plans for reform and that they were "for going a great way," including "placing Congress in loco of the King of Great Britain" and empowering it to veto state laws. As we have seen, Congress and two state legislatures did issue instructions that limited the convention to the "sole and express purpose" of revising the Articles. Some people clearly had an inkling that others aspired to a radical transformation of the Articles. Yet limiting instructions proved less efficacious than selecting differently minded delegates in the first place might have been.[423]

Thus, the lack of transparency in the convention's agenda probably influenced the cast of characters who came to Philadelphia. The lack of transparency within the convention itself probably influenced its handiwork. Because they met behind closed doors and had bound themselves to an oath of secrecy, the delegates were able to candidly express opinions that, had they been declared publicly, would have immediately mobilized resistance and probably would have had deleterious consequences for their public careers.[424]

Critics of the Constitution later complained of the convention's having met in "secret conclave," claiming that resistance might have developed sooner had the deliberations been public. The "genius of aristocracy," they charged, had "prompted the convention [delegates] to enjoin secrecy on their members, to keep their doors shut, their journals locked up, and none of the members to take any extracts." Jefferson criticized the convention's secrecy as manifesting "ignorance of the value of public discussions," but the delegates knew full well what they were doing: To open their proceedings to the public could kill their nationalist and antipopulist project before it had legs. Madison almost certainly was correct when he later observed that "no constitution would ever have been adopted by the convention if the debates had been public." The secrecy of the convention's proceedings was in stark contrast to the constitutional requirements of the very state in which the delegates assembled—namely, that legislative deliberations be conducted in public and that the Pennsylvania Assembly's votes and proceedings be published on a weekly basis.[425]

A relatively like-minded group of elite nationalists had gathered in Philadelphia under conditions that afforded them some space to maneuver independent of public opinion. The question immediately arose of how boldly they should challenge the nation's current political arrangements. In the run-up to the convention, as we have seen, Washington had told Madison that the delegates should "adopt no temporizing expedient" but instead should "probe the defects of the Constitution to the bottom and provide radical cures, whether they are agreed to or not." Randolph had told Madison that the convention should pursue "what is best in itself, not merely what can be obtained from the assemblies."[426]

Concurring with such views, Madison had devised a stunningly nationalist and antipopulist plan, around which the Virginia delegates then coordinated. Presenting that plan to the convention, Randolph repudiated Lansing's admonition that "[g]reat changes can only be gradually introduced." Instead, he urged his colleagues to seize this opportunity to accomplish as much as possible: "He would not as far as depended on him leave anything that seemed necessary undone. The present moment is favorable, and is probably the last that will offer." King agreed that this would "be the last opportunity of providing" for the nation's liberty and happiness. Hamilton warned that this was the "critical moment" for establishing a strong and stable government: "It is a miracle that we were now here exercising our own tranquil and free deliberations on the subject. It would be madness to trust to future miracles. A thousand causes must obstruct a reproduction of them."[427]

Over the course of the convention, the task of those delegates with a nationalist and antipopulist bent became easier when some of their opponents, in the words of Pennsylvania Antifederalists, "retired, hopeless, from the convention." Robert Yates and John Lansing, Jr., of New York, whom Madison had suspected from the time of their appointment of leaning "too much towards state considerations to be good members of an assembly," left Philadelphia early and resisted importunings to return. As they later explained to Governor George Clinton, they had departed because they faced "the disagreeable alternative of either exceeding the powers delegated to us, and giving our assent to measures which we conceived destructive to the political happiness of the citizens of the United States, or opposing our opinion to that of a body of respectable men, to whom those citizens had given the most unequivocal proofs of confidence."[428]

Their departure, which left only Hamilton representing New York, deprived that state of its influence because of the prevailing norm—explicitly embraced in the Articles of Confederation—that the vote of a state delegation would count only if at least two of its members were present. Two Maryland delegates who criticized the convention's nationalist bent, Luther Martin and John Francis Mercer, also left Philadelphia early (as noted previously, Mercer had attended the convention for only about ten days)—just at the time that James McHenry was trying to mobilize the Maryland delegation around an effort to convince the convention to amend rather than scrap the Articles. Such early departures simply enhanced the clout of those delegates who backed a nationalist and antipopulist agenda.[429]

Madison was depressed over the outcome of the convention. He had lost several key battles—over the apportionment of the Senate, the method of selecting its members, and the proposed federal power to veto state laws. The last of these defeats seemed to weigh most heavily on Madison because he feared that without such a veto, the federal government would be powerless to check the tendencies of state legislatures to capitulate to populist demands for debt

JOHN LANSING
Nat 1754 – Ob 1829.

Figure 3.11 John Lansing, Jr., mayor of Albany and later one of the leading opponents of ratification at the New York ratifying convention. (Photography © New-York Historical Society)

and tax relief. As Madison reported to Jefferson after the convention, it was the evils of such legislation that "contributed more to that uneasiness which produced the convention and prepared the public mind for a general reform" than those arising "from the inadequacy of the confederation to its immediate objects." A constitutional reform that failed adequately to protect private rights within the states thus must be "materially defective."[430]

Madison did not believe that judicial enforcement of the Article I, Section 10, ban on paper money emissions and debtor relief legislation would be a sufficient substitute for the defeated federal veto. It was "more convenient to prevent the passage of a law than to declare it void after it is passed," and individuals harmed by such laws might be "unable to support an appeal against a state to the Supreme Court." Most important, state legislatures were too creative to be stymied by words on a piece of paper: "Injustice may be effected by such an infinitude of legislative expedients that where the disposition exists it can only be controlled by some provision which reaches all cases whatsoever."[431]

Although in *The Federalist* Madison celebrated the Constitution for its "partly national, partly federal" mélange, he actually would have preferred a far more nationalist scheme than he had been able to secure in Philadelphia. Toward the end of the convention, he wrote Jefferson that the powers to be granted to Congress in the Constitution would "neither effectually answer its national object nor prevent the local mischiefs which everywhere excite disgusts against the state governments."[432]

Hamilton, who had favored tenure during good behavior for senators and presidents and would have preferred thoroughly to subordinate states to the national government, also was dissatisfied with the Constitution. On the last day of the convention, he declared that "[n]o man's ideas were more remote from the plan than his own were known to be" (although he signed the Constitution, believing that the choice was "between anarchy and convulsion on one side, and the chance of good to be expected from the plan on the other"). According to a subsequent report by Jefferson (which must be taken with a substantial grain of salt, given his animosity toward his political arch-rival), Hamilton described the Constitution as a "shilly-shally thing of mere milk and water, which could not last, and was only good as a step to something better." Gouverneur Morris, a friend and ally of Hamilton's and thus a more credible source, later confirmed that Hamilton "disliked" the Constitution, "believing all republican government to be radically defective."[433]

Madison's and Hamilton's disappointment that the Constitution was not even more nationalist and antipopulist seems extraordinary, given the vast distance traveled from both the Articles of Confederation and the state constitutions. Late in the convention, a disaffected Elbridge Gerry warned that "[t]he people who have been so lately in arms against Great Britain for their liberties will not easily give them up" and would regard the Constitution "with a very suspicious eye." Gerry thought it unlikely "the people will ever agree" to a system with such a strong "aristocratic" bent. Could the Framers persuade the nation to ratify a constitution that was such a radical departure both from the status quo and from the general expectations of what the Philadelphia convention would propose? Before turning to that question, however, it is necessary to consider another momentous issue that had confronted the convention: how to deal with the institution of slavery.[434]

4

Slavery and the Constitutional Convention

As we saw in chapter 3, the Philadelphia convention nearly dissolved amid conflict between small and large states over how to apportion representation in the national legislature. James Madison had sought to sidestep that conflict by reminding the delegates that "the great division of interests in the United States ... did not lie between the large and small states; it lay between the northern and southern." That sectional disparity of interests "resulted partly from climate, but principally from the effects of their [the states'] having or not having slaves."[1]

Madison pointed out that votes in Congress over the preceding decade—such as on whether to reinstruct Secretary for Foreign Affairs John Jay on his negotiations with Spain over American navigation rights on the Mississippi River—revealed that the states were mostly divided "by the geography of the country, not according to the size of the states." As far back as 1782, in the context of congressional debates over the admission of Vermont to the union as an independent state, Madison had noted that northern states supported admission "principally from the accession of weight they will derive from it in Congress," while southern states opposed admission because of "an habitual jealousy of a predominance of [northern] interests." At the Philadelphia convention, Hamilton largely agreed with Madison, observing that "[t]he only considerable distinction of interests lay between the carrying and non-carrying states"—a distinction that substantially overlapped with, but was not identical to, that between northern and southern states. Rufus King and Charles Pinckney also concurred with Madison on this point.[2]

With regard to this sectional conflict of interest, Madison believed that "every peculiar interest whether in any class of citizens, or any description of states, ought to be secured as far as possible. Wherever there is danger of attack there ought be given a constitutional power of defense." Thus, "if any defensive power were necessary, it ought to be mutually given" to the northern and

southern states. Accordingly, Madison told the convention that he had considered proposing that instead of one branch of the national legislature being
apportioned according to population and states' enjoying equal voting power
in the other, one branch should be apportioned according to the states' free
population, while the other should be apportioned according to their total
populations, with slaves counting the same as free persons. Madison's notion
was similar to a proposal made half a century later by the preeminent southern statesman John C. Calhoun, who suggested that the North and the South
ought to have "a concurrent voice in making and executing the laws, or a veto
on their execution."[3]

Indeed, southern delegates in Philadelphia felt that the South's interests
were sufficiently distinctive and sufficiently at risk that they repeatedly threatened that they would walk out of the convention—and that their states would
refuse to ratify the Constitution—if adequate safeguards for slavery were not
provided. Southerners had been making similar threats ever since a union was
first established to fight for independence from Great Britain. In 1776, as the
Continental Congress debated how to apportion tax obligations and military
service quotas among the states, a South Carolina delegate warned that if it
was "debated whether their [southerners'] slaves are their property, . . . there
is an end of the Confederation." At the Philadelphia convention of 1787, southern threats were similarly successful at extracting safeguards for slavery.[4]

Background

Regional differences over slavery had been much less pronounced in the early
colonial era. In the first decades after the American colonies were founded in
the early seventeenth century, northern colonies had as many slaves as southern ones, and neither had very many. But that situation changed dramatically
over time. The longer growing season in the South enabled the cultivation of
export crops such as tobacco, rice, and indigo. The demand for nearly year-
round labor to produce such crops made slavery more profitable in the South.
In addition, by the end of the seventeenth century, black mortality rates in
the colonies were falling, and the supply of white indentured servants from
England was diminishing—making investments in slavery even more profitable. Slaves grew from 7 percent of Virginia's population in 1680 to 28 percent in 1700 and to 46 percent in 1750. In South Carolina, slaves were 17 percent of the population in 1680, 44 percent in 1700, and more than 60 percent
by 1720.[5]

By contrast, slaves in the North often performed labor that was not clearly
distinguishable from that performed by whites. Northern slaves toiled on

farms alongside whites, and many acquired the skills necessary to become independent farmers. In northern cities, slaves worked in taverns, on ships, and as artisans and house servants. Because slaves in the North did not labor in large gangs on isolated plantations, they were gradually assimilated to the languages, customs, and religions of their masters. During the eighteenth century, the percentage of slaves in the northern population never approached the numbers reached in the South. In 1750, slaves were 14 percent of New York's population, 10 percent of Rhode Island's, and 7 percent of New Jersey's.[6]

The Revolutionary War had a profound effect on American slavery. The ideology of the Declaration of Independence—that "all men are created equal"—caused at least some Americans to reflect upon the injustice of human bondage. The man who wrote those words, Thomas Jefferson, owned well over one hundred slaves. He also thought that blacks were probably inferior to whites in reason and imagination, and he believed that "[d]eep rooted prejudices entertained by the whites" and the hatred many black slaves had developed for their white masters made it impossible for the two races to live together without "the extermination of the one or the other." Still, Jefferson admitted, "I tremble for my country when I reflect that God is just." Moreover, he had little doubt as to what the future portended with regard to slavery: "Nothing is more certainly written in the book of fate . . . than that these people are to be free."[7]

Many Americans, black and white, drew concrete connections between the natural-rights ideology of the Revolutionary cause and the injustice of slavery. In 1765, as the Sons of Liberty marched through the streets of Charleston chanting "liberty, liberty," slaves joined them and took up the chant, leading to the city's being placed under force of arms for a week. In 1773, four blacks published a leaflet in Massachusetts, purporting to speak for all the slaves in the state: "We expect great things from men who have made such a noble stand against the designs of their fellow men [the British] to enslave them." The following year, Abigail Adams wrote to her husband, Revolutionary leader John Adams, that it had "always appeared a most iniquitous scheme to me—fight ourselves for what we are daily robbing and plundering from those who have as good a right to freedom as we have."[8]

By the time fighting broke out, Pennsylvania Quakers were already emancipating their slaves and had founded the nation's first abolitionist society in Philadelphia. As the British military occupied coastal cities in the South during the Revolutionary War, many thousands of slaves seized the opportunity to flee their masters in what one historian has called "the greatest slave insurgency in North American history." British promises to free those slaves who fought against the colonists—such as that contained in the famous proclamation of Lord Dunmore, the royal governor of Virginia, in 1775—pressured

Americans to offer similar inducements.* After initial hesitancy, both the Continental Congress and most northern states allowed blacks into the Continental Army and the state militias. Some slave masters offered freedom to slaves who enlisted, often receiving government compensation for doing so. Perhaps as many as nine thousand blacks—most of them recently freed slaves—fought against the British during the Revolutionary War.[9]

Observing that slavery was "disgraceful to any people, and more especially to those who have been contending in the great cause of liberty themselves," the Pennsylvania Assembly in 1780 adopted the nation's first gradual emancipation scheme. The law freed children born to a slave mother after its enactment once they reached the age of twenty-eight. Permitting masters to maintain ownership of the slaves they already possessed and of those slaves' children until they reached the age of maturity was deemed compensation for the perceived invasion of property rights inherent in coerced emancipation; through their labor, slaves paid the price of their own liberation. Even many nonslaveholding whites were concerned about the use of government power to interfere with conventional property rights. Although slaves were less than 3 percent of Pennsylvania's population at the time, nearly 40 percent of state legislators voted against the gradual emancipation bill, and most slaveholders strongly opposed it.[10]

Several New England states quickly followed Pennsylvania's lead. While the Massachusetts legislature was considering an abolition bill in 1783, the state's Supreme Judicial Court interpreted the clause of the state constitution's Declaration of Rights announcing that all men are born "free and equal" as barring slavery—an interpretation that its drafters probably had not intended. Chief Justice William Cushing explained that even though slavery had been established by custom in Massachusetts, it could no longer exist because "sentiments more favorable to the natural rights of mankind, and to that innate desire of liberty which heaven, without regard to complexion or shape, has planted in the human breast, have prevailed since the glorious struggle for our rights began."[11]

In 1784, legislatures in Connecticut and Rhode Island adopted gradual emancipation schemes. In New York and New Jersey, however, where slaves were more numerous—according to the 1790 census, New York had

---

* British proclamations of emancipation primarily sought to advance war aims, not the goal of abolition, which would have been inconsistent with their strong commitment to slavery in the Caribbean sugar islands. Slaves of American Loyalists were not freed, and the British commander-in-chief warned that blacks who were captured wearing American uniforms would be sold back into slavery. Some British officers claimed captured slaves as property and sold them in the West Indies.

twenty-one thousand slaves, which was not many fewer than Georgia had—and slave owners were more politically powerful, legislatures rejected efforts to enact gradual emancipation statutes until 1799 in New York and 1804 in New Jersey.[12]*

The natural-rights ideology of the Revolution, the contributions made by black soldiers to the war effort, and economic forces ignited or accelerated by the war—including increases in the supply of white nonindentured laborers from Europe—put slavery on the road to extinction in northern states. As early as 1785, Jefferson reported that in the states north of Maryland, where there were "but few slaves" and people could "easily disencumber themselves of them," emancipation was already "put into such a train that in a few years there will be no slaves." Although Jefferson exaggerated, and northern slavery continued to linger well into the nineteenth century, by 1830 less than 1 percent of the northern black population was enslaved.[13]

Yet northern states were no racial paradise. Concern for protecting property rights ensured that gradual emancipation laws liberated no slaves already living when the laws were enacted. Moreover, many of these laws provided for delayed implementation to give owners an opportunity to transport their slaves out of state before the laws took effect. Even after they became effective, most such laws had weak enforcement provisions, which meant that owners usually could sell their slaves to southerners before the date of emancipation arrived. Disinclined to add to the number of free blacks in their states, most northern whites did not care enough about the welfare of slaves to support strong enforcement measures. In addition, for decades after enacting gradual emancipation, most northern states willingly cooperated with owners in the return of escaped slaves to the jurisdictions from which they had fled. Racism was pervasive in the North, manifesting itself in many varieties of discrimination against blacks, including disfranchisement, exclusion from militia and jury service, and unwritten barriers to many occupations.[14]

The Revolutionary War also induced a spate of slave manumissions in the Upper South. In 1782, the Virginia legislature authorized masters to emancipate slaves without receiving special permission from the legislature, as had been previously required. Maryland and Delaware soon adopted similar laws and even debated proposals for gradual emancipation. Reasoning that those who have "contributed towards the establishment of American liberty and independence should enjoy the blessings of freedom as a reward for their toils and labours," the Virginia legislature in 1783 freed slaves who had served as

---

* In 1785, the New York legislature passed a gradual emancipation law, but it was vetoed by the council of revision on the ostensible grounds that it disfranchised anyone with a small amount of black ancestry. One house of the legislature voted to overturn the veto but not the other.

substitutes for their masters in the state militia. Largely as a result of these laws, Virginia's free black population increased from twenty-eight hundred to more than twelve thousand in just eight years.[15]

Some Virginia statesmen now spoke optimistically of the possibility that slavery would be gradually abolished. In 1785, Jefferson told a British friend that in Maryland and Virginia, "the bulk of the people" approved of emancipation in theory, and "a respectable minority are ready to adopt it in practice, a minority which for weight and worth of character preponderates against the greater number, who have not the courage to divest their families of a property which however keeps their consciences inquiet." Jefferson was certain that the cause of justice was "gaining daily recruits from the influx into office of young men grown and growing up [who] have sucked in the principles of liberty as it were with their mother's milk" and would determine "the fate of this question." In 1785, Methodists petitioned the Virginia legislature to enact a gradual emancipation law. The following year, George Washington wrote that he intended to buy no more slaves—unless extraordinary circumstances intervened—and that he hoped "to see some plan adopted by the legislature by which slavery in this country may be abolished by slow, sure, and imperceptible degrees."[16]

Yet despite opposition to slavery grounded in religious conviction and revolutionary ideology, the economic reality of tremendous investments in slave property, coupled with racist fears of creating large populations of free blacks, would render abolition an uphill struggle even in an Upper South state such as Virginia. In the Deep South states of Georgia and South Carolina, there was little support among whites for abolition.[17]

Under the Articles of Confederation, a consensus existed that slavery was one of the issues on which the states retained complete sovereignty. Indeed, America's victory in the Revolutionary War had given southern slave owners substantially greater control over the institution of slavery. Slave owners had been a relatively small minority in an empire where local laws were subject to regulatory vetoes by an imperial government in which they had no direct representation. After independence, however, they constituted the political and economic elite that governed nearly half of a nation in which control of "domestic" institutions such as slavery was relegated to local governance. Adding to the clout of slave owners was the continuing growth in the slave population of the United States, which increased by more than 50 percent during the 1770s and 1780s.[18]

American slavery was in transition in 1787, becoming a distinctively regional phenomenon. Several northern delegates to the Philadelphia convention, including Benjamin Franklin and Alexander Hamilton, played prominent roles in their states' antislavery movements. But no northern legislature had given its delegation instructions to take action against slavery. White northerners who had been unwilling to appropriate money to prevent circumvention of their own states' gradual emancipation laws were not about to incur political costs to challenge slavery in the South. Northern delegates were far more interested in how slavery would influence convention decisions involving taxation and congressional representation than they were in using the Constitution to attack slavery in the South.[19]

Many delegates from the Upper South—especially Virginians, such as Washington, Madison, Mason, and Randolph—regarded slavery as a temporary evil that hopefully could be eliminated soon (through the actions of slave owners and state legislatures, not Congress). For example, Mason, one of the largest slaveholders at the convention, denounced slavery in a speech to the delegates on the grounds that it discouraged arts and manufacturing, taught poor whites to "despise labor," deterred the immigration of whites who would "enrich and strengthen a country," produced "the most pernicious effect on manners" by turning every slave master into "a petty tyrant," and brought "the judgment of heaven on a country."[20]

But the men representing the states of the Deep South in Philadelphia did not speak this way about slavery. With economies that were hugely dependent on slave labor, these states were voracious in their appetite for additional slaves to replace the many thousands who had emancipated themselves during the war. One of South Carolina's first Revolutionary-era governors, Rawlins Lowndes, observed soon after the convention that "[w]ithout negroes, this state would degenerate into one of the most contemptible in the union." Between 1783 and 1785, slave traders had carried about eleven thousand slaves from Africa and the Caribbean islands into Georgia and South Carolina.[21]

South Carolina appointed as delegates to the Philadelphia convention four enormously wealthy slave owners. These men spoke neither of the hope nor of the expectation that slavery would disappear any time soon. Moreover, rather than criticizing the institution, they argued, in the words of Charles Pinckney, that slavery was "justified by the example of all the world," including ancient Greece and Rome. Some of them probably even agreed with Lowndes, who went so far as to defend the foreign slave trade—considered barbaric even by many defenders of slavery—"on the principles of religion, humanity and justice; for certainly to translate a set of human beings from a bad country to a better, was fulfilling every part of these principles."[22]

Twenty-five of the delegates to the Philadelphia convention owned slaves, including some northerners who used them as household servants. For sixteen southern delegates, slaves were critical to their livelihoods and constituted a significant proportion of their wealth. Washington owned more than two hundred slaves and brought three of them with him to the convention;

he was not the only delegate to do so. Madison owned nine slaves (and would inherit more than a hundred more upon his father's death in 1801), and as he made clear in a subsequent letter, he was keenly aware that those to whom he owed his "public station" were known "to be greatly interested in that species of property." Rejecting a plea in 1791 that he support a gradual emancipation scheme in Virginia, Madison declared, "I might be chargeable at least with want of candor, if not of fidelity, were I to make use of a situation in which their [Madison's constituents'] confidence has placed me, to become a volunteer in giving a public wound, as they would deem it, to an interest on which they set so great a value."[23]

Although slavery had nothing to do with the calling of the convention, it played an enormous role in the proceedings. Establishing precisely the sense in which this was so is critical. That the Philadelphia convention would write an antislavery constitution was never in the cards (although South Carolina delegate Pierce Butler did insist at one point that southern states needed security against a compulsory emancipation). At the time of the convention, slaves constituted about 40 percent of the population of the five southernmost states and about one-third of their tangible "wealth." Accordingly, it was inconceivable that southern delegates would have agreed to an antislavery constitution or that southern states, where slave owners were politically dominant, would have ratified one.[24]

Even those northern delegates who opposed slavery were disinclined to press for an antislavery constitution. With just one or two exceptions, the northern states—even those that were in the process of abolishing slavery in 1787—had significant numbers of slaves, and even most opponents of slavery believed in the sanctity of property rights. In addition, most white northerners shared the fears of white southerners about creating large populations of free blacks, which would prove a much more vexing problem with regard to southern than to northern emancipation. Most important, even those northern delegates who opposed slavery aspired to establish a permanent union with southerners, who would never have agreed to a constitution that threatened slavery.[25]

Yet, while neither northern nor southern delegates were inclined to write an antislavery constitution, many of them had qualms about authoring one that was too explicitly proslavery. Many delegates were queasy about tainting the nation's organic document with linkages to slavery—an institution that Madison described at the convention as "the most oppressive dominion ever exercised by man over man" and that Gouverneur Morris denounced as a "nefarious institution—. . . the curse of heaven on the states where it prevailed."[26]

Thus, as Madison later explained, some of the delegates "had scruples against admitting the term 'slaves' into the instrument [i.e., the Constitution]."

In its place, they insisted that the document use euphemisms, such as "other persons." Thus, for example, the Constitution requires the return not of "fugitive slaves" but of "person[s] held to service or labour." John Dickinson of Delaware noted that the convention's omission of the word "slavery" from the Constitution would "be regarded as an endeavor to conceal a principle of which we are ashamed." Luther Martin later made the same point when opposing ratification of the Constitution—mostly on other grounds—in Maryland: Convention delegates had "anxiously sought to avoid the admission of expressions which might be odious in the ears of Americans, although they were very willing to admit into their system those things which the expressions signified."[27]

In a sense, the delegates were drafting two separate constitutions. As practical politicians who understood that slavery would not disappear any time soon, they wrote a constitution that protected the interests of slave owners. As idealists who were not oblivious to their historical reputations, they wrote a constitution that would require little amendment should slavery one day be abolished, as many of them hoped and expected it would be. As Abraham Lincoln later claimed, the Framers had hoped that the Constitution would last forever and did not wish anything in it to suggest "that such a thing as negro slavery had ever existed among us."[28]

How to Count Slaves in Apportioning National Political Power

Slavery was controversial at the Philadelphia convention, not because any of the delegates seriously considered abolishing it in the Constitution but rather because, as Madison repeatedly noted, northern and southern states had conflicting interests on a variety of issues—partly as a result of their very different levels of investment in the institution of slavery. In the 1780s, the southern economy was based largely on the production of agricultural staples for export—mainly tobacco, rice, and indigo (cotton became a substantial export crop only after the invention of the cotton gin in the 1790s). The South had few manufacturers and no significant merchant marine; it imported most of its manufactured goods and hired others to carry its imports and exports. Accordingly, the economic interests of southerners inclined them toward free trade. The North had a more diversified economy, including many more shippers, merchants, and manufacturers, who often favored various mercantilist restrictions on trade. In addition, as we have seen, conflicting sectional interests with regard to Secretary for Foreign Affairs John Jay's negotiations with Spain in 1786–87 had nearly torn the union asunder.[29]

Because northern and southern states had different economic interests, they cared greatly about how much power their respective regions would exercise within the new national government. The Constitution's treatment of slavery would affect that allocation of power. Most southern delegates were far more committed to securing constitutional protection for southern political power than to obtaining explicit textual safeguards against emancipation.[30]

Most of the delegates at the Philadelphia convention thought of the union as consisting of five southern states and eight northern ones; the northern border of Maryland was the dividing line. In 1787, those five southern states had almost precisely the same population as the eight northern states—if slaves were included in the counting. Therefore, if slaves were counted the same as free persons for purposes of apportioning representation in the House, the North and South would have equal power within that branch of the national government. If slaves counted for less, however, the South would be greatly outnumbered in the House—at least in the short term—as roughly 40 percent of its population was enslaved. In addition, if the Senate were apportioned equally among the states, rather than according to population, the southern states would be vulnerable to being constantly outvoted there as well.[31]

Delegates from southern and northern states could no more agree on how much slave populations ought to count in apportioning representation in the national legislature than delegates from small states and large states could agree upon whether population ought to be the sole basis of that apportionment. By providing that representation in the national legislature "ought to be proportioned to the quotas of contribution, [which would probably reflect the wealth produced by slave labor], or to the number of free inhabitants, as the one or the other rule may seem best in different cases," the Virginia Plan had avoided taking a position on whether and how slaves ought to count for apportionment purposes.[32]

On just the second day of the convention's substantive deliberations, Madison objected to a proposal to base apportionment of the House solely on "the number of free inhabitants," which would not count slaves at all. Desperate to establish broad support for rejecting the principle of equal state representation in Congress that had prevailed under the Articles, Madison could not afford to have southern state delegations join the small-state delegations in opposing his plan. Instead, he successfully urged that the convention replace equal state representation with the principle of "an equitable ratio of representation," which the delegates could flesh out later.[33]

In 1787, most elite statesmen believed that political representation ought to reflect wealth as well as population. Several state constitutions provided for legislative apportionment based partly on wealth. At the Philadelphia

convention, the South Carolinians—among the wealthiest men in America—
were the most strenuous in insisting that congressional representation ought
to reflect wealth, among other things. Observing that "[p]roperty was certainly the principal object of society," John Rutledge insisted that wealth deserved representation in the legislature. Charles Cotesworth Pinckney agreed
that the South's "superior wealth" ought to have "its due weight in the government."* Noting that "money is strength," Butler argued that "every state ought
to have its weight in the national council in proportion to the quantity it possesses." Mason of Virginia agreed that "slaves were valuable"—increasing the
value of land, augmenting exports, and potentially serving as soldiers in time
of emergency—and thus "they ought not to be excluded from the estimate of
representation."[34]

Many northern delegates sympathized with the notion that wealth should
play a role in apportioning representation in the national legislature. Agreeing
that "property was the primary object of society" and thus ought to factor into
representation, Rufus King of Massachusetts explained that he "had always
expected that as the southern states are the richest, they would not league
themselves with the northern unless some respect were paid to their superior
wealth. If the latter expect those preferential distinctions in commerce and
other advantages which they will derive from the connection, they must not
expect to receive them without allowing some advantages in return." Because
of the different interests of southern and northern states, King was prepared
"to yield something in the proportion of representation for the security of the
southern." Gouverneur Morris of Pennsylvania agreed that property, as "the
main object of government," deserved representation in the national legislature. He especially feared that if population were the sole basis of apportionment, then soon-to-be-admitted western states, whose economic radicalism
he feared, would come to dominate Congress.[35]

Yet one did not have to believe that apportionment should be based directly on wealth (or on "quotas of contribution," which would probably reflect
wealth) to conclude that slaves ought to count for purposes of apportioning
congressional representation. Charles Pinckney argued that apportionment
based on land values had proved "impracticable" under the Articles and that
apportionment based on quotas of contribution would prove too "changeable" and difficult to calculate. He concluded that apportionment based on
the number of inhabitants was "the only just and practicable rule," but he saw
no reason why black slaves ought not "to stand on an equality with whites" in
such an apportionment. Slaves were "the laborers, the peasants of the southern

---

* By one estimate, at the time of the Revolutionary War, per capita income (among free persons) in the South was twice what it was in the North.

states; they are as productive of pecuniary resources as those of the northern states. They add equally to the wealth, and considering money as the sinew of war, to the strength of the nation."[36]

Whether the apportionment of representation in the House was based on wealth or on population, the South Carolinians insisted that slaves ought to count the same as free persons. Some northern delegates took the opposite position: Slaves ought not to count at all. Elbridge Gerry of Massachusetts argued that if "blacks, who were property in the South," counted for apportionment purposes, then so should "the cattle and horses of the North."* Morris similarly objected to the notion that among all sorts of property, only that in slaves should count for apportionment purposes. He predicted that citizens of his state, Pennsylvania, would "revolt at the idea of being put on a footing with slaves." "Are they [slaves] men?" Morris asked. If so, "[t]hen make them citizens and let them vote. Are they property? Why then is no other property included? The houses in this city (Philadelphia) are worth more than all the wretched slaves which cover the rice swamps of South Carolina."[37]

Moreover, northerners argued that if southern states did not count slaves in apportioning representation in their own legislatures, then slaves ought not to count for purposes of apportioning representation in Congress. William Paterson of New Jersey asked, "Has a man in Virginia a number of votes in proportion to the number of his slaves? And if Negroes are not represented in the states to which they belong, why should they be represented in the general government?"[38]

Northerners also protested that counting slaves in the apportionment of congressional representation would simply encourage southerners to continue importing them. Yet most convention delegates considered the foreign slave trade barbaric and wished to end it. Thus, Morris objected that counting slaves for apportionment purposes would ensure that "the inhabitant of Georgia and South Carolina who goes to the coast of Africa, and in defiance of the most sacred laws of humanity tears away his fellow creatures from their dearest connections and damns them to the most cruel bondages, shall have more votes in a government instituted for protection of the rights of mankind, than the citizen of Pennsylvania or New Jersey who views with a laudable horror so nefarious a practice." Paterson agreed that the convention must not give "an indirect encouragement of the slave trade."[39]

---

* Under the Confederation, when the issue with regard to counting slaves was apportioning federal financial obligations rather than representation, it was southerners who insisted that their slaves were property and ought to count no more than the "land, sheep, cattle, and horses" of the North.

Figure 4.1 Gouverneur Morris, who had been assistant superintendent of finance under the Confederation, was the single most frequent speaker at the Philadelphia convention and, as a member of the Committee of Style, was the delegate most responsible for the final language of the Constitution. (Courtesy of Independence National Historical Park)

The convention rejected by lopsided margins of eight to two and seven to three the South Carolinians' proposals to count slaves equally in apportioning the House. Yet while delegates from the Upper South did not support the South Carolinians' position, neither were they willing to accept slaves' counting for nothing at all. Hugh Williamson of North Carolina declared that he could not "concur in either extreme." Mason thought that while "slaves were valuable" and thus "ought not to be excluded from the estimate of representation," he did not "regard them as equal to freemen and could not vote for them as such." Madison pondered proposing a compromise: One house of the national legislature would be apportioned according to free population and the other based on total population. Wilson actually proposed a different compromise: Representation would be based on free population plus three-fifths of the rest.[40]

The three-fifths figure was familiar to the delegates because an amendment that had been proposed to the Articles in 1783, when ten of the delegates had been in Congress, had used that fraction. Under the Articles, congressional financial requisitions upon the states were supposed to be apportioned according to land values—largely because a proposal in 1776 to apportion them based on population (excluding only Indians not taxed) had occasioned insuperable disagreements over how to count slaves. However, in the absence of a reliable land census, which the states had declined to undertake, such an apportionment proved impossible.[41]

At the behest of delegates from New England, where land was relatively more valuable because it was more likely to have been improved, Congress had proposed "a more convenient and certain rule of ascertaining the proportions to be supplied by the states respectively to the common treasury." Under the proposed amendment, which Madison had suggested, requisitions would be apportioned according "to the whole number of white and other free citizens and inhabitants, of every age, sex and condition, including those bound to servitude for a term of years, and *three-fifths of all other persons* not comprehended in the foregoing description."[42]

The proffered reason for counting only three-fifths of the slaves for purposes of apportioning financial requisitions was that slave labor was less efficient than free labor—that because slaves had "no interest in their labor," they did "as little as possible." In congressional debates over this amendment—which involved taxation rather than representation—New Englanders had advocated counting slaves the same or nearly the same as free persons, while southerners had insisted that they count as only a small fraction, perhaps as little as one-quarter or one-third.* Eleven of the thirteen states—all but New Hampshire and Rhode Island—had approved this proposed amendment, but of course the Articles required unanimity for amendments to become law (which did not stop Congress from using the population amendment as the basis for apportioning post-1783 financial requisitions).[43]

Two weeks into the Constitutional Convention—a time when large-state delegates cared more about rejecting the principle of equal state representation in Congress than figuring out precisely what an "equitable" apportionment might be—the delegates agreed to the three-fifths compromise by a vote of nine states to two. The only negative votes came from small states—New

---

* Thus, at the Philadelphia convention, Massachusetts delegate Nathaniel Gorham accused southerners of inconsistency for demanding that slaves count equally for purposes of apportioning congressional representation when in 1783 they had argued against counting even three-fifths of the slaves for purposes of apportioning financial requisitions. Williamson of North Carolina responded that northern delegates were being equally inconsistent, arguing that slaves should not count at all for purposes of apportioning representation when four years earlier they had argued that slaves should count equally for purposes of apportioning requisitions.

Jersey and Delaware—whose delegates did not acknowledge the legitimacy of population-based apportionment of representation. Yet in early July, as the convention neared final decisions on how to apportion the Senate and how to allocate representatives in the first House, that compromise nearly came undone.[44]

As we saw in chapter 3, on July 5, a grand committee composed of one delegate per state, which was chaired by Gerry, proposed a scheme that became known to history as the Connecticut Compromise: Each state would have the same number of senators, and the House would be apportioned according to a ratio of no more than one representative for every forty thousand inhabitants, counting only three-fifths of the slaves. The convention then quickly appointed another committee to allocate representatives among the states in the first House—a challenging enterprise in the absence of reliable census data on the states' populations.* Both northern and southern delegates declared that this committee ought to consider wealth as well as population in making its allocations.[45]

When that committee proposed an initial allocation of representatives for the House, it also suggested that the Constitution grant Congress discretion both to increase the number of representatives and to change the initial allocation based on fluctuations in the states' relative wealth and populations. Those delegates who were unhappy with the committee's allocation of representatives demanded to know the formula on which it had been based. Morris, who had been a member of the committee, explained that the allocation was "little more than a guess," based mostly on conjecture as to population, although wealth was "not altogether disregarded."[46]

The committee's allocation of representatives proved so controversial that the convention immediately appointed a grand committee, chaired by King, to revise it. The King committee's allocation gave the eight northern states an advantage of thirty-six to twenty-nine over the five southern states in the sixty-five-person House. Several southern delegates expressed unhappiness. For example, they objected that New Hampshire would be overrepresented and North Carolina underrepresented. Williamson declared that "the southern interest must be extremely endangered by the present arrangement," and Charles Cotesworth Pinckney protested the South's "form[ing] so considerable a minority."[47]

Yet given the dominant assumption that the South's population would grow much more quickly than the North's, an initial apportionment of the House

---

* Indeed, under the Articles, some states, such as North Carolina, had possessed strong incentives not to accurately report their populations to Congress, for fear that doing so would result in an increase in their quota of financial requisitions.

that favored northerners did not trouble most southern delegates enough for them to flatly reject it. The convention voted by nine states to two—only Georgia and South Carolina dissenting—in favor of the King committee's allocation of seats in the first House. Yet several southern delegates expressed concern that an initial northern majority in Congress would endeavor to entrench itself in power. Southerners' fears of being outnumbered in the House even after the demographic advantage had swung in their favor were compounded by their dawning realization that the small states were about to succeed in their mission to secure equal representation in the Senate—another allocation of political clout that was generally perceived to disadvantage the South.[48]

To protect themselves against the risk of a northern majority's entrenching itself in power in the House, several southern delegates now demanded that the Constitution require a periodic census and that Congress be mandated to reapportion representation based on it. Mason declared, "According to the present population of America, the northern part of it had a right to preponderate, and he could not deny it. But he wished it not to preponderate hereafter when the reason no longer continued." Leaving reapportionment to the discretion of Congress was a bad idea, Mason said, because "those who have power in their hands will not give it up while they can retain it." Thus, southern states, even after they held a clear majority of the population, might "complain from generation to generation without redress." Madison similarly ridiculed the notion that southern states should have "implicit confidence" in the northern majority when "all men who have power ought to be distrusted to a certain degree."[49]

Unsurprisingly, delegates from northern states proved far more willing to entrust reapportionment to Congress's discretion. Sherman was "against shackling the legislature too much." Morris opposed limiting Congress's discretion on the grounds that only "very urgent" reasons, which could not be foreseen and specified in advance, would induce Congress to resist a subsequent reapportionment of representation. However, southerners won on this issue: The apportionment of representatives in the future would be based on a census, which the Constitution would require Congress to undertake within three years of its first meeting and then again once every decade.[50]

But the delegates continued to disagree about what precisely that census should measure. Even though the committee that had initially allocated seats in the first House had supposedly been guided by the three-fifths rule tentatively approved earlier in the convention, it had proposed that subsequent reallocations of congressional representation be based upon the states' "wealth and number of inhabitants." Randolph's motion to require that Congress conduct a periodic census used that same formulation.[51]

But other southern delegates objected to its vagueness. If southerners could not trust a northern-dominated Congress to voluntarily reapportion itself, why should they entrust it with the administration of an amorphous reapportionment formula? Mason worried that by "requiring of the legislature something too indefinite and impracticable," they would be affording it "a pretext for doing nothing." The reapportionment standard must be "precise." Williamson proposed, as an amendment to Randolph's motion, that the yardstick for measuring "population and wealth" be simply the states' free population plus three-fifths of their slave populations.[52]

Randolph now conceded error: The committee's first stab at an apportionment of congressional representation had been based on "mere conjecture." He was unwilling to entrust a subsequent reapportionment based on a vague formula to a northern-dominated Congress. Especially given that some northern delegates had recently voiced opposition to slaves' counting at all in the apportionment formula, Randolph insisted that this matter not be left to Congress's discretion; the apportionment standard must explicitly require that three-fifths of the slaves be counted.[53]

With southerners expressing dissatisfaction with the King committee's allocations of seats in the first House and unwillingness to leave reapportionment to the discretion of a Congress that probably would be dominated by northerners, tempers flared and some northern delegates reassessed their willingness to count slaves at all in apportioning representation in Congress. King, who had previously agreed that the South's greater wealth ought to be reflected in the apportionment of the House, now warned that while northerners were "very desirous of uniting with their southern brethren," he did not "think it prudent to rely so far on that disposition as to subject them to any gross inequality." Morris similarly protested that southern states were demanding "more than their [fair] share of representation." Many northern delegates now withdrew their support for the three-fifths compromise, which was rejected on July 11 by a vote of six states to four. All the northern states except Connecticut voted against it, as did South Carolina, whose delegates were still insisting that slaves count the same as free persons for apportionment purposes.[54]

In response to that vote, William Davie of North Carolina declared that "it was high time now to speak out." His state "would never confederate on any terms that did not rate them [slaves] at least as three fifths," and he warned that if "some gentlemen" continued to seek "to deprive the southern states of any share of representation for their blacks," then "the business [of the convention] was at an end."[55]

Resenting that threat, Morris replied that he "verily believed the people of Pennsylvania will never agree to a representation of Negroes [i.e., slaves]."

Although he considered "groundless" the notion that southern and northern states had fundamentally conflicting interests, he could now see that "the southern gentlemen will not be satisfied unless they see the way open to their gaining a majority in the public councils." Morris asked, "[W]hat security will the northern and middle states" have once North Carolina, South Carolina, and Georgia had a majority of the population, which would be the case "in a little time?" A "transfer of power" to the southern and western states would result in "an oppression of commerce" in favor of the "landed interest" and probably "a war with Spain for the Mississippi." If regional interests were as disparate and conflicting as southerners seemed to think, Morris declared, then "instead of attempting to blend incompatible things, let us at once take a friendly leave of each other."[56]

Such statements by northern delegates, in turn, provoked the South Carolinians to reiterate their demand that slaves count equally with free persons in the apportionment of congressional representation. In direct response to Morris, Butler explained, "The security the southern states want is that their Negroes may not be taken from them, which some gentlemen within or without doors have a very good mind to do." Charles Pinckney argued that southern slaves were as productive of wealth as northern farmers, and because war required money, those slaves therefore contributed as much as freemen to the nation's strength. Yet only the delegations from South Carolina and Georgia voted to count slaves equally in apportioning the House.[57]

While some delegates on both sides of this debate were taking extreme positions and issuing threats, others were still calling for a compromise. A few days before the issue came to a head, King had dropped a hint as to how it might be reframed to make a compromise more palatable to both sides. As we have just seen, in the mid-1780s, eleven states had agreed to a proposed amendment to the Articles providing that three-fifths of the slaves be counted, in addition to all free inhabitants, in apportioning congressional financial *requisitions*, and most Americans agreed that taxation and representation should be linked. Amid fevered declamations regarding the rule for apportioning representation in the House, Morris now proposed that the clause that would empower Congress in the future to alter the allocation of representatives based on shifts in wealth and population be amended to provide also that taxation be apportioned according to representation.[58]

Several delegates—northern and southern—applauded the "justice" of Morris's proposal, though some of them also noted the impracticability of apportioning indirect taxes, such as import duties and excises. Morris quickly agreed to modify his proposal, limiting it to direct taxes, such as those on land

and polls.* Morris's aim, as Madison observed in his notes, was probably "to lessen the eagerness on one side and the opposition on the other to the share of representation claimed by the southern states on account of the Negroes."† Once the delegates had unanimously agreed to Morris's revised proposal for linking taxation and representation, Oliver Ellsworth of Connecticut suggested amending it to provide that "the rule of contribution by direct taxation" be the number of white inhabitants and three-fifths of all others, "until some other rule that shall more accurately ascertain the wealth of the several states can be devised and adopted by the legislature."[59]

Wilson explained why this proposal was attractive to northern delegates: Their constituents might take "less umbrage" to admitting slaves into the rule of representation if it were accomplished "indirectly." Slaves would be part of the formula for apportioning direct taxes because they were a significant component of the South's wealth. Representation, in turn, ought to reflect tax burdens. When a proposal was made late in the convention to strike the direct-taxes provision from the section of the Constitution apportioning representation in the House, Morris opposed on the grounds that its insertion there had been meant "to exclude the appearance of counting the Negroes in

---

* The delegates defined "direct" taxes only by example. A tax on persons or on land clearly qualified as such. But they did not specify criteria to inform the determination of which other taxes might qualify as direct. When King asked later in the convention for a definition of direct taxes, nobody responded.

When the Supreme Court first confronted this question in 1796, the justices proved equally perplexed. They stated that only a tax on land or polls would definitely qualify as a direct tax. On the specific question before them—whether a tax on carriages qualified as direct—the justices offered an odd definition that focused only on the feasibility of a particular tax's being apportioned: "[A]s all direct taxes must be apportioned, it is evident that the Constitution contemplated none as direct but such as could be apportioned."

Nor did the delegates in Philadelphia give much thought to how the apportionment of direct taxes would operate in practice. Some of them apparently imagined that Congress would simply stipulate the amount of money it wished to raise through direct taxes, and then states would be requisitioned based on the apportionment formula, though the states would be free to determine for themselves on which objects to levy the taxes. A second possibility, explicitly envisioned by John Marshall at the Virginia ratifying convention, was that Congress would stipulate a specific amount of money to be raised, which would be apportioned among the states according to the three-fifths rule, but Congress would then levy different direct taxes in different states, perhaps leaving the formulation of the tax in each state up to its congressional delegation. Yet another possibility apparently envisioned by some people was that Congress would frame its own taxes on, for example, land or slaves, which Congress itself would then collect, though the collective liability of each state's citizens would be based on the apportionment formula.

† Indeed, a couple of weeks later, Morris expressed the hope that the Committee of Detail would strike out this provision for apportioning direct taxes on the grounds that he had "only meant it as a bridge to assist us over a certain gulf; having passed the gulf, the bridge may be removed." But the committee nevertheless adhered to this provision.

the representation. The including of them may now be referred to the object of direct taxes and incidentally only to that of representation."[60]

Southern delegates were also generally happy to accede to the Morris-Ellsworth proposal. Perhaps most of them considered increased representation in the House worth the price of a larger burden in direct taxes.* More important, southern delegates probably understood, as Morris himself acknowledged late in the convention, that it would be impractical for the federal government to impose direct taxes: "It is idle to suppose that the general government can stretch its hand directly into the pockets of the people scattered over so vast a country." In this view, only duties on imports and exports, and excises on manufactured goods, were plausible sources of revenue for the federal government. Thus, the concession on direct taxes would cost the South very little, which may explain why all southern delegations agreed to it.[61]

In the end, the state delegations unanimously agreed that for purposes of apportioning direct taxes and representation in the House, three-fifths of the slave population would be added to the free population. Sherman observed that this compromise—embodied in what became known as the Three-Fifths Clause of the Constitution—had been approved only "after much difficulty and deliberation," and he strongly opposed reconsidering it later in the convention when other slavery-related issues provoked rancorous debate.[62]

Over time, the three-fifths compromise that the convention had approved became increasingly objectionable to many northerners. After the presidential election of 1800, some Federalists attributed Jefferson's narrow victory over John Adams to the three-fifths rule, which led them to disparage Jefferson as the "Negro president."[63†]

Northerners' dissatisfaction with the Three-Fifths Clause only grew when, in 1803, President Jefferson consummated the Louisiana Purchase, which vastly extended the geographic scope of the United States, adding territory that was ripe for the expansion of slavery. In a letter written that year, Rufus King called the Three-Fifths Clause one of the Constitution's "greatest blemishes," and he urged northerners to treat the clause as inapplicable to states added to the union as a result of Jefferson's bargain with Emperor Napoleon. King also insisted that northerners had been "injudiciously led to concede to this unreasonable provision" on the supposition that Congress "must resort to direct taxes," in combination with "the maxim that taxation and representation

---

* Some southerners may also have regarded the requirement that direct taxes be apportioned among the states according to population as an indirect protection for slavery because it limited Congress's ability to force emancipation through an exorbitant tax imposed on slaves.

† On the other hand, had slaves counted the same as free persons for purposes of apportioning the electoral college, Jefferson would have been elected president over Adams in 1796.

are inseparable." In 1804, the Massachusetts legislature proposed repeal of the Three-Fifths Clause, though only Connecticut and Delaware supported such a constitutional amendment.[64]

By 1820, the Three-Fifths Clause was in effect translating into eighteen additional southern congressional representatives, and it had become a consistent target of northern criticism. That year, when Congress was consumed by heated sectional debate over the admission of Missouri to the union as a slave state, King acknowledged in the US Senate that "the disproportionate power and influence allowed to the slaveholding states was a necessary sacrifice to the establishment of the Constitution," and that "faith and honor stand pledged not to disturb it." Yet he insisted that "the extension of this disproportionate power to the new states would be unjust and odious"—especially since none of the Founders had "anticipated the fact that the whole of the revenue of the United States would be derived from indirect taxes which cannot be apportioned."[65]

In a speech to the House of Representatives, Charles Pinckney responded that it was with "extreme astonishment" that he discovered that northerners thought "a great concession" had been made to the South in counting three-fifths of the slaves for purposes of apportioning the House. This supposition was a "great and unpardonable error," Pinckney insisted, as it was "the southern members [who were] unjustly deprived of any representation for a large and important part of our population."[66]

Slavery and Economic Issues

The Philadelphia convention confronted several other issues that directly implicated slavery. Should Congress be empowered to regulate—restrict or even prohibit—the foreign slave trade? Should the power to regulate foreign commerce, if granted to Congress, be qualified by a supermajority requirement in order to protect southerners whose slaves mainly produced staples for export, and thus were vulnerable to being disadvantaged by commercial regulations, such as the granting of preferences to domestic shipping (a trade dominated by northerners)? Should Congress have the authority to impose export taxes, which would be borne most heavily by southern planters and which could possibly be used as an indirect means of regulating or even abolishing slavery? These various issues involving trade and commerce ultimately provided the occasion for another, more complicated set of compromises over slavery at the convention.[67]

Convention delegates were vexed over how to handle the foreign slave trade. Before the Revolutionary War, many colonies had endeavored to enact taxes to suppress it, only to have those efforts vetoed in London. In his draft of the Declaration of Independence, Jefferson had complained of the king's "prostitut[ing] his negative for suppressing every legislative attempt to prohibit or to restrain this execrable commerce." The foreign slave trade "waged cruel war against human nature itself, violating its most sacred rights of life and liberty in the persons of a distant people who never offended him [the king], captivating and carrying them into slavery in another hemisphere or to incur miserable death in their transportation thither." Delegates to the Continental Congress from South Carolina and Georgia pressured Congress into deleting this harsh indictment of the foreign slave trade. The trade temporarily ceased under the general nonimportation policy adopted by Congress in 1774. But once the Revolutionary War ended, the Confederation Congress lightly dismissed Quaker petitions calling upon it to end the foreign slave trade, and the states of the Deep South resumed their importation of slaves from Africa.[68]

For several reasons, northern delegates to the Philadelphia convention were willing to take a stronger stand against the foreign slave trade than against domestic slavery. First, they saw the slave trade as more horrific; Morris denounced it at the convention as contravening "the most sacred laws of humanity." Second, they believed that banning it did not pose the same difficulties that abolishing slavery would: interfering with property rights and creating a large population of free blacks in America. Indeed, to allow the foreign slave trade to continue heightened the risk of slave insurrections, which the national government—not just southern importers of slaves—would bear the costs of suppressing. Finally, northern delegates worried that the Three-Fifths Clause, by tying the representation of southern states in Congress to their slave populations, would encourage the continuation of the foreign slave trade.[69]

Unlike with regard to their position on other issues related to slavery, such as whether slaves ought to count in apportioning representation in the national legislature, southerners were internally divided over the foreign slave trade. In 1787, only the Carolinas and Georgia still permitted it (and South Carolina, in March of that year, barred slave imports for three years as part of a debtor relief measure).* Virginia and Maryland, where slave owners already earned substantial profits by selling their slaves to the Deep South where they were more valuable, had prohibited the foreign slave trade. If the Constitution were to protect the trade, the prices that Upper South slave owners could charge the Deep South purchasers of their slaves would inevitably decline. Thus, delegates from Virginia and Maryland argued strongly in favor of the Constitution's banning the foreign slave trade—though, of course, their stated

---

* In 1786, the North Carolina legislature imposed a prohibitive tax on the foreign slave trade, but it did not formally prohibit it until 1798.

arguments concerned the inhumanity of the slave trade and the danger of slave insurrections, not the economic interests of slave owners in those states.[70]

By contrast, dominant opinion in South Carolina and Georgia strenuously opposed any federal restrictions on the foreign slave trade. As colonies, these two, unlike the rest, had not attempted to limit the importation of slaves in the years immediately preceding the Revolutionary War. During the war, many thousands of slaves had escaped from these two states, increasing the demand for slave imports from Africa, where the cost of obtaining slaves was significantly lower than it was in Maryland and Virginia. In the Deep South, where the climate and malarial low-country swamps discouraged free labor, slavery was deemed essential to economic prosperity for whites. As Charles Cotesworth Pinckney later explained, South Carolina "would soon be a desert waste" without slave labor. Under the Articles of Confederation, there was no limit on these states' ability to continue importing slaves. In the mid-1780s, when the South Carolina and Georgia legislatures approved the proposed amendment to the Articles that would empower Congress to regulate foreign commerce in certain ways, they explicitly exempted restrictions on the slave trade from that grant of power.[71]

Thus, at the Philadelphia convention, Charles Cotesworth Pinckney declared that "South Carolina and Georgia cannot do without slaves." While Pinckney acknowledged that a tax on the importation of slaves would be reasonable, just like any other import duty, to bar the foreign slave trade entirely would mean "an exclusion of South Carolina from the union." He also argued that "the importation of slaves would be for the interest of the whole union. The more slaves, the more produce to employ the carrying trade."[72]

Southern delegates also sought to prohibit Congress from imposing export taxes. Because most of the South's wealth derived from exports, it was particularly vulnerable to such taxes, especially if northerners were to generally enjoy majorities in both the House and the Senate.[73]

Thus, Pierce Butler of South Carolina declared himself "strenuously opposed to a [congressional] power over exports as unjust and alarming to the staple states." Mason insisted that those states required some "security" for their produce. Observing that in the first Congress northern states would have an eight-to-five majority in the Senate and a thirty-six to twenty-nine advantage in the House, he warned that "a majority when interested will oppress the minority." While the level of imports would be similar throughout the nation, exports would vary significantly, which gave the southern states good "ground for their suspicions." Williamson declared that his state, North Carolina, "would never agree" to giving Congress this power. If the convention insisted on doing so, then "it would destroy the last hope of an adoption of the plan." Southern delegates resisted even compromise proposals that would

Figure 4.2 Charles Cotesworth Pinckney of South Carolina, who rose to the rank of general during the Revolutionary War and later was, twice, the Federalist Party's candidate for president. (National Portrait Gallery, Smithsonian Institution/Art Resource, NY)

have provided only qualified protection against export taxes—such as requiring congressional supermajorities for their imposition or allowing Congress to use them solely for revenue-raising purposes.[74]

By contrast, most northern delegates opposed a constitutional ban on congressional export taxes because they believed such duties could be useful in terms of both raising revenue and retaliating against European trade restrictions. Thus, Wilson objected to depriving the national government of "half the regulation of trade"—especially the half that he thought "might be more effectual . . . in obtaining beneficial treaties of commerce." Morris considered a ban on export taxes "radically objectionable." Such taxes would often be more "easy and proper" than import duties. He also noted that all nations imposed export taxes on goods over which they monopolized production, and that such taxes could prove "of critical importance" for imposing embargoes in time of war. Morris denied that southern staples would be the only objects of export taxes; lumber and livestock from the North also could be subjected to such duties.

Finally, Morris warned that in the absence of federal export taxes, southerners would never have to contribute their fair share of federal revenues. Congress was unlikely to impose direct taxes any time soon because they would "push them [Americans] into revolts," and the South was unlikely to pay significant amounts in import duties or excise taxes because such a large percentage of its population was enslaved.[75]

Among southern delegates, Madison was virtually alone in defending a grant of power to Congress to tax exports. He insisted that the convention should be governed by "national and permanent views" and noted that export taxes might be expedient in the future, even if not at present. In addition to making some of the same points as Wilson and Morris, Madison expressed concern that if Congress were denied power over exports, the authority to regulate them would remain with the states, where it would be used in ways that fostered animosities among neighboring states (as state import duties had done under the Articles, when states with better natural ports had effectively shifted a substantial share of the costs of their governments onto the shoulders of their neighbors). Finally, Madison argued that because southern states were the ones "most in danger and most needing naval protection," they could hardly "complain if the [tax] burden should be somewhat heaviest on them."[76]

The last of the economic issues directly concerning slavery that confronted the convention also involved potential limits on Congress's power to regulate foreign commerce. As we saw in chapter 1, southerners feared that Congress would use such a power to pass laws protecting northern shippers from foreign competition for the South's carrying trade and to enact protective tariffs for the benefit of northern manufacturers. As agricultural exporters with little manufacturing of their own, southerners generally favored free trade and low shipping costs. Southerners' concerns about vesting Congress with power to regulate foreign commerce were exacerbated as it became increasingly clear at the convention that the South would be—at least initially—a minority in both the House and the Senate.[77]

Thus, after the King committee's report allocating seats in the first House left the southern states with a "considerable" minority, Charles Cotesworth Pinckney objected that if "the regulation of trade is to be given to the general government, they [southerners] will be nothing more than overseers for the northern states." Mason likewise warned that the disparate interests of the North and the South necessitated some "precautions in the case of regulating navigation, commerce, and imposts." Unless some check were provided against "a bare majority," Charles Pinckney concluded, regional diversity of interests "would be a source of oppressive regulations" for the South.[78]

One way to protect southern interests would be to require a supermajority vote for congressional regulations of commerce. Yet for some northern delegates, such as Nathaniel Gorham of Massachusetts, the principal "motive to union [was] a commercial one." Why should northern states remain in the union if Congress was to be "so fettered as to be unable to relieve the[m]?" Moreover, the South "had the most reason to dread" disunion because it was the most vulnerable to foreign attack. According to Gorham, northern and mid-Atlantic states "were not afraid of external danger, and did not need the aid of the southern states." George Clymer of Pennsylvania observed that "[t]he northern and middle states will be ruined, if not enabled to defend themselves against foreign [trade] regulations." Although Madison's notes do not record either Gorham or Clymer elaborating on the state of the northern economy, all the delegates presumably knew that the northern shipbuilding industry and seamen involved in the carrying trade had been especially hard hit by British trade restrictions following the war. Under such circumstances, to fetter Congress's ability to regulate foreign commerce with a supermajority requirement was to jeopardize northern support for the Constitution.[79]

Madison was something of an outlier among southern delegates with regard to the supermajority requirement for commercial legislation, just as he was with regard to Congress's power over export taxes. One benefit of allowing Congress to enact commercial legislation by a simple majority vote, Madison noted, was that foreign nations would be less able to exert "corrupt influence" to impede American retaliation against their discriminatory trade restrictions. Abuse of the commerce power would be "rendered improbable" by the requirement that both houses of Congress and the president concur in all legislation. In addition, Madison noted that a congressional majority in favor of legislation to protect northern shippers from foreign competition was by no means certain, given that two northern states—Connecticut and New Jersey—had mostly agricultural interests, which would incline them to oppose legislation to raise freight rates, and that future western states would also be primarily agricultural. Even if Congress did pass such legislation, Madison argued, at worst it would lead to a temporary increase in the freight rates paid by southern producers, before eventually having the effect of inducing the South to increase its own shipping capacity. Finally, Madison observed that "vulnerable" southern states—particularly Virginia*—"would derive an essential advantage in the general security afforded by the increase of our maritime strength" that would result from congressional legislation extending special benefits to domestic shippers.[80]

---

* As the Revolutionary War was beginning, Madison wrote to a friend that slavery was "the only part in which this colony [Virginia] was vulnerable, and if we should be subdued, we shall fall like Achilles by the hand of one that knows that secret."

During the first two months of the convention's deliberations, delegates had spent little time on these economic issues concerning slavery: the foreign slave trade, congressional export taxes, and Congress's power over foreign commerce. But when, on July 23, Gerry moved for the appointment of a committee to convert the resolutions thus far approved by the convention into a draft of the Constitution to be further reviewed by the delegates, Charles Cotesworth Pinckney "reminded the convention that if the committee should fail to insert some security to the southern states against an emancipation of slaves, and taxes on exports, he should be bound by duty to his state to vote against [its] report."[81]

On August 6, the Committee of Detail—composed of Gorham, Ellsworth, Wilson, Randolph, and Rutledge—issued a report that was widely perceived to be highly favorable to the South (even though three of its five members were northerners). In addition to the Three-Fifths Clause for apportioning direct taxes and representation in the House, Congress would be barred from taxing or prohibiting the foreign slave trade; export taxes would also be forbidden; and a two-thirds majority of both houses of Congress would be required for the enactment of "navigation" laws (i.e., restrictions on the use of foreign ships to carry American goods).[82]

The committee's report elicited howls of protest from several northern delegates. King now objected to the Three-Fifths Clause, which had been agreed upon weeks earlier. Counting slaves in apportioning representation was "a most grating circumstance to his mind, and he believed would be so to a great part of the people of America." King explained that hitherto he had accepted this concession to the South, which he had hoped "would have produced a readiness which had not been manifested to strengthen the general government and to mark a full confidence in it." The committee report, however, had "put an end to all these hopes." Under the committee's proposal, King complained, the North would be obligated to defend the South, which would "be at liberty . . . to increase its own danger" of slave insurrections by importing more slaves, without receiving any "compensation for the burden," because of the Constitution's ban on congressional imposition of taxes on exports and the foreign slave trade. King warned, "There was so much inequality and unreasonableness in all this, that the people of the northern states could never be reconciled to it." If no time limit were placed on the continuation of the foreign slave trade, then he would oppose counting slaves for purposes of apportioning representation in the House.[83]

Morris likewise condemned the committee report as too biased toward the South. Counting slaves for apportioning representation without barring the foreign slave trade would simply encourage southern slave owners to continue a practice that horrified most northerners. What compensation would northerners receive "for a sacrifice of every principle of right, of every impulse of humanity?" Perversely, they would have to "march their militia for the defense of the southern states" in case of slave insurrection, and they would have to "supply vessels and seamen in case of foreign attack," to which the already vulnerable southern states would be rendered even more susceptible after weakening themselves by importing additional slaves. Finally, Morris objected that Congress was to be barred from imposing export taxes, which would have the potential to raise significant revenue in the South, but that it was to have "indefinite power" to raise import and excise taxes, "both of which will fall heavier on [northern] than on the southern inhabitants."[84]

Delegates from Maryland and Virginia joined northerners in condemning the committee's proposal to ban congressional interference with the foreign slave trade. Luther Martin, who later became a founding member of the Maryland Society for the Abolition of Slavery, viewed that trade as "inconsistent with the principles of the revolution and dishonorable to the American character." He warned that the Three-Fifths Clause would encourage Deep South states to continue importing slaves, and he thought it unfair that slave imports "weakened one part of the union which the other parts were bound to protect" by contributing to the expense of suppressing slave insurrections.[85]

Mason likewise attacked the foreign slave trade as "infernal traffic," which he claimed had "originated in the avarice of British merchants" and which he blamed the British government for not allowing the colonies to end. Slave importations affected the entire union, not just the southern states. Mason argued that "[t]he evil of having slaves was experienced during the late war," when they might have proved "dangerous instruments" in the enemy's hands if dealt with more adroitly. Lamenting that some northerners "had from a lust of gain embarked in this nefarious traffic," he declared it "essential in every point of view that the general government should have power to prevent the increase of slavery."[86]

Such denunciations of the foreign slave trade elicited strong rejoinders from the South Carolinians. John Rutledge announced that he would happily exempt other states from any obligation to protect the South from slave insurrections. He also insisted, "Religion and humanity had nothing to do with this question. Interest alone is the governing principle with nations." Rutledge declared that "[t]he true question at present is whether the southern states shall or shall not be parties to the union." He warned: "If the convention thinks that North Carolina, South Carolina, and Georgia will ever agree to the plan, unless their right to import slaves be untouched, the expectation is vain. The people of those states will never be such fools as to give up so important an interest." He also observed that "[i]f the northern states consult their interests,

Figure 4.3 Luther Martin, who was the longtime attorney general of Maryland, became one of the leading opponents of ratification of the Constitution and later was one of the nation's most prominent lawyers and represented Justice Samuel Chase in his impeachment trial in 1805 and former vice president Aaron Burr in his treason trial in 1807. (Courtesy of Independence National Historical Park)

they will not oppose the increase of slaves which will increase the commodities of which they will become the carriers."[87]

The Pinckneys backed Rutledge. Charles Cotesworth Pinckney argued that Mason's denunciation of the slave trade was hypocritical: Virginia would "gain by stopping the importations" because "[h]er slaves will rise in value, and she has more than she wants." It would be unfair, Pinckney observed, "to require South Carolina and Georgia to confederate on such unequal terms." Conceding that Congress ought to be able to impose import duties on slaves, Pinckney insisted that authorizing Congress to bar the foreign slave trade entirely would mean "an exclusion of South Carolina from the union." Pinckney's cousin Charles warned that even if the state's delegation acquiesced in such a prohibition at the convention, the South Carolina legislature would "never receive the plan if it prohibits the slave trade." He also observed that "[i]f the states be all left at liberty on this subject, South Carolina may perhaps by degrees do of herself what is wished [i.e., bar the foreign slave trade], as Virginia and Maryland have already done."[88]

Hugh Williamson of North Carolina and Abraham Baldwin of Georgia supported the South Carolinians. Williamson warned that "the southern states could not be members of the union" if the clause barring congressional interference with the foreign slave trade was rejected, and he argued that "it was wrong to force anything down, not absolutely necessary, and which any state must disagree to." Baldwin insisted that the convention should deal with "national objects alone" and that the question of whether a state continued to import slaves was "of a local nature." He also warned that Georgia was naturally suspicious of "yielding national powers" because its distance from the center of the nation "would preclude [it] from equal advantage." This skeptical predisposition would not incline Georgia to favorably regard "an attempt to abridge one of her favorite prerogatives [i.e., the importation of slaves]." By contrast, if left to its own devices, Georgia "might probably put a stop to the evil."[89]

Several northern delegates seemed inclined to call the bluff of the Deep South states. King declared that "[i]f two states will not agree to the Constitution" without safeguards for the foreign slave trade, he could "affirm with equal belief . . . that great and equal opposition would be experienced from the other states" if the Constitution afforded such protection. Wilson observed that if South Carolina and Georgia were genuinely inclined to bar slave importations themselves, as their delegates had suggested they might be, then "they would never refuse to unite because importation might be prohibited [by Congress]." Dickinson likewise "could not believe that the southern states would refuse to confederate" if Congress were empowered to bar the foreign slave trade, "especially as the power was not likely to be immediately exercised by the general government."[90]

Yet, in fact, the delegates from the Deep South states probably cared more about preserving the option for their states to continue the foreign slave trade than the delegates from the other states cared about barring the trade in the Constitution or empowering Congress to do so. As Madison told Jefferson after the convention, South Carolina and Georgia "were inflexible on the point of the slaves." Thus, threats by Deep South delegates to walk out of the convention if the Constitution did not grant some protection to the foreign slave trade had to be taken seriously.[91]

Perhaps looking to broker another compromise, the Connecticut delegates evinced the strongest support of any northern delegation for the Deep South's position on the foreign slave trade. Ellsworth argued that "[t]he morality or wisdom of slavery are considerations belonging to the states themselves. What enriches a part enriches the whole, and the states are the best judges of their particular interest." He also noted that terminating the foreign slave trade would be unfair to the Deep South. In Maryland and Virginia, where the life expectancy of slaves was greater, it was cheaper to breed slaves than to import them, while "in the sickly rice swamps, foreign supplies are necessary." In any event, Ellsworth predicted that the issue would soon disappear, for "as population increases, poor laborers will be so plent[iful] as to render slaves useless," and thus "[s]lavery in time will not be a speck in our country."[92]

Sherman agreed that "it was better to let the southern states import slaves than to part with them, if they made that a sine qua non." Although he disapproved of the foreign slave trade, "as the states were now possessed of the right to import slaves, as the public good did not require it to be taken from them, and as it was expedient to have as few objections as possible to the proposed scheme of government, he thought it best to leave the matter as we find it." Sherman also agreed with Ellsworth that "the abolition of slavery seemed to be going on in the United States and that the good sense of the several states would probably by degrees complete it."[93]

Morris, who had recently launched into a diatribe against slavery, now proposed referring all of the clauses involving economic issues relating to slavery to a committee, where "[t]hese things may form a bargain among the northern and southern states." Randolph agreed that they must try to find "some middle ground" that would prevent the two Deep South states from being "lost to the union," but without repelling "the Quakers, the Methodists, and many others in the states having no slaves." The delegates approved the appointment of a grand committee, to which they assigned the provisions barring Congress from taxing or prohibiting the foreign slave trade, requiring a supermajority in both houses of Congress for the enactment of navigation acts, and requiring that "capitation" taxes (head taxes) be apportioned according to population (consistent with the Three-Fifths Clause).[94]

Although some delegates wanted also to commit the provision barring congressional export taxes, that provision, which the convention had approved the previous day, was not assigned to the committee. Believing that such taxes were an important tool for managing the national economy as well as an easy source of national revenue, Madison had sought to replace the ban with a provision requiring two-thirds majorities in both houses of Congress for the imposition of such taxes. Similarly seeking to preserve some congressional authority over export taxes, Clymer of Pennsylvania had sought to limit the ban to export taxes designed only for the purpose of raising revenue (which would have permitted Congress to enact export taxes aimed solely at regulating trade). Yet both of these efforts were defeated, and the outright ban on export taxes was approved.[95]

The committee to which the other slavery-related provisions were referred then proposed that Congress be barred from forbidding the foreign slave trade only until 1800 and that the supermajority requirement for navigation acts be eliminated. (The requirement for apportionment of capitation taxes was left untouched.) Martin, who was on the committee and soon would become an ardent critic of the Constitution, reported during the ratifying contest that the northern states, despite their professed aversion to slavery, "were very willing to indulge the southern states" on a temporary continuation of the foreign slave trade, so long as the supermajority requirement for navigation laws was removed.[96]

Although the committee proposal would not permit Congress to forbid the foreign slave trade until 1800, it did allow Congress to impose a nonprohibitive tax on imported slaves—"at a rate not exceeding the average of the duties laid on imports" (language that was quickly replaced with a concrete figure of ten dollars per slave). Madison later explained that allowing such a tax would give congressional representatives "an opportunity of evidencing their sentiments on the policy and humanity" of the foreign slave trade and would force southerners to bear their fair share of import duties.[97]

When the delegates debated this provision, Sherman objected that authorizing such a tax acknowledged the principle that men were property. Several delegates who had served on the committee quickly responded that this provision had been part of a quid pro quo and should not be tampered with. Gorham told Sherman that he should consider the authorized duty on slave imports not as an acknowledgment that slaves were property but as a disincentive to the foreign slave trade, while Mason argued that forbidding such a tax would be equivalent to providing a subsidy to the importation of slaves, given that other sorts of imports would be subject to taxation. The delegates then agreed to this provision authorizing a congressional tax on the importation of slaves.[98]*

Charles Cotesworth Pinckney proposed that the year in which the foreign slave trade would no longer be protected from congressional prohibition be changed from 1800 to 1808. This would enable the Deep South states to enjoy at least another twenty years in which they would be free to import slaves from Africa. Madison opposed the change in year, arguing that "[t]wenty years will produce all the mischief that can be apprehended from the liberty to import slaves. So long a term will be more dishonorable to the national character

---

* Congress never did impose the ten-dollar tax on the importation of slaves that the Constitution authorized. When a Virginia representative proposed such a tax in the first session of Congress, representatives from South Carolina and Georgia erupted in anger at the hypocrisy of Virginians, who already had all the slaves they needed. The proposal then died in committee and was never revived.

than to say nothing about it in the Constitution." But Madison was defeated by a vote of seven states to four.* He later explained that Massachusetts, New Hampshire, and Connecticut—states that had already abolished or begun to abolish slavery—voted in favor of the change of year with the motive of reconciling the Deep South delegations to the unqualified grant of power to Congress to regulate commerce, "against which they felt, as did some other states, a very strong repugnance."[99]

The "earnestness"—as Madison called it—of the Deep South states on the issue of the foreign slave trade manifested itself once again late in the convention. During discussion of the provision governing amendments to the Constitution, Rutledge proposed that the provision on the foreign slave trade be made unamendable, explaining that "he never could agree to give a power by which the articles relating to slaves might be altered by the states not interested in that property and prejudiced against it." In other words, under Rutledge's proposal, which the delegates approved on an unrecorded vote, no constitutional amendment could be enacted before 1808 to authorize Congress immediately to bar the foreign slave trade.[100]

The other key piece of the grand committee's proposal—removing the requirement of two-thirds majorities in both houses of Congress for the enactment of navigation laws—proved more difficult to pass. After the committee had made its recommendations, Charles Pinckney moved, in lieu of this part of the committee's proposal, to require that *all* congressional regulations of commerce, foreign or interstate, be subject to a two-thirds supermajority requirement. He warned that without such a safeguard, the North's distinctive commercial interests would result in the oppression of the South. Williamson backed Pinckney, denying that any "useful measure" had been lost in the Confederation Congress due to the Articles' requirement of supermajority support for certain important congressional actions. Nor was Williamson persuaded by the argument that the South should defer to the North on this issue because of the southern states' supposed need for northern military protection. He was confident that the "sickliness" of the southern climate would deter invaders.[101]

However, several northern delegates opposed Pinckney and spoke strongly in favor of the committee's proposal to eliminate the supermajority requirement for navigation acts. Morris argued that shipping required public support

---

* Morris was so aggrieved by the change in year that he proposed explicitly limiting the right to import slaves to North Carolina, South Carolina, and Georgia, partly so that everyone would understand that this constitutional provision had been a capitulation to the demands of those states. When Mason opposed this suggestion on the grounds that it might offend persons in those states, Morris withdrew his motion.

and that navigation acts would facilitate the creation of a navy, which would be especially vital to the protection of the more vulnerable southern states. In addition, Congress's granting preferences to American ships would create incentives to build more of them, and the ensuing increase in competition for the carrying trade would then reduce the freight rates paid by southern producers. Wilson argued more generally that majorities ought to control legislatures and that the supermajority requirement in the Articles had caused "[g]reat inconveniences."[102]

One of the southern delegations, South Carolina's, also endorsed the committee's proposal to eliminate the supermajority requirement for navigation acts, which enabled it to pass. Observing that "it was the true interest of the southern states to have no regulation of commerce," Charles Cotesworth Pinckney explained why he nonetheless was voting to remove the supermajority requirement: "[C]onsidering the loss brought on the commerce of the eastern states by the revolution, their liberal conduct towards the views of South Carolina, and the interest the weak southern states had in being united with the strong eastern states, he thought it proper that no fetters should be imposed on the power of making commercial regulations." Implicitly referring to New Englanders' support of South Carolina on the issue of the foreign slave trade, Pinckney admitted that he had entertained "prejudices against the eastern states before he came here, but would acknowledge that he had found them as liberal and candid as any men whatever." His constituents, "though prejudiced against the eastern states, would be reconciled to this liberality" for the same reason. Butler confirmed that a deal had been made: Although he believed the interests of northern and southern states "to be as different as the interests of Russia and Turkey," he was "desirous of conciliating the affections of the eastern states." In an editorial note appended to his reporting of these statements, Madison observed simply: "An understanding on the two subjects of navigation and slavery had taken place between those parts of the union."[103]

Virginians Mason and Randolph were upset with this deal, neither part of which directly benefited their state. Mason denounced majority control over navigation acts, which he declared would deliver southerners "bound hand and foot to the eastern states." He warned that a navigation act would enable a "few rich merchants" in northern cities to monopolize the trade in southern staples, siphoning off as much as half of their value. Randolph warned that "there were features so odious in the Constitution as it now stands that he doubted whether he should be able to agree to it." Abandoning the supermajority requirement for navigation acts "would complete the deformity of the system." Neither of these men would sign the Constitution on the last day of the convention, partly because of this bargain over the foreign slave trade and Congress's power to enact navigation laws.[104]

In the long term, the constitutional provision authorizing Congress eventually to abolish the foreign slave trade may have been momentous, though not in a way that most of the delegates in Philadelphia probably would have anticipated. Some of the Founding generation apparently believed that terminating the foreign slave trade at a future date would eventually lead to the end of slavery in the United States because they thought the natural rate of reproduction among slaves was not high enough to be self-sustaining. History proved that assumption badly mistaken. In 1790, the US population included 700,000 slaves. The foreign slave trade—which Georgia, South Carolina, and North Carolina all permitted at some point between 1788 and 1808—added approximately 150,000 more over the next twenty years. However, by 1860, the nation had 4 million slaves.[105]

At the first opportunity permitted under the Constitution—in 1808—and at President Jefferson's urging, Congress prohibited the foreign slave trade. This did not, of course, extinguish slavery in the United States, but it did affect the geographic distribution of slaves. After 1808, only an illegal slave trade could continue to transport slaves from Africa to the United States. Therefore, in the absence of a cheap supply of foreign slaves, slave owners in newly created and fertile states such as Alabama, Louisiana, and Mississippi bought hundreds of thousands of slaves from owners in eastern states, such as Maryland and Virginia. As vast numbers of slaves left the states of the Upper South, those states became less committed to the institution of slavery and developed stronger economic relationships with the North. As a result, while their southern brethren seceded in 1860–61, residents of the four slave states of Kentucky, Maryland, Delaware, and Missouri chose to remain in the union. Had they not done so, the Civil War might well have turned out differently.[106]

Other Issues Involving Slavery

The last of the Constitution's provisions dealing directly with slavery provoked far less controversy at the convention. Just one day before consummation of the bargain over the foreign slave trade and Congress's power to enact navigation laws, two South Carolinians—Butler and Charles Pinckney—moved, in the context of a discussion of the obligation of states to return fugitives from justice to the states from which they had absconded, "to require fugitive slaves and servants to be delivered up like criminals." In other words, they wanted the Constitution to guarantee slave owners the right to recover slaves who escaped to other states. The Articles of Confederation contained no such provision, although northern states in the 1780s did not generally resist the recapture and return of fugitive slaves to their out-of-state owners.[107]

The demand of southern delegates for a fugitive slave provision may have been provoked by an antislavery movement that had accelerated in the years during and immediately after the Revolutionary War, leaving southern slave owners feeling less secure about their property in slaves. In addition, the 1772 decision in *Somerset v. Stewart* may have been a contributing factor. The *Somerset* case involved a slave who had been brought by his owner from Virginia to England, then had escaped and been recaptured, and was about to be shipped to Jamaica for sale when a legal action for his freedom was brought on his behalf. The court ruled that Somerset's status was to be determined by English law, which was the common law and made no provision for slavery. Slavery could lawfully exist, ruled Lord Mansfield, the celebrated Lord Chief Justice of the King's Bench, only where established by statute. Before *Somerset*, slaveholders in the British Empire had believed they had a right to recapture fugitive slaves wherever they were found. After *Somerset*, they had no clear right to reclaim escaped slaves in free jurisdictions that did not provide by law for the return of fugitive slaves.[108]

Precedent for a provision guaranteeing slave owners a right to recapture fugitive slaves who escaped to other jurisdictions existed in the Northwest Ordinance of 1787, which, as discussed later in this chapter, Congress enacted while the Philadelphia convention was sitting. That ordinance barred slavery (except as a punishment for crime) in the extensive federal territory north of the Ohio River, but it also provided that slaves escaping into that territory from the United States could be "lawfully reclaimed and conveyed" to their owners. In 1856, Edward Coles, a former secretary to Madison and the second governor of Illinois, recalled that Madison had told him that many "conferences and intercommunications" were taking place in the summer of 1787 between members of the Philadelphia convention and delegates to the Confederation Congress sitting in New York, as several people sat in both bodies and were fully aware of their parallel proceedings. Madison had reported to Coles that southerners in Congress had agreed to ban slavery in the Northwest Territory in exchange for the agreement of northerners to guarantee the return of captured fugitive slaves in both the ordinance and the Constitution.[109]

The South Carolinians' proposal that the Constitution provide for the capture and return of fugitive slaves elicited little opposition from northern delegates, just two of whom voiced any objection. Wilson protested that such a provision would "oblige the executive of the state to do it, at the public expense." Why should northern states have to pay the costs of capturing and returning the escaped slaves of southern masters? Sherman declared that he "saw no more propriety in the public seizing and surrendering a slave or servant than a horse." At this point, Butler withdrew his motion so that a provision could be drafted to deal specifically with the return of fugitive slaves, rather than handling them under the general constitutional provision involving the return of fugitives from justice.[110]

When the Fugitive Slave Clause was introduced the following day, not a single delegate voted against it. Because no debate was recorded, we can only speculate as to the reasoning of northern delegates who raised no objection to this provision. For one thing, even those northerners who generally opposed slavery respected property rights in regard to slaves, and most northern states still had significant slave populations in 1787. In addition, the gradual emancipation laws enacted by several northern states in the 1780s provided for the return of fugitive slaves to their out-of-state owners. Thus, the Fugitive Slave Clause simply codified at the national level the existing practice of most or all northern states. It is also possible that northern delegates regarded the Fugitive Slave Clause as an additional part of the bargain over the foreign slave trade and Congress's power to enact navigation laws.[111]

Unlike the Three-Fifths Clause and the provision protecting the foreign slave trade from congressional interference for twenty years, the Fugitive Slave Clause does not appear to have been a sine qua non of any southern delegate's support for the Constitution. Yet in the early nineteenth century a myth arose that southerners would not have approved the Constitution without it. Most notably, Supreme Court justice Joseph Story stated in his *Commentaries on the Constitution*, published in 1833, that the absence of a fugitive slave provision under the Articles of Confederation "was felt as a grievous inconvenience by the slaveholding states, since, in many states, no aid whatsoever would be allowed to the owners, and sometimes, indeed, they met with open resistance." When a decade later, in 1842, Story wrote the opinion of the Court in *Prigg v. Pennsylvania*, which rejected a constitutional challenge to the Fugitive Slave Act of 1793 and struck down a Pennsylvania antikidnapping law that provided greater procedural protections to alleged fugitive slaves than those afforded by federal law, Story repeated the myth: "[I]t cannot be doubted that it [i.e., the Fugitive Slave Clause] constituted a fundamental article, without the adoption of which the union could not have been formed."[112]

This myth probably reflected the state of public opinion at the time Story wrote these passages better than it did historical reality. By the 1830s and 1840s, a repeal of the federal Fugitive Slave Act might well have provoked the southern states to secede from the union. By contrast, in 1787, southern delegates at the Philadelphia convention do not appear to have been terribly concerned about slave owners' fugitive slaves not being returned to them. Story published his *Commentaries* just after South Carolinians had threatened to nullify the federal tariff and to secede from the union if President Andrew Jackson dared to use force in response to their threats. In that context, Story strenuously endeavored to convince southerners that northern delegates to the

Philadelphia convention had made "many sacrifices of opinion and feeling" to the South. His stated goal was to "forever repress the delusive and mischievous notion that the [S]outh has not at all times had its full share of benefits from the union."[113]

Ironically, the Fugitive Slave Clause, which was not controversial at the Philadelphia convention or for a couple of decades thereafter, provoked enormous controversy by the middle of the nineteenth century. Its enforcement regularly generated riots in northern communities in the 1840s and 1850s, as abolitionists sought to block the return of fugitive slaves to the South, and the federal government occasionally dispatched troops to enforce the federal Fugitive Slave Act. When southern states seceded from the union in 1860–61, near the top of their list of grievances was the charge that northern states had reneged on their constitutional obligation to return fugitive slaves to their owners.[114]

In addition to the Three-Fifths Clause, the Foreign Slave Trade Clause, and the Fugitive Slave Clause, the Constitution contained several indirect safeguards for slavery. As already noted, the ban on congressional export taxes was a concession to southern planters whose slaves primarily produced agricultural goods for export.[115]

Another indirect protection for slavery was the constitutional provision empowering the national government, at the request of state legislatures—or executives, if the legislatures could not be convened—to suppress "domestic violence." Whenever the delegates to the Philadelphia convention discussed this provision, they focused explicitly on revolts by debtors and taxpayers, such as Shays's Rebellion. But the possibility of a slave insurrection cannot have been far from their minds. Indeed, as we have seen, northern delegates frequently criticized the foreign slave trade as increasing the risk of slave insurrections, which northern states would have to contribute men and money to suppressing.[116]

Another implicit constitutional protection for slavery was the restriction of the national government to enumerated powers. It is likely that every delegate in Philadelphia believed that regulating a domestic institution such as slavery would exceed the delegated powers of Congress. Indeed, southern delegates felt so secure in the Constitution's explicit and implicit protections for slavery that they declined to endorse a small-state proposal for an unamendable constitutional guarantee that "no state shall without its consent be affected in its internal police."[117]

The most divisive political issue in the nation in the 1850s and the proximate cause of the Civil War was whether Congress possessed the constitutional authority to regulate slavery in federal territories. Article IV, Section 3, of the Constitution authorizes Congress to make "needful rules and regulations" for the federal territories but does not say anything specifically about slavery. However, the issue of slavery in federal territories had arisen under the Articles of Confederation. Indeed, as was just noted, the Confederation Congress took action against slavery in federal territories at the very moment that the Constitutional Convention was sitting—in the form of the Northwest Ordinance. Such action can be considered part of the Founders' original understanding with regard to slavery.[118]

In 1784, congressional delegate Thomas Jefferson had proposed an ordinance to bar slavery from all territories held by the federal government—southern as well as northern—beginning in 1800. Most southern congressional delegates opposed this proposal—which northern delegates unanimously approved—and it was narrowly defeated, falling one delegation short of the number required to enact it. Yet even if Jefferson's proposal had passed Congress, it probably could not have been effectively implemented. By the mid-1780s, slave owners had taken many thousands of slaves across the Appalachian Mountains into what would become, in the 1790s, the states of Kentucky and Tennessee. North Carolina and Georgia probably would have refused to cede their western lands to Congress—and Virginia might have tried to rescind the cession it had already made of the land north of the Ohio River that would become the Northwest Territory—had Congress enacted Jefferson's ordinance. Indeed, just months after Jefferson's proposal, North Carolina explicitly conditioned cession of its western lands to Congress on slaves not being emancipated there. When North Carolina ultimately did cede its western lands to Congress in 1789, it reiterated that condition, and Congress acquiesced.[119]

In July 1787, at almost precisely the same moment that the Philadelphia convention tentatively agreed to the Three-Fifths Clause for apportioning representation in the House, the Confederation Congress sitting in New York City addressed the issue of slavery in the Northwest Territory—the region that would become, in the nineteenth century, the states of Ohio, Indiana, Illinois, Michigan, and Wisconsin. (By contrast, Jefferson's 1784 draft proposal had dealt with slavery in *all* federal territories.) Congress rarely enjoyed an operating quorum that summer, partly because so many delegates had been called away to the Philadelphia convention. In late May, Virginia congressional delegate William Grayson had told James Monroe that "the draft made from Congress on members for the convention has made [Congress] very thin and no business of course is going on here." Grayson predicted that Congress would remain inactive until the convention had completed its work, which he projected would take several months. Several other observers made similar predictions as to Congress's continued inactivity that summer.[120]

However, in early July, delegates from Georgia and North Carolina left the convention to travel to New York City, probably for the purpose of supplying Congress with a quorum that would enable passage of the Northwest Ordinance. One of the North Carolina delegates, William Blount, told his governor that he and Benjamin Hawkins, another member of the state's congressional delegation who happened to be in Philadelphia at the time, had received a letter from the secretary of Congress informing them that their presence was required for a quorum, which "was absolutely necessary for the great purpose of the union." Indeed, the arrival in New York of these delegates from the Philadelphia convention allowed Congress to meet and pass the ordinance organizing the Northwest Territory and prohibiting slavery there.[121]

Notably, the Northwest Ordinance passed Congress with only one dissenting voice (that of Abraham Yates of New York). Those southern delegates present unanimously supported it. There was an implicit quid pro quo: Barring slavery north of the Ohio River implied permitting it in the territories south of the river, which Congress later explicitly did. It is likely as well that some southern planters favored excluding slavery from the Northwest Territory to suppress economic competition. As Grayson told Monroe a few weeks after the ordinance passed, "The clause respecting slavery was agreed to by the southern members for the purpose of preventing tobacco and indigo from being made on the northwest side of the Ohio as well as for several other political reasons." In addition, as just noted, the Northwest Ordinance granted slave owners a right to the recovery of their escaped slaves—and perhaps there was an implicit understanding that the Constitution would also provide for such a right. It is even possible that the ordinance's ban on slavery was part of a package deal in which southerners received the Constitution's Three-Fifths Clause.[122]

Although the Northwest Ordinance's ban on slavery easily passed, most contemporaries agreed that Congress had no express power to enact it because the Articles made no provision for Congress's establishing governments for territories or prescribing the conditions for the admission of new states into the union (other than Canada or other "colon[ies]"). The Constitution, by contrast, directly addresses that gap in congressional power by granting Congress the explicit authority to "make all needful rules and regulations" for the territories. Once the Constitution was ratified, the first Congress promptly re-enacted the Northwest Ordinance. This time, nobody denied that Congress had the power to do so.[123]

However, over the decades, southerners began to distinguish between Congress's power to bar slavery in territories that existed within the United States in 1787 and in those that were subsequently acquired.* By the time

* The technical legal argument was that the Constitution did not contemplate the national government's acquiring territory beyond that already in its possession, or in the possession of

Congress debated Missouri's admission to the union as a slave state in 1819–21, most southern statesmen took the position that Congress lacked the authority to bar slavery in federal territories acquired after the ratification of the Constitution—such as the territory purchased from Emperor Napoleon during the Jefferson administration in 1803 (the Louisiana Purchase). The Supreme Court ultimately vindicated the southerners' position in the infamous *Dred Scott* decision of 1857.[124]

The ban on slavery in the Northwest Territory would prove critical to the history of slavery in the United States. White southerners were the first to migrate in large numbers to the region north of the Ohio River, and they probably would have brought slaves with them had the law permitted them to do so. If slavery was economically viable in Missouri, where just over 15 percent of the population was held in bondage in 1820, it would have been equally so in at least the southern counties of Indiana and Illinois. For decades after the enactment of the Northwest Ordinance, land speculators tried to persuade Congress—and later the Illinois legislature—to permit slavery there. In 1824, an Illinois referendum on whether to permit slavery failed by just 54 to 46 percent. The Northwest Ordinance—not any "natural" geographic or climate-based limits on the spread of slavery—kept the institution out of Indiana and Illinois. Had they become slave states, the nation's political balance of power would have shifted in favor of the South, and the history of slavery in America might have turned out very differently.[125]

Slavery and Ratification

Slavery was frequently discussed in the debates over ratification of the Constitution. (The ratification debate in general is treated in chapter 6.) Because the ratifying contest was conducted independently in each state, supporters and opponents of the Constitution could make different—even contradictory—arguments in different parts of the nation.[126]

Some prominent southern opponents of ratification professed grave concern that the Constitution would threaten the survival of slavery. Patrick Henry, who claimed to abhor slavery but believed that "prudence forbids its

---

the states, in 1787. Thus, Congress's power over subsequently acquired territory, if any, derived not from its enumerated power to govern federal territories but from another of its enumerated powers—that of admitting new states into the union. Southerners then applied to this latter grant of power what had become by the early nineteenth century their typical strict constructionist approach to constitutional interpretation. They argued that the "new states" provision authorized Congress's doing only what was strictly necessary for admitting new states, which included appointing a territorial government but not regulating domestic institutions such as slavery.

abolition," wondered why "it was omitted [in the Constitution] to secure us that property in slaves which we held now," and he darkly hinted that the "omission was done with design." Henry warned the Virginia ratifying convention that because "[t]he majority of Congress is to the North, and the slaves are to the South," Congress might tax slavery out of existence or abolish slavery as a wartime conscription measure under the Necessary and Proper Clause. Mason likewise warned that nothing in the Constitution would "prevent the northern and eastern states from meddling with our whole property of that kind" or restrain Congress from imposing a tax on slaves so prohibitive as "might totally annihilate that kind of property."[127]

In the Deep South, some opponents of ratification objected to the constitutional provision authorizing Congress eventually to prohibit the foreign slave trade (whereas at the Virginia ratifying convention, Mason criticized the Constitution's failure to immediately abolish this "diabolical" trade). One of the leading opponents of ratification in South Carolina, former governor Rawlins Lowndes, criticized this provision on the grounds that slave labor was indispensable to South Carolina's economy. He warned that even during the twenty years in which Congress was forbidden from barring the foreign slave trade, South Carolina could be made to "pay for this indulgence" (by a tax not exceeding ten dollars per imported slave). Lowndes concluded: "Negroes were our wealth, our only natural resource; yet behold how our kind friends in the North were determined soon to tie up our hands, and drain us of what we had!"[128]

Some delegates to northern ratifying conventions expressed agreement that the Constitution threatened the survival of slavery, and they approved of it for this very reason. These northern Federalists argued that even though the Constitution protected slavery in the short term, it would eventually help to extinguish it—a position later embraced by Abraham Lincoln, who insisted that the Framers had "expected and intended that it [slavery] should be in the course of ultimate extinction." Thus, Thomas Dawes told the Massachusetts ratifying convention that "we may say that, although slavery is not smitten by an apoplexy, yet it has received a mortal wound, and will die of consumption." Another Massachusetts Federalist, writing pseudonymously, agreed that the Philadelphia convention "went as far as policy would warrant or practicability allow. The friends to liberty and humanity may look forward with satisfaction to the period, when slavery shall not exist in the United States."[129]

Such northerners especially celebrated the constitutional provision enabling Congress to bar the foreign slave trade after twenty years. At the Massachusetts ratifying convention, Federalists declared that "the step taken in this article towards the abolition of slavery was one of the beauties of the Constitution." James Wilson told the Pennsylvania convention that this provision laid "the foundation for banishing slavery out of this country," whereas under the Articles of Confederation, states could admit slaves "as long as they please." Even before 1808, Wilson noted, Congress was authorized to impose a tax on the importation of slaves, which would "operate as a partial prohibition." Finally, Wilson noted (accurately) that the twenty-year prohibition on Congress's barring the foreign slave trade did not apply to federal territories or newly created states, where he predicted (inaccurately) that "slaves will never be introduced."[130]

By contrast, other northerners believed that the Constitution had unduly entrenched slavery, and they opposed ratification for that reason. For example, Congregationalist theologian and abolitionist Samuel Hopkins asked in despair, "How does it appear in the sight of Heaven . . . that *these states*, who have been fighting for liberty and consider themselves as the highest and most noble example of zeal for it, cannot agree in any political constitution, unless it indulge and authorize them to enslave their fellow-men?" Antifederalist delegates at the Massachusetts ratifying convention objected that the Constitution made "merchandise of the bodies of men" and that "there was not even a proposition that the Negroes ever shall be free." Concurring in this assessment of the Constitution as a fundamentally proslavery document, one important group of later abolitionists denounced it as a "covenant with death" and an "agreement with hell."[131]

A few of these antislavery northerners complained specifically of the Fugitive Slave Clause and of the Constitution's possibly forcing them against their consciences to help suppress southern slave insurrections. Rhode Island Quaker Moses Brown objected that the Constitution "was designed to destroy the present asylum" that Massachusetts, which had abolished slavery, offered to escaped slaves. Pennsylvania Antifederalist Benjamin Workman, a math tutor at the University of Pennsylvania who wrote pseudonymously, protested that a Philadelphia Quaker, conscientiously opposed both to bearing arms and to slavery, could be forced under the Constitution to serve in the state militia and then ordered by Congress to participate in suppressing an insurrection of southern slaves "prompted by the love of sacred liberty."[132]

Yet most northerners who criticized the Constitution as overly protective of slavery focused on the Three-Fifths Clause and the twenty-year prohibition on Congress's banning the foreign slave trade. Melancton Smith of New York objected to the former provision on the grounds that the proper principle of representation was that "every free agent should be concerned in governing himself," yet "slaves have no will of their own." Why should "certain privileges" be conferred upon "those people who were so wicked as to keep slaves?" Another northerner wrote that in apportioning representation in Congress, slaves should be counted no more than "the beasts of the field or trees of the forest." Moreover, antislavery northerners objected, the Three-Fifths Clause would simply give southerners an incentive to continue the foreign slave trade. Others argued that the ostensible quid pro quo for enhanced southern representation in Congress under the Three-Fifths Clause—that is, counting only three-fifths of the slaves for purposes of apportioning direct taxes—would prove worthless because direct taxes would never be imposed by the national government (a prediction that would be proved largely accurate by the course of events before the Civil War).[133]

The Foreign Slave Trade Clause elicited the most venomous attacks from those northerners who criticized the Constitution on slavery-related grounds. Dr. Benjamin Gale, a Connecticut Antifederalist, objected to the "sly, cunning, and artful" euphemism for slavery used in this provision to hide its offense against "the rights of human nature." A leading New Hampshire Antifederalist, Joshua Atherton, warned that the Constitution would make northerners "partakers in the sin and guilt of this abominable traffic, at least for a certain period, without any positive stipulation that it should even then be brought to an end." He objected to his state's "lend[ing] the aid of our ratification to this cruel and inhuman merchandise, not even for a day." The foreign slave trade, according to Atherton, involved "the most barbarous violation of the sacred laws of God and humanity." Three Massachusetts Antifederalists called it "monstrous indeed" for a government established to protect natural rights to become "an engine of rapine, robbery, and murder." Why should those who objected to Algerians' kidnapping and enslaving American sailors off the coast of Africa feel better about slave traders' capturing and enslaving Africans?[134]

In response to the argument that residents of South Carolina and Georgia had lost much of their property during the war when British troops seized their slaves or encouraged them to run away, Massachusetts Antifederalists observed that because slavery violated natural law, slave owners "lost no property because they never had any [in their slaves]," and, in any event, northerners had lost their own property during the war. Moreover, wartime losses did not give Americans "a right to make inroads upon another nation, pilfer and rob [it], in order to compensate ourselves." Another Massachusetts Antifederalist distinguished between the foreign slave trade under the British Empire, which Americans had possessed no power to control, and the Constitution's authorization of the continuation of the trade, which did indeed make them "partakers of each other's sins." Some antislavery northerners also argued that the Philadelphia convention had offered South Carolina and Georgia greater protection for slavery than was necessary to induce them to ratify the Constitution; the threat of economic boycotts would have sufficed to impel those states to remain in the union.[135]

Many southern supporters of the Constitution shared the view that it was strongly proslavery—but they extolled it for this reason. One of their arguments was that the Constitution secured southerners, as Charles Cotesworth Pinckney explained in South Carolina, "a right to recover our slaves in whatever part of America they may take refuge, which is a right we had not before." Madison made the same point at the Virginia ratifying convention—that the Constitution was a clear improvement upon the Articles in this regard.[136]

Southern Federalists also emphasized that the Constitution conferred upon Congress no power to interfere with slavery in the states. As Charles Cotesworth Pinckney explained in South Carolina, the South had "a security that the general government can never emancipate them [slaves], for no such authority is granted; and it is admitted, on all hands, that the general government has no powers but what are expressly granted by the Constitution."* James Iredell, a prominent North Carolina Federalist, emphasized that Congress's power over slavery was limited to barring the foreign slave trade after twenty years; it had no authority to abolish slavery in the states. Southern statesmen would later treat the absence of an explicit congressional power over slavery—as contrasted with Congress's expressly delegated power over the foreign slave trade, beginning in 1808—as a sacred component of the original compact.[137]

Southern Federalists bragged of other protections afforded to slavery by the Constitution. In case of emergency, states would be authorized to call upon the federal government's assistance in suppressing slave insurrections. Moreover, the Constitution guaranteed that the representation of southern states in the House and the electoral college would reflect their slave populations. As Charles Cotesworth Pinckney explained, this meant that the northern states had "allowed us a representation for a species of property which they have not among them." The requirement that direct taxes, such as a tax on slaves, be apportioned according to population and the qualification that only three-fifths of the slaves count in calculating that population were, according to Madison, "an insuperable bar against disproportion." Finally, southern Federalists argued that the supermajority requirements imposed by Article V for enacting constitutional amendments protected southerners from having any antislavery amendments foisted upon them without their consent.[138]

To be sure, the Constitution empowered Congress eventually to end the foreign slave trade, which it could not do under the Articles. Yet this concession had been unavoidable, Charles Cotesworth Pinckney explained in the South

---

* Contrary to Pinckney's claim, and as we shall see in chapter 5, it was certainly not "admitted on all hands" that Congress was limited to expressly granted powers. Notwithstanding that misstatement, however, Pinckney was right that virtually nobody in 1787 thought that Congress possessed a general authority to emancipate slaves.

Carolina legislature, because of "the religious and political prejudices of the eastern and middle states and . . . the interested and inconsistent opinion of Virginia, who was warmly opposed to our importing more slaves." Moreover, Pinckney continued, opponents of the foreign slave trade at the Philadelphia convention had objected that slaves were "a dangerous species of property which an invading enemy could easily turn against ourselves" and that the Three-Fifths Clause would encourage the South to continue importing slaves. As Federalist David Ramsay of South Carolina observed, if northerners were "bound to protect us from domestic violence," they might reasonably believe that "we ought not to increase our exposure to that evil by an unlimited importation of slaves."[139]

Yet Pinckney also noted that the Constitution did not *require* Congress to abolish the foreign slave trade as soon as it was authorized to do so. By 1808, southern states might possess sufficient political power to block any congressional effort to end the foreign slave trade. Moreover, as Robert Barnwell of South Carolina noted, northern shippers, who would become the "carriers of America," might discover it to be in "their interest to encourage exportation to as great an extent as possible." Fearing that a ban on importing slaves might reduce southern exports, these shippers might prefer not to "dam up the sources from whence their profit is derived." Unless South Carolina itself chose to bar by state law the importation of additional slaves from Africa, Barnwell predicted, "the traffic for Negroes will continue forever."[140]

Charles Cotesworth Pinckney summed up his defense of the Constitution from the perspective of southern slave owners: "In short, considering all circumstances, we have made the best terms for the security of this species of property [slaves] it was in our power to make. We would have made better if we could; but, on the whole, I do not think them bad."[141]

The best evidence of whether contemporary actors believed that the Constitution securely protected the interests of slaveholders is not what was actually *said* in the ratifying debates. As we shall see in the next chapter, once someone had decided to support or oppose the Constitution, he generally made whatever arguments he thought would advance that cause, regardless of whether they had actually influenced his position. Thus, for example, although Patrick Henry warned Virginians that slavery would not be safe under the Constitution, his decision to oppose ratification was almost certainly more attributable to his resentment at northerners for being willing to sacrifice American navigation rights on the Mississippi River, which were important to the South.[142]

The best evidence of how contemporaries viewed the Constitution with regard to slavery lies rather in what was *not* said. In South Carolina and Georgia, which were the states most strongly committed to the indefinite perpetuation of slavery, very few voices criticized the Constitution as insufficiently protective of the institution. Georgia's convention unanimously ratified the Constitution, which would have been inconceivable had serious doubts existed about whether the safeguards for slavery were adequate. In South Carolina, nobody challenged Pinckney's statement that the southern delegates in Philadelphia had secured a good deal for slave owners. Opponents of ratification in South Carolina, of whom there were a great many, rarely argued that the Constitution inadequately protected slavery. Given the state economy's utter dependence on slavery, critics of the Constitution certainly would have emphasized this argument had it seemed even minimally convincing. Indeed, in South Carolina, the low-country planters, who had by far the greatest investment in slavery, were among the most fervent supporters of ratification in the nation.[143]

To have expected the Constitution to be less protective of slavery than it was probably would have been unrealistic. Because all the delegates to the Constitutional Convention wished to preserve the union, southerners enjoyed considerable bargaining power. When Mason declared at the Virginia ratifying convention that the delegates in Philadelphia should have barred the foreign slave trade even if doing so would have led Georgia and South Carolina to reject the Constitution, Madison responded that the consequences of such an action might have been "dreadful to them and to us." As "[g]reat as the evil" of the foreign slave trade was, "a dismemberment of the union would be worse." At the Pennsylvania ratifying convention, Thomas McKean, chief justice of the state supreme court, criticized those who protested against the Foreign Slave Trade Clause for not being "well acquainted with the business of [a] diplomatic body [such as the Philadelphia convention], or they would know that an agreement might be made that did not perfectly accord with the will and pleasure of any one person."[144]

At the New York ratifying convention, Melancton Smith, after criticizing the Three-Fifths Clause as "founded on unjust principles" and "utterly repugnant to his feelings," conceded that "it was the result of accommodation," which probably could not have been avoided "if we meant to be in union with the southern states." Hamilton concurred: The Three-Fifths Clause was "one result of the spirit of accommodation which governed the convention; and without this indulgence no union could possibly have been formed." Moreover, establishing a union without the participation of the Deep South states hardly would have improved the welfare of slaves residing in those states.[145]

To be sure, northern delegates had occasionally uttered their own threats to walk out of the convention over issues involving slavery. Those threats simply had not proved credible. In the end, the reason that the Constitution was proslavery was that southern delegates generally were more intent upon protecting slavery than northern delegates were upon undermining it. In fact, most northern delegates cared far more about how southern slavery would affect the political power and economic interests of the North than they cared about eliminating the institution. Moreover, even those northerners who could be fairly characterized as antislavery believed in the sanctity of property rights. As Thomas Dawes observed at the Massachusetts ratifying convention, "It would not do to abolish slavery by an act of Congress, in a moment, and so destroy what our southern brethren consider as property."[146]

Antislavery northerners also worried about creating large free black populations. As Oliver Ellsworth, writing as "A Landholder," observed during the ratifying debates, "[A]ll good men wish the entire abolition of slavery as soon as it can take place with safety to the public." A Massachusetts Federalist argued that "even in this laudable pursuit" of emancipating slaves, "we ought to temper the feelings of humanity with political wisdom. Great numbers of slaves becoming citizens might be burdensome and dangerous to the public." A few years later, Vice President John Adams denied that "[j]ustice to the Negroes would require that they should . . . be abandoned by their masters and turned loose upon a world in which they have no capacity to procure even a subsistence" and would have to "live by violence or theft or fraud." Eventually, Adams thought, "the increasing population of the country shall have multiplied the whites to such a superiority of numbers that the blacks may be liberated by degrees, with the consent both of master and servant."[147]

Finally, the principle of state sovereignty enabled many antislavery northerners to reconcile themselves to the Constitution. At the Massachusetts ratifying convention, William Heath argued that because "[e]ach state is sovereign and independent to a certain degree" and thus free to regulate its "own internal affairs," joining a union with slaveholders did not make northerners "partakers of other men's sins." New Hampshire Antifederalist Joshua Atherton noted derisively that a commitment to federalism enabled supporters of ratification to simply wash their hands of slavery. Even northerners who could not countenance the Constitution's protection of the foreign slave trade did not "esteem [them]selves under any necessity to go . . . to the Carolinas to abolish the detestable custom of enslaving the Africans." In the end, very few northerners were sufficiently aggrieved by the Constitution's proslavery features to oppose its ratification on that basis.[148]

Critics of the Constitution

The Antifederalists

In the fortnight immediately following the Philadelphia convention, Alexander Hamilton contemplated whether the Constitution was likely to be ratified and listed the factors militating in either direction. One circumstance strongly supporting ratification was the "very great weight of influence of the persons who framed it, particularly in the universal popularity of General Washington."* In addition, Hamilton believed that "the goodwill of the commercial interest throughout the states will give all its efforts to the establishment of a government capable of regulating, protecting, and extending the commerce of the union."[1]

In Hamilton's estimation, other likely supporters of the Constitution included "most men of property in the several states who wish a government of the union able to protect them against domestic violence and the depredations which the democratic spirit is apt to make on property." Those who were "anxious for the respectability of the nation" also would probably endorse ratification, as would creditors of the United States, who wished for a national government that would possess the means to pay its debts. Finally, "a strong belief in the people at large of the insufficiency of the present confederation to preserve the existence of the union and of the necessity of the union to their safety and prosperity" augured well for ratification.[2]

Hamilton also enumerated the factors likely to generate resistance to ratification. The three men who had refused to sign the Constitution at the end of the Philadelphia convention—Mason, Randolph, and Gerry—probably would feel

---

* Washington's former aide-de-camp David Humphreys concurred in this assessment, telling Washington that "[w]hat will tend, perhaps, more than anything to the adoption of the new system will be a universal opinion of your being elected president of the United States, and an expectation that you will accept it for a while." It is hard to overstate the extent to which most Americans at the time revered Washington.

Figure 5.1 Alexander Hamilton, one of the true geniuses of his or any other generation of American political leaders, who authored a majority of the numbers of *The Federalist*, led the ratifying campaign in New York, and then became the nation's first and most important secretary of the treasury. (Courtesy National Gallery of Art, Washington)

"pledged to defeat the plan." Hamilton also feared "the influence of many inconsiderable men in possession of considerable offices under the state governments who will fear a diminution of their consequence, power and emolument by the establishment of the general government and who can hope for nothing there."[3]

Other circumstances that might hinder ratification were "the disinclination of the people to taxes and of course to a strong government" and "the opposition of all men much in debt who will not wish to see a government established, one object of which is to restrain the means of cheating creditors." Hamilton also worried about "the democratical jealousy of the people, which may be alarmed at the appearance of institutions that may seem calculated to place the power of the community in few hands and to raise a few individuals to stations of great preeminence." Finally, Hamilton noted "the influence of some foreign powers who from different motives will not wish to see an energetic government established throughout the states."[4]

Given such competing considerations, Hamilton thought it "difficult to form any judgment whether the plan will be adopted or rejected. It must be essentially a matter of conjecture." While "the probability seems to be on the side of its adoption," he wrote, the factors impeding ratification were "powerful and there will be nothing astonishing in the contrary [result]."[5]

Preliminaries

Historians have long sought to identify the considerations that led some Americans to favor ratification of the Constitution and others to oppose it. Supporters of the Constitution, who quickly appropriated for themselves the label "Federalists," tended to disparage the motives and question the loyalty of their opponents, whom they called "Antifederalists."*

Federalists accused critics of the Constitution of being covert Loyalists whose real goal was to reunite with Great Britain. They called Antifederalists "Shaysites" and "[d]ebtors in desperate circumstances, who have not resolution to be either honest or industrious." Most frequently, Federalists disparaged Antifederalists as disgruntled state officeholders, "who have provided well for themselves and dread any change lest they should be injured by its [the Constitution's] operation." Explaining opposition to ratification of the Constitution in Pennsylvania, Gouverneur Morris complained of "the wicked industry of those who have long habituated themselves to live on the public, and cannot bear the idea of being removed from the power and profit of state government, which has been and still is the means of supporting themselves, their families and dependents." Not surprisingly, Antifederalists resented such aspersions on their motives for opposing ratification.[6]

For several reasons, discerning the true motivations of those who opposed ratification is difficult. First, the better educated and more affluent Antifederalists—people such as Richard Henry Lee and George Mason of Virginia and Elbridge Gerry of Massachusetts—left far more detailed records of their thinking in newspaper essays, ratifying convention speeches, and private correspondence than did small farmers and frontiersmen. On some issues, such as the desirability of government responsiveness to populist politics and

---

* "Federalists" was an ironic label for supporters of ratification given that, as their opponents pointed out, Federalists wanted "entirely to destroy the confederation!" At the New York ratifying convention, leading Antifederalist Melancton Smith expressed the wish that the gentlemen on the other side would be willing "to exchange names with those who disliked the Constitution." Having appropriated their preferred term to describe themselves, Federalists quickly labeled their opponents "Antifederalists," which they intended as a term of derision.

of loose fiscal and monetary policy, these two segments of Antifederalist opinion held widely disparate views. Thus, the surviving records probably do not fully capture the range of Antifederalist concerns about the Constitution and the prevalence of particular objections.[7]

Second, even those Antifederalists who left detailed records of their thinking offered widely varying reasons for opposing ratification. Thus, some Antifederalists objected primarily to the omission of a bill of rights from the Constitution. Others criticized Congress's vastly expanded powers of taxation and its unrestricted authority to create standing armies in peacetime and to summon state militias into federal service. Still others objected to the constraints imposed on state economic policy by Article I, Section 10, of the Constitution. When Federalists complained that Antifederalist critiques of the Constitution were inconsistent with one another, they had a point: Different Antifederalists raised very different objections.[8]

Third, it is dubious to infer actual motives for opposing (or supporting) the Constitution from arguments made against (or in favor of) its ratification. Thus, when Madison sent Jefferson a pamphlet listing many of the Antifederalists' proposed amendments to the Constitution, he warned that "[v]arious and numerous as they appear, they certainly omit many of the true grounds of opposition." Federalists frequently charged their opponents with making arguments outside of state ratifying conventions that they were unwilling to make inside.[9]

Some motives for opposing ratification were widely deemed less respectable than others and thus were less likely to be candidly avowed. For example, many delegates from the counties of Maine at the Massachusetts ratifying convention may have opposed ratification because they believed that Maine would be less likely to secure independent statehood under the Constitution, but they did not make that argument in public debate. Instead, they criticized the omission of a bill of rights and Congress's vastly expanded taxing power. Similarly, farmers in central and western Massachusetts, who might have opposed the Constitution partly because of the Article I, Section 10, restrictions on paper money emissions and debtor relief laws, were disinclined to raise that objection explicitly (perhaps because almost nobody wished to associate himself with Rhode Island's infamous monetary schemes).[10]

Federalist David Ramsay of South Carolina, writing as "Civis," called for a careful examination of "the character and circumstances" of those who opposed the Constitution. Hostility toward Article I, Section 10, was "the real ground of the opposition of some of them," Ramsay insisted, "though they may artfully cover it with a splendid profession of zeal for state privileges and general liberty." Madison likewise complained to Hamilton that Virginians who were indebted to British creditors "secretly felt" concerns about the scope of federal court jurisdiction under Article III, but they "would not make the acknowledgment and would choose to ground their vote against the Constitution on other motives."[11]

Even aside from wishing to cloak questionable motives, Antifederalists (and their opponents) had an incentive to make the arguments most likely to appeal to swing delegates at ratifying conventions—regardless of whether such arguments represented their true motives for opposing (or, for their adversaries, supporting) ratification. Thus, for example, in New England, where slavery was generally disfavored, Antifederalists emphasized the Constitution's proslavery provisions. By contrast, in the Deep South, where slavery was solidly entrenched, Antifederalists sought to sow doubts about whether the Constitution sufficiently safeguarded slavery. Yet, as we saw in chapter 4, in neither the North nor the South did attitudes toward slavery determine many people's positions on the Constitution. Similarly, at the Virginia ratifying convention, as we shall see, both Federalists and Antifederalists devoted considerable attention to whether American navigation rights on the Mississippi River would be more or less secure under the Constitution. This was not because the Mississippi issue was the determining factor on ratification for most delegates but because it was foremost on the minds of the delegates from the Kentucky region, who were generally thought to hold the balance of power at the convention.[12]

Finally, Antifederalists held a spectrum of positions—not a unitary stance—on how to respond to the perceived deficiencies of the Constitution. Some Antifederalists, such as Patrick Henry of Virginia and Luther Martin of Maryland, probably favored rejecting the Constitution entirely and adhering instead to the blueprint of the Articles of Confederation, with perhaps a slight expansion of Congress's powers. Thus, for example, Rawlins Lowndes of South Carolina applauded the Articles' guarantee of state sovereignty, recommended "add[ing] strength to the old confederation, instead of precipitately adopting another," and wondered "whether a man should be looked on as wise, who, possessing a magnificent fabric, upon discovering a flaw, instead of repairing the injury should pull it down, and build another." Similarly, one Georgia Antifederalist could not fathom why the Philadelphia convention had "thought fit to destroy such a useful fabric as the Articles of Confederation."[13]

Other Antifederalists—perhaps the majority—readily admitted the flaws in the Articles and conceded, along with "Cato" of South Carolina, that the Constitution was "teeming with many blessings," but they nonetheless wished a few changes to be made before ratification, such as limiting Congress's power to levy direct taxes and to regulate congressional elections. Admitting that "an efficient government was indispensably necessary" and that the Constitution contained much of merit, Elbridge Gerry nonetheless insisted that "proper amendments" were required before ratification would be acceptable. Similarly,

"Federal Farmer," observing that the Constitution included "many good things" while also suffering from "many important defects," declared that it could make a "tolerable good" system "with several alterations."[14]

Still other Antifederalists objected to the Constitution mainly because of the absence of a bill of rights. One delegate to the South Carolina ratifying convention, Patrick Dollard, declared that his constituents almost unanimously opposed ratification for that reason. He explained that the people did not object to vesting Congress with "ample and sufficient powers," but they could "never agree" to conferring upon Congress, "or any set of men, their birthright, comprised in Magna Charta, which this Constitution absolutely does." A Philadelphia Antifederalist thought it "inexplicable" that the Constitution provided no guarantee for religious liberty, while one Massachusetts Antifederalist declared that a bill of rights was necessary "to secure the minority against the usurpation and tyranny of the majority." Even among Antifederalists who demanded a bill of rights, there was disagreement as to whether it should be an antecedent condition of ratification or whether Federalist promises to support a bill of rights after ratification should suffice.[15]

Most, if not all, Federalists conceded that the Constitution was imperfect, and many of them ultimately supported amendments, though not as an antecedent condition of ratification. Washington told his nephew Bushrod Washington (later a justice on the US Supreme Court), "The warmest friends to and the best supporters of the Constitution do not contend that it is free from imperfections." In another letter, Washington admitted that he himself was "not a blind admirer" of the Constitution, though he was "fully persuaded it is the best that can be obtained at this day." Given such Federalist admissions, opinion on the Constitution should be seen as existing along a continuous spectrum rather than being neatly divided into two opposing camps.[16]

With such qualifications in mind, let us consider, first, the Antifederalists' stated objections to the Constitution and the Federalists' responses. Then, we shall investigate the considerations that seemed genuinely to influence the positions people took on ratification.

The Legitimacy of the Constitution

To a considerable extent, the Antifederalists set the terms of the substantive debate over ratification. (The Federalists, as we shall see, had done a brilliant job of determining the procedural rules that would govern ratification.) The Antifederalists raised a wide variety of arguments against the Constitution, to which the Federalists responded.[17]

In addition to challenging many substantive provisions of the Constitution, the Antifederalists raised a preliminary objection to the *process* by which it had been proposed. The Articles of Confederation specified how amendments should be enacted, and no provision was made for a constitutional convention, such as the one that had taken place in Philadelphia. Even if the irregularity of holding a convention in contravention of the Articles could be cured by the acquiescence of Congress and the state legislatures that appointed delegates to it, there was the additional problem that those delegates had ignored their limiting instructions. Congress had approved a convention for the "sole and express purpose of *revising* the Articles of Confederation," and two state legislatures had similarly restricted their delegations. Yet the Philadelphia convention had scrapped the Articles from the outset.[18]

Furthermore, the convention had stipulated in Article VII that the Constitution would go into effect upon the ratification of nine states (although those states could bind only themselves). This was a clear departure from the Articles' requirement that amendments be approved unanimously by the thirteen states. In addition, the Articles had specified that amendments be approved by state *legislatures*, while the Constitution required action by special state ratifying *conventions*.[19]

For all these reasons, Antifederalists frequently charged that both the Constitutional Convention itself and its handiwork—the Constitution—were illegitimate. Once the Philadelphia convention had sent the Constitution to the Confederation Congress, which in turn was supposed to pass it on to state legislatures to call ratifying conventions, Richard Henry Lee, who represented Virginia in Congress, raised just such an objection. Although the Articles conferred upon Congress "no right to recommend a plan subverting the government," Lee protested, the Constitution "proposes to destroy the confederation of thirteen and to establish a new one of nine." Yet even Lee concluded that because twelve states had sent delegates to the convention and "respected characters" had agreed upon the Constitution there, it would "be indecent not to send it to the states" to decide whether to ratify it.[20]

In state ratifying conventions, Antifederalists frequently objected to the Philadelphia convention's having exceeded its charge to simply revise the Articles. In Pennsylvania, Robert Whitehill argued that the delegates to the Constitutional Convention had been authorized only to propose an augmentation of Congress's powers, "but it never was in the contemplation of any man that they were authorized to dissolve the present union, to abrogate the state sovereignties, and to establish one comprehensive government." In Virginia, Patrick Henry declared it "perfectly clear" that the convention had exceeded its authority. The Constitution perpetrated "the utter annihilation of the most solemn engagements of the states" and established "nine states into a confederacy, to the eventual exclusion of four." Henry demanded an account from Virginia's delegates to the Philadelphia convention of the dangers that were "of such awful magnitude as to warrant a proposal so extremely perilous as this."[21]

To such charges, Federalists offered several rejoinders. First, they noted that the Articles themselves were of dubious legitimacy because they had been enacted, as James Wilson told the Pennsylvania ratifying convention, "without the authority of the people, who alone possess the supreme power." (State legislatures—not special ratifying conventions—had approved the Articles.) Second, a few Federalists argued that the Articles were a treaty among the states that was no longer binding because it had been breached. According to the law of nations, as Madison explained, "a breach of any one article, by any of the parties, absolved the other parties from the whole obligation." Madison argued that breaches of the Articles had been "numerous and notorious"—the most egregious having been New Jersey's express refusal in 1786 to comply with a congressional requisition. Because such breaches nullified the binding force of the Articles, the states were free to replace them with a new constitution.[22]

Third, as Wilson explained, the delegates to the Philadelphia convention had simply made a proposal, which was "exercis[ing] no power at all" and thus could not be illegitimate. As presented by the Philadelphia convention, the Constitution "claims no more than a production of the same nature would claim, flowing from a private pen." By contrast, the convention that had written the Pennsylvania constitution in 1776 had simply proclaimed it to be law without submitting it for approval by the people.[23]

Fourth and relatedly, some Federalists argued that any irregularities in the process leading up to ratification could be cured by the assent of the sovereign people. When delegates to the Philadelphia convention had discussed how the Constitution should be put into operation, some of them objected to the use of special ratifying conventions, which were not provided for in state constitutions. Madison had responded that "[t]he people were in fact the fountain of all power and by resorting to them, all difficulties were got over. They could alter constitutions as they pleased."[24]

At the state ratifying conventions, Federalists offered the same response to Antifederalist charges of procedural irregularities. The president of the Virginia ratifying convention, Edmund Pendleton, who supported ratification, refused to allow debate on Patrick Henry's motion to read Congress's limiting instructions to the Constitutional Convention on the grounds that the people had the power to cure any defects in the process of drafting the Constitution. Likewise, James Wilson told the Pennsylvania ratifying convention that "supreme, absolute and uncontrollable power remains in the people."

As a consequence, "the people may change the constitutions whenever and however they please. This is a right of which no positive institution can ever deprive them."[25]

Finally, some Federalists defended procedural irregularities in terms of necessity. Prior to the Philadelphia convention, Washington had stated that "[t]he legality of this convention I do not mean to discuss." The national government lacked essential powers, and "the shortest course to obtain them will, in my opinion, under present circumstances, be found best. Otherwise, like a house on fire, whilst the most regular mode of extinguishing it is contending for, the building is reduced to ashes." At the Philadelphia convention, Edmund Randolph had similarly argued that "[t]here are great seasons when persons with limited powers are justified in exceeding them and a person would be contemptible not to risk it." Randolph repeated that justification for procedural irregularities at the Virginia ratifying convention: The Articles of Confederation had proved a "political farce," the delegates to the Philadelphia convention "[o]n a thorough contemplation of the subject . . . found it impossible to amend that system," and it would have been "treason" for the delegates "to return [home] without proposing some scheme to relieve their distressed country."[26]

In the end, the charge of procedural irregularity would have to be adjudicated by the people. What would they make of the Constitution written for them in Philadelphia?

Was Fundamental Reform Necessary?

Antifederalists generally portrayed the stakes of the ratifying contest as enormous: "We are now publicly summoned to determine whether we and our children are to be freemen or slaves." The nation should deliberate carefully before taking "an awful step which may involve in its consequences the ruin of millions yet unborn." To adopt the Constitution without changes would be to "lose more than all that we have fought for and gained in a glorious and successful war of seven years." Acknowledging that Congress must be invested with adequate powers, Antifederalists nonetheless warned that "[r]elinquishing a hair's breadth in a constitution is a great deal, for by small degrees has liberty in all nations been wrested from the hands of the people."[27]

Governor George Clinton of New York noted that although he had always supported an "energetic government," he nonetheless worried that "the people are too apt to vibrate from one extreme to another." The "feebleness of the confederation" must not "drive the people into an adoption of a constitution dangerous to our liberties." Richard Henry Lee likewise deprecated the tendency of the human mind "to rush from one extreme to another." When the Articles of Confederation had been proposed, "the universal apprehension was of the too great, not the defective, powers of Congress." Yet now "the cry is power, give Congress power." Every free nation, Lee warned, "has lost its liberty by the same rash impatience."[28]

Antifederalists insisted that their opponents bore the burden of demonstrating, in Patrick Henry's words, that "the dangers that awaited us" justified repudiating the Articles—"the most solemn engagements of the states"—and replacing them with "a great consolidated government, instead of a confederation." The nation was at peace, Antifederalists argued, and Federalist claims that a war with Great Britain or France was imminent were absurd, because those nations were too suspicious of one another to lightly commence hostilities with the United States. Moreover, the risk of the union's dissolving because of flaws in the Articles was minimal, given the strong ties of interest and affection that bound the nation together. At the Virginia ratifying convention, William Grayson disparaged as "merely imaginary" and "ludicrous in the extreme" Federalist depictions of the civil war that was likely to unfold if the Constitution were not ratified.[29]

Antifederalists also denied that the nation's financial situation was desperate: Foreign creditors were willing to lend the United States even more money, despite its failure to make timely interest payments on existing loans, and the sale of western lands was rapidly diminishing the domestic debt. A "Columbian Patriot" thought there was no doubt that, if a "free government" were maintained, "time and industry will enable both the public and the private debtor to liquidate their arrearages in the most equitable manner." At the New York ratifying convention, Melancton Smith even denied that state legislatures had behaved as badly as the Federalists claimed, although he admitted that Rhode Island, an extreme example of "political depravity," deserved to be condemned. Smith insisted that any bad laws enacted by the state legislatures were attributable more to the difficulty of the times than to any "want of honesty or wisdom."[30]

A few Antifederalists even went so far as to praise the Articles of Confederation. In South Carolina, Lowndes offered "a glowing eulogy on the old constitution [i.e., the Articles]" and celebrated its drafters, who "were eminent for patriotism, virtue, and wisdom." In Virginia, Patrick Henry insisted that the Articles deserved the highest praise for carrying the nation through "a long and dangerous war" and securing to the United States "a territory greater than any European monarch possesses." Even if the Articles were deficient, Antifederalists asked, why could they not be amended by granting Congress a few additional powers? Grayson wondered how the Federalists had progressed from the limited objective in the mid-1780s of granting the national government the powers to levy a 5 percent impost duty and to regulate trade to revolutionizing the government.[31]

Moreover, some Antifederalists insisted that whatever current difficulties the nation experienced were not attributable to flaws in the Articles, which were being exploited "as an instrument to make way for the proposed system." New York Antifederalists argued that "a long and expensive war" had burdened the people with oppressive public and private debts, but the economy was swiftly improving, and soon even the much vilified system of requisitions would satisfy the nation's financial needs. At the Virginia ratifying convention, Mason blamed Congress for creating economic havoc by demanding more gold and silver in requisitions than existed in the entire United States.[32]

Other Antifederalists blamed the nation's predicament, such as it was, not on the Articles but on the flawed character of Americans. Since the war, according to New York Antifederalist John Williams, "luxury and dissipation overran the country," as people imported European goods beyond their ability to pay. He noted disapprovingly, "How many thousands are there daily wearing the manufactures of Europe, when, by a little industry and frugality, they might wear those of their own country!" Blaming also "the dissipation" caused by "the immoderate use of spirits," Williams observed that men could not be hired "in time of harvest without giving them, on an average, a pint of rum per day." Richard Henry Lee agreed that "present discontents" were more attributable to the "vicious manners" of Americans than to any defect in their form of government.[33]

How did Federalists respond to these various points? For starters, they agreed with their opponents that the decision whether to ratify the Constitution would have momentous consequences—a rare point of consensus between the two sides. For example, Hamilton in *The Federalist No. 1* declared, "The subject speaks for its own importance, comprehending in its consequences nothing less than the existence of the union, the safety and welfare of the parts of which it is composed, [and] the fate of an empire in many respects the most interesting in the world." Unsurprisingly, Federalists were irritated by their opponents' insistence that only Antifederalists were committed to defending the liberties of generations unborn. Wilson wondered if Antifederalists really believed that supporters of ratification were "contending for the doctrines of tyranny and slavery" for their "own posterity." At the Virginia ratifying convention, Henry Lee insisted that Federalists were "true republicans and by no means less attached to liberty than those who oppose it [the Constitution]."[34]

Federalists strongly countered their opponents' denials that the nation faced a genuine crisis that called for abandoning the Articles. They argued that the credit of the United States could not be maintained under the Articles, as the failed system of requisitions had forced Congress to borrow money to pay the interest on the foreign debt. To renege on that debt would authorize creditor nations under international law to go to war to enforce payment. Congress had failed to raise a navy to rescue American sailors from Algerian pirates, and it probably could not have raised an army in the event of an enemy invasion. The British refused to relinquish their western forts because the United States could not enforce its treaty obligations on recalcitrant states. Foreign trade discrimination, against which Congress was powerless to retaliate, had proved devastating to American shippers and farmers alike. Insurrections by debtors and taxpayers were pervasive across the nation. A vital impost amendment acquiesced in by twelve states had been blocked by tiny and irresponsible Rhode Island. If the Constitution were not ratified, Federalists warned, the nation would probably disintegrate into separate confederacies, which would constantly be at war with one another.[35]

The problem with the Articles, Federalists insisted, was not that Congress lacked one or two important powers but that the entire concept of a confederation was deficient. Without material alterations in the Articles, Edward Rutledge told the South Carolina House of Representatives as it debated whether to call a ratifying convention, "the sun of American independence would indeed soon set—never to rise again." The "radical vice" in the Confederation, Hamilton explained to the New York ratifying convention, was that the laws of the union applied only to the states in their corporate capacities, not to individuals. Under such an arrangement, states would invariably evaluate federal measures according to their own "particular conveniency or advantage," and when they chose to disregard those measures, the only remedy was coercion, which would probably lead to civil war. However, once it was decided to vest Congress with the power to act on individuals, a "totally different" form of government became necessary because such power could not be safely entrusted to a unitary body such as the Confederation Congress.[36]

Although Federalists agreed with their opponents that the decision whether to ratify the Constitution was momentous, in at least one sense they sought to lower the stakes: Even if the Constitution was imperfect, which most of them conceded, it could be amended with relative ease. Thus, many Federalists celebrated the wisdom of the Philadelphia convention in providing for amendments through Article V—one of the Constitution's many "excellencies." In other nations, according to one delegate to the Massachusetts convention who ultimately supported ratification, "great or important change" in government had always "been written in blood." By contrast, under the Constitution, "[i]f, in the course of its operation, this government shall appear to be too severe, here are the means [i.e., Article V] by which this severity may be attempered and corrected." Indeed, some Federalists argued, it would be easier to ratify the Constitution and then amend it than to reject ratification and start all over again in an attempt to amend the Articles, which would require unanimity among the states.[37]

Consolidation

The Antifederalists' substantive objections to the Constitution fell into two broad categories. First, the Constitution contained no bill of rights. Nothing in the document explicitly forbade Congress from abridging the liberty of conscience or freedom of the press, dispensing with jury trials in federal civil cases, or authorizing cruel and unusual punishments for violators of federal criminal law. Even the few explicit rights protections contained in the Constitution seemed inadequate to many Antifederalists. For example, why was the power to suspend the writ of habeas corpus in cases of rebellion or invasion not limited to a certain period of time? Why did the right to a jury trial in criminal cases provided for in Article III not require that the jury be selected from the vicinity of the crime?[38]

The Antifederalists' other principal set of objections to the Constitution focused on the structure and powers of the federal government.* Antifederalists thought the Constitution granted too much power to the federal government and imposed too few checks and balances to effectively guard against tyranny.[39]

With regard to the federal government's powers, Antifederalists charged generally that the authority vested in Congress was "so unlimited in its nature, . . . so comprehensive and boundless" that "this alone would be amply sufficient to annihilate the state governments and swallow them up in the grand vortex of general empire." Pennsylvania Antifederalist William Findley warned that the extension of congressional power to "internal objects . . . leaves us no means of relief or protection in the state governments." Melancton Smith predicted that the state governments would "soon dwindle into insignificance and be despised by the people themselves," if all that was left for them to do was to meet once a year "to make laws for regulating the height of your fences and the repairing of your roads."[40]

---

* To be sure, Antifederalists would not have embraced the sharp distinction between structural provisions and individual-rights protections that comes naturally to modern analysts. For example, many Antifederalists, as we shall see, believed that Congress's power over the times, places, and manner of federal elections—a structural provision—threatened the people's right to vote for congressional representatives. Similarly, Antifederalists objected that the small size of the House—another structural provision—jeopardized the people's right to representation.

Antifederalists believed that states were critical to safeguarding the people from possible oppression by the federal government, yet the Constitution left the states with no power of self-defense. The federal government would win the competition with state governments for the support of the people, Antifederalists predicted, because its officers would probably be more influential men who received higher salaries. Moreover, Congress could use its vastly expanded powers of taxation to deprive states of revenue and call up the states' militias into federal service, thus undermining the states' capacity to defend themselves.[41]

Thus, for example, Patrick Henry objected to giving Congress "unlimited authority over the national wealth" and "an unbounded control over the national strength." At a minimum, Antifederalists argued, the Constitution should have imposed some limits on the federal taxing power in order to leave the states sufficient resources to survive. Grayson warned that state governments would be "despised as soon as they give up the power of direct taxation." More generally, Antifederalists denied that two concurrent powers could long subsist within the same jurisdiction, and they predicted that the states would soon be destroyed under the Constitution.[42]

"The most essential danger from the present system," Richard Henry Lee told Patrick Henry, arose "from its tendency to a consolidated government instead of a union of confederated states." Consolidation was objectionable because, as Mason explained to the Virginia ratifying convention, no national government would "suit so extensive a country, embracing so many climates, and containing inhabitants so very different in manners, habits, and customs." No law imposed over such a heterogeneous nation could ever be uniform in its operation throughout the land, and national legislators would not be sufficiently familiar with distant parts of the country to legislate effectively for them. Nor could one assume, according to two prominent New York Antifederalists, that representatives so remote from their constituents and probably enjoying a "permanency of office" would "be uniformly actuated by an attention to their [constituents'] welfare and happiness."[43]

Liberty was the power of self-government, a South Carolina Antifederalist observed, yet under the Constitution the people would be delivering their governance "into the hands of a set of men who live one thousand miles distant." Antifederalists invoked the French political philosopher Montesquieu for the proposition that all governments in history that extended over a large geographic area had eventually destroyed the liberties of their people. The national government, according to "Brutus" (one of the most highly regarded Antifederalist essayists, who was probably Melancton Smith), would be too distant from the people to secure their "confidence, respect, and affection." Without such confidence, people would question legislators' motives and be suspicious of their every measure. Only coercion—a standing army—could induce the people to follow the laws of such a government. But standing armies, "Brutus" observed, had proved to be "the destruction of liberty and are abhorrent to the spirit of a free republic."[44]

To avoid the dangers of consolidation, Antifederalists argued, a clear line must be drawn between the authority of the national and state governments. Melancton Smith told the New York ratifying convention that such a demarcation was necessary "to maintain harmony between the governments, and to prevent the constant interference which must either be the cause of perpetual differences, or oblige one to yield, perhaps unjustly, to the other." Another New York Antifederalist, John Williams, similarly expressed the wish that "little or no latitude might be left to the sophistical constructions of men who may be interested in betraying the rights of the people and elevating themselves upon the ruins of liberty."[45]

However, as Elbridge Gerry objected, some of Congress's enumerated powers were "ambiguous," while others were "indefinite and dangerous." Grayson agreed with that assessment, declaring that he did not believe "there existed a social compact upon the face of the earth so vague and so indefinite as the one now on the table." Clarity in the grants of power to Congress was especially important, Antifederalists insisted, because the ultimate arbiters of the limits of those powers were federal judges, who would have an incentive to construe ambiguities in favor of expanding the scope of congressional power—both because they were officers of the federal government and because broader federal legislative power would translate into broader federal judicial power (and perhaps larger salaries and greater fees), given that federal courts were to exercise jurisdiction in cases "arising under" federal law.[46]

Therefore, observing that experience had shown that gentlemen could "put what construction they please upon words," many Antifederalists demanded a constitutional amendment limiting Congress to expressly delegated powers. Mason argued that such a provision, which the Articles of Confederation contained, was even more necessary under the Constitution, which vested Congress with much greater power than the Articles had. One North Carolina Antifederalist objected that "[t]he omission of this clause makes the power [of Congress] so much greater."[47]

To the Antifederalists' invocation of Montesquieu's notion that republican government could not thrive in a large geographic area, Federalists offered a variety of responses. At the Virginia ratifying convention, Francis Corbin noted that Montesquieu's insight would condemn the republican experiment not only for the nation but also for any state larger than Delaware or Rhode Island. Edmund Randolph argued that Montesquieu's observations were irrelevant because "the science of politics" had "greatly improved" in the decades since Montesquieu wrote, and the theory of representation—the source of American and English liberty—"was a thing not understood in its full extent till very lately." Charles Pinckney stated that since no attempt had ever been made to establish a republic over as large a geographic area as the United States, while people might have opinions about whether it would work, they had no experience from which to draw firm conclusions.[48]

Other Federalists, conceding that a consolidated government might not succeed over so large a geographic sphere as the United States, denied that consolidation or the destruction of state governments was their aim. They insisted that the Constitution embraced a "confederate republic"—a government "of a mixed nature"—which was unprecedented in the history of the world. It was federal in some respects and consolidated in others. Federalists emphasized several features of the Constitution that illustrated its federal nature: States could not be bound to the Constitution without their individual consent; state legislatures picked senators, who represented the states as states; and Congress was limited to enumerated powers while state legislatures remained governments of inherent power (subject to only a few constitutional limits).[49]

Going even further, some Federalists, such as Madison and Charles Pinckney, turned Montesquieu's theory on its head, arguing that republican government would work much better over a large geographic area. The principal danger inherent in republican government was the formation of majority factions that would oppress minorities. In a small society, Pinckney explained, the people were "easily assembled and inflamed." Larger geographic areas, by contrast, featured greater heterogeneity of interest, which rendered more difficult the formation of majority factions on single issues. Even if such factions existed, they would find it harder to organize their supporters over broader distances. Moreover, representation over a larger geographic area would be superior, both because of the larger pool of people to choose from and because representatives who served larger constituencies would be more insulated from direct populist pressure. According to Pinckney, Rhode Island's deplorable political situation attested to the truth of these propositions. In this smallest state of the union, licentiousness had seized the reins of government and "oppress[ed] the people by laws the most infamous that have ever disgraced a civilized nation."[50]

Federalists also denied that the federal government would have either the incentive or the capacity to destroy state governments, which were essential to its operations. Because, under the Constitution, state legislatures chose US senators and specified the method by which presidential electors were selected, the federal government would not exist without the cooperation of state legislatures. Nor, Federalists insisted, could Congress destroy state governments by prohibiting them from raising revenue because its power over taxation—except with regard to import duties—was concurrent rather than exclusive. By Hamilton's estimate, states retained access to two-thirds of the country's tax resources. Federalists also argued that two distinct legislative powers could coexist in the same jurisdiction so long as they had different objects. If revenue could be simultaneously collected for the distinct purposes of state and county governments, Madison asked, why could it not be simultaneously raised through state and federal taxes?[51]

Federalists argued that, far from expanding its power at the expense of the states, Congress was likely to suffer encroachments by state governments or prove so subject to their influence that local considerations would predominate. History demonstrated, according to Hamilton, that "members of republics have been, and ever will be, stronger than the head." One reason not to be worried about congressional usurpation of power, Federalists argued, was that state governments would play a role in selecting federal officeholders but not vice versa. Another reason was that the people would feel a greater attachment to the state governments, which had responsibility for their more immediate interests. By contrast, the national government's powers related primarily to external objects, which did not directly implicate most people's concerns, and its powers mainly would be exercised in time of war, which Federalists predicted would prove infrequent.[52]

Moreover, Federalists argued, because there would be more state legislators than congressional representatives, the former would exercise proportionately greater personal influence. The state governments would also employ much larger numbers of people, who would, in consequence, be attached to the states' interests. State legislatures could potentially exercise influence over congressional representatives through the promise of appointment to lucrative state offices, as the Constitution restricted only the eligibility of federal legislators for appointment to federal offices. For all these reasons, Federalists insisted, state governments would be able to stymie any congressional attempt to usurp power. Randolph assured the Virginia ratifying convention that the federal government would be "cautiously watched. The smallest assumption of power will be sounded in alarm to the people and followed by bold and active opposition."[53]

To the Antifederalist charge that Congress's enumerated powers were too ambiguous, Federalists sometimes conceded that the line between national and state power could not be "drawn with mathematical precision" because of the nature of language. Nonetheless, they insisted that Congress's powers were "as minutely enumerated and defined as was possible." At a minimum, Congress plainly had not been delegated power to "intermeddle with the local, particular affairs of the states."[54]

The Taxing Power

Regarding Congress's expanded powers, Antifederalist criticism began with the so-called Sweeping Clause, which granted Congress the authority "to make all laws which shall be necessary and proper for carrying into execution" its enumerated powers. "Brutus" warned that this power left "the legislature at liberty to do everything which in [its] judgment is best" and might "be exercised in such manner as entirely to abolish the state legislatures." For example, Congress might justify repealing state taxes as "necessary and proper" to the federal government's raising revenue for itself. Mason warned that this clause would permit Congress to "grant monopolies in trade and commerce, constitute new crimes, [and] inflict unusual and severe punishments." Congress might even justify suppressing criticism of itself as "necessary and proper" to the exercise of its enumerated powers—especially in the absence of an express constitutional guarantee of freedom of speech.[55]

Federalists responded that the Necessary and Proper Clause did not, in the words of Randolph, "in the least increase the powers of Congress. It is only inserted for greater caution and to prevent the possibility of encroaching upon the powers of Congress." Madison declared that this provision was "at most but explanatory: For when any power is given, its delegation necessarily involves authority to make laws to execute it." Because "the limits of human capacity" would not permit specification of every essential federal power, Madison explained, the Philadelphia convention had enumerated important powers but left the "minute specification" of their implementation to Congress's discretion.[56]*

Antifederalists also objected to the language in Article I empowering Congress to lay and collect taxes "to pay the debts and provide for the common defence and general welfare of the United States." The power to "provide for the . . . general welfare," Antifederalists warned, might be construed as entirely independent of the power to tax. Thus, Richard Henry Lee objected that this power would seem to cover "every possible object of human legislation." The Antifederalist "Deliberator" warned that Congress could use the General

---

* Chief Justice John Marshall's latitudinarian interpretation of the Necessary and Proper Clause in *McCulloch v. Maryland* in 1819—enabling Congress to pass laws "convenient or useful" to the implementation of its enumerated powers—confirms the prescience of the Antifederalists. Responding to *McCulloch*, former president Madison conceded that it "was foreseen at the birth of the Constitution that difficulties and differences of opinion might occasionally arise in expounding terms and phrases necessarily used in such a charter." Nonetheless, Madison insisted—rightly—that a frank avowal in the Constitution of Marshall's broad and "pliant" rule of construction would "have prevented its ratification."

Welfare Clause to establish a national religion. Even if the power to provide for the general welfare were construed to be inseparable from the taxing power, "Brutus" objected, Congress would still be "the sole judge of what is necessary to provide for the general welfare," and thus the power to lay and collect taxes would be "unlimited."[57]

In response, Randolph insisted that it was "treason against common language" to construe Congress's power to provide for the general welfare as independent of its power to lay and collect taxes. Madison pointed out that the "general welfare" language was taken from the Articles of Confederation—where it appeared, along with language about providing for the states' "common defense" and securing their "liberties," as one of the objects of the union. Nobody would have dreamed, Madison insisted, of the Confederation Congress's invoking such language as justification for exceeding its enumerated powers.[58]

In terms of other congressional powers, one of the Antifederalists' principal objections to the Constitution was its grant of vastly expanded taxing power to Congress. Capitalizing on what John Jay had previously described as the "disinclination in too many [Americans] to any mode of government that can easily and irresistibly open their purses," Antifederalists warned against affording the federal government "free access to our pockets." Gerry predicted that if the Constitution were ratified, "the people will bleed with taxes at every pore," and "the wealth of the continent will be collected . . . [at] the seat of the federal government." Melancton Smith called it a "settled truth" that all governments taxed and spent to the limits of their revenue-raising capacity.[59]

Observing that had anybody "proposed such a Constitution as this [in 1775], it would have been thrown away at once," one Massachusetts Antifederalist expressed astonishment at how a people that had gone to war with Great Britain over "a right to tax us" was now being asked to confer upon the federal government the power to "take away . . . all our property." Another Antifederalist wondered how the same nation that just a few years earlier had denied Congress the authority to levy a 5 percent impost could now be expected to grant it such vastly expanded powers of taxation.[60]

Not only would the federal government's nearly unfettered taxing power be used oppressively to appropriate the people's wealth, Antifederalists warned, but it would also leave the states bereft of their own revenue. Pennsylvania Antifederalists insisted that because the Constitution reserved no specific modes of taxation to the states, Congress could "monopolize every source of revenue and thus indirectly demolish the state governments, for without funds they could not exist." Because two competing sovereigns could not "have a coequal command over the purses of the citizens," a "struggle for the spoils" was inevitable. Either the union would be "destroyed by a violent struggle," or the states' sovereignty would be "swallowed up by silent encroachments into a universal aristocracy."[61]

Although a few Antifederalists spoke fondly of the Articles' requisition system for raising federal revenue—Smith denied that requisitions were "such poor, unproductive things as is commonly supposed"—most of them conceded that Congress ought to be granted some coercive taxing authority. Yet Antifederalists insisted that limits be imposed on the kind of taxes that Congress could levy. Patrick Henry noted that "oppression" arose "not from the amount but from the mode" of taxes. Thus, many Antifederalists suggested limiting Congress's taxing authority to import duties, which were both easier to administer and less offensive in principle than other taxes because they were imposed on consumption.[62]

Other Antifederalists would have acquiesced to Congress's imposing not only import duties but also excise taxes on domestically produced goods—which are, again, consumption taxes—but would have stopped short of allowing the imposition of direct taxes, such as on land or persons. Direct taxes were widely seen to be more coercive because they were very difficult to evade and, if not paid, rendered property subject to seizure. Nobody ever lost his farm from failure to pay an import duty. Direct taxes also required more revenue officers to collect them and created more opportunities for conflict with the states over revenue sources, given the states' heavy reliance on such taxes. Finally, Antifederalists noted that direct taxes were severely regressive, as they imposed the same financial burden on the poor as the wealthy. Believing "it almost morally certain that this new government will be administered by the wealthy," New York Antifederalist John Williams warned that Congress would probably impose an "oppressive" capitation tax, which would "heap all the support of the government upon the poor."[63]

A Virginia Antifederalist later wrote Madison that "the opposition to the federal constitution is in my opinion reduced to a single point, the power of direct taxation."* James Monroe told the Virginia ratifying convention that he could accept every enumerated power of Congress except that over direct taxation. Monroe considered such a power both a "subversion of liberty" and unnecessary, given the federal government's reduced expenses after the war and its ability to raise substantial revenue from the impost and the sale of western lands. Grayson warned that for the states to relinquish the power of direct taxation was to "give up everything, as it is the highest act of sovereignty."[64]

---

* State bondholders had a powerful vested interest in opposing the federal government's authority to levy direct taxes, which were a major source of state revenue with which to pay the interest and principal on state bonds. However, because of the possibility that the new federal government might assume the states' war-related debts, state bondholders had conflicting incentives with regard to the federal taxing power.

Still other Antifederalists would have acquiesced to Congress's imposing direct taxes, but only if other revenue sources first proved insufficient. Even with that qualification, they wished to condition the power on states being afforded an initial opportunity to raise such taxes themselves in pursuance of a federal requisition. Only if the states' efforts failed would Congress then be authorized to collect the direct taxes itself through federal officials. Mason considered a constitutional amendment in such terms to be "indispensable" and a "sine qua non of ratification."[65]

Antifederalists insisted that only the state governments were closely enough connected to the people to appreciate how much of a tax burden they could bear. Patrick Henry declared that "a thorough acquaintance with the condition of the people is necessary to a just distribution of taxes." State governments, according to Mason, would employ the method of taxation that was "the most easy and least oppressive to the people" because those governments were most familiar with the people's "condition and circumstances."[66]

By contrast, Congress would be "unacquainted with our private circumstances," warned a Georgia Antifederalist. Congressional representatives, selected from enormous districts and serving lengthy terms in office without provision for mandatory rotation, would be "independent of the sentiments and resentment of the people" and thus disinclined to relieve them from "oppression and tyranny." Especially in light of "the importance of taxation" as a cause of the recent Revolutionary War, "Federal Farmer" could "scarcely believe we are serious in proposing to vest the powers of laying and collecting internal taxes in a government so imperfectly organized for such purposes."[67]

In addition to criticizing the Constitution's failure to impose limits on the *modes* of taxation permitted to Congress, Antifederalists warned that ratification would vastly increase the *amount* of the people's taxes. Patrick Henry spoke of the "enormous and extravagant expenses ... of this great consolidated government." There would be "[d]ouble sets of collectors," custom house officers to be paid, and the "splendid maintenance of the president" to be subsidized. Pennsylvania Antifederalists predicted that a government that would "not enjoy the confidence of the people" but could be sustained only by force would be "a very expensive and burdensome government," with vast numbers of tax collectors and revenue officers, who would "swarm over the land, devouring the hard earnings of the industrious, like the locusts of old." Massachusetts Antifederalist Amos Singletary warned that politically powerful merchants would block the imposition of import duties, forcing Congress to lay a tax "on the land and take all we have got."[68]

Federalists, by contrast, adamantly opposed any limits on Congress's taxing authority beyond the few imposed by the Constitution (such as the ban on export taxes and the requirement that direct taxes be apportioned according to population). Power over taxation, according to Virginia Federalist Francis Corbin, was "the lungs of the Constitution"; without it, the whole system was "consumptive and must soon decay." Federalists ridiculed the Articles' requisition system. Chancellor Robert R. Livingston of New York disparaged requisitions as "pompous petitions for public charity, which have made so much noise and brought so little cash into the treasury."[69]

Federalists noted the collective-action problems that had plagued the requisition system. According to Hamilton, the self-interested nature of human beings doomed requisitions: "States will contribute or not according to their circumstances and interests. They will all be inclined to throw off their burdens of government upon their neighbors." Madison later explained how experience under the Articles had demonstrated the inherent defects of a requisition system imposed on multiple entities:

> If some states contribute their quotas and others do not, justice is violated; the violation of justice is the ground of disputes among states as well as among individuals. . . . Those who furnish most will complain of those who furnish least. From complaints on one side will spring ill will on both sides; from ill will, quarrels; from quarrels, wars; and from wars a long catalogue of evils including the dreadful evils of disunion and a general confusion.

Moreover, if requisitions had proved a failure even during the Revolutionary War, a time of dire necessity, one could not possibly expect them to succeed in peacetime. Nor, Federalists maintained, was state noncompliance attributable simply to wartime sufferings, as Antifederalists claimed. New Hampshire had barely suffered at all from the war, yet it had paid almost nothing into the US treasury.[70]

Nor would it suffice simply to grant Congress power to lay indirect taxes—imposts and excises. Madison declared that Congress's ability to levy direct taxes was "essential to the salvation of the union." While indirect taxes might generally suffice in time of peace, Robert R. Livingston told the New York ratifying convention, "a constitution should be calculated for all circumstances—for the most critical and dangerous conjunctures." Hamilton explained that the ratio of government expenses during war and peace was at least fourteen to one and that "[u]nexpected invasions [and] long and ruinous wars may demand all the possible abilities of the country," as revenue from the impost would decline as war disrupted trade. Even if the United States wished to remain neutral in the event of a war between Great Britain and France, Madison observed, "[a] neutral nation ought to be respectable or else it will be insulted and attacked." To be respectable, it must "be known that our government can command the whole resources of the union," which would include the capacity to raise direct taxes quickly in response to an enemy attack or invasion.[71]*

Federalists also disparaged the Antifederalists' proposed amendment to require Congress to requisition funds from the states before imposing direct taxes itself. Wartime requisitions would be too slow to be effective; state legislatures might not be in session, or they might not be punctual about paying. If requisitions were made in support of future preparedness, moreover, would "the least exposed states exert themselves equally?" Federalists warned that congressional efforts to coerce compliance with requisitions once states had defaulted would excite the hatred of the people against the federal government. State legislatures that had refused to comply with requisitions would certainly resist Congress's efforts to levy direct taxes on their citizens. Resort to the sword would be more likely, Federalists insisted, if Congress were limited to requisitions than if it could impose taxes directly upon individuals. Moreover, Congress would have to pay higher interest rates to borrow money if its power to levy direct taxes were conditioned upon states' first failing to satisfy requisitions.[72]

Federalists insisted that if foreign adversaries possessed unlimited powers of taxation, then so too must the US government. Because "[w]ars have now become rather war[s] of the purse than of the sword," Connecticut Federalist Oliver Ellsworth explained, the federal government must be able "to command all the resources of the country." Limits on Congress's taxing power would enable "a hostile nation [to] look into our Constitution, see what resources are in the power of government and calculate to go a little beyond us." Ellsworth concluded, "A government which can command but half its resources is like a man with but one arm to defend himself."[73]

Madison added the observation that war required "borrowing, as sufficient money cannot be raised in a year's worth of taxes." Borrowing, in turn, required an efficacious system of taxation, as "who could be expected to lend to a government which depended on the punctuality of a dozen or more governments for the means of discharging even the annual interest of the loan?" Federalists conceded that any power could be used for tyrannical purposes, but they insisted that without an unlimited taxing power, Congress could not adequately defend the nation from a foreign invasion, which would also threaten freedom. Overall, Federalists seemed to think that war was more

---

* Indeed, just as the Federalists had promised, the national government, until after the Civil War, resorted to direct taxes only during times of war—the undeclared naval war with France in the late 1790s, the War of 1812, and the Civil War. For most of the nation's first century, the vast majority of the national government's tax revenue derived from import duties.

Figure 5.2 Oliver Ellsworth, a Connecticut delegate to the Philadelphia convention, who was an important molder of Federalist thought in the ratifying debates, principal author of the 1789 Judiciary Act in his capacity as one of Connecticut's original US senators, and later the third Chief Justice of the United States. (Collection of the Supreme Court of the United States)

likely than Antifederalists did. One Massachusetts Federalist observed that the nation was "circumscribed with enemies from Maine to Georgia."[74]

Federalists also argued that limits on Congress's taxing power that might make sense at the present moment could be rendered inconvenient by changed circumstances. Conceding that states must have their own sources of revenue, Hamilton nonetheless argued against specifying them in the Constitution because such documents "must necessarily be permanent" and thus could not "calculate for the possible changes of things." When New York Antifederalists proposed a ban on congressional excise taxes in order to protect the state's manufacturers in their infancy, Chancellor Livingston replied that future population increases might make the United States a manufacturing nation, at which point revenue from import duties would decline and other objects of taxation would become vital. Madison made the same argument at the Virginia ratifying convention.[75]

Although Federalists insisted that Congress must be vested with a vastly expanded taxing authority, they offered assurances that considerations of self-interest would impel it to rely mainly upon import duties and, if necessary, excise taxes on domestically produced goods such as liquor. At the Virginia ratifying convention, Madison observed that it could be "of little advantage to those in power to raise money in a manner oppressive to the people." Import duties raised revenue "easily and insensibly," Oliver Ellsworth told the Connecticut ratifying convention, and all nations had found them "the most fruitful and easy way" to go. As consumption taxes, import duties were, in a sense, voluntary. Moreover, they taxed a person only when he was "taking his pleasure and feels generous"—when he was "laying out a shilling for superfluities." Because the tax blended with the price of the commodity, the person bearing its incidence was often unaware of it. Finally, because import duties were imposed at the port of entry, they would "not fill the country with revenue officers."[76]

By contrast, Ellsworth explained, direct taxes required people to save money, "[b]ut you cannot make people thus provident." Capitation taxes—taxes on persons—were "abhorrent to the feelings of human nature," one Massachusetts Federalist insisted, and thus would "never be adopted by Congress." At the Massachusetts ratifying convention, Nathaniel Gorham predicted that under the Constitution the wealthy would pay high import duties on European luxury items, while "the middling and the poor parts of the community, who live by their industry, will go clear." If in a time "of great danger and distress" Congress were forced to levy direct taxes, Hamilton told the New York ratifying convention, it would "undoubtedly adopt such measures as are most conformable to the laws and customs of each state," including the use of state revenue collectors.[77]

Why would anyone assume that Congress would be more likely to impose "tyrannical" poll taxes, Hamilton asked, than would the New York legislature, which was not barred by the state constitution from doing so? A North Carolina Federalist noted that poor people should prefer that the national government be empowered to impose direct taxes during wartime because the alternative would have been for it simply to impress needed provisions and horses, which would be "unequal and oppressive" to the poor. Moreover, since the vast majority of Americans were farmers, only their own inattentiveness to politics could result in the election of national representatives who would impose land taxes. Another safeguard against oppressive taxation, George Nicholas told the Virginia ratifying convention, was that taxes imposed by Congress would affect congressional representatives and their friends the same as anybody else.[78]

In response to Antifederalist warnings that ratification would lead to tax increases, Federalists insisted that most Americans would pay lower taxes under the Constitution, both because the federal government would derive most of its revenue from import duties and the sale of western lands and because states would dramatically reduce internal taxes in the absence of federal requisitions. Oliver Ellsworth declared that the import duties collected by the three states with the largest ports—Massachusetts, New York, and Pennsylvania— would alone cover the entire interest on the foreign debt as well as nearly all of the federal government's other annual expenditures. James Wilson told the Pennsylvania ratifying convention that the total taxes paid by Americans might decline despite the greater expenses of a larger federal government because the incidence of import duties fell partly on foreign merchants, and the federal government might prove to be a more efficient taxer than the states. North Carolina Federalists predicted that taxes would decline because the federal government, which would enjoy a better credit rating once vested with vastly expanded taxing authority, would be able to borrow money at lower interest rates.[79]

Military Powers

In addition to their objections to Congress's vastly expanded taxing power, many Antifederalists protested the lack of constitutional constraints on its military powers—the authority to raise armies and navies and to call the state militias into federal service. Antifederalists conceded that Congress must have the power to raise an army during wartime, but they proposed limiting its authority to do so in time of peace to instances of necessity. The Radical Whigs of the British opposition, who had greatly influenced the political thought of American revolutionaries, considered a standing army in peacetime a temptation to the king to use it for domestic purposes, such as suppressing political dissent. American colonials were first introduced to the dangers of a peacetime army when the Boston Massacre in 1770 cost five people their lives.[80]

Not surprisingly, then, the deployment of a standing army in peacetime without the consent of local legislatures was one of the grievances articulated in the Declaration of Independence. Several state constitutions explicitly warned of the danger of standing armies. For example, the Virginia constitution of 1776 declared that "standing armies, in time of peace, should be avoided, as dangerous to liberty: and . . . in all cases, the military should be under strict subordination to, and governed by, the civil power." Congress discharged the Revolutionary Army after the peace treaty with Great Britain was signed in 1783, and subsequent proposals in the Confederation Congress to establish a peacetime standing army failed because of the traditional concerns. When, in 1784, Congress decided to raise an army of seven hundred men to guard military stores and provide security to frontier settlements, the Massachusetts delegation dissented on the grounds that if Congress had the power to raise an army in peacetime, "it would sooner or later terminate in the subversion of our liberties."[81]

Thus, most Antifederalists condemned peacetime standing armies as "the nursery of vice and the bane of liberty." A Massachusetts Antifederalist observed that "seven-eighths of the once free nations of the globe [have] been brought into bondage" through the use of standing armies. Other Antifederalists warned that "[a] standing army in the hands of a government placed so independent of the people may be made a fatal instrument to over-turn the public liberties." Such a government would have no choice but to use "the bayonet" to execute its measures, including collection of "the most op-pressive taxes." The Confederation Congress, by contrast, even if it did possess the power to create a peacetime army—which was contestable—could do so only by requisitioning troops from state legislatures, which might refuse to comply if the people were opposed.[82]

Some Antifederalists proposed limits on the size of any peacetime army, while others suggested that for Congress to raise a standing army in time of peace should require supermajority approval. Others proposed that Congress be prevented from forcing people to quarter the troops of a standing army in their homes.[83]

What need did Americans have for standing armies anyway, Antifederalists asked, when "[w]e fear no foe" and militiamen at Lexington and Concord had demonstrated in 1775 the ability of Americans to defend themselves with-out a professional military? Many Antifederalists regarded the state militias as a vital check upon potential usurpations of power by the national govern-ment. Any government wishing to invade the rights and liberties of its people would "attempt to destroy the militia and raise an army on its ruins." One Antifederalist warned that a "government which possesses all the powers of raising and maintaining armies, of regulating and commanding the militia, . . . must be supreme and will (whether in twenty or in one year, it signifies little to the event) naturally absorb every subordinate jurisdiction."[84]

To prevent the national government from monopolizing the nation's mili-tary force, many Antifederalists proposed limits on Congress's authority to call state militias into federal service. One such amendment would have re-quired the consent of a state legislature to deploy that state's militia beyond the state's borders for a period exceeding six weeks. Pennsylvania Antifederalists objected to Congress's having the power to march their state's militia to New England or Virginia "to quell an insurrection occasioned by [even] the most galling oppression." At the Pennsylvania ratifying convention, William Findley warned, "[W]hen the militia of one state has quelled insurrections and destroyed the liberties, the militia of the last state may, at another time, be employed in retaliating on the first."[85]

Other Antifederalists warned that, "in order to have a pretense of establishing a standing army," Congress might eviscerate state militias by declining to exercise its enumerated power to organize, arm, and discipline them. Virginia Antifederalists proposed a constitutional amendment empowering states to assume such functions themselves should Congress omit or neglect to perform them. Mason repeatedly expressed the related concern that Congress would use its power to discipline the militia to "inflict severe and ignominious punishments" upon members, which would "induce them to wish its abolition, which would afford a pretense for establishing a standing army." As a partial solution, he suggested an amendment to forbid Congress's subjecting the militia to martial law, except when in actual service in time of war, invasion, or rebellion.[86]

Some Antifederalists also objected that Congress's power to call up state militias extended not only to suppressing insurrections and repelling invasions but also to executing federal laws—a power that they feared would completely supplant civil authority with military power. Virginia Antifederalists further warned that Congress's power over state militias could be construed to be exclusive, which would mean that states could not use their own militias to suppress internal insurrections. Antifederalists in western regions worried that Congress's power to call up state militias would leave them defenseless against "the ravages of the merciless savages." Many Antifederalists additionally favored prohibiting Congress from disarming the people, warning that once the national government monopolized military force, it would rule supreme and the states would be destroyed.[87]

A few Antifederalists also objected to Congress's power to establish a navy—especially at a time when, according to Grayson, "[t]he riches of America are not sufficient to bear [its] enormous expense." Moreover, Grayson argued, an American navy would threaten the maritime powers of Europe, whose wealth derived mainly from commerce and navigation, and it would be unwise to "precipitately provoke" their resentment. At a minimum, the Constitution should limit the size of the navy to that which would be sufficient to protect American trade.[88]

In response to the Antifederalists' criticisms of the military powers conferred upon Congress by the Constitution, many Federalists professed to share their opponents' disdain of standing armies but nonetheless defended Congress's power to create them as necessary to deter foreign nations with professional armies from attacking the United States. Wilson told the Pennsylvania ratifying convention that because every other nation in the world had the power to raise a standing army, the United States must as well: "[W]e are not in the millennium. Wars may happen." Moreover, a standing army would save money in the long term, Wilson argued, by discouraging other nations from attacking the United States. Madison similarly observed that "[w]eakness will invite insults," and only a respectable government able to raise armies and navies would "be a security against attacks."[89]

Federalists emphasized that, in contrast to European nations, the United States would require only a small standing army because the Atlantic Ocean provided a barrier against most foreign invasions. Yet they insisted that the size of an American army could be determined only in response to the strengths and policies of European nations, which could not be determined in advance, thus rendering any constitutional limits ill-advised.[90]

While Federalists generally tended to downplay the domestic uses of a standing army, some of them cautioned that troops might be necessary to pacify Indian tribes on the frontier or in response to incidents such as Shays's Rebellion, when "[t]he flames of internal insurrection were ready to burst out in every quarter." "A Landholder" observed that while the power to raise a standing army in peacetime could be abused, just like any other power, it could also be "necessary to restrain the violence of seditious citizens." Daniel Shays might have become "the monarch and tyrant of America" if left unchecked.[91]

Federalists also downplayed the risks posed by a standing army in the United States. The English Bill of Rights forbade a standing army in time of peace only if Parliament did not consent to it. Because the Constitution authorized only Congress to raise armies, the principle of representation ought to protect the people from military oppression. Moreover, because the Constitution barred Congress from appropriating military funds for longer than two years, the people would have an early opportunity to remove those representatives who abused their power to raise an army. In any event, why would Congress be inclined to raise an army unnecessarily, especially as the control of the army would belong to the president? Finally, as Massachusetts Federalist Theodore Sedgwick noted, how could even a standing army "subdue a nation of free men, who know how to prize liberty, and who have arms in their hands?"[92]

Federalists disparaged the idea that the power to co-opt state militias could be a viable alternative to empowering Congress to raise an army. One Virginia Federalist observed that citizens who constituted the militia were "unacquainted with the hardships and unskilled in the discipline of war." Hamilton insisted that the notion that militia were an adequate military force had nearly "lost us our independence." Invoking his own experience during the Revolutionary War, Henry ("Light-Horse Harry") Lee told the Virginia ratifying convention that he had seen "incontrovertible evidence that militia cannot always be relied upon."[93]

Although disdainful of the notion that militias alone were adequate for national defense, Federalists nonetheless argued that the best way to avoid standing armies, which were expensive and inevitably posed some threat to liberty, was to vest Congress with unqualified control over state militias. Wilson expressed surprise that Antifederalists objected to this grant of power, which to some extent would "supersede the necessity of raising or keeping up standing armies." Moreover, if Congress was to have the power to co-opt state militias, it obviously must be authorized to impose uniformity on them. Anyone with military experience, Wilson observed, would know that "men without a uniformity of arms, accoutrements, and discipline, are no more than a mob in a camp." So long as states appointed militia officers, as the Constitution provided, Hamilton insisted there could be no danger posed by empowering Congress to discipline the militia while in national service.[94]

In response to the New York Antifederalists' proposed amendment to require Congress to secure the consent of a state legislature before sending its militia out of state for more than six weeks, Hamilton observed that during the Revolutionary War, states such as Virginia had been remiss about permitting their militias to assist other states until the battle lines had drawn near. In response to a similar proposal in Virginia, Madison asked why a federal government in which the people chose the members of one branch and state legislatures selected members of the other would be likely to "drag the militia unnecessarily to an immense distance," thus "exciting the universal indignation of the people." In response to the Antifederalists' criticism that Congress ought not to be empowered to use the militia for simple enforcement of federal law, Madison noted that popular resistance falling short of that qualifying as an "insurrection" could impede the administration of law. Congress obviously had to be able, just like any state legislature could, to compel the execution of its laws—by force, if necessary. Would Antifederalists prefer that it use a standing army to do so?[95]

Federalists also dismissed the notion that Congress's power over state militias was exclusive—an idea that would have enabled Congress to leave the states defenseless by failing to arm or discipline their militias. Because state governments did not derive their powers from the Constitution, Federalists argued, only those grants of power to Congress that were explicitly made exclusive had the effect of denying concurrent powers to the states.[96]

With regard to Congress's power to "provide and maintain a navy," South Carolina Federalist Edward Rutledge insisted that the United States could not "become a great nation until we were powerful on the waters." Noting that Great Britain had barred the United States from trading with some parts of the West Indies while European nations remained free to do so, Rutledge lamented that "we must hold our country by courtesy unless we have a navy."

Hamilton observed that American neutrality rights would "only be respected when they are defended by an adequate power," and thus without a strong navy, American commerce would "be a prey to the wanton intermeddlings of all nations at war with each other." Moreover, as John Jay noted, without a navy to protect it, American commerce in the Mediterranean Sea was at the mercy of Algerian pirates, who in 1785 had captured American sailors and were still holding them for ransom—much to the nation's consternation and embarrassment.[97]

The Commerce Power and the Treaty-Making Power

Some southern Antifederalists—but not northern ones—also objected to Congress's enumerated power to regulate commerce with foreign nations and among the states. Southerners worried that Congress would use the commerce power to provide a monopoly over the American carrying trade to northern shippers—to the detriment of agricultural exporters, such as southern planters. The generally prevailing assumption that northerners would control both houses of Congress, at least in the short term, rendered this concern especially acute.[98]

Thus, in Virginia, Mason objected to the simple majority requirement for commercial legislation on the grounds that northern states would demand "an exorbitant freight," and "the five southern states will be ruined." Richard Henry Lee similarly warned of the northern states' using Congress's commerce power to foist "the most oppressive monopoly upon the five southern states." Accordingly, southern Antifederalists revived proposals that had been at least partially approved during a portion of the Philadelphia convention— only to be abandoned before the convention ended—to require supermajorities in Congress for the enactment of commercial legislation.[99]

For similar reasons, southern Antifederalists expressed concern about the treaty-making power. The Constitution provides that for treaties to have the force of law, they must be made by the president with the "advice and consent" of two-thirds of the Senate. At the Virginia ratifying convention, Antifederalist John Dawson objected that the treaty-making power could be "highly injurious to the southern states." Southerners had "already seen a diabolical attempt made to surrender the navigation" of the Mississippi River, "on which depends the importance of the southern part of America." Under the Constitution, Dawson warned, the president, together with two-thirds of the Senate, could make a treaty "by which any territory may be ceded, or the navigation of any river surrendered."[100]

In response to this concern, some Antifederalists—mostly, but not exclusively, southerners—proposed that the two-thirds requirement for Senate approval of treaties be applied to the entire number of senators rather than the number who happened to be present for a particular vote on a treaty, as required by the Constitution. Otherwise, ten senators, representing just five states, could ratify a treaty—because fourteen would be a quorum in a twenty-six-person Senate (assuming two senators for each of the original thirteen states), and ten out of fourteen would satisfy the two-thirds requirement. Such a scenario left the South much more vulnerable under the Constitution than under the Articles of Confederation, which required the approval of nine states for treaty ratification. Some southern Antifederalists also proposed ratcheting up the supermajority requirement to three-fourths for those treaties that, among other things, restrained or suspended American claims to the navigation of rivers, and to restrict such treaties to instances of "the most urgent and extreme necessity." They also proposed that treaties not become operational without congressional legislation to implement them. Such a proposal would ensure that the House of Representatives, whose population-based apportionment was considered likely to favor the South over time, would participate in the enforcement of treaties.[101]

Federalists, however, strongly defended both Congress's power to regulate foreign and interstate commerce and the Constitution's treaty-making provision. Hamilton found the "least room to entertain a difference of opinion" with regard to the commerce power. Because the Confederation Congress lacked power over foreign trade, New Jersey Federalist Lambert Cadwalader observed, other nations "sacrificed our interest in every instance to their own in full expectation of our inability to counteract them." Most notably, European powers excluded Americans from the carrying trade—especially with their colonies in the West Indies—and the US government was powerless to respond in kind. As a result, John Jay told New Yorkers, American shipyards "have almost ceased to disturb the repose of the neighborhood by the noise of the axe and hammer." Recapturing some of that trade, Massachusetts Federalist Thomas Russell argued, would "furnish us with a great nursery of seamen [and] give employment not only to the mechanics in constructing the vessels, and the trades dependent thereon, but to the husbandman in cutting down trees for timber and transporting them to the places of building."[102]

In addition, under the Articles of Confederation, American goods were being "utterly excluded" from most foreign ports, or else "loaded down with [exorbitant] duties and customs," according to one Connecticut Federalist. Thomas Dawes declared at the Massachusetts ratifying convention that Americans were suffering "ignominious burdens" rather than trusting their own representatives with the power necessary to help them. While American states might be "independent of each other," they were "slaves to Europe." As a result, David Ramsay of South Carolina lamented, "our ships have rotted, our commerce has either been abandoned or carried on to our prejudice." James Wilson advised the Pennsylvania ratifying convention, "Go along the wharves of Philadelphia and observe the melancholy silence that reigns." Such was the consequence of denying Congress power over foreign commerce.[103]

Granting such power to Congress, Hamilton promised, would "oblige foreign countries to bid against each other for the privileges of our markets." Because the United States was mostly committed to agriculture, he argued, American markets were becoming increasingly valuable to manufacturing nations. In exchange for free access to American markets, those nations ought to be forced to open theirs to American agricultural products, which would increase the value of American farmland.[104]

In addition, Congress's power to regulate foreign commerce could be used—especially, but not exclusively, in the future—to impose tariffs on foreign imports, which might provide critical support to domestic manufacturers in their infancy. Massachusetts Federalist Dawes argued that recent immigration of foreign artisans, combined with natural resources such as water power, could make manufacturing an increasingly important part of the American economy. Congress must have the power to encourage it behind tariff barriers. Thus, one Pennsylvania Federalist wrote, "Heavy duties will be laid on all foreign manufactures which can be manufactured in this country, and bounties will be granted on [the] exportation of our commodities. The manufactories of our country will flourish—our mechanics will lift up their heads, and rise to opulence and wealth."[105]

Congress's power to regulate *interstate* trade was necessary, Madison explained, for "the relief of the states which import and export through other states, from the improper contributions levied on them by the latter." Unless Congress blocked such vexatious impositions, they "would nourish unceasing animosities, and not improbably terminate in serious interruptions of the public tranquility." Madison noted that even the loose confederacies of Europe, such as Switzerland and Germany, forbade discriminatory trade practices among member states.[106]

Federalists offered several responses to southerners' concerns that they would be outnumbered in Congress and thus were vulnerable to commercial regulations that would advantage the northern majority. First, they argued that the South's vulnerability to the higher freight rates likely to result from navigation laws was limited because "a spirit of competition would call forth the resources" of northern and middle states, which would compete for the southern carrying trade. At most, according to South Carolina Federalist Robert Barnwell, southern agricultural exporters would be injured "in a trifling degree" for a few years. In addition, Madison noted, because several northern states were not major carriers themselves, navigation acts might not command a northern majority in Congress.[107]

Federalists also argued that because southerners received certain countervailing benefits from the union, they ought to be willing to grant northerners "some privileges with regard to their [i.e., southerners'] shipping." One such benefit consisted of the concessions that northerners had made to slavery at the Philadelphia convention. As David Ramsay pointed out to Benjamin Lincoln of Massachusetts, "[y]our delegates never did a more political thing than in standing by those of South Carolina about Negroes [i.e., slaves]" at the Philadelphia convention, as this had generated much "liberality of sentiment" toward the North in South Carolina.[108]

Southern Federalists cited additional benefits that the South derived from the union, which they argued would justify affording the North certain commercial advantages under the Constitution. Being more vulnerable to both foreign invasions and domestic (slave) insurrections, the South benefited

Figure 5.3 David Ramsay, a physician and one of the first historians of the American Revolution, was one of South Carolina's leading Federalists. (Courtesy of Independence National Historical Park)

disproportionately from the physical security provided by a stronger union. Thus, at the Virginia ratifying convention, Madison argued against a supermajority requirement for commercial legislation on the grounds that northern states, which were better able to protect themselves, could not be expected to commit to defending the South if they were "left at the mercy of the minority for commercial advantages."[109]

Southern Federalists observed that northern troops had rescued the South during the Revolutionary War, and also that weaker southern states would benefit disproportionately in the future from "a common navy paid out of the federal treasury," which navigation laws would facilitate by encouraging shipping and developing seamen. "As the war has turned out so much in our favor, and so much against them [i.e., the northern states]," Ramsay reasoned, "ought we to begrudge them the carrying of our produce, especially when it is considered, that by encouraging their shipping, we increase the means of our own defense?" Fellow South Carolinian Charles Cotesworth Pinckney agreed that northerners had "assisted us in establishing our freedom," yet they had been "the greatest sufferers in the union by our obtaining our independence." Their shipbuilding trade had been "annihilated," their fisheries were "trifling," and their mariners were starving. "[E]very tie of justice, friendship and humanity" obliged the South to "relieve their distresses" and allow northerners to "partake of our prosperity."[110]

Federalists offered yet one additional response to assuage southerners' concerns that their minority status rendered them vulnerable to disadvantageous commercial regulations: Any immediate political advantage that the North would enjoy in Congress—which, they also noted, was no greater than the advantage northern states already possessed in the Confederation Congress—would not last long. As population shifted rapidly to the South and the West, northerners would lose their majority in the population-apportioned House. As those demographic changes translated into the creation of new states, the North's initial advantage in the Senate would also be erased.[111]

Thus, southern Federalists emphasized that the Constitution required a periodic census and congressional reapportionment based on it, which would soon reflect the "immense" demographic shifts they predicted. New England was small and its land was poor, Ramsay argued, while the southern states had a "vast extent of uncultivated country," which was "daily receiving new settlers." As a result, the South's "influence in the general government will be constantly increasing," and within fifty years it would "have a great ascendancy over the eastern [states]."[112]

In response to southern Antifederalists' concerns about the treaty-making power, Federalists argued that the South was better protected under the Constitution than under the Articles. The Constitution required that the president concur in treaties for them to become law—a check that did not exist under the Articles, which did not provide for an executive branch to counterbalance Congress—and southern states were likely to exercise great influence in selecting the president, given their anticipated population growth. Federalists defended excluding the House from participation in treaty making on the grounds that it could not act "with sufficient secrecy, dispatch and decision, which can only be found in small bodies."[113]

In response to the Antifederalists' concern that only two-thirds of the senators present were required to ratify treaties, which could amount in practice to the senators of just five states, Federalists noted how unlikely it was that so many senators would absent themselves from votes on measures as important as the ratification of treaties. Moreover, they argued, the Constitution's requirement that treaties be ratified by two-thirds of the senators present would probably in practice better protect southern interests, once the northern states of Vermont and Maine were added to the union, than did the Articles' nine-state requirement for treaty making.[114]

Antifederalists had also expressed concern that the president and the Senate might together approve treaties to dismember the empire. In response, Madison noted that the Constitution was no more threatening in this regard than the Articles of Confederation, which also imposed no subject-matter limitations on the treaty-making power. At the same time, he denied that this constitutional power could be validly used for objects inconsistent with its purpose, which meant that treaties could not alienate "any great essential right," such as free navigation of the Mississippi River. North Carolina Federalist James Iredell added the observation that if the Constitution were to impose substantive limits on the treaty-making power that other nations did not labor under, then the United States would be disadvantaged in its treaty negotiations. Finally, Federalists observed, in the words of Hugh Williamson of North Carolina, that the Mississippi River was "shut not by right but by the hand of power and that under the existing government we are never likely to be able to open it." Iredell believed that only "an efficient government," under which "we shall certainly have some ships of war," would be able to pressure Spain to allow Americans to export goods down the Mississippi River.[115]

Other Congressional Powers

Antifederalists also objected to other grants of power to Congress that would strike most modern observers as innocuous. One frequent object of criticism was Congress's power under Article I, Section 4, of the Constitution to "make or alter" state legislative regulations of "the times, places and manner of holding elections for senators and representatives."* At the Philadelphia convention, Madison had defended this grant of revisionary power to Congress on the grounds that state legislatures might manipulate the regulation of federal elections to promote "a favorite measure" or otherwise abuse the power in ways that were "impossible to foresee."[116]

During the ratifying contest, Antifederalists warned that Congress would use this "reprehensible" power to make itself "omnipotent." Writing to a college friend, the young Antifederalist (and future president) John Quincy Adams objected to giving members of Congress the power "of prescribing the manner of their own appointments." Adams considered this power especially "insidious because it appears trivial, and yet will admit of such construction as will render it a very dangerous instrument in the hands of such a powerful body of men." North Carolina Antifederalist Timothy Bloodworth worried that Congress might "make the time of election so long, the place so inconvenient, and the manner so oppressive, that it will entirely destroy representation."[117]

Specifically, Antifederalists warned that congressional representatives might set the "time" of elections as never, or at least postpone them and "by degrees render themselves absolute and perpetual." If members of the British Parliament in 1716 had been able to extend their term in office from three to seven years, then it was not inconceivable that congressional representatives might try something similar.[118]

Congress might choose as the "place" of a state's congressional elections the extremities of the state, to which most people would have difficulty traveling. Alternatively, Congress might order elections to be held in large cities, where Federalist candidates would have the electoral advantage. One Pennsylvania Antifederalist warned that Congress might order the state's congressional elections to "take place in the city of Philadelphia in the middle of winter," thus preventing 90 percent of the state's population from exercising its suffrage rights.[119]

Congressional control over the "manner" of federal elections could be used, according to Antifederalists, to reserve to Congress the power to fill vacancies or to dictate to states whether candidates needed to win pluralities or majorities of the vote in order to be elected. Congress might also require that congressional elections take place "at large"—that is, in multimember districts covering a large geographic area—which would probably advantage Federalist candidates because of their generally greater wealth and name recognition. Indeed,

---

* Congress's revisionary power does not extend to "the *places* of choosing senators." Federalists explained that, as the Constitution reposed the power to choose senators in state legislatures, Congress ought not to be empowered to force state lawmakers to make that choice in a location different from their usual meeting place.

New York Antifederalist Melancton Smith proposed a constitutional amend-ment to require that congressional elections be conducted in single-member districts rather than at large. Antifederalists also warned that Congress would use its power over the manner of federal elections to set property qualifications for voting. Patrick Henry declared that Congress might make "the vote of one gentleman go as far as the votes of 100 poor men."[120]

Federalists might deny that any such abuses were likely, but Antifederalists demanded to know why one should assume "that we shall be blessed with im-peccable rulers." It made no sense, Antifederalists insisted, to leave "a door open to improper regulations."[121]

In response to such charges, Federalists argued that every government ought to have the authority to preserve itself, and they noted that state law-makers exercised, without objection, the power to set the times, places, and manner of their own elections. Congress must have revisionary authority over the regulation of federal elections, Federalists insisted, because states might, for example, be unable to call federal elections due to an invasion, or refuse to do so in order to obstruct congressional action.* Indeed, Federalists alleged that Rhode Island in the summer of 1787 had deliberately withheld its congressional delegates, thus depriving Congress of a quorum, which re-sulted in the obstruction of a lucrative deal for the sale of western lands. Under Article I, Section 4, however, "that trifling state would not have withheld its representation."[122]

Federalists also defended this revisionary power as essential to checking those state legislatures that were determined to undermine fair representa-tion, as through malapportionment. In addition, they argued that Congress ought to have the power to insist on some uniformity in federal elections. For example, to prevent corruption or undue influence, Congress should be able to insist that congressional elections take place throughout the United States on the same day. Likewise, Federalists argued, Congress should have the power to require that all congressional elections be conducted either by ballot or by voice vote and not by a haphazard combination of the two.[123]

Federalists denounced as absurd the idea that the power to regulate the time of elections could be rationally construed to enable House members to serve

---

* Antifederalists replied that if the revisionary power was needed to deal with instances of emergency or state obstructionism, then it should be explicitly limited to such occasions. In sev-eral state ratifying conventions, they proposed that this power be restricted to instances in which a state legislature "shall neglect, refuse, or be disabled by invasion or rebellion to prescribe" regu-lations to govern the times, places, and manner of federal elections. When such an amendment was proposed in the first Congress, Madison opposed it as tending "to destroy the principles and the efficacy of the Constitution."

more than two years or senators more than six. Nor, they said, could the power to regulate the manner of congressional elections plausibly be interpreted to extend to imposing voter qualifications when the Constitution plainly specified that the qualifications of persons voting for congressional representatives were to be tied to the qualifications imposed by state law on "electors of the most numerous branch of the state legislature."[124]

In addition, Federalists argued that vesting state legislatures with too much control over the election of House members when they already picked senators would weaken the House's ability to check the Senate. They also insisted that senators selected by state legislatures would never agree to abusive congressional regulations of the times, places, and manner of federal elections.[125]

Finally, Federalists accused their opponents of paranoia in conjuring up such implausible abuses of congressional power. Madison observed that if Congress required people to travel to a single city to participate in congressional elections, it "would be execrated for the infamous regulation." One Massachusetts Federalist questioned the assumption that Congress, when exercising the revisionary power over congressional elections, would "act as bad as possible." Another asked whether it was not more likely that the people would elect to Congress "good men" than "men to ruin us."[126]

Some Antifederalists also criticized the constitutional provision authorizing Congress "[t]o exercise exclusive legislation in all cases whatsoever" over a district "not exceeding ten miles square," that would be ceded by states to become the seat of the new national government. Delegates to the Philadelphia convention had thought that Congress plainly needed a home that was not within the jurisdiction of any state in order to insulate it from pernicious influence, which had been a frequent complaint under the Articles. Moreover, as Rufus King had noted at the convention, Congress required a *permanent* residence: "The mutability of place had dishonored the federal government and would require as strong a cure as we could devise."[127]

During the ratifying debates, however, Antifederalists conjured up images of a tyrannical government taking advantage of its federal enclave to violate the people's liberties. "A Columbian Patriot"—who was Mercy Otis Warren, one of the few women to publicly, though pseudonymously, participate in the debates over independence and the ratification of the Constitution—denounced the idea of a "federal city whose 'cloud capped towers' may screen the state culprit from the hand of justice, while its exclusive jurisdiction may protect the riot of armies encamped within its limits." At the Virginia ratifying convention, Mason called this provision one of the most dangerous in the Constitution. He warned that such a federal enclave would become "the sanctuary of the blackest crimes," as state laws would be "set at defiance" within the district. Securing justice against federal officers who "attempt to oppress the people, or should actually perpetrate the blackest deed" would prove impossible in the district, where Congress would exercise its influence on judges and juries.[128]

Other Antifederalists raised different concerns about this provision. Grayson observed that because the district was not a state, neither the Fugitive Slave Clause nor the Fugitives from Justice Clause would apply, and thus slaves and felons who escaped there would not have to be surrendered. He also expressed concern that Congress would grant "exclusive privileges of commerce" to district residents. Denouncing this provision as "a wanton grasp of power," Patrick Henry similarly warned that Congress might excuse district residents "from all the burdens imposed on the rest of the society" and confer on them "exclusive emoluments to the great injury of the rest of the people."[129]

Federalists offered several defenses of the constitutional provision authorizing Congress to exercise exclusive legislation over the nation's capital. Congress needed a permanent residence, where it could establish archives and deposit state papers. No state would want another to house Congress and thus possibly exercise undue influence over its proceedings. In addition, according to the Federalists' controversial account, in 1783 the Confederation Congress had been forced to flee Philadelphia when the Pennsylvania government declined to call up state militia to protect Congress from a mutiny by Pennsylvania soldiers in the Revolutionary Army—"a disgraceful scene" that had treated the sovereignty of the United States with "indignity," according to James Iredell.[130]

Moreover, Madison observed, if states were genuinely concerned about abuses of this power, they were free to impose stipulations when ceding to Congress the territory that would constitute the district. At the Virginia ratifying convention, Henry Lee asked why "the members of the general government, who were freely chosen by the people," would allow the district they inhabited to become "crowded with rogues." He also wondered how a district "not exceeding ten miles square" could plausibly pose a threat to subjugate a vast nation.[131]

Antifederalists also objected to the constitutional provision allowing each house of Congress to publish the journal of its proceedings (which it was required to keep) only "from time to time," and authorizing exceptions from the publication requirement for "such parts as may in their judgment require secrecy." Patrick Henry warned the Virginia ratifying convention that Congress would take advantage of the vagueness of these exceptions and decline to publish any of its proceedings, thus preventing the people from knowing what was happening in Congress. Other Antifederalists objected that "from time to time" could mean never. Why not require Congress, as the Articles of Confederation did, to publish its journal on a monthly basis and limit the secrecy exception to portions of the proceedings relating to treaties, alliances, and military operations?[132]

Antifederalists raised similar objections to the constitutional requirement that "a regular statement and account of the receipts and expenditures of all public money shall be published from time to time." Henry criticized this as a "very indefinite" expression and warned that "the national wealth is to be disposed of under the veil of secrecy, for the publication from time to time will amount to nothing." Mason told the Virginia ratifying convention that the people had a right to know how their money was being spent, yet "[t]his expression was so loose, it might be concealed forever from them and might afford opportunities of misapplying the public money and sheltering those who did it."[133]

In response, Madison defended the open-ended secrecy provision in the clause requiring the publication of congressional journals on the grounds that it was impossible to enumerate everything that ought to be kept secret. He also noted that this power was enjoyed by all state legislatures and the British House of Commons. Requiring that a statement of receipts and expenditures be published occasionally rather than in specified short intervals, according to Federalists, would both facilitate a more thorough comprehension of the statement and make errors easier to detect. Federalists also noted that the people would simply evict from office those representatives who abused their positions in seeking to evade responsibility by refusing to keep the public apprised of their legislative actions.[134]

More generally, the extreme conspiratorial visions of some Antifederalists—Hamilton referred derisively to their "distempered imagination," which turned "the most distant and doubtful conjectures" of abuse of power into "inevitable realities"—elicited several different responses from Federalists. While acknowledging that "[j]ealousy in a free government ought to be respected," Iredell told the North Carolina ratifying convention that it could be "carried to too great an extent." It was impossible to "guard against all possible danger of people's choosing their officers indiscreetly. If they have a right to choose, they may make a bad choice." Similarly, John Marshall (who later became the most important Chief Justice of the United States in history) observed at the Virginia convention that because the people could not possibly transact their business in person, "if you repose no confidence in delegates, because there is a possibility of their abusing it, you can have no government, for the power of doing good is inseparable from that of doing some evil."[135]

Their opponents' extreme suspicions were especially absurd, Federalists insisted, in a system where the people elected—directly or indirectly—government officials, who in turn were governed by the rules they made.

Washington, like many Federalists, was enormously frustrated that everyone seemed to concede that the federal government required additional powers, yet "the instant these are delegated, . . . the persons holding them, as if their natures were immediately metamorphosed, are denominated tyrants and no disposition is allowed them but to do wrong." This was in spite of the fact that "those who are entrusted with the administration are taken from the people— return shortly to them again—and must feel [themselves] the bad effects of oppressive measures."[136]

Exasperated by the Antifederalists' extraordinary conjectures of congressional abuses of power, Francis Corbin asked the Virginia ratifying convention, "how, in the name of God," were representatives who "were to return every second year to mingle with their fellow citizens" going to "make laws to destroy themselves?" The Federalist governor of North Carolina, Samuel Johnston, observed that the congressional representatives whom the Antifederalists insisted would conspire to destroy the people's liberties were to be "chosen from among ourselves" and would "be in the same situation with us. They are to be the bone of our bone and the flesh of our flesh. They cannot injure us without injuring themselves." Some Federalists also argued that security against abuse of power was greater under the Constitution than the Articles, where all the federal government's power was vested in a single body over which the people exercised no direct control.[137]

Other Federalists, such as Hamilton, emphasized that state legislatures, which would have "the confidence of the people" and would be "jealous of federal encroachments," would be "the most powerful obstacle to the members of Congress betraying the interests of their constituents." Massachusetts Federalist Theophilus Parsons similarly observed that "none but mad men would attempt a usurpation" upon well-organized state legislatures that possessed "the means as well as inclination successfully to oppose it." Indeed, Edmund Randolph asked, why would state legislatures in the first place elect as senators "those desperados and horrid adventurers which they are represented to be" by the Antifederalists?[138]

In addition to arguing that the federal government could be trusted with power, Federalists insisted, in the words of Oliver Ellsworth, that their opponents' "jealousy in excess is a delirium of the imagination, by no means favorable to liberty." Washington noted that "great evils result from too much jealousy, as from the want of it," and Madison agreed that where government power was necessary and could be safely lodged, it was "imprudent and unsafe to withhold it." To relax "the bands of government" too much, which Madison believed was the invariable tendency in America, was to produce anarchy and, eventually, despotism.[139]

Thus, Richard Morris, chief justice of the New York Supreme Court, told his state's ratifying convention that the Antifederalists had wrongfully concluded that "all the danger is derived from a fancied tyrannical propensity in their rulers," whereas careful consideration "should teach us that vigor in government is as necessary to the protection of freedom as the warmest attachment to liberty in the governors." At the Pennsylvania convention, Wilson asserted that "liberty has a formidable enemy" in "licentiousness" as much as in "tyranny" and that the government must have "proper powers" to guard against the former danger. Benjamin Rush, a prominent Pennsylvania Federalist, wrote that in "cherishing jealousies of our rulers," the Antifederalists were "too apt to overlook the weaknesses and vices of the people," whereas only a "vigorous and efficient government can prevent their degenerating into savages or devouring each other like beasts of prey." If nothing else, according to Morris, the Antifederalists, "in all their zeal for liberty, do not seem to see the danger to be apprehended from foreign power."[140]

Yet Antifederalists were deeply skeptical of government power, which they assumed to be corrupting. "Brutus" observed that the "unerring experience of ages" proved that "every body of men, invested with power, are ever disposed to increase it, and to acquire a superiority over everything that stands in their way." Henry told the Virginia ratifying convention that "in all parts of the world" the "predominant thirst of dominion . . . has invariably and uniformly prompted rulers to abuse their powers." Three Massachusetts Antifederalists asked, "Does not the experience of past ages teach that men have generally exercised all the powers they had given them and even have usurped upon them in order to accomplish their own sinister and avaricious designs?"[141]

Antifederalists refused to assume that federal government officials would be good men; all humans were fallible and thus ought to be suspect. While Melancton Smith admitted that not all men were dishonest, he considered it safer when forming a constitution to "presume this" than the opposite. That assumption was especially warranted, "Brutus" observed, because "as this government is constituted, there is little reason to expect that the interest of the people and their rulers will be the same." Indeed, if "the habits and sentiments of the people are to be relied upon as the sole security against encroachments of their rulers," "Brutus" asked, then what was the point of placing any restrictions at all in the Constitution? Moreover, because government power was dynamic, Antifederalists argued, even a slight miscalculation in the Constitution's initial allocations of power would be compounded over time. As Henry explained, "It is easier to supply deficiencies of power than to take back excess of power," and he therefore warned that "a wrong step made now will plunge us into misery, and our republic will be lost."[142]

Antifederalists believed they needed to be especially vigilant about innocuous-looking provisions of the Constitution because, as Mason cautioned, Congress could "finally destroy the state governments more effectually by insidious, underhanded means, than such as could be openly practiced." In their extreme suspicion of government power, the Antifederalists shared the political perspective of the American revolutionaries of a decade earlier, who had embraced equally conspiratorial visions of the British government's supposedly oppressive designs upon them.[143]

The Federal Judiciary

The Antifederalists' fear of consolidation also inspired some of their objections to Article III, which Henry called the most dangerous provision in the Constitution and which Madison later described as one of the "most criticized." Article III provided for a federal judiciary—a US Supreme Court and, at the discretion of Congress, "inferior" federal courts as well—vested with what Antifederalists denounced as a "boundless" jurisdiction. At the Virginia ratifying convention, Mason warned that allowing Congress to create as many lower federal courts as it wished with a virtually unlimited jurisdiction would "impair and ultimately destroy the state judiciaries," as well as lead "slowly and imperceptibly rather than all at once" to the establishment of "one great, national, consolidated government."[144]

Antifederalists warned that federal judges would have the means and the incentive to expand congressional power. "Brutus" worried that because federal courts had jurisdiction in cases in "law and equity" that arose under the Constitution, and because equity jurisprudence did not allow for "established rules and fixed principles," federal courts would have enormous discretion to determine "the reason and spirit of the Constitution" and thus "to mold the government into almost any shape they please." In addition, because of the Necessary and Proper Clause, the Constitution "itself strongly countenances" a "latitude of interpretation" in Congress's powers.[145]

More important, because "[e]very body of men invested with office [is] tenacious of power," "Brutus" predicted that federal judges would be inclined to construe the Constitution in ways that would "enlarge the sphere of their own authority." Because federal judicial power was directly tied to federal legislative power through the former's extension in Article III to all cases "arising under" federal law, federal judges would "lean strongly in favor of the general government and will give such an explanation to the Constitution as will favor an extension of its jurisdiction." Every expansion of Congress's powers would increase "the dignity and importance of the judges." In addition, the more business the federal courts transacted, the more likely it would be that Congress would increase the pay of federal judges (which the Constitution permits).[146]*

The scope of the federal judicial power was especially worrisome because, as "Brutus" observed, "those who are to be vested with it are to be placed in a situation altogether unprecedented in a free country. They are to be rendered totally independent, both of the people and the legislature, both with respect to their offices and salaries."[147]†

Antifederalists proposed amendments to limit the federal judiciary to a supreme court and lower courts restricted to admiralty jurisdiction. A Georgia Antifederalist warned of the Constitution's "introducing strange and new courts of almost any denomination into any of the states, whereby our own courts will soon be annihilated."[148]

Antifederalists also favored drastically curtailing the jurisdiction assigned to federal courts under Article III. The federal judicial power, according to Antifederalists, should be limited to instances in which a federal arbiter was indispensable—for example, cases arising under federal treaties, lawsuits involving foreign ambassadors, disputes to which the United States was a party, controversies between two or more states, and incidents arising on the high seas. However, the jurisdiction of the federal judiciary under Article III was so extensive, Pennsylvania Antifederalists warned, that "by legal ingenuity [it] may be extended to every case and thus absorb the state judiciaries." Mason thought it "disgraceful" that a state court in Virginia was not to be trusted to adjudicate a dispute between a foreign citizen and a Virginian.§ Jurisdiction over cases "arising under" federal law, Mason warned, would enable federal judges to insulate from liability federal revenue collectors even if they "should

---

* The Constitution permits Congress to increase, but not decrease, the salary of federal judges (whereas Congress cannot change the president's salary in either direction). Some Antifederalists objected that Congress's power to increase the salaries of federal judges gave it too much influence over them. Moreover, because the Constitution's Incompatibility Clause—barring members of Congress from simultaneously holding federal executive office—does not cover federal judges, the prospect of appointment to lucrative executive offices could also influence their rulings.

† In contrast to federal judges, who enjoyed tenure during good behavior and could be removed from office only through impeachment for wrongdoing, judges in many states held very short terms of office and were easily removable by legislatures.

§ Article III's grant of jurisdiction to federal courts in controversies between citizens of a state and the citizens or subjects of a foreign nation seemed to open the door to British creditors' suing to collect on prewar debts, which was a subject of enormous controversy in southern states, especially Virginia and Maryland. Many southerners considered these prewar debts to be unjust because British mercantilist policy had deprived them of a considerable portion of the value of their agricultural exports. Antifederalist concerns about this aspect of Article III jurisdiction were vindicated in 1796 when the Supreme Court ruled that a Virginia law that effectively nullified

be guilty of the greatest oppressions, or behave with the most insolent and wanton brutality to a man's wife or daughter."[149]

Antifederalists also charged that by establishing federal court jurisdiction over cases in which citizens of different states were parties—even if the cases involved ordinary matters of state law, such as contractual disputes—the Constitution would enable creditors to force debtors to travel long distances (because federal trial courts would presumably be scarce) to defend lawsuits at great expense, which would "tend to oppress the middling and lower class of people." To prevent such potential abuses, Antifederalists proposed limiting federal court jurisdiction to cases involving more than a prescribed dollar amount. They even suggested a constitutional amendment clarifying that federal jurisdiction could not be concocted through fictions or collusion—such as simply assigning a contract claim to an out-of-state party. Broad appellate jurisdiction in the Supreme Court, Antifederalists similarly warned, put it "in the power of the wealthy to recover unjustly of the poor man, who is not able to attend at such extreme distance and bear such enormous expense as it must produce."[150]

Antifederalists also objected that the federal judicial power extended to cases in "equity" as well as "law." (As noted in chapter 3, courts of equity handled lawsuits in which plaintiffs sought remedies other than money damages, such as an injunction.) Pennsylvania Antifederalists warned that "rich and wealthy suitors would eagerly lay hold of the infinite mazes, perplexities, and delays" that characterized courts of equity. In the British chancery (equity) courts, these Antifederalists observed, the wealthy always prevailed over the poor because of the "monstrous expense and inconveniences" of equity proceedings.[151]

Antifederalists further criticized the Constitution's failure to protect the right to jury trials in civil cases. Juries were "the bulwarks of our rights and liberty," one North Carolina Antifederalist insisted, and only "twelve honest, disinterested men" could be entrusted with cases that affected people's property. Moreover, the Constitution gave the US Supreme Court appellate jurisdiction over matters of fact as well as law, which meant, according to Pennsylvania Antifederalists, that it could usurp the function of local juries, resulting in "the loss of the invaluable right of trial by an unbiased jury, so dear to every friend of liberty." Some Antifederalists suggested that Supreme Court review of facts should be limited to cases appealed from chancery and admiralty courts, which generally functioned without juries, and should be barred in cases appealed from common-law courts where juries found the facts. Antifederalists

recovery of such debts was invalid under the Treaty of Paris of 1783. The federal courts generally proved to be receptive forums for the claims of British creditors.

also objected that the Supreme Court's appellate review of trial court findings of fact would require litigants to bear considerable expense in transporting their evidence and witnesses to the Court. As such, New York Antifederalists claimed, this review power would operate as a "powerful engine in the hands of the rich to oppress and ruin the poor."[152]

Even the right to a jury trial in criminal cases, which Article III explicitly protected, could be "evaded [and] rendered of little value" because the Constitution required neither that federal criminal trials take place in the vicinity of the alleged crime—only in the same state—nor that the jury be locally empaneled. Thus, in a large state, a person might be tried for a crime five hundred miles from where it had allegedly been committed—and thus be deprived of the benefit of a local jury that knew his character and the character of the witnesses. Antifederalists could not believe that Americans, who had vociferously protested Great Britain's occasional practice of transporting colonists accused of certain legal violations to Britain for trial or of deploying in the colonies vice-admiralty courts that sat without juries, would tolerate this deprivation of the right to local criminal trials with locally empaneled juries.[153]

Nor did the Constitution mandate that federal criminal prosecutions proceed with common-law protections, such as grand jury indictments or the requirement that defendants be afforded the rights to be represented by counsel, to confront their accusers, to cross-examine witnesses, to not incriminate themselves, and to be free from cruel and unusual punishments. Under the Constitution, according to one Massachusetts Antifederalist, Congress could "institute judicatories little less inauspicious than ... that diabolical institution, the Inquisition," and it could authorize punishments with "racks and gibbets."[154]

Lastly with regard to Article III, Antifederalists objected that states would lose their traditional sovereign immunity, meaning that they could be sued and forced to make good on depreciated securities and other paper they had issued during and after the war. Patrick Henry warned that under the Constitution the states' paper money "must be discharged, shilling for shilling," because states could be sued without their consent in federal court under Article III, and would be barred from impairing the obligation of their contracts under Article I, Section 10.* At the Virginia ratifying convention, Mason objected to

---

* Both of these Antifederalist interpretive claims were debatable. Whether states could be sued without their consent in federal court was resolved in *Chisholm v. Georgia* in 1793, which is briefly discussed later in this chapter. In 1810, the Supreme Court ruled in *Fletcher v. Peck* (10 U.S. 87 (1810)) that the Contracts Clause did indeed prevent states from retrospectively impairing their own contracts, not just those of private parties—a controversial reading of Article I, Section 10.

states' being forced to bear "this mortification" of being "brought to the bar of justice like a delinquent individual."[155]

Federalists responded vigorously to these various criticisms of Article III and the federal judicial power. To the Antifederalist charge that federal courts would have an incentive to broadly construe Congress's enumerated powers in order to expand their own "arising under" jurisdiction, Federalists insisted, to the contrary, that federal courts would strike down legislation that exceeded Congress's enumerated powers. James Wilson argued that because of their lifetime tenure and protection against salary diminution, federal judges would block congressional usurpations of power "with intrepidity." Federalists defended tenure during good behavior for federal judges on the grounds that only an independent judiciary could reliably protect personal liberty and private property. Federalists also defended the constitutional provision permitting increases in the salaries of federal judges—but not of presidents—during their term of office, despite its opening the door to congressional influence, on the grounds that the value of money was far more likely to change during a judge's tenure for good behavior than during a president's four-year term.[156]

At the Virginia ratifying convention, Edmund Pendleton explained why the Constitution afforded Congress discretion over the creation of lower federal courts. Fixing a specific number of such courts in the Constitution would have been unwise given the difficulty of accurately predicting certain developments, such as the rapidity of population growth in the West. Pendleton insisted that Congress must be able to act "as experience shall dictate."[157]

Yet Pendleton and other Federalists also offered assurances that it was "highly probable" that the first Congress would invest state courts with most of the inferior federal jurisdiction, as this would be "best calculated to give general satisfaction and answer economical purposes." Madison agreed, noting that the Confederation Congress, rather than establishing its own courts to try piracies and felonies committed on the high seas, as authorized by the Articles, had instead invested state admiralty courts with such jurisdiction.[158]

Federalists also defended the jurisdictional provisions of Article III. Wilson acknowledged that the grant of jurisdiction to federal courts in cases brought by citizens or subjects of foreign states probably occasioned greater criticism than all the other jurisdictional provisions in Article III combined. Yet he defended this provision on the grounds that foreigners must have access to "a just and impartial tribunal" if public and private credit were to be restored in the United States. Wilson and other Federalists observed that the denial of justice in lawsuits brought by foreign creditors would be a just cause of war. Thus, William Davie told the North Carolina ratifying convention that "[i]f these controversies were left to the decision of particular states, it would be in their power, at any time, to involve the continent in a war, usually the greatest of all national calamities."[159]

Federalists defended the "arising under" jurisdiction of the federal judiciary on the grounds that "if there were any political axiom under the sun, it must be that the judicial power ought to be coextensive with the legislative." Such jurisdiction was critical to the federal government's ability to defend itself, particularly in conjunction with the enforcement of federal revenue laws and federal treaties. If the interpretation of treaties were left to thirteen separate judiciaries, Davie argued, there would "necessarily be unjust and contradictory decisions," which might involve the nation in war. When federal and state law conflicted, state judges—paid by state legislatures and dependent upon them for their tenure in office—could hardly be trusted to be impartial.[160]

Federal jurisdiction over admiralty and maritime cases—as well as suits affecting foreign ambassadors—was also critical to ensuring uniformity in the nation's foreign policy. Pendleton conceded, by contrast, that federal jurisdiction over lawsuits involving citizens of different states might not be critical to federal interests in most instances, but he insisted such jurisdiction would be essential to protecting an out-of-state creditor from being forced by a Rhode Island court to accept depreciated currency in payment of a Rhode Islander's debt. Moreover, according to New York Federalists, the defendants in these diversity-of-citizenship cases, who would have to face the potential inconvenience of travel to a distant federal court, would "in all probability, be men of property, merchants and great landholders, and not poor men."[161]

In response to Antifederalist concerns that broad appellate jurisdiction in the Supreme Court might force litigants to travel long distances in cases involving small sums of money, Federalists offered assurances that Congress would impose minimum dollar amounts on the lawsuits that were eligible for adjudication by federal courts. Congressional representatives, Pendleton observed, would not wish to subject their constituents to "oppressions of that dangerous kind." Federalists argued that Congress could be trusted to act reasonably on this issue because every state except those most proximate to the seat of the national government would have the same interest in curtailing possible abuses. Federalists even suggested that Congress might require the Supreme Court to rotate its sessions across different parts of the country—just as the Confederation Congress had done with the appellate prize court that it established. Such a practice would protect litigants from the inconvenience of having to travel to the national capital for appellate review of their cases.[162]

Federalists defended the Constitution's omission of a right to jury trials in civil cases on the grounds that wide variation in state practices with regard to civil juries rendered a unitary federal constitutional rule impracticable.* At a

* Antifederalists responded that if the Framers had been genuinely concerned about inconsistent state practices regarding jury trials in civil cases, they could have simply provided in the

minimum, not all states provided for jury trials in equity cases or in admiralty cases involving maritime captures. Thus, a requirement of jury trials in all federal civil cases would have been inconvenient in many states.[163*]

In addition, Federalists noted that while the Constitution did not guarantee the right to a jury trial in federal civil cases, Congress retained discretion to provide by statute for such trials.[†] Charles Pinckney doubted that it would be "the interest or intention of the general government to abuse one of the most invaluable privileges a free country can boast," especially given that congressional representatives would put their own fortunes at risk by failing to provide for jury trials in federal civil cases. To eliminate such a right in cases in which the right was popular, Iredell insisted, "would draw down on [Congress] the resentment and detestation of the people" and would be "instantly resisted."[164]

Federalists also observed that while jury trials in criminal cases might be essential to prevent overreaching by the government—because the government was the instigator of most criminal prosecutions—the vast majority of civil cases involved disputes between private parties. Accordingly, there was little reason to constrain government discretion over which civil cases should be tried by juries. Finally, some Federalists noted that jury trials might be inappropriate in some federal cases involving citizens of different states because the jurors might be partial to one of the parties. Thus, Wilson asked Pennsylvania Antifederalist William Findley if he would really want the fate of "a great part of his fortune" determined by a jury from Rhode Island.[165]

The Constitution did not require that juries in federal criminal cases be chosen from the vicinity of the alleged crime, Madison explained, because trials might have to be relocated in instances of rebellion. North Carolina Federalist Samuel Johnston pointed out, in addition, that state practices of assembling criminal juries were too disparate to permit of a single constitutional rule for the nation.[166]

Constitution that jury requirements in federal civil cases should mirror those of the courts in the state in which a particular federal court sat. Antifederalists also observed that, despite disparate state practices with regard to certain aspects of jury trials in criminal cases, the Framers had somehow managed to explicitly protect that right in the Constitution.

* Charles Cotesworth Pinckney explained to the South Carolina legislature that under the Articles of Confederation, Congress had experimented with jury trials in admiralty cases involving capture—a practice contrary to that of most nations. The experiment had proved a disaster, according to Pinckney, as juries condemned indiscriminately the property of friends, enemies, and citizens from other states. As a result, Congress had wisely ended the experiment—a step it could not have taken had the Articles mandated jury trials in all civil cases.

† The first federal Congress did in fact provide that juries would try issues of fact in all cases in federal district court—including civil cases, with the exception of those falling within the courts' admiralty and maritime jurisdiction.

In response to the Antifederalists' objection that the Supreme Court ought not to exercise appellate jurisdiction over questions of fact, Pendleton confided that he wished the language authorizing this had been excised from Article III, which would have "silenced the greatest objections against the section." Yet he also defended such jurisdiction on the grounds that in appeals from chancery or admiralty courts, where judges rather than juries usually found the facts, it was customary for appellate tribunals to review factual determinations. Madison said that Congress would probably enact regulations to ensure that the privilege of jury trials would not be nullified by the Supreme Court's over-turning the factual findings of juries on appeal. Further, Wilson noted that if the Supreme Court were not empowered to reverse those jury findings of fact that might infringe on the law of nations, the United States could find itself at war as a result.[167]

To their opponents' objection that under the Constitution states could be forced to redeem their paper currency at face value, many Federalists denied that states could be sued without their consent in federal court.[168]*

The House of Representatives

In addition to objecting to the broad-ranging powers of the federal government and to various aspects of the federal judiciary that would interpret the scope of those powers, Antifederalists raised a number of objections to other struc-tural features of the federal government. One principal criticism along these lines was the size of the House of Representatives. Initially consisting of sixty-five members (assuming all thirteen states ratified the Constitution and thus joined the new union), the House would be one-eighth the size of the British House of Commons and much smaller than most lower branches of state legis-latures, even though Congress was obviously representing a country that was vastly larger—in terms of both geography and population—than the biggest states. Thus, for example, in 1787, the lower house of the Massachusetts legis-lature contained 266 delegates, each of whom represented roughly 1,425 state inhabitants (based on the state's population according to the 1790 census). By contrast, in 1789, each of the 65 House members would represent about 50,000 people.[†] The enormous relative size of congressional constituencies

---

* When the Supreme Court ruled in *Chisholm v. Georgia* in 1793 that Article III permitted states to be sued without their consent in federal court, critics complained of a bait-and-switch. *Chisholm* was quickly overruled by the Eleventh Amendment.

† For a sense of perspective, consider that in 2016, the average member of the House repre-sents well over 700,000 people.

was especially striking, given that state legislatures had nearly doubled their number of seats in the 1780s in an effort to shrink the size of each legislator's constituency.[169]

Moreover, while the Constitution created a ceiling on the size of the House, it created only a very low floor. Each state is guaranteed at least one congressional representative, but beyond that the Constitution provides only that states can have no *more* than one congressional representative for every thirty thousand inhabitants. Indeed, the Philadelphia convention had initially set the minimum size of House constituencies at forty thousand, but this was reduced at the last minute to thirty thousand, possibly in an effort to improve the prospects of ratification. Because the only floor on the size of the House was provided by the guarantee of at least one representative per state, Congress was free to reduce the number of representatives far below sixty-five—indeed, all the way down to thirteen (until more states were admitted to the union).[170]

Antifederalists were convinced that congressional representatives would never agree to dilute their individual clout by supporting an increase in the size of the House (to the extent that the ceiling of one representative per every thirty thousand inhabitants would permit one). Furthermore, Antifederalists predicted that the small states, whose relative influence in the House would be slightly diluted if the body's size were increased, would use their influence in the Senate, where the states were equally represented, to block such an expansion.* New York Antifederalists proposed an amendment to fix the number of congressional representatives at one per twenty thousand inhabitants—until the House consisted of at least three hundred representatives, at which point the ratio would be altered. Virginia Antifederalists favored guaranteeing one representative for every thirty thousand people until the size of the House reached two hundred.[171]

To Antifederalists, a sixty-five-person House afforded "the mere shadow of representation," "a mere shred or rag of representation," "a mere burlesque." "Brutus" charged that "[n]o free people on Earth who have elected persons to legislate for them ever reposed that confidence in so small a number."[172]

Antifederalists believed that effective representation required that legislators have an intimate familiarity with the local circumstances of their

---

* Because of their very small populations, Delaware and Rhode Island, which were guaranteed at least one congressional representative under the Constitution, probably would not gain a second representative until the size of the House substantially exceeded one hundred members. Thus, they would exercise less relative influence in a House of one hundred members than in one of sixty-five. Accordingly, their congressional delegations would have some incentive to resist proposals to expand the size of the House—which is probably why, as we shall see, Delaware rejected a constitutional amendment that was proposed by Congress in 1789 to mandate an increase in the size of the House.

constituents. Smith told the New York ratifying convention that in a republican government, representatives should "resemble those they represent. They should be a true picture of the people, possess a knowledge of their circumstances and their wants, sympathize in all their distresses, and be disposed to seek their true interests." At the Virginia convention, Mason explained that representatives "ought to mix with the people, think as they think, feel as they feel."[173]

A mere sixty-five congressional representatives, Mason protested, could not "possibly know the situation and circumstances of all the inhabitants of this immense continent." Similarly, Samuel Chase of Maryland objected that so few congressional representatives could not "represent the opinions, wishes, and interests of great numbers" or "be acquainted with the sentiments and interests of the United States, which contains many different classes or orders of people—[m]erchants, farmers, planters, mechanics, and gentry." Indeed, Mason maintained that "a full and adequate representation in the general government" was simply impossible because "it would be too expensive and too unwieldy." He also argued that power should be given "with a sparing hand to a government thus imperfectly constructed."[174]

Inadequate representation was especially troubling, Mason contended, in the context of taxation. The modes of taxation, although "of the utmost consequence," were to be determined under the Constitution by federal representatives possessed of neither "common interest with us nor a fellow feeling for us." Smith similarly warned of the danger of affording the federal government "free access to our pockets" when it did not provide for "a genuine and fair representation of the people."[175]

Large districts not only would make it difficult for representatives to acquire familiarity with local circumstances but also would make it harder for those who, in Smith's words, "walk in the plain and frugal paths of life" to get elected. Mason warned that a House of sixty-five members would consist of "the great—the wealthy—the well-born." Such a House "must form an aristocracy, and will not regard the interests of the people." Smith observed that when the number of offices was small, "the office will be highly elevated and distinguished." Only men renowned for "birth, education, talents, and wealth" would be deemed worthy of holding office by "the common people," who respected such characteristics. In addition, only "conspicuous military, popular, civil or legal talents" would possess the influence necessary to carry elections in districts containing thirty or forty thousand inhabitants.[176]

Observing that in the English shires men of enormous fortune would spend £30,000 or £40,000 to get themselves elected to Parliament, Henry predicted that poor men would have no chance of competing in large congressional districts. The risk of aristocracy would be compounded if, as John Tyler warned at the Virginia ratifying convention, Congress fixed salaries for its members so low that only rich men could afford to seek office. Increasing the size of the House, by contrast, would "open a door for the admission of the substantial yeomanry of your country" and prevent the government's falling "into the hands of the few and the great."[177]

Smith conceded that able representation required "extensive political and commercial information, such as is acquired by men of refined education, who have leisure to attain to high degrees of improvement." Yet, he insisted, sound representation also required "that kind of acquaintance with the common concerns and occupations of the people, which men of the middling class of life are, in general, much better competent to than those of a superior class." With regard to taxation, for example, a competent representative must have not only "an acquaintance with the abstruse parts of the system of finance" but also "a knowledge of the circumstances and ability of the people in general" and of "how the burdens imposed will bear upon the different classes." Members of the middling class, Smith argued, could be trusted not to lay excessive burdens on the poor because doing so would affect them as well, and also not to enact laws that rendered property insecure because they, too, owned property. Indeed, Smith went so far as to argue that the middling class might make better representatives because they would be "more temperate, of better morals and less ambition than the great."[178]*

Finally with regard to the size of the House, Antifederalists argued that a smaller number of representatives would be more easily corrupted by bribery or foreign intrigue than a larger one. "Corruption" of House members by the president could be a special problem, Patrick Henry warned, because the Constitution disqualified congressional representatives from appointment only to those offices created—or for which salaries had been increased—during their terms in office. Representatives remained eligible for appointment to all other federal offices, which left presidents with ample enticements to influence susceptible legislators.[179]

A House that Antifederalists believed afforded only a shadow of representation was all the more troubling because the Constitution also departed from the usual American practice of annual elections for members of the lower

* This last point was too much for New York chancellor Robert R. Livingston to bear. He strongly objected to what he described as Smith's denunciation of the wealthy as "vicious and intemperate," and he insisted that they were as "honest and virtuous as any class in the community." He also wondered if the Antifederalists genuinely wished to exclude from governance "the learned, the wise, [and] the virtuous," and he sarcastically asked if the best way to populate Congress would be to "go out into the highways, and pick up the rogue and the robber . . . and bring in the poor, the blind and the lame."

house of a legislature. "A Columbian Patriot" criticized the shift from annual to biennial elections on the grounds that "a frequent return to the bar of their constituents" was "the strongest check against the corruptions to which men are liable, either from the intrigues of others of more subtle genius or the propensities of their own hearts." Another Massachusetts Antifederalist referred to annual elections, which had always been the practice in the Commonwealth, as "the safeguard of the liberties of the people" and warned that abandoning such elections was "the avenue through which tyranny will enter." Some Antifederalists favored an even shorter congressional term of six months, which was the tenure in office for the lower houses of the state legislatures of Connecticut and Rhode Island.[180]

Federalists offered rebuttals to their opponents' various criticisms of the design of the House. John Jay defended its being smaller than most state legislative assemblies on the grounds that Congress was entrusted mostly with objects that "comprehend the interests of the states in relation to each other and in relation to foreign powers." To successfully pursue such objectives, a representative did not require an intimate familiarity with the interests and needs of local communities. "[F]ive or ten honest and wise men from each state," according to the Federalist "Landholder," would be "more competent than a hundred." By contrast, state legislatures dealt with local issues, including petitions from individuals and towns. The just resolution of such matters, Jay explained, required more "minute and local information."[181]

Even in fields in which Congress would necessarily intrude on local matters—such as tax policy—Federalists argued that only a general knowledge of agriculture, manufacturing, and commerce was required for wise legislation, not familiarity with intimate local detail. Some Federalists also defended the small size of the House on the grounds that it would save money.* Finally, Federalists questioned why their opponents would prefer the Confederation Congress, to which most states sent even fewer delegates, to the House of Representatives designed by the Constitution.[182]

Although they defended a relatively small size for the House, Federalists adamantly denied that Congress would ever try to reduce the number of representatives below sixty-five or that it would unreasonably resist a proposed increase. At the New York ratifying convention, Hamilton admitted that the Constitution did not explicitly bar Congress from reducing the size of the House, while insisting that "the true and genuine construction of the clause gives Congress no power" to do so. Other Federalists went further and offered

---

* In response to the argument that a small House would save taxpayers money, Melancton Smith noted that the amount involved was small and insisted that "[t]he man who would seriously object to this expense to secure his liberties does not deserve to enjoy them."

reassurances that Congress would treat the ratio of one representative per thirty thousand people as a floor as well as a ceiling, which meant that the size of the House would probably increase to at least 100 members after the first census was taken in 1790 (in fact, it increased to 105).[183]

In the absence of any consensus as to the ideal size of a representative assembly—New York's lower house had 65 members, South Carolina's 100, and Massachusetts's well over 250—Hamilton argued that Congress must have discretion to set the proper ratio of constituents to representatives. In response to their opponents' charge that self-interested congressional representatives would never agree to dilute their individual clout by increasing the size of the House, Federalists argued that Congress would be powerless to resist public demands for such a change. In addition, they noted that congressional representatives would have an offsetting incentive to increase the House's size: Doing so would afford them additional opportunities to run for office. Only a few small-state delegations, Federalists insisted, would have any vested interest in resisting an expansion of the House.[184]

Federalists also defended biennial elections for the House. Contrasting the two-year terms of the House of Representatives with the seven-year terms of the British House of Commons, Madison insisted that biennial elections would be sufficient to ensure "sympathy" and "fellow feeling" between representatives and their constituents. Wilson argued that "in a government as large as that of the United States," where a delegate from Georgia would have to travel nearly a thousand miles to the seat of the federal government, annual elections would be impractical. In addition, many Federalists observed that one-year terms in office would not permit representatives to acquire, in the words of Theodore Sedgwick of Massachusetts, "a general knowledge of such extensive and weighty matters" as would concern the nation.[185]

Furthermore, biennial elections, according to Federalist Fisher Ames of Massachusetts, would be "an essential security to liberty" by ensuring that "the sober, second thought of the people," rather than "the momentary impulse of the public mind," would become law. Ames added that limiting congressional representatives to annual terms would have disabled the House from "bear[ing] some proportion in point of importance" to the Senate, whose members served six-year terms. Federalists further observed that because the people, in all the states but two, played no direct role in selecting delegates to the Confederation Congress, the Constitution represented an advance in popular governance, no matter how long the term of congressional representatives was. Finally, Federalists offered reassurances that expanding representatives' terms in office from one year to two hardly made it inevitable that there would be additional expansions in the future—to five or seven years or even to tenure during good behavior—as their opponents charged.[186]

Federalists also denied that large House constituencies would necessarily result in the election of "aristocrats." Hamilton insisted that voters were free to elect to office whomever they pleased; nothing in the Constitution made "a rich man more eligible than a poor one" for public office. Chancellor Robert R. Livingston agreed: In a republican government, "[w]e are all equally aristocrats. Offices, emoluments, honors are open to all." Indeed, Livingston went even further, arguing that the wealthy would be comparatively disadvantaged in seeking political office because "[t]he rich are ever objects of envy," which would operate "as a bar to their advancement." At the Virginia ratifying convention, Randolph asked why the people would be any more likely to elect to federal office than to state office representatives who did not share "fellow-feeling" with them.[187]

The Senate

Antifederalists also raised numerous objections to the Senate—its apportionment, its size, the form of its representation, and its powers. Large-state Antifederalists criticized the fact that states were equally represented in the Senate. It was "quite ridiculous," one Massachusetts Antifederalist observed, that "little Delaware" should count as much in national debates as Massachusetts, one of the most populous states. When Federalists defended the Senate's departure from population-based apportionment as a compromise critical to the success of the Philadelphia convention, one southern Antifederalist professed not to be assuaged by "its being brought about by the inflexibility of the small, pitiful states to the North." Many of the large-state Antifederalists' other objections to the Senate probably were driven in part by what they perceived as the injustice of its apportionment.[188]

A few Antifederalists objected to the small size of the Senate. Thus, one North Carolina Antifederalist worried about "giving such extensive powers to so few men." The Senate's small size, according to Samuel Chase, would open the door to "bribery and corruption."[189]

More frequently, Antifederalists objected to the six-year terms of senators, which would, they charged, "destroy their responsibility and induce them to act like the masters and not the servants of the people." Massachusetts Antifederalists warned that senators would "forget their dependence on the people and be loath to leave their places." Six years was "too long to trust any body of men with power." In that amount of time, senators could create enough offices and obtain sufficient influence to ensure their re-elections. Six-year terms might easily evolve, according to "A Columbian Patriot," into "an appointment for life, as the influence of such a body over the minds of the people will be co-equal to the extensive power with which they [senators] are vested."[190]

Many Antifederalists also criticized the Constitution for not requiring mandatory rotation in office for senators, as the Articles had for congressional delegates. Mason declared, "Nothing is so essential to the preservation of a republican government as a periodical rotation. Nothing so strongly impels a man to regard the interests of his constituents as the certainty of returning to the general mass of the people, from whence he was taken, where he must participate in their burdens." New York Antifederalist Gilbert Livingston worried that because senators would be walled off in a federal town, associating "only with men of their own class" and becoming "strangers to the condition of common people," they would be "apt to forget their dependence, lose their sympathy, and contract selfish habits." Mandatory rotation in office, according to John Lansing, Jr., would "revive that sympathy with their [fellow citizens], which power and an exalted station are too apt to efface from the minds of rulers."[191]

Moreover, Melancton Smith argued, by creating more opportunities to become a senator, mandatory rotation would "bring forward into office the genius and abilities of the continent." Thus, Smith supported the constitutional amendment proposed by his ally Gilbert Livingston, which would bar senators from serving more than six years in any twelve. Without such an amendment, Smith said, "there is no doubt that the senators will hold their office perpetually," which would be "inconsistent with the established principles of republicanism."[192]

Some Antifederalists also lamented the absence of any provision in the Constitution authorizing state legislatures to recall senators—as the Articles had provided for congressional delegates. At the New York ratifying convention, Smith and Lansing contended that if the purpose of the Senate was to protect the independence of the states, then state legislatures ought to have the power to recall senators who were not adequately fulfilling that role. Even if members of the House should not be subject to recall because "the impulses of the multitude are inconsistent with systematic government," Smith stated, state legislatures would not "possess the qualities of a mob." Moreover, the fact that under the Articles no state had ever actually recalled its congressional delegates demonstrated that state legislatures could be trusted with such a power.[193]

One Massachusetts Antifederalist neatly captured the concern of many with regard to the Constitution's provisions for representation generally and for the Senate specifically. The Articles had provided three different checks on congressional delegates: one-year terms in office, mandatory rotation, and state legislative recall. The Constitution removed all three, while conferring vast new powers upon federal legislators, which might enable them to become the people's "masters and not servants."[194]

Antifederalists also objected to many of the powers that the Constitution conferred on the Senate. Although the Constitution did not permit the Senate to originate money bills, it did permit senators to amend them. Antifederalists demanded to know why, if the British House of Lords could not alter money bills originating in the House of Commons, the Senate was not similarly restricted.[195]

Antifederalists objected as well to the joint exercise of the treaty-making power by the Senate and the president. Why should the House of Representatives, which more directly represented the people, not be included in treaty making? Some Antifederalists also objected to the absence of "any constitutional bounds" on the treaty-making power. While the Constitution stipulated that treaties were part of "the supreme law of the land," "Federal Farmer" protested, it did not even require—unlike with regard to federal statutes—that treaties be "made in pursuance of the Constitution."[196]

In addition, many Antifederalists objected to the Constitution's vesting in the Senate the power to try impeachments of federal officers. At the Virginia ratifying convention, Patrick Henry repeatedly complained of the absence of "true responsibility" in the new federal government. In Great Britain, government ministers who advised the Crown to pursue illegal measures were subject to impeachment by Parliament. Yet if US senators did "anything derogatory to the honor or interest of their country"—such as taking bribes to ratify a treaty contrary to the nation's interests—"they are to try themselves," which Henry said was an absurdity.[197]

Antifederalists also denied that senators, whose advice and consent were necessary for the ratification of treaties, could be relied upon to convict a president whom the House had impeached for negotiating a treaty that bartered away the nation's interests. How likely was it, William Grayson asked, that senators would convict a president on an impeachment when they had been his "partners in crime"? Moreover, while in England the consequence of conviction on an impeachment might be severe criminal punishment—"blocks and gibbets," Henry admiringly noted—under the Constitution the sanction upon conviction was limited to removal from office and future disqualification from holding federal office (though there was no bar on subsequent criminal prosecution).[198]

Reflecting upon the Senate's shared powers over legislation, appointments, treaty making, and impeachments, one North Carolina Antifederalist worried that this branch of the federal government had been given "such an enormity of power, and with such an overbearing and uncontrollable influence, as is incompatible with every idea of safety to the liberties of a free country, and is calculated to swallow up all other powers, and to render that body a despotic aristocracy."[199]

Federalists offered various responses to the Antifederalists' criticisms of the Senate. Acknowledging that equal state representation in the upper house was unjust, large-state Federalists emphasized the population-based apportionment of the House, which was an improvement upon the Articles of Confederation. At his state's ratifying convention, Edmund Pendleton approvingly observed that under the Constitution, Virginia would no longer have to pay one-sixth of the expenses of the union while enjoying no more influence in the public councils than Delaware.[200]

Federalists offered multiple justifications for the six-year terms of senators. Hamilton argued that every republic required "some permanent body to correct the prejudices, check the intemperate passions, and regulate the fluctuations of a popular assembly." Although the people were generally well intentioned, they did not "possess the discernment and stability necessary for systematic government" and were "frequently misguided by ignorance, by sudden impulses, and the intrigues of ambitious men." Madison similarly observed that the Senate could act "as a defense to the people against their own temporary errors and delusions" by "suspend[ing] the blow meditated by the people against themselves, until reason, justice, and truth can regain their authority over the public mind."[201]

In addition, Federalists noted that lengthy terms in office would afford senators "due acquaintance with the objects and principles of legislation." The Senate, together with the president, was to manage the nation's foreign affairs, which required knowledge that Hamilton insisted "is not soon acquired." Longer terms in office would enable the Senate to pursue longer-term projects and to supply what Madison called the requisite "sense of national character" that foreign nations would demand in their negotiations with the United States.[202]

Federalists also observed that six-year terms were just two years longer than those of state senators in New York and one year longer than those of senators in Maryland. In addition, Federalists denied that six-year terms were likely to evolve into tenure during good behavior. A six-year absence from state government, they argued, would diminish senators' influence with state legislatures, thus reducing their chances of reappointment.[203]

Federalists defended the Constitution's omission of mandatory rotation in office for senators. Roger Sherman of Connecticut argued that ineligibility for re-election would "abridge the liberty of the people" to choose their own representatives* and "remove one great motive to fidelity in office." In addition, Sherman noted that "nothing renders government more unstable than

---

* Antifederalists replied that age and citizenship restrictions on federal officeholding equally impinged upon the people's right to choose representatives, yet nobody seemed to oppose such restrictions.

a frequent change of the persons that administer it." In the New York ratifying convention, Robert R. Livingston denounced mandatory rotation as "an absurd species of ostracism—a mode of proscribing eminent merit and banishing from stations of trust those who have filled them with the greatest faithfulness." Hamilton warned that a man who knew he was about to be rotated out of office would "turn his attention chiefly to his own emolument" and might even be tempted "to perpetuate his power by unconstitutional usurpations."[204]

Federalists also defended the Constitution's failure to vest state legislatures with the power to recall senators. Livingston insisted that senators should represent not only the interests of state governments but also those of the union, yet this "could never be done if there was a power of recall, for sometimes it happens that small sacrifices are absolutely indispensable for the general good and safety of the confederacy, but if a senator should presume to consent to these sacrifices, he would be immediately recalled." Richard Morris, a fellow New York Federalist, agreed that subjecting senators to recall "would create a slavish subjection to the contracted views and prevailing factions of the state governments" rather than "firmness and vigor in the national operations." Reminding the New York ratifying convention of Rhode Island's experiment in monetary and fiscal radicalism, Hamilton warned that a power of recall would make state legislatures, which were constituted so as to feel the people's "prejudices and passions," a vehicle "in which the evil humors may be conveyed into the national system." For similar reasons, Federalists defended the Constitution's denying state legislatures the power to set senators' salaries.[205]

Federalists denied their opponents' charges that the Constitution conferred dangerous powers on the Senate. The House's exclusive power to originate money bills would enable it to "do everything," James Iredell of North Carolina insisted, because "[a] government cannot be supported without money." Charles Pinckney called the House "the moving spring of the system" because it controlled the power of the purse, upon which depended the raising of armies and navies and the payment of government salaries. By threatening to withhold supplies from the government, Federalists argued, the House could compel the Senate to agree to its proposals. Madison defended, against Antifederalist criticisms, the Senate's power to amend money bills—even if it could not initiate them—as essential to avoiding "disagreeable disputes" between the two branches. He also noted (inaccurately) that most of the state constitutions that barred upper houses of legislatures from initiating money bills did not prohibit them from offering amendments.[206]

Federalists also defended the Constitution's vesting the Senate with shared responsibility over treaties, while the House was excluded altogether from the treaty-making process. Wilson explained that at least some treaty negotiations had to be conducted in secret, which meant that only a smaller body such as the

Senate could be entrusted with the task. Moreover, treaty negotiations involving nations that were thousands of miles apart—which would usually be the case when the United States was one of the parties—were bound to be time-consuming, yet the House was unlikely to be in session for lengthy periods of time. Furthermore, Wilson noted, even if the House could not directly participate in treaty making, it could effectively block treaties that it found objectionable by declining to enact legislation to implement them. In any event, Senate abuses of the treaty-making power would be checked by the president.[207]

Federalists denied that vesting the power to try impeachments in the Senate undermined the accountability of the federal government. At the time of the ratifying contest, it was unclear whether members of Congress qualified as "officers of the United States," who were the only permissible objects of the impeachment power. However, Federalists insisted that even if senators could not be impeached, they could be criminally prosecuted for any abuses of office.[208]

Moreover, Federalists argued, if senators were eventually deemed to be among the federal officeholders liable to impeachment, Antifederalists were mistaken to think that senators would never convict their colleagues in impeachment trials. Iredell observed that the grounds for impeachment were limited to corruption or some other "wicked motive"—not merely the exercise of bad judgment—and he insisted that senators would not hesitate to remove colleagues from office if such serious wrongdoing were proved. Charles Cotesworth Pinckney noted, in addition, that turnover in office would ensure that many of the senators called upon to try an impeachment of their colleagues for, say, ratifying a treacherous treaty would have played no role in its approval and thus could serve as impartial judges.[209]

Although large-state Federalists often conceded that the Philadelphia convention—at the behest of small-state delegations—had granted the Senate greater power than they would have liked, they nonetheless insisted that the Senate's power was not dangerous. For one thing, as Iredell observed, any concerns arising from senators "not immediately" representing the people ought to be ameliorated by their representing "the representatives of the people, who are annually chosen." Furthermore, he noted, in their legislative capacity, senators could "do nothing without the concurrence of the House of Representatives, and we need look no further than England for a clear proof of the amazing consequence which representatives of the people bear in a free government." The British House of Lords—with its hereditary nobility, vast fortunes, and complete independence from the people—was far more potentially dangerous than the US Senate. Yet, in practice, the Lords' power had proved, according to Iredell, "far inferior to that of the Commons." Finally, Wilson charged that objections to the Senate's powers came "with a bad grace" from Antifederalists who purported to favor conferring expanded powers on a unicameral Confederation Congress that was neither popularly elected nor checked by either a president or a judiciary.[210]

The President

Many Antifederalists also objected to the executive department created by the Constitution. A single magistrate with the military at his disposal, according to one Pennsylvania Antifederalist, would be "in fact an elective king." Patrick Henry similarly objected that the Constitution "squints towards monarchy." Mason warned that the nation should not assume that all presidents would be as "disinterested and amiable" as Washington, and he proposed a constitutional amendment to require the consent of both houses of Congress before the president assumed personal command of armies in the field. Mason also objected that permitting the president to grant pardons even in cases of treason was dangerous because he might pardon crimes "which were advised by himself."[211]

Antifederalists charged that the electoral college system for selecting the president was a "deception" to delude the American people into believing that they were making the choice. Given the relatively small number of electors, "A Columbian Patriot" argued, such a system was "nearly tantamount to the exclusion of the voice of the people in the choice of their first magistrate. It is vesting the choice solely in an aristocratic junto, who may easily combine in each state to place at the head of the union the most convenient instrument for despotic sway." Antifederalists further warned that after Washington had ceased to be a candidate, the House of Representatives would in fact choose the president in forty-nine elections out of fifty. Because the House would select from among the top five vote getters when no candidate received the votes of a majority of the appointed electors, it would be possible to become president while receiving relatively few electoral votes. Furthermore, according to Grayson, the president would rarely be chosen "without the interposition of foreign powers," much as European nations had intervened in the appointment of executives in Poland and Sweden to protect their trade and preserve the balance of power in Europe.[212]

In large states such as Virginia, Antifederalists objected to the small states' disproportionate influence in choosing the president when the selection fell to the House, where voting would be by state delegation. Grayson warned that "the seven eastern states will always elect" the president, which meant that he was likely to make treaties that favored the interests of the carrying states over those of the staples-exporting states.[213]

Antifederalists regularly objected to the Constitution's omission of mandatory rotation in office for the president. In South Carolina, "Cato" warned that the president's eligibility for re-election would transform the office into one of tenure during good behavior. When combined with the president's great powers, this would give him many of the qualities of a king. Mason declared that the president's eligibility for re-election violated "the great fundamental principle of responsibility in republicanism." Although voters were free not to re-elect him, "the experience of all other countries and even our own" suggested that the president would "be continued in office for life" because "great" men were always re-elected.[214]

Upon first receiving a copy of the Constitution in Paris, Jefferson likewise identified as a principal flaw the absence of mandatory rotation in office for the president. "Experience concurs with reason in concluding," Jefferson told Madison, that "the first magistrate will always be reelected if the Constitution permits it," thus becoming "an officer for life." In a letter to John Adams, Jefferson objected, "Once in office and possessing the military force of the union, without either the aid or check of a council, he [the president] would not be easily dethroned." Jefferson predicted that this "perpetual re-eligibility of the president" would "be productive of cruel distress in our country." He explained to Edward Carrington of Virginia why the omission of a provision for mandatory rotation in office for the president "has scarcely excited an objection in America": "Our jealousy is only put to sleep by the unlimited confidence we all repose in the person to whom we all look as our president [i.e., Washington]. After him inferior characters may perhaps succeed and awaken us to the danger which his merit has led us into."[215*]

Reflecting such concerns, Virginia Antifederalists proposed a constitutional amendment to require mandatory rotation in office for the president. Their New York counterparts suggested limiting the president to a single seven-year term, as the Philadelphia convention had tentatively agreed upon several times.[216]

Federalists, responding to their opponents' charges that the president would become an elective king, defended a unitary executive on the grounds of greater accountability; the president could not, in Wilson's words, "roll upon any other person the weight of his criminality." Especially in the context of military operations, Iredell argued, "secrecy, dispatch, and decision" required vesting the executive power in a single person.[217]

---

* In a similar vein, Gouverneur Morris told Washington that "should the idea prevail that you would not accept the presidency, it would prove fatal in many parts." People were willing to place Washington in an elevated office because of his "great and decided superiority," but they "would not willingly put any other person in the same situation because they feel the elevation of others as operating (by comparison) the degradation of themselves."

Yet Federalists emphasized that, unlike the British king, the president did not have the power to declare war, raise armies and navies, or call up the militia, and he could not appoint people to office or make treaties without the acquiescence of the Senate. Moreover, Federalists noted, the president's veto power was qualified, while the king's was absolute. The president served only four-year terms, while a king served for life. Federalists also argued that if the British House of Commons, which had less of a popular backing than would the House of Representatives, had proved capable of resisting encroachments by the king, then surely the president could pose no threat to the liberties of the American people. Moreover, even if all other checks failed, the president—unlike the British king—could always be impeached and removed from office.[218]

Federalists also defended the electoral college system for selecting the president. Given that the electors would cast ballots in their own states on the same day, corruption would be almost impossible. Although small states might have the advantage in the House's selection of the president—on those occasions, widely assumed to be frequent, when no candidate won the votes of a majority of the appointed electors—large states would have greater influence over the electoral college's "nomination" of the candidates from whom the House would choose. To the objection that state legislatures might retain for themselves the power to choose presidential electors, some Federalists replied that denying this right to the people would be obviously inappropriate, even if technically not forbidden by the Constitution. Finally, Federalists protested that their adversaries were quick to criticize the electoral college system—which the Philadelphia convention had agreed upon only after agonizing for weeks over the method of selecting the president—but slow to propose a superior alternative.[219]

Checks and Balances

Antifederalists also objected to the Constitution's system of checks and balances. The Reverend James Madison, who was the president of the College of William and Mary, told his cousin James Madison that "the quantum of power proposed to be given to the new Congress" was less objectionable than the fact that this power was not "distributed in such a manner as might preserve, instead of threaten destruction to, the liberties of America." Specifically, the Framers had departed from a pristine separation of powers. For example, the Constitution gave the president a share of the legislative power through the veto, and the Senate a share of the judicial power through the trial of impeachments and a share of the executive power through the ratification of treaties.[220]

Thus, Pennsylvania Antifederalists objected to the "undue and dangerous mixture of the powers of government."* They argued that, according to
Montesquieu's teachings, combining "[s]uch various, extensive, and important
powers . . . in one body of men [the Senate] is inconsistent with all freedom."
Virginia Antifederalists favored an amendment declaring that the legislative,
executive, and judicial powers "should be separate and distinct."[221]

Antifederalists especially objected to the constitutional provisions that
"dangerously connected" the president with the Senate—jointly empowering
the two branches with regard to treaty making and the appointment of federal
officeholders. Although Madison's cousin generally praised the work of the
Philadelphia convention, he nonetheless considered it "essential to every free
government that the legislative and executive departments should be entirely
distinct and independent." Uniting the powers of these branches "threatens
ruin to republicanism itself" because such a "government must soon degenerate into a tyranny." Mason likewise objected to the "alarming dependence and
connection" between the Senate and the president. These branches would be
"continually supporting and aiding each other" and would "form a combination that cannot be prevented by the representatives [i.e., the House]."[222]

Some Antifederalists, such as Elbridge Gerry, worried that such a blending of powers would give the president "undue influence over the legislature."
Others worried that the president would become too dependent upon the
Senate. Thus, one North Carolina Antifederalist predicted that the president's
"firmness" could not "long prevail against the overbearing power and influence of the Senate."[223]

Antifederalists similarly charged that the Constitution, by making the vice
president the president of the Senate, "dangerously blend[s] the executive and
legislative powers." Mason called the vice president "not only an unnecessary but a dangerous officer." Virginia Antifederalist Arthur Lee, the brother
of Richard Henry Lee and an American diplomat during the Revolutionary
War, objected that the vice president's "sole business seems to be to intrigue."
Antifederalists would have preferred that the Senate choose its own presiding
officer from among its members.[224]

Rather than splitting a power—such as that over appointments—between
the president and the Senate, many Antifederalists would have preferred that
the Constitution give the president alone the power but make him subject
to the constraint of an executive council. Mason especially objected to the
Constitution's omission of such a council—he had repeatedly raised the same
objection at the Philadelphia convention—which was "a thing unknown in any

---

* They were being more than a little disingenuous, given their strong support for the
Pennsylvania state constitution, which created a unicameral legislature and a weak governor.

safe and regular government." Mason declared that "power and responsibility are two things essential to a good executive, the first of which cannot be safely given, nor the latter ensured, where the legislative Senate [rather than a council] form a part of the executive." Under the Constitution, Mason objected, "the guilty try themselves," as the president's impeachment would be tried by his "counsellors" in the Senate. By contrast, an executive council subject to removal from office through Senate trials of impeachments would have provided "real responsibility." Such a council, in Mason's view, should ideally consist of six members, two chosen from each of the three regions of the country by votes of the states and the House. Another proposal, offered by a North Carolina Antifederalist, was for an executive council consisting of one member per state (which would mimic the apportionment of the Senate).[225]

Antifederalist concerns about possible coordination between the Senate and the president were particularly acute because these were seen as the more aristocratic branches of the government. Antifederalists worried that the indirect methods of selecting presidents and senators, their lengthy tenures in office, and the vast constituencies they represented would hugely advantage "aristocrats" in the competition for these offices, whereas many Antifederalists believed that the "middling sort" were perfectly competent to administer the government.[226]

Thus, despite the Constitution's explicit prohibition on the granting of "titles of nobility" by either Congress or the state governments, one of the Antifederalists' principal criticisms of the Constitution was that it would foster an aristocracy. Even the elite Virginia Antifederalists raised this objection. Richard Henry Lee worried that the Constitution "in its first principles" was "highly and dangerously oligarchic." Grayson declared that the Constitution was organized so as "to form an aristocratic body." Mason had similarly warned at the Philadelphia convention that "the dangerous power and structure of the government" would probably culminate in "a tyrannical aristocracy."[227]

Not surprisingly, "middling" Antifederalists and their backwoodsmen allies were even more prone toward raising this objection to the Constitution. "Centinel" (probably Samuel Bryan of Pennsylvania), who embraced a conspiratorial view of the Constitution, warned that ratification would lead to "a permanent aristocracy"—rule by the "wealthy and ambitious, who in every community think they have a right to lord it over their fellow creatures." Pennsylvania Antifederalists predicted that "lordly and high minded" officers of the national government would have "a perfect indifference for, and contempt of," the people. Although conceding defects in the Articles, one Georgia Antifederalist nonetheless worried that the Constitution would pave the way for "an aristocratical government whereby about 70 nabobs would lord over three millions of people as slaves." Another Antifederalist sharply observed that if the Constitution were ratified, "we shall in future be perfectly contented if our tongues be left us to lick the feet of our wellborn masters."[228]*

Some Antifederalists blamed the Constitution's aristocratic bent on the elitist sensibilities of the delegates attending the Philadelphia convention. According to one Pennsylvania Antifederalist, although Wilson was admittedly a man of "sense, learning, and extensive information, . . . [t]he whole tenor of his political conduct has always been strongly tainted with the spirit of high aristocracy." Wilson despised "what he calls the inferior order of the people," and "popular assemblies offer to his exalted imagination an idea of meanness and contemptibility which he hardly seeks to conceal." According to this critic, Wilson believed that "[m]en of sublime minds . . . were born a different race from the rest of the sons of men," and to them only "high heaven intended to commit the reins of earthly government." The rest of mankind "were born to serve, to administer food to the ambition of their superiors and become the footstool of their power."[229]

Federalists offered responses to the separation-of-powers objections of their opponents. In reply to the Antifederalist charge that the Constitution improperly blended legislative, executive, and judicial powers, William Davie assured the North Carolina ratifying convention that Montesquieu had meant only that the *entirety* of such powers ought not to be combined in a single branch. Wilson likewise told the Pennsylvania convention that the Constitution's departures from a strict separation of powers were "but few, and they are not dangerous." Indeed, some such departures were critical to enabling each branch to fend off depredations by the others. Even those state constitutions that explicitly mandated a complete separation of powers, Wilson observed, had departed from that ideal in practice—for example, by empowering legislatures to select governors and their executive councils. Moreover, Federalists noted, the British system, which was the object of Montesquieu's great admiration, departed even further than the Constitution did from a pristine separation of powers: The House of Lords acted in both legislative and judicial capacities, and the king possessed, at least in theory, a veto power over legislation, as well as the power to appoint Lords and—in effect—Commoners as well (through the creation of "rotten boroughs" with very few constituents).[230]

---

* Twenty-year-old John Quincy Adams expressed similar views, explaining why the man with whom he was reading law, Theophilus Parsons, favored ratification (which Adams distinctly did not): "Nor do I wonder at all that he [Parsons] should approve of it [the Constitution], as it is calculated to increase the influence, power and wealth of those who have any already. If the Constitution be adopted it will be a grand point gained in favor of the aristocratic party. There are to be no titles of nobility, but there will be great distinctions, and those distinctions will soon be hereditary, and we shall consequently have nobles, but no titles."

Federalists also defended the Constitution's division of the treaty-making power between the Senate and the president. In most countries, they observed, the executive alone exercised this power. However, elected presidents were more vulnerable to foreign bribes than were unelected monarchs, who presumably could not live in greater splendor in a country other than their own and whose interests were inextricably tied with those of their nation. Thus, presidents could not be safely delegated the entirety of the treaty-making power. In addition, while large-state Federalists conceded that awarding tiny Rhode Island the same influence over treaty ratification in the Senate as mighty Virginia or Massachusetts violated every principle of justice, they explained that the Philadelphia convention would have failed unless concessions were made to small-state delegations over the apportionment and powers of the Senate.[231]

Federalists also responded to their adversaries' charge that the Constitution eliminated true responsibility from the government by making the president triable for impeachment by senators with whom he shared various powers. Madison insisted that the American Constitution created greater accountability than the British one by subjecting the president to impeachment, whereas only the king's ministers—and not the king himself—could be impeached. Iredell argued that the Senate could be relied upon to remove a treacherous president from office. Because impeachment and conviction would be warranted "only for an error of the heart and not of the head," the president could not be removed from office simply for negotiating an unwise treaty. Yet, Iredell insisted, if bribery or some "other corrupt motive" had induced him to agree to such a treaty, and through "artifices and misrepresentation" he had managed to conceal that motive from senators, then they would happily remove him from office once his "villainy" was revealed, especially because they would resent his having made them "the instrument of his treacherous purposes."[232]

Federalists defended the Framers' decision not to establish an executive council. If the president were barred from acting without the acquiescence of such a council, then the "[s]ecrecy, vigor, dispatch, and responsibility" required of the executive would be undermined. Iredell explained that the presence of an executive council would make it "difficult often to know whether the president or counsellors were most to blame. A thousand plausible excuses might be made, which would escape detection." Moreover, Edmund Randolph noted, if the president were "a man of dexterity," he would simply control his council, thus nullifying its checking function.[233]

In addition, according to Iredell, devising a good executive council would have proved difficult. States would have been jealous if councilors were chosen from only a few states or regions, which might result in favoritism. Yet to avoid that problem by providing for one councilor per state would have resulted in great expense, as "A Landholder" observed, especially because the council would have been "composed of great characters, who could not be kept attending without great salaries."[234]

Iredell explained that the Antifederalists' desire for an executive council derived from British practice and that people were generally resistant to departures from tradition. Yet under the British constitution, because the king could do no wrong, he could be neither impeached nor criminally prosecuted for his actions. Thus, it was "of the utmost moment" that the king have advisers who "should be personally responsible" for their advice. Yet because the president was in fact punishable by law for his crimes and subject to removal from office by impeachment for treason, bribery, or other high crimes and misdemeanors, there was not "the same reason here for having a council which exists in England."[235]

Still, Iredell conceded that the president had "such extensive and important business to perform" that he must have "the means of some assistance to enable him to discharge his arduous employment." The president's power to require the opinions of his principal executive officers was, "in some degree, substituted for a council." That the advice must be in writing, as required by the Constitution, would induce his cabinet members to be more cautious in giving it and create greater responsibility.[236]

Federalists adamantly denied the charge that the Constitution would further the creation of an American aristocracy. Noting the prohibition on titles of nobility and the guarantee to each state of a republican form of government, Madison asked what "further proof" would be required "of the republican complexion of this system." So long as all of the federal government's powers derived "directly or indirectly from the great body of the people," Madison insisted that no aristocracy was possible. South Carolina Federalist David Ramsay similarly observed that the Constitution barred "[a]ll distinctions of birth, rank and titles" and that "no privileges are conferred on the rich or the few, but what they hold in common with the poor and the many."[237]

Wilson professed not even to understand the term "natural aristocracy." Every office in the US government was "open to the poor as to the rich." If natural aristocracy meant a government administered by "those most noted for their virtue and talents," who could possibly object? Admitting that large concentrations of wealth in a few hands could be dangerous, Charles Cotesworth Pinckney denied cause for such concern in the United States. Most states had eliminated primogeniture; property would be divided equally among children; uncultivated frontier land would prevent "dangerous distinctions of fortune"; and, outside of the South, property was "almost equally divided."[238]

Some Federalists went so far as to criticize their opponents' charges of aristocracy as "uncandidly calculated to alarm and catch prejudices." Federalists accused Antifederalists of drawing false distinctions between classes of men while claiming to be advocates for the middling and lower classes. One Pennsylvania Federalist objected to a New York Antifederalist's writing under the pseudonym "Plebeian," given that the Constitution would create a "free and equal government, which rejects every preposterous distinction of blood or titles."[239]

Article I, Section 10

Some Antifederalists also criticized Article I, Section 10, which, among other things, barred states from issuing paper money, making anything but gold or silver legal tender, or impairing the obligation of contracts. Observing that the Constitution would forbid the states from issuing paper money, South Carolina Antifederalist Rawlins Lowndes asked, "[B]ut what evils had we ever experienced by issuing a little paper money to relieve ourselves from any exigency that pressed us?" Lowndes recalled that South Carolina had issued paper bills every year and recalled them every five "with great convenience and advantage." Paper money "carried us triumphantly through the war, extricated us from difficulties generally supposed to be insurmountable, and fully established us in our independence."[240]

The Pennsylvania Antifederalist "Deliberator" warned that under Article I, Section 10, "[n]o state can give relief to insolvent debtors, however distressing their situation may be." At the New York ratifying convention, Melancton Smith argued against depriving states of potentially useful powers over the economy simply because "some bad laws have been passed in most of the states" as a result of "the difficulty of the times." The Massachusetts Antifederalist "Candidus" proposed amending the Constitution to allow states, with Congress's consent, to adopt the measures forbidden by Article I, Section 10. Concurring with that proposal, Luther Martin declared that Maryland and other states "had formerly received great benefit from paper emissions" and that it was "impossible to foresee that events may not take place which shall render paper money of absolute necessity."[241]

In response, most Federalists did not hesitate to disparage paper money and debtor relief laws, and they openly celebrated Article I, Section 10. Charles Cotesworth Pinckney declared that paper money "had corrupted the morals of the people; it had diverted them from the paths of honest industry to the ways of ruinous speculation; it had destroyed both public and private credit, and had brought total ruin on numberless widows and orphans." His cousin Charles Pinckney explained that paper money "always carrie[d] the gold and silver out of the country and impoverishe[d] it," discouraged foreign merchants from participating in trade with America, undermined commerce between the states, and enabled "debtors in the [legislative] assemblies" to defraud their creditors. New York Federalists declared it "high time" to abolish that "wicked and fraudulent system of paper money," which had opened a door "to fraud, villainy and discord."[242]

Federalists praised Article I, Section 10, as "the soul of the Constitution" and its "best" provision. It would "produce respectability" among the states and "teach them to cultivate those principles of public honor and private honesty which are the sure road to national character and happiness." "[F]ounded on the strongest principles of justice," Article I, Section 10, would also "restore credit, and credit is a mine of real wealth." Virginia Federalist Bushrod Washington predicted that Article I, Section 10, would "restore confidence between individuals and bring into circulation a considerable quantity of money which fear and diffidence had locked up."[243]

Yet Federalists generally denied the charge that the Constitution would force states to pay off their existing paper currency at face value. They insisted that Article I, Section 10, did not apply retrospectively and indeed that to interpret the Constitution to force states to redeem their paper currency at par would itself be a kind of ex post facto law, prohibited by the Constitution.[244]

Actual Motivations

These were the principal arguments Antifederalists raised against the Constitution and the Federalists' responses. Yet participants in the ratifying contest frequently made whatever arguments they thought would be most likely to influence those voters and convention delegates who were undecided on ratification. Thus, the arguments made in favor of and against ratification do not necessarily correspond to the true reasons that some people supported the Constitution in 1787–88 and others opposed it. What, if anything, can be determined about the factors that genuinely explain people's stances on ratification?[245]

Over the course of the last century, historians have proposed a variety of factors or considerations to account for the division between Federalists and Antifederalists over ratification. Early in the twentieth century, Charles Beard famously offered an economic interpretation of the conflict over the Constitution. In his view, supporters of ratification were mostly creditors determined to suppress state debtor relief laws and inflationary monetary schemes, as well as speculators in government securities who stood to make a fortune from the creation of a powerful national government possessed of sufficient taxing power to pay off its debt at face value. Antifederalists, according to Beard, were mostly debtor farmers.[246]

Beard occasionally seemed to be charging the Framers with lining their own pockets: "The overwhelming majority of members [of the Philadelphia Convention] . . . were immediately, directly, and personally interested in the outcome of their labors at Philadelphia, and were to a greater or lesser extent economic beneficiaries from the adoption of the Constitution." At other times, however, he suggested only that the Framers advanced the economic interests of the class to which they belonged: "The purpose of [this] inquiry is not, of course, to show that the Constitution was made for the personal benefit of the members of the Convention. Far from it. . . . The only point here considered is: Did they represent distinct groups whose economic interests they understood and felt in concrete, definite form through their own personal experience with identical property rights . . . ?" The crux of Beard's argument, which relied on the propensity of government securities holders to support the Constitution, was convincingly refuted in the 1950s.[247]

Some subsequent historians have offered revised economic interpretations of the division between Federalists and Antifederalists. Jackson Turner Main argued that the contest over ratification divided those who participated in the market economy from those who did not. Merchants, urban tradesmen, and those farmers who supplied cities or produced surplus crops for export tended to be Federalists. Those farmers who were more isolated from commercial markets tended to be Antifederalists.[248]

Other historians, most notably Gordon Wood, have preferred a social explanation of the division between Federalists and Antifederalists. According to this view, supporters of ratification were predominantly affluent, well-educated, and mostly well-born persons who were distressed at having been displaced from political power over the preceding decade by the "middling" classes, such as shopkeepers, tavern owners, and skilled craftsmen.[249]

Thus, for example, in 1777, one member of the Georgia elite, objecting to the character of a delegate appointed to the Continental Congress, lamented that the better sort of people had "lost that influence they otherways would have had," and government had "got into the hands of those whose ability or situation in life does not entitle them to it." Such persons "must ruin the country if not timely prevented by some alteration" in the scheme of government. In 1787, Theodore Sedgwick objected to the men "of stupidity, vice, [and] meanness" who inhabited the Massachusetts legislature. At the Philadelphia convention, Elbridge Gerry likewise observed that in Massachusetts "the worst men get into the legislature"; several of them "had lately been convicted of infamous crimes." Gerry charged that "[m]en of indigence, ignorance and baseness spare no pains, however dirty, to carry their point against men who are superior to the artifices practiced." Madison agreed that "unfit characters" were having "too great success" at getting elected to the Virginia legislature.[250]

In this view, upper-crust Federalists were determined to use constitutional reform to restore what they saw as the natural order of things. Through the use of large constituencies, indirect elections, and longer terms in office, the Constitution would ensure that the "better sort" of people were elected to national office. Conversely, by this account, the middling and lower classes tended to oppose the Constitution because they understood it as part of a conspiracy to subjugate them politically by establishing a more "aristocratic" government.[251]

In the early 1960s, Stanley Elkins and Eric McKitrick offered a generational explanation of the divisions over ratification, observing that, on average, Federalists were about ten to twelve years younger than Antifederalists. The median age of the delegates to the Philadelphia convention was forty-three, and several of the most prominent delegates were in their mid-thirties or even younger. The formative experiences of this younger generation—people such as Hamilton, Madison, Gouverneur Morris, and Charles Pinckney—were service in the Revolutionary Army and in the Confederation Congress. Such nationalizing experiences had left these relatively young men favorably inclined toward more centralized government power. Unhappy experiences dealing with obstreperous state governments during the war had left soldiers such as Washington and Henry Knox (and a young John Marshall) profoundly skeptical as to whether states had any constructive role to play in the new government framework.[252]

By contrast, according to this interpretation, the formative experiences of Antifederalist elder statesmen—people such as Patrick Henry, George Mason, and Samuel Adams—were the various political confrontations with Great Britain that began with colonial resistance to the Stamp Act in 1765. Many of these older men had played little or no role in the Confederation Congress— at least after its early years. Their service in colonial governments, which had effectively mobilized resistance to British rule, left them more favorably disposed toward local government authority and gravely concerned about the risk of distant governmental power turning tyrannical.[253]

Thus, for example, as soon as fifty-five-year-old Richard Henry Lee formulated his critique of the Constitution, he instinctively sent it to sixty-five-year-old Samuel Adams, assuming that his fellow Revolutionary-era patriot and "dear friend," with whom he had toiled "in the vineyard of liberty," would concur with his concerns about a powerful centralized government. Indeed, many of the older Antifederalists explicitly warned during the ratifying debates that the country was at risk of enacting the same policies that had inspired it to revolt against Great Britain a decade earlier. Antifederalist Amos

Singletary, who was sixty-six years old in 1788, told the Massachusetts rati-fying convention that "if anybody had proposed such a Constitution as this in [1775], it would have been thrown away at once." Likewise, one New York Antifederalist observed that the Constitution "departed widely from the prin-ciples and political faith of '76, when the spirit of liberty ran high."[254]*

Other scholars have argued that disagreements over political philosophy—rather than disparate economic or social interests—best explain the division between Federalists and Antifederalists. From this perspective, opponents of ratification simply agreed with Montesquieu's maxim that republican govern-ment could thrive only in small, relatively homogeneous communities that fostered citizens' virtue—that is, the willingness to subordinate self-interest to the greater good of the community—and enabled tight connections be-tween representatives and their constituents. As Samuel Adams asked Richard Henry Lee, "Can this national legislature be competent to make laws for the free internal government of one people, living in climates so remote and whose 'habits and particular interests' are and probably always will be so different?"[255]

By contrast, according to this interpretation, Federalists tended to embrace Madison's theory of the large republic, which rejected Montesquieu's un-derstanding. As we have seen, Madison argued that an extended geographic sphere would expand the heterogeneity of the population's interests, which was the best safeguard against the formation of majority factions that would oppress minorities. In addition, greater physical distance would ensure looser ties between representatives and their constituents, which would enable rep-resentatives to "refine and enlarge" the interests of their constituents, thus further reducing the risk of majority oppression. That this political-theory in-terpretation does not explain why Madison happened to hold the ideas he did while Mason and Lee held very different ones hardly refutes the notion that differences in ideas—and not just in interests—may partially explain the divi-sion between Federalists and Antifederalists.[256]

In a similar vein, Max Edling has recently argued that Federalists and Antifederalists were mainly divided over the wisdom of conferring upon the national government the sort of taxing and war-making powers that would be necessary to turn lightly governed America into a powerful nation-state in the modern European mold.[257]

---

* As one aspiring poet colorfully put the point:

> Tho' British armies could not here prevail
> Yet British politics shall turn the scale;
> In five short years of freedom weary grown
> We quit our plain republics for a throne.

Although no single factor can fully explain why some people became Federalists and others Antifederalists, it is possible to confidently identify a few factors of explanatory weight—most important, urban versus rural; creditor versus debtor; East versus West; North versus South; and religious affiliation.

Residents of the largest cities—which were not very populous by modern standards (Philadelphia was the largest, with roughly thirty thousand people)— overwhelmingly supported the Constitution, regardless of class. In Baltimore, a grand procession in honor of Maryland's ratification attracted more than three thousand participants of all economic strata. In Boston, when word reached tradesmen and mechanics that one of their delegates to the Massachusetts ratifying convention, Samuel Adams, was inclined to oppose ratification, more than 380 of them attended a meeting that unanimously declared their strong support for the Constitution. Indeed, the day after ratification by the Massachusetts convention, Henry Jackson, who had been an officer in the Continental Army, reported to his close friend Henry Knox that thousands of people of "every class" had assembled in Boston's State Street "to express their joy."[258]

In Philadelphia and environs, Federalist candidates for the state ratifying convention outpolled Antifederalists by roughly five to one. In New York City, the margin was closer to twenty to one. Even in southern cities, such as Richmond, Norfolk, and Charleston, support for the Constitution was strong. A month after the Philadelphia convention ended, Randolph told Madison that "[t]he people of this town [Richmond] are still in rage for the Constitution."[259]

Urban opinion was so enthusiastic for ratification that dissenting voices were sometimes forcibly suppressed. One Philadelphia Federalist reported such "enthusiastic zeal" for the Constitution that an opponent "hazards ill-usage and insult." Indeed, Pennsylvania legislators who voted against calling a ratifying convention were attacked in their homes and in a lodging house by stone-wielding mobs that, according to one source, both abused them and frightened their wives. Similarly, in Boston, according to one newspaper report, the Constitution was "so very popular" that it was "dangerous to speak against it."[260]

What made the Constitution so popular in cities? Most urban merchants probably favored the Constitution because it would both enable Congress to foster free trade across the nation by suppressing protectionist state legislation and constrain loose monetary policy in the states, which had harmed merchants by enabling debtors to repay loans in depreciated currency. Indeed, in May 1787, Providence merchants and tradesmen had urged the Philadelphia convention to provide for free interstate trade and not to neglect "the consideration of a general currency throughout the United States."[261]

Urban shipping interests—including the workers who made, maintained, supplied, and manned ships—seem to have overwhelmingly supported the Constitution, probably because it empowered Congress to threaten retaliatory trade restrictions through its power to regulate foreign commerce, which would help secure to Americans their fair share of the carrying trade. Thus, the *Maryland Journal* observed that "merchants and those concerned in shipbuilding" supported the Constitution because they were "contemplating a revival, extension, and protection of trade and navigation" under it. Likewise, small manufacturers, "anticipating, under the new government, an increase of their different manufactures from the operations of uniform duties on similar articles imported into the United States," seem generally to have supported ratification. Even outside of cities, those involved in large-scale agricultural export, such as the South's largest planters—as well as the merchants and lawyers who were intertwined in commercial networks with them—tended to support the Constitution.[262]

Because Article I, Section 10, barred states from issuing paper money and secured debt agreements against retrospective impairment by state legislatures, most large creditors had strong incentives to support ratification, and it is likely that most of them did so. At the Philadelphia convention, Gouverneur Morris had warned that the "monied interests" would oppose ratification if paper money emissions were not barred by the Constitution, and Oliver Ellsworth had predicted that by refraining from authorizing Congress to issue paper money, the Constitution would gain many "friends of influence."[263]

During the ratifying contest, South Carolina Antifederalist Lowndes confirmed the accuracy of such predictions: "[A] great number of gentlemen were captivated with this new Constitution because those who were in debt would be compelled to pay; others pleased themselves with the reflection that no more confiscation laws would be passed." Enumerating the various features of the Constitution that different parties were applauding in the Philadelphia procession celebrating ratification by the requisite number of states on July 4, 1788, Benjamin Rush observed that "the man of wealth realized once more the safety of his bonds and rents against the inroads of paper money and tender laws." Writing from Petersburg, Virginia, in the fall of 1787, two mercantile partners declared, "If the new Constitution should not be adopted or something similar, we are of opinion such is the interest and influence of debtors in our state that every thing will be at risk." Of course, one need not view creditors supporting the Constitution as acting solely out of self-interest; most of them surely believed that Article I, Section 10, reflected uncontroversial principles of justice.[264]

Those creditors holding government securities—who were concentrated in northeastern cities and mainly consisted of merchants, lawyers, and other professionals—had an even stronger incentive to support ratification.* As one of them stated, "As a public creditor, and weighing, like many good citizens, my own private advantage against the public good, I ought to wish for the most speedy adoption of the proposed plan." Philadelphia businessman and political economist Pelatiah Webster explained, "[O]nly from a federal treasury can public creditors, of all descriptions, expect substantial and permanent justice." The Constitution's grant of a robust taxing power would enable Congress to raise sufficient revenue to pay off its debts. Moreover, the Philadelphia convention had agreed to a constitutional provision stating that "[a]ll debts contracted and engagements entered into before the adoption of this Constitution shall be as valid against the United States under this Constitution as under the Confederation."[265]

Indeed, the convention had initially agreed to an even stronger provision, which would have declared that Congress "*shall* fulfill the engagements and discharge the debts of the United States." However, several delegates had raised objections to this provision. Pierce Butler did not think that Congress should be obliged to make payments "as well to the blood suckers who had speculated on the distresses of others as to those who had fought and bled for their country." Mason agreed that there was "a great distinction between original creditors and those who purchased fraudulently of the ignorant and distressed," and he worried that imposing a mandatory duty on Congress to discharge its debts would "beget speculations and increase the pestilent practice of stock jobbing." Mason acknowledged the difficulty in distinguishing between those who had fairly bought federal debt on the open market and those who had taken advantage of the "ignorant and distressed," but he did not wish to preclude Congress from attempting to draw such a line. After Gerry defended the "stock-jobbers" for bolstering the value of government securities by creating a market for them, the convention overwhelmingly voted to substitute the provision that was ultimately adopted, which would neither increase nor diminish creditors' entitlements from what they had been under the Articles of Confederation.[266]

Wishing to go much further, John Rutledge had proposed to the convention the appointment of a grand committee "to consider the necessity and expediency of the United States assuming all the state [war] debts." Rutledge argued that adding a provision to the Constitution for the federal assumption

---

* Beard was not wrong to claim that government creditors—especially creditors of the *federal* government—had strong incentives to support ratification. His mistake was in overstating the extent to which those who drafted and ratified the Constitution held government securities at the time of their actions, as opposed to having purchased them by the time of Secretary of the Treasury Hamilton's funding operation, beginning in 1790.

of the states' war-related debts would be "just" because those debts had been "contracted in the common defense." Such a provision was "necessary" because the Constitution would require states to give up "the only sure source of revenue"—the impost—to the federal government. The provision would also be "politic, as by disburdening the people of the state debts, it would conciliate them to the plan." Rufus King strongly supported Rutledge's motion, noting that without such a constitutional provision, the state creditors might become "an active and formidable party" opposing ratification, out of fear that the Constitution would deprive the states of the best sources of revenue for repaying their own debts. King observed that under the Articles state creditors had been the strongest opponents of granting Congress the power to levy an impost for precisely this reason.[267]

The convention agreed to appoint the committee that Rutledge had suggested, and the committee proposed that Congress have the power to discharge the war debts of the states as well as those of the federal government. However, Gerry now objected that the states had devoted varying degrees of effort to sinking their own war-related debts, and those that had done the most would be "alarmed if they were now to be saddled with a share of the debts of states which had done least." The delegates agreed to postpone consideration of the matter, and when they returned to it just one day later, the language in this provision pertaining to the states' war debts had mysteriously been dropped (without any recorded deliberation). Hamilton later recalled that he and Madison had discussed this issue during "an afternoon's walk" while the convention was temporarily adjourned. According to Hamilton's recollection, although "perfectly agreed in the expediency and propriety" of a constitutional provision guaranteeing the federal government's assumption of the states' war debt, he and Madison "were both of opinion that it would be more advisable to make it a measure of administration than an article of constitution, from the impolicy of multiplying obstacles to its reception on collateral details."[268]

Yet few astute observers could have doubted that if the Constitution were ratified and Federalists elected to power, they would press for the federal government's assumption of the states' war debt. Of course, government bondholders who supported ratification need not have been acting solely out of self-interest. Undoubtedly, they were among those Americans most committed to the notion that governments must pay their debts—both as a matter of justice and as a means of maintaining a strong credit rating.[269]

Because most people believed that the federal government would fund the war debt if the Constitution were ratified, the price of federal securities rose as each step was taken toward the Constitution's fruition. As one North Carolina Antifederalist observed, speculators looked at the Constitution and saw "they are to be paid in gold and silver." The price of federal securities rose by a few cents on the dollar when the Philadelphia convention met and then increased more as states began to ratify the Constitution. A New York merchant who was actively speculating in government securities noted that the price rose when Massachusetts became the sixth state to ratify the Constitution early in February 1788, then fell two weeks later when the New Hampshire convention unexpectedly adjourned without ratifying. The price of federal securities rose even more once the requisite number of states had ratified the Constitution. Then, in the first months of President Washington's administration, as Secretary of the Treasury Hamilton's plans for funding the debt became clear, the price skyrocketed.[270]

In the end, the bondholders had calculated correctly—indeed, some of them, late in the process, were trading with inside information. Hamilton succeeded in funding the federal government's debt at par value, overcoming opposition from those (led by Madison in Congress) who favored discriminating against speculators who had purchased their securities from soldiers and government suppliers at much lower prices. Against even more substantial opposition, Hamilton also succeeded in funding the vast majority of the states' war-related debt.[271]*

By the time Hamilton's funding operation was consummated, government war debt had been concentrated into fewer and fewer hands. For example, just sixteen individuals owned 50 percent of the federal debt held by Marylanders. Two hundred eighty individuals scattered across the nation held nearly two-thirds of all government securities, both state and federal. Although many securities holders would have purchased their paper after the Constitution was ratified, those whose holdings dated farther back had a powerful incentive to support ratification.[272]

---

* Ironically, in 1790, Madison led the (initially successful) opposition in Congress to federal assumption of the states' war-related debts. Hamilton regarded this as a betrayal, given Madison's support for assumption, both in 1783 when they were in Congress together and—according to Hamilton's recollection—in their private conversation during the Philadelphia convention. Madison justified his switch on the grounds that he had favored federal assumption of state war debts as they stood at the end of the Revolutionary War, but not as they stood in 1790, by which time the states had devoted very different amounts of effort to retiring those debts. However, Hamilton was convinced that such a rapid change in Madison's views could only be explained by Jefferson's pernicious influence and by Madison's having been "seduced by the expectation of popularity."

A congressional deadlock over the assumption issue was broken by a famous bargain between Madison and Hamilton that was brokered by Jefferson. Hamilton got federal assumption of state debts in exchange for Philadelphia's becoming the nation's temporary capital (which induced a couple of members of Pennsylvania's divided congressional delegation to support assumption) and the permanent capital being established on the Potomac River (which secured the votes of a couple of Virginia and Maryland congressmen).

At the opposite end of the socioeconomic spectrum, small farmers from sparsely populated counties that were not well integrated into commercial networks seem mostly to have opposed ratification. For some of these people, as King wrote to Madison during the Massachusetts ratifying convention, their objections to the Constitution were grounded less in specific provisions than in a general sense that "the rich and ambitious" were plotting to exploit "the poor and illiterate." Indeed, the Pennsylvania Antifederalist "Centinel" accused "the wealthy," through the guise of the Constitution, of the "most daring attempt to establish a despotic aristocracy among freemen that the world has ever witnessed."[273]

Yet for many of the poor and middling farmers who opposed ratification, the critical factor may have been Article I, Section 10, which presumably would bar the sort of relief programs that a majority of states had enacted in the mid-1780s and that many farmers probably believed (or knew) had saved them from bankruptcy. Thus, the Pennsylvania Antifederalist "Deliberator" warned that under the Constitution, states could not grant relief to distressed debtors because they would be "expressly prohibited from passing any law impairing the obligation of contracts." When Antifederalists exalted the state governments for enjoying the confidence of the people and warned that the federal government could inspire allegiance only through fear, many of them probably had in mind the fiscal and monetary disputes of the 1780s.[274]

At the Philadelphia convention, Nathaniel Gorham of Massachusetts had predicted that "an absolute prohibition of paper money would rouse the most desperate opposition from its partisans." In his conjectures on whether the Constitution would be ratified, Hamilton agreed with Gorham, predicting opposition from "all men much in debt who will not wish to see a government established, one object of which is to restrain the means of cheating creditors."[275]

Writing to Madison during the Massachusetts ratifying convention, Gorham confirmed the accuracy of his earlier prediction: "[A]ll men who are in favor of paper money and tender laws" were opposing the Constitution. Madison reported to Jefferson that the provisions barring states from issuing paper money and impairing the obligation of contracts (together with the provision on treaties) "created more enemies [to the Constitution] than all the errors in the system positive and negative put together." Writing from New Hampshire, Washington's private secretary Tobias Lear observed that "[t]he opposition here (as has generally been the case) was composed of men who were involved in debt, and of consequence would be adverse to any government which was likely to abolish their tender laws and cut off every hope of accomplishing their favorite plan of introducing a paper currency."[276]

To be sure, one cannot fully credit Federalist estimates of the amount of opposition to ratification that derived from dishonest debtors who were seeking to "defraud their creditors." Federalists had obvious incentives—both political and psychological—to disparage the motives of their adversaries. Yet some Antifederalists agreed that "the principal weight of opposition" to ratification derived from Article I, Section 10. More significantly, several academic studies have found strong correlations between the voting patterns of state legislators and towns on the issues of paper money emissions and tax and debt relief in the mid-1780s and on ratification of the Constitution in 1787–88: The vast majority of those who had supported relief measures became Antifederalists.[277]

When Rhode Island voters rejected ratification in a referendum in March 1788, one of the principal reasons was almost certainly concern that Article I, Section 10, would prevent the state from completing its program of redeeming the state debt in vastly depreciated paper currency, given that other provisions of the Constitution—most notably, the apportionment of the Senate and Congress's power to regulate commerce—would obviously benefit Rhode Island. In addition, as we shall see in chapter 6, Article I, Section 10, elicited considerable criticism at the first North Carolina ratifying convention, which rejected unconditional ratification by a margin of greater than two to one. One of Washington's correspondents observed that "[w]hatever ostensible reasons may be offered" in North Carolina and Rhode Island "for the rejection of this Constitution, . . . the true one is the inhibition of paper money." Delegates from the central counties of Massachusetts, where support for Shays's Rebellion had been strongest, voted by 86 percent to 14 percent against ratification at the state's convention. Indeed, King reported to Madison from that convention that "the same infatuation, which prevailed not many months since in several counties of this state, and which emboldened them to take arms against the government, seems to have an uncontrollable authority over a numerous part of our convention."[278]

The perspectives and interests of those less affluent debtor farmers who disliked Article I, Section 10, were not well represented by the elite Antifederalists, who tended to share their opponents' disdain of tax and debt relief. For example, William Grayson, an elite Antifederalist leader from Virginia, had told Madison before the Philadelphia convention that a particular state legislative proposal to issue paper money was "one of the most iniquitous things I ever saw in my life." Grayson could think of no "greater act of despotism than that of issuing paper to depreciate for the purpose of paying debts on easy terms." Similarly, Richard Henry Lee, another member of the Virginia gentry who opposed ratification, had privately observed while the Constitution was being drafted that individual debt "almost universally arises from idleness and extravagance" and would only be "remedied by industry and economy." Thus, debtors had "no right to complain of" their plight.[279]

Because the upper-echelon Antifederalists who wrote most of the newspaper essays and gave most of the speeches opposing ratification tended to share their opponents' disapproval of paper money and debtor relief laws, they rarely criticized Article I, Section 10, for banning such measures. Thus, for example, barely a word of criticism was directed at that provision during the Virginia ratifying convention, even though proposals for tax and debt relief had commanded considerable political support in that state in the mid-1780s. Because elite Antifederalists and their more ordinary allies had such disparate perspectives on relief legislation, it is probably impossible to know with certainty how much of the opposition to ratification across the nation was driven by Article I, Section 10.[280]

Nonetheless, at least some of the debtor farmers who had backed paper money and debt relief in the mid-1780s did support ratification, despite Article I, Section 10. For example, many New Hampshire towns that had elected legislators in the mid-1780s who voted to issue paper money chose ratifying convention delegates in 1788 who supported the Constitution, which would ban such legislation in the future. One possible explanation for this seemingly paradoxical behavior is that relief measures may have lost some of their appeal by the time of the ratifying contest, both because the economy was starting to improve and because Rhode Island's extremist monetary policy had ignited a backlash against paper money.[281]

Perhaps more important, many past defenders of relief legislation may simply have found enough attractive features in the Constitution to outweigh any dislike they had of Article I, Section 10. As we have seen, Federalists campaigned aggressively to convince ordinary farmers that their tax burdens would decline under the Constitution, and with it their need for relief legislation. Federalists argued that the federal government would derive most of its revenue from import duties, the brunt of which, they said, would be borne by the wealthy. Federalists also promised that regressive state taxes, which had proved so burdensome to farmers in the 1780s, would decline under the Constitution because states no longer would have to meet federal requisitions. Moreover, if the federal government were to assume states' war-related debts, as seemed possible or even probable, then state tax burdens would diminish even further. Federalists may also have persuaded some farmers that the Constitution would raise the value of their land by empowering Congress to use its power over foreign commerce to pry open foreign markets with the threat of retaliatory trade restrictions.[282]

Thus, for example, a prominent New Jersey politician who had supported relief legislation in the past explained that he had decided not to oppose the Constitution because it would generate "immense sums" through import duties that would "ease the farmer and landholder and make the burden light."

Other advantages conferred by the Constitution in particular states—equality of voting power in the Senate for small states, protection against New York's impost for New Jersey and Connecticut, and security against violent conflict with Indian tribes for Georgia—probably convinced many past backers of relief legislation to support the Constitution despite Article I, Section 10.[283]

Another factor influencing opinion on ratification was regional: both East versus West and, to a lesser degree, North versus South. With regard to the former, Americans living along the coast tended to be far more enthusiastic about the Constitution than those inhabiting western counties. For example, in South Carolina, a crowd of twenty-eight hundred people marched through Charleston to celebrate the state's ratification of the Constitution. By contrast, in the state's backcountry, where leading Antifederalist Aedanus Burke reported that "all is disgust, sorrow, and vindictive reproaches against the system and those who voted for it," the people had "a coffin painted black, which borne in funeral procession, was solemnly buried as an emblem of the dissolution and internment of public liberty." One Pennsylvania Antifederalist declared that west of the Susquehanna River, "at least nine out of every ten [people] would at the risk of their lives and property be as willing to oppose the new Constitution as they were the British in their late designs."[284]

Westerners not only tended to be more supportive of the debtor relief measures that the Constitution prohibited but also reflexively opposed any measures endorsed by easterners, who flaunted their polished manners and superior educations and outvoted westerners in malapportioned legislatures. Had westerners known how close the Philadelphia convention came to explicitly discriminating against new western states in their congressional representation, their suspicions of the Constitution would only have been exacerbated.[285]

Objecting to a constitutional requirement that Congress reapportion representation every ten years in response to a census, Gouverneur Morris had highlighted "the danger of throwing . . . a preponderancy into the western scale." Fear that "the poor but numerous inhabitants of the western country will destroy the Atlantic states" led Morris to argue that easterners should have the power "to keep a majority of votes in their own hands." The backcountry was "always most averse to the best measures" and could not "furnish men equally enlightened to share in the administration of our common interests." In addition, Morris worried that westerners would be less "scrupulous of involving the community in wars, the burdens and operations of which would fall chiefly on the maritime states."[286]

During this debate at the Philadelphia convention, Gerry had likewise noted "the dangers apprehended from western states," which he predicted would abuse power and "oppress commerce and drain our wealth." By contrast, Virginia delegates Mason and Madison had resisted the idea of subjecting newly admitted western states to "degrading discriminations" and "unfavorable distinctions." By the narrow margin of five states to four—with New Jersey joining the four southern states in the majority—the convention had rejected a proposal by Gerry that the number of representatives in the House from newly admitted states should not exceed the total from the states that originally approved the Constitution.[287]

Westerners in Virginia and North Carolina, who inhabited the regions that would become the independent states of Kentucky and Tennessee in the 1790s, had what they believed was a powerful additional reason to oppose ratification: They feared that the new national government would use its treaty power to bargain away their claim of navigation rights to the Mississippi River, as Secretary for Foreign Affairs John Jay had attempted to do in 1786. Blocking river access would inhibit the region's growth and reduce the value of its land. The Mississippi River issue came up repeatedly at the Virginia ratifying convention, where the Kentucky region's delegation eventually voted ten to three against ratification.[288]

To be sure, not all westerners in the southern states opposed ratification. For example, John Brown, a Virginia congressional delegate from the Kentucky region who was described as "zealously attentive to the interests of the western settlers," assiduously defended the Constitution in letters to the region's delegates to the Virginia ratifying convention.[289]

Among those westerners supporting ratification, many were convinced of the need for a strong federal government that could raise an effective army to control Indian tribes. John Brown expressed hope that despite "the ill-advised attempt" to cede navigation rights on the Mississippi River, which had "laid the foundation for the dismemberment of the American empire by destroying the confidence of the people in the western country in the justice of the union," Congress might still be able to "conciliate their minds and to secure their attachment to the confederacy." Because there was "great reason to apprehend a general Indian war," Brown hoped that Kentuckians might "see the danger and impropriety of breaking off from the union at this time." Some residents of Pittsburgh, Pennsylvania, who supported ratification observed that the weakness of the Confederation Congress had prevented its taking "proper measures with the courts of Spain and Britain," which had left westerners both "deprived of the advantages of the Mississippi trade, which is our natural right," and "liable to the incursions of the savages" because the western forts had not yet been relinquished by the British, as required by the 1783 Treaty of Paris.[290]

The North-South axis was another regionally based factor explaining divisions over the Constitution, as ratifying conventions in southern states supplied a much higher percentage of votes against the Constitution than did those in the North. In South Carolina, Antifederalist Lowndes warned that under the new Constitution, the South would not have "the smallest chance of receiving adequate advantages," and "the influence of the northern states would be so predominant against us, as to divest us of even the shadow of a republic." If the Constitution were to be adopted, Lowndes predicted, "the sun of those southern states [would] set, never to rise again." Similarly, former governor Benjamin Harrison of Virginia told Washington, "[I]f the Constitution is carried into effect, the states south of [the] Potomac will be little more than appendages to those to the northward of it." Northern Antifederalists did not generally criticize the Constitution in this apocalyptic fashion.[291]

While some southern Antifederalists warned that slavery would be at risk under the Constitution, the principal basis of their opposition seems to have been fear that northerners would control the national government and use its powers—especially those over commerce and treaty making—to the detriment of southern economic interests. As we have seen, the controversy over Jay's negotiations with Spain regarding American navigation rights on the Mississippi River had left southerners profoundly distrustful of a northern-dominated Congress. Grayson told the Virginia ratifying convention that the Mississippi issue would determine "whether one part of the continent shall govern the other." He declared, "God and nature have intended, from the extent of territory and fertility of soil, that the weight of population should be on this [the southern] side of the continent." Yet northerners were determined to stymie western migration in order to block the formation of new southern states and thus retain control of the national government. Another Virginia Antifederalist, John Dawson, noting the recent "diabolical attempt" to surrender American navigation rights on the Mississippi River, "on which depends the importance of the southern part of America," told his state's convention that he would oppose ratification without antecedent amendments in order to secure against any similar attempts in the future.[292]

Partly because of the recent experience of southern states having been outvoted by northern states in Congress on Jay's reinstruction, southern Antifederalists were especially troubled by two features of the Constitution: equal state representation in the Senate and the absence of a supermajority requirement for commercial legislation. Explaining to Virginians his refusal to sign the Constitution in Philadelphia, Edmund Randolph called these the two "most repugnant" features of the document. Fellow Virginian Grayson warned that the interest of the northern carrying states was "strikingly different from that of the [southern] productive states," and he predicted that "this government will operate as a faction of seven states to oppress the rest of the union." In South Carolina, Lowndes warned that a Congress dominated by northerners would "fritter away the value of our produce to little or nothing by compelling payment of exorbitant freightage." A North Carolina Antifederalist worried, simply, that the North "will always outvote us."[293]

Even if southerners were likely eventually to gain control over Congress as population flowed southward and westward and new states joined the union, Mason pointed out that it was a peculiar argument "that we should cheerfully burn ourselves to death in hopes of a joyful and happy resurrection." Southern Antifederalists therefore proposed constitutional amendments to require two-thirds majorities in Congress for the enactment of commercial legislation and three-fourths majorities for the ratification of treaties ceding navigational claims.[294]

Additional factors may partially explain the greater opposition to ratification in the South than in the North. As we have seen, most people assumed that if the Constitution were ratified, the new federal government would fund its debt—and probably at par value. Yet southerners held a very small percentage of that debt. For example, southerners owned as little as 7 percent of the final settlement certificates issued by the federal government to civilian creditors during the war and only about 16 percent of the total federal debt. Furthermore, southern planters who were indebted to British creditors feared that the federal court system to be established under the Constitution would be less sympathetic to their interests than were more politically accountable state courts.[295]

One final factor accounting for a small share of divisions over the Constitution was religion. Religious dissenters—especially Baptists in states such as Virginia, North Carolina, and Massachusetts—disproportionately opposed ratification. In Massachusetts, about two-thirds of the Baptist delegates attending the state ratifying convention (of whom there were at least twenty) voted against the Constitution. As the ratifying contest heated up in Virginia early in 1788, Madison's father told him that most of the Baptists in Madison's home county of Orange were opposing ratification. Many Virginia Baptists, who had suffered religious persecution as recently as the 1770s, regarded the Constitution, which omitted any explicit safeguard for religious liberty, as a step backward from the Virginia Statute for Religious Freedom, which they had struggled for years to enact in Virginia, finally succeeding in 1786. Similarly in North Carolina, Baptist minister Henry Abbot insisted at the state's ratifying convention that Americans not "be deprived of the privilege of worshipping God according to their consciences."[296]

Perhaps ironically, some religiously devout persons argued against ratification on the opposite grounds—that the Constitution afforded *too much* protection for religious liberty by forbidding any religious test for federal officeholders. Such persons believed that republican government required a virtuous citizenry and that virtue was best instilled through Protestant Christianity.

Thus, for example, in New Hampshire, the state constitution explicitly declared the religious foundations of republican government—"morality and piety, rightly grounded on evangelical principles, will give the best and greatest security to government, and will lay in the hearts of men the strongest obligations to due subjection"—and required that the principal state officeholders be Protestants. One delegate to the Massachusetts convention who voted against ratification argued that "a person could not be a good man without being a good Christian," and thus rulers ought to take an oath that they believed in Christ or at least in God.[297]

Antifederalists of this ilk believed that the Constitution had gone too far in the direction of religious toleration. One Massachusetts Antifederalist "shuddered at the idea that Roman Catholics, papists and pagans might be introduced into office." In the North Carolina ratifying convention, one Antifederalist expressed the wish "that the Constitution had excluded Popish priests from offices," while another objected that the absence of a religious test for officeholding would constitute "an invitation for Jews and pagans of every kind to come among us," and thus might "endanger the character" of the nation.[298*]

During the ratifying contest, Federalists frequently complained that their opponents raised, "out of doors," arguments against the Constitution that they were unwilling to embrace openly in ratifying conventions. Yet the Federalists themselves often defended particular constitutional provisions in very different terms than the Framers had at the Philadelphia convention.[299]

On occasion, when this happened, a particular Federalist was simply making the best of a bad situation, defending a constitutional provision that he

---

* Federalists offered two different sorts of responses to such objections. First, a few of them argued strongly in favor of broad religious toleration. In this view, the United States was characterized by extraordinary religious diversity, and nobody should be excluded from federal office simply for holding viewpoints that were outside the mainstream. Thus, James Iredell of North Carolina declared, "[A] man may be of different religious sentiments from our own, without being a bad member of society." Religious qualifications for officeholding, according to Isaac Backus, a Baptist minister who supported ratification in Massachusetts, had been "the greatest engine of tyranny in the world."

Second, some Federalists agreed with their adversaries that atheists, pagans, and perhaps others were not suited to hold office, but nonetheless maintained that religious oaths were an ineffective means of excluding them. Atheists, for example, did not dread the vengeance of God and thus would not hesitate to take a false oath. For this reason, voters would have to be trusted to select only persons of good moral character to represent them. In addition, these Federalists offered reassurances that Protestant voters were unlikely to elect Jews, Muslims, and infidels to political office even in the absence of religious tests.

himself had opposed in Philadelphia. Madison and Hamilton were frequently confronted with this problem in writing *The Federalist*.

Thus, in the ratifying contest, Madison defended the Constitution's peculiar blend of federalist and nationalist features, whereas in Philadelphia he had argued for a much more consistently nationalist approach and had been despondent when his colleagues repeatedly outvoted him. For example, in Philadelphia, Madison had strongly opposed state legislatures' selecting senators, but at the Virginia ratifying convention he lauded the national government's dependence on states for the selection of its officeholders as a safeguard against oppression. At the New York ratifying convention, Antifederalist John Lansing, Jr., criticized Hamilton for arguing in Philadelphia for the subordination of the state governments while defending those governments in Poughkeepsie as essential to the preservation of the people's liberties.* With regard to various features of the presidency as well— the four-year term of office, the qualified veto power, and the limited share of the appointment power—Hamilton, in the debates over ratification, treated as virtues what he had disparaged as vices in Philadelphia.[300]

On many other occasions, however, Federalists were simply being disingenuous, refusing to defend particular constitutional provisions during the ratifying contest in the same terms that they had in Philadelphia for fear of alienating voters and ratifying convention delegates. Let us consider a few of the most striking examples of this phenomenon.

The delegates to the Philadelphia convention had gone to great lengths to create a national government that would be insulated from populist political pressure through mechanisms such as lengthy terms in office, indirect elections, and enormous constituencies. Even with regard to the House of Representatives, where the people's influence would be most direct, the Framers had sought to weaken that influence by omitting provision for instruction, recall, and mandatory rotation in office and securing the possibility of Congress mandating at-large elections through its power to regulate the times, places, and manner of federal elections. By contrast, in the ratifying debates, Federalists responded to every charge that the federal government would become oppressive by emphasizing its utter dependence

---

* When Hamilton denied the charge of inconsistency, he veered close to an outright lie. In Philadelphia, he had favored empowering the national government to appoint state officeholders. In his private "Speculations on the Constitution," he had gone even further, expressing the hope that after the Constitution was ratified, the federal government would eventually "triumph altogether over the state governments and reduce them to an entire subordination, dividing the larger states into smaller districts."

on the people. In response to criticisms of the Senate and the presidency, Federalists emphasized that the House would operate as a safeguard against possible abuse.[301]*

At the Philadelphia convention, most of the delegates not only had sought to reduce populist influence on the federal government but also had emphasized the importance of establishing mechanisms to ensure that offices were held by the "better sort." By contrast, in the ratifying debates, Federalists criticized their opponents for suggesting that anything in the Constitution would preclude the people from electing ordinary citizens to federal office. Thus, for example, in South Carolina, Charles Cotesworth Pinckney objected to the charge that under the Constitution, "everything would in future be managed by great men," and he insisted that nothing in the document "prevents the president and senators from being taken from the poor as well as the rich." In Philadelphia, however, he had argued against paying salaries to US senators, so that "the wealthy alone would undertake the service."[302]

At the Philadelphia convention, several delegates had argued that the Senate ought to "represent the wealth of the nation," possess the "aristocratic spirit," and mimic the British House of Lords. Lengthy terms in office were necessary so that senators could act "as a check on the democracy." By contrast, in the ratifying debates, Federalists insisted on "the republican complexion" of the Constitution, which barred titles of nobility and guaranteed to each state a republican form of government (which meant that anyone seeking to convert the government into an aristocracy would be committing treason). Federalists now denied that the Senate would foster aristocracy, and they defended six-year terms for senators primarily on the grounds that developing the foreign policy expertise necessary to advise the president wisely on treaty making required considerable experience.[303]

On many smaller issues as well, Federalists offered very different defenses of particular constitutional provisions in ratifying conventions than they had in Philadelphia. In the ratifying contest, Federalists sometimes defended the small size of the House as a cost-saving measure, whereas in Philadelphia they had argued that it would facilitate the election of the "better sort" of people.

---

* Only rarely during the ratifying contest did Federalists openly disparage popular participation in government, as the delegates to the Philadelphia convention had frequently done. At the New York convention, Chancellor Robert R. Livingston declared that the people "in many instances could not know their own good" and that "they were rarely competent to judge of the politics of a great nation or the wisdom of public measures." Also in New York, the Federalist "Caesar" (who may have been Hamilton) denied that ordinary people could "judge with any degree of precision concerning the fitness of this new constitution." However, most Federalists chose—wisely, no doubt—not to openly disparage the abilities of the people, who would be voting for delegates to ratifying conventions.

In the ratifying debates, some Federalists celebrated as a crucial safeguard the constitutional provision requiring that money bills be initiated in the House, whereas in Philadelphia many delegates had disparaged that provision as meaningless. In Philadelphia, the Framers had defended staggering the terms of senators as necessary to reduce populist influence, while in the ratifying contest they argued that this provision would remove "all danger of an aristocratic influence" and put "a stop to intrigues."[304]

While Federalists often defended constitutional provisions during the ratifying contest in very different terms than had the delegates in Philadelphia, Antifederalists frequently offered fancy theoretical justifications for positions that were probably driven mostly by considerations of interest. (Federalists, of course, did this too.) Virginia Antifederalists regularly objected to the consolidationist tendencies of Article III, but their pressing concern seems to have been that federal courts would compel southern planters to pay their prewar debts to British creditors, as the Treaty of Paris seemed to require. Frequently invoking Montesquieu for the proposition that republican government could not thrive in a vast, heterogeneous country such as the United States, Antifederalists seem mostly to have been worried that the federal government created by the Constitution would be unlikely to afford tax relief to financially strapped farmers, as state governments had done in the 1780s. Much of George Mason's professed unhappiness with the Constitution's blending of powers between the Senate and the president may have derived from his conviction that mighty Virginia had been unfairly deprived of its due influence in the Senate by the Connecticut Compromise.[305]

None of this is to deny that differences in ideas played some role in dividing people over the Constitution. For example, some Antifederalists were simply more worried than their Federalist adversaries that a powerful, unitary executive would become tyrannical. Similarly, although Mason and Richard Henry Lee were wealthy and elite, just like their Virginian political adversaries Washington and Madison, they seemed to worry a good deal more about the Constitution's fostering a dangerous aristocracy.

One can generalize to a certain extent about which sorts of people supported and opposed ratification. City dwellers, across class lines, overwhelmingly endorsed the Constitution, while backwoodsmen largely opposed it. Small farmers whose land was encumbered with debt were vastly more likely to oppose ratification than were lawyers and merchants, and their objections were frequently stated in class-conscious terms. Westerners were substantially more likely to oppose ratification than were easterners, and northerners supported the Constitution more than southerners. Small states, as we shall see in chapter 6, produced very few Antifederalists relative to large states.[306]

Yet at the level of particular individuals, it is hard to tell what explained attitudes toward the Constitution. Wealthy and elite Virginians who had a great deal in common with one another nonetheless divided sharply over whether the Constitution ought to be ratified. As we have seen, Patrick Henry proved to be a diehard opponent of ratification. He raised dozens of objections to the Constitution at the Virginia ratifying convention. Yet it is impossible to know his real reasons for opposing it, which might have been as trivial as his not having participated in its drafting. Perhaps had Henry accepted his appointment to the Philadelphia convention—and we cannot know his real reasons for declining that appointment either—he would have been inclined to support ratification of the document that he would have played a role in drafting (though, of course, that constitution might also have looked very different because of his involvement).

6

The Ratifying Contest

Proponents of a powerful national government relatively insulated from populist political influence had overcome great obstacles both in bringing about the Constitutional Convention and in carrying it to a successful conclusion. But could they convince Americans to ratify a document that so profoundly altered the nature of the union and the power and structure of the federal government?[1]

Soon after the Philadelphia convention ended, Madison told Jefferson that "[t]he final reception which will be given by the people at large to the proposed system can not yet be decided." Hamilton worried that the people's "democratical jealousy" would render them suspicious of a constitution that seemed to concentrate power in relatively few hands. Congressional delegate Stephen Mix Mitchell similarly doubted whether "those indomitable spirits" who had made the revolution possible "will ever give up so much of their natural or acquired liberty as is absolutely necessary in order to form a strong and efficient federal government."[2]

For the Federalists, the stakes were enormous. Even allowing for their obvious incentive to exaggerate the extent of the nation's current predicament, Federalists seemed genuinely—as confirmed by their private correspondence—to regard ratification as critical to the future well-being of the United States. Washington told the Marquis de Lafayette that the ratification contest would "determine the political fate of America for the present generation and probably produce no small influence on the happiness of society through a long succession of ages to come." Roger Sherman predicted "deplorable circumstances" should ratification fail: "Our credit as a nation is sinking. The resources of the country could not be drawn out to defend against a foreign invasion nor the forces of the Union to prevent a civil war." Madison declared that if the nation rejected the Constitution, it would fall into "anarchy and disunion."[3]

Hamilton's private speculations as to the likely consequences should the Constitution not be ratified were even more foreboding: "[I]t is probable the discussion of the question will beget such struggles, animosities, and heats in the community that this circumstance, conspiring with the real necessity of an essential change in our present situation, will produce civil war." Such an event, regardless of which parties eventually prevailed, would probably produce "governments very different from the present in their principles." Even the establishment of "monarchies in different portions of" the former republic was possible. Hamilton worried that even if civil war did not occur, several "confederacies [will] be established between different combinations of the particular states." Even a "reunion with Great Britain, from universal disgust at a state of commotion, is not impossible."[4]

Many Americans noted that the ratifying contest would have vast implications not only for their own country but for the entire world. As Hamilton noted in the first number of *The Federalist*, "It has been frequently remarked that it seems to have been reserved to the people of this country, by their conduct and example, to decide the important question, whether societies of men are really capable or not of establishing good government from reflection and choice, or whether they are forever destined to depend for their political constitutions on accident and force." A Connecticut Federalist, Governor Samuel Huntington, observed that "[n]ever before did a people, in time of peace and tranquility, meet together by their representatives, and, with calm deliberation, frame for themselves a system of government. This noble attempt does honor to our country."[5]

Although Federalists deemed ratification imperative, it was in no sense inevitable. As we shall see, Rhode Island initially rejected the Constitution, and North Carolina declined to ratify until amendments were secured. New Hampshire probably would have taken one of these paths as well had Federalists not deftly adjourned the first meeting of the state's ratifying convention before a vote on ratification could be taken. Only severe malapportionment in its ratifying convention enabled South Carolina to approve the Constitution.

In three other large and critical states, the Constitution's fate remained uncertain well into the ratification process, and the final margins in favor were razor-thin: 187 to 168 in Massachusetts, 89 to 79 in Virginia, and 30 to 27 in New York. Rejecting the Constitution had obviously been a genuine possibility in these states. Had three of the five largest states—perhaps even just one or two of them—chosen not to participate, the union almost certainly could not have succeeded.[6]

The Nature of the Debate

The contest over ratification was a great national debate, the likes of which the world had never previously witnessed. Within six weeks of the end of the

Philadelphia convention, nearly every newspaper in the country had reprinted the Constitution. One newspaper observed that Americans—a notably religious people—were reading newspapers more avidly than the Bible in search of information about the proposed Constitution. This consuming passion was aided by the fact that literacy rates were higher in the United States than anywhere else in the world—an estimated 90 percent of white males in New England and 60 to 70 percent in the mid-Atlantic states. Citizen interest in whether the Constitution was ratified resulted in a comparatively high voter turnout in the elections for delegates to state ratifying conventions.[7]

In December 1787, Madison told Jefferson that "[t]he Constitution proposed by the late convention engrosses almost the whole political attention of America." One Massachusetts resident observed that "[l]ittle else, among us, is thought or talked of." The Constitution, according to a Virginia planter, "affords matter for conversation to every rank of beings from the governor to the door keeper." An ardent Massachusetts Federalist declared, "I can bring myself to think of nothing but this important matter [ratification]; it is the last of my thought[s] when I go to bed and the first in the morning when I wake." So many people wanted to hear the deliberations of the Massachusetts ratifying convention that spectators had to line up an hour in advance to get a seat, even though the venue had seating for nearly a thousand people.[8]

Debate over the Constitution took place in taverns, boarding houses, stagecoaches, and political clubs. Brothers disagreed with one another over the merits of the Constitution, as did fathers with sons, and best friends with one another. Men kept their wives and fiancées informed with regard to developments in the ratifying contest, and one woman, Mercy Otis Warren, pseudonymously contributed one of the Antifederalists' most widely circulated pamphlets critiquing the Constitution. College students spent their summer vacations attending the debates in state ratifying conventions. Preachers delivered sermons on the Constitution, pro and con. Governor Hancock of Massachusetts declared a day of public thanksgiving to encourage people to pray for the wisdom of the delegates to the state's ratifying convention.[9]

While some of the debate over ratification was high-toned—one thinks, for example, of *The Federalist* and *Letters to the Republican* by "Federal Farmer"— much of it was characterized by invective and personal insult. One New York Antifederalist wrote that "[a] monkey has more unexceptionable claims to reason than the 'Examiner' [a Federalist author] to elegance or satire" and "every scavenger and chimneysweeper in the city" have more claim to wit. One Pennsylvania Antifederalist reported that the only supporters of ratification in Westmoreland County were "half-pay officers, Cincinnati, attorneys-at-law, public defaulters, and Jews."[10]

Figure 6.1 Mercy Otis Warren, a political propagandist of the American Revolution and later one of its first historians, authored one of the most widely circulated and influential pamphlets opposing ratification of the Constitution. (Museum of Fine Arts, Boston)

Federalists, in turn, gave as good as they got. One supporter of ratification in Massachusetts opined that "[t]he proper definition of the word antifederalism is anarchy, confusion, rebellion, treason, sacrilege, and rapine," while "the word federalism . . . combined national honor, dignity, freedom, happiness, and every republican privilege." A New York Federalist compared one of the opposition's essayists to "a certain animal, described in *Gulliver's Travels*, whose delight was, after hiding himself among the branches of a tree, to surprise the unwary passenger with a discharge of his excrements."[11]

Not infrequently, the invective turned into outright character assassination. Federalists compared their opponents to Revolutionary War Loyalists and Tories, who had opposed the Declaration of Independence as premature in the same way that Antifederalists now criticized the Constitution as premature. Federalists in New Hampshire charged Joshua Atherton, the leading Antifederalist in that state, who had been a Loyalist during the Revolutionary War, with wishing "to prevent the adoption of a system only because it will put it out of the power of Britain to subjugate us." Massachusetts Federalists compared leading Antifederalist Elbridge Gerry to Benedict Arnold. Of another prominent Antifederalist, they asked, "Where was Mr. Mason from 1775 to 1783? What was the part he then took? Of his colleague, who did sign the Constitution [Washington], the admiring world well knows."[12]

Antifederalists also assailed the character of their adversaries. In Massachusetts, they denounced Federalist Nathaniel Gorham, who represented the state at both the Philadelphia convention and the state ratifying convention, as "[a] timid Whig before the war, and a cold friend to the revolution—till the danger was over. He has learned his politics in London, and is now (in America) going to give us the first fruits of his travels." In Virginia, Antifederalists mocked Federalist Alexander White as a man of "notorious timidity" who had refused to fight for his country during the Revolutionary War but now dared to write newspaper essays attacking "respectable" Pennsylvania Antifederalists—"at the secure distance of 200 miles."[13]

The abusiveness of the debate over ratification occasionally prompted less partisan observers to protest the lack of decorum. "A Citizen" of Georgia wrote that, while he had expected "cool and dispassionate inquiry" on "a subject of such magnitude and importance," the public had been presented instead with "personal abuse and scurrility as though there were no other mode of proving the goodness of the proposed plan of government than by calumniating and vilifying the characters of its opposers." Benjamin Franklin grew so weary of "the spirit of rancor, malice, and hatred" that characterized his state's newspaper coverage of the ratifying contest that he submitted an essay, entitled "On the Abuse of the Press," to the *Pennsylvania Gazette*. Reading the state's newspapers, Franklin observed, left the impression that Pennsylvania was "peopled by a set of the most unprincipled, wicked, rascally, and quarrelsome scoundrels upon the face of the globe." (The *Gazette*, which Franklin had founded, declined to publish his essay.)[14]

Vituperative assaults on one's adversaries were not limited to the newspapers. At the Pennsylvania ratifying convention, Federalist delegate Stephen Chambers insulted opposition leader William Findley by noting that Findley had received just two votes when the Pennsylvania Assembly had balloted members to appoint delegates to the Constitutional Convention—evidence of the "insignificance of his [Findley's] character," according to Chambers. In response, Findley noted Chambers's tendency "to discourse without reason and to talk without argument," which afforded little "occasion to take much notice of anything that dropped from that quarter." Chambers replied that he had "a perfect contempt both for Mr. Findley's arguments and person."[15]

In another episode at the Pennsylvania convention, Findley produced a copy of William Blackstone's *Commentaries on the Laws of England* to support his refutation of a particular historical claim made by Federalist leader James Wilson. Findley gratuitously added the observation that if his son "had been at the study of the law for six months and was not acquainted with the passage in Blackstone, I should be justified in whipping him." The following day, Wilson replied contemptuously that "those whose stock of knowledge is limited to a few items may easily remember and refer to them." He also quoted Sir John Maynard's famous put-down of a petulant student who had reproached Maynard for his ignorance of a trivial point: "Young man, I have forgotten more law than ever you learned."[16]

Occasionally, exchanges between delegates at ratifying conventions became so heated that a duel seemed to be in the offing. When Edmund Randolph objected to the "aspersions" and "insinuations" that Patrick Henry leveled against him at the Virginia ratifying convention because Randolph had changed his mind on whether the Constitution should be unconditionally ratified, some observers anticipated that a challenge was about to ensue. Similarly, when John Lansing, Jr., disputed whether Alexander Hamilton's

Figure 6.2 William Findley of Pennsylvania, one of the most prominent "middling" Antifederalists in the nation and later a longtime member of the US House of Representatives. (Courtesy of Independence National Historical Park)

statements at the New York ratifying convention about the role of state governments under the Constitution were consistent with what Hamilton had said on that subject at the Philadelphia convention, "disputations" took place, according to one Federalist delegate, which it was feared might "terminate seriously." Antifederalist leader Elbridge Gerry and Federalist delegate Francis Dana nearly came to blows at the Massachusetts ratifying convention when Dana protested Gerry's attempt, as an invited guest of the convention, to speak without a formal query being directed to him. (Gerry had chosen not to stand for election as a convention delegate but was invited by the convention to attend some of its sessions to answer questions about what had transpired at the Philadelphia convention.)[17]

During the ratifying contest, both sides claimed—and, judging from private correspondence, genuinely believed—that reason was on their side, while their opponents appealed to passion and prejudice. From the perspective of George Washington, the Antifederalists had "a desire to inflame the passions and to alarm the fears by noisy declamations rather than to convince the understanding by some arguments or fair and impartial statements." The Antifederalist "Philadelphiensis" returned the favor, accusing Federalists of answering "reason and argument with scurrility and personal invective."[18]

Each side attacked the motives of the other. Federalists denounced their adversaries as state officeholders who "dread the lessening [of] their own power," "friends of paper money," Shaysites, and disunionists. Massachusetts Federalists accused Elbridge Gerry of opposing the Constitution because its ratification would cause a marked deterioration in the value of the state certificates he was said to hold in vast quantities. A New England Federalist attributed Virginian Richard Henry Lee's opposition to the Constitution to his "low envy of the brilliant virtues and unbounded popularity of that illustrious character [Washington]."[19]

Antifederalists, in turn, charged that those who wish "the people [to] gulp down the gilded pill blind-fold, whole, and without any qualification whatever . . . consist generally of the noble order of Cincinnatus, holders of public securities, men of great wealth and expectations of public office, brokers and lawyers." Rhode Island Antifederalists asserted that the Connecticut Federalist essayist "Landholder," who was Oliver Ellsworth, was "a public defaulter," who held "large sums of public money, unaccounted for—and which the new Constitution will secure in his pocket" (presumably because the clause in the Constitution barring ex post facto laws would preclude efforts to hold him to account).[20]

Both Federalists and Antifederalists accused their opponents of resorting to "chicanery" and "Machiavellian conduct," even while indulging in similarly underhanded tactics themselves.* Antifederalists regularly charged that Federalist sympathizers in the post office tampered with their mail and delayed circulation of their publications. For example, the Pennsylvania Antifederalist "Centinel" declared that post office officials, by suppressing the circulation of newspapers, had "prostituted their offices to forward the nefarious design of enslaving their countrymen, by thus cutting off all communication by the usual vehicle between the patriots of America." In Massachusetts, Antifederalists charged that "a bag of money had been sent down to Boston to quiet the members of convention in opposition to the new constitution." Responding in kind, Federalists alleged that Governor George Clinton of New York, an indefatigable opponent of ratification, had offered half of the proceeds of his state's impost to New Jersey if it would reject the Constitution. In the elections for delegates to the New York ratifying convention, both sides printed fake or misleading ballots in an effort to befuddle the opposition.[21]

Both sides also published fake letters and essays in the newspapers. For example, Federalists in Pennsylvania published a fictitious letter purportedly written by Daniel Shays, the leader of the Massachusetts debtors' rebellion, that was addressed to Philadelphia Antifederalists and urged them to "write letters to the frontier counties, where the people [are] most easily deceived, and alarm them with a number of hard words, such as *aristocracy, monarchy, oligarchy*, and the like, none of which they will understand." Antifederalists used the same device. Madison, referring to "an arrant forgery" in the newspapers reporting that John Jay had become an opponent of ratification, complained to Washington that "[t]ricks of this sort are not uncommon with the enemies of the new Constitution."[22]

In addition, both parties occasionally doctored—to their own advantage, of course—material that they published. For example, when Antifederalists had George Mason's objections to the Constitution published in Massachusetts, they deliberately omitted the paragraph in which he objected to the absence of a supermajority requirement for the exercise of Congress's power to regulate commerce—an objection that would have ill served the cause of northern Antifederalists. In New York, Antifederalists republished Randolph's letter to the Virginia House of Delegates explaining his misgivings about the Constitution but omitted the penultimate paragraph in which he pledged his devotion to the union and declared his willingness, if necessary to prevent its dissolution, to accept the Constitution without amendments. "A Federalist"

---

* When Federalist Theophilus Parsons bragged of his party's chicanery at the Massachusetts ratifying convention, his law pupil, John Quincy Adams, who was an ardent Antifederalist, disapproved of Parsons's making "of the science of politics the science of little, insignificant intrigue, and chicanery." Adams thought that many of the Massachusetts Federalists "exhibit a meanness [of] which I scarcely should expect a man would boast."

promptly condemned this "most daring effrontery to the public," which was also a "great injustice to that liberal patriot [i.e., Randolph]."[23]

Neither side was averse, if all else failed, to hint at a resort to violence should it lose the contest over ratification. For example, Pennsylvania Antifederalists warned that if the Constitution were put into operation despite the considerable opposition still existing in the state after the Pennsylvania ratifying convention had approved it, "[a] civil war with all its dreadful train of evils will probably be the consequence." New York City Federalists likewise predicted a civil war if the state's ratifying convention failed to unconditionally approve the Constitution, and they stated their resolve "to defend the constitution by force."[24]

Indeed, occasionally, each side went beyond intimating at violence to actually employing it. On the night of elections to choose ratifying convention delegates in Pennsylvania, a mob in Philadelphia attacked the private homes of local Antifederalists, as well as the boarding house where assemblymen and councilors from the state's western counties were lodged. According to the account provided by a local physician, the officeholders were "abused, their wives frightened, etc." "Does not this give us a foretaste," he wondered, "of this blessed Constitution?" Returning the favor, Antifederalists in Carlisle, Pennsylvania, rioted in the days after Christmas 1787, disrupting their opponents' celebration of the state's ratification of the Constitution and burning in protest both a copy of the Constitution and effigies of leading Federalists James Wilson and Chief Justice Thomas McKean.[25]

By the summer of 1788, violent disagreement over the Constitution was also erupting in New York. In June, the *New York Morning Post* reported that "the rage of party, relating to the new Constitution, has [risen] to alarming heights in some of the counties in this state" and that "several bloody affrays have taken place in consequence thereof, in one of which, it is said, a Col. Hartshorn of Fishkill, lost his life." On July 4 in Albany, as Federalists celebrated the Constitution and Antifederalists burned a copy of it, "a general battle took place, with swords, bayonets, clubs, stones, etc., which lasted for some time, both parties fighting with the greatest rage." Several participants were badly injured in the fray.[26]

In sum, while the contest over ratification of the Constitution was an extraordinary event in American and world history, it was generally fought with the tools of ordinary politics.

The Federalists' Advantages in the Ratifying Contest

A public debate over the Constitution, characterized by mass participation, was not something the Federalists relished. Most of them agreed with Madison's privately stated view that "there are subjects to which the capacities of the bulk of mankind are unequal, and on which they must and will be governed by those with whom they happen to have acquaintance and confidence. The proposed Constitution is of this description." However, given the broad suffrage rights already existing in the states, the Federalists had no choice but to appeal to the people with regard to ratification. Ironically, they were forced to ask ordinary Americans to ratify a constitution, one of the principal objectives of which was to constrain the influence of public opinion upon government.[27]

Although they did not relish the contest, the Federalists enjoyed a number of advantages in it: malapportionment in their favor in some ratifying conventions, the fact that several conventions were held in large coastal cities, the relative ease with which Federalists organized their supporters, newspaper bias in their favor, the division of opinion over ratification along lines of class and education, and Article VII of the Constitution (described later in this chapter). Some of these advantages Federalists had engineered themselves—for example, the fact that ratification, as provided in Article VII, was to be decided upon by special ratifying conventions rather than by state legislatures or in referenda. Other Federalist advantages would have existed regardless of the procedures they had devised for ratification.

One significant Federalist advantage was malapportionment of state conventions, an imbalance that favored ratification in as many as eight states. In South Carolina, New York, and Rhode Island, the convention delegates who ultimately formed the majority in favor of ratification represented a minority of those states' populations. Malapportionment was particularly severe in South Carolina, where strongly Federalist coastal districts containing fewer than thirty thousand white people, according to the 1790 census, were represented by 143 delegates at the ratifying convention. By contrast, the state's backcountry, with nearly four times that white population, had only 93 delegates at the convention. Although South Carolina's convention ultimately ratified the Constitution by a margin of roughly two to one, a majority of the state's residents almost certainly opposed ratification. To be sure, there were a few states where malapportionment benefited Antifederalists, though generally not enough to influence the outcome of the ratifying conventions.[28]

A second Federalist advantage derived from the location of several of the ratifying conventions: eastern cities—Boston, Philadelphia, Annapolis, and Charleston—where support for the Constitution was nearly universal. In South Carolina, the legislature decided by a single vote to hold the ratifying convention in coastal Charleston, even though legislators had recently voted to move the state capital to Columbia—in the middle of the state. One South Carolina Antifederalist objected to holding the convention in a "city where there are not fifty inhabitants who are not friendly to it [the Constitution]."

Pennsylvania Antifederalists believed that if they could situate their state's ratifying convention in Lancaster or Carlisle rather than Philadelphia, they could defeat ratification. In Massachusetts, Antifederalists proposed holding the convention in Worcester or York, Maine, while Federalists insisted on Boston.[29]

One reason that the location of ratifying conventions mattered was that it was expensive for western districts where Antifederalism was strong to send delegates to coastal cities—a factor that may have cost Massachusetts Antifederalists dozens of delegates at the state ratifying convention. Another reason that location mattered was that conventions were open to the public, and the audiences in attendance were not shy about voicing their opinions. For example, when Antifederalist delegates spoke at the Connecticut ratifying convention in Hartford, a predominantly Federalist audience, according to one Antifederalist's report, engaged in "shuffling and stamping of feet, coughing, talking, spitting and whispering." By contrast, because New York's convention was held in Poughkeepsie—not in New York City—local opinion on the Constitution was divided, as were the sympathies of the crowd attending the convention.[30]

Delegates were subject to influence not only by the spectators attending convention debates but also by the general population of the cities in which they assembled. When conventions adjourned in the evenings, delegates gathered at inns and taverns, where they mingled with the local population—which, in major cities, was overwhelmingly supportive of the Constitution. Charleston's wealthy merchants and planters held open houses during the South Carolina convention, undoubtedly filling delegates' ears with paeans to the wisdom of the Constitution.[31]

Another Federalist advantage stemmed from the geographic distribution of the Constitution's supporters and opponents. Because supporters tended to be concentrated in larger cities and along the eastern seaboard generally, they were easier to organize than their adversaries, whose strength was greatest along the frontier and outside of commercial networks. In other words, even if Federalists and Antifederalists had had equal numbers of supporters, the Federalists probably would have enjoyed the advantage because of the relative ease with which their backers could be coordinated.

Thus, Antifederalist leaders such as Richard Henry Lee of Virginia, who endeavored to coordinate opposition to ratification across states, derived little benefit from their organizing efforts. One Pennsylvania Antifederalist complained that his comrades in the central part of the state were at "a great loss . . . for intelligence" and that their allies in Philadelphia took "the least notice of us while our adversary carries on a constant intercourse with their confederates everywhere." Patrick Henry, too, lamented "the inconveniences arising from our dispersed situation." Seeking to capitalize on their organizational advantage, Federalists generally pushed for quick votes on ratification, while Antifederalists sought delay. Thus, in Massachusetts, Elbridge Gerry warned that "the supporters of the Constitution [aimed] to carry it through by surprise," and, in the fall of 1787, he expressed hope that the state legislature could be persuaded to wait until its next session to call a convention and "thus give to the people an opportunity to consider of the Constitution before they are called on to adopt it."[32]

Federalists enjoyed another enormous advantage in press coverage, which was slanted strongly in favor of the Constitution. In the late 1780s, more than 90 percent of the American population lived outside of urban areas, but almost all newspapers were published in cities—where, as we have seen, the population overwhelmingly supported ratification. Reflecting the views of both their readers and their advertisers, most publishers and editors strongly favored the Constitution and were predisposed to publish mostly—in some cases, *only*—essays supporting its ratification. Even those rare newspaper editors who believed that the concept of a free press obliged them to present both sides of important political debates often had to relent—or were fired for refusing to do so—in the face of economic boycotts launched by their overwhelmingly Federalist advertisers and readers. Federalists also tended to control printing offices and taverns, the latter of which served as unofficial post offices and thus could block circulation of Antifederalist pamphlets.[33]

Of the more than ninety American newspapers then in circulation, only twelve published any significant amount of material criticizing the Constitution. In Connecticut and New Hampshire, newspapers essentially became Federalist propaganda outlets, publishing almost nothing critical of the Constitution. One Connecticut Antifederalist complained that the state's newspapers were "evidently shut against all those that would dare and presume to write . . . against the new Constitution."* In South Carolina, leading

* Federalist publishers in Connecticut defended themselves from the charge of partisanship. The publisher of the *Connecticut Courant*, while acknowledging his private support for ratification, pledged his commitment to "the liberty of the press" and promised to publish any Antifederalist tracts that would "not disgrace [his] paper." However, he insisted that he had "not received a single essay upon the subject which contained the smallest objection [to the Constitution]." As for his not reprinting newspaper essays by Antifederalists from other states, he explained that most of these were "of a controversial nature [and] a publication of what was written on one side would be absurd, and in some cases unintelligible, except [as] it was explained by publications of what was written on the other side." In any event, he claimed to "prefer original essays whenever they can be obtained."

Likewise, the editor of the *New York Journal* dismissed as "groundless" the "many ill-natured and injudicious" assaults on his impartiality and insisted that "every performance that may be

Antifederalist Aedanus Burke complained that "the whole weight and influence of the press" was on the side of the Constitution. In Pennsylvania, Federalist publishers went so far as to deliberately distort the published account of the state ratifying convention's debates to make it appear as if the Constitution had been unopposed there. Pennsylvania Antifederalist "Centinel" objected that "the newspapers with few exceptions have been devoted to the cause of despotism," which resulted in "falsehood and deception hav[ing] had universal circulation, without the opportunity of refutation."[34]

The division of opinion on the Constitution along lines of class and education also played to the Federalists' advantage. While the relatively poor and less well-educated backwoods farmers generally were skeptical of the Constitution, the "better sort" of people—affluent, well educated, and well born—overwhelmingly supported it.[35]

Thus, Madison reported to Jefferson that in the northern and mid-Atlantic states, "the men of intelligence, patriotism, property and independent circumstances" were, with only a few exceptions, "zealously attached to the proposed Constitution." At the Massachusetts ratifying convention, one Antifederalist complained that all the "best men in the state"—the clergy, judges, and ablest lawyers—were "exerting their utmost abilities" to "gloss" the Constitution in support of its ratification. John Langdon, a New Hampshire political leader who had represented his state at the Philadelphia convention and strongly supported ratification, reported that in New Hampshire "almost every man of property and abilities" favored the Constitution. In South Carolina, Federalist David Ramsay similarly observed that with the exception of former governor Rawlins Lowndes, "the whole of the gentlemen of abilities in this state are uniformly in favor of the new constitution."[36]

The one prominent exception to this generalization was Virginia, where Madison noted that "men equally respectable in every point of character are marshaled in opposition to each other." Prominent Virginia Antifederalists included elite statesmen such as Patrick Henry, George Mason, William Grayson, and Richard Henry Lee.[37]

As a result of opinion regarding the Constitution dividing substantially along class lines (at least outside of the cities), Federalists enjoyed several distinct advantages in the ratifying conventions. Delegates selected by voters to represent them at ratifying conventions were generally better educated and more affluent than the average citizen, meaning that they were also more likely to personally support ratification. Thus, Federalists could expect the

---

written with decency [would be given] free access to his journal." Federalist printers in Boston similarly objected to charges of bias.

Constitution to fare better in ratifying conventions than in voter referenda or town meetings, which some New England Antifederalists had suggested should directly render verdicts on ratification.* Indeed, many delegates elected from districts with Antifederalist majorities ended up voting in favor of ratification—an outcome that Antifederalists regularly denounced during the ratifying campaign. One Federalist expressed confidence heading into the New York ratifying convention, despite the Antifederalists' clear majority of delegates there, because "no instance has yet happened of a federal turning antifederal, and numerous ones to the contrary."[38]

In addition, because Antifederalist delegates were, on average, poorer than their opponents, they generally found it more burdensome to be absent from home for lengthy periods of time. In the ratifying conventions that were closely contested, the fact that Antifederalist delegates were more likely to depart before a vote was taken obviously advantaged their adversaries. Thus, during the New York ratifying convention, one leading Antifederalist worried that if the business were "retarded to the disappointment of our country friends with whom it is now [late June] the busy season," then "numbers of [them] will return to their homes."[39]

Perhaps most important, the Federalists' greater education translated into a major oratorical advantage at the ratifying conventions. Backwoodsmen were neither particularly inclined nor especially able to hold their own in intellectual jousts with classically educated patricians, who could quote the ancient political philosophers in the original Greek or Latin.[40]

Thus, the Antifederalist "Centinel" complained that his adversaries had "every advantage which education, the science of government and of law, the knowledge of history and superior talents and endowments" could confer. Lamenting that his opponents had "almost all the best writers (as well as speakers) on their side," a Connecticut Antifederalist observed that his allies at the state ratifying convention "were browbeaten by many of those Ciceroes, as they think themselves, and others of superior rank, as they call themselves." At the Massachusetts ratifying convention, Antifederalist Amos Singletary complained of "[t]hese lawyers, and men of learning and moneyed men, that talk so finely, and gloss over matters so smoothly, to make us poor illiterate people swallow down the pill." In South Carolina, the aristocratic Lowndes explained that he spoke against the Constitution in the legislature because "a number of respectable members [legislators], men of good sense, though not in the habit of speaking in public," had requested that he do so.[41]

---

* This phenomenon was simply one manifestation of Madison's general maxim that better public policy—from the Federalists' perspective—would result from a political system that "refined and enlarged" public opinion.

In addition to being more skilled oratorically, Federalist speakers often received a measure of deference from the backcountry and middling Antifederalists, who were disinclined to challenge their social superiors directly. Moreover, partly to encourage such deference from ordinary citizens, the Federalist press tended to portray the Philadelphia convention as an assemblage of demigods. Indeed, some Antifederalists defended anonymous or pseudonymous newspaper contributions as essential to leveling the playing field by undermining the deference that would otherwise be extended to the social elite. Reflecting the same calculation, some Federalist newspaper publishers refused to accept unsigned contributions.[42]

Because the Federalists were generally better speakers and because many Antifederalists were intimidated into silence by a sense of inferiority regarding their talents and social status, the debates at some ratifying conventions were rather one-sided affairs. To be sure, not all ratifying conventions were genuinely deliberative bodies to begin with, as some delegates came fettered with instructions from their constituents, and others—although technically unfettered—had definitively made up their minds about the Constitution in advance.[43]

Yet in those conventions where the views of a significant number of delegates were genuinely in flux, the higher social status and superior oratorical abilities of Federalist speakers almost certainly influenced some delegates to support ratification. Thus, leading New York Antifederalist Melancton Smith expressed concern that "[t]he better sort have means of convincing those who differ with them." Similarly, New York Antifederalist Charles Tillinghast worried about the Massachusetts ratifying convention, even though Gerry had reported that a majority of the delegates there were Antifederalists, because "the more honest, though less informed, will be the more likely to be duped and cajoled by the designing ones, who will treat them with dinners, etc., etc.," and by the many Federalist clergymen who were delegates and would exercise influence "on the minds of the more ignorant, though not less virtuous, part of the community." Indeed, in several of the ratifying conventions—most notably, those of Massachusetts, New Hampshire, and New York—Antifederalists proved unable to maintain throughout the course of the proceedings the strength they had manifested in elections for convention delegates.[44]

Recognizing that genuinely deliberative conventions were to their advantage, Federalists generally opposed the practice of constituents' issuing binding instructions to convention delegates. Thus, for example, Madison worried that delegates to the Virginia ratifying convention from the region of Kentucky might "come fettered not only with prejudices but with instructions." A North Carolina Federalist sought to convince his fellow citizens that binding instructions for convention delegates were an "absurdity" because they put "a negative on the proposed constitution before debate."[45]

In Massachusetts, Federalists worried that their oratorical advantage at conventions would go for naught if town meetings simply voted upon the Constitution themselves rather than electing delegates to a ratifying convention. To encourage town meetings to support the calling of a convention, which some of them might have opposed because of the expense involved in paying their delegates, Federalists in the state legislature proposed—and the legislature agreed—that the state would pay such expenses. Partly because they knew that convention deliberations favored their cause, Federalists boycotted the one popular referendum on ratification—in Rhode Island, where voters overwhelmingly rejected the Constitution.[46]

Federalists enjoyed one other significant advantage in the ratifying contest—one they had created for themselves: the genius of Article VII of the Constitution. Under the Articles of Confederation, unanimous state consent was required for amendments—a requirement that Massachusetts congressional delegates had described in 1785 as "effectually prevent[ing] innovations in the Articles by intrigue or surprise." As we saw in chapter 1, on more than one occasion, a single holdout state had defeated a proposed amendment to confer vital revenue-raising authority on Congress. Just months before the Constitutional Convention assembled, Henry Knox had declared, "[I]t is next to an impossibility that all the states should agree to an efficient government." The delegates in Philadelphia were determined, however, not to allow the Articles' unanimity requirement to defeat their project of reform.[47]

To be sure, a few delegates to the Philadelphia convention had insisted on preserving the unanimity requirement and making the Constitution operational only upon the ratification of every state (which is what the Annapolis convention had explicitly provided for when it called for the Philadelphia convention). Thus, Roger Sherman "doubted the propriety of authorizing less than all the states to execute the Constitution, considering the nature of the existing confederation." When Rufus King proposed that ratification by nine states should be sufficient to implement the Constitution, Gerry protested "the indecency and pernicious tendency of dissolving in so slight a manner, the solemn obligations of the articles of confederation." (By this point in the convention, Gerry had decided that he would not sign the Constitution, so his support for making ratification difficult is unsurprising.)[48]

Yet with Rhode Island refusing even to participate in the convention, most delegates thought that abiding by the Articles' unanimity requirement was obviously impractical. Nathaniel Gorham declared it manifestly unreasonable that "all the states are to suffer themselves to be ruined if Rhode Island should persist in her opposition to general measures."* He also observed that "the current advantage which New York seems to be very attached to of taxing her neighbors (by the regulation of her trade) makes it very probable that she will [oppose ratification]." James Wilson agreed that the convention must not allow its handiwork "to be defeated by the inconsiderate or selfish opposition of a few states." Thus, he "hoped the provision for ratifying would be put on such a footing as to admit of such a partial union, with a door open for the accession of the rest." In the end, only Maryland's delegation voted to abide by the Articles' requirement that amendments be unanimously approved by the states.[49]

In place of unanimity, Wilson proposed that ratification by a bare majority of seven states should be sufficient to implement the Constitution. Preferring to require the concurrence of both a majority of the states and a majority of the people, Madison suggested instead that ratification by seven states should be sufficient only if those states collectively would be entitled to more than half of the representatives in the newly designed House. Other delegates suggested that the approval of ten states should be required.[50]

Urging that the convention stick with "ideas familiar to the people," Mason proposed a requirement of nine states, which was the supermajority needed for most "great" actions under the Articles. In the end, most of the delegates concurred with Mason. However, they also overwhelmingly agreed that the nine ratifying states should be able to commit only themselves. No state ought to be bound by the Constitution against its will.[51]

Notwithstanding the qualification that the nine ratifying states could bind only themselves, Article VII's rejection of a unanimity requirement dramatically altered the calculations of prospective holdout states. When, in 1786, New York had been the sole state yet to ratify the 1783 impost amendment, its legislature had tried to bargain with Congress, insisting that it would approve the amendment only if state officials collected the revenue and New York's paper money was accepted as payment. By contrast, the last states deciding whether to ratify the Constitution—after the approval of nine others had already made it operational—faced the prospect of being excluded from the

---

* At the Virginia ratifying convention, Edmund Randolph justified the Constitution's departure from the Articles' unanimity requirement on the grounds that Rhode Island, a state that had "plunder[ed] all the world by her paper money" and that was "in rebellion against integrity," should not be permitted to block enactment of the Constitution by itself. At the North Carolina ratifying convention, Richard Dobbs Spaight, who had also been a delegate to the Philadelphia convention, observed that "[t]he very refractory conduct of Rhode Island, in uniformly opposing every wise and judicious measure, taught us how impolitic it would be to put the general welfare in the power of a few members of the Union."

union, denied federal military protection, and subjected to trade sanctions.* Moreover, only those states that had ratified the Constitution would be allowed to participate in important decisions to be made by the first federal Congress, such as choosing the nation's permanent capital and possibly proposing amendments to the Constitution.[52]

As we shall see, New York's ratifying convention, which contained a decisive majority of Antifederalists, ratified the Constitution only because the requisite nine states—ten, in fact—had already done so before New York's decision was made. Thus, the choice confronting the New York convention was not whether to put the Constitution into effect but whether to become part of the new union. As Massachusetts Antifederalist Nathan Dane observed to his New York ally Melancton Smith, the longer New York and other holdout states remained outside of the new union, "the more the affections and friendship for each other" among the states would diminish, the greater the "disposition for coercive measures" would become, and the higher the likelihood of "recourse to arms . . . at no very distant period."[53]

After initially rejecting unconditional ratification, North Carolina and Rhode Island eventually changed course when they confronted the pressures that Dane described. Even at the Virginia ratifying convention, which began its deliberations when only eight states had approved the Constitution (although New Hampshire's convention was scheduled to reassemble shortly thereafter and was widely expected to ratify), some delegates probably shared Randolph's conviction that the ratification process was too far along for Virginia to reject the Constitution without jeopardizing the union.[54]

In addition to eliminating the unanimity requirement for changes to the Articles, the Constitution provided for ratification by special conventions called by state legislatures rather than by those legislatures themselves. Most of the state constitutions of the 1770s were written by legislatures, not specially elected conventions, and until the Massachusetts constitution of 1780 was submitted for ratification to town meetings, every state had implemented its constitution through legislative action.[55]

To be sure, a few delegates at the Philadelphia convention argued that state legislatures were the proper entities to pass judgment on the Constitution. Sherman contended that "a popular ratification [was] unnecessary, the Articles of Confederation providing for changes and alterations with the assent of Congress and ratification of state legislatures." Oliver Ellsworth agreed: When the Confederation Congress had sought amendments to expand its power,

---

* New York Antifederalists later objected that the threats made against those states resisting ratification after nine others had put the Constitution into effect were "the language of tyrants and an insult on the understandings of a free people."

those proposals had gone to state legislatures for approval, not to the people, as assembled in special conventions. The Philadelphia convention must not ignore the fact, Ellsworth insisted, that the United States existed "as a federal society, united by a charter, one article of which is that alterations therein may be made by the legislative authority of the states." Maryland delegates Luther Martin and Daniel Carroll objected that their state's constitution, which would be effectively amended by the federal Constitution, made no provision for alterations through popularly elected conventions. Gerry warned against referring the Constitution to conventions because the people of New England currently had "the wildest ideas of government in the world"—an allusion to Shays's Rebellion. Gouverneur Morris proposed that states be allowed to choose their own method of ratification.[56]

Yet other delegates strongly disagreed. Even before the Philadelphia convention, Madison had told Jefferson, who had himself objected that the 1776 Virginia constitution was not subject to a requirement of popular ratification, that it would be "expedient in the first place to lay the foundation of the new system in such a ratification by the people themselves of the several states." As Madison explained in his essay on the Articles' vices, because the Articles had been ratified only by state legislatures, it was "at least questionable" which law should prevail when state legislation conflicted with federal. At the Philadelphia convention, Madison argued that ratification of the Constitution by popularly elected conventions would clarify that congressional legislation enacted in pursuance of delegated powers was "legally paramount to the acts of the states."[57]

Madison and other delegates noted additional theoretical advantages to ratification of the Constitution by special conventions. The proposed Constitution "would make essential inroads on the state constitutions," Madison observed, "and it would be a novel and dangerous doctrine that a legislature could change the constitution under which it held its existence." Mason agreed that state legislatures were "the mere creatures of the state constitutions" that had established them and that those state constitutions conferred no powers upon legislatures to ratify a federal constitution. Thus, it was necessary to look to the people, "with whom all power remains that has not been given up in the constitutions derived from them." Mason also noted that state legislatures had no authority to bind their successors—thus the Constitution, if ratified only by legislatures, "would stand in each state on the weak and tottering foundation of an act of assembly."[58]

Madison also argued that the choice of whether the Constitution would be ratified by state legislatures or by special conventions represented "the true difference between a league or treaty and a constitution." In turn, there were two "important distinctions" between a treaty and a constitution. First, judges would feel obliged to invalidate laws violating a constitution but not those in-consistent with a treaty. Second, under the law of nations, one party's breach of any article in a treaty "frees the other parties from their engagements." By con-trast, "a union of people under one Constitution ... has always been under-stood to exclude such an interpretation." Because Madison wanted judges to invalidate unconstitutional laws and did not wish states to be free to dissolve the union simply because the Constitution had been violated, he preferred that the Constitution not be regarded as a mere treaty, which led him to favor rati-fication by special conventions.[59]

In sum, Madison considered it "indispensable" that the Constitution be ratified "by the supreme authority of the people themselves." Mason agreed that referring the Constitution to the people—popular sovereignty—was "one of the most important and essential" aspects of the scheme. Although believ-ing that state legislatures were competent to decide upon ratification, King also preferred a reference to special ratifying conventions "as the most certain means of obviating all disputes and doubts concerning the legitimacy of the new Constitution."[60]

Delegates to the Philadelphia convention also made the pragmatic point that state legislatures would be less inclined to approve the Constitution than would special ratifying conventions. Randolph thought it would be "highly imprudent" to refer the Constitution to state legislatures, which were more subject to influence by "the local demagogues who will be degraded by it [the Constitution] from the importance they now hold." Madison agreed that, "the powers given to the general government being taken from the state govern-ments, the legislatures would be more disinclined [to ratify] than conventions composed in part at least of other men." King went even further, noting that to refer ratification to state legislatures, which would be the "most likely to raise objections" because they would be losing power under the Constitution, would be "equivalent to giving up the business altogether."[61]

Moreover, state legislatures—with the exception of those in Pennsylvania and Georgia—were bicameral, while ratifying conventions would be unicam-eral. Consequently, Gorham observed, it would be "more difficult ... to get the plan through the legislatures than through a convention." In addition, he explained that legislatures were likely to be "interrupted with a variety of little business," which "designing men" might "artfully press" to supply the "means to delay from year to year, if not to frustrate altogether the national system." Finally, Gorham argued that "many of the ablest men [were] excluded from the legislatures"—such as clergymen, who were barred from serving in legis-latures in several states on the grounds of the separation of church and state— "but may be elected into a convention." King agreed that conventions were "the most likely means of drawing forth the best men in the states to decide on it." Because the "best men" were disproportionately likely to support ratification, as we have seen, this was yet another reason why special conventions would be more likely than state legislatures to approve the Constitution.[62]

In sum, the Federalists enjoyed numerous advantages in the ratifying contest. Some of those advantages derived from good luck or the way in which public opinion happened to divide over the Constitution. Still other advantages were attributable to the manner in which the Federalists themselves had structured the ratifying process. Yet despite all their advantages, the Federalists barely managed to convince the American people to approve the Constitution.[63]

First Steps Toward Ratification

Let us turn our attention now to the story of the Constitution's ratification. The delegates to the Philadelphia convention had agreed that the Constitution would first be transmitted to the Confederation Congress in New York City. However, they disagreed as to whether Congress should be treated as a mere messenger to pass the Constitution along to the states or as an actor of genuine consequence that would be invited to approve or disapprove the document it was transmitting.[64]

The report of the convention's Committee of Detail had provided that the Constitution would be laid before Congress "assembled for [its] approbation." Gerry strongly defended this provision: Not requiring Congress's approval would give "just umbrage to that body." Hamilton, who rarely saw eye to eye with Gerry during the convention, agreed "as to the indecorum of not requiring the approbation of Congress."[65]

However, Gouverneur Morris moved to strike that requirement, and Charles Pinckney seconded his motion. Thomas FitzSimons of Pennsylvania argued that eliminating this provision would "save Congress from the necessity of an act inconsistent with the Articles of Confederation under which [Congress] held [its] authority." Wilson argued strongly against requiring congressional approval. For one thing, it would be "worse than folly to rely on the concurrence of the Rhode Island members of the Congress in the plan." In addition, given that New York had not had a voting delegation at the convention since early July and that many delegates from other states had spoken against the Constitution, could "it be safe to make the assent of Congress necessary?" Wilson warned that "[a]fter spending four or five months in the laborious and arduous task of forming a government for our country, we are ourselves at the close throwing insuperable obstacles in the way of its success." The convention then voted by eight states to three against requiring congressional approbation.[66]

In the end, the Philadelphia convention resolved instead that the Constitution "be laid before the United States in Congress assembled" and that it was the convention's "opinion . . . that it should afterwards be submitted to a convention of delegates, chosen in each state by the people thereof, under the recommendation of its legislature, for their assent and ratification." By this declaration, neither Congress nor the state legislatures were invited to debate or express an opinion on whether the Constitution should be ratified. One Antifederalist later called it "remarkable" that the convention would treat Congress and the state legislatures as mere "vehicles of conveyance" precluded from "passing their judgments on the system." What right did the convention have to tell either Congress or the state legislatures what to do?[67]

The Framers' plan immediately encountered difficulties. Even before Congress began to consider the Constitution, Virginia congressional delegate Edward Carrington warned Madison that "the same schism which unfortunately happened in our state in Philadelphia"—an allusion to the refusal of Randolph and Mason to sign the Constitution—"threatens us here [i.e., in Congress] also." Carrington reported that Richard Henry Lee was formulating "propositions for essential alterations in the Constitution, which will, in effect, be to oppose it." In addition, Carrington noted, another of Virginia's congressional delegates, William Grayson, "dislikes it" and was, "at best, for giving it only a silent passage to the states." Carrington warned that "[a] lukewarmness in Congress will be made a ground of opposition by the unfriendly in the states."[68]

When Congress turned its attention to the Constitution in late September 1787, Federalists strongly opposed any debate on the merits of the document. Worried that lengthy congressional debates and roll-call votes on particular provisions would only rally opposition to ratification, Federalists argued that Congress should simply forward the Constitution to the states—hopefully, with its approbation. Massachusetts congressional delegate Nathan Dane, who had serious objections to the Constitution, reported that its "warmest friends . . . appeared to be extremely impatient to get it through Congress, even the first day that it was taken up; they wanted Congress to approve of it, but objected to any examinations of it by paragraphs in the usual mode of doing business."[69]

Congressional delegates faced two principal questions regarding their posture toward the Constitution. First, should they consider amendments to it? Second, should they *approve* the Constitution or simply *transmit* it to the states?

Richard Henry Lee argued that Congress should treat the document drafted by the Philadelphia convention as it would any committee report—which it would be free to amend in any way it liked. Lee urged that before

Congress forwarded the Constitution to the states, it should propose amendments to accompany it—especially a bill of rights. The idea that Congress could propose no amendments was the "strangest doctrine he ever heard." Denying that "all wisdom centers in the convention," Lee also argued that for Congress to propose amendments would enhance the prospect of state ratification by removing objections to the Constitution. Finally, Lee wondered if the Federalists intended to preclude the states—as well as Congress—from offering amendments. Privately, he complained to Mason that "[i]t was with us, as with you [at the convention], this or nothing; and this urged with a most extreme intemperance."[70]

The Federalists, for their part, were determined to prevent Congress from proposing amendments. Although Madison, who had traveled from Philadelphia to New York City to join the Virginia congressional delegation (for the first time since he had been rotated out of office in 1783), at first contested Congress's right to suggest amendments, he eventually agreed that Congress could amend the Constitution but offered extensive arguments against its doing so.[71]

Madison explained those arguments in a letter to Washington. Because the "introduction of Congress as a party to the reform was intended by the states merely as a matter of form and respect," it would be improper for Congress to propose amendments to the handiwork of a convention that had originated with the states. Moreover, the states approving the call for the convention had intended that "the plan to be proposed should be the act of the Philadelphia convention with the assent of Congress, which could not be the case if alterations were made, the convention being no longer in existence to adopt them." Thus, if Congress did propose amendments, there would effectively be two proposed constitutions, and some states might ratify one and some the other, and "confusion and disappointment will be the least evils that could ensue." Furthermore, if Congress were to alter the Constitution, then it would become the act of Congress, not the convention, and the Articles of Confederation would then apply, meaning that the *unanimous* consent of state *legislatures* would be required for ratification.[72]

Finally, Madison made the practical argument that Congress would never agree on which amendments were necessary. As he explained to Washington, "[I]t was evident from the contradictory objections which had been expressed by the different members who had animadverted on the plan, that a discussion of its merits would consume much time, without producing agreement even among its adversaries." Madison also insisted that there was nothing unusual about proposing systems of government on a take-it-or-leave-it basis. The Continental Congress, he noted, had refused to recognize amendments to the Articles of Confederation that many states had proposed when ratifying the Articles.[73]

The Federalists not only wished to avoid amendments but even wanted to secure what Richard Henry Lee referred to as "respectful marks of approbation" from Congress when it transmitted the Constitution to the states. Madison told Congress that if it "does not agree [with the Constitution], it implies a disagreement. . . . The question is, whether on the whole it is best to adopt it, and [we] ought to say so." Carrington then introduced a motion that indicated that Congress, in transmitting the Constitution to the states, "agree[d]" with it. Madison later explained to Washington that obtaining Congress's approval "would have been of advantage in this [New York] and some other states, where stress will be laid on the agency of Congress in the matter."[74]

However, the Antifederalists' position, in Madison's words, was that "there was a constitutional impropriety in [Congress's] taking any positive agency in the work" because the Constitution "subverted these Articles altogether." Indeed, Dane had begun these congressional debates by proposing a motion declaring that Congress, while agreeing to transmit the Constitution to the states out of deference to the people and an acknowledgment of the issue's importance, criticized the Philadelphia convention for clearly exceeding its authority and, consequently, refused to express an opinion on the merits of the Constitution.[75]

To that argument, Federalists responded, as Madison explained to Washington, that because Congress "had recommended the Convention as the best mean[s] of obtaining a firm national government" and because "the powers of the Convention were defined by [Congress's resolution endorsing it] in nearly the same terms with the powers of Congress given by the Confederation on the subject of alterations, Congress [was] not more restrained from acceding to the new plan than the convention [was] from proposing it." Furthermore, even if the convention had exceeded its authority in proposing the Constitution, "the same necessity which justified the Convention would justify Congress" in approving the Constitution. This would not be the first time, Madison told his fellow congressional delegates, that Congress had recommended something that was beyond its powers to recommend.[76]

The fact that ten of the thirty-three congressional delegates present had participated in the Philadelphia convention certainly helped the Federalists get most of what they wanted from Congress. In a letter to Samuel Adams, Richard Henry Lee objected that a Congress containing so many delegates from the Philadelphia convention could not give "a dispassionate and impartial consideration" to the Constitution. Nevertheless, Lee was determined to propose amendments, including a bill of rights, and he initially demanded that a vote on them be recorded in Congress's journal—a demand that he told Randolph seemed "to alarm" his opponents.[77]

After two days of debate, which Madison told Washington had "threatened a serious division in Congress," a compromise was reached. Lee abandoned his demand for a vote on amendments—a vote he clearly would have lost, given the composition of Congress. Moreover, any mention of opposition to the Constitution that had been voiced in Congress was to be stricken from its journals. In exchange, Federalists agreed that Congress would simply "transmit" the Constitution to state legislatures "in order to be submitted" to special ratifying conventions, in conformity with the resolutions of the Philadelphia convention. As Lee explained, this transmission would occur "without a syllable of approbation or disapprobation." However, Federalists then managed to add the word "unanimously" to the resolution on transmission. Lee complained that while unanimity had characterized only the act of transmission, Federalists hoped "to have it mistaken for a unanimous approbation of the thing."[78]

Although Madison triumphantly reported to Washington that "[t]he circumstance of unanimity must be favorable everywhere," he complained to Jefferson of the "very serious effort" in Congress made by Lee and Dane "to embarrass" the convention's plan. Though Lee's proposal for amendments had been easily defeated, "[i]n order, however, to obtain unanimity, it was necessary to couch the resolution in very moderate terms."[79]

In reply, Washington assured Madison that a unanimous, albeit "feeble," vote by Congress on the Constitution was preferable to one with "stronger marks of approbation" that lacked unanimity. He was confident that "[t]his apparent unanimity will have its effect. Not everyone has opportunities to peep behind the curtain; and as the multitude often judge from externals, the appearance of unanimity in that body, on this occasion, will be of great importance." Indeed, the Antifederalist "Sidney" later complained that while Congress had "barely" agreed to transmit the Constitution to state legislatures, without its endorsement, newspapers had reported Congress's "unanimous consent" to the Constitution.[80]

The resolution drafted by the Philadelphia convention to accompany the Constitution provided that once Congress transmitted it to the states, it should "be submitted to a convention of delegates, chosen in each state by the people thereof, under the recommendation of its legislature, for their assent and ratification." Only these ratifying conventions, as Madison reflected years later, could breathe "life and validity" into the Constitution, which was "nothing more than the draft of a plan, nothing but a dead letter" when proposed by the Philadelphia convention.[81]

At the convention, Gouverneur Morris had proposed amending the resolution that would accompany the Constitution to provide that state legislatures ought to call conventions "as speedily as circumstances will permit." Morris explained that his "object was to impress in stronger terms the necessity of calling conventions in order to prevent enemies to the plan from giving it the go by." Yet the convention had rejected Morris's motion by a vote of seven states to four. The majority of delegates may have been leery of the convention's adopting too peremptory a tone toward state legislatures. After all, even if Morris's proposal had passed, the convention had no means of forcing state legislatures to comply with its will.[82]

Yet, despite John Lansing's warning at the convention that "[t]he states will never sacrifice their essential rights to a national government," every state legislature but Rhode Island's fairly quickly agreed to call a ratifying convention (and even the Rhode Island legislature conducted a referendum on ratification). Even in states that would manifest formidable opposition to ratification, legislatures easily—often unanimously—agreed to call conventions.[83]

In a letter to Washington, Morris offered an explanation of why they did so. Observing that a majority of legislators in New York probably wished to reject the Constitution, Morris predicted that they would nonetheless call a ratifying convention because they could not "assign to the people any good reason for not trusting them with a decision on their own affairs." Indeed, when the New York legislature later debated whether to summon a convention, Federalist senator James Duane asked, "Is there a man among us so hardy as to say that the people shall not have an opportunity of judging for themselves? In such case, would not the legislature exhibit a high stretch of arbitrary power? And instead of being the guardians, they would be the tyrants of the people." Similarly, when the Massachusetts House of Representatives debated summoning a convention, one member stated that it was "impossible that we can refuse to the people what I think is their unquestionable right," and another declared that "we have no right to deprive them of this privilege, unless we will undertake to think for them in this instance, which they never employed us to do, and which they have reserved for themselves."[84]

Meeting at different times, state legislatures called for elections of delegates to special ratifying conventions, which were scheduled to meet over a period of roughly nine months, from the late fall of 1787 through the summer of 1788. Legislatures in several of the smaller states—Connecticut, Delaware, Georgia, and New Jersey—acted quickly on the Constitution simply because they happened to be in session soon after the Philadelphia convention ended. Within weeks of the convention's conclusion, these legislatures had scheduled elections for delegates to ratifying conventions, which were set to assemble within a couple of months.[85]

The conventions in these small states, in turn, quickly and decisively ratified the Constitution. Indeed, the conventions in Delaware, New Jersey, and Georgia *unanimously* approved it, and the margin in favor of ratification in

Connecticut was more than three to one—a "very smooth and easy" verdict, as Madison had predicted. Even though these states had endured deep political divisions over various issues in the 1780s, including fiscal and monetary policy—differences that had occasionally erupted into violence—opinion on the Constitution was overwhelmingly favorable.[86]

There are several reasons why the smaller states so easily determined to ratify the Constitution. First and probably most important, their delegations had extracted a tremendous concession at the Philadelphia convention in the form of equal state representation in the Senate. When Roger Sherman and Oliver Ellsworth, two of Connecticut's delegates to the Philadelphia convention, sent their report on the Constitution and the convention to their governor, they emphasized that "this state's proportion of suffrage [in Congress] remained the same" as under the Articles and that "[t]he equal representation of the states in the Senate and the voice of that branch in the appointment to offices will secure the rights of the lesser as well as the greater states." A New Jersey delegate to Congress told a Delaware legislator that "when I reflect that the smaller states are admitted to an equal representation in the Senate with the larger, it appears to me a circumstance much more favorable than I could have expected and ought to satisfy your state in particular." When New Hampshire's ratifying convention initially adjourned without approving the Constitution, Washington expressed surprise because the proposed system "holds out advantages to the smaller states equal, at least, to their most sanguine expectations." Conversely, in large states such as Massachusetts and Virginia, Antifederalists regularly criticized the Constitution on the grounds that it was "quite ridiculous" that "petty states" such as Delaware and Rhode Island should enjoy equal voting power in the Senate.[87]

Second, while a large state such as Virginia might have been able to survive outside of the union—or at least could credibly threaten to do so—small states such as Delaware and Georgia obviously could not. Imbalances in power between the differently sized states, which had vexed small-state political leaders before and during the Constitutional Convention, would be greatly exacerbated should the Constitution be rejected and the union consequently dissolved. The need for physical security from the possible depredations of their larger neighbors and foreign nations supplied small states with a powerful incentive to ratify the Constitution.[88]

Thus, the Federalist "Landholder" told New Hampshire residents that "the adoption of this Constitution is the only probable means of saving the greatest part of your state from becoming an appendage of Canada or Nova Scotia," for "[s]hould a disunion of the states tempt Britain to make another effort for recovering her former greatness, you will be the first to fall under her sway." In the summer of 1788, the Rhode Island Federalist "Phocion" explained that the "natural and powerful reason" why the smaller states had been "much more unanimous on the question of ratifying the new Constitution than the larger ones" was that they "clearly saw that if the Constitution was rejected, in the hurly-burly of confusion and anarchy which would arise, they should be swallowed up by their more powerful neighbors."[89]

Third, certain small states had their own particular reasons for supporting ratification. One of the Constitution's principal attractions to Delaware, New Jersey, and Connecticut was the promise of being liberated from the hated impost duties paid to neighboring states blessed with better ports of entry—specifically, New York City and Philadelphia. As Gorham had explained at the Philadelphia convention, if the union dissolved because no constitution was agreed upon, "the fate of New Jersey would be worst of all. She has no foreign commerce and can have but little. Pennsylvania and New York will continue to levy taxes on her consumption."[90]

Under the Constitution, by contrast, only the federal government would be allowed to lay import duties, which meant that consumers of foreign imports in these small states would no longer have to subsidize the operating expenses of their neighbors' governments. Thus, "Landholder" urged New Hampshire residents to ratify the Constitution to secure their "just share in that revenue" that would inevitably "be collected in the great importing towns," none of which were located in New Hampshire. He similarly argued for ratification in Connecticut on the grounds that the Constitution would end New York's ability to "draw an annual tribute of forty thousand pounds from the citizens of Connecticut." One Massachusetts Antifederalist lamented that Connecticut had ratified the Constitution "more from irritation and resentment to a sister state . . . than from a comprehensive view of the system."[91]

Under the Confederation, 72 percent of the expenditures of Delaware's government had gone to obligations that would disappear under the Constitution: interest payments on soldiers' certificates, congressional requisitions, and payment of congressional delegates' salaries. Without a major port through which to extract import duties and lacking western lands to sell, Delaware had been forced to raise most of its revenue from internal taxes. Under the Constitution, by contrast, Congress would raise revenue from its own impost and the sale of western lands that had been ceded to it, and states would not have to pay requisitions. Moreover, if Congress were to assume the states' wartime debts, Delaware would be able to further reduce the tax burden on its citizens.[92]

The hope of being chosen as the site of the new national capital—which, according to one Massachusetts Antifederalist, would "naturally attract the intercourse of strangers, the youth of enterprise, and the wealth of the nation to the central states"—also generated support for the Constitution in Delaware and New Jersey (as well as in the large state of Pennsylvania). Just before the Philadelphia convention, Madison noted that southerners had long resented the "very eccentric position of Congress"—since 1785, in New York City, well north of the nation's latitudinal center—which produced "very substantial inconveniences . . . to the southern states from their remoteness from the seat of government." In addition to travel difficulties, which discouraged the attendance in Congress of delegates from distant states, Madison observed that "from the nature of things, the interests and views of the states nearest to Congress will always press more on [its] attention." Thus, Madison believed that had Congress sat in Pittsburgh, it was "morally certain . . . that a surrender of the Mississippi would not have had two votes."* He also predicted that congressional delegates from the southern states would "seize the first moment" for changing the site of Congress.[93]

Indeed, in the spring of 1787, just before the Philadelphia convention assembled, a proposal by southern delegates in Congress to move its residence back to Philadelphia from New York City had failed by just one delegation's vote. The Constitutional Convention had then broached the subject when some southern delegates defended a provision permitting the two houses of Congress to agree to adjourn to another place without the president's consent. While King of Massachusetts objected that "[t]he mutability of place had dishonored the federal government and would require as strong a cure as we could devise," Spaight of North Carolina argued that without such a provision, Congress would "never be able to remove [from New York], especially if the president should be a northern man." During this debate, Madison observed that a central location, which would enable Congress to "contemplate with the most equal eye and sympathize most equally with every part of the nation," would be even more critical under the new government that the convention was designing, which would have greater power and more members representing interior parts of the nation, who could not easily travel to Congress.[94]

During the ratifying contest, many political leaders in the mid-Atlantic states seemed to believe that quick and decisive votes in favor of ratification would enhance the prospects of their states being chosen to house the new national capital. A substantial majority of the delegates at Delaware's ratifying convention agreed to cede land on behalf of the people of the state to

---

* In the mid-1780s, those opposed to Robert Morris's schemes for expanding the national government's powers over public finance had sought to move Congress from Philadelphia because, as "the bosom of Toryism," that city exerted an "unhealthy and dangerous" influence over national politics. Arthur Lee, a congressional delegate from Virginia, thought that "Mr. Robert Morris's undue and wicked influence depends so much upon [Congress's] residence here [in Philadelphia]."

entice Congress to locate the federal capital there. Benjamin Franklin had recommended a similar ploy to the Pennsylvania Assembly the day after the Constitutional Convention ended, and the Pennsylvania ratifying convention followed his advice; the New Jersey ratifying convention did the same. At the Virginia convention, Patrick Henry complained that Delaware's desire to become the national capital—"with all [its] concomitant emoluments"—had "operated so powerfully" as to lead it to ratify the Constitution "without taking time to reflect."[95]

The small state of Georgia had its own additional reason for ratifying the Constitution: It desperately needed federal military assistance in its violent confrontations with Indian tribes. As Georgians migrated westward in great numbers in the 1770s and 1780s—under its royal charter, Georgia claimed territory all the way to the Mississippi River—they increasingly encroached on the lands of Creek Indians, who were unwilling to cede them without a fight. The Georgia legislature that called a ratifying convention in the fall of 1787 had been summoned into special session to deal with what the governor called an "unavoidable" war with the Creeks, and it passed a law to raise an army of several thousand men. A New Hampshire congressional delegate observed at the time that his Georgia colleagues were "under the greatest apprehensions of an open war with the Creek nation, which . . . consists of seven or eight thousand fighting men." Joseph Clay, a Savannah merchant and Georgia political leader, declared that he had "reason to apprehend that we are involved in a general Indian war." Dozens of people had already been killed on both sides, and continuation of the war portended, according to Clay, "the most ruinous consequences to this state."[96]

Soon after the conclusion of the Philadelphia convention, William Grayson predicted that ratification was "highly probable" in Georgia, which was "at present very much embarrassed with an Indian war, and in great distress." Likewise, Washington declared that if Georgia, "a weak state, with powerful tribes of Indians in its rear, and the Spaniards on its flank [i.e., in Florida]," did not "embrace a strong general government there must, I should think, be either wickedness or insanity in [its] conduct."[97]

Indeed, Georgia's ratifying convention unanimously approved the Constitution after less than two full days of deliberation. The Antifederalist "A Columbian Patriot" lamented that "Georgia, apprehensive of a war with the savages, has acceded [to the Constitution] in order to insure protection." Even though Georgians were generally suspicious of centralized government power—the Georgia legislature had initially voted against even sending delegates to the Philadelphia convention—they believed that ratification of the Constitution, as Clay observed, was essential to "avoid[ing] this great evil, an Indian war."[98]

While these four small states acted quickly on the Constitution, the large state of Pennsylvania was actually the first state to call a ratifying convention. So determined were Pennsylvania Federalists for a quick victory that they nearly overplayed their hand.

Of all the state legislatures, only that of Pennsylvania was in session when the Constitutional Convention ended its business on September 17, 1787. (Indeed, the Pennsylvania Assembly had had to vacate its chamber for the use of the convention.) But the Assembly was set to adjourn on September 29. The day before adjournment, Federalists introduced resolutions to call a state ratifying convention, even though word had not yet arrived from New York City as to Congress's disposition toward the Constitution. Currently in control of the Assembly, Federalists did not wish to wait another several months for the next legislative session in order to initiate the ratifying process, especially given that intervening state elections might cost them their legislative majority. Arguing that Congress's posture toward the Constitution was irrelevant to the Assembly's decision, Federalist legislators insisted on an immediate call for a ratifying convention—even though copies of the Constitution had not yet circulated throughout the state's western counties.[99]

Antifederalists, wishing to delay action until after the state legislative elections and the meeting of the new Assembly, questioned the need for such a precipitate response. They argued that the Assembly should await Congress's verdict on the Constitution, that the people of the state required time to consider the proposed Constitution, and that the upcoming state elections would essentially enable voters to instruct their representatives on ratification. Because the Constitution "ought to be dispassionately and deliberately examined," the Antifederalist "Centinel" objected to the "frenzy of enthusiasm that has actuated the citizens of Philadelphia [who had petitioned the Assembly for quick action] in their approbation of the proposed plan before it was possible that it could be the result of a rational investigation into its principles."[100]

To slow down the rush toward ratification, nineteen Antifederalists absented themselves from the Assembly, depriving it of the necessary two-thirds quorum.* The Federalists responded by sending the Assembly's sergeant-at-arms to force the return of two assemblymen to meet the quorum. This was accomplished—with the assistance of a mob. The Assembly then set elections in early November—a concession by Federalists, who had initially pushed for an even earlier date—for a convention to meet two weeks afterward.[101]

---

* One Federalist later denounced this "seceding from the legislature" as an abandonment of duty and "the most bare-faced act of tyranny and wickedness."

Most contemporaries predicted that ratification in Pennsylvania would be closely fought. In October, Gouverneur Morris told Washington that the outcome in Pennsylvania was uncertain. Philadelphia and its environs were "enthusiastic in the cause," but Morris feared "the cold and sour temper of the back counties" as well as "the wicked industry" of state officeholders. Around the same time, Madison told Jefferson that Pennsylvania would be "divided," with backers of the Constitution including Philadelphians, critics of the state constitution, Quakers,* and most Germans, while the western country and defenders of the state constitution would be opposed. William Shippen, Jr., the brother-in-law of Richard Henry Lee and a prominent Philadelphia physician, predicted before the outcome of the elections for convention delegates was known that Federalists would win a slender majority of no more than "five or six," but that "a very respectable minority" would offer "a severe and pointed protest."[102]

The ratifying contest in Pennsylvania proved to be largely an extension of a decade-long battle in state politics. Pennsylvania's constitution of 1776 was the most radically democratic in the nation. It abolished property requirements for both voting and officeholding, which meant that roughly 90 percent of the adult male population could participate in politics. It also established a weak executive and a unicameral legislature that was required to hold public sessions, to publish records of its proceedings, and to have bills published for a period of time before they could be enacted. Pennsylvania conservatives had been trying to amend the state constitution virtually since it had been adopted; their primary objectives were to secure a second house for the legislature, a stronger executive, and a more independent judiciary.[103]

In 1787, Pennsylvania conservatives hoped that a sizable victory for ratification would enable them to secure sufficient control over state politics to adopt a new state constitution. Most of the opposition to the federal Constitution in the state came from the "constitutionalists"—those who supported the 1776 state constitution. Thus, the Federalist "Landholder" observed that the fight over the Constitution in Pennsylvania was just the "old warfare carried on with different weapons." When one faction declared in favor of the federal Constitution, that was "a sufficient motive for the other to oppose it." Likewise, Madison reported to Jefferson that "[t]he cause of the inflammation

---

* After James Neal, a Quaker preacher from Maine, had criticized the Constitution at the Massachusetts ratifying convention because of the provision forbidding Congress to bar the foreign slave trade for twenty years, Massachusetts Federalist Jeremy Belknap had inquired of his Pennsylvania ally Benjamin Rush how Pennsylvania's Quakers were disposed toward ratification. Rush replied that with just a few exceptions, Pennsylvania's Quakers were "highly Federal." Indeed, all eight of the Quakers at the Pennsylvania ratifying convention supported ratification.

[in Pennsylvania] . . . is much more in their state factions than in the system proposed by the Constitution."[104]

Federalists won a much larger victory in the election for convention delegates than was generally expected. Newspapers estimated that they would enjoy a majority of two to one at the convention.* Not surprisingly, the election also revealed a stark regional division, with the eastern portion of the state voting overwhelmingly for Federalist candidates and the western counties for Antifederalists.[105]

During the convention's three weeks of deliberations that began on November 20, Antifederalists repeatedly challenged the "precipitancy" of the proceedings. On the merits, they raised the usual Antifederalist objections to the Constitution: its "consolidationist" tendencies, the excessive power granted to Congress, the departure from annual elections, the inadequacy of representation in the federal government which would promote a tendency toward "aristocracy," and the omission of a bill of rights.[106†]

Antifederalists, recognizing that they were badly outnumbered and had no chance to defeat ratification, argued that at least they ought to be permitted to propose amendments. However, Federalists insisted that the convention had the power only to approve or reject the Constitution, not to "alter and amend" it.[107]

Some Antifederalists also proposed adjourning the convention for several months on the grounds that the people needed time to "examine . . . with care and attention" a system of government that "contains a total abolition of the existing Confederation" and that was so radically different from what was "generally expected" of the Philadelphia convention. Such a delay, they argued, could not "occasion any delay to the union," since several states were not holding their conventions for another six months or so. In addition, an adjournment would enable the people of Pennsylvania to consider what amendments to the Constitution they might favor and to learn what amendments other states proposed. Federalists, however, easily defeated the motion for adjournment.[108]

In the end, Federalists would not even permit their adversaries to record on the convention journal their reasons for objecting to the Constitution or their

---

* Antifederalists attributed their poor showing in the election to the fact that "the greater part of the people had [not] sufficiently recovered from their surprise" at what the Philadelphia convention proposed "to know what part to take in it, or how to give their suffrages. They therefore remained inactive."

† James Wilson, the only member of the Pennsylvania delegation to the Constitutional Convention to serve as a delegate to the state ratifying convention, dominated the proceedings from the Federalist side. One sympathetic observer reported to Thomas Jefferson that Wilson exerted himself to "the astonishment of all hearers. The powers of Demosthenes and Cicero seemed to be united in this able orator."

proposed amendments to it. To note the Antifederalists' reasons for opposing ratification on the journal, Federalists argued, would needlessly increase
the cost to taxpayers of printing it, and listing their proposed amendments
on the journal would make it appear as if opposition to the Constitution in
Pennsylvania was greater than was actually the case. On December 13, 1787,
by a vote of forty-six to twenty-three, the Pennsylvania ratifying convention became the second in the country—after Delaware's—to approve the
Constitution.[109]

However, the aggressive tactics that Pennsylvania Federalists had used to
secure a quick ratification proved costly. Antifederalists, in light of the mis-
treatment they felt they had endured ever since the legislature had first taken
up the Constitution, did not regard their defeat at the convention as a sufficient
reason to abandon their cause. Dissenting members of the convention filed an
address that circulated across the country and attracted special attention because of the coercive tactics used against its authors. They complained specifically of the "violence and outrage" used to assemble a legislative quorum to
enable the calling of a convention and more generally of the "tar and feathers
[that] were liberally promised to all those who would not immediately join in
supporting the proposed government."[110]

Pennsylvania Antifederalists also launched a petition campaign to condemn the Constitutional Convention for exceeding its powers and to call upon
the Pennsylvania Assembly to refuse to confirm the results of the state ratifying convention. By the end of March 1788, petitions containing more than six
thousand signatures had been submitted to the Assembly.[111]

Federalists denounced their opponents' unwillingness to acquiesce to the
majority's verdict on the Constitution as "downright rebellion" and as "obstinate, base, and politically wicked." Yet they also worried, as Madison told
Washington a few weeks after the Pennsylvania convention ended, that the
Antifederalists were "very restless under their defeat" and would "endeavor
to undermine what has been done there" if they could regain control of the
Assembly. Madison was especially worried because the ratifying convention
had now assembled in Massachusetts, and if it rejected the Constitution, the
Pennsylvania dissenters "will probably be emboldened to make some more
rash experiment."[112]

Running into Snags in New England

The quick and relatively easy ratifications by Pennsylvania and several of the
smaller states helped build momentum in favor of the Constitution. For example, newspapers in Connecticut, which would become the fifth state to ratify,

reported on the unanimous votes in favor of the Constitution in Delaware and New Jersey, thus creating a drumbeat of positive news on ratification. Both sides in the ratifying contest understood that one state's decision on ratification—especially if it was a large state's—would influence the choice of states deciding later. Reflecting on the significant number of states (eight) that had ratified the Constitution by the time of the Virginia convention, Washington told Madison, "I do not mean that numbers alone [are] sufficient to produce conviction in the mind, but I think [they are] enough to produce some change in the conduct of any man who entertains a doubt of his infallibility." Because of this influence that states' actions had upon one another, both Federalists and Antifederalists urged their allies across the nation to keep them closely apprised of positive developments in the ratification process.[113]

Furthermore, the states that ratified early in the process established a precedent for unconditional ratification—that is, ratification without antecedent amendments. As Massachusetts Antifederalist Nathan Dane later reflected, "[W]hen a few states had adopted without any alterations, the ground was materially changed." Had one of the states that were quick to decide rejected the Constitution or insisted on amendments before approval, the chances of defeating ratification would have been materially enhanced.[114]

The Federalists' campaign for ratification hit its first significant snags in New England. To be sure, on January 9, 1788, Connecticut became the fifth state to ratify the Constitution—much to the relief of Massachusetts Federalists, whose ratifying convention assembled that same day and most of whom had been following the Connecticut proceedings with great avidity. Massachusetts and New Hampshire were the sixth and seventh states to hold ratifying conventions. Massachusetts was the second of the large states—Pennsylvania had been the first—to hold a convention and the first of any state in which the outcome was seriously in doubt.[115]

Across the country, interested observers anxiously awaited the result of the Massachusetts convention, which they widely assumed would greatly influence the outcome of the larger ratifying contest. Gouverneur Morris informed a friend that with five states having already approved the Constitution, Federalists "wait impatiently the result of their deliberations in Massachusetts. Should that state also adopt it, . . . there will then be little doubt of a general acquiescence." Edward Carrington wrote Madison that "everything seems to depend" on Massachusetts. Even if nine other states ratified the Constitution, Massachusetts was "so important" that, along with Virginia, it "would be able, if not to prevent the effects of the government altogether, to hold it in suspense longer than the state of our affairs can well admit of." Madison predicted that a defeat in Massachusetts would probably reduce the chances of ratification in Virginia and give new life to the dissenters in Pennsylvania; he told King that "[i]t is impossible to express how much depends on the result of the deliberations of your body." In New York, where it was uncertain whether the legislature would even summon a ratifying convention, Federalists looked to Massachusetts "for our political salvation," while Antifederalists proclaimed that the decision of Massachusetts "will certainly have great influence on the final issue of the business." The stage was set for one of the decisive episodes in the ratification struggle.[116]

For several reasons, ratification in Massachusetts was bound from the start to be a challenge. First, the counties of the state that had provided the greatest support for Shays's Rebellion sent dozens of delegates to the ratifying convention in Boston—Gorham estimated that as many as eighteen or twenty of the delegates actually had served in Shays's army—and they overwhelmingly opposed ratification. As we saw in chapter 2, the suppression of the rebellion had resulted in the political mobilization of its supporters, whose inclination would be to oppose the Constitution simply because it was supported by the eastern political elite. As King explained to Madison:

> Notwithstanding the superiority of talents in favor of the Constitution, yet the same infatuation, which prevailed not many months since in several counties of this state, and which emboldened them to take arms against the government, seems to have an uncontrollable authority over a numerous part of our convention. Their objections are not directed against any part of the Constitution, but their opposition seems to arise from an opinion, that is immovable, that some injury is plotted against them, that the system is the production of the rich and ambitious; that they discern its operation, and that the consequence will be the establishment of two orders in the society, one comprehending the opulent and great, the other the poor and illiterate. The extraordinary union in favor of the Constitution in this state of the wealthy and sensible part of it, is in confirmation of their opinion; and every exertion hitherto made to eradicate it, has been in vain.[117]

In addition, delegates from the region of Maine, of whom there were nearly fifty at the convention, were generally inclined to oppose ratification. Gorham explained to Madison that "many of them and their constituents are only squatters upon other people's land and they are afraid of being brought to account." Moreover, many of the Maine delegates thought—erroneously, according to Gorham—that "their favorite plan of being a separate state will be defeated" if the Constitution were ratified. In addition, Nantucket, which was inhabited mostly by Quakers, would decline to appoint the five delegates to which it was entitled because the Quakers' pacifism—"foolish religious whims," according to Gorham—led them to oppose the Constitution, which granted Congress the authority to raise armies.[118]

Another factor generating resistance to the Constitution in Massachusetts was the long experience its citizens had with localist democracy, annual elections, and small legislative constituencies—all of which the Constitution repudiated at the federal level. As Grayson ruefully observed in the spring of 1787 (before the Constitution was written and thus before he had developed an Antifederalist predisposition), although Shays's Rebellion might have convinced the New England elite to favor "a very strong government" and to be willing "to prostrate all the state legislature[s]," the great bulk of the people of Massachusetts believed the government was already too strong and were "about rebelling again, for the purpose of making it more democratical." Furthermore, as a large state, Massachusetts would be disadvantaged by the Constitution's guarantee of equal state representation in the Senate.[119]

Despite the existence of these factors suggesting that the campaign for ratification would encounter substantial hurdles in Massachusetts, the initial Federalist predictions out of Boston, perhaps influenced by the overwhelming support for the Constitution manifested in that city, were very optimistic. Christopher Gore, a Federalist lawyer and legislator, wrote King that "[t]he federal plan is well esteemed and as far as can be deduced from present appearances the adoption will be easy." Similarly, Henry Jackson, a Boston merchant and former colonel in the Continental Army, told Henry Knox that "[t]he Constitution as proposed will most certainly be adopted by this state." From the reports Madison was receiving in New York City, he concluded that even "[t]he party in Boston which was thought most likely to make opposition are warm in espousing it."[120]

One major wild card in the Massachusetts ratifying contest was the posture to be assumed by the prominent statesman Elbridge Gerry, who had represented the state at the Philadelphia convention and refused to sign the Constitution. One month after the Constitutional Convention ended, Gerry wrote a letter to the Massachusetts legislature—which was soon published and then widely reprinted—in which he explained his actions in Philadelphia. Conceding that much of the Constitution had "great merit" and acknowledging that it was "painful" for him to disagree with his esteemed colleagues at the convention on a matter of such importance, Gerry nonetheless insisted that as "the liberties of America were not secured by the system, it was my duty to oppose it." The principal flaws he identified were the "ambiguous" and "dangerous" powers granted to Congress, the inadequacy of representation in the federal government, the blending of legislative and executive powers, an "oppressive" judicial department, and the absence of a bill of rights.[121]

Federalists immediately expressed concern that Gerry's letter would damage their cause. Madison wrote Washington that Gerry's objections would "shake the confidence of some, and embolden the opposition of others in that state," and Edward Carrington predicted the letter would "work some probable mischief." However, the Massachusetts legislature, rejecting Gerry's thinly veiled request to appear before it to further explain his objections to the Constitution, easily voted to call a ratifying convention.[122]

Within a month of its publication, it was clear, as Gorham wrote Knox, that Gerry's letter had "done infinite mischief." Writing in the *Massachusetts Centinel*, a self-described "plain countrym[a]n" noted that he had been "very much pleased" with the new Constitution upon first analysis and that "I and all my neighbors [were] determined to vote for it." However, Gerry's letter "has quite alarmed us, for fear our liberties are in danger." Henry Jackson, who had been supremely confident before the publication of Gerry's letter that Massachusetts would easily approve the Constitution, was now distraught. He wrote Knox that Gerry "has done more injury to this country by that infamous letter than he will be able to make atonement in his whole life. . . . You have not an idea what a turn this letter has given to the federal Constitution nor could have given it so severe a stab. . . . Damn him. Damn him. Everything looked well and had the most favorable appearance in this state, previous to this, and now I have my doubts." Another Massachusetts Federalist observed that if the Constitution "should be rejected, we must thank Mr. Gerry. Of how much importance, sometimes, is the voice of a single man!"[123]

Madison, who was reading such reports from Massachusetts Federalists as they arrived in New York City, was beginning to have doubts whether Massachusetts would ratify the Constitution. In December, he told Jefferson that there was "great uncertainty" in the matter. He also wrote to Washington to delicately suggest, if "a proper occasion offered, . . . an explicit communication of your good wishes for the plan" in Washington's correspondence with Massachusetts Federalists.[124]

Meanwhile, the views of another eminent Massachusetts statesman were also potentially important to the fate of ratification in Massachusetts. In early December 1787, when Massachusetts voters selected delegates to the state's ratifying convention, Samuel Adams, the Revolutionary hero, had yet to take a public position on the Constitution. Privately, however, he told his old colleague from the Continental Congress, Richard Henry Lee, that he opposed ratification because the Constitution created "a national government, instead of a federal union of sovereign states" and, he worried, would foster aristocracy.[125]

By late December, however, after Boston voters had elected Adams as one of their delegates to the state's ratifying convention, newspapers were reporting

Figure 6.3 Samuel Adams, one of the leaders of the revolutionary movement in Massachusetts and the nation, who later became the state's lieutenant governor and governor. (Museum of Fine Arts, Boston)

rumors that he was "an enemy to the new plan of government." Federalist delegate Christopher Gore, noting reason to believe that Adams had written the recently published Antifederalist essay "Helvidius Priscus," reported that Adams "is out full against it [the Constitution]" and warned against the Federalists' discussing their convention strategy in Adams's presence.[126]

On January 3, 1788, six days before the Massachusetts convention was set to assemble, former governor James Bowdoin entertained most of the Boston delegates at his home, and all of those present except Adams expressed support for ratification. According to Gore's report of the evening's conversation, Adams was "open and decided against" the Constitution on the grounds that the country was too large for a single government, "that internal taxes ought not to be given to the union, [and] that the representation was inadequate." The only amendments that Adams believed would ameliorate his objections would, in Gore's estimation, "totally destroy" the system. Gore concluded that

Adams, unless something happened to change his mind, would "be indefatigable and constant in all ways and means to defeat [ratification]."[127]

As rumors spread of Adams's statements critical of the Constitution, Boston tradesmen organized—in Gorham's words—"the most numerous caucus ever held in Boston to consider what was to be done" in response. On January 7, 380 of them gathered and unanimously passed resolutions denying "false and groundless" rumors that the tradesmen opposed ratification. Expressing their strong support for the Constitution, which they said was "well calculated to . . . guard the rights of the citizens of America" as well as to "revive and increase . . . trade and navigation," the tradesmen warned that any Boston delegate to the ratifying convention who failed to support unconditional ratification would be acting "contrary to their best interest, . . . strongest feelings, and warmest wishes." Several Federalists predicted that the tradesmen's resolutions, which had been targeted principally at Adams, would influence his posture at the convention.[128]

The Massachusetts convention assembled on January 9, 1788. Demand for spectator seating was so great that the venue had to be changed from the Boston statehouse to a large church nearby. Experience in the late 1770s had accustomed Massachusetts citizens to playing an active role in considering, criticizing, and amending proposed state constitutions. Thus, the Federalists' strong preference in general for quick ratification with little discussion was a nonstarter in Massachusetts. Especially given the Antifederalists' obvious strength at the convention—many delegates had been instructed by constituents either to reject ratification outright or to demand amendments—Federalists had little choice but to acquiesce to a laborious paragraph-by-paragraph consideration of the Constitution. In any event, as Federalist delegate Theophilus Parsons observed, this mode of proceeding might be "the most favorable way for us, as it will give us time to exert our influence, before the great question."[129]

One of the principal issues at the convention was the nature of representation in the federal government. Delegates criticized the small size of the House and the use of biennial elections for representatives—both dramatic departures from Massachusetts's practice. One Antifederalist worried that the Constitution adopted the "widely different" customs of the southern states, where elections "were not so free and unbiased." Many delegates also expressed concern that Congress would use its power over the times, places, and manner of federal elections for improper purposes, such as advantaging Federalist candidates.[130]

In addition, the convention devoted considerable attention to Congress's taxing power—and, specifically, whether it ought to extend to the imposition of direct taxes. Several delegates also criticized the Senate's apportionment as unfair to the most populous states, such as Massachusetts. Other significant topics of debate included the Constitution's stance toward slavery—and especially the foreign slave trade—and its failure to require religious oaths for federal officeholders, which occasioned much criticism. Federalist delegates repeatedly emphasized the importance of the grant of power to Congress to regulate commerce, which they portrayed as vital to reviving the New England economy.[131]

One of the most striking features of the Massachusetts convention, which many participants commented upon, was the extreme disparity in the oratorical skills of the two sides.* Nathaniel Barrell, an Antifederalist delegate from Maine, professed himself—with a certain amount of sarcasm—"[a]wed in the presence of this august assembly, conscious of my inability to express my mind fully on this important occasion, and sensible how little I must appear in the eyes of those giants in rhetoric, who have exhibited such a pompous display of declamation." Disclaiming any pretension "to talents above the simple language adapted to the line of my calling"—that of "plain husbandman"—Barrell declared himself unable to speak with "the pleasing eloquence of Cicero or the blaze of Demosthenian oratory." Another Massachusetts Antifederalist, Benjamin Randall, expressed hope that the convention would not be "biased by the best orators," and he facetiously noted that if "these great men" who defended the Constitution "would speak half as much against it, we might complete our business and go home in 48 hours." King reported to Madison from the convention that Antifederalists "complain that the lawyers, judges, clergymen, merchants and men of education are all in favor of the Constitution, and that for this reason they appear to be able to make the worst appear the better cause."[132]

Protests against their elitist domination of the debates were so frequent that exasperated Federalists felt compelled to deny that "those gentlemen who have had the superior advantages of education were enemies to the rights of their country." One Federalist declared that the insinuations of "a combination of the rich, the learned, and those of liberal professions to establish and support an arbitrary form of government" were "uncharitable and unchristian." A self-confessed "plain man" who got his "living by the plough" even felt compelled to stand up for the "lawyers and men of learning and monied men," noting that "we must all swim or sink together" and insisting that he would not "think the worse of the Constitution [simply] because [they] . . . are fond of it."[133]

---

* Compounding the usual Antifederalist disadvantage in elite representation was the fact that several Massachusetts Antifederalists who were part of the elite—men such as Elbridge Gerry, James Warren, and James Winthrop—could not secure election to the ratifying convention because they lived in commercial towns that overwhelmingly supported ratification.

During the first two weeks of the convention, ratification was very much in doubt. On January 16, Gorham told Knox that "the prospect [is] not very good. Numbers are at present against us and the opposition leaders say they are sure of the victory." On January 18, Federalist delegate Theodore Sedgwick wrote, "At the time the convention met there was doubtless a majority against the constitution. It is certain that several converts have been made in the course of the debates. Which side now possess[es] a majority it is impossible to determine." Two days later, King told Madison that the Antifederalists "affirm to each other that they have an unalterable majority on their side; the Friends doubt the strength of their adversaries but are not entirely confident of their own." Indeed, on January 22, Antifederalist Samuel Nasson of Maine predicted that the Constitution would be defeated by a hefty margin of nearly fifty votes.[134]

Fearing defeat, Federalist leaders made a critical decision: They would abandon their adamant opposition to any amendments whatsoever. Rather than insisting on an unvarnished ratification, which is what the previous conventions had approved, they would accept ratification with a call for constitutional amendments to follow.

On January 23, King wrote Madison, "Our prospects are gloomy, but hope is not entirely extinguished." He explained that Federalists were "now thinking of amendments to be submitted not as a condition of our assent and ratification, but as the opinion of the convention subjoined to [its] ratification." King thought that this scheme "may gain a few members, but the issue is doubtful."[135]

A few days later, Gorham offered Madison a substantially similar—albeit slightly more optimistic—report. Despite what he considered the Federalists' vastly superior abilities, Gorham was "pretty well satisfied we shall lose the question, unless we can take off some of the opposition by amendments. I do not mean those to be made the condition of the ratification—but recommendatory only. Upon this plan I flatter myself we may possibly get a majority of 12 or 15—and not more."[136]

On January 26, the Antifederalist "Hampden," writing in the *Massachusetts Centinel*, made the first public suggestion that the convention ratify the Constitution on the condition of antecedent amendments. The following day, King told Knox that the Antifederalists gave this proposal "some countenance," which revealed that they were "not so confident of their numbers, since hitherto they have reprobated the suggestion of amendments, and insisted among their party on a total rejection of the Constitution." Federalist delegate Benjamin Lincoln (who, as we saw in chapter 2, had led the army that suppressed Shays's Rebellion) assured Washington that the proposal for conditional ratification "will not be attended to," though it was "possible if we adopt it [the Constitution] absolutely that the convention may recommend certain amendments."[137]

Figure 6.4 Governor John Hancock of Massachusetts, a wealthy Boston merchant who served as president of the Second Continental Congress and signed the Declaration of Independence. (Museum of Fine Arts, Boston)

Calculating that proposed amendments coming from them would only stoke Antifederalist suspicions, Federalists chose instead to use intermediaries: John Hancock and Samuel Adams. As Federalist Jeremy Belknap, pastor of the church in which the convention was sitting, explained, "Hancock is the ostensible puppet in proposing amendments; but they are the product of the Feds in concert, and it was thought that coming from him they would be better received than from any other person."[138]

Governor John Hancock, whose name headed the list of signatories to the Declaration of Independence, had been chosen president of the Massachusetts ratifying convention, but a preexisting gout condition had prevented his attending the first three weeks of deliberations. Hancock's views on ratification were unknown, although King told Knox, "[H]e appears to me to wish well to the Constitution but doesn't care to risk anything in its favor."* However,

---

* King also believed that Hancock's gout attack was politically convenient and that "he will improve in his health as soon as a majority shows itself on either side of the convention."

according to another Federalist's report, the Antifederalists had taken advantage of Hancock's absence to "industriously report that his Excellency was opposed to the Constitution and advised [the convention] to reject it." Adams, as we have seen, had strongly opposed ratification before the convention. However, the Boston tradesmen's impressive rally in support of ratification may have had its intended effect of pressuring Adams to reconsider his views.[139]

The Federalists approached Hancock with appeals to his patriotism but also offers of political support. As King explained to Knox, Hancock, in his gubernatorial re-election bid, would "receive the universal support of [former governor] Bowdoin's friends." Moreover, Hancock was told "that if Virginia does not unite, which is problematical, . . . he is considered as the only fair candidate for President." (If Virginia did not ratify the Constitution, George Washington would be ineligible for the presidency.) Federalist delegate Tristram Dalton, a merchant and state legislator, reported that the Federalists had "sacrifice[d] everything but moral honesty to carry our point."[140]

Hancock accepted the Federalists' overtures, and on January 30, he appeared on the floor of the convention for the first time, and the following morning he spoke. Acknowledging the possible impropriety of his intervention, given that "through painful indisposition of body, he had been prevented from giving his attendance in his place," Hancock assured the delegates that he had been receiving information and following the debates through the newspapers. Noting the "great dissimilarity of sentiments" revealed in the convention's deliberations, Hancock proposed amendments "[t]o remove the objections of some gentlemen." These amendments would, among other things, restrict Congress to expressly delegated powers; limit its control over the times, places, and manner of federal elections; curtail its authority over direct taxes; and require juries in federal civil cases and grand jury indictments in federal criminal prosecutions.[141]

Adams seconded Hancock's proposal. Admitting to some concerns about the Constitution, he argued that the proposed amendments would "have a tendency to remove such doubts and to conciliate the minds of the convention." Adams also predicted that the proposal, "coming from Massachusetts, from her importance, [would] have its weight" and would "have the most salutary effect throughout the union," including in "greatly agitated" Pennsylvania.[142]

In the days that followed, some Antifederalists protested that the convention had no authority to propose amendments, and they questioned whether the five states that had already ratified the Constitution would be likely now to support amendments. Federalists responded that the ratifying convention, as "the fullest representation of the people ever known," had ample authority to recommend amendments. They also predicted that, given "the influence of

Massachusetts" and the fact that the proposed amendments were "general and not . . . calculated for the peculiar interest of this state," other states would eagerly support them and the first Congress would approve them.[143]

Several Federalists now privately predicted victory. Dalton wrote that the endorsement of the Constitution by Hancock and Adams would "settle the matter favorably." Henry Van Schaack, a Federalist in western Massachusetts who was receiving reports from Boston, told his brother that Hancock's actions "had an amazing influence over a great number of wavering members" and that "the opposition [now] despaired of success." Gorham predicted a Federalist majority of about fifteen on the final question. A more measured King reported to Madison that "our hopes are increasing," although he worried that Hancock, whose "character is not entirely free from a portion of caprice," might still "disappoint our present expectations."[144]

Yet the governor delivered on his promise. The convention sent his proposal to a large committee—which was supposed to be balanced between the parties but nonetheless had a Federalist majority—which then recommended amendments very similar to the ones Hancock had proposed. On the final day of the convention, Hancock would endorse ratification "in full confidence that the amendments proposed will soon become a part of the system."[145]

Sensing defeat, Antifederalists proposed adjourning the convention. As one Antifederalist essayist explained, an adjournment would "not only ripen the judgment of our own citizens, but give them an opportunity of benefiting by the opinions of those states [especially Virginia], which are attentive to, but not extravagantly zealous, in this matter." Federalists fended off this tactical maneuver, however, defeating the motion to adjourn on February 5 by a margin of 214 to 115.[146]

Before the final vote was called on February 6, some Antifederalist delegates rose to explain why they would be voting in favor of ratification. William Symmes, Jr., a 1780 graduate of Harvard College who had identified "great defects" in the Constitution but feared the consequences of "a total rejection," declared that Governor Hancock's intervention "in the character of a mediator" had been like "a ray of hope shone in upon the gloom that overspread [his] heart," leading him to support ratification with recommended amendments. Another Antifederalist delegate, Charles Turner of Scituate, noted that he had "been averse to the reception of the Constitution while it was considered merely in its original form," but his "mind [was] reconciled" by the proposal to recommend certain amendments. Because of the "respect due to the hoary head of Massachusetts" and the "catholic nature and complexion" of the proposed amendments, Turner expressed confidence that they would be "universally accepted."[147]

In the end, the Massachusetts convention ratified the Constitution by the slender margin of 187 to 168. It simultaneously recommended "certain amendments and alterations" in order to "remove the fears and quiet the apprehensions of many of the good people of this Commonwealth."[148]

Not only had the Federalists won, but immediately after the final vote, several of their opponents rose to declare themselves, in the words of Antifederalist delegate John Taylor, "fairly beaten." To the Federalists' delight, Taylor expressed "his determination to go home and endeavor to infuse a spirit of harmony and love among the people." Another Antifederalist delegate, William Widgery, similarly stated that he would inform his constituents that he had opposed the Constitution but been defeated "by a majority of wise and understanding men," and that he would "endeavor to sow the seeds of union and peace among the people he represented." As King wrote Madison later that day, "the minority are in a good temper"—unlike their counterparts in Pennsylvania—and given the Antifederalists' "magnanimity," he was confident that "ratification will be very cordially and universally approved through our state."[149]

Indeed, numerous reports from around Massachusetts in the months following the convention suggest that these Antifederalist pledges were mostly honored and that agitation against the Constitution in the Commonwealth largely ceased. For example, in late March 1788, Antifederalist convention delegate Silas Lee reported from Biddeford, Maine: "[A]t present we seem to be at peace. Many who have been much opposed to the Constitution are become warm advocates of it."[150]

That spring's election results seemed to confirm that public opinion in Massachusetts strongly endorsed the outcome of the state ratifying convention. Federalists, as they had promised, did not field a candidate against the incumbent governor, Hancock. Gerry was a reluctant Antifederalist candidate, and Hancock trounced him, winning 81 percent of the vote. Federalists also won the lieutenant governorship and large majorities in both houses of the state legislature, leading Henry Van Schaack to conclude that "federalism has gained so amazingly that the Constitution is not even opposed in private conversation."[151]

The largely positive outcome of the Massachusetts convention was an enormous accomplishment for the state's Federalists.* In a letter to Washington,

---

* They celebrated with a procession in Boston on February 8 in which forty-five hundred people participated—the largest such event in American history to that date. Other large cities—Baltimore, New York, and Charleston—subsequently sought to outdo Boston in their processions celebrating their states' ratifications of the Constitution. Philadelphia bested them all in its Fourth of July celebration of the Constitution's having been ratified by the requisite number of states.

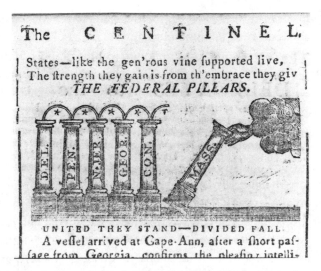

The C E N T I N E L.

States—like the gen'rous vine fupported live,
The ftrength they gain is from th'embrace they giv
, THE FEDERAL PILLARS.

UNITED THEY STAND—DIVIDED FALL.
A veffel arrived at Cape-Ann, after a fhort paf-
fage from Georgia, confirms the pleafing intelli-

Figure 6.5 Massachusetts, the Sixth Pillar of the "Grand Republican Superstructure," in the popular metaphor originated by Benjamin Russell, the printer of the *Massachusetts Centinel.* (Library of Congress)

Knox summarized how it had come about. Noting that it was "now no secret that on the opening of the convention, a majority were prejudiced against it [the Constitution]," Knox explained how the Federalists had "proceeded most cautiously and wisely, debated every objection with the most guarded good nature and candor but took no questions on the several paragraphs and thereby prevented the establishment of parties." In addition, as Henry Jackson told Knox, if Governor Hancock, who had "gained himself immortal honor in his conduct on this occasion," had not taken "a very active part in favor of adoption, we [the Federalists] should never have gained a vote in favor of it." The popular Hancock's embrace of ratification with recommended amendments may have provided Antifederalist delegates with political cover to change their positions on the Constitution.[152]

While Massachusetts Federalists were proud of their accomplishment, Madison viewed the outcome of the Massachusetts convention as more of a mixed bag. The size of the Antifederalist vote was "very disagreeably large," yet the good temper of the losers was "some atonement." The recommended amendments were "a blemish," but at least they were "in the least offensive form"—that is, they were not conditions of ratification.[153]

Randolph shared Madison's mixed reaction to the latest intelligence. On the one hand, he considered Massachusetts a "paltry snare" and not yet "fairly enlisted," given that some of its proposed amendments were "inadmissible." On the other hand, he acknowledged that had Massachusetts rejected the Constitution, it "would have damned it here [in Virginia]."[154]

The reaction of many other Federalists to the news from Massachusetts was far more celebratory. Washington told Madison that Massachusetts's ratification would prove "a severe stroke to opponents of the proposed Constitution in this state [Virginia]," and he wrote King that it would "be productive of good effects in other states, whose determination may have been problematical." Edward Carrington called "[t]he decision of Massachusetts ... perhaps the most important event that ever took place in America, as upon her in all probability depended the fate of the Constitution—had she rejected I am certain there would not have been the most remote chance for its adoption in Virginia." More than one Federalist agreed with the judgment of the young French diplomat Victor DuPont that, "Massachusetts having accepted, the new constitution can be regarded as having been accepted for all America."[155]

Developments in New Hampshire, where the state ratifying convention assembled just one week after Massachusetts's ended, quickly put a stop to such talk. Since the end of the Philadelphia convention, nearly everyone had been predicting quick and easy ratification in New Hampshire. In November 1787, John Langdon, who had been one of New Hampshire's two delegates to the Philadelphia convention and was a former governor of the state, told Washington that he had "not heard a single person [in the state] object to the plan and very few find fault even with a single sentence, but all express their greatest desire to have it established as soon as may be." The following month, Madison wrote Jefferson that "New Hampshire from every account ... will pretty certainly be on the affirmative side."[156]

By virtue of their control of the state government, New Hampshire Federalists created additional advantages for themselves in the ratifying process. The state's chief executive, President John Sullivan, called a special legislative session in December 1787, which Federalists controlled. The legislature chose Exeter, the heartland of New Hampshire Federalism, as the convention's venue. It also provided that the state law excluding officeholders from the legislature would not apply to the ratifying convention, which meant that influential Federalists, such as state treasurer John Taylor Gilman and the chief justice of the state's superior court, Samuel Livermore, could serve as delegates. Finally, the Federalists defeated their opponents' motion to double the size of the convention.[157]

Once the Massachusetts convention ratified the Constitution on February 6, a Federalist victory in New Hampshire seemed even more certain. Langdon had spent several days attending the Massachusetts ratifying convention and confidently told Federalists in Boston, according to one report, that "if Massachusetts adopted the Constitution, New Hampshire would not be one week in session." Immediately upon Massachusetts's ratification, King wrote Madison that "New Hampshire will undoubtedly decide in favor," and Madison then reassured Washington that there could "be no question" but that New Hampshire would become the "seventh pillar . . . to the federal temple."[158]

However, just two days before the New Hampshire convention assembled, Sullivan reported that the prospects of ratification were "not so favorable as I expected." Langdon, in a subsequent letter to Washington, explained what had happened:

> Contrary to the expectation of almost every thinking man, a small majority of (say four persons) appeared [in the convention] against the system. . . . Just at the moment of choice for members of our convention (in one of our principal counties), . . . a report was circulated by a few designing men who wished for confusion that [the] Massachusetts convention who had just met were against the plan and would certainly refuse it, the liberties of the people were in danger, and that the great men (as they call them) were forming a plan for themselves.

This report, Langdon observed, "together with a thousand other absurdities, . . . frightened the people almost out of what little senses they had," leading them to choose delegates opposed to the Constitution and, in many cases, issuing instructions to reject it.[159]

At the ratifying convention, the proceedings of which were not well reported, the principal stated grounds of opposition to the Constitution were the lengthy terms in office for federal legislators, the scope of Congress's powers, the Constitution's compromises with slavery, and its failure to require federal officeholders to take a religious oath. The convention's debates apparently convinced some delegates to rethink their opposition to ratification, yet they were reluctant to defy their constituents' instructions. As Langdon subsequently reported to King, "[A]fter spending ten days in the arguments, a number of opponents came to me and said they were convinced and should be very unhappy to vote against the Constitution which they (however absurd) must do, in case the question was called for." The preference of these delegates, Langdon wrote Washington, was for "an opportunity to lay the matter before their constituents."[160]

Fearing they might lose if the convention took a vote on ratification, Federalists moved instead to adjourn. As a result of their having arrived early in Exeter, before some Antifederalist delegates straggled in, Federalists had dominated the convention's rules committee and secured procedural rules favorable to their cause, including priority for motions to adjourn and anonymity for all votes except the one on the final question (which might embolden

some Antifederalist delegates to defy their constituents' instructions on preliminary votes, such as a motion to adjourn). According to Langdon's account,
the Antifederalists "greatly opposed" the adjournment motion, but they lost
that vote by a margin of fifty-six to fifty-one. The New Hampshire convention would reassemble in Concord (an inland venue more favorable to the
Antifederalists) in mid-June—after spring legislative elections.[161]

For the Federalists to avoid an outright defeat at this stage of the ratifying
contest was important, given that the prospects for ratification were uncertain in New York, North Carolina, Rhode Island, and Virginia, and Federalists
tried to put the best face possible on the New Hampshire adjournment. Still,
given the previous widespread assumption that New Hampshire would easily
ratify, the adjournment of its convention was generally perceived as a loss for
the Federalists. Langdon considered the result "mortifying" and "astonishing." Especially after ratification in Massachusetts and in view of the fact that
"almost every man of property and abilities [had been] for it," how could New
Hampshire, with "everything to gain, and nothing to lose, by the adoption of
the government," have failed to approve it?[162]

Across the country, many Federalist leaders were distressed by the news from
New Hampshire. Madison told Randolph that the adjournment was "no small
check to the progress of the business." Opponents of ratification in Virginia
would "take new spirits"—after ratification in Massachusetts "had almost extinguished their hopes"—and New Hampshire's adjournment meant that nine
states could not possibly have ratified the Constitution by the time Virginia's
convention assembled. Madison also noted that Pennsylvania's unchastened
Antifederalists "will probably be equally encouraged." Nicholas Gilman, one
of New Hampshire's congressional delegates (and the brother of John Taylor
Gilman), reported to Sullivan the "pernicious effects our convention business has produced in a number of states," as Antifederalists "augmented their
forces, took possession of their old ground, and seemed determined to maintain it at all hazards." The price of federal securities fell in New York after the
adjournment of the New Hampshire convention, and the French vice-consul
confirmed in his report home that the Federalists had suffered a "dangerous
defeat," which had "the most unfortunate effect on the people of the states of
New York, Maryland, Virginia, and the two Carolinas," where the opposition
"has taken on new strength."[163]

Indeed, it was around this time that the Rhode Island legislature, still under
the control of the party responsible for its radical fiscal and monetary policies,
rejected a motion even to summon a ratifying convention. By way of explanation, Antifederalist legislators observed that "the citizens of other states had,
by the means of appointing conventions, been decoyed into an adoption of the
Constitution," when "at least two-thirds" of their citizens opposed ratification.

Instead, the legislature provided for a referendum on the Constitution to take place on March 24, 1788. Federalists in larger towns, such as Newport and Providence, boycotted that referendum, which consequently yielded a ten-to-one margin against ratification.[164]

Maryland and South Carolina

To this point, among southern states, only Georgia had held a ratifying convention, but Maryland's was scheduled for late April 1788. Madison had initially told Jefferson that he had it on "pretty good authority" that "[t]he voice of Maryland" was, "as far as it has been declared, strongly in favor of the Constitution." Yet two months later, he reported "more formidable opposition" in Maryland than in most of the early-adopting states.[165]

The state's paper money faction, led by Samuel Chase and William Paca, sought to rally opposition to ratification. They and several other Maryland Antifederalist leaders had speculated in confiscated Loyalist estates, and without a paper money emission—which the Constitution would forbid—to enable them to pay off their mortgages in depreciated currency, they would face likely financial ruin. They were joined by Luther Martin, who had been a disaffected Maryland delegate to the Philadelphia convention. In an appearance before the state legislature—which, apparently at the behest of Antifederalist legislators, had summoned the state's delegates to the Philadelphia convention to appear before it in November 1787 to discuss the Constitution—and subsequently in newspaper essays, Martin described a "monarchical party" at the Philadelphia convention that had wished to abolish the state governments entirely.[166]

In the mid-1780s, Maryland politicians had been bitterly divided over tax and debt relief, which might lead one to predict similar divisions over the Constitution because of Article I, Section 10. Yet most of the state's political elite agreed that Maryland, a less populous state whose small geographic size had always made its leaders feel vulnerable within the union, would greatly benefit from equal state representation in the Senate. Thus, former governor Thomas Johnson wrote Washington that the "scale of power" between "the great and small states" had been "very properly adjusted" in the Constitution. Moreover, lacking any western land claims, most Marylanders did not feel the same outrage that other southerners did over Jay's willingness to trade away American navigation rights on the Mississippi River.[167]

Maryland Antifederalists calculated that their best chance of success would be, in the words of one of their opponents, to "push first for an adjournment till the determination of Virginia is known," hoping that a defeat for the

Figure 6.6 Samuel Chase, a signer of the Declaration of Independence and one of Maryland's leading Antifederalists, later became a partisan Federalist and Supreme Court justice, and was nearly removed from office by the Jeffersonians through impeachment in 1805. (Courtesy of Independence National Historical Park)

Constitution in Virginia would influence swing delegates at the Maryland ratifying convention. Learning of these plans, Virginia Federalist George Nicholas, who feared that an adjournment in Maryland would adversely impact the cause of ratification in Virginia, urged Madison and (indirectly) Washington to use their influence in Maryland to counteract the scheme, and both of them complied.[168]

Washington wrote Johnson that an adjournment in Maryland would "be tantamount to the rejection of the Constitution" and "would have the worst tendency imaginable" on the South Carolina convention, which was the only other one scheduled to meet before Virginia's. Madison voiced a similar view in letters to Maryland Federalists Daniel Carroll and James McHenry. A letter from McHenry to Washington written just before McHenry left for the Maryland convention in Annapolis reveals that he was aware of the Antifederalists' plans, in coordination with their allies in Virginia, "to push for an adjournment under the pretext of a conference with [the Virginia convention] respecting amendments." Agreeing with the view that an adjournment would be equivalent to a rejection, McHenry promised Washington to "do every thing in my power to prevent it."[169]

However, it turned out the Federalists had little cause for concern. The election for ratifying convention delegates in Maryland that took place on the four days beginning April 7 gave them a majority of greater than five to one, even though they had failed to convince the legislature to select the earlier date for elections they preferred or to impose a higher property qualification for delegates than that imposed on members of the lower house of the state legislature.[170]

Capitalizing on their decided numerical advantage once the convention assembled on April 21, Federalists rejected their opponents' motion for paragraph-by-paragraph consideration of the Constitution, explaining that everyone at the convention "was perfectly master of the subject, having had sufficient time to study it and make up his mind on it before he came there." However, not wishing to press their advantage too far, Federalists did not seek an immediate vote on ratification, instead allowing their opponents to speak their piece, while mostly remaining silent themselves. After several days of perfunctory debate, the convention, whose deliberations were not well reported, voted on April 26 to approve the Constitution by a margin of sixty-three to eleven.[171]

To that point in the proceedings, Federalists had adamantly opposed consideration of amendments, ostensibly on the grounds that their constituents had not instructed them on that issue. However, after the ratification vote, they agreed to the appointment of a committee to consider amendments, though only on the condition that any amendments to be recommended by the convention would come with the endorsement of the delegates acting solely in their capacity as private citizens. It turned out that the Federalists, who had a large majority on the committee, were almost unanimously willing to approve several of the amendments discussed, though some of them insisted that they were acting more from a desire to accommodate the Antifederalists than from a conviction that the Constitution was genuinely in need of amendment.[172]

The amendments to which the Federalists provisionally agreed were mainly addressed to soothing Marylanders' concerns about the federal courts— concerns that probably were attributable to the fact that Maryland planters were more indebted to British creditors than were residents of any other state but Virginia. For example, proposed amendments would have required jury trials in certain federal civil cases, limited the jurisdiction of the federal judiciary in various ways, and guaranteed the state courts concurrent jurisdiction over certain cases falling within the federal judicial power. Yet the Federalists were unwilling to support other amendments proposed by their opponents, such as ones restricting Congress's powers to regulate congressional elections, levy direct taxes, and create a standing army.[173]

However, when Antifederalists demanded that the entire convention consider certain of the amendments that had failed to garner majority support in the committee, exasperated Federalists decided to abandon the entire project of amendments. Some of them may also have been concerned that for the Maryland convention to propose amendments would harm the prospects for ratification in Virginia.[174]

After the convention adjourned on April 29, Antifederalists quickly published an address to the people of Maryland that included a call for amendments. Antifederalist delegate John Francis Mercer, who had briefly attended the Philadelphia convention as a Maryland delegate, also wrote to the New York and Virginia ratifying conventions to "prevent your forming unjust conclusions from the adoption of the Constitution in the state of Maryland by so large a majority of the convention and the subsequent dissolution of that body without proposing any amendments." He insisted that "four-fifths of the people of Maryland are now in favor of considerable alterations and amendments and will insist on them."[175]

South Carolina was the next state to consider ratification. In November 1787, the French interim consul in Charleston, Jean-Baptiste Petry, had reported that the Constitution "seems generally approved of by the principal inhabitants of this city." However, he also noted that some concerns had been expressed over the provision authorizing Congress after twenty years to bar the foreign slave trade and, more generally, at "sacrifices" that the southern states had made to northern interests and at the "preponderance" that northerners would enjoy, at least initially, in Congress.[176]

Two months later, Petry reported that the Pennsylvania dissenters had "spared neither money nor effort in order to flood this state and its neighbors with [their] pamphlets and writings against this Constitution," which he thought might have an "effect in the back country which is not very learned in politics and in matters of government." Petry had learned that some Federalists were determined to force the opposition, "under the pretext of enlightening the people, . . . to show itself in broad daylight" at the legislature's session in January, in order to combat "objections with the same reason which convinced the deputies of the several states in Philadelphia."[177]

Indeed, in response to a motion in the South Carolina House of Representatives to thank the state's delegates to the Philadelphia convention for their service, those delegates—all four of whom held seats in the House— insisted that it would be inappropriate to thank them before the legislature had discussed the merits of the Constitution. Antifederalists objected, but Federalists had the numbers. Thus, for three days in mid-January, former governor Rawlins Lowndes, indicating that he was representing the views of backcountry members uncomfortable with public oratory, raised objections to the Constitution, and eight or ten Federalist speakers responded.[178]

At the conclusion of these debates, the legislature unanimously called for a ratifying convention. The House and Senate initially disagreed about its timing, but eventually they set April 11 and 12 as the dates to elect delegates to a convention, which would meet on May 12. By a single vote, the House determined that the convention would meet in Charleston rather than an interior location more favorable to the Antifederalists.[179]

Federalists initially worried that their opponents' organizing efforts—"great pains [being] taken in the back-country to poison the minds of the people," according to one Federalist—would produce a closely divided convention. Soon after the legislature had summoned the convention, one Federalist observed that opposition to ratification was "heavy and increasing" because the state's farmers "entertain jealousies that it [the Constitution] is a scheme to favor the mercantile interest." Just before the elections for ratifying convention delegates took place, Arthur Bryan, the son and brother of leading Pennsylvania Antifederalists, reported that "[a]ccounts from the back counties say it [the Constitution] is universally reprobated."[180]

However, the elections produced a secure Federalist majority for the convention. One Federalist reported that, judging from the election returns, "there is not a shadow of doubt but the Constitution will be ratified by a considerable majority." The severe malapportionment in the legislature had been reproduced in the ratifying convention: Low-country planters, who overwhelmingly favored ratification, were drastically overrepresented in both bodies.[181]

In the debates over the Constitution that took place in both the South Carolina House and the state ratifying convention, Antifederalists offered many of the standard objections that their political allies raised virtually everywhere, such as the illegitimacy of the Philadelphia convention's abrogation of the Articles and the Constitution's grants of excessive power to Congress. But South Carolina Antifederalists also raised some distinctively southern objections. They criticized the Constitution on the grounds that northerners would dominate the national government and use its powers over commerce and treaty making to the disadvantage of the South. They also objected to the constitutional provision authorizing Congress to forbid the foreign slave trade after twenty years.[182]

Federalists responded by emphasizing the many safeguards for slavery provided in the Constitution. They also argued that population flow to the Southwest would quickly dissipate any initial northern advantage in Congress. Moreover, even if northerners did use their temporary ascendancy in Congress to give themselves a monopoly over the South's carrying trade, this was the least to which they were entitled given their sacrifices on behalf of the South during the war. Finally, the Federalists noted that South Carolina would especially benefit from a powerful national government because of its unique vulnerability to foreign invasion.[183]

When news reached the Charleston convention on May 15 that Maryland had ratified the Constitution, the Antifederalists—according to a subsequent account offered by one of them—began "losing ground," with "numbers going over to the enemy, on an idea that further opposition was useless." Despairing of an outright victory, Antifederalists sought to adjourn the convention until October, which would afford them additional time to mobilize opposition, but their adjournment motion was defeated on May 21 by a vote of 135 to 89.[184]

Two days later, the South Carolina convention voted by 149 to 73 to ratify the Constitution. To placate their opponents, Federalists agreed to propose amendments limiting Congress to expressly delegated powers and restricting its authority to impose direct taxes and regulate federal elections. After the convention, one of the Antifederalist leaders, Aedanus Burke, insisted that a clear majority of South Carolinians opposed the Constitution—a claim that was very likely true—because of its "evil tendency." Burke also asserted that "if a fair opportunity offers itself to our back countrymen they will join heart and hand to bring ruin on the new plan unless it be materially altered." Finally, Burke predicted that if "either Virginia or New York state reject it, the system will fall to pieces."[185]

South Carolina was the eighth state to ratify the Constitution. Only one more state's approval was necessary for the Constitution to become operational. Virginia's ratifying convention was set to meet on June 2 and New York's on June 17, while the adjourned New Hampshire convention was scheduled to resume its deliberations on June 18. Georgia congressional delegate Abraham Baldwin, not feeling very confident about the Federalists' chances in Virginia or New York and not daring to "hope much good" from New Hampshire after it had "acted so ill before," reflected that "[w]here we are to go for the ninth, [to] set all the mighty wheels in motion, time must determine. I fear it will be delayed too long."[186]

In the months since February, when Federalists had adjourned the New Hampshire convention for fear of losing the vote on ratification, the state's Federalist-dominated press had conducted a formidable propaganda campaign in favor of the Constitution. In March, Madison told Washington that it was "fully expected that some of the instructed members will prevail on their towns to unfetter them." Though such efforts mostly came to naught, five Antifederalist delegates who had attended the convention in February were absent—for unknown reasons—when it resumed its deliberations. In addition, some towns that had gone unrepresented in February sent Federalist delegates to the convention in June.[187]

Based on reassurances they had received from their New Hampshire allies, Federalists across the nation were supremely confident that the reassembled New Hampshire convention would ratify the Constitution. For example, Rufus King told Hamilton that "[t]hose who are best informed of the situation of the question in New Hampshire are positive that the decision will be such as we wish."[188]

Events proved the Federalists' confidence justified. On June 21, the fourth and final day of the reassembled convention, Federalists defeated motions to make ratification conditional upon antecedent amendments and to adjourn the convention. Then, by a vote of fifty-seven to forty-seven, the delegates ratified the Constitution unconditionally, making New Hampshire the ninth state to do so. The convention also recommended essentially the same amendments that the Massachusetts convention had proposed. Without the last-minute decision by Federalists to support recommended amendments, the convention might have rejected ratification.[189]

Virginia

New Hampshire's ratification came after the Virginia convention had been meeting for more than two weeks, but that result did not detract from the drama and significance of the Virginia proceedings because news of it did not reach Richmond until after the delegates had voted on ratification. Thus, while the Virginia convention was meeting, the delegates believed that the fate of the Constitution remained undetermined, and Federalist George Nicholas had told Madison that he worried that "some of them [the delegates] will fear to give the last hand to the business." Moreover, even after nine other states had ratified, Virginia's approval would remain critical because the union probably could not succeed without the participation of its largest and wealthiest state. Finally, as Richard Henry Lee wrote to Mason before the Virginia convention, the states that had yet to consider the Constitution would likely "depend much upon Virginia for their determination" whether to ratify.[190]

Whether Virginia would ratify the Constitution had been deeply uncertain from the very start. About three weeks after the Philadelphia convention ended, Washington wrote Madison that the first accounts he had received from southern and western Virginia were favorable to ratification, and he doubted that "any powerful opposition will be made to the Constitution's being submitted to a convention." By late October, however, Randolph was reporting to Madison that "[t]he first raptures in favor of the Constitution were excessive" and "the tide is turning" against ratification in Virginia. New objections were being "daily started," "the final event seems uncertain," and "strong exertions" would be required to "carry it through." In mid-November, Grayson, who opposed ratification, noted "very considerable opposition" to the Constitution in Virginia and professed himself "at a loss to determine how the matter will be ultimately closed." Judging from the information he was receiving in Paris, Jefferson concluded that "the presumption is that Virginia will reject it."[191]

For several reasons, the Constitution was bound to encounter significant opposition in Virginia. First, most residents of the far-western part of the state were deeply opposed to ratification. For one thing, the Jay imbroglio had caused them to fear that a northern-dominated Congress would abandon American claims to navigation rights on the Mississippi River, which would stymie westward migration and reduce the value of their lands. Washington complained to Knox, "The Kentucky district will have great weight in deciding this question [Virginia's ratification]; and . . . no pain is spared to inculcate a belief that the government proposed will—without scruple or delay—barter away the right of navigation to the River Mississippi." Similarly, Nicholas warned Madison that "[t]he only danger" he apprehended to ratification in Virginia was "from the Kentucky members, and one consideration only has any weight with them: a fear that if the new government should take place, that their navigation would be given up."[192]

Yet Kentuckians had other concerns about the Constitution as well. According to a circular letter opposing ratification that was written by several prominent Kentuckians, they worried that westerners would be "dragged by the power of the federal court six or eight hundred miles" to adjudicate lawsuits involving contested land titles. In addition, they feared that Kentucky "never shall be able to encourage manufactures"—especially hemp—because the Constitution barred states from imposing import duties. Finally, according to Washington, the idea of the Constitution's "becoming an impediment to its [Kentucky's] separation"—most Kentuckians wanted to become a state independent of Virginia—"has got hold of them."[193]

In addition to the Kentuckians' discontent with the Constitution, Virginians generally—as residents of the nation's most populous state—felt aggrieved by the provision for equal state representation in the Senate. Virginians had also been disadvantaged by both parts of the compromise at the Philadelphia convention that allowed the foreign slave trade to continue for a generation while removing the supermajority requirement for the enactment of navigation laws by Congress.[194]

Furthermore, many Virginians feared that the broad jurisdiction and independence of the federal courts, together with the omission of a right to a jury trial in federal civil cases, would render them vulnerable to lawsuits by British creditors seeking payment of prewar debts. Even before the Philadelphia convention, Virginia legislator John Dawson wrote Madison that "a large majority of the citizens of this state are warmly opposed to the payment of British debts." A month after the convention, Randolph told Madison that "the most vulnerable and odious part of the Constitution" in Virginia was "the danger of every defendant being hurried sooner or later to the seat of the federal government" at the behest of British creditors. Another Virginia legislator, John Pierce, confirmed that "[t]he popular objection [to the Constitution] is that the British debts must be paid if it is adopted."[195]

Lastly, the fact that two of the three delegates who had refused to sign the Constitution on the last day of the Philadelphia convention—Mason and Randolph—were from Virginia signaled the state's citizens that they had reason to fear the Constitution and emboldened the state's Antifederalists. Madison believed that had Mason and Randolph (and Patrick Henry) supported ratification, Virginia "would have been as zealous and unanimous as she is now divided on the subject." Carrington wrote Jefferson that there might be "some difficulty" with ratification in Virginia because "two of her members in convention whose characters entitle them to the public confidence refused to sign the report."[196]

Late in the Philadelphia convention, Mason had declared that he would "sooner chop off his right hand than put it to the Constitution as it now stands." In the convention's final days, he wrote down his objections to the Constitution. Among other things, there was no declaration of rights, the House offered only "the shadow" of representation, the jurisdiction of the federal judiciary was too broad, commercial legislation that would injure the interests of the southern states could be passed by a simple majority of both houses of Congress, the powers of the national government's branches were blended together, Congress was barred from interfering with the foreign slave trade for twenty years, and the president was not constrained by an executive council. Mason also warned that the Constitution would eventually lead to "a monarchy or a corrupt, tyrannical aristocracy."[197]

Mason left Philadelphia, according to Madison, "in an exceeding ill humor indeed." Madison explained to Jefferson, "A number of little circumstances arising in part from the impatience which prevailed towards the close of the business conspired to whet his acrimony," and Mason returned to Virginia with a "fixed disposition to prevent the adoption of the plan if possible." In the weeks after the convention, Mason revised and enlarged his objections and, according to one Federalist Virginia legislator, took "the utmost pains to disseminate" them. Tobias Lear reported that Mason circulated his objections "in manuscript to persons in all parts of the country where he supposed they would make an impression." Beginning in November, Mason's objections were published and then widely republished in newspapers and pamphlets through-out the nation.[198]

However, the good news from the Federalists' perspective was that Mason had assured Washington that he was "most decidedly of opinion" that the Virginia legislature ought to submit the Constitution to a ratifying convention and that "should any attempt be made to prevent the calling [of] such a convention here, such a measure shall have every opposition in my power to give it."* In addition, Nicholas later reported that Mason had said publicly, "immediately after his return [from the convention] . . . that notwithstanding his objections to particular parts of the plan, he would take it as it was rather than lose it altogether."[199]

Randolph, too, had declared late in the Philadelphia convention that he would not be able to sign the Constitution, which "irreconcilably departed" from the Virginia Plan proposals and would, he predicted, "end in tyranny." Among other things, Randolph objected to the small size of the House, Congress's unrestricted power to raise standing armies, the Necessary and Proper Clause, the absence of a supermajority requirement for navigation laws, and the indistinct boundaries drawn between the powers of the federal and state legislatures and the jurisdiction of their judiciaries. "The only mode in which his embarrassments could be removed," Randolph explained in Philadelphia, was to authorize the state ratifying conventions to propose amendments to be submitted, in turn, to "another general convention with full power to adopt or reject the alterations proposed by the state conventions."[200]

However, Madison, who was in touch with Randolph soon after the convention, was not expecting "inveterate" opposition to ratification from him. Madison wrote Jefferson that Randolph's opposition was mostly grounded in his "unwillingness to commit himself, so as not to be at liberty to be governed by further lights on the subject." Carrington told Jefferson that Randolph "has declared that his refusal to sign shall not be followed by hostility against the measure—that his wish is to get the exceptionable parts altered if practicable, but if not, then he will join in its support from the necessity of the case."[201]

Patrick Henry's opposition to the Constitution would prove a much more formidable barrier to ratification in Virginia. As we saw in chapter 3, Henry had declined his appointment to the Philadelphia convention for reasons that

---

* Indeed, Mason's constituents in Fairfax County instructed him as one of their delegates to the Virginia House to support an immediate call for a ratifying convention. Because of the strongly Federalist bent of his constituents, Mason could not be elected as a delegate to the Virginia ratifying convention from his home county and instead had to represent Stafford County, where he also owned property.

are not entirely clear, though his agitation over Jay's willingness to barter away American navigation rights on the Mississippi River—Henry called it an "iniquitous" project that would "crush all our hopes of prosperity for the western country"—may have been among them.[202]

After the Philadelphia convention ended, Henry's views on the Constitution were initially unknown. Madison, who thought "[m]uch will depend" on Henry's position, told Jefferson that he took it "for granted from a variety of circumstances that he [Henry] would be in the opposition." Washington similarly observed that while Henry's views remained undeclared, many people conceived that, "as the advocate of a paper emission, he cannot be friendly to a Constitution which is an effectual bar." On October 19, Henry removed any uncertainty, writing Washington that his concern about the Constitution "is really greater than I am able to express." Henry had already begun announcing his views publicly, as the Virginia legislature assembled for its fall session in mid-October.[203]

Around this time, George Lee Turberville, a member of the Virginia House of Delegates who had serious doubts about the Constitution, summarized the opinions he had heard expressed about it, which "appear to be as various as the persons possessing them":

> The enthusiastic admirers of the thing in toto . . . appear the least considerable. A vast consolidated squadron is composed of those who view the plan as an admirable frame wanting only some few amendments to render it desirable. And a pretty considerable band consists of those who hold it as the engine of destruction and never think or speak of it but with detestation and abhorrence.

Many other observers confirmed that there was "formidable" opposition to ratification in Virginia and that proponents seemed to be "losing ground" over time.[204]

On October 15, Governor Randolph sent the Constitution to the legislature, without comment. Ten days later, delegates in the House debated whether to call a ratifying convention. While they were deeply divided over the merits of the Constitution—and Henry, according to several reports, was seizing every opportunity to criticize it—they manifested little opposition to summoning a convention. However, critics of the Constitution, led by Mason and Henry, insisted that the resolution calling a convention make clear that the convention had the power to propose amendments to remedy defects in the Constitution. By contrast, Federalists, although they did not deny that a convention would be entitled to propose amendments, wished to avoid any action implying that the legislature believed the Constitution stood in need of changes.[205]

After debate, Federalist delegate John Marshall devised a compromise measure, which, once formalized into a motion, called for submission of the Constitution "to a convention of the people for their full and free investigation and discussion." The legislature unanimously approved this resolution, which neither foreclosed amendments nor implied the legislature's disapproval of the Constitution as it stood. This outcome pleased Washington, who had feared that the legislature would brand the Constitution "with the mark of disapprobation" in order "to bias the public mind." Madison agreed that the Virginia legislature had given the Constitution "a more prompt and general approbation than could well have been expected."[206]

The legislature also had to resolve the issue of timing, and, after debate, it scheduled elections for delegates in March for a convention to meet in early June. One member of the House of Delegates, David Stuart, reported to Washington that on the issue of timing, "the variety of sentiments . . . was almost infinite, neither friends nor foes agreeing to any one period." Some Federalist-leaning counties had instructed their delegates to call a quick convention, but Federalist legislators, according to one of them, John Pierce, were "willing to delay it—to see what other states would do." Some Federalists may also have agreed with the judgment of delegate John Dawson, who eventually voted against ratification, that an early convention, if confronted with the question of whether to approve the Constitution without amendments, would probably have rejected ratification.[207]

In turn, some Antifederalist legislators may have hoped that delaying the Virginia convention would enable them to coordinate with allies in other states in a campaign for antecedent amendments and that the identification of constitutional defects by other states' conventions would rally opposition in Virginia. James Monroe, who had concerns about the Constitution but initially favored ratification, only to subsequently change his mind and vote against ratification at the Virginia convention, offered a slightly different explanation for the delay. He told Madison, "[T]he object in the postponement of our convention to so late a day was to furnish an evidence of the disposition of the other states to that body when it would be assembled." If many other states had rejected ratification, then, Monroe explained, Virginia "might mediate between contending parties and lead the way to a union more palatable to all." If, however, all the other states had ratified the Constitution, then "the knowledge of that circumstance [ought to] have its weight" in the deliberations of the Virginia convention.[208]

Whatever the precise thinking behind calling a late convention had been, the choice ultimately had dramatic consequences. As we shall see, by delaying its convention so long, Virginia both deprived itself of influence over the ratifying decisions of most other states and ensured that its convention confronted a very different calculus than it would have had it assembled earlier.[209]*

The fall session of the Virginia legislature had other business to transact besides calling a ratifying convention, and Patrick Henry searched for additional opportunities to criticize the Constitution and send a message to other states that Virginians had grave doubts about unconditional ratification. According to reports from Federalist delegate Pierce, Henry "fires his shot at the new Constitution [at] every opportunity." For example, even though the Virginia legislature the previous year had already remonstrated against Jay's handling of the Mississippi River issue, Henry proposed another such resolution, in order "to show in a forcible manner how the commercial interests of the southern states are sacrificed by the northern whenever it suits their convenience." Similarly, when the House of Delegates debated Congress's recent resolution calling on states to repeal any of their laws that were inconsistent with the 1783 peace treaty, Henry, according to Pierce, seized the opportunity to "attack the Constitution of the union in the strongest terms and endeavored to sow the seeds of jealousy against the federal court, the New England states and the spirit of the union itself."[210]

In December, Henry got his best chance to convey to the nation the Virginia legislature's support for amendments to the Constitution. When the legislature in late October had passed the resolution summoning a convention, it had neglected to authorize payment of expenses for convention delegates. When the House of Delegates turned its attention to redressing that omission, Henry and his allies proposed that the legislature also authorize defraying the expenses of both delegates to a second constitutional convention, "should such a convention be judged necessary," and of deputies sent to confer with the conventions of other states, should the Virginia convention "deem it proper" to appoint them. Henry, according to the report of Archibald Stuart, a Federalist delegate, had defended this proposal on the grounds that Virginia's "southern neighbors might be driven to despair" unless they saw "a door open to safety should they disapprove of the new Constitution."[211]

This proposal, Stuart wrote Madison, confirmed that many Virginia legislators opposed the Constitution "as it now stands," and he feared that the Antifederalists, "hav[ing] discovered their strength, ... will adopt other measures tending to its [the Constitution's] prejudice." In light of such

* When John Breckinridge, a former state legislator who was ambivalent about the Constitution, learned of the late date set for the ratifying convention, he (presciently) wrote that the convention delegates "will have little to deliberate on by the time they meet. Nearly all the states will have met before June, and this state will agree with the majority."

developments, Stuart declared himself "happy to find most of the states will have decided on the question before Virginia, for I now have my doubts whether she would afford them as usual a good example."[212]

While Federalists were able to defeat their adversaries' proposal, which would have made clear the legislature's support for a second convention, they could not prevent the enactment on December 12 of a law authorizing payment of expenses should the Virginia convention "deem it necessary to hold any communications with any of the sister states or the conventions thereof" for the purpose of securing "the greatest unanimity . . . during the deliberations concerning the great and important change of government which has been proposed by the federal convention." The Virginia legislature, by this act, had clearly indicated its interest in coordinating with other states in support of constitutional amendments. Two weeks later, the legislature voted to instruct Governor Randolph to send a copy of this statute to the other states.[213]

Rufus King, who was in New York City and probably was privy to the reports Madison was receiving there from Richmond, now reported that "[t]he nabobs of Virginia begin to be alarmed." Indeed, Virginia Federalists were increasingly worried that even if most Virginians supported ratification, their views might be altered, as Madison told Jefferson, "by the united influence and exertions" of Henry, Mason, and Randolph. While Madison believed that Randolph and Mason probably could be reconciled to the Constitution with amendments providing "a few additional guards in favor of the rights of the states and of the people," he considered Henry "the great adversary who will render the event precarious." Madison believed that Henry, at a minimum, favored "the principle of the existing confederation" and thus would probably "contend for such [amendments] as strike at the essence of the [new] system." At the worst, Henry preferred "a partition of the union into several confederacies."[214]

Madison's allies in Virginia confirmed his alarming description of Henry's position. In January 1788, Edward Carrington reported that Henry was insisting upon amendments prior to ratification and that he was prepared to "leave the fate of the measure to depend on all the other states conforming to the will of Virginia." Henry was saying, according to Carrington, that "the other states cannot do without us and therefore we can dictate to them what terms we please." If other states resisted, then Virginia "may alone enter into foreign alliances. The value of our tobacco is such that any nation will be ready to treat with us separately."[215]

A few weeks later, after travels on circuit had taken him "pretty much within the neighborhood of Mr. Henry," Carrington confirmed that it was "fairly to be concluded that his [Henry's] views are a dismemberment of the union." Moreover, Henry's opposition to the Constitution had "been so industriously propagated that the people are much disposed to be his blind followers." Carrington told Madison that "demagogues in opposition" to ratification were drowning out Federalists, who thought "it prudent to suppress their opinions or at least to advance them with caution." The one optimistic note struck by Carrington was that other Virginia Antifederalists seemed "alarmed at the probable extent of Mr. Henry's views" and professed "a determination to do nothing which may even endanger the union."[216]

Other Virginia Federalists offered similar reports of the evolution in Henry's views. In April, George Nicholas reported that Henry had become "almost avowedly an enemy to the union, and therefore will oppose every plan that would cement it." However, Nicholas hoped that if Henry's "real sentiments" were exposed, then other Virginia Antifederalists, who unlike Henry were genuinely "friends to the union," would cease to support his call for antecedent amendments. That month, Madison confirmed that Henry seemed "to aim at disunion" and was resorting to "desperate measures."[217]

Meanwhile, the two Virginians who had refused to sign the Constitution in Philadelphia, Mason and Randolph, were moving in directions opposite to one another. In the fall of 1787, Federalist legislator Archibald Stuart had reported that Randolph, after initially reacting with "much anxiety" when he was "coolly received" in Richmond because of his refusal to sign the Constitution, had begun criticizing it with "more confidence" upon learning of opposition from around the state. Randolph himself complained to Madison that "[t]he conjectures [in Virginia] of my reasons for refusing to sign were extraordinary, and so far malicious as to suppose that I was chagrined at not carrying every point in my own way [at the convention], or that I sought for popularity."[218]

Randolph said little publicly about the Constitution in the months after the Philadelphia convention. (As governor, it would probably have been inappropriate for him to do so.) In early December, four House delegates, stating that they had heard rumors that Randolph's reasons for disapproving the Constitution "no longer exist," asked for permission to publish the objections to the Constitution that he claimed to have written earlier for the benefit of the legislature (but had never sent to it). Randolph acquiesced, and the delegates had his objections published in late December as a pamphlet, which was widely reprinted in newspapers throughout the country.[219]

In his published letter, Randolph began by explaining that once his fellow delegates in Philadelphia had convinced him that the Articles were seriously defective, he had supported the creation of a powerful national government, which could collect taxes, retaliate against foreign trade discrimination, and enforce treaties within the states. The alternative to forming such a government, he warned, was dissolution of the union, which he thought would spell disaster.[220]

However, Randolph, in his published letter, insisted that despite his admiration for his Virginia colleagues at the convention and his reverence for Washington, his conscience would not permit him to sign a defective constitution. Amendments were needed, and the best mechanism for obtaining them—which Randolph had proposed in Philadelphia, only to have the convention overwhelmingly reject it—was to allow state ratifying conventions to propose amendments and then to call a second national convention to consider them. Such amendments should precede ratification, Randolph explained, both because "a bad feature in government becomes more and more fixed every day" and because "a bare majority of states" would suffice for the approval of antecedent amendments—Randolph did not explain why this was the case—whereas the Constitution would require a three-fourths majority of the states for the enactment of subsequent amendments.[221]

Randolph also noted that his two principal objections to the Constitution were the provision for equal state representation in the Senate and the absence of a supermajority requirement for commercial legislation. In addition, he objected to certain "ambiguities of expression"—such as in the boundaries established between national and state power—as well as to the absence of mandatory rotation in office for the president, the Senate's power to try impeachments and make treaties (in conjunction with the president, but to the exclusion of the House), and the president's power to pardon persons convicted of treason.[222]

Yet Randolph concluded his published letter on a very different note. His "most fervent prayer" was for "the establishment of a firm, energetic government," and he opined that "the most inveterate curse which can befall us is a dissolution of the union." He would "cling to the union as the rock of our salvation," and "if after our best efforts for amendments they cannot be obtained," he pledged to "accept the Constitution" as it was.[223]

Across the country, Federalists generally regarded Randolph's letter as favorable to their side, and Antifederalists condemned it. From New York City, Madison wrote Washington, "It is generally understood here that the arguments contained in it in favor of the Constitution are much stronger than the objections which prevented his assent." From Richmond, Virginia legislator Turberville reported that Randolph's letter "has been of great service in promoting the adoption of it [the Constitution]." By contrast, the Virginia Antifederalist "Plain Dealer" criticized Randolph, the governor "of a free republican government," for his willingness to approve a constitution that he had previously warned was likely to end in "either a monarchy or an aristocracy."[224]

Because Randolph's position was to seek antecedent amendments only so long as obtaining them was practicable, he was subject to being swayed by developments on the ground. In late February 1788, after learning that

Massachusetts had become the sixth state to ratify, Randolph confirmed, in a letter to Madison, that he believed Virginia would have no choice but to endorse the Constitution if nine other states had done so before its convention met. Madison responded by trying to convince Randolph that the time to make ratification conditional on amendments had already passed and that "the only ground" for "a coalition among all the real Federalists" was "[r]ecommendatory alterations." In reply, Randolph acknowledged that "the hope of obtaining them [antecedent amendments] might be frustrated by the assent of too many states."[225]

In addition, both Madison and Washington sought to persuade Randolph to abandon his long-held enthusiasm for a second convention. Washington told him that such a gathering "would be productive of more heat and greater confusion than can well be conceived," and Madison warned that a second convention would either fail entirely or produce a document even further removed from Randolph's preferences. By late April, Madison was reporting to Jefferson that Randolph was "so temperate in his opposition and goes so far with the friends of the Constitution that he cannot properly be classed with its enemies."[226]

While Randolph was moving in the direction of the Federalists, Mason's opposition to ratification seemed to be intensifying—for two reasons, according to Virginia Federalist George Nicholas. The first was the "irritation he feels from the hard things that have been said of him." Second, Mason had come to entertain "a vain opinion . . . (which has industriously been supported by some particular characters) that he has influence enough to dictate a constitution to Virginia, and through her to the rest of the union."[227]

Madison agreed that Mason appeared to be "ripening fast for going every length. His licentiousness of animadversion it is said, no longer spares even the moderate opponents of the Constitution." Madison told Jefferson that "Colonel Mason is growing every day more bitter and outrageous in his efforts to carry his point, and will probably in the end be thrown by the violence of his passions into the politics of Mr. Henry." Hugh Williamson, a North Carolina Federalist, reported that in a courthouse speech in Stafford County, Virginia, where Mason was running for election as a delegate to the Virginia convention, Mason had denied that the Philadelphia convention was "an assemblage of great men," insisting instead that the eastern delegates were "knaves and fools," the delegates representing states south of Virginia were "a parcel of coxcombs," and "not a few" of the mid-Atlantic delegates were "office hunters."[228]

Elections for delegates to Virginia's ratifying convention finally took place in March. Soon after the Philadelphia convention, Washington had urged Madison to stand for election to the state ratifying convention, noting that explanations of the Constitution "will be wanting [and] none can give them with more precision than yourself." Federalist legislator Archibald Stuart similarly informed Madison that "it is generally considered necessary that you should be at the convention" and implored him, "[F]or God's sake do not disappoint the anxious expectations of your friends and let me add of your country." Warning that "the federal system is roughly handled by some very able men in this state," yet another friend and political ally, Lawrence Taliaferro, also pleaded with Madison to run.[229]

However, Madison initially professed reluctance to serve in the convention on the grounds that "the final decision" upon the Constitution "should proceed from men who had no hand in preparing and proposing it." Later, he told Washington that participating in the convention "will involve me in very laborious and irksome discussions," require "public opposition to several very respectable characters whose esteem and friendship I greatly prize," and subject his views to "disagreeable misconstructions."[230]

In the end, Madison agreed to stand for election, explaining to his brother that many other members of the Philadelphia convention had become delegates to their states' ratifying conventions, that "very respectable friends" had implored him to run, and that his service in Philadelphia would enable him "to contribute some explanations and information which may be of use" in addressing "misconception[s]" about the Constitution and explaining how parts of it that Virginians might consider objectionable had come about. Yet Madison remained reluctant to return to Virginia to campaign. He had always hated electioneering,* and he would have preferred to remain in New York City, where he was attending Congress and working on *The Federalist*. Madison told Washington that he preferred not to return to Orange County, Virginia, to campaign, for he wished "to avoid apparent solicitude on the occasion," as well as "a journey of such lengths at a very unpleasant season." Yet he would do so if "informed that my presence at the election in the county be indispensable."[231]

Throughout the winter, Madison's family and political allies beseeched him to return home for the election. Taliaferro wrote Madison, "You will be greatly surprised to hear that it is reported that you are opposed to the system [the Constitution] and I was told the other day that you were actually writing a piece against it." Only Madison's presence could prevent men "from being led into an error." Randolph bluntly told Madison that he "must come" or else "hazard it [his election] by being absent at the time." Madison's father warned him that the district's Baptists, who were numerous, were now "generally opposed" to ratification and that some of the planters had turned against the Constitution after visiting Richmond to sell their tobacco and hearing many

---

* In 1777, Madison lost the only popular election of his life when he refused to provide his constituents with the customary alcohol on the hustings.

legislators' denunciation of it. He implored Madison to return home to defend the Constitution, as some of his friends and neighbors "suspend their opinion till they see you and wish for an explanation."[232]

Yielding to the importuning of his friends and family, Madison returned to Orange County. However, "[t]he badness of the roads and some other delays," as he explained, resulted in his reaching home only the day before the election. He then discovered to his chagrin that the county was "filled with the most absurd and groundless prejudices against the federal Constitution." Madison found himself obliged "to mount for the first time in my life the rostrum before a large body of the people and to launch into a harangue of some length in the open air and on a very windy day."[233]

In the election results, Madison headed the list of four candidates (who were competing for two slots) with 202 votes. The other Federalist candidate also was elected to the convention with 187 votes. The two Antifederalists polled only 56 and 34 votes. Madison concluded that it was "very probable that a very different event would have taken place as to myself if the efforts of my friends had not been seconded by my presence," though his substantial margin of victory renders that claim dubious.[234]

In most of the contests for seats in the Virginia ratifying convention, candidates ran on a platform of supporting or opposing the Constitution. The election results revealed a state starkly divided by region over ratification. Madison reported to Jefferson that almost all counties in the Northern Neck (the far northeastern part of the state) had elected Federalists, while counties south of the James River had chosen Antifederalists. The "intermediate district is much chequered in this respect." Counties between the Blue Ridge and Allegheny Mountains had chosen Federalists "without a single exception," while counties just west of the Alleghenies had "generally though not universally pursued the same rule." Farther west, however, the Kentucky region was thought to be divided.[235]

After the election results were published, nearly all observers on both sides of the debate predicted a narrowly divided convention. Nicholas told Madison that he believed a majority of the delegates would be Federalists, "but that majority if it exists will be but small." Mason wrote Jefferson that the delegates would be "so equally divided upon the subject that no man can, at present, form any certain judgment of the issue." Randolph actually thought that a narrow majority of the delegates favored antecedent amendments.[236]

Many people judged the parties so evenly balanced that they predicted the fourteen Kentucky delegates, whose views were initially less well known, would determine the outcome of the convention. For example, Madison declared that "[a] good deal may depend on the vote of Kentucky," and he worried that those delegates "may come fettered not only with prejudices but with instructions." He told Washington that he had written "several letters" to Kentucky correspondents "with a view to counteract antifederal machinations." Washington agreed that the Kentucky delegation would "have great weight in deciding this question."[237]

As Madison acquired additional information about the predispositions of the Kentucky delegates, he grew increasingly pessimistic. In April, he had told Jefferson, "Kentucky, it is supposed, will be divided." Yet as the Richmond convention assembled early in June, Madison confided to Washington that "Kentucky has been extremely tainted, is supposed to be generally adverse, and every piece of address is going on privately to work on the local interests and prejudices of that and other quarters." About a week later, he told King that "the vote of Kentucky will turn the scale, and there is perhaps more to fear than to hope from that quarter," as those delegates had arrived in Richmond "generally under an adverse bias produced by a combination of efforts to mislead them."[238]

In early June 1788, according to one North Carolina Federalist, "all eyes . . . [were] looking with hope or fear towards Virginia." The ratifying convention in Richmond, which assembled on June 2, featured titans on both sides, as Virginia Antifederalists put forward a more talented and elite lineup of speakers than did their allies in other states. Leading the opposition was Patrick Henry, who was regarded by Jefferson, who despised him, as "the greatest orator that ever lived."* Two decades earlier, Henry's early and strident opposition to British efforts to exert greater control over the colonies had made him a national hero. By calling the king's actions tyrannical, Henry had even risked a prosecution for treason.[239]

Now, Henry in effect declared war on the Constitution. He dominated the Virginia ratifying convention, speaking nearly every day and holding the floor for as much as one-quarter of the entire proceedings.† Liberally brandishing

---

* William Short, a Virginian who was serving as Jefferson's private secretary in Paris, thought that while Federalists would have "a great weight of abilities" in Richmond, "the powers of Henry in a large assembly are incalculable." James Breckinridge, a Virginia Federalist who witnessed the first week of the convention's deliberations, wrote that Henry's "eloquence and oratory far exceeded my conception. In such an assembly he must, to be sure, be better adapted to carry his point and lead the ignorant people astray than any other person upon earth." After attending portions of the convention, Martin Oster, the French vice-consul in Virginia, wrote that Henry had "displayed a popular eloquence and an astonishing resource of genius and abilities."

† David Robertson, a prominent Petersburg lawyer, attended the entirety of the Virginia convention and took shorthand notes, which were later published. Consequently, the proceedings were reported more copiously than those of any other state. However, Antifederalists charged Robertson with bias, and some prominent Federalists also questioned the accuracy of his reporting.

Figure 6.7 Patrick Henry, who was one of the leaders of the revolutionary movement in Virginia and the state's first postcolonial governor, led the opposition to the ratification of the Constitution in Virginia but later became a Federalist and declined invitations from President Washington to serve as secretary of state and as Chief Justice of the Supreme Court. (Courtesy of Independence National Historical Park)

his credentials as a Revolutionary hero and passionate defender of liberty, Henry held his audience in rapt attention. He also refused to be constrained by convention rules that required paragraph-by-paragraph consideration of the Constitution, repeatedly wandering into general denunciations that were technically out of order.[240]

Even before the convention, Federalists had expressed concern, in Carrington's words, that "a great proportion of the Assembly [i.e., convention] will be so overborn by the declamatory powers of Mr. Henry as to be deceived into his measures although their ultimate views may be entirely different." Now, at the convention, Federalists complained that Henry discarded "solid argument and strong reasoning" in favor of "throwing those bolts, which he has so peculiar a dexterity at discharging." Indeed, in his desperation to defeat ratification in Virginia, Henry was not above resorting to personal invective, disingenuousness, and outright demagoguery—as the following examples illustrate.[241]

In one controversial tactic, Henry quoted from a letter written by Jefferson urging that, after nine states had ratified the Constitution, which would "secure to us the good it contains," the other four should "refuse to accede to it, till a declaration of rights be annexed." Henry urged serious consideration of "the counsel of this enlightened and worthy countryman of ours."[242]

Several Federalists strongly objected to Henry's invocation of Jefferson's name. Chancellor Edmund Pendleton, who was the president of the convention, observed that Jefferson was simply "a private individual, however enlightened," and as such his opinion "ought not to influence our decision." Madison insisted that convention delegates should be able to follow their "own reason," that Jefferson's "feelings [would] be wounded" by the mention of his name, and that Jefferson "would be for the adoption of the Constitution" were he present at the Richmond convention. Moreover, if Antifederalists insisted on invoking "the opinion of an important character . . . to weigh on this occasion, could we not adduce a character equally great on our side?"—meaning Washington. Randolph pointed out that since the required nine states had not yet ratified the Constitution, Jefferson's logic would have led him to favor Virginia's ratification "to prevent a schism in the union"—which was, as we shall see, precisely Randolph's position.[243]*

In perhaps his most demagogic tactic, Henry played on white Virginians' paranoia with regard to slavery. Observing that northerners were likely to dominate Congress, Henry warned that "[a]mong ten thousand implied powers which [Congress] may assume" was the authority to "liberate every one of your slaves" by conscripting them into military service in the event of a war. He also alluded to a dark design behind the Framers' failure to explicitly protect slave property in the Constitution. Finally, Henry warned that Congress's power over state militias would be construed to be exclusive, which would mean that Virginia could not suppress its own slave insurrections without congressional acquiescence.[244]

Henry's principal allies at the convention were George Mason, William Grayson, and James Monroe.† Virginia's Antifederalists made the usual

---

* Although the delegates could not know it because of the slowness of transatlantic mail, Jefferson had changed his mind by the time of the Virginia convention, telling Carrington that undecided states should pursue the "far preferable" Massachusetts strategy of unconditional ratification with a call for subsequent amendments.

† After the convention, Monroe explained to Jefferson that although he had had some "strong objections" to the Constitution from the beginning, he had not publicly stated his views until the convention. In fact, however, Monroe's initial impressions of the Constitution, conveyed in a letter to Madison in October 1787, had been, on balance, favorable to ratification: "There are in my opinion some strong objections against the project. . . . But under the predicament in which the Union now stands, and this state in particular with respect to this business, they are overbalanced

arguments against ratification: the absence of a bill of rights, the Constitution's consolidationist tendencies, Congress's vastly expanded power over taxation, the small size of the House, and the broad jurisdiction of the federal judiciary.[245]

Yet Virginia Antifederalists also made their own distinctively southern and Virginian arguments against the Constitution. Because delegates from Kentucky were thought to hold the balance of power at the convention, Antifederalists repeatedly invoked Secretary for Foreign Affairs John Jay's apparent willingness to abandon American claims to navigation rights on the Mississippi River as a reason for rejecting ratification. Madison reported to King that a great deal was being made of the Mississippi issue during the convention—"particularly out of doors where the chief mischief is effected." Antifederalists raised the topic so often that their opponents protested at the "very reprehensible" attempts being made to appeal to "local interests" and "partial considerations."[246]

Thus, Henry argued that ratifying the Constitution would lead to "the loss of the navigation" of the Mississippi, which northern states had "the interest and inclination ... to relinquish." Although Henry expressed resentment at being accused of "scuffling for Kentucky votes and attending to local circumstances," in fact he had written to several prominent Kentuckians to warn that ratification would jeopardize their claim to the Mississippi River.[247]

Grayson, too, warned that northern states would wish to keep the Mississippi River closed in order to halt western migration, "retain their inhabitants, [and] preserve their superiority and influence" over the South. Monroe agreed that "the northern states would not fail of availing themselves of the opportunity given them by the Constitution of relinquishing that river, in order to depress the western country, and prevent the southern interest from preponderating." He warned that while the Articles did not permit the consummation of a treaty abandoning the American claim to navigation rights on the Mississippi River without the acquiescence of nine states, the Constitution would permit the ratification of such a treaty by two-thirds of the senators present, which could, depending on attendance, amount to the senators of fewer than seven states.[248]

Antifederalists also complained that equal state representation in the Senate would benefit the North to the detriment of Virginia. Henry demanded

---

by the arguments in its favor." In the months that followed, Monroe did not commit himself—publicly or privately—one way or the other on the Constitution. In April 1788, Madison wrote Jefferson: "Monroe is considered by some as an enemy [to the Constitution], but I believe him to be a friend, though a cool one." Just before the convention, Monroe wrote a pamphlet expressing strong objections to the Constitution, but he decided at the last minute not to have it published, partly because, upon reflection, he found his arguments "loosely drawn" and partly because he thought it might be improper to intervene in the debate so close to the convention.

to know why "[t]he two petty states of Rhode Island and Delaware, which, together, are infinitely inferior to this state in extent and population, have double her weight, and can counteract her interest." Northerners might control the presidency as well as the Senate, Henry warned, because if the electoral college failed to produce a majority for any candidate, the House would choose the president, with each state's delegation casting an equal vote. Operating in tandem with one another, a northern-dominated Senate and a northern-leaning president could enact treaties that advantaged the northern carrying states over the staples-exporting southern states.[249]

Grayson warned that "the produce of the southern states will be carried by the northern states on their own terms" and that northerners would use their dominance in Congress to channel federal spending in their direction—for example, subsidizing shipbuilding for a navy. He linked the issues of northern domination of Congress and navigation rights on the Mississippi: Keeping the river closed would stymie western migration and ensure that no new states were formed in that region, thus preserving northern control over Congress. Grayson concluded that Virginia, which was "rich" and of "vast consequence," would "lose her importance" under the Constitution. Virginia was giving up an "immense" amount, but "[w]hat does she get in return?"[250]

Similarly, Henry protested that under the Constitution, the national government would "subject everything to the northern majority," rendering the South vulnerable to "the most oppressive mode of taxation." To ratify the Constitution would be to confer "unbounded power over our property in hands not having a common interest with us." For example, northerners might use their control of Congress to pay off at face value the continental currency that New England speculators had bought for a pittance. Indeed, Henry argued that the Constitution's clause prohibiting ex post facto laws would require Congress to do so, resulting in what Mason contended would be "the destruction and annihilation of all the citizens of the United States to enrich a few."[251]

Virginia Antifederalists also maintained that the jurisdiction of the federal courts to hear lawsuits between foreigners and American citizens, combined with the absence of a right to a jury trial in federal civil cases, rendered Virginia debtors vulnerable to lawsuits by British creditors. Henry wondered why delegates to the Virginia convention would "venture to ruin their own citizens" by subjecting them to "unjust and vexatious suits and appeals" in tribunals that did not exist when the debts were undertaken. Grayson agreed that when such debts were contracted, suit could be brought only in state court, where both parties probably contemplated "procrastination and delays" in a venue that would naturally be favorable to the Virginia debtors. The Treaty of Paris specified only that states impose no hindrances to the collection of prewar debts; it did not require that creditors be put in a more advantageous position.[252]

Insisting that everyone knew he had always spoken in favor of the payment of prewar debts to British creditors, Mason nonetheless declared that the Constitution ought not to confer upon those creditors the "power to gratify private malice to our injury." He observed, "There are a thousand instances where [such] debts have been paid, and yet must by this appellate cognizance be paid again." In addition, Mason thought it "disgraceful" that citizens of other states could "arraign" Virginia, "like a culprit," and drag the state into federal court to adjudicate claims regarding the disposition of its western lands or other controversies.[253]

As the convention proceeded paragraph by paragraph through the Constitution, the Antifederalists—Henry especially—criticized virtually every provision. When Mason objected that the Constitution required Congress to publish a statement of its accounts only "from time to time," an exasperated Henry Lee disparaged the concern as "trivial." Madison, too, grew weary of the Antifederalists' supposing that congressional representatives "will do every mischief they possibly can, and that they will omit to do every good which they are authorized to do." Why not assume instead that voters of "virtue and intelligence" would select as their representatives "men of virtue and wisdom"? Federalist delegate James Innes likewise objected to the Antifederalists' mode of argument: "[H]orrors have been called up, chimeras suggested, and every terrific and melancholy idea adduced" to oppose ratification. The Antifederalists, Zachariah Johnston complained, had put "the strained construction ... on every word and syllable, in endeavoring to prove oppressions which can never possibly happen."[254]

Madison, who had proved instrumental in bringing about the Philadelphia convention and setting its agenda, led the Federalists in Richmond, taking "the principal share" in the pro-ratification argument, according to the account Monroe subsequently provided to Jefferson. Madison was slight of stature, timorous, frequently ill, and so soft-spoken in public debate that the convention's stenographer frequently could not hear his words.* Yet Madison overcame what he called a "bilious attack" that left him "extremely feeble" and confined to his room for two days, as well as the "extreme heat of the weather,"

---

* Jefferson had anticipated that Madison would be the "main pillar" of the Constitution at the Virginia ratifying convention. While he expected Madison to be "an immensely powerful" champion of ratification, he thought it "questionable" whether Madison could "bear the weight of such a host."

to battle toe to toe with the formidable Henry.* Madison's principal allies at the convention were Edmund Pendleton, Henry Lee, George Nicholas, and Francis Corbin.[255]

Randolph proved to be another important proponent of ratification at the Virginia convention. As noted earlier, Randolph had refused to sign the Constitution at the end of the Philadelphia convention, and several months later, he was still insisting on the need for antecedent amendments, while expressing approval of many features of the Constitution. Less than two months before the convention, Madison was still uncertain as to "which party will have most of his [Randolph's] aid." Many of the delegates in Richmond were eager to discover their governor's current position on ratification.[256]

What the delegates witnessed was a "curious spectacle," as Monroe described it: "[H]aving refused to sign the paper [in Philadelphia,] everybody supposed him [Randolph] against it. But he afterwards had written a letter and having taken a part which might be called rather vehement than active he was constantly laboring to show that his present conduct was consistent with that letter and the letter with his refusal to sign."[257]

On June 4, the convention's first day of substantive deliberations, Randolph rose to explain his actions, although he refused to "apologize to any individual" for obeying "the impulse of duty." At the Philadelphia convention, he explained, he had felt that he could not bind himself to support the Constitution until he had observed the public reaction to it. Although he wished "for a firm energetic government," he thought the Constitution in need of amending. "Wholly to adopt or wholly to reject it" was "too hard an alternative." Moreover, he had worried that to insist on an up-or-down vote would result in the Constitution's defeat. While he favored "any practical scheme of amendments," he would never "assent to any scheme that will operate a dissolution of the union." For Randolph, "the only question has ever been between previous and subsequent amendments."[258]

Yet by postponing "this convention to so late a day," Randolph felt that the Virginia legislature had "extinguished the probability" of antecedent amendments "without inevitable ruin to the union, and the union is the anchor of our political salvation." Randolph declared, "I will assent to the lopping of this limb (meaning his arm) before I assent to the dissolution of the union." Because eight states had already unconditionally ratified the Constitution, Randolph concluded that Virginia must ratify as well to preserve the union. As

---

* For several years, Madison and Henry had been doing battle in the Virginia House of Delegates over issues such as tax policy, the payment of prewar debts to British creditors, and public subsidies for the Episcopal Church. That Henry and Madison were longtime political adversaries possibly played some role in Henry's decision to declare war on the Constitution.

Madison reported to Washington, Randolph had "thrown himself fully into the federal scale."[259]*

In Richmond and across the nation—and especially in New York, where two-thirds of the delegates recently elected to the state's ratifying convention opposed unconditional ratification of the Constitution—Federalists were delighted with Randolph's conversion into a full-throated ally, which they considered immensely important to the success of their cause. Patrick Henry, by contrast, was furious with Randolph. Three days after Randolph's speech, Henry observed that it was "very strange and unaccountable that that which was the object of his [Randolph's] execration should now receive his encomiums. Something extraordinary must have operated so great a change in his opinion." In turn, Randolph forcefully objected to this attack upon his character—Henry seemed to be implying a corrupt motive for Randolph's conversion—which he declared incompatible "with the least shadow of friendship."[260]

Madison and the other Federalist delegates—with Randolph now firmly ensconced on their side—responded to each of their opponents' principal criticisms of the Constitution. In reply to Henry's allegation that ratification would put slavery at risk, Madison declared himself "struck with surprise," because it would be an obvious "usurpation of power" for the federal government to emancipate slaves. Moreover, why would that government wish to "discourage and alienate the affections of five thirteenths of the union?" Another "great security" for slavery, Madison explained, was the fact that in addition to the five southern states that "were greatly interested in that species of property," three others—New York, New Jersey, and Connecticut—still had significant numbers of slaves and thus would probably oppose any efforts to abolish slavery. Any concern that Congress might severely tax owners for their property in slaves should be alleviated by the constitutional requirement that direct taxes be apportioned according to population—a safeguard that Madison thought "ought to satisfy all reasonable minds."[261]

Nicholas added that Virginians actually gained protection for slavery under the Constitution, relative to what they enjoyed under the Articles of Confederation, through the provision empowering states to call upon the federal government to assist them in suppressing insurrections. Randolph emphasized that nobody in the Virginia or South Carolina delegations to the Philadelphia convention "had the smallest suspicion of the abolition of slavery." Several Federalists noted the paradox that some of their Virginia adversaries

---

* On June 4, William Grayson reported that "two unlucky circumstances happened today— Governor Randolph declared in favor of adopting the Constitution and news has come that South Carolina has ratified."

complained that slavery would be abolished under the Constitution, while others objected that the Foreign Slave Trade Clause would encourage the perpetuation of slavery. How could the Constitution be "opposed for being promotive and destructive of slavery" at the same time?[262]

To assuage the concern of Kentucky delegates that the American claim to navigation rights on the Mississippi River would be abandoned under the Constitution, Virginia Federalists noted several points. For starters, Madison insisted that Jay's negotiations with Spain had been abandoned and would never be revived, due to the strong repugnance southerners had manifested toward them. He also contended that northern states would ultimately recognize that opening the river would serve their own economic interests. For example, open access to the Mississippi River would enhance the value of those western lands held by the United States and thus would facilitate repayment of the national debt.[263]

Federalists also argued that as more northerners emigrated westward, the friends and families they left behind would become advocates for insisting upon American navigation rights on the Mississippi. Moreover, only a strong federal government, such as that created by the Constitution, could force Spain to open the river, as well as pressure the British to honor their treaty obligation to abandon the western forts, at which point they could no longer instigate Indian attacks on settlers from Virginia and other states. Finally, Virginia Federalists noted that because the Constitution required the president's acquiescence for treaties to become law, the claim of Americans to navigation rights on the Mississippi would be harder to abandon under the Constitution than under the Articles.[264]

In response to the Virginia Antifederalists' charge that the South would be oppressed by a northern-dominated national government, Federalists argued that northerners would not be so blind to their own interests as to jeopardize the union by enacting legislation that would alienate the affections of southerners. Moreover, they cautioned, the "general spirit of jealousy with respect to our northern brethren" being voiced by Antifederalists at the Richmond convention would have proved fatal during the Revolutionary War, when Virginia would have been destroyed without the assistance of northern states. The South still needed the union, the Federalist delegates argued, because its long navigable rivers, lack of shipbuilding capacity, and large slave population all rendered it vulnerable to foreign invasion.* The South's "situation and circumstances"—that is, its large slave population—also rendered it dependent upon the national government for assistance in suppressing insurrections.[265]

---

* In the event of a foreign invasion, southern slaves were likely to flock to the enemy, as many thousands of them had done when the British army invaded the South during the Revolutionary War.

Furthermore, the South had little to fear from northern domination, Federalist delegate Nicholas argued, because Virginia's population would soon exceed that of New England. "[A]s their country is well settled, and we have very extensive uncultivated tracts," the new federal government, which he hoped would "last to the remotest ages, will be very shortly in our favor." Similarly, Madison predicted that representatives from soon-to-be admitted western states, who would mostly be southern in their orientations, would quickly come to dominate the House of Representatives. In any event, the Constitution's scheme of checks and balances, together with its implicit reservation of unenumerated powers to the states, would protect the South from any abuse of national government powers.[266]

In response to Antifederalist concerns that federal courts would favor British creditors in their efforts to recover on prewar debts, Randolph insisted that those debts "ought to be paid," and he hoped "the honest convention of Virginia will not oppose it." If the Constitution provided foreign creditors with better access to federal court than Virginia creditors, as Antifederalists complained, it was only because some states had refused to provide justice to foreign litigants, thus necessitating a remedy in the form of federal tribunals. Madison argued that granting federal courts jurisdiction over lawsuits brought by foreigners against American citizens would minimize the occasions for war. He also noted that foreigners' inability to "get justice done them in these [state] courts . . . has prevented many wealthy gentlemen from trading or residing among us."[267]

To the Antifederalist warning that under the Constitution Virginians would face a massive tax increase so that Congress could pay off northern speculators in continental currency, Madison and other Federalists responded that Article VI provided that claims against the United States were no more or less valid than they had been under the Articles. If the old Congress could redeem its vastly depreciated currency on a scale, then so could the new Congress. Federalists also insisted that the clause in the Constitution forbidding ex post facto laws applied only in criminal cases and thus would not require Congress to redeem its currency at face value. Moreover, because nothing in the Constitution makes Congress suable in federal court, whether and how to redeem its currency would remain entirely a matter of congressional discretion. Indeed, because nothing in the Articles prevented Congress's redeeming its money at face value, the Constitution left southerners in no worse a position.[268]

In addition to debating the merits of the Constitution, the delegates had to confront the fundamental question of amendments. Although Madison at this time preferred that there be no amendments at all, he realized that a majority of delegates would not ratify the Constitution unless the convention proposed some. Indeed, a week before the convention met, Mason had told Jefferson that there seemed to be "a great majority for amendments"; the only question was whether the convention would insist that the amendments be adopted prior to ratification. Late in the convention, Madison explained to Hamilton that given "the nice balance of numbers, and the scruples entertained by some who are in general well affected," the Federalists had decided "to preface the ratification with some plain and general truths that cannot affect the validity of the act and to subjoin a recommendation which may hold up amendments as objects to be pursued in the constitutional mode."[269]

Henry insisted that Virginia should stay out of the union until amendments had been proposed either by Congress or by a second convention, and that it was irrelevant that eight states had already approved the Constitution. Even if "twelve states and a half had adopted it," Henry declared that he would, "with manly firmness, and in spite of an erring world, reject it." The states that had already ratified, which Henry believed had been "egregiously misled," could "hardly stand on their own legs." Moreover, even those states were having "heart-burnings and animosity and repent their precipitate hurry." Henry insisted that "[t]here were very respectable minorities [opposed to ratification] in several of them." It was inconceivable that Virginia, "the greatest and most mighty state," would be excluded forever from the union just because it "propose[d] certain amendments as the conditions on which [it] should ratify." Other states would surely "be willing to indulge" Virginia if its "aversion is founded on just grounds."[270]

By contrast, if Virginia followed the example of Massachusetts and simply recommended amendments to be considered after ratification, Henry predicted only "some small possibility" that they would ever be enacted. He argued forcefully that amendments must be antecedent to ratification: "I should be led to take that man to be a lunatic, who should tell me to run into the adoption of a government avowedly defective, in hopes of having it amended afterwards." Henry concluded: "Evils admitted in order to be removed subsequently, and tyranny submitted to in order to be excluded by a subsequent alteration, are things totally new to me."[271]

Other Virginia Antifederalists also insisted that amendments should be an antecedent condition of ratification. Monroe declared that if Virginia demanded prior amendments "with manly fortitude," it would produce "harmony and perfect concord" rather than "disunion and national confusion." Other states had as much of an interest "to be united with Virginia, as it could be her interest to be in union with them." Indeed, Monroe went so far as to argue that "[d]isunion is more to be apprehended from the adoption of a system reprobated by some, and allowed by all to be defective." Unconditional ratification, he warned, would lead to the Constitution's "never be[ing] amended, not even when experience shall have proved its defects."[272]

Grayson agreed that "the idea of subsequent amendments is preposterous." The Federalists were undervaluing Virginia's importance. North Carolina would probably follow Virginia's lead, and if neither of them ratified without antecedent amendments, the northern states would become "carrying states, without having anything to carry." Grayson also ridiculed the notion that other states could afford to abandon the union, should Virginia hold out for antecedent amendments: Small states were too weak to disunite, the New England states held their fisheries "by a hair," and New York and Pennsylvania needed the British out of the forts on their western frontiers in order to recapture the fur trade. Antifederalist Benjamin Harrison V (the father and great-grandfather of future presidents) denied that the union would be dissolved if Virginia insisted upon antecedent amendments because he believed that several other states would support such a demand. In Massachusetts, only the "artifice of the Federalists" had prevailed upon the convention to ratify without prior amendments; New York and North Carolina, whose conventions had yet to meet, would reject the Constitution without antecedent amendments; and there was much support for such amendments even in states that had already ratified, such as Maryland and South Carolina.[273]

Madison responded by denying that nine ratifying states (in fact, only eight states were known to have ratified by this point) would submit to "the demand of a single state." He disputed Henry's claim that even the states that had already adopted the Constitution were experiencing "heart-burnings." To the contrary, Madison insisted, the evidence suggested that satisfaction with the Constitution in those states "is increasing every day." Moreover, only the "mutual deference and concession" displayed at the Philadelphia convention had rendered possible the creation of the Constitution. By contrast, it would demonstrate "neither . . . confidence nor respect" for Virginia to "call on a great majority of the states to acknowledge that they have done wrong" and to question whether those states would subsequently agree to proposed amendments that were said to be necessary "for the preservation of the common liberty." If Virginia blocked the Constitution's ratification, Madison warned, Antifederalists in different parts of the country would never agree on the changes that should be made. Finally, he argued, given how much support existed for particular amendments in the various states, it would surely not be difficult to enact them after ratification.[274]

Randolph agreed that the states that had already ratified the Constitution would not reverse their stands "to gratify Virginia." Rather, they would be irritated at Virginia's trying to arrogate to itself "a right to dictate what ought to be done." Acknowledging that the Constitution was defective and in need of amending, Randolph declared that Henry's proposal for antecedent amendments would have appealed to him if "there were peace and tranquility in this land, and . . . there was no storm gathering which would burst." Yet if Virginia insisted on antecedent amendments now, he predicted that "the union will be dissolved, the dogs of war will break loose, and anarchy and discord will complete the ruin of this country."[275]

Moreover, if nine other states formed a union and Virginia remained outside of it, Randolph warned, "jealousy, rivalship, and hatred would subsist between" those states and Virginia. Nations that shared common borders but were not united into a greater union almost invariably went to war with one another, as had England and Scotland before combining into Great Britain. In addition, without the security provided by the union, Randolph observed, Virginia would be vulnerable to foreign invasions. The Chesapeake Bay rendered Virginia susceptible to penetration by water; the state had little manufacturing with which to make war materiel; its slaves made it especially vulnerable to wartime insurrections; and hostile Indians on the western frontier could be bribed by foreign gold to attack Virginians. Randolph also argued that a conditional ratification, which would leave Virginia outside of the union at least temporarily, would deprive it of influence while important national policy decisions were being made in the first federal Congress.[276]

Other Virginia Federalists denied that the idea of subsequent amendments was as fanciful as their opponents claimed. If Virginia and Massachusetts, the two "most populous, wealthy, and powerful states in the union," recommended amendments, their joint influence would probably be sufficient to carry them. Finally, Federalists warned that if the convention rejected ratification, the state's Northern Neck might secede from Virginia.[277]

Both Federalist and Antifederalist delegates believed that the outcome would turn on just a few votes, and each side claimed to have a majority. About halfway through the convention, Madison wrote Washington, "The majority will certainly be very small on whatever side it might finally lie, and I dare not encourage much expectation that it will be on the favorable side." He told King that the outcome was "more doubtful than was [previously] apprehended" and that "the event is as ticklish as can be conceived." About the same time, Mason reported to John Lamb, one of New York's leading Antifederalists, that while the Virginia delegates generally agreed on the need for amendments, they were "so equally divided with respect to the time and manner of obtaining them, that it cannot now be ascertained whether the majority will be on our side or not."[278]

A week later, on June 20, Madison told Hamilton that the Federalists probably had a majority of three or four, although there remained "a very disagreeable uncertainty in the case, . . . as there is a possibility that our present strength may be miscalculated," and "the smallness of the majority suggests the danger from ordinary casualties which may vary the result." Madison also worried that the Antifederalists might seek an adjournment, which would enable them to better coordinate with their allies in New York. "[A]nother circumstance that ought to check our confidence," Madison observed, was that "[i]t unluckily happens that our legislature, which meets at this place tomorrow, consists of a considerable majority of antifederal members. . . . As individuals they may have some influence, and as coming immediately from the people at large they can give any color they please to the popular sentiments at this moment, and may in that mode throw a bias on the representatives of the people in convention."[279]

Because the convention had yet to take any formal votes, neither side could be entirely confident of its numbers. The first such ballot came on June 25, when the delegates voted by a margin of eighty-eight to eighty to reject a resolution to ratify contingent upon the enactment of antecedent amendments. The delegates then voted to ratify unconditionally by a margin of eighty-nine to seventy-nine.[280]

The form of ratification they agreed upon provided that "the powers granted under the Constitution, being derived from the people of the United States may be resumed by them whensoever the same shall be perverted to their injury or oppression."* It also declared that "among other essential rights, the liberty of conscience and of the press cannot be cancelled, abridged, restrained or modified by any authority of the United States." With "these impressions," and "under the conviction that, whatsoever imperfections may exist in the Constitution ought rather to be examined in the mode prescribed therein [i.e., Article V], than to bring the union into danger by a delay, with a hope of obtaining amendments previous to the ratification," the convention ratified the Constitution.[281]

Before the convention adjourned, however, a committee headed by Federalist George Wythe, which had a Federalist majority and included Madison and Henry, deliberated for two days over which amendments to recommend, before proposing forty of them. Half of these dealt with protections for individual rights—"certain natural rights of which men when they form a social compact cannot [be] deprive[d]." These included freedom of speech, freedom of the press, the free exercise of religion, and many of the other rights that eventually were incorporated into the Bill of Rights.[282]

The other half of the proposed amendments consisted of limits on Congress's powers and structural changes to the federal government. This category included proposals to explicitly secure nondelegated powers to the

---

* In 1860–61, when southern states purported to secede from the union, this language in the Virginia form of ratification was one of many sources white southerners invoked to justify the constitutionality of secession.

states, specify a minimum size for the House, require mandatory rotation in office for the president, require a two-thirds supermajority of both houses of Congress for the enactment of commercial regulations and the raising of a standing army in time of peace, require a three-quarters supermajority of both houses of Congress to ratify treaties that ceded territorial or navigational claims, and restrain Congress from imposing direct taxes until states had first enjoyed an opportunity to raise their proportional share of a requisition through their own methods. The convention then approved the amendments proposed by the committee and also enjoined the state's representatives and senators in the first federal Congress to pursue ratification of these amendments through the mechanism provided in Article V.[283]

"The convention broke up," according to Federalist delegate Archibald Stuart, "in friendship and amity, although our majority was a very small one. The minority, with a few exceptions, have promised their aid to the new government." In contrast to other cities, where large processions to celebrate ratification were becoming the norm, in Richmond the victorious Federalists, according to one report, were "either wise enough, or polite enough, to make no procession or other parade."[284]

Madison, as was his wont during the ratifying contest, was in no celebratory mood. He told Hamilton that many of the amendments proposed by the convention were "highly objectionable." Moreover, despite what Madison described as the "fair professions" by Henry that "he should submit as a quiet citizen" after his defeat at the convention, Madison predicted that Henry's "ill will to the Constitution will produce . . . every peaceable effort to disgrace and destroy it." He told Washington that Henry's strategy would probably be "to engage 2/3 of the [state] legislatures in the task of undoing the work, or to get a Congress appointed in the first instance that will commit suicide on [its] own authority."[285]

Monroe, who had opposed ratification without antecedent amendments, told Jefferson that only the known support and influence of Washington had "carried this government." Although Washington never made a formal statement in support of ratification, he had been promoting a significant expansion of the powers of the federal government for the better part of a decade, had served as president of the Philadelphia convention, and had signed the Constitution. Moreover, his privately voiced opinion "that there is no alternative between the adoption of [the Constitution] and anarchy" had eventually found its way into the public domain and been reproduced in no fewer than forty-nine newspapers. Virginians' desire to make Washington the nation's first president, which would have been impossible without Virginia's participation in the union, might also have been a sufficient consideration to swing the balance at the ratifying convention in favor of the Constitution.[286]

Virginia's ratification, coming when it did, was hugely important to the success of the ratifying campaign. On June 25, reporting from New York, where that state's ratifying convention was a week into its deliberations, Virginia congressional delegate John Brown observed (a week before he had received word of Virginia's ratification), "We wait with fear and trembling to hear the determination of Virginia respecting the new Constitution. Both Federalists and Antifederalists agree in opinion that its fate [in New York] depends upon her decision." Thomas Tudor Tucker, a South Carolina congressional representative and a strong critic of the Constitution, observed a month later that if Virginia had refused to ratify the Constitution, New York would "certainly have rejected it," and North Carolina probably "would have followed the example."[287]

New York

While the Virginia convention was sitting, New Hampshire became the ninth state to ratify the Constitution, thus ensuring that it would become operational. Virginia, the largest and most influential state, became the tenth to ratify. Yet despite these developments, ratification in New York remained very much in doubt.

Earlier in this chapter, we saw that conventions in New Jersey and Connecticut readily ratified the Constitution, partly because it would nullify New York's ability to use its import duties to extract tax revenue from residents of those states. For this same reason, New Yorkers could be expected to oppose ratification. The state impost had supplied a substantial proportion of New York's revenue in the mid-1780s, enabling the legislature to keep other taxes low and largely avoid the farm foreclosures and debtor unrest that afflicted other states. Accordingly, New York's small farmers generally supported the status quo under the Articles and opposed the Constitution. Federalists regularly derided the opponents of ratification in New York as being motivated—and financed—by the state impost. Indeed, John Lamb, collector of the impost, used his customs office to disseminate Antifederalist literature and to coordinate Antifederalist opposition across the country.[288]*

---

* The French vice-consul stationed in New York City speculated that New York state officeholders had additional "personal motives for preserving the complete and full direction of the affairs of the state for as long as possible. The application of money arising from [state] import duties to the funding of public securities on which they speculate is of major importance for their fortunes."

Moreover, in the 1780s, New York had confiscated a great deal of land owned by Loyalists, which arguably violated the 1783 treaty with Great Britain. Ignoring that treaty with impunity would be more difficult under the Constitution, which explicitly guaranteed the supremacy of federal treaties over state law in cases of conflict and created a federal court system to enforce that supremacy.[289]

Alluding to such considerations, "A Columbian Patriot," writing from Boston, noted that New York had motives "that will undoubtedly lead her to a rejection." Less than two weeks after the Philadelphia convention ended, Madison wrote Washington from New York City, "The general voice of this city seems to espouse the new constitution. It is supposed nevertheless that the party in power [in the state] is opposed to it." In November 1787, William Grayson reported, also from New York City, that "there is a great majority against" ratification in the state of New York. As an early indication of opposition in New York, when Congress received the Constitution from the Philadelphia convention, the three New York congressional delegates who were present argued in favor of adding a bill of rights before transmitting it to the states.[290]

The fate of the Constitution in New York was thought to depend significantly on the actions of Governor George Clinton, whom one Federalist described as wielding "astonishingly great" influence in the backcountry. Clinton, who had been governor since 1777, had pursued fiscal and monetary policies that were favorable to small farmers and therefore were generally opposed by the wealthy manor lords, merchants, and lawyers of the state. The long-standing policy differences between these factions were largely reproduced in their stances toward ratification of the Constitution, with Clinton's backers generally becoming Antifederalists.[291]

Although Clinton carefully refrained from making public statements regarding the Constitution during the fall of 1787, reports circulated that, privately, he was "violently opposed to the plan," and he was generally believed to have authored the "Cato" essays criticizing the Constitution. Indeed, while the Philadelphia convention was still sitting, New York Federalists had charged in the newspapers that Clinton was "secretly hostile to such measures as were conceived absolutely necessary to the support of a substantial federal government." Throughout the fall, Clinton refused to call the legislature into special session to consider summoning a ratifying convention, which meant that the issue would be deferred until the legislature convened for its regularly scheduled session in January 1788. When New York delegates Robert Yates and John Lansing, Jr., wrote a public letter to the governor explaining why they had left the Philadelphia convention early—principally noting that they had objected to the convention delegates' decision, contrary to their instructions, to jettison

Figure 6.8 George Clinton, who led the Antifederalists in New York, served more than twenty years as the state's governor, and then was vice president of the United States under Thomas Jefferson and James Madison. (Photography © New-York Historical Society)

the Articles and pursue a "consolidated" government—at least one New York Federalist assumed that Clinton had "had a hand in it."[292]

When the legislature finally met, many Federalists worried that their opponents would try to block the calling of a ratifying convention and might have sufficient strength in the Senate to accomplish that goal. A Federalist lawyer in Albany wrote that the Constitution's "best friends [doubted] whether we shall have a convention called by a legislative act; the opposition are determined to make their first stand here." Antifederalists in the Assembly apparently prepared a resolution to express the legislature's disapprobation of the Constitution but then decided not to submit it. Egbert Benson, the state's Federalist attorney general and an assemblyman, commented that "if the whole [Antifederal] party had had nerves, they would have made the attempt, but some of the most prudent found it would not do."[293]

In place of a resolution criticizing the Constitution, Antifederalist assemblymen proposed one condemning the Philadelphia convention for, rather than "revising and reporting alterations [to] provisions in the Articles of Confederation," instead producing "a new Constitution for the United States, which if adopted, will materially alter the constitution and government of this state, and greatly affect the rights and privileges of the people thereof." Federalists strongly opposed this resolution, claiming that it would send the Constitution "from the legislature with a very dangerous influence," by "throwing an odium on the members of the Convention" in declaring "that they had gone beyond their powers." The people of New York were "as well informed as we are" and "not hoodwinked," Federalists insisted, and should be left to decide for themselves "whether the Convention had exceeded [its] powers or not." Antifederalists replied that their resolution "was a simple detail of facts, which no one could deny," and that the people should be informed that the Philadelphia convention had exceeded its authority. After debate, Federalist assemblymen managed to defeat this proposal by a margin of just two votes.[294]

Federalists also displayed unexpected strength in the New York legislature on the issue of selecting the state's new congressional delegation. They secured four of the five slots when Antifederalist incumbents John Lansing, Jr., and Melancton Smith were not reappointed, and the arch-nationalist Hamilton was chosen as one of their replacements. One Antifederalist leader noted that Hamilton's appointment was "a very considerable point gained over the opponents to the new Constitution, as his election holds up an idea of the approbation of the legislature respecting his late conduct in [the Philadelphia] convention," and "implie[d] an indirect censure" on Yates and Lansing for leaving the convention early.[295]

In the end, Antifederalists in the New York legislature chose not to oppose the calling of a ratifying convention. Perhaps most of them agreed with James Duane, a New York Federalist senator, who warned that for legislators to refuse to summon a ratifying convention would "exhibit a high stretch of arbitrary power," making them "tyrants" rather than "guardians" of the people.[296]

Still, Antifederalist assemblymen introduced a resolution to instruct delegates to the ratifying convention that the Constitution was submitted for "their free investigation, discussion, and decision"—language that was intended to signify that the convention had the authority to propose amendments. Federalists countered that the legislature's charge to the ratifying convention should confine itself to the words used by the Philadelphia convention, which the Confederation Congress had now approved, with regard to transmitting the Constitution to the states—that is, that the Constitution should be submitted to conventions, chosen in each state by the people thereof, "for their assent and ratification." By contrast, Federalists insisted, the Antifederalists' proposed resolution would be "a reflection on Congress," conveying the impression that Congress "had sent to the states a vague and undefined resolution."

This time, Federalists defeated their adversaries' proposal by a margin of five votes.[297]

Without explanation, the legislature broadened the eligibility requirements for voting in the election of delegates to the ratifying convention. While the New York constitution imposed property qualifications for voting in legislative elections, now, for the first time ever in the state, all free males over the age of twenty-one would be eligible to vote in the election of ratifying convention delegates. Across the country, it was generally assumed that broader eligibility for voting advantaged Antifederalists, but in New York it was Federalists who proposed expanding the suffrage, and Antifederalists did not resist. The legislature also chose Poughkeepsie as the convention's venue, a location where both parties would be amply represented in the galleries.[298]

The election for delegates to the convention would take place over several days, beginning in late April, with the convention to assemble in mid-June. One Federalist observed that the "distant day" appointed for the convention revealed that the Antifederalists, who evidently calculated that delaying the convention would enhance their chances of defeating ratification, had done "a good thing with a bad grace." If the Antifederalists had indeed supposed that delay was their friend, their calculation turned out to be, as we shall see, egregiously wrong.[299]

The battle over ratification in New York generated unprecedented levels of political activity and voter interest. Although Federalists dominated the newspapers in the state, as they did elsewhere in the nation, New York Antifederalists were more successful in getting their views publicly circulated than were their counterparts in most other states. Both parties established county committees to supervise the nomination of candidates for the ratifying convention and to coordinate with allies across the state. Henry Oothoudt, an Antifederalist leader, observed, "[S]ince the settlement of America, such exertions have not been made upon a question of any kind as the present upon the new Constitution. Those who advocate the measure are engaged from morning until evening. They travel both night and day to proselytize the unbelieving Antifederals. They have printed . . . hand bills . . . by thousands."[300]

In February 1788, as we have seen, Massachusetts became the sixth state to ratify the Constitution, which was enormously important to the ratifying contest in New York because it made the eventual approval of nine states seem highly probable. In particular, New York Federalists used the Massachusetts convention's recommendation of amendments to their advantage. In *An Impartial Address* to New Yorkers, the Albany Federal Committee congratulated Massachusetts for leading "the way in recommending amendments" for later consideration, perhaps in a convention that could be "easily" assembled "to agree upon amendments after the adoption of the system." By contrast, "the specious . . . idea of previous amendments" would "defeat a system which you shudder at the thought of wholly rejecting."[301]

Similarly, John Jay, who was still the Confederation's secretary for foreign affairs, wrote an important pseudonymous address to the people of New York just before the election of convention delegates, in which he admitted that the Constitution was imperfect but doubted that Americans were likely to get a better one in time to save themselves from their current predicament. The second convention that Antifederalists sought, Jay predicted, would feature delegates who would be less inclined to compromise and more likely to come under foreign influence. Instead, Jay advised, New Yorkers should "give the proposed Constitution a fair trial" and then "mend it as time, occasion and experience may dictate."[302]

"Plebeian," who was possibly Melancton Smith, responded to the Federalists by warning that "we shall hear nothing of amendments from most of the warm advocates for adopting the new government, after it gets into operation." Those persons holding "places of great honor and emolument" under the new government would be reluctant to support amendments detracting from its power. Once the government was in operation, "Plebeian" predicted, it would "acquire strength by habit [and] steal by insensible degrees one right from the people after another." The history of the world revealed few, if any, instances "in which the rulers have been persuaded to relinquish their powers to the people." Thus, it would be "much easier, as well as safer, to enlarge the powers of . . . rulers, if they should prove not sufficiently extensive, than it is to abridge them if they should be too great."[303]

Heading into the balloting, both sides were predicting a close contest. Rufus King reported from New York City that "[i]t is exquisitely problematical what the issue of the business will be in this state—both parties are indefatigable and each seems confident of success." Henry Knox wrote that "it is probable that the parties are nearly balanced."[304]

Although the election for convention delegates took place from April 29 to May 3, under New York election law, county supervisors were barred from opening the boxes and counting the ballots until May 27. By June 5, election results from all counties but one had been reported in the New York newspapers. The results were shocking. In a contest featuring two well-organized political parties holding nearly opposite views on ratification, Antifederalists had won forty-six seats at the ratifying convention, to the Federalists' nineteen. Federalists dominated in New York City and ran evenly in the neighboring counties, but they were defeated everywhere else in the state. New York's Antifederalist leaders were so elated by their margin of victory that they immediately wrote letters touting it to Antifederalists in the states that had yet to decide upon ratification.[305]

With the extent of the Federalists' defeat clearly apparent, Hamilton wrote a long letter to Madison speculating on what might happen at the New York ratifying convention, which was set to assemble on June 17. Hamilton believed that the Antifederalist leaders were hostile to the union but were worried that an outright rejection of the Constitution "would bring matters to [a] crisis between this state and the states which had adopted the Constitution and between the parties in the state," as well as possibly inducing New York City to secede from the state. The Antifederalists' solution might well be to seek "a long adjournment [until the following spring or summer] as the safest and most artful course to effect their final purpose."* Hamilton believed that Antifederalist leaders were calculating that once the federal government commenced operations, it would have to adopt unpopular revenue measures that enemies of the union could exploit to bolster their ranks. If, however, the federal system turned out instead to operate "smoothly and the sentiments of our own people should change, they can then elect to come into the union." Hamilton was uncertain how far the Antifederalist rank and file would follow their leaders' disunionism, but he told Madison that he feared civil war if the states that had yet to decide on the Constitution rejected it, and he concluded by stating, "God grant that Virginia may accede."[306]

The Antifederalists' majority was "so great and so determined" that, according to William Bingham, a Pennsylvania congressional delegate writing from New York City, even "[t]he most sanguine advocates for the federal system only flatter themselves with the hopes that the Convention will adjourn and not reject." However, some Federalists continued to hold out hope that if nine states were to ratify before the New York convention ended, "the ground of opposition, if any, will be entirely altered," and Antifederalists at that point would not dare to block New York's ratification and leave the state "surrounded by enemies." Further, according to New York City Federalist William Duer, the possibility that Antifederalists "cannot agree amongst themselves" with regard to the form that proposed amendments should take "may create a division in favor of the Federalists."[307]

News that South Carolina had become the eighth state to ratify the Constitution reached New York on June 4 and bolstered the Federalists' hopes that a ninth state—either New Hampshire or Virginia—would have ratified before the New York convention had to make its decision. Federalist reports from Richmond describing the early days of the Virginia ratifying convention

---

* If nothing else, a lengthy delay in New York's ratification would enable the state—and holders of state securities, who were a powerful lobbying force—to continue to enjoy the revenue from state import duties, which would instead flow to Congress once the Constitution was ratified and New York joined the new union.

and confidently predicting victory also bolstered the hopes of some New York Federalists.[308]

As the date set for the ratifying convention approached, Antifederalists caucused among themselves in order to, as one of their leaders put it, "form a plan of operations which would promote our object and systematize the business." Antifederalist leaders wished to embolden their supporters to insist on nothing less than conditional ratification and to resist Federalist efforts to pressure them, through threats of coercion by the federal government and of secession by New York City, into supporting ratification with recommended amendments.[309]

Many Antifederalist leaders expressed confidence heading into the convention. Abraham Lansing (the brother of John Lansing, Jr., who had represented New York at the Philadelphia convention) told Abraham Yates, Jr., one of the party's leaders in the New York legislature, that it was "the opinion of all those whom I have conversed with [in the northern part of the state] that the Constitution will be effectually amended previous to its adoption [by the convention]—or that it will be totally rejected." Yates expressed similar confidence, telling Abraham Lansing, "I don't feel very uneasy about consequences. What steps the federals mean to take in reality I cannot imagine." Yates supposed "from common conversation" that the Federalists "had some hopes that the Anties would be taken in by their [the Federalists'] superior ability either to adopt or to adjourn" and that the Antifederalists would not dare to insist on conditional ratification, which would be tantamount to rejection now that so many states had ratified without conditions. Yates predicted that such Federalist arrogance might even stiffen the Antifederalists' resolve for antecedent amendments. Antifederalists in New York City, Yates reported, "seem determined not to adopt (without previous amendments) though all the others [i.e., states] should."[310]

A few days after this exchange, Robert Yates (the nephew of Abraham Yates, Jr.), who had been another of New York's delegates to the Philadelphia convention, wrote to George Mason of Virginia to reassure him of "our fixed determination that we shall not adopt the present Constitution without previous amendments." Confident in the Antifederalists' superior numbers at the convention, Yates promised Mason that "neither sophistry, fear, [n]or influence will affect any change in [our] sentiments." Around the same time, an Antifederalist lawyer in New York City reported that "[u]nanimity and harmony reigns among the Anties," who were determined "to bend their force to the same point," thus "shut[ting] out hope, in the Federalists, of creating divisions."[311]

But New York Federalists recognized that their best chance of victory lay in exploiting whatever divisions might exist within Antifederalist ranks. Most

Federalists believed, as Jay explained to Washington, that the Antifederalists' "principal leaders are very far from being solicitous about the fate of the union [and t]hey wish and mean (if possible) to reject the Constitution with as little debate and as much speed as may be." Yet, Jay suggested, it was "doubtful whether the leaders will be able to govern the party. Many in the opposition are friends to union and mean well." In a similar assessment, William Duer told Madison that while Antifederalist leaders such as Governor Clinton might "hazard everything rather than agree to any system which tended to a consolidation of our government," many of his followers "avowed themselves friends to the union." Because the Antifederalists "cannot agree amongst themselves," it might be possible to "create a division in favor of the Federalists."[312]

Eight states had already ratified the Constitution when New York's convention assembled on June 17; the Virginia convention was still meeting, and New Hampshire's adjourned convention was set to reassemble the following day. New York Federalists calculated that they must extend their convention's deliberations until word (they hoped it would be favorable) had arrived from those states. Hamilton told Madison that the New York Federalists' "only chances will be the previous ratification by nine states, which may shake the firmness of his [Clinton's] followers." Accordingly, it was "of vast importance that an exact communication should be kept up between" Federalists in those three states, and Hamilton hired at his own expense express riders to carry news from the ratifying conventions of Virginia and New Hampshire.[313]

Alexander Hamilton and Melancton Smith* led the two competing sides in Poughkeepsie, a town of about twenty-five hundred people in 1788, located one mile east of the Hudson River, about halfway between New York City and Albany. While Smith was an extremely able exponent of the Antifederalist case for antecedent amendments, Hamilton's superior brilliance in debate was widely acknowledged. (One Federalist admirer referred to Hamilton's "elegant speeches" and called him "one of the most remarkable geniuses of the age.") Smith was ably assisted in Poughkeepsie by Robert Yates, John Lansing, Jr., and Governor George Clinton. Hamilton's most important allies were Jay and Chancellor Robert R. Livingston. Jay, a seasoned diplomat, was adept at conciliating opponents. By contrast, Livingston was perceived as arrogant and

---

* Smith was born in 1744 on western Long Island. His parents were farmers, he was educated at home, and at an early age he became a store clerk in Poughkeepsie. In 1776, Smith became captain of the Dutchess County militia and was appointed one of New York's commissioners for detecting Loyalist conspiracies. During the Revolutionary War, he profited from government contracting and the purchase of confiscated Loyalist estates, and emerged a wealthy man.

In the mid-1780s, Smith moved to New York City, took up the practice of law, and continued his mercantile activities. He also assumed a more active role in politics, becoming a confidant of longtime New York governor George Clinton. Appointed by the New York legislature as a

condescending, and as a result got into heated altercations with his opponents at the convention, who tired of his attempts "to ridicule the opposition out of their arguments."[314]

The Federalists' strategy in Poughkeepsie, as already noted, was to drag out the proceedings until news could arrive from the conventions of New Hampshire and Virginia, and so on the first day of the convention's substantive deliberations Federalist leaders proposed that the Constitution be examined clause by clause before any votes were taken. (This was the opposite of Federalist strategy in those state conventions where supporters of ratification commanded a clear majority of the delegates.) Some Antifederalists were apprehensive, as Abraham Lansing explained, that their cause would "eventually be injured by delay, notwithstanding the[ir] decided majority," because "Federalists would operate upon the hopes or fears of some [convention delegates]." In addition, Lansing worried that "procrastinat[ing] the business" would increase the likelihood that some of the Antifederalists' "country friends" would have to go home to tend to their harvests. Nonetheless, as Robert Yates explained to George Mason, the Antifederalists, secure in their majority, decided to yield on the issue of extended debate "to prevent the opposition from charging us with precipitation." That decision ultimately proved critical.[315]

For more than two weeks, the convention proceeded through the Constitution by sections. The Antifederalists proposed many amendments—a procedure Federalists had agreed to as the price for delaying any votes until the entire Constitution had been examined. Progress was slow. For example, the delegates spent several days discussing a proposed amendment to limit Congress's power to levy excise taxes and direct taxes—a marathon debate arising from the Antifederalists' concern that Congress would deprive states of essential revenue while also imposing regressive taxes.[316]

Antifederalists also objected to Congress's power over the times, places, and manner of congressional elections and to the size of the House, which was

---

delegate to the Confederation Congress in 1785, Smith played a prominent role in drafting and securing passage of the Northwest Ordinance of 1787.

After his failed effort to defeat ratification of the Constitution in New York—discussed in the following pages—Smith became, in the 1790s, a member of the Democratic-Republican party of Thomas Jefferson and James Madison, which formed in opposition to the administrations of George Washington and John Adams. Smith was the first president of the New York Society for Encouraging Manufacturing and a member of various humanitarian organizations, including the Humane Society and the Emigrant Aid Society. He died in 1798, a victim of a yellow fever epidemic. Chancellor James Kent described Smith as "a man of remarkable simplicity, and of the most gentle, liberal, and amiable disposition," and another Federalist adversary described him as a "good and able man."

Figure 6.9 Robert R. Livingston, who served twenty-five years as the first chancellor of the state of New York, was a member of the Continental Congress's committee that drafted the Declaration of Independence, served as the Confederation's first secretary for foreign affairs, and later helped negotiate the Louisiana Purchase as minister to France. (Photography © New-York Historical Society)

said to be too small for adequate representation. They criticized as well the absence of provisions for mandatory rotation and recall in the Senate, an institution that Antifederalists warned would foster aristocracy. On the other side of the debate, probably because eight states had already ratified the Constitution, the Federalists sought to demonstrate how vulnerable New York would be if the union dissolved or if the state were excluded from it: New York City had proved susceptible to attack by land and sea during the Revolutionary War, the Hudson River was a source of weakness in time of invasion, and both the British and the Indians continued to pose a threat to the state's northwestern regions.[317]

On June 21, New Hampshire became the ninth state to ratify the Constitution, and word reached Poughkeepsie three days later. Chancellor Livingston immediately announced in convention that "the circumstances of the country were greatly altered, and the ground of the present debate changed." As one Federalist essayist now noted, the question confronting the convention "is materially different from what it was at first. It is now reduced to this single point—whether we shall unite with the other states in adopting this new form of government, or separate ourselves entirely from them?"[318]

By contrast, Antifederalist leaders denied that anything of significance had changed. Immediately after Livingston's speech, Smith rose to insist that whatever "solemn effect" the news from New Hampshire may have had on Livingston, "it had not altered his [Smith's] feelings or wishes on the subject." Supporting Smith, Lansing declared that "it is still our duty to maintain our rights." New York Antifederalists must not, Lansing maintained, allow fears of a dissolution of the union "to force us to adopt a system which is dangerous to liberty."[319]

Privately, New York Antifederalists conveyed the same message. Governor Clinton reported that the news from New Hampshire had not had "the least effect" upon the Antifederalist delegates, who "are firm and I hope and believe will remain so to the end." Abraham Yates told inquiring congressional delegates that New York Antifederalists would do "the same they would have done if New Hampshire had not adopted it"; they would insist on antecedent amendments even "if all the twelve states were to come in."[320]

Hamilton confirmed, in a letter to Madison, that New Hampshire's ratification seemed to have little effect on New York's Antifederalists, and he declared that "our only chance of success depends on you [i.e., Virginia]." In another letter to Madison written a few days later, Hamilton reiterated that there was "more and more reason to believe that our conduct will be influenced by yours." Although the Federalists' arguments on the merits of the Constitution were not influencing their adversaries, Hamilton thought that some Antifederalist leaders (though not Governor Clinton) appear "to be convinced by circumstances and to be desirous of a retreat." Antifederalist Abraham Lansing seemed to confirm Hamilton's supposition, expressing concern that Virginia's ratification would have a "more serious effect" upon "the spirits and determinations" of New York Antifederalists than had New Hampshire's.[321]

Virginia ratified the Constitution on June 25, and the news reached Poughkeepsie on July 2. Elated Federalists made no effort to stifle their cheers, as many of them had long predicted that ratification by Virginia would have "a vast influence" on New York Antifederalists. One observer in the gallery reported, "Joy and hilarity were painted in the faces of the Federalists."[322]

Yet Antifederalist delegates at least tried to appear unmoved by the latest intelligence. Another spectator reported that the Antifederalists "took no more notice of it [the news from Virginia] than if the most trifling occurrence had been mentioned." Governor Clinton's nephew, De Witt Clinton, a precocious nineteen-year-old who was already contributing pseudonymous newspaper essays in the battle over ratification, similarly reported that the news from Virginia had made "no impressions" on the Antifederalists. In private correspondence as well, some New York Antifederalists insisted that Virginia's ratification was irrelevant to their decision-making. The day the news arrived, Antifederalist delegate Cornelius C. Schoonmaker wrote, "I trust that our deliberations will not in the least be affected or changed, in consequence of the states of New Hampshire and Virginia acceding to the Constitution." Another Antifederalist delegate, Nathaniel Lawrence, told John Lamb, New York's leading Antifederalist organizer, that "the information from Virginia seems to have no effect on us." A few days later, Lamb replied that he was delighted to hear that the Antifederalists "stand firm" and expressed hope that "they will remain so, in spite of their opponents' endeavors to disunite them."[323]

Jay reported to Washington that while news of Virginia's ratification had "disappointed the expectations" of the Antifederalists, their opposition to unconditional ratification "nevertheless continues pertinacious." Federalists were beside themselves. A Federalist congressional delegate from North Carolina considered it "astonishing" that New York Antifederalists seemed "determined to dispute the ground inch by inch" when the ratification of the Constitution by ten states rendered New York's "concurrence sooner or later not only expedient but unavoidable." Writing from Poughkeepsie, one Federalist observed that while he had "fondly (but in vain) expected that the ratification of Virginia would have a serious effect on the minds of the antifederal party," instead Antifederalists seemed "intent on pursuing" a "destructive" path.[324]

The one undeniable effect in Poughkeepsie of Virginia's ratification was on the strategy of Federalist convention delegates. The day after the news arrived, one Antifederalist delegate observed that while his adversaries had previously "disputed every inch of ground, . . . today they have quietly suffered us to propose our amendments without a word of opposition to them." Although the Federalists did not explain their change of strategy, they had probably concluded that, with the conventions of New Hampshire and Virginia having ratified the Constitution, further delay in Poughkeepsie would produce no additional benefits for them.[325]

The Federalists' change of strategy had a dramatic impact on the pace of the convention proceedings. It had taken the delegates nearly two weeks to get through the provisions in Article I of the Constitution, but once the Federalists stopped responding to their opponents' objections and proposed amendments, Articles II and III together were dispensed with in just three days and the rest of the Constitution in less than one day. On July 7, Lansing proposed a series of individual-rights amendments to supplement the structural amendments already proposed along the way by the Antifederalists.[326]

At this point, nobody was quite certain what to expect next. The Antifederalists had proposed a plethora of amendments, but what they planned to do with them was, as one Federalist delegate observed, "difficult to determine." Would these amendments be offered as antecedent conditions of ratification, or would they simply be recommended for future adoption, which is how other ratifying conventions had treated their amendments? The Poughkeepsie convention was adjourned for two days as the Antifederalist delegates caucused among themselves.[327]

Federalist leaders privately expressed hope that the Antifederalists were now divided and that it might be possible to exploit their divisions. Indeed, with this expectation, Federalist leaders had been lobbying Antifederalist delegates outside of formal proceedings since the convention began. On July 8, Hamilton told Madison, "We have good reason to believe that our opponents are not agreed, and this affords some ground of hope. Different things are thought of—conditions precedent, or previous amendments; conditions subsequent, or the proposition of amendments upon condition, that if they are not adopted within a limited time, the state shall be at liberty to withdraw from the union; and lastly recommendatory amendments." That same day, Jay offered a similarly hopeful assessment to Washington, while adding the observation that "the unanimity" of New York's southern counties in favor of the Constitution and "their apparent determination to continue under the wings of the union operates powerfully on the minds of the opposite party."[328]

The Antifederalist delegates were indeed divided. Although they publicly denied it, the news of ratification by the New Hampshire and Virginia conventions had in fact influenced the thinking of at least some of them. The Constitution had become operational; the Poughkeepsie convention was no longer deciding whether there would be a new federal government but only whether New York would participate in it.[329]

On July 9, Abraham Lansing reported having "received some accounts from our friends, which savor much of division among them respecting the mode of introducing the amendments." Most important, Melancton Smith, the Antifederalists' principal spokesperson and manager at the convention, had begun to change his mind about conditional ratification. A few days after receiving word of New Hampshire's ratification, Smith wrote to Massachusetts Antifederalist Nathan Dane, expressing hope that the news would convince New York Antifederalists to consider "what is proper to be done in the present situation of things." Yet Smith had been disappointed: He could "scarcely perceive an effect it has had," and he feared that there would "not be a sufficient degree of moderation in some of the most influential men, calmly to consider the circumstances in which we are and to accommodate our decisions to those circumstances."[330]

Dane quickly replied to Smith, arguing forcefully that because ten states had now ratified the Constitution, "there can be no previous amendments" proposed by the remaining three. The time had arrived, Dane argued, for those who continued to regard the Constitution as defective "to unite in their exertions in making the best of the Constitution now established," including participating in the efforts that would be made in the first session of the new Congress to amend it. Smith replied that although he entirely agreed with Dane, other New York Antifederalists "do not accord in sentiments." The task of convincing them to support unconditional ratification would be "arduous and disagreeable," though with "time and great industry," he was "not without hopes we shall become of one mind." One New York Federalist publicly expressed a concern similar to Smith's: Even if Antifederalists were now "convinced of the necessity of adopting [the Constitution], yet as they have acted on the opposition so long, and with such warmth, they cannot with a good grace immediately give their assent."[331]

The Antifederalist caucus that took place on July 8 and 9 was characterized by heated debate, according to one newspaper report. By this point in the convention, few Antifederalist delegates still supported outright rejection of the Constitution, but significant disagreement remained over the form that a conditional ratification, which is still what most Antifederalists preferred, should take.[332]

On July 10, Lansing unveiled to the convention the compromise that the Antifederalist delegates had formulated in their caucus. The amendments they had proposed over the preceding three weeks were now organized into three categories: explanatory, recommended, and conditional. New York's form of ratification, according to the proposal, would begin with a list of nearly thirty "explanations" of what Antifederalists considered, in the words of De Witt Clinton, "some important parts of the constitution which were either equivocal or too latitudinal." For example, one explanatory amendment provided that "nothing in the Constitution is to be construed to prevent" legislatures from dividing their states into congressional districts rather than electing congressional representatives at large. Another explanatory amendment provided that "no power is to be exercised by Congress but such as is expressly given by the said Constitution." Included in this list of explanatory amendments were most of the individual-rights provisions that ultimately made their way into the Bill of Rights (discussed in chapter 7), including freedom of the press, the free exercise of religion, and the right of the people to peaceably assemble.[333]

In addition to the explanatory amendments, Lansing's proposed form of ratification included twenty major structural amendments that were to be called to the attention of the first Congress. For example, one of these amendments would bar Congress from raising a standing army without the concurrence of two-thirds of the members present in both houses, and another would subject US senators to mandatory rotation in office and recall by state legislatures. According to the proposed form of ratification, New York would approve the Constitution "in confidence" that its recommended amendments would be submitted to a general convention of the states as soon as possible. In addition, New York's representatives in the new Congress would be enjoined "to exert all their influence and use all reasonable means to obtain a ratification" of these amendments and to secure the enactment of legislation "in the meantime to conform to the spirit of the said amendments as far as the Constitution will admit."[334]

Finally, and most important, New York's ratification would be *on the condition* that Congress refrain from exercising three of its delegated powers in particular ways until New York's recommended amendments had been submitted to, and determined upon, by a general convention. Specifically, Congress would not be able to order New York's militia out of the state for longer than six weeks without the consent of the state legislature. Congress would also be barred from altering the New York legislature's regulations of the times, places, and manner of congressional elections unless the legislature had neglected or refused to make such regulations. Finally, Congress would not be able to impose excise taxes on articles grown or manufactured in New York, or to levy direct taxes in New York without first requisitioning the state to raise its proportion of a national levy in the manner deemed best by the state legislature. One attraction of this form of conditional ratification, from the perspective of Antifederalists, was that New York would not have to forgo representation in Congress while awaiting a second convention.[335]

The Lansing proposal represented a significant retreat from the demand for antecedent amendments as an absolute condition of ratification with which most Antifederalist delegates had begun the convention. The Antifederalists declared that their new proposal was offered in "a spirit of amity and mutual concession"—a close paraphrase of words used in Washington's letter transmitting the Constitution to Congress at the end of the Philadelphia convention. Indeed, some Antifederalists believed, according to De Witt Clinton, that their caucus had "conceded too much." The Lansing proposal was said to be the "ne plus ultra" of the party's concessions. Clinton expressed confidence that "the antis will keep together now" under the banner of Lansing's scheme.[336]

The response of Federalists to the Lansing proposal was negative. They disparaged the idea of ratification conditioned upon Congress's temporarily forbearing from the exercise of certain powers as a "gilded rejection" that Congress would surely reject. The day after Lansing introduced the Antifederalists' proposal, Jay presented the Federalists' version of a compromise. Hamilton

had told Madison that while New York Federalists would insist on an unconditional ratification that would ensure Congress's acceptance of New York
into the union, they were prepared to "concur in rational recommendations" and would "go as far as [they could] . . . without invalidating the act
[of ratification]." Now, Jay proposed that New York unconditionally ratify the
Constitution while appending explanatory and recommended amendments,
though at this point he did not say what those would be. Chancellor Livingston
touted the Federalists' proffered compromise: "We will have our Constitution;
you will have your amendments."[337]

In reply, Antifederalists suggested the appointment of a committee, consisting of members of both parties, to arrange the proposed amendments and
reach some accommodation on the form of ratification. The convention appointed such a committee, but after only one hour of deliberations, Federalists
called a halt to the proceedings on the grounds that the Antifederalists made
conditional ratification an ultimatum.[338]

Many convention delegates and observers now predicted that the proceedings would conclude within days (not the two weeks that were ultimately required), and at least some Federalists assumed that they would lose the final
vote. For example, on July 12, Federalist delegate Abraham Bancker wrote to
his uncle, "I believe it to be a settled point that they [the Antifederalists] are
fixed and determined, and farther that they have pledged their faith and their
honor to adhere to this resolution [the Lansing proposal], which was the result
of their deliberations, in a secret conclave." Matters had "drawn to a crisis,"
Bancker was expecting the final question to be put within three or four days,
and he was "apprehensive" he would be "among the minority."[339]

The delegates spent the next few days debating whether Lansing's scheme
was a conditional ratification, whether the convention had the power to
propose it, whether Congress could and would accept it, and what the consequences would be if Congress rejected it. For starters, Federalists argued
that the ratifying convention, as constituted by the New York legislature, had
power only to accept or reject the Constitution, and not to propose a conditional ratification. Hamilton observed that the legislature had submitted the
Constitution to a convention chosen by the people of New York "in conformity to the resolves of the [Philadelphia] convention," which in turn had called
on state legislatures to submit the Constitution to conventions of the people
"for their assent and ratification." The power "to assent," Hamilton argued,
"implies a power to reject," but "no more."[340]

Federalists also argued that Lansing's proposal was, in Hamilton's
words, "utterly anti-constitutional," as Congress had no authority under the
Constitution to abdicate its discretion over the exercise of its powers—and
especially not with regard to great powers, such as those of taxation. Jay noted

the incongruity, under Lansing's proposal, that Congress could impose direct taxes on other states while being permitted only to make a requisition upon New York, and that Congress could call other states' militias into out-of-state service for lengthy periods of time while New York's could be sent out of state for only six weeks without the legislature's consent. Because such an arrangement was obviously unconstitutional, Jay argued, Congress would have no choice but to reject a ratification taking the form of Lansing's proposal, and thus New York would remain outside of the union. Hamilton noted, in addition, that the Confederation Congress had rejected New York's conditional ratification of the impost amendment in 1786 and predicted that it would reject the state's conditional ratification of the Constitution as well.[341]

Even if Congress had the power to accept ratification along the lines of the Lansing proposal, Federalists argued, it probably would choose not to do so. Other states would resent New York's attempt to dictate terms to them. Jay urged that New York conduct "joint counsels" with other states about amendments, rather than trying to "dictate and insist that the other states should come down to our terms." The fact that "the best men" of ten other states had rendered verdicts in favor of the Constitution was "strong circumstantial evidence of the expediency" of adopting it. Jay asked, "Are the other states less attentive to their rights than we? Are they less wise to discover their rights?"[342]

In addition, Federalists noted, some states already in the new union would have an incentive to block New York's admission because New York's interests conflicted with their own on issues such as the location of the new nation's capital. Indeed, Hamilton pointed out, some states would like to see New York dismembered. Federalists observed that neighboring states already resented New York for exercising a form of commercial tyranny over them and for permitting its local concerns to trump the national interest on issues such as the impost amendment; these states would seize any opportunity to retaliate against New York.[343]

Because so many state ratifying conventions had already recommended amendments, Federalists contended, New York could probably secure adoption of its proposed amendments by joining the union and pressing for constitutional change via the mechanism specified in Article V of the Constitution. Given that, Federalist delegate Richard Harison observed, "prudence will dictate to leave out the conditions and unite in recommendations." Indeed, Federalists argued that the Lansing proposal was especially risky because it required New York's amendments to be considered by a constitutional convention, yet nothing in the Constitution authorized Congress to summon such a convention until two-thirds of the states had petitioned for one.[344]

Antifederalist leaders, of course, responded to these arguments. In reply to the Federalist claim that the ratifying convention had the authority only to approve or reject the Constitution, they insisted that the sovereign people of New York, as represented in convention, could agree to the Constitution "under any restrictions and qualifications which should be thought expedient." Melancton Smith noted that the Antifederalist delegates represented people "opposed to the Constitution" and had an obligation to "satisfy them."[345]

Antifederalists also insisted that Congress could and would admit New York to the union under the conditions specified in the Lansing proposal. Asking Congress to forbear from exercising powers that it would probably have little occasion to exercise immediately—why lay excise taxes on New York manufacturing at a time when little of it existed?—was not a very onerous condition. Indeed, Smith went so far as to deny that Lansing's proposal imposed any conditions at all. According to Smith, even Federalists admitted that it was permissible for the convention to offer "explanations" of constitutional provisions that were subject to competing interpretations. The so-called conditions in Lansing's proposal, Smith maintained, were simply explanations, worded "so that Congress might exercise those powers in a particular mode which [Congress] by the Constitution might otherwise exercise in various modes."[346]

Even if the "conditions" in Lansing's proposal were conceded to be conditions, however, Smith wondered what was so exceptionable about Congress's agreeing for a limited period of time to suspend the exercise of certain of its powers. Surely Congress could, for example, enact a rule that it would temporarily refrain from imposing a poll tax. Nor was there anything objectionable about a sovereign legislature—either Congress or a state legislature—choosing to lay different taxes in different jurisdictions under its control. Finally, Smith noted the irony that Federalists were so concerned about Lansing's proposed form of ratification violating "a compact [the Constitution] . . . because agreed to by nine states" when the Constitution itself was "directly in breach of the . . . solemn compact of the Confederation."[347]

Antifederalists also denied that Lansing's proposed form of ratification would be widely construed as an attempt by New York to dictate terms to other states. Lansing himself insisted that New York Antifederalists only wished to submit the Constitution's "imperfections to the wisdom of the people," gathered in a second convention. Smith emphasized that he and his allies were prepared to accept the results of that convention, whatever they might be. In response to the argument that New York should submit to the wisdom of the ten states that had already adopted the Constitution, Antifederalists maintained that each state was sovereign and therefore must decide upon the Constitution for itself. Their constituents wanted the proposed amendments, Smith explained, yet to demonstrate "affection to our sister states, we have gone as far as duty to ourselves and our constituents and conscience will permit."[348]

Federalists, in addition to denying that the convention had the power to propose a conditional ratification or that Congress had the authority to accept one, emphasized the "evil consequences" that New York would suffer, should Congress reject a ratification along the lines of the Lansing proposal. According to one newspaper account, Chancellor Livingston in particular "appealed to the apprehensions and passions of the convention, paint[ing] in the most glowing colors the unavoidable convulsions of our state," should Congress reject its form of ratification. New York Federalists made three principal arguments regarding the deleterious consequences of New York's remaining outside of the union.[349]

First, so long as New York failed to ratify the Constitution, Congress would enact important laws without the state's participation. Jay explained, "This government will be organized and we have no hand in it. Many important laws will and must then be passed. They may affect our rights and interests." One of the first measures the new Congress was likely to consider would be constitutional amendments, and nobody from New York would be there to explain and advocate for its proposals. Nathan Dane had made this same point about a week earlier in a letter to Melancton Smith, urging New York's unconditional ratification: Only the ratifying states would "immediately have a voice in the federal councils . . . during the most interesting period," when "some of the most important laws [would] be made in the first Congress, and essential amendments [would] be recommended by it."[350]

The second adverse consequence that Federalists predicted would ensue if Congress rejected New York's form of ratification was the removal of Congress from New York City. Immediately upon receiving news of the ratifications by the New Hampshire and Virginia conventions, Congress, which was in session in New York City, began to arrange elections for the new national government, as the Philadelphia convention had instructed it to do once nine states had approved the Constitution. However, congressional delegates temporarily deferred the controversial question of where the first federal Congress would sit, pending the New York convention's decision on ratification.[351]

Jay warned the delegates in Poughkeepsie that if New York did not approve the Constitution, New York City could not possibly remain the home of Congress, as it had been for the last three and a half years. The departure of Congress would cost New York City at least $100,000 in annual federal government spending, which Jay insisted comprised most of the hard currency circulating in the city. Chancellor Livingston, mentioning the same dollar amount, warned that the loss of so much specie would cause a drastic depreciation in the value of New York's paper money, and he declared that agents were already in New York City pressing for the relocation of Congress to Philadelphia.[352]

Antifederalist leaders Smith and Samuel Jones were hearing this same message privately from Samuel Osgood, a member of the Confederation's Board of Treasury and a Massachusetts Antifederalist. Osgood reported from New York City that "[t]he anxiety of the citizens [here] is probably greater than you would imagine." If the New York convention held out against ratification, Osgood warned, the Antifederalists would "have all the blame laid at their door for forcing Congress to leave this city." There was no doubt that "Philadelphia . . . is desirous New York may not come in, for the purpose of getting Congress removed." Another Federalist declared that he did "not believe the life of the Governor and his party would be safe in this place [New York City]" if the convention rejected the Constitution. Nineteen out of twenty voters in New York City had cast their ballots for Federalist delegates to the Poughkeepsie convention, and in July, city leaders planned a procession with "extraordinary pomp"—five thousand people ended up participating—to celebrate the Constitution's ratification by the requisite nine states and to pressure the New York convention into approving unconditional ratification.[353]

Third, and relatedly, because support for the Constitution was nearly universal in New York City and because city leaders desperately wished to keep the Congress located there, a real possibility existed that the city and its environs—Staten Island, Long Island, and Westchester County—would secede from the state if Congress rejected the convention's form of ratification. Even before the New York convention began, Jay had told Washington that "an idea has taken air, that the southern part of the state will at all events adhere to the union, and if necessary to that end seek a separation from the northern. This idea has influence on the fears of the [Antifederal] party."[354]

Chancellor Livingston in particular sought to exploit that fear in Poughkeepsie. If the convention insisted on the form of ratification in the Lansing proposal and Congress rejected it, Livingston asked, "Would not the southern part of the state say you set out with an act of injustice? We have a right to separate." Such a separation, Livingston warned, would be almost certain to result in a civil war. Outside of the convention, newspapers were filled with talk of the possibility of secession, should New York fail to unconditionally ratify. Statements in private correspondence—including observations by foreign ministers who had no incentive to exaggerate the risk—confirm that, if New York's ratification had failed, secession by New York City and the state's southern counties was a serious possibility, not just a rhetorical threat.[355]

Ultimately, it would be precisely such dire predictions that proved most effective with Antifederalist delegates. As Hamilton had earlier written to Madison, Federalist "arguments confound, but do not convince," yet some Antifederalist leaders appear "to be convinced by circumstances."[356]

Nonetheless, initially, Federalist depictions of the adverse consequences that would ensue if Congress rejected the form of New York's ratification appeared to have little influence on the Antifederalist delegates. After several days of debate on Lansing's proposal, some Antifederalists demanded that the question be called. On July 15, Smith formally moved for ratification along the lines of Lansing's proposal for ratification with explanatory and recommended amendments, and on the condition that Congress not exercise certain powers until a second convention had been assembled to consider New York's proposed amendments. The predominant mood among Federalists at this time was gloomy. Based on information received from Poughkeepsie, Connecticut congressional delegate Jeremiah Wadsworth reported that New York Federalists "despair of an unconditional adoption of the Constitution," and Secretary at War Henry Knox predicted that New York would either reject the Constitution altogether or insist on antecedent amendments.[357]

Fearing defeat, the Federalists decided that adjourning the convention would be, as one of their delegates privately explained, "the only probable means of preventing the mischief which threatened us." On July 16, Federalist delegate John Sloss Hobart, a justice on the state supreme court, moved that the convention adjourn until the first week of September. Federalists justified the adjournment motion on the grounds that "things have changed since we came here"—that is, the Constitution had been made operational by the ratification of the requisite number of states—and "consult[ing] our constituents" was the "decent" thing to do. Some Federalists may have calculated, as one of their New Hampshire allies theorized, that "it would not be so consistent for them [Antifederalist delegates] to give it [the Constitution] their affirmative in the same session they have so violently opposed it; and a short recess may at least put a better coloring to their acceding to it. A little time and cool conversation with their friends at home, no doubt will have a good effect."[358]

One of New York's Antifederalist leaders, Abraham Yates, who was not a delegate at the convention but was in close contact with many who were, had worried since the start of the convention that an adjournment would simply provide Federalists with "a farther opportunity to show their dexterity at management." Now, in response to Hobart's motion, Antifederalist delegates insisted that they already knew "the mind of [their] constituents," who would "not accept without amendments," and that an adjournment, "without giving evidences of a change of sentiment," would be "an affront to the house." In addition, they noted that an adjournment motion would have been more appropriate coming from them, "as the reasons mentioned in the resolution hold up the idea of change of sentiment in our side of the house, which does not appear." Federalist delegates lined up behind the motion, but Antifederalists still commanded the numbers to easily defeat it, by a margin of forty to twenty-two.[359]*

After the Federalists' adjournment motion failed on July 17, Hamilton made a motion for unconditional ratification with explanatory and recommended amendments, but the Antifederalists easily defeated it. The delegates then voted to resume consideration of the Lansing proposal, as previously formalized into a motion by Smith.[360]

At this point, however, Smith stunned the delegates by taking another step in the Federalists' direction, abandoning his support for the Lansing proposal on the grounds that the Federalists' arguments had convinced him that Congress would probably reject it as an invalid form of ratification. The delegates' two main goals, Smith reminded them, were to "secure an admission into the union and procure a consideration of amendments by the people of America," and he now believed that he had come upon a plan that would "avoid the objections on both sides."[361]

According to Smith's new proposed form of ratification, the New York convention would declare that a majority of delegates "cannot approve the whole of the said Constitution without amendments" for a variety of reasons that included the "general, indefinite and ambiguous" manner in which Congress's powers were stated and the lack of "sufficient precision" with which the boundaries between the powers of the state and federal governments were marked. In addition, Smith's proposed form of ratification noted specific objections to the Constitution—substantially overlapping those stated in the Lansing proposal—including the inadequate size of the first House, the failure to sufficiently protect states in their ability to raise revenue, and the grant of power to Congress to regulate the times, places, and manner of congressional elections. It continued: "For these and various other reasons, this Convention would be induced not to accede to this Constitution, did not other weighty considerations interpose; but the strong attachments they feel to their sister states, and their regard to the common good of the union impel them to preserve it."[362]

---

* Abraham Lansing, an Antifederalist leader in Albany, believed that if the adjournment motion carried, "all the exertions we have made and the anxiety we have experienced for the liberty of our country will end in nothing." He worried that "[t]he baneful manor interest will be exerted to obtain instructions to the delegates, and the poor deluded well-meaning yeomanry of our country, not having it in their power to follow the dictates of their own consciences, will be compelled to sign these instructions to keep well with their masters." By contrast, Antifederalists "will decline signing counter instructions, by the maneuvers of the Federalists who will hold out every circumstance they can to alarm and intimidate." Much as he opposed ratification without antecedent amendments, Lansing said that he would prefer that outcome to an adjournment, and he decided to organize a letter from Albany Antifederalists to their allies at the convention to "recommend them by all means to push the business to a close before they rise."

Smith's critical contribution came toward the end of the proposal: New York would ratify the Constitution, "in the firmest confidence that an opportunity will be speedily given to revise and amend the said Constitution in the mode pointed out in [Article V], *expressly reserving nevertheless to this state a right to recede and withdraw from the said Constitution, in case such opportunity be not given within ____ years.*" (Smith's proposal did not specify the number of years, but Jay later stated the number as four.) In addition, according to Smith's proposal, the convention would recommend that the New York legislature request the first session of Congress to call a constitutional convention to consider amendments, and the convention would also approve a circular letter to the states inviting them to make the same request to Congress. Acknowledging that his proposal might "not please either side of the house," Smith nonetheless insisted that it "avoids all the objections of any weight made against the other [i.e., Lansing's proposal]" and would accomplish the principal objectives of both sides.[363]

Some Federalists were heartened by Smith's proposal. Federalist delegate Abraham Bancker wrote that, while previously his "mind was filled with gloomy discontent" and "every gleam of hope appeared to be lost," Smith's proposal was "a favorable omen," which had "gained [him] much credit" with the Federalists. Jay told the convention that Smith's latest proposal was "less evil than the former" and that he would vote to make it the basis of discussion. Antifederalist delegate Cornelius C. Schoonmaker thought that the Federalists would probably agree to Smith's plan "as the most favorable to them, and having no great hopes of a better."[364]

By contrast, Antifederalists were deeply divided over Smith's proposal. Some of them were apparently now searching for a form of ratification that would "save their reputations with their constituents," and Smith's proposal might fit the bill. De Witt Clinton, who strongly opposed the scheme, noted in his journal that many Antifederalists supported it and that "if it is not agreed to, its friends will I expect vote with the Feds for unconditional adoption and allege this as an excuse" (indeed, Clinton observed, "[s]ome of the violent [Antifederalists] ungenerously suppose this was designed"). Clinton also reported that one Antifederalist leader, Samuel Jones, who represented Queens County at the convention and was hearing pro-ratification sentiments from his constituents, now "comes openly out and declares we must join the union sooner or later and we might as well [do so] now and trust to future amendments."[365]

However, Governor Clinton and John Lansing, Jr., opposed Smith's proposal, and other Antifederalists were, according to De Witt Clinton, "enraged" at Smith, even to the point that "[s]ome detest Smith as much as Hamilton." Clinton wrote in his journal, "If any divisions take place in the party, I must impute the principal blame to ... Smith," who "goes so much among the Federalists that he has raised jealousies against him." Angrily, De Witt Clinton noted the contrast between Smith's current position and the views Smith had expressed in a letter written to Governor Clinton the preceding winter, in which Smith had declared that New York should reject the Constitution even if all twelve other states had assented to it.[366]

Antifederalist delegate Schoonmaker, who opposed Smith's proposal as "very little short of an absolute adoption," feared that it would pass if Federalists supported it as "the lesser evil of the two" and Antifederalists divided over it. But when the question was put on July 18 whether to replace Lansing's proposal with Smith's, Jay reported to Washington, "[a] long silence ensued," and the Antifederalists "seemed embarrassed—fearful to divide among themselves, and yet many of them very averse to the new plan." Antifederalists then managed to adjourn the convention for the day to consider the matter in their caucus.[367]

At this point, Hamilton wrote to Madison asking if he thought Congress would accept New York's ratification on the terms of Smith's proposal. However, the Antifederalists themselves rejected Smith's proposal in their caucus, and on the following day, July 19, Smith moved to withdraw it from consideration (although one newspaper nevertheless reported that the proposal might still "afford the groundwork of an adoption"). The convention then voted by a margin of forty-one to eighteen to postpone consideration of all other plans to focus on Lansing's proposal.[368]

Over the next several days, the convention debated the merits of the rights provisions and structural amendments in Lansing's proposal, deferring the question of whether New York would ratify only on the condition that Congress forbear from exercising certain specified powers within New York until the state's proposed amendments were considered by a national convention. Antifederalists still commanded the majorities necessary to defeat Federalist efforts to delete or alter the terms of Lansing's amendments. For example, Antifederalists easily beat back Federalist attempts to eliminate the amendment providing for mandatory rotation in office and recall for senators, and the amendment requiring a two-thirds majority in both houses of Congress to create a standing army.[369]

At this point, nobody could confidently predict what the outcome of the convention would be. De Witt Clinton reported that "the political sky is so frequently overcast and so variable in appearance that I am oftentimes at a loss what to think or what to say." From New York City, Madison informed Edmund Randolph that it was "not yet certain that ratification will take any final shape that can make New York immediately a member of the new union. The opponents can not come to that point without yielding a complete victory to the

Federalists, which must be a severe sacrifice of their pride." Federalist delegate Isaac Roosevelt (the great-great-grandfather of Franklin Delano Roosevelt) reported that the convention was now divided into four factions: one favoring ratification with antecedent conditions, one favoring ratification with the reservation of a right to secede if no second convention to consider amendments materialized, one favoring unconditional ratification, and one favoring adjournment. Roosevelt hoped that Antifederalists' "diversity of sentiments" would work to the Federalists' advantage.[370]

The critical vote came on July 23. Samuel Jones, who had started out as a staunch opponent of unconditional ratification, now proposed that New York ratify the Constitution "in full confidence"—instead of "on the express condition"—that Congress would forbear from exercising certain powers within New York until amendments had been considered by a second convention. Jones's motion carried by thirty-one votes to twenty-nine. Clinton, Yates, and Lansing all opposed it, but, critically, Smith voted in favor. A dozen Antifederalist delegates, most of them representing the southern counties of Queens and Suffolk, had deserted party ranks.[371]

In a speech defending his vote as consistent with his prior positions, Smith explained that he continued to regard the Constitution as "radically defective." However, once Virginia had ratified, Smith explained, antecedent amendments had become impracticable. Therefore, he had determined "to quit his first ground," while continuing to "pursue his important and favorite object of amendments with equal zeal as before, but in a practicable way, which was only in the mode prescribed by the Constitution." At first, he had thought that Lansing's plan "might have answered the purpose," but Federalists had persuaded him that Congress would not accept a ratification in that form. Thus, that plan "must now be abandoned as fallacious." Smith described a desperate situation if New York were not admitted to the union, with "convulsions in the northern part, factions and discord in the rest." As a result, he had concluded that "a proper discharge of his public duty as well as the most advisable way of obtaining the great end of his opposition" required that he vote against any form of ratification that Congress was unlikely to accept.[372]

A Federalist victory now seemed all but assured, though a cautious Jay told Washington that the Antifederalists "mean to rally their forces and endeavor to regain that ground." Indeed, the following day, July 24, Lansing moved to take up Smith's recent (but now abandoned) proposal that New York ratify the Constitution with recommended amendments while reserving a right to secede if a second convention to consider amendments had not materialized by a certain date. Lansing explained that, while he still preferred his earlier proposal that Congress ratify on the condition that Congress forbear from the exercise of certain powers until a second convention had been assembled,

Smith's scheme at least offered "some security," as it would enable New York to "resist without being rebels," should a second convention not take place within the allotted time. Supporting Lansing, Governor Clinton insisted that fairness required that the delegates be afforded an opportunity to vote on this proposal, given that many Antifederalists had "heretofore voted under an impression that this question would be put."[373]

Sensing that victory was near at hand, Federalists naturally opposed Lansing's motion, even though one week earlier many of them had been intrigued when Smith had first made the proposal. Hamilton now argued that Congress would reject a ratification in this form because "the terms of the Constitution import a perpetual compact between the different states; this certainly is not." He also noted that the proposal "implied a distrust of the other states" and thus "would awaken their pride and other passions unfriendly to the object of amendments." Other Federalists similarly insisted that threats were not the best way to secure amendments.[374]

Hamilton also read to the convention a letter from Madison declaring that a reservation of the right to secede would render New York's ratification conditional and thus unacceptable to Congress.* Lansing denigrated Madison's statement as "an impression of the moment—or as an opinion," and insisted that the only reason he had relented on antecedent conditions was the assumption that New York would have an escape clause.[375]

The following day, the convention rejected Lansing's motion by a margin of thirty-one to twenty-eight. Smith voted against the very proposal that he had recently championed. Antifederalist delegate Schoonmaker reported that while the measure had never been "supposed to be of great importance by" most Antifederalists, Smith had "most strenuously heretofore advocated the principle" yet now was, curiously, "convinced that it will not do at all." Smith's own explanation for his change of course was that he had submitted the proposal as "a middle ground and hoped both sides of the house would be pleased with it," only to discover that "neither will be pleased."[376][†]

After rejecting Lansing's proposal, the convention voted, in the committee of the whole, to approve the Constitution with explanatory provisions and recommended amendments, but without conditions. The convention accepted

---

* Madison explained: "Compacts must be reciprocal, this principle would not in such a case be preserved. The Constitution requires an adoption in toto, and forever. It has been so adopted by the other states. An adoption for a limited time would be as defective as an adoption of some of the articles only. In short, any condition whatever must vitiate the ratification."

† Many Antifederalists were furious with Smith for abandoning his previous ground and accepting an unconditional ratification. Antifederalist resentment over his change of heart probably later cost Smith a seat in the first US Senate.

the report of the committee of the whole and appointed another committee to prepare a circular letter to the states urging them to petition Congress for a second convention. Smith had first proposed the idea of a circular letter a week earlier, and Federalists had decided to support it as a conciliatory gesture.[377]

The following day, July 26, the convention voted by a margin of thirty to twenty-seven in favor of the committee of the whole's recommendation for unconditional ratification.* The convention sent a record of its proceedings to the New York legislature and "earnestly requested" it to cooperate with the other states in measures for obtaining a general convention to consider amendments.[378]

The convention also unanimously approved a circular letter, which Governor Clinton was instructed to send to the other states' executives. That letter began by observing that several provisions in the Constitution appeared "so exceptionable to a majority of us [convention delegates] that nothing but the fullest confidence of obtaining a revision of them, by a general convention, and an invincible reluctance to separating from our sister states, could have prevailed upon a sufficient number to ratify it, without stipulating for previous amendments." The "apprehensions and discontents" occasioned by the Constitution could not be allayed unless "effectual measures be immediately taken for calling a convention, to meet at a period not far remote." Because Article V required that two-thirds of the states petition Congress before it could call for such a convention, the New York delegates "earnestly exhort[ed] and request[ed]" the state legislatures to "take the earliest opportunity of making" that appeal. After the circular letter was approved, Governor Clinton concluded the proceedings by noting that, while those New Yorkers who had opposed ratification "would not be satisfied" with the work of the convention, he would use his "power and influence" to "keep up peace and good order" in the state.[379]

New York Federalists had won an extraordinary victory. At the start of the New York ratifying convention, Federalist delegates had been outnumbered more than two to one by Antifederalists, at least a few of whom favored outright rejection of the Constitution and all of whom appeared determined not to ratify without antecedent amendments. Over the course of the convention, the Federalists, as one of their adversaries explained, had "brought [the Antifederalists] down from one point to another till we are brought to an unconditional adoption." First, the Antifederalists had relinquished their demand for antecedent amendments and accepted ratification contingent upon Congress's

---

* The twenty-seven delegates opposing ratification represented more New Yorkers than did the thirty voting in favor.

forbearing from exercising certain powers until a second constitutional convention was assembled. Then, under Federalist pressure, Antifederalists had retreated even further, agreeing to ratify the Constitution while reserving a right to secede from the union should a second convention fail to materialize within a certain number of years. Finally, enough Antifederalists had abandoned even that compromise position to create a majority in favor of unconditional ratification with explanatory and recommended amendments, and a circular letter calling upon the other states to support a second convention.[380]

Just a couple of days before the Federalist victory was complete, one Federalist delegate offered an accurate account of how it was rendered possible: Through "patience, moderation and calmness on the[ir] part," the Federalists had "delay[ed] a rash decision and give[n] time [for] reflection and finally caused a division of sentiments" among their opponents. While this Federalist delegate also noted that "much precious breath [had] been spent in speeches and debates," it bears emphasis that the Federalists had not persuaded their adversaries of the Constitution's merits through eloquent argument. Rather, they had exploited changed circumstances to convince the Antifederalists that New York's failure to ratify would have severe adverse consequences for the state.[381]

Specifically, conditional ratification, which the Federalists insisted Congress would not accept, would leave New York out of the union, at least temporarily. As a result, New York would be unrepresented in the first Congress, where important decisions—such as choosing the permanent site of the nation's capital and deciding which constitutional amendments, if any, to propose—would be made. In addition, with New York out of the union, Congress would have no choice but to relocate from New York City, which would cost the city's residents $100,000 a year in federal spending. Moreover, New York's failure to ratify would probably lead New York City and its neighboring counties to secede from the state and might produce a civil war, both within New York and between New York and its neighbors. As one Antifederalist explained, the convention's ultimate vote for unconditional ratification was based "on principles of expediency—that ten states have adopted and the government will be put into operation," and that New York's failure to acquiesce would result in "great difficulties and embarrassments."[382]

The pressure of circumstances had caused a dozen Antifederalist delegates to relent and accept unconditional ratification. Gilbert Livingston, who was one of those delegates, explained on the final day of the convention that he had arrived in Poughkeepsie "fully determined on previous amendments." Over the course of the proceedings, however, he had been persuaded that "the most essential interests of my country" required "another ground." Because he continued to regard the Constitution as unsafe unless amended, Livingston explained, the only question remaining for him was "which was the most eligible mode to ensure a general convention of the states to reconsider it, to have the essential amendments ingrafted into it." The convention's deliberations had persuaded him that, "considering our present situation with respect to our sister states, the wisest and best measure we can possibly pursue" would be unconditional ratification with recommended amendments and a call for a second convention. Describing this as the "most important transaction of my life" and knowing that it would be "strictly scrutinized," Livingston expressed the hope that his constituents "soon will, if they at present do not, see the propriety of the measure here pursued." Whether or not that proved to be the case, though, Livingston declared that, most important, he had an "approving conscience" and could vouch "for the rectitude of my intentions."[383]

Despite the impressive accomplishment of his New York allies, however, Madison was distraught by the issuance of the circular letter, which he called "a matter of as much regret, as the unanimity with which it passed is matter of surprise." He told Washington that the New York Federalists' "determination to purchase an immediate ratification in any form and at any price" to maximize New York City's chances of remaining, at least temporarily, the residence of Congress was the only explanation he could fathom for their agreeing to such a letter, which he worried might "prove more injurious than a rejection would have done." New York's rejection of the Constitution, Madison wrote, "would have rather alarmed the well meaning Antifederalists elsewhere, would have had no ill effect on the other party, would have excited the indignation of the neighboring states, and would have been necessarily followed by a speedy reconsideration of the subject." By contrast, the circular letter was "everywhere, and particularly in Virginia, laid hold of as the signal for united exertions in pursuit of early amendments."[384]

North Carolina and Rhode Island

With New York's ratification in late July 1788, eleven states had approved the Constitution—two more than were required to put it into effect. One month earlier, when news that New Hampshire had become the ninth state to ratify reached New York City, congressional delegates had immediately turned their attention to setting up the new national government, which required selecting a temporary home for the federal Congress, and choosing dates both for its first meeting and for the selection and convening of presidential electors. However, two states—North Carolina and Rhode Island—remained outside of the new union, as the ratifying states had no power under Article VII of the Constitution to bind anyone but themselves.[385]

In December 1787, the North Carolina legislature, possibly at the behest of Antifederalists who believed they needed time to rally opposition to the Constitution, had arranged for the state's ratifying convention to meet late in the process—July 1788. Washington—and many others—believed that North Carolina legislators had postponed their state's convention until after Virginia's because "of a disposition to take her tone" from her neighbor.[386]

For a variety of reasons, the ratifying campaign faced an uphill struggle in North Carolina. As in other states, persons involved in commerce—merchants, traders, lawyers—generally favored the Constitution in North Carolina. Yet because of its treacherous coastline and lack of a major port, North Carolina had relatively fewer such persons than most other states. Because of its relatively poor soil and the consequent lack of large-scale commercial agriculture, North Carolina also had relatively fewer men of wealth and education—the type of person who generally supported ratification. The state had no large cities and consisted mostly of relatively isolated settlements with little outside contact. Western North Carolinians had a long history, dating back to the colonial era, of populist resistance to the imposition of legal mandates by distant governments. Those North Carolinians who lived in the western region that would soon become the independent state of Tennessee were reluctant to expand federal government power because of the recent imbroglio over Secretary for Foreign Affairs John Jay's negotiations with Spain.[387]

North Carolina held its election for ratifying convention delegates in late March, and Antifederalists won a big victory: When the convention assembled in Hillsborough on July 21, 1788, they would enjoy an advantage in delegates of greater than two to one. Antifederalist sentiment had proved so strong in North Carolina that two Federalists who had been among the state's delegates to the Philadelphia convention were defeated in elections for the ratifying convention.[388]

As soon as the convention began, some Antifederalists, seizing upon their large numerical advantage, urged a quick vote on the Constitution without debate, arguing that this would save the state and the delegates a good deal of time and money. In response, leading Federalist James Iredell expressed surprise at the suggestion that the convention vote without deliberation. He denied that delegates had come to Hillsborough "predetermined for or against the Constitution." They were there to acquire "information and to judge, after all that can be said upon it, whether it [the Constitution] really merits [our] attachment or not." Iredell declared that, although some people "may arrogate infallibility to themselves, and conclude deliberation to be useless," he had "scarcely ever conversed on the subject with any man of understanding, who has not thrown some new light upon the subject which escaped me before."

The expense of extended deliberations was a "trivial consideration compared to the consequences of a rash proceeding upon this important question."[389]

Although the Antifederalists relented on the issue of voting without debate, most of them chose simply to remain silent during the convention, allowing Federalists single-handedly to explicate the Constitution—even to the extent of raising their own objections before refuting them. When one Antifederalist objected to the impropriety of "the friends of the new system making objections, when none were urged by its opposers," Federalist William Davie criticized his adversaries for "suppressing their objections" and declared it "highly improper to pass over in silence any part of this Constitution which has been loudly objected to [out of doors]." Throughout the convention, Federalists objected to "the precipitancy with which we go through the business."[390]

When the Antifederalist delegates did deign to speak, they raised the same sorts of objections to the Constitution as their compatriots had elsewhere— especially with regard to the absence of a bill of rights; the aristocratic nature of the Senate; the broad jurisdiction of the federal courts; and the virtually unlimited grants of power to Congress to impose direct taxes and to revise state regulations of the times, places, and manner of federal elections. Yet the North Carolina convention was the only one to date in which Antifederalists unashamedly defended states' emission of paper money in the mid-1780s and criticized Article I, Section 10, of the Constitution for prohibiting them from doing so in the future.[391]

One Antifederalist argued that because of the "extreme scarcity of specie" during the war, "[o]ur political existence must have been destroyed" had it not been for paper money. He also asked if federal taxes—which he predicted would increase under the Constitution—could be paid in paper money, as "the poor man has not the money locked up in his chest." Another Antifederalist defended South Carolina's installment laws and North Carolina's paper money emissions as necessary "to save vast numbers of people from ruin." In times of widespread distress, "public measures must be accommodated to their circumstances with peculiar delicacy and caution" or else an "insurrection may be the consequence." Antifederalist leader Timothy Bloodworth warned that North Carolina "ought to be particular in adopting a constitution which may destroy our currency, when it is to be the supreme law of the land and prohibits the emission of paper money."[392]

Several Antifederalists expressed concern that the Constitution would not only forbid future emissions of paper money but also subject North Carolina to lawsuits in federal court seeking to compel it to redeem in gold and silver the paper it had already issued. In reply, Federalist delegates, seeking to reassure those Antifederalists representing debtors who might otherwise oppose ratification out of concern that the paper money already in circulation would

Figure 6.10 William Davie, who represented North Carolina at the Philadelphia convention, was one of the leading Federalists at that state's two ratifying conventions, and later sponsored the bill in the state legislature that chartered the University of North Carolina, for which he is known as its founder. (Courtesy of Independence National Historical Park)

no longer be considered legal tender for existing debts, insisted that Article I, Section 10, would have no retroactive effect. Federalist reassurances proved unavailing, however, and North Carolina Antifederalists proposed a constitutional amendment barring Congress, "directly or indirectly, either by [itself] or through the judiciary, [from] interfer[ing] with any one of the states in the redemption of paper money already emitted and now in circulation."[393]

Toward the end of the convention, the delegates' focus shifted from the merits of the Constitution to the form that proposed amendments should take, and Antifederalists demanded that amendments be approved prior to ratification. In reply, Federalist Richard Dobbs Spaight, who had been one of the state's delegates to the Philadelphia convention, noted that the question confronting the convention was not "whether the Constitution be good, but whether we will or will not confederate with the other states." Iredell asked why the North Carolina convention should "suppose [its] knowledge and wisdom to be superior" to those of the states that had already ratified. He also insisted that North Carolina had "no right to make a conditional ratification" and that doing so would result in its exclusion from the union, with no guarantee "of an easy admission at a future day."[394]

Iredell declared that "the impossibility of existing out of the union must be obvious to every thinking man." North Carolina would "have no share or agency in [congressional] transactions, though we may be ultimately bound by them," and the first session of Congress would "probably be the most important of any for many years." If North Carolina had as much to fear from northern states as some Antifederalists charged, Davie asked, why should it stay out of the union and allow those states to implement their favored policies unimpeded? Another Federalist, Governor Samuel Johnston, who was president of the convention, warned that Congress would probably impose discriminatory tariffs upon North Carolina if it refused to ratify. Although Iredell considered the Constitution "perfectly safe" as it was, he promised to support "any [subsequent] amendments which do not destroy the substance of the Constitution, but will tend to give greater satisfaction," and he predicted that such amendments were likely to win approval, given the strong demand for them in other states.[395]

Yet Antifederalists insisted that convention delegates should decide "as if no state had adopted it [the Constitution]," exercise their "own judgments and act independently," and refuse to ratify without antecedent amendments. Willie Jones, one of the Antifederalists' leaders, denied the plausibility of any of the "dreadful consequences" of which the Federalists foretold, should North Carolina remain temporarily out of the union, and he insisted the state would "run no risk of being excluded from the union when [it] think[s] proper to come in." Antifederalists also argued that New York—which North Carolinians did not realize had just ratified—would probably hold out for antecedent amendments as well. Moreover, the other southern states would have a strong interest in ensuring that Congress eventually admitted North Carolina.[396]

Although the convention spanned thirteen days, Antifederalist leader Jones declared that "no person had changed his opinion." Bloodworth similarly observed, "Many words have been spoken, and long time taken up; but with me, they [the Federalists' arguments] have gone in at one ear, and out at the other." In the end, the convention voted by a margin of 184 to 83 against ratification until Congress had called a convention of the states to consider a declaration of rights and other amendments directed at the "most ambiguous and exceptionable parts of the said Constitution." The convention also supplied Congress and the other states with a list of North Carolina's desired amendments, which were similar to those proposed by the Virginia convention. The goal of North

Carolina Antifederalists was plainly to secure favored amendments, not to reject the union forever.[397]

Federalist leaders across the nation were gravely disappointed with the outcome of the North Carolina convention, especially because, as Madison told Jefferson, it had been "generally expected" after Virginia's ratification that North Carolina "would in some form or other have fallen into the general stream." Blaming the adverse result largely on the influence of Patrick Henry, Madison expressed concern that North Carolina's refusal to ratify, combined with what he expected would be the pernicious influence of the New York convention's circular letter, "has somewhat changed the aspect of things and has given fresh hopes and exertions to those who opposed the Constitution." The Antifederalists' current objective, Madison surmised, was "to effect an early convention composed of men who will essentially mutilate the system, particularly in the article of taxation, without which in my opinion the system cannot answer the purposes for which it was intended."[398]

North Carolina Federalists made gains in the state elections that occurred soon after the close of the Hillsborough convention, and they signed petitions requesting the legislature at its fall session to call a second state convention. After considerable wrangling, the legislature in November 1788 defeated Antifederalist efforts to block the call for a second state convention, but it also rejected Federalist attempts to set an early date for elections to choose delegates to that convention. Instead, elections were set for August to choose delegates to a convention to meet in Fayetteville in November 1789—a full year after the legislature's action. In the meantime, Federalists took advantage of their domination of the press to unleash an assault on the "strange, imprudent, and outrageous proceedings at the late convention in Hillsborough." They emphasized the state's need for federal government protection from Indian attacks, the risk that federal tariffs would discriminate against North Carolina's trade, and the ignominy of being linked in people's minds with the much maligned state of Rhode Island as holdouts.[399]

In May 1789, the governor and executive council of North Carolina wrote to President Washington congratulating him on ascending to the presidency and expressing the "pleasing hope" of their state's joining the union as soon as amendments—such "as will remove the apprehensions of many of the good citizens of this state for those liberties for which they have fought and suffered in common with others"—had been proposed. When Madison pushed for a bill of rights in the first Congress that summer—as discussed in the next chapter—North Carolina Federalist Davie wrote that "nothing ever gave me so much pleasure," because it would refute Antifederalist prophecies that Congress "would never propose an amendment." Davie told Madison it was critical that Congress actually approve amendments before North Carolina's second ratifying convention assembled in November.[400]

By the fall of 1789, the national government had been in operation for six months and Congress had proposed a bill of rights. Letters appeared in North Carolina newspapers predicting that the second state ratifying convention would approve the Constitution because the amendments proposed by Congress would "undoubtedly satisfy the minds of all its enemies." In October, Washington reported to Gouverneur Morris that opposition to the Constitution "is either no more, or hides its head," and he predicted that "the non-acceding states will very soon become members of the union." He had "no doubt" about North Carolina. "Nor would there be of Rhode Island, had not the majority of that people bid adieu, long since, to every principle of honor, common sense, and honesty."[401]

By the time North Carolina's second convention met, the speaker of the state senate was reporting an "amazing change in the sentiments of the people." After several days of deliberation—which was not reported—the delegates defeated an Antifederalist motion for ratification on the condition of previous amendments and then voted on November 21, 1789, by a margin of 194 to 77, in favor of unconditional ratification (though the convention did recommend for Congress's consideration several amendments in addition to the ones Congress had approved in September). According to one of Iredell's correspondents, most Antifederalists seemed to "acquiesce cheerfully" in that result—not so much because "their doubts and fears have been fully removed" but rather because the Constitution met with "the approbation of a majority of their countrymen."[402]

Rhode Island proved a tougher nut for the Federalists to crack. As we have seen, because of concerns that the Constitutional Convention might impose constraints on the states' ability to issue paper money and provide debt relief, the Rhode Island legislature had declined to appoint a delegation to Philadelphia (which had proved a cause for celebration elsewhere in the nation). While the Philadelphia convention was still meeting, a joint committee of the two houses of the Rhode Island legislature protested against the "many severe and unjust sarcasms propagated against" Rhode Island and explained that the state had refused to appoint delegates because of a "love of true constitutional liberty." The committee insisted that the Articles of Confederation set forth a procedure for amendments, and that departing from that procedure would endanger the people's liberties. To avoid the appearance of legitimizing Congress's actions on the Constitution, the Rhode Island legislature even declined to send delegates to the session of the Confederation Congress to which the Philadelphia convention forwarded the Constitution.[403]

In the fall of 1787, with Rhode Island's fears regarding how the Framers would handle paper money and debt relief confirmed by Article I, Section 10, of the Constitution, the state legislature also refused to summon a ratifying convention, leading a Federalist merchant in Philadelphia to observe that the "unhappy deluded state still adds infamy to infamy." Earlier that year, the Rhode Island legislature, under the control of the country party, which had come to power in the spring of 1786 on a platform of relieving distressed debtors, had passed a law to redeem the state war debt in installments. The law required public creditors to submit their certificates to be paid in paper money, which had vastly depreciated in value, or else forfeit their claims. Until this scheme to pay off the public debt at little cost to the state's taxpayers had been completed, the country party would not permit the Constitution to be ratified in Rhode Island.* According to the outraged editor of the Federalist *Newport Herald*, the country party seemed "to view a dissolution of the federal compact as of no magnitude, when placed in competition with their favorite paper money."[404]

By the time the Rhode Island legislature reassembled in late February 1788, six states had ratified the Constitution, and the *Newport Herald* was urging the legislature to "act wisely" by calling a convention rather than "persist in our obstinacy and be the butt of ridicule." However, the General Assembly, still dominated by deputies of the country party, again rejected calling a convention, by a margin of forty-three to fifteen. Instead, the legislature called for a referendum on the Constitution by voters participating in town meetings in late March. Country party leaders argued that, since "by the proposed Constitution, the people were called upon to surrender a part of their liberties, ... they were the best judges what part they ought to give up." A referendum was

---

* In a letter written to President George Washington in 1790, Rhode Island governor Arthur Fenner offered the best public defense of the country party's scheme for effectively repudiating the state's war debt. According to Fenner, the Rhode Island legislature had failed to levy adequate taxes to support the public securities issued during the war for personal services and property, leading to a vast decline in their market value. Many of the original holders then sold their securities at small fractions of par value "to the richer, the more speculating, and enterprising part of the community, who availed themselves of the then low price." The legislature's subsequent decision to raise taxes in order to pay interest on the securities led to "discussions of the reasonableness and justice of the public paying so much more than the purchasers had given for the securities." Because "many of the purchasers had been instrumental in depreciating the securities and at the time of purchasing had made use of the argument of the uncertainty of their ever being paid to induce the original holders or earners to part with them at a low price," many Rhode Islanders resented the tax increase and demanded a policy of discrimination in favor of the original holders of the securities and a liquidation of securities that had been transferred. Fenner noted that similar arguments had prevailed in Congress in 1780, when it had depreciated the continental currency at a rate of forty paper dollars to one dollar of specie.

"the only mode by which the true sentiments of the people could be collected." Party leaders were confident that a majority of Rhode Islanders, who had repeatedly endorsed through elections the party's schemes of paper money and public-debt repudiation, would reject ratification.[405]

By contrast, Rhode Island's mercantile party, whose members were Federalists, criticized the referendum on the Constitution as "without precedent on the face of the earth." They argued that Rhode Island "ought to pay some deference to the opinions" of the other twelve states, all of which had appointed ratifying conventions, even when Antifederalists controlled the legislatures. One Federalist newspaper ridiculed the notion that the people in "one afternoon" could determine "the merits of a system of federal government, which employed the talents of a convention of the ablest politicians from 12 states four months [of] unremitted attention to frame." The people did not possess "either leisure or opportunity to examine the proposed Constitution, so as to be competent to form an adequate judgment on this very momentous question." In a convention, however, "all the light and information which may be collected from every part of the state will be afforded." Moreover, Federalists observed, even if Rhode Island voters approved the Constitution in a referendum, Congress would consider this an invalid form of ratification because it was inconsistent with the procedures prescribed by Article VII, and thus the state legislature eventually would have to call a convention anyway.[406]

Accordingly, Federalist leaders urged their supporters to boycott the referendum and instead instruct their town's deputies in the General Assembly to call a ratifying convention, which they said would be free to propose amendments to address any flaws in the Constitution that Antifederalists might identify. The strongest bastions of Federalist support—Newport, Providence, and Bristol—either did instruct their deputies to call a convention or else signed petitions asking the legislature to do so. With most supporters of the Constitution thus abiding by their leaders' call to boycott the referendum, only two of the state's thirty towns endorsed ratification, and Rhode Island voters overall rejected the Constitution by a margin of 2,714 to 238.[407]

After confirming the referendum result, the General Assembly voted by a wide margin to reject a motion to call a ratifying convention. Reporting the referendum results to Congress, Rhode Island's governor defended the state's choice to use a referendum rather than a ratifying convention as consistent with "pure republican principles." He also observed that, while Rhode Islanders had serious qualms about the Constitution, they would "heartily acquiesce" in granting Congress the powers to regulate commerce and to levy impost duties and excise taxes for the purpose of discharging the national debt.[408]

The Rhode Island legislature took no further action on the Constitution during its sessions in May and June 1788, and after the latter session it stood adjourned until October. Late in June, as we have seen, New Hampshire became the ninth state to ratify the Constitution.* In July, the New York ratifying convention approved the Constitution, an event some Federalists had predicted would "have a considerable effect" on Rhode Island. The *Newport Herald* now announced that "the last hopes of the Antifederal junto in this state" had been "blasted," and many Federalists again demanded that the Rhode Island legislature call a convention, some even predicting that it would do so.[409]

In newspaper essays, Federalists argued that Rhode Island could not possibly hold out long as an independent state. "Phocion" wrote, "We shall then be left in a contending world, to shift for ourselves, surrounded by great, powerful and confederated neighbors." The United States would boycott trade with Rhode Island, "A Friend to the Union" noted, and the idea of a foreign nation's intervening to protect Rhode Island was "chimerical." "Rhodiensis" warned that Congress would sooner strip Rhode Island of its sovereignty and partition it between Massachusetts and Connecticut than permit the state to become "a nest for smugglers or a receptacle for the ships of an enemy." Were Rhode Island to join the union, by contrast, its well-situated harbors and disproportionately coastal population would turn the state into "the great entrepot and mart of New-England." Federalists also pointed out that if Rhode Island insisted on its independence, Congress would demand payment of the state's share of the national government's debt, resulting in the imposition of burdensome direct taxes on the very farmers who largely constituted the country party. If the Constitution needed amending, Federalists argued, then Rhode Island could better influence the amendment process if it were represented in the first federal Congress.[410]

In response to such arguments, some Antifederalists suggested that if Rhode Island remained independent of the union, it could monopolize European trade by declaring its harbor towns to be free ports. If the United States sought to coerce Rhode Island, Antifederalists maintained, the state could look to Great Britain or another European power for protection.[411]

At its session in the fall of 1788, the Rhode Island legislature once again refused, by a margin of nearly three to one, to call a ratifying convention, ignoring dire Federalist warnings that "an obstinate opposition to the federal government must terminate in the ruin of the inhabitants and the utter annihilation

---

* When Federalists in Providence sought to combine their traditional Fourth of July festivities with a celebration of the Constitution's ratification by the requisite nine states, the country party gathered a force of several hundred men on the outskirts of town to block the event, which they deemed an insult to Rhode Island's Antifederalist majority. Violence was narrowly averted when Federalists promised to limit themselves to a celebration of the nation's independence.

of the state." The legislature also continued to implement its policy of paying off the state debt with paper money, which by then had sunk to one-eighth of its face value. Finally, the legislature forwarded to the towns the circular letter and the proposed constitutional amendments of the New York ratifying convention, together with a recommendation that the towns instruct their Assembly deputies on whether to support New York's call for a second national constitutional convention.[412]

The Rhode Island legislature would meet seven times in 1789, and, on four of those occasions, it defeated motions to summon a state ratifying convention. One Antifederalist leader, expressing confidence that Rhode Island could be admitted to the union any time it pleased, argued in favor of waiting to see if the new national government actually produced the benefits that Federalists promised it would. Antifederalists also expressed doubts that Congress would subject Rhode Island to trade discrimination if it persisted in remaining outside of the union.[413]

By the spring and summer of 1789, Rhode Island Federalists were beginning to grow desperate. Regarding themselves as "the virtuous and oppressed minority," Federalists—especially in Newport and Providence—discussed the possibility of their towns' seceding from Rhode Island. In April, the Newport town meeting warned that if Rhode Island remained outside the union, the "wretched situation" of the town's inhabitants would "oblige them, as the last alternative, to apply to the federal government for relief and protection." Rhode Island Federalists, explaining that secession "would be certain" to elicit "the vengeance" of the Rhode Island government in retaliation, turned to members of Congress and even to Vice President John Adams for guarantees of protection should their towns secede from the state. In June, during congressional debates on the Bill of Rights (discussed in chapter 7), Congressman James Jackson of Georgia announced that he would support Rhode Island's mercantile towns, who were "firm friends of the union," should they petition Congress to assert jurisdiction over them.[414]

William Ellery, a Newport lawyer and one of the state's leading Federalists (who had signed the Declaration of Independence as a Rhode Island delegate to the Continental Congress), had long predicted that the country party would "stand out to the end" and that "nothing but necessity will compel them to embrace a measure which will put it out of their power to do mischief." By the spring of 1789, Ellery was privately calling upon members of Congress to impose trade sanctions on Rhode Island—tonnage fees on its shipping and duties on its exports to the other states (mainly lime, cheese, and barley). Other Federalists called publicly for the imposition of trade sanctions. George Benson, a Providence merchant, took a different tack, informing Massachusetts congressman Theodore Sedgwick that while Rhode Island's Antifederalists treated "with contemptuous levity every address from an insulted minority," they would take more seriously a congressional resolution demanding that Rhode Island summon a ratifying convention.[415]

By September 1789, the state debt had been "redeemed," on schedule, in nearly worthless paper currency. Some Rhode Island Federalists had predicted that, once this scheme was accomplished, the country party would "veer about." Furthermore, significant gains by the mercantile party in the August elections for the General Assembly had led many Federalists to predict that the legislature would call a ratifying convention when it met in October.[416]

However, such was not to be the case. To counter that very possibility, the governor called a special session of the legislature in September, and it passed a bill calling town meetings for October to instruct Assembly deputies on whether to call a ratifying convention.[417]*

The special session of the legislature also sent a letter to Congress and President Washington explaining why Rhode Island had yet to ratify the Constitution. Acknowledging "themselves to be a handful comparatively viewed," legislators recalled the collective hardships endured by the thirteen states during the Revolutionary War and noted their constituents' reluctance to approve a constitution that many of them considered inconsistent with the principles for which the war had been fought. Rhode Islanders, the letter continued, wished to observe the new federal system in operation "to see what further checks and securities would be agreed to and established by way of amendments." Those amendments passed by the House of Representatives in August had "already afforded some relief and satisfaction to the minds of the people of this state," and Rhode Islanders looked forward to the day when they could be safely reunited with their sister states. In conclusion, the legislature expressed the hope that Rhode Islanders would not be "altogether considered as foreigners" and declared the state's willingness to pay its share of the national debt. Many Federalists deemed this letter "a gross insult" to Congress.[418]

In the meantime, Congress was deliberating upon when to begin imposing trade sanctions on Rhode Island commerce. In mid-September 1789, Congress set January 15, 1790, as the deadline for Rhode Island to ratify the Constitution or else face discriminatory tonnage duties on its shipping. Later

---

* The country party proved more willing to compromise, now that the state debt had been redeemed or forfeited, on the three-year-old tender law, which had required creditors to accept paper money at par value as legal tender for debts, upon threat of forfeiture. The special session of the legislature in September 1789 repealed this law and substituted one that made real and personal property at an appraised value, or paper money at a discount of fifteen paper dollars to one silver dollar, a legal tender for debts. Since at this point Rhode Island paper money was trading on the market at a rate of closer to twenty to one, this tender law still disadvantaged creditors, though not nearly as much as the repealed law had.

that fall, President Washington conspicuously avoided Rhode Island during his New England tour.[419]

Congress's decision to postpone the imposition of trade sanctions until early 1790 was widely interpreted as an act of lenity. One Federalist disparaged the measure for attempting to draw in Rhode Island "by the cords of love"—an effort he predicted the state's Antifederalists would "despise." For a variety of reasons, though, most members of Congress were reluctant to take harsh measures against Rhode Island. Some opposed coercion for ideological reasons or out of concern that such steps might backfire. In addition, one of Congress's most effective levers for pressuring Rhode Island—the imposition of tonnage duties on its shipping—would, perversely, harm the mercantile interests of Newport and Providence, where support for the Constitution was strong, much more than it would affect the interests of inland farmers, who were the backbone of the country party. Finally, members of Congress who represented southern and mid-Atlantic states were not, in the words of Vice President Adams, "unanimously zealous at this moment to give New England two additional senators." Specifically, the addition of senators from Rhode Island might prove decisive in northerners' efforts to keep Congress in New York City, at least temporarily.[420]

However, in private correspondence, Adams warned that the postponement of trade sanctions was "the greatest length" to which Congress was likely to go in indulging Rhode Island. If the state had not ratified the Constitution by the January 15 deadline, "something much more serious than has ever yet been done or talked of will most probably be undertaken." Further, Adams threatened "very speedy and very bitter" consequences if the "rumors of correspondences between the Antis in [Rhode Island] and those in Massachusetts, New York, Virginia, North Carolina, etc. and even with insinuations of intrigues with British emissaries" turned out to be true. Adams concluded by urging Rhode Islanders to "open their eyes before it is too late."[421]

The town meetings summoned by the Rhode Island legislature's special session in September to instruct deputies on whether to call a ratifying convention resulted in a majority of deputies' being instructed to oppose a convention. Accordingly, even though a majority of deputies elected in August had seemed inclined to support calling a convention, the Assembly's regular session in October voted by a margin of thirty-nine to seventeen against calling one—the eighth such rejection in two years. The Assembly then adjourned until January 1790.[422]

Some Federalists had predicted that Rhode Island would ratify the Constitution once North Carolina had done so, and Rhode Island's newspapers closely followed the proceedings of the second North Carolina convention, which met in November 1789. When that convention ratified the

Constitution, President Washington reflected that Rhode Island was now left "entirely alone." Jabez Bowen, a wealthy Providence Federalist and former deputy governor of Rhode Island, told Vice President Adams that "our Antes are thunderstruck at the news" from North Carolina, "especially as the majority was so large." (The North Carolina convention ratified the Constitution by a margin of 194 to 77.) Whether North Carolina's ratification would ultimately persuade the Rhode Island legislature to summon a convention was anybody's guess.[423]

With the Rhode Island legislature set to convene in January 1790, one Federalist essayist warned that the choice is "either voluntarily and immediately to unite with the twelve confederated states; or, by obstinately standing out, forfeit what remains of our commerce . . . and finally, like refractory fools, be compelled to do that which both interest and honor require us to perform." Federalists also reiterated threats that if the legislature did not call a convention, the larger seaport towns would probably secede from Rhode Island and look to Congress for protection.[424]

Finally capitulating to the pressure, the Rhode Island General Assembly at its January session voted by a margin of thirty-four to twenty-nine to call a ratifying convention. However, the upper house (whose members were known as "assistants") narrowly rejected the Assembly's bill, preferring instead that the legislature again ask the towns to instruct deputies with regard to calling a convention. But it happened that one assistant, who had voted against calling a convention, had to leave the legislative session before its conclusion, resulting in a tie vote in the upper house, which Governor John Collins had to break. Noting the "extreme distress" that Rhode Island would suffer if it continued to defy the United States, Collins cast the decisive vote in favor of calling a convention. The legislature then summoned the convention to meet in South Kingston on March 1, 1790.* It also instructed the governor to apply to Congress for a further suspension of trade sanctions.[425]

Elated Rhode Island Federalists expressed confidence that they had won the war. One of them declared, "The Federal Temple will now soon be completed and peace, joy, and plenty, I hope, pervade the land." Jabez Bowen assured President Washington that the Constitution would be "finally adopted by a respectable majority" at the ratifying convention. Henry Marchant, a prominent Federalist lawyer and former attorney general of Rhode Island, told Vice President Adams that he had "not a reasonable doubt but the constitution will be adopted," as the Antifederalists had "promised they would

---

* The country party then declined to renominate Collins for governor in the April election, at which point he turned to President Washington with a request to be appointed to a post in the federal government as a reward for the personal sacrifice he had made on behalf of the union.

give no further opposition." Marchant also urged Adams to press Congress to extend its deferral of trade sanctions against Rhode Island, which he predicted would "have a tendency to reconcile hundreds of our people" to the Constitution and be worth "at least ten votes in our convention." On February 8, Congress granted the requested extension, though for "no longer" than until April 1.[426]

Also on February 8, Rhode Island voters gathered in their towns to elect delegates for the state ratifying convention. To the Federalists' astonishment and consternation, voters returned an Antifederalist majority variously estimated at between six and ten delegates. The caucus of Antifederalist delegates then agreed that rather than rejecting ratification altogether, they would seek to adjourn the convention.[427]

Rhode Island Federalists turned in desperation to federal officials for help. Some of them wrote to Vice President Adams to urge that Congress enact measures before the ratifying convention assembled that would convince Antifederalists that "Congress will not be dallied with any longer."* One of them suggested that Congress require Rhode Island to satisfy its debts to the union through direct taxes, which would immediately and adversely impact the state's farmers. Another Federalist proposed that Congress simply declare Rhode Island to be part of the United States; those residents who preferred not to live under the federal government's jurisdiction would be free to sell their estates and move away.[428]

Rhode Island Federalists also appealed directly to their adversaries through newspaper essays. They pointed out that the Rhode Island legislature, in its January letter to Congress, had given "every reason to hope that this state would in a short time accede to the federal union" if granted a temporary reprieve from trade sanctions, which Congress had provided. If the convention nonetheless adjourned without ratifying the Constitution, Congress would "consider the legislature as having trifled with them." Trade sanctions would be certain to follow, as Congress would never "suffer a single refractory state to embarrass its great, necessary national measures." Such sanctions, Federalists warned, would only compound the "various distresses" of the mercantile towns and accelerate Rhode Island's loss of population to western migration. Federalists also reiterated that the convention's failure to ratify the Constitution would lead Congress to force Rhode Island to pay its share of the

---

* In his reply to a letter from Bowen, Adams noted that it "would not be prudent" for him to predict Congress's response should the Rhode Island convention refuse to ratify the Constitution. Still, Adams went on to say that he doubted Congress would ever "beg or pray or exhort your Antis to come in," and he warned that the US government might "take severe measures" at Rhode Island's expense just to prove that it was capable of punishing those who opposed it.

federal government's debt and operating expenses, and induce Newport and Providence to secede from the state and seek federal protection.[429]

Secure in their majority, however, Antifederalist delegates at the ratifying convention proved impervious to Federalist appeals. They framed a bill of rights and drew up a list of numerous additional amendments, consisting mainly of ones already proposed by the conventions of other states, and ordered these printed and laid before the towns at their regularly scheduled April meetings, when state legislators and executive officials would be elected. Then, the Antifederalists moved to adjourn the convention. However, their opponents denied that the convention, which had been appointed by the legislature for a "full and free investigation and *decision*" on whether to ratify the Constitution, had the power to adjourn itself. Federalists also argued that adjournment would be inexpedient because Congress would regard it as an insult and thus would immediately impose trade sanctions.[430]

Antifederalist delegates defended adjournment on the grounds that North Carolina and New Hampshire had adjourned their ratifying conventions, and that the people of Rhode Island had a right to be consulted on the bill of rights and other amendments to be proposed by the convention. Antifederalist delegates also argued that, since a majority of Rhode Islanders continued to oppose the Constitution, they would have no choice but to vote against ratification if the convention forced a vote on that question. Because rejecting the Constitution altogether would be dangerous, Antifederalists maintained, their opponents should prefer an adjournment, which would allow the people additional time for consideration. The Antifederalists then carried their motion to adjourn the convention by a margin of forty-one to twenty-eight.[431]

Federalists had hoped that, if they could not prevent an adjournment, at least they could ensure that it would not last beyond April 1, the date on which Congress's postponement of trade sanctions against Rhode Island was set to expire. Arguing against adjournment to a date later than that, one leading Federalist delegate disparaged the need for further delay given that "every man has made up his mind on the subject," and warned against "trifling" with Congress. Another Federalist threatened that if the convention adjourned beyond April 1, his constituents would petition Congress to join Massachusetts.[432]

However, the Federalists' appeals to "reason, duty, necessity, and every other argument" were "to no purpose," as noted in one report. Antifederalists, contending that "the people are frightened by the anxiety which is shown for the adoption," insisted on a longer adjournment. Expressing confidence that Congress would grant a further postponement of trade sanctions, Antifederalists defeated a motion to adjourn the convention only until the end of March and then carried a motion to adjourn until May 24—several weeks after the April elections for state legislators and executive officials.[433]

One of the Antifederalists' main reasons for adjourning the convention was partisan. By redeeming the state's debt with vastly depreciated paper money and enforcing the paper-money tender law to the advantage of debtors for several years, the country party had largely fulfilled its original raison d'être. With those goals accomplished, opposition to the Constitution had become the party's principal campaign issue—but ratification would of course eliminate that issue as well. Thus, one prominent Federalist reported that country party leader and deputy governor Daniel Owen, who also served as president of the ratifying convention, "did not hesitate to say out of doors that an adjournment of the convention was necessary to insure their election." According to Federalists, the ratifying convention had framed a bill of rights and other amendments to submit to the town meetings only to "cover their design," which was to ensure that the party could continue to campaign in the April elections on a platform of opposition to the Constitution.[434]

In addition to partisan motives, some Antifederalists had ideological reasons for continuing their opposition to ratification. Many Rhode Islanders were deeply disaffected by what they regarded as the exorbitant salaries voted by members of the first federal Congress to themselves and other federal officeholders—salaries that contrasted starkly with the relative pittance that Rhode Island paid its legislators and executive officials. In addition, many Rhode Island Antifederalists considered the proposal of Secretary of the Treasury Alexander Hamilton to fund the national debt at close to par value to be "pernicious" because it would "fix a grievous land-tax on you [Rhode Island farmers] for the payment of unjust interest, which will realize ill-gotten securities in the hands of wicked speculators." According to one report, a "powerful reason" for adjourning the convention was "an expectation that the report of the Secretary of the Treasury would create great uneasiness in the states in the union, which would terminate in insurrections, and thereby would establish the antifederal power in this state and make it the center of opposition." According to one prominent Rhode Island Federalist, the Antifederalists planned to continue adjourning the state's ratifying convention to give Congress time to "do so many unjust things that several of the great states will be ready to revolt and . . . Rhode Island, remaining a free and independent state, will put herself at their head."[435]

Rhode Island Antifederalists had one final reason for adjourning the ratifying convention. As Rhode Island Federalists had repeatedly observed to their allies in the national government, the burden of any trade restrictions imposed by Congress on Rhode Island would probably fall, at least initially, "entirely on our friends." That is, while tonnage fees imposed on Rhode Island ships would have an immediate adverse impact on the interests of Federalist merchants in the coastal towns, duties levied on Rhode Island agricultural exports to the other states would not be felt by Antifederalist farmers until their crops were harvested and sold in the fall. After nearly four years of bitter partisan warfare over state monetary and fiscal policy, Rhode Island farmers, according to one Federalist, seemed to "care not how much the [merchants] suffer, provided they [the farmers] are unhurt." Another Federalist thought the farmers would "glory in effecting their [the merchants'] ruin."[436]

Federalists in Congress had warned that if Rhode Island Antifederalists adjourned the state's ratifying convention, "which, after so long [a] time to reflect on the subject, will be only a delicate mode of rejection," the federal government would be "justified even to the discerning people in Rhode Island in pursuing measures that in other circumstances might be thought severe." Thus, after the adjournment, Federalists in Congress decided to take seriously their Rhode Island allies' prediction that the state's Antifederalists would approve the Constitution only "upon the most urgent necessity." As the May 24 date for the Rhode Island convention to reassemble grew near, Federalists in the US Senate—led by northerners who wanted Rhode Island to join the union partly to enhance the North's advantage in Congress—passed a coercive measure. The bill forbade, after July 1, 1790, the importation into the United States by land or water of any Rhode Island produce or manufacturing, barred US vessels from Rhode Island ports and waters and Rhode Island ships from US ports and waters, and established harsh penalties for violations of these provisions. In addition, the bill declared that Rhode Island must pay the federal government, no later than December 1, 1790, $25,000 toward discharging its share of the national debt. Because direct taxes would be necessary to raise so much revenue so quickly, the brunt of this last requirement would be borne primarily by the state's farmers.[437]

The Senate bill to coerce Rhode Island proved controversial in both houses of Congress. One congressional representative called it "tyrannical and arbitrary in the highest degree," while another reported that "many merciful men among us . . . choose to wait to see the result of the next session of [the Rhode Island] convention" and would not "agree to any coercive measures with the little sister until they are convinced of her final obstinacy." A Virginia congressman, John Page, declared it "sadly unbecoming a free state to make anything like threats" and observed that the Senate bill revealed "a malevolence resembling that which Great Britain showed" when it closed Boston harbor in response to the Boston Tea Party, thus rallying support for independence across the colonies. Rhode Island citizens ought to be as free to deliberate upon the Constitution as citizens of the other states had been, Page argued, and Congress ought to "show a generous indulgence to that jealous, cautious republican spirit, which indeed we should cherish and revere." Moreover, Page warned, the bill was essentially a declaration of war against Rhode Island and thus might push the state to seek assistance from foreign nations. At the very least, the measure was likely to backfire by provoking "the indignation" of the delegates to the Rhode Island ratifying convention, who "would esteem them-selves contemptible to accede to the new constitution under the influence of threatening measures." Even if the bill succeeded in pressuring Rhode Island into ratifying the Constitution, the state would "come with so bad a grace into the union that she must be ashamed when she enters it."[438]

The Senate bill also elicited a strong protest from Rhode Island's governor, Arthur Fenner, who complained to President Washington of "a measure of such an hostile appearance and so degrading to this state." Fenner assured the president that, as a result of twelve states' having ratified the Constitution and many of them also having approved the Bill of Rights, "many persons of influ-ence who have heretofore opposed the adoption of the new Constitution here have withdrawn their opposition." He predicted that the Constitution "will be very soon adopted in this state," though he warned that measures such as the Senate bill, "which have the appearance of coercion," might produce an "alien-ation of affection."[439]

On May 18, the Senate passed the coercion bill by a vote of thirteen to eight. Then, "carefully managed delays" in the House—as one astute observer, the French consul general, put it—ensured that the bill would remain pending when the Rhode Island convention reassembled on May 24. Rhode Island newspapers publicized the bill, and several members of Congress wrote public letters calling attention to it and urging Rhode Islanders not to be deceived into thinking that their state's independence from the union would be toler-ated for long. Rhode Island Federalist George Benson told Congressman Theodore Sedgwick that the Senate bill had "made a very alarming impression on the antifederal minds." No other event had "produced effects so apparently auspicious to our wishes," and Benson reported "the most sanguine expecta-tions" for ratification.[440]

In the days before May 24, Rhode Island Federalists predicted that if the Constitution were not ratified, their supporters would "become desperate and a dissolution of government may be expected." The town of Providence instructed its convention delegates that, if ratification failed, they should co-ordinate with delegates from Newport and other towns to apply to Congress for protection. Rhode Island Federalists also renewed their appeals to allies in the national government for guarantees of protection against violence should secession become necessary. In response to one such appeal—by William Ellery—Congressman Benjamin Huntington of Connecticut declared that, while he could not commit Congress as a body, he knew of many congressmen who would be receptive to an application for protection. Vice President Adams went even further in his response to a similar missive from Ellery: "If the inland part of your people are so abandoned as to refuse still to ratify the Constitution, there will be no part left for the seaports, but to do what I think they ought to have done long ago, meet and adopt the Constitution for themselves and petition Congress to be received and protected."[441]

Just before the convention reassembled, Ellery reported that the Antifederalists "have talked more favorably respecting an accession," but he thought that the point of such discussion was "only to amuse." He predicted that the Antifederalists would continue to adjourn the convention until Congress actually implemented coercive legislation. Another prominent Rhode Island Federalist noted that he had "strong hopes but not without some fears."[442]

Antifederalist delegates were still in the majority when the convention reassembled. However, the Federalists considered it a "happy circumstance" that the reassembled convention met in Newport, which had been selected by the margin of a single vote at the convention's March session. Newport "had the largest federal interest and little influence of the country anties."[443]

After the Federalists had endured several days filled with "anxiety, labor and assiduity, hope and fear," delegates from the towns of Portsmouth and Middletown dramatically announced that they would vote to ratify the Constitution if they could first obtain favorable instructions from their constituents. On May 29, meetings of those two towns clarified and changed, respectively, their delegates' instructions so as to support ratification. The convention then voted by a margin of thirty-four to thirty-two* to ratify the Constitution. The form of ratification offered "explanations" of several controversial provisions in the Constitution and expressed "confidence" that the amendments proposed by the convention would receive "an early and mature consideration," and that Congress would refrain from exercising certain delegated powers until the amendments had been approved. The convention also recommended to the state legislature that it ratify all but one of the amendments in the Bill of Rights passed by Congress the previous fall.[444]

---

* Federalists insisted that their margin of victory would have been greater had more delegates been able to communicate with their towns to obtain changed instructions before casting a vote. Apparently, the threats of trade sanctions by Congress and of secession by the towns of Newport and Providence had convinced many wavering delegates that ratification would be prudent. Indeed, Senator Oliver Ellsworth of Connecticut attributed Rhode Island's accession to "a pretty bold measure taken in Congress which would have exposed me to some censure had it not produced the effect which I expected it would and which in fact it has done. But all is well that ends well."

After nearly three years of struggle, Rhode Island Federalists had finally achieved victory. A Boston newspaper headline proclaimed, "The American Union Completed." That summer, President Washington traveled to Newport and Providence to celebrate Rhode Island's accession to the union.[445]

The Federalists' Great Fears: Conditional Ratification and a Second Convention

Throughout the ratifying contest, Federalists strenuously opposed either conditional ratification or a second constitutional convention. As we have seen, when the Confederation Congress considered whether to forward the Constitution to the states, Federalists had denied that Congress had the authority to propose amendments. In addition, the letter drafted by the Philadelphia convention to accompany the Constitution had called upon state legislatures to submit it to ratifying conventions for "their assent and ratification." The meaning of those words, as Edmund Randolph later explained, was "allowed universally to be that the [state ratifying] convention must either adopt the Constitution in the whole or reject it in the whole and is positively forbidden to amend."[446]

Indeed, in early state ratifying conventions, Federalists had insisted on up-or-down votes on the Constitution and rejected the notion of amendments, whether conditional or merely recommended. However, beginning with the Massachusetts convention, Federalists had accepted the idea of ratification with recommended amendments, realizing that, without such a concession, they would lose. Still, they remained resolutely opposed to anything that smacked of conditional ratification—a notion that Madison called "pregnant with such infinite dangers, that I cannot contemplate it without horror."[447]

A second national convention was even more of an anathema to Federalists than ratification contingent upon amendments. Near the end of the Philadelphia convention, Randolph and George Mason had proposed that state ratifying conventions be permitted to propose amendments to the Constitution, which would then be considered by a second national convention. As Mason explained, such a convention would "know more of the sense of the people and be able to provide a system more consonant to it." Moreover, he argued that "[i]t was improper to say to the people, take this or nothing." Randolph agreed that "holding out this plan with a final alternative to the people, of accepting or rejecting it in toto, would really produce . . . anarchy and civil convulsions."[448]

Even after the Virginia ratifying convention, Randolph continued to support a second national convention, on the grounds that "the theory of the people" was entitled to "equal respect" with "the theory of the convention." Richard Henry Lee also endorsed a second convention, telling Washington that although the Constitution "abounds with useful regulations," there were "fundamentally strong" objections to it. These could be dealt with quickly by a second convention, thus producing general satisfaction without abridging "the exercise of a very confident federal power." In Paris, Jefferson too was intrigued with the idea of holding a second convention after the Constitution had been "duly weighed and canvassed by the people," thus revealing "the parts they generally dislike, and those they generally approve." Even after Virginia and New York had unconditionally ratified the Constitution and it had become operational, legislatures in those states continued to advocate strongly for a second convention. The circular letter issued by the New York ratifying convention exhorted other states to petition Congress to quickly call another convention to propose amendments to address concerns occasioned by the Constitution.[449]

In response to Mason's proposal in Philadelphia for a second convention, Charles Pinckney had objected that "[n]othing but confusion and contrariety could spring from the experiment." Pinckney warned his colleagues that "[c]onventions are serious things and ought not to be repeated." Madison told Jefferson that a second convention was "in every view to be dreaded," and he despaired over the New York circular letter calling for one. Madison feared that a second convention would "contain men who secretly aimed at disunion" and could easily further their goal by insisting "on points popular in some parts [of the country], but known to be inadmissible in others."[450]

Why were the Federalists so determined to avoid any changes to their handiwork—through either antecedent amendments or a second convention? Federalists offered legal arguments for resisting such proposals. James Innes told the Virginia ratifying convention that it was not authorized to consider antecedent amendments, which might "radically change" the document, because the people "have seen the Constitution and sent us hither to adopt or reject it." Subsequent amendments were different, according to Innes, because they "would not operate till the people had an opportunity of considering and altering them, if they thought proper."[451]

Madison made a different argument: Conditional ratification would not be legally effective because all states had to ratify the same document, and other states had already unconditionally ratified the Constitution. Thus, if Virginia ratified on the condition of antecedent amendments, every state that had already ratified would have to appoint another convention to begin anew. For this reason, conditional ratifications, another Virginia Federalist explained, would mean that the states would be "eternally revolving and de-vising expedients without coming to a final decision." In response to the pro-posal of New York Antifederalists that the Poughkeepsie convention ratify the Constitution while reserving New York's right to withdraw from the union if a second convention did not take place within a few years, Madison objected that "[t]he Constitution requires an adoption in toto, and forever. It has been so adopted by the other states. An adoption for a limited time would be as de-fective as an adoption of some of the articles only." James Iredell and Robert R. Livingston made similar legal arguments against conditional ratification at their states' conventions.[452]

As to a second national convention, Madison argued that once the Constitution had been ratified by the requisite number of states, Congress was powerless to accede to the Antifederalists' request that it call one. Under Article V of the Constitution, Congress could assemble a convention only upon the application of two-thirds of the state legislatures.[453]

Federalists also made policy arguments—as distinct from their legal arguments—against conditional ratification and a second convention. Arguing against conditional ratification by his state's convention, Madison asked Jefferson what reason there was to expect "that the states which have ratified will reconsider their determinations and submit to the alterations pre-scribed by Virginia." Madison was also certain that supporters of amendments in the different states "would find themselves as much at variance in detail as they are agreed in the general plan of amendments. Or if they could agree at all it would be only on a few points of very little substance." In addition, at the Virginia convention, John Marshall warned that if antecedent amendments were pursued, "enemies of the union" would propose "amendments which are local in their nature" to block agreement and thus destroy the union.[454]

Arguing against a second convention as a policy matter, Washington noted that its delegates would be "more discordant or less conciliatory" than were those at the Philadelphia convention. Similarly, Madison told Jefferson that "if a second convention should be formed, it is as little to be expected that the same spirit of compromise will prevail in it as produced an amicable result to the first." Federalists warned that delegates attending a second convention would probably be extremists disinclined to compromise, or they would come fettered with instructions that would render compromise impossible. John Jay even warned that foreign nations might seek to influence the deliberations of a second convention.[455]

Federalists also stressed that a second convention would take time—time for states to petition Congress to summon it, time to select delegates, time to hold the convention, and time to secure ratification of its proposals by the states. Such delay might prove fatal to the union, the affairs of which, according to Jay, were "daily going on from bad to worse." Jay warned that other nations would use the delay "to perfect their restrictive systems of commerce." Even worse, creating additional opportunities for "discord to alienate the hearts of our citizens from one another" would only "encourage new Cromwells to bold exploits." Madison expressed concern that foreign creditors would be unwilling to lend additional money to the US government if the scope of its taxing power remained unresolved. Rather than risking the delay inherent in a second convention, Federalists concluded, amendments should be pursued within Congress, which could act much more quickly.[456]

These were not bad arguments. Yet, in rejoinder, Antifederalists made several effective points in support of both conditional ratification and a second convention.

As we have seen, most Antifederalists admitted that the Articles of Confederation were flawed and that Congress's power ought to be expanded. Richard Henry Lee spoke for the majority of Antifederalists when he conceded that the Constitution "has a great many excellent regulations in it" and declared that "if it could be reasonably amended, [it] would be a fine system." Yet many Antifederalists also agreed with Lee's warning that without amendments to the Constitution, "either a tyranny will result from it, or it will be prevented by a civil war."[457]

Antifederalists found it galling that their opponents sought to force an up-or-down vote on the Constitution. In a letter to Mason, Richard Henry Lee objected to "the very arbitrary mode that has been pursued in some states, that is, to propose a question of absolute rejection or implicit admission." Lee declared that "every temperate man must agree that neither the convention, nor any set of men upon earth, have or had a right to insist upon such a question of extremity. To receive the good and reject the bad is too necessary and inherent a right to be parted with." At the Virginia ratifying convention, James Monroe observed that the delegates in Philadelphia could not possibly have designed a flawless system and that it was "presumable that by subsequent attempts we shall make it more complete and perfect." At the New York convention, Melancton Smith objected to most states' having considered the Constitution "in such a manner that no opportunity was afforded of bringing forward and discussing [amendments]."[458]

Antifederalists bridled at their opponents' suggestion that they be satisfied with recommended amendments to be enacted following ratification. At the Virginia ratifying convention, Henry wondered who would be so foolish as to "enter into a compact first, and afterwards settle [its] terms." "A Columbian Patriot" thought it absurd to ask Antifederalists to trust in "the precarious hope of amendments and redress, after we have voluntarily fixed the shackles on our own necks." Leading New Hampshire Antifederalist Joshua Atherton warned that "to ratify, and then propose amendments, is to surrender our all, and then to ask our new masters, if they will be so gracious to return to us some, or any part of our most important rights and privileges." A Virginia Antifederalist warned that Congress would have little incentive to propose constitutional amendments that would diminish its own power. Moreover, on what authority did the Federalists insist that Congress could not accept a conditional ratification? At the New York convention, Antifederalist John Lansing, Jr., wondered from where Congress or the Philadelphia convention had derived the power to prescribe rules of conduct for a state convention representing the sovereign people.[459]

Antifederalists also questioned what all the rush was about. It was "very reprehensible," "A Columbian Patriot" declared, that the Federalists were attempting to force the Constitution upon the nation "before it could be thoroughly understood." What could account for "the mad zeal of some to precipitate a blind adoption of the measures of the late federal convention, without giving opportunity for better information to those who are misled by influence or ignorance into erroneous opinions?" Another Massachusetts Antifederalist, observing that "important transactions" such as approving a new scheme of government required "cool deliberation," lamented that the Constitution was being "hurried on . . . very furiously" in some states. Mason told Elbridge Gerry that the Federalists, by "attempting to force the new government upon the people, betray their consciousness of its not bearing the test of impartial examination." Rather than "be terrified by imaginary dangers," the New York Antifederalist "Plebeian" wrote, it was essential to "take time to deliberate and amend."[460]

Antifederalists charged their opponents with exaggerating when they warned that the nation faced a dire emergency that necessitated quick ratification of the Constitution. Pennsylvania Antifederalists declared that their opponents "were busily employed in alarming the fears of the people with dangers which did not exist." According to the Antifederalist "Centinel," "our situation is represented to be so critically dreadful, that, however reprehensible and exceptionable the proposed plan of government may be, there is no alternative between the adoption of it and absolute ruin." At the Virginia ratifying convention, Monroe denied that the United States faced any current danger of war with European nations or that "a conditional ratification would in the most remote degree endanger the union." Thus, the people should consider themselves free to "calmly and dispassionately" examine the Constitution before ratifying it.[461]

Patrick Henry likewise wondered why "precipitate measures" were being taken "to hurry the people into adoption" of the Constitution. The experiment of ratification without antecedent amendments could not be justified "[u]nless there be great and awful dangers." Yet until the Philadelphia convention had roiled politics, Henry insisted, "a general peace and a universal tranquility prevailed in this country." Why, when the situation was "calm and tranquil," should the nation be "wandering on the great ocean of human affairs?" Henry also disparaged claims that the union was genuinely at risk. Only "an imprudent adoption" of the Constitution "in its defective and dangerous state" would produce such "a schism."[462]

Richard Henry Lee also protested the Federalists' plan "to push the business on with great dispatch and with as little opposition as possible," so that the Constitution would be approved "before it has stood the test of reflection and due examination." No war or internal discord prevented "the most cool, collected, full and fair discussion of this all important subject." Lee argued that ratifying the Constitution would have "immense consequences," given that it was "neither prudent [n]or easy to make frequent changes in government, and as bad governments have been generally found the most fixed." Thus, he was mystified as to why, on this "business of such infinite moment to the happiness of millions," the Federalists seemed determined in "the most rash and violent proceeding in the world to cram" the Constitution down the nation's throat.[463]

Moreover, Lee could not fathom why, "[i]f with infinite ease, a convention was obtained to prepare a system," another convention could not "with equal ease be procured to make proper and necessary amendments." A second convention made sense, Rawlins Lowndes of South Carolina argued, because "the general sense of America appeared well understood, every objection could be met on fair grounds, and adequate remedies applied where necessary." A Pennsylvania Antifederalist asked why "the opinions of thirty-nine men" (the number who signed the Constitution)—"secluded from the rest of the world" and enjoying no opportunity to correct their errors—should be permitted to control "the collective wisdom of a great nation." The New York Antifederalist "Plebeian" similarly observed that because the debates of the Philadelphia convention "were kept an impenetrable secret, and no opportunity was given for well-informed men to offer their sentiments upon the subject," a second convention was essential to correcting the "material errors" that had been identified now that the Constitution had been "the object of universal attention."[464]

These were good arguments, and Federalists were less than fully candid in their reasons for rejecting them. The fact is that Federalists did not really wish to consult the people on whether the Constitution should be amended before it was ratified. They understood how difficult—probably impossible—it would be to recreate the conditions that had enabled the Philadelphia convention to produce the nationalist and democracy-constraining document that it had. Madison confided that he "should tremble for the result of a second [convention]," given "the difficulties and dangers experienced by the first convention, which assembled under every propitious circumstance." He told Randolph that a second convention "would of course be formed under the influence and composed in great measure of the members of opposition in the several states." Thus, "a second experiment would be either wholly abortive, or would end in something much more remote from your ideas and those of others who wish a salutary government, than the plan now before the public."[465]

The lack of transparency that had proved so critical to the handiwork of the first convention could not possibly have been replicated at a second one: The cat was out of the bag. The agenda of a second convention would have been known in advance, whereas that of the first had pretty much existed only in Madison's head. Antifederalists would surely have contested the choice of delegates to a second convention, whereas state legislatures had mainly just selected their states' most prominent citizens as delegates to the first. Antifederalists who were chosen as delegates to a second convention almost certainly would have attended, unlike many of their counterparts who had been selected for the first. Delegates to a second convention would probably have been more fettered with binding instructions than those to the first had been. Given a better understanding of what was at stake, Antifederalist delegates would not have been so quick to depart a second convention simply because it was trending against their preferences, as Yates and Lansing had the first. Delegates to a second convention would have found it much harder to keep secret what they were doing than those at the Philadelphia convention had. In retrospect, Randolph was almost certainly right when he told his colleagues at the outset of the Philadelphia convention that this might be their last opportunity to secure revolutionary changes in the nature of the federal government.[466]

After the delegates to the Philadelphia convention had produced a constitution that they liked,* Federalists sought to force the nation into a simple up-or-down vote on it. Federalists plainly appreciated that although most Americans might favor the Constitution over the status quo of an obviously flawed Articles of Confederation, they might also prefer—if given the choice—an amended Constitution to the one designed in Philadelphia. Precisely for this reason, at the Pennsylvania ratifying convention, Federalists rejected their opponents' demands for a separate vote on each article and insisted that the Constitution be approved or rejected as a whole.[467]

Especially in ratifying conventions that were deeply divided—such as those of Massachusetts, Virginia, and New York—a majority of delegates almost

---

* It bears repeating that many of the delegates were disappointed that the Constitution was not even more nationalist and democracy-constraining.

certainly would have preferred the Constitution with certain amendments over the one they were presented with. Thus, for example, most delegates to the Virginia ratifying convention apparently preferred, if that were the only choice, that Congress have vastly expanded taxing power, rather than that it be denied all independent revenue-raising authority, as under the Articles. Yet it was also clear from a vote that was taken that a majority of convention delegates would have preferred even more that, rather than granting Congress such enormous taxing authority, the Constitution should require Congress to requisition states before imposing direct taxes. Precisely the same thing was true of the New York ratifying convention.[468]

Even in state conventions that unanimously ratified the Constitution, such as those of New Jersey and Delaware, delegates did not necessarily prefer the unamended Constitution to one with certain amendments. For example, all delegates to the New Jersey ratifying convention presumably considered the Constitution an improvement over the Articles insofar as it barred New York from enacting impost duties that indirectly forced the people of New Jersey to subsidize New York's government. Yet many of those delegates might have liked even better a constitution that accomplished this change without simultaneously barring states from enacting debtor relief legislation or departing quite so dramatically from the populist features of the state constitutions. Paper money supporters remained in control of New Jersey politics during the ratifying contest. That they did not oppose ratification does not mean that their views on paper money had changed. Perhaps they simply concluded that the Constitution's virtues outweighed its vices.* Yet the Constitution with certain amendments might have appealed to them even more.[469]

To the extent possible, Federalists were determined to prevent Americans from enjoying such choices. When Randolph proposed to Madison before the Philadelphia convention that the constitution about to be drafted be presented to the country in a fashion allowing its provisions to be "detached from each other [so] as to permit a state to reject one part without mutilating the whole," Madison quickly dismissed the idea. He and most Federalists doubted that the people were sufficiently calm, wise, or well informed to play a responsible role in devising their own system of government. For example, late in 1787, Madison told Jefferson, "In Virginia, where the mass of people have been so accustomed to be guided by their rulers on all new and intricate questions," the matter of whether to ratify the Constitution "certainly surpasses the judgment of the greater part of them." In a similar vein, arguing

---

* Similarly, in Georgia, the Savannah merchant Joseph Clay worried about the "great" powers conferred on the federal government yet still considered the Constitution the lesser of "two evils" because "[u]nder such a government we should have avoided this great evil, an Indian war."

against constituents' instructing their delegates to the state ratifying convention, one North Carolina Federalist was stunningly candid in telling his readers that "[t]he greatest part of you have not the means of information, and being unaccustomed to think of government, few of you are competent judges of it."[470]

From the Federalists' perspective, the less popular participation in the ratifying process, the better. Antifederalists did not greatly exaggerate in accusing their opponents of "despis[ing] the general opinion of the multitude."[471]

The Federalists also seemed convinced that time was not on their side. At the Philadelphia convention, Gouverneur Morris had predicted that when the Constitution was first publicly unveiled, "with the sanction of this convention, the people will be favorable to it." However, "[b]y degrees the state officers and those interested in the state governments will intrigue and turn the popular current against it." Luther Martin, who after the convention became a leading Antifederalist in Maryland, agreed with Morris that time did not favor the Federalists, though he disagreed about the reason: Martin was convinced that the people "would not ratify it [the Constitution] unless hurried into it by surprise." During the ratifying contest, the Antifederalist "Centinel" similarly charged that the Federalists, aware of the danger that "allowing time for a rational investigation would prove fatal to their designs, precipitated the establishment of the new Constitution with all possible celerity."[472]

Whether "intrigue," "surprise," or some other factor was at work, Federalists were convinced that the more time the people had to learn about the Constitution and deliberate upon it, the less likely they would be to ratify it without substantial changes. The secrecy rule at the Philadelphia convention had prevented Antifederalists from getting wind of what was in store and securing a head start at rallying opposition. Once the ratifying contest had begun, leading Federalists such as Morris, Washington, and Madison repeatedly expressed grave concern about any delays in the process.[473]

In several states, Federalists sought to secure quick elections for delegates to ratifying conventions. As we have seen, Pennsylvania Federalists were in such a rush to secure ratification that they pressed the legislature into calling a convention even before the Constitution had been formally received. "Centinel" complained, more generally, that despite the advantages the Federalists enjoyed in terms of education and talent, they nonetheless had "exerted all their power and influence to prevent all discussion of the subject."[474]

Finally, Federalists were determined that if they could not prevent amendments altogether, at least the changes ought to be proposed by Congress rather than a second convention. At the Philadelphia convention, the ultranationalist Hamilton had recognized that the sorts of constitutional amendments that nationalists would favor were more likely to come from Congress than from a constitutional convention. The Virginia Plan had provided that subsequent amendments to the Constitution ought not to require the assent of the national legislature, and the Committee of Detail report had authorized only one route to amendments—two-thirds of the state legislatures' applying to Congress to call a constitutional convention. Hamilton had objected that state legislatures would probably petition for a convention only to consider amendments that would expand their own powers, and he proposed that Congress also be empowered to summon a convention, without having to depend on states' applying for one. In the end, Article V provided two different routes to constitutional change—amendments could be proposed either by Congress itself (if two-thirds of both houses agreed) or by a constitutional convention that Congress would be obliged to summon once two-thirds of the state legislatures had petitioned for it. (In either event, to become law, amendments would have to be ratified by three-quarters of the states—either through their legislatures or through special ratifying conventions, whichever Congress provided for on a particular occasion.)[475]

During the ratifying contest, Federalists acted on the assumption that—as Madison put it—Congress would "probably be careful not to destroy or endanger" the federal government by proposing the sorts of structural amendments that Antifederalists were demanding. Although Jefferson thought more amendments were necessary than Madison did, he agreed that a second convention would be dangerous. By contrast, Jefferson declared, if amendments were proposed by Congress, then he would "not fear any dangerous innovation in the plan." Madison and Washington especially worried that a second convention would propose limits on Congress's taxing powers. Antifederalists favored a second convention for precisely the same reason that their adversaries opposed one: They were certain that Congress would not support the sort of amendments they believed were necessary. As we shall see in the next chapter, they were right.[476]

Federalists had won an enormous victory in heading off conditional ratification and a second convention.[477]

Interpreting Ratification

On July 4, 1788, an estimated seventeen thousand people in Philadelphia— much more than half of the city's population—participated in a celebration of the Constitution's ratification. Describing the event in the *Pennsylvania Mercury*, Benjamin Rush, a leading Federalist, observed that hundreds of participants had remarked that "[h]eaven was on the federal side of the question." Rush himself declared that for the requisite number of states to ratify the Constitution in less than ten months, despite "the influence of local prejudices, opposite interests, popular arts, and even the threats of bold and desperate men, is a solitary event in the history of mankind." He concluded that the drafting and ratification of the Constitution had been "as much the work of a divine providence as any of the miracles recorded in the Old and New Testament were the effects of a divine power." On the eve of the Virginia ratifying convention—with approval of the Constitution by nine states easily within reach—Washington similarly told the Marquis de Lafayette that the Federalists' accomplishment was "so much beyond anything we had a right to imagine or expect eighteen months ago that it will demonstrate as visibly the finger of Providence, as any possible event in the course of human affairs can ever designate it."[478]

How had the Federalists managed to secure the ratification of a constitution that was so vastly different from what most Americans would have expected or wanted from the Philadelphia convention? The Federalists had a lot of luck, but they also made their own luck. Their victory was so narrow—one North Carolina Antifederalist rightly noted the "very trifling" margins of victory in "several great adopting states"—that a small shift in any of a large number of circumstances and choices might have altered the outcome.[479]

As we have seen, Federalists benefited enormously from having the press mostly on their side, and in a couple of states—especially South Carolina—they were aided by malapportionment of the ratifying conventions. In addition, Antifederalists had a more difficult time organizing their disproportionately backwoods and western constituencies. Federalists also benefited from having the best educated and most eloquent speakers on their side at ratifying conventions, where they could influence undecided delegates. That many conventions were held in coastal cities where people across class lines overwhelmingly and enthusiastically supported ratification also advantaged Federalists. Indeed, the very process of ratifying through conventions rather than referenda or town meetings benefited Federalists by removing the decision one step from direct popular participation—in precisely the same way Federalists anticipated that a federal government partially insulated from populist pressure would enact the sort of policies they preferred.[480]

The delegates to the Philadelphia convention had created another critical advantage for the Federalists in Article VII of the Constitution. Whereas the Articles of Confederation had required unanimity for amendments, the Constitution would go into effect, according to its own terms, upon the ratification of nine of the thirteen states. Although those ratifying states could bind only themselves, the last four states to consider ratification would face enormous pressure to join a union already in operation. Just six weeks after the Philadelphia convention ended, Madison told Washington there was "a very strong probability that nine states at least will pretty speedily concur in establishing it [the Constitution]," and then the "tardy remainder" would be "either left as outcasts from the society to shift for themselves, or be compelled to come in, or must come in of themselves when they will be allowed no credit for it." Henry Knox was almost certainly correct when he told the Marquis de Lafayette in May 1788, when the Federalist campaign for ratification was nearing a successful conclusion, that "[w]ere the new Constitution to have required the unanimous assent of all the states, it would never have been adopted."[481]

Although nationalists such as Madison and James Wilson had detested granting small states equal representation in the Senate, it was this feature of the Constitution that, in substantial part, induced the speedy and nearly unanimous ratifications by several of the smaller states, quickly establishing momentum in favor of the Constitution. Federalists kept that momentum going in New England with shrewd tactics. In Massachusetts, they avoided an adjournment or even an outright defeat by altering their initial strategy and agreeing to recommend amendments to the Constitution in exchange for an unconditional ratification. Without that concession, the Massachusetts convention would probably have refused to ratify. Then, in New Hampshire, Federalists deftly adjourned a convention that probably would have rejected the Constitution if forced to take a vote on it.[482]

The Federalists' victory was also partly attributable to their opponents' miscalculations in New York and Virginia. As Antifederalist De Witt Clinton noted late in the New York proceedings, "[i]t was a great error in policy that our convention was not called sooner." By the time the New York and Virginia conventions assembled in June 1788, eight states had ratified the Constitution and New Hampshire was about to become the ninth to do so. Thus, delegates to these two conventions faced a very different choice than they would have had their conventions met earlier in the ratifying process. As one newspaper explained, the decision facing the New York ratifying convention after New Hampshire and Virginia had become the ninth and tenth states, respectively, to ratify was whether to "adopt the new Constitution with its defects under a prospect of future corrections" or to "hazard the consequences of being repudiated from the grand American confederacy." Randolph similarly told the Virginia convention that, from the beginning, the only real issue had been whether amendments to the Constitution should be antecedent or subsequent, and that postponing the convention to so late in the day had eliminated the possibility of securing antecedent amendments without jeopardizing the union, which he was unwilling to do.[483]

Given how narrowly the conventions in Virginia and New York voted to approve the Constitution, it seems almost certain that they would have rejected ratification without antecedent amendments had they made their decisions earlier. Such outcomes would have disrupted the momentum in favor of unconditional ratification and possibly altered the result in other states that followed. In some of those other states, Antifederalists had been hoping to delay decisions until after Virginia or New York had decided, because they believed that a defeat for the Constitution in one of those important states would have bolstered the opposition cause in their own states. Thus, leading New Hampshire Antifederalist Atherton told New York Antifederalists, just before the adjourned New Hampshire convention reassembled in mid-June 1788, that if New York refused to ratify without antecedent amendments, he had "not the least doubt" that a "great majority" of the New Hampshire convention "would immediately close with your views and wishes." Similarly, Patrick Henry told the Virginia convention that only a rejection of unconditional ratification by an important state such as Virginia would be sufficient to influence less formidable states that might be inclined in that direction to take such a decisive step.[484]

In addition, had one early-deciding state rejected ratification without antecedent amendments, Antifederalists in other states might have been able to coordinate their opposition to the Constitution around the particular amendments demanded by that state. Antifederalists would have been in a far stronger position to appeal to swing delegates at ratifying conventions had they been able to present a specific plan as an alternative to the Constitution, which could have served as a rejoinder to Federalist criticisms that their adversaries did not "pretend to offer a better system for the government of our country."[485]

Indeed, New York Antifederalists sought to organize precisely such a scheme for securing antecedent amendments. In May 1788, the chairman of the Federal Republican Committee of New York (an Antifederalist organization), John Lamb, wrote to Antifederalist leaders in six or seven other states, proposing that they "open a correspondence and maintain a communication" in order to "unite in the amendments" they would demand prior to ratification.* Several of these Antifederalists responded favorably to the concept, while lamenting that the plan had been conceived too late in the ratifying

---

* The New York Antifederalists used Eleazer Oswald, the fiery Antifederalist editor of the Philadelphia *Independent Gazetteer*, as a courier to carry correspondence between New York City and Richmond because they distrusted the US postal service, which they believed had Federalist leanings.

process to be practicable.* For example, South Carolina Antifederalist leader Lowndes replied to Lamb:

> Had your plan been proposed in time, I doubt not it might have produced very good effect in this country: A strong systematic opposition, wherein the opinions and sentiments of the different states were concentrated, and directed to the same specific objects, would have had a weight, which the advocates for the Constitution must have submitted to, and have removed the force of an objection, strongly insisted upon, arising from the seeming diversity and dissimilarity of the several amendments contended for.

Richard Henry Lee similarly told Lamb that his proposal "would have produced salutary consequences" had it reached Virginia earlier.[486]

The Federalists enjoyed one other important advantage in the ratifying contest—one that they did not create but that they shrewdly exploited. In 1787, most Americans probably agreed that the Articles of Confederation were badly flawed and required amending. At a minimum, Congress should have

---

* One reason this effort at coordination by New York Antifederalists got underway so late is that a similar scheme initiated earlier by their Virginia counterparts had gone awry. As we have seen, in December 1787, the Virginia legislature resolved to authorize expenses for the delegates to its ratifying convention to communicate with other states' conventions. The legislature instructed Governor Randolph to transmit news of this resolution to the other states' governors, and he did so in late December. However, Randolph's letter to Governor George Clinton of New York was not received, according to Clinton, until March 7, 1788—ten weeks after it was sent (the cause of the delay was never identified) and too late in the New York legislature's session to be acted upon.

When Governor Clinton wrote back to Randolph on May 8, he noted that the New York convention, set to assemble on June 17, would "with great cordiality hold a communication with any sister state on the important subject" of the Constitution. Clinton continued, "Friendly communications on the subject and temperate discussions would, it is to be presumed, have had a most happy tendency in accommodating it [the Constitution] much more to the sentiments and wishes of the people of America, than is likely to be the case in the form it is offered by the general [i.e., Philadelphia] convention and acceded to by some of the states." Because the Virginia convention was scheduled to begin two weeks before the New York convention, Clinton presumed that the Virginians would "commence the measures for holding such communications as shall be deemed necessary."

Clinton's letter reached Governor Randolph while the Virginia ratifying convention was in session, but Randolph chose not to share its contents with the delegates on the grounds that, as a formal communication to the governor, the letter must first be presented to the legislature, which would then direct him how to proceed. However, the Virginia legislature's summer session convened only as the ratifying convention was concluding its business. The delegates never saw Clinton's letter, and some Virginia Antifederalists later condemned Randolph for his failure to show it to the convention.

some independent revenue-raising authority, the power to retaliate against foreign trade discrimination, and the authority to force states to comply with national treaties. By proposing an alternative to an admittedly flawed status quo, the Federalists—to a certain extent—shifted the burden of persuasion to their opponents.[487]*

Thus, for example, one Massachusetts Federalist observed, "As objections may be made without end as well as without reason, and as some constitution must be adopted, it is justly observed that the objectors, should not only pull down but also build up. Show us a constitution that is free of imperfections." At the Massachusetts ratifying convention, Charles Turner, who chose to support ratification with recommended amendments even though the Constitution contained "several imperfections in it, and some which give me pain," explained his decision by noting that unless the country could obtain soon "a constitution preferable to the Confederation, . . . we shall be an undone people."[488]

This tactic of switching the burden of persuasion may have proved especially effective because the Constitution, in Article V, appeared to be much easier to amend than the Articles had proved to be. Thus, Joseph Barrell, a Federalist merchant from Boston, who expressed "mortification" that his brother Nathaniel, a Maine farmer, had been elected as an Antifederalist delegate to the Massachusetts ratifying convention, offered "one consideration alone" that he hoped would induce his brother to support ratification even if opposed to the Constitution in principle—

> viz: because the present Confederation cannot be altered, unless all the 13 states agree and I was going to say Heaven and Earth may pass away before that event will take place! While the Constitution now proposed may be altered when ever nine states shall require it. Is it not therefore better to adopt this Constitution (even if it was not the best) which may be altered rather than to retain the present wretched system which never can?

On the last day of the Massachusetts ratifying convention, Nathaniel Barrell switched sides and voted for ratification, explaining that the Constitution, "with all its imperfections," was "excellent" as compared with the "essentially deficient" Articles of Confederation, and that it would be "more difficult" to amend the Articles than to reform the Constitution.[489]

---

* Antifederalists naturally preferred to frame the issue facing the nation in the opposite way, as Melancton Smith did at the New York convention: "But the question was not whether the present confederation be a bad one but whether the proposed Constitution be a good one."

Having presented the nation with a choice between the Articles and the Constitution, Federalists strenuously resisted their opponents' efforts to offer—through either antecedent amendments or a second convention—an intermediate option: the Constitution with significant alterations made prior to ratification. Most Americans probably would have favored that intermediate position had it been available to them.* Thus, at the New York convention, Melancton Smith had questioned why the appropriate remedy for the Articles' failure to grant Congress sufficient power was to move "into the contrary and a more dangerous extreme." Opinion in the nation had not changed so drastically over the several years since the Articles had been ratified, and most Americans probably did not approve of the extreme nationalizing and democracy-constraining aspects of the Constitution. John Dawson, a swing delegate at the Virginia convention who professed his support for an energetic federal government but not a consolidated one, probably was correct when he declared that had the Constitution "been presented to our view ten years ago, . . . it would have been considered as containing principles incompatible with republican liberty and therefore doomed to infamy."[490]

The Federalists managed—barely—to keep intermediate options off the table. With the nation's choice limited to the Articles of Confederation and the unamended Constitution, the Federalists—again, barely—won the contest.

---

* Lachlan McIntosh, a Georgian who had been a general in the Revolutionary War, favored an intermediate position, albeit of a slightly different sort. On the one hand, McIntosh acknowledged that the Constitution revealed "great judgment and abilities" and that the "exigencies of our national affairs requires some speedy and effectual remedy." He also doubted that a second convention would feature the same "illustrious members" as the first, whom he deemed "the wisest and best that this or perhaps any other nation ever produced."

On the other hand, he did not consider the Framers "infallible," and he worried that their popularity was "so great that the public voice seems to be for adopting the Constitution in the lump on its first appearance as a perfect system without inquiry or limitation of time or matter." Yet, McIntosh believed, "[s]uch hasty resolutions have occasioned all the misfortunes that ever happened in governments." Moreover, he considered the objections raised to the Constitution by Antifederalists such as Gerry and "Centinel" to be "very weighty." Finally, McIntosh worried that unconditional ratification now would make it impossible to obtain amendments later because a northern majority, "once fixed in their saddles," would resist changes.

McIntosh therefore proposed a compromise solution—a sunset provision—that he hoped would "avoid the rocks on both sides of the question." Instead of "binding ourselves and posterity forever to adopt the Constitution," Georgians should ratify "only for a certain period of time during which they will have a fair trial of its effects." Once that time had expired, they would "have it in their own power to adopt it again if they please for another period, either without or with any amendments they may find necessary."

The Bill of Rights

Soon after the Philadelphia convention ended, James Madison sent a copy of the Constitution to his good friend and mentor, Thomas Jefferson, who was in Paris serving as American minister to France. Jefferson generally approved of what he saw in the document, though he noted one glaring omission: "[A] bill of rights is what the people are entitled to against every government on earth, general or particular, and what no just government should refuse, or rest on inference." Jefferson had in mind constitutional provisions guaranteeing rights such as freedom of religion, freedom of the press, and jury trials in civil cases (not just criminal ones), as well as restrictions on standing armies and government-granted monopolies. John Adams, who was serving in London as American minister to Great Britain, had a similar reaction: He generally approved of the Constitution but thought that a declaration of rights should have "preceded the model."[1]

In a subsequent letter, Jefferson described his preferred strategy for obtaining such a bill of rights: "I wish with all my soul that the nine first conventions may accept the new Constitution, because this will secure to us the good it contains, which I think great and important. But I equally wish that the four latest conventions, whichever they be, may refuse to accede to it till a declaration of rights be annexed." Jefferson thought this strategy would "command the offer of such a declaration," which would "give to the whole fabric, perhaps, as much perfection as any one of that kind ever had."[2]*

A few months later, however, Jefferson changed his mind and decided that the Massachusetts convention's approach of unconditional ratification with a recommendation of subsequent amendments was "far preferable, and will I hope be followed by those who are yet to decide." Jefferson thought that if other states followed this strategy, "it is impossible but they must obtain the

---

* As we saw in chapter 6, it was from this letter that Patrick Henry quoted at the Virginia ratifying convention, eliciting a strong rebuke from Federalist delegates.

essential amendments." He also stated that "[i]t will be more difficult if we lose this instrument, to recover what is good in it, than to correct what is bad after we shall have adopted it."[3]

Madison disagreed with Jefferson and Adams about the importance of a bill of rights. In a lengthy letter written to Jefferson in the fall of 1788, discussed in greater detail later in this chapter, Madison explained that while he did not object to a declaration of rights—provided that it was carefully framed—he had never considered "the omission a material defect," and he thought the only substantial reason in favor of one was that many people strongly desired it. Madison believed that a declaration of rights against a government that was limited to enumerated powers, such as the new federal government, would be superfluous. He also thought that "the jealousy of the subordinate [i.e., state] governments" would provide a greater security against federal usurpation of power than would a bill of rights. Most important, though, Madison believed that experience had demonstrated that words on a piece of paper would not deter committed majorities from trampling individual rights.[4]

Yet Madison acknowledged that a bill of rights might nonetheless serve two useful purposes. First, a formal declaration of important rights might educate public opinion. Second, a bill of rights might provide a focal point around which to rally community sentiment in opposition to an oppressive government.[5]

In his reply to Madison, Jefferson observed that a bill of rights, even if not completely efficacious, would nonetheless be useful. He also objected that in Madison's "arguments in favor of a declaration of rights, you omit one which has great weight with me, the legal check which it puts into the hands of the judiciary. This is a body, which if rendered independent, and kept strictly to their own department merits great confidence for their learning and integrity." That Madison neglected to consider the point about judicial enforceability is stunning from a modern perspective but perhaps understandable given how little the subject of judicial review was discussed at the Philadelphia convention or in the state ratifying debates. Even when Antifederalists protested the omission of a bill of rights from the Constitution, which was often, they rarely said anything about judicial review.[6]

Given Madison's initial resistance to a bill of rights, it is greatly ironic that without his efforts, the Constitution probably would not have been amended to include one. It is also ironic that some critics of the Constitution, who demanded a bill of rights as the price of supporting ratification, regarded the amendments that eventually were adopted as "little better than whip-syllabub, frothy and full of wind."[7]

The Arguments Pro and Con

Five days before the Philadelphia convention ended, George Mason, the principal author of Virginia's Declaration of Rights, suggested that a bill of rights be added to the Constitution, which he said would "give great quiet to the people." Elbridge Gerry agreed and moved for the appointment of a committee to prepare a bill of rights. Earlier in the convention, Charles Pinckney had unsuccessfully proposed a few provisions to safeguard particular rights, such as liberty of the press and the right not to have soldiers quartered in one's home without one's consent during time of peace. By contrast, the convention had approved Pinckney's proposal to protect yet another individual right— the writ of habeas corpus (except in "cases of rebellion or invasion" when "the public safety" might require its suspension).[8]

After a brief debate on Gerry's motion, not a single delegation supported adding a bill of rights to the Constitution. The delegates' dismissive reaction

Figure 7.1 George Mason, who was principal author of the Virginia Declaration of Rights, a prominent participant in the deliberations of the Philadelphia convention, and then one of the nation's leading Antifederalists. (Courtesy of Independence National Historical Park)

to his proposal may have been what Mason was referring to when he later told Jefferson that he had been offended "by the precipitate and intemperate, not to say indecent manner, in which the business was conducted during the last week of the Convention, after the patrons of this new plan found they had a decided majority in their favor."[9]

When Mason and Gerry subsequently refused to sign their names to the Constitution—"upon the most mature consideration . . . and for motives of sincere patriotism," as Mason assured Jefferson—one of their principal stated objections was the omission of a bill of rights. With the aid of hindsight, it is clear that the Federalists had made a major tactical blunder in not taking the proposal of Mason and Gerry more seriously.[10]

As we shall see in a moment, at the Philadelphia convention and in the state ratifying debates, Federalists made a series of arguments against adding a bill of rights to the Constitution. Whether they genuinely believed those arguments is an interesting question. According to James Wilson's recollection, the idea of a bill of rights "never entered the mind of many of them [the delegates in Philadelphia]," and nothing was said on the subject until a few days before the convention's adjournment. It seems likely, at that point, that most of the delegates would have opposed the proposal of Mason and Gerry simply out of fear of introducing new and contentious issues when they were so near to realizing their goal of securing a consensus in favor of a vastly more powerful and less populist federal government.[11]

The delegates had been in Philadelphia for four long, mostly very hot months; Pierce Butler noted that the summer's confinement had "injured my health much." Many of them were living in uncomfortable accommodations. In August, John Rutledge had noted "the extreme anxiety of many members of the convention to bring the business to an end." Although Mason insisted that a bill of rights could "be prepared in a few hours" by drawing upon the example of declarations of rights in state constitutions, other delegates probably thought the task of agreeing upon one would take much longer.[12]

Later, during the ratifying debates, Federalists simply parried all criticisms of the Constitution, including its omission of a bill of rights. At that point, they were determined to avoid anything less than unconditional ratification. Yet had a bill of rights been proposed earlier in the Philadelphia convention and then incorporated into the Constitution, the Federalists' position on this issue probably would have been very different.

In opposing a bill of rights, Federalists made three principal arguments: that it was unnecessary, that it was dangerous, and that it was useless. The argument that a bill of rights was unnecessary—an "idle and superfluous instrument," according to Pennsylvania Federalist Benjamin Rush—had several permutations. One reason for its being unnecessary, Federalists explained, was that the federal government was limited to the exercise of enumerated powers.[13]

Thus, for example, Federalists insisted that a constitutional ban on Congress's passing laws abridging freedom of the press would have been superfluous, given that the Constitution granted Congress no power in the first place to interfere with such freedom. At the North Carolina ratifying convention, James Iredell explained that adding rights limitations to grants of enumerated powers was like "saying at the end of a power of attorney . . . that the attorney should not exercise more power than was there given him"—a statement that was too obvious to bother including. As the Federalist "Landholder" more colorfully put it, the absence from the Constitution of explicit protection for liberty of the press should be of no more concern than the absence of protection for liberty "of burial of the dead." Congress had "no power to prohibit either, and can have no temptation."[14]

Indeed, explicitly providing for such rights by amendment would have been risky, Federalists argued, because doing so could have been interpreted to imply that the unamended Constitution had indeed conferred upon Congress a power to abridge such rights. As Hamilton explained in *The Federalist No. 84*, specifying rights limitations out of an abundance of caution was a dubious enterprise because it would furnish to men who were "disposed to usurp" a plausible "pretext to claim more [powers] than were granted. For why declare that things shall not be done which there is no power to do?"[15]

Federalists then explained why most state constitutions contained bills of rights, while the federal Constitution did not. Such protections were not superfluous in state constitutions because those charters treated states as governments of inherent—not enumerated—powers. That is, state constitutions presumed that all powers not denied to the state government had been granted to it, while the federal Constitution presumed the opposite with regard to the federal government.[16]

As for the several state constitutions that did *not* contain bills of rights,* Federalists explained that those states had reasonably concluded that paper guarantees were not essential to protecting liberty. Observing that the state constitutions of South Carolina, New Jersey, New York, Connecticut, and Rhode Island contained no bill of rights, Wilson asked, "[W]hence comes this notion that in the United States there is no security without [one]?" Moreover, if a bill of rights was "not an essential or necessary measure" in state

---

* Even state constitutions lacking a formal bill of rights contained scattered individual-rights protections. In this regard, they were similar to the federal Constitution.

constitutions that created governments of inherent power, then surely it was not only unnecessary but "highly imprudent" in a constitution creating a federal government authorized to exercise only enumerated powers.[17]

In response to the Federalist argument that no bill of rights was necessary in a constitution grounded on the principle of enumerated powers, Antifederalists convincingly observed that some of Congress's enumerated powers, such as that over taxation, could be used to interfere with some important liberties, such as freedom of the press. Without an amendment explicitly protecting that right, what would stop Congress, Mason asked, from imposing prohibitive taxes on newspapers that criticized the federal government? If a newspaper then challenged that tax as beyond Congress's powers, what would stop Congress—as a "necessary and proper" means of executing its taxing power—from mandating that the case be tried without a jury? Similarly, Patrick Henry warned that Congress's expressly delegated power to define certain crimes and punishments could be used—in the absence of explicit rights protections—to inflict cruel and unusual punishments and excessive fines. Especially given open-ended grants of power to Congress, such as the General Welfare Clause and the Necessary and Proper Clause, a bill of rights was vital. Without it, Mason told the Virginia ratifying convention, "implication might swallow up all our rights." Had the Constitution explicitly denied to Congress those powers that were not expressly delegated, one North Carolina Antifederalist allowed, then perhaps no bill of rights would have been necessary.[18]

Furthermore, Antifederalists noted that the enumerated-powers argument against a bill of rights was peculiar, given that the unamended Constitution actually did contain some explicit individual-liberties protections, such as the right to the writ of habeas corpus and the right to a jury trial in federal criminal cases. According to the Federalists' logic, such rights provisions were superfluous: Why should the Constitution guarantee a jury trial in criminal cases if Congress had been delegated no power to abridge that right?* If the answer to this objection was that these rights had simply been inserted for greater caution, then, Antifederalists argued, the same should be done for freedom of the press, the right to a jury trial in civil cases, and so forth. Even "if its necessity be doubtful," Patrick Henry noted, a bill of rights would "exclude the possibility of dispute." It would also "satisfy the minds of the people," according to a

---

* In response to this counterargument, some Federalists maintained that these particular rights had to be reserved because Congress might otherwise claim that specific delegated powers were broad enough to warrant interfering with these rights. Concretely, Congress's power to define federal crimes might be construed to authorize the elimination of jury trials, and its power over federal courts might be interpreted to authorize abrogation of the writ of habeas corpus.

North Carolina Antifederalist. Could the Federalists really be objecting that it would "consume too much paper?"[19]

A second reason that a bill of rights was unnecessary, Federalists explained, was that the United States had a republican form of government. In a monarchical system such as that of Great Britain, rights protections—such as those contained in the Magna Carta—were vitally important concessions from the king to the people. Yet in America, the people were sovereign, they had no rulers, and they retained all rights that had not been abdicated to the government's control. Thus it made no sense, as Rush explained to the Pennsylvania ratifying convention, to have "a formal declaration that our natural rights are acquired from ourselves." This was why, according to Wilson, many state constitutions did not contain bills of rights.[20]

Antifederalists responded—naturally enough—by asking why, according to this rationale, most state constitutions *did* contain bills of rights. Thus, Mason observed that even though the government of Virginia was "drawn from the people," the convention that wrote the state constitution in 1776 nonetheless drafted a declaration of "great and important rights." If such protections were deemed necessary against a state government in which "the people were substantially and fully represented," then they were even more critical in the context of a federal government that had been designed to be well insulated from popular influence. Patrick Henry likewise noted that providing for a bill of rights in state constitutions but not the federal one was to "arm yourselves against the weak and defenseless and expose yourselves naked to the armed and powerful."[21]

A few Federalists offered yet a third reason that a bill of rights was unnecessary. When Mason proposed one at the Philadelphia convention, Roger Sherman responded that it would be superfluous because "[t]he state Declarations of Rights are not repealed by this Constitution, and being in force are sufficient." This was a surprisingly weak argument, coming from someone as able as Sherman. As Mason immediately responded, under the Constitution's Supremacy Clause, a federal statute could lawfully abridge a right protected by a state constitution. Moreover, as already noted, several state constitutions contained no bill of rights. How a federal version could be superfluous in those states was hard to fathom.[22]

In addition to denying that a bill of rights was necessary, Federalists argued that it would be dangerous. Enumerating all the individual rights that warranted protection from government interference would be impossible. At the Pennsylvania ratifying convention, Wilson asked, "[W]ho will be bold enough to undertake to enumerate all the rights of the people?" Yet "if the enumeration is not complete," he warned, "everything not expressly mentioned will be presumed to be purposely omitted." In this way, Iredell explained, a bill of rights "might operate as a snare rather than a protection."[23]

The best solution to the problem that a partial enumeration of rights would be dangerous—which Madison later called "one of the most plausible arguments I have ever heard against the admission of a bill of rights"—was to include in the bill of rights a provision expressly precluding the inference that listing some rights implied the nonexistence of others. Interestingly, the Antifederalists failed to advocate such a provision in response to the Federalists' argument that a partial enumeration of rights would be dangerous. However, when Madison ultimately drafted the Bill of Rights in the first Congress, he inserted precisely such a provision, which, as amended, became the Ninth Amendment, declaring that "the enumeration in the Constitution of certain rights shall not be construed to deny or disparage others retained by the people."[24]

Finally, Federalists argued that a bill of rights would be useless because it would amount simply to a "parchment barrier," which would prove insufficient to restrain determined majorities from doing as they pleased, especially during times of war or emergency. As Madison observed to Jefferson, "Should a rebellion or insurrection alarm the people as well as the government, and a suspension of the habeas corpus be dictated by the alarm, no written prohibitions on earth would prevent the measure." As empirical support for this claim, Madison noted that bills of rights in state constitutions had not prevented "[r]epeated violations" by "overbearing majorities." The true safeguard against federal government oppression, Madison insisted, would lie not in words on a piece of paper but in vigilant state governments and the system of checks and balances within the federal government.[25]

Thus, at the Virginia ratifying convention, Federalist delegates noted that during the Revolutionary War, in spite of the command in the state Declaration of Rights that no man should be condemned without a fair trial, the legislature had in fact sentenced a man to death (a bill of attainder) and then seen him executed. In Connecticut, Sherman, like Madison, disparaged a bill of rights as a "parchment barrier"—"not worth even the trouble of writing." Genuine protection for rights, Sherman insisted, came from the people's exercising significant control over their government, thus ensuring that "rulers were interested in preserving the rights." Hamilton agreed that "the only solid basis of all our rights" must be "public opinion" and "the general spirit of the people and of the government." Disparaging Antifederalist fears of systematic rights violations by the federal government, Rush wondered if his political adversaries were imagining "that this government was immediately to be administered by foreigners, strangers to our habits and opinions, and unconnected with our interests and prosperity."[26]

Responding to the argument that a bill of rights would be useless was harder for Antifederalists because it represented a contestable empirical claim rather than an analytically flawed conceptual point. The best response was probably Jefferson's: "Half a loaf is better than no bread." Even if a bill of rights would not be "absolutely efficacious under all circumstances, it is of great potency always and rarely inefficacious." At the Pennsylvania ratifying convention, Antifederalist William Findley similarly wondered whether, "because all securities are broken, shall we have none? Is it not a new doctrine that because a good government, ill administered, produces mischief, therefore we ought to be indifferent about it?"[27]

Finally, a few southern Federalists added their own peculiar argument against a bill of rights. Charles Cotesworth Pinckney told the South Carolina House of Representatives that bills of rights generally began with declarations that all people are "by nature born free." Yet southerners could make that claim only "with a very bad grace, when a large part of our property consists in men who are actually born slaves."[28]

As we have seen, early in the ratifying contest, Federalists staunchly resisted all proposals for amending the Constitution—whether addressed to securing individual-rights protections or to changing the structure and limiting the powers of the federal government. To many Federalists, proposed amendments were simply a pretext for gutting the Constitution they had struggled so mightily to create.[29]

Early in 1788, Edward Carrington told Madison that because Patrick Henry had not "even once specified the amendments he would have in the project," it was fair to infer that his true objective was to divide the union. George Nicholas confirmed that while Henry was in fact an enemy to the union, he would "industriously conceal" his "real sentiments" and speak "only of amendments," so as not to alienate those who, while objecting "to particular parts of the Constitution," nonetheless opposed a dissolution of the confederacy. Madison told Randolph that Henry was "driving at a southern confederacy" and was "not farther concurring in the plan of amendments than as he hopes to render it subservient to his real designs." Madison noted how easy it would be for "those who secretly aim at disunion . . . to carry on their schemes under the mask of contending for alterations popular in some places and known to be inadmissible in others."[30]

Not until facing probable defeat at the Massachusetts ratifying convention did Federalists promise to recommend subsequent amendments, including a bill of rights, in exchange for swing delegates' support of unconditional ratification. The concession worked: Delegates who had earlier expressed opposition to the Constitution now voted to ratify it—with the recommendation of subsequent amendments.[31]

Massachusetts was the sixth state to ratify the Constitution. In every state but one (Maryland) that ratified afterward, the ratifying conventions, with the acquiescence of Federalists, recommended subsequent amendments. In several of these states, where votes were very close, the Federalists' concession was probably instrumental to securing ratification. For at least some undecided delegates, "the custom of recommending amendments with the adoptions" set their minds at ease. Indeed, the Virginia legislature might well have refused even to call a ratifying convention were the delegates' agenda not framed so as to permit the consideration of amendments. Even in a state such as South Carolina, where the Federalists' margin of victory was sufficiently large that the promise to support subsequent amendments probably had been unnecessary to securing ratification, Federalists still made the concession—perhaps with the goal of reconciling disgruntled Antifederalists to the Constitution.[32]

As we saw in chapter 6, once Federalists had conceded on the question of amendments, much of the subsequent debate—in other states, if not so much in Massachusetts—was over whether such amendments would be an antecedent condition of ratification or simply recommendations to be considered by Congress after the Constitution had gone into effect. Although most Antifederalists vigorously protested the notion of ratifying the Constitution on the mere recommendation of subsequent amendments, Federalists in every state successfully resisted anything resembling conditional ratification.[33]

The amendments recommended by the various state conventions fell into two general categories. One set consisted of safeguards for individual rights, such as those that dominate our Bill of Rights—for example, freedom of the press, free exercise of religion, the right to a jury trial in civil and criminal cases, and various additional procedural safeguards for criminal defendants.

The other category consisted of amendments to limit congressional powers and to alter the structure of the federal government. Among the amendments curtailing congressional power was a general one limiting Congress to expressly delegated powers and specific ones limiting its authority to tax; to create standing armies and call up state militias into federal service; and to set the times, places, and manner of federal elections. Among the amendments proposing structural changes to the federal government were ones increasing the size of the House, reducing the extent to which powers were shared between the Senate and the president, curtailing the jurisdiction of the federal courts, and imposing mandatory rotation in office for senators and presidents. For the most part, Federalists staunchly resisted the structural and power-limiting amendments, while acquiescing—with varying degrees of reluctance—to those amendments protecting individual rights.[34]

Madison's Election to Congress

Madison played a critical role in the adoption of the Bill of Rights, just as he had in bringing about the Constitutional Convention, setting its agenda, ensuring its success, and securing the ratification of its handiwork in Virginia. Without Madison's perseverance, there would not have been a Bill of Rights.[35]

In the final days of the Virginia ratifying convention, Patrick Henry had promised that he would be "a peaceable citizen," refrain from advocating violence, and seek to "remove the defects of that system [the Constitution] in a constitutional way." In fact, he turned his attention to retaliating against Madison—perhaps partly to avenge Henry's defeat at the Virginia convention and partly to prevent his adversary's seizing control over the project of constitutional amendments and steering it away from the proposals that Henry considered most important. According to the subsequent account of Henry's son-in-law, Spencer Roane (who was a longtime justice on Virginia's highest court), Henry's "prejudice against Madison always remained in some degree," as he had been "astonished that Madison would take the Constitution, admitting its defects, and in a season of perfect peace." Six months after Virginia's ratification of the Constitution, one of Madison's political allies reported to him that a majority of the Virginia legislature, under Henry's influence, was "disposed to do every thing they can to disappoint and hurt your feelings."[36]

Despite his defeat at the Virginia convention, Henry continued to exercise extraordinary political clout in the state. Madison called him "omnipotent" within the Virginia legislature. Washington remarked that Henry's "edicts" were meeting "with less opposition by the majority of that body than those of the Grand Monarch are in the Parliaments of France. He has only to say let this be law—and it is law."[37]

In October 1788, after visiting Mount Vernon, Carrington told Madison of Washington's concern that under Henry's influence, "anti-federalism will be the actuating principle" of the fall session of the Virginia legislature, and that "great circumspection is necessary to prevent very mischievous effects from a cooperation in the insidious proposition of New York" for a second convention. Madison was convinced that Henry's "enmity was levelled . . . against the whole system," and its destruction remained "the secret wish of his [Henry's] heart and the real object of his pursuit." Madison was also "certain that a clear majority of the Assembly are enemies to the [new federal] government."[38]

Indeed, Patrick Henry told Richard Henry Lee that fall, after the Confederation Congress had enacted an ordinance setting the date and place for the new national government to commence operations, that he remained determined to secure "substantial amendments" from Congress. Yet Henry believed that the Federalists possessed too little zeal for the preservation of liberty to support the sort of amendments he considered necessary—such as limiting Congress's power to impose direct taxes and summon state militias into federal service. Were Congress to reject such amendments, Henry predicted, resistance to the Constitution would not remain "temperate," and he "dread[ed] the consequences." Although professing a wish not to "see the day when it shall be the duty of whiggish Americans to seek for shelter under any other government than that of the United States," Henry insisted that "the American union depends on the success of amendments."[39]

When the Virginia legislature convened in October, Henry told the House of Delegates, according to an account provided to Washington by his lawyer, Charles Lee (a younger brother of Henry Lee and cousin of Richard Henry Lee), that he would "oppose every measure tending to the organization of the [federal] government unless accompanied with measures for the amendment of the Constitution," and that he favored assembling a second convention "as soon as practicable" for that purpose. Lee also reported that Henry was considering introducing a resolution containing "a direct and indecent censure on all those who have befriended the new constitution, holding them forth as the betrayers of the dearest rights of the people." According to Federalist delegate George Lee Turberville, Henry "launched into a field of declamation" in which he "brought all the imaginary horrors of the new government upon us."[40]

To advance his goal of securing substantial constitutional amendments, Henry was determined to keep Madison out of the US Senate. Washington, who was reportedly "alarmed from a prospect" that the Virginia legislature would select Antifederalist senators, was of the "decided opinion" that Madison, who was "very well established in the confidence of the people," should put himself forward as a candidate. Although Madison had failed to indicate to his allies in the Virginia legislature whether he even wished to be considered for an appointment to the Senate, they nonetheless, according to a report Henry Lee made to Madison, "exerted themselves [on] your behalf," which was a "strong testimonial of the unbounded attachment" they had for Madison.[41]

However, Patrick Henry, convinced that Virginia's efforts to secure amendments would be "to no purpose . . . if one of her senators had been found adverse to that scheme," reportedly declared that "no person who wishes the Constitution to be amended should vote for Mr. Madison to be in the Senate." Henry Lee told Madison that Patrick Henry "exclaimed against your political character and pronounced you unworthy of the confidence of the people in the station of senator." Reportedly, Henry even warned that Madison's "election would terminate in producing rivulets of blood throughout the land." A whispering campaign in the House of Delegates alleged that Madison had been "an advocate for the surrender of the navigation of the Mississippi"—a "misunderstanding [that] had the effect of reality," according to Henry Lee.[42]

Lee also reported that Patrick Henry's "declarations followed by artful management without doors were successful." The Virginia legislature selected two Antifederalists, Richard Henry Lee and William Grayson, as US senators. Madison ran third in the balloting, nine votes behind Grayson and twenty-one behind Lee. Patrick Henry gleefully reported that the result had "much displeased" the Federalists, who had "urged his [Madison's] election most warmly, claiming as a sort of right the admission of one Federal member." Madison told Randolph that, given the "present temper and disproportionate number of the Antifederal part of the Assembly," he was surprised he had won as many votes as he had. Washington reported that Federalists were "exceedingly mortified" by the result.[43]

Moreover, in response to the New York convention's circular letter, the Virginia House of Delegates voted by eighty-five to thirty-nine—with the Senate concurring—to petition Congress to call a second constitutional convention immediately, and the legislature sent a letter to other states urging them to do likewise. Henry Lee concluded that under Patrick Henry's influence, "every measure succeeds which menaces the existence of the [new federal] government." Madison's ally Turberville similarly declared that "[t]he triumph of anti-federalism is complete." He attributed the Antifederalists' large legislative majority less to public opinion in Virginia "verging towards Antifederalism" than to the disbanding and "unsuspicious inattention" of Federalists after their victory at the ratifying convention, which had rendered them vulnerable to the determined efforts of a "designing" minority.[44]

In addition to having the Virginia legislature elect Antifederalists to the US Senate and petition Congress for a second constitutional convention, Patrick Henry was determined to keep Madison out of the House of Representatives. Madison told Randolph that he was willing "to afford any service" that would help put the new government "into quiet and successful operation," but he confided that "the real object of my preference" was the House. Any service he could render there could "only be to the public, and not even in imputation, to myself." In addition, Madison supposed "the arrangements for the popular elections may secure me against any competition which would require on my part any step that would speak a solicitude which I do not feel, or have the appearance of a spirit of electioneering which I despise." Yet he worried that Antifederalists in the Virginia legislature would "be equally successful to shut the door of the other house against me."[45]

Madison was right to be concerned. Turberville reported to him from Richmond that, although it was unusual for the House of Delegates "to bend its utmost efforts against an individual," the majority's object was plainly to prevent Madison's election to the House as well. Carrington confirmed to Madison that "the Antis have leveled every effort at you."[46]

At Patrick Henry's urging, the legislature provided that Virginia's seats in the US House of Representatives would be contested in districts—rather than at large—and then gerrymandered* the district that included Madison's home county of Orange. According to Madison, Henry took "pains in forming the counties into districts" to combine Orange with those counties "most devoted to his [Henry's] politics and most likely to be swayed by the prejudices excited against me." After the gerrymander, Mason noted reports that Madison would lose if he ran, given the district's composition, and one of Madison's allies reported to him that his election was now "extremely doubtful."[47]

Henry also prevailed upon the legislature to impose a one-year district residency requirement on congressional candidates, which would preclude Madison from seeking election from a more favorably constituted House district.[†] Henry even persuaded the legislature to reappoint Madison as one of Virginia's delegates to the lame-duck session of the Confederation Congress, "with no other view," according to Turberville, but to keep Madison out of the state and preoccupied, while "some favored man, some minion of his [Henry's]" campaigned for the seat. Madison thought that he could not easily decline the reappointment without his actions being subject to "misinterpretation."[48]

Henry then recruited James Monroe, a popular Revolutionary War hero who had served with Washington at the battle of Trenton and possessed a commanding physical presence, to run against Madison, who was slight of stature and whose poor health had kept him out of combat duty during the war. Monroe, at the Virginia ratifying convention and in a formal statement of his views that he ultimately decided not to publish, had voiced the usual Antifederalist concerns about the Constitution—including Congress's vastly expanded taxing power, the omission of a bill of rights, the broad jurisdiction of the federal courts, and the insulation of senators and presidents from direct political accountability.[49]

Prior to the Philadelphia convention, Madison and Monroe had been friends and had even become partners in land speculation in upstate New York. But Monroe believed—there is no evidence he was right—that in the fall of 1786, Madison had helped to thwart Monroe's wish to be appointed by the Virginia

---

* The term "gerrymander" did not exist in 1788. It was named for Elbridge Gerry, whose political party (the Democratic-Republicans) had drawn state senate districts, including one shaped like a salamander, to their advantage when he was governor of Massachusetts in 1812.

† Because the Constitution requires only that congressional representatives reside in their state—not in their district—this law was arguably unconstitutional. In 1807, a House committee concluded that a similar Maryland law was unconstitutional.

JAMES MONROE
5T PRESIDENT OF THE UNITED STATES

Figure 7.2 James Monroe, who studied law under Thomas Jefferson and served as a Virginia delegate to the Confederation Congress, and later became secretary of state and secretary of war in the Madison administration and then the fifth president of the United States. (Library of Congress)

legislature to the state's delegation to the Philadelphia convention.* At the time, Monroe had complained to Jefferson that Madison, "upon whose friendship I have calculated, whose views I have favored and with whom I have held the most confidential correspondence," was "in strict league with [Governor Randolph] and has, I have strong reason to believe, concurred in arrangements unfavorable to me." The two Jefferson acolytes had then been on opposite sides at the Virginia ratifying convention. Thus, Monroe may have seen the congressional contest as an opportunity to avenge a perceived wrong.[50]

As the election contest unfolded, Madison was initially inclined to remain at his congressional post in New York City and leave electoral matters "to their own course in Virginia." In addition to his precarious health, which made travel difficult for him in general, Madison found the prospect of journeying home that winter "disagreeable" for other reasons as well. He worried that returning

---

* While Monroe believed that his suspicions were "supported by some strong circumstances," he conceded that he might be mistaken and hoped that he was.

to Orange County would have an "electioneering appearance," which he found objectionable. In addition, he was planning to devote the winter months to an unidentified project that required access to the papers of Congress, which were in New York.[51]

Yet Madison was receiving what he later described as "pressing exhortations" from friends and allies to return home "to counteract the machinations against my election into the House." One friend, Burgess Ball, told Madison that he "must take some trouble, however disagreeable it may be," and return "immediately." Only Madison's attendance at public meetings could frustrate the designs of "that *Great Man* [Henry]." Carrington likewise urged Madison to "come into this district at an early period in order to counteract a number of reports which may take hold upon the minds of the people—it is busily circulated that you declared in Convention that the Constitution required no alteration whatever." Madison ultimately took his friends' advice and returned home to campaign against Monroe.[52]

As we have seen, as late as October 1788, Madison continued to regard the omission of a bill of rights as, at most, a minor defect in the Constitution. In a letter to Jefferson that month, he enumerated the arguments against amending the Constitution to include one. Madison agreed with Wilson's point that a bill of rights was largely superfluous with regard to a government of enumerated powers, such as the federal government. He was also convinced that the "true grounds of opposition" to the Constitution had nothing to do with the absence of a bill of rights but rather derived from the provisions "relating to treaties, to paper money, and to contracts."[53]

Madison also feared "that a positive declaration of some of the most essential rights could not be obtained in the requisite latitude." Specifically, he worried that the rights of religious conscience, "if submitted to public definition, would be narrowed much more than they are likely ever to be by an assumed power." As evidence, Madison noted that some New Englanders had objected to the Constitution because it prohibited religious tests for federal office and thus opened the door to "Jews, Turks and infidels."[54]

Madison's principal objection to a bill of rights, however, was that it was unlikely to cure the pathologies of republican government. For Madison, "the danger of oppression" resided "[w]herever the real power in a government lies." In a republican system of government, "the real power lies in the majority of the community and the invasion of private rights is chiefly to be apprehended, not from acts of government contrary to the sense of its constituents, but from acts in which the government is the mere instrument of the major number of the constituents." In a monarchical system, where "abuses of power issu[e] from a very different quarter" and "the latent force of the nation is superior to that of the sovereign," a bill of rights could be of "great effect, as a standard for trying the validity of public acts, and a signal for rousing and uniting the superior force of the community." By contrast, in a republican government, where "the political and physical power may be considered as vested in the same hands"—those of the majority—there could be no "appeal to any other force within the community."[55]

Concretely, Madison believed that "experience proves the inefficacy of a bill of rights on those occasions when its control is most needed." He told Jefferson, "Repeated violations of these parchment barriers have been committed by overbearing majorities in every state." For example, in Virginia, the Declaration of Rights had been "violated in every instance where it has been opposed to a popular current." Despite the Declaration's explicit protection for liberty of conscience, Madison was certain that the legislature would have instituted a religious establishment had it discovered, as expected, that a majority of people favored one. As he had told the Virginia ratifying convention, "a bill of rights would be a poor protection for [religious] liberty" where a single majority sect existed. Freedom of religion derived "from that multiplicity of sects which pervades America." Where "there is such a variety of sects, there cannot be a majority of any one sect to oppress and persecute the rest." In the end, Madison was convinced that the restriction of Congress to enumerated powers, the greater variety of interests represented at the federal level, and the watchful eye of the state governments would afford greater security to individual liberty than could a bill of rights.[56]

Yet, despite all these reservations, Madison told Jefferson he was not adamantly opposed to adding a bill of rights to the Constitution, partly because "it is anxiously desired by others." He conceded that many of those arguing for amendments, "particularly in Virginia," did so "from the most honorable and patriotic motives." Even among Federalists, Madison noted, "there are some who wish for further guards to public liberty and individual rights."[57]

Indeed, in his letter to Jefferson, Madison went so far as to declare that a bill of rights "might be of use" and that his "own opinion ha[d] always been in favor of a bill of rights," provided it was carefully framed so as not to imply that Congress possessed powers beyond those that were enumerated. Madison identified two principal advantages to a bill of rights, "which, though less essential than in other governments, sufficiently recommend the precaution." First, "[t]he political truths declared in that solemn manner acquire by degrees the character of fundamental maxims of free government and as they become incorporated with the national sentiment, counteract the impulses of interest and passion." Second, even though the danger of oppression in republican governments derived mostly from "interested majorities," on the few occasions when government officials usurped power, a bill of rights would be "a good ground for an appeal to the sense of the community."[58]

Assuming that a bill of rights was appropriate, Madison was inclined to think that "absolute restrictions in cases that are doubtful or where emergencies may overrule them ought to be avoided." This was because "[t]he restrictions, however strongly marked on paper, will never be regarded when opposed to the decided sense of the public, and after repeated violations in extraordinary cases, they will lose even their ordinary efficacy."[59]

In addition to describing his thoughts on the merits of a bill of rights, Madison told Jefferson that it now appeared likely that one would be added to the Constitution. Two months later, in December 1788, Madison observed, again in a letter to Jefferson, that even Federalists were "generally agreed that the system [i.e., the Constitution] should be revised"—"some from an approbation of particular amendments, others from a spirit of conciliation." Yet Federalists wanted "the revisal to be carried no farther than to supply additional guards for liberty, without abridging the sum of power transferred from the states to the general government."[60]

Moreover, while many Federalists were now willing to support individual-rights amendments, they were resolutely opposed, according to Madison, to running "the risk of another convention." Although conceding that some of those who were "zealous for a second convention" were "no doubt friends to an effective government and even to the substance of the particular government in question," Madison was convinced "that there are others who urge a second convention with the insidious hope of throwing all things into confusion and of subverting the fabric just established, if not the union itself." He expressed hope that the first Congress would propose "every desirable safeguard for popular rights and by thus separating the well meaning from the designing opponents, fix on the latter their true character, and give to the government its due popularity and stability."[61]

During his congressional contest against Monroe in early 1789, Madison publicly advocated a bill of rights for the first time. He would quickly take over the campaign for one, much as he had seized the initiative in organizing the Philadelphia convention and in promoting ratification of the Constitution in Virginia. This is almost precisely what Patrick Henry had feared. Late in 1788, he had warned Richard Henry Lee that "[t]he universal cry is for amendments, and the Federal[ist]s are obliged to join in it; but whether to amuse, or conceal other views seems dubious." Henry believed that "the American union depends on the success of amendments" and that Antifederalists could not "trust their safety to those whose late proceedings, if they do not manifest enmity to public liberty, yet show too little solicitude or zeal for its preservation."[62]

In the congressional district that Madison was contesting, a bill of rights commanded strong support, especially among the many Baptists—Madison's friend Burgess Ball observed that "the Baptist interest seems every where to prevail"—who had been persecuted in Virginia for their religious views within the preceding decade. Federalist David Jameson, Jr., who represented Culpeper County in the House of Delegates, urged Madison to make a public address "to remove some false prejudices," which Jameson apprehended "were predominating in this county against you." With "evil minds using every measure which envy or malice can suggest to our prejudice," Jameson wrote, much depended on Madison's overcoming that natural "restraint we otherwise should feel."[63]

George Nicholas told Madison, "Every art has been used to prejudice the minds of the people against you." He accused Patrick Henry of spreading rumors that Madison had "tricked this country [i.e., Virginia] into the business by the manner in which you [Madison] first proposed a general convention to our legislature; that you had a chief hand in sending forth the Constitution from the convention without the amendments generally wished; and that you are now opposed to all amendments." The opposition to Madison's election, Nicholas argued, should be seen as "an attack on the Constitution itself." He urged Madison to write public letters declaring his views and to justify his doing so on the grounds that his absence from the district and the short time remaining before the election left him no other options for responding to Henry's slanders. Nicholas also encouraged Madison to state that, if elected, he would "consider it as [his] duty to procure the adoption" of all the amendments proposed by the Virginia ratifying convention, regardless of his "private opinion of any particular amendment."[64]

Madison complained to Washington that "[i]t has been very industriously inculcated that I am dogmatically attached to the Constitution in every clause, syllable and letter, and therefore not a single amendment will be promoted by my vote, either from conviction or a spirit of accommodation." He worried that such rumors, though "most likely to affect the election," were "most difficult to be combated with success, within the limited period."[65]

So Madison did as his friends urged. Reporting to Washington that he had made "great use of epistolary means," Madison wrote several letters, some of which were published in newspapers, that contradicted the erroneous rumors being circulated about him. The frail Madison also stumped across the district in harsh winter conditions. On one occasion, he suffered frostbite on his nose after traveling twelve miles to discuss constitutional issues with a group of Dutchmen at a church. Occasionally, he and Monroe even made joint appearances on the campaign trail.[66]*

---

* After the election, Madison told Jefferson that he and Monroe had managed to maintain the distinction "between political and personal views, and [thus] saved our friendship from the smallest diminution." Decades later, Madison recalled that "there never was an atom of ill will between" him and Monroe, despite their spending "days of considerable excitement" jointly addressing political gatherings.

With the question of whether to amend the Constitution to include a bill of rights becoming the dominant issue in the contest, Madison explained in his public letters that he had "thought it proper to give written communications of my real opinions" in order to "rectify the mistakes" circulating in the district. Contrary to the rumor that he was "a strenuous advocate for the perfection of the Constitution as it stands, and an inflexible opponent to the change of a single letter," Madison insisted that in fact he had always "thought it might be improved in several points." Indeed, he had been "an unsuccessful advocate in the general convention, which framed the instrument, for several of the very amendments since recommended by this and other states," such as requiring a periodic increase in the size of the House and limiting the jurisdiction of the federal courts. Yet Madison also acknowledged that he had never seen "those serious dangers which have alarmed many respectable citizens" with regard to the unamended Constitution.[67]

Furthermore, Madison explained that until the Constitution had been safely ratified, he had opposed antecedent amendments "as opening a door for endless and dangerous contentions among the states, and giving an opportunity to the secret enemies of the union to promote its dissolution." Yet now that the Constitution had been adopted, Madison believed that amendments, "if pursued with a proper moderation and in a proper mode, will be not only safe, but may serve the double purpose of satisfying the minds of well meaning opponents and of providing additional guards in favor of liberty." Madison emphasized that whether or not he personally favored particular amendments, he would feel himself bound "by the strongest motives to wish for such an alteration of it [the Constitution], as may banish the party heats, which have so long and so injuriously prevailed." However, Madison emphatically rejected the proposed amendment to limit Congress's power to impose direct taxes.[68]

In terms of how amendments should be pursued, Madison argued that it would be more "expeditious" and "certain" for Congress to propose them than for the states to call a second convention to recommend them (though he conceded that, under Article V of the Constitution, Congress had no discretion to refuse to call a convention if two-thirds of the states petitioned for one). Congress was scheduled to meet in March, Madison observed, and when it did, it could quickly prepare amendments and immediately submit them to the states, whereas a convention could not take place until the requisite number of states had assembled their legislatures and applied to Congress for one. Madison also argued that some state legislatures that would not support calling a convention would have no objection to particular amendments. Finally, he urged that securing amendments through Congress was "the safest mode" of proceeding because Congress would "probably be careful not to destroy or endanger" the new government. By contrast, a second convention, "meeting in the present ferment of parties and containing perhaps insidious characters from different parts of America, would at least spread a general alarm, and be but too likely to turn every thing into confusion and uncertainty."[69]

In his public letters, Madison also seized the opportunity to respond to rumors not only that he opposed all amendments but that he had "ceased to be a friend to the rights of conscience." Quite to the contrary, Madison insisted, it was now his "sincere opinion" that the first federal Congress ought to "recommend to the states for ratification the most satisfactory provisions for all essential rights," including specifically "the rights of conscience in the fullest latitude."[70]

Most of the Central Virginia Baptists, whose primary concern was the absence of any explicit constitutional protection for religious liberty, probably were inclined to believe Madison's promises. He had defended them from persecution by the state's Anglican establishment in the 1770s, supported a right of religious liberty in the Virginia Declaration of Rights of 1776, helped defeat a bill in the state legislature in 1785 that would have imposed a tax in support of teachers of the Christian religion, and played a critical role the following year in enacting Virginia's Statute for Religious Freedom. Such a consistent history of defending the rights of religious minorities gave Madison enormous credibility with the Virginia Baptists.[71]

The electoral contest was closely fought, and the outcome remained uncertain until the votes had been counted. In the end, Madison defeated Monroe by 57 to 43 percent among the roughly twenty-two hundred district residents who turned out to vote despite a heavy snowfall. Carrington wrote Madison that his "personal attendance in the district" had produced "an extensive change" in opinion, without which he probably would have lost. Madison agreed, telling Randolph that only his personal appearance had enabled him "to repel the multiplied falsehoods which circulated." Madison's endorsement of a bill of rights—not just his return to the district to campaign—probably had been critical to his victory. His triumph was important because, as Nicholas had observed, other states would interpret Madison's exclusion from both the House and the Senate as "an expression of dislike to the Constitution both by the [Virginia] legislature and the people."[72]

Madison and the Bill of Rights in Congress

Federalists had promised to support constitutional amendments in exchange for favorable votes on ratification by swing delegates at several state conventions. They had sought to reassure doubters that the Constitution, as one Massachusetts Federalist explained, "with the proposed amendments, which will certainly take place, will operate less injuriously than many suppose." Whether the Federalists would actually honor their promises for amendments after ratification had been accomplished, however, was anybody's guess.[73]

After his state's convention had ratified the Constitution, New Hampshire Federalist Tobias Lear told Washington that the amendments recommended by the convention "were drawn up more with a view of softening and conciliating the adoption to some who were moderate in their opposition than from an expectation that they would ever be engrafted in the Constitution." Many Antifederalists suspected as much. Early in 1789, New York Antifederalist leader Melancton Smith wrote, "The fair promises and pretensions of most of the leading men who were in favor of the new system are mere illusions. They intend to urge the execution of the plan in its present form." At the Virginia convention, Monroe had offered a similar prediction: "Adopt it now, unconditionally, . . . and it will never be amended, not even when experience shall have proved its defects. An alteration would be a diminution of [Congress's] power, and there will be great exertions made to prevent it." It was Madison who would ensure that the amendments became a reality.[74]

The first congressional elections would prove critical not only to the operation of the new national government but also to the prospects of a bill of rights. Soon after Virginia ratified the Constitution, Washington told James McHenry of Maryland that the Antifederalists remained committed to "obtaining great and essential changes" to the Constitution and that some of them were not above using "insidious means to prevent its [the federal government's] organization." The reports he received from visitors to Mount Vernon, Washington wrote, "lead me to expect that a considerable effort will be made to procure the election of Antifederalists to the first federal Congress" in order "to undo all that has been done." Thus, Washington considered it crucial that "the worthiest citizens" be elected to the House and to state legislatures, which would choose US senators.* To the first federal representatives would be entrusted a "point of no common delicacy": how to effect such "amendments as might be really proper and generally satisfactory without producing or at least fostering such a spirit of innovation as will overturn the whole system."[75]

Throughout the nation in the fall of 1788 and the winter of 1788–89, both in state legislative races and in contests for seats in the first House of Representatives, Antifederalists urged voters to support candidates who were committed to securing early amendments to the Constitution. This might be the "last opportunity," the Pennsylvania Antifederalist "Centinel"

---

* Others wrote to Washington to tell him, in Hamilton's words, that "on your acceptance of the office of president the success of the new government in its commencement may materially depend."

warned people, "to preserve their liberties, as the new Congress will have it in [its] power to establish despotism without violating the principles of the Constitution." By contrast, many Federalists urged voters not to support Antifederalists who had recently opposed ratification of the Constitution and would now (they charged) seek to block its implementation in Congress under the pretext of securing amendments. Thus, one Pennsylvania Federalist warned that if Antifederalists were permitted "to creep into the general [i.e., federal] government," they would "clog its wheels and retard its motions by endeavoring to foist in a train of amendments." He urged the people that, having enacted the Constitution "in name," they must now elect Federalists to Congress to ensure that it was adopted "in practice."[76]

In the contests for seats in the first Congress, Antifederalists won only eleven out of the fifty-nine that were at stake in the House, and only two of the twenty-two at issue in the Senate (the Virginia seats, which Patrick Henry had orchestrated). The failure of North Carolina and Rhode Island to ratify the Constitution yet meant that those states could not participate in the inaugural federal Congress, which probably deprived Antifederalists of several additional seats in the House and Senate. In addition, Federalists used their control of several state legislatures to mandate at-large elections for the House, which enabled them to sweep the congressional races in those states and contributed to the size of their majority in that body. Despondency or disillusionment over failing to block ratification may have led to low turnout among Antifederalist voters in congressional elections in several states. Finally, promises by some Federalist candidates to support amendments to the Constitution may also have neutralized the effectiveness of Antifederalist appeals to voters.[77]

As Madison prepared to enter the House—service that he was not relishing because he saw few among his fellow representatives who would be inclined to "share in the drudgery of business"—he anticipated that a bill of rights would emerge, despite the Antifederalists' surprisingly slim representation. He told Jefferson that he expected "some conciliatory sacrifices will be made, in order to extinguish opposition to the system, or at least break the force of it, by detaching the deluded opponents from their designing leaders." Another Virginia Federalist congressman, Richard Bland Lee, the younger brother of Henry and Charles Lee, had "little doubt that all the amendments tending to the greater security of civil liberty will be obtained." Even Patrick Henry seemed convinced at this point that amendments were likely, given that "our highest toned Federalists say we must have the[m]." However, he was not expecting the sort of structural amendments that he considered necessary.[78]

By contrast, Abraham Baldwin, a Federalist congressman from Georgia, surveyed the election results and concluded that "[t]he advocates for amendments will be but few." A Federalist senator from New Hampshire, Paine Wingate, opined that "[p]ossibly in a convenient time," Congress might consider and recommend some amendments "that may quiet the fears and jealousies of the well designing and not affect the essentials of the present system." Yet he was "rather inclined to suppose that this cannot be attended to immediately but must be postponed for other more important matters."[79]

In April 1789, Madison told Edmund Pendleton that securing amendments would depend "entirely on the temper of the Federalists, who predominate as much in both branches as could be wished." He was expecting "no great difficulty in obtaining reasonable ones," though he acknowledged to Randolph that, with some Federalist congressmen, "the concurrence will proceed from a spirit of conciliation rather than conviction."[80]

Indeed, some Federalist politicians saw advantages to the first Congress's proposing a bill of rights. Tench Coxe, an ardent Pennsylvania Federalist who would soon become assistant secretary of the treasury under Hamilton, thought that "[i]f due attention be paid to removing the jealousies and fears of the honest part of the opposition, we may gain strength and respectability without impairing one essential power of the Constitution." The amendments that Madison favored, according to Coxe, would "greatly tend to promote harmony among the late contending parties and a general confidence in the patriotism of Congress." In addition, once those amendments had been introduced, those opponents "who are not honest" would be "stripped of every rationale and most of the popular arguments they have heretofore used." Coxe also believed that "[s]ome declarations concerning the liberty of the press, of conscience, etc., ought perhaps to be frankly made parts of the Constitution." Richard Bland Lee thought that a bill of rights not only would "conciliate the affections" of the American people but also would be useful for squelching support for a second convention, which he reported Federalists in Congress were "almost unanimous against."[81]

Yet many other Federalist political leaders were strongly opposed to Congress's considering amendments at this time and made a variety of arguments against its doing so. Connecticut congressman Roger Sherman asked whether it would "not be best to make a fair trial of the Constitution before any attempts are made to alter it." William Ellery, the former chief justice of Rhode Island's high court and a longtime delegate to the Confederation Congress, agreed that "perhaps it would not be amiss to try whether the new government would not do without any alteration." Believing the Constitution to be "good and excellent," Ezra Stiles, a Congregationalist minister and the president of Yale University, suggested that no amendments be made for twenty years, or at least "not until by experience and cool judgment we should be able to discern what amendments are necessary."[82]

Other Federalists agreed with Senator Robert Morris of Pennsylvania that for Congress to consider amendments now would be a "waste of precious time." Senator Ralph Izard of South Carolina, one of the wealthiest men in the nation, thought that Congress should "go to work immediately about the finances and endeavor to extricate ourselves from our present embarrassed and disgraceful situation," rather than engage in "idle discussions about amendments [to] the Constitution." Congressman Abraham Baldwin considered Congress "too busy at present in cutting away at the whole cloth to stop to do anybody's patching."[83]

Moreover, Federalists warned that taking up amendments now might prove needlessly divisive. Writing pseudonymously in a New York newspaper, Federalist Noah Webster (the future lexicographer) wondered why, at a moment when the people were generally "disposed to acquiesce peaceably in the federal laws," Congress would consider amendments, which would "revive the spirit of party, spread the causes of contention through all the states, [and] call up jealousies which have no real foundation." Federalist newspaper publisher John Fenno argued that "[e]very movement of this kind unhinges the public mind, gives an opening to the artful, unprincipled, and disaffected, who are waiting with burning impatience for an opportunity to embroil and embarrass public affairs." William Ellery likewise warned that once amendments were proposed, "some degree of ill humor may take [the] place of that harmony which I am told prevails."[84]

Other Federalists urged—in Sherman's words—that the Constitution, as "the foundation of law and government, ought not to be changed without the most pressing necessity." Ellery worried that approving some amendments would lead to "expectations of further amendments," which might "unsettle the minds of the people and invalidate the force of the present government." Theodore Sedgwick, a Federalist congressman from Massachusetts, warned that considering amendments so soon after the new system had gone into operation would reveal "a frivolity of character very inconsistent with national dignity." Similarly concerned about Congress's demonstrating inconstancy, Sherman bluntly predicted that taking up amendments now would be "detrimental, if not fatal" to foreign credit.[85]

Still other Federalists queried why amendments would even be useful, given that, in the words of Congressman Baldwin, "[t]here is no such thing as antifederalism heard of [any more]." Richard Peters, the Federalist speaker of the Pennsylvania Assembly, could not understand why Madison favored "throw[ing] out tubs" unless he was "afraid of the whale"*—yet Antifederalist

---

* "A tub to the whale" was an allusion to Jonathan Swift's *Tale of a Tub* (1704). The idea was to protect a ship from whales that threatened it by distracting them with an object thrown into the sea.

Figure 7.3 Theodore Sedgwick, who was a Massachusetts lawyer and represented his state in the Continental Congress, and later served as US senator and Speaker of the US House of Representatives. (Museum of Fine Arts, Boston)

representation in Congress was too trivial to be concerned about. In any event, a bill of rights was unnecessary, according to Oliver Wolcott, Sr., the Federalist lieutenant governor of Connecticut, because "[t]o bind a government with fetters of iron which is founded on periodical elections is, in my opinion, to guard against evils of the most visionary nature." Jeremy Belknap, a Federalist minister and historian, found the Antifederalists' demands for amendments positively insulting: "Should a man tell me that he devoutly wished I might not break into his house and rob his desk, I think I should have a right to suspect that he viewed me in no better light than a burglar. So if a man publicly expresses a devout wish that the new government may not rob him of his personal and domestic rights, I think it not uncharitable to conclude that he has a jealousy of its intentions."[86]

During the first month of the federal Congress's inaugural session, representatives focused on raising revenue for the federal government, and the topic of amendments was not discussed on the floor. One leading Federalist reported that "[m]oney is indeed the first and most important object. Neither civil nor military wheels can turn easily without it." Even representatives who had been instructed by their states to pursue amendments were silent on the subject.[87]

In late April, Richard Henry Lee, one of Virginia's Antifederalist senators, told Samuel Adams that the Federalists were guilty of "deception and impudence" because they had secured ratification of the Constitution in Massachusetts by promising amendments but were now reneging on that commitment. He warned that "[d]eceit, whether in public or private life, seldom fails in the end to injure those who practice it." In light of the Federalists' domination of Congress, Aedanus Burke, an Antifederalist representative from South Carolina, was not expecting amendments. In May, he wrote that the "high flying monarchical gentry," whom he was sorry to discover "abound in New York as well as in Carolina," were determined to oppose all amendments. Indeed, Burke reported, "[t]he wealthy powerful families in general throughout the union ridicule the notion and will prevent if possible [amendments] taking place."[88]

Such Antifederalist pessimism regarding amendments proved unwarranted—largely owing to Madison. President Washington, it turned out, agreed with Madison that amendments, even if "not very essential, are necessary to quiet the fears of some respectable characters and well meaning men." As Washington's confidential adviser, Madison drafted the president's inaugural address, which was delivered on April 30, 1789. In it Washington called for Congress to consider constitutional amendments guaranteeing "the characteristic rights of freemen," while warning against the sort of structural amendments that might "endanger the benefits of a united and effective government." Then Madison, donning the hat of a congressional representative, helped draft the House's reply to the president's address, which promised that the topic of amendments would "receive all the attention demanded by its importance." Naturally, Washington then asked Madison to draft the president's response to the House's reply.[89]

Less than a week after Washington's inaugural address, Madison gave notice to the House that he would introduce amendments in late May, but the date was eventually postponed—as he explained to Jefferson—"in order that more urgent business may not be delayed." On June 8, Madison finally introduced his amendments.[90]

In his speeches to Congress that summer, Madison offered several arguments as to why the House should not "let the first session pass over without proposing to the state legislatures some things to be incorporated into the Constitution." First, Congress should consider a bill of rights if only "to quiet that anxiety which prevails in the public mind" and for the "salutary influence" it would have "on the public councils." Among those dissatisfied with the

Constitution were many persons who were "respectable for their talents and patriotism and respectable for the jealousy they have for their liberty, which, though mistaken in its object, is laudable in its motive." It would be prudent for the Federalists, Madison said, to seek to "extinguish from the bosom of every member of the community any apprehensions that there are those among his countrymen who wish to deprive them of the liberty for which they valiantly fought and honorably bled." Federalists must demonstrate that they were as "sincerely devoted to liberty and a republican government as those who charged them with wishing the adoption of this Constitution in order to lay the foundation of an aristocracy or despotism."[91]

Second, an even "stronger motive" for Congress to propose amendments, according to Madison, was to induce the holdout states, North Carolina and Rhode Island, to ratify the Constitution and join the union. Madison thought it "a desirable thing, on our part as well as theirs, that a reunion should take place as soon as possible."[92]

Indeed, Madison was receiving encouraging reports from Virginia and North Carolina that his efforts in the House to secure a bill of rights were having beneficial political effects. John Dawson, who had voted against ratification at the Virginia convention, reported that he rejoiced at Madison's speech calling for amendments, "which have been so ardently desired by many of the states." Amendments need not "materially affect the system," Dawson assured Madison, in order to render it "more secure and more agreeable in the eyes of those who were opposed to its establishment." Another Virginia ally, Archibald Stuart, told Madison that the growing likelihood of amendments—even if not the ones most desired by the Antifederalists—had eliminated "party spirit and political dissensions" in Stuart's part of the state. To preserve the political peace, he declared, it was critical that Congress approve at least some of Madison's proposed amendments.[93]

A leading North Carolina Federalist, William Davie, told Madison that critics of the Constitution in his state had accepted as fact "the uniform cant of the enemies of the government" that Congress would seek to squelch a second convention and refuse to propose any amendments that would diminish its authority. Yet Madison's notice to the House that he would introduce amendments had produced "almost universal pleasure" in North Carolina, where Federalists cited it "as a refutation of the gloomy prophecies of the leaders of the opposition." Davie also reported that "the honest part of our Antifederalists have publicly expressed great satisfaction on this event."[94]

Another prominent North Carolina Federalist, Benjamin Hawkins, similarly told Madison that Antifederalists had been predicting that "the friends to the new government would never consent to make any amendments" once Congress had been "possessed with power." Yet Madison's "motion on that great and delicate subject directly contradicts" such predictions. Both Davie and Hawkins deemed it critical that Congress actually pass amendments before North Carolina's second ratifying convention assembled in November 1789, as the Antifederalists were sure to "avail themselves of every thing to strengthen their party."[95]

Madison's third argument for a bill of rights was that Federalists had "something to gain" and "nothing to lose" from one, so long as they "proceed with caution." Unlike the position he had taken in some of his earlier writings and speeches on the topic, Madison now conceded that "the abuse of the powers of the general government may be guarded against in a more secure manner [i.e., a bill of rights] than is now done, while no one advantage, arising from the exercise of that power, shall be damaged or endangered by it."[96]

In a curious spectacle, Madison then proceeded to respond to the main arguments that Federalists—including him—had been making against a bill of rights for the last two years. In reply to the contention that "all paper barriers against the power of the community are too weak to be worthy of attention," Madison insisted that a bill of rights would have "a salutary effect against the abuse of power" because of its "tendency to impress some degree of respect for them [enumerated rights], to establish the public opinion in their favor, and rouse the attention of the whole community." Moreover, embracing Jefferson's argument as his own, Madison noted that if provisions safeguarding individual rights were incorporated into the Constitution, "independent tribunals of justice will consider themselves in a peculiar manner the guardians of those rights; they will be an impenetrable bulwark against every assumption of power in the legislature or executive." State legislatures, too, would "jealously and closely watch the operations of this government" for violations of the bill of rights.[97]

Madison admitted that the argument that a bill of rights was unnecessary in a system of enumerated powers was "not entirely without foundation." Yet he thought that argument "not conclusive to the extent which has been supposed" because of the "wide discretion" conferred upon Congress by provisions such as the Necessary and Proper Clause. For example, nothing in the unamended Constitution would prevent Congress's authorizing the use of general warrants as an appropriate means of protecting federal revenue from tax evaders.[98]

Addressing the claim that a bill of rights was unnecessary in the federal Constitution because many state constitutions contained one, Madison noted that some state constitutions lacked a bill of rights and that others featured ones that were "very defective" or else "absolutely improper." In response to the argument that a bill of rights was dangerous because enumerating certain rights would imply the nonexistence of others, Madison proposed adding a provision to expressly foreclose such an inference. In concluding his case for a bill of rights, Madison declared that "if we can make the Constitution better in the opinion of those who are opposed to it, without weakening its frame, or abridging its usefulness, in the judgment of those who are attached to it, we act the part of wise and liberal men to make such alterations as shall produce that effect."[99]

Congressman John Page, a fellow Virginia Federalist, added two of his own arguments in support of a bill of rights. Those "who dread the assembling of a [second] convention" ought to support congressional enactment of a bill of rights, which would obviate the need for such a convention. In addition, the many people who had supported the Constitution "in confidence of its being speedily amended" might "complain of being deceived" if the first Congress did not propose a bill of rights.[100]

However, many of Madison's Federalist colleagues in Congress were not impressed with his arguments for a bill of rights. With opposition to the Constitution seeming to evaporate, the Federalists dominating Congress, and the prospects for a second convention dimming as Federalists controlled at least one house of most state legislatures, many Federalists no longer considered it imperative to honor earlier pledges to support amendments. Indeed, some of them privately disparaged Madison for so avidly pursuing a bill of rights.[101]

Thus, Senator Robert Morris declared that "poor Madison got so cursedly frightened in Virginia that I believe he has dreamed of amendments ever since." Publisher Fenno, who considered amendments "a very unpropitious affair" at the moment, concluded that Madison, although "universally acknowledged a man of the first rate abilities," appeared to have "a mixture of timidity in his disposition." Acknowledging that Madison had "fair and honorable intentions" and "ardently wishes the prosperity of the public," Congressman Sedgwick nonetheless thought him "constantly haunted with the ghost of Patrick Henry" and lacking "that strength of nerves which will enable him to set at defiance popular and factious clamors." Noah Webster publicly charged Madison with parochialism for supporting amendments because of a promise to his constituents, when "amendments are not generally wished for."[102]

Accordingly, many Federalist congressmen rose to speak in opposition to Madison's proposal that the House consider constitutional amendments. Some of them argued that Congress simply had more pressing concerns at the moment. Noting that "without revenue the wheels of government cannot move," Representative James Jackson of Georgia suggested that the bill for collecting revenue be resolved first and the consideration of amendments postponed until the next session of Congress. John Vining of Delaware strongly opposed discussing amendments, which he thought might take months, before completing the revenue system and establishing the federal judiciary.

He insisted that the best way to "quiet the perturbation of the public mind will be to pass salutary laws." Observing that Connecticut had ratified the Constitution by a very great majority and desired no amendments, Sherman declared it "imprudent to neglect much more important concerns for this." Even the Antifederalist Burke, who thought amendments were desperately needed, considered the time inappropriate to discuss them, when the government required organizing and a law for collecting revenue was "immediately necessary."[103]

Several Federalists agreed with Sherman that "the necessity of amendments would be best pointed out by the defects, which experience may discover in the Constitution." Congressman John Laurance of New York asked whether they should "incur an absolute evil in order to rid themselves of an imaginary one." The people were "more anxious to see the government in operation than speculative amendments upon an untried constitution." Jackson declared that he would "like to stand on the sure ground of experience, and not be treading air," when considering amendments. He compared the Constitution to "a vessel just launched." If it turned out "she sails upon an uneven keel, let us right her by adding weight where it is wanting. . . . [B]ut if we proceed now to make alterations, we may deface a beauty, or deform a well proportioned piece of workmanship." Why enter upon a third "revolution in less than fourteen years . . . without necessity or propriety?" Jackson asked.[104]

Sherman also warned that "taking up the subject of amendments at this time would alarm more persons than would have their apprehensions quieted thereby." William Loughton Smith, a South Carolina congressman, went so far as to inform Madison that now that he "had done his duty" to his constituents "with ability and candor" and "was not to blame" if his efforts proved unsuccessful, he must allow the House to move on to more "important and pressing business of the government." According to the report of one of Virginia's US senators, Madison "was so embarrassed in the course of the business that he was once or twice on the point of withdrawing the motion," and the House did not peremptorily dismiss his proposal for amendments "more owing to personal respect than a love of the subject introduced."[105]

After Madison introduced his proposed amendments on June 8, the bill for collecting revenue and the measures to organize the federal judiciary and the executive branch fully occupied representatives' time for several weeks. Not until late July did the House refer Madison's amendments to a select committee. Whether Congress would have enough time to approve them before its first session ended was unclear.[106]

Despite the House's repeated deferrals, Madison would not relent in his pursuit of amendments. Expressing sympathy for the concern that the House had other urgent business to transact, Madison nonetheless warned that too many postponements "may occasion suspicions which, though not well founded, may tend to inflame or prejudice the public mind against [Congress's] decisions." It was imperative, Madison declared, that their constituents believe that Congress paid "a proper attention to a subject they have much at heart." Apologizing for "trespass[ing] upon the indulgence of this House," Madison insisted that he could not fulfill his duty to himself or his constituents by allowing "the subject [to] pass over in silence."[107]

Madison's Amendments

Having seized control of the amendments project, Madison powerfully influenced its shape and scope. When, during the ratifying contest, Federalists had resisted calls for amendments, their primary concern had been with proposals for structural change, such as limiting Congress's taxing and military powers, expanding the size of the House, and increasing the popular accountability of the president and the Senate. Such structural changes accounted for roughly half of the amendments proposed by state ratifying conventions in general and a much larger proportion of those recommended by some conventions, such as that of Massachusetts. Given Federalist domination of Congress in 1789, such amendments were nonstarters.[108]

In a letter written as Congress was about to take up his proposal for a bill of rights, Madison made it clear that he had no interest in such amendments: "The structure and stamina of the government" would be "as little touched as possible" by the changes he was recommending. Madison's political opponents had feared as much. As soon as Madison had announced in Congress his intention to pursue amendments, Maryland Antifederalist Samuel Chase declared himself to be "one of the number that expect no essential alterations." Although he hoped he was mistaken, Chase feared "that no check will be placed on the exercise of any of the powers granted." Richard Henry Lee told Patrick Henry that Madison's ideas of amendments and those of the Virginia ratifying convention were "not similar."[109]

When Madison unveiled his proposals in Congress, Pennsylvania Federalist representative George Clymer, who had been worried that Madison might "be so far frightened with the antifederalism of his own state as to attempt to lop off essentials," was relieved to discover that "he means merely a tub to the whale." Clymer observed that Madison, "[l]ike a sensible physician," had offered only "bread pills, powder of paste and neutral mixtures" for the "malades imaginaires" (hypochondriacs) among the Antifederalists. Federalist congressman Fisher Ames of Massachusetts, who disparaged the entire enterprise of amendments, thought that Madison's proposals "may do good towards quieting men who attend to sounds only."[110]

In the speech in which he presented his proposals to Congress, Madison declared that while he saw "no serious objection" to considering "provisions for the security of rights," he was unwilling "to see a door opened for a reconsideration of the whole structure of the government—for a reconsideration of the principles and the substance of the powers given." Were such a thorough review of the government's structure to be undertaken, Madison warned, it was not "very likely to stop at that point which would be safe to the government itself." Madison's Federalist colleagues agreed that only amendments consistent with "the principles of the government" ought to be considered.[111]

Thus, Madison refused to endorse the vast majority of the states' proposed structural amendments. He was especially determined to resist efforts to restrict the national government's taxing power, which had been the target of many amendments proposed by state conventions and was said to be Patrick Henry's "great desideratum." Similarly, Washington had confided to Jefferson that the only Antifederalist amendment to which he strongly objected was "that which goes to the prevention of direct taxation," although he admitted that this would be the one "most strenuously advocated and insisted upon."[112]

Conveniently, Madison argued that most of the structural proposals for which he had no sympathy—such as those allowing constituents to instruct their congressional representatives and limiting Congress's power to regulate the times, places, and manner of congressional elections—were simply too controversial to secure the requisite two-thirds majority in both houses of Congress and the approval of three-quarters of the state legislatures. He called himself "a friend to what is attainable." Equally conveniently, Madison opined that while "some respectable characters" favored structural amendments, "the great mass of the people who opposed it [the Constitution], disliked it because it did not contain effectual provisions against the encroachments on particular rights." Although Antifederalist Burke accused Madison of lacking candor on this point, Madison insisted that the amendments he proposed were "those most strenuously required by the opponents to the Constitution."[113]

When Antifederalist congressmen proposed structural amendments that Madison deemed potentially harmful, he sometimes converted them into individual-rights guarantees that he considered innocuous. Thus, while Antifederalists sought an amendment limiting Congress's power to raise standing armies in time of peace, Madison offered instead a guarantee of the right "to keep and bear arms" in connection with militia service. In response to proposals by the ratifying conventions of Virginia and North Carolina to protect the rights of assembly, speech, press, and the instruction of representatives, Madison retained the individual-rights guarantees but eliminated the structural provision for instruction, which would have significantly altered the nature of representation in the House.[114]

With just a few exceptions, Madison's proposed amendments were limited to safeguards for individual rights. One of those exceptions provided that the national legislature "shall never exercise the powers vested in the executive or judicial, nor the executive exercise the powers vested in the legislative or judicial, nor the judicial exercise the powers vested in the legislative or executive departments." Sherman raised the obvious objection that this provision, which appeared in several state constitutions, was "altogether unnecessary inasmuch as the Constitution assigned the business of each branch of the government to a separate department." Madison did not disagree, but he nonetheless supported this vacuous amendment because "the people would be gratified" by it. (This amendment was approved by the House but rejected by the Senate.)[115]

Madison proposed only a few structural amendments of any real significance. Responding to Antifederalist concerns that Congress might reduce—or at least resist an increase in—the size of the House, Madison suggested a provision that, as amended by the select committee and then the full House, stipulated a ceiling of thirty thousand constituents per representative until the House had grown to one hundred members, after which the ceiling would rise to forty thousand constituents per representative until the size of the House had reached two hundred. Madison also proposed an amendment providing that a law altering congressional pay not take effect until after an intervening election. Conceding that this amendment was not "absolutely necessary," Madison nonetheless supported it because "it was desired by a great number of the people of America." Although Congress ultimately approved both of these amendments, neither was ratified at the time by the requisite number of states. In response to Antifederalist concerns that ordinary citizens might be dragged long distances to defend appeals in the Supreme Court, Madison endorsed another amendment denying the Court appellate jurisdiction over cases involving sums of less than $1,000.[116]

Madison proposed yet another structural amendment that we know today as the Tenth Amendment, which reiterated the principle that the national government was one of enumerated—rather than inherent—powers. Although Madison considered this provision "superfluous," he saw "no harm in making such a declaration." Yet he substantially weakened the version of this amendment proposed by state ratifying conventions by omitting the word "expressly" from the amendment's reservation to the states of powers not delegated to Congress. When an Antifederalist congressman proposed adding the word "expressly," Madison successfully opposed the motion on the grounds that it would be "impossible to confine a government to the exercise of express powers . . . unless the Constitution descended to recount every minutiae."[117]

Of the individual-rights provisions that Madison proposed, some appeared in every—or, in some cases, almost every—state constitution, such as the right of religious conscience, freedom of the press, and the right to jury trials in criminal cases. Others were protected by very few state constitutions, such as freedom of speech, the right to a grand jury indictment in felony cases, and protection against double jeopardy in criminal prosecutions.[118]

Some of Madison's amendments that might appear, at first glance, to be about protecting individual rights were actually closet federalism safeguards. Madison's proposal, as amended by the joint committee, that "no religion be established by law," implicitly protected, against congressional interference, the established churches still existing in several states. The protection for the right "to keep and bear" arms, which ultimately became the Second Amendment, prevented Congress from disarming state militias, which Antifederalists deemed critical to blocking possible oppression by the national government.[119]

Those of Madison's proposals that genuinely concerned individual rights were mostly responsive to particular abuses in British or American colonial history. Many of those provisions were concerned more with the problem of government officials' abusing their authority in self-interested ways—the so-called agency problem of representative government—than with popular majorities oppressing minorities, which was the pathology Madison considered most characteristic of republican governments.[120]

For example, constitutional protection of the right to a jury trial was partly responsive to the British practice of using vice-admiralty courts, which operated without juries, to prosecute colonial smugglers, whom local jurors were often reluctant to convict. The right to freedom of the press was partly responsive to the 1735 episode in which the royal governor of New York had brought a seditious libel prosecution to suppress criticism of his administration by colonial publisher John Peter Zenger. The ban on Congress's establishing a religion—to the extent it was not simply a federalism protection, as just noted—was intended to insulate the federal government from the sort of religious and political strife, especially between Catholics and Protestants, that had engulfed Europe for centuries. Rights that we tend to think of today as criminal procedure safeguards—such as those against self-incrimination and unreasonable searches and seizures—mostly derived from particular episodes in eighteenth-century England in which the government had targeted political or religious dissidents. Many Americans would also have applauded limits on searches as important constraints on government's ability to enforce unpopular revenue measures.[121]

By virtue of seizing control of the amendments project, Madison was even able to propose one for which he had genuine enthusiasm—"the most valuable amendment in the whole list," he told the House. This amendment would have barred *state* governments from interfering with what Madison regarded as the most important individual liberties: equal rights of religious conscience, freedom of the press, and the right to a jury trial in criminal cases. For Madison, this amendment was a second-best substitute for his beloved federal veto, which, as we have seen, the Philadelphia convention rejected.[122]

Madison defended this proposal on the grounds that "there is more danger of those [rights] being abused by the state governments than by the government of the United States." From his experience with American politics during the 1780s, Madison had derived the lesson that it was state legislatures—directly elected to annual terms of office (at least in the lower houses) by relatively small constituencies, and unchecked by weak governors—that posed the greatest threat to individual liberty. Madison was much less concerned about possible abuses of power by the national legislature that he had helped to devise at the Philadelphia convention—one that was characterized by longer terms in office; large districts; indirect elections, in the case of the Senate; and the constraining influence of a presidential veto.[123]

In support of this proposal, Madison argued that because the unamended Constitution already barred the states from interfering with certain rights—such as through bills of attainder or ex post facto laws—the imposition of additional restrictions was neither unprecedented nor unwarranted. Thomas Tudor Tucker, an Antifederalist representative from South Carolina, objected to Madison's proposal on the grounds that the Constitution already interfered too much with state prerogatives. Yet the Federalist-dominated House approved this amendment.[124]

Although Madison triumphed on most matters involving the substance of the amendments, he was defeated on the question of form. Madison had proposed that amendments be interdelineated with the text of the original Constitution, rather than appearing collectively at the end. He argued that this approach would create less confusion because amendments would appear alongside the part of the Constitution that they were altering.[125]

Although some representatives denigrated the importance of this question of form, Congress devoted significant attention to it. Skeptical of the need for amendments altogether, Representative Clymer argued that they should be grouped together at the end of the document, so that people could see the "perfection of the original [Constitution] and the superfluity of the amendments." Sherman similarly argued that Congress "ought not to interweave" its amendments with the Constitution. Not only would doing so be potentially "destructive of the whole fabric," but Sherman doubted that Congress "had the right to propose amendments in this way," given that the Constitution was the "act of the people," while the amendments would be "the acts of the state governments." Sherman's position eventually prevailed. Madison described this outcome as "an unavoidable sacrifice to a few who knew their concurrence to be necessary, to the dispatch if not the success of the business."[126]

Antifederalist representatives were more concerned with the substance of the amendments than their form. They sought repeatedly—but without much success—to force the House to consider the more substantial structural amendments that they desired. Some of these representatives were under instruction from their state legislatures and ratifying conventions to ensure that the amendments proposed by their states' conventions were considered by Congress. (Madison himself was operating under such instructions.) These representatives insisted that their proposals be debated by the entire House and not simply by a select committee—and certainly not one that they believed to have been stacked against them. Because five of the eleven committee members had served as delegates to the Philadelphia convention, they had "already given their opinion with respect to the perfection of the work [i.e., the Constitution]," according to these Antifederalist congressmen, and thus were "improper agents to bring forward amendments." Indeed, as one Federalist representative privately described the committee's work, it had proposed such amendments as "might quiet the minds of the dissatisfied without injuring the Constitution."[127]

When Federalists sought to preempt debate of their opponents' preferred amendments on the House floor, the proceedings grew rancorous. Antifederalist Burke warned that "it would occasion a great deal of mischief" if the amendments were not discussed in a "satisfactory manner," while John Page objected to depriving members of their "freedom of debate." Tucker, who had insisted on antecedent amendments during the ratifying contest in South Carolina, warned that the House's refusal to seriously consider amendments proposed by state ratifying conventions "might tend to destroy that harmony which had hitherto existed, and which did great honor to their proceedings." Citizens expected the House to give a full hearing to these amendments, Tucker declared, and they would "feel some degree of chagrin at having misplaced their confidence in the general government." If state legislatures were disappointed in their expectations regarding amendments, they would "naturally recur to the alternative, and endeavor to obtain a federal convention; the consequence of this may be disagreeable to the union." Tucker predicted that such a convention would revive "party spirit" and rekindle "animosities," and "many of the valuable principles now established in the present Constitution" might be lost as a result.[128]

Tempers flared on what Federalist congressman Smith of South Carolina described as an "intensely hot" day in August. He reported that more "ill humor and rudeness [were] displayed today than has existed since the meeting of Congress." Another congressman noted that "[t]he hot weather and the subject of amendments . . . kept the House in bad temper." Indeed, "very high words passed in the House on this occasion, and what nearly amounted to direct challenges [i.e., duels]."* A third representative confirmed that "the political thermometer" had been "high each day" that the amendments were debated on the House floor.[129]

Yet Federalists had the votes, and they defeated by a margin of greater than two to one Gerry's motion that all amendments proposed by the state ratifying conventions that had not been approved by the select committee should be debated on the House floor. Even on the occasions in which Antifederalists were able to get their structural amendments considered by the full House, they could not pass them because of the Federalists' overwhelming majority. The House debated an Antifederalist proposal—which five state conventions had approved—to bar Congress from imposing direct taxes without first requisitioning funds from the states. Congressman Samuel Livermore of New Hampshire called this amendment "of more importance than any yet obtained" and insisted that it "ought to engage their most serious consideration." Yet the Federalist-dominated House defeated it by a margin of greater than four to one.[130]

By a similar margin, the House rejected a proposal to allow constituents to instruct their congressional representatives. Several state constitutions recognized such a right, which Antifederalists considered both inherent in popular sovereignty and an essential "check against abuses" by government officials. Yet Federalists feared the right of instruction would be used "[w]hen the passions of the people are excited" and would prove "utterly destructive of all ideas of an independent and deliberative body." What if the people, Congressman Vining asked, instructed their representatives to enact paper money legislation?[131]

On a few of the Antifederalists' structural proposals, the vote was closer. Even Federalist congressmen occasionally proved reluctant to vote against amendments recommended by their own states' ratifying conventions. Thus, for example, the proposal to restrict Congress's power over the times, places, and manner of federal elections to instances of state neglect or refusal to hold elections was defeated by a margin of only twenty-eight to twenty-three.[132]

Antifederalist congressmen were unimpressed with the amendments that were being approved by the House, which Burke described as "very far from giving satisfaction to our constituents." No man of "sense and candor," Burke

---

* A year later, Gerry explained what had happened on this occasion. Antifederalist Burke had resented a statement by Federalist Ames and "hinted an intention to call him out." Yet Ames then apologized, which ended their dispute. However, another Federalist congressman then expressed offense at something Gerry had said. Gerry responded, according to his subsequent account, that he had no objection to a challenge, but the matter was dropped.

insisted, could believe that these amendments bore much resemblance to those proposed by the state ratifying conventions. They were not "those solid and substantial amendments which the people expect; they are little better than whip-syllabub, frothy and full of wind, formed only to please the palate; or they are like a tub thrown out to a whale, to secure the freight of the ship and its peaceable voyage." Congressman Livermore declared that his constituents "would not value them [i.e., the House's amendments] more than a pinch of snuff; they went to secure rights never in danger." The people "would be dissatisfied," he warned, "[u]nless something more effectual was done to improve the Constitution."[133]

Antifederalists outside of the House had a similarly disparaging view of what Senator Pierce Butler of South Carolina called Madison's "milk and water" amendments. Patrick Henry thought that these amendments were "but a shadow"; they would "tend to injure rather than to serve the cause of liberty." Such amendments "answer no purpose but to lull suspicion totally on the subject" and thrust impediments in the way of those persons "who wish to retrench the exorbitancy of power granted away by the Constitution from the people." Senator William Grayson agreed: Madison's amendments were "good for nothing" and would "do more harm than benefit" because they did nothing to limit Congress's nearly plenary power over taxation and the broad jurisdiction of the federal courts.[134]

Antifederalist congressmen were so displeased with the amendments the House was proposing that they apparently decided they would prefer to have none at all. Thus, the House was treated to the "very curious" spectacle, as described by one Federalist congressman, of the Federalists having "to force" amendments on their opponents. John Brown, a Federalist representative from the Kentucky region of Virginia, noted that the Antifederalists "appear determined to obstruct and embarrass the business as much as possible," and he asked if it were "not surprising that the opposition should come from that quarter." Congressman William Smith of Maryland wondered if the amendments proposed by Madison and revised by the select committee could secure the requisite two-thirds majority in the House with the Antifederalists "oppos[ing] their being brought forward in every stage" and "making every exertion to put off the consideration of that business until the next session" because the amendments did not "go far enough." Congressman Frederick A. Muhlenberg of Pennsylvania concluded that the Antifederalists' strategy at this point was to impede the progress of the congressional debates with the goal of favoring "their darling question for calling a convention." After nearly ten days of debating amendments on the House floor, Madison described the work as "exceedingly wearisome, not only on account of the diversity of opinions that was to be apprehended, but of the apparent views of some to defeat by delaying a plan short of their wishes."[135]

In the end, however, over Antifederalist opposition, the House approved amendments that did not differ greatly from the ones first introduced by Madison. Federalist congressmen had increasingly evinced—in the words of Representative William Loughton Smith—a disposition to agree to some amendments, "which will more effectually secure private rights, without affecting the structure of the government." Madison's proposals, as revised by the select committee, were deemed "inoffensive" and indeed might "do some good on the other side." As Smith noted, "North Carolina only wants some pretext to come into the union, and we may afford that pretext by recommending a few amendments." Congressman Fisher Ames, who had initially been unsympathetic to the entire amendments project, was eventually persuaded to support the proposed amendments, in part so that Antifederalists, if they dared to say that the amendments were "of no consequence" after having "protested that the principles were important," could be "reproached with their opposition to the government." Congressman Benjamin Goodhue of Massachusetts thought the amendments would "quiet the honest part of the dissatisfied" without "weakening the Constitution." Rhode Island Federalist William Ellery, while still opposing the idea of amendments, conceded that the ones about to be approved by the House were "very innocent, and the admission of them might gratify the pride of some opposers of the new government and facilitate their embracing it."[136]

Yet the amendments also had to pass the Senate before they could be sent on to the states for ratification, and their fate in the upper house was difficult to predict. Goodhue was uncertain what the Senate would do, and he worried that it might defer consideration of the amendments until its next session. Indeed, a couple of ardent Federalists in the Senate, Ralph Izard and John Langdon, proposed doing exactly that, while—according to one account—speaking "contemptuously" of the House amendments. Having always doubted Madison's commitment to genuine structural reform of the Constitution, Virginia senator Richard Henry Lee had promised Patrick Henry that "when the plan comes to the Senate, we shall prepare to abridge, or enlarge [it], so as to effect, if possible" the Antifederalists' proposed amendments. Lee was hopeful that if they could not "gain the whole loaf, we shall at least have some bread."[137]

The Federalist-dominated Senate did alter the amendments—in ways that Madison thought detrimental to the "most salutary articles." Much to his disappointment, the Senate rejected the amendment that Madison had proposed to constrain the states with regard to what he considered the most important rights. That rejection was probably a reflection of the facts that senators owed their appointments to state legislatures and that one-third of them enjoyed only a two-year respite before their terms would expire.* Madison was also disappointed that the Senate eliminated two of the concessions made to localism by his proposed amendments—namely, that cases involving sums of less than $1,000 would not be appealable to the US Supreme Court and that juries in federal criminal cases would be drawn from the vicinage of the alleged crime.[138†]

Madison reported that Federalist senators objected to the first of these localist amendments because it might prove "embarrassing in questions of national or constitutional importance in their principle though of small pecuniary amount." They resisted the vicinage requirement, Madison explained, because it was "too vague if depending on limits to be fixed by the pleasure of the law" and "too strict if limited to the county," which would be a departure from the general practice of states to select juries from larger geographic areas. At least partially because of these Senate changes to the localist amendments that a Federalist congressman had called "the darling objects [of] the Virginians," the two Antifederalist senators from Virginia concluded, in Grayson's words, that the amendments proposed by the House had been "so mutilated and gutted that in fact they are good for nothing."[139]

As for any other structural amendments that they cared about, the Antifederalists were clearly not going to secure them from a Federalist-dominated Senate. Senators Lee and Grayson of Virginia nonetheless presented their proposals for consideration, but they were hopelessly outnumbered, and the Senate simply approved the rest of the House's amendments—with relatively minor changes—and proposed no additional amendments itself. After a joint committee resolved the differences, Congress sent the amendments to the

---

* Although the Constitution stipulates six-year terms for senators, in order to accomplish the staggering of terms that the Framers desired, it also provides that one-third of the first class of senators would vacate their seats after two years and another one-third after four years.

† The Senate struck out the jury requirement in criminal cases altogether, probably because such a requirement already existed in Article III, but the joint conference committee reinstated it. However, the committee's version stipulated for juries to be drawn only from the "district," not the "vicinage," of the crime. (The House then added—and the Senate concurred—the requirement that juries be drawn from the state where the crime was allegedly committed, as well as from the district.) In practice, federal judicial districts, as drawn by the 1789 Judiciary Act, were largely coextensive with states—with only two states, Virginia and Massachusetts, containing more than one federal judicial district, and the other eleven states each comprising a district by themselves.

states for ratification in late September 1789. There were twelve amendments altogether—the ten that ultimately became known as the Bill of Rights, plus the ones on increasing the size of the House and requiring intervening elections before changes in congressional pay could go into effect.[140]

Lee and Grayson assured the Virginia legislature that "nothing on our part has been omitted to procure the success of those radical amendments proposed by the [Virginia ratifying] convention" and expressed their "grief" that the amendments passed by Congress were "inadequate to the purpose of real and substantial amendments." Lee also observed, separately, that the "great points" of Congress's control over federal elections and its vastly expanded powers over taxation and standing armies had gone unaddressed in Congress's proposed amendments, thus revealing the Federalists' promises of amendments subsequent to ratification to have been "delusion altogether." He conceded that "[s]ome valuable rights" had been stated yet insisted that the powers that remained uncurbed were ample to render those rights "nugatory at pleasure." The "most essential danger" remained: the system's "tendency to a consolidated government, instead of a union of confederated states."[141]

Lee seemed genuinely distraught: "What with design in some and fear of anarchy in others, it is very clear, I think, that a government very different from a free one will take place e're [i.e., before] many years are passed." His only solace lay in the hope that a sufficient number of state legislatures would soon call for a second convention. When, a couple of weeks later, the legislature of Rhode Island reaffirmed that the state would remain out of the union until what Lee called "effectual amendments" were passed, he wistfully remarked to Patrick Henry that Virginia "ought in common prudence to have done the same."[142]

Not all Antifederalists were as disappointed as Lee, Grayson, and Henry in the amendments Congress had passed. George Mason reported "much satisfaction from the amendments" (although he said this before he had seen the Senate's changes to the House's proposed amendments). Mason declared that with just a few further additions—such as limiting the jurisdiction of the federal judiciary, curtailing Congress's power over federal elections, imposing a supermajority requirement for commercial legislation, and adding an executive council—he would be willing to "cheerfully put my hand and heart to the new government."[143]

For the amendments approved by Congress to become part of the Constitution, they had to be ratified by three-quarters of the state legislatures (which translated to at least ten out of the thirteen). Within four months, half a dozen states had ratified, but then the road got tougher. Georgia rejected the

Figure 7.4 Richard Henry Lee, who was a leader of the revolutionary movement in Virginia, signed the Declaration of Independence and the Articles of Confederation, and served as president of the Confederation Congress in the mid-1780s. (National Portrait Gallery, Smithsonian Institution/Art Resource, NY)

amendments, and the bicameral legislatures of Massachusetts and Connecticut divided over whether to ratify them.* Because rejection by just four states would suffice to block ratification, Virginia's support became critical.[144]

When Virginia's US senators transmitted the amendments approved by Congress to their state's legislature, they disparaged them as inadequate to protect civil liberty and expressed confidence that a second convention remained a genuine possibility. Madison told Washington that the transmittal letter was "well calculated to keep alive the disaffection to the government and is accordingly applied to that use by the violent partisans." Indeed, convinced that Congress would consider more fundamental structural amendments only if ratification of the ones already approved was blocked, Patrick Henry sought to

---

* Surprisingly little information has survived with regard to the state ratifying debates on the Bill of Rights, with the sole exception of the deliberations in the Virginia House of Delegates, as noted in the text.

prevent Virginia's endorsement of the amendments. Ratification would prove an uphill battle in the Virginia legislature, where many Antifederalists took umbrage at Congress's apparent disdain for the amendments proposed by the Virginia ratifying convention, which the legislature had explicitly endorsed.[145]

For the next two years, the Virginia legislature stalemated over whether to ratify the amendments approved by Congress. In the fall of 1789, Henry moved to have consideration of the amendments deferred to the next session of the legislature, in order—according to Edward Carrington's report to Madison—"that the people might give their sentiments whether they were satisfactory, alleging that in his [Henry's] opinion they were not." Discovering that the House of Delegates was not sympathetic to his resolution for deferral, Henry moved that it lie on the table and then, according to Carrington, "went away without ever calling it up again."[146]

Henry's early departure from Richmond may have proved significant to the fate of the amendments. On three separate occasions during the fall session, the House voted on a resolution urging that Congress reconsider and adopt all the amendments proposed by the Virginia ratifying convention. Initially, a great majority of delegates rejected the resolution, but the second vote was closer. On the third ballot, only the Speaker's tie-breaking vote killed the resolution. Henry probably would not have left the session early had he realized that opinion in the House on amendments would trend in his direction.[147]

When the Virginia House debated whether to approve the twelve amendments passed by Congress, delegates manifested little opposition to any except the last two. These provided, respectively, that "[t]he enumeration in the Constitution of certain rights shall not be construed to deny or disparage others retained by the people," and that "[t]he powers not delegated to the United States by the Constitution, nor prohibited to it by the states, are reserved to the states respectively, or to the people."

Edmund Randolph, who supported all the other amendments proposed by Congress, led the opposition to these two, which he considered unclear and worried might be interpreted to imply that Congress had the power to interfere with unenumerated rights. As recounted by one of Madison's allies in the Virginia House, Hardin Burnley, Randolph's argument was that the rights specifically enumerated in the first ten amendments did not exhaust those that a free people should enjoy, yet there was no specified criterion by which to determine whether any other particular right had been retained by the people. Accordingly, Randolph preferred, according to Burnley, who confessed that he was not certain that he followed Randolph's reasoning, that "this reservation against constructive power should operate rather as a provision against extending the powers of Congress by their own authority than as a protection to rights reducible to no definitive certainty."[148]

Madison told Washington that the opposition in the House of Delegates to the last two amendments was "really unlucky and the more to be regretted as it springs from a friend to the Constitution." Randolph's opposition was "a still greater cause of regret" because the distinction he drew between reservations of rights and limitations on powers struck Madison as "altogether fanciful." What was the difference between declaring that rights "shall not be abridged" and declaring that powers "shall not be extended"? Moreover, even if Randolph's distinction was "just," Madison did not think it "of sufficient importance to justify the risk of losing the amendments, of furnishing a handle to the disaffected and of arming North Carolina with a pretext, if she be disposed, to prolong her exile from the union."[149]

At one point that fall, the Virginia House of Delegates narrowly rejected the two amendments to which Randolph objected. According to Burnley, who favored ratification of all of Congress's proposed amendments, that vote brought the entire package of amendments "into hazard," as some of the "decided friends" to the other ten amendments thought it "unwise" to adopt them without the last two—a position that was hard to quarrel with, given that the whole point of the first of the two controversial amendments had been to rebut the inference that enumerating certain rights implied the nonexistence of others. However, after initially rejecting these two amendments, the House quickly reversed itself. By contrast, the Senate refused to acquiesce in several of the proposed amendments, probably because they did not go as far as the amendments recommended by the ratifying conventions of Virginia and other states (and perhaps mainly because of the absence of an amendment limiting Congress's power to levy direct taxes). A joint conference committee failed to produce agreement, so the entire set of amendments failed during that legislative session.[150]

In the end, Virginia did ratify Congress's proposed amendments—though not until two years later, in December 1791. By then, support for a second constitutional convention had largely evaporated, which left Virginia little to lose by ratifying. With Virginia's ratification, the proposed amendments became part of the Constitution—with two exceptions. The requisite number of states did not ratify the amendment that would have ensured an increase in the size of the House or the one mandating that congressional pay alterations not take effect until after an intervening election. Soon after Virginia's ratification, Secretary of State Thomas Jefferson declared ten of the twelve proposed amendments duly enacted.[151]*

---

* One of the eleven states to ratify ten of the amendments was Delaware. (By the time of Virginia's ratification late in 1791, Vermont had been admitted to the union as an independent state, which meant that the approval of eleven states, not ten, was required for the amendments

Interpreting the Enactment of the Bill of Rights

As what he called "the nauseous project of amendments" was about to wrap up in the House of Representatives in August 1789, Madison wrote a long letter to Richard Peters of Pennsylvania, an ardent Federalist who had been battling to reform Pennsylvania's exceptionally democratic constitution for the last decade, in which Madison reflected on his reasons for supporting a bill of rights. He began by insisting—a bit disingenuously—that he had "never opposed a constitutional provision in favor of essential rights." Although a bill of rights "may be less necessary in a republic than a monarchy" and in a confederation than in a simple republic, Madison observed, it was "in some degree rational in every government, since in every government, power may oppress, and declarations on paper, though not an effectual restraint, are not without some influence."[152]

Aside from this lukewarm endorsement of a bill of rights on its merits, the reasons Madison expressed for supporting one were entirely political. Many states, he reminded Peters, had ratified the Constitution "under a tacit compact in favor of some subsequent provisions on this head." Indeed, Madison was certain that Virginia would have rejected ratification without such assurances. As an "honest man," he felt himself "bound by this consideration." Madison also considered it relevant that at least some Federalist candidates in Virginia's congressional races—including himself—almost certainly would have been defeated had they "not taken this conciliatory ground at their election."[153]

Next, Madison observed that their political opponents would have proposed amendments if the Federalists had not, and it was "certainly best that they [i.e., the amendments] should appear to be the free gift of the friends of the Constitution rather than to be extorted by the address and weight of its enemies." In addition, a bill of rights would "kill the opposition everywhere

proposed by Congress to be duly ratified.) Of those eleven states, Delaware alone rejected the amendment to increase the size of the House, undoubtedly for the reason that its relative influence in that body would have diminished as a result of the amendment. Indeed, as soon as he had proposed this amendment in the House, Madison reported that "[t]he small states betray already a coolness towards it."

As to the pay-alteration amendment, only six states ratified it before the end of 1791. However, in the early 1980s, an undergraduate student at the University of Texas began a campaign to persuade additional state legislatures to ratify it—the Constitution saying nothing about a contemporaneity requirement for state ratifications of amendments. When Michigan became the thirty-eighth state to ratify the amendment in 1992—three-fourths of fifty states is thirty-eight—Congress and the archivist of the United States declared the amendment duly ratified, and it became part of the Constitution, a little more than two hundred years after Congress had proposed it.

and by putting an end to the disaffection to the government itself, enable the administration to venture on measures not otherwise safe."[154]

By contrast, if Federalists had declined to propose amendments, Antifederalists would have insisted that their earlier warnings of Federalist duplicity had been validated. Had Federalists not introduced amendments in Congress, Madison observed, Antifederalists would have "blow[n] the trumpet for a second convention" at the upcoming fall sessions of state legislatures. In Virginia specifically, where a majority of the legislature was already "bitterly opposed" to the federal government, Congress's failure to approve amendments in its inaugural session would lead even "great numbers" of Federalists to "complain of being deceived." Finally, Madison reported that political leaders in North Carolina had assured him that congressional approval of a bill of rights was necessary to secure ratification of the Constitution there.[155]

In his reply, Peters wrote that while Madison had made the strongest possible case for a bill of rights, he remained unpersuaded. Peters believed that "a firmness in adhering to our Constitution 'till at least it had a longer trial would have silenced Antifederalists sooner than magnifying their importance by acknowledgments on our part and of ourselves holding up a banner for them to rally to." The Antifederalists would not be satisfied with what Madison had offered, Peters noted, and while "there are among them good characters," many of the Antifederalist leaders simply wanted "to make or keep themselves heads of a party" and thus would continue the "clamor" for amendments. Peters also worried that "[o]ur character abroad will never acquire consistency while foreigners see us wavering even in our government about the very instrument under which that government acts." In sum, Peters feared "worse consequences from the good disposition of the conciliators" than from "an adherence to the system."[156]

The Bill of Rights was another huge personal victory for Madison. Congress would not have seriously considered constitutional amendments in 1789 had it not been for his persistence; the Federalists had such large majorities in both houses that they did not need to offer any concessions to their adversaries. Over initial opposition from both sides of the aisle, Madison maneuvered the Bill of Rights to passage.[157]

Moreover, by taking charge of the amendments scheme, Madison was able to control it. The amendments passed by Congress were the ones he had proposed—with relatively minor modifications. Madison ignored or helped to defeat the proposed amendments that the Antifederalists cared the most about—the ones limiting the power of the federal government or restructuring it. Those amendments—which Madison thought went to "the very essence of the proposed government"—would have undermined much of what he had fought so hard to establish, first in Philadelphia and then in Richmond.[158]

By delivering the Bill of Rights, Madison accomplished several related political objectives: He divided his opponents' ranks, soothed the concerns of the less irredeemable Antifederalists, convinced the country that the Federalists were good to their word, and stifled talk of a second convention. When Madison had begun his conversion to Bill of Rights enthusiast, he told Jefferson that on no other point were the Antifederalists "so much divided" as on the "importance and . . . propriety" of a bill of rights. Once Randolph learned that Madison had promised his constituents to pursue amendments if elected to Congress, he approvingly declared, "Although I am convinced that nothing will soften the rancor of some men, I believe that a moderate and conciliating conduct in our federal rulers will detach from their virulence, those who have been opposed [to the Constitution] from principle." Hamilton agreed that carefully designed amendments would "satisfy the more considerate and honest opposers of the Constitution, and with the aid of time will break up the party [i.e., the Antifederalists]." This is precisely what Antifederalist leaders had feared. Grayson warned Patrick Henry that the Federalists, their object being "unquestionably to break the spirit of the [Antifederalist] party by divisions," would "support amendments that affect personal liberty only, leaving the great points of the judiciary and direct taxation, etc., to stand as they are."[159]

During the ratifying contest, Federalists had repeatedly and unequivocally promised to support amendments once the Constitution was ratified. To renege on such explicit promises might have severely compromised their credibility with the citizenry. William Davie, a leading North Carolina Federalist, observed that before Madison had given notice to the House that he would propose a bill of rights, Antifederalists had been "remarking with great triumph the fulfillment of their prophecies with respect to Congress never taking up the subject of amendments." Yet Madison's action had, according to Davie, "confounded the Anties exceedingly." In August 1789, as it became clear that the House would pass amendments, Carrington reported that the people of Virginia were becoming "well reconciled to the new government" and that Madison was "becoming popular with the Antis, who say they believe he is to be depended upon for procuring amendments."[160]

The following month, Edmund Pendleton predicted to Madison that the amendments proposed by the House would have "a good effect in quieting the minds of many well meaning citizens." Pendleton derived "some degree of pleasure in discovering . . . that the public are indebted for the measure to the friends of government, whose elections were opposed under pretense of their being averse to amendments." Also in September, Rhode Island's governor reported to Congress and President Washington that the amendments proposed by Congress "have already afforded some relief and satisfaction to the minds of the people of this state" (though he also noted that the time had not yet arrived when Rhode Island might "with clearness and safety be again united with [its] sister states"). In November, Madison told Washington, "One of the principal leaders of the Baptists lately sent me word that the amendments had entirely satisfied the disaffected of his sect, and that it would appear in their subsequent conduct." In April 1790, just months after returning to the United States from France, Jefferson observed that "almost all" of the Antifederalists had become supporters of the Constitution, and he credited the amendments proposed by Congress for this conversion.[161]

Although without Madison there very likely would have been no Bill of Rights, he never did figure out why other people seemed to have much greater faith than he did in "parchment barriers." Many of his Federalist colleagues similarly acquiesced to a bill of rights more because they deemed it harmless and possibly of political use than because they believed it important for safeguarding individual rights.[162]

Thus, Congressman Roger Sherman declared that the amendments proposed by Congress would "probably be harmless and satisfactory to those who are fond of bills of rights." Representative Lambert Cadwalader of New Jersey regarded Madison's amendments as "of little or no consequence," though he conceded that they might "calm the turbulence of the opposition in Virginia and some of the other states, and certainly bring North Carolina into the union." Although Congressman Thomas Hartley of Pennsylvania did not consider an enumeration of rights essential, he "was disposed to gratify" the states that had recommended amendments, so long as their proposals were "not incompatible with the general good." Offering this concession "would tend to obtain the confidence of the people in the government."[163]

By contrast, most Antifederalist leaders disparaged Madison's proposed amendments, which they considered positively harmful because their enactment would be likely to reduce the prospects of securing the sort of amendments they deemed necessary. Congressman Thomas Tudor Tucker described Madison's amendments as "calculated merely to amuse, or rather to deceive." Gerry considered them plainly irrelevant to whether the "Constitution will preserve its theoretical balance" or else tilt toward aristocracy or monarchy, and he thought the amendments would serve no purpose other than "to reconcile those who had no adequate idea of the essential defects of the Constitution." Richard Henry Lee believed that Congress had been "wonderfully scrupulous . . . in stating rights," but that "right without power to protect it is of little avail."[164]

According to Noah Webster, Federalists and Antifederalists agreed that "paper declarations of rights are trifling things and no real security to liberty." Webster was right: Very few people at the time of the Founding considered the provisions of the Bill of Rights to be "fundamental safeguards of liberty," as the Supreme Court under Chief Justice Earl Warren would proclaim them to be. Hamilton's view, stated roughly a decade after the ratification of the Bill of Rights, probably came nearer to capturing the predominant sentiments of that era: Madison's amendments met "scarcely any of the important objections which were urged, leaving the structure of the government and the mass and distribution of its powers where they were, [and] are too insignificant to be, with any sensible man, a reason for being reconciled to the system if he thought it originally bad."[165]

8

Conclusion

Contingency

Because the Constitution has become so critical to the self-conception of Americans, it is difficult to accept the uncertainty and contingency of its adoption. Yet nothing about the process that produced the Constitution was inevitable.[1]

The Annapolis convention that preceded the Constitutional Convention had failed to generate sufficient interest among the states to accomplish any substantive results. There was not much reason to expect the Philadelphia convention to fare any better. Were it not for widespread anxiety among the nation's elite caused by Shays's Rebellion and the radical economic populism of Rhode Island, both Congress and several state legislatures might have declined to endorse the convention. In addition, George Washington nearly declined to attend the convention, and his absence would have deprived it of his extraordinary legitimizing influence.[2]

Once convened, the Philadelphia assemblage—to quote the subsequent recollection of one important participant, Charles Pinckney—was "repeatedly in danger of dissolving without doing anything." Even after the convention produced a constitution, whether it would be ratified was far from certain. Ratifying contests in several states were too close for participants to forecast the outcomes with any confidence. Tactical savvy and considerable good fortune enabled the Federalists to win the ratifying contest—barely. They only narrowly fended off calls for conditional ratification or a second convention. Even after the Constitution had been approved, the addition of a bill of rights seemed unlikely.[3]

James Madison played a critical role at almost every stage of this process. Partly at his initiative, the Virginia legislature issued a call for the Annapolis convention. When that convention failed, Madison and the few other commissioners who attended boldly decided to invite states to another convention—one with a broader mandate—to assemble in Philadelphia the following spring. Madison then drafted the bill in the Virginia legislature appointing delegates to the Philadelphia convention, which, once enacted, was circulated to every state as a clarion call to appoint delegates to that convention. He also helped persuade Washington to participate in the convention.[4]

Almost single-handedly, Madison shaped the convention's initial agenda. Alone among the delegates, he had systematically reflected upon the vices of the Articles of Confederation and the pathologies of the state governments and devised a scheme of government that he believed would remedy them. Then he persuaded his fellow Virginia delegates to arrive early in Philadelphia so that they could coordinate behind a plan that would become the convention's blueprint.[5]

At the convention itself, Madison was one of the three or four most able and frequent contributors to the deliberations. In William Pierce's character sketches of convention delegates, he noted that Madison, who was always "the best informed man of any point in debate," took the lead "[i]n the management of every great question." Although Madison lost on many issues about which he cared deeply, his role in shaping the Constitution was at least as important as anyone else's.[6]

Without Madison's tireless organizing efforts and his Herculean service at the Richmond ratifying convention, Virginia—by far the largest and most important state—might well have rejected the Constitution. Madison then orchestrated and shaped—again almost single-handedly—the Bill of Rights passed by the first federal Congress. Rarely if ever in American history has a single individual played such an instrumental role in an event as important as the nation's founding.[7]

What might have happened had the process of constitutional revision set in motion in the late 1780s failed? Obviously, one cannot know for certain. Yet some dire developments were eminently plausible.

Most American political leaders believed the Articles were a decisive failure. In the summer of 1786, Rufus King observed that "it is not possible that the public affairs can be in a much worse situation." Congressional delegate James Manning of Rhode Island reported that all members of Congress agreed that "things are come to a crisis with the federal government," and that "without a speedy reform in the policy of the states, the federal government must be no more." Two months before the Philadelphia convention assembled, Virginia congressional delegate John Brown observed that the prospect of a new constitution "had already damned the present government in the estimation of the world. [I]t cannot—it will not—drag on much longer, and should the new be rejected, God only knows what will be the event."[8]

One possibility is that, without the Constitution, the Confederation would have dissolved. The month before the Philadelphia convention assembled,

Madison observed that leading statesmen were openly discussing the possibility of "the partition of the empire into rival and hostile confederacies."
The imbroglio over what one Virginian described as Secretary for Foreign
Affairs John Jay's "diabolical attempt to surrender the navigation of [the
Mississippi] river" had led many southerners and westerners to question the
value of the union. Virginia governor Patrick Henry had reportedly declared
that "he would rather part with the Confederation than relinquish the navigation of the Mississippi," and Virginia congressional delegate Henry Lee had
voiced alarm that "gentlemen talk so lightly of a separation and dissolution
of the Confederation." The failed effort to ratify a proposed amendment to
vest Congress with the authority to regulate foreign commerce had similarly
led many northerners to contemplate the possibility of their forming, in the
words of Rufus King, "a sub-confederation" to remedy their commercial
difficulties.[9]

Had the Constitutional Convention dissolved in contentiousness or the
Constitution not been ratified, the prospects of the Confederation surviving would have been even grimmer than had no fundamental reform of the
Articles been attempted in the first place. One of Georgia's delegates to the
Philadelphia convention, William Few, later reflected that had the delegates
adjourned the convention "without doing anything" after "weeks of deliberation and debating"—as they had "serious thoughts" of doing—then "the dissolution of the union of the states seemed inevitable." Hamilton conjectured that
if the Constitution, once drafted, was not ratified, "it is probable the discussion
of the question will beget such struggles, animosities, and heats in the community that this circumstance, conspiring with the real necessity of an essential
change in our present situation, will produce civil war." At the Virginia ratifying convention, Randolph similarly predicted that if the ratification effort
failed, "the union will be dissolved, the dogs of war will break loose, and anarchy and discord will complete the ruin of this country."[10]

Another dire possibility, without the Constitution, was that many elite
Americans would have abandoned their commitment to republican government. Shays's Rebellion and the capitulation of most state legislatures to populist demands for fiscal and monetary relief had caused extreme consternation
among the upper classes. In the months before the Philadelphia convention,
Madison told Randolph that "many individuals of weight, particularly in the
eastern district [i.e., New England], are suspected of leaning towards monarchy." Washington similarly observed that "even respectable characters speak
of a monarchical form of government without horror." One week after the
Massachusetts convention ratified the Constitution, a Boston Federalist noted
with relief that he had "dreaded the consequences of a rejection by this state,"
which he said would have left "no other alternative" than a dissolution of the

union, followed by "anarchy and confusion," and "in the course of a few years, some despot [ruling] over us with a rod of iron."[11]

The drafting and ratification of the Constitution prevented such contingencies from developing. Republican government—albeit of a less populist variety—was preserved, and so was the union, although it would be severely tested again in a few generations' time.

Contingency characterized not just the adoption of the Constitution but also many of the substantive provisions in it. The Constitutional Convention nearly decided against authorizing any federal courts other than the US Supreme Court. In addition, the delegates in Philadelphia adopted the Constitution's mechanism for selecting the president—through a college of electors who are appointed in a manner specified by state legislatures—only after first overwhelmingly repudiating that method and after considering and rejecting numerous alternatives. Indeed, before its final rejection, one of those alternative methods of choosing the president—selection by Congress—had been tentatively but repeatedly embraced by the convention. How to choose the president was a vitally important question: If the president were selected by Congress, the US government might have become more like the parliamentary democracies that dominate the modern world, in which the executive is heavily dependent upon the legislature. Yet the Philadelphia convention resolved this issue through incessant deliberations that seemed, in the end, to produce an almost random solution.[12]

Because so many of the issues confronted by the convention were intertwined with one another, particular decisions made tentatively during deliberations produced path dependencies, which in turn led to more highly contingent resolutions. For example, once the Connecticut Compromise had produced equal state voting in the Senate, some large-state delegates, including Madison, voted to shift powers that had been provisionally allocated to the Senate—over appointments and treaty making—to the president. At the same time, many small-state delegates, now having secured equal state voting in the Senate, favored expanding the powers of the national government—something they had resisted before the Connecticut Compromise. Delegates took positions based on compromises that had been provisionally agreed upon; had those compromises unraveled, many matters of importance would again have been up for grabs.[13]

Indeed, without the various compromises negotiated at the convention—especially between small states and large states, and between slave states and mostly free states—no constitution would have been possible. Yet those compromises deprived the Constitution of its internal coherence. As Madison explained in *The Federalist No. 37*, the need for such compromises compelled the convention "to sacrifice theoretical propriety to the force of extraneous considerations," which ensured that the final product deviated "from that artificial structure and regular symmetry which an abstract view of the subject might lead an ingenious theorist to bestow on a constitution planned in his closet or in his imagination." Equal state representation in the Senate fitted awkwardly in a national government ostensibly grounded in popular sovereignty. For purposes of apportioning the House of Representatives, slaves—who by the year 1800 would constitute nearly 19 percent of the US population—counted neither as nothing at all nor as full human beings. Congress was authorized to forbid the foreign slave trade—but not until another generation had elapsed.[14]

Interests

The compromises undertaken in Philadelphia also illustrate the extent to which the Constitution was a product of clashing interests rather than dispassionate political philosophizing. George Mason was right to remark upon the extraordinary talent of his fellow delegates in Philadelphia: "America has certainly, upon this occasion, drawn forth her first characters, . . . many gentlemen of the most respectable abilities." Yet while these were remarkable men, their interests were rather ordinary. As Benjamin Franklin keenly observed, any assembly of men, no matter how talented, bring with them "all their prejudices, their passions, their errors of opinion, their local interests and their selfish views."[15]

One need not deny that the Framers, as Mason and Madison insisted, had "the purest intentions" in order to believe that—inevitably—they also had interests. Unsurprisingly, supporters of the Constitution preferred to believe that they were disinterested, while their opponents were motivated by selfish concerns. To the Federalists, only the natural aristocracy of virtue, talent, and education—men like themselves—could rise above narrow self-interest.[16]

Thus, Hamilton complained to Madison that because the Antifederalists used "every species of influence and artifice," the Federalists could "count little on overcoming opposition by reason." Madison, too, attributed most of the opposition to the Constitution to "designing, illiberal, and unthinking minds." According to Washington, the Antifederalists raised objections "better calculated to alarm the fears than to convince the judgment" and permitted "their local views" to trump arguments that did "not accord with their present or future prospects." Yet while the Federalists considered themselves disinterested, in reality they simply held different interests than their political opponents.[17]

Conflicts of interest had torpedoed efforts to amend the Articles in the 1780s and led to a crisis over the union. First Rhode Island and then New York had vetoed an amendment to empower Congress to raise revenue through an impost, because those states wished to preserve a status quo that enabled them to shift much of the incidence of their own import duties to citizens of neighboring states. New York's refusal to unconditionally ratify the 1783 impost amendment had led New Jersey to threaten not to pay its congressional requisitions and to actually take retaliatory measures against New York; the president of Congress believed that "bloodshed" was close at hand. Many southerners had resisted an amendment to authorize Congress to regulate foreign commerce because they feared such a power would be used primarily to benefit northern shippers and manufacturers at the expense of southern planters. In 1786–87, during the controversy over Secretary for Foreign Affairs John Jay's negotiations with Spanish envoy Don Diego de Gardoqui, northerners had favored a commercial treaty, while southerners had demanded the assertion of American navigation rights on the Mississippi River. Dissension in Congress over Jay's instructions had led many statesmen to despair over the fate of the union.[18]

Such conflict over opposing interests did not suddenly disappear during the process of constitutional reform: The Philadelphia convention was a veritable smorgasbord of conflicting interests. At one point in the proceedings, Hugh Williamson bemoaned to a political ally back home in North Carolina that "[t]he diverse and almost opposite interests that are to be reconciled occasion us to progress very slowly." As the convention seemed about to implode over the question of how to apportion representation in the national legislature, Elbridge Gerry "lamented that instead of coming here like a band of brothers, belonging to the same family, we seemed to have brought with us the spirit of political negotiators." Although Gouverneur Morris professed to serve in Philadelphia as "a representative of America"—indeed, "as a representative of the whole human race"—he regretted that most of the delegates were acting as if they were there "to truck and bargain for our particular states."[19]

Most delegates sought to secure to their own states as much power within the new national government as possible.* A state delegation's interest sometimes had to do with the size of the state: Delegates from Delaware, the least populous state, favored equal state representation in at least one branch of the national legislature, while delegates from Virginia, the most populous state, wanted both houses of Congress apportioned according to population. On other occasions, the interests of a state's delegation were mainly a function of

---

* Perhaps the starkest illustration of this phenomenon was the quibbling over allocation of seats in the first House, which was exacerbated by the absence of any reliable population census.

the state's region: Delegates from southern states wanted as much representation as possible in the House on account of their slaves, while northern state
delegations preferred that slaves count as little as possible for apportionment
purposes.[20]

Illustrating how regional interest could sometimes trump narrowly defined state interest, at one point Madison explained that he had voted against
increasing by one Virginia's allotment of representatives in the first House
because he cared more about increasing that of South Carolina and North
Carolina by one apiece. When the convention considered on the penultimate
day of its proceedings whether to increase by one the size of North Carolina's
delegation in the first House, all five southern states voted in favor, only to be
defeated by the solid bloc of six northern delegations still in attendance.[21]

Delegates pursued their states' interests with hardball tactics. Representatives of small states and slave states threatened to walk out of the convention if they could not secure concessions on the issues they deemed most
important. Their opponents on these issues made similar—if somewhat less
credible—threats.[22]

To be sure, a few issues do not appear to have implicated particularistic
concerns in the way that others did. For example, how worried an individual
delegate was about executive tyranny does not appear to have been correlated
with his state or region. In addition, Madison sometimes appeared to be an
exception to the rule of delegates' pursuing the specific interests of their states.
On certain important issues, his votes differed from those of both the other
Virginia delegates and the other southern delegations. Thus, Madison was
one of the only southern delegates to vote against the proposed constitutional
provisions to ban export taxes and to require a supermajority in Congress for
the enactment of navigation laws. On these votes, Madison proclaimed that
he was taking "national and permanent" views instead of parochial and shortsighted ones.[23]

Yet, on closer scrutiny, both of these exceptions—the delegates' concerns
about executive power and Madison's unorthodox voting pattern—are more
apparent than real. Although the delegates' abstract concerns about executive
usurpation of power do not appear to have been correlated with their state or
region, their willingness to repose particular powers in the presidency—such
as those over appointments and treaty making—often reflected how their
states had fared in the Connecticut Compromise. Moreover, debates over how
to select the executive very much reflected the conflicts—between small and
large states, and between slave states and mostly free states—that dominated
much of the convention's proceedings.[24]

Similarly, the apparent exceptionalism of Madison's voting pattern reveals not an imperviousness to interest but rather a broader field of vision in

assessing the relevant interests. For example, Madison believed that the higher costs that southern agricultural producers were likely to bear as a result of a northern-dominated Congress's probable use of the commerce power to provide a legal monopoly to northern shippers was a fair exchange for the greater security that a more vulnerable South would enjoy within a stronger union. On other issues, moreover—such as how to allocate the powers of appointment and treaty making after the Connecticut Compromise—Madison's votes reflected more consistently his status as a delegate from a large southern state.[25]

Although positions that were driven by interest were often dressed up as if they were about political principle, this did not make them any less interest-driven. Gunning Bedford of Delaware was right to express skepticism when large-state delegates insisted, in his words, upon "the purity of their principles and the rectitude of their intentions" while defending population-based apportionment of both houses of the national legislature.[26]

Yet Bedford failed to turn an equally skeptical eye upon the rationalizations of his small-state colleagues. They, too, argued from principle in defending equal state representation in the Senate. For example, they insisted that small states required protection against large states' coordinating with one another to dominate them in Congress. In reality, though, the small-state delegates were mostly just seeking to secure for their states as much power as possible within the new federal government. In debating how to apportion representation in Congress, the delegates spent weeks discussing the nature of sovereignty, theories of representation, and which groups deserved political protection against majoritarian domination. Yet in the end, no minds were changed; the small-state delegates won the battle simply because they drove a harder bargain.[27]

Similarly, delegates conducted a philosophical debate over whether ratification of the Constitution by special state conventions—rather than legislatures—would confer greater legitimacy upon it. In fact, however, delegates ultimately chose the convention route mostly to maximize the chances of the Constitution's being ratified.[28]

Likewise, Madison's theory of the large republic—that better government decision-making would occur over a larger geographic area, both because a greater multiplicity of interests would exist and because representatives would have greater opportunities to "refine and enlarge" their constituents' views through a system of indirect elections, large constituencies, and lengthy terms in office—was in fact mainly inspired by his wish to design a system that would suppress paper money emissions and debtor relief laws. Madison essentially admitted as much during one very candid moment at the convention, when he noted that the fundamental challenge facing a republican form of government was figuring out how to prevent power "slid[ing] into the hands" of those who "sigh for a more equal distribution of [property]."[29]

To an astonishing degree, the drafting and ratification of the Constitution were shaped by conflicts of interest that derived from fairly transient episodes and disputes. While such conflicts would quickly recede in significance, the Constitution they shaped has lasted for centuries.

The controversy over Jay's willingness to bargain away the American claim to free navigation of the Mississippi River profoundly influenced southerners' thinking on issues as diverse as the value of the union, how to apportion representation in Congress, and the limits that should be placed on the national government's powers over commerce and treaty making. Yet the issue itself was largely a moot point by the time the ratification process had concluded. Opposition to British creditors' collecting on their prewar debts—another fairly transient issue—rendered the federal court system, in the words of Edmund Randolph, "the most vulnerable and odious part of the Constitution" to Virginians. New York's ability to extract tax revenue from neighboring states through import duties—not a transient issue but an intensely particularistic one—had an enormous effect both on the ways in which delegates to the Philadelphia convention from New Jersey and Connecticut thought about expanding congressional power over taxes and trade and on the posture of those states toward ratification of the Constitution.[30]

The rebellion of taxpayers and debtors led by Daniel Shays and others in Massachusetts in 1786–87 profoundly influenced the Philadelphia convention and the Constitution. The insurrection generated vital support in Massachusetts for sending a delegation to the convention, and it may have determined Washington's decision to participate. Still more important, Shays's Rebellion influenced the views of many convention delegates on how powerful and responsive to populist influence the new federal government should be. In his conversations with New England congressional delegates on the eve of the convention, William Grayson of Virginia had been shocked to discover the extent of their support "for a very strong government" and their "wish to prostrate all the state legislature[s] and form a general system out of the whole." Mason, too, was astonished when he arrived in Philadelphia at the "extraordinary" extent to which the New Englanders had become antirepublican. At the convention itself, delegates constantly alluded to Shays's Rebellion. Gerry was referring to it when he declared that the people of New England had "the wildest ideas of government in the world," and so was Hamilton when he noted "the amazing violence and turbulence of the democratic spirit."[31]

Had a constitutional convention taken place in the year before Shays's Rebellion rather than the year after, it probably would have produced a very different constitution. In the spring of 1786, before the rebellion, Grayson had told Madison that New Englanders were interested only in giving Congress power to regulate commerce and would not even agree that "Congress should have the power to prevent states from cheating one another as well [as] their own citizens by means of paper money." Two years later, while opposing ratification of the Constitution, Grayson made a similar point, ruefully reflecting that prior to Shays's Rebellion, it was only Virginians who had supported fundamental reform of the federal system, while New Englanders had been "well aware of the dangers" of revolutionary changes in government. Indeed, at the Massachusetts ratifying convention, it was clear, as one Antifederalist delegate put it, that "many men who, within a few years past, were strenuous opposers of an augmentation of the power of Congress are now the warmest advocates of power so large as not to admit of a comparison with those which they opposed."[32]

Rhode Island's monetary radicalism also played a significant role in giving paper money a bad name, mobilizing the nation's economic elite in opposition, and thus paving the way for the Constitution. According to the Federalist "Landholder," by allowing "public injustice [to] be exhibited in its greatest degree and most extreme effects," Rhode Island's "apostasy from all the principles of good and just government" had "silence[d] such opposition as might be made" to constitutional reform at the national level. Even Melancton Smith, who criticized Article I, Section 10, at the New York ratifying convention, would not defend his neighboring state's policies: "[A]s for Rhode Island, I do not mean to justify her; she deserves to be condemned. If there were in the world but one example of political depravity, it would be hers. And no nation ever merited or suffered a more genuine infamy than a wicked administration has attached to her character." During the ratifying contest, one Pennsylvania Federalist observed that Rhode Island's initial rejection of the Constitution in a referendum would "amount to a greater proof of its excellence" than "the best reasons yet given by the wisest politicians in favor of [it]," and he predicted that "[m]any worthy men in the different states hitherto opposed to the federal government will now attach themselves to it" to avoid the shame of being associated "with men who for years have been a disgrace to human nature by their fraudulent proceedings."[33]

Trying to explain to a friend in London why the Constitution was "less democratic than might be expected from a people who are so fond of liberty," a Unitarian minister from Boston noted that among the various causes that had "conspired to render republican sentiments unfashionable" were a recent "insurrection in the state of Massachusetts and the corrupt proceedings of the legislature of Rhode Island." Similarly, while the Philadelphia convention was assembled, a prominent Boston merchant, Samuel Breck, told Secretary at War Henry Knox that Rhode Island's "villainous conduct," together with

Shays's Rebellion, demonstrated "the necessity of parting with a greater share of our privileges . . . than we have been willing to do at any former time."[34]

It is hard to overstate the extent to which the state crises over tax and debt relief in the 1780s influenced the agenda of the Philadelphia convention.* The Framers overwhelmingly saw relief legislation as craven capitulations by overly responsive state legislatures to the illegitimate demands of lazy and dissolute farmers. Such legislation was "wicked and fraudulent"; it "corrupted the morals of the people"; and it "destroyed both public and private credit."[35]

Yet, in fact, the relief seekers had valid arguments in support of the policies for which they advocated. In a time of severe economic distress, they were being forced to pay heavy and regressive taxes in scarce hard currency to pay off government securities that had been scooped up (sometimes from them) at a fraction of par value by speculators who now stood to make a financial killing. Relief measures had been necessary, according to one North Carolina Antifederalist, "to save vast numbers of people from ruin." That perspective was one for which neither the delegates at the Philadelphia convention nor the more elite Antifederalist leaders in state ratifying contests had much sympathy. Among the clearest losers in the interest-group conflicts surrounding the adoption of the Constitution were advocates for a loosening of monetary and fiscal policies in times of economic crisis.[36]

The Constitution was designed, in part, to suppress such relief legislation. Article I, Section 10, expressly forbade states from issuing paper currency or impairing the obligation of contracts (i.e., enacting debtor relief laws). The Constitution also empowered Congress to suppress domestic insurrections— a provision that was implicitly addressed, at least in part, to revolts by taxpayers and debtors, such as the recent one in Massachusetts.[37]

Hostility Toward Democracy

Because the Framers blamed relief legislation on "democratic licentiousness," they designed the federal government to be insulated from the populist politics that had produced such measures in the states. Thus, they opted for huge districts for congressional representatives, and indirect elections and lengthy terms in office for both senators and presidents. They also rejected, for federal legislators, instruction, mandatory rotation, and recall. In addition, they created a powerful executive armed with a veto power that could be used to block

---

* To the extent these crises were simply a function of a war-devastated economy, as Antifederalists sometimes insisted, the Framers' most fundamental choices on questions of constitutional design were influenced by transitory conditions.

any populist economic measures that might somehow sneak through a legislature designed to squelch them. To the extent that the Framers were thinking
about judicial review at all, they mostly conceived of it as another potential
check on such relief legislation.[38]

Indeed, most of the delegates to the Philadelphia convention would have
preferred a constitution that shielded the federal government even more
from populist pressures. Yet their choices were constrained by the role
that popularly elected state ratifying conventions would play in deciding
whether to approve the Constitution. To the limited extent that the Framers
cared about public opinion, it was mainly because of this constraining influence of the ratifying process. It is this consideration that possibly explains
their rejection of Madison's proposal for a national veto on state legislation,
which was replaced with explicit constraints on state relief measures to be
enforced by judges under the Supremacy Clause. The delegates, also for this
reason, agreed on significantly shorter terms in office for congressmen, senators, and presidents than most of them would have liked. Likewise, even
though most of the Framers favored property qualifications for voting and
officeholding, they did not impose any in the Constitution, partly because
they understood that doing so would jeopardize ratification in states that
had already reduced such property qualifications more than the Framers
were inclined to do.[39]

The Antifederalists were not off base when they charged the Framers with
seeking to establish an aristocracy of sorts. The Federalists' response—that
the Constitution prohibited titles of nobility and that "no privileges are conferred on the rich or the few"—was disingenuous. In fact, the Federalists had
little confidence in the ability of ordinary people to participate in government
decision-making. The people, in the Federalists' view, had "little sense," and
"intricate questions" of governance "certainly surpass the judgment of the
greater part of [them]." Most of the Framers wanted the federal government
to be administered by the "better sort" of people—the well-educated and well-
born elite, which had ceased to dominate politics at the state level in the 1780s.
Behind the closed doors of the Philadelphia convention, the delegates were
often quite candid about that objective. For example, the Senate was expressly
designed to be "the aristocratic part of our government," to "represent the
wealth of the country," and to bear "as strong a likeness to the British House
of Lords as possible." Allowing the people to directly choose the president,
Mason told the convention, would be like referring "a trial of colors to a blind
man."[40]

Of course, during the ratifying contest, the Federalists could not defend the
Constitution in such terms. The trend toward democracy in American politics
had been too strong, and it was the people who would select the delegates to

the state ratifying conventions that would, in turn, pronounce judgment upon the Constitution.[41]

So instead of defending the Constitution in openly aristocratic terms, the Federalists invoked popular sovereignty as a cure-all for every manner of alleged flaw. In response to Antifederalist charges of "consolidation," Federalists argued that all power derived from the people, and it was "of little moment" to the people whether that portion of power "which they must for their own happiness lodge in their rulers" was reposed in the state government or the federal one. When Antifederalists criticized the Constitution for compromising state sovereignty, Federalists responded that only the people had ever exercised sovereign power.[42]

To those who charged that the Constitution was illegal because it had been devised through a process not countenanced by the Articles of Confederation, the Federalists argued popular sovereignty: The people were "the most certain means of obviating all disputes and doubts concerning the legitimacy of the new Constitution," Rufus King told the Philadelphia convention. To those who worried that the Constitution had the effect of altering state constitutions—for example, by limiting the ability of state legislatures to enact debtor relief legislation—without complying with the methods specified by those charters for their own amendment, the Framers again invoked popular sovereignty. As Madison explained, "The people were in fact the fountain of all power and by resorting to them, all difficulties were got over. They could alter constitutions as they pleased." The power of the people, James Wilson told the Pennsylvania ratifying convention, was "supreme, absolute, and uncontrollable." They "may change the constitutions whenever and however they please."[43]

Yet despite the Framers' regular professions of devotion to popular sovereignty, their deep distrust of the people was evident, as we have seen, in nearly every substantive choice made in the Constitution that bore on the new federal government's susceptibility to popular influence. As Madison pointed out, one of the beauties of popular sovereignty was that it did not mandate any particular political arrangement, so long as the people endorsed the overall system. Even lifetime tenure for unelected government officeholders such as federal judges was consistent with republicanism, Madison argued, so long as the government's powers derived "directly or indirectly from the great body of the people." Criticizing that perspective a generation later, Jefferson explained that political thought regarding republican government was still in its "infancy" at the time of the Founding, and "we imagined everything republican which was not monarchy." The Founders had yet, according to Jefferson, to penetrate "to the mother principle" that governments are "republican only in proportion as they embody the will of their people and execute it."[44]

The Framers even argued that ostensibly undemocratic practices were justified in the name of preserving republican government. The relief legislation produced by the populist politics of the 1780s had begun to sour many political leaders on popular participation in government, and some even questioned whether any form of government short of monarchy or aristocracy could adequately defend property and preserve public order. Alluding to such concerns at the Philadelphia convention, Madison defended lengthy terms in office for congressional representatives on the grounds that "if our amendments should fail of securing their [the people's] happiness, they will despair it can be done in this way [i.e., through republican government] and incline to monarchy." Populist influence on government, according to Madison, had to be sacrificed in the name of republicanism![45]

Finally, during the ratifying contest, the Federalists disingenuously offered justifications for the Constitution's most aristocratic features that differed from the arguments they had made in Philadelphia for including those provisions in the Constitution in the first place. Thus, for example, in ratifying debates, Federalists justified long terms in office for senators as conducive to developing the foreign policy expertise necessary to properly advise presidents on treaty making, not—as delegates to the Philadelphia convention had argued—as essential to blocking paper money legislation or defending "the wealth of the nation." Similarly, at the Philadelphia convention, the Framers had justified departing from annual elections for the House as necessary to insulate it from popular passions, whereas in the ratifying contest, they tended to argue instead that the enormous geographic scope of the nation necessitated a longer term in office for congressional representatives.[46]

Ratification as Ordinary Politics

The ratifying contest posed a quandary for the Federalists. Just as the Philadelphia convention was getting underway, Grayson had told James Monroe that "[t]he people of America don't appear to me to be ripe for any great innovations" that would require them "to pay money or part with power." During the convention, Gerry had warned that those delegates supporting "a plan of vigorous government" were "pushing the experiment too far" and that others "of a more democratic cast will oppose it with equal determination." How could the Federalists possibly convince the people to approve through a reasonably democratic ratifying process a constitution that went so far toward constraining democracy?[47]

The ratifying campaign revealed the Federalists to be shrewd tacticians, but they also benefited from some luck, and from circumstances they played no role in creating. The press was overwhelmingly Federalist, and many newspapers declined to present the Antifederalist side of the debate. Most ratifying conventions were held in eastern cities, where the vast majority of the population—across class lines—approved of the Constitution. Antifederalists had a harder time organizing their supporters, who disproportionately lived in western districts and in backwoods regions that were relatively isolated from commercial networks. The South Carolina ratifying convention was so badly malapportioned in favor of Federalist districts that it approved the Constitution by a margin of two to one even though a majority of the state's residents almost certainly opposed ratification. In most states, the political and economic elite—the sort of people who could make eloquent speeches at ratifying conventions and perhaps influence swing delegates—strongly supported ratification. Antifederalists in New York and Virginia made a serious tactical blunder by scheduling their states' ratifying conventions so late in the process that they became mostly irrelevant to the larger outcome. Had those states instead held their conventions earlier, they might well have rejected the Constitution or insisted upon amendments prior to ratification, which would have disrupted the momentum behind unconditional ratification and possibly influenced other states deciding after them.[48]

On top of such built-in advantages and miscalculations by their adversaries, the Federalists made some of their own luck. Had the delegates to the Philadelphia convention not trimmed the sails on their nationalizing and democracy-constraining enterprise, the constitution they drafted might have proved impossible to ratify. Thus, for example, awarding the selection of senators to state legislatures—instead of to the House of Representatives, as proposed in the Virginia Plan—might have been critical to the willingness of state legislatures even to call ratifying conventions. Reducing the minimum population of House districts on the last day of the convention was another tactical concession made by the Framers to enhance the prospects of ratification.[49]

The Framers made choices at the convention that appeased not only state legislatures but also various interest groups that might otherwise have opposed ratification. When Mason proposed that the Constitution forbid the seat of the national government from being in a city that was also its state's capital—in order to prevent jurisdictional squabbles—Gouverneur Morris shrewdly observed that, while this might be a good idea in principle, it would needlessly convert the residents of New York City and Philadelphia into enemies of the Constitution, because they hoped that their cities would become the nation's capital. Mason then withdrew his motion. Likewise, the Framers may have omitted a provision guaranteeing the federal government's assumption of the states' war debt to avoid—as Hamilton recalled—"multiplying obstacles to its [i.e., the Constitution's] reception on collateral details." A proposal made late in the convention by Madison to empower Congress to charter corporations in certain circumstances was withdrawn after it was pointed out that such a provision would mobilize state banking interests—which would not wish to endure competition from a federally chartered bank—in opposition to the Constitution.[50]

The Framers' most important tactical choice for enhancing the prospects of ratification was probably Article VII, which provided that ratification by nine states would suffice to put the Constitution into operation, even though those states could bind only themselves. The upshot of this ground rule was to put enormous pressure to ratify on those states' manifesting the greatest resistance to the Constitution, which tended to decide last. Whereas the unanimity requirement for approving amendments under the Articles had awarded tremendous bargaining power to prospective holdouts, under Article VII of the Constitution, such states risked being excluded from a union that was already in operation, denied federal military protection, and subjected to trade discrimination. Had it not been for this feature of the Constitution, Virginia and New York would very likely have refused to ratify without antecedent amendments.[51]

Despite all their advantages and shrewd tactical decisions, Federalists probably could not have won the battle over ratification had a great many Americans not agreed with Randolph's assessment that the Articles of Confederation had "proved totally inadequate to the purpose for which it was devised" and had become a "political farce" that needed to be drastically revised or replaced. Capitalizing upon widespread dissatisfaction with the status quo, Federalists insisted upon presenting the country with a stark choice between the admittedly flawed Articles, which they said put the nation at risk of descending into anarchy, and the vastly different Constitution—which, though concededly imperfect, contained many features that represented a significant improvement over the Articles in most people's eyes. Moreover, the Federalists made the plausible argument that rectifying flaws in the Constitution through subsequent amendments would be easier than starting again from scratch to amend the Articles. Thus, at the Virginia ratifying convention, Madison challenged Patrick Henry: "Would the honorable gentleman agree to continue the most radical defects in the old system, because the petty state of Rhode Island would not agree to remove them?"[52]

That many Americans preferred the Constitution, which they considered flawed but susceptible to amendment, to the Articles of Confederation, which had been revealed to be both obviously deficient and practically impossible to amend, does not mean that they would not have preferred an intermediate option had one been available to them. For example, many Americans who agreed that Congress should have an independent revenue-raising authority would have preferred that certain limits be imposed on its ability to levy direct taxes. Similarly, many Americans who were willing to grant Congress the power to raise armies would have liked limits to be imposed on its ability to do so during peacetime. Further, many Americans would have preferred that the more powerful national government designed by the delegates to the Philadelphia convention not be so insulated from popular political influence. Yet the Federalists resolutely and successfully sought to deny Americans any intermediate options—that is, points along the spectrum between the flawed Articles and the vastly more nationalist and democracy-constraining Constitution.[53]

The Federalists' shrewd strategizing illustrates how the ratifying contest was a political campaign not very different from ordinary politics, much more than it was an abstract debate between proponents of competing political philosophies. Both sides in the contest pursued any political advantage they could find. If one party believed it had the votes to win at a ratifying convention, it favored a quick up-or-down vote with minimal deliberation. If that same side made a different calculation in another state, then there it favored an extended paragraph-by-paragraph consideration of the Constitution. If one party thought it might lose a convention vote, then it favored an adjournment to preserve its chances of winning at a later date. But if in a different state, that same side believed it had the votes to win, then there it staunchly opposed an adjournment. Federalists denied that state ratifying conventions had the power to propose amendments to the Constitution—until they discovered at the Massachusetts convention that recommending amendments was the only way to secure ratification. Then, they defended the convention's power—as "the fullest representation of the people ever known"—to propose amendments.[54]

The ratifying contest was not just a political campaign but one characterized by bare-knuckle tactics. In the Pennsylvania Assembly, Federalists forcibly rounded up two of their opponents to achieve the quorum necessary to call a ratifying convention. Federalist newspapers in Pennsylvania distorted their accounts of that state's ratifying convention debates to make it appear as if nobody had criticized the Constitution. Federalist promises of future political support may have influenced Governor John Hancock's critical decision at the Massachusetts ratifying convention to endorse the Constitution with recommended amendments. Governor Edmund Randolph, who had decided to support unconditional ratification of the Constitution, chose not to show the Virginia convention a letter from New York governor George Clinton proposing that the two states coordinate efforts to make antecedent amendments a condition of ratification. In both Rhode Island and New York, residents of cities that strongly backed the Constitution threatened to secede if their states did not ratify it. A Federalist-controlled Congress eventually threatened Rhode Island with trade sanctions unless it approved the Constitution.[55]

Of course, Antifederalists were not above using similarly aggressive tactics when they had the opportunity to do so. When New York Antifederalists anthologized Randolph's objections to ratification without antecedent amendments, they excised the penultimate paragraph in which he declared that he would prefer an unamended Constitution to dissolution of the union. When Antifederalists had Mason's objections to the Constitution published in Massachusetts, they similarly omitted a paragraph in which he criticized the Constitution for allowing Congress to enact commercial legislation by a simple majority vote (an objection that would not have benefited the Antifederalist cause in northern states). In Virginia, Patrick Henry went to extraordinary lengths—including gerrymandering a congressional district and enacting a (probably unconstitutional) district residency requirement for congressional candidates—to keep Madison out of the first Congress, where Henry (rightly) suspected he would obstruct efforts to secure meaningful constitutional amendments.[56]

The ratifying contest resembled ordinary politics not just in the tactics that were used but also in the sorts of arguments that were made. Both sides disparaged the motives of their opponents, attacked their characters, and appealed to the interests of voters and ratifying convention delegates.

Thus, for example, the Federalist "Landholder" derided opponents of the Constitution as "[d]ebtors in desperate circumstances, who have not resolution to be either honest or industrious." A Federalist lawyer in Philadelphia declared that opponents of ratification consisted of "a few interested placemen whose offices and profits will diminish whenever the federal government takes place." Massachusetts Federalist Christopher Gore observed that "[i]ntegrity, abilities and patriotism seem to declare for adopting the Constitution, while vice and poverty, with few exceptions, mark the opposition."[57]

On the other side of the debate, Connecticut Antifederalist Benjamin Gale charged that Federalists' complaints about the weakness of the Confederation Congress were "only a specious pretense to cover the artful schemes of designing men" to secure redemption at face value of federal securities they had purchased at a fraction of par. New York Antifederalists charged that "the rich and wellborn" were "indefatigable" in their efforts to promote ratification because "they and their friends and connections expect to possess some of the many lucrative offices under the new government." Both sides took umbrage at their opponents' constantly questioning their motives.[58]

Federalists and Antifederalists alike appealed to the material interests of voters and convention delegates. For example, Federalists frequently promised farmers—which is what the vast majority of Americans were at the time—that demand for their produce would grow and the value of their land would increase as Congress used its newly granted power over commerce to pry open foreign markets by threatening retaliatory trade restrictions. Federalists also told urban tradesmen and laborers involved in shipping that the "almost annihilated trade" of their towns would be "revived, invigorated, and expanded to all quarters of the earth," as Congress used its power over commerce to secure northern states their fair share of the international carrying trade.[59]

In several states, Federalists urged that ratification of the Constitution, by producing a more powerful national government, would supply the military protection necessary to secure those states' particularistic interests. Thus, Virginia Federalists tried to convince ratifying convention delegates from the Kentucky district that the navigation rights of Americans on the Mississippi River would be better secured under the Constitution than the Articles because the new national government could more credibly threaten war with Spain. The Federalist "Landholder" appealed to citizens of New Hampshire to ratify the Constitution to protect themselves from the British in Canada, who wish "nothing more than your submission to [their] laws" and whose "force may easily be pointed through your whole territory." Chancellor Robert R. Livingston told the Poughkeepsie convention that New York, which had been a major theater of the last American war and (he said) probably would be in the next as well, had a special interest in ratifying the Constitution because only a powerful national government could extract the tax revenue necessary to successfully fight a war. Desperate for the assistance of a national military force in its violent conflict with Indian tribes, Georgia sought to persuade other states to approve the Constitution by promising to cede to Congress thirty million acres of western lands it claimed, on the condition that the Constitution be ratified.[60]

Antifederalists made the same sort of appeals to material interests. For example, in Virginia, they warned Kentuckians that the northern-dominated Congress likely to result from the Constitution would abandon American claims to navigation rights on the Mississippi River. They also predicted that federal courts would force Virginia debtors to pay their prewar debts to British creditors, and that Virginia planters would have to pay exorbitant freight rates to northern shippers once Congress had used the commerce power to grant those shippers a monopoly over the nation's carrying trade. In Massachusetts, the Antifederalist "Agrippa" warned holders of state certificates that Congress's vastly expanded taxing power under the Constitution would leave the state with "no adequate fund" to pay them.[61]

Perhaps the most frequent appeals to interest, made by both sides, had to do with taxes. Federalists promised farmers that their taxes would decline under the Constitution because the new federal government would raise most of its revenue from the impost and the sale of western lands, and states would no longer have to pay congressional requisitions, which would enable them to reduce or eliminate regressive land and head taxes. In Virginia, Madison argued that the Constitution's requirement that direct taxes be apportioned according to population, with only three-fifths of the slaves being counted, would be "an insuperable bar against" oppressive taxation of southern slave owners. Federalist James Iredell told North Carolinians that their taxes would decline under the Constitution because import duties would go into the federal treasury rather than into the coffers of states blessed with better ports.[62]

Conversely, Antifederalists warned that under the Constitution, "the people will bleed with taxes at every pore" because of the "enormous and extravagant expenses . . . of this great and consolidated government." A distant and remotely accountable federal government not only would impose higher taxes but also would be more severe in exacting them than more politically accountable state governments had been in the 1780s. Pennsylvania Antifederalists warned that tax collectors would "swarm over the land, devouring the hard earnings of the industrious, like the locusts of old." At the Richmond convention, Patrick Henry and George Mason warned that Virginians would be "taxed for centuries" by a northern-dominated Congress, which would be compelled by the Constitution's ban on ex post facto legislation to pay off in gold and silver "rapacious speculators" from "a few particular states"—mostly in New England—who had "collected and barrelled up" nearly worthless continental currency that had been trading at "a thousand to one." In Poughkeepsie, Governor George Clinton warned that New Yorkers would have to pay higher state taxes if the Constitution were ratified because the state could no longer derive revenue from import duties, the incidence of which was partly borne by consumers in neighboring states. At the Founding—as during the Revolution and most of subsequent American history—much of the political debate turned on which side could be better trusted to reduce taxes for most Americans.[63]

Although it is impossible to know for sure why ratifying convention delegates voted as they did on the Constitution, it certainly appears as if calculations of material interest were a vitally important factor. Small states ratified quickly—three of them unanimously—in significant part, no doubt, because they had secured such a good deal in the Senate's apportionment. Delegates to ratifying conventions in several mid-Atlantic states apparently calculated that quick ratification would enhance the prospects of their states becoming home to the nation's capital, which promised significant economic benefits. In deciding how to vote on ratification, delegates from western regions of southern states seem to have balanced whether securing federal military protection against Indian tribes, which could enhance the value of their land (and their lives), outweighed concerns that the Constitution would foster aristocracy, forbid states from issuing paper money and enacting debtor relief legislation, and possibly jeopardize their claims to navigation rights on the Mississippi River. More southerners than northerners opposed ratification, probably because they feared that northern domination of both houses of Congress—at least in the short term—would lead to the imposition of commercial regulations that would advantage northern shippers and manufacturers at the expense of southern planters. Deep divisions in a state ratifying convention such as Virginia's signified disparate calculations as to where the state's interests lay, not an absence of interest-based thinking.[64]

Excluding Intermediate Alternatives

Federalists had initially rejected the idea of any amendments at all to the handiwork of the Philadelphia convention, but Antifederalists commanded sufficient strength at the Massachusetts ratifying convention that they were able to extract an important concession: In exchange for unconditional ratification, Federalists promised to recommend amendments for Congress's consideration after the Constitution had become operational. In the ratifying conventions that followed, much of the contest was over whether proposed amendments should be simply recommendatory or an antecedent condition of ratification.[65]

The Antifederalists made a strong case for conditional ratification, arguing that their opponents would have little incentive to deliver on their promises to support amendments once the Constitution had been unconditionally ratified. For their part, Federalists were adamant that ratification be unconditional. Although the Federalists made legal and policy arguments against conditional ratification, their real concern may have been that the amendments most sought by the Antifederalists would weaken the national government or render it more susceptible to populist influence.[66]

Federalists were especially determined to resist Antifederalist calls for a second constitutional convention. Again, they offered legal and policy arguments in support of their position. Yet the Federalists' real concern was probably that they knew they could never reproduce at a second convention what they had accomplished at the first.[67]

The lack of transparency in the process leading to the drafting of the Constitution had enabled the Framers to devise a system of government very different from the one that most Americans would have expected or desired from the Philadelphia convention. Most people probably anticipated that the convention would propose adding a few grants of power to Congress's arsenal—principally, the authority to raise revenue independently of state requisitions and to regulate commerce. They had no reason to expect that the convention would create a true national government (empowered to act directly upon individual citizens), insulate it from populist influence, and impose direct constraints on the state governments. As the New York Antifederalist "Plebeian" observed, "Previous to the meeting of the convention, the subject of a new form of government had been little thought of and scarcely written upon at all." While Americans expected the Philadelphia convention to propose changes to the Articles, "Plebeian" wrote, "it never was in the contemplation of one in a thousand of those who had reflected on the matter, to have an entire change in the nature of our federal government—to alter it from a confederation of states, to that of one entire government, which will swallow up that of the individual states." Yet the convention delegates had taken Randolph's advice not to "leave anything that seemed necessary undone," as "[t]he present moment is favorable and is probably the last that will offer."[68]

Because it would have been difficult to predict the tack taken in Philadelphia—the convention's agenda, it turned out, existed only in Madison's head—and because the Articles' unanimity requirement for amendments seemed to provide security against radical reform efforts, populists and those committed to preserving state sovereignty had not mobilized to oppose the convention or to participate in it. The secrecy of the convention's proceedings further delayed any efforts to organize in opposition to what was transpiring in Philadelphia. In addition, several of the relatively small number of convention delegates who resisted the nationalizing and democracy-constraining efforts of the majority made the dubious tactical choice to leave the convention early, so as not to legitimize its handiwork.[69]

By contrast, if a second convention were held, everyone would immediately understand the stakes. Antifederalists would aggressively contest the selection of delegates, bind them with instructions, and ensure that they remained present until the convention's bitter end. In addition, given that Antifederalists had a harder time mobilizing their forces to begin with, a second convention would play to their advantage because it would be an extension of the initial struggle over ratification, in which Antifederalists had demonstrated greater strength over time.

The Federalists triumphed on the issues of both conditional ratification and a second convention. Thus, they managed to avoid offering the American people the option that most of them probably would have favored: ratification of the Constitution together with amendments to significantly limit the power of the new national government and to alter its structure to permit greater populist influence. The Federalists' professed commitment to popular sovereignty did not extend so far as to permit the people to suggest amendments to the

Constitution before approving it. Most Federalists agreed with Madison that "the capacities of the bulk of mankind are unequal" to the task of informed and intelligent debate on the Constitution.[70]*

Just as the Constitution represented a significant substantive departure from the more democratic norms of governance that prevailed in the states at the time, so did the *process* of ratification depart from existing norms— especially in New England—of how important governance decisions were to be made. The Revolutionary War had made ordinary Americans more confident in their ability to govern themselves. New England town meetings were accustomed to exerting direct influence over government decisions such as declaring independence from Great Britain, levying taxes, and—beginning in the late 1770s—ratifying state constitutions. Indeed, when in 1780, a Massachusetts convention submitted a draft state constitution to the towns for ratification, it had declared, "It is your interest to revise it with the greatest care and circumspection, and it is your undoubted right, either to propose such alterations and amendments as you shall judge proper, or to give it your own sanction in its present form, or totally to reject it."[71]

By contrast, in 1787–88, Federalist leaders—recognizing that the more participatory the ratifying process was, the lower their chances of success— sought to minimize direct popular influence on the decision over ratification. They favored state conventions over referenda or decisions by town meetings, opposed the instruction of delegates to ratifying conventions, resisted the adjournment of conventions for the purpose of consulting constituents, and opposed efforts to alter the Constitution they had drafted by conditioning ratification upon prior amendments. Only a ratifying process that was less participatory than the governance norms employed in many states could have secured endorsement of a constitution that was less democratic in its substance than were all state constitutions of the era.[72]

In sum, what most Federalists wanted was not a genuine national debate on the merits of the Constitution but simply its ratification. During the ratifying contest, they generally sought to preempt debate, recognizing that the longer the process lasted and the more people learned about the Constitution, the worse were their chances of winning. In the early stages of the ratifying contest especially, they pushed for conventions to be held quickly. At those conventions, they generally opposed paragraph-by-paragraph consideration of the Constitution and urged quick up-or-down votes, seeking to foreclose all

---

* By contrast, Randolph told Madison that even though he feared that "the Constitution may be enervated" by a second convention—specifically, Congress's power over direct taxation "may be too much weakened"—if such was "the will of America," he did not believe it should be thwarted.

discussion of possible amendments. Outside of conventions, they sought to stifle open and robust debate on the Constitution by threatening to withhold their subscriptions and advertising from newspapers that dared to publish the Antifederalist side of the argument.[73]

Once having secured ratification of the Constitution, the Federalists—largely through the efforts of Madison—were able to devise amendments that alleviated some of their adversaries' concerns while protecting the Constitution from any significant structural changes. Most Antifederalists had wanted amendments to limit congressional power and to alter the structure of the federal government to render it more susceptible to populist and state influence. Madison channeled those demands into a bill of rights that mainly consisted of individual-rights guarantees that neither Federalists nor Antifederalists deemed of any great significance. Madison and his allies ensured that Congress never seriously considered the sort of amendments that would have materially altered the work product of the Philadelphia convention.[74]

The Decline of Legitimacy Objections

As we have seen, Antifederalists could and did raise legitimacy objections to the process that produced the Constitution. Yet such criticism quickly dissipated, as most freemen seemed to rally around the Constitution after its ratification. In New York, where Antifederalists had largely controlled state politics before ratification, voters in 1789 elected Federalists to four of the state's six House seats, and the legislature selected Federalists as the state's first two US senators.[75]

Similarly in Virginia, Antifederalists had constituted nearly half of the delegates to the state's ratifying convention in June 1788, and political observers had predicted that the legislature's gerrymandering of congressional districts would favor Antifederalists in the elections for the first House. Yet voters returned seven or eight Federalists—depending on how one of the representatives was counted—for the state's ten congressional seats. In the spring of 1789, Edward Carrington reported to Madison that even Antifederal districts in Virginia had "become perfectly calm."[76]

Indeed, as we have seen, Federalists dominated both the House and the Senate in the first federal Congress. Virginia's Antifederalist senator Grayson reported to Patrick Henry not only that both houses were "almost wholly composed of Federalists" but also that even the few Antifederalists in Congress were "so extremely lukewarm as scarcely to deserve the appellation."[77]

Opposition to the Constitution had also diminished in North Carolina, where a second convention easily ratified it in the fall of 1789. Around the same time, Washington reported, more generally, that opposition to the new national government "is either no more or hides its head," as that government had apparently been organized "to the satisfaction of all parties." In the spring of 1790, Thomas Jefferson similarly observed, "The opposition to our new constitution has almost totally disappeared."[78]

Given that perhaps as many as half of all Americans had opposed ratification in 1787–88, what could explain this rapid decline in opposition to the Constitution? As discussed in chapter 7, Congress's approval of the Bill of Rights in the summer of 1789—at Madison's behest—was probably a significant factor.[79]

The surging economy probably played a role as well. Early in 1790, Congressman Abraham Baldwin reported, "People say the times are good and praise the new government." To the extent that the Constitution inspired business confidence and facilitated trade by empowering Congress to regulate commerce, it may have played a role in legitimizing itself. Yet the Constitution was certainly not the sole cause of improving economic conditions. The American economy benefited greatly from European crop failures and from the nation's ability to maintain political neutrality in the European wars that began in the early 1790s and continued almost uninterrupted for the next quarter of a century. Trade with Europe boomed, which was good for American farmers, and much of that commerce was carried in American vessels, which was good for American shippers and shipbuilders.[80]

Whatever its cause, the booming economy helped Federalists deliver upon their promises to reduce the tax burden on struggling farmers. As much as 90 percent of federal tax revenue in the 1790s derived from import duties. Moreover, states were able to dramatically reduce direct taxes—by as much as 85 or 90 percent—once the federal government, under Hamilton's direction of the Treasury, assumed the vast majority of states' war-related debts. Substantial tax relief helped reconcile rural America to the Constitution.[81]

Yet lower taxes and a burgeoning economy were not the only reasons that attacks on the Constitution's legitimacy all but disappeared in the years following its ratification. In addition, and of critical significance, former Antifederalists quickly discovered that working within the new system would be at least as effective as attacking its legitimacy.[82]

Although the delegates to the Philadelphia convention had resolved many controversial issues, political disputes of the 1790s that raised questions of constitutional interpretation quickly revealed how many fundamental matters the Framers had left unresolved—either by choice or through failure to anticipate them. Most of the Framers probably agreed with Edmund Randolph, who noted in connection with his work on the convention's Committee of Detail that drafters of constitutions ought "to insert essential principles only, lest the operations of government should be clogged by rendering those provisions permanent and unalterable, which ought to be accommodated to times and events." Whatever the cause, however, the Constitution proved sufficiently open-ended that Antifederalists found they could effectively marshal it in support of their preferred policy positions, and thus had no reason to continue questioning its legitimacy.[83]

Thus, as two political parties began to take shape in the 1790s—largely as a result of conflicts over Secretary of the Treasury Hamilton's fiscal policies and the appropriate stance for the United States to adopt in the war between France and Great Britain—most Antifederalists became Jeffersonian Democratic-Republicans. (Ironically, that political party was jointly led by Madison, who had been Hamilton's staunchly nationalist colleague at the time of the Founding.) The Jeffersonians challenged the Federalists' broad interpretations of the federal government's powers. They denied the constitutionality of Hamilton's national bank, disputed his broad interpretation of the General Welfare Clause in the context of his proposal for Congress to subsidize American manufacturers, rejected the notion of a federal common law of crimes,* and denied the constitutionality of the Federalists' Alien and Sedition Acts of 1798.[†] None of these positions required the Jeffersonians to challenge the legitimacy of the Constitution. Rather, they argued that the best interpretation of the document was inconsistent with the Federalists' broad constructionism.[84]

Jefferson and his Virginia acolytes, Madison and Monroe, won all six of the presidential elections conducted from 1800 to 1820. Their political party

---

* The question here was whether federal law contemplated the existence of crimes beyond those defined by federal statute. For example, could one be prosecuted under federal law for seditious libel or for bribing a federal official in the absence of a federal statute specifically criminalizing such activity? Federalists, insisting that every sovereign government enjoyed the protection of a common law, argued in favor of a federal common law of crimes. Jeffersonians, emphasizing that the federal government was one of enumerated rather than inherent powers, argued strenuously against such a notion.

† In 1798, as the nation fought an undeclared naval war with France, Federalist majorities in Congress passed, and President John Adams signed, the Alien and Sedition Acts. The Alien Acts, of which there were three, extended the naturalization period for aliens from five to fourteen years and gave the president broad authority, without any judicial proceedings, to remove or incarcerate aliens—both alien friends and alien enemies. The Sedition Act, in turn, provided criminal punishment for those who made "false, scandalous, and malicious" statements against the US government with intent, among other things, to defame it, to bring it "into contempt or disrepute," or to incite "the hatred of the people of the United States" against it. Jeffersonians denied the constitutionality of both sets of laws. While the constitutionality of the Alien Acts was not litigated at the time, every constitutional challenge raised against the Sedition Act was rejected by the (all-Federalist) federal judiciary.

was committed to strict constructionism—denying, for example, that the federal government had the constitutional authority to build a national infrastructure of roads, bridges, and canals. Beginning in the 1820s, under the banner of the Jacksonian Democratic Party, the intellectual and political descendants of these Founding-era Virginians rallied opposition to Chief Justice John Marshall's latitudinarian interpretations of federal government power. Running on a platform that rejected the constitutionality of the national bank, national support for internal improvements, and congressional regulation of slavery in federal territories, the Jacksonian party dominated national politics for most of the remainder of the antebellum period. After Marshall and his Federalist colleagues on the bench began to die or retire in the late 1820s and the first half of the 1830s, Jacksonian Democrats also came to dominate the Supreme Court—the last branch of the federal government to submit to their control. In short, the Antifederalists' descendants did not need to challenge the legitimacy of the Constitution because, for much of the antebellum period, their political dominance enabled them to control its interpretation.[85]

How the Constitution Did and Did Not Adapt to Democracy

Because of various fortuities in its drafting, the Constitution could be adapted—without formal amendment—to the powerful democratic trends of the Jacksonian era (trends that ultimately decimated the political fortunes of the Federalists, who had been largely responsible for the drafting and ratification of the Constitution). For example, although nearly all the delegates to the Philadelphia convention had favored property qualifications for voting and officeholding, the Constitution does not impose any, largely because the great variability in property qualifications across states made a federal rule too difficult to devise. Instead, the Framers simply tied voter qualifications for elections to the House of Representatives (the only federal offices for which the people directly cast ballots under the original Constitution) to those prescribed in the states for elections to the more numerous branch of their legislatures. Because of that linkage, no federal constitutional amendment was necessary early in the nineteenth century to liberalize access to federal suffrage and officeholding. As Jacksonian Democrats embraced "universal" suffrage— for white men, at least—at the state level, they automatically did so at the federal level as well.[86]

The same dynamic operated with regard to at least part of the electoral college system for choosing presidents. Article II of the Constitution provides that state legislatures are to specify the manner in which presidential electors are chosen. The Framers probably contemplated that the predominant method of selection would be appointment by state legislatures rather than election by voters. Yet state legislators who had to earn the people's support at the polls found it difficult to resist popular demands for direct input into the selection of the president. Within a couple of decades of the Founding, most state legislatures had provided for direct popular election of presidential electors (although South Carolina would hold out against this trend until the Civil War). Had the Framers written Article II to mandate, rather than simply authorize, what most of them wanted and expected—that state legislatures themselves would select presidential electors—then a federal constitutional amendment would have been necessary to enable direct popular participation in the choice of the nation's chief executive.[87]

The manner in which state legislatures regulated elections for the US House of Representatives offers yet a third illustration of how choices made by the Framers to leave certain issues unresolved unintentionally enabled democratic forces to influence the Constitution's implementation without a formal amendment. Although the Constitution stipulates rules for how representation in the House is apportioned among the states and specifies a floor on the population of each House district, the choice among various methods of districting a state's House seats is left up to its legislature (subject to the exercise of Congress's revisionary authority). At the time of the Founding, Federalists strongly preferred at-large elections—that is, all of a state's congressional delegation being elected in a statewide contest—to single-member districts. This was both because they assumed that elections conducted over larger geographic areas would result in victories for "the characters most noted for wisdom and virtue" and because they favored looser connections between representatives and their constituents, which would enable elected officials "to refine and enlarge"—in Madison's words—popular sentiment. Antifederalists naturally had the opposite preference: They wanted representatives selected from smaller districts both because ordinary citizens would have a better chance of winning such contests and because representatives selected in such a manner would be more likely to mirror—rather than launder—their constituents' preferences.[88]

Arguing that single-member districts were "contrary to the true spirit of the Constitution," several Federalist-controlled state legislatures provided for at-large elections for their states' first delegations to the House of Representatives. Yet because the *letter* of the Constitution, regardless of its spirit, allows states to regulate the manner of federal elections—subject to congressional revision— it was possible for democratic forces quickly to pressure state legislatures into providing for House seats generally to be contested in single-member districts. Had the Framers instead written their preference for at-large elections explicitly into the Constitution, an amendment would have been necessary to implement procedures to accord with this shift in democratic sensibilities.[89]

Perhaps most important, the Framers' decision to include a Necessary and Proper Clause among Congress's powers, along with Madison's successful opposition to including the word "expressly" in the Tenth Amendment, enabled the Supreme Court under Chief Justice John Marshall to adopt very broad interpretations of congressional power. Extremely controversial at the time, those interpretations elicited the condemnation of Patrick Henry's son-in-law Spencer Roane, who denounced Marshall for adding "[a] new mode of amending the Constitution . . . to the ample ones provided in that instrument."[90]

Although, as just noted, the dominant political party for the remainder of the antebellum period—the Jacksonian Democrats—rejected Marshall's broad constructionism, over the very long term his approach to constitutional interpretation would triumph. As the world changed in ways that demanded greater regulatory authority at the federal level—technological advances, the increasing mobility of the American people, the growth of national and international markets, and an expanding role for the United States in international affairs—the federal government rose to meet the challenges by exercising greater power. What had been a gradual shift assumed a new dimension in the 1930s with the New Dealers' legislative response to the Great Depression. In his inaugural address in 1933, President Franklin D. Roosevelt argued that the extraordinary expansion of national power that he proposed was consistent with the original Constitution—if construed in the manner endorsed by John Marshall. After briefly resisting Roosevelt's efforts, the Supreme Court eventually acquiesced. A revolution in the national government's powers had occurred without any formal constitutional amendment to authorize it.[91]

Controversial as such developments were, this is all as it should be: Every generation must govern itself. Yet the enormous barriers constructed against constitutional amendments by Article V threaten to disable current majorities from escaping constitutional constraints imposed by their predecessors. Rarely in American history has it been possible to mobilize the extraordinary popular support necessary for formal constitutional amendments. Since the Bill of Rights was ratified in 1791, the Constitution has been amended only seventeen times in well over two hundred years. Without the open texture of the constitutional provisions just described—and the Supreme Court's latitudinarian interpretations of congressional power—Americans would have needed either to formally amend the Constitution much more frequently than they have done, or else to scrap it as of merely antiquarian interest.[92]

Yet some constitutional provisions were written with such specificity that they resist evasion—even under the guise of broad construction. Such provisions, if left formally unamended, continue to exert their influence over time—and often in ways that are difficult to square with democracy.

One historical example of such a provision was the Three-Fifths Clause, which pegged representation in the House partly to the amount of property that a state's inhabitants held in human beings. Although northerners occasionally called for an amendment to eliminate this provision, nobody seemed to believe that it could be circumvented through construction (though some northerners did briefly argue that the Three-Fifths Clause did not apply to states added to the union after the Founding). Only the formal abolition of slavery by the Thirteenth Amendment, enacted after the Civil War, terminated this most undemocratic of practices, which the Framers had foisted upon their descendants.[93]*

A second historical example of an undemocratic constitutional provision that was too specific in its language to be circumvented through construction was the one specifying that state legislatures choose US senators. Deeply in tension with Jacksonian trends toward greater popular participation in governance, this provision proved highly resistant to amendment. Not until the late nineteenth century was there a serious effort made to change it, and even then senators were able to block for decades an amendment providing for their popular election, even though most Americans clearly supported it, as evidenced by its repeated passage in the popularly elected House. Senators apparently either feared alienating the state legislatures that had appointed them to office or else doubted that the skill set enabling them to thrive in back-room negotiations (such as characterized state legislative selection of US senators) would translate well into success on the hustings. Not until 1913 was the Constitution finally amended to end this undemocratic practice.[94]

Another very precise, yet undemocratic, constitutional provision is of greater relevance today: the electoral college system. As already noted, one potentially undemocratic feature of this system—the authorizing of state

---

* Indeed, the entrenchment of slavery as an institution—not just as a component of apportioning representation in the House—was almost accomplished by a constitutional amendment that northerners offered to southerners in 1860–61 as an inducement to remain in the union. The so-called Corwin amendment—named for the Republican congressman from Ohio who proposed it—would have forever protected slavery in existing states from congressional interference. Republicans, including Lincoln, accepted this amendment because they did not see it as conceding anything valuable: Even without the amendment, they believed that Congress lacked the constitutional authority to interfere with slavery in existing states. To bolster its value to southerners, sponsors of the amendment included a provision making it unamendable. In other words, had the Corwin amendment been enshrined in the Constitution—ironically, it would have become the Thirteenth Amendment—it would have theoretically prevented subsequent majorities at the national level from ever abolishing slavery.

legislatures to provide for the selection of presidential electors in some manner other than direct popular election—was elided in an era more democratic than the Founding by legislatures' stipulating direct popular election as the mode of selection. However, another feature of this system—the apportionment of electors among states in a manner not proportional to their population (because each state's number of electors consists of its representatives plus its senators, and every state, regardless of size, has two senators)—cannot be so easily circumvented. Four times in American history, the candidate winning the most popular votes did not ascend to the presidency because he failed to win in the electoral college.* That result is difficult to reconcile with democratic principles: The votes of citizens in different states do not count equally in presidential elections. Yet an amendment to alter this aspect of the system would be virtually impossible to enact—both because the even more drastically malapportioned US Senate would very likely never pass it and because the smaller states, which benefit from the malapportionment, would never ratify it.[95]

More significantly, the malapportionment of the US Senate, in which each state enjoys equal representation, was difficult to justify in 1787 and is impossible to defend in a more democratic age that seems to take for granted—in most other contexts—the principle of one person, one vote. To be sure, democratic theory does not require that minorities go unprotected from majority oppression. Yet on no viable theory of minority rights do people living in sparsely populated states qualify as the sort of minority group deserving special protection. Historically, to the extent that the Senate's malapportionment has served the interests of minorities other than simply the residents of underpopulated states, it has generally advantaged the wrong sort of minorities: first, southern slaveholders, and later, southern white supremacists. Today, malapportionment of the Senate mostly ensures that people living in thinly populated states receive far more than their per capita share of federal spending, and it advantages a Republican Party that is widely perceived to better reflect the values of rural America.[96]

Ironically, while other undemocratic features of the original Constitution— such as protections for slaveholders and state legislative selection of senators— have been eliminated over time, the Senate's malapportionment has grown significantly worse. In 1787, the largest state (Virginia) had roughly twelve

---

* To be sure, some of the gap between popular vote totals and electoral college results is attributable not to the malapportionment of the electoral college but to the system's use of winner-take-all contests at the state level. Thus, a presidential candidate can win the national popular vote but lose in the electoral college simply because of the manner in which that candidate's popular votes are distributed.

times the population of the smallest (Delaware). By 2010, the population of California, the largest state, was more than sixty-five times that of Wyoming, the smallest. Moreover, the constitutional provision that malapportions the Senate by guaranteeing each state two senators is expressly rendered unamendable without the consent of every state—a truly extraordinary instance of dead-hand control that we should not expect to see eliminated even if we live a very long time.[97]

Tenure during good behavior (which is, effectively, lifetime tenure) for unelected federal judges is another feature of the Constitution that is both difficult to reconcile with democracy and impossible to circumvent without an amendment. At the time of the Founding, several state constitutions authorized legislatures to remove judges—many of whom enjoyed tenures much briefer than "good behavior"—on grounds falling short of the criteria specified for impeachment, which under the Constitution is the only way to remove federal judges from office. By the middle of the nineteenth century, the accountability gap between state and federal judges had grown even greater, as all newly created states and many existing ones were providing for the popular election of state judges to finite terms in office. The federal system probably would have moved in that same direction at roughly the same time had federal constitutional amendments not been so difficult to secure.[98]

Since the Founding, there has been a dramatic shift in the way that judges have exercised the power of judicial review. At most, the Framers would have anticipated courts' striking down laws that were clearly unconstitutional or that especially affected the judiciary, such as restrictions on the right to a jury trial. By contrast, today's unelected, life-tenured federal judges resolve many of society's most contested social and political issues—abortion, affirmative action, gay marriage, school prayer, gun control, campaign finance reform, and the death penalty, to name only a few. Moreover, today's Supreme Court generally resolves such issues by five-to-four votes that divide the justices along largely consistent and predictable political lines, which strongly suggests that ideology plays a substantial role in the justices' constitutional interpretations. Empowering unelected and remotely accountable government officials with this much political discretion seems very difficult to reconcile with democracy.[99]

The Constitution contains one other undemocratic feature that is too specific to be circumvented through creative construction and is unlikely ever to be amended: the Article V provision specifying that constitutional amendments require the approval of two-thirds of both houses of Congress (or a proposal by a constitutional convention called by Congress at the behest of two-thirds of the state legislatures) and ratification by three-quarters of the state legislatures (or by three-quarters of special state ratifying conventions, if so specified by Congress). This provision blocks constitutional changes that are supported even by large majorities of the American people. Thirty-four senators from the seventeen smallest states—together representing as little as 7 percent of the nation's population—can defeat a constitutional amendment. So can the legislatures of the thirteen smallest states, which together constitute less than 4 percent of the nation's population. Were it not for the extraordinary difficulty of enacting constitutional amendments, popular majorities probably would long ago have adopted measures guaranteeing equality without regard to sex, allowing voluntary nondenominational prayer in public schools, and permitting governments to criminalize the burning of the American flag as an act of symbolic speech.[100]

From the Perspective of Today

Most of the delegates to the Philadelphia convention would have been astonished to learn that most of the Constitution they wrote in 1787 remains in place more than 225 years later. Nathaniel Gorham of Massachusetts, for one, was incredulous at the idea "that this vast country including the western territory will 150 years hence remain one nation."[101]

The Framers did not think they were perfect. During the convention, George Mason observed that the Constitution the delegates were drafting "will certainly be defective, as the Confederation has been found on trial to be." During the ratifying contest, Elbridge Gerry noted that even "the greatest men may err." Federalist Noah Webster considered it "consummate arrogance" to presume that the Founders had "all possible wisdom," could "foresee all possible circumstances," or could "judge for future generations better than they can judge for themselves." Because they understood their own imperfections and limitations, the Framers deliberately fashioned Article V to make amendments easier to obtain than they had been under the Articles of Confederation.[102]

On a few occasions, the Framers simply made mistakes. For example, the electoral college system they devised required electors to cast two votes for different candidates but did not permit them to designate one of those votes for president and the other for vice president. Not anticipating the rise of political parties, which nonetheless happened almost immediately, the Framers did not imagine party tickets that combined a candidate for president with one for vice president. Yet by coordinating support for candidates among the electors, political parties fostered the realistic possibility of tie votes in the electoral college, as each party's electors cast their two (undifferentiated) votes for the presidential and vice presidential nominees of their parties.[103]

This gaffe by the Framers nearly led to a debacle in the presidential election of 1800, when Thomas Jefferson and Aaron Burr, both Democratic-Republicans, received the same number of electoral votes. Although everyone knew that Jefferson had been the party's choice for president and Burr for vice president, it remained uncertain for weeks who would become president. Even worse, members of the opposition party—the Federalists—controlled the decisive votes in the House of Representatives that would determine which of their adversaries' candidates would become the nation's third president.[104]

The Framers' mistaken assumptions meant that the system they had designed sometimes worked very differently in practice than they had anticipated. For example, the Framers assumed that political actors in different branches of the national government would have self-interested incentives to challenge each other's assertions of power. Yet the existence of political parties, which the Framers did not contemplate, drastically altered the practical operation of the system of checks and balances. Specifically, while the Framers expected the president and Congress to be adversaries competing for power, the rise of political parties meant that the two branches—if controlled by the same party—might be more likely to coordinate their efforts than to compete with one another.[105]

Similarly, the development of political parties radically altered the practical workings of the electoral college system. The Framers assumed that presidential candidates would rarely command majorities in the electoral college, and thus "nineteen times in twenty," the House of Representatives would have to pick the president (from among the top five vote getters in the electoral college). Yet with the rise of political parties, one candidate has almost always won a majority in the electoral college, and only two presidents in American history—Thomas Jefferson in the election of 1800 and John Quincy Adams in the election of 1824—have been chosen by the House.[106]

The Framers also made demographic assumptions that, although they turned out to be badly flawed, nonetheless shaped the convention's handiwork in significant ways. At the time of the Founding, virtually everyone assumed that the South's population would grow much more quickly than the North's. Thus, at the Philadelphia convention and in the ratifying contest, southerners believed that the rejection of population-based apportionment for the Senate would disadvantage them over the long term. Much of the work done by the Philadelphia convention after the consummation of the Connecticut Compromise in mid-July—for example, the compromises involving slavery and the decision about how to select the president—was influenced by this assumption.[107]

Yet because European immigrants, not wishing to live in a slave society or to compete with slave labor, mostly steered away from the South, the North's population grew much more quickly than the South's during the antebellum period. Ironically, the equally apportioned Senate turned out to be the bastion of support for southern slaveholders, while the population-apportioned House repeatedly posed a threat to them. By the 1850s, southern statesmen warned of civil war if the balance of power they had eventually secured and preserved in the Senate—there were fifteen free states and fifteen slave states before the admission of California in 1850—were thrown out of kilter by the admission of too many additional free states.[108]

Other constitutional provisions have simply been rendered obsolete or antiquated in the face of dramatically changed social and economic conditions. The Constitution provided for the first session of each new Congress to assemble in December because the Framers assumed most legislators would be farmers, who would find a summer session inconvenient. Technological developments in transportation have also rendered certain constitutional provisions obsolete. The Constitution empowers the president to make recess appointments to federal offices because the Framers assumed—in an era of relatively primitive transportation—that senators representing distant states would have to be absent from the capital for months when the Senate adjourned. In addition, one reason that the Constitution provides that a quorum for conducting business in either house shall consist of a majority of its members is that the Framers worried that any lesser requirement would jeopardize the interests of distant states with disparate interests. Such concerns seem quaint in the modern era of rapid transportation.[109]

In addition to their mistakes, faulty assumptions, and concerns that were later rendered obsolete, the Framers were constrained by history to make certain choices that differed from those they might have considered ideal. Most notably, a constitution that was devised by delegates who represented states, and that would be subject to ratification by state conventions, would inevitably include many federalism provisions that may not have been theoretically optimal. Thus, the Framers provided that state legislatures would select US senators, choose the method of selecting presidential electors, and regulate—subject to congressional override—the times, places, and manner of federal elections. They also restricted the jurisdiction of federal courts and limited Congress to enumerated powers, while treating states as governments of inherent power (subject only to the limitations of Article I, Section 10). Among democratic nations in the world today, only those sharing a similar history of evolution from confederation to nation have included similar federalism provisions in their constitutions.[110]

Finally, the Framers held certain values that are abhorrent to most Americans today. Most of them accepted that human beings could be held as property, and they believed that African Americans and Native Americans were inferior in various ways to Caucasians. None of them thought that women should enjoy full political or civil rights. Most of them doubted that poor people should be permitted to vote or hold political office. The purpose of such observations is not to criticize the Framers but simply to note, as Benjamin Franklin did at the Philadelphia convention, that they—like all human beings—were influenced by the passions and prejudices of their era. How likely is it that persons holding values so radically different from our own would have written a constitution that perfectly suits our needs today?[111]

In the final analysis, the Constitution—like any governmental arrangement—must be defended on the basis of its consistency with our basic (democratic) political commitments and the consequences that it produces. That it has been around for a very long time or that its authors were especially wise and virtuous should not be sufficient to immunize it against criticism.[112]

Toward the end of his long life, Thomas Jefferson, who played no direct role in either the drafting or the ratification of the Constitution, sagely observed that because "laws and institutions must go hand in hand with the progress of the human mind" and because each generation has "a right to choose for itself the form of government it believes most promotive of its own happiness," constitutions ought not to receive "sanctimonious reverence" and be deemed, "like the ark of the covenant, too sacred to be touched." As Jefferson would have recognized, those who wish to sanctify the Constitution are often using it to defend some particular interest that, in their own day, cannot in fact be adequately justified on its own merits.[113]

NOTES

Introduction

1. Benjamin Franklin at Philadelphia convention, Sept. 17, 1787 (Madison's Notes), in *The Records of the Federal Convention of 1787* (Max Farrand, ed., rev. ed. 1966), 2:642 [hereinafter, "*Farrand*"]. Madison's notes from the Philadelphia convention are the most extensive, but several other delegates also took notes. All subsequent references to Farrand are to Madison's notes, unless specifically noted otherwise.
2. *New York Times*, Mar. 7, 1928, p. 27; Michael Kammen, *A Machine that Would Go of Itself: The Constitution in American Culture* (New York, 1986), 225; Robert A. Dahl, *How Democratic Is the American Constitution?* (New Haven, CT, 2nd ed. 2003), 122; Sanford Levinson, *Constitutional Faith* (Princeton, NJ, 1988), 14; see also Jack N. Rakove, *Original Meanings: Politics and Ideas in the Making of the Constitution* (New York, 1996), 367; James H. Hutson, "Country, Court, and Constitution: Antifederalism and the Historians," *William and Mary Quarterly* (July 1981), 38:342.
3. *The Federalist No. 37* (Madison), at 230–1 (Clinton Rossiter, ed., New York, 1961) ("[i]t is impossible"); Madison to Jefferson, Oct. 24, 1787, *The Papers of James Madison* (Congressional Series) (Robert R. Rutland and William M. E. Rachal, eds., Chicago, 1977), 10:208 [hereinafter, "*PJM* (C.S.)"] ("consider the degree"); see also Richard Beeman, *Plain, Honest Men: The Making of the American Constitution* (New York, 2009), 179.
4. "The Landholder" X, *Connecticut Courant*, Mar. 3, 1788, *The Documentary History of the Ratification of the Constitution* (John P. Kaminski and Gaspare J. Saladino, eds., Madison, WI, 1986), 16:306 [hereinafter, "*DHRC*"] ("[t]he unexpected harmony"); David Ramsay, Oration, Charleston *Columbian Herald*, June 5, 1788, *DHRC*, 18:160 ("Heaven smiled"); Rush at Pennsylvania convention, Dec. 12, 1787, *DHRC*, 2:593 ("the hand of God"); Benjamin Rush, Observations on the Fourth of July Procession in Philadelphia (July 15, 1788), *DHRC*, 18:266 ("as much the work" and "of heaven"); see also Levinson, *Constitutional Faith*, 13; Beeman, *Plain, Honest Men*, 179.
5. Madison at Philadelphia convention, June 12, 1787, *Farrand*, 1:215 ("The respectability"); Madison to Randolph, Jan. 10, 1788, *PJM* (C.S.), 10:355 ("Had the Constitution"); Alexander Hamilton, Conjectures About the New Constitution (Sept. 17–30, 1787), *DHRC*, 13:277.
6. *Pennsylvania Gazette*, Aug. 22, 1787, *DHRC*, 13:190 ("[s]uch a body" and "entitled"); "An Admirer of Anti-Federal Men," *New York Daily Advertiser*, July 26, 1787, *DHRC*, 19:15 ("surely will never," "[r]est assured," "worthies," and "have the good"). For other such statements made while the convention was still sitting, see, e.g., "An American," *Massachusetts Centinel*, Aug. 4, 1787, *DHRC*, 13:185; "Observator" V, *New Haven Gazette*, Sept. 20, 1787, *DHRC*, 3:349; see also John K. Alexander, *The Selling of the Constitutional Convention: A History of News Coverage* (Madison, WI, 1990), 27–8, 58–62, 202–4, 213–4.

Even Jefferson, who was harder to impress, referred to the convention as "an assembly of demigods"; to John Adams, Aug. 30, 1787, *The Papers of Thomas Jefferson* (Main Series) (Julian P. Boyd et al., eds., Princeton, NJ, 1955), 12:68 [hereinafter, "*PTJ* (M.S.)"].

7. *Pennsylvania Packet*, Sept. 22, 1787, *DHRC*, 13:222 ("[b]ear witness") (emphasis in original); New York *Daily Advertiser*, Sept. 24, 1787, *DHRC*, 19:51 ("the duty" and "to cultivate"); Alexander White, "To the Citizens of Virginia," *Winchester Gazette* [Virginia], Feb. 29, 1788, *DHRC*, 8:443–4 ("a Washington," "whose philosophical," and "could conspire"). For additional uses of this rhetorical technique by Federalists, see, e.g., *A Citizen of New-York: An Address to the People of the State of New York* (John Jay) (Apr. 15, 1788), *DHRC*, 20:931; *Essex Journal*, Nov. 21, 1787, *DHRC*, 4:292; *Massachusetts Centinel*, Nov. 10, 1787, ibid., 214.

8. "Centinel" I, Philadelphia *Independent Gazetteer*, Oct. 5, 1787, *DHRC*, 13:330 ("too apt to yield"); "Sydney," *Albany Gazette*, Jan. 24, 1788, *DHRC*, 20:646 ("as infidels" and "their approbation"); Findley to William Irvine, Mar. 12, 1788, *DHRC*, 16:374 ("addressing our reason" and "address[ing] our implicit faith"); Elbridge Gerry to the Massachusetts General Court, *Massachusetts Centinel*, Nov. 3, 1787, *DHRC*, 13:549 ("that an implicit confidence" and "however respectable"). For other similar Antifederalist statements, see "Centinel" VIII, Philadelphia *Independent Gazetteer*, Jan. 2, 1788, *DHRC*, 15:233; "Centinel" XV, Feb. 22, 1788, ibid., 16:190; Consider Arms, Malachi Maynard, and Samuel Field: Dissent to the Massachusetts Convention, Northampton, Mass. *Hampshire Gazette*, Apr. 16, 1788, *DHRC*, 17:52–3; "An Officer of the Late Continental Army" (possibly William Findley), Philadelphia *Independent Gazetteer*, Nov. 6, 1787, *DHRC*, 2:214; "The Republican Federalist" II, *Massachusetts Centinel*, Jan. 2, 1788, *DHRC*, 5:590–1; "Rusticus," *New York Journal*, May 23, 1788, *DHRC*, 20:1108–9; Luther Martin, Genuine Information I, Baltimore *Maryland Gazette*, *DHRC*, 11:133.

   At the Massachusetts ratifying convention, one Antifederalist, Samuel Nasson, confessed that, given "the list of illustrious names annexed to it," he was "suspicious of [his] own judgment" when he viewed the Constitution as "pregnant with danger" (Massachusetts convention, Feb. 1, 1788, *DHRC*, 6:1397).

   A note to readers: For reasons that are beyond my limited technological capacity to comprehend, it is either impossible or extremely difficult to use endnotes within footnotes. Thus, throughout this book, I will append the references that support a particular footnote to the end of the endnote whose call number in the text immediately follows the call for that particular footnote. (Because of the vagaries of the relative placement of footnotes and endnotes, sometimes the call for the endnote containing the references for a particular footnote will appear on the same page as the footnote, and sometimes on the following page.)

   For the references supporting the preceding footnote, see "A Citizen of Philadelphia" (Pelatiah Webster), *Pennsylvania Gazette*, Jan. 23, 1788, *DHRC*, 2:658 ("Can human nature"); "Cassius" V, *Massachusetts Gazette*, Nov. 30, 1787, *DHRC*, 4:340 ("unprincipled" and "who for eight years"); see also Olney Winsor to Mrs. Olney (Hope) Winsor, Mar. 31, 1788, *DHRC*, 8:523.

9. Kammen, *Machine that Would Go of Itself*, 142, 315.

10. Ibid., 68 ("fetishism"), 205 ("fetishism"); Jefferson to "Henry Tompkinson" (Samuel Kercheval), July 12, 1816, *The Papers of Thomas Jefferson* (Retirement Series) (J. Jefferson Looney, ed., Princeton, NJ, 2014), 10:226 [hereinafter, "*PTJ* (R.S.)"] ("a wisdom" and "constitutions").

11. *The Federalist No. 49* (Madison), at 314–5 (quotations); see also Madison to Jefferson, Feb. 4, 1790, *PJM* (C.S.), 13:19; Drew R. McCoy, *The Last of the Fathers: James Madison and the Republican Legacy* (New York, 1989), 54–8; Rakove, *Original Meanings*, 140–1.

12. Michael Vorenberg, *Final Freedom: The Civil War, the Abolition of Slavery, and the Thirteenth Amendment* (Cambridge, England, 2001), 107–8 ("stood around" at p. 108); Kammen, *Machine that Would Go of Itself*, 191 ("greatest jewel"), 219–23, 283 ("Shrine of the Constitution"); Jeff Shesol, *Supreme Power: Franklin Roosevelt vs. the Supreme Court* (New York, 2010), 107–8.

13. Kammen, *Machine that Would Go of Itself*, 24.

Chapter 1

1. Roger H. Brown, *Redeeming the Republic: Federalists,*
   Constitution (Baltimore, 1993), 24–7; see also Edmund
   vention, May 29, 1787, *Farrand*, 1:18–9; Randolph (Yates
   (McHenry's Notes), ibid., 24–8; Randolph at Virginia c(
   9:931–6; Charles Pettit to Jeremiah Wadsworth, May
   Congress, 1774–1789 (Paul H. Smith ed., Washington, D(
   "*LDC*"].
2. See sources cited in the preceding note.
3. Madison to Edmund Randolph, Feb. 25, 1787, *PJM* (C.!
   "unanimously agree"); Madison to Edmund Pendleton, F
   ther has," "No money," and "It is not possible"); Madison
   1787, ibid., 297 ("losing all confidence").
4. Randolph to Washington, Nov. 24, 1786, *The Papers of George Washington* (Confederation
   Series) (W. W. Abbot, ed., Charlottesville, VA, 1995), 4:395 [hereinafter, "*PGW* (C.S.)"]
   ("nerves of government"); Randolph to Washington, Dec. 6, 1786, ibid., 445 ("alarm");
   Grayson to Madison, Mar. 22, 1786, *PJM* (C.S.), 8:510 ("that the present Confederation");
   Grayson to Short, Apr. 16, 1787, *LDC*, 24:226 ("American affairs"). For additional state-
   ments to similar effect, see Roger Alden to Jonathan Trumbull, Jr., Mar. 23, 1787, ibid.,
   168 9; Stephen Mix Mitchell to William Johnson, Sept. 14, 1786, *LDC*, 23:526 n. 11; New
   York *Daily Advertiser* (Hamilton), July 21, 1787, *DHRC*, 19:11–4; *The Federalist No. 15*
   (Hamilton), at 106.
5. Jack N. Rakove, *The Beginnings of National Politics: An Interpretive History of the Continental
   Congress* (New York, 1979), 17–8; Joseph L. Davis, *Sectionalism in American Politics, 1774–*
   1787 (Madison, WI, 1977), 12–3; David C. Hendrickson, *Peace Pact: The Lost World of the
   American Founding* (Lawrence, KS, 2003), 26–7.
      For the preceding footnote, see American National Biography Online.
6. Gordon S. Wood, *The Creation of the American Republic, 1776–1787* (Chapel Hill, NC,
   1969), 355; Rakove, *Beginnings of National Politics*, 144–5, 155. For the delay in Congress's
   finalizing a draft of the Articles, which was caused by the intervention of military hostilities, see Introduction, *DHRC*, 11:xl. For a good account of the disputes involved in the
   drafting of the Articles, see Hendrickson, *Peace Pact*, ch. 18.
7. Madison, Preface to Debates in the Convention of 1787, *Farrand*, 3:542 (quotations)
   [hereinafter, "Preface to Debates"]; Rakove, *Beginnings of National Politics*, 177–8, 186–7;
   Hendrickson, *Peace Pact*, 150. The states did propose many amendments to the Articles,
   but Congress chose to ignore them. For these amendments, see volume 1 of *DHRC*.
8. Madison, Preface to Debates, *Farrand*, 3:542 (quotation); see also Madison to Edmund
   Pendleton, Apr. 23, 1782, *PJM* (C.S.), 4:178; Madison, Observations Relating to the
   Influence of Vermont and the Territorial Claims on the Politics of Congress (May 1,
   1782), ibid., 200–2; Richard Dobbs Spaight to Alexander Martin, Apr. 30, 1784, *LDC*,
   21:567; David Ramsay to Nathanael Greene, Sept. 10, 1782, *LDC*, 19:143; Introduction,
   DHRC, 11:xli–xlvi; Gaspare J. Saladino, "Delaware: Independence and the Concept of a
   Commercial Republic," in Michael Allen Gillespie and Michael Lienesch, eds., *Ratifying
   the Constitution* (Lawrence, KS, 1989), 34–5; Peter S. Onuf, "Maryland: The Small
   Republic in the New Nation," in ibid., 174–5; Peter S. Onuf, *The Origins of the Federal
   Republic: Jurisdictional Controversies in the United States, 1775–1787* (Philadelphia, 1983),
   13–4; Rakove, *Beginnings of National Politics*, 187–90; Hendrickson, *Peace Pact*, 132–3,
   140–1, 146; Willi Paul Adams, *The First American Constitutions: Republican Ideology and the
   Making of the State Constitutions in the Revolutionary Era* (Chapel Hill, NC, 1980), 284–5.
9. Act of Confederation of the United States of America (1781), Art. II, *DHRC*, 1:86 (quotation) [hereinafter, "Articles of Confederation"]; Wood, *Creation of the American Republic*,
   354–9; Rakove, *Beginnings of National Politics*, 158–60, 170–2; Hendrickson, *Peace Pact*,
   28, 134, 138–9, 144–5, 179; but cf. Onuf, *Origins of the Federal Republic*, 5–7.
10. Madison to Washington, Dec. 9, 1785, *PJM* (C.S.), 8:438 ("Nothing but"); Hamilton
    at New York convention, June 24, 1788, *DHRC*, 22:1861 ("the great object"); Rakove,

Original Meanings, 206–7; Hendrickson, *Peace Pact*, 135; Max Edling, "A More Perfect Union: The Framing and Ratification of the Constitution," in Edward G. Gray and Jane Kamensky, eds., *The Oxford Handbook of the American Revolution* (New York, 2013), 391.

11. Gouverneur Morris to Matthew Ridley, Aug. 6, 1782, *Papers of Robert Morris* (John Catanzariti and E. James Ferguson, eds., Pittsburgh, 1984), 6:148 [hereinafter, "*PRM*"] ("rapid" and "daily"); Robert Morris to Matthew Ridley, Oct. 6, 1782, ibid., 512 ("a patriot" and "a continuance"); Hamilton to Jay, July 25, 1783, *The Papers of Alexander Hamilton* (Harold C. Syrett, ed., New York, 1961), 3:416 [hereinafter, "*PAH*"] ("[e]very day"); see also Davis, *Sectionalism in American Politics*, 44, 54–5; Rakove, *Beginnings of National Politics*, 310; Merrill Jensen, *The New Nation: A History of the United States During the Confederation, 1781–1789* (New York, 1950), 66.

    For the preceding footnote, see John P. Kaminski and Timothy D. Moore, *An Assembly of Demigods: Word Portraits of the Delegates to the Constitutional Convention by Their Contemporaries* (Madison, WI, 2012), 133–9 (quoting William Pierce's *Sketches* ("one of those geniuses") at p. 136; Madison to Jared Sparks, Apr. 8, 1831 ("the finish") at p. 139; George Mason to James Monroe, Jan. 30, 1792 ("a man") at p. 138; Washington to Gouverneur Morris, Jan. 28, 1792 ("mode of expression") at p. 137; John Laurens to Hamilton, Dec. 18, 1779 ("[T]he world") at p. 135; James Kent to Mrs. Elizabeth Hamilton, Dec. 10, 1832 ("very commanding," "noble head," and "majestic mien") at p. 139; John Jay to Robert Morris, Sept. 16, 1780 ("Gouverneur's leg") at p. 135); Beeman, *Plain, Honest Men*, 45–9 ("consummate philanderer" at p. 48); American National Biography Online.

12. E. James Ferguson, *The Power of the Purse: A History of American Public Finance, 1776– 1790* (Chapel Hill, NC, 1961), xv, 111 (quotation); Articles of Confederation, Art. VIII; Hamilton to James Duane, Sept. 3, 1780, *PAH*, 2:401, 404; Rakove, *Beginnings of National Politics*, 320; Robin L. Einhorn, *American Taxation, American Slavery* (Chicago, 2006), 18–9.

13. Max E. Edling, *A Revolution in Favor of Government: Origins of the U.S. Constitution and the Making of the American State* (New York, 2003), 150; Ferguson, *Power of the Purse*, 7–8; Stephen Mihm, "Funding the Revolution: Monetary and Fiscal Policy in Eighteenth-Century America," in Gray and Kamensky, eds., *American Revolution*, 332.

14. Ferguson, *Power of the Purse*, 26; Mihm, "Funding the Revolution," 332.

15. Ferguson, *Power of the Purse*, 19, 26–7, 29–30; Thomas K. McCraw, *The Founders and Finance: How Hamilton, Gallatin, and Other Immigrants Forged a New Economy* (Cambridge, MA, 2012), 65; Einhorn, *American Taxation*, 126–7; Mihm, "Funding the Revolution," 332–4.

16. Ferguson, *Power of the Purse*, 32 tbl., 33, 48; Rakove, *Beginnings of National Politics*, 210.

17. Ferguson, *Power of the Purse*, 33–6, 39. On the failure of states to conduct a land census, see, e.g., Charles Thomson to John Dickinson, July 19, 1785, *LDC*, 22:520; see also Rufus King at Massachusetts convention, Jan. 19, 1788, *DHRC*, 6:1255; Einhorn, *American Taxation*, 128, 134–5.

18. Madison to Jefferson, May 6, 1780, *PJM* (C.S.), 2:20.

19. Washington to Joseph Jones, May 31, 1780, *The Writings of George Washington* (Jared Sparks, ed., New York, 1834), 7:67 ("One state"); Madison to John Page (?), May 8, 1780, *PJM* (C.S.), 2:21 ("[o]ur great danger"); Madison to Jefferson, Apr. 16, 1781, ibid., 3:71 ("most capable" and "shameful"); see also Madison to Jefferson, May 6, 1780, ibid., 2:19; Robert Morris to Benjamin Franklin, Sept. 27, 1782, *PRM*, 6:449; Abner Nash to James Iredell, Jan. 8, 1783, *LDC*, 19:565; James M. Varnum to William Greene, Apr. 2, 1781, *LDC*, 17:115; Rakove, *Beginnings of National Politics*, 207–8; Edling, *Revolution in Favor of Government*, 155–7. On the much lighter taxes paid by American colonists than Europeans, see Jeremy Atack and Peter Passell, *A New Economic View of American History from Colonial Times to 1940* (New York, 2nd ed., 1994), 68 tbl. 3.4; Einhorn, *American Taxation*, 21; Mihm, "Funding the Revolution," 328.

20. Madison to Randolph, Jan. 22, 1783, *PJM* (C.S.), 6:55 ("operate" and "the mutual jealousies"); Madison to George Thompson, Jan. 29, 1789, ibid., 11:433–4 ("[i]f some states"); see also Madison to Jefferson, Oct. 3, 1785, ibid., 8:374; *The Federalist No. 15* (Hamilton), 112; George Read to John Dickinson, Jan. 17, 1787, *LDC*, 22:592; Nathaniel Gorham to

Caleb Davis, Mar. 1, 1786, *LDC*, 23:167; "A Freeholder," *Providence Gazette*, Nov. 9, 1782, p. 2. Robin Einhorn argues that it was the absurdity of Article VIII's reliance on land values for apportioning requisitions that ensured the failure of the requisition system, but whatever method of apportionment was used, the same collective-action problem would have plagued the system (*American Taxation*, 145).

21. Editorial Note, Report on Payment of New Jersey Troops, Oct. 1, 1782, *PJM* (C.S.), 5:173 ("common justice"); see also Ferguson, *Power of the Purse*, 221–3; Davis, *Sectionalism in American Politics*, 42; Lance Banning, *The Sacred Fire of Liberty: James Madison and the Founding of the Federal Republic* (Ithaca, NY, 1995), 27; Sara M. Shumer, "New Jersey: Property and the Price of Republican Politics," in Gillespie and Lienesch, eds., *Ratifying the Constitution*, 79; Edwin J. Perkins, *American Public Finance and Financial Services, 1700–1815* (Columbus, OH, 1994), 145–6.
    For the preceding footnote, see *DHRC*, 19:14 n. 4.

22. Madison, Notes on Debates, Dec. 4, 1782, *PJM* (C.S.), 5:363 ("not only a breach," "followed," and "our bond"); Report on Payment of New Jersey Troops, Oct. 1, 1782, ibid., 174; Rufus King to W. Coleman, Feb. 9, 1817, *The Life and Correspondence of Rufus King* (Charles R. King, ed., New York, 1900), 6:54 [hereinafter, "*LCRK*"] ("increased the financial"); see also *Journals of the Continental Congress* (Gaillard Hunt, ed., Washington, DC, 1914), 23:629–31 (Oct. 1, 1782) [hereinafter, "*JCC*"]; Stephen Mix Mitchell to Jeremiah Wadsworth, Jan. 24, 1787, *LDC*, 24:74; Monroe to Madison, Feb. 11, 1786, *PJM* (C.S.), 8:492 & n. 2; Monroe to Jefferson, June 16, 1785, *PTJ* (M.S.), 8:215; Massachusetts Delegates to James Bowdoin, Aug. 23, 1785, *LDC*, 22:592; John Paul Kaminski, "Paper Politics: The Northern State Loan Offices During the Confederation, 1783–1790" (PhD diss., University of Wisconsin, 1972), 148; Introduction, *DHRC*, 3:123; Perkins, *American Public Finance*, 150–2.

23. Morris to Washington, Aug. 29, 1782, *PRM*, 6:282 ("like preaching"); Dane to King, Oct. 8, 1785, *LCRK*, 1:68 ("a mere recommendatory" and "so long as"); Washington to John Jay, Aug. 15, 1786, *PGW* (C.S.), 4:212–3 ("[R]equisitions"); see also Robert Morris, Circular to the Governors of the States, May 12, 1783, *PRM*, 8:31–2; June 5, 1783, ibid., 171; Robert Morris to President John Dickinson of Pennsylvania, Jan. 20, 1783, *PRM*, 7:342–3; North Carolina delegates to Governor Alexander Martin, Oct. 22, 1782, *LDC*, 19:293; McCraw, *The Founders and Finance*, 71; Brown, *Redeeming the Republic*, 15–6; Calvin H. Johnson, *Righteous Anger at the Wicked States: The Meaning of the Founders' Constitution* (New York, 2005), 15; Edling, *Revolution in Favor of Government*, 94.

24. Morris to Matthew Ridley, Aug. 6, 1782, *PRM*, 6:148 (quotation); Brown, *Redeeming the Republic*, 12, 24–5, 70, 97, 117–8, 122; see also James Madison, Vices of the Political System of the United States, *PJM* (C.S.), 9:351 [hereinafter, "Madison, Vices"]; Robert Morris to Matthew Ridley, Oct. 6, 1782, *PRM*, 6:511–3; *JCC*, 30:70 (Feb. 15, 1786); Rufus King's Address, Oct. 17, 1785, *LDC*, 23:588–9.

25. Brown, *Redeeming the Republic*, 25, 155; Madison to James Madison, Sr., Feb. 25, 1787, *PJM* (C.S.), 9:297 ("payments"); Madison to Jefferson, Oct. 24, 1787, ibid., 10:218 ("[i]t may well"); Madison to Jefferson, Dec. 20, 1787, ibid., 332 ("[t]he treasury board"); North Carolina delegates to the North Carolina Assembly, Dec. 15, 1787, *LDC*, 24:585 ("we are at the eve"); see also Theodore Sedgwick to Caleb Strong, Aug. 6, 1786, *LDC*, 23:437; Roger Alden to Jonathan Trumbull, Jr., Mar. 23, 1787, *LDC*, 24:168; Madison to Washington, Feb. 21, 1787, *PJM* (C.S.), 9:285; Board of Treasury Report, Feb. 7, 1787, *JCC*, 32:33–4; David Humphreys to Washington, Nov. 1, 1786, *PGW* (C.S.), 4:325.

26. John Jay Address to Congress, Aug. 3, 1786, *JCC*, 31:484 ("destitute"); Carrington to Randolph, Apr. 13, 1787, *LDC*, 24:219 ("[t]he reduced state" and "considerably"); Madison to Jefferson, Dec. 20, 1787, *PJM* (C.S.), 10:332 ("probably bring on"); Gilman to President John Sullivan, Nov. 7, 1787, *DHRC*, 3:262 ("efficient" and "become contemptible"); North Carolina delegates to the North Carolina General Assembly, Dec. 15, 1787, *LDC*, 24:585 ("reduced to," "[t]he deception," and "[o]ur friends"); see also Jay to Jefferson, Dec. 14, 1786, *PTJ* (M.S.), 10:597; Secretary of Congress Charles Thomson to Governor Samuel Huntington of Connecticut, Dec. 27, 1787, *LDC*, 24:599; Rhode Island delegates to Governor John Collins, Sept. 28, 1786, *LDC*, 23:570; Board of Treasury Report, June 22,

1786, *JCC*, 30:365; Charles Pinckney motion, Feb. 7, 1786, *JCC*, 30:50–1; New York *Daily Advertiser* (Hamilton), July 21, 1787, *DHRC*, 19:12; "Primitive Whig" No. 1 (Governor William Livingston), *New Jersey Gazette*, Jan. 9, 1786, at 1; Boston *Independent Chronicle*, Sept. 7, 1786, at 1; Brown, *Redeeming the Republic*, 18–19, 33, 228. In June 1787, John Adams, the American minister plenipotentiary to Holland (and also the American minister to Great Britain), signed a loan agreement with Dutch bankers, which would enable the United States to pay the interest due on earlier Dutch loans. See Board of Treasury Report, July 25, 1787, *JCC*, 33:412–5; Congressional Resolution, Oct. 11, 1787, ibid., 649; see also editorial note, *DHRC*, 20:1149 n. 3.

27. Pendleton to Madison, Apr. 7, 1787, *PJM* (C.S.), 17:516 ("independent" and "upon the various"); Lee to George Mason, May 15, 1787, *Papers of George Mason* (Robert Allen Rutland, ed., Chapel Hill, NC, 1970), 2:878 [hereinafter, "*PGM*"] ("so unpardonably remiss"); Washington to Madison, Mar. 31, 1787, *PGW* (C.S.), 5:115 ("[M]y opinion"); see also Thomas Johnson to Washington, Dec. 11, 1787, ibid., 484; Boston *Independent Chronicle*, Sept. 7, 1786, at 1. Calvin Johnson argues that it was the Founders' anger at the states for failing to pay their requisitions that, more than any other cause, led to the enactment of the Constitution (*Righteous Anger at the Wicked States*, 2–3).

28. Report of the Committee on Dispatches from Foreign Ministers, Sept. 25, 1783, *LDC*, 20:701 (quotations); Edling, *Revolution in Favor of Government*, 85–8; Frederick Marks III, *Independence on Trial: Foreign Affairs and the Making of the Constitution* (Baton Roge, LA, 1973), 52–9, 110–2; Curtis P. Nettels, *The Emergence of a National Economy, 1775–1815* (New York, 1962), 65–6; Albert Anthony Giesecke, *American Commercial Legislation Before 1789* (New York, 1910), 127; Hendrickson, *Peace Pact*, 200–1; Forrest McDonald, *Novus Ordo Seclorum: The Intellectual Origins of the Constitution* (Lawrence, KS, 1985), 105; Forrest McDonald, *We the People: The Economic Origins of the Constitution* (Chicago, 1958), 367, 382; Jensen, *New Nation*, 157–63; editorial note, *DHRC*, 4:398 n. 2; Introduction, *DHRC*, 1:24; see also John Adams to Elbridge Gerry, Sept. 11, 1785, in James T. Austin, *The Life of Elbridge Gerry* (Boston, 1828), 482–6; "A," *Essex Journal*, Oct. 10, 1787, *DHRC*, 4:66; Nathaniel Peaslee Sargeant to Joseph Badger, 1788 (precise date unknown), *DHRC*, 5:564–5. Merrill Jensen denies that the British restrictions had much impact in practice, and he argues that American politicians overstated their significance as a means of rallying support for expanding Congress's powers over trade (*New Nation*, 165–6, 175, 198–200). For a rejoinder to Jensen, see Marks, supra, 56–8.

29. Madison to Richard Henry Lee, July 7, 1785, *PJM* (C.S.), 8:315 ("the most visible"); Thomas Dawes, Jr., at Massachusetts convention, Jan. 21, 1788, *DHRC*, 6:1288 ("freight" and "money"); Madison to Jefferson, Mar. 18, 1786, *PJM* (C.S.), 8:502 ("[a]nother unhappy effect" and "by draining"); Monroe to Jefferson, Aug. 15, 1785, *PTJ* (M.S.), 8:382 ("daily declining"); see also McDonald, *Novus Ordo Seclorum*, 104. For British monopolization of American trade under the mercantilist system, which was one of the colonists' grievances leading to the Revolutionary War, see Woody Holton, *Forced Founders: Indians, Debtors, Slaves, and the Making of the American Revolution in Virginia* (Chapel Hill, NC, 1999), 45–60; Atack and Passell, *New Economic View*, 55–65. On the extent of Great Britain's monopolization of the South's carrying trade under the Confederation, see *Newport Herald*, Oct. 25, 1787, *DHRC*, 24:39.

30. Proceedings of the Continental Congress, Apr. 30, 1784, *JCC*, 26:318 ("with similar"); Grant of Temporary Power to Regulate Commerce, Apr. 30, 1784, *DHRC*, 1:154 ("never command"); Washington to James McHenry, Aug. 22, 1785, *PGW* (C.S.), 3:198–9 ("professedly" and "in a ridiculous"); King to Gerry, July 6, 1786, *LDC*, 23:390 ("most explicit" and "why should we"); Jefferson to Madison, Feb. 8, 1786, *PJM* (C.S.), 8:486 ("would produce" and "insult and war"); see also Madison to Monroe, Aug. 7, 1785, ibid., 334; Washington to Madison, Nov. 30, 1785, ibid., 429; Nathaniel Gorham to James Warren, Mar. 6, 1786, *LDC*, 23:181; John Adams to Robert R. Livingston, July 16, 1783, *Papers of John Adams* (Gregg L. Lint et al., eds., Cambridge, MA, 2010), 15:123–4.

31. David Brian Robertson, *The Constitution and America's Destiny* (New York, 2005), 59; Giesecke, *American Commercial Legislation*, 128–9; Brown, *Redeeming the Republic*, 147–8; Allan Nevins, *The American States During and After the American Revolution, 1775–1789*

(New York, 1924), 556, 558–9; Davis, *Sectionalism in American Politics*, 99–100; Marks, *Independence on Trial*, 80–2; Madison to Jefferson, Oct. 3, 1785, *PJM* (C.S.), 8:375. On artisan demands for protection from British imports in the mid-1780s, see Marks, supra, 77–9.

32. Madison to Monroe, Aug. 7, 1785, *PJM* (C.S.), 8:333 ("they could separately"); Madison to Jefferson, Dec. 9, 1787, ibid., 10:313 ("little short of madness"); Proceedings of the Continental Congress, Mar. 28, 1785, *JCC*, 28:203 ("must prove" and "avail themselves"); Carrington to Edmund Randolph, Apr. 2, 1787, *LDC*, 24:193 ("surreptitious views"); see also Washington to David Stuart, Nov. 30, 1785, *PGW* (C.S.), 3:423; Monroe to Madison, July 26, 1785, *PJM* (C.S.) 8:329–30; Madison to Jefferson, Oct. 3, 1785, ibid., 375.

33. Giesecke, *American Commercial Legislation*, 126 n. 15, 134–5; Saladino, "Delaware," 36; Brandon P. Denning, "Confederation-Era Discrimination Against Interstate Commerce and the Legitimacy of the Dormant Commerce Clause," *Kentucky Law Journal* (2005), 94:62; Davis, *Sectionalism in American Politics*, 92, 101; Marks, *Independence on Trial*, 82; Kaminski, "Paper Politics," 97–8; see also Thomas Dawes, Jr., at Massachusetts convention, Jan. 18, 1788, *DHRC*, 6:1245; "One of the Middle-Interest," *Massachusetts Centinel*, Dec. 5, 1787, *DHRC*, 4:387.

34. Carrington to Randolph, Apr. 2, 1787, *LDC*, 24:193 ("the impossibility"); Madison to Jefferson, Jan. 22, 1786, *PJM* (C.S.), 8:476 ("The necessity"); March 18, 1786, ibid., 502 ("in the belief"); Nevins, *American States During and After the Revolution*, 564; see also Banning, *Sacred Fire*, 47–9; Madison, Preface to Debates, *Farrand*, 3:547–8.

35. Monroe to Jefferson, June 16, 1785, *PTJ* (M.S.), 8:215 ("very mischievous"); Madison, Vices, *PJM* (C.S.), 9:350 ("though not contrary"); Dawes at Massachusetts convention, Jan. 21, 1788, *DHRC*, 6:1288; Madison, Preface to Debates, *Farrand*, 3:547; Tench Coxe to the Virginia Commissioners at Annapolis, Sept. 13, 1786, *PJM* (C.S.), 9:124–6.

36. Gorham to James Warren, Mar. 6, 1786, *LDC*, 23:180 ("the restraining hand"); Randolph at Virginia convention, June 6, 1788, *DHRC*, 9:985–6 ("jealousy"); Madison to Jefferson, Jan. 22, 1786, *PJM* (C.S.), 8:476; see also "A Pennsylvanian to the New York Convention" (Tench Coxe), *Pennsylvania Gazette*, June 11, 1788, *DHRC*, 20:1143, 1149 n. 1; editorial note, *DHRC*, 25:359 n. 4; Robertson, *The Constitution and America's Destiny*, 59–60; Denning, "Interstate Commerce," 47–8, 62–4, 75; John P. Kaminski, *George Clinton: Yeoman Politician of the New Republic* (Madison, WI, 1993), 91; but cf. Giesecke, *American Commercial Legislation*, 134–5.

37. Duane to Washington, Jan. 29, 1781, *LDC*, 16:633 ("The day" and "however reluctantly"); Hamilton to Clinton, Jan. 12, 1783, *PAH*, 3:240 ("Every day"); Washington to the Executives of the States (June 1783), *DHRC*, 13:64 ("give such a tone" and "relax the powers"); see also Oliver Ellsworth to Governor Jonathan Trumbull of Connecticut, July 10, 1783, in Henry Flanders, *The Lives and Times of the Chief Justices of the Supreme Court of the United States* (Philadelphia, 1881), 2:114; James M. Varnum to Governor William Greene of Rhode Island, Apr. 2, 1781, *LDC*, 17:117; Hamilton to Jay, July 25, 1783, *PAH*, 3:416–7; Washington to Hamilton, Mar. 4, 1783, ibid., 279.

38. Proceedings of the Continental Congress, Mar. 6, 1781, *JCC*, 19:236 ("full and explicit"); May 2, 1781, ibid., 20:470 ("most consonant" and "fulfill"); infra pp. 46–7; see also Rakove, *Beginnings of National Politics*, 289–90. The issue of whether, and on what conditions, the Confederation Congress should grant statehood to Vermont also caused Madison to struggle with the question of when "plausible pretexts, if not necessary occasions, of assuming power should occur" (to Pendleton, Jan. 22, 1782, *PJM* (C.S.), 4:39).

39. Articles of Confederation, Art. XIII, *DHRC*, 1:93; Hamilton to Jay, July 25, 1783, *PAH*, 3:416–7 ("The road"); Charles Pinckney, *Observations on the Plan of Government Submitted to the Federal Convention* (pre–Oct. 14, 1787), *DHRC*, 27:28 ("the depressed" and "absurd") [hereinafter, "Charles Pinckney, *Observations*"].

40. Proceedings of the Continental Congress, Feb. 1, 1781, *JCC*, 19:105 ("indispensably necessary"); Dec. 18, 1780, ibid., 18:1157–64; Feb. 3, 1781, ibid., 19:112–3; Madison to Pendleton, May 29, 1781, *PJM* (C.S.), 3:140 ("republican jealousy"); see also Brown, *Redeeming the Republic*, 22; Einhorn, *American Taxation*, 132–3.

41. Abraham Clark to John Cleves Symmes and Josiah Hornblower, Dec. 9, 1785, in Richard P. McCormick, "New Jersey Defies the Confederation: An Abraham Clark Letter,"

Journal of the Rutgers University Library (June 1950), 13:47 ("the most easy"); Brown, *Redeeming the Republic*, 83 ("[a]rticles which" and "the industrious farmer") (quoting Report of Ways and Means Committee, Rhode Island Session Laws, Nov. 1782); see also Eliphalet Dyer to Jonathan Trumbull, Sr., Mar. 18, 1783, *LDC*, 20:45; Einhorn, *American Taxation*, 133, 148; Max M. Edling and Mark D. Kaplanoff, "Alexander Hamilton's Fiscal Reform: Transforming the Structure of Taxation in the Early Republic," *William and Mary Quarterly* (Oct. 2004), 61:740–1. Einhorn especially emphasizes another virtue of the impost as a revenue-raising measure: It enabled Congress to avoid inevitably com-bustible discussions of how much of the tax burden slaveholders should bear (*American Taxation*, 118–20, 128, 134).

42. Morris to Nathaniel Appleton, Apr. 16, 1782, *PRM*, 5:4 ("We cannot," "in order," and "do justice"); Hamilton to Clinton, May 14, 1783, *PAH*, 3:355 ("shocking"); see also Robert Morris, Report on Public Credit, July 29, 1782, *PRM*, 6:60–1, 63; Morris, Circular to the Governors of Massachusetts et al., July 27, 1781, ibid., 1:397–400; Ferguson, *Power of the Purse*, 146.

43. Thomas Thacher at Massachusetts convention, Feb. 4, 1788, *DHRC*, 6:1416 ("a negative"); Madison, Notes on Debates, Feb. 19, 1783, *PJM* (C.S.), 6:259 (Hamilton statement); Madison to Randolph, May 27, 1783, ibid., 7:89; Hamilton to Clinton, May 14, 1783, *PAH*, 3:354; see also Abner Nash to James Iredell, Jan. 8, 1783, *LDC*, 19:565; Rakove, *Beginnings of National Politics*, 313–4; Brown, *Redeeming the Republic*, 22–3; Giesecke, *American Commercial Legislation*, 142; Einhorn, *American Taxation*, 134. For a detailed discussion of rejection of the impost, see Irwin H. Polishook, *Rhode Island and the Union, 1774–1795* (Evanston, IL, 1969), 60–80; see also Jensen, *New Nation*, 63–5. Several states attached conditions, which might have made it difficult to determine if ratification was effective, but Rhode Island's rejection rendered that issue moot. See editorial note, *PRM*, 1:396.

  For the preceding footnote, see Proceedings of the Continental Congress, Feb. 7, 1781, *JCC*, 19:124–5; Einhorn, *American Taxation*, 134, 296 n. 27; editorial note, *PRM*, 1:396.

44. Objections to the impost in Rhode Island from David Howell, c. July 31–Aug. 2, 1782, *PRM*, 6:113–4; Howell to Governor William Greene, July 30, 1782, *LDC*, 18:679–80; see also North Carolina delegates to Governor Alexander Martin, Oct. 22, 1782, *LDC*, 19:290. On the extensive property damage caused by British troops in Rhode Island during the war, see Kaminski, "Paper Politics," 1; see also ibid., 169.

45. Davis, *Sectionalism in American Politics*, 37–9 ("derogat[ion]" at p. 39); Rhode Island del-egates to Governor William Greene, Oct. 15, 1782, *LDC*, 19:262 ("The object"); see also "A Free Holder," *Providence Gazette*, Nov. 9, 1782, p. 2; Polishook, *Rhode Island*, 63–6, 69, 71, 82–3; Einhorn, *American Taxation*, 119.

46. Randolph to Madison, Dec. 13, 1782, *PJM* (C.S.), 5:401 ("amidst"); see also Polishook, *Rhode Island*, 78–80, 87–8; Banning, *Sacred Fire*, 28. On the uncertainty regarding the rea-sons for Virginia's rescission, see Governor Benjamin Harrison to Washington, Mar. 31, 1783, in George Bancroft, *History of the Formation of the Constitution of the United States of America* (New York, 1882), 1:301–2 [hereinafter, "Bancroft, *History of the Formation of the Constitution*"]; Pendleton to Madison, Dec. 31, 1781, *PJM* (C.S.), 3:347, 349 n. 7; Madison to Randolph, Dec. 30, 1782, ibid., 5:472; Randolph to Madison, Feb. 7, 1783, ibid., 6:207.

  For the preceding footnote, see John Adams to Jabez Bowen, Feb. 27, 1790, *DHRC*, 26:743.

47. Nash to James Iredell, Jan. 8, 1783, *LDC*, 19:565 ("[a] deputation"); Dyer to Jonathan Trumbull, Sr., Mar. 18, 1783, *LDC*, 20:43 ("thrown out" and "at the point"); see also Robert Morris to Benjamin Franklin, Jan. 11, 1783, *PRM*, 7:294; Madison to Randolph, Dec. 30, 1782, *PJM* (C.S.), 5:473, 474–5 n. 8; Madison to Randolph, Feb. 25, 1783, ibid., 6:286. For background to the conflict over the officers' pension claims, see Introduction, *DHRC*, 3:318–30. On the "Newburgh conspiracy" generally, see Richard H. Kohn, *Eagle and Sword: The Federalists and the Creation of the Military Establishment in America, 1783–1802* (New York, 1975), ch. 2.

48. Arthur Lee to Samuel Adams, Jan. 29, 1783, *LDC*, 19:639 (quotation); see also Arthur Lee to St. George Tucker, July 21, 1783, *LDC*, 20:436; Kohn, *Eagle and Sword*, 18–25; Rakove, *Beginnings of National Politics*, 318.

49. Morris to Knox, Feb. 7, 1783, *PRM*, 7:417 ("The same principle"); Madison, Notes on Debates, Feb. 19, 1783, *PJM* (C.S.), 6:260–1 (quoting Williamson) ("did not wish"); see also Gouverneur Morris to Jay, Jan. 1, 1783, *PRM*, 7:257; Washington to Hamilton, Apr. 16, 1783, *PAH*, 3:330; Editorial Note, *PRM*, 7:412–20; Kohn, *Eagle and Sword*, 24; Davis, *Sectionalism in American Politics*, 44–50; Jensen, *New Nation*, 69–72; Banning, *Sacred Fire*, 31–2; Ferguson, *Power of the Purse*, 155–6, 161–3; Max M. Mintz, *Gouverneur Morris and the American Revolution* (Norman, OK, 1970), 157–61. Hamilton, too, supported "importunity, if temperate, from the army" (to Washington, Mar. 17, 1783, *PAH*, 3:291); see also Hamilton to Washington, Feb. 13, 1788, ibid., 254–5.

For the preceding footnote, see Madison, Notes on Debates, Feb. 19, 1783, *PJM* (C.S.), 6:259–61 ("avert"); Hamilton to Washington, Apr. 8, 1783, *PAH*, 3:318 ("It is in vain").

50. Knox to McDougall, quoted in Editorial Note, *PRM*, 7:416; Washington to the President of Congress, Mar. 12, 1783, *JCC*, 24:294; Washington, General Order No. 3, Mar. 11, 1783, ibid., 297–8; see also Washington to Hamilton, Mar. 11, 1783, *PAH*, 3:286–7; Kohn, *Eagle and Sword*, 25–30.

51. Robert Morris, Report on Public Credit, July 29, 1782, *PRM*, 6:65–8; see also North Carolina delegates to Governor Alexander Martin, Oct. 22, 1782, *LDC*, 19:290–1. Hamilton had been urging since 1780 that Congress be empowered to impose land and poll taxes (to James Duane, Sept. 3, 1780, *PAH*, 2:404).

52. Madison, Notes on Debates, Feb. 21, 1783, *PJM* (C.S.), 6:272, 273 (quoting Lee) ("a rope" and "pregnant"); Madison to Randolph, Feb. 4, 1783, ibid., 193 ("convinced" and "enormous"). For additional statements of ideological opposition to investing Congress with permanent revenue-raising authority, see Arthur Lee to Samuel Adams, Jan. 29, 1783, *LDC*, 19:639; Samuel Osgood to Stephen Higginson, Feb. 2, 1784, *LDC*, 21:328–9; see also Ferguson, *Power of the Purse*, 153; Davis, *Sectionalism in American Politics*, 39, 46, 54–5.

53. Jones to Washington, Feb. 27, 1783, *LDC*, 19:745 ("[D]ifficulties"); see also North Carolina delegates to Governor Alexander Martin, Oct. 22, 1782, ibid., 290–1; Einhorn, *American Taxation*, 145–8; Ferguson, *Power of the Purse*, 165.

54. Proceedings of the Confederation Congress, Apr. 18, 1783, *JCC*, 24:258 (quotations); Madison, Notes on Debates, Feb. 19, 1783, *PJM* (C.S.), 6:261; see also Ferguson, *Power of the Purse*, 161, 166–7; Einhorn, *American Taxation*, 138–40; Rakove, *Beginnings of National Politics*, 322; Polishook, *Rhode Island*, 98. Congress also proposed an amendment to change the formula for apportioning requisitions among the states. Rather than using land values, the proposed amendment would apportion requisitions according to population, with three slaves counting the same as five free persons. This formula would prove handy for the delegates at the Philadelphia convention, who used it as the method for apportioning representation, and direct taxes, among the states. For further discussion, see infra pp. 265–77.

55. Hamilton to Clinton, May 14, 1783, *PAH*, 3:354–5 (quotations); Ferguson, *Power of the Purse*, 161, 167.

56. Rakove, *Beginnings of National Politics*, 338; Davis, *Sectionalism in American Politics*, 53–4; Kaminski, "Paper Politics," 220; see also Thomas Rodney's Diary, May 3, 1786, *LDC*, 23:263; William Grayson to Madison, Mar. 22, 1786, *PJM* (C.S.), 8:508; Monroe to Madison, Mar. 19, 1786, ibid., 507; Nathan Dane Address to Massachusetts House of Representatives, Nov. 9, 1786, *LDC*, 24:16–7; Rufus King to John Adams, May 5, 1786, *LCRK*, 1:172. Rhode Island rejected the second impost amendment in 1784 before approving it in 1785 (Polishook, *Rhode Island*, 99, 110).

57. John P. Kaminski, "New York: The Reluctant Pillar," in Stephen L. Schechter, ed., *The Reluctant Pillar: New York and the Adoption of the Federal Constitution* (Troy, NY, 1985), 50–1 (quotation); Cecil L. Eubanks, "New York: Federalism and the Political Economy of the Union," in Gillespie and Lienesch, eds., *Ratifying the Constitution*, 304–5.

58. "Sidney" (Abraham Yates), *Loudon's New-York Packet*, Mar. 17, 1785, at 2 ("sacrifice" and "imperceptible"); "Rough Hewer" (Abraham Yates), ibid., Apr. 21, 1785, at 2 ("mighty continental legislat[ure]" and "merge and swallow"); see also Kaminski, *George Clinton*,

90; Linda Grant De Pauw, *The Eleventh Pillar: New York State and the Federal Constitution* (Ithaca, NY, 1966), 35; Kaminski, "New York," 56–7.

59. Kaminski, "New York," 51–2; Eubanks, "New York," 305; Brown, *Redeeming the Republic*, 135; Rakove, *Beginnings of National Politics*, 338; Edling and Kaplanoff, "Alexander Hamilton's Fiscal Reform," 720 tbl. 1, 722; see also Timothy Pickering to John Pickering, Dec. 29, 1787, *DHRC*, 19:482. In the New York legislature, assemblymen from towns tended to support the impost amendment, while the greatest opposition came from assemblymen farthest removed from urban centers. See Jackson Turner Main, *Political Parties Before the Constitution* (Chapel Hill, NC, 1973), 139.

60. Kaminski, *George Clinton*, 91 ("privilege Providence") (quoting state senator John Williams); Monroe to Madison, Feb. 11, 1786, *PJM* (C.S.), 8:492 ("[t]he more extensive"); see also Nathaniel Gorham to Caleb Davis, Feb. 23, 1786, *LDC*, 23:161; Alfred E. Young, *The Democratic Republicans of New York: The Origins, 1763–1797* (Chapel Hill, NC, 1967), 57.

61. Washington to Madison, Mar. 31, 1787, *PGW* (C.S.), 5:116 (quotations). On the British occupation of the western forts and its impact on New Yorkers' involvement in the fur trade, see *Hudson Weekly Gazette*, June 17, 1788, *DHRC*, 21:1199; ibid., 1200 ("robbed"); "An American," *New York Packet*, May 27, 1788, *DHRC*, 20:1113; Charleston *City Gazette*, Apr. 14, 1788, ibid., 916; see also Marks, *Independence on Trial*, 9; Alexander, *The Selling of the Constitutional Convention*, 18. On New York's efforts to secure Congress's help in its dealings with Vermont, see Introduction, *DHRC*, 19:xxxii; Kaminski, "New York," 53.

62. Madison to Monroe, Jan. 22, 1786, *PJM* (C.S.), 8:484 (quotation); Pauline Maier, *Ratification: The People Debate the Constitution, 1787–1788* (New York, 2010), 324–5; Kaminski, *George Clinton*, 92–4; Kaminski, "New York," 56–7; De Pauw, *Eleventh Pillar*, 36–43; see also Timothy Bloodworth to the Governor of North Carolina, Aug. 24, 1786, *LDC*, 23:521; Monroe to Madison, Sept. 12, 1786, *PJM* (C.S.), 9:122; Proceedings of the Confederation Congress, Aug. 22, 1786, *JCC*, 31:531–5, 558–61.

63. Abraham Clark to John Cleves Symmes and Josiah Hornblower, Dec. 9, 1785, in McCormick, "New Jersey Defies the Confederation," 47 (quotation); see also Richard P. McCormick, *Experiment in Independence: New Jersey in the Critical Period, 1781–1789* (New Brunswick, NJ, 1950), 239–40; Kaminski, *George Clinton*, 91; Kaminski, "Paper Politics," 96–7; Robertson, *The Constitution and America's Destiny*, 119 n. 49.

64. Proceedings of the New Jersey Assembly, Feb. 20, 1786, in *Votes and Proceedings of the Tenth General Assembly of the State of New-Jersey* (1786), 99:11 (quotations); see also Nathaniel Gorham to Caleb Davis, Mar. 1, 1786, *LDC*, 23:166; Monroe to Madison, Mar. 19, 1786, *PJM* (C.S.), 8:506–7; Rakove, *Beginnings of National Politics*, 341–2.

65. Grayson to Madison, Mar. 22, 1786, *PJM* (C.S.), 8:508 ("a good deal"); Gorham to James Warren, Mar. 6, 1786, *LDC*, 23:180 ("work the end"); Beatty to Josiah Hornblower, Mar. 6, 1786, in *Proceedings of the New Jersey Historical Society* (1883), Series 2, 7:218–9 ("mortifying," "extremely reprehensible," "to the dissolving," "unfavorable," and "attempt[ing]"); Madison to Monroe, Apr. 9, 1786, *PJM* (C.S.), 9:25 ("certainly" and "furnish fresh pretexts"); see also Henry Lee to Washington, Mar. 2, 1786, *LDC*, 23:171–2; McCormick, *Experiment in Independence*, 241.

66. Proceedings of the Confederation Congress, Mar. 7, 1786, *JCC*, 30:97 ("fatal consequences"); McCormick, *Experiment in Independence*, 241–3 ("breach" at p. 242); Rakove, *Beginnings of National Politics*, 341–2.

67. Board of Treasury Report, June 22, 1786, *JCC*, 30:366 ("bankruptcy").

68. Report of the Committee on Dispatches from Foreign Ministers, Sept. 25, 1783, *LDC*, 20:701–2 ("of the highest" and "a general power"); Thomson to John Dickinson, July 19, 1785, *LDC*, 22:521 ("[t]he conduct" and "from the embarrassed"); see also Monroe to Jefferson, Apr. 12, 1785, *PTJ* (M.S.), 8:77; Nathan Dane to Rufus King, Oct. 8, 1785, *LCRK*, 1:69; John Jay to the Marquis de Lafayette, July 15, 1785, *The Correspondence and Public Papers of John Jay* (Henry P. Johnston, ed., New York, 1891), 3:161 [hereinafter, "*CPPJJ*"].

69. Grant of Temporary Power to Regulate Commerce, Apr. 30, 1784, *DHRC*, 1:153–4.

70. Proceedings of the Confederation Congress, Mar. 28, 1785, *JCC*, 28:201 ("of regulating"); Monroe to Jefferson, June 16, 1785, *PTJ* (M.S.), 8:215–6 ("absolute investment" and "[t]he measures"); see also Monroe to Madison, July 26, 1785, *PJM* (C.S.), 8:329–30; Madison to Jefferson, Oct. 3, 1785, ibid., 374; Davis, *Sectionalism in American Politics*, 89–92. On the campaign by northern merchants for a commerce amendment, see Marks, *Independence on Trial*, 72–5.

71. Monroe to Madison, July 26, 1785, *PJM* (C.S.), 8:330 ("dangerous"); Proceedings of the Confederation Congress, Mar. 28, 1785, *JCC*, 28:201 ("not be restrained" and "all such duties"); see also Davis, *Sectionalism in American Politics*, 92.

72. Monroe to Jefferson, June 16, 1785, *PTJ* (M.S.), 8:215 (quotation); see also Monroe to Madison, July 26, 1785, *PJM* (C.S.), 8:329–30; Massachusetts delegates to Governor James Bowdoin, Aug. 18, 1785, *LDC*, 22:571; Davis, *Sectionalism in American Politics*, 92–3; editorial note, *DHRC*, 1:154–5.

73. For the list of state ratifications and the terms thereof, see Proceedings of the Confederation Congress, Oct. 23, 1786, *JCC*, 31:907–9; Mar. 3, 1786, ibid., 30:93–4. See also Davis, *Sectionalism in American Politics*, 105–8; Banning, *Sacred Fire*, 71; Giesecke, *American Commercial Legislation*, 143; Marks, *Independence on Trial*, 90 n. 79.

74. Lance Banning, "Virginia: Sectionalism and the Common Good," in Gillespie and Lienesch, eds., *Ratifying the Constitution*, 267; Robertson, *The Constitution and America's Destiny*, 60–1; McCraw, *The Founders and Finance*, 49; Davis, *Sectionalism in American Politics*, 85.

75. Pendleton to Madison, Dec. 9, 1786, *PJM* (C.S.), 9:202.

76. Lee to Madison, Aug. 11, 1785, *PJM* (C.S.), 8:340 (quotations); see also Richard Henry Lee to George Mason, May 15, 1787, *PGM*, 3:878. Madison called Lee an "inflexible adversary" to the proposed commerce amendment (to Jefferson, Oct. 3, 1785, *PJM* (C.S.), 8:374). For a prominent Marylander's similar statement of opposition to conferring upon Congress the power to regulate commerce, see James McHenry to Washington, Aug. 1, 1785, *PGW* (C.S.), 3:167–8.

 For the preceding footnote, see American National Biography Online. For the dispute over the authorship of the *Letters to the Republican*, see *DHRC*, 19:204–5.

77. Washington to Madison, Nov. 30, 1785, *PJM* (C.S.), 8:429 ("so self-evident" and "at a loss"); Madison to Monroe, Aug. 7, 1785, ibid., 334–5 ("passive victim" and "a case"); see also Washington to McHenry, Aug. 22, 1785, *PGW* (C.S.), 3:197–8; Davis, *Sectionalism in American Politics*, 91. For the argument that Madison's support for a national power over foreign commerce was tied to a broader vision of a mainly agrarian political economy, see Drew R. McCoy, *The Elusive Republic: Political Economy in Jeffersonian America* (Chapel Hill, NC, 1980), 125–6, 131–2.

78. Madison to Monroe, Aug. 7, 1785, *PJM* (C.S.), 8:335–6.

79. Ibid., 335–6 (quotations); see also Madison to Jefferson, Aug. 20, 1785, ibid., 344.

80. Madison to Jefferson, Jan. 22, 1786, ibid., 476 (quotations); see also Madison to Washington, Dec. 9, 1785, ibid., 438.

81. Monroe to Madison, Sept. 3, 1786, ibid., 9:114 ("always considered"); Madison to Monroe, Aug. 7, 1785, ibid., 8:334 ("not only because" and "long respect"); Madison to Jefferson, Aug. 20, 1785, ibid., 344 ("of a regular remedy," "the strongest motives," and "as much from the hope"); see also Rakove, *Beginnings of National Politics*, 367–8.

82. King to John Adams, May 5, 1786, *LCRK*, 1:172–4 ("Our commerce" at p. 172); King to Adams, Nov. 2, 1785, ibid., 112 ("bitter regret" and "the false"); King to Jonathan Jackson, June 11, 1786, *LDC*, 23:352 ("[h]ow long"). For the disproportionate impact of the British trade restrictions on northern states, see Davis, *Sectionalism in American Politics*, 85, 106–7; Marks, *Independence on Trial*, 62–5; Jensen, *New Nation*, 164, 191–2; see also Samuel Osgood to Stephen Higginson, Feb. 2, 1784, *LDC*, 21:327.

 For the preceding footnote, see American National Biography Online; Kaminski and Moore, *An Assembly of Demigods*, 50–4 (quoting John Bayard to Samuel Bayard, Dec. 1, 1785 ("unrivaled influence" at p. 50); William Pierce's *Sketches* ("most distinguished" and "ranked among" at pp. 50–1); Thomas B. Wait to George Thatcher, Aug. 9, 1789 ("a man of genius" at p. 52); Brissot de Warville, *New Travels in the United States of America* (1788) ("the most eloquent man" at p. 51)).

83. King to Adams, Nov. 2, 1785, *LCRK*, 1:113.
84. King to Jonathan Jackson, June 11, 1786, *LDC*, 23:352 ("the imaginary interests"); Madison to Jefferson, Oct. 3, 1785, *PJM* (C.S.), 8:373 ("frustrated"); Madison to Washington, Dec. 9, 1785, ibid., 438–9 ("[T]he difficulty," "caprice," and "increase with").
85. Proceedings of the Confederation Congress, Aug. 7, 1786, *JCC*, 31:497 (quotations); U.S. Constitution, Arts. V, VII.
86. Articles of Confederation, Art. IX, *DHRC*, 1:92.
87. Grayson to Madison, Aug. 21, 1785, *PJM* (C.S.), 8:348 ("the states"); Mar. 22, 1786, ibid., 508 ("in a kind of"); Gorham to James Warren, Mar. 6, 1786, *LDC*, 23:180 ("great inattention" and "matters in which"); Jay to Jefferson, Aug. 18, 1786, *CPPJJ*, 3:210 ("often experiences"); see also Rakove, *Beginnings of National Politics*, 355–6; Marks, *Independence on Trial*, 128–9. For similar statements noting and criticizing the poor attendance of congressional delegates, which made it difficult to assemble a quorum for doing business, see, e.g., Madison to Washington, Mar. 18, 1787, *PJM* (C.S.), 9:315; Madison to James Madison, Sr., Apr. 1, 1787, ibid., 358; Jay to Jacob Reed, Dec. 12, 1786, *CPPJJ*, 3:221; John Brown to James Breckinridge, Jan. 28, 1788, *LDC*, 24:630; Stephen Mix Mitchell to Jeremiah Wadsworth, Jan. 24, 1787, ibid., 73; Charles Pettit to Jeremiah Wadsworth, May 27, 1786, *LDC*, 23:316.
88. Grayson to Madison, May 28, 1786, *PJM* (C.S.), 9:61 (quotation); Rakove, *Beginnings of National Politics*, 199, 220–2, 236–7; see also Kenneth Coleman, *The American Revolution in Georgia, 1763–1789* (Athens, GA, 1958), 254.
89. Fleming to Jefferson, May 10, 1779, *LDC*, 12:449 ("besides" and "shortly find"); Bland to Jefferson, June 3, 1781, *LDC*, 17:288 ("the anxiety"); see also Rakove, *Beginnings of National Politics*, 236–7. For similar complaints by other congressional delegates, see James Manning to Nathan Miller, June 12, 1786, *LDC*, 23:354; Virginia delegates to Thomas Nelson, Sept. 18, 1781, *LDC*, 18:60; John Francis Mercer to Madison, Nov. 26, 1784, *PJM* (C.S.), 8:152–3; Madison to James Madison, Sr., May 20, 1782, ibid., 4:256.
90. Unsubmitted Resolution Calling for a Convention to Amend the Articles of Confederation, resolution 11 (July 1783), *PAH*, 3:424.
91. Madison to Jefferson, Oct. 3, 1785, *PJM* (C.S.), 8:374. Only the legislatures of Rhode Island and Connecticut provided for popular election of congressional delegates. See, e.g., *DHRC*, 26:740 n. 6.
92. Proceedings of the Confederation Congress, Apr. 30, 1784, *JCC*, 26:318 ("that a free people"); Washington to James Warren, Oct. 7, 1785, *PGW* (C.S.), 3:299 ("[I]t is one"); Washington to Jay, Aug. 15, 1786, ibid., 4:212 ("the very climax" and "very timidly"); see also Rakove, *Beginnings of National Politics*, 364–5.
93. "Nestor: To the People of the United States," Philadelphia *Independent Gazetteer*, June 3, 1786, at 2 ("custom" and "a science"); see also William Samuel Johnson to Hugh Williamson, Mar. 31, 1787, *LDC*, 24:189.
94. Madison, Vices, *PJM* (C.S.), 9:351.
    For the preceding footnote, see Madison to Randolph, May 27, 1783, *PJM* (C.S.), 7:89 ("a change"); Madison, Notes on Debates, Jan. 6, 1783, ibid., 6:16 ("experience").
95. Definitive Treaty of Peace Between the United States of America and His Britannic Majesty (Jan. 14, 1784), Arts. IV ("creditors"), V ("earnestly recommend"), and VI, *JCC*, 26:26.
96. John Jay, Office for Foreign Affairs Report, Oct. 13, 1786, *JCC*, 31:784–91 [hereinafter, "Jay, Foreign Affairs Report"]; Mason to Patrick Henry, May 6, 1783, *PGM*, 2:771; see also Grayson to Madison, May 28, 1786, *PJM* (C.S.), 9:62–3; Rakove, *Beginnings of National Politics*, 343–4; Eubanks, "New York," 305; Young, *Democratic Republicans of New York*, 66–7; Marks, *Independence on Trial*, 5–15. On confiscation as a revenue-raising scheme for financially strapped states, see Main, *Political Parties*, 45, 47; Kaminski, "New York," 52–3; Perkins, *American Public Finance*, 138, 146; Coleman, *American Revolution in Georgia*, 201; McDonald, *We the People*, 289; Introduction, *DHRC*, 11:xxxvii. On payment of prewar debts to British creditors, see Emory G. Evans, "Private Indebtedness and the

Revolution in Virginia, 1776 to 1796," *William and Mary Quarterly* (July 1971), 28:349–74; infra pp. 454–5, 470–1.

97. Madison, Vices, *PJM* (C.S.), 9:352 ("Courtiers"); Madison to Monroe, Dec. 30, 1785, ibid., 8:466 ("no pains"); Grayson to Madison, May 28, 1786, ibid., 63.

98. Articles of Confederation, Art. XIII, *DHRC*, 1:93 (quotation); Jay, Foreign Affairs Report, *JCC*, 31:798; Grayson to Madison, May 28, 1786, *PJM* (C.S.), 9:62; Rakove, *Beginnings of National Politics*, 295–6, 344–5; see also Mason to Henry, May 6, 1783, *PGM*, 2:770–1; Charles Cotesworth Pinckney in South Carolina House, Jan. 16, 1788, *DHRC*, 27:103; John Rutledge, ibid., 103–4; Charles Cotesworth Pinckney, Jan. 17, ibid., 117; Nathan Dane Address to the Massachusetts House of Representatives, Nov. 9, 1786, *LDC*, 24:18.

99. Washington to Jay, Aug. 15, 1786, *PGW* (C.S.), 4:213 (quotation); Grayson to Madison, May 28, 1786, *PJM* (C.S.), 9:63.

100. Articles of Confederation, Art. IX, *DHRC*, 1:89; *The Federalist No. 80* (Hamilton), at 476. For background on how the provision on prewar debts got into the treaty, see Jensen, *New Nation*, 16–7.

101. Jay to Washington, June 27, 1786, *CPPJJ*, 3:203 ("to deceive" and "better fairly"); Jay, Foreign Affairs Report, *JCC*, 31:799–833, 851–62, 870; Proceedings of the Confederation Congress, Mar. 21, 1787, *JCC*, 32:124–5.

102. Jay to Jefferson, Apr. 24, 1787, *CPPJJ*, 3:244 ("[s]ome of the states"); Grayson to William Short, Apr. 16, 1787, *LDC*, 24:227 ("create great" and "so many people"); see also infra pp. 454–5, 470–1.

103. Washington to Jay, Aug. 15, 1786, *PGW* (C.S.), 4:213 ("well grounded"); Definitive Treaty of Peace Between the United States of America and His Britannic Majesty (Jan. 14, 1784), Art. VII, *JCC*, 26:27; see also Randolph to Madison, Apr. 4, 1787, *PJM* (C.S.), 9:364.

104. Jay, Foreign Affairs Report, *JCC*, 31:784 (quoting British response to Adams's complaint of British treaty violations, Feb. 28, 1786). On British motives for holding onto the forts, which had mostly to do with protecting British fur traders, see Jensen, *New Nation*, 169–70.

105. Jay to John Adams, Nov. 1, 1786, *CPPJJ*, 3:214 ("there has not been"); Madison to Pendleton, Apr. 22, 1787, *PJM* (C.S.), 9:395 ("were not only"); Jay, Foreign Affairs Report, *JCC*, 31:867; see also Grayson to Madison, May 28, 1786, *PJM* (C.S.), 9:62–3.

106. Proceedings of the Continental Congress, Mar. 6, 1781, *JCC*, 19:236 ("full and explicit"); May 2, 1781, ibid., 20:470 ("to employ the force"); Madison to Jefferson, Apr. 16, 1781, *PJM* (C.S.), 3:71 ("the whole confederacy"); see also Rakove, *Beginnings of National Politics*, 289–90; Kaminski, "New York," 50–1; Banning, *Sacred Fire*, 21.

107. Madison to Jefferson, Oct. 3, 1785, *PJM* (C.S.), 8:374 (quotation); see also Madison to Jefferson, Apr. 16, 1781, ibid., 3:72.

108. Rakove, *Beginnings of National Politics*, 290.

109. Report of the Grand Committee, Aug. 7, 1786, *JCC*, 31:497; infra pp. 164–6.

110. Washington to James McHenry, Aug. 22, 1785, *PGW* (C.S.), 3:199 ("enter" and "means of carrying"); Thatcher to Pierse Long, Apr. 23, 1788, *LDC*, 25:65 n. 1, 66 ("exhibited"); Report of Committee, Mar. 28, 1785, *JCC*, 28:202; see also Brown, *Redeeming the Republic*, 230–1; Eliga H. Gould, *Among the Powers of the Earth: The American Revolution and the Making of a New World Empire* (Cambridge, MA, 2012), 126–9.

111. For one such criticism, see "Solon, junior," Providence *United States Chronicle*, Mar. 4, 1790, *DHRC*, 26:750.

112. Hamilton to James Duane, Sept. 3, 1780, *PAH*, 2:404–5 ("defect," "the want," "kept the power," and "Congress"); Hamilton to Morris, Apr. 30, 1781, ibid., 604 ("administration" and "would speedily").

113. Jay to Jefferson, Aug. 18, 1786, *CPPJJ*, 3:210 (quotations); Washington to Henry Knox, Feb. 3, 1787, *PGW* (C.S.), 5:9; see also Jay to Jefferson, Apr. 24, 1787, *CPPJJ*, 3:243; Dec. 14, 1786, ibid., 223; Feb. 9, 1787, ibid., 231–2; Jay to Adams, Feb. 21, 1787, ibid., 234; Eric Nelson, *The Royalist Revolution: Monarchy and the American Founding* (Cambridge, MA, 2014), 169. For the first several years of Congress's existence, traditionally executive functions were performed, first, by standing committees composed of congressional

delegates, and then by boards, some of whose members came from outside of Congress. In 1781, Congress replaced this system with one of departments headed by individuals—Foreign Affairs, Finance, and War (the Post Office had been headed by an individual from the beginning)—but the officials who headed these departments were appointed by Congress, were dependent upon it for their tenure in office, and for the most part remained under its tight control. (In 1784, after Robert Morris left office, the position of superintendent of finance was replaced by the three-person Board of Treasury.) See generally Jennings B. Sanders, *Evolution of Executive Departments of the Continental Congress, 1774–1789* (Chapel Hill, NC, 1935); see also Jensen, *New Nation*, 55–7.

114. Davis, *Sectionalism in American Politics*, 10 ("two grand republics") (quoting John McKesson to Governor George Clinton, June 10, 1775). For the account of the Mississippi River controversy that follows, I have relied, in addition to the primary sources cited throughout, on the secondary accounts in Davis, *Sectionalism in American Politics*, ch. 7; H. James Henderson, *Party Politics in the Continental Congress* (New York, 1974), 387–99; Arthur Preston Whitaker, *The Spanish-American Frontier, 1783–1795* (1927; rpr. Gloucester, MA, 1962), 63–77; Marks, *Independence on Trial*, 23–36; Calvin Jillson and Rick K. Wilson, *Congressional Dynamics: Structure, Coordination, and Choice in the First American Congress, 1774–1789* (Stanford, CA, 1994), 268–73; Eli Merritt, "Sectional Conflict and Secret Compromise: The Mississippi River Question and the United States Constitution," *American Journal of Legal History* (Apr. 1991), 35:117–71; editorial note, *DHRC*, 13:149–52; Editorial Note, *PJM*, 8:100–2.

115. Treaty of Paris (Feb. 10, 1763), Art. VII.

116. Definitive Treaty of Peace Between the United States of America and His Britannic Majesty (Jan. 14, 1784), Art. VIII, *JCC*, 26:27; James Monroe at Virginia convention, June 13, 1788, *DHRC*, 10:1230–1; Madison at Virginia convention, June 12, 1788, ibid., 1207–8; Davis, *Sectionalism in American Politics*, 21, 25–7, 77, 109; Whitaker, *Spanish-American Frontier*, 65; Banning, *Sacred Fire*, 18–9; Jillson and Wilson, *Congressional Dynamics*, 269; see also Madison to Joseph Jones, Nov. 25, 1780, *PJM* (C.S.), 2:202–4; Motion on Navigation of Mississippi, Feb. 1, 1781, ibid., 302–3.

117. King to Jonathan Jackson, Sept. 3, 1786, *LDC*, 23:542 ("yearly making"); Letter from a Gentleman at the Falls of Ohio to his Friend in New England, Dec. 4, 1786, *JCC*, 32:197 n. 8, 198–9 ("a barren country," "the most luxurious," "and that in the midst," and "the quantities"); J. M. Opal, "The Republic in the World, 1783–1803," in Gray and Kamensky, eds., *American Revolution*, 596; see also Jensen, *New Nation*, 112–4.

118. Opal, "The Republic in the World," 595–6 (quotations); Jay, Foreign Affairs Report, Feb. 28, 1786, *JCC*, 30:85; Nettels, *Emergence of a National Economy*, 68; Whitaker, *Spanish-American Frontier*, 63, 67, 69–70; Davis, *Sectionalism in American Politics*, 119, 215 n. 43.

119. Louis Guilluame Otto to Comte de Vergennes, Sept. 10, 1786, in Bancroft, *History of the Formation of the Constitution*, 2:392 (quotations); Davis, *Sectionalism in American Politics*, 115; Nettels, *Emergence of a National Economy*, 68; Henderson, *Party Politics*, 387; Whitaker, *Spanish-American Frontier*, 71.

120. Report of the Committee, July 20, 1785, *JCC*, 29:562 ("propositions"); Jay to the President of Congress, Aug. 15, 1785, *JCC*, 29:628 ("exceedingly embarrassing"); Report of the Committee, Aug. 25, 1785, ibid., 658 ("particularly"); see also Proceedings of the Confederation Congress, June 3, 1784, *JCC*, 27:529–30; Henderson, *Party Politics*, 387–8.

   For the preceding footnote, see Jay to President John Adams, Jan. 2, 1801, *CPPJJ*, 4:284–6 (quotation at p. 285); American National Biography Online.

121. Mason to George Mason, Jr., Jan. 8, 1783, *PGM*, 2:761 ("extremely uneasy," "a natural right," and "strong enough"); Madison to Monroe, June 21, 1786, *PJM* (C.S.), 9:82 ("the right"); Memorial of the Delegates Representing in General Assembly the Counties in this Commonwealth upon the Western Waters, Nov. 17, 1786, in ibid., 183 n. 1 ("from nature"); Muter to Madison, Feb. 20, 1787, ibid., 280 ("not met"); see also Harry Innes to John Brown, Dec. 7, 1787, *DHRC*, 8:221; Davis, *Sectionalism in American Politics*, 119.

   For the preceding footnote, see American National Biography Online; Maier, *Ratification*, 39–44 ("content" and "the smiles" at p. 40; "etiquette" at p. 41); Kaminski and Moore, *An Assembly of Demigods*, 187–9 (quoting Pierce's *Sketches*, at p. 187 ("a gentleman"); Jefferson, *Autobiography*, at p. 189 ("a man")); Mason at Philadelphia convention, Aug. 31, 1787, *Farrand*, 2:479 ("he would sooner").

122. Edward J. Cashin, "Georgia: Searching for Security," in Gillespie and Lienesch, eds., *Ratifying the Constitution*, 104 ("incredible") (quoting James Habersham to Thomas Brown, Aug. 5, 1785); Madison to Lafayette, Mar. 20, 1785, *PJM* (C.S.), 8:251 ("a foreign people" and "a bone of our bone"); Monroe to Madison, May 31, 1786, ibid., 9:69 ("we separate"); Banning, "Virginia," 265; Banning, *Sacred Fire*, 58, 62. For a broader connection—especially in Madison's thinking—between westerners' access to markets and their moral and political development, see McCoy, *Elusive Republic*, 122–5.

123. Washington to Henry Lee, June 18, 1786, *PGW* (C.S.), 4:117–8 (quotations); see also Washington to James Warren, Oct. 7, 1785, ibid., 3:288, 290; Washington to Benjamin Harrison, ibid., 2:86–96 (including editorial note); Davis, *Sectionalism in American Politics*, 110–1, 118–9; Stuart Leibiger, *Founding Friendship: George Washington, James Madison, and the Creation of the American Republic* (Charlottesville, VA, 1999), 35–40; Kenneth R. Bowling, *The Creation of Washington, D.C.: The Idea and Location of the American Capital* (Fairfax, VA, 1991), 110–9. Jefferson also strongly supported improvements to the Potomac River, which he said would "pour into our lap the whole commerce of the western world" (to Washington, Mar. 15, 1784, *PGW* (C.S.), 1:217).

124. Lee to Washington, July 3, 1786, *PGW* (C.S.), 4:148. Lee, it turns out, was being paid by the Spanish, so perhaps it is not altogether surprising that his position on the Mississippi River differed from that of most southerners. See Jon Kukla, *A Wilderness So Immense: The Louisiana Purchase and the Destiny of America* (New York, 2003), 99–100.

125. Lee to Washington, July 15, 1787, *PGW* (C.S.), 5:259.

126. Instructions to the Hon. Elbridge Gerry, Esq; and Others, Delegates in Congress from This State, Acts and Laws of the Commonwealth of Massachusetts, ch. 109 (Mar. 8, 1785) (quotation); Davis, *Sectionalism in American Politics*, 116.

127. King to Elbridge Gerry, June 4, 1786, *LCRK*, 1:176 ("every emigrant" and "the United States"); King to Jonathan Jackson, Sept. 3, 1786, *LDC*, 23:542 ("Nature has severed" and "[t]he states situated"); see also Louis Guillaume Otto to Comte de Vergennes, Sept. 10, 1786, in Bancroft, *History of the Formation of the Constitution*, 2:390; Whitaker, *Spanish-American Frontier*, 74–5; Davis, *Sectionalism in American Politics*, 118; Banning, "Virginia," 265.

128. Grayson to Washington, Apr. 15, 1785, *PGW* (C.S.), 2:500–1 (quotation); Davis, *Sectionalism in American Politics*, 117.

129. Henry Lee to Washington, Oct. 11, 1786, *PGW* (C.S.), 4:290–1 (quotations); Davis, *Sectionalism in American Politics*, 116, 118, 214 n. 35; Nevins, *American States During and After the Revolution*, 565–6; Jillson and Wilson, *Congressional Dynamics*, 270; Whitaker, *Spanish-American Frontier*, 74–5.

130. Madison to Jefferson, Aug. 12, 1786, *PJM* (C.S.), 9:96.

131. Jay to the President of Congress, May 29, 1786, *JCC*, 30:323 (quotations); Monroe to Madison, May 31, 1786, *PJM* (C.S.), 9:68–9; Monroe to Henry, Aug. 12, 1786, *Papers of James Monroe* (Daniel Preston, ed., Westport, CT, 2006), 2:333; see also Monroe at Virginia ratifying convention, June 13, 1788, *DHRC*, 10:1232; Davis, *Sectionalism in American Politics*, 116; Henderson, *Party Politics*, 388, 392; Merritt, "Sectional Conflict," 129.

132. Monroe to Jefferson, July 16, 1786, *LDC*, 23:404–5 ("Jay has managed," "an intrigue," and "the most illiberal"); Monroe to Henry, Aug. 12, 1786, *Papers of James Monroe*, 2:333 ("This is one"); see also Banning, *Sacred Fire*, 67–8; Henderson, *Party Politics*, 388–9. For Monroe's evolution on the Mississippi issue, from a stance of relative indifference to one of insistence on American navigation rights, see Davis, *Sectionalism in American Politics*, 120. During the Revolutionary War, Jay had staunchly defended American navigation rights to the Mississippi River during his negotiations with Spain. See Joseph J. Ellis, *The Quartet: Orchestrating the Second American Revolution, 1783–1789* (New York, 2015), 68, 84; see also Hendrickson, *Peace Pact*, 199–200.

133. Madison to Monroe, June 21, 1786, *PJM* (C.S.), 9:82 ("shortsighted," "amazement," and "a voluntary barter"); Bloodworth to North Carolina Assembly, Dec. 16, 1786, *LDC*, 24:51 ("pay the price"); see also Theodorick Bland to Arthur Lee, Nov. 20, 1786, in *Life of Arthur Lee* (Richard Henry Lee, ed., Boston, 1829), 2:332–6; Banning, *Sacred Fire*, 68– 9. For Madison's resistance to abandoning American claims to Mississippi River access during the Revolutionary War, see Madison to Joseph Jones, Nov. 25, 1780, *PJM* (C.S.), 2:202–4; Dec. 5, 1780, ibid., 224; Banning, *Sacred Fire*, 58–9.

134. Speech by John Jay, Aug. 3, 1786, *JCC*, 31:474 (quotations); see also Gardoqui to Jay, May 25, 1786, ibid., 470.

135. Speech by John Jay, Aug. 3, 1786, ibid., 477; Gardoqui to Jay, undated, ibid., 468.

136. Speech by John Jay, Aug. 3, 1786, ibid., 480 (quotation); see also Henderson, *Party Politics*, 391.

137. Speech by John Jay, Aug. 3, 1786, *JCC*, 31:481, 484 (quotations); Monroe at Virginia ratifying convention, June 13, 1788, *DHRC*, 10:1232–3.

138. John Campbell to Madison, Feb. 21, 1787, *PJM* (C.S.), 9:287.

139. A Letter from a Gentleman at the falls of Ohio to his friend in New England, Dec. 4, 1786, *JCC*, 32:197–9 (all quotations but "the ill-advised"); Brown to Jefferson, Aug. 10, 1788, *LDC*, 25:283 ("the ill-advised attempt"). For other similar statements, see Resolutions Reaffirming American Rights to Navigate the Mississippi, Nov. 29, 1786, *PJM* (C.S.), 9:183 n. 1; Extract of a letter from Wilmington, North Carolina (Feb. 2), Charleston *City Gazette*, Feb. 11, 1788, *DHRC*, 27:225.

140. Madison to Jefferson, Aug. 12, 1786, *PJM* (C.S.), 9:96 ("be an unnatural" and "to seize an"); Jefferson to Madison, Jan. 30, 1787, ibid., 248 ("the act," "honest," and "who"); Washington to Henry Lee, Oct. 31, 1786, *PGW* (C.S.), 4:319 ("have on the minds" and "be influenced"); see also June 18, 1786, ibid., 118; Madison to Washington, Mar. 18, 1787, *PJM* (C.S.), 9:316; Madison to Jefferson, Mar. 19, 1787, ibid., 319–20.

141. Monroe to Henry, Aug. 12, 1786, *Papers of James Monroe*, 2:333 (quotations); see also Davis, *Sectionalism in American Politics*, 13–4; Banning, "Virginia," 265–6. On the point about northern states wishing to keep up the value of their own vacant lands, see Madison to Randolph, Apr. 2, 1787, *PJM* (C.S.), 9:361.

142. Bloodworth to Governor Richard Caswell of North Carolina, Aug. 24, 1786, *LDC*, 23:520–1 ("the policy"); Sept. 29, 1786, ibid., 573 ("well known" and "determined").

143. Louis Guillaume Otto to Comte de Vergennes, Sept. 10, 1786, in Bancroft, *History of the Formation of the Constitution*, 2:392.

144. Resolutions Reaffirming American Rights to Navigate the Mississippi, Nov. 29, 1786, *PJM* (C.S.), 9:182–3 ("in the most decided" and "the just resentments"); Monroe at Virginia ratifying convention, June 13, 1788, *DHRC*, 10:1234 ("warmly opposed").

145. Charles Pinckney's Speech, Aug. 16, 1786, *JCC*, 31:938–42, 945–6; Charles Thomson's Notes of Debates, Aug. 16, 1786, *LDC*, 23:485 (reporting Grayson's speech); see also Henderson, *Party Politics*, 392–3; Merritt, "Sectional Conflict," 130–1.

146. Charles Pinckney's Speech, Aug. 16, 1786, *JCC*, 31:943 ("check"), 945–6 ("upon principles," "great reason," and "the impropriety"); Charles Thomson's Notes of Debates, Aug. 16, 1786, *JCC*, 23:485 (quoting Grayson) ("separate the interest," "destroy," and "their deepest").

147. King to Gerry, June 4, 1786, *LCRK*, 1:177 ("be of vast importance"); Aug. 13, 1786, ibid., 188 ("rival," "France," "embarrass[ing]," and "embroil"); see also Henderson, *Party Politics*, 392.

148. Charles Thomson's Notes of Debates, Aug. 16, 1786, *LDC*, 23:486 (quoting King) ("ungrateful," "draw from," and "of the utmost consequence"); Aug. 18, 1786, ibid., 497 (quoting St. Clair) ("the immediate," "quickly," and "redound").

149. Aug. 16, 1786, ibid., 486 (quoting King).

150. Aug. 18, 1786, ibid., 497 (quoting St. Clair); see also Henry Lee to Washington, Oct. 11, 1786, *PGW* (C.S.), 4:292 (describing the arguments of the northern delegates).

151. Charles Thomson's Notes of Debates, Aug. 18, 1786, *LDC*, 23:497–8 (quoting Symmes); Henderson, *Party Politics*, 392. Symmes was heavily invested in land in the Northwest Territory and thus had a personal stake in the issue.

152. Monroe at Virginia ratifying convention, June 13, 1788, *DHRC*, 10:1232.
153. Virginia Delegates' Motion, Aug. 16, 1786, *LDC*, 23:487 ("the establishment"); Bloodworth to Governor Richard Caswell of North Carolina, Sept. 29, 1786, ibid., 573 ("precedent dangerous" and "seven states"); Sept. 4, 1786, ibid., 549 ("the confederated compact" and "dissolution").
154. Monroe at Virginia ratifying convention, June 13, 1788, *DHRC*, 10:1233 (quotation); see also Bloodworth to Caswell, Aug. 24, 1786, *LDC*, 23:520–1; Aug. 16, 1786, ibid., 474.
155. Madison, Notes on Debates, Apr. 25, 1787, *PJM* (C.S.), 9:405 (quotation); Proceedings of the Confederation Congress, Sept. 1, 1786, *JCC*, 31:621 (procedural rule change); Sept. 28, 1786, ibid., 697 (secrecy injunction); Bloodworth to Caswell, Sept. 29, 1786, *LDC*, 23:573; see also Sept. 4, 1786, ibid., 549; Monroe to Madison, Sept. 3, 1786, *PJM* (C.S.), 9:113; Henderson, *Party Politics*, 393–6; Rakove, *Beginnings of National Politics*, 350; Davis, *Sectionalism in American Politics*, 124.
156. Otto to Vergennes, Sept. 10, 1786, in Bancroft, *History of the Formation of the Constitution*, 2:391.
157. Monroe to Henry, Aug. 12, 1786, *Papers of James Monroe*, 2:333, 334 (all quotations except "gentlemen"); Charles Thomson's Notes of Debates, Aug. 18, 1786, *LDC*, 23:496 (quoting Henry Lee) ("gentlemen"); Monroe to Madison, Sept. 3, 1786, *PJM* (C.S.), 9:113–4; see also Sept. 12, 1786, ibid., 122–3; Henderson, *Party Politics*, 394.
158. Sedgwick to Caleb Strong, Aug. 6, 1786, *LDC*, 23:436 (quotations); see also Henderson, *Party Politics*, 394.
159. Madison to Randolph, Mar. 11, 1787, *PJM* (C.S.), 9:308 ("[t]he negotiations"); Carrington to Madison, Dec. 18, 1786, ibid., 218; Bloodworth to the North Carolina Assembly, Dec. 16, 1786, *LDC*, 24:51 ("reason to fear"); see also Madison to Washington, Nov. 1, 1786, *PJM* (C.S.), 9:155; Monroe to Jefferson, Oct. 12, 1786, *LDC*, 23:596. On Jay's continuing negotiations with Gardoqui, see Jay to the President of Congress, Apr. 11, 1787, *JCC*, 32:184–9.
160. Monroe to Madison, Oct. 7, 1786, *PJM* (C.S.), 9:142 ("inclined," "made a different," "the narrative," and "by those"); Proceedings of the Confederation Congress, Mar. 30, 1787, *JCC*, 32:147–8; Madison, Notes on Debates, Apr. 18, 1787, *PJM* (C.S.), 9:389 ("much embarrassed"); Jay to Jefferson, Dec. 14, 1786, *PTJ* (M.S.), 10:596 ("[m]ischief has been" and "the western people"); see also Louise Irby Trenholme, *The Ratification of the Federal Constitution in North Carolina* (New York, 1932), 107.
161. Madison to Jefferson, Feb. 15, 1787, *PJM* (C.S.), 9:269 ("not ventured"); Madison, Notes on Debates, Mar. 13, 1787, ibid., 310 ("would not listen" and "Spain"); Madison to Jefferson, Mar. 19, 1787, ibid., 319 ("arrested"); see also Madison, Notes on Debates, Mar. 29, 1787, ibid., 337–9.
162. Jay, Foreign Affairs Report, Apr. 12, 1787, *JCC*, 32:204 ("a treaty disagreeable"); Jay to the President of Congress, Apr. 11, 1787, ibid., 186 (several drafts); Madison, Notes on Debates, Apr. 26, 1787, *PJM* (C.S.), 9:407 ("it was considered"); Apr. 18, 1787, ibid., 389; see also Madison to Randolph, Apr. 15, 1787, ibid., 380; Madison to Jefferson, Apr. 23, 1787, ibid., 400; Grayson to Monroe, Apr. 30, 1787, *LDC*, 24:262; Proceedings of the Confederation Congress, July 4, 1787, *JCC*, 32:299–300; Whitaker, *Spanish American Frontier*, 76–7; Banning, *Sacred Fire*, 106.
163. John Brown to James Breckinridge, Jan. 28, 1788, *LDC*, 24:630 (quotations); see also ibid., June 21, 1788, *DHRC*, 10:1662. Van Cleve argues that abandoning the negotiations with Spain was the quid pro quo demanded by southerners in the summer of 1787 in return for their agreement to the Northwest Ordinance, which barred slavery in the territory north of the Ohio River (George William Van Cleve, *A Slaveholders' Union: Slavery, Politics, and the Constitution in the Early American Republic* (Chicago, 2010), 158–63; see also infra pp. 294–7).
164. Proceedings of the Confederation Congress, Sept. 16, 1788, *JCC*, 34:534–5 ("a clear and essential"); Madison to Randolph, Sept. 24, 1788, *PJM* (C.S.) 11:263 ("well calculated"); Madison to Jefferson, Sept. 21, 1788, ibid., 257; Williamson to Governor Samuel Johnston of North Carolina, Sept. 17, 1788, *LDC*, 25:377 ("no power," "perfectly convinced," and "increase"); see also Madison to John Brown, Sept. 26, 1788, *PJM* (C.S.),

11:266–7; Banning, *Sacred Fire,* 268. In 1795, a treaty between the United States and Spain opened the Mississippi River to American navigation.

165. Monroe to Madison, Oct. 7, 1786, *PJM* (C.S.), 9:143 ("this intrigue"); Madison to Randolph, Apr. 2, 1787, ibid., 361, 362 n. 3; Madison to James Madison, Sr., Apr. 1, 1787, ibid., 359, 360–1 n. 3 (declaration by New Jersey legislature); Monroe to Madison, Sept. 12, 1786, ibid., 122–3; Abraham Clark to Madison, Nov. 23, 1786, ibid., 177 & n. 1; see also Randolph at Virginia ratifying convention, June 13, 1788, *DHRC,* 10:1253–4; Henderson, *Party Politics,* 396–7; Whitaker, *Spanish-American Frontier,* 76–7.

166. Madison to Jefferson, Aug. 12, 1786, *PJM* (C.S.), 9:96–7 (quotations); Davis, *Sectionalism in American Politics,* 154–5; Rakove, *Original Meanings,* 43.

167. Henry Lee to Washington, Aug. 7, 1786, *PGW* (C.S.), 4:200–1 (all quotations but the last); Charles Thomson's Notes on Debates, Aug. 16, 1786, *LDC,* 23:496 (quoting Henry Lee) ("the powers").

168. Madison to Washington, Nov. 1, 1786, *PJM* (C.S.), 9:155 ("on the federal spirit"); Resolutions Affirming American Rights to Navigate the Mississippi River, Nov. 29, 1786, ibid., 183 n. 1 ("greatly alarmed," "unconstitutional and dangerous," "the just resentments," and "that confidence").

169. Madison to James Madison, Sr., Nov. 1, 1786, ibid., 154 ("excited much heat" and "a great bar"); Madison to Washington, Dec. 7, 1786, ibid., 200 ("most federal," "extremely soured" and "unless the project"); Washington to Henry Knox, Dec. 26, 1786, *PGW* (C.S.), 4:482 ("a prompt disposition" and "if the unlucky stirring"); Madison to Jefferson, Dec. 4, 1786, *PJM* (C.S.), 9:189 ("very pointed"); see also Mar. 19, 1787, ibid., 319; George Muter to Madison, Feb. 20, 1787, ibid., 280; Henderson, *Party Politics,* 398; Davis, *Sectionalism in American Politics,* 119.

170. Pendleton to Madison, Dec. 9, 1786, *PJM* (C.S.), 9:202–3 ("suppress" and "the project"); Hugh Williamson to Madison, June 2, 1788, *LDC,* 25:136 ("the navigation"); Bloodworth to Caswell, Sept. 4, 1786, *LDC,* 23:549 ("unhappy dispute" and "out of view"); see also Rakove, *Beginnings of National Politics,* 371–2; Davis, *Sectionalism in American Politics,* 13, 139–40; Banning, *Sacred Fire,* 425 n. 85; Marks, *Independence on Trial,* 91.

171. Madison to Randolph, Feb. 25, 1787, *PJM* (C.S.), 9:299 ("radical"); Madison to Pendleton, Feb. 24, 1787, ibid., 295 ("the danger"); see also Madison at Virginia convention, June 12, 1788, *DHRC,* 10:1208–9; Banning, "Virginia," 266.

172. *State Gazette of South Carolina,* Sept. 14, 1786, at 2 (reprinting intelligence from New York, Aug. 24) ("hourly falling" and "[a]s well ye may"); Boston *Independent Chronicle,* Sept. 7, 1786, at 2; Washington to Jay, Aug. 15, 1786, *PGW* (C.S.), 4:212 ("go on in" and "the very climax"); Jay to Jefferson, Dec. 14, 1786, *CPPJJ,* 3:223 ("if it may be called"); see also Jay to Adams, July 4, 1787, ibid., 248–9; Jay to William Carmichael, Jan. 4, 1787, ibid., 225; Providence *United States Chronicle,* Mar. 29, 1787, *DHRC,* 13:76; Present Situation of Affairs, Philadelphia *American Museum,* Apr. 4, 1787, ibid., 76–7.

173. Grayson to William Short, Apr. 16, 1787, *LDC,* 24:227 ("the more slack" and "ripe"); Lear to Benjamin Lincoln, June 4, 1787, microformed on Benjamin Lincoln Papers, P-40, Reel 8 (Mass. Historical Society) ("[I]n a country"); Mitchell to William Samuel Johnson, Sept. 18, 1787, *DHRC,* 3:347 ("those indomitable spirits" and "easily and efficaciously"); see also Charles Thomson to John Dickinson, July 19, 1785, *LDC,* 22:520; Henry Lee to Washington, Sept. 8, 1786, *PGW* (C.S.), 4:241; Grayson to Monroe, May 28, 1787, *Farrand,* 3:30.

174. Supra pp. 24–41; Rakove, *Beginnings of National Politics,* 329.

175. Hamilton to James Duane, Sept. 3, 1780, *PAH,* 2:407; Hamilton to Robert Morris, Apr. 30, 1781, ibid., 630 ("futile and senseless" and "complete sovereignty"); Hamilton to Robert Morris, July 22, 1782, ibid., 3:115 ("be brought to cooperate"); see also Hamilton to George Clinton, Jan. 12, 1783, ibid., 240; Resolution of the New York Legislature Calling for a Convention of the States to Revise and Amend the Articles of Confederation, July 20, 1782, ibid., 113; Unsubmitted Resolution Calling for a Convention to Amend the Articles of Confederation, July 1783, ibid., 420; Ferguson, *Power of the Purse,* 148; Ron Chernow, *Alexander Hamilton* (New York, 2004), 139, 157, 171, 183; Rakove, *Beginnings of National Politics,* 325–6; McCraw, *The Founders and Finance,* 77; Davis, *Sectionalism in*

American Politics, 50–1; Banning, *Sacred Fire*, 38, 415 n. 97; Kaminski, "New York," 50. On the early support for a constitutional convention by Rhode Island congressional delegate James Mitchell Varnum, see his letter to Gov. William Greene, Apr. 2, 1781, *LDC*, 17:117; Davis, supra, 33. On Washington's support for a convention, see Washington to William Gordon, July 8, 1783, in *The Writings of George Washington* (John C. Fitzpatrick, ed., Washington, DC, 1938), 27:49–50.

176. Grayson to Madison, May 28, 1786, *PJM* (C.S.), 9:64; see also Rakove, *Beginnings of National Politics*, 373.

177. Massachusetts delegates to Governor James Bowdoin, Sept. 3, 1785, *LDC*, 22:610 ("premature"); Aug. 18, 1785, ibid., 571 ("no cause"); Madison to Monroe, Mar. 19, 1786, *PJM* (C.S.), 8:505–6; Rakove, *Beginnings of National Politics*, 293–5.

178. Thomson to John Dickinson, July 19, 1785, *LDC*, 22:521–2 (quotations); see also Robert Morris to Franklin, Sept. 27, 1782, *PRM*, 6:449–50.

179. Massachusetts delegates to Bowdoin, Sept. 3, 1785, *LDC*, 22:612; see also Davis, *Sectionalism in American Politics*, 103–4; Rakove, *Beginnings of National Politics*, 348.

180. Rakove, *Beginnings of National Politics*, 380; Ferguson, *Power of the Purse*, 242–3.

For the preceding footnote, see John Adams to Abigail Adams, Apr. 14, 1776, in *Adams Family Correspondence* (L. H. Butterfield et al., eds., Cambridge, MA, 1963), 1:381 ("gentry" and "[t]his inequality"); Howell to Welcome Arnold, Aug. 3, 1782, *LDC*, 19:6 ("as you go," "the common people," and "In New England"); see also Samuel Osgood to Stephen Higginson, Feb. 2, 1784, *LDC*, 21:326; Davis, *Sectionalism in American Politics*, 59–60, 69. For the argument that American governments were more democratic and more efficacious where slavery was only a marginal institution, see Einhorn, *American Taxation*, 7. On the extent to which the governments of Virginia and South Carolina were dominated by planter elites, see Main, *Political Parties*, 11, 13.

Chapter 2

1. Knox to Washington, Oct. 23, 1786, *PGW* (C.S.), 4:300 ("determined"); Knox to Mercy Otis Warren, May 30, 1787, *Collections of Massachusetts Historical Society* (Boston, 1925), 73:294 ("anarchy"); Henry Lee to Washington, Oct. 17, 1786, *PGW* (C.S.), 4:295 ("the malcontents," "their object," and "we are all").

2. Washington to Henry Lee, Oct. 31, 1786, *PGW* (C.S.), 4:318 ("mortified," "equally to be," and "exhibit"); Washington to Madison, Nov. 5, 1786, *PJM* (C.S.), 9:161 ("no morn"); Washington to Humphreys, Oct. 22, 1786, *PGW* (C.S.), 4:297 ("ridiculous").

3. Lee to Washington, Sept. 8, 1786, ibid., 241 ("[w]eak and feeble"); Washington to Madison, Nov. 5, 1786, *PJM* (C.S.), 9:161 ("Without some").

4. Madison at Philadelphia convention, June 6, 1787, *Farrand*, 1:134 (quotations); Rakove, *Original Meanings*, 29–30; Wood, *Creation of the American Republic*, 465.

5. Adams, *First American Constitutions*, 59, 61–2, 79; Michael A. McDonnell, "The Struggle Within: Colonial Politics on the Eve of Independence," in Gray and Kamensky, eds., *American Revolution*, 114. On the greater popular participation in governance generally, see Main, *Political Parties*, 15–7; Alfred F. Young, *Liberty Tree: Ordinary People and the American Revolution* (New York, 2006), 185–6, 188. On the democratizing effect of the Revolutionary War more generally, see Gordon S. Wood, *The Radicalism of the American Revolution* (New York, 1992), ch. 13.

6. Rakove, *Beginnings of National Politics*, 121–2 (quoting Carroll and Livingston); Holton, *Forced Founders*, 193–4 (Braxton quotation at p. 193); see also John Adams to Horatio Gates, Mar. 23, 1776, *LDC*, 3:431; Adams, *First American Constitutions*, 158; Davis, *Sectionalism in American Politics*, 11; McDonnell, "The Struggle Within," 115; Young, *Liberty Tree*, 189, 192.

For the preceding footnote, see Louis Guillaume Otto to Comte de Vergennes, Oct. 10, 1786, in Bancroft, *History of the Formation of the Constitution*, 2:399.

7. Woody Holton, *Unruly Americans and the Origins of the Constitution* (New York, 2007), 26–8; Edling, *Revolution in Favor of Government*, 84–6; Brown, *Redeeming the Republic*,

39; McCraw, *The Founders and Finance*, 47–8, 375 n. 4; Kaminski, "Paper Politics," 1–3; John P. Kaminski, "Rhode Island: Protecting State Interests," in Gillespie and Lienesch, eds., *Ratifying the Constitution*, 369; Terry Bouton, "The Trials of the Confederation," in Gray and Kamensky, eds., *American Revolution*, 374; Peter H. Lindert and Jeffrey G. Williamson, "American Incomes Before and After the Revolution," *Journal of Economic History* (Sept. 2013), 73:741, 752–3. For a very different view of the state of the American economy in the mid-1780s, see Jensen, *New Nation*, chs. 8–10, 12.

8. Holton, *Unruly Americans*, 28; Edling, *Revolution in Favor of Government*, 84–6; Robertson, *The Constitution and America's Destiny*, 52; Terry Bouton, *Taming Democracy: "The People," the Founders, and the Troubled Ending of the American Revolution* (New York, 2007), 91; Kaminski, "Paper Politics," 14; Davis, *Sectionalism in American Politics*, 80–1.

9. Hamilton to Morris, Aug. 13, 1782, *PAH*, 3:135 (quotation); Kaminski, "Paper Politics," 10–18, 139; McCraw, *The Founders and Finance*, 48, 53–4; Bouton, *Taming Democracy*, 78; Brown, *Redeeming the Republic*, 39.

10. Holton, *Unruly Americans*, 29, 40–2, 81; Edling, *Revolution in Favor of Government*, 155–6; Brown, *Redeeming the Republic*, 33, 69; Leonard L. Richards, *Shays's Rebellion: The American Revolution's Final Battle* (Philadelphia, 2002), 81–2; Bouton, *Taming Democracy*, 86; Edling and Kaplanoff, "Alexander Hamilton's Fiscal Reform," 714, 724, 729; *Proceedings of the House of Assembly of the Delaware State 1781–1792* (Claudia L. Bushman et al., eds., Cranbury, NJ, 1988), 379–80 [hereinafter, "*Delaware House Proceedings*"].

11. Edling, *Revolution in Favor of Government*, 56–8; Brown, *Redeeming the Republic*, 36–7; Shumer, "New Jersey," 86; Richards, *Shays's Rebellion*, 82–3; Main, *Political Parties*, 57; Edling and Kaplanoff, "Alexander Hamilton's Fiscal Reform," 720–3. Poll taxes were less regressive in the South, where they had to be paid on slaves as well as free male members of the household, and thus operated, in part, as taxes on wealth. See Einhorn, *American Taxation*, 38.

12. Clark to John Cleves Symmes and Josiah Hornblower, Dec. 9, 1785, in McCormick, "New Jersey Defies the Confederation," 47 (quotations); Brown, *Redeeming the Republic*, 39, 69, 149; *Minutes of the Council of the Delaware State from 1776 to 1792* (June 16, 1786) (Dover, 1887), 122 [hereinafter, "*Delaware Council Minutes*"]; *Delaware House Proceedings*, 356–7. On Congress's refusal to accept payment of requisitions in paper money, see Proceedings of the Confederation Congress, Sept. 18, 1786, *JCC*, 31:663–4; Rhode Island delegates to Governor John Collins, Sept. 28, 1786, *LDC*, 23:570.

13. John Dawson to Madison, Apr. 15, 1787, *PJM* (C.S.), 9:381 (quotation); Holton, *Unruly Americans*, 43–5; Bouton, *Taming Democracy*, 92, 99–100; Brown, *Redeeming the Republic*, 55, 71.

14. Edling, *Revolution in Favor of Government*, 56–7; Holton, *Unruly Americans*, 55; Alexander Keyssar, *The Right to Vote: The Contested History of Democracy in the United States* (New York, 2000), 24–5. For some examples of relief petitions, see Bouton, "Trials of the Confederation," 376.

15. Kaminski, "Paper Politics," 98–9, 139, 170, 174 ("flint-hearted" and "lying in wait" at p. 174); Grayson to Madison, Mar. 22, 1786, *PJM* (C.S.), 8:509; *Delaware House Proceedings*, 349 (June 15, 1786) ("deeply impressed" and "devise"); ibid., 310 (Jan. 14, 1786); John A. Munroe, *Federalist Delaware, 1775–1815* (New Brunswick, NJ, 1954), 141–2; Perkins, *American Public Finance*, ch. 7; Holton, *Unruly Americans*, 77, 81; see also Madison to Jefferson, Aug. 12, 1786, *PJM* (C.S.), 9:94–5.

16. *Delaware House Proceedings*, 349 (June 15, 1786) (quotation); ibid., 341 (June 8, 1786); *Delaware Council Minutes*, 122 (June 16, 1786); Munroe, *Federalist Delaware*, 141–3; Robertson, *The Constitution and America's Destiny*, 53.

17. Brown, *Redeeming the Republic*, 60–71, 91 ("relieve the distressed" at p. 91); Madison to Jefferson, Dec. 4, 1786, *PJM* (C.S.), 9:191 ("This indulgence"); Kaminski, "Paper Politics," 25, 50–1, 113, 177–8; Perkins, *American Public Finance*, 160, 162; Polishook, *Rhode Island*, 124; Shumer, "New Jersey," 79; see also Madison to Washington, Dec. 7, 1786, *PJM* (C.S.), 9:200; Madison to Jefferson, Oct. 3, 1785, ibid., 8:375.

18. *Delaware House Proceedings*, 349 (June 15, 1786) ("happy effects"); ibid., 356 (June 17, 1786) ("happy concurrence"); Kaminski, "Paper Politics," 51–2, 107, 110, 115, 147, 152, 173–4, 178–9; Perkins, *American Public Finance*, ch. 7; Brown, *Redeeming the Republic*,

79–81, 151; Ferguson, *Power of the Purse*, 5, 16–9; James R. Morrill, *The Practice and Politics of Fiat Finance: North Carolina in the Confederation, 1783–1789* (Chapel Hill, NC, 1969), 63; George William Van Cleve, "The Anti-Federalists' Toughest Challenge: Paper Money, Debt Relief, and the Ratification of the Constitution," *Journal of the Early Republic* (Winter 2014), 34:534. On colonial land banks, see Perkins, supra, ch. 2.

19. Kaminski, "Paper Politics," 24–5, 45, 50, 147–8, 152; Perkins, *American Public Finance*, ch. 7; Van Cleve, "Anti-Federalists' Toughest Challenge," 536 n. 11, 536–8, 541–2; Brown, *Redeeming the Republic*, 151–2; Holton, *Unruly Americans*, 131; Polishook, *Rhode Island*, 126; Coleman, *American Revolution in Georgia*, 214; Kaminski, "New York," 54–5; see also Grayson to Madison, Mar. 22, 1786, *PJM* (C.S.), 8:509; Madison to Jefferson, Aug. 12, 1786, ibid., 9:94–5. For the various permutations of tender laws, see Glossary of Frequently Used Terms, *DHRC*, 24:317. On Rhode Island's version, see Introduction, *DHRC*, 25:455.

20. Hamilton to Robert Morris, Apr. 30, 1781, *PAH*, 2:619–20.

21. American Intelligence, *State Gazette of South Carolina*, Sept. 14, 1786, at 2 ("pass[ing] universally equal"); Pieter Johan van Berckel to the Estates General, Sept. 12, 1786, in Bancroft, *History of the Formation of the Constitution*, 2:393 ("in the most solemn"); Madison to Jefferson, Aug. 12, 1786, *PJM* (C.S.), 9:94 ("the lead," "not considerable," and "funds"); Kaminski, "Paper Politics," 25, 79, 118–9, 123–4, 153–4, 158, 281–2; Perkins, *American Public Finance*, ch. 7; Morrill, *Fiat Finance*, 64–6, 83–4; Van Cleve, "Anti-Federalists' Toughest Challenge," 535–6, 538, 541; Brown, *Redeeming the Republic*, 151; Holton, *Unruly Americans*, 113; see also Timothy Bloodworth to Governor Richard Caswell of North Carolina, Sept. 4, 1786, *LDC*, 23:549; Rhode Island Legislature to President George Washington, Sept. 10–19, 1789, *PGW* (Presidential Series) [hereinafter "*PGW* (P.S.)"], 4:14.

22. Madison to Jefferson, July 18, 1787, *PJM* (C.S.), 10:105–6 (quotations); Kaminski, "Paper Politics," 26; Morrill, *Fiat Finance*, 70–1, 75, 85; Perkins, *American Public Finance*, 158; Coleman, *American Revolution in Georgia*, 214; Van Cleve, "Anti-Federalists' Toughest Challenge," 537; see also Madison to Jefferson, Aug. 12, 1786, *PJM* (C.S.), 9:94–5; Bloodworth to Caswell, Sept. 4, 1786, *LDC*, 23:549.

23. American Intelligence, *State Gazette of South Carolina*, Sept. 14, 1786, at 2 (quotation); Kaminski, "Paper Politics," 181–3; Polishook, *Rhode Island*, 126–7. Even during the colonial era, Rhode Island's paper money had depreciated in value far more dramatically than that issued by other colonies. See Atack and Passell, *New Economic View*, 65–6; Perkins, *American Public Finance*, 154–6, 164–5; Polishook, supra, 165; see also "A Citizen of United America" (Tench Coxe), Philadelphia *Federal Gazette*, Apr. 6, 1790, *DHRC*, 26:810–1, 815 n. 4.

24. Extract of a letter from a gentleman in Providence (July 1), *New Jersey Gazette*, Aug. 28, 1786, at 2 (all quotations except "in a sort"); Madison to Jefferson, Aug. 12, 1786, *PJM* (C.S.), 9:95 ("in a sort"); Kaminski, "Paper Politics," 183; see also Letter from Providence Merchants to President George Washington, Mar. 27, 1789, *PGW* (P.S.), 1:453; Bloodworth to Caswell, Sept. 4, 1786, *LDC*, 23:550; Brown, *Redeeming the Republic*, 151; Polishook, *Rhode Island*, 127.

25. Kaminski, "Rhode Island," 371–2, 374–5; Kaminski, "Paper Politics," 186; Polishook, *Rhode Island*, 128–9, 154–5, 178–9; editorial note, *DHRC*, 25:470 n. 1; *Worcester Magazine* (Oct. 1786), 2 (No. 30):366. On this case, *Trevett v. Weeden*, see James M. Varnum, *The Case, Trevett Against Weeden* (Providence, RI, 1787); see also Irwin H. Polishook, "Trevett vs. Weeden and the Case of the Judges," *Newport History* (Apr. 1965), 38:45–69; Patrick T. Conley, "Rhode Island: Laboratory for the Internal 'Lively Experiment,'" in Patrick T. Conley and John P. Kaminski, eds., *The Bill of Rights and the States: The Colonial and Revolutionary Origins of American Liberties* (Madison, WI, 1992), 136–43.

26. Brown, *Redeeming the Republic*, 40, 53, 64–5, 128; Robertson, *The Constitution and America's Destiny*, 110; Madison to Jefferson, Dec. 4, 1786, *PJM* (C.S.), 9:191.

27. Brown, *Redeeming the Republic*, 152, 163; Bouton, *Taming Democracy*, 118–9; *Delaware House Proceedings*, 346 (June 13, 1786).

28. Robertson, *The Constitution and America's Destiny*, 53, 110; Brown, *Redeeming the Republic*, 80–1, 90; Main, *Political Parties*, 63, 280, 335; see also Madison to Washington, Dec. 24, 1786, *PJM* (C.S.), 9:224–5; Munroe, *Federalist Delaware*, 143; Morrill, *Fiat Finance*, 62; Robert A. Becker, "Salus Populi Suprema Law: Public Peace and South Carolina Debtor Relief Laws, 1783–1788," *South Carolina Historical Review* (Jan. 1979), 80:66–72; Van Cleve, "Anti-Federalists' Toughest Challenge," 536; editorial note, *DHRC*, 27:114 n. 17. For an interesting account of the origins of South Carolina's 1787 installment law, see Henry W. DeSaussure to Jedidiah Morse, Feb. 11, 1788, ibid., 222–3.

29. Brown, *Redeeming the Republic*, 76–8 ("[t]he ravages," "greatly reduced," and "Let a medium"), 93 ("Many irreproachable characters"), 148; Van Cleve, "Anti-Federalists' Toughest Challenge," 542 ("help the feeble"); see also Holton, *Unruly Americans*, 42, 60–1, 274–5; Bouton, *Taming Democracy*, 106; Ferguson, *Power of the Purse*, xiv–xv.

30. Bouton, *Taming Democracy*, 84, 114–5 (quotations); Holton, *Unruly Americans*, 32; Kaminski, "Paper Politics," 177, 205; Polishook, *Rhode Island*, 114–5.

31. Richards, *Shays's Rebellion*, 74–81 (quotation at p. 79); Holton, *Unruly Americans*, 68–9. For resentment at the pensions paid to Continental Army officers, which was especially strong in New England, see Jensen, *New Nation*, 261; McDonald, *We the People*, 141; supra pp. 27–8.

32. Holton, *Unruly Americans*, 37–8, 55; Bouton, *Taming Democracy*, 84–5, 114–5; Munroe, *Federalist Delaware*, 143–4; Perkins, *American Public Finance*, 146–7; Polishook, *Rhode Island*, 116–8.

33. Holton, *Unruly Americans*, 37; Bouton, *Taming Democracy*, 85, 107; Richards, *Shays's Rebellion*, 75; see also Brown, *Redeeming the Republic*, 38. On the extraordinary extent to which state debt was concentrated in relatively few hands—often the hands of investors from out of state—by the time that the federal government assumed most of the states' war debts in 1790, see Whitney K. Bates, "Northern Speculators and Southern State Debts: 1790," *William and Mary Quarterly* (Jan. 1962), 19:32–8.

34. Holton, *Unruly Americans*, 130–1, 153.

35. Miscellany, *Massachusetts Centinel*, Nov. 11, 1789, at 65–6.

36. Jay to John Adams, Feb. 21, 1787, *CPPJJ*, 3:235 ("the treasury"); Rutledge to Arthur Middleton (Aug. 1782), in "Correspondence of Hon. Arthur Middleton," *The South Carolina Historical and Genealogical Magazine* (Joseph W. Barnwell ann., 1926), 27:21 ("it will be"); Brown, *Redeeming the Republic*, 142.

37. "The Primitive Whig" No. 1, *New-Jersey Gazette*, Jan. 9, 1786, at 1 (quotations); Brown, *Redeeming the Republic*, 48–9.

38. "The Primitive Whig" No. 1, *New-Jersey Gazette*, Jan. 9, 1786, at 1 ("idle spendthrifts"); Richard Henry Lee to Richard Lee, Sept. 13, 1787, *Letters of Richard Henry Lee* (James Curtis Ballagh, ed., New York, 1914), 2:436 ("almost universally" and "industry and economy") [hereinafter, "*LRHL*"]; Brown, *Redeeming the Republic*, 124 ("the exorbitant importation"), 160; *Delaware Council Minutes*, 975 ("very rarely," "inevitable misfortune," and "men's living"); *Virginia Independent Chronicle*, Sept. 7, 1786, at 2 ("gewgaws and trifles"); see also Kaminski, "Paper Politics," 102–4; Samuel Vaughan to Richard Price, Jan. 4, 1785, in *The Correspondence of Richard Price* (D. O. Thomas ed., Durham, NC, 1991), 2:253–4.

39. From the *Pennsylvania Gazette*: Thoughts on Paper Money, *New-Haven Gazette & Conn. Magazine* (July 27, 1786), 1 (No. 24):188 ("greatest evil" and "destroys the morals"); Grayson to Madison, Mar. 22, 1786, *PJM* (C.S.), 8:509 ("violently opposed" and "one of the most"); Letter from "Probus," in "Primitive Whig" No. IV, *New-Jersey Gazette*, Jan. 30, 1786, at 1 ("expressly calculated" and "acts conducing"); Brown, *Redeeming the Republic*, 120 (quoting Sedgwick to Nathan Dane, June 3, 1787 ["men of talents" and "firmly determined"] and Sedgwick to Dane, June 5, 1787 ["the dregs"], both in the Massachusetts Historical Society); see also Jay to Washington, June 27, 1786, *CPPJJ*, 3:204; David Ramsay to Benjamin Rush, Aug. 6, 1786, in "David Ramsay, 1749–1815: Selections from His Writings," *Transactions of the American Philosophical Society* (Aug. 1965) (Robert L. Brunhouse, ed., Philadelphia, 1965), 105; Gordon Wood, "Interests and Disinterestedness in the Making of the Constitution," in Richard Beeman, Stephen Botein, and Edward C.

Carter II, eds., *Beyond Confederation: Origins of the Constitution and American National Identity* (Chapel Hill, NC, 1987), 106–7.

40. Grayson to Madison, Mar. 22, 1786, *PJM* (C.S.), 8:509 (quotations); see also Letter from "Probus" to the "Primitive Whig," in "Primitive Whig" No. IV, *New-Jersey Gazette*, Jan. 30, 1786, at 2.

41. Ibid. (quotations); see also Ferguson, *Power of the Purse*, 249; Holton, *Unruly Americans*, 88; David Szatmary, *Shays' Rebellion: The Making of an Agrarian Insurrection* (Amherst, MA, 1980), 45.

42. "Primitive Whig" No. 14, *New-Jersey Gazette*, Jan. 30, 1786, at 1 (quotations); Munroe, *Federalist Delaware*, 142; Kaminski, "Rhode Island," 370; Brown, *Redeeming the Republic*, 149; Ferguson, *Power of the Purse*, 19; Holton, *Unruly Americans*, 59–60.

43. Morris, Report on Public Credit, July 29, 1782, *PRM*, 6:58 ("indolence"); David Stuart to Washington, Nov. 16, 1785, *PGW* (C.S.), 3:364 ("the people"); Madison to Jefferson, Mar. 18, 1786, *PTJ* (M.S.), 9:335; see also Charles Lee to Washington, Apr. 11, 1788, *PGW* (C.S.), 6:207; Brown, *Redeeming the Republic*, 34, 48–9, 53, 150; Holton, *Unruly Americans*, 98–9.

44. Brown, *Redeeming the Republic*, 92, 150, 276 n. 20 ("the present scarcity"); "The Primitive Whig" No. 1, *New-Jersey Gazette*, Jan. 9, 1786, at 1 ("into this breathing"); From the *Pennsylvania Gazette*: Thoughts on Paper Money, *New-Haven Gazette & Conn. Magazine* (July 27, 1786), 1 (No. 24):188; Holton, *Unruly Americans*, 110; see also Samuel Johnston at North Carolina ratifying convention, July 26, 1788, in Jonathan Elliot, ed., *The Debates in the Several State Conventions on the Adoption of the Federal Constitution* (5 vols., Washington, D.C., 1836–1845), 4:90 [hereinafter, "*Elliot*"]; Charles Pinckney at South Carolina ratifying convention, May 20, 1788, *DHRC*, 27:354.

45. Madison to James Madison, Sr., Nov. 1, 1786, *PJM* (C.S.), 9:154 ("unjust, impolitic"); Madison to Jefferson, July 18, 1787, ibid., 10:106 ("[n]othing but evil"); Aug. 12, 1786, ibid., 9:95 ("fictitious," "morally certain," "depreciation," "numerous ills," and "the same warfare"); see also *The Federalist No. 44* (Madison), at 281–2; Madison, Vices, *PJM* (C.S.), 9:349.

46. Madison to Jefferson, June 6, 1787, *PJM* (C.S.), 10:30 ("appetite for"); Jan. 22, 1786, ibid., 8:477 ("itch for"); Apr. 23, 1787, ibid., 9:401 ("itch"); Madison to Washington, Dec. 7, 1786, ibid., 200 ("not consonant to" and "a prudential compliance"); Madison to Jefferson, Aug. 12, 1786, ibid., 95 ("epidemic malady"); Madison to Washington, Dec. 24, 1786, ibid., 224 ("greater evil"); see also Madison to Jefferson, Sept. 6, 1787, ibid., 10:164.

47. Brown, *Redeeming the Republic*, 3, 91–2 ("revolution") (quoting Peregrine Foster to Dwight Foster, Apr. 24, 1786), 153–4; Rakove, *Original Meanings*, 41; Holton, *Unruly Americans*, 162–3; Wood, "Interests and Disinterestedness," 72–3.

48. Hamilton to Morris, Aug. 13, 1782, *PAH*, 3:135 ("the general disease"); Grayson to Madison, Mar. 22, 1786, *PJM* (C.S.), 8:509 ("Montesquieu"); Madison to James Madison, Sr., May 27, 1787, ibid., 10:10 ("the unruly temper" and "unwise and wicked"); see also Ferguson, *Power of the Purse*, 220 (quoting Theodore Sedgwick to Nathan Dane, July 5, 1787).

49. Richard Henry Lee to Francis Lightfoot Lee, July 14, 1787, *LRHL*, 2:424 ("from simple democracy" and "indispensably necessary"); Charles Lee to Washington, Apr. 11, 1788, *PGW* (C.S.), 6:207 ("more powerful"); Grayson to William Short, Apr. 16, 1787, *LDC*, 24:226 ("however excellent"); see also Boston *Independent Chronicle*, Sept. 7, 1786, at 2; Henry Knox to Mercy Otis Warren, May 30, 1787, in *Collections of Massachusetts Historical Society* (Boston, 1925), 73:295.

50. Boston *Independent Chronicle*, Sept. 7, 1786, at 2 ("firm and independent"); Hamilton to Morris, Aug. 13, 1782, *PAH*, 3:135 ("order that has"); Washington to Jay, Aug. 15, 1786, *PGW* (C.S.), 4:212 ("We have" and "that men"); see also Bouton, *Taming Democracy*, 159–63, 167; Brown, *Redeeming the Republic*, 161.

51. Extract of a Letter from Washington County, Rhode Island (May 1787), *Virginia Independent Chronicle*, June 20, 1787, at 1 ("villainy, rascality"); "A.M.," *Massachusetts Centinel*, May 17, 1786, p. 2 ("the other states"); Hartford (May 22), Providence *United States Chronicle*, June 1, 1786, at 2 ("the most extraordinary" and "the depravity"); see

also "Jonathan," From the *Boston Gazette*, ibid., May 25, 1786, at 3; Rhode Island delegates to Governor John Collins, Sept. 28, 1786, *LDC*, 23:571; James Mitchell Varnum to Washington, June 18, 1787, *Farrand*, 3:47–8; Jay to John Adams, Nov. 1, 1786, *CPPJJ*, 3:214–5; Kaminski, "Rhode Island," 371, 376; Holton, *Unruly Americans*, 77–81; Polishook, *Rhode Island*, 170–2.

52. "Jonathan," From the *Boston Gazette*, Providence *United States Chronicle*, May 25, 1786, at 2–3 ("Rogue Island" and "Fool Island"); To the Printer, Providence *Gazette*, Jan. 6, 1787, at 3 ("An Act"); James Mitchell Varnum to Samuel Ward, Jr., Apr. 2, 1787, *LDC*, 24:199 ("unneighborly"); Szatmary, *Shays' Rebellion*, 115–6; see also Edward Carrington to Governor Edmund Randolph, Apr. 2, 1787, *LDC*, 24:193; Polishook, *Rhode Island*, 165–8, 178; Kaminski, "Paper Politics," 172; Alexander, *The Selling of the Constitutional Convention*, 72; Introduction, *DHRC*, 24:xxxiii.

53. James Manning to Nathan Miller, June 12, 1786, *LDC*, 23:354–5 ("Rhode Island," "[t]he flagrant violations," "as the completion," and "a speedy reform"); Extract of a Letter from a Gentleman in the Southern States (Apr. 1), *Newport Herald*, Apr. 12, 1787, *DHRC*, 13:80 ("matters have come" and "to reduce you"); see also *Newport Herald*, Mar. 22, 1787, at 3; "The Landholder" XII (Oliver Ellsworth), *Connecticut Courant*, Mar. 17, 1788, *DHRC*, 16:406; Alexander, *The Selling of the Constitutional Convention*, 23–4, 71–4.

54. Humphreys to Washington, Sept. 24, 1786, *PGW* (C.S.), 4:265 (quotation); Brown, *Redeeming the Republic*, 76–8, 93; Holton, *Unruly Americans*, 145–52; Szatmary, *Shays' Rebellion*, 124–6; Bouton, *Taming Democracy*, 162–3; Perkins, *American Public Finance*, 162; Davis, *Sectionalism in American Politics*, 152, 154; Becker, "Public Peace and South Carolina Debtor Relief Laws," 67–8; editorial note, *DHRC*, 4:324 n. 4.

55. Richards, *Shays's Rebellion*, 68–74; Szatmary, *Shays' Rebellion*, 49. In New York, the governor was part of a "council of revision" that could veto legislation.

56. Brown, *Redeeming the Republic*, 108–11; Ferguson, *Power of the Purse*, 245; Michael Allen Gillespie, "Massachusetts: Creating Consensus," in Gillespie and Lienesch, eds., *Ratifying the Constitution*, 143; Richards, *Shays's Rebellion*, 74–5, 85–8; Perkins, *American Public Finance*, 166, 173–80; Kaminski, "Paper Politics," 22; Mihm, "Funding the Revolution," 340; Jensen, *New Nation*, 307–8.

57. Brown, *Redeeming the Republic*, 100, 108–9; Holton, *Unruly Americans*, 74–5; Richards, *Shays's Rebellion*, 82–3; Szatmary, *Shays' Rebellion*, 31–2; Perkins, *American Public Finance*, 180–2; Henderson, *Party Politics*, 400; Einhorn, *American Taxation*, 77; Edling and Kaplanoff, "Alexander Hamilton's Fiscal Reform," 724, 729.

58. Adams to Jefferson, Nov. 30, 1786, *PTJ* (M.S.), 10:557 ("The Massachusetts Assembly"); Brown, *Redeeming the Republic*, 111–3 (other quotations); Resolutions by the Hampshire, Massachusetts Delegates, in George Richards Minot, *History of the Insurrection of Massachusetts in 1786* (New York, reprint ed., 1971), 34, 36; Szatmary, *Shays' Rebellion*, 38–44; Main, *Political Parties*, 102–3, 115; Van Beck Hall, *Politics Without Parties: Massachusetts, 1780–1791* (Pittsburgh, 1972), 168, 170–1, 192, 194, 208–9.

59. Brown, *Redeeming the Republic*, 160–1 (quoting Webster); Lincoln to Washington, Dec. 4, 1786–Mar. 4, 1787, *PGW* (C.S.), 4:420 ("diverted," "the indolent," "idleness," and "of the weight"); see also Szatmary, *Shays' Rebellion*, 46–8, 53, 93; Hall, *Politics Without Parties*, 192–4, 199–200, 203. On the relative severity of the tax rate, see Perkins, *American Public Finance*, 180.

60. Summary of Late Intelligence, *Worcester Magazine* (Oct. 1786), 2 (No. 30):366 ("alarming"); Pieter Johan van Berckel to the States General, Sept. 12, 1786, in Bancroft, *History of the Formation of the Constitution*, 2:393 ("[i]n the state"); Ferguson, *Power of the Purse*, 247; Szatmary, *Shays' Rebellion*, 58–9; Holton, *Unruly Americans*, 134; see also King to Gerry, Aug. 5, 1786, *LCRK*, 1:188.

61. Richards, *Shays's Rebellion*, 1, 5, 9–12, 21–2, 48–50, 55–8, 63, 89–92, 95, 98, 102–8, 111–6; see also Szatmary, *Shays' Rebellion*, ch. 4; Hall, *Politics Without Parties*, 211–2; Brown, *Redeeming the Republic*, 113–5; Henry Knox to Washington, Dec. 17, 1786, *PGW* (C.S.), 4:460–1; Jan. 14, 1787, ibid., 519.

62. Richards, *Shays's Rebellion*, 16–8; Szatmary, *Shays' Rebellion*, 83–4; Hall, *Politics Without Parties*, 214–8; Brown, *Redeeming the Republic*, 115, 118–9; infra pp. 96–7; see also Lincoln to Washington, Dec. 4, 1786–Mar. 4, 1787, *PGW* (C.S.), 4:421–2.

63. Richards, *Shays's Rebellion*, 1, 5–6, 15–6, 23–5, 27–30, 78–9, 111; Szatmary, *Shays' Rebellion*, ch. 6; Hall, *Politics Without Parties*, 210, 222–3; see also Lincoln to Washington, Dec. 4, 1786–Mar. 4, 1787, *PGW* (C.S.), 4:422–7.

64. Grayson and Madison to Edmund Randolph, Feb. 12, 1787, *PJM* (C.S.), 9:266 (quotation); Knox to Washington, Mar. 19, 1787, *PGW* (C.S.), 5:95; Lincoln to Washington, Dec. 4, 1786–Mar. 4, 1787, ibid., 4:428–30; Richards, *Shays's Rebellion*, 31–2; Szatmary, *Shays' Rebellion*, 85–7, 104–8; Hall, *Politics Without Parties*, 224–5.

65. Richards, *Shays's Rebellion*, 32–3, 39–40; Hall, *Politics Without Parties*, 229–30; see also William Irvine to Josiah Harmar, Feb. 21, 1787, *LDC*, 24:123; Lincoln to Washington, Dec. 4, 1786–Mar. 4, 1787, *PGW* (C.S.), 4:431–2; infra pp. 97–8.

66. George Muter to Madison, Feb. 20, 1787, *PJM* (C.S.), 9:281 ("truly deplorable" and "distressing"); Henry Lee to Washington, Sept. 8, 1786, *PGW* (C.S.), 4:240–1 ("The period" and "[w]eak and feeble"); William Irvine to Josiah Harmar, Feb. 27, 1787, *LDC*, 24:123 ("feared"). On the important role of Shays's Rebellion in bringing about the Constitution, see Richards, *Shays's Rebellion*, 2–3, 132; Holton, *Unruly Americans*, 81–2, 218–20; Brown, *Redeeming the Republic*, 166–7, 172–4; Szatmary, *Shays' Rebellion*, 120, 123. But see Johnson, *Righteous Anger at the Wicked States*, 7.

67. Knox to the President of Congress, Oct. 18, 1786, *JCC*, 31:887 (quotations); see also Sept. 20, 1786, ibid., 676; Sept. 28, 1786, ibid., 698–9; Knox to the President of Congress, Oct. 3, 1786, in Papers of the Old Congress, No. 150, I:587–90; see also Richards, *Shays's Rebellion*, 129–31; Szatmary, *Shays' Rebellion*, 82.

For the preceding footnote, see Adams to Jefferson, Nov. 30, 1786, *PTJ* (M.S.), 10:557 ("be alarmed"); Jefferson to Abigail Adams, Feb. 22, 1787, ibid., 11:174 ("I like" and "spirit of resistance"); see also Jefferson to Madison, Jan. 30, 1787, ibid., 93; Dec. 20, 1787, ibid., 12:442.

68. King's Address, Oct. 17, 1786, *LDC*, 23:589–90 ("commotions"); Knox to Washington, Oct. 23, 1786, *PGW* (C.S.), 4:301–2 ("averting," "giving indisputable," "strengthen," and "fully impressed"); Proceedings of the Confederation Congress, Oct. 20, 1786, *JCC*, 31:891–2; see also Knox to the President of Congress, Feb. 12, 1787, *JCC*, 32:39–40; David Humphreys to Washington, Nov. 1, 1786, *PGW* (C.S.), 4:325; Grayson to Madison, Nov. 22, 1786, *PJM* (C.S.), 9:174; Hall, *Politics Without Parties*, 220, 262; Kohn, *Eagle and Sword*, 74; but cf. King to Gerry, Oct. 20, 1786, *LDC*, 23:607.

69. Knox to Washington, Oct. 23, 1786, *PGW* (C.S.), 4:300 ("arrested" and "are the ostensible"); Dec. 17, 1786, ibid., 460 ("in a considerable degree," "annihilate," and "to have a division"); see also David Humphreys to Washington, Nov. 9, 1786, ibid., 351; Lincoln to Washington, Dec. 4, 1786–Mar. 4, 1787, ibid., 421; Washington to Madison, Nov. 5, 1786, *PJM* (C.S.), 9:161.

70. Knox to Washington, Oct. 23, 1786, *PGW* (C.S.), 4:300 (quotations); see also Humphreys to Washington, Nov. 1, 1786, ibid., 325.

71. Lee to Washington, Oct. 17, 1786, ibid., 295 (all quotations but the last); Lee to Madison, Oct. 25, 1786, *PJM* (C.S.), 9:145 ("extensive national calamity"); see also Oct. 19, 1786, ibid., 144; Lee to Washington, Sept. 8, 1786, *PGW* (C.S.), 4:240; Oct. 1, 1786, ibid., 281–2. For other alarmed reports from congressional delegates, see Grayson to Madison, Nov. 22, 1786, *PJM* (C.S.), 9:174; Charles Pettit to President Benjamin Franklin of Pennsylvania, Oct. 18, 1786, *LDC*, 23:603.

72. Washington to Knox, Dec. 26, 1786, *PGW* (C.S.), 4:481, 483 ("those vague," "an unconcerned spectator," and "to foment the"); Washington to Humphreys, Dec. 26, 1786, ibid., 478 ("inconsistency and perfidiousness," "unsheathing," and "but the other"); Oct. 22, 1786, ibid., 297 ("[c]ommotions"); see also Washington to Henry Lee, Oct. 31, 1786, ibid., 318–9; Washington to Madison, Nov. 5, 1786, *PJM* (C.S.), 9:161; Washington to Knox, Feb. 3, 1787, *PGW* (C.S.), 5:7.

For the preceding footnote, see John Dawson to Madison, Apr. 15, 1787, *PJM* (C.S.), 9:381 ("they talk"); Tobias Lear to Benjamin Lincoln, July 30, 1787, microformed on

Benjamin Lincoln Papers, P-40, Reel 8 (Mass. Historical Society) ("three-quarters"); Madison to Jefferson, Sept. 6, 1787, *PJM* (C.S.), 10:164 ("wilfully burnt"); see also Szatmary, *Shays' Rebellion*, 125–6.

73. Madison to Edmund Pendleton, Jan. 9, 1787, *PJM* (C.S.), 9:245 ("ominous events" and "become formidable"); Madison to James Madison, Sr., Nov. 1, 1786, ibid., 154 ("great commotions," "as numerous," "profess to aim," and "an abolition"); Madison to George Muter, Jan. 7, 1787, ibid., 231 ("secretly stimulated," "not improbable," and "somewhat uncertain"); see also Banning, *Sacred Fire*, 104–5, 122. For widespread concerns about British subversion, which made allegations of their involvement in Shays's Rebellion plausible to many Americans, see Marks, *Independence on Trial*, 100–5.

74. Jay to Jefferson, Oct. 27, 1786, *PTJ* (M.S.), 10:488–9 (quotations); see also Dec. 14, 1786, ibid., 596.

75. Jefferson to Madison, Jan. 30, 1787, *PJM* (C.S.), 9:247 ("nature has formed" and "not founded"); Lee to Madison, Oct. 25, 1786, ibid., 145 ("the impotency" and "an encouragement"); Lee to Washington, Sept. 8, 1786, *PGW* (C.S.), 4:240–1 ("schemes portending"); Washington to Henry Lee, Oct. 31, 1786, ibid., 319 ("by which" and "all will be"); Jay to Jefferson, Oct. 27, 1786, *PTJ* (M.S.), 10:489 ("As the knaves"); see also Feb. 9, 1787, ibid., 11:129.

76. Knox to Washington, Dec. 21, 1786, *PGW* (C.S.), 4:470 ("The commotions"); Higginson to Knox, Nov. 12, 1786, in *Annual Report* of the American Historical Association for the Year 1896 (Washington, DC, 1897), 1:742 ("[t]he present moment" and "so very favorable"); see also Knox to Washington, Oct. 23, 1786, *PGW* (C.S.), 4:300–1.

77. Gore to King, June 28, 1787, *LCRK*, 1:227 ("our government" and "personal liberty"); Sedgwick to King, June 18, 1787, ibid., 224 ("Every man"); King to Sedgwick, Oct. 22, 1786, *LDC*, 23:612 ("the great body," "government free," and "countrymen"); King to Gerry, Feb. 11, 1787, *LDC*, 24:90 ("already mark"); see also Boston *Independent Chronicle*, Sept. 7, 1786, p. 2; Tobias Lear to Benjamin Lincoln, June 4, 1787, microformed on Benjamin Lincoln Papers, P-40, Reel 8 (Mass. Historical Society); Washington to Knox, Dec. 26, 1786, *PGW* (C.S.), 4:482; "Centinel" XV, Philadelphia *Independent Gazetteer*, Feb. 22, 1788, *DHRC*, 16:190; Henderson, *Party Politics*, 401.

78. Knox to Washington, Oct. 23, 1786, *PGW* (C.S.), 4:301; Ferguson, *Power of the Purse*, 249–50; Richards, *Shays's Rebellion*, 127–8.

79. Higginson to Knox, Nov. 25, 1786, in *Annual Report* of the American Historical Association for the Year 1896 (Washington, D.C., 1897), 1:743 ("so great," "tend much," and "we shall here"); Breck to Knox, July 14, 1787, in Henry Knox Papers, Reel 20 (Mass. Historical Society) ("[t]he danger" and "reduce the powers"); see also Wadsworth to Knox, Sept. 23, 1787, *DHRC*, 5:1078; Davis, *Sectionalism in American Politics*, 152; Hall, *Politics Without Parties*, 256–7, 262.

80. Brown, *Redeeming the Republic*, 120 n. 68 (quoting Sedgwick to Dane, June 3, 1787), 153.

81. Richards, *Shays's Rebellion*, 16–7; Hall, *Politics Without Parties*, 191, 214–8; Brown, *Redeeming the Republic*, 117; Holton, *Unruly Americans*, 155; Perkins, *American Public Finance*, 181; Jensen, *New Nation*, 310.

82. Grayson to Monroe, Nov. 22, 1786, *LDC*, 24:33 ("fearful"); Knox to Washington, Dec. 17, 1786, *PGW* (C.S.), 4:460 ("temporizing," "despise," "impotency," and "proceed"); Jan. 14, 1787, ibid., 519 ("lenient measures" and "the rebellion"); see also Humphreys to Washington, Nov. 16, 1786, ibid., 373; Higginson to Knox, Nov. 25, 1786, in *Annual Report* of the American Historical Association for the Year 1896 (Washington, D.C., 1897), 1:743; King to Sedgwick, Oct. 22, 1786, *LDC*, 23:612.

83. Madison to Washington, Apr. 16, 1787, *PJM* (C.S.), 9:386 ("We understand"); Madison to Pendleton, Apr. 22, 1787, ibid., 394 ("muster").

84. Ibid., 395 ("acknowledged merits" and "not a little"); *To the Free, Virtuous, and Independent Electors of Massachusetts* (Boston, 1787) ("[t]he insurgents" and "[t]he same spirit"); Madison to Washington, Apr. 16, 1787, *PJM* (C.S.), 9:386 ("the engine"); see also Virginia delegates to Governor Edmund Randolph, Mar. 19, 1787, ibid., 325; Madison to Jefferson, Apr. 23, 1787, ibid., 399; Brown, *Redeeming the Republic*, 119.

85. Madison to Monroe, Apr. 30, 1787, *PJM* (C.S.), 9:408. Historians disagree over whether the postelection policy changes should be interpreted as a major—or a minor—victory for the insurgents and their sympathizers. See, e.g., Brown, *Redeeming the Republic*, 119–20; Holton, *Unruly Americans*, 76–7; Main, *Political Parties*, 118; Gillespie, "Massachusetts," 143–4; Ferguson, *Power of the Purse*, 247; Szatmary, *Shays' Rebellion*, 114–5, 119; Hall, *Politics Without Parties*, 191, 228, 235–52, 277; Einhorn, *American Taxation*, 53; Perkins, *American Public Finance*, 184.

86. Lear to Lincoln, June 4, 1787, microformed on Benjamin Lincoln Papers, P-40, Reel 8 (Mass. Historical Society) ("What frenzy," "some measures," and "fast towards"); Jay to Jefferson, Apr. 24, 1787, *PTJ* (M.S.), 11:313 ("the spirit" and "operated powerfully"); see also Joseph Jones to Madison, July 6, 1787, *PJM* (C.S.), 10:95; Grayson to Monroe, Apr. 30, 1787, *LDC*, 24:262; Davis, *Sectionalism in American Politics*, 159–60; Hall, *Politics Without Parties*, 235, 255, 265.

87. Edling, *Revolution in Favor of Government*, 156.

88. Grayson to William Short, Apr. 16, 1787, *LDC*, 24:226 ("Connecticut"); Grayson to Monroe, May 29, 1787, ibid., 292 ("be elected"); Hamilton at Philadelphia convention, June 26, 1787, *Farrand*, 1:425 ("had entirely"); see also Madison, June 30, ibid., 485–6; Humphreys to Washington, Nov. 1, 1786, *PGW* (C.S.) 4:325; Donald S. Lutz, "Connecticut: Achieving Consent and Assuring Control," in Gillespie and Lienesch, eds., *Ratifying the Constitution*, 122; Introduction, *DHRC*, 3:322–4; Brown, *Redeeming the Republic*, 91–2, 120–1, 131; Holton, *Unruly Americans*, 154–5; Perkins, *American Public Finance*, 171.

89. Grayson to Monroe, May 29, 1787, *LDC*, 24:293 ("500 Shays"); Grayson to William Short, Apr. 16, 1787, ibid., 226 ("a considerable party," "payment," "showed itself," and "pressure"); see also Davis, *Sectionalism in American Politics*, 152.

90. Randolph (McHenry's Notes) at Philadelphia convention, May 29, 1787, *Farrand*, 1:27; Brown, *Redeeming the Republic*, 122, 145. On the South Carolina legislature's capitulation to populist demands for relief legislation to forestall an episode similar to Shays's Rebellion, see Becker, "Public Peace and South Carolina Debtor Relief Laws," 72–4. On New York's constitution, see Kaminski, "New York," 48.

91. Brown, *Redeeming the Republic*, 172–4.

92. Madison to George Muter, Jan. 7, 1787, *PJM* (C.S.), 9:231 ("furnish[es] new proofs"); Henry Lee to Washington, Sept. 8, 1786, *PGW* (C.S.), 4:240–1 ("officers," "that power," "fast approaching," and "submit to"); Washington to Madison, Nov. 5, 1786, ibid., 332 ("a liberal"); see also William Irvine to Josiah Harmar, Feb. 27, 1787, *LDC*, 24:123; George Muter to Madison, Feb. 20, 1787, *PJM* (C.S.), 9:281–2; "A Landholder" III (Oliver Ellsworth), *Connecticut Courant*, Nov. 19, 1787, *DHRC*, 14:139–40; Jay to Adams, July 4, 1787, *CPPJJ*, 3:249; James Wilson and Thomas McKean, *Commentaries on the Constitution* (London, 1792), 68.

93. King to Gerry, Feb. 11, 1787, *LDC*, 24:91 ("Events"); Lee to Francis Lightfoot Lee, July 14, 1787, *LRHL*, 2:424 ("the minds of men").

94. Supra pp. 86–7.

95. Brown, *Redeeming the Republic*, 176–7, 222–3 ("give up the idea" at p. 177; "I pray" at p. 176); "Letter from a Connecticut Man" (probably Noah Webster), in Extract of a Letter from a Member of the House of Delegates, Philadelphia *Independent Gazetteer*, Dec. 2, 1786 ("as strong," "a republic," "some of," and "should infinitely prefer"); see also James Mitchell Varnum to Samuel Ward, Jr., Apr. 2, 1787, *LDC*, 24:199; David Ramsay to Benjamin Rush, Aug. 6, 1786, in "David Ramsay, 1749–1815: Selections from His Writings," *Transactions* of the American Philosophical Society, Aug. 1965 (Robert L. Brunhouse, ed., Philadelphia, 1965), 105; Jonathan Smith at Massachusetts ratifying convention, Jan. 25, 1788, *DHRC*, 6:1346; Szatmary, *Shays' Rebellion*, 81–2; McDonald, *Novus Ordo Seclorum*, 180.

96. Jay to Washington, June 27, 1786, *PGW* (C.S.), 4:131–2.

97. Jay to Jefferson, Oct. 27, 1786, *CPPJJ*, 3:213 (quotations); see also Jay to Adams, Nov. 1, 1786, ibid., 214; Jay to Washington, Jan. 7, 1787, ibid., 227.

98. Washington to Jay, Aug. 15, 1786, *PGW* (C.S.), 4:213 (quotations); see also Washington to Madison, Mar. 31, 1787, ibid., 5:115.

99. Madison to Randolph, Feb. 25, 1787, *PJM* (C.S.), 9:299 ("[m]any individuals"); Madison to Pendleton, Feb. 24, 1787, ibid., 295 ("the late turbulent"); see also Madison to Jefferson, Mar. 19, 1787, ibid., 318; Madison, Notes on Debates, Feb. 21, 1787, ibid., 291–2; Madison, Preface to Debates, *Farrand*, 3:548–9; Banning, *Sacred Fire*, 105, 122–3.

100. Madison to Washington, Feb. 21, 1787, *PJM* (C.S.), 9:286; infra pp. 129–33.

101. Madison at the Philadelphia convention, June 12, 1787, *Farrand*, 1:219.

102. Monroe to John Sullivan, Aug. 16, 1786, *LDC*, 23:481 ("received"); Washington to Knox, Feb. 3, 1787, *PGW* (C.S.), 5:9 ("strongly inclined"); see also Monroe to Jefferson, Apr. 12, 1785, *PTJ* (M.S.), 8:76; New York *Daily Advertiser* (Hamilton), July 21, 1787, *PAH*, 4:231; Rakove, *Beginnings of National Politics*, 361, 372; Maier, *Ratification*, 19.

103. Grayson to Madison, May 28, 1786, *PJM* (C.S.), 9:63.

104. Proceedings of the Confederation Congress, Aug. 7, 1786, *JCC*, 31:494–8; Davis, *Sectionalism in American Politics*, 139–40.

105. Madison to Jefferson, Jan. 22, 1786, *PJM* (C.S.), 8:476 (quotations); Resolution Calling for the Regulation of Commerce by Congress, Nov. 14, 1785, ibid., 413; editorial note, ibid., 414–5 n. 1; Rakove, *Beginnings of National Politics*, 368–9; Banning, *Sacred Fire*, 56. See generally Editorial Note, Debates and Resolutions Related to the Regulation of Commerce by Congress, Including a Call for a Convention at Annapolis, Nov. 1785–Jan. 1786, *PJM* (C.S.), 8:406–9.

106. Madison to Jefferson, Jan. 22, 1786, ibid., 476–7 ("so far destroyed"); Madison to Washington, Dec. 9, 1785, ibid., 438, 440 n. 1 ("the hope," "visionary," "caprice," "impossible," and "better to trust"); Monroe to Madison, Dec. 26, 1785, ibid., 462 ("decisive," "prevent[ing] its renewal," and "avoid those stipulations"); see also Davis, *Sectionalism in American Politics*, 128–9.

107. Madison to Washington, Dec. 9, 1785, *PJM* (C.S.), 8:439 ("politico-commercial," "for the purpose," "have fewer enemies," and "naturally to grow"); Resolution Authorizing a Commission to Examine Trade Regulations, Jan. 21, 1786, ibid., 471 ("to consider"); Madison to Monroe, Jan. 22, 1786, ibid., 483; see also Dec. 9, 1785, ibid., 436; Madison, Preface to Debates, *Farrand*, 3:543–4; Davis, *Sectionalism in American Politics*, 129–30. For the Mount Vernon conference, see ibid., 113–4.

108. Supra pp. 70–1; see also Introduction, *DHRC*, 13:9–10; Lee to Madison, Nov. 26, 1784, *PJM* (C.S.), 8:151; John Francis Mercer to Madison, Nov. 26, 1784, ibid., 152; Madison, Preface to Debates, *Farrand*, 3:546.

109. Grayson to Madison, Mar. 22, 1786, *PJM* (C.S.), 8:509–10 (quotations); see also Nathaniel Gorham to Caleb Davis, Mar. 1, 1786, *LDC*, 23:167; Thomas Rodney's Diary, May 3, 1786, ibid., 262; Rakove, *Beginnings of National Politics*, 370; Davis, *Sectionalism in American Politics*, 137–9.

      For the preceding footnote, see American National Biography Online; Beeman, *Plain, Honest Men*, 92–8; Kaminski and Moore, *An Assembly of Demigods*, 159–62. For statements of annoyance by Madison and Washington at Pinckney's self-aggrandizing tendencies, see Washington to Madison, Oct. 22, 1787 and Madison to Washington, Oct. 28, 1787, in Kaminski and Moore, supra, 159. For Pinckney's effort to enlist Madison in his quest for a diplomatic post in the first Washington administration, see Pinckney to Madison, Aug. 6, 1791, ibid., 159–61.

110. Randolph to Madison, Mar. 1, 1786, *PJM* (C.S.), 8:495 (quotation); see also Madison to Jefferson, Mar. 18, 1786, ibid., 501–2; Madison, Preface to Debates, *Farrand*, 3:545.

111. Madison to Monroe, Mar. 19, 1786, *PJM* (C.S.), 8:505–6 (quotations); see also Madison to Monroe, May 13, 1786, ibid., 9:55.

112. Grayson to Madison, May 28, 1786, ibid., 64.

113. Supra pp. 32–3; Madison to Jefferson, Mar. 18, 1786, *PJM* (C.S.), 8:502 (quotation); see also Monroe to Madison, Mar. 19, 1786, ibid., 506–7.

114. Madison to Jefferson, Mar. 18, 1786, ibid., 502–3. Washington was much more optimistic about the prospects of the Annapolis convention, telling Lafayette, "All the legislatures which I have heard from have come into the proposition, and have made very judicious appointments; much good is expected from this measure" (Washington to Lafayette, May 10, 1786, *PGW* (C.S.), 4:42).

115. Madison to Jefferson, Mar. 18, 1786, *PJM* (C.S.), 8:503 ("foreign machinations," "the probability," and "bring sentiment[s]"); Madison to Monroe, Mar. 14, 1786, ibid., 498 ("nothing can be done" and "such a piece"). On Vermont's independence, see supra p. 32 & n. 61.

116. Madison to Jefferson, Aug. 12, 1786, *PJM* (C.S.), 9:96 (quotations); supra pp. 66–8; see also Washington to Lafayette, May 10, 1786, *PGW* (C.S.), 4:42; Davis, *Sectionalism in American Politics*, 134–8, 142; Rakove, *Beginnings of National Politics*, 374; Banning, *Sacred Fire*, 69–70.

117. King to Jonathan Jackson, June 11, 1786, *LDC*, 23:352–3. Only one month earlier, King had been much more optimistic about the Annapolis convention (to John Adams, May 5, 1786, *LCRK*, 1:172–3).

118. Sedgwick to Strong, Aug. 6, 1786, *LDC*, 23:436–7.

119. Monroe to President John Sullivan of New Hampshire, Aug. 16, 1786, ibid., 436 ("the source"); Monroe to Madison, Sept. 3, 1786, *PJM* (C.S.), 9:114 ("intrigues" and "a most important"); see also supra pp. 38–9, 64.

120. Jacob Broom to Tench Coxe, Aug. 4, 1786, in Coxe Family Papers, microfilm edition, series 2, Reel 49 ("no risk" and "[H]ow ridiculous"); Madison to Jefferson, Aug. 12, 1786, *PJM* (C.S.), 9:95 ("rendered obnoxious").

121. Carroll to Madison, Mar. 13, 1786, ibid., 8:496 (quotations); Davis, *Sectionalism in American Politics*, 132–3; Introduction, *DHRC*, 11:xlviii.

122. Madison to Monroe, May 13, 1786, *PJM* (C.S.), 9:55 (quotations); Rakove, *Beginnings of National Politics*, 374; Banning, *Sacred Fire*, 73.

123. Davis, *Sectionalism in American Politics*, 140–2; Henderson, *Party Politics*, 399; Introduction, *DHRC*, 4:xxxv–vii; editorial note, *DHRC*, 27:112 n. 3; see also Washington to Knox, Dec. 26, 1786, *PGW* (C.S.), 4:419; Knox to Washington, Jan. 14, 1787, ibid., 519; King to Jonathan Jackson, Sept. 3, 1786, *LDC*, 23:543.

124. Madison to Monroe, Sept. 11, 1786, *PJM* (C.S.), 9:121–2; see also Madison to Ambrose Madison, Sept. 8, 1786, ibid., 120; Davis, *Sectionalism in American Politics*, 143–4.

125. Address of the Annapolis Convention, Sept. 14, 1786, *PAH*, 3:687 (quotation); Rakove, *Beginnings of National Politics*, 374; Banning, *Sacred Fire*, 73–4.

126. Address of the Annapolis Convention, Sept. 14, 1786, *PAH*, 3:688–9 (quotations); see also King to Bowdoin, Sept. 17, 1786, *LDC*, 23:561; Madison, Preface to Debates, Farrand, 3:545.

127. Davis, *Sectionalism in American Politics*, 144–6; Rakove, *Beginnings of National Politics*, 374–5; Maier, *Ratification*, 3; Banning, *Sacred Fire*, 427 n. 106.

128. Tucker to Monroe, Sept. 18, 1786, *Papers of James Monroe*, 2:359 (all quotations but "terminated"); King to Adams, Oct. 2, 1786, *LDC*, 23:579 ("terminated").
    For the preceding footnote, see Louis Guillaume Otto to Comte de Vergennes, Oct. 10, 1786, in Bancroft, *History of the Formation of the Constitution*, 2:399–401.

129. Address of the Annapolis Convention, Sept. 14, 1786, *PAH*, 3:689 ("they have" and "motives"); Tucker to Monroe, Sept. 18, 1786, *Papers of James Monroe*, 2:359 ("a sense" and "induce them"); King to Adams, Oct. 2, 1786, *LDC*, 23:578; Rakove, *Beginnings of National Politics*, 375.

130. King Address to the Massachusetts House of Representatives, Oct. 11, 1786, *LDC*, 23:588 (quotations); see also King to Adams, Oct. 2, 1786, ibid., 579; Henderson, *Party Politics*, 402.
    For the preceding footnote, see Louis Guillaume Otto to Comte de Vergennes, Nov. 10, 1786, in Bancroft, *History of the Formation of the Constitution*, 2:403.

131. Dane Address to the Massachusetts House of Representatives, Nov. 9, 1786, *LDC*, 24:20–1 (quotations); see also Steven R. Boyd, *The Politics of Opposition: Antifederalists and the Acceptance of the Constitution* (Millwood, NY, 1979), 4.

132. Introduction, *DHRC*, 4:xxxviii; Introduction, *DHRC*, 3:325–6; see also David Humphreys to Washington, Jan. 20, 1787, *PGW* (C.S.), 4:527–8.

133. Madison to Pendleton, Nov. 30, 1786, *PJM* (C.S.), 9:186–7 ("the season" and "been brought forward"); Madison to Washington, Nov. 1, 1786, ibid., 155 ("to ferment"); see also Madison to Jefferson, Dec. 4, 1786, ibid., 189.

134. Madison to Jefferson, Dec. 4, 1786, *PJM* (C.S.), 9:189.
135. Madison to Washington, Nov. 8, 1786, *PJM* (C.S.), 9:166 ("give this subject," "earnestness," and "the liberty"); Madison to Washington, Dec. 7, 1786, ibid., 199 ("an invitation"); New York *Daily Advertiser* (Hamilton), July 21, 1787, *PAH*, 4:231 ("avail"); see also Maier, *Ratification*, 23–4, 68.
136. Washington to Joseph Jones, May 31, 1780, in *The Writings of George Washington*, 7:67 ("assumes them"); Washington to William Gordon, July 8, 1783, in Bancroft, *History of the Formation of the Constitution*, 1:320 ("[U]nless adequate powers"); Washington to James McHenry, Aug. 22, 1785, *PGW* (C.S.), 3:198 ("[w]e are either"); see also Washington to Hamilton, Mar. 31, 1783, *PAH*, 3:310.
137. Washington to Madison, Nov. 18, 1786, *PGW* (C.S.), 4:382–3 (quotations); see also Washington to Madison, Dec. 16, 1786, *PJM* (C.S.), 9:215, 217 n. 1; Washington to Randolph, Dec. 21, 1786, *PGW*, 4:472; Washington to Humphreys, Dec. 26, 1786, ibid., 479–80; Washington to Knox, Feb. 3, 1787, ibid., 5:8; Washington to Randolph, Apr. 9, 1787, ibid., 135; Holton, *Unruly Americans*, 219; Maier, *Ratification*, 1–2; Beeman, *Plain, Honest Men*, 31–2. For popular resentment of the Cincinnati, see Jensen, *New Nation*, 262–5.
138. Washington to the Executives of the States (June 1783), *DHRC*, 13:62 ("to pass"); Washington to Randolph, Apr. 9, 1787, *PGW* (C.S.), 5:135 ("inconsistent"); Maier, *Ratification*, 6–7.
139. Washington to Humphreys, Dec. 26, 1786, *PGW* (C.S.), 4:480 (quotations); see also Knox to Washington, Mar. 19, 1787, ibid., 5:96; Monroe to Jefferson, July 12, 1788, *PTJ* (M.S.), 13:352; Maier, *Ratification*, 20.
140. Madison to Washington, Dec. 7, 1786, *PJM* (C.S.), 9:199 ("the opinion" and "the peculiarity"); Randolph to Washington, Dec. 6, 1786, *PGW* (C.S.), 4:445 ("one ray," "dissolution," "to you," and "those who began"); see also Randolph to Washington, Jan. 4, 1787, ibid., 501.
141. Washington to Madison, Dec. 16, 1786, *PJM* (C.S.), 9:216 ("not for" and "remove"); Madison to Washington, Dec. 24, 1786, ibid., 224 ("in case"); see also Washington to Knox, Feb. 3, 1787, *PGW* (C.S.), 5:8.
142. Washington to Knox, Dec. 26, 1786, ibid., 4:482; Washington to Humphreys, Dec. 26, 1786, ibid., 477; see also Washington to Knox, Feb. 3, 1787, ibid., 5:7.
143. Knox to Washington, Jan. 14, 1787, ibid., 4:519–20.
144. Ibid., 520–1.
145. Ibid.
146. Humphreys to Washington, Jan. 20, 1787, ibid., 527–9.
147. Jay to William Carmichael, Jan. 4, 1787, *CPPJJ*, 3:225 ("the public mind" and "it is not clear"); Washington to Humphreys, Dec. 26, 1786, *PGW* (C.S.), 4:480 ("be considered"); see also Davis, *Sectionalism in American Politics*, 158–9; Henderson, *Party Politics*, 403; Boyd, *Politics of Opposition*, 4.
148. King to Gerry, Jan. 7, 1787, *LCRK*, 1:201 ("not alone because"); Madison to Randolph, Feb. 18, 1787, *PJM* (C.S.), 9:272 ("not augur well"); Madison to Washington, Feb. 21, 1787, ibid., 285 ("might be incommoded"); see also Madison to Jefferson, Feb. 15, 1787, ibid., 269; Kaminski, "New York," 58–9.
149. King to Gerry, Feb. 18, 1787, *LCRK*, 1:202; see also Jan. 7, 1787, ibid., 201; Henderson, *Party Politics*, 403.
150. Madison to Jefferson, Feb. 15, 1787, *PJM* (C.S.), 9:269 (quotations); Knox to Washington, Feb. 12, 1787, *PGW* (C.S.), 5:25–6.
151. King to John Adams, Oct. 2, 1786, *LDC*, 23:578–9 ("interfere" and "fully convinced"); Monroe to Madison, Oct. 2, 1786, *PJM* (C.S.), 9:139 ("the eastern states"); Oct. 7, 1786, ibid., 143; see also Henry Lee to St. George Tucker, Oct. 20, 1786, *LDC*, 23:608–9; Kaminski, "New York," 58. Washington later told Jay that a congressional endorsement of the convention might "give it a coloring" of legitimacy (Mar. 10, 1787, *PGW* (C.S.), 5:80). Jay had agreed with King and others that Congress ought not to endorse what he regarded as an illegitimate project. For his complicated, alternative mode of pursuing constitutional change, see Jay to Washington, Jan. 7, 1787, *PGW* (C.S.), 4:503.

152. Carrington to Madison, Dec. 18, 1786, *PJM* (C.S.), 9:218–9.

153. Ferguson, *Power of the Purse*, 248–9 ("ridiculous farce") (quoting *Massachusetts Centinel*, Nov. 11, 1789); Massachusetts delegates to Governor James Bowdoin, Sept. 3, 1785, *LDC*, 22:612 ("baleful aristocrac[y]"); Grayson to Monroe, Nov. 22, 1786, *Papers of James Monroe*, 2:265–6 ("The Massachusetts delegation"); see also Rakove, *Beginnings of National Politics*, 391–2; Szatmary, *Shays' Rebellion*, 127–8; Davis, *Sectionalism in American Politics*, 159–60; Henderson, *Party Politics*, 400, 403; McDonald, *Novus Ordo Seclorum*, 178; supra pp. 92, 96.

154. Madison to Washington, Feb. 21, 1787, *PJM* (C.S.), 9:285 ("much divided" and "taking an interest"); Madison, Notes on Debates, Feb. 21, 1787, ibid., 290 ("lending its sanction," "tend to weaken," and "the interposition"); see also Madison to Pendleton, Feb. 24, 1787, ibid., 294; Madison to Randolph, Feb. 18, 1787, ibid., 272. On Congress's difficulty in achieving a quorum, see Grayson to Madison, Nov. 22, 1786, ibid., 173, 174 n. 1; King to Gerry, Jan. 7, 1787, *LCRK*, 1:200; Stephen Mix Mitchell to Jeremiah Wadsworth, Jan. 24, 1787, *LDC*, 24:73–4; Jay to Jefferson, Feb. 9, 1787, *CPPJJ*, 3:231; Beeman, *Plain, Honest Men*, 20.

155. Madison to Washington, Feb. 21, 1787, *PJM* (C.S.), 9:285 ("some of the backward"); Knox to Washington, Feb. 22, 1787, *PGW* (C.S.), 5:47 ("take away"); see also Madison to Randolph, Feb. 18, 1787, *PJM* (C.S.), 9:271–2.

156. Madison, Notes on Debates, Feb. 21, 1787, ibid., 290 ("considerable difficulty"); Grand Committee report, Feb. 21, 1787, *JCC*, 32:71–2 ("as to the inefficiency" and "strongly recommend").

157. Madison, Notes on Debates, Feb. 21, 1787, *PJM* (C.S.), 9:291 ("in case Congress"); New York Assembly Resolution on the Call of a Convention of the States, Feb. 17, 1787, *PAH*, 4:93 ("for the purpose"); see also Kaminski, *George Clinton*, 116–7.

158. New York delegates' motion, Feb. 21, 1787, *JCC*, 32:72; Madison, Notes on Debates, Feb. 21, 1787, *PJM* (C.S.), 9:291 ("There was reason"); Madison to Pendleton, Feb. 24, 1787, ibid., 294, 296 n. 3 ("room to suspect" and "very federal"); Kaminski, *George Clinton*, 117; Kaminski, "New York," 58–9; New York Introduction, *DHRC*, 19:xxxix–xl, xlv–xlvi; see also Madison to Randolph, Feb. 25, 1787, *PJM* (C.S.), 9:299; Henderson, *Party Politics*, 403–4.

159. Irvine to James Wilson, Mar. 6, 1787, *Letters of Members of the Continental Congress* (Edmund Cody Burnett, ed., Washington, DC, 1936), 8:551 ("would be carried") [hereinafter "*LMCC*"]; Proceedings of the Confederation Congress, Feb. 21, 1787, *JCC*, 32:73–4 ("the most probable," "the sole," and "such alterations"); see also Kaminski, "New York," 59; Henderson, *Party Politics*, 404.

160. Irvine to James Wilson, Mar. 6, 1787, *LMCC*, 8:551 (quotation); Madison, Notes on Debates, Feb. 21, 1787, *PJM* (C.S.), 9:290–1.

161. Ibid., 291.

162. Madison to Washington, Feb. 21, 1787, ibid., 285, 286 n. 5 ("certainly accede," "similar information," and "interference"); Knox to Washington, Mar. 19, 1787, *PGW* (C.S.), 5:96 ("has had good effects" and "[i]t is now"); Carrington to Jefferson, Apr. 24, 1787, *PTJ* (M.S.), 11:311 ("unauthorized" and "remove[d] every"); see also Madison to Randolph, Feb. 25, 1787, *PJM* (C.S.), 9:299; Introduction, *DHRC*, 3:326.

163. Washington to Knox, Feb. 3, 1787, *PGW* (C.S.), 5:8 ("in confidence" and "some of the"); Randolph to Madison, Mar. 1, 1787, *PJM* (C.S.), 9:301 ("assayed every" and "fear[ed] ineffectually"); see also Randolph to Washington, Jan. 4, 1787, *PGW* (C.S.), 4:501; Mar. 11, 1787, ibid., 5:83.

164. Washington to Knox, Mar. 8, 1787, ibid., 74–5 (quotations); Washington to Humphreys, Mar. 8, 1787, ibid., 72–3; see also Maier, *Ratification*, 21–2.

    For the preceding footnote, see Washington to Madison, Mar. 31, 1787, *PGW* (C.S.), 5:115.

165. Humphreys to Washington, Mar. 24, 1787, ibid., 103. New York's two "anti-federal" delegates were Robert Yates and John Lansing, Jr. New York's other delegate was, of course, Alexander Hamilton. On New York's appointment of delegates, see Kaminski, "New York," 59–60; Davis, *Sectionalism in American Politics*, 166.

166. Humphreys to Washington, Mar. 24, 1787, *PGW* (C.S.), 5:103–4.

167. Knox to Washington, Mar. 19, 1787, ibid., 96.

168. Ibid., 97.

169. Knox to Washington, Apr. 9, 1787, ibid., 134.

170. Washington to Randolph, Mar. 28, 1787, ibid., 113; Washington to Lafayette, June 6, 1787, ibid., 222 ("The pressure"); see also Washington to Randolph, Apr. 9, 1787, ibid., 135–6. For the argument that Shays's Rebellion ultimately proved critical to Washington's decision to attend the convention, see Holton, *Unruly Americans*, 219–20; Richards, *Shays's Rebellion*, 3, 129–32.

171. Madison to James Madison, Sr., Apr. 1, 1787, *PJM* (C.S.), 9:359 ("not doubted" and "already resolved"); Madison to Randolph, Apr. 2, 1787, ibid., 362 ("Nothing").

　　For the preceding footnote, see Monroe to Jefferson, July 27, 1787, *PTJ* (M.S.), 11:631 ("the signature"); Morris to Washington, Oct. 30, 1787, *PGW* (C.S.), 5:399–400 ("been of infinite service" and "not attended"); Beeman, *Plain, Honest Men*, 193; Richards, *Shays's Rebellion*, 132.

172. *Massachusetts Centinel*, May 19, 1787, p. 71 ("a circumstance" and "cause of much"); Kaminski, "Rhode Island," 377 ("give grounds") (quoting Dana to Gerry); see also Carrington to Randolph, Apr. 2, 1787, *LDC*, 24:193; Extract of a letter from a gentleman in the southern states (Apr. 1), *Newport Herald*, Apr. 12, 1787, *DHRC*, 13:80; Alexander, *The Selling of the Constitutional Convention*, 23–4. There were three separate votes taken in the Rhode Island legislature on whether to send delegates to the Philadelphia convention. On March 24, the Assembly voted by a majority of twenty-three (out of seventy delegates) against sending a delegation. On May 5, the Assembly by a majority of two reversed course, but the upper house now voted against sending a delegation. On June 13, the upper house changed its position, but three days later the Assembly by a majority of seventeen refused to concur. See Kaminski, "Paper Politics," 259 n. 3; Polishook, *Rhode Island*, 184–5; Introduction, *DHRC*, 24:xxxv–vi; see also Governor Arthur Fenner to President George Washington, May 20, 1790, *DHRC*, 26:875.

173. Madison to Pendleton, Apr. 22, 1787, *PJM* (C.S.), 9:395 ("unpropitious" and "materially affect"); Madison to Jefferson, Apr. 23, 1787, ibid., 401 ("numerous" and "[t]he prospect of"); Act Electing and Empowering Delegates, May 17, 1787, *DHRC*, 1:215–6.

　　For the preceding footnote, see Letter from Several Gentlemen of Rhode Island to the Chairman of the General Convention, May 11, 1787, *Farrand*, 3:19 ("their regret" and "prevent any impressions"); Varnum to Washington, June 18, 1787, *PGW* (C.S.), 5:231–2 ("the measures" and "all the worthy citizens"); see also Rhode Island delegates to the Governor of Rhode Island, Apr. 24, 1787, *LDC*, 24:256; Polishook, *Rhode Island*, 189.

174. Madison to Pendleton, Feb. 24, 1787, *PJM* (C.S.), 9:294 ("that a meeting" and "inscrutable"); Washington to Humphreys, Dec. 26, 1786, *PGW* (C.S.), 4:479–80 ("to confess" and "to see any thing"); see also Washington to Jay, Mar. 10, 1787, ibid., 5:79.

175. Washington to Randolph, Apr. 9, 1787, ibid., 135–6 (quotation); Madison to Randolph, Mar. 11, 1787, *PJM* (C.S.), 9:307. For the limiting instructions of the Delaware delegates, see *Farrand*, 3:574–5. For instructions barring the delegates from New York and Massachusetts from going beyond revising the Articles, see ibid., 579, 584.

176. Grayson to William Short, Apr. 16, 1787, *LDC*, 24:227 (quotations); see also Davis, *Sectionalism in American Politics*, 163–4.

177. Varnum to Samuel Ward, Jr., Apr. 2, 1787, *LDC*, 24:198.

178. King to Theophilus Parsons, Apr. 8, 1787, *LDC*, 24:207 ("What the convention"); Lear to Lincoln, June 4, 1787, microformed on Benjamin Lincoln Papers, P-40, Reel 8 (Mass. Historical Society) ("Much, indeed" and "submit to"); see also William Samuel Johnson to Hugh Williamson, Mar. 31, 1787, *LDC*, 24:189; Jay to Jefferson, Apr. 24, 1787, *PTJ* (M.S.), 11:313; Knox to Mercy Otis Warren, May 30, 1787, in *Collections of Massachusetts Historical Society* (Boston, 1925), 73:295; Robert R. Livingston to Marquis de la Luzerne, Apr. 24, 1787, quoted in *DHRC*, 20:1088–9 n. 4; Rakove, *Beginnings of National Politics*, 378–9.

179. Madison to Randolph, Apr. 15, 1787, *PJM* (C.S.), 9:378.

180. Madison to Pendleton, Apr. 22, 1787, ibid., 395 ("The necessity"); Madison to James Madison, Sr., Apr. 1, 1787, ibid., 359 ("[t]he probable diversity," "no very sanguine,"

"[t]he existing embarrassments," "a spirit," and "general chaos"); see also Madison to Jefferson, Mar. 19, 1787, ibid., 318.

Chapter 3

1. Mason to George Mason, Jr., June 1, 1787, *PGM*, 3:892 ("The eyes"); Monroe to Madison, May 23, 1787, *PJM* (C.S.), 9:416 ("We all look"); see also Madison to William Short, June 6, 1787, ibid., 10:31; Madison to Jefferson, June 6, 1787, ibid., 29; Dawson to Madison, Apr. 15, 1787, ibid., 9:381; Jay to John Adams, July 4, 1787, *CPPJJ*, 3:248; Mason to George Mason, Jr., May 20, 1787, *PGM*, 3:880.

2. Knox to Washington, May 29, 1787, *PGW* (C.S.), 5:201 ("I have no hope"); Washington to Jefferson, May 30, 1787, ibid., 208 ("at an end"); Monroe to Jefferson, July 27, 1787, *PTJ* (M.S.), 11:630–1 ("The affairs"); see also Madison to William Short, June 6, 1787, *PJM* (C.S.), 10:31; Charles Pinckney at Philadelphia convention, July 2, 1787, *Farrand*, 1:511.

3. Randolph (James McHenry's Notes), May 29, *Farrand*, 1:26 ("on the eve"); Lear to Benjamin Lincoln, June 4, 1787, microformed on Benjamin Lincoln Papers, P-40, Reel 8 (Mass. Historical Society) ("some measures" and "a civil war"); Charles Pinckney, *Observations, Farrand*, 3:123 ("should the convention," "of providing," and "[t]hey might possibly"); see also David Humphreys to Washington, Nov. 1, 1786, *PGW* (C.S.), 4:325.

4. Madison to Randolph, Apr. 8, 1787, *PJM* (C.S.), 9:371 ("be organized efficiently" and "the partition"); Boston *Independent Chronicle*, Feb. 15, 1787, *DHRC*, 13:57 ("contempt" and "leave the rest"); Varnum to Samuel Ward, Jr., Apr. 2, 1787, *LDC*, 24:199 ("warm espousers"); see also *Massachusetts Centinel*, Apr. 18, 1787, at 35; Dawson to Madison, Apr. 15, 1787, *PJM* (C.S.), 9:381; Madison to James Madison, Sr., Apr. 1, 1787, ibid., 359; "Reason," New York *Daily Advertiser*, Mar. 24, 1787, *DHRC*, 13:57–8; "Lycurgus," Apr. 2, 1787, ibid., 58–9; Caleb Strong at Philadelphia convention, July 14, *Farrand*, 2:7; Jay to Adams, July 4, 1787, *CPPJJ*, 3:248; Nathan Dane to Rufus King, July 5, 1787, *Farrand*, 3:54–5; Hendrickson, *Peace Pact*, 3–4; Kaminski, "New York," 66; Alexander, *The Selling of the Constitutional Convention*, 25–6.

5. Madison to Randolph, Apr. 8, 1787, *PJM* (C.S.), 9:371 (quotation); see also Madison at Philadelphia convention, June 12, *Farrand*, 1:219.

6. Madison, June 26, ibid., 423 ("would decide"); Hamilton, ibid., 424 ("due stability"); Jay to Jefferson, Oct. 27, 1786, *CPPJJ*, 3:213 ("cause of liberty" and "little pains"); Morris, July 5, *Farrand*, 1:529 ("the whole human race"); see also Mason to George Mason, Jr., June 1, 1787, *PGM*, 3:892; McDonald, *Novus Ordo Seclorum*, 6–7; Brown, *Redeeming the Republic*, 223–4.

7. Mason to Beverley Randolph, June 30, 1787, *PGM*, 3:918 ("fundamental principles," "very doubtful," and "any sound"); Hamilton to Washington, July 3, 1787, *PAH*, 4:224 ("seriously and deeply" and "we shall let slip"); Washington to Hamilton, July 10, 1787, *PGW* (C.S.), 5:257 ("narrow minded," "under the influence," "if possible," and "I almost"); see also Jared Sparks to Madison, Mar. 30, 1831, *Farrand*, 3:498; Madison to Jared Sparks, Apr. 8, 1831, *The Writings of James Madison* (Gaillard Hunt, ed., New York, 1910), 9:449; see also Beeman, *Plain, Honest Men*, 163, 203.

8. Ibid., 40, 87, 156; Banning, *Sacred Fire*, 138–9; but cf. Nelson, *Royalist Revolution*, 202.

9. Madison to Washington, Feb. 21, 1787, *PJM* (C.S.), 9:286 ("a thorough reform"); Washington to Madison, Mar. 31, 1787, *PGW* (C.S.), 5:116 ("adopt no temporizing"). In a letter to Washington, Knox had urged a similar notion. If the convention made proposals only "for bracing up the present radically defective thing, so as [to] enable us to drag on with pain and labor, for a few years, then better had it been that the idea of the convention had never been conceived." Instead, Knox hoped, the convention would "possess the magnanimity to propose a wise modification of a national government, without regarding the present local and contracted views that the mass of the people in the respective states entertain of the subject" (Mar. 19, 1787, *PGW* (C.S.), 5:96).

10. Madison to Randolph, Apr. 8, 1787, *PJM* (C.S.), 9:369 ("In truth"); Madison to Washington, Apr. 16, 1787, ibid., 382–3 ("Temporizing applications").

11. Supra p. 99 & n. 93; William Pierce, Character Sketches of Delegates to the Federal Convention, *Farrand*, 3:94 (quotation) [hereinafter, "Pierce, Character Sketches"]; Madison, Vices, *PJM* (C.S.), 9:348–57; Editorial Note, ibid., 345–8; Rakove, *Beginnings of National Politics*, 379–80; Robertson, *The Constitution and America's Destiny*, 76; Hendrickson, *Peace Pact*, ch. 24.

12. Madison to John Page?, May 8, 1780, *PJM* (C.S.), 2:21 ("distress"); Madison, Vices, ibid., 9:348, 350 ("want" at p. 350); supra pp. 13–48; see also Madison to Randolph, Apr. 8, 1787, *PJM* (C.S.), 9:370.

13. Madison, Vices, ibid., 350; see also ibid., 348–9. On states' negotiating their own treaties with Indian tribes, see Marks, *Independence on Trial*, 4.

14. Madison, Vices, *PJM* (C.S.), 9:351–2.

15. Madison to Washington, Apr. 16, 1787, ibid., 384–5 ("the right," "the difficulty," "to the judiciary," and "the oaths"); Madison to Randolph, Apr. 8, 1787, ibid., 370 ("the intention").

16. Ibid., 369 ("principle of representation," "just," "safe," and "as the liberty"); Madison to Jefferson, Mar. 19, 1787, ibid., 318 ("the equality of votes" and "such an augmentation"); see also Madison to Washington, Apr. 16, 1787, ibid., 383.

17. Madison to Jefferson, Mar. 19, 1787, ibid., 318–9 ("[a] majority"); Madison to Randolph, Apr. 8, 1787, ibid., 371 ("by the actual," "the southern," "[t]his principle," and "yield"); see also Madison to Washington, Apr. 16, 1787, ibid., 383.

18. Madison, Vices, ibid., 353–7 (all quotations but "unjust" at pp. 353–4); Madison to James Madison, Sr., Nov. 1, 1786, ibid., 154 ("unjust"); see also Madison to Jefferson, Dec. 9, 1787, ibid., 10:313.

19. Madison, Vices, ibid., 9:354–5.

20. Ibid., 355, 357 (all quotations but the last two); Madison to Monroe, Oct. 5, 1786, ibid., 141 ("the interest" and "the majority"); see also Madison to Washington, Apr. 16, 1787, ibid., 383–4; Madison to Jefferson, Oct. 24, 1787, ibid., 10:212–4; *The Federalist No. 10* (Madison), especially pp. 72–3, 75; *The Federalist No. 51* (Madison), at 323–5; Rakove, *Original Meanings*, 313–6; Holton, *Unruly Americans*, 4–5.

21. Madison, Vices, *PJM* (C.S.), 9:356–7.

22. Ibid., 357 ("extract from"); Madison to Washington, Apr. 16, 1787, ibid., 384 ("There has not been").

23. Madison to Jefferson, Oct. 24, 1787, ibid., 10:212 ("in contradiction to").

24. Madison to Randolph, Apr. 8, 1787, ibid., 9:370 ("essential" and "a negative"); Madison to Jefferson, Mar. 19, 1787, ibid., 318 ("not only to guard," "paper money," "on paper," and "easily and continually"); Madison to Washington, Apr. 16, 1787, ibid., 384 ("the internal vicissitudes"); see also Madison at Philadelphia convention, June 8, *Farrand*, 1:164–5, 168; July 17, ibid., 2:27–8. The British Declaratory Act of 1766, on which Madison modeled the federal veto, had provided that Parliament had "full power" to make laws "to bind the colonies and people of America . . . in all cases whatsoever." See editorial note, *DHRC*, 24:266 n. 2.

25. Madison, June 6, *Farrand*, 1:134–5 (quotations); see also June 26, ibid., 421–3.

26. Madison to Randolph, Apr. 8, 1787, *PJM* (C.S.), 9:369 (quotations); see also Holton, *Unruly Americans*, 200–4, 206–7.

27. Madison to Randolph, Apr. 15, 1787, *PJM* (C.S.), 9:379 ("some materials"); Washington to Arthur Lee, May 20, 1787, *PGW* (C.S.), 5:191 ("to sour"); Mason to George Mason, Jr., May 20, 1787, *PGM*, 3:880; Randolph to the Speaker of the Virginia House of Delegates (dated Oct. 10; published Dec. 27, 1787), *DHRC*, 8:262 ("was not so eminently" and "destitute"); see also Madison to Noah Webster, Oct. 12, 1804, *PJM* (Secretary of State Series), 8:161 [hereinafter, "*PJM* (S.S.S.)"]; George Read to John Dickinson, May 21, 1787, *Farrand*, 3:25; Beeman, *Plain, Honest Men*, 57.

28. Mason to George Mason, Jr., May 20, 1787, *PGM*, 3:880 ("a total alteration"); Madison to Pendleton, May 27, 1787, *PJM* (C.S.), 10:12 ("[i]n general"); see also Mason to Arthur Lee, May 21, 1787, *PGM*, 3:882; Beeman, *Plain, Honest Men*, 52–4.

29. Benjamin Rush to Richard Price, June 2, 1787, *Farrand*, 3:33 ("the most august") (reporting Franklin's statement); Madison to William Short, June 6, 1787, *PJM* (C.S.), 10:31 ("in several instances"); see also Madison to James Madison, Sr., May 27, 1787, ibid., 10;

Madison to Pendleton, May 27, 1787, ibid., 12; Madison to Jefferson, June 6, 1787, ibid., 28; Beeman, *Plain, Honest Men*, 57.

30. Madison to Monroe, June 10, 1787, *PJM* (C.S.), 10:43 ("If her deputies"); Madison to Jefferson, June 6, 1787, ibid., 29 ("the state treasury"); see also Jacob Broom to Thomas Collins, May 23, 1787, *Farrand*, Supp.:16; Mason to George Mason, Jr., May 27, 1787, ibid., 3:28.

31. Ibid.; Randolph to Beverley Randolph, June 6, 1787, ibid., 36 ("a very long"); North Carolina convention delegates to Governor Richard Caswell, June 14, 1787, ibid., 46 ("a summer's campaign"); see also Grayson to Monroe, May 29, 1787, *Papers of James Monroe*, 2:385; Jay to Adams, July 4, 1787, *CPPJJ*, 3:248; but cf. Benjamin Rush to Richard Price, June 2, 1787, *Farrand*, 3:33 (reporting Franklin statement).

32. May 25, *Farrand*, 1:2–6; May 28, ibid., 7–14 (Mason quotation at p. 10); May 29, ibid., 16–7; see also Beeman, *Plain, Honest Men*, 82. The significance of the delegates' decision to give each state delegation an equal vote is discussed infra pp. 201–2.

For the preceding footnote, see Mary Sarah Bilder, *Madison's Hand: Revising the Constitutional Convention* (Cambridge, MA, 2015), passim, esp. pp. 1–5, 19, 60–2, 66–84, 89, 91, 96, 101, 104, 114–8, 122–4, 127, 134, 137, 141–2, 146–50, 154–5, 179–92, 198–200, 214–8, 223, 226–8; see also James H. Hutson, "The Creation of the Constitution: The Integrity of the Documentary Record," *Texas Law Review* (1986), 65:9–12, 24–35; infra pp. 242–3 n. *.

33. Official Journal, May 29, *Farrand*, 1:15 (quotation); Beeman, *Plain, Honest Men*, 83; see also Bilder, *Madison's Hand*, 55–6.

34. Jefferson to Adams, Aug. 30, 1787, *PTJ* (M.S.), 12:69.

35. Mason to George Mason, Jr., May 27, 1787, *PGM*, 3:884 ("a proper precaution"); Madison to Monroe, June 10, 1787, *PJM* (C.S.), 10:43 ("prudent," "effectually secure," and "save both"); Beeman, *Plain, Honest Men*, 83; see also Mason to George Mason, Jr., June 1, 1787, *PGM*, 3:893; Madison to Jefferson, June 6, 1787, *PJM* (C.S.), 10:29; Alexander Martin to Caswell, July 27, 1787, *Farrand*, 3:64.

36. Journal of Jared Sparks, Apr. 19, 1830, *Farrand*, 3:479 (quotations); Beeman, *Plain, Honest Men*, 91–2; Clinton Rossiter, *1787: The Grand Convention* (New York, 1966), 167–8.

37. Randolph, May 29, *Farrand*, 1:18–23; see also Madison to Noah Webster, Oct. 12, 1804, *PJM* (S.S.S.), 8:161; Beeman, *Plain, Honest Men*, 86–91. On Madison's influence in the drafting of the Virginia Plan, see Editorial Note, *PJM* (C.S.), 10:12–3.

For the preceding footnote, see American National Biography Online; Kaminski and Moore, *An Assembly of Demigods*, 190–4 (quotations from Benjamin Harrison to George Washington, July 23, 1775 ("one of the cleverest") at p. 190; Louis-Guillaume Otto's *Biographies* (fall 1788) ("one of the most distinguished") at p. 192; William Pierce's *Sketches* ("a young gentleman") at p. 190; Jefferson to Madison, Aug. 11, 1793 ("the poorest chameleon") at p. 192).

38. Randolph, May 29, *Farrand*, 1:18–9 ("the jealousy" and "the havoc"); Randolph (McHenry's Notes), ibid., 26 ("wise and great men").

39. Ibid., 18–9.

40. Randolph, May 29, ibid., 19 ("republican"); Virginia Plan, resolution 1, ibid., 20 ("common defense") (paraphrasing Article III of the Articles of Confederation).

41. Virginia Plan, resolutions 2–3, ibid., 20. "Quotas of contribution" connotes requisitions, which suggests that the drafters of the Virginia Plan had not entirely repudiated that feature of the Articles.

42. Resolutions 4–5, ibid., 20.

43. Resolution 6, ibid., 21.

44. Resolutions 7–8, ibid.

45. Resolution 9, ibid., 21–2. On the indeterminate number of inferior tribunals, see editorial note, *PJM*, 10:18 n. 4.

46. Resolutions 10–11, 13–15, *Farrand*, 1:22. Article XI of the Articles of Confederation provided for the admission of Canada if it approved the Articles, and of other "colon[ies]" if their admission was approved by nine states. The Articles said nothing about admitting new states either from territory belonging to the United States or from territory carved out of existing states. See, e.g., John Brown to Archibald Stuart, June 25, 1788, *DHRC*, 10:1678.

47. Virginia Plan, resolution 1, *Farrand*, 1:20 (quotation); see also Beeman, *Plain, Honest Men*, 91. On the complete novelty of the federal veto, see John Lansing, Jr., June 16, *Farrand*, 1:250. As previously noted, there was no independent executive under the Articles. The officials who headed the Departments of Foreign Affairs, Finance, War, and the Post Office were appointed by Congress and were entirely within its control. See supra pp. 47–8.

48. Randolph, May 30, *Farrand*, 1:33 ("merely federal," "national," and "supreme"); Morris, ibid., 34 ("a mere" and "a complete"); see also Official Journal, ibid., 30; Yates's Notes, ibid., 38–9; McHenry's Notes, ibid., 41.

49. Pinckney (McHenry's Notes), ibid., 41 ("declaring"); Pinckney (Yates's Notes), ibid., 39 ("their business"); Gerry (McHenry's Notes), ibid., 42–3 ("questionable not only"); see also Beeman, *Plain, Honest Men*, 99–102; Merrill Jensen, *The Making of the American Constitution* (Princeton, NJ, 1964), 41–2.

    For the preceding footnote, see American National Biography Online; Maier, *Ratification*, 50–1; Beeman, *Plain, Honest Men*, 111–4; Kaminski and Moore, *An Assembly of Demigods*, 37–48 (quoting Adams to James Warren, July 15, 1776 ["a man of immense worth" and "If every" at p. 37]; William Pierce, *Sketches* ["hesitating" at p. 40]). See generally George Athan Billias, *Elbridge Gerry: Founding Father and Republican Statesman* (New York, 1976).

50. Lansing, June 16, *Farrand*, 1:249 ("decidedly"); Paterson, June 9, ibid., 178 ("the people" and "usurpation"); Paterson (Yates's Notes), ibid., 182 ("give a complexion," "as the deputies," and "consolidate"); see also Gunning Bedford (Yates's Notes), June 30, ibid., 501–2; Paterson, June 16, ibid., 250; Lansing, June 20, ibid., 336.

51. Randolph, June 16, *Farrand*, 1:255 (quotations); see also Randolph (Paterson's Notes), ibid., 273.

52. Hamilton, June 18, ibid., 283 ("[W]e owed it"); Hamilton (Yates's Notes), ibid., 294 ("a good government"); Wilson, June 16, ibid., 253 ("With regard").

53. May 30, ibid., 35 (the vote); Abraham G. Lansing to Abraham Yates, Aug. 26, 1787, *Farrand*, Supp.:243 ("no prospect" and "whether") (reporting what John Lansing told him). For additional statements rejecting the legitimacy concerns, see George Read, June 6, ibid., 1:136–7; Charles Pinckney, *Observations, Farrand*, 3:108; Charles Pinckney, June 16, ibid., 1:255; King, June 19, ibid., 324; Mason, June 20, ibid., 338.

54. Madison to Jefferson, Oct. 24, 1787, *PJM* (C.S.), 10:207 (quotation); Lance G. Banning, "The Constitutional Convention," in Leonard W. Levy and Dennis J. Mahoney, eds., *The Framing and Ratification of the Constitution* (New York, 1987), 113–4; Brown, *Redeeming the Republic*, 184; see also Charles Pinckney at South Carolina ratifying convention, Jan. 16, 1788, *DHRC*, 27:93.

55. Ellsworth (Yates's Notes), June 30, *Farrand*, 1:496 ("because"); ibid., 502 ("depends"); Paterson, June 9, ibid., 178 ("a national" and "[a] confederacy"); Dickinson, June 2, ibid., 86 ("had no idea," "The happiness," and "required"). For additional statements to similar effect, see Lansing, June 16, ibid., 249; Lansing (Yates's Notes), June 20, ibid., 345; Mason, June 7, ibid., 155; Ellsworth (Yates's Notes), June 25, ibid., 414, 417; Luther Martin, June 27, ibid., 437; Roger Sherman, May 30, ibid., 34–5; Pierce Butler, May 31, ibid., 53; Madison's Notes, June 14, ibid., 242 n. *.

56. Charles Pinckney and John Rutledge, May 31, ibid., 53 ("an exact"); Randolph, ibid. ("indefinite"); Sherman, June 6, ibid., 133 ("the objects"); see also May 31 (Pierce's Notes), ibid., 59–60; Beeman, *Plain, Honest Men*, 121. On Sherman, see Robertson, *The Constitution and America's Destiny*, 123–7.

    For the preceding footnote, see Kaminski and Moore, *An Assembly of Demigods*, 251; Introduction, *DHRC*, 3:327.

57. Wilson (Pierce's Notes), May 31, *Farrand*, 1:60 ("it would be impossible"); Madison, ibid., 53 ("a strong bias," "doubts concerning," and "had become stronger"); ibid., 54 (nine-to-zero vote, with one delegation divided); Madison (Yates's Notes), June 21, ibid., 364 ("not be done"); Hamilton, June 19, ibid., 323 ("boundary," "gradually subvert," and "indefinite authority"); see also Hamilton (Yates's Notes), June 18, ibid., 298. Banning strongly rejects the view that Madison ever had intended this broad formulation of Congress's powers to be written into the Constitution (*Sacred Fire*, 160, 454–5 nn. 64 and 68).

For the first of the two preceding footnotes, see Kaminski and Moore, *An Assembly of Demigods*, 150–3 (quoting Pierce's *Sketches*, at p. 150; John Adams to Abigail Adams, Mar. 5, 1796 ["ardent speculations"] at p. 52; James Iredell to Hannah Iredell, Aug. 11, 1797 ["absconding"] at p. 153; and Jacob Rush to Benjamin Rush, Sept. 8, 1798 ["What a miserable"] at p. 153).

For the second of the two preceding footnotes, see Madison to John Tyler (undated and unsent), *Farrand*, 3:526–7.

58. Randolph, July 17, ibid., 2:26; Committee of Detail report, Art. VII, Aug. 6, ibid., 157, 158–9; Beeman, *Plain, Honest Men*, 266–7, 274, 288; Banning, *Sacred Fire*, 161.

For the preceding footnote, see Beeman, supra, 246–7, 263–76.

59. Hamilton, June 18, *Farrand*, 1:286 (quotations); supra pp. 13–21.

60. Mason, May 30, ibid., 34; Madison, ibid. ("very cogently"); Virginia Plan, resolution 6, May 29, ibid., 21 ("call forth"); Madison, May 31, ibid., 54 ("the more" and "against"); see also Madison, June 19, ibid., 320; Mason (King's Notes), June 20, ibid., 349; Madison, July 14, ibid., 2:9; Madison to Jefferson, Oct. 24, 1787, *PJM* (C.S.), 10:207; Banning, *Sacred Fire*, 119, 140–1.

For the preceding footnote, see James Buchanan, Fourth Annual Message (Dec. 3, 1860), in *Works of James Buchanan* (John Bassett Moore, ed., Philadelphia, 1910), 11:18–9; see also Jesse T. Carpenter, *The South as a Conscious Minority, 1789–1861: A Study in Political Thought* (New York, 1930), 214–6.

61. Hamilton (King's Notes), June 18, *Farrand*, 1:302 (quotations); see also Hamilton at New York ratifying convention, June 20, 1788, *DHRC*, 22:1724; Edling, *Revolution in Favor of Government*, 73–4.

62. Mason, Aug. 18, *Farrand*, 2:326–7 ("perpetual revenue"); Sherman, July 17, ibid., 26 ("power of levying" and "the power"); ibid. (eight-to-two vote against Sherman proposal); Martin, Aug. 31, ibid., 359 ("cases of absolute"); ibid. (eight-to-one vote, with one delegation divided, against Martin proposal); see also New Jersey Plan, resolutions 2–3, June 15, ibid., 1:243; Robertson, *The Constitution and America's Destiny*, 188–93; Edling, *Revolution in Favor of Government*, 74; Ferguson, *Power of the Purse*, 290–1; McDonald, *Novus Ordo Seclorum*, 263.

63. Articles of Confederation, Art. IX, *DHRC*, 1:91; Pinckney, Aug. 18, *Farrand*, 2:332 ("a scanty faith," "[t]he United States," and "rapid approaches"); Morris to Moss Kent, Jan. 12, 1815, ibid., 3:420 ("[t]hose who"). In 1780, after the defeat suffered by General Horatio Gates at Camden, South Carolina, Hamilton had written, "His passion for militia, I fancy, will be a little cured, and he will cease to think them the best bulwark of American liberty" (to James Duane, Sept. 6, 1780, *PAH*, 2:420).

64. Gerry, Aug. 18, *Farrand*, 2:329 (quotations); Martin, ibid., 330; ibid. (motion of Martin and Gerry rejected without dissent); Sherman, Sept. 4, ibid., 509; Gerry, ibid. For Gerry's opposition in Congress to a peacetime standing army, see Kohn, *Eagle and Sword*, 52–3, 59–60, 77–8; Billias, *Elbridge Gerry*, 106–13.

65. Hamilton (Yates's Notes), June 18, *Farrand*, 1:298 ("raise no troops"); Dayton, Aug. 18, ibid., 2:330; Langdon, ibid.; Committee of Unfinished Parts report, presented by David Brearley, Sept. 5, ibid., 508 (two-year limit on military appropriations); Sept. 14, ibid., 616–7 ("the liberties") (nine-to-two vote against Mason proposal); Edling, *Revolution in Favor of Government*, 226. In 1783, Hamilton had expressed concern that Article VI was "susceptible of a construction which would . . . preclude the United States from raising a single regiment or building a single ship, before a declaration of war, or an actual commencement of hostilities." He considered this a "dangerous" principle, "leaving the United States at all times unprepared for the defense of their common rights, obliging them to begin to raise an army and to build and equip a navy at the moment they would have occasion to employ them." Unsubmitted Resolution Calling for a Convention to Amend the Articles of Confederation (July 1783), *PAH*, 3:422. Whether the Articles permitted Congress to raise troops in peacetime was ambiguous, and Hamilton's statement at the Philadelphia convention that the Articles plainly prohibited Congress from doing so was disingenuous (Kohn, *Eagle and Sword*, 49, 87).

66. Mason, Aug. 18, *Farrand*, 2:326; Pinckney, ibid., 330.

67. Ellsworth, ibid., 331 ("states would pine"); Sherman, ibid., 332 ("the states"); Dickinson, ibid., 331 ("the states never").
68. Madison, ibid., 332.
69. Report of the Committee of Eleven, presented by William Livingston, Aug. 21, ibid., 356; Gerry, Aug. 23, ibid., 384 (quotations); Martin, ibid., 387.
70. Madison, ibid., 386–7; Randolph, ibid., 387 ("court[ing] popularity"); ibid., 387–8 (nine-to-two vote in favor of Committee of Eleven proposal); ibid., 388 (eight-to-three vote against Madison's proposal); see also Charles Pinckney, *Observations*, ibid., 3:118–9; Robertson, *The Constitution and America's Destiny*, 186; Kohn, *Eagle and Sword*, 78–80.
71. Supra pp. 21–4; Madison to J. C. Cabell, Feb. 13, 1829, *Farrand*, 3:478 (quotation).
72. Madison, Aug. 28, ibid., 2:441; ibid. (seven-to-four vote against Madison's motion).
73. Pinckney, Aug. 29, ibid., 449 ("the true interest" and "to have no regulation"); Mason, ibid., 451 ("Is it to be expected"); McHenry's Notes, Aug. 7, ibid., 211 ("the dearest interests") (reporting McHenry's conversation with fellow Maryland delegate Daniel Carroll). On the extent of northern manufacturing in the 1780s, see Jensen, *New Nation*, 219–27.
74. Clymer, Aug. 29, *Farrand*, 2:450 ("[t]he northern"); Morris, ibid. ("most precarious," "multiply them," "[a] navy," and "by a navigation act"); Madison, ibid., 451–2 ("temporary rise," "increase of southern," and "removal"). For similar views expressed by Madison in the mid-1780s, see supra p. 37.
75. Pinckney, Aug. 29, *Farrand*, 2:449; Sherman, ibid., 450 ("was always embarrassing"); Williamson, ibid., 450–1 ("the southern people").
76. Infra pp. 277–91; Madison, Sept. 15, *Farrand*, 2:625 ("more and more"); Sherman, ibid. ("[T]here is no danger"). On the so-called dormant commerce clause issue in the antebellum Supreme Court, see Felix Frankfurter, *The Commerce Clause: Under Marshall, Taney, and Waite* (Chapel Hill, NC, 1937), 28–9, 50–6.
77. Committee of Detail report, Art. VII, Aug. 6, *Farrand*, 2:182; Aug. 20, ibid., 344–5 (vote agreeing to the clause without dissent); infra p. 322; Rakove, *Original Meanings*, 84, 180; Beeman, *Plain, Honest Men*, 274, 288–9; Jensen, *Making of the American Constitution*, 84. Toward the end of the convention, the three delegates who would ultimately refuse to sign the Constitution objected to the Necessary and Proper Clause. See Randolph, Sept. 10, *Farrand*, 2:563; Gerry, Sept. 15, ibid., 633; Mason, ibid., 640.
78. June 15, *Farrand*, 1:242 n. *; Beeman, *Plain, Honest Men*, 172, 227–8; Brown, *Redeeming the Republic*, 194; see also William R. Casto, *The Supreme Court in the Early Republic: The Chief Justiceships of John Jay and Oliver Ellsworth* (Columbia, SC, 1995), 12–4.
79. Brearley, June 9, *Farrand*, 1:177 ("astonished," "alarmed," and "come to"); Dickinson, June 15, ibid., 242 n. * ("friends"); Read, July 10, ibid., 570 ("the objects"); Madison to Van Buren, May 13, 1828, ibid., 3:477 ("[t]he threatening contest"); see also Gunning Bedford, July 17, ibid., 2:26; Read, June 29, ibid., 1:463; June 6, ibid., 136; Wilson, June 30, ibid., 484.
80. New Jersey Plan, June 15, ibid., 242–5 ("revise and "correct" in resolution 1 at p. 242); Paterson, June 14, ibid., 240 ("purely federal"); June 15, ibid., 242 n. *; Lansing (Yates's Notes), ibid., 246.
81. Alexander Hamilton, Address of the Annapolis Convention, Sept. 14, 1786, *PAH*, 3:687 (quotations); Introduction, *DHRC*, 3:122–4; Robertson, *The Constitution and America's Destiny*, 119–20; McCormick, "New Jersey Defies the Confederation," 45.
82. Pinckney, June 16, *Farrand*, 1:255 ("Give New Jersey"); George Bancroft, *History of the United States of America: From the Discovery of the Continent* (New York, 1888), 6:269 ("From the day"); see also Madison to Theodore Sedgwick, Jr., Feb. 12, 1831, *Farrand*, 3:496; Madison to unidentified recipient, Mar. 1836, ibid., 538; Brown, *Redeeming the Republic*, 193; Rakove, *Original Meanings*, 63; Beeman, *Plain, Honest Men*, 227–8; Rossiter, *1787: The Grand Convention*, 176.
83. Donald L. Robinson, *Slavery in the Structure of American Politics, 1765–1820* (New York, 1971), 209–10, 213; infra pp. 191–2. For one particularly striking example of such southern nationalism, see Charles Pinckney, June 8, *Farrand*, 1:164.
84. Virginia Plan, resolution 6, May 29, ibid., 21.

85. Madison, July 17, ibid., 2:27 ("to pursue" and "continue to disturb"); June 19, ibid., 1:316–7, 319 ("same tendency" and "dreadful class"); see also June 8, ibid., 164.

86. Madison, July 17, ibid., 2:27–8 (all quotes but the last); June 8, ibid., 1:164 ("the only remedy"); Aug. 28, ibid., 2:440; Rakove, *Original Meanings*, 171–7; see also Madison, Sept. 12, *Farrand*, 2:589; Wilson, Aug. 23, ibid., 390–1.

87. Ibid., 391 ("[t]he power" and "the key-stone"); Charles Pinckney, ibid., 390; Hamilton, June 18, ibid., 1:293 ("contrary to"); Jay to Washington, Jan. 7, 1787, *PGW* (C.S.), 4:503; May 31, *Farrand*, 1:54 (unanimous vote in favor of the principle of the veto). It is puzzling that the convention would unanimously endorse the principle of the veto but then evince such strong and repeated opposition to specific instantiations of it.

88. Pinckney, June 8, ibid., 164 (quotations); Charles Pinckney, *Observations*, ibid., 3:112–3.

89. Madison, June 8, ibid., 1:164 ("an indefinite"); Wilson, ibid., 166 ("impracticable" and "most safely"); ibid., 168 (the vote); supra pp. 132–3; see also Dickinson, June 8, *Farrand*, 1:167; Banning, *Sacred Fire*, 451 n. 30.

90. The convention discussed the veto on several occasions. To my mind, the best way to organize discussion of the issue is conceptually rather than chronologically.

91. Sherman, June 8, *Farrand*, 1:166 ("the cases"); Williamson, ibid., 165 ("a power"); Gerry, ibid. ("extend" and "enslave"); Jefferson to Madison, June 20, 1787, *PJM* (C.S.), 10:64 ("Prima facie," "It fails," and "concern[s]").

92. Morris, July 17, *Farrand*, 2:27, 28 (quotations); see also Sherman, ibid., 28. Morris made this speech the day after the Connecticut Compromise passed, when he was in a sour, obstructionist mood. See infra p. 204.

93. Bedford (King's Notes), June 8, *Farrand*, 1:172. Gerry made a more generalized version of Bedford's argument: The proposed veto might "enable the general government to depress a part for the benefit of another part." For example, Congress might block the inducements offered by some states to their manufacturers. Gerry (King's Notes), ibid., 171–2.

94. June 8, ibid., 168 (seven-to-three vote against Pinckney's motion, one delegation divided); July 17, ibid., 2:28 (seven-to-three vote against the limited version of the veto); see also Aug. 23, ibid., 391 (six-to-five vote against referring an unlimited veto to the Committee of Eleven). In the vote on July 17, North Carolina, which was in fact the third most populous state, joined Virginia and Massachusetts in supporting the veto, while Pennsylvania voted against.

95. Butler (King's Notes), ibid., 1:168; see also Rakove, *Original Meanings*, 174, 337.

96. Mason, Aug. 23, *Farrand*, 2:390 ("Is no road"); Bedford, June 8, ibid., 1:167 ("Are the laws"); Lansing, June 20, ibid., 337; see also Martin, July 17, ibid., 2:27.

97. Madison, June 8, ibid., 1:168 (quotations); see also July 17, ibid., 2:28.

98. Rutledge, Aug. 23, ibid., 391 ("If nothing else"); Gerry, June 8, ibid., 1:165 ("[s]uch an idea" and "never be"); see also Lansing, June 16, ibid., 250; Morris, July 17, ibid., 2:28; Brown, *Redeeming the Republic*, 198–9.

99. Madison, July 17, *Farrand*, 2:27 (quotation); Charles Pinckney, Aug. 23, ibid., 390 (supermajority requirement for the exercise of the veto power); Williamson, ibid., 391 (waste of time); Madison to Jefferson, Oct. 24, 1787, *PJM* (C.S.), 10:209.

100. Madison to John Tyler (1833) (unsent), *Farrand*, 3:527 ("The necessity"); Madison, June 19, ibid., 1:316 ("been manifested" and "if not prevented").

101. New Jersey Plan, resolution 6, June 15, ibid., 245.

102. Martin, July 17, ibid., 2:28–9; ibid., 29 (agreed to without dissent); Committee of Detail report, Art. VIII, Aug. 6, ibid., 183; Aug. 23, ibid., 389 (Rutledge amendment to Supremacy Clause agreed to, again without dissent); see also Rakove, *Original Meanings*, 173–4; Charles F. Hobson, "The Negative on State Laws: James Madison, the Constitution, and the Crisis of Republican Government," *William and Mary Quarterly* (Apr. 1979), 36:228–9.

103. Holton, *Unruly Americans*, 186; Rakove, *Original Meanings*, 175; Larry D. Kramer, *The People Themselves: Popular Constitutionalism and Judicial Review* (New York, 2004), 75; Robertson, *The Constitution and America's Destiny*, 229.

104. Wood, *Creation of the American Republic*, 453–4, 456.

105. Letter from "Probus" to the "Primitive Whig," in "Primitive Whig" IV, *New-Jersey Gazette*, Jan. 30, 1786, at 2 ("laws directly"); Grayson to Madison, Mar. 22, 1786, *PJM* (C.S.), 8:509 ("surely paper money" and "an attack"); see also Polishook, "Trevett vs. Weeden," 47, 67; Kaminski, "Paper Politics," 188–9; Conley, "Rhode Island: Laboratory for the Internal 'Lively Experiment,'" 136–43. David Howell, who was one of the judges in the Rhode Island case, *Trevett v. Weeden*, invoked his role there as a credential for appointment to federal office when lobbying the Washington administration for a job in 1790 (to Jefferson, June 3, 1790, *DHRC*, 26:1026).

106. Gerry, June 4, *Farrand*, 1:97; Madison, July 17, ibid., 2:28. For the threat of impeachment in *Trevett* and the wide publicity given to that case around the nation, see Polishook, "Trevett vs. Weeden," 47, 64–5, 67–8 & n. 43. For similar controversy surrounding the first instances of judicial review in New Hampshire in the mid-1780s, see Frank C. Mevers, "New Hampshire Accepts the Bill of Rights," in Conley and Kaminski, eds., *The Bill of Rights and the States*, 172–3. For discussion of the state cases generally, see Wood, *Creation of the American Republic*, 454–63; Julius Goebel, Jr., *History of the Supreme Court of the United States: Antecedents and Beginnings to 1801* (New York, 1971), 125–42; Charles Groves Haines, *The American Doctrine of Judicial Supremacy* (New York, 2nd ed., 1932), 88–121. For the claim that judicial review was still a novel and controversial concept in 1787, see Sylvia Snowiss, *Judicial Review and the Law of the Constitution* (New Haven, CT, 1990), 13–44; Leonard W. Levy, "Judicial Review, History, and Democracy: An Introduction," in *Judicial Review and the Supreme Court* (Leonard W. Levy, ed., New York, 1967), 10; Kramer, *The People Themselves*, 78.

107. See supra p. 157; see also Kramer, *The People Themselves*, 76–7.

108. Virginia Plan, resolution 8, May 29, *Farrand*, 1:21 ("a convenient"); Gerry, June 4, ibid., 97 ("have a sufficient check"); Martin, July 31, ibid., 2:76 ("a dangerous innovation," "a double negative," and "will come").

109. Morris, Aug. 15, ibid., 299 ("should be"); Mercer, ibid., 298 ("disapproved" and "laws ought to be"); ibid., 299 (Dickinson) ("strongly impressed" and "no such power"); Madison, Aug. 28, ibid., 440 ("oblige the judges"); see also Wilson, July 21, ibid., 73; Madison, ibid., 84; Mason, ibid., 78; Madison, July 23, ibid., 93; Morris, ibid., 92; see also P. Allan Dionisopoulos and Paul Peterson, "Rediscovering the American Origins of Judicial Review: A Rebuttal to the Views Stated by Currie and Other Scholars," *John Marshall Law Review* (1984), 18:56; Ralph L. Ketcham, "James Madison and Judicial Review," *Syracuse Law Review* (1957), 8:159; Kramer, *The People Themselves*, 73 & n. 1.

110. Gerry, June 8, *Farrand*, 1:165 (quotation); see also Steven R. Boyd, "The Contract Clause and the Evolution of American Federalism, 1789–1815," *William and Mary Quarterly* (July 1987), 44:532.

111. U.S. Constitution, Art. I, § 10 (quotation); see also Bouton, *Taming Democracy*, 178. On the limitation of Article I, Section 10, to *retrospective* impairments of contract, see Wilson, Aug. 28, *Farrand*, 2:440.

112. Committee of Detail report, Art. XIII, Aug. 6, ibid., 187; Gorham, Aug. 28, ibid., 439 ("an absolute prohibition"); Sherman, ibid. ("a favorable crisis"); ibid. (eight-to-one vote, with one delegation divided, in favor of making the prohibition absolute).

    For the preceding footnote, see Holton, *Forced Founders*, 62–4; Atack and Passell, *New Economic View*, 67; Bouton, "Trials of the Confederation," 374.

113. Gerry, June 8, *Farrand*, 1:165; Mason, Aug. 16, ibid., 2:309; Randolph, ibid., 310; see also Robertson, *The Constitution and America's Destiny*, 112, 194; Jensen, *Making of the American Constitution*, 96–7; Wood, "Interests and Disinterestedness," 107. For the lack of discussion on the specific provisions in Article I, Section 10, see *Farrand*, 2:442–3.

114. Committee of Detail report, Art. VII, Aug. 6, ibid., 182; Morris, Aug. 16, ibid., 309 ("[m]onied interest"); Mason, ibid. ("mortal" and "could not foresee"); Mercer, ibid. ("It was impolitic").

    For the preceding footnote, see Unsubmitted Resolution Calling for a Convention to Amend the Articles of Confederation (July 1783), *PAH*, 3:422.

115. All statements on Aug. 16, *Farrand*, 2:309–10; ibid., 310 (nine-to-two vote to strike the language authorizing Congress to emit bills of credit).

116. Mercer, Aug. 16, ibid., 309 ("a friend"); William Samuel Johnson to Hugh Williamson, Mar. 31, 1787, *LDC*, 24:189 ("iniquitous"); Madison to James Madison, Sr., Nov. 1, 1786, *PJM* (C.S.), 9:154; see also Saladino, "Delaware," 36, 46; Kaminski, *Paper Politics*, 23, 106; Brown, *Redeeming the Republic*, 129; Hall, *Politics Without Parties*, 264, 266–7; but cf. Robertson, *The Constitution and America's Destiny*, 110 n. 32. McDonald emphasizes that about one-quarter of the delegates at the Philadelphia convention had voted for paper money or debt relief as state legislators (*We the People*, 37, 349; see also ibid., 107–8). But that figure is misleading, since he counts as part of this number the four incredibly wealthy South Carolina delegates, who had supported such measures under very unusual circumstances: low-country aristocrats who found themselves heavily in debt as they endeavored to rebuild their plantations and replenish their supply of slave laborers after suffering economic devastation during the Revolutionary War and then enduring successive years' crop failures in the mid-1780s (ibid., 35, 210–1). These South Carolinians bore little resemblance to the small farmers who had sought tax and debt relief in most states. McDonald also counts in this category those delegates who had voted for a relief measure in their state legislature to head off something more drastic, which again seems misleading. See Jackson Turner Main, "Charles Beard and the Constitution: A Critical Review of Forrest McDonald's *We the People*," *William and Mary Quarterly* (Jan. 1960), 17:92 n. 6, 100.

   For the preceding footnote, see Kenneth W. Dam, "The Legal Tender Cases," *Supreme Court Review*, 1981:367–412.

117. U.S. Constitution, Art. I, § 8, cl. 15; Art. I, § 9, cl. 2; Art. IV, § 4; Randolph (Yates's Notes), June 16, *Farrand*, 1:263 (quotation); Holton, *Unruly Americans*, 157–8, 218, 243; Szatmary, *Shays' Rebellion*, 130–1; supra p. 93. On the linkage between insurrections and the clause guaranteeing each state a republican form of government, see Wilson and Randolph, July 18, *Farrand*, 2:47; Wilson, ibid., 48–9.

118. Daniel Carroll, July 18, ibid., 47 ("essential"); statements by Mason, Randolph, William Houston, Martin, Gorham, and Wilson, ibid., 47–9; see also Gerry to Monroe, June 11, 1787, ibid., 3:45.

119. Committee of Detail report, Art. VII, Aug. 6, ibid., 2:182; Morris, Aug. 17, ibid., 317 ("very strange," "first form," and "with such a power"); Langdon, ibid. ("have a salutary"); see also Dickinson and Dayton, Aug. 30, ibid., 466–7.

120. Gerry, Aug. 17, ibid., 316–7 ("was against," "more blood," and "intermeddled"); Martin, ibid. ("dangerous").

121. Ibid., 318 (dividing four to four on Charles Pinckney's motion to strike out the requirement of state consent); Ellsworth, Aug. 17, ibid., 317 (proposing inclusion of the executive); Aug. 30, ibid., 467 (voting eight to two, with one delegation divided, to permit application by the executive as an alternative to the legislature); see also Aug. 30, ibid., 467 (rejecting by an eight-to-three vote another effort to strike the requirement of state consent); Sept. 15, ibid., 628–9 (limiting the provision allowing application by the state executive to instances in which the legislature was unable to meet).

122. Randolph, July 18, ibid., 46; Madison to Washington, Apr. 16, 1787, *PJM* (C.S.), 9:384; Madison to Randolph, Apr. 8, 1787, ibid., 370.

123. Jefferson to Madison, June 20, 1787, ibid., 10:64 (quotations); see also Casto, *The Supreme Court in the Early Republic*, 31, 45–6.

124. New Jersey Plan, resolutions 2 and 5, June 15, *Farrand*, 1:243–4; June 4, ibid., 95, 104–5 (vote approving without recorded dissent the Virginia Plan resolution to establish a federal judiciary); see also Casto, *The Supreme Court in the Early Republic*, 10.

125. Virginia Plan, resolution 9, May 29, *Farrand*, 1:21 ("supreme"); New Jersey Plan, resolutions 2 and 5, June 15, ibid., 243–4; Sherman, June 5, ibid., 125 ("the supposed"); July 18, ibid., 2:46.

126. Rutledge, June 5, ibid., 1:124 ("ought to be left," "sufficient," "an unnecessary encroachment," and "unnecessary obstacles"); Butler, ibid., 125 ("[t]he people" and "follow"); Martin, July 18, ibid., 2:45–6 ("create jealousies"); Mason, Sept. 15, ibid., 638 ("to absorb"); see also Butler, July 18, ibid., 45; Carpenter, *The South as a Conscious Minority*, 62–3; Casto, *The Supreme Court in the Early Republic*, 10–11.

127. Madison, June 5, *Farrand*, 1:124.
128. Ibid. ("[a]n effective" and "would be"); Gorham, July 18, ibid., 2:46 ("essential"); King, ibid., 1:125 ("the establishment"); see also Madison, July 17, ibid., 2:27–8; Robertson, *The Constitution and America's Destiny*, 228.
129. U.S. Constitution, Art. III, § 1; Art. I, § 8, cl. 9 ("tribunals"); June 5, *Farrand*, 1:125 (five-to-four vote, with two delegations divided, defeating motion that the Constitution create lower federal courts; eight-to-two vote, one delegation divided, in favor of the proposal by Wilson and Madison that the Constitution give Congress discretion to create such tribunals); July 18, ibid., 2:46 (agreeing without dissent to empower Congress to create inferior federal courts). For the compromises over the federal courts' jurisdiction in the 1789 Judiciary Act, see Casto, *The Supreme Court in the Early Republic*, ch. 2.
130. Official Journal, June 13, *Farrand*, 1:223–4 (quotation); Randolph (Yates's Notes), ibid., 238; ibid. (unanimous agreement to this resolution); July 18, ibid., 2:46 (unanimous agreement to a somewhat different statement of jurisdictional principles); Committee of Detail report, Art. XI, Aug. 6, ibid., 186; see also Aug. 27, ibid., 428–32 (discussion of Article XI); Aug. 28, ibid., 437–8 (same).
131. Articles of Confederation, Art. IX, *DHRC*, 1:89; U.S. Constitution, Art. 3, § 2; Wilson, June 5, *Farrand*, 1:124; see also Casto, *The Supreme Court in the Early Republic*, 7–8.
132. U.S. Constitution, Art. III, § 2; see also Casto, *The Supreme Court in the Early Republic*, 6, 8–9.
133. U.S. Constitution, Art. III, § 2.
134. The Declaration of Independence, para. 2 (1776); Adams, *First American Constitutions*, 268–9.
135. U.S. Constitution, Art. III, § 1 ("during good behavior"); Dickinson, Sherman, Rutledge, Wilson, and Randolph, Aug. 27, *Farrand*, 2:428–9 (other quotations); ibid., 429 (rejecting Dickinson's motion by a vote of seven to one); July 18, ibid., 44 (voting without dissent in favor of tenure during good behavior).
136. Madison, July 18, ibid., 44, 45; Morris, ibid., 44, 45; Franklin, ibid., 44–5; ibid., 45 (voting six to two against Madison's proposal to bar increases in federal judges' salaries during their terms in office); ibid. (voting without dissent to protect federal judges from diminutions in their salaries during their terms in office); July 20, ibid., 69 (voting without dissent that the executive ought to have "fixed compensation"); U.S. Constitution, Art. II, § 1; see also Casto, *The Supreme Court in the Early Republic*, 18.
137. U.S. Constitution, Art. II, § 4 ("high crimes"); Art. 1, § 3 (two-thirds requirement for removal from office); Wood, *Creation of the American Republic*, 161 & n. 65; Adams, *First American Constitutions*, 269; Jed Handelsman Shugerman, *The People's Courts: Pursuing Judicial Independence in America* (Cambridge, MA, 2012), 20; Don E. Fehrenbacher, *Constitutions and Constitutionalism in the Slaveholding South* (Athens, GA, 1989), 17; Shumer, "New Jersey," 78; Kaminski, "Rhode Island," 189–90; Polishook, "Trevett vs. Weeden," 66; Main, *Political Parties*, 68–9; Madison, July 17, *Farrand*, 2:27–8; *An Additional Number of Letters from the Federal Farmer to the Republican*, Letter VI, Dec. 25, 1787, *DHRC*, 20:987; Pennsylvania Constitution of 1776, Art. II, § 23; New Jersey Constitution of 1776, Art. XII; Maryland Constitution of 1776, Art. XXX; South Carolina Constitution of 1776, Art. XX.
138. June 5, *Farrand*, 1:119–21; infra pp. 221–4.
139. U.S. Constitution, Art. III, § 2, cl. 3 (jury trials required in federal criminal cases); Gerry, Sept. 15, *Farrand*, 2:633 (quotation); Williamson, Gorham, Gerry, and Mason, Sept. 12, ibid., 587; motion by Charles Pinckney and Gerry, Sept. 15, ibid., 628; Gorham, King, and Charles Cotesworth Pinckney, ibid.
140. Official Journal, May 31, ibid., 1:45–6 & n. 3; Madison's Notes, ibid., 48; Yates's Notes, ibid., 55; Beeman, *Plain, Honest Men*, 110–1; Wood, *Creation of the American Republic*, 163, 230–1. Vermont, which Congress had yet to recognize as an independent state, had also adopted a unicameral legislature in its 1777 constitution.
141. Paterson (Yates's Notes), June 16, *Farrand*, 1:260 ("legislative objects"); Wilson, ibid., 254 ("danger" and "within").

142. Madison, May 31, ibid., 49–50 (all quotations but the last); June 6, ibid., 134; Jefferson to Madison, Dec. 20, 1787, *PJM* (C.S.), 10:336 ("inviolate").

143. Gerry, May 31, *Farrand*, 1:48 ("the dupes" and "daily misled"); Sherman, ibid.; June 6, ibid., 133 ("preserve harmony"); Pinckney, ibid., 137 ("notoriously" and "some sense"); see also Gerry, May 31, ibid., 50; Rutledge, June 21, ibid., 359; Mercer, Aug. 7, ibid., 2:205; Beeman, *Plain, Honest Men*, 111, 113–4.

144. Mason, May 31, *Farrand*, 1:49 ("to attend to," "we had been," and "afraid we should"); June 21, ibid., 359 ("it must"); Wilson, ibid. ("the cornerstone"); Michael Lienesch, "North Carolina: Preserving Rights," in Gillespie and Lienesch, eds., *Ratifying the Constitution*, 351; see also Dickinson, June 6, *Farrand*, 1:136; Robertson, *The Constitution and America's Destiny*, 205–6; Beeman, *Plain, Honest Men*, 117–8; Rakove, *Original Meanings*, 221–2.

145. Wilson, May 31, *Farrand*, 1:49.

146. Madison, June 6, ibid., 134 ("too great"); Mason, ibid., 134 ("send to"); ibid., 137–8 (rejecting by a vote of eight to three Pinckney's proposal that state legislatures choose members of the lower house); King, June 21, ibid., 359 ("would constantly choose"); Wilson, ibid. ("by an official sentiment"); May 31, ibid., 49; Official Journal, ibid., 46 (six-to-two vote, with two delegations divided, in favor of Virginia Plan provision for direct election of members of the lower house); Official Journal, June 21, ibid., 353 (six-to-four vote, with one delegation divided, against Pinckney proposal that members of the lower house be selected in a manner directed by state legislatures; then, nine-to-one vote, one delegation divided, in favor of popular election of members of the lower house); see also Charles Pinckney (Pierce's Notes), May 31, ibid., 59.

147. Madison (King's Notes), June 6, ibid., 143–4 (quotations); Madison (King's Notes), May 31, ibid., 56; Wood, *Creation of the American Republic*, 167, 510–4; Holton, *Unruly Americans*, 201–3, 206, 210; Rakove, *Original Meanings*, 222.

148. Wilson, June 6, *Farrand*, 1:133 ("There is no"); Mercer, Aug. 7, ibid., 2:205 ("unite their votes"); see also Mason, June 6, ibid., 1:134. At the Pennsylvania ratifying convention, Wilson argued that only "real weight of character can give a man real influence over a large district," and he blamed the small districts of the Massachusetts legislature for its inclination "to show very little disapprobation of the conduct of the [Shays] insurgents" (Dec. 4, 1787, *DHRC*, 2:489). Similarly, at the South Carolina convention, Charles Pinckney observed that in large constituencies, there was greater opportunity for "the more temperate and prudent part of the society to correct the licentiousness and injustice of the rest." Thus, he thought it was no accident that in Rhode Island, the smallest state, the paper money faction had "seize[d] the reins of government, and oppress[ed] the people by laws the most infamous that have ever disgraced a civilized nation" (May 14, 1788, *DHRC*, 27:331).

149. Grand committee report, presented by King, July 10, *Farrand*, 1:563 (proposing House of sixty-five members); July 16, ibid., 2:15–6 (the vote in favor of the committee's report); Holton, *Unruly Americans*, 200. Incredibly, Sherman of Connecticut argued for an even smaller House (July 10, *Farrand*, 1:569).

150. Madison, July 10, ibid., 568–9 ("would not possess" and "too inconsiderable"); Gerry, ibid., 569; ibid., 570 (nine-to-two vote to reject Madison's motion to double the size of the first House); see also Holton, *Unruly Americans*, 204.

151. Williamson, Madison, and Hamilton, Sept. 8, *Farrand*, 2:553–4; ibid., 554 (six-to-five vote against Williamson's proposal to increase the size of the House by an unspecified amount); Williamson, Sept. 14, ibid., 612; ibid. (six-to-five vote against Williamson's proposal to increase the size of the House by about 50 percent); George Mason, Objections to the Constitution of Government, Sept. 15, ibid., 638 ("not the substance") [hereinafter, "Mason, Objections"]; infra pp. 355–8.

152. Washington and Gorham, Sept. 17, *Farrand*, 2:643–4; see also Holton, *Unruly Americans*, 204–5.

153. U.S. Constitution, Art. 1, § 4 ("times, places"); Madison, Aug. 9, *Farrand*, 2:240 ("sometimes fail"); infra pp. 341–2, 623–4.

154. Saul Cornell, *The Other Founders: Anti-Federalism and the Dissenting Tradition in America, 1788–1828* (Chapel Hill, NC, 1999), 149, 151 ("a good") (quoting Clymer in the Pennsylvania Assembly in 1788, at p. 149); Madison to Jefferson, Oct. 8, 1788, *PJM* (C.S.), 11:276 ("confine the choice"); Nathaniel Appleton to Noah Webster, Nov. 30, 1788, in *Documentary History of the First Federal Elections, 1788–1790* (Merrill Jensen and Robert A. Becker, eds., Madison, WI, 1976), 1:506 ("contrary to") [hereinafter, "*DHFFE*"]; Holton, *Unruly Americans,* 254–6.

155. Virginia Plan, resolution 4, May 29, *Farrand,* 1:20; Wood, *Creation of the American Republic,* 165–7; Adams, *First American Constitutions,* 242; Holton, *Unruly Americans,* 196.

156. Sherman, June 26, *Farrand,* 1:423 ("Frequent elections"); June 21, ibid., 362 ("ought to return home"); Wilson, ibid., 361 ("most familiar" and "an effectual representation"); Randolph, ibid., 360 ("[t]he people" and "the inconvenience"); see also Sherman and Ellsworth motion, June 12, ibid., 214; Ellsworth, June 21, ibid., 361.

157. Gerry, June 12, ibid., 214–5 (quotations); see also Gorham (Yates's Notes), June 22, ibid., 381; supra pp. 71–2 & n. *.

158. Jenifer, June 12, *Farrand,* 1:214 ("rendered"); Madison, ibid. ("great vices," "almost consumed," and "be necessary"); Hamilton, June 21, ibid., 362 ("in the other branches"); see also Dickinson, ibid., 360–1; Madison, ibid., 361.

159. Madison, June 12, ibid., 215.

160. Gerry, ibid.

161. Ibid. (the initial vote); Official Record, June 21, ibid., 353 (seven-to-three vote, with one delegation divided, to delete three-year terms, followed by unanimous approval of two-year terms); see also Caleb Strong at Massachusetts convention, Jan. 15, 1788, *DHRC,* 6:1189.

162. Articles of Confederation, Art. V, *DHRC,* 1:87; Virginia Plan, resolution 4, May 29, *Farrand,* 1:20; Hamilton (Yates's Notes), June 18, ibid., 298 ("come with"); June 12, ibid., 217 (agreeing, without dissent, to strike the Virginia Plan provision for recall).

163. Virginia Plan, resolution 4, May 29, ibid., 20; Pennsylvania Constitution of 1776, § 19 ("inconvenient aristocracy"); Resolutions of the Massachusetts Legislature, Mar. 8, 1785, in *Acts and Resolves of Massachusetts, 1784–85,* at 379 ("[t]he world cannot"); June 12, *Farrand,* 1:217 (agreeing, without dissent, to strike Virginia Plan provision for mandatory rotation in office for members of the lower house); Gerry, Aug. 14, ibid., 285; see also Maier, *Ratification,* 31; Holton, *Unruly Americans,* 188; Elaine K. Swift, *The Making of an American Senate: Reconstitutive Change in Congress, 1787–1841* (Ann Arbor, MI, 1996), 45; Adams, *First American Constitutions,* 249; "The Republican Federalist" I, *Massachusetts Centinel,* Dec. 29, 1787, *DHRC,* 5:552.

164. New Hampshire Constitution of 1784, Part 1, Art. XXXII (quotations); Holton, *Unruly Americans,* 175, 199; Wood, *Creation of the American Republic,* 190; Adams, *First American Constitutions,* 244–6; Jean Yarbrough, "New Hampshire: Puritanism and the Moral Foundations of America," in Gillespie and Lienesch, eds., *Ratifying the Constitution,* 238–9; Ray Raphael, "The Democratic Moment: The Revolution and Popular Politics," in Gray and Kamensky, eds., *American Revolution,* 122, 131–2; Swift, *The Making of An American Senate,* 44; infra p. 583.

165. Articles of Confederation, Art. V, *DHRC,* 1:87; Ellsworth, June 22, *Farrand,* 1:371; Williamson, ibid., 372 (quotation); see also Sherman, ibid., 373; Butler, Aug. 14, ibid., 2:290.

166. Hamilton, June 22, ibid., 1:373 ("strenuously" and "Those who pay"); Randolph, ibid., 372 ("a dependence"); Gorham, ibid. ("such a manner"); King, ibid.; Madison, ibid., 373; Wilson, ibid.; Mason, Aug. 14, ibid., 2:291 ("both houses"); Morris, ibid., 290; see also Langdon, ibid., 290–1; Madison, June 12, ibid., 1:215–6.

167. Ellsworth, June 22, ibid., 374 ("the general government"); ibid. (five-to-four vote, with two delegations divided, rejecting Ellsworth's proposal); Committee of Detail report, Art. VI, § 10, Aug. 6, ibid., 2:180; Ellsworth, Aug. 14, ibid., 290; Daniel Carroll, ibid., 292; ibid. (nine-to-two vote rejecting proposal of Committee of Detail).

168. Wilson, June 22, ibid., 1:373; Gorham, ibid., 372 (quotation); Broom, Aug. 14, ibid., 2:291.

169. King, June 22, ibid., 1:372 ("would excite" and "any sum"); Madison, ibid., 374 ("It would be indecent"); Ellsworth, Aug. 14, ibid., 2:292 ("for that purpose"); Sherman, ibid., 291–2; ibid., 293 (the vote, by an unrecorded margin, to have congressional salaries fixed by law).

170. Hamilton (Yates's Notes), June 18, ibid., 1:299 (quotation); Holton, *Unruly Americans*, 202; Wood, *Creation of the American Republic*, 168–9, 508–13; Rakove, *Original Meanings*, 214–5.

171. On the relaxation of suffrage qualifications as a political imperative of the war, see McDonnell, "The Struggle Within," 110–1, 114. On the states' property qualifications for voting, see Adams, *First American Constitutions*, 194–6, 315–27.

172. Morris, Aug. 7, *Farrand*, 2:202–3 ("[t]he ignorant," "abound," and "the secure"); Dickinson, ibid., 202 ("necessary defense"); Madison, ibid., 203–4 ("would be the safest," "a great majority," and "the tools"); see also Beeman, *Plain, Honest Men*, 279–80; Rakove, *Original Meanings*, 225.

173. Franklin, Aug. 7, *Farrand*, 2:204 ("should not"); Aug. 10, ibid., 249 ("dislike of everything" and "[s]ome of the greatest"); see also Franklin (McHenry's Notes), Aug. 7, ibid., 210.

174. Ellsworth, ibid., 201 ("the best judges" and "the people"); Wilson, ibid. ("difficult"); Mason, ibid., 201–2; Gorham, Aug. 8, ibid., 215–6; see also Rutledge, Aug. 7, ibid., 205.

175. Ibid., 206 (seven-to-one vote, with one delegation divided, rejecting Morris's motion to add a property qualification for voting in congressional elections); U.S. Constitution, Art. I, § 2; Holton, *Unruly Americans*, 196; Robertson, *The Constitution and America's Destiny*, 150.

176. Gerry, July 26, *Farrand*, 2:123 ("property be one object"); Mason, ibid., 121 ("in order to promote"); Morris, ibid., 121; Dickinson, ibid., 123; ibid. (amendment to extend the property requirement for officeholding to members of the federal executive and judiciary, proposed by Charles Pinckney and Charles Cotesworth Pinckney and agreed to without dissent). Mason and Madison also warned of persons with "unsettled accounts" with the government—many of whom would be public creditors rather than debtors—seeking to obtain public office for what Madison called "sinister purposes." See Mason, ibid.; Madison, ibid., 122; see also ibid., 125–6. On property requirements for officeholding under the state constitutions, see Adams, *First American Constitutions*, 315–27.

177. Dickinson, July 26, *Farrand*, 2:123 ("and a partial" and "a veneration"); King, ibid., 123 ("great danger"); see also Gorham, ibid., 122.

178. Madison, ibid., 123.

179. Official Record, ibid., 117 (the votes); see also Beeman, *Plain, Honest Men*, 256.

180. Committee of Detail report, Art. VI, § 2, Aug. 6, *Farrand*, 2:179; Rutledge, Aug. 10, ibid., 249 ("had reported"); Ellsworth, ibid. (all other quotations); see also Robertson, *The Constitution and America's Destiny*, 151; Rakove, *Original Meanings*, 225–6.

181. Madison, Aug. 10, *Farrand*, 2:249–50 ("an improper" and "fundamental articles"); Pinckney, ibid., 248 ("an undue aristocratic" and "be possessed").

182. Morris, Williamson, Rutledge, and Wilson, ibid., 250–1; ibid., 251 (seven-to-three vote to reject Committee of Detail proposal to explicitly authorize Congress to set property qualifications for both houses of the national legislature).

183. Madison to Jefferson, Oct. 24, 1787, *PJM* (C.S.), 10:215; Beeman, *Plain, Honest Men*, 150–1, 181–9.

184. Virginia Plan, resolution 2, May 29, *Farrand*, 1:20.

185. Madison to Jefferson, Mar. 19, 1787, *PJM* (C.S.), 9:319 (quotation); Madison (King's Notes), July 7, *Farrand*, 1:554.

186. Madison to Jefferson, Mar. 19, 1787, *PJM* (C.S.), 9:318–9; see also Madison to Washington, Apr. 16, 1787, ibid., 382; Robertson, *The Constitution and America's Destiny*, 93–4; Rakove, *Original Meanings*, 54; Maier, *Ratification*, 24. On the demographic assumption, see Staughton Lynd, "The Compromise of 1787," *Political Science Quarterly* (1966), 81:240–3; Banning, "Virginia," 269; Carpenter, *The South as a Conscious Minority*, 173–7; Hendrickson, *Peace Pact*, 227.

187. King, May 30, *Farrand*, 1:35–6; Hamilton, ibid., 36 ("free inhabitants"); Morris, July 5, ibid., 533 ("the main" and "it ought"); see also Beeman, *Plain, Honest Men*, 107–8.
188. Rutledge, July 5, *Farrand*, 1:534 ("property was certainly"); infra pp. 265–77; see also Rutledge and Butler, June 11, *Farrand*, 1:196; Rutledge, July 11, ibid., 582; Abraham Baldwin, June 29, ibid., 469–70.
189. Madison, May 30, ibid., 36 ("the equality"); Read, ibid., 37; Robertson, *The Constitution and America's Destiny*, 133.
190. Read to Dickinson, May 21, 1787, *Farrand*, 3:25–6 ("keep a strict watch"); Read to Dickinson, Jan. 17, 1787, in William Thompson Read, *Life and Correspondence of George Read* (Philadelphia, 1870), 438–9 (all other quotations) [hereinafter, "Read, *George Read*"].
191. Delaware delegates' instructions, May 25, *Farrand*, 1:4; Read, May 30, ibid., 37 ("retire"); Read to Dickinson, Jan. 17, 1787, in Read, *George Read*, 438 ("as a prudent" and "disagreeable"); Saladino, "Delaware," 38–9; see also Jacob Broom to Thomas Collins, May 23, 1787, *Farrand*, Supp.:17; Robertson, *The Constitution and America's Destiny*, 122; Beeman, *Plain, Honest Men*, 71–2.
192. Madison, June 29, *Farrand*, 1:464 ("confessedly unjust" and "subject the system"); July 14, ibid., 2:9 ("negative the will" and "extort measures").
193. Madison, May 30, ibid., 1:37; supra pp. 130–1.
194. Hamilton, June 18, *Farrand*, 1:286 ("shock" and "[i]t was not"); Wilson, June 9, ibid., 179 ("as all authority"); Wilson (Yates's Notes), June 20, ibid., 348 ("in the hour," "a sacrifice," and "the time"); Morris (King's Notes), July 7, ibid., 555 ("sacred compact"); see also Gerry, June 29, ibid., 467; Wilson, June 16, ibid., 253; June 20, ibid., 343; June 28, ibid., 449–50; King, July 14, ibid., 2:6; Wilson, ibid., 4.
195. Madison, June 19, ibid., 1:322 ("a more objectionable"); June 29, ibid., 464 ("must infuse"); Wilson, July 14, ibid., 2:10 ("A vice"); see also Madison, ibid., 9; Hamilton, June 18, ibid., 1:286–7.
196. Wilson, June 30, ibid., 483–4 ("under the weakness" and "leave"); Madison, ibid., 486 ("extort measures," "some great," and "impose").
197. Wilson, ibid., 483 ("Can we forget"); Hamilton, June 29, ibid., 466 ("the rights" and "artificial beings"). Wilson went so far as to deny that the states had ever been sovereign entities. When the colonies declared their independence from Great Britain, they did so, according to Wilson, "not individually but unitedly" (June 19, ibid., 324).
198. Madison, June 29, ibid., 463 ("too much stress"); July 14, ibid., 2:8–9 ("to act" and "a single instance"); see also June 28, ibid., 1:446–7; Williamson, June 9, ibid., 180; Rosemarie Zagarri, *The Politics of Size: Representation in the United States, 1776–1850* (Ithaca, NY, 1987), 75–6.
199. Wilson, June 21, *Farrand*, 1:355–6 ("reciprocal"); Madison, ibid., 357.
200. Wilson, ibid., 356 ("would be in"); Madison, ibid. ("to anarchy").
201. Madison (Yates's Notes), June 29, ibid., 476 ("real danger" and "defensive weapons"); June 28, ibid., 447–8 ("manners," "as dissimilar," and "rivalships"); Madison (Yates's Notes), ibid., 455 ("[w]here is"); see also June 30, ibid., 486; Zagarri, *Politics of Size*, 74–5; Rakove, *Original Meanings*, 55; Dahl, *How Democratic Is the American Constitution?*, 52; Beeman, *Plain, Honest Men*, 222.
202. Hamilton, June 29, *Farrand*, 1:466 ("there could not," "The only considerable," and "a contest"); June 19, ibid., 325 ("all the peculiarities"); Bedford, June 20, ibid., 491 ("to act from" and "held fast"); see also Brearley, June 9, ibid., 177; Wilson (Yates's Notes), June 30, ibid., 494–5.
203. Williamson, June 28, ibid., 445 ("would consequently"); Franklin, June 30, ibid., 488 ("their money"); see also Williamson (Yates's Notes), June 28, ibid., 456–7.
204. Madison, June 29, ibid., 464 (all quotations except "If the large states"); June 8, ibid., 168 ("If the large states"); see also June 19, ibid., 320; June 28, ibid., 448–9; Gorham, June 29, ibid., 462–3; Hamilton, ibid., 466–7; Hamilton (Yates's Notes), ibid., 473–4.
205. Morris, July 5, ibid., 530.
206. Paterson, June 8, ibid., 178 ("no power," "the people," and "must follow"); Sherman, June 20, ibid., 342; Ellsworth, June 29, ibid., 469 ("[W]as it meant"); see also Paterson

(Yates's Notes), June 9, ibid., 182; Paterson (King's Notes), ibid., 184; Paterson (Yates's Notes), June 16, ibid., 258–9; Martin, June 27, ibid., 437–8; Brearley, June 9, ibid., 176–7; Lansing (Yates's Notes), June 16, ibid., 257; supra p. 143.

207. Bedford, June 30, ibid., 491 ("right" and "interest"); Bedford (Yates's Notes), ibid., 500 ("endeavor"); Martin, June 27, ibid., 437–8 ("an equal vote" and "[s]tates, like individuals"); June 19, ibid., 324 ("in a state," "entered," and "they met"); Paterson (Yates's Notes), June 16, ibid., 259 ("When independent"); June 9, ibid., 178 ("no more reason"); see also Brearley (Yates's Notes), June 9, ibid., 181. See generally Zagarri, *Politics of Size*, 2, 62–73 (esp. 66–67), 142–3.

208. Johnson, June 29, *Farrand*, 1:461 ("so many," "in their political," and "armed"); Sherman, July 14, ibid., 2:5 ("not so much"); see also Sherman, June 11, ibid., 1:196; Sherman (Yates's Notes), ibid., 204; Johnson, June 21, ibid., 354–5.

For the preceding footnote, see Kaminski and Moore, *An Assembly of Demigods*, 244.

209. Martin, Aug. 30, ibid., 2:463–4 ("phantoms" and "political societies"); Paterson (Yates's Notes), June 16, ibid., 1:259 ("stock of land"); U.S. Constitution, Art. IV, § 3, cl. 1; see also Read, June 11, *Farrand*, 1:202.

210. Paterson, June 9, ibid., 177–9 ("at the existence," "be swallowed," and "never confederate"); Bedford, June 8, ibid., 167 ("a system in which" and "crush"); Martin, June 27, ibid., 438 ("a system of slavery" and "without a miraculous"); see also Ellsworth, June 30, ibid., 484–5; Ellsworth (Yates's Notes), ibid., 495–6; Sherman, June 11, ibid., 196; Brearley, June 9, ibid., 177; Bedford (Yates's Notes), June 30, ibid., 500; Zagarri, *Politics of Size*, 172–3.

211. Ellsworth (King's Notes), June 29, *Farrand*, 1:478 ("three or four"); June 30, ibid., 484–5; see also June 29, ibid., 469; Charles Pinckney, July 2, ibid., 510; Martin, June 27, ibid., 438; Bedford, June 8, ibid., 167.

212. Supra p. 157.

213. Virginia delegates to Governor Patrick Henry, Nov. 7, 1785, *LDC*, 23:7 ("against the dismemberment" and "wish for every facility"); Richard Dobbs Spaight to Governor Alexander Martin of North Carolina, Apr. 30, 1784, *LDC*, 21:567 ("[t]he little states"); Madison, Observations Relating to the Influence of Vermont and the Territorial Claims on the Politics of Congress, May 1, 1782, *PJM* (C.S.), 4:201 ("a lucrative desire" and "the envy"); see also Madison to Pendleton, Apr. 23, 1782, ibid., 178; Aug. 14, 1781, ibid., 3:224; Mason to Randolph, Oct. 19, 1782, *PGM*, 2:746–55; Zagarri, *Politics of Size*, 63–4; Brown, *Redeeming the Republic*, 192; Onuf, "Maryland," 181; Davis, *Sectionalism in American Politics*, 39–40; Banning, *Sacred Fire*, 22–4.

214. Read to Dickinson, Jan. 17, 1787, *Farrand*, 3:575 n. 6 ("the just claims"); Read (Yates's Notes), June 25, ibid., 1:412; Martin, Aug. 30, ibid., 2:463–4; Wilson, ibid., 462 ("to be torn asunder"); ibid., 462 (defeating, by an eight-to-three vote, which largely though not entirely tracked the division between small and large states, a motion to reject the requirement that states consent before Congress be enabled to divide them); see also North Carolina delegates to the North Carolina General Assembly, Dec. 15, 1787, *LDC*, 24:586.

215. Martin, June 28, *Farrand*, 1:445 (quotations); see also Lansing, June 20, ibid., 337.

216. Official Journal, June 11, ibid., 192–3; Bedford, June 30, ibid., 491 ("a small state" and "she is actuated"); see also Official Journal, June 29, ibid., 460 (reiterating commitment to "equitable ratio" in lower house by a vote of six to four, with one delegation divided).

217. Morris, July 13, ibid., 604–5 ("North Carolina"); Mason, July 11, ibid., 586 ("a few years"); see also Butler, July 13, ibid., 605; Madison, July 14, ibid., 2:10. On the South's growing population disadvantage over time, see Carpenter, *The South as a Conscious Minority*, 21–3; David M. Potter, *The Impending Crisis, 1848–1861* (New York, 1976), 475–6.

For the preceding footnote, see infra pp. 272, 388–9; Mason, July 11, *Farrand*, 1:579 ("subjected to").

218. Sherman, June 11, *Farrand*, 1:201 ("[t]he smaller states"); Ellsworth, June 29, ibid., 469 ("if there was no" and "would risk every"); Dickinson, June 15, ibid., 242 n. * ("would sooner"); Paterson, June 9, ibid., 179 ("rather submit"); see also Martin, June 28, ibid.,

445; Martin (Yates's Notes), June 30, ibid., 499; Paterson (King's Notes), July 7, ibid., 554; Martin, July 14, ibid., 2:4; Jonathan Dayton, ibid., 5.

219. King, ibid., 7 ("would never"); June 30, ibid., 1:489 ("fixed" and "there could not"); Wilson, ibid., 482 ("not abandon" and "[i]f the minority"); June 9, ibid., 180 ("[i]f the small" and "Pennsylvania"); see also Morris, May 30, ibid., 37; Gerry, June 29, ibid., 467.

220. Gerry to the Vice President of the Convention of Massachusetts, Jan. 21, 1788, *Farrand*, 3:264 ("so serious"); Madison to Jared Sparks, Apr. 8, 1831, in *Writings of James Madison*, 9:449 ("[g]reat zeal" and "not only"); see also Madison to George Nicholas, Apr. 8, 1788, *PJM* (C.S.), 11:12; Luther Martin, Genuine Information III, Baltimore *Maryland Gazette*, Jan. 4, 1788, *DHRC*, 11:149; Madison, June 15, *Farrand*, 1:242 n. *; Butler, June 25, ibid., 407–8.

221. Madison, June 30, ibid., 481 ("it was well understood"); Wilson, ibid.; ibid., 482 (rejecting by a five-to-two vote, with one delegation divided, the proposal by New Jersey delegates to appeal to New Hampshire to send its delegation immediately).

222. Pierce, Character Sketches, ibid., 3:92 ("warm"); Bedford, June 30, ibid., 1:491–2 ("interest," "ambition," "evidently seeking," and "the small"); Bedford (Yates's Notes), ibid., 500 ("*I do not*") (emphasis in original); see also Beeman, *Plain, Honest Men*, 184.

223. King, June 30, *Farrand*, 1:493 ("vehemence," "court," and "grieved"); Randolph, July 2, ibid., 515 ("the warm and rash"); Bedford, July 5, ibid., 531 ("warmth," "natural," "did not mean," "no man," and "the sword").

224. Franklin speech (read by Wilson), June 11, ibid., 197.

225. Franklin, June 28, ibid., 450–2 ("humbly applying" and "imploring"); Hamilton and several other delegates, ibid., 452 ("lead the public"); ibid., 452 & n. 16 (the resolution of the proposal); see also The Autobiography of William Few, in ibid., 3:423.

226. Dickinson, June 2, ibid., 1:83 ("must probably"); Sherman, June 11, ibid., 196; Johnson, June 29, ibid., 461 ("political societies" and "districts"); Sherman, July 7, ibid., 550; see also Johnson (King's Notes), June 29, ibid., 476–7; Ellsworth (Yates's Notes), June 29, ibid., 474–5; Sherman, June 20, ibid., 343; Beeman, *Plain, Honest Men*, 150–1, 163–4, 223–4.

227. Official Journal, July 2, *Farrand*, 1:509; ibid., 510; see also Beeman, *Plain, Honest Men*, 185–6; Coleman, *American Revolution in Georgia*, 268.

228. Franklin, June 30, *Farrand*, 1:488 ("part with"); Pinckney motion, July 2, ibid., 511; Sherman (Yates's Notes), ibid., 517 ("It seems we have"); Martin (Yates's Notes), ibid. ("You must"); Randolph (Yates's Notes), ibid., 519 ("no great hopes"); Lansing, ibid.; Sherman, ibid., 511 ("meant that" and "most likely"); Williamson, ibid., 515 ("if we do not" and "with more"); see also Gerry, ibid.; Madison to Jared Sparks, Apr. 8, 1831, *Farrand*, 3:500; Beeman, *Plain, Honest Men*, 187–9. For hints that the large-state coalition was beginning to fracture, see Gorham, June 25, *Farrand*, 1:404–5; see also Banning, *Sacred Fire*, 452 n. 38.

229. Wilson and Madison (Yates's Notes), July 2, *Farrand*, 1:519; July 5, ibid., 516 (nine-to-two vote to commit the apportionment issue to committee, followed by a ten-to-one vote to use a grand committee); Official Journal, May 28, ibid., 9 (rule for appointing committees); see also Beeman, *Plain, Honest Men*, 188–9; Robertson, *The Constitution and America's Destiny*, 141; Banning, *Sacred Fire*, 153–4; Bilder, *Madison's Hand*, 105; Rossiter, *1787: The Grand Convention*, 187.

230. Gerry, July 5, *Farrand*, 1:527; Yates's Notes, July 3, ibid., 522–3.

231. Gerry, June 13, ibid., 233 ("was more"); Gerry (Yates's Notes), ibid., 238 ("dislik[ing]" and "not be").

232. Butler, ibid., 233 ("the Senate should be degraded"); Madison, ibid. ("the Senate would be," "would easily prevail," "would be generally," and "it would be wrong"); Pinckney, ibid., 234 ("been a source"); Official Journal, ibid., 229 (the vote).

233. Gerry to the Vice President of the Convention of Massachusetts, Jan. 21, 1788, ibid., 3:265–6.

234. Madison (Yates's Notes), July 5, ibid., 1:535 ("nothing more"); Wilson, July 6, ibid., 544 ("a trifle"); Pinckney, ibid., 546; see also Madison, July 5, ibid., 527; Butler, ibid., 529; Charles Pinckney, July 6, ibid., 545; Wilson, July 14, ibid., 2:4.

235. Gerry, ibid., 5 ("of great consequence" and "the cornerstone"); Gerry, July 6, ibid., 1:545 ("the confidence" and "weight"); Mason, ibid., 544 ("the immediate"); ibid., 547 (by a vote of five states to three, with three delegations divided, keeping the origination clause in the committee's report).

The delegates reconsidered the origination clause on multiple occasions. Although the committee chaired by Gerry had initially conceived the clause as an inducement to large-state delegates to accept equal state representation in the Senate, some of those delegates continued to criticize the clause and to urge its elimination. Charles Pinckney argued that "[i]f the Senate can be trusted with the many great powers proposed, it surely may be trusted with that of originating money bills." Madison also wanted the clause eliminated, "considering it as of no advantage to the large states, as fettering the government, and as a source of injurious altercations between the two houses." See Pinckney, Aug. 8, ibid., 2:224; Madison, ibid.; see also Wilson, Ellsworth, and Madison, Aug. 9, ibid., 233; Morris, ibid., 234; Wilson, ibid.; Charles Pinckney, Aug. 11, ibid., 263.

With many prominent large-state delegates seemingly determined to reject the concession offered to them, some small-state delegates were disinclined to force it upon them (especially those small-state delegates who had never wanted to offer the concession in the first place because they wished to preserve the power of the Senate, where small states would exercise an equal vote). Thus, on August 8, the convention reversed itself, voting by seven delegations to four to eliminate the origination clause. Yet other large-state delegates immediately objected to the rescission of this part of the Connecticut Compromise. Williamson declared he was "surprised to see the smaller states forsaking the condition on which they had received their equality [in the Senate]." Randolph insisted that "the large states would require this compensation at least" for abandoning their commitment to population-based apportionment of the Senate, and he warned that eliminating this clause would "endanger the success of the plan." Randolph also argued that the origination clause would make the Connecticut Compromise more acceptable to the people, as "they will consider the Senate as the more aristocratic body and will expect that the usual guards against its influence be provided according to the example in Great Britain." See Aug. 8, ibid., 224–5 (the vote); Williamson, Aug. 9, ibid., 233 ("surprise"); Randolph, ibid., 230 ("endanger"); Randolph, Aug. 11, ibid., 263 ("the large states" and "they will consider"); see also Aug. 9, ibid., 232; Caleb Strong, ibid.; George Read, ibid., 232–3; Mason, ibid., 233; ibid., 234. For the strong opposition of one Maryland delegate to limiting the Senate's power over money bills, see Aug. 7 (McHenry's Notes), ibid., 210–1.

Several days later, Randolph and Mason sought to revive the origination clause by offering concessions to address the objections that had been raised against it. They now proposed limiting the scope of the clause to measures that had the *purpose* of raising revenue (or appropriating it), which would exclude from its coverage laws that had the unintended consequence of raising revenue. They also proposed giving the Senate a narrow scope to amend such bills (whereas the committee's proposal had permitted no Senate amendments). While the Senate, under their proposal, would not be permitted to increase or diminish the amount to be raised, or the mode of raising it, or the object of an appropriation, the Senate would (implicitly) be allowed to excise extraneous provisions that the House had tacked on to a bill raising revenue or appropriating it. See Randolph motion, Aug. 13, ibid., 273; Mason, ibid.

Wilson and Madison were no more impressed with the new version of the origination clause than they had been with the old one. Madison objected that some trade regulations were ambiguous as to whether their principal purpose was raising revenue, and he criticized the narrow scope for Senate amendments contemplated by the Randolph-Mason proposal because it would restrain the Senate from checking the House's "extravagance." He also worried that the Senate could "couch extraneous matter" under the guise of amendments, which would lead to vexatious disputes between the branches. See Madison, ibid., 276–7; Wilson, ibid., 274–5; see also Rutledge, ibid., 279–80.

However, Gerry, who had consistently been the convention's strongest proponent of an origination clause, warned that the Constitution "will inevitably fail [of ratification] if the Senate be not restrained from originating money bills," as the people would insist that only "their immediate representatives shall meddle with their purses." Dickinson, too, thought that "experience [has] verified the utility of restraining money bills to the immediate representatives of the people." He noted that eight states had such a provision in their constitution (though most of them permitted amendments by the upper house), and he warned that "all the prejudices of the people would be offended by refusing this exclusive privilege to the House of Representatives." Dickinson argued that an origination clause would be an important shield against critics of the Constitution, who would invoke "aristocracy" as their "shibboleth." Randolph similarly warned that an upper house already bearing "the countenance of an aristocracy" would raise enough alarms "without taking from [the people's] immediate representatives a right which has been so long appropriated to them." The delegates ought not, Randolph argued, increase the "numerous and monstrous" difficulties already facing ratification. Despite such appeals, the delegates rejected the amendment proposed by Randolph and Mason by the same seven-to-four vote by which they had recently rescinded the origination clause. See Gerry, ibid., 275; Dickinson, ibid., 278; Randolph, ibid., 278–9; ibid., 280.

    Yet Mason, Randolph, and Gerry would not give up. Eventually, they secured a compromise measure specifying that only the House could originate bills for raising revenue but allowing the Senate to amend them. However, their dissatisfaction with this watered-down version of the origination clause may partially explain their refusal to sign the Constitution at the end of the convention. See motion by Caleb Strong, seconded by Mason, Aug. 15, ibid., 297; Gorham, ibid.; Williamson, ibid.; Committee on Unfinished Parts Report, presented by Brearley, Sept. 5, ibid., 508–9; Official Journal, Sept. 8, ibid., 545. On Gerry's unhappiness with the compromise provision, see Gerry to the Vice President of the Convention of Massachusetts, Jan. 21, 1788, ibid., 3:265–6. For speculation regarding the part played by their unhappiness over the origination clause in the decision by Mason and Randolph not to sign the Constitution, see Banning, *Sacred Fire*, 154, 174–5, 452 n. 48.

236. Madison, July 5, *Farrand*, 1:527–8.
237. Butler, ibid., 529 ("evidently unjust"); Morris, ibid., 530 ("[T]he ties"); Wilson, July 7, ibid., 550 ("firmness"); see also Morris (Paterson's Notes), July 5, ibid., 537.
238. Ellsworth, ibid., 532 ("necessary" and "reasonable"); Gerry, ibid. ("material objections" and "if we do not"); Mason, ibid., 532–3 ("would bury"); July 6, ibid., 544 ("supposed"); Paterson, July 7, ibid., 551; see also Paterson (King's Notes), ibid., 554; Gerry, ibid., 550.
239. July 7, ibid., 550–1 (six-to-three vote, with two delegations divided, to include in the committee report the provision for equal state voting in the Senate). On the North Carolina delegation's abandonment of the large-state coalition, see Trenholme, *Ratification of the Federal Constitution in North Carolina*, 84–5.
240. Pinckney, June 7, *Farrand*, 1:155; Pinckney, Madison, Wilson, and Gerry, July 14, ibid., 2:5; ibid., 11 (six-to-four vote rejecting Pinckney's proposal); see also motion by Charles Pinckney and Rutledge, June 8, ibid., 1:169; Charles Pinckney motion, July 2, ibid., 511; Gorham, June 25, ibid., 404–5; see also Banning, *Sacred Fire*, 452 n. 38.
241. Franklin, June 30, *Farrand*, 1:489; Franklin (Yates's Notes), ibid., 499; Franklin proposal, ibid., 507–8; Randolph, July 2, ibid., 514; Randolph (Yates's Notes), ibid., 519; see also Edmund Randolph's Suggestion for Conciliating the Small States, July 10, ibid., 3:55.
242. King, July 14, ibid., 2:7 ("would never be"); Strong, ibid., 7–8 ("Congress," "considerable concession," and "might naturally").
243. July 16, *Farrand*, 2:15; Madison, Sept. 15, ibid., 631 (quotation); see also Beeman, *Plain, Honest Men*, 219, 355.
    For the preceding footnote, see Banning, *Sacred Fire*, 156; Rossiter, *1787: The Grand Convention*, 189.
244. Madison, July 16, *Farrand*, 2:19–20 ("inflexibility" and "differed"); Randolph, ibid., 17–8 ("the small states"); Rutledge, ibid., 19 ("he could see").
245. Wilson, July 2, ibid., 1:515; Wilson (Yates's Notes), June 30, ibid., 494; see also ibid., 482; July 14, ibid., 2:4.
246. May 28, ibid., 1:10–11 n. * ("the large states" and "conceiving that"); Madison to Jefferson, Mar. 19, 1787, *PJM* (C.S.), 9:319 ("the fewer"); see also Beeman, *Plain, Honest Men*, 55, 82; Rakove, *Original Meanings*, 60.

247. Williamson, Aug. 29, *Farrand*, 2:454.

248. Saladino, "Delaware," 34 ("decently" and "to an equal voice"); Gerry, June 29, *Farrand*, 1:467 ("The injustice"); see also Notes of Debates of the Continental Congress, July 30, 1776, *JCC*, 6:1079–80 (statements of Benjamin Franklin and John Witherspoon); Wood, *Creation of the American Republic*, 357; Zagarri, *Politics of Size*, 62–3; Rakove, *Beginnings of National Politics*, 140–1, 158–9; Hendrickson, *Peace Pact*, 138–9, 144–5, 223; Adams, *First American Constitutions*, 283.

249. Madison, Observations Relating to the Influence of Vermont and the Territorial Claims on the Politics of Congress, May 1, 1782, *PJM* (C.S.), 4:201.

250. Madison, July 14, *Farrand*, 2:9–10 (quotation); see also Rakove, *Original Meanings*, 77; supra pp. 191–2.

251. Madison, July 14, *Farrand*, 2:10 ("pretty well understood"); Morris, July 13, ibid., 1:604 ("[v]icious principle"); infra pp. 265–77.

252. Supra pp. 62–3; infra pp. 272, 388–9; Banning, *Sacred Fire*, 155; see also Hendrickson, *Peace Pact*, 231.

253. Randolph, July 16, *Farrand*, 2:17–8 (quotations). The delegates found Randolph's proposal for an adjournment ambiguous: Did he mean an adjournment until the next day or an adjournment sine die (during which the delegates would return home to consult their constituents)? Paterson announced that he would favor an adjournment sine die to lift the veil of secrecy surrounding the convention. By contrast, Charles Cotesworth Pinckney and Jacob Broom insisted that such an adjournment would be fatal to the entire enterprise of constitutional reform. Randolph then clarified that he meant only an adjournment until the next day, which, after debate, the delegates approved. Ibid., 18–9.

254. Morris, July 17, ibid., 2:25 ("in the abstract"); Virginia Plan, resolution 6, May 29, ibid., 1:21 ("the separate" and "the harmony"); Butler and Rutledge, July 16, ibid., 2:17; see also Beeman, *Plain, Honest Men*, 227–8.

255. Madison, July 7, Farrand, 1:551 (quotations); see also Robertson, *The Constitution and America's Destiny*, 158; Banning, *Sacred Fire*, 168–9.

256. Virginia Plan, resolution 9, May 29, *Farrand*, 1:21; Madison, June 5, ibid., 120 (quotations); infra pp. 223–4.

257. Madison, July 21, *Farrand*, 2:80–1 ("the second branch," "throw the appointments," and "would in general"); Aug. 23, ibid., 392 ("that the Senate"); Committee of Detail report, Art. IX, Aug. 6, ibid., 183.

258. Sherman, July 18, ibid., 41; Sherman motion, Aug. 25, ibid., 419. Sherman's motion with regard to the pardon power was overwhelmingly defeated. Ibid.

259. Madison, June 25, ibid., 408 n. * (quotations); see also Wilson (Yates's Notes), ibid., 413.

260. Madison, May 31, ibid., 52 (quotation); statements by Richard Dobbs Spaight, Butler, and Sherman, ibid., 51–2; ibid., 52 (the vote); see also Beeman, *Plain, Honest Men*, 119–20; Robertson, *The Constitution and America's Destiny*, 137.

261. Wilson, June 7, *Farrand*, 1:151 ("to establish" and "dissensions"); June 25, ibid., 406 ("introduce" and "[w]ith respect to"); Madison, June 30, ibid., 490 ("absolutely dependent").

262. Dickinson motion, June 7, ibid., 150 ("the most distinguished"); Sherman, ibid. ("interested" and "a due harmony"); Mason, ibid., 155 ("ought to have"); Sherman (Yates's Notes), June 11, ibid., 204 ("as the people" and "the legislature"); Ellsworth (Yates's Notes), June 25, ibid., 414 ("more competent" and "wisdom"); see also Dickinson, June 6, ibid., 137; Charles Pinckney, June 7, ibid., 155.

263. Gerry, ibid., 152 ("leave no," "chiefly composed," "some check," and "oppression"); Madison, ibid., 154 ("[t]he great evils," "a like propensity," and "promote"); Gerry, ibid., 154–5 ("the people" and "the commercial"); see also Holton, *Unruly Americans*, 203.

264. Dickinson, June 7, *Farrand*, 1:152–3 (quotations); Wilson, ibid., 153; see also Mason, June 25, ibid., 407.

265. June 7, ibid., 156 (ten-to-zero vote); June 25, ibid., 408 (nine-to-two vote); see also Jack N. Rakove, "The Madisonian Moment," *University of Chicago Law Review* (1988), 55:484–5; Robertson, *The Constitution and America's Destiny*, 108–9, 139.

266. Dickinson (King's Notes), June 7, *Farrand*, 1:158 (quotations); Madison, ibid.; Mason, July 23, ibid., 2:94.

267. Davie, June 30, ibid., 1:487–8; Wilson, ibid., 488.

268. Martin, July 23, ibid., 2:94; ibid., 94–5 (voting eight to one against a proposal for three senators per state; then agreeing without dissent to two senators per state); Martin, ibid.; ibid., 95 (voting nine to one in favor of per capita voting).

269. Ellsworth motion for state legislative payment of senators' salaries, June 26, ibid., 1:427; Committee of Detail report, Art. VI, § 10, Aug. 6, ibid., 2:180; Martin, Aug. 14, ibid., 292; Butler (Yates's Notes), June 26, ibid., 1:434 ("the aristocratic" and "must be controlled"); Aug. 14, ibid., 2:290 ("be so long").

270. Madison, June 26, ibid., 1:428 ("the mere agents"); Aug. 14, ibid., 2:291 ("could not see"); June 19, ibid., 1:319 ("the public business"); Aug. 14, ibid., 2:292 (nine-to-two vote rejecting Committee of Detail proposal to have state legislatures pay the salaries of members of both houses of Congress). For statements expressing sentiments similar to Madison's, see Dickinson, ibid.; Daniel Carroll, ibid.

271. Holton, *Unruly Americans*, 128–31, 174–5, 190; Kaminski, "Paper Politics," 114, 139, 146, 149, 178; Shumer, "New Jersey," 79–80; Van Cleve, "Anti-Federalists' Toughest Challenge," 541–3; Main, *Political Parties*, 133, 220–3. On the distinguishing features of the upper legislative houses, see Wood, *Creation of the American Republic*, 213–4.

272. Randolph (McHenry's Notes), May 29, *Farrand*, 1:26–7 ("[o]ur chief danger" and "provided sufficient"); June 12, ibid., 218 ("[t]he democratic licentiousness"); Morris, July 2, ibid., 512 ("to check"); July 19, ibid., 2:52 ("the propensity"); see also Ellsworth (Yates's Notes), June 25, ibid., 1:414; Randolph, May 31, ibid., 51; Hamilton (Yates's Notes), June 18, ibid., 299.

273. Madison, June 12, ibid., 218 ("that stability"); June 26, ibid., 422–3 ("labor under," "slide into," "sufficiently respectable," and "the preponderance"); Madison (Yates's Notes), June 12, ibid., 222 ("as a check"); see also June 7, ibid., 151; Rakove, "Madisonian Moment," 482. For an effort to place these sentiments of Madison in the broader context of his political economy, see McCoy, *Elusive Republic*, 128–30.

274. Madison, June 26, *Farrand*, 1:423 ("a considerable duration"); Madison to Jefferson, Aug. 12, 1786, *PJM* (C.S.), 9:95 ("universal" and "hitherto"); Holton, *Unruly Americans*, 190; Brown, *Redeeming the Republic*, 127–8; see also Madison, Aug. 14, *Farrand*, 2:291; Tobias Lear to Benjamin Lincoln, June 4, 1787, microformed on Benjamin Lincoln Papers, P-40, Reel 8 (Mass. Historical Society). For background to the fight over paper money in Maryland, see James Haw et al., *Stormy Patriot: The Life of Samuel Chase* (Baltimore, 1980), 136–43. As early as 1785, when he provided advice on the design of a constitution for Kentucky, Madison had treated the Maryland senate as a model (to Caleb Wallace, Aug. 23, 1785, *PJM* (C.S.), 8:351).

275. Virginia Plan, resolution 5, May 29, *Farrand*, 1:20 ("sufficient"); Spaight, June 12, ibid., 218; Pierce, ibid. ("[g]reat mischiefs"); Pinckney, June 25, ibid., 409 ("would fix" and "would acquire"); Sherman, June 26, ibid., 423 ("[f]requent elections"); Gerry, ibid., 425; see also Gorham, ibid., 408; Charles Cotesworth Pinckney, June 26, ibid., 421.

276. Randolph, June 12, ibid., 218 (quotation); ibid., 219 (eight-to-one vote, with two delegations divided, in favor of seven-year terms for senators).

277. Madison (King's Notes), June 7, ibid., 158 ("ought to come"); Dickinson, ibid., 150 ("distinguished for"); Butler (Yates's Notes), June 26, ibid., 434 ("the aristocratic part"); Pinckney, ibid., 426–7 ("meant to represent"); Robertson, *The Constitution and America's Destiny*, 134; see also Dickinson, June 6, *Farrand*, 1:136; Wood, *Creation of the American Republic*, 553–4.

278. Hamilton, June 18, ibid., 288–90 (all quotations except "[n]othing but"); Hamilton (Yates's Notes), ibid., 299 ("[n]othing but").

279. Morris, July 2, ibid., 512–4 (quotations); see also Madison to Jared Sparks, Apr. 8, 1831, in *Writings of James Madison*, 9:447–51.

280. Memorandum by N. P. Trist, Sept. 27, 1834, *Farrand*, 3:534 (quoting Madison) ("very extravagant" and "his usual fondness"); Pinckney, June 7, ibid., 1:155; Read and Robert Morris, June 25, ibid., 409; ibid. (rejecting seven-year terms by a seven-to-three vote, with one delegation divided; motion to substitute six years defeated by five-to-five vote, with one delegation divided; motion to substitute five years lost by the same

vote); Madison (Yates's Notes), June 26, ibid., 431 ("permanency"); Madison, ibid., 423; Wilson, ibid., 426 ("made respectable"); ibid. (rejecting by eight-to-three vote a proposal for nine-year terms with one-third of the senators to leave office every three years; then, voting by seven states to four in favor of six-year terms with one-third of the senators to leave office every two years); Official Journal, June 12, ibid., 210–1 (ten-to-one vote against mandatory rotation in Senate); see also Read, June 26, ibid., 421; Williamson and Sherman, June 25, ibid., 409; Jay to Washington, Jan. 7, 1787, *PGW* (C.S.), 4:503.

281. Madison to Jefferson, Aug. 12, 1786, *PJM* (C.S.), 9:95 ("the whole body" and "to be chosen"); Randolph, June 25, *Farrand*, 1:408 ("favorable"); see also Gorham, June 26, ibid., 421; Holton, *Unruly Americans*, 168–9. Randolph's point is not quite right. A Senate with staggered terms is, consistently, moderately independent of public opinion. By contrast, a Senate without staggered terms is very independent of public opinion at the beginning of the senators' term in office but extremely dependent at the end. I am grateful to Michael Coenen for this point.

282. Committee of Detail report, Art. IX, Aug. 6, *Farrand*, 2:183; Wilson motion, Sept. 7, ibid., 538; ibid. (ten-to-one vote, Pennsylvania dissenting, against Wilson's motion to include the House in treaty making).

283. Wilson, Sept. 8, ibid., 547–8; Williamson, ibid., 548; ibid., 549 (rejecting by nine-to-one vote, with one delegation divided, Wilson's motion to eliminate the supermajority requirement for Senate approval of treaties); ibid. (eight-to-three vote against proposal by Rutledge and Gerry to require approval of two-thirds of all senators for ratification of treaties); see also Wilson, Sept. 7, ibid., 540; Mason at Virginia ratifying convention, June 24, 1788, *DHRC*, 10:1488. For New Englanders' concerns about rights to these fisheries in the treaty ending the Revolutionary War, see Jensen, *New Nation*, 15–6; Hendrickson, *Peace Pact*, 181–3.

284. Madison, Sept. 7, *Farrand*, 2:540 ("would necessarily"); Butler, ibid., 541 ("a necessary security"); Gerry, ibid. ("dearest" and "the extremities"); Wilson, Sept. 8, ibid., 548 ("the minority"). On some New Englanders' willingness to trade to Great Britain, in negotiations to end the Revolutionary War, Georgia and South Carolina in exchange for Nova Scotia, see Hendrickson, *Peace Pact*, 189.

285. Sept. 7, *Farrand*, 2:541 (eight-to-three vote rejecting Madison's motion to exclude presidents from the making of peace treaties, followed by another eight-to-three vote in favor of exempting peace treaties from a supermajority requirement); Gerry, Sept. 8, ibid., 548 ("the essential rights"); Williamson, ibid. ("the power").

286. Morris, ibid. (quotations); ibid., 548–9 (eight-to-three vote to strike the exemption of peace treaties from the supermajority requirement for treaty making); see also Banning, *Sacred Fire*, 178.

287. Madison to Jefferson, Oct. 24, 1787, *PJM* (C.S.), 10:208 (quotation); see also Carroll, Aug. 15, *Farrand*, 2:300; Gorham, ibid.; Madison, June 1, ibid., 1:66–7; Dickinson (Pierce's Notes), ibid., 74.

288. Articles of Confederation, Art. IX, *DHRC*, 1:91; Beeman, *Plain, Honest Men*, 125; Rakove, *The Beginnings of National Politics*, 180, 356–7; Bowling, *The Creation of Washington, D.C.*, 61–2.

289. Rakove, *Original Meanings*, 249–50, 254–5; Beeman, *Plain, Honest Men*, 125, 137; The Declaration of Independence (1776), paras. 3–5. For the argument that an important segment of the Founding generation—including prominent Federalists such as Wilson, Hamilton, and James Iredell—had never embraced this deep suspicion of executive power and indeed had consistently favored, as colonials, the expansion of the king's prerogative power over Parliament, see Nelson, *Royalist Revolution*, 5–9, 35–7, 102–3, 149, 154–6. For criticism of Morris's administration of his office, see, e.g., Arthur Lee to Samuel Adams, Aug. 6, 1782, *LDC*, 19:25–6; infra p. 425 n. *.

290. Wood, *Creation of the American Republic*, 135–50, 155–9, 407, 434–6; Rakove, *Original Meanings*, 250–3; Nelson, *Royalist Revolution*, 146, 148, 308–9 n. 1; Robertson, *The Constitution and America's Destiny*, 35; Shumer, "New Jersey," 76–7; New York Constitution of 1777, Art. XXIII; Massachusetts Constitution of 1780, Pt. 2, Ch. 2, §§

IV, V, VIII, and IX. New York's constitution bound the governor to act in conjunction with an executive council only with regard to appointments.

291. Madison, July 17, *Farrand*, 2:35 ("Experience," "in general," "some expedient," "the instability," and "a revolution"); Morris, ibid., 35–6 ("the way to keep"); July 19, ibid., 52 ("to control"); see also Charles Pinckney at South Carolina ratifying convention, May 14, 1788, *DHRC*, 27:329–30; Robertson, *The Constitution and America's Destiny*, 215–6; Nelson, *Royalist Revolution*, 5–6, 179–81, 203, 215.

292. Madison to Washington, Apr. 16, 1787, *PJM* (C.S.), 9:385 (quotation); Beeman, *Plain, Honest Men*, 55–6, 126–7, 257; see also Madison to Randolph, Apr. 8, 1787, *PJM* (C.S.), 9:370; Nelson, *Royalist Revolution*, 199. In 1785, when Madison had been asked for his thoughts regarding a constitution for Kentucky, he had displayed a similar lack of certitude on the optimal design of the executive branch (to Caleb Wallace, Aug. 23, 1785, *PJM* (C.S.), 8:352).

293. Virginia Plan, resolutions 7–8, May 29, *Farrand*, 1:21.

294. Pinckney, June 1, ibid., 64 ("vigorous"); Morris, July 19, ibid., 2:52 ("an executive"); Wilson (King's Notes), June 1, ibid., 71 ("to require" and "manners"); Sherman, ibid., 65 ("nothing more"); see also Beeman, *Plain, Honest Men*, 55–6, 125–6.

295. Wilson, June 1, *Farrand*, 1:65 ("most energy"); Official Journal, ibid., 63 (motion by Wilson, seconded by Charles Pinckney, for unitary executive); Wilson (King's Notes), June 16, ibid., 266–7 ("if divided"); Rutledge, June 1, ibid., 65 ("feel the greatest"); Pinckney, June 2, ibid., 88 ("obvious" and "no member"); Wilson, June 4, ibid., 96; see also Butler, June 1, ibid., 88–9; Beeman, *Plain, Honest Men*, 56, 127, 129; Judith A. Best, "The Presidency and the Executive Power," in Levy and Mahoney, eds., *The Framing and Ratification of the Constitution*, 213–4; Nelson, *Royalist Revolution*, 185–6. On Wilson's consistent support, from the time of the revolution onwards, for broad executive power, see Nelson, *Royalist Revolution*, 35–7, 149, 164–5, 178–9.

296. Randolph, June 2, *Farrand*, 1:88 ("with great earnestness"); June 1, ibid., 66 ("the fetus" and "the British"); Williamson, July 24, ibid., 2:101 ("an elective king," "lay a train," and "pretty certain"); see also Madison to Jefferson, Oct. 24, 1787, *PJM* (C.S.), 10:208.

297. Dickinson, June 2, *Farrand*, 1:86–7 ("not consistent," "from the attachments," "one of the best," and "The spirit"); Mason, June 4, ibid., 101–2 ("genius"); New Jersey Plan, resolution 4, June 15, ibid., 244; see also Sherman, June 1, ibid., 65; Rakove, *Original Meanings*, 253, 257, 268–9; Beeman, *Plain, Honest Men*, 128, 134; Nelson, *Royalist Revolution*, 188, 195.

298. Randolph, June 2, *Farrand*, 1:88; Mason, June 4, ibid., 113 ("a more perfect" and "quiet the minds"); Williamson, July 24, ibid., 2:100–1 ("essential difference"); see also Randolph (King's Notes), June 1, ibid., 1:71; Williamson, ibid.

299. Wilson, June 4, ibid., 96 ("nothing but"); June 16, ibid., 254 ("contend among"); June 1, ibid., 66 ("unity" and "the manners"); Butler, June 2, ibid., 88–9 ("constant struggle" and "mischievous"); Butler (Yates's Notes), ibid., 90 ("delays, divisions"); see also Gerry, June 4, ibid., 97; Nelson, *Royalist Revolution*, 189–90.

300. June 1, *Farrand*, 1:66 (postponing the vote by common consent); June 2, ibid., 89 (postponing the vote in order to adjourn for the day); Official Journal, June 4, ibid., 93 (seven-to-three vote in favor of a unitary executive); Sherman, ibid., 97 (quotations); see also July 17, ibid., 2:29 (affirming, without dissent, a unitary executive); Aug. 24, ibid., 401 (same); Nelson, *Royalist Revolution*, 322 n. 14; Adams, *First American Constitutions*, 272.

301. Mason, Objections, Sept. 15, *Farrand*, 2:638–9 ("safe and proper"); Sept. 7, ibid., 541–2 ("an experiment"); Franklin, ibid., 542 ("a council"); Gerry, June 1, ibid., 1:66 ("in order to"); Ellsworth, Aug. 18, ibid., 2:328–9; see also Dickinson, Sept. 7, ibid., 542.

302. Pinckney, Aug. 18, ibid., 329 ("thwart" and "shelter"); Wilson, June 4, ibid., 1:97 ("to cover"); see also Gouverneur Morris, Sept. 7, ibid., 2:542.

303. Sept. 7, ibid., 541 (eight-to-three vote against Mason's motion to instruct the Committee on Unfinished Parts to prepare a provision for an executive council; then, all states but New Hampshire voted in favor of authorizing the president to call for written opinions from the heads of departments); Mason, Objections, Sept. 15, ibid., 638 (quotation); see also Rakove, *Original Meanings*, 268–70.

304. July 17, *Farrand*, 2:32 (the executive's power to execute national law agreed to without dissent); Banning, *Sacred Fire*, 100; Adams, *First American Constitutions*, 267, 271.

305. Virginia Plan, resolution 8, May 29, *Farrand*, 1:21; Sherman, June 4, ibid., 99 ("against"); Bedford, ibid., 100–1 ("it would be sufficient"); New Jersey Plan, resolution 4, June 15, ibid., 244.

306. Wilson, Aug. 15, ibid., 2:300–1 ("swallowing up" and "sufficient"); Morris, July 21, ibid., 76 ("in greater danger"); Mason, ibid., 78 ("would so much resemble"); Mercer, Aug. 15, ibid., 298 ("legislative usurpation"); see also Morris, ibid., 300; Madison, Sept. 12, ibid., 586–7; Rakove, "Madisonian Moment," 492.

307. Madison, July 21, *Farrand*, 2:74 ("as an additional check"); Morris, Aug. 15, ibid., 299 ("dwelt" and "this ruinous expedient"); see also Holton, *Unruly Americans*, 197.

308. Official Journal, June 4, *Farrand*, 1:94 (eight-to-two vote approving of executive veto, subject to a two-thirds override by both houses of Congress).

309. Virginia Plan, resolution 8, May 29, ibid., 21 ("convenient number"); Madison, July 21, ibid., 2:74 ("an additional opportunity" and "inspir[e] additional confidence"); New York constitution of 1777, Art. III; see also Madison (King's Notes), June 4, *Farrand*, 1:108; Madison (King's Notes), June 6, ibid., 144; Wilson (Yates's Notes), June 4, ibid., 105; James T. Barry III, "The Council of Revision and the Limits of Judicial Power," *University of Chicago Law Review* (1989), 56:244–5; Nelson, *Royalist Revolution*, 166; Rakove, "Madisonian Moment," 493. Madison had long been a fan of New York's council of revision (to Caleb Wallace, Aug. 23, 1785, *PJM* (C.S.), 8:351).

310. Madison, June 6, *Farrand*, 1:138–9 ("settled pre-eminence," "permanent stake," and "would both double"); July 21, ibid., 2:74 ("preserving a consistency"); Ellsworth, ibid., 73–4 ("give more wisdom" and "competent information"); see also Barry, "Council of Revision," 249–50; Rakove, *Original Meanings*, 261–2.

311. Morris, July 21, *Farrand*, 2:75–6.

312. Supra p. 160; Martin, July 21, *Farrand*, 2:76 ("a double negative"); Wilson, ibid., 73 ("weight" and "[l]aws may be"); Mason, ibid., 78 ("unjust").

313. King, June 6, ibid., 1:139; Gorham, July 21, ibid., 2:73 ("not to be presumed"); Gerry, ibid., 75 ("making statesmen"); Strong, ibid., 75; Pinckney, Aug. 15, ibid., 298; Sherman, ibid., 300 ("disapproved"); see also Gerry, June 4, ibid., 1:97; King, ibid., 98; Gerry, June 6, ibid., 139; Robertson, *The Constitution and America's Destiny*, 217–9; Barry, "Council of Revision," 253–7. Acknowledging some weight to the objection that judges might be biased in the interpretation of laws they had been involved in enacting, Madison responded, however, that only "a small proportion of the laws coming in question before a judge would be such wherein he had been consulted [and] that a small part of this proportion would be so ambiguous as to leave room for his prepossessions" (June 6, *Farrand*, 1:138).

314. Gerry, July 21, ibid., 2:75; Martin, ibid., 76; Madison, ibid., 77 (quotations).

315. Official Record, June 4, ibid., 1:104 (eight-to-two vote in favor of executive veto without the participation of the judiciary); Wilson and Madison motion to reconsider inclusion of judges in council of revision, June 6, ibid., 138; ibid., 140 (eight-to-three vote rejecting inclusion of judges); Wilson motion to include judges, July 21, ibid., 2:73; Madison, ibid., 74 (supporting the motion); Gerry, ibid. (expressing displeasure); ibid., 80 (rejecting Wilson's motion by four-to-three vote, with two delegations divided); Madison motion, seconded by Wilson, for separate vetoes to be exercised by executive and Supreme Court, Aug. 15, ibid., 298; Gerry, ibid. (objecting that this issue has already been resolved); ibid. (eight-to-three vote rejecting the motion); Robertson, *The Constitution and America's Destiny*, 217–9; Rakove, *Original Meanings*, 261–3.

316. Wilson and Hamilton motion for executive to exercise an absolute veto, June 4, *Farrand*, 1:98, 100 ("tempestuous"); Read motion for absolute veto, seconded by Morris, Aug. 7, ibid., 2:200; Wilson, Aug. 15, ibid., 300–1 ("prejudices"); Morris, ibid., 300; Rakove, *Original Meanings*, 258, 262; Nelson, *Royalist Revolution*, 189–91.

317. Gerry, June 4, *Farrand*, 1:98 ("the best"); Franklin, ibid., 99; Butler, ibid., 100 ("in a constant course," "a Cromwell," and "arise"); Mason, ibid., 101.

318. Virginia Plan, resolution 8, May 29, ibid., 21; Madison, June 4, ibid., 99–100 ("would certainly be" and "a proper proportion"); ibid., 103 (unanimous vote against absolute executive veto); ibid., 104 (eight-to-two vote in favor of an executive veto with a provision for override by two-thirds votes in both houses of Congress); Official Journal, July 21, ibid., 2:71 (executive veto with two-thirds override unanimously approved); Aug. 15, ibid., 301 (six-to-four vote, with one delegation divided, to change override requirement from two-thirds to three-fourths); Official Record, Sept. 12, ibid., 582 (six-to-four vote, with one delegation divided, to change the override requirement of three-fourths to two-thirds); Morris, ibid., 585 ("[t]he excess"); Charles Pinckney, ibid., 586 ("putting a dangerous power"); Hamilton, ibid., 585; see also Williamson, ibid.; Sherman, ibid.

319. Madison, Observations on Jefferson's Draft of a Constitution for Virginia, Oct. 15, 1788, *PJM* (C.S.) 11:290 ("the most difficult"); Mason, June 22, *Farrand*, 2:376.

320. Madison to Jefferson, Oct. 24, 1787, *PJM* (C.S.), 10:209.

321. Wilson, June 5, *Farrand*, 1:119 ("the impropriety" and "intrigue"); Randolph, July 21, ibid., 2:81 ("generally resulted" and "the responsibility"); Morris, ibid., 82 ("intercourse"); see also Aug. 23, ibid., 389; Wilson, July 18, ibid., 41; Morris, ibid.; Gorham, ibid., 42; Morris, Sept. 6, ibid., 524.

322. Rutledge, June 5, ibid., 1:119 ("so great" and "leaning"); Mason, July 18, ibid., 2:42 ("insensibly form"); see also Mason, July 21, ibid., 83. For references to judges' trying impeachments, see Randolph, July 20, ibid., 67; Madison, Sept. 8, ibid., 551.

323. Madison, June 5, ibid., 1:120 ("sufficiently stable"); Pinckney, July 21, ibid., 2:81; Sherman, July 18, ibid., 41, 43 ("ought to be" at p. 41); see also Madison, June 13, ibid., 1:232–3; Randolph, July 18, ibid., 2:43; Ellsworth, July 21, ibid., 81.

324. Virginia Plan, resolution 9, May 29, ibid., 1:21; Madison, June 1, ibid., 66–7 ("to appoint"); ibid., 67 (approving Madison's proposal unanimously, with one delegation divided); Official Journal, ibid., 63; Madison, June 5, ibid., 120 ("maturer"); ibid. (the vote to strike out "the legislature" and leave the appointing authority blank); June 13, ibid., 233 (appointment of federal judges by the Senate agreed to without dissent); see also Official Journal, July 17, ibid., 2:23 (unanimous vote confirming that the executive would make appointments to offices not otherwise provided for in the Constitution).

325. Supra pp. 204–5; Madison, July 21, *Farrand*, 2:80–1; see also Banning, "Virginia," 274. Disagreeing with Madison, Mason denied that "the difference of interest between the northern and southern states could be properly brought into this argument," and he continued to defend Senate appointment of federal judges (July 21, *Farrand*, 2:83).

326. Gorham, July 18, ibid., 41; Madison, ibid., 42–3 ("would unite"); July 21, ibid., 82; Mason, ibid., 83; Ellsworth, ibid., 81 (advocating reversing the procedure); Wilson, Sept. 7, ibid., 538–9 ("Good laws"); see also Morris, July 21, ibid., 82; Sept. 7, ibid., 539; Massachusetts Constitution of 1780, Pt. 2, Ch. 2, Art. IX.

327. Martin, July 18, *Farrand*, 2:41 (quotation); Sherman, ibid., 43; Bedford, ibid.; Official Record, July 21, ibid., 72 (six-to-three vote against the proposal for federal judges to be nominated by the president, subject to disapproval by the Senate; followed by a six-to-three vote in favor of Senate appointment of federal judges); Committee of Detail report, Art. IX, § 1 and Art. X, § 2, ibid., 183, 185; see also July 18, ibid., 38–9 (rejecting by a six-to-two vote a proposal to shift the power of appointing federal judges from the Senate to the president; then rejecting by an evenly divided vote of four-to-four Gorham's proposal for presidential appointment of judges with the advice and consent of the Senate).

328. Committee on Unfinished Parts report, presented by Brearley, Sept. 4, ibid., 498–9 ("with the advice"); Sept. 7, ibid., 539–40 (agreeing without dissent to this proposal with regard to ambassadors, other public ministers, and Supreme Court judges; voting nine-to-two in favor of this proposal with regard to "all other officers of the United States"); U.S. Constitution, Art. II, § 2, cl. 2.

329. Sept. 3, *Farrand*, 2:492 (agreeing, without dissent, to bar members of the national legislature from holding any other federal office). Nelson argues that the convention's debate over the ineligibility of members of Congress to appointment to other federal office mirrored the disagreement between British Whigs, who believed that the Crown had corrupted the British constitution by influencing Members of Parliament with the promise

of executive appointments, and Royalists, who believed that the Crown's prerogative to appoint legislators to executive office was its only remaining bulwark against parliamentary tyranny since the royal veto had gradually been emasculated through disuse (*Royalist Revolution*, 196–8).

330. June 12, *Farrand*, 1:217 (eight-to-two vote in favor of ineligibility of members of Congress for appointment to federal office for one year after the expiration of their term in office); resolutions of the Virginia Plan as amended and agreed to by the Committee of the Whole, June 13, ibid., 228–9; Butler, June 22, ibid., 376 ("precaution"); Mason (Yates's Notes), ibid., 380–1 (all other quotations); see also Rutledge, June 23, ibid., 386; Gerry, Aug. 14, ibid., 2:285–6; Randolph, ibid., 290.

331. King, June 22, ibid., 1:376 ("discourage merit"); Hamilton, ibid. ("passions" and "pure patriotism"); Morris (Yates's Notes), July 2, ibid., 518 ("the pursuit" and "proceed"); June 23, ibid., 390 (eight-to-two vote in favor of ineligibility during the term for which elected, followed by a six-to-four vote, one delegation divided, against extending that ineligibility for one year after the expiration of the term); see also Gorham, June 22, ibid., 375–6; Charles Pinckney, Aug. 14, ibid., 2:283–4; Wilson, ibid., 289; Committee of Detail report, Aug. 6, Art. VI, § 9, ibid., 180 (one year's ineligibility for the Senate but not for the House); Committee on Unfinished Parts report, presented by Brearley, Sept. 1, ibid., 484 (one year's ineligibility removed).

332. Madison motion, June 23, ibid., 1:386; Madison, ibid., 388–9 ("impulse," "too feeble," and "too great success"); Wilson (Yates's Notes), ibid., 393 ("ought not to shut"); see also ibid., 390 (eight-to-two vote, with one delegation divided, against Madison's proposal).

333. Mason (Yates's Notes), ibid., 392 ("[I]f we do not"); Gerry, ibid., 393 ("by admitting"); Sept. 3, ibid., 2:492 (defeating by an evenly divided vote of five to five King's motion to limit the ineligibility clause to newly created offices; then, by a vote of five to four, with one delegation divided, limiting the ineligibility clause to newly created offices and existing offices for which salaries had been increased during the term for which the member of Congress was elected). At the Virginia ratifying convention, Madison defended the ineligibility provision he had proposed in Philadelphia, noting that no state constitution barred sitting legislators from appointment to existing offices. He explained that the Philadelphia convention had adopted a middle path between two extremes. It had reduced Congress's incentive to create needless offices or increase the salaries of existing offices, while preserving the capacity of those who "had served their country with the greatest fidelity" to be appointed to office "on a par with their fellow citizens" (June 14, 1788, *DHRC*, 10:1262–3).

334. July 17, *Farrand*, 2:32 (agreeing, without dissent, to president's power to execute national laws); Committee of Detail report, resolution 10, Aug. 6, ibid., 185; Committee on Unfinished Parts report, presented by Brearley, Sept. 4, ibid., 498–9 (adding to the president's powers that of making treaties, with the advice and consent of the Senate); Sept. 7, ibid., 538 (agreeing without dissent to president's power to make treaties); see also Brown, *Redeeming the Republic*, 191.

335. Virginia Plan, resolution 7, May 29, *Farrand*, 1:21 ("enjoy"); Articles of Confederation, Art. IX, *DHRC*, 1:89 ("the sole"); Pinckney, June 1, *Farrand*, 1:64–5 ("vigorous executive" and "a monarchy"); Wilson, ibid., 65–6; Gerry, Aug. 17, ibid., 2:318 ("never expected"); see also Madison (King's Notes), June 1, ibid., 1:70.

336. Madison, Aug. 17, ibid., 2:318 ("the power to repel"); ibid., 319 (the vote); see also Gerry, ibid., 318; Charles Pinckney, ibid.; Mason, ibid., 319.

337. Wilson, Sept. 4, ibid., 501 (quotations); see also Wilson at Pennsylvania ratifying convention, Dec. 11, 1787, *DHRC*, 2:566–7; Madison to Jefferson, Oct. 24, 1787, *PJM* (C.S.), 10:208; Rakove, *Original Meanings*, 256; Beeman, *Plain, Honest Men*, 249, 297; Best, "The Presidency," 215.

338. Virginia Plan, resolution 7, May 29, *Farrand*, 1:21; Mason, June 1, ibid., 68 ("temptation"); July 26, ibid., 2:119–20 ("the very palladium" and "at fixed periods"); Randolph, July 19, ibid., 54–5; Wilson, ibid., 56; Rutledge, ibid., 57; June 2, ibid., 1:81 (eight-to-two vote in favor of legislative selection of the executive for a seven-year term); ibid., 88

(seven-to-two vote, with one delegation divided, in favor of making the executive ineligible for re-election); see also Williamson, July 17, ibid., 2:32; Gerry, July 24, ibid., 100.

339. Morris, July 17, ibid., 33 ("to destroy"); July 19, ibid., 53 ("the civil road" and "to make the most"); Morris (McHenry's Notes), Aug. 24, ibid., 407; Ellsworth, July 24, ibid., 101 ("the most eminent" and "if they foresee"); see also Morris, ibid., 104–5; King, July 19, ibid., 55.

340. Madison, July 25, ibid., 109 ("insuperable," "agitate," and "[m]inisters"); July 17, ibid., 34–5 ("essential"); July 19, ibid., 56; see also Madison to Jefferson, Oct. 24, 1787, *PJM* (C.S.), 10:208–9.

341. Butler, July 25, *Farrand*, 2:112 ("cabal"); Morris, Sept. 4, ibid., 500 ("danger of" and "indispensable"); Sherman, June 1, ibid., 1:68 ("absolutely" and "very essence"). For more statements opposing congressional selection of the executive, see Gerry, June 2, ibid., 80; June 9, ibid., 175; July 19, ibid., 2:57; Morris, July 17, ibid., 29, 31; July 24, ibid., 103.

342. Wilson, June 2, ibid., 1:80 ("produce more"); Morris, July 17, ibid., 2:29 ("to prefer" and "of continental"); Madison, July 19, ibid., 56 ("the fittest"); Massachusetts Constitution of 1780, Part 2, Ch. 2, Art. III; New York Constitution of 1777, Art. XVII; see also Wilson, June 1, *Farrand*, 1:68, 69; Wilson motion, June 2, ibid., 80; Morris, July 19, ibid., 2:53; King, ibid., 55–6; Wilson, ibid., 56; Madison, July 25, ibid., 110–1; Morris, ibid., 113; Dickinson, ibid., 114; Nelson, *Royalist Revolution*, 172, 187–8.

343. Gerry, July 25, *Farrand*, 2:114 ("radically vicious" and "ignorance"); Pinckney, July 17, ibid., 30 ("a few active"); Mason, ibid., 31 ("it would be as unnatural" and "it impossible"); see also Mason, July 26, ibid., 119; Gerry, June 2, ibid., 1:80; July 19, ibid., 2:57; Beeman, *Plain, Honest Men*, 129–31, 231–2, 252; Rakove, *Original Meanings*, 259.

344. Sherman, July 17, *Farrand*, 2:29 ("never be," "generally vote," and "the largest"); Madison, July 25, ibid., 111 ("to prefer"); Williamson, ibid., 113; see also Dickinson, ibid., 114; Charles Pinkney, July 17, ibid., 30; Williamson, ibid., 32.

345. Madison, July 19, ibid., 57 ("serious"); July 25, ibid., 111 ("local considerations," "must give way," and "was willing"); Wilson, June 1, ibid., 1:68 ("chimerical"); July 17, ibid., 2:32 (the vote); see also Williamson, ibid.; Aug. 24, ibid., 402 (again rejecting a proposal for direct popular election of the executive, this time by a vote of nine states to two).

346. Hamilton, June 18, ibid., 1:289 ("could be established" and "stability"); Morris, July 17, ibid., 2:33 ("great pleasure" and "[t]his was the way"); see also James McClurg, ibid.; Jacob Broom, ibid.

347. Mason, ibid., 35 ("a softer name" and "easy step"); Madison, ibid.; Sherman, ibid., 33 ("by no means").

348. Ibid., 36 (the vote), ibid., 36 n. * (quotation); see also Hamilton to Timothy Pickering, Sept. 16, 1803, *PAH*, 26:147–8. For the argument that Madison probably had an incentive to understate the amount of delegate support for an executive tenured during good behavior, see Nelson, *Royalist Revolution*, 194, 326–7 n. 57. For the unreliability of Madison's notes on this point, see Bilder, *Madison's Hand*, 114–5, 216–7.

349. Gerry, July 24, *Farrand*, 2:102; Martin, ibid.; Williamson, ibid., 101; Wilson, ibid., 102; Ellsworth, July 19, ibid., 59 ("firm"); Williamson, ibid. ("the best men"); supra p. 227; *Farrand*, 2:58–9 (eight-to-two vote against ineligibility, followed by a nine-to-one vote in favor of six-year terms); Wilson, June 1, ibid., 1:68; Sherman, ibid.; Bedford, ibid., 68–9; see also Broom, July 17, ibid., 2:33; Morris, July 19, ibid., 54; July 24, ibid., 105; Beeman, *Plain, Honest Men*, 249; Robertson, *The Constitution and America's Destiny*, 215.

350. Gerry, July 25, *Farrand*, 2:109 ("radically"); Madison, ibid., 110 ("had betrayed" and "infected"); Randolph, June 9, ibid., 1:176 ("national executive"); see also Gerry, June 2, ibid., 80; June 9, ibid., 176 (rejecting by a vote of nine to zero, with one delegation divided, Gerry's motion for the federal executive to be chosen by state executives); Gerry, July 19, ibid., 2:57; Gerry, July 24, ibid., 101; Mason, July 26, ibid., 118–20; Wilson, June 2, ibid., 1:69; Beeman, *Plain, Honest Men*, 135, 247–8, 254.

351. Ellsworth, July 25, *Farrand*, 2:108–9 ("deserving magistrate"); Charles Pinckney, ibid., 111–2; Mason, ibid., 112; Morris, ibid., 113 ("intrigue").

352. Gerry, July 24, ibid., 103 ("[w]e seem"); Wilson, ibid. ("a digested"); Wilson motion to this effect, ibid., 105; Morris, ibid. ("[i]t would be better"); Official Record, June 2, ibid.,

1:77–8 (eight-to-two vote in favor of congressional selection of the executive for a seven-year term; seven-to-two vote, with one delegation divided, in favor of making the executive ineligible for re-election); July 17, ibid., 2:32 (unanimous vote in favor of Congress's selecting the executive); Official Record, July 24, ibid., 97 (seven-to-four vote in favor of Congress's selecting the executive); Official Record, July 26, ibid., 116 (seven-to-three vote in favor of a seven-year term with ineligibility for re-election); Committee of Detail report, Art. X, § 1, Aug. 6, ibid., 185 (congressional selection of the president to a seven-year term with ineligibility for re-election); see also Best, "The Presidency," 215–6.

353. Brearley, Aug. 24, *Farrand*, 2:402 ("[t]he argument"); statements by Sherman, Gorham, Dayton, Wilson, Langdon, and Madison, ibid., 401–3; ibid., 403 (the vote); see also Gorham and Wilson, Aug. 7, ibid., 196–7.

354. Committee on Unfinished Parts report, presented by Brearley, Sept. 4, ibid., 497–8; Wilson motion, June 2, ibid., 1:80; Official Journal, ibid., 77 (rejecting Wilson's proposal by a vote of seven to two, with one delegation divided); King, July 19, ibid., 2:56; Paterson, ibid.; ibid., 58 (six-to-three vote, with one delegation divided, in favor of selecting president via system of electors; then voting eight to two in favor of state legislatures' choosing the electors); July 23, ibid., 95 (seven-to-three vote the next day to reconsider the electoral college system for selecting the president); July 24, ibid., 101 (seven-to-four vote in favor of returning to the method of congressional selection of the president); see also Dickinson to George Logan, Jan. 16, 1802, ibid., 3:301; Beeman, *Plain, Honest Men*, 135–6, 299–302; Rakove, *Original Meanings*, 264–5.

355. Strong, July 24, *Farrand*, 2:100 ("first characters" and "make the government"); Williamson, July 19, ibid., 58 ("the most respectable"); Morris, Sept. 4, ibid., 500 ("the great evil" and "impossible"); Wilson, ibid., 501–2; Madison, July 25, ibid., 110–1; July 19, ibid., 57; see also William Houston, July 24, ibid., 99.

356. Ellsworth, July 25, ibid., 111; Paterson, July 19, ibid., 56; Ellsworth motion, seconded by Broom, ibid., 57; July 20, ibid., 64 (voting by six states to four in favor of an apportionment of electors ranging from one to three per state); see also Official Record, June 8, ibid., 1:163 (Charles Pinckney proposal for a relatively flat apportionment of electors).

357. Committee on Unfinished Parts report, presented by Brearley, Sept. 4, ibid., 497.

358. Ibid., 498; Pinckney, Sept. 5, ibid., 511 ("not have sufficient"); Mason, Sept. 4, ibid., 500 ("nineteen").

359. Morris, ibid., 502; Sherman, Sept. 5, ibid., 512–3; see also King, ibid., 514; Beeman, *Plain, Honest Men*, 300–1; but see Morris, Sept. 5, *Farrand*, 2:512.

360. Mason motion, seconded by Williamson, proposing to eliminate the majority requirement, ibid., 512; ibid., 513 (nine-to-two vote against Mason proposal); Madison motion, seconded by Williamson, to replace "majority" with "one-third," ibid., 514; Gerry, ibid.; ibid. (nine-to-two vote against Madison's proposal); see also Hamilton, Sept. 6, ibid., 525.

361. Madison, Sept. 4, ibid., 500 ("the attention"); Wilson, ibid., 502; Mason motion, seconded by Gerry, to change "five" to "three," Sept. 5, ibid., 514; Sherman, ibid.; ibid. (eight-to-two vote against Mason's proposal); Spaight motion, seconded by Rutledge, to replace "five" with "thirteen," ibid., 515; ibid. (only North Carolina and South Carolina voting for Spaight proposal).

362. Committee on Unfinished Parts report, presented by Brearley, Sept. 4, ibid., 498–9; Wilson, Sept. 6, ibid., 523 ("will not be"); Mason, Sept. 5, ibid., 512 ("if a coalition"); Williamson, ibid. ("lays"); Randolph, ibid., 513; see also Charles Pinckney, ibid., 511; Rutledge, ibid.

363. Committee on Unfinished Parts report, presented by Brearley, Sept. 4, ibid., 499; Wilson (McHenry's Notes), Sept. 6, ibid., 530 ("combined and blended"); see also Wilson, Sept. 8, ibid., 522–3; Charles Pinckney, Sept. 4, ibid., 501; Madison to George Hay, Aug. 23, 1823, ibid., 3:458; Rakove, *Original Meanings*, 265; Banning, "Constitutional Convention," 130.

364. Wilson, Sept. 4, *Farrand*, 2:502; Randolph, ibid.; Wilson motion to replace "Senate" with "the legislature," Sept. 5, ibid., 513; Dickinson, ibid.; ibid. (Wilson motion defeated by a vote of seven to three, with one delegation divided); Sherman motion to replace "the

Senate" with "the House," Sept. 6, ibid., 527; Mason, ibid. ("the aristocratic influence"); ibid. (ten-to-one vote in favor of Sherman motion); Madison to George Hay, Aug. 23, 1823, ibid., 3:458 ("on account of" and "present greater obstacles"); see also Robertson, *The Constitution and America's Destiny*, 156–7; Beeman, *Plain, Honest Men*, 304–5; Rakove, *Original Meanings*, 265.

365. Committee on Unfinished Parts report, presented by Brearley, Sept. 4, *Farrand*, 2:497; see also Williamson, July 25, ibid., 113; Morris, ibid.; Gouverneur Morris to Lewis Morris, Dec. 10, 1803, ibid., 3:405.

366. Williamson, Sept. 7, ibid., 2:537 ("only for the sake" and "such an officer"); Sherman, ibid. ("be without employment"); Gerry, ibid., 536–7 ("the close intimacy"); Mason, ibid.; Gerry (King's Notes), Sept. 15, ibid., 635 ("destroy the independence").

367. Morris, Sept. 7, ibid., 537 (quotation); ibid., 538 (eight-to-two vote, with one delegation divided, in favor of making the vice president ex officio president of the Senate).

368. Committee on Unfinished Parts report, presented by Brearley, Sept. 4, ibid., 497; Sherman, Sept. 4, ibid., 499; Morris, ibid., 500; Wilson, ibid., 501–2; Sept. 6, ibid., 525 (eight-to-three vote against a motion to change the president's term from four years to seven, followed by a nine-to-two vote against changing it from four years to six); ibid. n. *. For the terms in office of state executives, see Adams, *First American Constitutions*, 243.

369. Maryland Constitution of 1776, Art. XXXI ("a long continuance"); Franklin, July 26, *Farrand*, 2:120 ("returning to" and "[i]n free governments"); Wood, *Creation of the American Republic*, 140; Adams, *First American Constitutions*, 251; see also Charles Pinckney, July 25, *Farrand*, 2:111–2.

370. Mason, June 2, ibid., 1:86 ("some mode"); Virginia Plan, resolutions 7 and 9, May 29, *Farrand*, 1:21, 22; Dickinson motion, seconded by Bedford, June 2, ibid., 85–6; New Jersey Plan, resolution 4, June 15, ibid., 244; see also Beeman, *Plain, Honest Men*, 141–2.

371. Sherman, June 2, *Farrand*, 1:85 ("at pleasure"); Mason, ibid., 86 ("opposed decidedly" and "the mere creature"); Madison and Wilson, ibid.

372. Official Journal, June 2, ibid., 78–9 (rejecting Dickinson proposal by a vote of nine to one and then approving Williamson motion, seconded by Davie, for impeachment for "malpractice or neglect of duty" by a vote that is unclear); Morris, July 20, ibid., 2:64–5 ("render the executive"); Pinckney, ibid., 66 ("effectually destroy"); King, ibid., 67 ("intermediate trial" and "tried for"); Morris, July 19, ibid., 53, 59; see also Randolph (King's Notes), June 1, ibid., 1:71.

373. Wilson, July 20, ibid., 2:64; Davie, ibid. ("essential security"); Mason, ibid., 65; Randolph, ibid., 67; Franklin, ibid., 65; Madison, ibid., 65–6 ("incapacity" and "fatal"); see also Morris, ibid., 68–9; July 24, ibid., 103–4.

374. July 20, ibid., 69 (the vote); Randolph, ibid., 67 ("excluding"); Committee of Detail report, Art. X, § 2, Aug. 6, ibid., 186; see also Robertson, *The Constitution and America's Destiny*, 157.

375. Committee on Unfinished Parts report, presented by Brearley, Sept. 4, ibid., 497, 499.

376. Madison, Sept. 8, ibid., 551 ("improperly dependent"); Pinckney, ibid. ("a favorite law").

377. Morris, Sept. 8, ibid. (quotation); Sherman, ibid.; ibid. (the vote).

378. Official Journal, June 2, ibid., 1:78; Official Record, July 20, ibid., 2:61; Committee of Detail report, Art. X, § 2, Aug. 6, ibid., 186 ("treason"); Morris, July 20, ibid., 68–9.

379. Committee on Unfinished Parts report, presented by Brearley, Sept. 4, ibid., 499; Mason, Sept. 8, ibid., 550 ("great and dangerous" and "other high crimes"); Madison, ibid. ("so vague"); ibid. (eight-to-three vote in favor of Mason's proposed change); Richard A. Posner, *An Affair of State: The Investigation, Impeachment, and Trial of President Clinton* (Cambridge, MA, 2000), 98–100, 170–4; Michael Les Benedict, *The Impeachment and Trial of Andrew Johnson* (New York, 1973), 26–36.

380. Best, "The Presidency," 209; see also Nelson, *Royalist Revolution*, 7, 186–7, 203, 324 n. 33.

381. Mason, June 4, *Farrand*, 1:101 ("the genius"); Pierce Butler to Weedon Butler, May 5, 1788, *DHRC*, 27:270 ("had not many"); see also James Thomas Flexner, *George Washington and the New Nation (1783–1793)* (Boston, 1970), 3:134; Beeman, *Plain, Honest Men*, 128; but cf. Rakove, *Original Meanings*, 244.

382. Franklin, Sept. 17, *Farrand*, 2:643 ("to doubt," "put his name," and "to make"); ibid., 646 ("prevent"); Hamilton, ibid., 645 ("A few characters"); Randolph, Sept. 15, ibid., 631; see also Sept. 10, ibid., 563–4.
    For the preceding footnote, see *DHRC*, 24:82 n. 1.
383. Morris, Sept. 17, *Farrand*, 2:645 ("the best" and "take it"); Williamson, ibid. (letter option); Charles Cotesworth Pinckney, ibid., 647 (point about disingenuousness); McHenry (McHenry's Notes), ibid., 649 ("many parts" and "I distrust"). On McHenry's background, see Introduction, *DHRC*, 11:li.
384. Randolph, *Farrand*, 2:645 ("himself free"); ibid., 646 ("dictated").
385. William Lewis to Thomas Lee Shippen, Oct. 11, 1787, *PTJ* (M.S.), 12:229 ("Grumbletonian"); see also infra pp. 433, 455–6, 461–2; Luther Martin to the Printer, *Maryland Journal*, Jan. 18, 1788, *DHRC*, 10:192–4 (explaining Gerry's grounds of opposition); Gerry, Sept. 15, *Farrand*, 2:632–3; Aug. 14, ibid., 285–6; Randolph, Sept. 15, ibid., 631; Sept. 10, ibid., 563–4; Mason, Objections, ibid., 637–40; Mason at the Virginia ratifying convention, June 24, 1788, *DHRC*, 10:1488; Banning, *Sacred Fire*, 174; Helen Hill Miller, *George Mason: Gentleman Revolutionary* (Chapel Hill, NC, 1975), 254; Mason to Randolph, Oct. 19, 1782, *PGM*, 2:752; Gerry to John Adams, Sept. 20, 1787, *DHRC*, 13:218.
386. Catherine Drinker Bowen, *Miracle at Philadelphia: The Story of the Constitutional Convention* (Boston, repub. 1986), 43; see also Madison to Jefferson, Sept. 6, 1787, *PJM* (C.S.), 10:163; Swift, *Making of an American Senate*, 32.
387. Gerry, June 12, *Farrand*, 1:215 ("[I]t was necessary"); Madison to Randolph, Apr. 8, 1787, *PJM* (C.S.), 9:369 ("unattainable"); Dahl, *How Democratic Is the American Constitution?*, 12; see also Extract of a letter from William Pierce to St. George Tucker (Sept. 28, 1787), *Gazette of the State of Georgia*, Mar. 20, 1788, *DHRC*, 16:442. For other acknowledgments during the convention of the practical constraint imposed by the need to secure ratification, see, e.g., Madison, June 4, *Farrand*, 1:100; Mason, ibid., 101; see also Robert E. Brown, *Charles Beard and the Constitution: A Critical Analysis of "An Economic Interpretation of the Constitution"* (Princeton, NJ, 1956), 40–2 & n. 26, 113; Young, *Liberty Tree*, 198–9, 202. The delegates were not particularly consistent in their invocations of this argument—meaning that they would also invoke it strategically when opposing a proposal they did not favor. See Robertson, *The Constitution and America's Destiny*, 108–9 n. 30.
388. Hamilton (Yates's Notes), June 18, *Farrand*, 1:296–7 (all quotations but the last); ibid., 287, 293 ("to shock" at p. 287); see also Chernow, *Hamilton*, 231–5. For an account of Hamilton's extreme nationalism that is rooted in his immigrant background, see McCraw, *The Founders and Finance*, 43–4.
389. Read, June 29, *Farrand*, 1:463 ("good general" and "must be"); June 11, ibid., 202 ("into one great"); June 6, ibid., 136–7; Butler (Yates's Notes), ibid., 144 ("abolishing"); King, June 19, ibid., 324 ("doubted" and "that much"); Dickinson, June 2, ibid., 85 ("some gentlemen"); but cf. William Samuel Johnson, June 21, ibid., 355.
390. Madison (Yates's Notes), June 29, ibid., 471 ("possessed" and "ought to be"); Charles Pinckney, *Observations*, ibid., 3:112 ("mere local"); Morris, Aug. 20, ibid., 2:342–3; Madison, Aug. 18, ibid., 325; Pinckney, ibid.; Madison, Sept. 14, ibid., 615; see also Madison to Jefferson, Oct. 24, 1787, *PJM* (C.S.), 10:209; Knox to Washington, Jan. 14, 1787, *PGW* (C.S.), 4:521–2; Extract of a letter from William Pierce to St. George Tucker (Sept. 28, 1787), *Gazette of the State of Georgia*, Mar. 20, 1788, *DHRC*, 16:442; Wood, *Creation of the American Republic*, 473. Banning does not deny that there were extreme consolidationists at the convention, but he insists that Madison was not one of them (*Sacred Fire*, 160–5 & 455 n. 73).
391. Supra pp. 137–40, 161; Madison to Jefferson, Oct. 24, 1787, *PJM* (C.S.), 10:215–6; Maier, *Ratification*, 47–8; Banning, *Sacred Fire*, 173; Miller, *George Mason*, 240. Hendrickson puts the point nicely: The nationalists of 1783 would have been thrilled with the nationalism of the New Jersey Plan and would never have dreamed of obtaining more than that (*Peace Pact*, 222–3).

392. Massachusetts delegates to Governor James Bowdoin, Sept. 3, 1785, *LDC*, 22:612 ("plans" and "our republican"); Davis, *Sectionalism in American Politics*, 141–2 ("esteemed great aristocrats") (quoting Higginson to John Adams, July 1786); Richard Henry Lee to Francis Lightfoot Lee, July 14, 1787, *LRHL*, 2:424 ("from simple democracy," "indispensably," "the minds," and "that this tendency"); Gerry, Aug. 23, *Farrand*, 2:388 ("a plan," "pushing," and "[o]thers"); supra pp. 71–2.

For the preceding footnote, see Madison to Andrew Stevenson, Mar. 25, 1826, *Farrand*, 3:473–4 ("unlimited or consolidated" and "theoretically than practically"); Madison to J. C. Cabell, Feb. 2, 1829, ibid., 477–8 ("crude and broken," "were of a," "before the rough," and "totally mistaken"); Madison to Joseph Gales, Aug. 26, 1821, ibid., 446–7 ("to an unfavorable" and "the strongest feelings"); see also Madison to J. G. Jackson, Dec. 27, 1821, ibid., 448–9; Madison to Thomas Cooper, Dec. 26, 1826, ibid., 474–5; Madison to John Tyler (not sent), ibid., 530–1; see also Bilder, *Madison's Hand*, 214–7, 226–7; Hutson, "The Creation of the Constitution," 9–12. For Madison's revisionism regarding his support for a federal veto at the convention, see Madison to N. P. Trist, Dec. 1831, *Farrand*, 3:516; Madison to W. C. Rives, Oct. 21, 1833, ibid., 522–3. For the differences arising between Hamilton and Madison in the 1790s, see, e.g., Stanley Elkins and Eric McKitrick, *The Age of Federalism: The Early American Republic, 1788– 1800* (New York, 1993), chs. 2, 3, and 7. For Madison's rejection of nullification in the 1830s, see Drew R. McCoy, *The Last of the Fathers: James Madison and the Republican Legacy* (New York, 1989), 130–51. For the Banning references in the preceding footnote, see *Sacred Fire*, 7–8, 17, 24–6, 34–5, 112, 115–6, 139–40, 158–62, 170–1, 190–1, 201.

393. Wilson, May 31, *Farrand*, 1:49 (quotation); see also Madison, June 5, ibid., 122–3; Holton, *Unruly Americans*, 193, 211.

394. Hamilton, June 18, *Farrand*, 1:289 ("[W]e ought"); Randolph (McHenry's Notes), May 29, ibid., 26–7 ("chief danger"); Gerry, May 31, ibid., 48 ("[t]he evils"); see also Bouton, *Taming Democracy*, 176–7; Holton, *Unruly Americans*, 233; Robertson, *The Constitution and America's Destiny*, 103.

395. Gerry, Sept. 17, *Farrand*, 2:647 ("the worst"); Sherman, May 31, ibid., 1:48 ("should have"); Hamilton (Yates's Notes), June 18, ibid., 299 ("[t]he voice"); Madison, June 12, ibid., 215; Randolph, June 22, ibid., 373 ("neither incumbent" and "popular prejudices"); see also Mercer, Aug. 7, ibid., 2:205; Beeman, *Plain, Honest Men*, 294–5; Edmund Morgan, *Inventing the People: The Rise of Popular Sovereignty in England and America* (New York, 1988), 271; Bouton, "Trials of the Confederation," 370, 372, 384–5.

396. Madison, May 31, *Farrand*, 1:50 (quotation); supra pp. 171–8.

397. Randolph, May 31, *Farrand*, 1:51 (quotations); supra pp. 208–11, 218–9, 228–9. On terms of office under state constitutions, see Adams, *First American Constitutions*, 242–3.

398. Robertson, *The Constitution and America's Destiny*, 232.

399. Hamilton, June 18, *Farrand*, 1:289 (quotation); supra pp. 209–11, 228–9; see also Holton, *Unruly Americans*, 196–7.

400. Gerry, May 31, *Farrand*, 1:48 ("had been taught"); Butler, July 6, ibid., 541–2 ("the great object"); supra pp. 74–88.

401. Mason, Aug. 16, *Farrand*, 2:309 ("mortal hatred"); June 6, ibid., 1:133–4; Holton, *Unruly Americans*, 276–7; supra pp. 155, 159–63, 206–11, 218–9.

402. "Federal Farmer," *Letters to the Republican* (Nov. 8, 1787), Letter I, *DHRC*, 14:23. Authorship of the *Letters* has generally been attributed to Richard Henry Lee, though this claim has been disputed. For some of the scholarship debating authorship, see ibid., 16; see also Cornell, *Other Founders*, 88 & n. 11; Rakove, *Original Meanings*, 228–9.

403. Rutledge, June 21, *Farrand*, 1:359.

404. Beeman, *Plain, Honest Men*, 190–2; Robertson, *The Constitution and America's Destiny*, 102 & n. 5; Miller, *George Mason*, 242–3; see also McDonald, *Novus Ordo Seclorum*, 167, 187; Ellis, *The Quartet*, 140–1. On the nationalizing effect of service in the Continental Army, see Kohn, *Eagle and Sword*, 10–13. New York was a notable exception to the rule. Its most prominent statesmen—men such as Chancellor Robert R. Livingston, James Duane, John Jay, and Governor George Clinton—were not delegates to the Philadelphia convention. See Kaminski, "New York," 60.

405. Beeman, *Plain, Honest Men*, 65–6; see also McDonald, *Novus Ordo Seclorum*, 220; McDonald, *We the People*, 86.

406. Mason to George Mason, Jr., June 1, 1787, *Farrand*, 3:32.

407. The Address and Reasons of Dissent of the Minority of the Convention of the State of Pennsylvania to Their Constituents, *DHRC*, 2:619 [hereinafter, "Pennsylvania Minority Dissent"]; "Federal Farmer," *Letters to the Republican* (Nov. 8, 1787), Letter I, *DHRC*, 14:23 ("those men"); see also The Address of the Seceding Assemblymen, *DHRC*, 2:112; Wood, "Interests and Disinterestedness," 72.

408. Madison to Jefferson, Oct. 24, 1787, *PJM* (C.S.), 10:208 ("it is impossible"); Washington to Lafayette, Feb. 7, 1788, *PGW* (C.S.), 6:95 ("little short"); see also Charles Pinckney letter, *State Gazette of South Carolina*, May 2, 1788, *Farrand*, 3:301; *The Federalist No. 37* (Madison), at 230; William Samuel Johnson at Connecticut ratifying convention, Jan. 4, 1788, *DHRC*, 3:546.

409. Mason to George Mason, Jr., May 20, 1787, *Farrand*, 3:23 ("greater unanimity"); Madison to Pendleton, May 27, 1787, *PJM* (C.S.), 10:12 ("[i]n general"); see also Brown, *Redeeming the Republic*, 184.

410. Randolph to the Speaker of the House of Delegates (dated Oct. 10; published Dec. 27, 1787), *DHRC*, 8:262 (quotations); see also *A Plebeian: An Address to the People of the State of New-York* (Apr. 17, 1788), *DHRC*, 20:951 [hereinafter, "*A Plebeian*"].

411. Hosea Humphry and Daniel Perkins in Connecticut General Assembly, May 12, 1787, *DHRC*, 13:108; Lutz, "Connecticut," 125; Alexander, *The Selling of the Constitutional Convention*, 32–3.

412. Madison to James Madison, Sr., Apr. 1, 1787, *PJM* (C.S.), 9:359 ("[b]eing conscious"); *Massachusetts Centinel*, May 19, 1787, vol. 4, p. 71 ("birds of a feather"); Kaminski, "Rhode Island," 376; Proceedings of Government, *Newport Herald*, Mar. 22, 1787, at 3; supra pp. 122–3.

413. Rhode Island delegates to the Governor of Rhode Island, Apr. 24, 1787, *LDC*, 24:256 ("momentous" and "common safety"); Dane to Smith, July 3, 1788, *DHRC*, 18:218 ("When measures"); see also A Narrative of the Proceedings of the General Assembly of the State of Rhode-Island and Providence Plantations, specially convened at Newport (Sept. 10), *Newport Herald*, Sept. 20, 1787, *DHRC*, 24:17.

414. Bedford (Yates's Notes), June 30, *Farrand*, 1:501 ("Why, then"); "Federal Farmer," *Letters to the Republican* (Nov. 8, 1787), Letter I, *DHRC*, 14:23 ("not one man"); Findley to William Irvine, Mar. 12, 1788, *DHRC*, 16:373; supra pp. 69–70; see also Charles Carroll to Daniel Carroll, Mar. 13, 1787, in Kate Mason Rowland, *The Life of Charles Carroll of Carrollton, 1737–1832* (New York, 1898), 2:105; Pennsylvania Minority Dissent, *DHRC*, 2:619; William Findley at Pennsylvania ratifying convention, Dec. 1, 1787, *DHRC*, 2:445; Thomas Rodney's Diary, May 3, 1786, *LDC*, 23:262–3; Bouton, *Taming Democracy*, 176; Brown, *Redeeming the Republic*, 179.

415. Paterson, June 9, *Farrand*, 1:178 ("never entered"); "A Columbian Patriot" (Mercy Otis Warren), *Observations on the Constitution* (Feb. 1788), *DHRC*, 16:282 ("had the most") [hereinafter, "A Columbian Patriot, *Observations*"]; Gerry, June 8, *Farrand*, 1:165–6 ("never been suggested"); see also Lansing, June 16, ibid., 250; William Grayson to William Short, Nov. 10, 1787, *DHRC*, 19:247; *A Plebeian*, *DHRC*, 20:951.

416. Washington to Madison, Mar. 31, 1787, *PJM* (C.S.), 9:344 ("if the delegates"); Lansing, June 16, *Farrand*, 1:249 ("New York"); Elbridge Gerry to Ann Gerry, Aug. 26, 1787, ibid., Supp.:241 ("have induced him"); see also Holton, *Unruly Americans*, 181; Bouton, *Taming Democracy*, 176; Rakove, *Beginnings of National Politics*, 377, 390; Davis, *Sectionalism in American Politics*, 163; Brown, *Redeeming the Republic*, 30.

417. Grayson to William Short, Apr. 16, 1787, *LDC*, 24:227 (quotations); see also John Roche, "The Founding Fathers: A Reform Caucus in Action," *American Political Science Review* (1961), 55:802; Boyd, *Politics of Opposition*, 6; Davis, *Sectionalism in American Politics*, 168.

418. Beeman, *Plain, Honest Men*, 92.

419. Randolph to Madison, Mar. 1, 1787, *PJM* (C.S.), 9:301 ("assayed"); Madison to Washington, Dec. 7, 1786, ibid., 200 ("the champion"); Madison to Jefferson, Mar. 19,

1787, ibid., 319 ("intended sacrifice" and "himself free"); June 6, 1787, ibid., 10:30 ("good reason," "hostile," and "either a partition"); Madison to Randolph, Mar. 25, 1787, ibid., 9:331, 332 n. 1 ("ominous"); see also Madison to Washington, Mar. 18, 1787, ibid., 316; Banning, "Virginia," 263. On Henry's consternation over Jay's possible abandonment of American navigation rights on the Mississippi River, see Henry to Mrs. Annie Christian [his sister], Oct. 20, 1786, in William Wirt Henry, *Patrick Henry: Life, Correspondence, and Speeches* (New York, 1891), 3:380; Henry to Joseph Martin, Oct. 4, 1786, ibid., 374.

420. Lee to Governor Edmund Randolph, Mar. 26, 1787, *LRHL*, 2:415 (quotations); Lee to Samuel Adams, Oct. 27, 1787, *DHRC*, 1:348; Lee to John Adams, Sept. 3, 1787, *DHRC*, 8:9.

421. Boyd, *Politics of Opposition*, 6, 30; Robertson, *The Constitution and America's Destiny*, 101 n. 1; Brown, *Redeeming the Republic*, 213–4. On Chase, see Haw et al., *Stormy Patriot*, 145; Introduction, *DHRC*, 11:xxxix, l. Several Marylanders on the other side of the paper money debate, such as former governor Thomas Johnson, also turned down their appointments to the Philadelphia convention, apparently for fear of what Chase might be able to accomplish in Annapolis in their absence. See J. B. Cutting to Jefferson, July 11, 1788, *PTJ* (M.S.), 13:332–3; Davis, *Sectionalism in American Politics*, 218 n. 20; McDonald, *We the People*, 31. On Clark's reason for not attending, see Jonathan Dayton to David Brearley, June 7, 1787, in *Farrand*, Supp.:59. On Willie Jones's declining his appointment, see Jones to Governor Richard Caswell, Feb. 4, 1787 in *State Records of North Carolina*, 20:611; Trenholme, *Ratification of the Federal Constitution in North Carolina*, 66. For criticism of Jones for not attending, see "A Citizen and Soldier: To the People of the District of Edenton," in *A Plea for Federal Union* (North Carolina, 1788), 47. All told, seventy-four delegates were appointed to the Philadelphia convention, but only fifty-five attended at least some portion of the proceedings. See *DHRC*, 24:82 n. 1. For a list of all those appointed delegates who chose not to attend, see McDonald, *We the People*, ch. 2.

422. Dane to Smith, July 3, 1788, *LDC*, 25:208 ("certain individuals" and "engrafted"); "Federal Farmer," *Letters to the Republican* (Nov. 8, 1787), Letter I, *DHRC*, 14:23 ("good republican," "a most unfortunate," and "the result").

   For the preceding footnote, see Erastus Wolcott to the Governor and General Assembly of Connecticut, May 15, 1787, *Farrand*, Supp.:3–4 & n. 1.

423. King to Gerry, Jan. 7, 1787, *LDC*, 24:64 ("for God sake"); House Substitute of 7 March for the Resolution of 22 February (Authorizing the Appointment of Delegates and Providing Instructions for Them), Mar. 7, 1787, *DHRC*, 1:207; Grayson to William Short, Apr. 16, 1787, *LDC*, 24:227 ("conversed freely," "going a great way," and "placing Congress"); Boyd, *Politics of Opposition*, 5–6; supra pp. 119, 141–2; see also Davis, *Sectionalism in American Politics*, 153–4; Kaminski, "New York," 59–60.

424. McCraw, *The Founders and Finance*, 78; Boyd, *Politics of Opposition*, 8. To be sure, there were a few leaks from the convention, and a handful of newspaper writers did challenge what they suspected the convention had in store for the nation. See Boyd, *Politics of Opposition*, 11–13.

425. Pennsylvania Minority Dissent, *DHRC*, 2:620 ("secret conclave"); Albany Anti-Federal Committee Circular, Apr. 10, 1788, *DHRC*, 21:1382 ("genius" and "prompted"); Jefferson to Adams, Aug. 30, 1787, *PTJ* (M.S.), 12:67 ("ignorance"); Jared Sparks, Journal, Apr. 19, 1830, *Farrand*, 3:479 ("no constitution") (quoting Madison); Pennsylvania Constitution of 1776, §§ 13, 14; see also Beeman, *Plain, Honest Men*, 20–1, 91; Rakove, *Beginnings of National Politics*, 399.

426. Washington to Madison, Mar. 31, 1787, *PJM* (C.S.), 9:344 ("adopt no temporizing" and "probe the defects"); Randolph to Madison, Mar. 27, 1787, ibid., 335 ("what is best"); supra pp. 128–9; see also Knox to Mercy Otis Warren, May 30, 1787, in *Collections of Massachusetts Historical Society* (Boston, 1925), 73:295; Davis, *Sectionalism in American Politics*, 161–2, 164.

427. Lansing (Yates's Notes), June 16, *Farrand*, 1:258 ("[g]reat changes"); Randolph, ibid., 255 ("He would not"); King, June 30, ibid., 490 ("be the last"); Hamilton, June 29, ibid., 467 ("critical" and "It is a miracle"); see also Madison to Washington, Feb. 21, 1787, *PJM*

(C.S.), 9:286; Hamilton to Washington, July 3, 1787, *PAH*, 4:223–4; Brown, *Redeeming the Republic*, 186.

428. Pennsylvania Minority Dissent, *DHRC*, 2:620 ("retired"); Madison to Randolph, Mar. 11, 1787, *PJM* (C.S.), 9:307 ("too much towards"); Robert Yates and John Lansing, Jr., to Governor George Clinton, Dec. 21, 1787, *DHRC*, 19:457 ("the disagreeable alternative"); William Paterson to John Lansing, Jr., July 27, 1787, *Farrand*, Supp.:195; Hamilton to King, Aug. 20, 1787, *PAH*, 4:235; see also Abraham G. Lansing to Abraham Yates, Jr., Aug. 26, 1787, *Farrand*, Supp.:242–3; Boyd, *Politics of Opposition*, 10; Kaminski, "New York," 63; editorial note, *DHRC*, 19:454–5.

429. McHenry's Notes, Aug. 6, *Farrand*, 2:190–1; Beeman, *Plain, Honest Men*, 203, 353; Boyd, *Politics of Opposition*, 10–11; Maier, *Ratification*, 92; Kaminski, "New York," 64; Introduction, *DHRC*, 11:xli; Articles of Confederation, Art. V, *DHRC*, 1:87. For background on Martin and his reasons for departing the convention early, see editorial note, *DHRC*, 11:126–7.

430. Madison to Jefferson, Oct. 24, 1787, *PJM* (C.S.), 10:212 (quotations); see also Editorial Note, ibid., 205–6; Maier, *Ratification*, 36; Rakove, *Original Meanings*, 197, 331; Edling, *Revolution in Favor of Government*, 227; Bilder, *Madison's Hand*, 10; but cf. Banning, *Sacred Fire*, 190–1.

431. Madison to Jefferson, Oct. 24, 1787, *PJM* (C.S.), 10:211–2.

432. *The Federalist No. 39* (Madison), at 246 ("partly national"); Madison to Jefferson, Sept. 6, 1787, *PJM* (C.S.), 10:163–4 ("neither effectually").

433. Hamilton, Sept. 17, *Farrand*, 2:645–6 ("[n]o man's ideas" and "between"); Thomas Jefferson, Notes of a Conversation with George Washington, Oct. 1, 1792, *PTJ* (M.S.), 24:435 ("shilly-shally"); Morris to Robert Walsh, Feb. 5, 1811, *Farrand*, 3:418 ("disliked" and "believing").

434. Gerry, Aug. 14, ibid., 2:285–6 (quotations); Rakove, *Original Meanings*, 139–40; see also Gerry to John Wendell, Nov. 16, 1787, *DHRC*, 4:251; Lansing, June 16, *Farrand*, 1:249–50.

Chapter 4

1. Madison, June 30, *Farrand*, 1:486.
2. Madison (Yates's Notes), June 29, ibid., 476 ("by the geography"); James Madison, Observations Relating to the Influence of Vermont and the Territorial Claims on the Politics of Congress, May 1, 1782, *PJM* (C.S.), 4:200–1 ("principally from"); Hamilton, June 29, *Farrand*, 1:466 ("[t]he only considerable"); King, July 10, ibid., 566; Pinckney, July 2, ibid., 510; see also Madison, July 13, ibid., 601–2; July 14, ibid., 2:9–10; Robertson, *The Constitution and America's Destiny*, 40 n. 24; Beeman, *Plain, Honest Men*, 183, 207; Hendrickson, *Peace Pact*, 225–6.
3. Madison, June 30, *Farrand*, 1:486 (quotations); July 9, ibid., 562; John C. Calhoun, *Disquisition on Government* (Richard K. Crallé, ed., Charleston, SC, 1851), 25, 35–8 ("a concurrent voice" at p. 25); see also Carpenter, *The South as a Conscious Minority*, 77, 102.
4. John Adams, Notes of Debates in the Continental Congress, in 1775 and 1776, *The Works of John Adams* (Charles Francis Adams, ed., Boston, 1850), 2:498 (quoting Thomas Lynch, July 30, 1776); Van Cleve, *Slaveholders' Union*, 48–9; see also Adams, *First American Constitutions*, 38.
5. Michael J. Klarman, *Unfinished Business: Racial Equality in American History* (New York, 2007), 11; Robinson, *Slavery in the Structure of American Politics*, 40–2; Edmund S. Morgan, *American Slavery, American Freedom* (New York, 1975), 180–1, 299; Robertson, *The Constitution and America's Destiny*, 38.
6. Ira Berlin, *Many Thousands Gone: The First Two Centuries of Slavery in North America* (Cambridge, MA, 1998), 369; Gary B. Nash and Jean R. Soderlund, *Freedom by Degrees: Emancipation in Pennsylvania and Its Aftermath* (New York, 1991), 8, 21.
7. Thomas Jefferson, *Notes on the State of Virginia* (William Peden, ed., Chapel Hill, NC, 1954), 138, 163 ("[d]eep rooted prejudices," "the extermination," and "I tremble"); Thomas

Jefferson, *The Autobiography of Thomas Jefferson* (Paul Leicester Ford, ed., Philadelphia, 2005), 77 ("Nothing is more"); Nash and Soderlund, *Freedom by Degrees*, 77–80.

8. Gary B. Nash, "The African-Americans' Revolution," in Gray and Kamensky, eds., *American Revolution*, 253–4 (quotations); see also Eric Slauter, "Rights," in ibid., 452–4, 458–9; Douglas R. Egerton, *Death or Liberty: African Americans and Revolutionary America* (New York, 2009), 43–7, 50, 58–64; but cf. Van Cleve, *Slaveholders' Union*, 40–1.

9. Nash, "African-Americans' Revolution," 254–60 ("the greatest" at p. 258); Egerton, *Death or Liberty*, ch. 3; Nash and Soderlund, *Freedom by Degrees*, 80–1; Robinson, *Slavery in the Structure of American Politics*, 114–8; Benjamin Quarles, *The Negro in the American Revolution* (Chapel Hill, NC, 1961), viii–x, 9–12, 15, 19–23, 52–6, 60, 113. For the latest research on slave escapes during the Revolutionary War, see Cassandra Pybus, "Jefferson's Faulty Math: The Question of Slave Defections in the American Revolution," *William and Mary Quarterly* (Apr. 2005), 62:243–64.

For the preceding footnote, see Nash, "African Americans' Revolution," 261–3; Christopher Leslie Brown, "The Problems of Slavery," in Gray and Kamensky, eds., *American Revolution*, 430–1; Gould, *Among the Powers of the Earth*, 148–9; Egerton, *Death or Liberty*, 73. For a more favorable assessment of British emancipation policy, see Pybus, supra, 264.

10. Ira Berlin, *Generations of Captivity: A History of African-American Slaves* (Cambridge, MA, 2003), 104 (quotation); Nash and Soderlund, *Freedom by Degrees*, 103; Robinson, *Slavery in the Structure of American Politics*, 31–2; Van Cleve, *Slaveholders' Union*, 61–4, 72–5; Egerton, *Death or Liberty*, 97–101.

11. Commonwealth v. Jennison (Mass. 1783), reported in W. Cushing, Notes of Cases Decided in the Superior and Supreme Judicial Court of Massachusetts, 1772–1789 (1789), 34, 34 verso (unpublished manuscript in Harvard Law School Library); Egerton, *Death or Liberty*, 93–5, 103–8; Leon F. Litwack, *North of Slavery: The Negro in the Free States, 1790–1860* (Chicago, 1961), 10–11; Robinson, *Slavery in the Structure of American Politics*, 26–7; Van Cleve, *Slaveholders' Union*, 66–7. In 1777, a proposal in the Massachusetts House of Representatives to abolish slavery was abandoned out of concern for offending southern states during the war. See Adams, *First American Constitutions*, 181; Hendrickson, *Peace Pact*, 180–1.

12. Litwack, *North of Slavery*, 3 n. 1; Van Cleve, *Slaveholders' Union*, 68–70; Egerton, *Death and Liberty*, 109–21.

13. Jefferson to Richard Price, Aug. 7, 1785, *PTJ* (M.S.), 8:356–7 (quotation); Litwack, *North of Slavery*, 4–7, 10; Van Cleve, *Slaveholders' Union*, 62–5, 69–71; William W. Freehling, "The Founding Fathers and Slavery," *American Historical Review* (Feb. 1972), 77:86, 89; Egerton, *Death or Liberty*, 95–6.

For the preceding footnote, see Van Cleve, *Slaveholders' Union*, 68–9.

14. Van Cleve, *Slaveholders' Union*, 60–4, 68–9, 74–5, 79–93, 99–100; Paul Finkelman, *An Imperfect Union: Slavery, Federalism, and Comity* (Chapel Hill, NC, 1981), 64 & n. 55, 70, 73, 75; Litwack, *North of Slavery*, 15–7; Egerton, *Death or Liberty*, 120–1.

15. 11 *Hening's Statutes at Large* 308 (Richmond, VA, 1823) (quotation); Don E. Fehrenbacher, *The Dred Scott Case: Its Significance in American Law and Politics* (New York, 1978), 18, 49, 610 n. 5; Egerton, *Death or Liberty*, ch. 5; Brown, "Problems of Slavery," 436.

16. Jefferson to Richard Price, Aug. 7, 1785, *PTJ* (M.S.), 8:356–7 ("the bulk," "a respectable," "gaining daily," and "the fate"); Madison to Jefferson, Jan. 22, 1786, *PJM* (C.S.), 8:477; Madison to Washington, Nov. 11, 1785, ibid., 403, 405 n. 4; Washington to John Francis Mercer, Sept. 9, 1786, *PGW* (C.S.), 4:243 ("to see some plan"); see also Zachariah Johnston at Virginia ratifying convention, June 25, 1788, *DHRC*, 10:1533; David Waldstreicher, *Slavery's Constitution: From Revolution to Ratification* (New York, 2009), 59; Egerton, *Death and Liberty*, 48–9, 130–3; Brown, "Problems of Slavery," 438–9; John P. Kaminski, ed., *A Necessary Evil? Slavery and the Debate over the Constitution* (Madison, WI, 1995), 33–4.

17. Van Cleve, *Slaveholders' Union*, 43, 93–4; Waldstreicher, *Slavery's Constitution*, 61; Egerton, *Death or Liberty*, 159–60; Berlin, *Generations of Captivity*, 124; see also Jefferson to Price, Aug. 7, 1785, *PTJ* (M.S.), 8:356.

18. Van Cleve, *Slaveholders' Union*, 40–1, 45–7, 103; Brown, "Problems of Slavery," 442.

19. Fehrenbacher, *Dred Scott*, 19; Van Cleve, *Slaveholders' Union*, 90, 109. On Hamilton's anti-slavery activities in New York, see Chernow, *Hamilton*, 214–6; McCraw, *The Founders and Finance*, 80.
20. Mason, Aug. 22, *Farrand*, 2:370 (quotations); Van Cleve, *Slaveholders' Union*, 93–4; Jefferson, *Notes on the State of Virginia*, 162. For Mason's much earlier criticism of slavery, see Extracts from the Virginia Charters (July 1773), *PGM*, 1:173 n. 7; Robert Allen Rutland, *George Mason: Reluctant Statesman* (Baton Rouge, LA, 1961), 53. Mason owned about three hundred slaves upon his death in 1792 (editorial note, *DHRC*, 3:492 n. 3).
21. Lowndes in South Carolina House, Jan. 16, 1788, *DHRC*, 27:108 (quotation); Egerton, *Death or Liberty*, 151–2, 154–6; Berlin, *Generations of Captivity*, 127; Brown, "Problems of Slavery," 432; Hendrickson, *Peace Pact*, 234–5. For recent estimates of the number of slaves that escaped from South Carolina and Georgia during the war, see Brown, supra, 442–3 n. 2; Pybus, "Jefferson's Faulty Math," 261.
22. Pinckney, Aug. 22, *Farrand*, 2:371 ("justified"); Lowndes in South Carolina House, Jan. 16, 1788, *DHRC*, 27:108 ("on the principles"); see also Robinson, *Slavery in the Structure of American Politics*, 298; Robert M. Weir, "South Carolina: Slavery and the Structure of the Union," in Gillespie and Lienesch, eds., *Ratifying the Constitution*, 209–10; Beeman, *Plain, Honest Men*, 59, 311, 315, 324; Speech by Rep. James Jackson (May 13, 1789), in Kaminski, *A Necessary Evil?*, 206.
23. Madison to Robert Pleasants, Oct. 30, 1791, *PJM* (C.S.), 14:91 (quotations); Beeman, *Plain, Honest Men*, 67–8, 308–10; Van Cleve, *Slaveholders' Union*, 94.
24. Butler, July 13, *Farrand*, 1:605; Weir, "South Carolina," 203, 208–9; Paul Finkelman, "Slavery and the Constitutional Convention: Making a Covenant with Death," in Beeman Botein, and Carter, eds., *Beyond Confederation*, 224; Robertson, *The Constitution and America's Destiny*, 38; Van Cleve, *Slaveholders' Union*, 22–3, 104; Beeman, *Plain, Honest Men*, 310–1, 315.
25. Freehling, "Founding Fathers and Slavery," 83; Van Cleve, *Slaveholders' Union*, 60; Fehrenbacher, *Dred Scott*, 18–9; Brown, "The Problems of Slavery," 428.
26. Madison, June 6, *Farrand*, 1:135 ("the most oppressive"); Morris, Aug. 8, ibid., 2:221 ("nefarious").
27. Madison to Robert Walsh, Nov. 27, 1819, *Farrand*, 3:436 ("had scruples"); U.S. Constitution, Art. IV, § 2, cl. 3 ("person[s]"); John Dickinson, Notes for a Speech (July 8, 1787), *Farrand*, Supp.:158 ("be regarded as"); Luther Martin, Genuine Information VII, Baltimore *Maryland Gazette*, Jan. 18, 1788, *DHRC*, 15:412 ("anxiously sought"); see also Madison, Aug. 25, *Farrand*, 2:417; Letter from Massachusetts, Oct. 17, 24, 1787, *DHRC*, 3:378–9; James Iredell at North Carolina ratifying convention, July 29, 1788, *Elliot*, 4:176.
28. Seventh Lincoln-Douglas Debate, Alton, Illinois (Oct. 15, 1858), in *Lincoln: Speeches and Writings 1832–1858* (Don E. Fehrenbacher, ed., New York, 1989), 801–2; Fehrenbacher, *Dred Scott*, 27; Freehling, "Founding Fathers and Slavery," 83–4; but cf. Finkelman, "Slavery and the Constitutional Convention," 222; Robinson, *Slavery in the Structure of American Politics*, 3–4.
29. Weir, "South Carolina," 208–9; Banning, "Virginia," 267; Robertson, *The Constitution and America's Destiny*, 37–8; see also Charles Pinckney, Aug. 29, *Farrand*, 2:449.
30. Van Cleve, *Slaveholders' Union*, 125; see also Beeman, *Plain, Honest Men*, 214; Mark A. Graber, *Dred Scott and the Problem of Constitutional Evil* (New York, 2006), 96, 101.
31. Fehrenbacher, *Dred Scott*, 19, 599 n. 20; Van Cleve, *Slaveholders' Union*, 119–20.
32. Virginia Plan, resolution 2, May 29, *Farrand*, 1:20.
33. Madison, May 30, ibid., 35–6 (quotation); see also Beeman, *Plain, Honest Men*, 107–8.
34. Rutledge, July 5, *Farrand*, 1:534 ("[p]roperty was certainly"); Pinckney, July 10, ibid., 567 ("superior wealth" and "its due weight"); Butler (Yates's Notes), June 11, ibid., 204 ("money is strength" and "every state"); Mason, July 11, ibid., 581 ("slaves were valuable" and "they ought not"); see also Rutledge, June 11, ibid., 196; Butler, July 6, ibid., 542; July 9, ibid., 562; Abraham Baldwin, June 29, ibid., 470; Weir, "South Carolina," 203, 210–1; Einhorn, *American Taxation*, 163–4. For state constitutions that used wealth in their apportionment formulas, see, e.g., South Carolina Constitution of 1778, Art. XV; Massachusetts Constitution of 1780, Ch. 1, § 2; New York Constitution of 1777, §§ V,

VII, XVI. Mason partly contradicted himself in the debate over the foreign slave trade, in which he insisted that slaves were dangerous to society. See infra p. 284.

For the preceding foonote, see Lindert and Williamson, "American Incomes," 741.

35. King, July 6, *Farrand*, 1:541 ("property was"); July 9, ibid., 562 ("had always expected"); July 10, ibid., 566 ("to yield"); Morris, July 5, ibid., 533–4 ("the main object"); July 11, ibid., 581–2, 583; see also Gerry, July 6, ibid., 541; William Samuel Johnson, July 12, ibid., 593; King, ibid., 595–6; Van Cleve, *Slaveholders' Union*, 116–7, 127–8.

36. Pinckney, July 6, *Farrand*, 1:542 ("impracticable," "changeable," "the only just," and "to stand"); July 12, ibid., 596 ("the laborers"); see also Johnson, ibid., 593; Butler, July 11, ibid., 580.

37. Gerry, June 11, ibid., 201 ("blacks" and "the cattle"); Morris, July 11, ibid., 583 ("revolt"); Aug. 8, ibid., 2:222 ("Are they" and "[t]hen make"); motion of Butler, seconded by Charles Cotesworth Pinckney, that slaves count equally for apportionment purposes, July 11, ibid., 1:580; Charles Pinckney, July 12, ibid., 596 (same); see also Wilson, July 11, ibid., 587.

For the preceding footnote, see John Adams, Notes of Debates in the Continental Congress, in 1775 and 1776, *Works of John Adams*, 2:498 (quoting Thomas Lynch of South Carolina, July 30, 1776).

38. Paterson, July 9, *Farrand*, 1:561.

39. Morris, Aug. 8, ibid., 2:222 ("the inhabitant"); Paterson, July 9, ibid., 1:561 ("an indirect"); see also Morris, July 11, ibid., 588. Van Cleve regards this argument as pretextual (*Slaveholders' Union*, 122).

40. July 12, *Farrand*, 1:596 (eight-to-two vote); July 11, ibid., 581 (seven-to-three vote); Williamson, ibid. ("concur"); Mason, ibid. ("slaves," "ought not," and "regard them"); Madison, June 30, ibid., 486–7; July 9, ibid., 562; Wilson, June 11, ibid., 205.

41. On the 1776 debate, see Einhorn, *American Taxation*, 120–4; see also Hendrickson, *Peace Pact*, 139–40, 147, 226; editorial note, *DHRC*, 26:948 n. 9.

42. Proceedings of the Confederation Congress, Apr. 18, 1783, *JCC*, 24:259–60 (emphasis added). Some New Englanders had opposed from the start the Articles' scheme for apportioning states' contributions to the federal government based on land values because it failed to take account of "that one third part of the wealth of the southern states which consists in negroes" (Nathaniel Folsom to Meshech Weare, Nov. 21, 1777, *LDC*, 8:299; see also Einhorn, *American Taxation*, 128–9).

43. Ibid., 138–45, 164, 172 (quotations at p. 143); Wilson, June 11, *Farrand*, 1:205; King, July 9, ibid., 562; editorial note, *DHRC*, 26:931 n. 1; editorial note, *DHRC*, 1:148–9; see also Madison to Randolph, Apr. 8, 1783, *PJM* (C.S.), 8:440; North Carolina delegates to Governor Alexander Martin, Mar. 24, 1783, *LDC*, 20:90–1; Charles Cotesworth Pinckey in South Carolina House, Jan. 17, 1788, *DHRC*, 27:116–24; Charles Pinckney in the House, Feb. 14, 1820, *Annals of Congress* (Joseph Gales, ed., Washington, DC, 1855), 36:1313; Rufus King speech before the US Senate (Mar. 1819), *Farrand*, 3:428–30; Kaminski, ed., *A Necessary Evil?*, 21–2; Van Cleve, *Slaveholders' Union*, 105–6; Robertson, *The Constitution and America's Destiny*, 56, 137 n. 14; Beeman, *Plain, Honest Men*, 154; Bilder, *Madison's Hand*, 30.

For the preceding footnote, see Gorham, July 11, *Farrand*, 1:580; Williamson, ibid., 581.

44. June 11, *Farrand*, 1:201 (the vote); see also Beeman, *Plain, Honest Men*, 155, 207–10; Banning, *Sacred Fire*, 148.

45. Supra pp. 195–7; Gerry, July 5, *Farrand*, 1:526; Morris, July 6, ibid., 540; King, ibid., 541; Butler, ibid., 541–2; ibid., 542 (seven-to-three vote, with one delegation divided, to appoint a committee to allocate representatives in the first House).

For the preceding footnote, see North Carolina delegates to Governor Richard Caswell, Sept. 18, 1787, *DHRC*, 13:216; Richard Dobbs Spaight at the North Carolina ratifying convention, July 24, 1788, *Elliot*, 4:31–2.

46. Morris, July 9, *Farrand*, 1:560 (quotations); committee report, ibid., 559; Sherman, ibid.; Gorham, ibid., 559–60; Martin, ibid., 560.

47. Ibid., 562 (nine-to-two vote to appoint a grand committee); King report for the committee, July 10, ibid., 566; Williamson, ibid., 567 ("southern interest"); Pinckney, ibid. ("form[ing] so considerable"); Rutledge motion, seconded by Charles Cotesworth

Pinckney, to reduce New Hampshire's representation from three to two, ibid., 566; ibid., 568 (motions—all of which fail—to reduce representation of New Hampshire and to increase that of North Carolina, South Carolina, and Georgia).

48. July 10, ibid., 570 (the vote); see also Beeman, *Plain, Honest Men*, 207–8; Banning, *Sacred Fire*, 173–4.

49. Mason, July 11, *Farrand*, 1:578 ("According to," "those who have," and "complain"); Madison, ibid., 584 ("implicit confidence" and "all men"); see also Randolph, ibid., 579; Mason, ibid., 586; Charles Cotesworth Pinckney, July 12, ibid., 592; Randolph, July 9, ibid., 561.

50. Sherman, July 11, ibid., 578 ("against shackling"); Morris, July 10, ibid., 571 ("very urgent"); July 12, ibid., 596 (eight-to-two vote to require a census every ten years, after a seven-to-three vote to reject a motion to require a census only every twenty years; also voting five-to-four, with one delegation divided, to require the first census within six years, instead of two, of the first meeting of Congress); Aug. 20, ibid., 2:350 (nine-to-two vote to require the first census to be held within three years, instead of six, of Congress's initial meeting); see also Morris, July 11, ibid., 1:581; Wilson, ibid., 583; Brown, *Redeeming the Republic*, 196.

51. Morris delivering the committee report, July 9, *Farrand*, 1:559 ("wealth"); Randolph motion, July 10, ibid., 570–1.

52. Mason, July 11, ibid., 582 ("requiring" and "a pretext"); ibid., 578 ("precise"); Williamson motion, ibid., 579.

53. Randolph, ibid. ("mere conjecture"); July 12, ibid., 594; Charles Cotesworth Pinckney, ibid., 593–4; Paterson, July 9, ibid., 561; Gorham, July 11, ibid., 583.

54. King, July 10, ibid., 566 ("very desirous" and "think it prudent"); Morris, ibid., 567; July 11, ibid., 588 (six-to-four vote against the three-fifths compromise); Beeman, *Plain, Honest Men*, 208–11.

55. Davie, July 12, *Farrand*, 1:593.

56. Morris, ibid. ("verily believed"); July 13, ibid., 604–5 (other quotations).

57. Butler, ibid., 605 ("The security"); Pinckney, July 12, ibid., 596; Butler, ibid., 592; ibid., 596 (the vote).

58. King, July 9, ibid., 562; Morris, July 12, ibid., 591–2; supra pp. 269–70.

59. Madison, July 24, ibid., 2:106 n. * ("to lessen"); Butler and Mason, July 12, ibid., 1:592 ("justice"); statements by Morris, Charles Cotesworth Pinckney, Wilson, and Morris again, ibid.; ibid., 592–3 (provision stating that direct taxation ought to be "proportioned to representation" agreed to without dissent); Ellsworth amendment, seconded by Butler, ibid., 594 ("the rule" and "until"); see also Madison, July 13, ibid., 602; Wilson, July 11, ibid., 587; Einhorn, *American Taxation*, 162–5; Beeman, *Plain, Honest Men*, 211–2.

   For the first of the two preceding footnotes, see King, Aug. 20, *Farrand*, 2:350; Hylton v. United States, 3 U.S. (3 Dall.) 171, 181 (1796); Marshall at Virginia ratifying convention, June 10, 1788, *DHRC*, 9:1127; Einhorn, supra, 158–60, 168, 182–3.

   For the second of the two preceding footnotes, see Morris, July 24, *Farrand*, 2:106; Committee of Detail report, Art. VII, § 3, Aug. 6, ibid., 182–3.

60. Wilson, July 12, *Farrand*, 1:595 ("less umbrage" and "indirectly"); Morris, Sept. 13, ibid., 2:607 ("to exclude"); U.S. Constitution, Art. I, § 2, cl. 3.

61. Morris, Aug. 8, *Farrand*, 2:223 (quotation); see also Beeman, *Plain, Honest Men*, 211; Robinson, *Slavery in the Structure of American Politics*, 238; Einhorn, *American Taxation*, 165–6, 168; Van Cleve, *Slaveholders' Union*, 116.

   For the preceding footnote, see Speech of Rep. Abraham Baldwin, Feb. 12, 1790, *Annals of Congress*, 1:1243; infra p. 301.

62. July 13, *Farrand*, 1:606 (unanimous vote, with one delegation divided); Sherman, Aug. 8, ibid., 2:220–1 (quotation).

63. Van Cleve, *Slaveholders' Union*, 139–40 ("Negro president" at p. 140) (quoting Massachusetts's Federalist senator Timothy Pickering); Fehrenbacher, *Dred Scott*, 20, 91; William W. Freehling, *The Road to Disunion*, vol. 1, *Secessionists at Bay, 1776–1854* (New York, 1990), 147. There was some opposition to the Three-Fifths Clause at northern state ratifying conventions, but not a great deal. See infra pp. 299–300.

64. King to Timothy Pickering, Nov. 4, 1803, *Farrand*, 3:400 (quotations); Robinson, *Slavery in the Structure of American Politics*, 270–1, 278–9; Van Cleve, *Slaveholders' Union*, 216–7; David E. Kyvig, *Explicit and Authentic Acts: Amending the U.S. Constitution, 1776–1995* (Lawrence, KS, 1996), 119–20.

65. Rufus King, Speech Before the U.S. Senate (Mar. 1819), *Farrand*, 3:420–30; see also William M. Wiecek, "The Witch at the Christening: Slavery and the Constitution's Origins," in Levy and Mahoney, eds., *The Framing and Ratification of the Constitution*, 180; Van Cleve, *Slaveholders' Union*, 249–50; 1 Freehling, *Road to Disunion*, 148; Graber, *Dred Scott*, 120.

66. Pinckney speech in the House, Feb. 14, 1820, *Annals of Congress*, 36:1311.

67. Madison to Jefferson, Oct. 24, 1787, *PJM* (C.S.), 10:214.

68. Notes of Proceedings in the Continental Congress (June 7 to Aug. 1, 1776), *PTJ* (M.S.), 1:317–8 (quotations); Proceedings of the Continential Congress, Oct. 20, 1774, *JCC*, 1:77; Apr. 6, 1776, ibid., 4:258; Oct. 8, 1783, ibid., 25:660 n. 1; Jan. 8, 1784, ibid., 26:13–4; Weir, "South Carolina," 206–7; Egerton, *Death or Liberty*, 57; Kaminski, ed., *A Necessary Evil?*, 2, 7, 26–7; James A. McMillin, *The Final Victims: Foreign Slave Trade to North America, 1783–1810* (Columbia, SC, 2004), 5–6; Van Cleve, *Slaveholders' Union*, 104; editorial note, *DHRC*, 26:933 n. 27; supra p. 263. For background to Great Britain's vetoes of colonial efforts to suppress the foreign slave trade, see Holton, *Forced Founders*, 66–73. For the impact of nonimportation on the foreign slave trade in Virginia in 1774, see ibid., 105.

69. Morris, Aug. 8, *Farrand*, 2:221–2 (quotation); see also Dickinson, Aug. 22, ibid., 372; Weir, "South Carolina," 228.

70. McHenry's Notes, Aug. 22, *Farrand*, 2:378; infra p. 284; Weir, "South Carolina," 208; Robinson, *Slavery in the Structure of American Politics*, 233; Van Cleve, *Slaveholders' Union*, 146–7; Brown, "Problems of Slavery," 432, 437–8; editorial note, *DHRC*, 27:114 n. 17. On South Carolina's 1787 law closing the slave trade, see Patrick S. Brady, "The Slave Trade and Sectionalism in South Carolina, 1787–1808," *Journal of Southern History* (Nov. 1972), 38:601–6.

    For the preceding footnote, see editorial note, *DHRC*, 26:934 n. 33; see also Mason, Aug. 22, *Farrand*, 2:370; Brady, supra, 602 n. 2.

71. Pinckney in South Carolina House, Jan. 17, 1788, *DHRC*, 27:123 (quotation); Notes of Proceedings in the Continental Congress (June 7 to Aug. 1, 1776), *PTJ* (M.S.), 1:314; Weir, "South Carolina," 202, 208; Brown, "Problems of Slavery," 429; Van Cleve, *Slaveholders' Union*, 110; Kaminski, ed., *A Necessary Evil?*, 2; McMillin, *Final Victims*, 7–8; see also James Iredell at North Carolina ratifying convention, July 26, 1788, *Elliot*, 4:101; McHenry's Notes, Aug. 22, *Farrand*, 2:378; Madison to Jefferson, Oct. 3, 1785, *PJM* (C.S.), 8:375.

72. Pinckney, Aug. 22, *Farrand*, 2:371–2.

73. Einhorn, *American Taxation*, 112. For an explanation of why South Carolinians opposed export taxes even at the state level, see Edward Rutledge to Samuel Myers, Nov. 8, 1787, *DHRC*, 27:36–7.

74. Butler, Aug. 21, *Farrand*, 2:360 ("strenuously opposed"); Mason, Aug. 16, ibid., 305–6 ("security"); Aug. 21, ibid., 362–3 ("a majority" and "ground"); Williamson, ibid., 360 ("would never agree" and "it would destroy"); see also Charles Cotesworth Pinckney, July 12, ibid., 1:592; Rutledge, Aug. 16, ibid., 2:306; Williamson, ibid., 307; Ellsworth, Aug. 21, ibid., 359–60; Aug. 21, ibid., 363 (six-to-five vote against two-thirds supermajority requirement for export taxes); Beeman, *Plain, Honest Men*, 318.

75. Wilson, Aug. 21, *Farrand*, 2:362 ("half the regulation" and "might be more"); Morris, Aug. 16, ibid., 306 ("radically objectionable" and "easy and proper"); ibid., 307 ("push"); Aug. 21, ibid., 360 ("of critical importance"); see also Hamilton, June 18, ibid., 1:286; John Langdon, Aug. 21, ibid., 2:359; Dickinson, ibid., 361; Thomas FitzSimons, ibid., 362; Rakove, *Original Meanings*, 86–7.

76. Madison, Aug. 21, *Farrand*, 2:361 ("national and permanent"); Aug. 16, ibid., 306–7 ("most in danger" and "complain"); see also Banning, *Sacred Fire*, 178–9.

77. Supra pp. 35–8.

78. Charles Cotesworth Pinckney, July 10, *Farrand*, 1:567 ("considerable" and "the regulation"); Mason, July 21, ibid., 2:83 ("precautions"); Charles Pinckney, Aug. 29, ibid., 449 ("a bare majority" and "would be a source"); see also Banning, "Virginia," 267.

79. Gorham, Aug. 22, *Farrand*, 2:374 ("motive" and "were not afraid"); Aug. 29, ibid., 453 ("so fettered" and "had the most"); Clymer, ibid., 450 ("[t]he northern"); see also Sherman, ibid.; infra pp. 336–7.

80. Madison, Aug. 29, *Farrand*, 2:451–2 (quotations); see also Banning, "Virginia," 275–6; Hendrickson, *Peace Pact*, 235–6.

    For the preceding footnote, see Madison to William Bradford, June 19, 1775, *PJM* (C.S.), 1:153.

81. Gerry, July 23, *Farrand*, 2:95; Pinckney, ibid. (quotation). The committee was appointed on July 24 (ibid., 106).

82. Committee of Detail report, Art. IV, § 3 and Art. VII, §§ 3–6, Aug. 6, *Farrand*, 2:179, 182–3; see also Van Cleve, *Slaveholders' Union*, 130–2; Waldstreicher, *Slavery's Constitution*, 90–2; Robinson, *Slavery in the Structure of American Politics*, 218–20; Robertson, *The Constitution and America's Destiny*, 179; Hendrickson, *Peace Pact*, 232; Banning, "Virginia," 270; Finkelman, "Slavery and the Constitutional Convention," 211.

83. King, Aug. 8, *Farrand*, 2:220.

84. Morris, ibid., 221–2.

85. Martin, Aug. 21, ibid., 364.

86. Mason, ibid., 370; see also Beeman, *Plain, Honest Men*, 320.

87. Rutledge, Aug. 21, *Farrand*, 2:364 (all quotations except "If the convention"); Aug. 22, ibid., 373 ("If the convention").

88. Charles Cotesworth Pinckney, ibid., 371–2 ("gain," "[h]er slaves," "to require," and "an exclusion"); Charles Pinckney, Aug. 21, ibid., 364–5 ("never receive" and "[i]f the states"); see also Aug. 22, ibid., 371. During the ratifying contest, Oliver Ellsworth, writing as "A Landholder," reiterated this charge of hypocrisy against Mason, who owned more than three hundred slaves but criticized the Constitution for not immediately ending the foreign slave trade ("A Landholder" VI, *Connecticut Courant*, Dec. 10, 1787, *DHRC*, 3:489–90).

89. Williamson, Aug. 22, *Farrand*, 2:373 ("the southern" and "it was wrong"); Baldwin, ibid., 372 (other quotations).

90. King, ibid., 373 ("[i]f two" and "affirm"); Wilson, ibid., 372 ("they would"); Dickinson, ibid., 372–3 ("could not" and "especially").

91. Madison to Jefferson, Oct. 24, 1787, *PJM* (C.S.), 10:214 (quotation); see also Madison at Virginia convention, June 17, 1788, *DHRC*, 10:1338–9. Finkelman argues that the Deep South delegates were bluffing and their bluff should have been called ("Slavery and the Constitutional Convention," 221). Other scholars take the walkout threats more seriously (Weir, "South Carolina," 212–3; Beeman, *Plain, Honest Men*, 332; Hendrickson, *Peace Pact*, 238).

92. Ellsworth, Aug. 21, *Farrand*, 2:364 ("[t]he morality"); Aug. 22, ibid., 371 ("in the sickly," "as population," "[s]lavery").

93. Sherman, ibid., 374 ("it was better"); ibid., 369–70 ("as the states" and "the abolition").

94. Morris, ibid., 374 ("[t]hese things"); Randolph, ibid. ("some middle" and "lost to"); ibid. (seven-to-three vote, with one delegation divided, assigning to a committee the provisions involving the foreign slave trade and the apportionment of capitation taxes); ibid., 375 (nine-to-two vote for also committing the provision requiring supermajority votes in Congress for the enactment of navigation laws); ibid. (appointment of the committee).

95. Butler, ibid., 374 (resisting sending the ban on export taxes to committee); Read, ibid. (insisting that the ban on export taxes be sent to committee); Sherman, ibid. (insisting that the provision had already been agreed to and thus could not be sent to committee); Aug. 21, ibid., 363 (Clymer motion defeated by a vote of seven to three); ibid. (Madison motion defeated by a vote of six to five); ibid., 363–4 (flat ban on export taxes approved by a vote of seven to four); see also Robinson, *Slavery in the Structure of American Politics*, 221–2; Beeman, *Plain, Honest Men*, 318–9.

96. Governor William Livingston, delivering the report of the Committee of Eleven, Aug. 24, *Farrand*, 2:400; Luther Martin, Genuine Information VII, Baltimore *Maryland Gazette*, Jan. 18, 1788, *DHRC*, 15:413 (quotation).

97. Governor William Livingston, delivering the report of the Committee of Eleven, Aug. 24, *Farrand*, 2:400 ("at a rate"); Aug. 25, ibid., 417 (substituting the ten-dollar figure without dissent); Madison speech in the House, May 13, 1789, *Annals of Congress*, 1:353 ("an opportunity").

98. Statements by Sherman, King, Langdon, Charles Cotesworth Pinckney, Mason, and Gorham, Aug. 25, *Farrand*, 2:416; ibid., 417 (approving the provision by an unrecorded vote).

99. Pinckney motion, ibid., 415; Madison, ibid. ("[t]wenty years"); ibid. (the vote); Madison to Robert Walsh, Nov. 27, 1819, *PJM* (Retirement Series) [hereinafter, "*PJM* (R.S.)"], 1:553 ("against which"); Van Cleve, *Slaveholders' Union*, 147, 150; Waldstreicher, *Slavery's Constitution*, 97–8.

    For the first of the two preceding footnotes, see Einhorn, *American Taxation*, 152–3; Kaminski, ed., *A Necessary Evil?*, 201–10; Robinson, *Slavery in the Structure of American Politics*, 299–301.

    For the second of the two preceding footnotes, see Aug. 25, *Farrand*, 2:415–6.

100. Madison to Robert Walsh, Nov. 27, 1819, *PJM* (R.S.), 1:553 ("earnestness"); Rutledge, Sept. 10, *Farrand*, 2:559 ("he never could").

101. Pinckney, Aug. 29, ibid., 449; Williamson, ibid., 450–1 (quotations).

102. Morris, ibid., 450; Wilson, ibid., 451 (quotation); see also Clymer, ibid., 450; Sherman, ibid.; Gorham, ibid., 453.

103. Pinckney, ibid., 449–50 ("it was," "[C]onsidering," "prejudices," and "though prejudiced"); Butler, ibid., 451 ("to be" and "desirous"); ibid., 449 n. * ("An understanding"); ibid. (seven-to-four vote not to take up Charles Pinckney's motion to reinstate the supermajority requirement for navigation acts, followed by agreement, without dissent, to this aspect of the committee's report); see also Madison to Robert Walsh, Nov. 27, 1819, *PJM* (R.S.), 1:553; Mason's Account of Certain Proceedings in Convention, Sept. 30, 1792, *Farrand*, 3:367.

104. Mason, Aug. 29, ibid., 2:451 ("bound hand and foot"); Randolph, ibid., 452 ("there were features" and "would complete"); Mason, Sept. 15, ibid., 631 ("few rich merchants"); see also "A Landholder" VI (Ellsworth), *Connecticut Courant*, Dec. 10, 1787, *DHRC*, 3:488; Beeman, *Plain, Honest Men*, 329; Waldstreicher, *Slavery's Constitution*, 100; Banning, "Virginia," 270–1.

105. Freehling, "Founding Fathers and Slavery," 88–90; McMillin, *Final Victims*, 48; Robinson, *Slavery in the Structure of American Politics*, 318–9; Van Cleve, *Slaveholders' Union*, 150 tbl. 4.1. Van Cleve is skeptical as to how many delegates in Philadelphia would have genuinely believed that barring the foreign slave trade would lead to the end of slavery in the United States (ibid., 147–9). On the reopening of the foreign slave trade in South Carolina from 1803 to 1807, see Brady, "The Slave Trade," 602, 612–6.

106. Freehling, "Founding Fathers and Slavery," 88–90, 92; 1 Freehling, *Road to Disunion*, 136–7.

107. Motion by Butler and Pinckney, Aug. 28, *Farrand*, 2:443; see also Beeman, *Plain, Honest Men*, 329–30. Van Cleve argues that provisions in the Articles were broad enough to bear the construction that states were, in fact, already under an obligation to capture and return slaves escaping from other states (*Slaveholders' Union*, 53–6).

108. Steven Lubet, *Fugitive Justice: Runaways, Rescuers, and Slavery on Trial* (Cambridge, MA, 2010), 17–9; Van Cleve, *Slaveholders' Union*, 31–7, 171; see also Egerton, *Death or Liberty*, 51–2.

109. Northwest Ordinance of 1787, Art. VI, July 13, 1787, *JCC*, 32:343 ("lawfully"); Van Cleve, *Slaveholders' Union*, 168–70; Edward Coles, "History of the Ordinance of 1787," *Farrand*, Supp.:321 ("conferences").

110. Wilson, Aug. 28, *Farrand*, 2:443 ("oblige"); Sherman, ibid. ("saw no more"); Butler, ibid.

111. Aug. 29, ibid., 453–4 (fugitive slave provision agreed to without dissent); Van Cleve, *Slaveholders' Union*, 61–2, 91–3, 143, 168; Weir, "South Carolina," 212–3. On the final wording of the Fugitive Slave Clause, see Sept. 15, *Farrand*, 2:628.

112. Joseph Story, *Commentaries on the Constitution of the United States* (Boston, 1833), 2:677 ("was felt"); Prigg v. Pennsylvania, 41 U.S. 539, 611 (1842) ("[I]t cannot be doubted"). For support for Story's perspective that the southern states might not have agreed to the Constitution without the Fugitive Slave Clause, see Van Cleve, *Slaveholders' Union*, 172.

113. Story, *Commentaries*, 2:677 ("many sacrifices" and "forever repress"); see also Paul Finkelman, "Story Telling on the Supreme Court: *Prigg v. Pennsylvania* and Justice Joseph Story's Judicial Nationalism," *Supreme Court Review* (1994), 265–6; Fehrenbacher, *Dred Scott*, 42.

114. Lubet, *Fugitive Justice*, 6–7, 47–9, 86–9, 134–56, 160–75, 208–16; H. Robert Baker, *The Rescue of Joshua Glover: A Fugitive Slave, the Constitution, and the Coming of the Civil War* (Athens, OH, 2006), 10, 20–3, 53–5; Potter, *Impending Crisis*, 133–5. On southern grievances at the time of secession regarding northern failures to enforce the fugitive slave law, see William W. Freehling and Craig M. Simpson, *Secession Debated: Georgia's Showdown in 1860* (New York, 1992), 7–8, 41–3.

115. Finkelman, "Slavery and the Constitutional Convention," 191; supra pp. 279–80.

116. U.S. Constitution, Art. IV, § 4; supra pp. 163–4, 278, 284; see also Aug. 30, *Farrand*, 2:467 (rejecting by a vote of six to five, with all southern states in the minority, a motion to replace "domestic violence" in Article IV, § 4, with "insurrections"); Finkelman, "Slavery and the Constitutional Convention," 222; Holton, *Unruly Americans*, 222; but cf. Robinson, *Slavery in the Structure of American Politics*, 218 n. *.

117. Sherman, Sept. 15, *Farrand*, 2:630 (quotation); ibid. (eight-to-three vote rejecting Sherman's motion); see also Sherman, July 17, ibid., 25–6; Finkelman, "Slavery and the Constitutional Convention," 192; Robinson, *Slavery in the Structure of American Politics*, 232; Graber, *Dred Scott*, 104.

118. U.S. Constitution, Art. IV, § 3, cl. 2 (quotation). On the issue of slavery in the territories as the proximate cause of the Civil War, see, e.g., James McPherson, *Battle Cry of Freedom: The Civil War Era* (New York, 1988), 8, 41, 51–77, 145–69, 195, 214–5; Fehrenbacher, *Dred Scott*, chs. 6, 19–21; Potter, *Impending Crisis*, passim; 1 Freehling, *Road to Disunion*, parts 6–7.

119. Fehrenbacher, *Dred Scott*, 76–9; Van Cleve, *Slaveholders' Union*, 104–5, 153; Robinson, *Slavery in the Structure of American Politics*, 379–80, 385–6; Lynd, "Compromise of 1787," 231–2.

120. Grayson to Monroe, May 29, 1787, *Farrand*, 3:30 (quotation); Rhode Island delegates to Governor John Collins, Apr. 24, 1787, *LDC*, 24:256; Madison to Pendleton, May 27, 1787, *PJM* (C.S.), 10:11; see also Richard Henry Lee to John Adams, Sept. 3, 1787, *LDC*, 24:423.

121. William Blount to Governor Richard Caswell, July 10, 1787, *Farrand*, 3:57 (quotation); see also Beeman, *Plain, Honest Men*, 216; Lynd, "Compromise of 1787," 227–8, 245; Van Cleve, *Slaveholders' Union*, 154.

122. Proceedings of the Confederation Congress, July 13, 1787, *JCC*, 32:343; Grayson to Monroe, Aug. 8, 1787, *LDC*, 24:393 (quotation); Nathan Dane to Rufus King, July 16, 1787, ibid., 358; Edward Coles, "History of the Ordinance of 1787," *Farrand*, Supp.:321; Lynd, "Compromise of 1787," 226, 232; Robinson, *Slavery in the Structure of American Politics*, 381–2, 385; Waldstreicher, *Slavery's Constitution*, 87–8; Fehrenbacher, *Dred Scott*, 79–81; Beeman, *Plain, Honest Men*, 217. Van Cleve argues instead that the quid pro quo for southern support of the antislavery provision in the Northwest Ordinance was northern abandonment of Secretary for Foreign Affairs John Jay's effort to barter American navigation rights on the Mississippi River for a commercial treaty with Spain (*Slaveholders' Union*, 158–66).

123. Articles of Confederation, Art. 10, *DHRC*, 1:93 ("colon[ies]"); U.S. Constitution, Art. IV, § 3, cl. 2 ("make all"); *The Federalist No. 38* (Madison), at 239; Van Cleve, *Slaveholders' Union*, 156–7; Fehrenbacher, *Dred Scott*, 83–4.

124. Fehrenbacher, *Dred Scott*, 102–13; Robinson, *Slavery in the Structure of American Politics*, 402–23; Dred Scott v. Sandford, 60 U.S. 393 (1857); see also Madison to Monroe, Feb. 23, 1820, *PJM* (R.S.), 2:16–7.

   For the preceding footnote, see Fehrenbacher, *Dred Scott*, 368–79; Robert R. Russel, "Constitutional Doctrines with Regard to Slavery in Territories," *Journal of Southern History* (Nov. 1966), 32:470–2.

125. Freehling, "Founding Fathers and Slavery," 87; Freehling, *Road to Disunion*, 1:138–41.

126. Waldstreicher, *Slavery's Constitution*, 108; Einhorn, *American Taxation*, 175–8; Graber, *Dred Scott*, 109.

127. Henry at Virginia convention, June 24, 1788, *DHRC*, 10:1477–8 ("prudence forbids" and "[t]he majority"); June 17, ibid., 1341 ("it was omitted" and "omission"); Mason, June 11, ibid., 9:1161 ("prevent the northern"); June 17, ibid., 10:1343 ("might totally"); see also Lachlan McIntosh to John Wereat, Dec. 17, 1787, *DHRC*, 3:260–1; Maier, *Ratification*, 283–4, 294–5; Waldstreicher, *Slavery's Constitution*, 143–5; Banning, "Virginia," 280.

128. Mason at Virginia convention, June 17, 1788, *DHRC*, 10:1338 ("diabolical"); Lowndes in South Carolina House, Jan. 16, 1788, *DHRC*, 27:108 ("pay for this" and "Negroes were"); see also Mason at Virginia convention, June 11, 1788, *DHRC*, 9:1161.

129. Abraham Lincoln, Reply to Douglas (Oct. 15, 1858), in *Abraham Lincoln: Speeches and Writings, 1832–1858*, at 802 ("expected"); Dawes at Massachusetts convention, Jan. 17, 1788, *DHRC*, 6:1245 ("we may say"); "Mark Antony," Boston *Independent Chronicle*, Jan. 10, 1788, *DHRC*, 5:677 ("went as far"); see also Thomas McKean at Pennsylvania convention, Nov. 28, 1787, *DHRC*, 2:417; James Wilson, Dec. 3, ibid., 463; Robinson, *Structure of Slavery in American Politics*, 243; Fehrenbacher, *Dred Scott*, 26–7; Freehling, "Founding Fathers and Slavery," 82–4, 87–91; Waldstreicher, *Slavery's Constitution*, 132.

130. Massachusetts convention, Jan. 25, 1788, *DHRC*, 6:1354 ("the step taken") (referring to "gentlemen" making this argument); Wilson at Pennsylvania convention, Dec. 3, 1787, *DHRC*, 2:463 ("the foundation," "as long as," "operate," and "slaves will never"); see also Dec. 4, 1787, ibid., 499; Isaac Backus at Massachusetts convention, Feb. 4, 1788, *DHRC*, 6:1422–3; "Philanthrop," Northampton, Mass. *Hampshire Gazette*, Apr. 23, 1788, *DHRC*, 4:1745; Benjamin Rush to Jeremy Belknap, Feb. 28, 1788, *DHRC*, 16:250–1; "An American Citizen IV: On the Federal Government" (Tench Coxe), Oct. 21, 1788, *DHRC*, 13:432; *The Federalist No. 42* (Madison), at 266–7; Kaminski, ed., *A Necessary Evil?*, 68–9, 112, 115–7; but see Van Cleve, *Slaveholders' Union*, 137–8.

131. Hopkins to Levi Hart, Jan. 29, 1788, *DHRC*, 14:528 ("How does it appear") (emphasis in original); James Neal at Massachusetts convention, Jan. 25, 1788, *DHRC*, 6:1354 ("makes merchandise"); unidentified speaker, ibid. ("there was not even"); Paul Finkelman, *Slavery and the Founders: Race and Liberty in the Age of Jefferson* (New York, 2nd ed., 2001), 3 ("covenant with death" and "agreement with hell"); see also Neal at Massachusetts convention, Jan. 31, 1788, *DHRC*, 6:1377; Waldstreicher, *Slavery's Constitution*, 115–6; Maier, *Ratification*, 188, 191, 195; Yarbrough, "New Hampshire," 248.

132. Brown to James Pemberton, Oct. 17, 1787, in Kaminski, ed., *A Necessary Evil?*, 70 ("was designed"); "Philadelphiensis" II (Workman), Philadelphia *Freeman's Journal*, Nov. 28, 1787, *DHRC*, 14:253 ("prompted"); see also Edmund Prior to Moses Brown, Dec. 1, 1787, *DHRC*, 19:340; Moses Brown to James Thornton, Sr., Nov. 13, 1787, *DHRC*, 24:54.

133. Smith at New York convention, June 20, 1788, *DHRC*, 22:1715 ("every free agent," "slaves have," "certain privileges," and "those people"); "The Republican Federalist" V, *Massachusetts Centinel*, Jan. 19, 1788, *DHRC*, 5:750 ("the beasts"); see also "Brutus" III (probably Melancton Smith), *New York Journal*, Nov. 15, 1787, *DHRC*, 19:254; Albany Anti-Federal Committee Circular, Apr. 10, 1788, *DHRC*, 21:1380; William Symmes, Jr., to Peter Osgood, Jr., Nov. 15, 1787, *DHRC*, 4:236–7; Silas Lee to George Thatcher, Jan. 23, 1788, *DHRC*, 5:781; Van Cleve, *Slaveholders' Union*, 135–6, 173.

134. Gale at Killingworth, Conn., Town Meeting, Nov. 12, 1787, *DHRC*, 3:425 ("sly, cunning," and "the rights"); Atherton at New Hampshire convention, undated, *Elliot*, 2:203–4 ("partakers," "lend[ing] the aid," and "the most barbarous"); Consider Arms, Malachi Maynard, and Samuel Field, Dissent to the Massachusetts Convention, Northampton, Mass., *Hampshire Gazette*, Apr. 9, 16, 1788, *DHRC*, 7:1738 ("monstrous"

and "an engine") [hereinafter, "Arms, Maynard, and Field, Dissent"]; A Letter from a Gentleman in a Neighboring State to a Gentleman in this City, *Connecticut Journal*, Oct. 17, 24, 1787, in Herbert Storing, ed., *The Complete Anti-Federalist* (Chicago, 1981), 4:12; "Adelos," Northampton, Mass., *Hampshire Gazette*, Feb. 6, 1788, *DHRC*, 5:872–3; see also Thomas Lusk at Massachusetts convention, Feb. 4, 1788, *DHRC*, 6:1421; Samuel Hopkins to Moses Brown, Oct. 22, 1787, *DHRC*, 24:37–8; Proceedings of Rhode Island ratifying convention, *Newport Herald*, Mar. 11, 1790, *DHRC*, 26:935; Proposed amendment of Rhode Island ratifying convention, Mar. 6, 1790, ibid., 981; Waldstreicher, *Slavery's Constitution*, 122; Van Cleve, *Slaveholders' Union*, 175–6.

135. Arms, Maynard, and Field, Dissent, *DHRC*, 7:1739 ("lost no property" and "a right"); "Phileleutheros," Northampton, Mass., *Hampshire Gazette*, May 21, 1788, *DHRC*, 4:1748 ("partakers"). For the view that the threats of disunion by the Deep South delegations were credible, see Hendrickson, *Peace Pact*, 238.

136. Pinckney in South Carolina House, Jan. 17, 1788, *DHRC*, 27:124 (quotation); Madison at Virginia convention, June 17, 1788, *DHRC*, 10:1339; see also Randolph, June 24, ibid., 1483–4; North Carolina delegates to Governor Richard Caswell, Sept. 18, 1787, *DHRC*, 13:216; Finkelman, *Prigg v. Pennsylvania*, 262–3.

137. Pinckney in South Carolina House, Jan. 17, 1788, *DHRC*, 27:124 (quotation); Iredell at North Carolina convention, July 26, 1788, *Elliot*, 4:102; Charles Pinckney in the House of Representatives, Feb. 25, 1820, *Congressional Globe* (House), 1316; see also Madison at Virginia convention, June 17, 1788, *DHRC*, 10:1339; June 24, ibid., 1503; Weir, "South Carolina," 227–8; but see Robinson, *Slavery in the Structure of American Politics*, 245–6.
    For the preceding footnote, see infra p. 322.

138. Pinckney in South Carolina House, Jan. 17, 1788, *DHRC*, 27:121 ("allowed us"); Madison at Virginia convention, June 12, 1788, *DHRC*, 10:1204 ("an insuperable bar"); see also June 17, ibid., 1343; George Nicholas, ibid., 1342; Edward Rutledge in South Carolina House, Jan. 16, 1788, *DHRC*, 27:112; William Davie at North Carolina convention, July 24, 1788, *Elliot*, 4:30–1.

139. Pinckney in South Carolina House, Jan. 17, 1788, *DHRC*, 27:123 ("the religious" and "a dangerous"); "Civis: To the Citizens of South Carolina" (David Ramsay), Charleston *Columbian Herald*, Feb. 4, 1788, *DHRC*, 16:25 ("bound to protect" and "we ought not") [hereinafter, " 'Civis' "].

140. Pinckney in South Carolina House, Jan. 17, 1788, *DHRC*, 27:123–4; Barnwell, ibid., 133 (quotations); see also "Civis," *DHRC*, 16:25; Van Cleve, *Slaveholders' Union*, 151–2, 178.

141. Pinckney in South Carolina House, Jan. 17, 1788, *DHRC*, 27:124.

142. Banning, "Virginia," 280; Robinson, *Structure of Slavery in American Politics*, 238–9; Maier, *Ratification*, 296; infra pp. 309, 456–7, 469.

143. Randolph at Virginia convention, June 24, 1788, *DHRC*, 10:1483; Weir, "South Carolina," 217, 221; Robinson, *Slavery in the Structure of American Politics*, 241, 243–4; Waldstreicher, *Slavery's Constitution*, 114–5; Brown, "Problems of Slavery," 432; see also David Ramsay to John Eliot, Jan. 19, 1788, *DHRC*, 27:206.

144. Madison at Virginia convention, June 17, 1788, *DHRC*, 10:1339 ("dreadful," "[g]reat," and "a dismemberment"); McKean at Pennsylvania convention, Dec. 10, 1787, *DHRC*, 2:539–40 ("well acquainted"); see also Iredell at North Carolina convention, July 26, 1788, *Elliot*, 4:100; Banning, *Sacred Fire*, 459–60 n. 48; Van Cleve, *Slaveholders' Union*, 177, 182–3; Weir, "South Carolina," 226; Brown, *Redeeming the Republic*, 197.

145. Smith at New York convention, June 20, 1788, *DHRC*, 22:1715–6 ("founded on," "utterly repugnant," "it was the result," and "if we meant"); Hamilton, ibid., 1728 ("one result"); see also Yarbrough, "New Hampshire," 249; Hendrickson, *Peace Pact*, 234.

146. Dawes at Massachusetts convention, Jan. 18, 1788, *DHRC*, 6:1245 (quotation); see also Robinson, *Slavery in the Structure of American Politics*, 232–3; Brown, "Problems of Slavery," 429. For walkout threats over slavery by northern delegates, see supra pp. 273, 286.

147. "A Landholder" VI (Ellsworth), *Connecticut Courant*, Dec. 10, 1787, *DHRC*, 3:490 ("[A]ll good men"); "Mark Antony," Boston *Independent Chronicle*, Jan. 10, 1788, *DHRC*, 5:676 ("even in this" and "we ought to temper"); Adams to Jeremy Belknap, Oct. 22, 1795,

in *Collections of Massachusetts Historical Society* (Boston, 1877), 5th Series, 3:416 ("[j]ustice," "live by violence," and "the increasing population"). On northern fears of creating large populations of free blacks as an obstacle to emancipation generally, see Van Cleve, *Slaveholders' Union*, 60, 71–2.

148. Heath at Massachusetts convention, Jan. 30, 1788, *DHRC*, 6:1371 ("[e]ach state," "own internal," and "partakers"); Atherton at New Hampshire convention, undated, *Elliot*, 2:203–4 ("esteem"); see also "Philanthrop," Northampton, Mass., *Hampshire Gazette*, Apr. 23, 1788, *DHRC*, 7:1745; "Mark Antony," Boston *Independent Chronicle*, Jan. 10, 1788, *DHRC*, 5:675; Van Cleve, *Slaveholders' Constitution*, 172–3, 176–7.

Chapter 5

1. Alexander Hamilton, Conjectures About the New Constitution, Sept. 17–30, 1787, *PAH*, 4:275 [hereinafter, "Hamilton, Conjectures"].

    For the preceding footnote, see Humphreys to Washington, Sept. 28, 1787, *DHRC*, 5:355 (quotation); see also St. Jean de Crevecoeur to William Short, Apr. 1, 1788, *DHRC*, 9:635–6; Charles M. Thruston to the Mayor of Winchester, Nov. 15, 1787, *DHRC*, 8:165; Abraham Bancker to Evert Bancker, Feb. 9, 1788, *DHRC*, 20:760; Thomas Wait to George Thatcher, Jan. 8, 1788, *DHRC*, 5:645.

2. Hamilton, Conjectures, *PAH*, 4:275.

3. Ibid.

4. Ibid., 275–6.

5. Ibid.

6. *Pennsylvania Gazette*, Oct. 10, 1787, *DHRC*, 13:app. 1, 584 ("Shaysites"); "A Landholder" II (Ellsworth), *Connecticut Courant*, Nov. 12, 1787, *DHRC*, 3:402 ("[d]ebtors"); "A Landholder" I, Nov. 5, 1787, ibid., 399 ("who have"); Gouverneur Morris to Washington, Oct. 30, 1787, *PGW* (C.S.), 5:399 ("the wicked industry"); see also "A Landholder" IX, *Connecticut Courant*, Dec. 31, 1787, *DHRC*, 3:516; "A Friend to Order and Peace," *Pennsylvania Mercury*, June 21, 1788, *DHRC*, 21:1206–7; New York *Daily Advertiser*, Dec. 4, 1787, *DHRC*, 19:353; James Duncanson to James Maury, Feb. 17, 1789, *DHFFE*, 2:405–6; John Vaughan to John Dickinson, July 26, 1788, *DHRC*, 21:1345; Maier, *Ratification*, 80, 93, 132, 208, 351; Robert Allen Rutland, *Ordeal of the Constitution: The Antifederalists and the Ratification Struggle of 1787–1788* (Norman, OK, 1966), 26–7; infra pp. 403, 613. For examples of Antifederalists' resenting the disparaging of their motives by their opponents, see, e.g., John Lansing, Jr., at New York convention, June 20, 1788, *DHRC*, 22:1708; *American Herald*, Jan. 7, 1788, *DHRC*, 5:547.

    For the preceding footnote, see "Sidney," *Albany Gazette*, Jan. 24, 1788, *DHRC*, 20:645 ("entirely to destroy"); Smith at New York convention, June 20, 1788, *DHRC*, 22:1713 ("to exchange"); see also *New York Journal*, May 26, 1788, *DHRC*, 20:1111; Jurgen Heideking, *The Constitution Before the Judgment Seat: The Prehistory and Ratification of the American Constitution, 1787–1791* (John P. Kaminski and Richard Leffler, eds., Charlottesville, VA, 2012), 112–3.

7. Cornell, *Other Founders*, 48, 51, 84, 120; Brown, *Redeeming the Republic*, 206; Jackson Turner Main, *The Antifederalists: Critics of the Constitution, 1781–1788* (Chapel Hill, NC, 1961), 166–7, 281; Edling, *Revolution in Favor of Government*, 34–5; Wood, *Creation of the American Republic*, 485–6.

8. *A Citizen of New-York: An Address to the People of the State of New York* (John Jay) (Apr. 15, 1788), *DHRC*, 20:933 [hereinafter, *A Citizen of New-York*]; Carrington to Jefferson, Oct. 23, 1787, *DHRC*, 8:94; Maier, *Ratification*, 56, 65, 119, 121, 160, 179–82, 224, 266, 282, 362–3, 370–1; Cornell, *Other Founders*, 26–7; Robert Allen Rutland, *The Birth of the Bill of Rights, 1776–1791* (Chapel Hill, NC, 1955), 119.

9. Madison to Jefferson, Oct. 17, 1787, *PJM* (C.S.), 11:297 (quotation); see also *A Citizen of New-York*, *DHRC*, 20:933; infra pp. 454, 469.

10. Maier, *Ratification*, 160–1; Gorham to Madison, Jan. 27, 1788, *DHRC*, 7:1552; infra p. 432.

11. "Civis," *DHRC*, 16:26 ("the character," "the real ground," and "though they may"); Madison to Hamilton, June 22, 1788, *PAH*, 5:61 ("secretly felt" and "would not make"); see also Madison to King, June 13, 1788, *DHRC*, 10:1619; "Plain Truth," Providence *United States Chronicle*, Nov. 29, 1787, *DHRC*, 24:65.

12. See supra pp. 297–304; infra pp. 469, 474.

13. Lowndes in South Carolina House, Jan. 17, 1788, *DHRC*, 27:127 ("add[ing] strength" and "whether a man"); "A Georgian," *Gazette of the State of Georgia*, Nov. 15, 1787, *DHRC*, 3:237 ("thought fit"); Cornell, *Other Founders*, 6–8, 22, 26–7; Maier, *Ratification*, 83, 91, 93, 157, 232; Heideking, *The Constitution Before the Judgment Seat*, 106–8, 174–5; see also Samuel Adams to Richard Henry Lee, Dec. 3, 1787, *DHRC*, 14:333; William Thompson at Massachusetts convention, Jan. 23, 1788, *DHRC*, 6:1316; George Clinton's Remarks Against Ratifying the Constitution, July 11, 1788, *DHRC*, 22:2142–7; Madison to Jefferson, Apr. 22, 1788, *PJM* (C.S.), 11:28.

14. "Cato," *State Gazette of South Carolina*, Nov. 26, 1787, *DHRC*, 27:45 ("teeming"); Elbridge Gerry to the Massachusetts General Court, *Massachusetts Centinel*, Nov. 3, 1787, *DHRC*, 13:549 ("an efficient" and "proper amendments"); "Federal Farmer," *Letters to the Republican* (Nov. 8, 1787), Letter V, *DHRC*, 14:49–50 ("many good," "many important," "tolerable good," and "with several"); see also Gerry to John Adams, Sept. 20, 1787, *DHRC*, 4:16; Mason to Washington, Oct. 7, 1787, *DHRC*, 8:43; John Dawson at Virginia convention, June 24, 1788, *DHRC*, 10:1489; Richard Harison at New York convention, June 23, 1788, *DHRC*, 22:1802; "Many Customers," Philadelphia *Independent Gazetteer*, Dec. 1, 1787, *DHRC*, 2:307–9; Maier, *Ratification*, 48, 66–7, 262–3, 301; Edling, *Revolution in Favor of Government*, 220; Eubanks, "New York," 328–9.

15. Dollard at South Carolina convention, May 22, 1788, *DHRC*, 27:379 ("ample," "never agree," and "or any set"); "Philadelphiensis" II, Philadelphia *Freeman's Journal*, Nov. 28, 1787, *DHRC*, 14:253 ("inexplicable"); "Agrippa" XVI, *Massachusetts Gazette*, Feb. 5, 1788, *DHRC*, 5:864 ("to secure"); see also "Agrippa" XV, Jan. 29, 1788, ibid., 822–6; Mason at Virginia convention, June 11, 1788, *DHRC*, 9:1162; Lee to Mason, Oct. 1, 1787, *DHRC*, 8:28; "M.C.," *Pennsylvania Herald*, Oct. 27, 1787, *DHRC*, 2:203–4; George Turner to Winthrop Sargent, Nov. 6, 1787, ibid., 209; Kaminski, "The Constitution Without a Bill of Rights," 23–5.

16. Washington to Bushrod Washington, Nov. 10, 1787, *PGW* (C.S.), 5:422 ("The warmest"); Washington to Charles Carter, Dec. 14, 1787, ibid., 492 ("not a blind" and "fully persuaded"); see also Bushrod Washington to Robert Carter, Nov. 4, 1787, *DHRC*, 8:143–4; Randolph to Madison, c. Oct. 29, 1787, ibid., 134; Robert R. Livingston to John Stevens, Sr., Dec. 8, 1787, *DHRC*, 19:381; David Ramsay to Benjamin Rush, Nov. 10, 1787, *DHRC*, 27:39; Richard Henry Lee to George Mason, May 7, 1788, *DHRC*, 9:785; Maier, *Ratification*, 93–4.

17. Edling, *Revolution in Favor of Government*, 31–3.

18. Supra pp. 119, 141–3.

19. U.S. Constitution, Art. VII; Articles of Confederation, Art. 13, *DHRC*, 1:93.

20. Melancton Smith's Notes on the Proceedings of Congress, Sept. 27, 1787, *DHRC*, 1:330 (quotations); see also Elbridge Gerry to the Massachusetts General Court, *Massachusetts Centinel*, Nov. 3, 1787, *DHRC*, 13:548–9; Madison to Washington, Sept. 30, 1787, *PJM* (C.S.), 10:179.

21. Whitehill at Pennsylvania convention, Nov. 28, 1787, *DHRC*, 2:394 ("but it never"); Henry at Virginia convention, June 4, 1788, *DHRC*, 9:929–31 ("perfectly clear," "the utter annihilation," "nine states," and "of such awful magnitude"); see also June 7, 1788, ibid., 1041; Grayson, June 24, ibid., 10:1496–7; Lowndes in South Carolina House, Jan. 17, 1788, *DHRC*, 27:127–8; William Lenoir at North Carolina convention, July 30, 1788, *Elliot*, 4:201; George Clinton at New York convention, July 11, 1788, *DHRC*, 22:2137; Albany Anti-Federal Committee Circular, Apr. 10, 1788, *DHRC*, 21:1380; "Vox Populi," *Massachusetts Gazette*, Nov. 6, 1787, *DHRC*, 4:201; "Portius," *American Herald*, Nov. 12, 1787, ibid., 217–8.

22. Wilson at Pennsylvania convention, Dec. 11, 1787, *DHRC*, 2:556 ("without the authority"); Madison at Philadelphia convention, June 5, 1787, *Farrand*, 1:122–3 ("a breach");

June 19, ibid., 315 ("numerous and notorious"); see also Robert R. Livingston at New York convention, July 11, 1788, *DHRC*, 22:2138; Davie at North Carolina convention, July 24, 1788, *Elliot*, 4:21; Iredell, July 31, ibid., 230; Charles Cotesworth Pinckney in South Carolina House, Jan. 18, 1788, *DHRC*, 27:151; Albany Federal Committee, *An Impartial Address* (c. Apr. 20, 1788), *DHRC*, 21:1388; "Examiner," *Massachusetts Gazette*, Nov. 9, 1787, *DHRC*, 4:211; *The Federalist No. 22* (Hamilton), at 152; Akhil Reed Amar, "The Consent of the Governed: Constitutional Amendment Outside Article V," *Columbia Law Review* (1994), 94:464–9.

23. Wilson at Pennsylvania convention, Dec. 4, 1787, *DHRC*, 2:483 (quotations); see also Edmund Pendleton at Virginia convention, June 5, 1788, *DHRC*, 9:945–6; Archibald MacLaine at North Carolina convention, July 24, 1788, *Elliot*, 4:24; Richard Dobbs Spaight, July 30, ibid., 206; Charles Cotesworth Pinckney in South Carolina House, Jan. 17, 1788, *DHRC*, 27:120–1; Albany Federal Committee, *An Impartial Address* (c. Apr. 20, 1788), *DHRC*, 21:1389.

24. Madison, Aug. 31, *Farrand*, 2:476 (quotation); see also Rakove, *Original Meanings*, 105.

25. Pendleton at Virginia convention, June 4, 1788, *DHRC*, 9:917; Wilson at Pennsylvania convention, Nov. 24, 1787, *DHRC*, 2:361–2 ("supreme, absolute" and "the people"); see also Dec. 4, 1787, ibid., 474; Iredell at North Carolina convention, July 31, 1788, *Elliot*, 4:230; Amar, "Consent of the Governed," 470–5.

26. Washington to Knox, Feb. 3, 1787, *PGW* (C.S.), 5:8 ("[t]he legality" and "the shortest course"); Randolph (Yates's Notes), June 16, *Farrand*, 1:262 ("[t]here are great seasons"); Randolph at Virginia convention, June 4, 1788, *DHRC*, 9:934–5 ("political farce," "[o]n a thorough," "treason," and "to return"); see also Madison to Washington, Sept. 30, 1787, *PJM* (C.S.), 10:179; supra p. 253.

27. "Philadelphiensis" II, Philadelphia *Freeman's Journal*, Nov. 28, 1787, *DHRC*, 14:251–2 ("We are now publicly summoned" and "lose more"); "An Officer of the Late Continental Army," Philadelphia *Independent Gazetteer*, Nov. 6, 1787, *DHRC*, 2:216 ("an awful step"); Charles Turner at Massachusetts convention, Jan. 17, 1788, *DHRC*, 6:1226 ("[r]elinquishing"); see also Joshua Atherton to John Lamb, June 11–14, 1788, *DHRC*, 18:46; Samuel Chase, Objections to the Constitution, Apr. 24–25, 1788, *DHRC*, 12:632 [hereinafter, "Chase, Objections"]; George Clinton's Remarks Against Ratifying the Constitution, July 11, 1788, *DHRC*, 22:2147; Patrick Henry at Virginia convention, June 4, 1788, *DHRC*, 9:930; Lowndes in South Carolina House, Jan. 18, 1788, *DHRC*, 27:154.

28. Clinton at New York convention, June 28, 1788, *DHRC*, 22:1979–80 ("energetic," "the people," "feebleness," and "drive the people"); Lee to Mason, May 15, 1787, *LRHL*, 2:421 ("to rush," "the universal," "the cry," and "has lost").

29. Henry at Virginia convention, June 4, 1788, *DHRC*, 9:929–30 ("the dangers," "the most solemn," and "a great"); Grayson, June 11, ibid., 1167 ("merely imaginary" and "ludicrous"); see also Lowndes in South Carolina House, Jan. 18, 1788, *DHRC*, 27:152; Lansing at New York convention, June 20, 1788, *DHRC*, 22:1707; Monroe at Virginia convention, June 10, 1788, *DHRC*, 9:1105–6; John Tyler, June 25, ibid., 10:1526–7; *A Plebeian*, *DHRC*, 20:946–8; Richard E. Labunski, *James Madison and the Struggle for the Bill of Rights* (New York, 2006), 102–3; Banning, *Sacred Fire*, 244–5; Hendrickson, *Peace Pact*, 11–12, 252–3.

30. "A Columbian Patriot," *Observations*, *DHRC*, 16:285 ("free government" and "time and industry"); Smith at New York convention, June 27, 1788, *DHRC*, 22:1924 ("political depravity" and "want of honesty"); see also Grayson at Virginia convention, June 11, 1788, *DHRC*, 9:1165–6; *A Plebeian*, *DHRC*, 20:947; "Agrippa" III, *Massachusetts Gazette*, Nov. 30, 1787, *DHRC*, 4:342–3; "Agrippa" VII, Dec. 18, 1787, ibid., 5:484; "A Correspondent," *American Herald*, Dec. 10, 1787, *DHRC*, 4:406.

31. Lowndes in South Carolina House, Jan. 17, 1788, *DHRC*, 27:125, 128 ("glowing eulogy" at p. 128; "were eminent" at p. 125); Henry at Virginia convention, June 5, 1788, *DHRC*, 9:952–3 ("a long" and "a territory"); Grayson, June 11, ibid., 1167; see also Lansing at New York convention, June 20, 1788, *DHRC*, 22:1705.

32. John Williams, June 21, 1788, ibid., 1746 ("as an instrument"); Smith, June 27, ibid., 1925; Lansing, June 28, ibid., 1999–2000; *A Plebeian*, *DHRC*, 20:946 ("a long"); Mason at

Virginia convention, June 4, 1788, *DHRC*, 9:938; see also "Federal Farmer," *Letters to the Republican* (Nov. 8, 1787), Letter I, *DHRC*, 14:20.

33. Williams at New York convention, June 21, 1788, *DHRC*, 22:1745–6 ("luxury," "How many thousands," "the dissipation," "the immoderate," and "in time"); Lee to Mason, May 15, 1787, *LRHL*, 2:419 ("present discontents" and "vicious manners"); see also Lansing at New York convention, June 20, 1788, *DHRC*, 22:1706; *A Plebeian, DHRC*, 20:946; "Candidus" I, Boston *Independent Chronicle*, Dec. 6, 1787, *DHRC*, 4:398; Heideking, *The Constitution Before the Judgment Seat*, 110–1.

34. *The Federalist No. 1* (Hamilton), at 33 ("The subject"); Wilson at Pennsylvania convention, Dec. 11, 1787, *DHRC*, 2:553 ("contending for" and "own posterity"); Henry Lee at Virginia convention, June 9, 1788, *DHRC*, 9:1073 ("true republicans"); see also Spaight at North Carolina convention, July 30, 1788, *Elliot*, 4:207.

35. Pendleton at Virginia convention, June 5, 1788, *DHRC*, 9:946–7; Randolph, June 4, ibid., 933–6; June 6, ibid., 971–89; Francis Corbin, June 7, ibid., 1008–9; Wilson at Pennsylvania convention, Dec. 11, 1787, *DHRC*, 2:581–4; Charles Cotesworth Pinckney in South Carolina House, Jan. 17, 1788, *DHRC*, 27:120; *The Federalist No. 15* (Hamilton), at 106–7; see also Heideking, *The Constitution Before the Judgment Seat*, 135–40; Hendrickson, *Peace Pact*, 7–10; infra pp. 597–8.

36. Rutledge in South Carolina House, Jan. 16, 1788, *DHRC*, 27:110 ("the sun"); Hamilton at New York convention, June 20, 1788, *DHRC*, 22:1722–5 ("radical vice" and "particular conveniency" at p. 1723; "totally different" at p. 1725); see also Robert R. Livingston, June 19, ibid., 1685–6; *The Federalist No. 15* (Hamilton), at 108–13.

37. Richard Law at Connecticut convention, Jan. 9, 1788, *DHRC*, 3:558 ("excellencies"); Charles Jarvis at Massachusetts convention, Jan. 31, 1788, *DHRC*, 6:1374 ("great," "been written," and "[i]f, in the course"); see also Pendleton at Virginia convention, June 5, 1788, *DHRC*, 9:945; Randolph, June 15, ibid., 10:1353–4; Iredell at North Carolina convention, July 29, 1788, *Elliot*, 4:176–7.

38. Pennsylvania Minority Dissent, *DHRC*, 2:630–1; George Mason's Objections to the Constitution of Government Formed by the Convention (Oct. 1787), *DHRC*, 8:43 [hereinafter, "Mason's Objections"]; Richard Henry Lee to Edmund Randolph, Oct. 16, 1787, ibid., 61; Samuel Nasson at Massachusetts convention, Feb. 1, 1788, *DHRC*, 6:1400; James White to Governor Richard Caswell of North Carolina, Nov. 13, 1787, *LDC*, 24:555; infra ch. 7.

39. Elbridge Gerry to the Massachusetts General Court, *Massachusetts Centinel*, Nov. 3, 1787, *DHRC*, 13:548; Mason's Objections, *DHRC*, 8:43–5; Cornell, *Other Founders*, 30–1.

40. Pennsylvania Minority Dissent, *DHRC*, 2:629 ("so unlimited" and "this alone"); William Findley to William Irvine, March 12, 1788, *DHRC*, 16:373 ("internal objects"); Smith at New York convention, June 25, 1788, *DHRC*, 22:1880 ("soon dwindle" and "to make"); see also "Brutus" I, *New York Journal*, Oct. 18, 1787, *DHRC*, 19:107; "A Columbian Patriot," *Observations, DHRC*, 16:285; Samuel Spencer at North Carolina convention, July 25, 1788, *Elliot*, 4:51; Lenoir, July 30, ibid., 202; Lowndes in South Carolina House, Jan. 17, 1788, *DHRC*, 27:125; Henry at Virginia convention, June 9, 1788, *DHRC*, 9:1068; Robert Whitehill at Pennsylvania convention, Nov. 30, 1787, *DHRC*, 2:425.

41. Grayson at Virginia convention, June 12, 1788, *DHRC*, 10:1188; Smith at New York convention, June 25, 1788, *DHRC*, 22:1881; Gilbert Livingston, July 2, ibid., 2058–60.

42. Henry at Virginia convention, June 16, 1788, *DHRC*, 10:1310 ("unlimited authority" and "an unbounded control"); Grayson, June 12, ibid., 1188 ("despised"); see also Mason, June 4, ibid., 9:936; Henry, June 5, ibid., 957; Monroe, June 10, ibid., 1110–1; Williams at New York convention, June 27, 1788, *DHRC*, 22:1935–6; Lansing, June 28, ibid., 2001; George Clinton's Remarks Against Ratifying the Constitution, July 11, 1788, *DHRC*, 22:2145.

43. Lee to Henry, Sept. 14, 1789, *LRHL*, 2:502 ("The most essential" and "from its tendency"); Mason at the Virginia convention, June 4, *DHRC*, 9:937 ("suit so extensive"); Robert Yates and John Lansing, Jr., to Governor George Clinton, Dec. 21, 1787, *DHRC*, 19:458 ("permanency" and "be uniformly actuated"); see also Grayson at Virginia convention, June 11, 1788, *DHRC*, 9:1167; Monroe, June 10, ibid., 1110; Richard Henry

Lee to Samuel Adams, Apr. 28, 1788, ibid., 765; Chase, Objections, *DHRC*, 12:632; Hendrickson, *Peace Pact*, 252; Cecelia Kenyon, "Men of Little Faith: The Anti-Federalists on the Nature of Representative Government," *William and Mary Quarterly* (Jan. 1955), 12:6–8.

44. James Lincoln in South Carolina House, Jan. 18, 1788, *DHRC*, 27:155 ("into the hands");"Brutus" I, *New York Journal*, Oct. 18, 1787, *DHRC*, 19:112 ("confidence, respect" and "the destruction"); see also Mason at Virginia convention, June 4, 1788, *DHRC*, 9:937; Spencer at North Carolina convention, July 25, 1788, *Elliot*, 4:51–2; Lansing at New York convention, June 20, 1788, *DHRC*, 22:1707; Smith, June 27, ibid., 1924; Pennsylvania Minority Dissent, *DHRC*, 2:625–6; William Shippen, Jr., to Thomas Lee Shippen, Dec. 12, 1787, ibid., 602; William Findley to William Irvine, March 12, 1788, *DHRC*, 16:373; Bernard Bailyn, *The Ideological Origins of the American Revolution* (Cambridge, MA, enlarged ed., 1992), 347–9.

45. Smith at New York convention, June 27, 1788, *DHRC*, 22:1922 ("to maintain"); Williams, ibid., 1936 ("little").

46. Elbridge Gerry to the Massachusetts General Court, *Massachusetts Centinel*, Nov. 3, 1787, *DHRC*, 13:548 ("ambiguous" and "indefinite"); Grayson at Virginia convention, June 23, 1788, *DHRC*, 10:1469 ("there existed"); see also Pennsylvania Minority Dissent, *DHRC*, 2:629; "Brutus" I, *New York Journal*, Oct. 18, 1787, *DHRC*, 19:107; Tyler at Virginia convention, June 25, 1788, *DHRC*, 10:1525; Cornell, *Other Founders*, 11, 59, 134.

47. Timothy Bloodworth at North Carolina convention, July 29, 1788, *Elliot*, 4:167–8 ("put what construction"); Mason at Virginia convention, June 16, 1788, *DHRC*, 10:1326; Lenoir at North Carolina convention, July 30, 1788, *Elliot*, 4:206 ("[t]he omission"); see also Spencer, July 28, ibid., 137; Lansing at New York convention, July 3, 1788, *DHRC*, 22:2089.

48. Corbin at Virginia convention, June 7, 1788, *DHRC*, 9:1011; Randolph, June 10, ibid., 1096 ("the science," "greatly improved," and "was a thing"); Pinckney at South Carolina convention, May 14, 1788, *DHRC*, 27:330; see also Hamilton at New York convention, June 27, 1788, *DHRC*, 22:1957; Wilson at Pennsylvania convention, Nov. 24, 1787, *DHRC*, 2:342.

49. Ibid., 352 ("confederate republic"); Madison at Virginia convention, June 6, 1788, *DHRC*, 9:995 ("mixed nature"); Pendleton, June 5, ibid., 947; Davie at North Carolina convention, July 24, 1788, *Elliot*, 4:22; Iredell, July 25, ibid., 53; Davie, ibid., 58; Charles Pinckney in South Carolina House, Jan. 16, 1788, *DHRC*, 27:99; "A Pennsylvanian to the New York Convention" (Tench Coxe), *Pennsylvania Gazette*, June 11, 1788, *DHRC*, 20:1141–3; Alexander White, "To the Citizens of Virginia," *Winchester Gazette* [Virginia], Feb. 29, 1788, *DHRC*, 8:438; see also Hendrickson, *Peace Pact*, 12–3.

50. Pinckney in South Carolina convention, May 14, 1788, *DHRC*, 27:331 (quotations); *The Federalist No. 10* (Madison), at 77–84; ibid., *No. 51*, at 323–5.

51. Hamilton at New York convention, June 28, 1788, *DHRC*, 22:1982–3; Madison at Virginia convention, June 6, 1788, *DHRC*, 9:996; June 12, ibid., 10:1203–4; Pendleton, June 5, ibid., 9:948; Iredell at North Carolina convention, July 25, 1788, *Elliot*, 4:53; Wilson at Pennsylvania convention, Nov. 28, 1787, *DHRC*, 2:400–2; Increase Sumner at Massachusetts convention, Jan. 22, 1788, *DHRC*, 6:1298–9; Theophilus Parsons, Jan. 23, ibid., 1327; Ellsworth at Connecticut convention, Jan. 7, 1788, *DHRC*, 3:548, 552; Richard Law, Jan. 9, ibid., 559; Robert R. Livingston at New York convention, June 27, 1788, *DHRC*, 22:1942–3; Hamilton, ibid., 1957–8.

52. June 27, ibid., 1958–9 (quotation); Charles Pinckney in South Carolina House, Jan. 16, 1788, *DHRC*, 27:96, 98; "America: To the Dissenting Members of the Late Convention of Pennsylvania" (Noah Webster), New York *Daily Advertiser*, Dec. 31, 1787, *DHRC*, 19:491.

53. Randolph at Virginia convention, June 10, 1788, *DHRC*, 9:1102 (quotation); Hamilton at New York convention, June 24, 1788, *DHRC*, 22:1864; Madison at Virginia convention, June 11, 1788, *DHRC*, 9:1151–2; June 6, 1788, ibid., 997–8; Wilson at Pennsylvania convention, Dec. 4, 1787, *DHRC*, 2:478; Alexander White, "To the Citizens of Virginia," *Winchester Gazette* [Virginia], Feb. 29, 1788, *DHRC*, 8:439; "Poplicola," *Massachusetts Centinel*, Oct. 31, 1787, *DHRC*, 4:181.

54. Wilson at Pennsylvania convention, Dec. 4, 1787, *DHRC*, 2:496 ("drawn with" and "as minutely"); Pendleton at Virginia convention, June 5, 1788, *DHRC*, 9:947 ("intermeddle"); see also Jasper Yeates at Pennsylvania convention, Nov. 30, 1787, *DHRC*, 2:435; Alexander White, "To the Citizens of Virginia," *Winchester Gazette* [Virginia], Feb. 29, 1788, *DHRC*, 8:442.

55. U.S. Constitution, Art. I, § 8, cl. 18; "Brutus" XI, *New York Journal*, Jan. 31, 1788, *DHRC*, 20:684 ("the legislature"); "Brutus" I, *New York Journal*, Oct. 18, 1787, *DHRC*, 19:109 ("be exercised"); Mason's Objections, *DHRC*, 8:45 ("grant monopolies"); see also John Tyler at Virginia convention, June 17, 1788, *DHRC*, 10:1340; Mason, June 16, ibid., 1325–6; Spencer at North Carolina convention, July 29, 1788, *Elliot*, 4:152; "An Old Whig" II, Philadelphia *Independent Gazetteer*, Oct. 17, 1787, *DHRC*, 13:401–2.

56. Randolph at Virginia convention, June 10, 1788, *DHRC*, 9:1102 ("in the least"); Madison, June 16, ibid., 10:1323 ("at most," "the limits," and "minute"); see also Wilson at Pennsylvania convention, Dec. 4, 1787, *DHRC*, 2:482; Banning, *Sacred Fire*, 331.

57. U.S. Constitution, Art. I, § 1, cl. 1; Lee to Randolph, Oct. 16, 1787, *DHRC*, 8:62 ("every possible object"); "Deliberator," Philadelphia *Freeman's Journal*, Feb. 20, 1788, in Storing, ed., *The Complete Anti-Federalist*, 3:179 [hereinafter, " 'Deliberator' "]; "Brutus" I, *New York Journal*, Oct. 18, 1787, *DHRC*, 19:107 ("the sole judge" and "unlimited"); see also Henry at Virginia convention, June 7, 1788, *DHRC*, 9:1046; Williams at New York convention, June 26, 1788, *DHRC*, 22:1917–8; "A Countryman" V (De Witt Clinton), *New York Journal*, Jan. 17, 1788, *DHRC*, 20:623–4; Silas Lee to George Thatcher, Jan. 23, 1788, *DHRC*, 5:782.

    For the preceding footnote, see McCulloch v. Maryland, 17 U.S. 316, 413 (1819) ("convenient"); Madison to Judge Roane, Sept. 2, 1819, *PJM* (R.S.), 1:500–3 (quotations at p. 502).

58. Randolph at Virginia convention, June 17, 1788, *DHRC*, 10:1350 (quotation); *The Federalist No. 41* (Madison), at 263–4; see also Nicholas, June 16, *DHRC*, 10:1326–7; Randolph, June 10, ibid., 1484. For Madison's interesting and convincing explanation of how the General Welfare Clause got into the Constitution, see Madison to Andrew Stevenson, Nov. 17, 1830, *Farrand*, 3:483–8.

59. Jay to John Adams, Feb. 21, 1787, *CPPJJ*, 3:235 ("disinclination"); Smith at New York convention, June 21, 1788, *DHRC*, 22:1755 ("free access"); Gerry to James Warren, Oct. 18, 1787, *DHRC*, 4:94 ("the people" and "the wealth"); Smith at New York convention, June 27, 1788, *DHRC*, 22:1922; see also William Symmes, Jr., to Peter Osgood, Jr., Nov. 15, 1787, *DHRC*, 4:239.

60. Amos Singletary at Massachusetts convention, Jan. 25, 1788, *DHRC*, 6:1345 ("proposed," "a right," and "take away"); Symmes, Jan. 22, ibid., 1307–8; see also William Goudy at North Carolina convention, July 26, 1788, *Elliot*, 4:93.

61. Pennsylvania Minority Dissent, *DHRC*, 2:627 ("monopolize"); "An Officer of the Late Continental Army," Philadelphia *Independent Gazetteer*, Nov. 6, 1787, ibid., 211 ("have a coequal," "struggle," "destroyed," and "swallowed up"); see also Robert Whitehill at Pennsylvania convention, Nov. 28, 1787, ibid., 396; Melancton Smith at New York convention, June 27, 1788, *DHRC*, 22:1922; Williams, ibid., 1936–7; Mason at Virginia convention, June 4, 1788, *DHRC*, 9:936–7; "Brutus" I, *New York Journal*, Oct. 18, 1787, *DHRC*, 19:108; Chase, Objections, *DHRC*, 12:636; Samuel Osgood to Samuel Adams, Jan. 5, 1788, *DHRC*, 5:618–9; Edling, *Revolution in Favor of Government*, 180, 184, 221.

62. Smith at New York convention, June 27, 1788, *DHRC*, 22:1925 ("such poor"); Henry at Virginia convention, June 12, 1788, *DHRC*, 10:1215 ("oppression" and "not from the amount"); see also Richard Harison at New York convention, June 23, 1788, *DHRC*, 22:1802 (noting Antifederalist concession that requisitions were inadequate); "Federal Farmer," *Letters to the Republican* (Nov. 8, 1787), Letter III, *DHRC*, 19:224–5; Edling, *Revolution in Favor of Government*, 164, 194, 202–5; Einhorn, *American Taxation*, 149.

63. Williams at New York convention, June 27, 1788, *DHRC*, 22:1937 ("almost morally certain," "oppressive," and "heap"); see also Mason at Virginia convention, June 4, 1788, *DHRC*, 9:936; June 11, ibid., 1156; William Widgery at Massachusetts convention, Jan. 18, 1788, *DHRC*, 6:1251; Jan. 25, ibid., 1353; Ebenezer Peirce, Jan. 23, ibid., 1313–4; Pennsylvania Minority Dissent, *DHRC*, 2:635–6; "A Georgian," *Gazette of the State of Georgia*, Nov. 15, 1787, *DHRC*, 3:237.

64. Hardin Burnley to Madison, Nov. 28, 1789, *PJM* (C.S.), 12:456 ("the opposition"); Monroe at Virginia convention, June 10, 1788, *DHRC*, 9:1109 ("subversion"); Grayson, June 11, 1788, ibid., 1170 ("give up everything"); see also Madison, June 6, ibid., 996–7.

    For the preceding footnote, see Thomas FitzSimons to Samuel Meredith, Aug. 20, 1788, *DHFFE*, 1:253; *Pennsylvania Gazette*, Sept. 3, 1788, ibid., 265; infra pp. 382–3.

65. Mason at Virginia convention, June 4, 1788, *DHRC*, 9:928, 940 (quotations); see also June 11, ibid., 1156; Henry, June 12, ibid., 10:1215–6; June 5, ibid., 9:961–2; Williams's proposed amendment at New York convention, June 26, 1788, *DHRC*, 22:1919; New York *Daily Advertiser*, July 25, 1788, ibid., 2262; "Deliberator," in Storing, ed., *The Complete Anti-Federalist*, 3:179; Thomas Tudor Tucker's proposed constitutional amendment, Aug. 22, 1789, *Annals of Congress*, 1:803; Maier, *Ratification*, 362.

66. Henry at Virginia convention, June 12, 1788, *DHRC*, 10:1215 ("a thorough acquaintance"); Mason, June 11, ibid., 9:1156 ("the most easy" and "condition"); see also Spencer at North Carolina convention, July 25, 1788, *Elliot*, 4:76–7.

67. "A Georgian," *Gazette of the State of Georgia*, Nov. 15, 1787, *DHRC*, 3:239 ("unacquainted"); Pennsylvania Minority Dissent, *DHRC*, 2:636 ("independent" and "oppression"); "Federal Farmer," *Letters to the Republican* (Nov. 8, 1787), Letter III, *DHRC*, 19:226 ("the importance" and "scarcely believe"); see also Henry at Virginia convention, June 5, 1788, *DHRC*, 9:962–3; Melancton Smith at New York convention, June 27, 1788, *DHRC*, 22:1924; Nathaniel Barrell to George Thatcher, Jan. 15, 1788, *DHRC*, 5:719; Hall, *Politics Without Parties*, 281–2.

68. Henry at Virginia convention, June 7, 1788, *DHRC*, 9:1045 ("enormous," "[d]ouble sets," and "splendid"); June 12, ibid., 1218; Pennsylvania Minority Dissent, *DHRC*, 2:639 ("not enjoy," "a very expensive," and "swarm"); Singletary at Massachusetts convention, Jan. 25, 1788, *DHRC*, 6:1345 ("on the land"); see also Benjamin Gale at Killingworth, Conn., Town Meeting, Nov. 12, 1787, *DHRC*, 3:422–3; Joseph M'Dowall at North Carolina convention, July 26, 1788, *Elliot*, 4:87; Williams at New York convention, June 26, 1788, *DHRC*, 22:1918; Smith, June 27, ibid., 1924; Gilbert Livingston, July 2, ibid., 2059; Lowndes in South Carolina House, Jan. 18, 1788, *DHRC*, 27:153; Pierce at Massachusetts convention, Jan. 23, 1788, *DHRC*, 6:1313–4.

69. Corbin at Virginia convention, June 7, 1788, *DHRC*, 9:1012 ("the lungs" and "consumptive"); Robert R. Livingston at New York convention, June 27, 1788, *DHRC*, 22:1940 ("pompous petitions"); see also Randolph at Virginia convention, June 7, 1788, *DHRC*, 9:1016–8.

70. Hamilton at New York convention, June 28, 1788, *DHRC*, 22:1986 ("States will contribute"); Madison to George Thompson, Jan. 29, 1789, *PJM* (C.S.) 11:433–4 ("if some states"); Robert R. Livingston at New York convention, June 27, 1788, *DHRC*, 22:1941; see also Hamilton, June 20, ibid., 1724; Rufus King at Massachusetts convention, Jan. 21, 1788, *DHRC*, 6:1286–7; Randolph at Virginia convention, June 7, 1788, *DHRC*, 9:1017–8; William Samuel Johnson at Connecticut convention, Jan. 4, 1788, *DHRC*, 3:545–6.

71. Madison at Virginia convention, June 11, 1788, *DHRC*, 9:1143–4 ("essential," "[a] neutral nation," and "be known"); Robert R. Livingston at New York convention, June 27, 1788, *DHRC*, 22:1941–2 ("a constitution"); Hamilton, ibid., 1956 ("[u]nexpected invasions"); see also Thomas Dawes at Massachusetts convention, Jan. 18, 1788, *DHRC*, 6:1245–6; Francis Dana, ibid., 1250; James Wilson at Pennsylvania convention, Dec. 11, 1787, *DHRC*, 2:558; Carrington to Jefferson, Apr. 24, 1788, *DHRC*, 9:755; Edling, *Revolution in Favor of Government*, 163–4, 172–3, 195.

72. Madison at Virginia convention, June 11, 1788, *DHRC*, 9:1145 (quotation); Dawes at Massachusetts convention, Jan. 21, 1788, *DHRC*, 6:1289; Christopher Gore, Jan. 22, ibid., 1300–1; Pendleton at Virginia convention, June 5, 1788, *DHRC*, 9:948–9; Randolph, June 7, ibid., 1018–9; Iredell at North Carolina convention, July 25, 1788, *Elliot*, 4:91–2; Robert R. Livingston at New York convention, June 27, 1788, *DHRC*, 22:1942; Hamilton, ibid., 1955–6; June 20, ibid., 1723–4; *The Federalist No. 30* (Hamilton), at 190–2; Edling, *Revolution in Favor of Government*, 166–7; Maier, *Ratification*, 272–3.

    For the preceding footnote, see Einhorn, *American Taxation*, 157–8.

73. Ellsworth at Connecticut convention, Jan. 7, 1788, *DHRC*, 3:548 (quotations); see also "A Landholder" V (Ellsworth), *Connecticut Courant*, Dec. 3, 1787, ibid., 481–2; Corbin at Virginia convention, June 7, 1788, *DHRC*, 9:1011; Randolph, ibid., 1016; Edling, *Revolution in Favor of Government*, 171, 226–7.

74. Madison to George Thompson, Jan. 29, 1789, *PJM* (C.S.), 11:435 ("borrowing" and "who could be"); Christopher Gore at Massachusetts convention, Jan. 22, 1788, *DHRC*, 6:1300–1 ("circumscribed"); see also Madison at Virginia convention, June 6, 1788, *DHRC*, 9:996–7; *The Federalist No. 30* (Hamilton), at 192; Edling, *Revolution in Favor of Government*, 171–4.

75. Hamilton at New York convention, June 28, 1788, *DHRC*, 22:1984, 1988 (quotations at p. 1984); Livingston, June 27, ibid., 1939; Madison at Virginia convention, June 12, 1788, *DHRC*, 10:1206–7.

76. June 6, ibid., 9:996 ("of little advantage"); Ellsworth at Connecticut convention, Jan. 7, 1788, *DHRC*, 3:549–50 (other quotations); see also "Connecticutensis: To the People of Connecticut," *American Mercury*, Dec. 31, 1787, ibid., 512–3; Wilson at Pennsylvania convention, Dec. 4, 1787, *DHRC*, 2:481; Jasper Yeates, Nov. 30, 1787, ibid., 436; King at Massachusetts convention, Jan. 21, 1788, *DHRC*, 6:1287; Theodore Sedgwick, ibid., 1290; *The Federalist No. 21* (Hamilton), at 142–3.

77. Ellsworth at Connecticut convention, Jan. 7, 1788, *DHRC*, 3:549 ("[b]ut you cannot"); Dana at Massachusetts convention, Jan. 18, 1788, *DHRC*, 6:1250–1 ("abhorrent" and "never be"); Gorham, Jan. 25, ibid., 1353 ("the middling"); Hamilton at New York convention, June 21, 1788, *DHRC*, 22:1790 ("of great danger" and "undoubtedly"); see also Randolph at Virginia convention, June 7, 1788, *DHRC*, 9:1027; John Marshall, June 10, ibid., 1121–2; Edling, *Revolution in Favor of Government*, 202–3.

78. Hamilton at New York convention, June 28, 1788, *DHRC*, 22:1984 ("tyrannical"); John Steele at North Carolina convention, July 26, 1788, *Elliot*, 4:87 ("unequal and oppressive"); Wilson Nicholas at Virginia convention, June 6, 1788, *DHRC*, 9:999–1000; Dawes at Massachusetts convention, Jan. 21, 1788, *DHRC*, 6:1289; Yeates at Pennsylvania convention, Nov. 30, 1787, *DHRC*, 2:436; see also Albany Federal Committee, *An Impartial Address* (c. Apr. 20, 1788), *DHRC*, 21:1391.

79. Ellsworth at Connecticut convention, Jan. 7, 1788, *DHRC*, 3:550; Wilson at Pennsylvania convention, Dec. 11, 1787, *DHRC*, 2:576; Samuel Johnston at North Carolina convention, July 25, 1788, *Elliot*, 4:90–1; Iredell, ibid., 92; Archibald MacLaine, July 29, ibid., 188–9; Iredell, July 30, ibid., 220; see also Corbin at Virginia convention, June 7, 1788, *DHRC*, 9:1012; Wilson Nicholas, June 6, ibid., 999–1000; George Nicholas, June 10, ibid., 1136; Edling, *Revolution in Favor of Government*, 197–200.

80. "Deliberator," in Storing, ed., *The Complete Anti-Federalist*, 3:179; Samuel Nasson at Massachusetts convention, Feb. 1, 1788, *DHRC*, 6:1399–400; see also William Symmes, Jr., to Peter Osgood, Jr., Nov. 15, 1787, *DHRC*, 4:240; Aedanus Burke's proposed amendment, Aug. 17, 1789, *Annals of Congress*, 1:780; Kohn, *Eagle and Sword*, 2–6.

81. Virginia Constitution of 1776, Art. 13 ("standing armies"); Massachusetts delegates to Governor James Bowdoin, Aug. 23, 1785, *LDC*, 22:592 ("it would"); Proceedings of the Confederation Congress, Oct. 18, 1783, *JCC*, 25:703; June 3, 1784, ibid., 27:530–1; see also Monroe to Jefferson, Apr. 12, 1785, *PTJ* (M.S.), 8:77; "Brutus" IX, *New York Journal*, Jan. 17, 1788, *DHRC*, 15:396, 397 n. 7; Samuel Nasson to George Thatcher, July 9, 1789, in Helen E. Veit et al., eds., *Creating the Bill of Rights: The Documentary Record from the First Federal Congress* (Baltimore, 1991), 261; Edling, *Revolution in Favor of Government*, 44, 82, 90, 101–5; Kohn, *Eagle and Sword*, 40–6, 52–62.

82. "A Columbian Patriot," *Observations*, *DHRC*, 16:280 ("the nursery"); Nasson at Massachusetts convention, Feb. 1, 1788, *DHRC*, 6:1399 ("seven-eighths"); Pennsylvania Minority Dissent, *DHRC*, 2:637 ("[a] standing army" and "the most oppressive"); Lowndes in South Carolina House, Jan. 17, 1788, *DHRC*, 27:128 ("the bayonet"); see also "Brutus" VIII, *New York Journal*, Jan. 10, 1788, *DHRC*, 15:335; "Brutus" IX, Jan. 17, 1788, ibid., 394, 395–6; "A Son of Liberty," *New York Journal*, Nov. 8, 1787, *DHRC*, 13:481–2; Mason at Virginia convention, June 14, 1788, *DHRC*, 10:1271; Albany Anti-Federal Committee Circular, Apr. 10, 1788, *DHRC*, 21:1381; Kohn, *Eagle and Sword*, 81–2.

83. Proposed Amendment No. 9 at Virginia convention, June 27, 1788, *DHRC*, 10:1554; Lansing's proposed amendment at New York convention, July 3, 1788, *DHRC*, 22:2088; Henry at Virginia convention, June 16, 1788, *DHRC*, 10:1299–300; see also "Brutus" IX, *New York Journal*, Jan. 17, 1788, *DHRC*, 15:397–8; Chase, Objections, *DHRC*, 12:636; Aedanus Burke's proposed amendment, Aug. 17, 1789, *Annals of Congress*, 1:780; Edling, *Revolution in Favor of Government*, 91.

84. Nasson at Massachusetts convention, Feb. 1, 1788, *DHRC*, 6:1400 ("[w]e fear no foe"); Gerry in the US House, Aug. 17, 1789, *Annals of Congress*, 1:749–50 ("attempt to destroy"); Whitehill at Pennsylvania convention, *DHRC*, 2:396 ("government which possesses"); see also "Cincinnatus IV: To James Wilson," *New York Journal*, Nov. 22, 1787, *DHRC*, 14:186; "A Democratic Federalist," *Pennsylvania Herald*, Oct. 17, 1787, *DHRC*, 2:197; *Massachusetts Gazette*, Oct. 9, 1787, *DHRC*, 4:61; Edling, *Revolution in Favor of Government*, 106–7, 125–6; Kohn, *Eagle and Sword*, 6–9, 82–3.

85. Pennsylvania Minority Dissent, *DHRC*, 2:638 ("to quell"); Findley at Pennsylvania convention, Dec. 7, 1787, ibid., 509 ("[W]hen the militia"); Lansing's proposed amendment at New York convention, July 10, 1788, *DHRC*, 22:2122; see also Albany Anti-Federal Committee Circular, Apr. 10, 1788, *DHRC*, 21:1381; "A Son of Liberty," *New York Journal*, Nov. 8, 1787, *DHRC*, 13:482; Luther Martin, Genuine Information VII, Baltimore *Maryland Gazette*, Jan. 18, 1788, *DHRC*, 11:188.

86. Proposed Amendment No. 11 at Virginia convention, June 27, 1788, *DHRC*, 10:1554; Mason, June 16, 1788, ibid., 1304 ("severe and ignominious" and "induce them"); June 14, ibid., 1271–2, 1289; June 16, ibid., 1312, 1314; see also Henry, June 5, ibid., 9:957–8; June 14, ibid., 10:1276; Luther Martin, Genuine Information VII, Baltimore *Maryland Gazette*, Jan. 18, 1788, *DHRC*, 11:189–90; Kohn, *Eagle and Sword*, 83.

87. U.S. Constitution, Art. I, § 8, cl. 15; Samuel McDowell et al., circular letter to the Fayette County Court in Danville, Kentucky, Feb. 29, 1788, *DHRC*, 8:435 ("the ravages"); Charles Clay at Virginia convention, June 14, 1788, *DHRC*, 10:1294; Henry, June 16, ibid., 1304–5, 1310; Grayson, ibid., 1305–6; Luther Martin, Genuine Information VII, Baltimore *Maryland Gazette*, Jan. 18, 1788, *DHRC*, 11:189; Edling, *Revolution in Favor of Government*, 92; Kohn, *Eagle and Sword*, 83.

88. Grayson at Virginia convention, June 16, 1788, *DHRC*, 10:1314–6; see also June 12, ibid., 1188–9; Melancton Smith at New York convention, July 1, 1788, *DHRC*, 22:2047.

89. Wilson at Pennsylvania convention, Dec. 11, 1787, *DHRC*, 2:576 ("[W]e are not"); Madison at Virginia convention, June 12, 1788, *DHRC*, 10:1206 ("[w]eakness" and "be a security"); see also June 6, ibid., 9:993; Marshall, June 10, ibid., 1120; Randolph, June 14, ibid., 10:1289; William Phillips, Sr., at Massachusetts convention, Jan. 22, 1788, *DHRC*, 6:1301–2; Iredell at North Carolina convention, July 25, 1788, *Elliot*, 4:95–6; Charles Pinckney in South Carolina House, Jan. 16, 1788, *DHRC*, 27:97–8; *The Federalist No. 41* (Madison), at 256–7; Edling, *Revolution in Favor of Government*, 69–70, 97, 99; Kohn, *Eagle and Sword*, 84.

90. Iredell at North Carolina convention, July 25, 1788, *Elliot*, 4:96–7; *The Federalist No. 8* (Hamilton), at 70–1; *No. 41* (Madison), ibid., 258; Edling, *Revolution in Favor of Government*, 122–3.

91. Wilson at Pennsylvania convention, Dec. 11, 1787, *DHRC*, 2:577 ("[t]he flames"); "A Landholder" V, *Connecticut Courant*, Dec. 3, 1787, *DHRC*, 3:482 ("necessary to restrain" and "the monarch"); see also Iredell at North Carolina convention, July 26, 1788, *Elliot*, 4:96; Albany Federal Committee, *An Impartial Address* (c. Apr. 20, 1788), *DHRC*, 21:1392.

92. U.S. Constitution, Art. I, § 8, cl. 12; Sedgwick at Massachusetts convention, Jan. 24, 1788, *DHRC*, 6:1337 (quotation); see also Wilson at Pennsylvania convention, Dec. 11, 1787, *DHRC*, 2:576–7; "An American Citizen" IV (Tench Coxe), *On the Federal Government* (Oct. 21, 1787), *DHRC*, 13:435; "Plain Truth: Reply to an Officer of the Late Continental Army," Philadelphia *Independent Gazetteer*, Nov. 10, 1787, *DHRC*, 2:220.

93. Nicholas at Virginia convention, June 14, 1788, *DHRC*, 10:1278 ("unacquainted"); *The Federalist No. 25* (Hamilton), at 166 ("lost us"); Henry Lee at Virginia convention, June 9, 1788, *DHRC*, 9:1073 ("incontrovertible"); see also Madison, June 6, ibid., 993; Edling, *Revolution in Favor of Government*, 80–1, 97–8, 125–7; Kohn, *Eagle and Sword*, 9–10, 85.

94. Wilson at Pennsylvania convention, Dec. 11, 1787, *DHRC*, 2:577–8 (quotations); Extract of a letter from Poughkeepsie (July 22), New York *Daily Advertiser*, July 26, 1788, *DHRC*, 23:2262 (reporting Hamilton speech at New York convention on July 21); see also Madison at Virginia convention, June 14, 1788, *DHRC*, 10:1272–4; Randolph, ibid., 1289; "A Pennsylvanian: To the New York Convention" (Tench Coxe), *Pennsylvania Gazette*, June 11, 1788, *DHRC*, 20:1142; Alexander White, "To the Citizens of Virginia," *Winchester Gazette* [Virginia], Feb. 29, 1788, *DHRC*, 8:441; *The Federalist No. 29* (Hamilton), at 182–3.

95. Extract of a letter from Poughkeepsie (July 22), New York *Daily Advertiser*, July 25, 1788, *DHRC*, 23:2262–3, 2264 n. 4 (summarizing speeches of Hamilton and Jay at New York convention on July 21); Madison at Virginia convention, June 14, 1788, *DHRC*, 10:1272–4 (quotations at p. 1272); Nicholas, ibid., 1279–80; Madison, ibid., 1294–5; June 16, ibid., 1301–2; Marshall, ibid., 1308; Albany Federal Committee, *An Impartial Address* (c. Apr. 20, 1788), *DHRC*, 21:1392; *The Federalist No. 29* (Hamilton), at 183.

96. Marshall at Virginia convention, June 16, 1788, *DHRC*, 10:1306–7; George Nicholas, ibid., 1314; Randolph, June 10, ibid., 9:1102.

97. U.S. Constitution, Art. I, § 8, cl. 13 ("provide"); Rutledge in South Carolina House, Jan. 17, 1788, *DHRC*, 27:135 ("become" and "we must hold"); *The Federalist No. 11* (Hamilton), at 86–7 ("only be respected" and "be a prey"); *A Citizen of New-York* (Jay), *DHRC*, 20:931; see also James Innes at Virginia convention, June 25, 1788, *DHRC*, 10:1522. On the Algerian pirates' ransoming of American sailors, see Marks, *Independence on Trial*, 36–45.

98. For examples of northern Antifederalists supporting the commerce power, see "Agrippa" III, *Massachusetts Gazette*, Nov. 30, 1787, *DHRC*, 4:343; Melancton Smith at New York convention, June 21, 1788, *DHRC*, 22:1756; see also Main, *Antifederalists*, 149.

99. Mason's Objections, *DHRC*, 8:45 ("an exorbitant" and "the five southern"); Lee to Randolph, Oct. 16, 1787, ibid., 63 ("the most oppressive"); Proposed Amendment No. 8, Virginia convention, June 27, 1788, *DHRC*, 10:1554; *Address of the Antifederalist Minority of the Maryland Convention* (May 1, 1788), *DHRC*, 12:666; see also Grayson to Short, Nov. 10, 1787, *DHRC*, 8:151; Mason at Virginia convention, June 24, 1788, *DHRC*, 10:1488; Henry, ibid., 1479; supra pp. 281–2, 289–90.

100. U.S. Constitution, Art. II, § 2, cl. 2 ("advice"); Dawson at Virginia convention, June 24, 1788, *DHRC*, 10:1493 (other quotations); see also Monroe, June 10, ibid., 9:1115; William Porter at North Carolina convention, July 28, 1788, *Elliot*, 4:115; Grayson to Short, Nov. 10, 1787, *DHRC*, 14:82.

101. Proposed Amendment No. 7, Virginia convention, June 27, 1788, *DHRC*, 10:1554 (quotation); Grayson, June 12, ibid., 1192; Henry, June 13, ibid., 1246; Mason, June 18, ibid., 1380; June 19, ibid., 1390; Henry, ibid., 1393–5; Lowndes in South Carolina House, Jan. 16, 1788, *DHRC*, 27:102; William Symmes, Jr., to Peter Osgood, Jr., Nov. 15, 1787, *DHRC*, 4:241; *Cumberland Gazette*, Nov. 22, 1787, ibid., 296 & n. 1.

102. *The Federalist No. 11* (Hamilton), at 84 ("least room"); Cadwalader to George Mitchell, Oct. 8, 1787, *DHRC*, 13:353 ("sacrificed"); *A Citizen of New-York* (Jay), *DHRC*, 20:930 ("have almost ceased"); Russell at Massachusetts convention, Feb. 1, 1788, *DHRC*, 6:1404 ("furnish us"); see also Dawes, Jan. 21, ibid., 1288; Yeates at Pennsylvania convention, Nov. 30, 1787, *DHRC*, 2:436; John Howard to George Thatcher, Feb. 27, 1788, *DHRC*, 20:819; "An American," *New York Packet*, May 27, 1788, ibid., 1113. For a particularly strong statement of the importance of the commerce power to northerners, see William Phillips, Sr., at the Massachusetts convention, Jan. 22, 1788, *DHRC*, 6:1301.

103. "Social Compact," *New Haven Gazette*, Oct. 4, 1787, *DHRC*, 13:310–1 ("utterly excluded"); Dawes at Massachusetts convention, Jan. 21, 1788, *DHRC*, 6:1288 ("ignominious," "independent," and "slaves"); David Ramsay, Oration, Charleston *Columbian Herald*, June 5, 1788, *DHRC*, 18:163 ("our ships") [hereinafter, "Ramsay, Oration"]; Wilson at Pennsylvania convention, Dec. 11, 1787, *DHRC*, 2:580 ("Go along"); see also Gorham at Massachusetts convention, Jan. 25, 1788, *DHRC*, 6:1353–4; *A Citizen of New-York*, *DHRC*, 20:930–1.

104. *The Federalist No. 11* (Hamilton), at 85 (quotation); see also *A Citizen of New-York*, *DHRC*, 20:931; "A Farmer: To the Farmers of Connecticut," *New Haven Gazette*, Oct. 18, 1787, *DHRC*, 3:393–4.

105. Dawes at Massachusetts convention, Jan. 21, 1788, *DHRC*, 6:1289; One of the People, *Pennsylvania Gazette*, Oct. 17, 1787, *DHRC*, 2:188 (quotation); see also John Howard to George Thatcher, Feb. 27, 1788, *DHRC*, 20:819.

106. *The Federalist No. 42* (Madison), at 267–8 ("the relief" and "would nourish"); see also Dawes at Massachusetts convention, Jan. 21, 1788, *DHRC*, 6:1288 ("domestic traffic"); "Phocion," Providence *United States Chronicle*, July 17, 1788, *DHRC*, 25:354.

107. Russell at Massachusetts convention, Feb. 1, 1788, *DHRC*, 6:1404 ("a spirit"); Barnwell in South Carolina House, Jan. 17, 1788, *DHRC*, 27:132 ("in a trifling degree"); Madison at Virginia convention, June 12, 1788, *DHRC*, 10:1209; see also Tobias Lear to John Langdon, Oct. 19, 1787, *DHRC*, 8:81; James Hughes to Horatio Gates, Nov. 20, 1787, ibid., 169; Iredell at North Carolina convention, July 29, 1788, *Elliot*, 4:186.

108. Charles Cotesworth Pinckney in South Carolina House, Jan. 17, 1788, *DHRC*, 27:122 ("some privileges"); David Ramsay to Benjamin Lincoln, Jan. 29, 1788, *DHRC*, 15:487 ("[y]our delegates" and "liberality").

109. Madison at Virginia convention, June 24, 1788, *DHRC*, 10:1503 (quotation); see also Robert Barnwell in South Carolina House, Jan. 17, 1788, *DHRC*, 27:132. On the South's greater vulnerability during wartime, see Robinson, *Slavery in the Structure of American Politics*, 103–4.

110. "Civis" (Ramsay), *DHRC*, 16:23, 25 ("a common navy," "As the war," and "ought we to"); Charles Cotesworth Pinckney in South Carolina House, Jan. 17, 1788, *DHRC*, 27:122–3 (other quotations); see also Edward Rutledge, ibid., 135; Charles Pinckney at South Carolina convention, May 14, 1788, ibid., 335; Pierce Butler to Weedon Butler, May 5, 1788, *DHRC*, 17:383–4; Barnwell in South Carolina House, Jan. 17, 1788, *DHRC*, 27:129.

111. For the point that the South was just as vulnerable in the Confederation Congress, see Barnwell in South Carolina House, Jan. 17, 1788, *DHRC*, 27:129.

112. Rutledge in South Carolina House, Jan. 16, 1788, ibid., 111–2 ("immense"); "Civis" (Ramsay), *DHRC*, 16:23 ("vast extent," "daily," "influence," and "have a great"); see also Iredell at North Carolina convention, July 29, 1788, *Elliot*, 4:186.

113. Corbin at Virginia convention, June 19, 1788, *DHRC*, 10:1391 (quotation); George Nicholas, June 10, ibid., 9:1130; Pendleton, June 12, ibid., 10:1200; Nicholas, June 13, ibid., 1251.

114. Johnston at North Carolina convention, July 28, 1788, *Elliot*, 4:115–6; George Nicholas at Virginia convention, June 18, 1788, *DHRC*, 10:1380–1; Charles Cotesworth Pinckney in South Carolina House, Jan. 16, 1788, *DHRC*, 27:103; Hugh Williamson to Madison, June 2, 1788, *LDC*, 25:135–6; *The Federalist No. 75* (Hamilton), at 453–4.

115. Madison at Virginia convention, June 19, 1788, *DHRC*, 10:1395 ("any great, essential right"); Iredell at North Carolina convention, July 28, 1788, *Elliot*, 4:128–9; Hugh Williamson to Madison, June 2, 1788, *LDC*, 25:136 ("shut not" "an efficient," and "we shall certainly"); see also Pendleton at Virginia convention, June 12, 1788, *DHRC*, 10:1200.

116. Madison at Philadelphia convention, Aug. 9, 1787, *Farrand*, 2:240–1.
     For the preceding footnote, see Madison at Virginia convention, June 14, 1788, *DHRC*, 10:1259–60; "An American Citizen" IV (Tench Coxe), *On the Federal Government* (Oct. 21, 1787), *DHRC*, 13:436.

117. Samuel Spencer at North Carolina convention, July 25, 1788, *Elliot*, 4:51 ("reprehensible"); Nasson at Massachusetts convention, Feb. 1, 1788, *DHRC*, 6:1399 ("omnipotent"); John Quincy Adams to William Cranch, Oct. 14, 1787, *DHRC*, 4:73 ("of prescribing" and "insidious"); Bloodworth at North Carolina convention, July 25, 1788, *Elliot*, 4:55 ("make the time"); see also Charles Turner at Massachusetts convention, Jan. 17, 1788, *DHRC*, 6:1224–5; William Widgery, Jan. 16, ibid., 1218–9; Henry at Virginia convention, June 5, 1788, *DHRC*, 9:964; Main, *Antifederalists*, 149–51.

118. Arms, Maynard, and Field, Dissent, *DHRC*, 7:1734 (quotation); David Caldwell at North Carolina convention, July 25, 1788, *Elliot*, 4:62; see also Pennsylvania Minority Dissent, *DHRC*, 2:628–9; Robert Whitehill at Pennsylvania convention, Nov. 30, 1787, ibid., 395–6. On Parliament's action, see editorial note, *DHRC*, 22:2141–2 n. 4.

119. "Deliberator," in Storing, ed., *The Complete Anti-Federalist*, 3:179 (quotation); Turner at Massachusetts convention, Jan. 17, 1788, *DHRC*, 6:1224–5; see also Ebenezer Peirce, Jan. 16, ibid., 1213–4; Henry at Virginia convention, June 5, 1788, *DHRC*, 9:964; "Vox Populi," *Massachusetts Gazette*, Oct. 30, 1787, *DHRC*, 4:169–70.

120. Smith's proposed amendment, New York convention, June 25–26, 1788, *DHRC*, 22:1907, 1910; Henry at Virginia convention, June 9, 1788, *DHRC*, 9:1071 (quotation); "Federal Farmer," *Letters to the Republican* (Nov. 8, 1787), Letter III, *DHRC*, 19:220; see also Bloodworth at North Carolina convention, July 25, 1788, *Elliot*, 4:55–6; Pierce at Massachusetts convention, Jan. 16, 1788, *DHRC*, 6:1213; John Taylor, Jan. 21, ibid., 1278; Rakove, *Original Meanings*, 231; Eubanks, "New York," 322.

121. Arms, Maynard, and Field, Dissent, *DHRC*, 7:1734 ("that we shall"); "Federal Farmer," *Letters to the Republican* (Nov. 8, 1787), Letter III, *DHRC*, 19:220 ("a door open").

122. William Davie at North Carolina convention, July 25, 1788, *Elliot*, 4:60 ("trifling"); Iredell, ibid., 53–4; Jay at New York convention, June 25, 1788, *DHRC*, 22:1905; Richard Morris, ibid., 1907; Increase Sumner at Massachusetts convention, Jan. 17, 1788, *DHRC*, 6:1226; Nicholas at Virginia convention, June 4, 1788, *DHRC*, 9:920; Wilson at Pennsylvania convention, Dec. 11, 1787, *DHRC*, 2:565; "A Pennsylvanian to the New York Convention," *Pennsylvania Gazette*, June 11, 1788, *DHRC*, 20:1144–6; "America: To the Dissenting Members of the Late Convention of Pennsylvania," New York *Daily Advertiser*," Dec. 31, 1787, *DHRC*, 19:486; *The Federalist No. 59* (Hamilton), at 361–3. On the Rhode Island point specifically, see Rufus King and Nathaniel Gorham at Massachusetts convention, Jan. 16, 1788, *DHRC*, 6:1214–5; see also editorial note, ibid., 1212–3 n. 5; ibid., 7:1674 n. 2; *Newport Herald*, Mar. 6, 1788, *DHRC*, 24:122–3; Providence *United States Chronicle*, Feb. 28, 1788, ibid., 126. On the need to change the place of elections in Rhode Island because of the British occupation of major towns during the Revolutionary War, see editorial note, *DHRC*, 26:932 n. 12.

    For the preceding footnote, see Proposed Amendment No. 16, Virginia convention, June 27, 1788, *DHRC*, 10:1555 ("shall neglect"); Proposed Amendment No. 3, Massachusetts convention, Feb. 6, 1788, *DHRC*, 6:1477; Samuel Jones's proposed amendment, New York convention, June 25, 1788, *DHRC*, 22:1904–5; Aedanus Burke's proposed amendment in House of Representatives, Aug. 21, 1789, *Annals of Congress*, 1:797; Madison, ibid., 800 ("to destroy"); see also Phanuel Bishop at Massachusetts convention, Jan. 16, 1788, *DHRC*, 6:1214; William Goudy at North Carolina convention, July 25, 1788, *Elliot*, 4:56.

123. Davie at North Carolina convention, July 25, 1788, *Elliot*, 4:60–1; Thomas McKean at Pennsylvania convention, Nov. 28, 1787, *DHRC*, 2:413; Wilson, ibid., 402; King at Massachusetts convention, Jan. 21, 1788, *DHRC*, 6:1279; Nicholas at Virginia convention, June 4, 1788, *DHRC*, 9:920–1; Madison, June 14, ibid., 10:1260; *The Federalist No. 61* (Hamilton), at 375.

124. U.S. Constitution, Art. I, § 2, cl. 1 (quotation); Iredell at North Carolina convention, July 25, 1788, *Elliot*, 4:53; Davie, ibid., 60–1; John Steele, ibid., 71; King at Massachusetts convention, Jan. 21, 1788, *DHRC*, 6:1279.

125. George Cabot in Massachusetts convention, Jan. 16, ibid., 1216–7; Theophilus Parsons, ibid., 1217–8; Wilson at Pennsylvania convention, Nov. 28, 1787, *DHRC*, 2:403.

126. Madison at Virginia convention, June 14, 1788, *DHRC*, 10:1295 ("execrated"); Sumner at Massachusetts convention, Jan. 17, 1788, *DHRC*, 6:1226 ("act as bad"); Samuel West, ibid., 1227 ("good men" and "men to ruin"); see also Isaac Snow, ibid., 1228; John Coffin Jones, Jan. 16, ibid., 1219; *The Federalist No. 60* (Hamilton), at 367. On the Federalists' more general charge that their opponents were conjuring up implausible scenarios of abuse by elected representatives, see infra pp. 345–6.

127. U.S. Constitution, Art. I, § 8, cl. 17 ("[t]o exercise" and "not exceeding"); King at Philadelphia convention, Aug. 10, 1787, *Farrand*, 2:261 ("The mutability"); see also Mason motion, July 26, ibid., 127; Gerry, ibid. On concerns that the Confederation

Congress had been unduly influenced by the states in which it sat, see Stephen Higginson to Samuel Adams, Aug. 21, 1783, *LDC*, 20:573.

128. "A Columbian Patriot," *Observations, DHRC*, 16:285 ("federal city"); Mason at Virginia convention, June 16, 1788, *DHRC*, 10:1317 ("the sanctuary," "set at defiance," and "attempt to oppress"); see also William Lenoir at North Carolina convention, July 30, 1788, *Elliot*, 4:203; Rutland, *Ordeal of the Constitution*, 30–1, 97; Bowling, *The Creation of Washington, D.C.*, 81–3.

129. Grayson at Virginia convention, June 16, 1788, *DHRC*, 10:1319–20; ibid., 1316–7 ("exclusive privileges"); Henry, ibid., 1321–2 ("a wanton grasp," "from all the burdens," and "exclusive emoluments"); see also Proposed Amendment, New York convention, July 22, 1788, *DHRC*, 23:2269–70; John Taylor at Massachusetts convention, Jan. 24, 1788, *DHRC*, 6:1339; Maier, *Ratification*, 283; Bowen, *Miracle at Philadelphia*, 209–10.

130. Iredell at North Carolina convention, July 30, 1788, *Elliot*, 4:219–20 (quotation); Madison at Virginia convention, June 16, 1788, *DHRC*, 10:1318; Randolph, June 9, ibid., 9:1084; Caleb Strong at Massachusetts convention, Jan. 24, 1788, *DHRC*, 6:1338–9; Caleb Davis, ibid., 1339; King, ibid., 1340; Bowling, *The Creation of Washington, D.C.*, 83–5. On the 1783 "mutiny" that allegedly drove Congress out of Philadelphia (but that mostly existed in the minds of nationalist congressional delegates who sought to use the episode to their political advantage), see Bowling, supra, 30–4, 77; see also "A True American," *Maryland Journal*, June 29, 1783, p. 1; Oliver Ellsworth to Governor Jonathan Trumbull, Sr., of Connecticut, July 10, 1783, *LDC*, 20:413–4; Davis, *Sectionalism in American Politics*, 60; Jensen, *New Nation*, 83; Kohn, *Eagle and Sword*, 50.

131. Madison at Virginia convention, June 16, 1788, *DHRC*, 10:1319; Henry Lee, ibid., 1321 ("the members" and "crowded"); U.S. Constitution, Art. 1, § 8, cl. 17 ("not exceeding"); see also Albany Federal Committee, *An Impartial Address* (c. Apr. 20, 1788), *DHRC*, 21:1397.

132. U.S. Constitution, Art. I, § 5, cl. 3 (quotation); Articles of Confederation, Art. IX, *DHRC*, 1:92; Henry at Virginia convention, June 14, 1788, *DHRC*, 10:1286; Mason, ibid., 1291; Widgery at Massachusetts convention, Jan. 21, 1788, *DHRC*, 6:1283; John Graham at North Carolina convention, July 26, 1788, *Elliot*, 4:72; William Symmes, Jr., to Peter Osgood, Jr., Nov. 15, 1787, *DHRC*, 4:238–9.

133. U.S. Constitution, Art. I, § 9, cl. 7 ("a regular statement"); Henry at Virginia convention, June 5, 1788, *DHRC*, 9:965 ("very indefinite"); Mason, June 17, ibid., 10:1344 ("[t]his expression"); Henry, ibid., 1346 ("the national wealth"); see also Proposed Amendments 10 and 11, Rhode Island convention, Mar. 6, 1790, *DHRC*, 26:980.

134. Madison at Virginia convention, June 14, 1788, *DHRC*, 10:1295–6; June 17, ibid., 1344–5; Henry Lee, June 9, ibid., 9:1079; Davie at North Carolina convention, July 26, 1788, *Elliot*, 4:72.

135. Hamilton at New York convention, June 21, 1788, *DHRC*, 22:1787 ("distempered imagination," "the most distant," and "inevitable realities"); Iredell at North Carolina convention, July 30, 1788, *Elliot*, 4:195 ("[j]ealousy," "carried," and "guard against"); Marshall at Virginia convention, June 10, 1788, *DHRC*, 9:1118 ("if you repose"); see also Henry Lee, June 16, 1788, ibid., 10:1320–1; Madison, June 14, ibid., 1295; Lee, ibid., 1292; "Examiner," *Massachusetts Gazette*, Nov. 2, 1787, *DHRC*, 4:192; Bailyn, *Ideological Origins*, 352–4, 369–70.

136. Washington to Bushrod Washington, Nov. 9, 1787, *PGW* (C.S.), 5:423.

137. Corbin at Virginia convention, June 16, 1788, *DHRC*, 10:1305 ("how, in the name," "were to return," and "make laws"); Johnston at North Carolina convention, July 25, 1788, *Elliot*, 4:57 ("chosen" and "be in the same"); Theophilus Parsons at Massachusetts convention, Jan. 23, 1788, *DHRC*, 6:1324; Tristram Dalton, Jan. 25, ibid., 1352; see also Christopher Gore, Jan. 30, ibid., 1368; James Bowdoin, Jan. 23, ibid., 1321–2; George Nicholas at Virginia convention, June 16, 1788, *DHRC*, 10:1327; Iredell at North Carolina convention, July 28, 1788, *Elliot*, 4:130; Alexander White, "To the Citizens of Virginia," *Winchester Gazette* [Virginia], Feb. 29, 1788, *DHRC*, 8:444; *The Federalist No. 57* (Madison), at 352.

138. Hamilton at New York convention, June 21, 1788, *DHRC*, 22:1790 ("the confidence," "jealous," and "the most powerful"); Parsons at Massachusetts convention, Jan. 23, 1788, *DHRC*, 6:1328 ("none but mad men" and "the means"); Randolph at Virginia convention, June 17, 1788, *DHRC*, 10:1354 ("those desperados").

139. "The Landholder" X (Ellsworth), *Connecticut Courant*, Mar. 3, 1788, *DHRC*, 16:306 ("jealousy in excess"); Washington to Bushrod Washington, Nov. 9, 1787, *PGW* (C.S.), 5:423 ("great evils"); Madison at Virginia convention, June 14, 1788, *DHRC*, 10:1283 ("imprudent" and "the bands"); see also Randolph, June 6, ibid., 9:975; Hamilton at New York convention, June 25, 1788, *DHRC*, 22:1890–1.

140. Morris at New York convention, June 24, 1788, *DHRC*, 22:1854–5 ("all the danger," "should teach," and "in all their zeal"); Wilson at Pennsylvania convention, Nov. 28, 1787, *DHRC*, 2:400 ("liberty," "licentiousness," "tyranny," and "proper powers"); Rush to Jeremy Belknap, Feb. 28, 1788, *DHRC*, 16:251 ("cherishing," "too apt," and "vigorous"); see also Bowdoin at Massachusetts convention, Jan. 23, 1788, *DHRC*, 6:1320; Thomas Thacher, Feb. 4, 1788, ibid., 1420; Pendleton at Virginia convention, June 12, 1788, *DHRC*, 10:1193; Madison, June 6, ibid., 9:990.

141. "Brutus" I, *New York Journal*, Oct. 18, 1787, *DHRC*, 19:109 ("unerring experience" and "every body"); Henry at Virginia convention, June 16, 1788, *DHRC*, 10:1321 ("in all parts" and "predominant"); Arms, Maynard, and Field, Dissent, *DHRC*, 7:1735 ("Does not experience"); see also Pierce at Massachusetts convention, Jan. 16, 1788, *DHRC*, 6:1214; Symmes, Jan. 22, ibid., 1310; John Lansing, Jr., at New York convention, June 28, 1788, *DHRC*, 22:2000–1; Henry at Virginia convention, June 5, 1788, *DHRC*, 9:952; "An Old Whig" II, Philadelphia *Independent Gazetteer*, Oct. 17, 1787, *DHRC*, 13:401; Luther Martin, Address No. IV, *Maryland Journal*, Apr. 4, 1788, *DHRC*, 12:481–2; Bailyn, *Ideological Origins*, 345–6.

142. Smith at New York convention, June 25, 1788, *DHRC*, 22:1882 ("presume this"); "Brutus" IX, *New York Journal*, Jan. 17, 1788, *DHRC*, 15:395 ("as this government" and "the habits"); Henry at Virginia convention, June 14, 1788, *DHRC*, 10:1275 ("It is easier"); June 4, ibid., 9:930 ("a wrong step"); "Brutus" I, *New York Journal*, Oct. 18, 1787, *DHRC*, 19:109; see also Caldwell at North Carolina convention, July 29, 1788, *Elliot*, 4:187; William Thompson at Massachusetts convention, Jan. 17, 1788, *DHRC*, 6:1227–8; Nathan Dane to Samuel Adams, May 10, 1788, *DHRC*, 20:1093.

143. Mason at Virginia convention, June 16, 1788, *DHRC*, 10:1303 (quotation); see also John Smilie at Pennsylvania convention, Nov. 28, 1787, *DHRC*, 2:407; Bailyn, *Ideological Origins*, 331–51; Rakove, *Original Meanings*, 16–7, 150–2; Edling, *Revolution in Favor of Government*, 40–1, 66–7; Wood, *Creation of the American Republic*, 520–1.

144. Henry at Virginia convention, June 20, 1788, *DHRC*, 10:1419; Madison to Samuel Johnston, July 31, 1789, *PJM* (C.S.), 12:317 ("most criticized"); "A Columbian Patriot," *Observations*, *DHRC*, 16:279 ("boundless"); Mason at Virginia convention, June 19, 1788, *DHRC*, 10:1407 ("impair"); ibid., 1402 ("slowly" and "one great"); see also Mason's Objections, *DHRC*, 8:44; George Clinton's Remarks Against Ratifying the Constitution, July 11, 1788, *DHRC*, 22:2145–6.

145. U.S. Constitution, Art. III, § 2, cl. 1 ("law and equity"); "Brutus" XI, *New York Journal*, Jan. 31, 1788, *DHRC*, 15:514, 515, 517 (other quotations); see also George Clinton's Remarks Against Ratifying the Constitution, July 11, 1788, *DHRC*, 22:2145–6.

146. "Brutus" XI, *New York Journal*, Jan. 31, 1788, *DHRC*, 15:513, 515, 516; see also George Clinton's Remarks Against Ratifying the Constitution, July 11, 1788, *DHRC*, 22:2145–6. A case falls within the "arising under" jurisdiction of the federal courts, according to the Supreme Court's subsequent interpretation in *Osborne v. Bank of the United States*, 22 U.S. (9 Wheat.) 738 (1824), if federal law forms "an ingredient" in the case, under either the plaintiff's claim or the defendant's defense. Thus, the broader the reach of federal law—which includes statutes enacted by Congress—the broader the potential jurisdiction of the federal courts. In this way, the "arising under" jurisdiction links the powers of Congress and the federal courts.

147. "Brutus" XI, *New York Journal*, Jan. 31, 1788, *DHRC*, 15:512 (quotation); see also Benjamin Gale at Killingworth, Conn., Town Meeting, Nov. 12, 1787, *DHRC*, 3:428; The

Society of Western Gentlemen Revise the Constitution, *Virginia Independent Chronicle*, Apr. 30, May 7, 1788, *DHRC*, 9:771; Melancton Smith to Abraham Yates, Jr., Jan. 23, 1788, *DHRC*, 20:638.

For the preceding footnote, see Grayson at Virginia convention, June 21, 1788, *DHRC*, 10:1445; see also McKean at Pennsylvania convention, Dec. 10, 1787, *DHRC*, 2:534 (summarizing Antifederalist objections).

148. "A Georgian," *Gazette of the State of Georgia*, Nov. 15, 1787, *DHRC*, 3:241 (quotation); Proposed Amendment No. 14, Virginia convention, June 27, 1788, *DHRC*, 10:1555; Samuel Jones's proposed amendment, New York convention, July 5, 1788, *DHRC*, 22:2100; see also Mason at Virginia convention, June 19, 1788, *DHRC*, 10:1401; Grayson to Short, Nov. 10, 1787, *DHRC*, 14:82; Albany Anti-Federalist Committee Circular, Apr. 10, 1788, *DHRC*, 21:1383.

149. Pennsylvania Minority Dissent, *DHRC*, 2:629 ("by legal ingenuity"); Mason at Virginia convention, June 19, 1788, *DHRC*, 10:1402–4 ("disgraceful" at p. 1402; "should be guilty" at p. 1404); see also Henry, June 23, ibid., 1464; William Symmes, Jr., to Peter Osgood, Jr., Nov. 15, 1787, *DHRC*, 4:242; Richard Henry Lee to Samuel Adams, Apr. 28, 1788, *DHRC*, 9:766.

For the preceding footnote, see Main, *Political Parties*, 76; infra pp. 454–5, 470–1; Ware v. Hylton, 3 U.S. (3 Dall.) 199 (1796); Casto, *The Supreme Court in the Early Republic*, 98–101; Holton, *Forced Founders*, 50–1, 210–1; Evans, "Private Indebtedness and the Revolution in Virginia," 370–2.

150. Mason at Virginia convention, June 23, 1788, *DHRC*, 10:1470 ("tend to oppress"); Amendments proposed by William Paca at Maryland convention, Apr. 26, 1788, *DHRC*, 12:651; Joseph M'Dowall at North Carolina convention, July 30, 1788, *Elliot*, 4:211 ("in the power"); see also Mason at Virginia convention, June 19, 1788, *DHRC*, 10:1404; Henry, June 12, ibid., 1312–3; William Lancaster at North Carolina convention, July 30, ibid., 214; "A Georgian," *Gazette of the State of Georgia*, Nov. 15, 1787, *DHRC*, 3:241–2; "Federal Farmer," *Letters to the Republican* (Nov. 8, 1787), Letter III, *DHRC*, 19:229; "Candidus" I, Boston *Independent Chronicle*, Dec. 6, 1787, *DHRC*, 4:397; Samuel Osgood to Samuel Adams, Jan. 5, 1788, *DHRC*, 5:619; Ralph A. Rossum, "The Courts and the Judicial Power," in Levy and Mahoney, eds., *The Framing and Ratification of the Constitution*, 239.

151. Pennsylvania Minority Dissent, *DHRC*, 2:630, 633 (quotations); see also Melancton Smith to Abraham Yates, Jr., Jan. 23, 1788, *DHRC*, 20:639; "Federal Farmer," *Letters to the Republican* (Nov. 8, 1787), Letter III, *DHRC*, 19:229; Rossum, "The Courts and the Judicial Power," 238.

152. Samuel Spencer at North Carolina convention, July 29, 1788, *Elliot*, 4:154 ("the bulwarks" and "twelve honest"); Pennsylvania Minority Dissent, *DHRC*, 2:630, 632–4 ("the loss of" on p. 633); Albany Anti-Federalist Committee Circular, Apr. 10, 1788, *DHRC*, 21:1381, 1382 ("powerful engine"); John Pierce to Henry Knox, Oct. 26, 1787, *DHRC*, 8:123–4; Proposed Amendments Nos. 11 and 14, Virginia convention, June 27, 1788, *DHRC*, 10:1552, 1555; see also Federal Farmer, *Letters to the Republican* (Nov. 8, 1787), Letter III, *DHRC*, 19:229; Henry at Virginia convention, June 20, 1788, *DHRC*, 10:1420; Grayson, ibid., 1416; Bloodworth at North Carolina convention, July 28, 1788, *Elliot*, 4:143; Cornell, *Other Founders*, 59–60; Rakove, *Original Meanings*, 321; Bailyn, *Ideological Origins*, 341. On the use of jury trials in admiralty cases under the Confederation, see editorial note, *DHRC*, 27:159 n. 9. The absence of a right to a jury trial in civil cases could be an important means of protecting foreign creditors from having their rights to recover on debts nullified in practice. See Holton, *Unruly Americans*, 187; Cornell, *Other Founders*, 66–7.

153. Pennsylvania Minority Dissent, *DHRC*, 2:634 (quotation); Abraham Holmes at Massachusetts convention, Jan. 30, 1788, *DHRC*, 6:1366–7; Federal Farmer, *Letters to the Republican* (Nov. 8, 1787), Letter III, *DHRC*, 19:229; Spencer at North Carolina convention, July 29, 1788, *Elliot*, 4:154; see also Henry at Virginia convention, June 20, 1788, *DHRC*, 10:1424.

154. Holmes at Massachusetts convention, Jan. 30, 1788, *DHRC*, 6:1638 (quotations); see also "Brutus" XIV, *New York Journal*, Feb. 28, 1788, *DHRC*, 20:821–3; Henry at Virginia convention, June 16, 1788, *DHRC*, 10:1330.

155. June 17, ibid., 1356 ("must be discharged"); Mason, June 19, ibid., 1406 ("this mortification" and "brought"); see also Grayson, June 21, ibid., 1448; James Galloway at North Carolina convention, July 29, 1788, *Elliot*, 4:190; Bloodworth, ibid., 184; Samuel Jones's proposed amendment, New York convention, July 5, 1788, *DHRC*, 22:2100; Proposed Amendment No. 3, Rhode Island convention, Mar. 6, 1790, *DHRC*, 26:979; "Federal Farmer," *Letters to the Republican* (Nov. 8, 1787), Letter III, *DHRC*, 19:230–1; "Lycurgus," *Boston Gazette*, Nov. 19, 1787, *DHRC*, 4:277; *American Herald*, Nov. 19, 1787, ibid.

156. Wilson at Pennsylvania convention, Dec. 1, 1787, *DHRC*, 2:451 ("with intrepidity"); Dec. 4, ibid., 495; Dec. 7, ibid., 517; McKean, Dec. 10, ibid., 540–1; Madison at Virginia convention, June 20, 1788, *DHRC*, 10:417–8; Ellsworth at Connecticut convention, Jan. 7, 1788, *DHRC*, 3:553; *The Federalist No. 78* (Hamilton), at 464–72; ibid., *No. 79*, at 473.

157. Pendleton at Virginia convention, June 19, 1788, *DHRC*, 10:1398 (quotation); see also June 20, ibid., 1426; Marshall, ibid., 1430.

158. Pendleton, June 18, ibid., 1398 ("highly probable" and "best calculated"); Madison, June 20, ibid., 1417; editorial note, ibid., 1439–40 n. 3; Marshall, ibid., 1431; Archibald MacLaine at North Carolina convention, July 28, 1788, *Elliot*, 4:140; "A Citizen of New Haven" (Roger Sherman), *Connecticut Courant*, Jan. 7, 1788, *DHRC*, 3:527.

159. Wilson at Pennsylvania convention, Dec. 7, 1787, *DHRC*, 2:518–9 ("a just"); Davie at North Carolina convention, July 29, 1788, *Elliot*, 4:158–9 ("[i]f these controversies"); see also Madison at Virginia convention, June 20, 1788, *DHRC*, 10:1414–5; *The Federalist No. 80* (Hamilton), at 476–7.

160. Davie at North Carolina convention, July 29, 1788, *Elliot*, 4:158 (quotations); Richard Dobbs Spaight, July 28, ibid., 139; Iredell, ibid., 145–6; MacLaine, July 29, ibid., 172; Madison at Virginia convention, June 20, 1788, *DHRC*, 10:1413; Wilson at Pennsylvania convention, Dec. 7, 1787, *DHRC*, 2:517.

161. Pendleton at Virginia convention, June 20, 1788, *DHRC*, 10:1427–8; Albany Federal Committee, *An Impartial Address* (c. Apr. 20, 1788), *DHRC*, 21:1395 (quotation); Madison at Virginia convention, June 20, 1788, *DHRC*, 10:1413–4; Randolph, June 21, ibid., 1451; Wilson at Pennsylvania convention, Dec. 7, 1787, *DHRC*, 2:519; Davie at North Carolina convention, July 29, 1788, *Elliot*, 4:159; "An American Citizen" IV, *On the Federal Government* (Oct. 21, 1787), *DHRC*, 13:434; *The Federalist No. 80* (Hamilton), at 477–8.

162. Pendleton at Virginia convention, June 19, 1788, *DHRC*, 10:1400–1 (quotation); Madison, June 20, ibid., 1416–7; editorial note, ibid., 1439 n. 2; Marshall, ibid., 1431–3; Iredell at North Carolina convention, July 28, 1788, *Elliot*, 4:145–7; "A Citizen of New Haven," *Connecticut Courant*, Jan. 7, 1788, *DHRC*, 3:527.

163. Wilson at Pennsylvania convention, Dec. 11, 1787, *DHRC*, 2:575; Dec. 7, ibid., 516–7; Iredell at North Carolina convention, July 29, 1788, *Elliot*, 4:170; Spaight, July 28, ibid., 144; Gore at Massachusetts convention, Jan. 30, 1788, *DHRC*, 6:1369; Thomas Dawes, ibid., 1369–70; Randolph at Virginia convention, June 6, 1788, *DHRC*, 9:974; "An American Citizen" IV, *On the Federal Government* (Oct. 21, 1787), *DHRC*, 13:434.

For the preceding footnote, see Spencer at North Carolina convention, July 29, 1788, *Elliot*, 4:154–5; Bloodworth, ibid., 167; William Findley at Pennsylvania convention, Dec. 7, 1787, *DHRC*, 2:522; "One of the Common People," *Boston Gazette*, Dec. 3, 1787, *DHRC*, 4:369; see also "A Democratic Federalist," *Pennsylvania Herald*, Oct. 17, 1787, *DHRC*, 2:194.

164. Charles Pinckney in South Carolina House, Jan. 16, 1788, *DHRC*, 27:97 ("the interest"); Iredell at North Carolina convention, July 28, 1788, *Elliot*, 4:148 ("would draw down" and "instantly resisted"); July 29, ibid., 171; Albany Federal Committee, *An Impartial Address* (c. Apr. 20, 1788), *DHRC*, 21:1394; Wilson at Pennsylvania convention, Dec. 7, 1787, *DHRC*, 2:516; Randolph at Virginia convention, June 6, 1788, *DHRC*, 9:974; "America: To the Dissenting Members of the Late Convention of Pennsylvania," New York *Daily Advertiser*, Dec. 31, 1787, *DHRC*, 19:488.

For the first of the two preceding footnotes, see Pinckney in South Carolina House, Jan. 18, 1788, *DHRC*, 27:150–1; see also editorial note, *DHRC*, 5:611–2 nn. 3–4.

For the second of the two preceding footnotes, see Judiciary Act of 1789, ch. 20, § 9, 1 Stat. 76–7.

165. Wilson at Pennsylvania convention, Dec. 11, 1787, *DHRC*, 2:574 (quotation); Dec. 7, ibid., 516; Iredell at North Carolina convention, July 29, 1788, *Elliot*, 4:171.

166. Madison at Virginia convention, June 20, 1788, *DHRC*, 10:1418; Johnston at North Carolina convention, July 28, 1788, *Elliot*, 4:150.

167. Pendleton at Virginia convention, June 19, 1788, *DHRC*, 10:1399 (quotation); Madison at Virginia convention, June 20, 1788, *DHRC*, 10:1415; Wilson at Pennsylvania convention, Dec. 11, 1787, *DHRC*, 2:573; see also Dec. 7, 1787, ibid., 520; *The Federalist No. 81* (Hamilton), at 490. Henry insisted that Congress had no constitutional authority to enact the regulations that Madison predicted it would (June 20, 1788, *DHRC*, 10:1420).

168. Madison at Virginia convention, June 20, 1788, *DHRC*, 10:1414; Marshall, ibid., 1433; *The Federalist No. 81* (Hamilton), at 487–8.

169. Mason at Virginia convention, June 11, 1788, *DHRC*, 9:1154–5; Henry, June 5, ibid., 968; Grayson, June 11, ibid., 1171; Smith at New York convention, June 20, 1788, *DHRC*, 22:1717; Lansing, June 21, ibid., 1783; "Federal Farmer," *Letters to the Republican* (Nov. 8, 1787), Letter III, *DHRC*, 19:219–20; Pennsylvania Minority Dissent, *DHRC*, 2:632; Robertson, *The Constitution and America's Destiny*, 35–6.

For the first of the two preceding footnotes, see Casto, *The Supreme Court in the Early Republic*, 188–202; Charles Warren, *The Supreme Court in United States History*, vol. 1, *1789–1835* (Boston, 1926), 93–102.

170. U.S. Constitution, Art. I, § 2, cl. 3; Philadelphia convention, Sept. 17, 1787, *Farrand* 2:644 (agreeing, without dissent, to the proposal made by Gorham and supported by Washington to change 40,000 to 30,000); Report of the Committee of Eleven, presented by Gerry, July 5, ibid., 1:526 (providing for one representative for every 40,000 inhabitants); Mason at Virginia convention, June 4, 1788, *DHRC*, 9:939; Henry, June 5, ibid., 953; see also Rakove, *Original Meanings*, 228.

171. Mason at the Virginia convention, June 4, 1788, *DHRC*, 9:939; Proposed Amendment No. 2, June 27, ibid., 10:1553; Smith's proposed amendment, New York convention, June 20, 1788, *DHRC*, 22:1718; Smith, June 21, ibid., 1749; Lansing, June 23, ibid., 1806; Pennsylvania Minority Dissent, *DHRC*, 2:632; see also Labunski, *James Madison*, 83.

172. Mason's Objections, *DHRC*, 8:43 ("the mere shadow"); Smith at New York convention, June 21, 1788, *DHRC*, 22:1740–50, 1753, 1754 ("shadow" at p. 1753); Richard Henry Lee to Randolph, Oct. 16, 1787, *DHRC*, 8:62 ("a mere shred"); "Brutus" III, *New York Journal*, Nov. 15, 1787, *DHRC*, 19:257 ("a mere burlesque" and "[n]o free people"); see also John Taylor at Massachusetts convention, Jan. 17, 1788, *DHRC*, 6:1237; Elbridge Gerry's Objections to the Constitution, *Massachusetts Centinel*, Nov. 3, 1787, *DHRC*, 13:548 [hereinafter, "Gerry's Objections"].

173. Smith at New York convention, June 21, 1788, *DHRC*, 22:1749–55 ("resemble" at p. 1750); June 20, ibid., 1715–6; Mason at Virginia convention, June 4, 1788, *DHRC*, 9:937–40 ("ought to mix" at p. 938); see also Henry, June 12, 1788, ibid., 10:1217; "Federal Farmer," *Letters to the Republican* (Nov. 8, 1787), Letter II, *DHRC*, 19:214–5; Chase, Objections, *DHRC*, 12:633; Kenyon, "Men of Little Faith," 10–13.

174. Mason at Virginia convention, June 4, 1788, *DHRC*, 9:937–9 ("possibly know," "a full," "it would be," and "with a sparing"); Chase, Objections, *DHRC*, 12:633 ("represent" and "be acquainted"); see also Clinton at New York convention, June 21, 1788, *DHRC*, 22:1784–5.

175. Mason at Virginia convention, June 4, 1788, *DHRC*, 9:937 ("of the utmost" and "common interest"); Smith at New York convention, June 21, 1788, *DHRC*, 22:1755 ("free access" and "a genuine"); see also "Federal Farmer," *Letters to the Republican* (Nov. 8, 1787), Letter III, *DHRC*, 19:219.

176. Smith at New York convention, June 21, 1788, *DHRC*, 22:1751–2 ("walk in," "the office," "birth," "the common people," and "conspicuous"); Mason at Virginia convention, June 11, 1788, *DHRC*, 9:1155–8 ("the great" at p. 1158; "must form" at p. 1155); see also Pennsylvania Minority Dissent, *DHRC*, 2:631–2; Chase, Objections, *DHRC*, 12:633;

Henry at Virginia convention, June 12, 1788, *DHRC*, 10:1217; "Brutus" III, *New York Journal*, Nov. 15, 1787, *DHRC*, 19:255–6; "Federal Farmer," *Letters to the Republican* (Nov. 8, 1787), Letter III, ibid., 219–20; Rakove, *Original Meanings*, 228–9; Cornell, *Other Founders*, 45, 98.

177. Henry at Virginia convention, June 12, 1788, *DHRC*, 10:1217; Tyler, June 14, ibid., 1263; Smith at New York convention, June 21, 1788, *DHRC*, 22:1749–51 (quotations).

178. Ibid., 1750, 1752 (quotations); see also Benjamin Gale at Killingworth, Conn., Town Meeting, Nov. 12, 1787, *DHRC*, 3:423; Cornell, *Other Founders*, 40, 97; Rakove, *Original Meanings*, 233; Maier, *Ratification*, 354–5.

179. Henry at Virginia convention, June 14, 1788, *DHRC*, 10:1285–6; John Williams at New York convention, June 21, 1788, *DHRC*, 22:1746–7; Smith, June 20, ibid., 1717; Pennsylvania Minority Dissent, *DHRC*, 2:631; "Brutus" III, *New York Journal*, Nov. 15, 1787, *DHRC*, 19:256.

For the preceding footnote, see Robert R. Livingston at New York convention, June 23, 1788, *DHRC*, 22:1811–2.

180. "A Columbian Patriot," *Observations*, *DHRC*, 16:278 ("a frequent" and "the strongest"); Taylor at Massachusetts convention, Jan. 14, 1788, *DHRC*, 6:1185 ("the safeguard" and "the avenue"); see also Abraham White, ibid., 1186; Williams at New York convention, June 21, 1788, *DHRC*, 22:1747; William Lenoir at North Carolina convention, July 30, 1788, *Elliot*, 4:202; Robert Whitehill at Pennsylvania convention, Nov. 28, 1787, *DHRC*, 2:395–6; John Quincy Adams to William Cranch, Oct. 14, 1787, *DHRC*, 4:72; "Cornelius," *Hampshire Chronicle* [Massachusetts], Dec. 11, 18, 1787, ibid., 411–2.

181. Jay at New York convention, June 23, 1788, *DHRC*, 22:1823 ("comprehend" and "minute"); Hamilton, June 21, ibid., 1789; "A Landholder" IV, *Connecticut Courant*, Nov. 26, 1787, *DHRC*, 3:478–9 ("[F]ive or ten" and "more competent"); see also Corbin at Virginia convention, June 7, 1788, *DHRC*, 9:1013; Wilson at Pennsylvania convention, Nov. 30, 1787, *DHRC*, 2:442; *The Federalist No. 56* (Madison), at 346–8; Rakove, *Original Meanings*, 240–1; Edling, *Revolution in Favor of Government*, 201.

182. Madison at Virginia convention, June 11, 1788, *DHRC*, 9:1147; Corbin, June 7, ibid., 1013; Francis Dana at Massachusetts convention, Jan. 17, 1788, *DHRC*, 6:1238; Richard Harison at New York convention, June 23, 1788, *DHRC*, 22:1802–3; Hamilton, June 21, ibid., 1770–1; Wilson at Pennsylvania convention, Dec. 4, 1787, *DHRC*, 2:489; Nov. 30, ibid., 442; Albany Federal Committee, *An Impartial Address* (c. Apr. 20, 1788), *DHRC*, 21:1390; *The Federalist No. 36* (Hamilton), at 218. All states were entitled to send seven delegates to the Confederation Congress—who would collectively cast their state's one vote—but none of them in fact sent that many, and many states regularly failed to send even the two delegates that were required for a state's vote to count. See supra p. 41.

For the preceding footnote, see Smith at New York convention, June 21, 1788, *DHRC*, 22:1749.

183. Hamilton, June 20, ibid., 1728–9 (quotation); Nicholas at Virginia convention, June 4, 1788, *DHRC*, 9:921; *The Federalist No. 55* (Madison), at 343.

184. Hamilton at New York convention, June 20, 1788, *DHRC*, 22:1729–30; June 21, ibid., 1768; Jay, June 23, ibid., 1823; Nicholas at Virginia convention, June 6, 1788, *DHRC*, 9:1000–1; June 4, ibid., 921–2; *The Federalist No. 55* (Madison), at 341–2; ibid., *No. 58*, at 356–61.

185. Madison at Virginia convention, June 14, 1788, *DHRC*, 10:1283–4 ("sympathy" and "fellow feeling"); Wilson at Pennsylvania convention, Dec. 4, 1787, *DHRC*, 2:479 ("in a government"); Sedgwick at Massachusetts convention, Jan. 14, 1788, *DHRC*, 6:1185 ("a general knowledge"); see also Fisher Ames, Jan. 15, ibid., 1191–2; Dawes, Jan. 14, ibid., 1186; John Brooks, Jan. 15, ibid., 1195–6; Rufus King, ibid., 1202–3; Thomas McKean at Pennsylvania convention, Dec. 11, 1787, *DHRC*, 2:535–6; Nicholas at Virginia convention, June 4, 1788, *DHRC*, 9:924; MacLaine at North Carolina convention, July 24, 1788, *Elliot*, 4:29; *The Federalist No. 53* (Madison), 332–5.

186. Ames at Massachusetts convention, Jan. 15, 1788, *DHRC*, 6:1192–3 (quotations); Christopher Gore, Jan. 15, ibid., 1201–2; see also "A Democratic Federalist," Philadelphia *Independent Gazetteer*, Nov. 26, 1787, *DHRC*, 2:297. In Connecticut and Rhode Island, the legislatures had provided for popular votes on the selection of congressional

delegates, but in other states the people played no direct role in the selection process (editorial note, *DHRC*, 22:1698 n. 9).

187. Hamilton at New York convention, June 21, 1788, ibid., 1771–2 ("a rich man"); Robert R. Livingston, June 23, ibid., 1811–2 ("[w]e are all," "[t]he rich," and "as a bar"); Randolph at Virginia convention, June 7, 1788, *DHRC*, 9:1024–5 ("fellow-feeling"); Alexander White, "To the Citizens of Virginia," *Winchester Gazette* [Virginia], Feb. 29, 1788, *DHRC*, 8:439; *The Federalist No. 57* (Madison), at 350–1; ibid., *No. 60* (Hamilton), at 371.

188. William Symmes, Jr., to Peter Osgood, Jr., Nov. 15, 1787, *DHRC*, 4:240 ("quite ridiculous" and "little Delaware"); Joseph M'Dowall at North Carolina convention, July 28, 1788, *Elliot*, 4:124 ("its being brought"); see also Joseph Jones to Madison, Oct. 29, 1787, *PJM* (C.S.), 10:228; infra pp. 433, 469–70.

189. M'Dowall at North Carolina convention, July 28, 1788, *Elliot*, 4:124 ("giving such"); Chase, Objections, *DHRC*, 12:634 ("bribery and corruption"); see also "An Officer of the Late Continental Army," Philadelphia *Independent Gazetteer*, Nov. 6, 1787, *DHRC*, 2:212; Gilbert Livingston at New York convention, June 24, 1788, *DHRC*, 22:1836–7.

190. Albany Anti-Federal Committee Circular, Apr. 10, 1788, *DHRC*, 21:1380 ("destroy"); William Jones at Massachusetts convention, Jan. 19, 1788, *DHRC*, 6:1255 ("forget their dependence"); Samuel Nasson, Feb. 1, 1788, ibid., 1398 ("too long"); "A Columbian Patriot," *Observations*, *DHRC*, 16:281 ("an appointment"); see also Mason at Virginia convention, June 14, 1788, *DHRC*, 10:1292; Taylor at Massachusetts convention, Jan. 19, 1788, *DHRC*, 6:1257–8; Gilbert Livingston at New York convention, June 24, 1788, *DHRC*, 22:1837; Stephen Cabarrus at North Carolina convention, July 25, 1788, *Elliot*, 4:37; Luther Martin, Genuine Information IV, Baltimore *Maryland Gazette*, Jan. 8, 1788, *DHRC*, 11:159–60; Nathaniel Barrell to George Thatcher, Jan. 15, 1788, *DHRC*, 5:719.

191. Mason at Virginia convention, June 17, 1788, *DHRC*, 10:1366 ("Nothing is"); Gilbert Livingston at New York convention, June 24, 1788, *DHRC*, 22:1837 ("only with," "strangers," and "apt to forget"); Lansing, ibid., 1849 ("revive"); see also Nasson at Massachusetts convention, Feb. 1, 1788, *DHRC*, 6:1398; Eubanks, "New York," 234.

192. Smith at New York convention, June 25, 1788, *DHRC*, 22:1878 (quotations); Gilbert Livingston's proposed amendment, June 24, ibid., 1838.

193. Smith at New York convention, June 25, ibid., 1880 (quotations); Gilbert Livingston, June 24, ibid., 1837–8; Lansing, ibid., 1841; ibid., 1850; see also Henry at Virginia convention, June 13, 1788, *DHRC*, 10:1247–8; Mason, June 14, ibid., 1292; "A Plain Dealer," *Virginia Independent Chronicle*, Feb. 13, 1788, *DHRC*, 8:365; Proposed Amendment No. 18, Rhode Island convention, May 29, 1790, *DHRC*, 26:1002; Kenyon, "Men of Little Faith," 29.

194. Martin Kingsley at Massachusetts convention, Jan. 21, 1788, *DHRC*, 6:1291 (quotation); see also Taylor, Jan. 19, ibid., 1257–8; Mason at Virginia convention, June 14, 1788, *DHRC*, 10:1292.

195. Grayson, ibid., 1267; editorial note, ibid., 1297 n. 7; Arthur Lee to Edward Rutledge, Oct. 29, 1787, *DHRC*, 8:131; "Cincinnatus IV: To James Wilson," *New York Journal*, Nov. 22, 1787, *DHRC*, 14:188; Silas Lee to George Thatcher, Feb. 7, 1788, *DHRC*, 5:874.

196. Federal Farmer, *Letters to the Republican* (Nov. 8, 1787), Letter IV, *DHRC*, 19:232 (quotations); William Porter at North Carolina convention, July 28, 1788, *Elliot*, 4:115; "Many Customers," Philadelphia *Independent Gazetteer*, Dec. 1, 1787, *DHRC*, 2:309; see also Lansing's proposed amendment, New York convention, July 7, 1788, *DHRC*, 22:2108.

197. Henry at Virginia convention, June 5, 1788, *DHRC*, 9:965 ("true responsibility"); June 19, ibid., 10:1394 ("anything derogatory" and "they are"); see also Mason, June 14, ibid., 1290; Henry Pendleton in South Carolina House, Jan. 16, 1788, *DHRC*, 27:100; Joseph Taylor at North Carolina convention, July 24, 1788, *Elliot*, 4:32; M'Dowall, July 28, ibid., 119; The Society of Western Gentlemen Revise the Constitution, *Virginia Independent Chronicle*, Apr. 30, May 7, 1788, *DHRC*, 9:770.

198. U.S. Constitution, Art. I, § 3, cl. 7; Grayson at Virginia convention, June 18, 1788, *DHRC*, 10:1374 ("partners"); Henry, June 19, ibid., 1394 ("blocks"); June 14, ibid., 1285; Samuel Spencer at North Carolina convention, July 28, 1788, *Elliot*, 4:117; ibid., 124–5;

"Cincinnatus IV: To James Wilson," *New York Journal*, Nov. 22, 1787, *DHRC*, 14:189; Luther Martin, Genuine Information IX, Baltimore *Maryland Gazette*, Jan. 29, 1788, *DHRC*, 11:215–6; Arthur Lee to Edward Rutledge, Oct. 29, 1787, *DHRC*, 8:131.

199. Spencer at North Carolina convention, July 28, 1788, *Elliot*, 4:118 (quotation); see also Arthur Lee to Edward Rutledge, Oct. 29, 1787, *DHRC*, 8:131; "Cincinnatus IV: To James Wilson," *New York Journal*, Nov. 22, 1787, *DHRC*, 14:187–8.

200. Wilson at Pennsylvania convention, Dec. 11, 1787, *DHRC*, 2:565; Pendleton at Virginia convention, June 5, 1788, *DHRC*, 9:948–9; see also *The Federalist No. 62* (probably Madison), 377.

201. Hamilton at New York convention, June 24, 1788, *DHRC*, 22:1861–2 ("some permanent," "possess," and "frequently"); *The Federalist No. 63* (probably Madison), at 384 ("as a defense" and "suspend[ing]"); see also ibid., *No. 62* (probably Madison), at 378–9; Iredell at North Carolina convention, July 25, 1788, *Elliot*, 4:40–1; July 28, ibid., 133; "Marcus" (James Iredell), Answers to Mr. Mason's Objections to the New Constitution, *Norfolk and Portsmouth Journal*, Feb. 20, 1788, *DHRC*, 16:166.

202. *The Federalist No. 62* (probably Madison), at 379 ("due acquaintance"); Hamilton at New York convention, June 24, 1788, *DHRC*, 22:1866 ("is not soon"); *The Federalist No. 63* (probably Madison), at 382 ("sense of"); see also ibid., *No. 64* (Jay), at 392; Robert R. Livingston at New York convention, June 24, 1788, *DHRC*, 22:1844; King at Massachusetts convention, Jan. 19, 1788, *DHRC*, 6:1257; McKean at Pennsylvania convention, Dec. 10, 1787, *DHRC*, 2:535–6.

203. James Bowdoin at Massachusetts convention, Feb. 1, 1788, *DHRC*, 6:1391; William Davie at North Carolina convention, July 28, 1788, *Elliot*, 4:122–3; Alexander White, "To the Citizens of Virginia," *Winchester Gazette* [Virginia], Feb. 29, 1788, *DHRC*, 8:440.

204. "A Citizen of New Haven" (Sherman), Mar. 24, 1789, in Veit et al., eds., *Bill of Rights*, 221 ("abridge," "remove," and "nothing"); Robert R. Livingston at New York convention, June 24, 1788, *DHRC*, 22:1845 ("an absurd species"); Hamilton, June 25, ibid., 1894 ("turn his" and "to perpetuate"); see also Theophilus Parsons at Massachusetts convention, Jan. 23, 1788, *DHRC*, 6:1325–6.

For the preceding footnote, see Smith at New York convention, June 25, 1788, *DHRC*, 22:1879.

205. Robert R. Livingston, June 24, ibid., 1844 ("could never"); Richard Morris, ibid., 1854 ("would create" and "firmness"); Hamilton, June 25, ibid., 1891 ("prejudices" and "in which"); Madison at Virginia convention, June 14, 1788, *DHRC*, 10:1262; see also Theophilus Parsons at Massachusetts convention, Jan. 23, 1788, *DHRC*, 6:1327.

206. Iredell at North Carolina convention, July 28, 1788, *Elliot*, 4:129 ("do everything" and "[a] government"); Pinckney at South Carolina convention, May 14, 1788, *DHRC*, 27:333–4 ("the moving spring"); Madison at Virginia convention, June 14, 1788, *DHRC*, 10:1267–8 ("disagreeable"); editorial note, ibid., 1298 n. 8; see also Theophilus Parsons at Massachusetts convention, Jan. 23, 1788, *DHRC*, 6:1327; "Cassius" VI, *Massachusetts Gazette*, Dec. 18, 1787, *DHRC*, 5:480.

207. Wilson at Pennsylvania convention, Dec. 11, 1787, *DHRC*, 2:562–3; see also Charles Cotesworth Pinckney in South Carolina House, Jan. 16, 1788, *DHRC*, 27:101; Corbin at Virginia convention, June 19, 1788, *DHRC*, 10:1391–2; *The Federalist No. 64* (Jay), at 392–3; ibid., *No. 75* (Hamilton), at 453–4.

208. On the uncertainty as to whether members of Congress could be impeached, see Iredell at North Carolina convention, July 28, 1788, *Elliot*, 4:127; see also Michael J. Gerhardt, *The Federal Impeachment Process: A Constitutional and Historical Analysis* (Chicago, 2000), 75–81. For the point about criminal prosecution, see Wilson at Pennsylvania convention, Dec. 4, 1787, *DHRC*, 2:491. For another defense of empowering the Senate to try impeachments, see *The Federalist No. 65* (Hamilton), at 396–401.

209. Iredell at North Carolina convention, July 28, 1788, *Elliot*, 4:128 ("wicked motive"); Charles Cotesworth Pinckney in South Carolina House, Jan. 16, 1788, *DHRC*, 27:101–2.

210. "Marcus" (Iredell), Answers to Mr. Mason's Objections to the New Constitution, *Norfolk and Portsmouth Journal*, Feb. 20, 1788, *DHRC*, 16:165 ("not immediately," "the representatives," and "do nothing"); Iredell at North Carolina convention, July 28, 1788, *Elliot*, 4:129 ("far inferior"); Wilson at Pennsylvania convention, Dec. 4, 1787, *DHRC*,

2:491 ("with a bad grace"); see also Davie at North Carolina convention, July 28, 1788, *Elliot*, 4:120; James Wilson's Speech in the State House Yard (Philadelphia), Oct. 6, 1787, *DHRC*, 2:169–70; "A Democratic Federalist," Philadelphia *Independent Gazetteer*, Nov. 26, 1787, ibid., 296–7; "A Pennsylvanian: To the New York Convention," *Pennsylvania Gazette*, June 11, 1788, *DHRC*, 20:1141; *The Federalist No. 63* (probably Madison), at 389.

211. "An Officer of the Late Continental Army," Philadelphia *Independent Gazetteer*, Nov. 6, 1787, *DHRC*, 2:212 ("in fact"); Henry at Virginia convention, June 5, 1788, *DHRC*, 9:963 ("squints"); Mason, June 18, ibid., 1378–9 ("disinterested" and "which were advised"); see also Luther Martin, Genuine Information II, Baltimore *Maryland Gazette*, Jan. 1, 1788, *DHRC*, 11:136–7; Genuine Information IX, Jan. 29, 1788, ibid., 214–5; Lenoir at North Carolina convention, July 30, 1788, *Elliot*, 4:204; Albany Anti-Federal Committee Circular, Apr. 10, 1788, *DHRC*, 21:1381; William Symmes, Jr., to Peter Osgood, Jr., Nov. 15, 1787, *DHRC*, 4:241; William Short to William Grayson, Jan. 31, 1788, *DHRC*, 8:343; Nelson, *Royalist Revolution*, 214–5, 221–2. The New York ratifying convention proposed constitutional amendments requiring congressional consent for the president to pardon in cases of treason or to assume personal command of an army in the field (New York's Recommendatory Amendments, July 26, 1788, *DHRC*, 23:2332). For Iredell's interesting defense of the president's power to pardon even in cases of treason, see North Carolina convention, July 28, *Elliot*, 4:112–3; see also *The Federalist No. 74* (Hamilton), at 448–9.

212. Mason at Virginia convention, June 18, 1788, *DHRC*, 10:1375 ("deception"); "A Columbian Patriot," *Observations*, *DHRC*, 16:281 ("nearly tantamount"); Grayson at Virginia convention, June 18, 1788, *DHRC*, 10:1373 ("without the interposition"); editorial note, ibid., 1376 nn. 2–3; Lowndes in the South Carolina House, Jan. 17, 1788, *DHRC*, 27:126; see also George Lee Turberville to Arthur Lee, Oct. 28, 1787, *DHRC*, 13:506.

213. Grayson at Virginia convention, June 18, 1788, *DHRC*, 10:1374 (quotation); James Monroe, ibid., 1372; see also William Symmes, Jr., to Peter Osgood, Jr., Nov. 15, 1787, *DHRC*, 4:237.

214. "Cato," *State Gazette of South Carolina*, Nov. 26, 1787, *DHRC*, 27:46, 47–8; Mason at Virginia convention, June 17, 1788, *DHRC*, 10:1365 (quotations); see also Grayson, June 18, ibid., 1374; Monroe, June 10, ibid., 9:1114; Reverend James Madison to Madison, c. Oct. 1, 1787, *PJM* (C.S.), 10:184; Albany Anti-Federal Committee Circular, Apr. 10, 1788, *DHRC*, 21:1381; Luther Martin, Genuine Information IX, Baltimore *Maryland Gazette*, Jan. 29, 1788, *DHRC*, 11:213.

215. Jefferson to Madison, Dec. 20, 1787, *PJM* (C.S.), 10:337 ("Experience concurs," "the first magistrate," and "an officer"); Jefferson to Adams, Nov. 13, 1787, *PTJ* (M.S.), 12:351 ("Once in office"); Jefferson to Alexander Donald, Feb. 7, 1788, ibid., 571 ("perpetual reeligibility" and "be productive"); Jefferson to Carrington, May 27, 1788, ibid., 13:208–9 ("has scarcely" and "Our jealousy").

216. Proposed Amendment No. 5, Virginia convention, June 27, 1788, *DHRC*, 10:1551; Smith's proposed amendment, New York convention, July 4, 1788, *DHRC*, 22:2095; see also Gilbert Livingston's proposed amendment, July 22, ibid., 23:2265; Smith's proposed amendment, seconded by Jay, ibid.; John Williams, ibid.

   For the preceding footnote, see Morris to Washington, Oct. 30, 1787, *PGW* (C.S.), 5:399–400.

217. Wilson at Pennsylvania convention, Dec. 4, 1787, *DHRC*, 2:495 ("roll upon"); Iredell at North Carolina convention, July 28, 1788, *Elliot*, 4:107–8 ("secrecy"); see also Richard Dobbs Spaight, ibid., 114–5; Charles Pinckney at South Carolina convention, May 14, 1788, *DHRC*, 27:333; *The Federalist No. 70* (Hamilton), at 424.

218. Ibid., *No. 69*, at 415–23; ibid., *No. 71*, at 434; Henry Lee at Virginia convention, June 5, 1788, *DHRC*, 9:950–1; Albany Federal Committee, *An Impartial Address* (c. Apr. 20, 1788), *DHRC*, 21:1394; "An American Citizen" I (Tench Coxe), On the Federal Government, Philadelphia *Independent Gazetteer*, Sept. 26, 1787, *DHRC*, 2:140–1; "Caroliniensis," Charleston *City Gazette*, Apr. 1, 2, 1788, *DHRC*, 27:236–9; Nelson, *Royalist Revolution*, 217–25.

219. Madison at Virginia convention, June 18, 1788, *DHRC*, 10:1376–7; Iredell at North Carolina convention, July 26, 1788, *Elliot*, 4:105; Davie, ibid.; Wilson at Pennsylvania convention, Dec. 11, 1787, *DHRC*, 2:567; *The Federalist No. 68* (Hamilton), at 412–3.

220. Reverend James Madison to Madison, c. Oct. 1, 1787, *PJM* (C.S.), 10:184 ("the quantum" and "distributed"); Pennsylvania Minority Dissent, *DHRC*, 2:634–5; Spencer at the North Carolina convention, July 28, 1788, *Elliot*, 4:116, 118; "Federal Farmer," *Letters to the Republican* (Nov. 8, 1787), Letter III, *DHRC*, 19:222; see also Proposed Amendment No. 19, Virginia convention, June 27, 1788, *DHRC*, 10:1556; Cornell, *Other Founders*, 31, 270.

221. Pennsylvania Minority Dissent, *DHRC*, 2:634–5 ("undue and dangerous" and "[s]uch various"); Proposed Bill of Rights at Virginia convention, resolution 5, June 27, 1788, *DHRC*, 10:1551 ("should be separate"); Richard Henry Lee to Randolph, Oct. 16, 1787, *DHRC*, 9:64; see also George Lee Turberville to Arthur Lee, Oct. 28, 1787, *DHRC*, 13:506; Joseph Jones to Madison, Oct. 29, 1787, *PJM* (C.S.), 10:228; "Cincinnatus IV: To James Wilson," *New York Journal*, Nov. 22, 1787, *DHRC*, 14:189–90.

   For the preceding footnote, see Wilson at Pennsylvania convention, Dec. 4, 1787, *DHRC*, 2:474.

222. Pennsylvania Minority Dissent, ibid., 635 ("dangerously"); Reverend James Madison to Madison, c. Oct. 1, 1787, *PJM* (C.S.), 10:184 ("essential," "threatens ruin," and "government"); Mason's Objections, *DHRC*, 8:44 ("alarming"); Mason at Virginia convention, June 18, 1788, *DHRC*, 10:1376 ("continually" and "form"); see also Lenoir at North Carolina convention, July 24, 1788, *Elliot*, 4:27; James McClurg to Madison, Oct. 31, 1787, *PJM* (C.S.), 10:233.

223. Gerry's Objections, *DHRC*, 13:548 ("undue influence"); Spencer at North Carolina convention, July 28, 1788, *Elliot*, 4:118 ("firmness" and "long prevail"); see also Monroe at Virginia convention, June 10, 1788, *DHRC*, 9:1115; William Symmes, Jr., to Peter Osgood, Jr., Nov. 15, 1787, *DHRC*, 4:241; Nelson, *Royalist Revolution*, 204–5; Kenyon, "Men of Little Faith," 26–7.

224. Mason's Objections, *DHRC*, 8:44 ("dangerously blend[s]"); Mason at Virginia convention, June 17, 1788, *DHRC*, 10:1367 ("not only"); Arthur Lee to John Adams, Oct. 3, 1787, *DHRC*, 8:34 ("sole business"); see also Monroe at Virginia convention, June 18, 1788, *DHRC*, 10:1373; David Caldwell at North Carolina convention, July 24, 1788, *Elliot*, 4:26.

225. Mason's Objections, *DHRC*, 8:44 ("a thing"); Mason to John Lamb, June 9, 1788, *DHRC*, 9:818 ("power and responsibility"); Mason at Virginia convention, June 18, 1788, *DHRC*, 10:1376 ("the guilty," "counsellors," and "real responsibility"); Spencer at North Carolina convention, July 28, 1788, *Elliot*, 4:116–7; see also Monroe at Virginia convention, June 18, 1788, *DHRC*, 10:1372; John Smilie at Pennsylvania convention, Dec. 6, 1787, *DHRC*, 2:508; Pennsylvania Minority Dissent, ibid., 635; Reverend James Madison to Madison, Aug. 15, 1789, in Veit et al., eds., *Bill of Rights*, 277; Joseph Jones to Madison, Oct. 29, 1787, *PJM* (C.S.), 10:228; Arthur Lee to John Adams, Oct. 3, 1787, *DHRC*, 8:34.

226. On the Antifederalists' concerns about aristocracy, see Main, *Antifederalists*, 130–8; Wood, *Creation of the American Republic*, 487–92.

227. U.S. Constitution, Art. I, § 9, cl. 8 ("titles"); ibid., § 10, cl. 1 ("titles"); Lee to Randolph, Oct. 16, 1787, *DHRC*, 8:62 ("in its first" and "highly and dangerously"); Grayson at Virginia convention, June 16, 1788, *DHRC*, 10:1308–9 ("to form"); Mason at Philadelphia convention, Sept. 15, 1787, *Farrand*, 2:632 ("the dangerous" and "a tyrannical"); see also Mason's Objections, *DHRC*, 8:43–4; Richard Henry Lee to Mason, Oct. 1, 1787, ibid., 28; Arthur Lee to John Adams, Oct. 3, 1787, ibid., 34; Beeman, *Plain, Honest Men*, 355–6, 372.

228. "Centinel" I, Philadelphia *Independent Gazetteer*, Oct. 5, 1787, *DHRC*, 13:330, 335 ("a permanent" and "wealthy"); editorial note, ibid., 326–7; Pennsylvania Minority Dissent, *DHRC*, 2:637 ("lordly" and "a perfect"); "A Georgian," *Gazette of the State of Georgia*, Nov. 15, 1787, *DHRC*, 3:236 ("an aristocratical"); "John Humble, Address of the Lowborn," Philadelphia *Independent Gazetteer*, Oct. 29, 1787, *DHRC*, 2:206 ("we shall"); see also Amos Singletary at Massachusetts convention, Jan. 25, 1788, *DHRC*, 6:1345–6; Patrick

Dollard at South Carolina convention, May 22, 1788, *DHRC*, 27:379; James Lincoln in South Carolina House, Jan. 18, 1788, ibid., 155–6; "Cato" IV, *New York Journal*, Nov. 8, 1787, *DHRC*, 19:198; *A Plebeian*, *DHRC*, 20:958; "A Republican," *New York Journal*, Sept. 6, 1787, ibid., 19; Cornell, *Other Founders*, 40, 100–1; Eubanks, "New York," 311; Beeman, *Plain, Honest Men*, 377–8.

229. "An Officer of the Late Continental Army," Philadelphia *Independent Gazetteer*, Nov. 6, 1787, *DHRC*, 2:213 (quotations); see also "Federal Farmer," *Letters to the Republican* (Nov. 8, 1787), Letter I, *DHRC*, 19:211–2; Cornell, *Other Founders*, 52; Eubanks, "New York," 312.

For the preceding footnote, see John Quincy Adams Diary, Oct. 12, 1787, *DHRC*, 4:67; see also John Quincy Adams to William Cranch, Dec. 8, 1787, ibid., 402.

230. Davie at North Carolina convention, July 28, 1788, *Elliot*, 4:121–2; Wilson at Pennsylvania convention, Dec. 4, 1787, *DHRC*, 2:494 (quotation); Dec. 11, ibid., 561; Alexander White, "To the Citizens of Virginia," *Winchester Gazette* [Virginia], Feb. 29, 1788, *DHRC*, 8:441; *The Federalist No. 66* (Hamilton), at 401–2; see also Adams, *First American Constitutions*, 273.

231. Charles Cotesworth Pinckney in South Carolina House, Jan. 16, 1788, *DHRC*, 27:100–1; Wilson at Pennsylvania convention, Dec. 11, 1787, *DHRC*, 2:563; Davie at North Carolina convention, July 28, 1788, *Elliot*, 4:121–2; *The Federalist No. 75* (Hamilton), at 450–2.

232. Madison at Virginia ratifying convention, June 19, 1788, *DHRC*, 10:1396–7; Iredell at North Carolina convention, July 28, 1788, *Elliot*, 4:125–6 (quotations).

233. "A Landholder" VI, *Connecticut Courant*, Dec. 10, 1787, *DHRC*, 3:489 ("[s]ecrecy"); Iredell at North Carolina convention, July 28, 1788, *Elliot*, 4:110 ("difficult"); Randolph at Virginia convention, June 10, 1788, *DHRC*, 9:1092 ("a man"); *The Federalist No. 70* (Hamilton), at 424–8.

234. Iredell at North Carolina convention, July 28, 1788, *Elliot*, 4:110; ibid., 134; "A Landholder" VI, *Connecticut Courant*, Dec. 10, 1787, *DHRC*, 3:489 (quotation).

235. Iredell at North Carolina convention, July 28, 1788, *Elliot*, 4:108–9; see also *The Federalist No. 70* (Hamilton), at 429.

236. Iredell at North Carolina convention, July 28, 1788, *Elliot*, 4:108–9.

237. *The Federalist No. 39* (Madison), at 241–2 ("further proof," "of the republican," and "directly"); Ramsay, *Oration*, *DHRC*, 18:160 ("[a]ll distinctions" and "no privileges"); Iredell at North Carolina convention, July 30, 1788, *Elliot*, 4:195; see also Spaight, ibid., 207; Charles Cotesworth Pinckney in South Carolina House, Jan. 17, 1788, *DHRC*, 27:120.

238. Wilson at Pennsylvania convention, Dec. 11, 1787, *DHRC*, 2:579 ("open"); Dec. 4, ibid., 488 ("those most noted"); Charles Pinckney at South Carolina convention, May 14, 1788, *DHRC*, 27:326 ("dangerous" and "almost equally"); see also Albany Federal Committee, *An Impartial Address* (c. Apr. 20, 1788), *DHRC*, 21:1397; "An American Citizen" IV, *On the Federal Government* (Oct. 21, 1787), *DHRC*, 13:432; Wood, *Creation of the American Republic*, 492–3.

239. Iredell at North Carolina convention, July 28, 1788, *Elliot*, 4:132 ("uncandidly calculated"); "A Pennsylvanian: To the New York Convention," *Pennsylvania Gazette*, June 11, 1788, *DHRC*, 20:1146 ("free and equal"); see also Charles Cotesworth Pinckney in South Carolina House, Jan. 17, 1788, *DHRC*, 27:119–20; Pendleton at the Virginia ratifying convention, June 12, 1788, *DHRC*, 9:1194; "A Dialogue Between Mr. Z and Mr. &," *Massachusetts Gazette*, Oct. 31, 1787, *DHRC*, 4:177.

240. Lowndes in South Carolina House, Jan. 17, 1788, *DHRC*, 27:127.

241. "Deliberator," in Storing, ed., *The Complete Anti-Federalist*, 3:180 ("[n]o state can"); Smith at New York convention, June 27, 1788, *DHRC*, 22:1924 ("some bad laws" and "the difficulty"); "Candidus" II (Benjamin Austin), Boston *Independent Chronicle*, Dec. 20, 1787, *DHRC*, 5:494; Luther Martin, Genuine Information VIII, Baltimore *Maryland Gazette*, Jan. 22, 1788, *DHRC*, 15:435–6 ("had formerly" and "impossible"); see also William Symmes, Jr., to Peter Osgood, Jr., Nov. 15, 1787, *DHRC*, 4:240–1; Albany Anti-Federal Committee Circular, Apr. 10, 1788, *DHRC*, 21:1381; Maier, *Ratification*, 160, 224–5; Boyd, "Contract Clause," 536; infra pp. 385, 512–3.

242. Charles Cotesworth Pinckney in South Carolina House, Jan. 18, 1788, *DHRC*, 27:150 ("had corrupted"); Charles Pinckney at South Carolina convention, May 17, 1788, ibid., 353 ("carrie[d] the gold" and "debtors"); Albany Federal Committee, *An Impartial Address* (c. Apr. 20, 1788), *DHRC*, 21:1392 ("high time," "wicked," and "to fraud"); see also Jasper Yeates at Pennsylvania convention, Nov. 30, 1787, *DHRC*, 2:436; Henry Lee at Virginia convention, June 9, 1788, *DHRC*, 9:1074; Wilson at Pennsylvania convention, Dec. 4, 1787, *DHRC*, 2:500; "Cassius" VI, *Massachusetts Gazette*, Dec. 18, 1787, *DHRC*, 5:482.

243. Charles Pinckney at South Carolina convention, May 17, 1788, *DHRC*, 27:353 ("the soul" and "teach them"); Davie at North Carolina convention, July 29, 1788, *Elliot*, 4:191 ("best" and "[F]ounded"); Yeates at Pennsylvania convention, Nov. 30, 1787, *DHRC*, 2:436 ("produce respectability"); Ramsay, Oration, *DHRC*, 18:162 ("restore credit"); Bushrod Washington to Robert Carter, Nov. 4, 1787, *DHRC*, 8:144 ("restore confidence"); see also Thomas McKean at Pennsylvania convention, Nov. 28, 1787, *DHRC*, 2:418; Benjamin Rush to Jeremy Belknap, Feb. 28, 1788, *DHRC*, 16:251; Holton, *Unruly Americans*, 228–9.

244. See infra pp. 475, 512–3.

245. Supra pp. 308–9.

246. Charles Beard, *An Economic Interpretation of the Constitution of the United States* (New York, 2nd ed., 1935), 253–91. For a short summary of the historiographic debates, see Brown, *Redeeming the Republic*, 201–3. For a more thorough, albeit now dated, review of the historiography, see James H. Hutson, "Country, Court, and Constitution: Antifederalism and the Historians," *William and Mary Quarterly* (July 1981), 38:337–68.

247. Beard, *Economic Interpretation*, 73, 149 (quotations); Brown, *Charles Beard and the Constitution*; McDonald, *We the People*. Brown's book is a punishing, point-by-point critique of Beard's work, though it is much more devastating, I think, with regard to Beard's specific research and methodology than with regard to the general effort to interpret the struggle over the Constitution in terms of conflicting economic interests. For the point about Beard's inconsistency in how he characterized his own argument, see Brown, supra, 73. McDonald's data-rich study also demolishes Beard's specific argument that holders of government securities were driving the adoption of the Constitution, both in Philadelphia and at the state ratifying conventions, though much of his argument complicates, rather than refutes, an economic interpretation of the Constitution (*We the People*, passim, esp. pp. 90–1, 95, 100–1, 106, 109–10, 161–2, 181, 234–5, 242, 253, 283, 310, 321, 340–1, 354–8). For an effort to partially rehabilitate Beard from McDonald's assault, see Jackson Turner Main, "Charles Beard and the Constitution: A Critical Review of Forrest McDonald's *We the People*," *William and Mary Quarterly* (Jan. 1960), 17:86–102.

248. Main, *Antifederalists*, 280–1; see also Main, *Political Parties*, 111.

249. Wood, *Creation of the American Republic*, 483–8, 497–9; see also Gordon S. Wood, *The Radicalism of the American Revolution* (New York, 1992), 254–5. On the large number of farmers, artisans, and shopkeepers who sat in state legislatures in the 1780s, see Main, *Political Parties*, xx, 16–7, 25 tbl. 2.2, 93 tbl. 4.2.

250. Joseph Clay to Mr. Bright and Mr. Pechin, July 2, 1777, in *Letters of Joseph Clay, Merchant of Savannah, 1776–1793* (Savannah, GA, 1913), 35 ("lost," "got into," and "must ruin"); Sedgwick to Rufus King, June 18, 1787, *LCRK*, 1:224 ("of stupidity"); Gerry at Philadelphia convention, June 6, 1787, *Farrand*, 1:132 ("the worst," "had lately," and "[m]en of indigence"); Madison, June 23, ibid., 388 ("unfit" and "too great"); see also Main, *Political Parties*, 402; Kaminski, *George Clinton*, 25; Young, *Liberty Tree*, 188, 191.

251. On such conspiracy theories, see Heideking, *The Constitution Before the Judgment Seat*, 182–3; see also supra pp. 371–2.

252. Stanley Elkins and Eric McKitrick, "The Founding Fathers: Young Men of the Revolution," *Political Science Quarterly* (June 1961), 76:200–6; see also Beeman, *Plain,*

Honest Men, 64–5; Ron Chernow, *Washington: A Life* (New York, 2010), 327–8, 369; R. Kent Newmyer, *John Marshall and the Heroic Age of the Supreme Court* (Baton Rouge, LA, 2001), 24–6; Kohn, *Eagle and Sword*, 10–13; Main, *Political Parties*, 32. For strong statements to this effect by Washington, see Washington to William Gordon, July 8, 1783, in Bancroft, *History of the Formation of the Constitution*, 1:320–3; Washington to Hamilton, Mar. 31, 1783, *PAH*, 3:310.

253. Elkins and McKitrick, "Young Men of the Revolution," 203–4; Beeman, *Plain, Honest Men*, 65; Maier, *Ratification*, 163, 185; Edling, *Revolution in Favor of Government*, 179; Miller, *George Mason*, 275–7.

254. Lee to Adams, Oct. 5, 1787, *DHRC*, 8:36 ("dear friend" and "in the vineyard"); Singletary at Massachusetts convention, Jan. 25, 1788, *DHRC*, 6:1345 ("if anybody"); Thomas Tredwell speech at New York convention (not delivered), *Elliot*, 2:401 ("departed widely"); see also Lincoln in South Carolina House, Jan. 18, 1788, *DHRC*, 27:155–6; James Freeman to Theophilus Lindsey, Mar. 29, 1788, *DHRC*, 16:504; William Smith to Abraham Yates, Jr., June 12, 1788, *DHRC*, 20:1150–1; "Helvidius Priscus" I (possibly Samuel Adams), Boston *Independent Chronicle*, Dec. 27, 1787, *DHRC*, 5:537–8; Nathaniel Barrell to George Thatcher, Jan. 15, 1788, ibid., 718; Cornelius C. Schoonmaker to William Smith, July 7, 1788, *DHRC*, 22:2115–6; Bailyn, *Ideological Origins*, 331–51.

255. Adams to Lee, Dec. 3, 1787, *DHRC*, 14:333 (quotation); Kenyon, "Men of Little Faith," 3–43; see also Henry at Virginia convention, June 9, 1788, *DHRC*, 9:1059; Samuel Adams to Gerry, Aug. 22, 1789, in Veit et al., eds., *Bill of Rights*, 285; supra pp. 318–9.

For the preceding footnote, see On the New Constitution, *State Gazette of South Carolina*, Jan. 28, 1788, *DHRC*, 27:210.

256. Supra pp. 131–2, 319–20.

257. Edling, *Revolution in Favor of Government*, 8–10, 55–7, 73–88, 163–74, 219–27; see also Marks, *Independence on Trial*, passim, esp. chs. 4–5.

258. *Maryland Journal*, May 6, 1788, *DHRC*, 12:703–4; Editorial Note, The Meeting of the Tradesmen of Boston on the Constitution (Jan. 7, 1788), *DHRC*, 5:629–31; Jackson to Knox, Feb. 6, 1788, *DHRC*, 7:1580 (quotations); see also Madison to Jefferson, Oct. 24, 1787, *PJM* (C.S.), 10:216; Nathaniel Gorham to Henry Knox, Jan. 6, 1788, *DHRC*, 5:628–9; Daniel Carroll to Madison, Oct. 28, 1787, *DHRC*, 11:25; Brown, *Redeeming the Republic*, 214; Young, *Liberty Tree*, 61–3, 206–8. On the Baltimore procession specifically, see Procession Committee Broadside, pre–May 1, 1788, *DHRC*, 12:697–9; *Maryland Journal*, May 6, 1788, ibid., 703–4.

259. Randolph to Madison, c. Oct. 29, 1787, *DHRC*, 8:134 (quotation); see also Samuel Blachley Webb to Joseph Barrell, Jan. 13, 1788, *DHRC*, 20:608; Young, *Democratic Republicans of New York*, 90, 100–1; Kaminski, "New York," 80; infra pp. 406–7, 501.

260. Charles Swift to Robert E. Griffiths, Oct. 18, 1787, *DHRC*, 2:199 ("enthusiastic" and "hazards"); William Shippen, Jr., to Thomas Lee Shippen, Nov. 7–18, 1787, ibid., 235; *Pennsylvania Gazette*, Oct. 10, 1787, *DHRC*, 13:584 ("so very popular" and "dangerous"); Maier, *Ratification*, 100.

261. Rhode Island Committee to James Mitchell Varnum, May 14, 1787, *Farrand*, Supp.:2 (quotation); see also William Constable to William Chalmers, Dec. 10, 1787, *DHRC*, 19:381–2; Brown & Benson to Hewes & Anthony, Apr. 24, 1788, *DHRC*, 24:256–7; Brown & Benson to Champion & Dickson, Dec. 17, 1788, *DHRC*, 25:452; John Pintard to Elisha Boudinot, Sept. 22, 1787, *DHRC*, 19:47; Brown, *Redeeming the Republic*, 214–5; Robertson, *The Constitution and America's Destiny*, 66–7.

262. *Maryland Journal*, May 6, 1788, in Bernard Bailyn, ed., *The Debate on the Constitution* (New York, 1993), 2:430 (quotations); see also "A," *Essex Journal*, Oct. 10, 1787, *DHRC*, 4:66; Newport Mechanics' Meeting (c. Mar. 20–22, 1788), *Newport Herald*, Mar. 27, 1788, *DHRC*, 24:119; Hamilton, Conjectures, *PAH*, 4:275; Brown, *Redeeming the Republic*, 208–9, 215; Maier, *Ratification*, 164, 217, 405; Heideking, *The Constitution Before the Judgment Seat*, 248–9; Norman K. Risjord, *Chesapeake Politics, 1781–1800* (New York, 1978), 23, 42; Lienesch, "North Carolina," 348; Young, *Democratic Republicans of New York*, 100–1. For the widespread demands for protectionist

legislation made by artisans and tradesmen in parades celebrating ratification, see Heideking, supra, 362–3; see also *Pennsylvania Packet*, Dec. 15, 1787, *DHRC*, 2:607.

263. Morris at Philadelphia convention, Aug. 16, 1787, *Farrand*, 2:309 ("monied"); Ellsworth, ibid. ("friends"); Holton, *Unruly Americans*, 228–9; see also Thomas Goadsby to Kirkman, Holmes and Co., July 3, 1788, *DHRC*, 21:1259.

264. Lowndes in South Carolina House, Jan. 16, 1788, *DHRC*, 27:109 ("[A] great"); Benjamin Rush, Observations on the Fourth of July Procession in Philadelphia, *Pennsylvania Mercury*, July 15, 1788, *DHRC*, 18:263 ("the man"); Logan & Story to Stephen Collins, Nov. 2, 1787, *DHRC*, 8:141 ("If the new"); see also Minton Collins to Stephen Collins, Mar. 16, 1788, ibid., 504; May 8, 1788, quoted in editorial note, ibid. n. 3; Theodore Foster to Dwight Foster, Aug. 7, 1788, *DHRC*, 25:380–1; Adam Gilchrist to Collin McGregor, Feb. 11, 1788, *DHRC*, 27:224–5; Ramsay, Oration, *DHRC*, 18:161–2; "Federal Farmer," *Letters to the Republican* (Nov. 8, 1787), Letter I, *DHRC*, 19:211; Brown, *Redeeming the Republic*, 226–7.

265. George Turner to Winthrop Sargent, Nov. 6, 1787, *DHRC*, 2:209 ("As a public"); "A Citizen of Philadelphia" (Pelatiah Webster), *Pennsylvania Gazette*, Jan. 23, 1788, ibid., 660 ("[O]nly from"); U.S. Constitution, Art. VI, cl. 1 ("[a]ll debts"); Philadelphia convention, Aug. 25, 1787, *Farrand*, 2:414 (agreeing by ten states to one to this provision, which had been proposed by Randolph); see also Hamilton, Conjectures, *PAH*, 4:275; Holton, *Unruly Americans*, 239; Main, *Antifederalists*, 163.

For the preceding footnote, see Ferguson, *Power of the Purse*, 340–1.

266. Official Journal, Aug. 23, *Farrand*, 2:382 ("*shall* fulfill") (emphasis added); Butler, ibid., 392 ("as well to"); Mason, Aug. 25, ibid., 413 ("a great distinction" and "beget speculations"); Gerry, ibid. ("stock-jobbers"); see also statements by Madison, Randolph, and Gerry, and the motion by Morris, Aug. 22, ibid., 377; Madison to Andrew Stevenson, Nov. 17, 1830, ibid., 3:485; Madison at Virginia convention, June 17, 1788, *DHRC*, 10:1354.

267. Rutledge, Aug. 18, *Farrand*, 2:327 (all quotations but "an active"); King, ibid., 327–8 ("an active"); see also July 14, ibid., 6; Robertson, *The Constitution and America's Destiny*, 108, 196–7; Hall, *Politics Without Parties*, 266; McDonald, *We the People*, 106, 141.

268. Aug. 18, *Farrand*, 2:328 (six-to-four vote, with one delegation divided, to appoint a grand committee to consider federal assumption of the states' war debts); Committee of Eleven report, presented by William Livingston, Aug. 21, ibid., 355–6; Gerry, ibid., 356 ("alarmed"); Aug. 22, ibid., 377 (reference to states' war-related debts has disappeared from the provision proposed by the Committee of Eleven); Hamilton to Carrington, May 26, 1792, *PAH*, 11:428 ("perfectly agreed" and "were both"); see also Gerry in House of Representatives, Feb. 25, 1790, *Annals of Congress*, 1:1409–10; Ferguson, *Power of the Purse*, 219; editorial note, *PJM* (C.S.), 10:234 n. 2. To be sure, it is possible that Hamilton's recollection of his conversation with Madison during the convention was colored by his subsequent irritation with Madison for opposing, in Congress, Hamilton's plan for the federal government to assume the states' war debt.

269. On the likelihood of the federal government's assuming the states' war debts, see Matthew M'Connell to William Irvine, Sept. 20, 1787, *DHRC*, 2:132; Archibald Stuart to Madison, Dec. 2, 1787, *PJM* (C.S.), 10:291; see also Van Cleve, "Anti-Federalists' Toughest Challenge," 554–6; Richards, *Shays's Rebellion*, 124–5; but cf. Extract of a Letter from Richmond (June 26), *Pennsylvania Packet*, July 3, 1788, *DHRC*, 10:1699–700; Edling, *Revolution in Favor of Government*, 160–1.

270. James Galloway at North Carolina convention, July 29, 1788, *Elliot*, 4:190 (quotation); Collin McGregor to Neil Jamieson, Mar. 4, 1788, *DHRC*, 20:843; Ferguson, *Power of the Purse*, 256–7; see also Charles Lee to Washington, April 11, 1788, *DHRC*, 9:734–5; George Thatcher to Pierse Long, Apr. 23, 1788, *DHRC*, 17:199–200; Collin McGregor to Neil Jamieson, Oct. 10, 1787, *DHRC*, 19:77; Feb. 18, 1788, ibid., 20:786; June 4, 1788, ibid., 1128; Peter Collin to Nicholas Low, June 18, 1788, quoted in editorial note, ibid., 1129 n. 2.

271. Ferguson, *Power of the Purse*, chs. 13–14; McCraw, *The Founders and Finance*, ch. 9; Chernow, *Hamilton*, chs. 15–16. On the allegations and facts regarding insider trading, see Bates, "Northern Speculators and Southern State Debts," 40–2.

272. The figures are from Ferguson, *Power of the Purse*, 275, 284–5, though he emphasizes in conclusion that most of the speculation took place after the Constitution had been ratified (ibid., 285–6; see also Bates, "Northern Speculators and Southern State Debts," 32–8). One of the main problems with Beard's analysis is that he inferred securities holdings in 1787–88 from data derived from the funding operation of the early 1790s (Brown, *Charles Beard and the Constitution*, 48–9, 57–8, 74).

    For the preceding footnote, see Hamilton to Carrington, May 26, 1792, *PAH*, 11:440 (quotation); Bowling, *The Creation of Washington, D.C.*, chs. 5–7; Banning, *Sacred Fire*, 294–6, 312–21; Chernow, *Hamilton*, 226–31.

273. King to Madison, Jan. 27, 1788, *PJM* (C.S.), 10:437 ("the rich" and "the poor"); "Centinel" I, Philadelphia *Independent Gazetteer*, Oct. 5, 1787, *DHRC*, 13:330–2 ("the wealthy" and "most daring"); see also Main, *Antifederalists*, 280–1; Brown, *Redeeming the Republic*, 208–9; Hall, *Politics Without Parties*, xv–xvi, 294–5; Maier, *Ratification*, 76, 217; Lutz, "Connecticut," 122–3, 125, 129.

274. "Deliberator," in Storing, ed., *The Complete Anti-Federalist*, 3:180 (quotation); Brown, *Redeeming the Republic*, 202, 204–5, 210; Maier, *Ratification*, 160, 224; but cf. Van Cleve, "Anti-Federalists' Toughest Challenge," 547.

275. Gorham, Aug. 28, *Farrand*, 2:439 ("an absolute"); Hamilton, Conjectures, *PAH*, 4:275 ("all men").

276. Gorham to Madison, Jan. 27, 1788, *PJM* (C.S.), 10:435 ("[A]ll men"); Madison to Jefferson, Oct. 17, 1788, ibid., 11:297 ("created more"); Lear to Washington, June 22, 1788, *PGW* (C.S.), 6:349–50 ("[t]he opposition"); see also Knox to Washington, Dec. 11, 1787, ibid., 5:485; Ramsay to Rush, Apr. 21, 1788, *DHRC*, 27:261; "Civis" (Ramsay), *DHRC*, 16:26; Ramsay to Benjamin Lincoln, Jan. 29, 1788, *DHRC*, 15:487.

277. "Civis," *DHRC*, 16:26 ("defraud"); William Symmes, Jr., to Peter Osgood, Jr., Nov. 15, 1787, *DHRC*, 4:240 ("the principal"); Main, *Political Parties*, 104–9, 113, 140, 202, 292, 315, 357–8, 406; Owen S. Ireland, *Religion, Ethnicity, and Politics: Ratifying the Constitution in Pennsylvania* (University Park, PA, 1995), xv, xviii–xix, 211–6, 256, 265; Hall, *Politics Without Parties*, 227–9, 256–8, 286–93; Brown, *Redeeming the Republic*, 201–2; Nathaniel Joseph Eiseman, "Ratification of the Federal Constitution by the State of New Hampshire" (master's thesis, Columbia University, 1937), 105; Orin Grant Libby, "The Geographical Distribution of the Vote of the Thirteen States on the Federal Constitution, 1787–8," *Bulletin of the University of Wisconsin* (June 1894), 1:50–69.

278. Thomas Ruston to Washington, Aug. 17, 1788, *DHRC*, 18:335 ("[w]hatever ostensible" and "for the rejection"); King to Madison, Jan. 27, 1788, *PJM* (C.S.), 10:436–7 ("the same infatuation"); Van Cleve, "Anti-Federalists' Toughest Challenge," 547, 559; Kaminski, "Rhode Island," 378–9; Gillespie, "Massachusetts," 158; Libby, "Geographical Distribution of the Vote," 12; see also James Duncanson to James Maury, Feb. 17, 1789, *DHFFE*, 2:405; David Sewall to George Thatcher, Feb. 11, 1788, *DHRC*, 7:1691; *Massachusetts Centinel*, Aug. 20, 1788, *DHRC*, 25:393; July 23, ibid., 361–2; William Ellery to Ebenezer Hazard, Jan. 12, 1789, ibid., 460; infra pp. 512–3. Although acknowledging that paper money and debtor relief were an undercurrent in many state ratifying contests, Van Cleve denies that these issues "played an important role in public debate or . . . materially influenced ratification outcomes in most states" ("The Anti-Federalists' Toughest Challenge," 547–8; see also Kenyon, "Men of Little Faith," 30–2). I agree with Van Cleve that Rhode Island's monetary and fiscal radicalism had produced a significant backlash by the time of the Philadelphia convention. Nonetheless, I think he understates both the amount of open resistance Antifederalists offered to Article I, Section 10, and the extent to which clandestine opposition to this provision drove opposition to ratification.

279. Grayson to Madison, Mar. 22, 1786, *PJM* (C.S.), 8:509–10 ("one of" and "greater act"); Richard Henry Lee to Richard Lee, Sept. 13, 1787, *LRHL*, 2:436 ("almost universally," "remedied," and "no right"); see also Richard Henry Lee to Mason, May 15, 1787, *PGM*,

3:878; Mason to Jefferson, May 26, 1788, *PTJ* (M.S.), 13:206; "Federal Farmer," *Letters to the Republican* (Nov. 8, 1787), Letter III, *DHRC*, 19:229; Brown, *Redeeming the Republic*, 206; Hall, *Politics Without Parties*, 264, 266–7; Van Cleve, "Anti-Federalists' Toughest Challenge," 558.

280. Grayson at Virginia convention, June 21, 1788, *DHRC*, 10:1447; Main, *Antifederalists*, 166–7, 281; Holton, *Unruly Americans*, 232–3; Kaminski, "Paper Politics," 23; but see Henry at Virginia convention, June 9, 1788, *DHRC*, 9:1055.

281. Van Cleve, "Anti-Federalists' Toughest Challenge," 552–3, 555; John H. Flannagan, Jr., "Trying Times: Economic Depression in New Hampshire, 1781–1789" (PhD diss., Georgetown University, 1972), 349–50; McDonald, *We the People*, 212, 373.

282. Supra pp. 329–30, 336–7; infra pp. 613–5; Holton, *Unruly Americans*, 240–2; Bouton, *Taming Democracy*, 182; Edling, *Revolution in Favor of Government*, 192–5; Maier, *Ratification*, 132; Brown, *Redeeming the Republic*, 230.

283. Lambert Cadwalader to George Mitchell, Oct. 8, 1787, *DHRC*, 13:353 (quotations); Brown, *Redeeming the Republic*, 212–4; Holton, *Unruly Americans*, 242.

284. Aedanus Burke to John Lamb, June 23, 1788, *DHRC*, 18:56 ("all is disgust" and "a coffin"); Richard Bard to John Nicholson, Feb. 1, 1788, *DHRC*, 2:712 ("at least"); see also Madison to Randolph, Oct. 7, 1787, *PJM* (C.S.), 10:186; Bouton, *Taming Democracy*, 182–3; Maier, *Ratification*, 160, 207–8; Gillespie, "Massachusetts," 158; Lienesch, "North Carolina," 348; Trenholme, *Ratification of the Federal Constitution in North Carolina*, 108, 115, 161–2; Weir, "South Carolina," 201; Libby, "Geographical Distribution of the Vote," 43–4, 46–9; editorial note, *DHRC*, 18:158–9.

285. On the antieastern biases of westerners in North Carolina specifically, see Maier, *Ratification*, 405–6.

286. Morris at the Philadelphia convention, July 10, 1787, *Farrand*, 1:571 ("the danger" and "to keep"); Morris (King's Notes), July 5, ibid., 536 ("the poor"); July 11, ibid., 583 ("always most" and "furnish"); July 5, ibid., 533 ("scrupulous"). Morris had long worried about the consequences of western expansion for eastern interests. During discussions over treaty negotiations to end the Revolutionary War, he had opposed the United States' claiming boundaries all the way to the Mississippi River and navigation rights on the river (editorial note, *PRM*, 7:258–9 n. 3).

287. Gerry, July 14, *Farrand*, 2:2–3 ("the dangers" and "oppress"); Mason, July 11, ibid., 1:579 ("degrading"); Madison, ibid., 584 ("unfavorable"); July 14, ibid., 2:3 (five-to-four vote, with one delegation divided, against Gerry's motion); see also Rutledge and Mason, July 5, ibid., 1:534. However, the delegates later rejected a proposal to *require* Congress to admit new (western) states on equal terms with the original states, preferring instead to leave the issue to Congress's discretion (Aug. 29, ibid., 2:454 [nine-to-two vote against requiring Congress to admit new states on an equal footing]). See also Robinson, *Slavery in the Structure of American Politics*, 204–5; Robertson, *The Constitution and America's Destiny*, 144; Hendrickson, *Peace Pact*, 228.

288. Supra pp. 48–69; infra pp. 469, 474; William Porter at North Carolina convention, July 28, 1788, *Elliot*, 4:115; Timothy Bloodworth, July 29, ibid., 167–8; William Grayson to Nathan Dane, June 18, 1788, *DHRC*, 10:1636; Hugh Williamson to Madison, June 2, 1788, *LDC*, 25:135; Tench Coxe to Madison, Apr. 21, 1789, *PJM* (C.S.), 12:93; Maier, *Ratification*, 237–8, 276–8, 296, 301; Labunski, *James Madison*, 94, 111–2, 295–6 n. 98; Patricia Watlington, *The Partisan Spirit: Kentucky Politics, 1779–1792* (New York, 1972), 150, 156; Charles Gano Talbert, "Kentuckians in the Virginia Convention of 1788," *Register of the Kentucky Historical Society* (July 1960), 58:188.

289. Carrington to Madison, June 25, 1788, *LDC*, 25:189. For Brown's enthusiastic support of ratification, see Brown to Madison, June 7, 1788, *PJM* (C.S.), 11:89–90 & n. 2. For biographical information on Brown, see *DHRC*, 21:1226 n. 1.

290. Brown to Jefferson, Aug. 10, 1788, *LDC*, 25:283 ("the ill-advised," "laid the foundation," "conciliate," "great reason," and "see the danger"); Pittsburgh Meeting (Nov. 9), *Pittsburgh Gazette*, Nov. 17, 1787, *DHRC*, 2:286 ("proper measures," "deprived," and "liable"); see also Madison to Nicholas, May 17, 1788, *PJM* (C.S.), 11:49–50; Hugh Williamson to Madison, June 2, 1788, ibid., 72; Nicholas Gilman to President John

Sullivan of New Hampshire, Nov. 7, 1787, *DHRC*, 3:262; Holton, *Unruly Americans*, 244–8; McDonald, *We the People*, 264.

291. Lowndes in South Carolina House, Jan. 16, 1788, *DHRC*, 27:107–8 ("the smallest," "the influence," and "the sun"); Harrison to Washington, Oct. 4, 1787, *DHRC*, 8:36 ("[I]f the Constitution"); see also Grayson to William Short, Nov. 10, 1787, *DHRC*, 14:81; William Lenoir at North Carolina convention, July 30, 1788, *Elliot*, 4:205; Michael Allen Gillespie and Michael Lienesch, "Introduction," in Gillespie and Lienesch, eds., *Ratifying the Constitution*, 20–1; Rutland, *Ordeal of the Constitution*, 172–3.

292. Supra pp. 48–69, 335; Grayson at Virginia convention, June 14, 1788, *DHRC*, 10:1258 ("whether" and "God"); Dawson, June 24, ibid., 1493 ("diabolical"); see also Maier, *Ratification*, 296; Gillespie and Lienesch, "Introduction," 21; Lienesch, "North Carolina," 355; Trenholme, *Ratification of the Federal Constitution in North Carolina*, 161–2.

293. Randolph to the Speaker of the House of Delegates (dated Oct. 10; published Dec. 27, 1787), *DHRC*, 8:273 ("most repugnant"); Grayson at Virginia convention, June 11, 1788, *DHRC*, 9:1171 ("strikingly" and "this government"); Lowndes in South Carolina House, Jan. 17, 1788, *DHRC*, 27:126 ("fritter away"); Bloodworth at North Carolina convention, July 29, 1788, *Elliot*, 4:185 ("will always"); see also Mason's Objections, *DHRC*, 8:45; Monroe at Virginia convention, June 10, 1788, *DHRC*, 10:1115; Grayson, June 23, ibid., 1471; Richard Henry Lee to Randolph, Oct. 16, 1787, *DHRC*, 8:63; Grayson to Short, Nov. 10, 1787, *DHRC*, 14:82; Banning, "Virginia," 272, 297.

294. Mason at Virginia convention, June 11, 1788, *DHRC*, 9:1159 (quotation); Proposed Amendments Nos. 7 and 8, Virginia convention, June 27, ibid., 10:1554; Proposed Amendments Nos. 7 and 8, North Carolina convention, Aug. 1, 1788, *Elliot*, 4:245. Lowndes denied that migrants would flock to South Carolina in view of the "excessive heat." He predicted that once the foreign slave trade ended, South Carolina's representation in Congress would decrease (in South Carolina House, Jan. 18, 1788, *DHRC*, 27:152).

295. On the point about ownership of federal debt, see Ferguson, *Power of the Purse*, 183; Davis, *Sectionalism in American Politics*, 74; see also Hamilton to George Clinton, May 14, 1783, *PAH*, 3:354; Banning, *Sacred Fire*, 311–2. On the British debts and the federal courts, see supra p. 349 n. §; infra pp. 454–5, 470–1, 475.

296. James Madison, Sr., to Madison, Jan. 30, 1788, *PJM* (C.S.), 10:446; Abbot at North Carolina convention, July 30, 1788, *Elliot*, 4:191 (quotation); Isaac Backus Diary, *DHRC*, 7:1594; see also Joseph Spencer to Madison, Feb. 28, 1788, *DHRC*, 8:424; editorial notes, ibid., 426 nn. 2–3; Maier, *Ratification*, 207, 225; Introduction, *DHRC*, 6:1112–3; Lienesch, "North Carolina," 348; Trenholme, *Ratification of the Federal Constitution in North Carolina*, 155–6; Heideking, *The Constitution Before the Judgment Seat*, 193. On persecution of Baptists in Virginia, see Steven Waldman, *Providence, Politics, and the Birth of Religious Freedom in America* (New York, 2008), 135–8. However, Heideking emphasizes that Protestant ministers generally were strong proponents of ratification (*The Constitution Before the Judgment Seat*, 191–4).

297. New Hampshire Constitution of 1784, Art. VI ("morality"); William Jones at Massachusetts ratifying convention, Jan. 31, 1788, *DHRC*, 6:1376–7 ("a person"); Yarbrough, "New Hampshire," 237; see also Robertson, *The Constitution and America's Destiny*, 152 n. 54.

298. Thomas Lusk at Massachusetts convention, Feb. 4, 1788, *DHRC*, 6:1421 ("shuddered"); Wilson at North Carolina convention, July 30, 1788, *Elliot*, 4:212 ("that the Constitution"); David Caldwell, ibid., 199 ("an invitation" and "endanger"); see also Abbot, ibid., 192; Madison to Jefferson, Oct. 17, 1788, *PJM* (C.S.), 11:297; Amos Singletary at Massachusetts convention, Jan. 19, 1788, *DHRC*, 6:1255; reporter's statement, Jan. 31, 1788, ibid., 1375; James Innes at Virginia convention, June 25, 1788, *DHRC*, 10:1523; Maier, *Ratification*, 152, 176–7, 420–1.

299. For examples of this Federalist objection, see supra pp. 308–9.

　　For the preceding footnote, see Iredell at North Carolina convention, July 30, 1788, *Elliot*, 4:192–3 ("[A] man"); Backus at Massachusetts convention, Feb. 4, 1788, *DHRC*, 6:1421–2 ("the greatest"); see also Theophilus Parsons, Jan. 23, 1788, ibid., 1325; Daniel

Shute, Jan. 31, ibid., 1375; Phillips Payson, ibid., 1377; "Caroliniensis," Charleston *City Gazette,* Jan. 3, 1788, *DHRC,* 27:61.

300. *The Federalist No. 39* (Madison), at 240–6; Madison at Virginia convention, June 6, 1788, *DHRC,* 9:998; supra pp. 146–7, 155–6, 206, 254–5; Lansing at New York convention, *DHRC,* 22:2002; Nelson, *Royalist Revolution,* 217–8; see also Fisher Ames at Massachusetts convention, Jan. 19, 1788, *DHRC,* 6:1260; Hendrickson, *Peace Pact,* 221. Banning denies that Madison was being disingenuous and claims instead that Madison's contributions to *The Federalist* demonstrate how much his views had changed as a result of his having been educated by the discussions at the Philadelphia convention (*Sacred Fire,* 139–40, 170–2). On the altercation between Lansing and Hamilton at the New York convention, see infra pp. 402–3.

For the preceding footnote, see Hamilton, Conjectures, *PAH,* 4:276 (quotation).

301. Supra pp. 171–81, 244–5, 345–6, 365, 374.

302. Charles Cotesworth Pinckney in South Carolina House, Jan. 17, 1788, *DHRC,* 27:119–20 ("everything" and "prevents"); Pinckney at Philadelphia convention, June 26, 1787, *Farrand,* 1:426–7 ("the wealthy"); see also Randolph at Virginia convention, June 7, 1788, *DHRC,* 9:1024–5; Rufus King and Theodore Sedgwick at Massachusetts convention, Jan. 17, 1788, *DHRC,* 6:1236; supra pp. 171–2, 206, 209–11, 361, 374.

For the preceding footnote, see Robert R. Livingston at New York convention, June 25, 1788, *DHRC,* 22:1899 ("in many" and "they were rarely"); "Caesar" II, New York *Daily Advertiser,* Oct. 17, 1787, *DHRC,* 19:94 ("judge"); see also *Connecticut Courant,* Jan. 7, 1788, *DHRC,* 3:533–4; Heideking, *The Constitution Before the Judgment Seat,* 185; Eubanks, "New York," 311–2; supra p. 244.

303. Supra pp. 208–11, 361, 364, 374; "An American Citizen" IV, *On the Federal Government* (Oct. 21, 1787), *DHRC,* 13:431–2; Holton, *Unruly Americans,* 251; Swift, *The Making of an American Senate,* 13; see also Iredell at North Carolina convention, July 28, 1788, *Elliot,* 4:129.

304. On the small size of the House, compare supra pp. 171–3 with supra p. 359. On the initiation clause, compare supra p. 198 with supra p. 365. On the staggering of senators' terms, compare supra p. 211 with Charles Pinckney at South Carolina convention, May 14, 1788, *DHRC,* 27:333 ("all danger"); Madison at Virginia convention, June 6, 1788, *DHRC,* 9:998 ("a stop"); Iredell at North Carolina convention, July 25, 1788, *Elliot,* 4:42; Wilson at Pennsylvania convention, Dec. 11, 1788, *DHRC,* 2:579–80; *Aratus: To the People of Maryland* (post–Nov. 2, 1787), *DHRC,* 11:33.

305. Supra pp. 317–9, 348–50, 370–1; infra pp. 454–5, 470–1.

306. Infra pp. 422–6.

Chapter 6

1. Edling, *Revolution in Favor of Government,* 57.

2. Madison to Jefferson, Oct. 24, 1787, *PJM* (C.S.), 10:216 ("[t]he final reception"); Hamilton, Conjectures, *PAH,* 4:275–6 ("democratical jealousy"); Mitchell to William Samuel Johnson, Sept. 18, 1787, *DHRC,* 3:347 ("those indomitable spirits" and "will ever"). For other statements by Framers indicating uncertainty regarding the Constitution's fate in the ratifying contest, see Madison to Jefferson, Sept. 6, 1787, *PJM* (C.S.), 10:164; Washington to Lafayette, Sept. 18, 1787, *PGW* (C.S.), 5:334.

3. Washington to the Marquis de Lafayette, May 28, 1788, *PGW* (C.S.), 6:298–9 ("determine the political fate"); Sherman to William Floyd (undated), *DHRC,* 3:353 ("deplorable circumstances" and "Our credit"); Madison to George Nicholas, Apr. 8, 1788, *PJM* (C.S.), 11:12 ("anarchy and disunion"). For similar statements, see Madison to Pendleton, Feb. 21, 1788, ibid., 10:532–3; John Brown to James Breckinridge, Jan. 28, 1788, *DHRC,* 15:485; "Civis," *DHRC,* 16:22; "A Landholder" IX, *Connecticut Courant,* Dec. 31, 1787, *DHRC,* 3:516; "Monitor," Northampton, Mass., *Hampshire Gazette,* Oct. 24, 1787, *DHRC,* 4:116–7; Iredell at North Carolina convention, July 31, 1788, *Elliot,* 4:228; *The Federalist No. 41* (Madison), at 254–5.

4. Hamilton, "Conjectures," *PAH*, 4:276; see also Hamilton to Madison, June 8, 1788, *PJM* (C.S.), 11:99–100.

5. *The Federalist No. 1* (Hamilton), at 1 ("It has been"); Huntington at Connecticut convention, Jan. 9, 1788, *DHRC*, 3:556 ("[n]ever before"). For other similar statements, see Madison at Virginia convention, June 24, 1788, *DHRC*, 10:1499–500; Wilson at Pennsylvania convention, Nov. 24, 1787, *DHRC*, 2:353; Dec. 11, ibid., 584; Charles Pinckney at South Carolina convention, May 14, 1788, *DHRC*, 27:335.

6. Maier, *Ratification*, 97, 125–6, 207, 305, 326, 396; Wood, *Creation of the American Republic*, 498–9; see also Carrington to Madison, Feb. 10, 1788, *PJM* (C.S.), 10:494.

7. Edling, *Revolution in Favor of Government*, 25; Maier, *Ratification*, xi, 140; Cornell, *Other Founders*, 26 n. 11; Heideking, *The Constitution Before the Judgment Seat*, 63–5, 194–5. On the claim that newspapers were being read more avidly than the Bible, see "A Friend for Liberty," *Massachusetts Centinel*, Nov. 14, 1787, *DHRC*, 4:231. For another statement describing how the newspapers had "become prolific indeed" on the Constitution, see Roger Alden to Samuel William Johnson, Dec. 31, 1787, *DHRC*, 19:483.

8. Madison to Jefferson, Dec. 9, 1787, *PJM* (C.S.), 10:311 ("[t]he Constitution"); Samuel P. Savage to George Thatcher, Jan. 11, post-14, 1788, *DHRC*, 5:692 ("[l]ittle else"); George Lee Turberville to Arthur Lee, Oct. 28, 1787, *DHRC*, 13:505 ("affords matter"); Henry Van Schaack to Theodore Sedgwick, Feb. 4, 1788, *DHRC*, 7:1577 ("I can bring"). For additional statements to similar effect, see Matthew Cobb to George Thatcher, Jan. 24, 1788, *DHRC*, 5:796; Madison to Jefferson, Apr. 22, 1788, *PJM* (C.S.), 11:27–8; John Dawson to Madison, Sept. 25, 1787, ibid., 10:173; Monroe to Madison, Feb. 7, 1788, ibid., 481; James Freeman to Theophilus Lindsey, Mar. 29, 1788, *DHRC*, 16:504; *Hudson Weekly Gazette*, July 8, 1788, *DHRC*, 21:1300; James Kent to Nathaniel Lawrence, Dec. 8, 1787, *DHRC*, 19:379; Hugh Hughes to Ephraim Kirby, Apr. 3, 1788, *DHRC*, 20:890; Cornell, *Other Founders*, 19–20. For the point about seating at the Massachusetts convention, see Henry Jackson to Henry Knox, *DHRC*, 7:1536–7.

9. For debates in political clubs, see The Union Society Considers the Constitution, *DHRC*, 8:170–3; The Political Club of Danville, Kentucky, ibid., 408–17. For examples of brothers disagreeing, see Joseph Barrell to Nathaniel Barrell, Dec. 20, 1787, *DHRC*, 5:490; see also Washington to Madison, Jan. 10, 1788, *DHRC*, 8:292 (Richard Henry Lee and Francis Lightfoot Lee). For examples of good friends disagreeing, see Thomas B. Wait to George Thatcher, Jan. 8, 1788, ibid., 645; John Quincy Adams to William Cranch, Oct. 14, 1788, *DHRC*, 4:72; Dec. 8, 1788, ibid., 400; William Cranch to John Quincy Adams, Nov. 26, 1788, ibid., 318. For a man keeping his fiancée apprised of developments at the New York ratifying convention, see, e.g., Samuel Blachley Webb to Catherine Hogeboom, June 24–25, 1788, *DHRC*, 21:1222; July 13, ibid., 1314. For husbands keeping their wives informed, see, e.g., John Jay to Sarah Jay, July 5, 1788, *DHRC*, 22:2098; July 16, ibid., 23:2370; Oliver Ellsworth to Abigail Ellsworth, June 7, 1790, *DHRC*, 3:1040; Isaac Backus to Susanna Backus, Jan. 17, 1788, *DHRC*, 7:1531. The pamphlet by Mercy Otis Warren is "A Columbian Patriot," *Observations on the Constitution* (Feb. 1788), *DHRC*, 16:285. For another instance of women's involvement in private debate over the Constitution, see Maier, *Ratification*, 156. For a Columbia College student attending the New York ratifying convention on his summer holiday, see David S. Bogart to Samuel Blachley Webb, July 8, 1788, *DHRC*, 21:1296. For preachers sermonizing on the Constitution, see Richard Terrill to Garret Minor, Dec. 6, 1787, *DHRC*, 8:208; James Manning to Isaac Backus, Oct. 31, 1787, *DHRC*, 24:41. On the day of thanksgiving, see Governor John Hancock: Proclamation for a Day of Public Thanksgiving, Oct. 25, 1787, *DHRC*, 4:146.

10. "A Friend to Common Sense," *New York Journal*, Dec. 19, 1787, *DHRC*, 19:442–3 ("[a] monkey" and "every scavenger"); Extract of a letter from a gentleman of veracity in Franklin County (Mar. 2), Philadelphia *Freeman's Journal*, Mar. 19, 1787, *DHRC*, 2:723 ("half-pay officers").

11. *Massachusetts Gazette*, Jan. 18, 1788, *DHRC*, 5:744 ("[t]he proper definition" and "the word federalism"); *Albany Gazette*, Dec. 20, 1787, *DHRC*, 19:445 ("a certain animal"). For other examples of invective and insult, see *Albany Gazette*, Dec. 20, 1787, *DHRC*, 19:444; "A Bostonian," *Massachusetts Gazette*, Nov. 23, 1788, *DHRC*, 4:234; "Philanthrop: To the

People," *American Mercury*, Nov. 19, 1787, *DHRC*, 3:467. The French chargé d'affaires in New York reported that "the two parties abuse each other in the public papers with a rancor which sometimes does not even spare insults and personal invectives" (Louis Guillaume Otto to Comte de Montmorin, Nov. 26, 1787, *DHRC*, 19:309).

12. Daniell, "Ideology and Hardball," 15 ("to prevent"); From a correspondent, *Massachusetts Gazette*, Jan. 22, 1788, *DHRC*, 5:773 (Benedict Arnold); *Massachusetts Centinel*, Nov. 28, 1787, *DHRC*, 4:284 ("Where was"); Southwark, *Pennsylvania Gazette*, Oct. 3, 1787, *DHRC*, 2:157. For other examples of Federalists disparaging their adversaries for their Revolutionary War loyalties, see David Ramsay to Benjamin Rush, Feb. 17, 1788, *DHRC*, 27:227; Lansingburgh *Northern Centinel*, Nov. 27, 1787, *DHRC*, 19:310; An extract of a letter from a gentleman in South Carolina (Jan. 30), Poughkeepsie *Country Journal*, Mar. 11, 1788, *DHRC*, 20:853. Antifederalists sometimes responded by invoking their own Revolutionary War credentials as a testament to their patriotism. See, e.g., "An Old Soldier," Lansingburgh *Northern Centinel*, Sept. 10, 1787, *DHRC*, 19:24. For a defense of Mason, see "Candor," *American Herald*, Dec. 3, 1787, *DHRC*, 4:284.

13. "Z," *American Herald*, Dec. 31, 1787, *DHRC*, 5:559 ("[a] timid Whig"); Editorial Note, *DHRC*, 8:401 ("notorious timidity") (quoting "Dion," Winchester *Virginia Gazette*). A New England Federalist accused Virginian Richard Henry Lee, "the owner of several hundred Negroes," of hypocrisy for the "unusual anxiety for our liberties" that he displayed in opposing ratification ("New England: To the Honorable Richard Henry Lee, Esquire," *Connecticut Courant*, Dec. 24, 1787, *DHRC*, 3:508).

14. "A Citizen," *Gazette of the State of Georgia*, Dec. 6, 1787, *DHRC*, 3:252–3 ("cool and dispassionate," "a subject," and "personal abuse"); Introduction, *DHRC*, 2:645 ("the spirit" and "peopled"). For other objections to the pervasive invective and insult, see "Lycurgus," *Massachusetts Gazette*, Oct. 23, 1787, *DHRC*, 4:114; Winchester *Virginia Gazette*, Feb. 29, 1788, *DHRC*, 8:445; A Marylander, Baltimore *Maryland Gazette*, Feb. 12, 1788, *DHRC*, 11:298.

15. Newspaper Report of a "Warm Altercation" (*Pennsylvania Herald*, Dec. 12, 1787), *DHRC*, 2:530 (quotations). On another occasion, Findley complained that Federalist William Jackson, who had been secretary to the Philadelphia convention and was in the gallery at the Pennsylvania ratifying convention, had been "laughing for some time at everything I have said." Findley attributed this conduct not to "a superiority of understanding, but [to] the want of a sense of decency and order" (Pennsylvania convention, Dec. 12, 1787, ibid., 587). For valuable background on Findley, see Wood, "Interests and Disinterestedness," 94–100.

16. Findley, Dec. 10, 1787, *DHRC*, 2:532 ("had been at the study"); Wilson, Dec. 11, ibid., 551 ("those whose stock" and "Young man").

17. On the exchange between Hamilton and Lansing, see Abraham Bancker to Evert Bancker, June 28, 1788, *DHRC*, 21:1231 (quotations); John Lansing, Jr., to Abraham Yates, Jr., June 28, 1788, *DHRC*, 22:2010–1; Christopher P. Yates to Abraham Yates, Jr., June 30, 1788, ibid., 2011; Proceedings at New York convention, June 28, 1788, ibid., 2005. The exchange between Randolph and Henry is discussed further infra p. 473; see also Miller, *George Mason*, 291. On the altercation between Gerry and Dana, see Editors' Note, Elbridge Gerry and the Massachusetts Convention, Jan. 23–28, 1788, *DHRC*, 5:787; see also Jeremy Belknap to Ebenezer Hazard, Jan. 20, 1788, *DHRC*, 7:1534–5; Nathaniel Gorham to Henry Knox, Jan. 20, 1787, ibid., 1536; King to Madison, Jan. 20, 1788, ibid., 1539–40; Benjamin Lincoln to Washington, Jan. 20, 1787, ibid., 1541; Hall, *Politics Without Parties*, 282; Billias, *Elbridge Gerry*, 213. For another exchange of accusations and denials that at least raised the possibility of a duel, see the editorial note and correspondence involving John Francis Mercer and William Tilghman of Maryland at *DHRC*, 12:759–63.

18. Washington to John Armstrong, Sr., Apr. 25, 1788, *DHRC*, 9:760 ("a desire"); "Philadelphiensis" I, Philadelphia *Freeman's Journal*, Nov. 7, 1787, *DHRC*, 2:281 ("reason and argument"). For more such statements by Federalists, see Madison to Tench Coxe, June 11, 1788, *PJM* (C.S.), 11:102–3; Samuel Holden Parsons to Roger Alden, Dec. 24, 1787, *DHRC*, 3:501; Samuel Blachley Webb to Catherine Hogeboom, June 24–25, 1788, *DHRC*, 21:1222; James Duncanson to James Maury, Mar. 11, 1788, *DHRC*, 8:479; Joseph

Barrell to Samuel Blachley Webb, May 4, 1788, *DHRC*, 20:1086. For another such statement by an Antifederalist, see Nathan Dane to Samuel Adams, May 10, 1788, ibid., 1094.

19. Jeremiah Wadsworth to Henry Knox, Sept. 23, 1787, *DHRC*, 3:351 ("dread"); "A Citizen of Philadelphia," *Pennsylvania Gazette*, Jan. 23, 1788, *DHRC*, 2:658 ("friends"); "New England: To the Honorable Richard Henry Lee, Esquire," *Connecticut Courant*, Dec. 24, 1787, *DHRC*, 3:508 ("low envy"). For more examples of Federalists disparaging their opponents' motives, see John Francis to Nicholas Brown, July 23, 1788, *DHRC*, 21:1336; *Boston Gazette*, Oct. 15, 1787, *DHRC*, 4:80–1; Knox to Washington, Feb. 14, 1788, *DHRC*, 7:1698; "A Dialogue Between Mr. Z and Mr. &," *Massachusetts Centinel*, Nov. 7, 1787, ibid., 203; "One of the People," *Massachusetts Centinel*, Nov. 17, 1787, ibid., 262; see also supra p. 307 & n. 6; infra p. 613. For another similar charge against Lee, see Extract of a Letter from Wilmington (Nov. 17), *Pennsylvania Gazette*, Nov. 21, 1787, *DHRC*, 3:94.

On the accusation against Gerry, see *Massachusetts Centinel*, Nov. 10, 1787, *DHRC*, 4:214, 215 n. 2; see also "A Landholder" VIII, *Connecticut Courant*, Dec. 24, 1787, *DHRC*, 3:504–5; Billias, *Elbridge Gerry*, 132–5. Antifederalists naturally objected to the "very dishonorable" treatment of "the worthy" Gerry by the "aristocratical party." See "The Yeomanry of Massachusetts," *Massachusetts Gazette*, Jan. 25, 1788, *DHRC*, 5:804; see also Luther Martin to the Printer, *Maryland Journal*, Jan. 18, 1788, *DHRC*, 11:193–4; Luther Martin, Reply to Maryland "Landholder" X, *Maryland Journal*, Mar. 10, 1788, ibid., 371–8; "Ocrico," *Massachusetts Gazette*, Dec. 21, 1787, *DHRC*, 5:504. For Gerry's urgings at the Philadelphia convention that specific provision be made in favor of the payment of public creditors, see Aug. 18, 1787, *Farrand*, 2:326; Aug. 21, ibid., 356; Aug. 25, ibid., 413.

20. "A Federalist," *Boston Gazette*, Nov. 26, 1787, *DHRC*, 4:322 ("the people"); "A Real Federalist," Providence *United States Chronicle*, Mar. 27, 1788, *DHRC*, 24:244 ("a public defaulter" and "large sums"). For more examples of Antifederalists disparaging their opponents' motives, see Albany Anti-Federal Committee Circular, Apr. 10, 1788, *DHRC*, 21:1382; Hugh Ledlie to John Lamb, Jan. 15, 1788, *DHRC*, 3:580–1; Charles Tillinghast to Hugh Hughes, Jan. 27–28, 1788, *DHRC*, 20:668; *New York Journal*, June 20, 1788, *DHRC*, 10:1660. For the response to the attack on "Landholder," which apparently was not penned by Ellsworth, see "Landholder," May 8, 1788, Providence *United States Chronicle*, *DHRC*, 24:259. For similar charges of misappropriation of public funds made by Pennsylvania Antifederalists, see Introduction, *DHRC*, 2:643; Editorial Note, *DHRC*, 16:217–8; "Centinel," XVI, Philadelphia *Independent Gazetteer*, Feb. 26, 1788, ibid., 218–20.

21. Abraham G. Lansing to Abraham Yates, Jr., June 22, 1788, *DHRC*, 21:1208 ("chicanery"); Extract of a letter (Dec. 7), *Massachusetts Centinel*, Dec. 19, 1787, *DHRC*, 14:157 ("Machiavellian conduct"); "Centinel" XI, Philadelphia *Independent Gazetteer*, Jan. 16, 1788, *DHRC*, 16:543 ("prostituted"); (Col. William Donnison), "To the Public," *Boston Gazette*, Jan. 28, 1788, *DHRC*, 5:763 ("a bag of money"); *Pennsylvania Journal*, Dec. 19, 1787, *DHRC*, 19:444 (charge against Governor Clinton); Kaminski, "New York," 80, 89–90 (New York election example). On Antifederalist allegations of tampering with the mails, which were pervasive, see Introduction, *DHRC*, 2:643; Introduction, *DHRC*, 20:736; Abraham G. Lansing to Abraham Yates, Jr., June 1, 1788, ibid., 1121; Abraham Yates, Jr., to George Clinton, July 1, 1788, *DHRC*, 21:1244; editorial note, *DHRC*, 7:1711 (Elbridge Gerry complaints of mail tampering); "Centinel" IX, Philadelphia *Independent Gazetteer*, Jan. 8, 1788, *DHRC*, 16:542; "Centinel" XVIII, Apr. 9, 1788, ibid., 580–1; see also Rutland, *Ordeal of the Constitution*, 62, 128–32. A change in post office policy, which had cost-saving rather than partisan motivations, explains at least some of the delay in the circulation of newspapers across the country that editors complained of throughout 1788. See New York Journal and the Post Office, Jan. 10–Mar. 25, 1788, *DHRC*, 20:582–5; Newspapers and the Post Office, Jan. 28–Feb. 21, 1788, *DHRC*, 5:818–9; *New York Journal*, Jan. 23, 1788, *DHRC*, 20:585–6. The Antifederalist editor of the Philadelphia *Independent Gazetteer* publicly attacked Postmaster General Ebenezer Hazard, who privately dismissed the "whole noise" as "an antifederal maneuver." Eleazer Oswald's Statement, Philadelphia *Independent Gazetteer*, Mar. 12, 1788, *DHRC*, 16:557–9; Hazard

to Jeremy Belknap, Mar. 5, 1788, ibid., 554–5. For Hazard's public defense, see his letter to the editor (Mar. 19), *New York Journal*, ibid., 587–8. For more on the (unsubstantiated) bribery charges, see The Alleged Bribery and Corruption of the Delegates to the Massachusetts Convention, Jan. 21–Feb. 6, 1788, *DHRC*, 5:759; "Centinel: Bribery and Corruption!," *Boston Gazette*, Jan. 21, 1788, *DHRC*, 5:760. For the charge that the delegates from the region of Maine had been bribed with the promise of independent statehood for voting in favor of ratification at the Massachusetts convention, see *New York Journal*, Feb. 23, 1788, in *DHRC*, 7:1593 n. 3.

For the preceding footnote, see John Quincy Adams Diary, Feb. 11, 1788, *DHRC*, 7:1691.

22. Daniel Shays to the Antifederal Junto in Philadelphia, Philadelphia *Independent Gazetteer*, Sept. 25, 1787, *DHRC*, 2:136 ("write letters") (emphasis in the original); Madison to Washington, Dec. 20, 1787, *DHRC*, 8:254 ("an arrant forgery" and "[t]ricks"). On fake letters and essays generally, see Introduction, *DHRC*, 2:644.

23. "A Federalist," Poughkeepsie *Country Journal*, Apr. 22, 1788, *DHRC*, 20:899 (quotation); Editors' Note, ibid., 580; George Mason's Objections to the Constitution, Nov. 21–Dec. 19, 1787, *DHRC*, 4:287. Madison objected to the Massachusetts Antifederalists' "mutilati[on]" of both Mason's speech and Benjamin Franklin's valedictory address to the Philadelphia convention, which they altered to make Franklin sound like a lukewarm supporter of ratification (to Washington, Dec. 20, 1787, *DHRC*, 8:254 & nn. 7–8). The report of Franklin's speech to which Madison was referring is "Z," Boston *Independent Chronicle*, Dec. 6, 1787, *DHRC*, 14:358–60.

24. Philadelphia *Independent Gazetteer*, Jan. 22, 1788, *DHRC*, 2:657 ("[a] civil war"); Richard Penn Hicks to John Dickinson, July 15, 1788, *DHRC*, 21:1318 ("to defend"); see also Samuel Blachley Webb to Catherine Hogeboom, July 13, 1788, ibid., 1314; Alexander, *The Selling of the Constitutional Convention*, 184. When George Mason returned to Alexandria, Virginia, from the Philadelphia convention, according to one newspaper report, the mayor and other town leaders, who were upset at his refusal to sign the Constitution, warned him "to withdraw from that town within an hour, for they could not answer for his personal safety, from an enraged populace, should he exceed that time" (*Pennsylvania Journal*, Oct. 17, 1787, *DHRC*, 8:70). For a denial of this report, see *Massachusetts Gazette*, Nov. 20, 1787, *DHRC*, 4:283. Mason himself warned of "the most alarming consequences" if "a system so replete with defects" were enacted, and he "dreaded popular resistance to its operation" (at Virginia convention, June 23, 1788, *DHRC*, 10:1471; see also Madison to Washington, June 23, 1788, ibid., 1668–9).

25. William Shippen, Jr., to Thomas Lee Shippen, Nov. 7–18, 1787, *DHRC*, 2:235 (quotations); see also The Election of Convention Delegates, ibid., 225; Introduction, ibid., 129. On the Carlisle riot and its aftermath, see ibid., 670–708, and especially John Montgomery to James Wilson, Mar. 2, 1788, ibid., 701–4; see also Bouton, *Taming Democracy*, 185; Rutland, *Ordeal of the Constitution*, 63–5, 143–7.

26. *New York Morning Post*, June 17, 1788, *DHRC*, 21:1202 ("the rage" and "several bloody"); Extract of a letter from Poughkeepsie (July 8), New York *Daily Advertiser*, July 10, 1788, ibid., 1266 ("a general battle"). For the violence in Albany, see Albany, Albany County, ibid., 1264–5. Later, a mob celebrating New York's ratification damaged the print shop of Thomas Greenleaf, New York City's leading Antifederalist publisher (The Controversy over Thomas Greenleaf's Description of the Procession, July 24–31, 1788, ibid., 1614–9). For violence related to the ratifying contest in North Carolina, see Editors' Note, The New York Reporting of the Election Riot in Dobbs County, N.C., May 20, 1788, *DHRC*, 20:1106–7; Trenholme, *Ratification of the Federal Constitution in North Carolina*, 113. One newspaper reported the death of one of the participants in a duel over the Constitution that took place in Richmond while the Virginia ratifying convention was in session there (Paragraph of a letter from a gentleman in Petersburg, Virginia (June 15), Charleston *City Gazette*, July 9, 1788, *DHRC*, 10:1700).

27. Madison to Randolph, Jan. 10, 1788, *PJM* (C.S.), 10:355 (quotation); Rakove, *Original Meanings*, 139–40.

28. Charles W. Roll, Jr., "We, Some of the People: Apportionment in the Thirteen State Conventions Ratifying the Constitution," *Journal of American History* (June 1969),

56:22, 26, 30–4; Introduction, *DHRC*, 27:300; Maier, *Ratification*, 250, 252; Holton, *Unruly Americans*, 249; Weir, "South Carolina," 222; James W. Ely, Jr., " 'The Good Old Cause': The Ratification of the Constitution and Bill of Rights in South Carolina," in *The South's Role in the Creation of the Bill of Rights* (Robert J. Haws, ed., Jackson, MS, 1991), 101, 109–10 [hereinafter, "Ely, 'Ratification of the Constitution' "]. On malapportionment in the South Carolina legislature, see Main, *Political Parties*, 268; McDonald, *We the People*, 210. For a contemporary observation on South Carolina's legislative malapportionment, see Madison at Virginia convention, June 14, 1788, *DHRC*, 10:1260. In New York, the Antifederalists won a much larger percentage of the delegates to the ratifying convention than they did of the popular vote for convention delegates, but this was apparently a function of the at-large nature of the county contests—which meant that narrow popular majorities translated into electoral sweeps—not of malapportionment. Hamilton told Madison that the Antifederalists had won only four-sevenths of the popular vote but well over two-thirds of the convention delegates (June 8, 1788, *PJM* (C.S.), 11:99).

29. Aedanus Burke to John Lamb, June 23, 1788, *DHRC*, 18:55 (quotation); Proceedings of the Pennsylvania Assembly, Sept. 29, 1787, *DHRC*, 2:100–1, 109 (Lancaster and Carlisle); Introduction, *DHRC*, 4:125 (Worcester and York); Introduction, *DHRC*, 27:74 (Charleston); Maier, *Ratification*, 102; Boyd, *Politics of Opposition*, 24, 26, 38; Weir, "South Carolina," 222, 225; Ely, "Ratification of the Constitution," 109; see also William Shippen, Jr., to Thomas Lee Shippen, Nov. 7–18, 1787, *DHRC*, 2:235–6; "Centinel" XV, Philadelphia *Independent Gazetteer*, Feb. 22, 1788, *DHRC*, 16:191.

30. Main, *Antifederalists*, 209; Szatmary, *Shays' Rebellion*, 133; Hugh Ledlie to John Lamb, Jan. 15, 1788, *DHRC*, 3:576 ("shuffling"); Maier, *Ratification*, 345; see also John Smilie at Pennsylvania convention, Dec. 10, 1787, *DHRC*, 2:547–8.

31. Aedanus Burke to John Lamb, June 23, 1788, *DHRC*, 18:55; Introduction, *DHRC*, 27:300; Maier, *Ratification*, 250; Ely, "Ratification of the Constitution," 119; Rutland, *Ordeal of the Constitution*, 167.

32. William Petrikin to John Nicholson, Feb. 24, 1788, *DHRC*, 2:694–5 ("a great loss" and "the least notice"); Henry to John Lamb, June 9, 1788, *DHRC*, 18:40 ("the inconveniences"); Gerry to James Warren, Oct. 18, 1787, *DHRC*, 13:407 ("the supporters" and "thus give"); Wood, *Creation of the American Republic*, 485–6. On Lee's extensive efforts to coordinate opposition across states, see Lee to Gerry, Sept. 29, 1787, *DHRC*, 8:25; to William Shippen, Jr., Oct. 2, 1787, ibid., 32; to Samuel Adams, Oct. 5, 1787, ibid., 36; to George Mason, Oct. 1, 1787, ibid., 28; ibid., May 7, 1788, *DHRC*, 3:784; see also William Shippen, Jr., to Thomas Lee Shippen, Nov. 7–18, 1787, *DHRC*, 2:235; Boyd, *Politics of Opposition*, 20; Labunski, *James Madison*, 39–40. On a more substantial effort by New York Antifederalists to coordinate opposition to ratification across the states, see infra pp. 542–3 & n. 486.

33. Maier, *Ratification*, 70–5, 83, 130, 137, 142, 218, 333; Jeffrey L. Pasley, *"The Tyranny of Printers": Newspaper Politics in the Early American Republic* (Charlottesville, VA, 2001), 42–5; Bouton, *Taming Democracy*, 181; Cornell, *Other Founders*, 122; Heideking, *The Constitution Before the Judgment Seat*, 90; Rutland, *Ordeal of the Constitution*, 72–4, 135; "Centinel" XII, Philadelphia *Independent Gazetteer*, Jan. 23, 1788, *DHRC*, 15:448–9. For statements by newspaper editors strongly endorsing the idea of a free press equally accessible to both parties in the debate, see *New York Journal*, July 17, 1788, *DHRC*, 21:1324; Nathaniel Willis' Editorial Announcement, Mar. 14, 1788, *DHRC*, 8:469. South Carolina Antifederalist Aedanus Burke explained that in Charleston the printers were, "in general, British journeymen or poor citizens who are afraid to offend the great men, or merchants, who could work their ruin" (to John Lamb, June 23, 1788, *DHRC*, 18:55).

34. Hugh Ledlie to John Lamb, Jan. 15, 1788, *DHRC*, 3:576 ("evidently shut"); Burke to John Lamb, June 23, 1788, 18:55 ("the whole weight"); "Centinel" XV, Philadelphia *Independent Gazetteer*, Feb. 22, 1788, *DHRC*, 16:190 ("the newspapers" and "falsehood"); see also "Centinel" XII, Jan. 23, 1788, ibid., 3:448; "A Federalist," *Boston Gazette*, Nov. 26, 1787, *DHRC*, 4:321; Maier, *Ratification*, 74, 100–1, 137, 218; Lutz, "Connecticut," 128–9; Yarbrough, "New Hampshire," 250; Cornell, *Other Founders*, 104, 122; Heideking, *The*

Constitution Before the Judgment Seat, 90–2; Introduction, *DHRC*, 3:329–30. For an extensive discussion of the role of newspapers in the ratification debate, see Heideking, supra, 74–93. The Albany Anti-Federal Committee, noting the Federalist bias of newspapers in upstate New York, unsuccessfully endeavored to set up its own Antifederalist paper (to Melancton Smith, Mar. 1, 1788, *DHRC*, 20:834–5; see also Abraham G. Lansing to Abraham Yates, Jr., Mar. 2, 1788, ibid., 835).

For the preceding footnote, see *Connecticut Courant*, Dec. 10, 1787, *DHRC*, 3:492–3; see also *Connecticut Courant and American Mercury*, Dec. 24, 1787, ibid., 493. For the *New York Journal*, see Oct. 4, 1787, *DHRC*, 19:73. For the Federalist printers of Boston, see, e.g., Responses to "An Old Whig" I, *Massachusetts Centinel*, Oct. 31, 1787, *DHRC*, 4:179; *American Herald*, Dec. 17, 1787, ibid., 48.

35. Heideking, *The Constitution Before the Judgment Seat*, 266–73; Maier, *Ratification*, 157, 185.

36. Madison to Jefferson, Dec. 9, 1787, *DHRC*, 8:227 ("the men" and "zealously"); Benjamin Randall at Massachusetts convention, Jan. 18, 1788, *DHRC*, 6:1244 ("best men," "exerting," and "gloss"); Langdon to Washington, Feb. 28, 1788, *PGW* (C.S.), 6:132 ("almost every"); Ramsay to Benjamin Lincoln, Mar. 31, 1788, *DHRC*, 27:234 ("the whole"); see also James Freeman to Theophilus Lindsey, Mar. 29, 1788, *DHRC*, 16:504; Gouverneur Morris to Washington, Oct. 30, 1787, *PGW* (C.S.), 5:399; Tobias Lear to Washington, June 22, 1788, ibid., 6:349; Madison to Washington, Mar. 3, 1788, *DHRC*, 8:454; Madison to Pendleton, Feb. 21, 1788, *PJM* (C.S.), 10:533.

37. Madison to Archibald Stuart, Dec. 14, 1787, ibid., 326 (quotation); see also Madison to Pendleton, Feb. 21, 1788, ibid., 533; Maier, *Ratification*, 232; Heideking, *The Constitution Before the Judgment Seat*, 271–2; Rutland, *Ordeal of the Constitution*, 171; Banning, "Virginia," 287.

38. John Vaughan to John Langdon, June 6, 1788, in *DHRC*, 21:1346 n. 3 (quotation); Boyd, *Politics of Opposition*, 39, 123; Maier, *Ratification*, 146. On the possibility of submitting the Constitution directly to town meetings, see William Thompson at Massachusetts convention, Jan. 24, 1788, *DHRC*, 6:1336; infra p. 412. For a couple of examples of delegates elected as Antifederalists changing their minds over the course of the Massachusetts ratifying convention, see Nathaniel Barrell, Feb. 5, 1788, *DHRC*, 6:1449–50; William Symmes, Jr., Feb. 6, 1788, ibid., 1474–5. On the generally elite nature of delegates to state ratifying conventions, see Heideking, *The Constitution Before the Judgment Seat*, 264–6.

39. Abraham G. Lansing to Abraham Yates, Jr., June 22, 1788, *DHRC*, 21:1207 (quotations); see also John Lansing, Jr., to Abraham Yates, Jr., June 19, 1788, *DHRC*, 22:1702. At the Massachusetts convention, some Antifederalist delegates complained that their lengthy absences from home were causing financial difficulties, to which Samuel Adams replied that they ought not "to be stingy of their time or the public money, when so important an object demanded them." See Samuel Nasson, William Widgery, and Tristram Dalton at Massachusetts convention, Jan. 23, 1788, *DHRC*, 6:1333; Adams, Jan. 24, 1788, ibid., 1335; see also Heideking, *The Constitution Before the Judgment Seat*, 254–5.

40. Maier, *Ratification*, 137, 157, 184–6, 345–7; Heideking, *The Constitution Before the Judgment Seat*, 275–7; Cornell, *Other Founders*, 104–5; Wood, *Creation of the American Republic*, 486; Young, *Democratic Republicans of New York*, 52.

41. "Centinel" VIII, Philadelphia *Independent Gazetteer*, Jan. 2, 1788, *DHRC*, 15:233 ("every advantage"); Hugh Ledlie to John Lamb, Jan. 15, 1788, *DHRC*, 3:576–7 ("almost all" and "were browbeaten"); Amos Singletary at Massachusetts convention, Jan. 25, 1788, *DHRC*, 6:1345–6 ("[t]hese lawyers"); Lowndes in South Carolina House, Jan. 17, 1788, *DHRC*, 27:125 ("a number"); see also Alexander Tweed at South Carolina convention, May 20, 1788, ibid., 380–1; Dawson at Virginia convention, June 24, 1788, *DHRC*, 10:1488–9; Joseph Taylor at North Carolina convention, July 25, 1788, *Elliot*, 4:46; Maier, *Ratification*, 137, 301. The disparity in abilities was especially notable at the Massachusetts convention. See infra p. 437.

42. Rakove, *Original Meanings*, 135–6; Wood, *Creation of the American Republic*, 486; Cornell, *Other Founders*, 105; Heideking, *The Constitution Before the Judgment Seat*, 76; Pasley, "The Tyranny of Printers," 44; but see Gillespie, "Massachusetts," 147–8. For one illustration of a Federalist's invoking deference to the "worthy characters" of the convention, "with

the illustrious Washington at their head," see "Monitor," Northampton, Mass., *Hampshire Gazette*, Oct. 24, 1787, *DHRC*, 4:117–8; see also supra pp. 2–3. For a strong rejection of the claim that any such deference was shown by ordinary Americans to a social elite by the mid-eighteenth century, see Michael Zuckerman, "The Polite and the Plebeian," in Gray and Kamensky, eds., *American Revolution*. For the decision of Federalist printers in Boston to stop accepting pseudonymous publications on the grounds that "foreign and domestic enemies" ought not to be "allowed to publish their dark and alarming fears, while they are concealed," see "A Citizen," *Massachusetts Gazette*, Oct. 16, 1787, *DHRC*, 4:45 (quotation); see generally The Boston Press and the Constitution, Oct. 4–Dec. 22, 1787, ibid., 41–4. Many Antifederalist authors who were intent on preserving anonymity were more worried about avoiding physical and economic reprisals than about failing to manifest sufficient deference to the "better sort." For a strong protest against this policy of Federalist printers, which Antifederalists tended to regard as inconsistent with liberty of the press, see "Philadelphiensis" I, Philadelphia *Freeman's Journal*, Nov. 7, 1787, *DHRC*, 2:281–4.

43. On the instruction of delegates, which was the exception rather than the rule everywhere, though much less exceptional in New England, see Libby, "Geographical Distribution of the Vote," ch. 4; Maier, *Ratification*, 134–6, 147; Introduction, *DHRC*, 5:890; Heideking, *The Constitution Before the Judgment Seat*, 200–1; William Lenoir at North Carolina convention, July 30, 1788, *Elliot*, 4:202. Edling takes more seriously than I would some speakers' claims to be open to persuasion (*Revolution in Favor of Government*, 22). At the North Carolina convention, where Antifederalists had a secure majority, they delighted in noting how Federalist arguments had gone "in at one ear, and out at the other" (Timothy Bloodworth, July 28, 1788, *Elliot*, 4:143). The Pennsylvania convention was not a genuinely deliberative body either. See Maier, *Ratification*, 106; Heideking, supra, 278–9.

44. Smith to Abraham Yates, Jr., Jan. 28, 1788, *DHRC*, 20:672 ("[t]he better sort"); Tillinghast to Hugh Hughes, Jan. 27–28, 1788, ibid., 668 ("the more honest" and "on the minds"); Boyd, *Politics of Opposition*, 123, 130; Heideking, *The Constitution Before the Judgment Seat*, 318; see also Henry, *Patrick Henry*, 2:377. For the view that the Antifederalist cause "suffered exceedingly" in the Massachusetts convention by virtue of its "being conducted by unskillful hands," see John Bacon to Elbridge Gerry, Feb. 27, 1788, *DHRC*, 7:1712. One of New York's leading Antifederalists, Abraham Yates, Jr., was constantly worried about the Federalists' "dexterity at management" (to George Clinton, July 1, 1788, *DHRC*, 21:1245; see also Abraham Yates, Jr., to Abraham G. Lansing, June 29, 1788, ibid., 1240). Unsurprisingly, Federalists attributed their ability to change the minds of former doubters to their "virtue, knowledge and abilities," which "tended to dispel the mists of ignorance and prejudice," rather than to their skills at duping "the more ignorant." See Tench Coxe to James Madison, June 11, 1788, *DHRC*, 20:1138 ("virtue"); Extract of a letter from Richmond, Philadelphia *Federal Gazette*, Apr. 12, 1788, *DHRC*, 9:737 ("tended to dispel").

   Some delegates' minds clearly changed at the New Hampshire convention. See John Langdon to Rufus King, Feb. 23, 1788, *DHRC*, 16:183; see also infra p. 445. The Massachusetts convention was also a genuinely deliberative body. See Maier, *Ratification*, 168; Gorham to Knox, Jan. 20, 1788, *DHRC*, 5:752; infra pp. 436–42. Perhaps as many as 10 percent of the delegates at the Virginia ratifying convention were undecided at the outset. See Heideking, supra, 283. In Connecticut as well, some Antifederalist leaders changed their minds during the convention and voted for ratification. See, e.g., "A Connecticut Man," New York *Daily Advertiser*, Feb. 9, 1788, *DHRC*, 3:597–8. Those Antifederalists who changed their minds at the New York ratifying convention were plainly more influenced by changes in circumstances than by Federalist arguments regarding the merits of the Constitution. See infra pp. 508–10.

45. Madison to Nicholas, May 17, 1788, *PJM* (C.S.), 11:51 ("come fettered"); "Publicola: An Address to the Freemen of North Carolina," *State Gazette of North Carolina*, Mar. 20, 1788, *DHRC*, 16:438 ("absurdity" and "a negative"); Heideking, *The Constitution Before the Judgment Seat*, 201–4; Edling, *Revolution in Favor of Government*, 18–9; Maier, *Ratification*, 146–7.

46. Introduction, *DHRC*, 4:125; *Massachusetts Centinel*, Oct. 27, 1787, ibid., 138; Maier, *Ratification*, 143, 223; Boyd, *Politics of Opposition*, 26; Rutland, *Ordeal of the Constitution*, 23, 126; Hall, *Politics Without Parties*, 272–3. On the Rhode Island referendum, see infra pp. 446–7, 517–8.

47. Massachusetts delegates to James Bowdoin, Sept. 3, 1785, *LDC*, 22:612 ("effectually prevent[ing]"); Knox to Stephen Higginson, Feb. 25, 1787, in William Winslow Crosskey and William Jeffrey, Jr., *Politics and the Constitution in the History of the United States* (Chicago, 1980), 3:503 app. I ("[I]t is next to an"); supra pp. 24–33.

48. Sherman, Aug. 31, *Farrand*, 2:475 ("doubted"); King, Sept. 10, ibid., 561; Gerry, ibid. ("the indecency"); Beeman, *Plain, Honest Men*, 293, 339–40; see also Luther Martin and Daniel Carroll, Aug. 31, *Farrand*, 2:477 (unanimity); Gerry, ibid., 478 (same); William Paterson, June 16, ibid., 1:250 (same). On the Annapolis convention's explicit invocation of the Articles' unanimity requirement for amendments, see supra p. 109.

49. Gorham, July 23, *Farrand*, 2:90 ("all the states" and "the current advantage"); Wilson, June 5, ibid., 1:123 ("to be defeated" and "hoped"); Aug. 31, ibid., 2:477 (the vote rejecting unanimity); see also Wilson (Paterson's Notes), June 16, ibid., 1:272; Rakove, *Original Meanings*, 103–5.

    For the preceding footnote, see Randolph, June 4, 1788, *DHRC*, 9:935; Spaight, July 30, 1788, *Elliot*, 4:207.

50. Wilson, Aug. 30, *Farrand*, 2:468; Madison, Aug. 31, ibid., 475. For the proposal to require ten states, see Sherman, Aug. 30, ibid., 468–9; Sherman and Jonathan Dayton, Aug. 31, ibid., 477.

51. Mason, ibid. (quotations); ibid. (eight-to-three vote in favor of requiring nine states for ratification to be effective); see also Beeman, *Plain, Honest Men*, 294. The convention voted by nine states to one to confine the operations of the new government to the states that had ratified it (Aug. 31, *Farrand*, 2:475).

52. Supra p. 32; infra pp. 477–8, 498–501, 509–10, 513–4, 521–30. After the convention, Madison noted that once nine states had ratified the Constitution, "the tardy remainder must be reduced to the dilemma of either shifting for themselves, or coming in without any credit for it" (to Edmund Pendleton, Oct. 28, 1787, *PJM* (C.S.), 10:224). On the incentive of holdout states to ratify once the union was already in operation, so as to be able to influence amendments in Congress and to support a petition for a second convention, see Nathan Dane to Melancton Smith, July 3, 1788, *DHRC*, 18:218; "Solon, Jr.," *Providence Gazette*, Aug. 23, 1788, *DHRC*, 25:399–400.

    For the preceding footnote, see Albany Anti-Federal Committee Circular, Apr. 10, 1788, *DHRC*, 21:1382.

53. Dane to Smith, July 3, 1788, *DHRC*, 18:215–6 (quotations); see also "A Pennsylvanian to the New York Convention," *Pennsylvania Gazette*, June 11, 1788, *DHRC*, 20:1147–8; "Solon, jun.," *Providence Gazette*, July 5, 1788, *DHRC*, 25:347; Maier, *Ratification*, 378, 382.

54. Infra pp. 472–3, 477–8, 510–30; Randolph at Virginia convention, June 4, 1788, *DHRC*, 9:932–3, 936; Maier, *Ratification*, 457–9.

55. Rakove, *Original Meanings*, 97–8; Adams, *First American Constitutions*, 61–2, 69–73, 76–7, 84–9.

56. Sherman, June 5, *Farrand*, 1:122 ("a popular ratification"); Gerry, ibid., 123 ("the wildest ideas"); Ellsworth, July 23, ibid., 2:91 ("as a federal society"); Morris and Carroll, Aug. 31, ibid., 475; Martin, ibid., 476; see also Ellsworth and Paterson, July 23, ibid., 88; Ellsworth, June 20, ibid., 1:335; Beeman, *Plain, Honest Men*, 245–6.

57. Madison to Jefferson, Mar. 19, 1787, *PJM* (C.S.), 9:318 ("expedient"); Madison, Vices, ibid., 352–3 ("at least questionable"); Madison, June 19, *Farrand*, 1:317 ("legally paramount"); see also Randolph (McHenry's Notes), May 29, ibid., 26; Madison to Randolph, Apr. 8, 1787, *PJM* (C.S.), 9:370; Banning, *Sacred Fire*, 132. The convention voted by seven delegations to three against referring the Constitution to state legislatures (July 23, *Farrand*, 2:93). For Jefferson's criticism of the 1776 Virginia constitution on the grounds that it had not been ratified by the people, see Merrill D. Peterson, *Thomas Jefferson and the New Nation* (New York, 1970), 101–2.

58. Madison, July 23, *Farrand*, 2:92–3 ("would make essential inroads" and "and it would be"); Mason, ibid., 88 ("the mere creatures," "with whom," and "would stand"); see also Madison to Washington, Apr. 16, 1787, *PJM* (C.S.), 9:385; Madison to Pendleton, Apr. 22, 1787, ibid., 395. Jay agreed that state legislatures were bound by their own constitutions and that "alterations in the government" must be "deducible from the only source of just authority—the people." But from this insight, he drew the conclusion that special state conventions—not state legislatures—should have made the appointment of delegates to the Philadelphia convention (to Washington, Jan. 7, 1787, *PGW* (C.S.), 4:503–4).

59. Madison, July 23, *Farrand*, 2:92–3 (quotations); see also Madison, Vices, *PJM* (C.S.), 9:352–3.

60. Madison, June 5, *Farrand*, 1:122–3 ("indispensable" and "by the supreme authority"); Mason, July 23, ibid., 2:88 ("one of the most"); King, ibid., 92 ("as the most certain"); see also Wood, *Creation of the American Republic*, 382–3; Rakove, *Original Meanings*, 100–1.

61. Randolph, July 23, *Farrand*, 2:88 ("highly imprudent" and "the local demagogues"); Madison, Aug. 31, ibid., 476 ("the powers given"); King, ibid. ("equivalent"); June 5, ibid., 1:123 ("most likely"); see also Gorham, July 23, ibid., 2:90; Rakove, *Original Meanings*, 103–4; Beeman, *Plain, Honest Men*, 245; Robertson, *The Constitution and America's Destiny*, 159–60; Heideking, *The Constitution Before the Judgment Seat*, 26–7.

62. Gorham, July 23, *Farrand*, 2:90 (all quotations except "the most likely"); King, ibid., 92 ("the most likely"); see also Hugh Williamson, ibid., 91; King, June 5, ibid., 1:123. The convention voted by nine states to one in favor of ratification by special conventions (July 23, ibid., 2:94).

63. Cf. Holton, *Unruly Americans*, 249–50.

64. Rakove, *Original Meanings*, 106.

65. Committee of Detail report, resolution XXII, Aug. 6, *Farrand*, 2:189 ("assembled"); Gerry, Sept. 10, ibid., 559–60 ("just umbrage"); Hamilton, ibid., 560 ("as to the indecorum"); see also Beeman, *Plain, Honest Men*, 339–40.

66. Morris motion, Pinckney second, and eight-to-three vote, Aug. 31, *Farrand*, 2:472; FitzSimons, Sept. 10, ibid., 560 ("save Congress"); Wilson, ibid., 562 ("worse than folly," "it be safe," and "[a]fter spending"); see also King, ibid., 563. The convention rejected Gerry's motion to reconsider this vote on September 10 by a margin of seven states to three, with one state divided. During the ratifying contest, Maryland Antifederalist Luther Martin protested that, at the Philadelphia convention, "the warm advocates of this system" had struck out the requirement for congressional approval, "fearing it [the Constitution] would not meet with the approbation of Congress" (Genuine Information XII, Baltimore *Maryland Gazette*, Feb. 8, 1788, *DHRC*, 16:90).

67. Resolutions of the Convention Recommending the Procedures for Ratification, Sept. 17, 1788, *DHRC*, 1:317 ("be laid before" and "opinion"); "The Republican Federalist" V, *Massachusetts Centinel*, Jan. 19, 1788, *DHRC*, 5:749 ("remarkable," "vehicles," and "passing"); see also Labunski, *James Madison*, 14.

68. Carrington to Madison, Sept. 23, 1787, *DHRC*, 8:14.

69. Dane to Caleb Strong, Oct. 10, 1787, *DHRC*, 4:63 (quotation); see also Madison to Washington, Sept. 30, 1787, *PJM* (C.S.), 10:179–80; Rakove, *Original Meanings*, 109–10. Dane thought that had Congress "taken time to examine it, as so respectable a body ought always to do [in] such important cases," it was "highly probable that Congress would have very fully approved of the plan proposed and on the principles which actuated the convention."

70. Melancton Smith's Notes, Sept. 27, 1787, *DHRC*, 1:336–7 (Lee) ("strangest doctrine" and "all wisdom"); Lee to Mason, Oct. 1, 1787, *DHRC*, 8:28 ("[i]t was with us"); Maier, *Ratification*, 56; Rakove, *Original Meanings*, 108–9. Lee's proposed amendments appear in *DHRC*, 1:337–9; see also John P. Kaminski, "The Constitution Without a Bill of Rights," in Patrick T. Conley and John P. Kaminski, eds., *The Bill of Rights and the States: The Colonial and Revolutionary Origins of American Liberties* (Madison, WI, 1992), 24.

71. For the Federalist opposition to amendments in Congress, see, e.g., Melancton Smith's Notes, Sept. 27, 1787, *DHRC*, 1:333 (Pierce Butler), 339 (Carrington).

72. Madison to Washington, Sept. 30, 1787, *PJM* (C.S.), 10:180 (all quotations); see also Melancton Smith's Notes, Sept. 27, 1787, *DHRC*, 1:335–7 (Madison and King); Maier, *Ratification*, 55.

73. Madison to Washington, Sept. 30, 1787, *PJM* (C.S.), 10:180. The states' proposed amendments to the Articles are collected in *DHRC*, 1:140–74.

74. Lee to Mason, Oct. 1, 1787, *DHRC*, 8:29 ("respectful marks"); Melancton Smith's Notes, Sept. 27, 1787, *DHRC*, 1:332 (Madison) ("does not agree"); ibid., 333 (William Samuel Johnson); Edward Carrington's Motion, ibid., 334–5 ("agree[d]"); Madison to Washington, Sept. 30, 1787, *PJM* (C.S.), 10:180 ("would have been").

75. Ibid., 179 (quotation); Nathan Dane's Motion, Sept. 26, 1787, *DHRC*, 1:328; see also Richard Henry Lee's Motion, Sept. 27, ibid., 329–30. As Lee explained the Antifederalists' argument, congressional delegates who opposed unconditional ratification believed that the Articles' unanimity requirement for amendments "precluded us from giving an opinion concerning a plan subversive of the present system and eventually forming a new confederacy of nine instead of thirteen states" (to Mason, Oct. 1, 1787, *DHRC*, 8:28–9).

76. Madison to Washington, Sept. 30, 1787, *PJM* (C.S.), 10:179 (quotations); Melancton Smith's Notes, Sept. 27, 1787, *DHRC*, 1:332 (Madison). When pressed by Richard Henry Lee, Madison offered the Northwest Ordinance as an example of the Confederation Congress's exceeding its powers (ibid., 333).

77. Lee to Samuel Adams, Oct. 27, 1787, *DHRC*, 1:348 ("a dispassionate"); Lee to Randolph, Oct. 16, 1787, *DHRC*, 8:64 ("to alarm"). On the number of convention delegates then sitting in Congress, see Arthur Lee to John Adams, Oct. 3, 1787, ibid., 34; The Confederation Congress and the Constitution, Sept. 26–28, 1787, *DHRC*, 13:229.

78. Madison to Washington, Sept. 30, 1787, *PJM* (C.S.), 10:180 ("threatened"); Journals of Congress, Sept. 28, 1787, *JCC*, 33:549 ("transmit," "in order to be," and "unanimous"); Lee to Randolph, Oct. 16, 1787, *DHRC*, 1:64 ("without a syllable"); Lee to Mason, Oct. 1, 1787, *DHRC*, 8:29 ("to have it mistaken"); see also Editors' Note, The Confederation Congress and the Constitution, Sept. 26–28, 1788, ibid., 21; Arthur Lee to John Adams, Oct. 3, 1787, ibid., 34; Labunski, *James Madison*, 17–8; Maier, *Ratification*, 58; Rakove, *Original Meanings*, 109–10.

79. Madison to Washington, Sept. 30, 1787, *PJM* (C.S.), 10:181 ("[t]he circumstance"); Madison to Jefferson, Oct. 24, 1787, ibid., 217 ("very serious effort," "to embarrass," and "[i]n order"). Carrington similarly explained that "a great majority in Congress" would have given the Constitution "a warm approbation," but Federalists thought it best to secure unanimous consent to a "bare" transmission (to Jefferson, Oct. 23, 1787, *DHRC*, 8:93).

80. Washington to Madison, Oct. 10, 1787, *PJM* (C.S.), 10:189 ("feeble," "stronger marks," and "[t]his apparent unanimity"); "Sidney," *Albany Gazette*, Jan. 24, 1788, *DHRC*, 20:646 ("barely" and "unanimous"); see also "Centinel" II, Philadelphia *Freeman's Journal*, Oct. 24, 1787, *DHRC*, 13:467–8; Heideking, *The Constitution Before the Judgment Seat*, 33. Carrington agreed with Washington that "people do not scrutinize terms" and that "the unanimity of Congress in recommending a measure to their consideration naturally implies approbation" (to Jefferson, Oct. 23, 1787, *DHRC*, 8:93).

81. Resolutions of the Convention Recommending the Procedures for Ratification, Sept. 17, 1787, *DHRC*, 1:318 ("be submitted"); Madison in the House of Representatives, Apr. 6, 1796, *Annals of Congress*, 5:776 ("life and validity" and "nothing more").

82. Morris, Aug. 31, *Farrand*, 2:478 (quotations); ibid., 479 (the vote).

83. Lansing (Yates's Notes), June 16, *Farrand*, 1:258. For unanimous votes to summon ratifying conventions even in state legislatures where Antifederalists commanded significant support, see, e.g., South Carolina House of Representatives Proceeding, Jan. 19, 1788, *DHRC*, 27:161; Newspaper Reports of Virginia House of Delegates' Proceedings and Debates, Oct. 25, 1788, *DHRC*, 8:114.

84. Morris to Washington, Oct. 30, 1787, *PGW* (C.S.), 5:399 ("assign to the people"); Newspaper Reports of Senate Debates (New York), Feb. 1, 1788, *DHRC*, 20:717 (Duane) ("Is there a man"); *Massachusetts Centinel*, Oct. 27, 1787, *DHRC*, 4:136–7 ("impossible" and "we have no right") (speeches of Charles Jarvis and Thomas Dawes, Jr., respectively); see also Heideking, *The Constitution Before the Judgment Seat*, 51–2; Boyd, *Politics of*

Opposition, 40. In Rhode Island, a Federalist newspaper editor observed that the legislature's repeated refusals to call a ratifying convention "strongly impl[y] that the people are not fit to be trusted with so important a subject as the establishment of a government" (*Newport Herald*, June 11, 1789, *DHRC*, 25:536).

85. For detailed discussions of the state legislatures' calling of conventions, see Boyd, *Politics of Opposition*, ch. 2; Heideking, *The Constitution Before the Judgment Seat*, ch. 1. The large state of Pennsylvania actually was the first to call a convention. See infra p. 427.

86. Madison to Jefferson, Oct. 24, 1787, *PJM* (C.S.), 10:216 (quotation); Beeman, *Plain, Honest Men*, 382–4; Maier, *Ratification*, 122–4, 137–8; Saladino, "Delaware," 41; Shumer, "New Jersey," 71–4; Cashin, "Georgia," 95. In none of these small states were the convention proceedings well reported. The relatively little information that exists is collected in volume 3 of *DHRC*.

87. Sherman and Ellsworth to Governor Huntington, Sept. 26, 1787, *DHRC*, 3:352 ("this state's" and "[t]he equal representation"); Lambert Cadwalader to George Mitchell, Oct. 8, 1787, *DHRC*, 13:352–3 ("when I reflect"); Washington to John Langdon, Apr. 2, 1788, *PGW* (C.S.), 6:187 ("holds out advantages"); William Symmes, Jr., to Peter Osgood, Jr., Nov. 15, 1787, *DHRC*, 4:237 ("quite ridiculous"); Henry at Virginia convention, June 12, 1788, *DHRC*, 10:1218 ("petty states"); see also "Phocion," Providence *United States Chronicle*, July 17, 1788, *DHRC*, 25:358; Gillespie and Lienesch, "Introduction," 20; Saladino, "Delaware," 43, 44; Shumer, "New Jersey," 71.

88. Onuf, "Maryland," 185, 194; McDonald, *We the People*, ch. 5; Gorham at Philadelphia convention, June 29, Farrand, 1:462.

89. "The Landholder" X, *Connecticut Courant*, Mar. 3, 1788, *DHRC*, 16:305–6 ("the adoption" and "[s]hould a disunion"); "Phocion," Providence *United States Chronicle*, July 17, 1788, *DHRC*, 25:357–8 ("natural," "much more," and "clearly saw"); see also Ellsworth at Connecticut convention, Jan. 4, 1788, *DHRC*, 3:541–2.

90. Gorham, June 29, Farrand, 1:462 (quotation); supra pp. 31–3, 151.

91. "The Landholder" XI, *Connecticut Courant*, Mar. 10, 1788, *DHRC*, 16:368 ("just share" and "be collected"); "A Landholder" IX, *Connecticut Courant*, Dec. 31, 1787, *DHRC*, 3:516 ("draw an annual tribute"); "A Columbian Patriot," *Observations*, *DHRC*, 16:287 ("more from irritation"); see also Ellsworth at Connecticut convention, Jan. 4, 1788, *DHRC*, 3:544; "A Farmer: To the Farmers of Connecticut," *New Haven Gazette*, Oct. 18, 1787, ibid., 393; *A Plebeian*, *DHRC*, 20:954; Maier, *Ratification*, 122–3; Holton, *Unruly Americans*, 240–1; Brown, *Redeeming the Republic*, 211–2; Saladino, "Delaware," 45; Gillespie and Lienesch, "Introduction," 20; Lutz, "Connecticut," 134; Shumer, "New Jersey," 86.

92. McDonald, *We the People*, 119–20; Saladino, "Delaware," 45.

93. "A Columbian Patriot," *Observations*, *DHRC*, 16:87 ("naturally attract"); Madison to Randolph, Apr. 15, 1787, *PJM* (C.S.), 9:379 (all other quotations). On battles over the location of Congress during the Confederation period, see Davis, *Sectionalism in American Politics*, ch. 4; Bowling, *The Creation of Washington, D.C.*, chs. 1–2.

For the preceding footnote, see Davis, *Sectionalism in American Politics*, 59, 61–2 ("the bosom" at p. 59 [quoting Arthur Lee]; "unhealthy" at p. 61 [quoting Rhode Island congressional delegate David Howell]); Arthur Lee to St. George Tucker, July 21, 1783, *LDC*, 20:436 ("Mr. Robert Morris's"); see also Bowling, supra, 29–30, 36, 39–40; Banning, *Sacred Fire*, 46; Kohn, *Eagle and Sword*, 50; Samuel Osgood to Stephen Higginson, Feb. 2, 1784, *LDC*, 21:324–5.

94. King, Aug. 11, Farrand, 2:261 ("[t]he mutability"); Spaight, ibid. ("never be able"); Madison, ibid. ("contemplate"); see also Williamson and Carroll, ibid., 262; Bowling, *The Creation of Washington, D.C.*, 79–80. For the efforts to change the residence of Congress in the months before the Philadelphia convention, see William Irvine to James Wilson, Mar. 6, 1787, *LDC*, 24:129; Nathaniel Mitchell to Gunning Bedford, Feb. 10, 1787, ibid., 89; William Grayson to William Short, Apr. 16, 1787, ibid., 228; Davis, *Sectionalism in American Politics*, 156–7; Bowling, supra, 70–2.

95. Henry at Virginia convention, June 9, 1788, *DHRC*, 9:1056 (quotations); The Delaware Convention, *DHRC*, 3:105; Convention Resolution Recommending Cession of Land for Federal Capital, Dec. 7, 1787, ibid., 109; Proceedings of the Pennsylvania Assembly, Sept.

18, 1787, *DHRC*, 2:60–1 (Franklin); Proceedings of Pennsylvania convention, Dec. 15, 1787, ibid., 611–2; The New Jersey Convention, *DHRC*, 3:177; Proceedings of the New Jersey convention, Dec. 20, 1788, ibid., 187–8; see also Saladino, "Delaware," 40, 44; Maier, *Ratification*, 59, 122.

Disputes over relocating the national capital continued to embroil Congress in the summer of 1788, when the Constitution had been put into operation by the ratification of nine states. After the failure of several efforts in Congress to move the seat of the national government from New York City, Madison, who considered New York an "extremely objectionable" location, wrote Washington that "[i]t is truly mortifying that the outset of the new government should be immediately preceded by such a display of locality, as portends the continuance of an evil which has dishonored the old, and gives countenance to some of the most popular arguments which have been inculcated by the southern Antifederalists" (Aug. 24, 1788, *PJM* (C.S.), 11:240–1). See also Madison to Jefferson, Sept. 21, 1788, ibid., 258; Aug. 23, 1788, ibid., 239; Aug. 10, 1788, ibid., 226; Carrington to Monroe, Sept. 15, 1788, *LDC*, 25:372; Bowling, *The Creation of Washington, D.C.*, 80, 87–96.

96. Governor George Mathews to the Speaker of the Assembly, Oct. 18, 1787, *DHRC*, 3:225 ("unavoidable"); Nicholas Gilman to President John Sullivan of New Hampshire, Nov. 7, 1787, ibid., 261 ("under the greatest apprehensions"); Clay to John Pierce, Oct. 17, 1787, ibid., 232 ("reason to apprehend" and "the most ruinous"); The Georgia Assembly Calls the State Convention, ibid., 220; Secretary of Congress Charles Thomson to Connecticut Governor Samuel Huntington, Dec. 27, 1787, *LDC*, 24:599 (the law raising troops); see also Extract of a Letter from Augusta, Charleston *Columbian Herald*, Oct. 15, 1787, *DHRC*, 3:223; Cashin, "Georgia," 105; Holton, *Unruly Americans*, 245–6; Coleman, *American Revolution in Georgia*, 269; McDonald, *We the People*, 129. For background to the conflict between Georgia and the Creek Indians, see Coleman, supra, ch. 15.

97. Grayson to Short, Nov. 10, 1787, *DHRC*, 14:82 ("highly probable" and "at present"); Washington to Samuel Powel, Jan. 18, 1788, *PGW* (C.S.), 6:45–6 ("a weak state" and "embrace"); see also Washington to Knox, Jan. 10, 1788, ibid., 28; Madison to Jefferson, Oct. 24, 1787, *PJM* (C.S.), 10:219.

98. "A Columbian Patriot," *Observations*, *DHRC*, 16:287 ("apprehensive"); Clay to Pierce, Oct. 17, 1787, *DHRC*, 3:232 ("avoid[ing] this great evil"); The Georgia Convention, Dec. 25, 1787–Jan. 5, 1788, ibid., 269; Holton, *Unruly Americans*, 244–5; see also "The Landholder" X, *Connecticut Courant*, Mar. 3, 1788, *DHRC*, 16:305; Maier, *Ratification*, 123–4; Coleman, *American Revolution in Georgia*, 270–1; Brown, *Redeeming the Republic*, 213; Beeman, *Plain, Honest Men*, 383–4; Heideking, *The Constitution Before the Judgment Seat*, 226; Cashin, "Georgia," 108.

99. Pennsylvania Assembly Debates, Sept. 28, 1787, *DHRC*, 2:68–9 (Resolutions of George Clymer on Calling a Convention); ibid., 70–1, 71–2 (Daniel Clymer); ibid., 72 (Gerardus Wynkoop); ibid., 79–81 (Hugh Brackenridge); Boyd, *Politics of Opposition*, 23; Beeman, *Plain, Honest Men*, 376; Maier, *Ratification*, 59–60; Heideking, *The Constitution Before the Judgment Seat*, 36–7.

100. "Centinel" I, Philadelphia *Independent Gazetteer*, Oct. 5, 1787, *DHRC*, 13:329 (quotations); Assembly Debates, Sept. 28, 1787, *DHRC*, 2:69 (Robert Whitehill); ibid., 71 (William Findley); ibid., 74–5 (Whitehill); ibid., 82–5 (Findley); ibid., 92 (Findley); see also Pennsylvania Minority Dissent, ibid., 620–1; Boyd, *Politics of Opposition*, 23; Maier, *Ratification*, 60–1; Rutland, *Ordeal of the Constitution*, 20.

101. Introduction, *DHRC*, 2:54–5; Pennsylvania Assembly Debates, Sept. 28–29, 1787, ibid., 96–108; Tench Coxe to Madison, Sept. 28–29, 1787, ibid., 121–2; Samuel Hodgdon to Timothy Pickering, Sept. 29, 1787, ibid., 122–3; Charles Swift to Robert E. Griffiths, Oct. 18, 1787, ibid., 199; see also Maier, *Ratification*, 63–4; Beeman, *Plain, Honest Men*, 376–7; Bouton, *Taming Democracy*, 180; Heideking, *The Constitution Before the Judgment Seat*, 37–8. When George Mason learned of what had happened in the Pennsylvania Assembly, he predicted that "such intemperate and violent measures" would result in the defeat of the Constitution because they would "betray [the Federalists'] consciousness of its not bearing the test of impartial examination" (to Elbridge Gerry, Oct. 20, 1787,

DHRC, 8:87). See also Thomas B. Wait to George Thatcher, Jan. 8, 1788, *DHRC*, 5:645; Nathan Dane to Caleb Strong, Oct. 10, 1787, *DHRC*, 4:63.

   For the preceding footnote, see "America: To the Dissenting Members of the Late Convention of Pennsylvania," New York *Daily Advertiser*, Dec. 31, 1787, *DHRC*, 19:492.

102. Morris to Washington, Oct. 30, 1787, *PGW* (C.S.), 5:399 ("enthusiastic," "the cold," and "the wicked"); Madison to Jefferson, Oct. 24, 1787, *PJM* (C.S.), 10:216 ("divided"); William Shippen, Jr., to Thomas Lee Shippen, Nov. 7–18, 1787, *DHRC*, 2:235 ("five or six," "a very respectable," and "a severe"); see also Arthur Lee to Edward Rutledge, Oct. 29, 1787, *DHRC*, 8:131; Madison to Randolph, Oct. 21, 1787, *PJM* (C.S.) 10:199; Maier, *Ratification*, 97.

   For the preceding footnote, see Belknap to Rush, Feb. 12, 1788, *DHRC*, 7:1588; Rush to Belknap, Feb. 28, 1788, *DHRC*, 16:250, 251–2 nn. 2–3 ("highly Federal" at p. 250).

103. Ireland, *Ratifying the Constitution in Pennsylvania*, xv, 215; Main, *Political Parties*, 174–81, 202; Bouton, *Taming Democracy*, 5–6, 52–3, 194; Adams, *First American Constitutions*, 177, 246, 248; Wood, *Creation of the American Republic*, 226–7, 231–2; Rakove, *Original Meanings*, 111; Maier, *Ratification*, 66, 98–9; Graham, "Pennsylvania," 52.

104. "A Landholder" VIII, *Connecticut Courant*, Dec. 24, 1787, *DHRC*, 3:506 ("old warfare" and "a sufficient motive"); Madison to Jefferson, Feb. 19, 1788, *PJM* (C.S.), 10:519 ("[t]he cause of the inflammation"); see also Grayson to Short, Nov. 10, 1787, *DHRC*, 14:82; Charles Swift to Robert E. Griffiths, Oct. 18, 1787, *DHRC*, 2:199; Timothy Pickering to John Gardner, Dec. 11, 1787, ibid., 586.

105. For recognition during the convention that Federalists enjoyed roughly a two-to-one advantage, see Timothy Pickering to John Pickering, Nov. 29, 1787, ibid., 423; William Shippen, Jr., to Thomas Lee Shippen, Nov. 29, 1787, ibid., 424; see also Editorial Note, ibid., 129. On the election results generally, see Heideking, *The Constitution Before the Judgment Seat*, 207–8. Madison reported that the election results had "reduced the adoption of the plan in that state [Pennsylvania] to absolute certainty" (to Randolph, Nov. 18, 1787, *PJM* (C.S.), 10:252). The election occasioned more violence in Philadelphia, where a mob attacked some of the western assemblymen in their lodgings. See William Shippen, Jr., to Thomas Lee Shippen, Nov. 7–18, 1787, *DHRC*, 2:235.

   For the preceding footnote, see Philadelphia County Petition to the Pennsylvania Convention, Dec. 11, 1787, ibid., 318; see also "Columbus," *Pennsylvania Herald*, Dec. 8, 1787, ibid., 314.

106. For challenges to the precipitancy of the proceedings, see John Smilie, Nov. 24, ibid., 336 ("precipitancy"); Findley, Dec. 12, ibid., 587; Smilie, ibid., 600. For some of the principal Antifederalist speeches criticizing the substance of the Constitution, see Whitehill, Nov. 28, ibid., 393–8; Smilie, ibid., 407–10; Whitehill, Nov. 30, ibid., 425–8; Findley, ibid., 439–40; Smilie, Dec. 4, 1787, ibid., 465–6; Findley, Dec. 6, ibid., 510. For discussions of the Pennsylvania convention's proceedings, see Heideking, *The Constitution Before the Judgment Seat*, 285–7; Maier, *Ratification*, 101–20.

107. Thomas McKean, Nov. 24, *DHRC*, 2:337 ("alter and amend"); Thomas Hartley, Nov. 27, ibid., 370; McKean, Dec. 12, 1787, ibid., 596; see also Whitehill, ibid. (presenting petition from Cumberland County opposing ratification without prior amendments).

   For the preceding footnote, see Kaminski and Moore, *An Assembly of Demigods*, 150 (quoting Francis Hopkinson, a Philadelphia Federalist and signer of the Declaration of Independence).

108. Philadelphia County Petition to the Pennsylvania Convention, Dec. 11, *DHRC*, 2:317 (quotations); Findley, Dec. 12, ibid., 587; motion for adjournment, ibid., 589; Whitehill, ibid., 597–9; Smilie, ibid., 600; ibid. (voting by forty-six to twenty-three against adjournment).

109. For the debate and the vote on the Antifederalist motion to allow delegates to record on the journal the reasons for their votes, see Nov. 27, ibid., 369–79. For the Federalists' refusal to allow the amendments proposed by the Antifederalists to be entered on the journal, see Dec. 13, ibid., 603; see also Wilson, Dec. 11, ibid., 552–3.

110. Pennsylvania Minority Dissent, ibid., 620–1 ("violence and outrage" and "tar and feathers"); see also Maier, *Ratification*, 64–5; Rakove, *Original Meanings*, 111–2. Antifederalist

leader William Findley explained that the Federalists' methods of "violence and deception" had excited "resentments" (to William Irvine, Mar. 12, 1788, *DHRC*, 16:374).

111. *DHRC*, 2:709–25; Boyd, *Politics of Opposition*, 95–7; Rutland, *Ordeal of the Constitution*, 143–6; Graham, "Pennsylvania," 67–8.

112. "A Citizen of Pennsylvania," *Pennsylvania Gazette*, Jan. 23, 1788, *DHRC*, 2:660 ("downright rebellion"); "America: To the Dissenting Members of the Late Convention of Pennsylvania," New York *Daily Advertiser*, Dec. 31, 1787, *DHRC*, 19:485 ("obstinate"); Madison to Washington, Jan. 20, 1788, *PJM* (C.S.), 10:399 ("very restless," "endeavor," and "will probably"); see also Madison to Jefferson, Feb. 19, 1788, ibid., 519. For additional reports of the continuing unrest in Pennsylvania, see John Armstrong, Sr., to Washington, Feb. 20, 1788, *DHRC*, 8:385; Nicholas Gilman to John Sullivan, Mar. 22, 1788, *DHRC*, 16:462; Samuel Adams at Massachusetts convention, Jan. 31, 1788, *DHRC*, 6:1384.

113. Washington to Madison, June 8, 1788, *DHRC*, 10:1586 (quotation); Lutz, "Connecticut," 128. On the importance of momentum in the ratifying contest generally, see Maier, *Ratification*, 155, 241–3, 247, 315, 382. For contemporary recognition of the extent to which one state's actions would affect another's, see, e.g., Abraham G. Lansing to Abraham Yates, Jr., June 1, 1788, *DHRC*, 20:1121; King to Madison, Jan. 6, 1788, *DHRC*, 5:625; King to Jeremiah Wadsworth, Jan. 6, 1788, ibid., 626; Christopher Gore to Wadsworth, Jan. 9, 1788, ibid., 657–8; Collin McGregor to Neil Jamieson, Feb. 18, 1788, *DHRC*, 20:785–6; infra pp. 443–4, 446, 448–9, 453, 481.

114. Dane to Melancton Smith, July 3, 1788, *DHRC*, 21:1258.

115. Maier, *Ratification*, 155; Gillespie, "Massachusetts," 138; Introduction, *DHRC*, 5:1077. On Massachusetts Federalists' eagerness for news from Connecticut, see King to Wadsworth, Jan. 6, 1788, *DHRC*, 5:626; Knox to Wadsworth, ibid., 626; Christopher Gore to Wadsworth, Jan. 9, 1788, ibid., 657–8. On the hope of Massachusetts Federalists that Connecticut's ratification would have a positive influence on the Massachusetts convention, see, e.g., Jeremy Belknap to Ebenezer Hazard, Jan. 13, 1788, *DHRC*, 3:605; Samuel Breck to Wadsworth, Jan. 12, 1788, ibid., 603–4; Winthrop Sargent to Knox, Jan. 12, 1788, ibid., 604.

116. Gouverneur Morris to James LaCaze, Feb. 21, 1788, *DHRC*, 16:171 ("wait impatiently"); Carrington to Madison, Feb. 10, 1788, *PJM* (C.S.), 10:494 ("everything seems," "so important," and "would be able"); Madison to Washington, Jan. 20, 1788, ibid., 399; Madison to King, Jan. 23, 1788, ibid., 409 ("[i]t is impossible"); Samuel Blachley Webb to Joseph Barrell, Jan. 13, 1788, *DHRC*, 3:605 ("for our political salvation"); Melancton Smith to Abraham Yates, Jr., Jan. 23, 1788, *DHRC*, 20:638 ("will certainly"). For another statement of the importance of Massachusetts's decision to the ultimate outcome of the ratifying contest, see John Brown to James Breckinridge, Jan. 28, 1788, *DHRC*, 5:1090. For statements of the importance of the Massachusetts outcome to the fate of the Constitution in Virginia, see John Dawson to Madison, Feb. 18, 1788, *PJM* (C.S.), 10:518; Washington to Madison, Mar. 2, 1788, ibid., 553; Joseph Jones to Madison, Feb. 14, 1788, *DHRC*, 8:368. For similar statements from New York, see Introduction, *DHRC*, 20:687; Editors' Note, the Importance of Massachusetts Ratification to New York, Feb. 6, 1788, ibid., 747–50; Charles Tillinghast to Hugh Hughes, Jan. 27–28, 1788, ibid., 668; Madison to Randolph, Jan. 20, 1788, *PJM* (C.S.), 10:398. For the claim that the outcomes in both Virginia and New York would turn on the result of the Massachusetts convention, see Cyrus Griffin to Thomas FitzSimons, Jan. 13, 1788, *DHRC*, 5:705; William Robinson, Jr., to John Langdon, Feb. 4, 1788, ibid., 849; Joseph Jones to Madison, Feb. 14, 1788, *DHRC*, 8:368.

117. King to Madison, Jan. 27, 1788, *DHRC*, 7:1554 (quotation); Gorham to Madison, Jan. 27, 1788, ibid., 1552. For other statements noting that the presence of so many Shaysites at the convention—Knox called them "[t]he vile insurgents"—would render ratification difficult, see Knox to Wadsworth, Jan. 13, 1788, *DHRC*, 3:605; Benjamin Lincoln to Washington, Feb. 3, 1788, *DHRC*, 7:1573; Jeremy Belknap to Ebenezer Hazard, Jan. 25–26, 1788, ibid., 1547; see also David Sewall to George Thatcher, Feb. 11, 1788, ibid., 1691–2. For the number of Shaysites at the convention and their overwhelming

opposition to ratification, see Richards, *Shays's Rebellion*, 144–7; Szatmary, *Shays' Rebellion*, 131–3; Richard D. Brown, "Shays's Rebellion and the Ratification of the Federal Constitution in Massachusetts," in Beeman, Botein, and Carter, eds., *Beyond Confederation*, 122–7; see also Hall, *Politics Without Parties*, 277–9; Libby, "Geographical Distribution of the Vote," 57. Knox thought that the former insurgents "deriv[ed] fresh strength and life from the impunity with which the rebellion of last year was suffered to escape" (to Washington, Feb. 10, 1788, *DHRC*, 7:1587).

118. Gorham to Madison, Jan. 27, 1788, *DHRC*, 7:1552 ("many of them" and "their favorite plan"); Gorham to Henry Knox, Jan. 6, 1788, *DHRC*, 5:629 ("foolish religious whims"). For additional observations that the delegates from Maine seemed inclined to oppose ratification, see Christopher Gore to King, Jan. 6, 1788, ibid., 627; Gore to Wadsworth, Jan. 9, 1788, ibid., 603; Samuel Breck to Wadsworth, Jan. 12, 1788, ibid., 697; Knox to Washington, Jan. 14, 1788, ibid., 707. However, over the course of the convention, Federalist leaders managed to convince many of the Maine delegates that their chances of securing independent statehood were at least as good under the Constitution as under the Articles, and in the end, delegates from the three counties of Maine voted by a margin of twenty-five to twenty-one in favor of ratification (*Pennsylvania Herald*, Feb. 9, 1788, ibid., 884–5 & n. 3). On the Federalists' lobbying of the Maine delegates, see Introduction, *DHRC*, 6:1112.

119. Grayson to Monroe, May 29, 1787, *Farrand*, 3:30 (quotations). For objections at the Massachusetts convention to the Constitution's departures from localist democracy and its provision for equal state representation in the Senate, see infra p. 436.

120. Gore to King, Oct. 7, 1787, *DHRC*, 4:57 ("[t]he federal plan"); Jackson to Knox, Oct. 21, 1787, ibid., 109 ("[t]he Constitution"); Madison to Randolph, Oct. 7, 1787, ibid., 58 ("[t]he party"); see also Jackson to Knox, Oct. 28, 1787, ibid., 142; King to Knox, Oct. 28, 1787, ibid., 155; Gillespie, "Massachusetts," 144. Theodore Sedgwick was more pessimistic, predicting "great opposition" to ratification in Massachusetts (to unidentified recipient, Oct. 28, 1787, *DHRC*, 4:156). Gorham's assessment was in the middle, noting that "[t]hings look pretty well though there is an opposition preparing" (to Knox, Oct. 30, 1787, ibid., 168).

121. Elbridge Gerry to the Massachusetts General Court, *Massachusetts Centinel*, Nov. 3, 1787, *DHRC*, 13:548–9 (quotations); see also Gerry to James Warren, Oct. 18, 1787, *DHRC*, 18:407; Gerry to John Wendell, Nov. 16, 1787, *DHRC*, 4:251; Billias, *Elbridge Gerry*, 208–9. On the wide reprinting of Gerry's letter, see *DHRC*, 4:96; Introduction, ibid., 149.

122. Madison to Washington, Nov. 18, 1787, *PJM* (C.S.), 10:254 ("shake"); Carrington to William Short, Nov. 11, 1787, *LDC*, 24:554 ("work some"). Madison explained that legislators declined Gerry's offer to appear "either from a supposition that they have nothing further to do in the business, having handed it over to the convention, or from an unwillingness to countenance Mr. Gerry's conduct, or from both these considerations" (to Washington, supra). The vote in the Assembly to call a convention was 129 to 32. See Jackson to Knox, Oct. 28, 1787, *DHRC*, 4:142. On the legislature's calling of the convention, see Introduction, ibid., 124–5.

123. Gorham to Knox, Dec. 4, 1787, ibid., 380 ("done infinite"); "A Friend for Liberty," *Massachusetts Centinel*, Nov. 14, 1787, ibid., 231 ("plain countrym[a]n," "very much pleased," "I and all," and "has quite alarmed"); Jackson to Knox, Nov. 5, 1787, ibid., 193 ("has done more"); From Tristram Dalton, Jan. 20, 1788, *DHRC*, 7:1536 ("should be rejected"); see also Jackson to Knox, Nov. 11, 1787, *DHRC*, 5:215; Nov. 18, 1787, ibid., 264. For another Federalist's observation that Gerry's letter "has done harm," see Gore to King, Dec. 30, 1787, ibid., 556. For the view of historians that Gerry's letter helped to rally significant opposition to the Constitution in Massachusetts, see Rutland, *Ordeal of the Constitution*, 23–4, 74–5; Gillespie, "Massachusetts," 144. Gorham and King prepared a point-by-point rejoinder to Gerry's letter but never published it (*DHRC*, 4:97). "Landholder" insisted that Gerry's motivation for dissenting from the Constitution was pique at the convention's rejection of his alleged proposal to redeem at face value continental currency, of which he allegedly held large quantities. "A Landholder" VIII, *Connecticut Courant*, Dec. 24, 1787, *DHRC*, 3:504–5; see also McDonald, *We the People*, 387 n. 22; supra p. 403 & n. 19.

124. Madison to Jefferson, Dec. 9, 1787, *PJM* (C.S.), 10:311 ("great uncertainty"); Madison to Washington, Dec. 20, 1787, ibid., 334 ("a proper occasion"); Maier, *Ratification*, 126. Washington replied that he "had no regular correspondent in Massachusetts" or else he would have had "no objection" to such a communication (to Madison, Jan. 10, 1788, *PJM* (C.S.), 10:358). Two weeks before asking Washington to intervene in Massachusetts, Madison had offered him a more optimistic assessment, reporting that the Constitution's "friends there continue to be very sanguine of victory" (to Washington, Dec. 7, 1787, ibid., 295).

125. Adams to Lee, Dec. 3, 1787, *DHRC*, 14:333 (quotation). In October, Gorham had noted that Adams "has not declared himself," and Madison had reported that Adams "objects to one point only, viz. the prohibition of a religious test." See Gorham to Knox, Oct. 30, 1787, *DHRC*, 4:168; Madison to Randolph, Oct. 7, 1787, ibid., 58.

126. Extract of a letter from a gentleman in Salem (Dec. 23), *Massachusetts Gazette*, Dec. 25, 1787, *DHRC*, 5:518 ("an enemy"); Gore to King, Dec. 30, 1787, ibid., 556 ("is out full"); see also Extract of a letter from a gentleman in Salem (Dec. 26), *Massachusetts Gazette*, Dec. 28, 1788, ibid., 543; editorial note, ibid., 630. Adams may have been the author of the four Antifederalist essays written by "Helvidius Priscus," but it is not certain that he was (editorial note, ibid., 534–5).

    In an earlier letter to King, Gore explained why Federalists had "feared the consequences of opposing Sam Adams's election" even though uncertain of his views on ratification. First, they worried that, if Adams were opposed, his "mortification" would lead him to "openly declare himself against it and endeavor to make proselytes." By contrast, "an election by his townsmen, under an idea that he was really its advocate, might damp his opposition, for he is too old not to know his dependence is more on the people than theirs on him." In addition, some Federalists believed that Adams's arguments against ratification "could be opposed with greater probability of success while he was a member [of the convention] than if he was absent, suggesting objections to small circles of delegates" (Dec. 23, 1787, ibid., 506).

127. Gore to King, Jan. 6, 1788, ibid., 627 (quotations); see also editorial note, ibid., 630. For additional statements the same day reporting Adams's strong opposition to ratification, see King to Wadsworth, ibid., 626; Gorham to Knox, ibid., 628–9; Thomas L. Winthrop to John Todd, ibid., 626.

128. Gorham to Knox, ibid., 629 ("the most numerous"); Resolutions of the Tradesmen of the Town of Boston, *Massachusetts Gazette*, Jan. 7, 1788, ibid., 631–2 (other quotations); Editors' Note, The Meeting of the Tradesmen of Boston on the Constitution, Jan. 7, 1788, ibid., 630–1. For Federalist speculations about the impact of the tradesmen's resolutions on Adams's thinking, see Gore to George Thatcher, Jan. 9, 1788, ibid., 656; Jackson to Knox, Jan. 20, 1788, *DHRC*, 7:1538; Henry Van Schaack to Peter Van Schaack, Jan. 20, 1788, *DHRC*, 5:755.

129. Parsons to Michael Hodge, Jan. 14, 1788, ibid., 708 (quotation); Massachusetts Convention Journal, Jan. 14, 1788, *DHRC*, 6:1182; convention proceedings, Jan. 17, 1788, ibid., 1229; Introduction, ibid., 1109, 1111; *DHRC*, 5:657 n. 3; Maier, *Ratification*, 138–9, 141, 165–6, 169; Beeman, *Plain, Honest Men*, 387; Gillespie, "Massachusetts," 153; Hall, *Politics Without Parties*, 279–80. On the convention's relocating three times owing to a combination of acoustics problems and inadequate spectator seating, see Jackson to Knox, Jan. 20, 1788, *DHRC*, 7:1536–7. For examples of Antifederalist delegates who were instructed to reject ratification, see Boyd, *Politics of Opposition*, 57–60; see also Theophilus Parsons to Michael Hodge, Jan. 14, 1788, *DHRC*, 5:708. On Massachusetts's history of using a participatory process for enacting state constitutions, see Adams, *First American Constitutions*, 86–93; infra p. 618. On the agreement for paragraph-by-paragraph consideration, see King to Madison, Jan. 16, 1788, *DHRC*, 7:1530; Isaac Backus to Susanna Backus, Jan. 17, 1788, ibid., 1531. After the convention, Federalist Jeremy Belknap claimed that the consideration of the Constitution by paragraphs is what enabled Federalists to "protract the debates . . . til they were sure of a majority" (to Ebenezer Hazard, Feb. 10, 1788, ibid., 1583). For detailed discussions of the Massachusetts ratifying convention, see Maier, *Ratification*, chs. 6–7; Heideking, *The Constitution Before the Judgment Seat*, 290–9; Gillespie, "Massachusetts," 147–58.

130. Benjamin Randall at Massachusetts convention, Jan. 22, 1788, *DHRC*, 6:1303 ("widely different" and "were not so"). For criticism of the small size of the House, see John Taylor, Jan. 16, ibid., 1237. For criticism of biennial elections, see, e.g., Taylor, Jan. 14, ibid., 1185; Abraham White, ibid., 1186. For criticism of Congress's power over the times, places, and manner of federal elections, see, e.g., William Jones, Jan. 16, ibid., 1219; Samuel Nasson, Feb. 1, ibid., 1397–9.

131. On Congress's taxing power, see Massachusetts convention, Jan. 18, 1788, *DHRC*, 6:1245–6, 1250–1; see also Hall, *Politics Without Parties*, 281–2. On Senate apportionment, see Francis Dana, Jan. 17, *DHRC*, 6:1232–3; Samuel Nasson, Feb. 1, ibid., 1398. On slavery, see, e.g., James Neal, Jan. 25, ibid., 1354; Thomas Lusk, Feb. 4, ibid., 1421; Thomas Dawes, Jan. 18, ibid., 1244–5. On religious oaths, see, e.g., Lusk, supra; Daniel Shute, Jan. 31, ibid., 1375–7. On Federalists' celebrating the commerce power, see Thomas Russell, Feb. 1, ibid., 1403–4; Thomas Dawes, Jan. 21, ibid., 1287–9. For a good summary of Massachusetts Antifederalists' objections to the Constitution, see William Symmes, Jr., to Peter Osgood, Jr., Nov. 15, 1787, *DHRC*, 4:236–7. Gerry explained to the convention that, in Philadelphia, he had acquiesced in the unfair apportionment of the Senate only in exchange for the clause requiring that money bills originate in the House, which had later been watered down over his objection (to the Vice President of the Convention of Massachusetts, Jan. 21, 1788, *Farrand*, 3:265–7).

132. Barrell, Feb. 5, 1788, *DHRC*, 6:1448 ("[a]wed in the presence," "to talents above," "plain husbandman," and "the pleasing eloquence"); Randall, Jan. 18, 1788, ibid., 1244 ("biased," "these great men," and "would speak half as much"); King to Madison, Jan. 27, 1788, *DHRC*, 7:1554 ("complain"); see also George R. Minot Journal, ibid., 1599; Amos Singletary at Massachusetts convention, Jan. 25, 1788, *DHRC*, 6:1345–6. The Pennsylvania Antifederalist "Centinel" similarly described a "very unequal" contest in Massachusetts in which "well meaning, though uninformed men, were opposed to great learning, eloquence and sophistry in the shape of lawyers, doctors and divines, who were capable and seemed disposed to delude by deceptive glosses and specious reasoning" ("Centinel" XV, Philadelphia *Independent Gazetteer*, Feb. 22, 1788, *DHRC*, 16:190–1). The Massachusetts Antifederalist "Helvidius Priscus," acknowledging that the Federalist speakers had been more "improved by education" and "brightened by study and experience," nonetheless insisted that they used their talents mostly "to find evasion and sophistry," and he maintained that an "impartial observer" would find "the boldness of truth in the short, unadmired speeches" of the Antifederalists ("Helvidius Priscus" IV, *Massachusetts Gazette*, Feb. 5, 1788, *DHRC*, 5:858; see also Heideking, *The Constitution Before the Judgment Seat*, 279).

     For the preceding footnote, see Hall, *Politics Without Parties*, 275.

133. Francis Dana, Jan. 18, *DHRC*, 6:1250 ("those gentlemen"); Peter Thatcher, Feb. 4, ibid., 1420 ("a combination" and "uncharitable"); Jonathan Smith, Jan. 25, ibid., 1347 ("plain man," "living," "lawyers," "we must all," and "think worse"); see also William Phillips, Jan. 22, ibid., 1302.

134. Gorham to Knox, Jan. 16, 1788, *DHRC*, 5:730 ("the prospect"); Sedgwick to Henry Van Schaack, Jan. 18, 1788, ibid., 740 ("At the time"); King to Madison, Jan. 20, 1788, *DHRC*, 7:1539 ("affirm"); Nasson to George Thatcher, Jan. 22, 1788, ibid., 1545. For other statements expressing doubt that the convention would ratify, see Matthew Cobb to George Thatcher, Jan. 24, 1788, *DHRC*, 5:796; Theophilus Parsons to Michael Hodge, Jan. 14, 1788, ibid., 708; Madison to Randolph, Jan. 20, 1788, *PJM* (C.S.), 10:398. Federalist Henry Jackson was much more optimistic about the prospects for ratification (to Knox, Jan. 23, 1788, *DHRC*, 7:1546; Jan. 20, ibid., 1537). New York Antifederalist Melancton Smith, observing that "the information received from Massachusetts differs according to the sentiments of the men who give it" and that both parties claimed to have a majority, concluded that it was "impossible . . . to form an opinion that may be relied upon" (to Abraham Yates, Jr., Jan. 28, 1788, *DHRC*, 20:671–2). For other statements describing the outcome in Massachusetts as impossible to predict, see Gorham to Knox, Jan. 20, 1788, *DHRC*, 5:752; John Jackson to Keith Spence, Jan. 20, 1788, ibid., 752; Benjamin Lincoln to Washington, Jan. 9[–13], 1788, *PGW* (C.S.), 6:22.

135. King to Madison, Jan. 23, 1788, *DHRC*, 7:1546.
136. Gorham to Madison, Jan. 27, 1788, ibid., 1552 (quotations); see also Gorham to Knox, Jan. 30, 1788, ibid., 1561; Tristram Dalton to Stephen Hooper, Jan. 31, 1788, ibid., 1563; Jeremy Belknap to Ebenezer Hazard, Jan. 25–26, 1788, ibid., 1548–9.
137. "Hampden" (possibly James Sullivan), *Massachusetts Centinel*, Jan. 26, 1788, *DHRC*, 5:807–9; King to Knox, Jan. 27, 1788, *DHRC*, 7:1553 ("some countenance" and "not so confident"); Lincoln to Washington, Jan. 27, 1788, ibid., 1555 ("will not be" and "possible"); editorial note, *DHRC*, 5:806–7; see also Introduction, *DHRC*, 6:1116–7. Specifically, "Hampden" proposed that Massachusetts ratify on the condition that the first substantive act of the new Congress would be to consider the amendments proposed by the ratifying conventions of Massachusetts and the other states. A joint session of Congress, voting by state delegations, would be empowered to enact amendments by the vote of just seven state delegations. The specific amendments proposed by "Hampden" were some of the same ones favored by Antifederalists everywhere—for example, restricting Congress's taxing power, limiting its authority over the times, places, and manner of congressional elections, and expanding protections for the right to trial by jury.
138. Belknap to Ebenezer Hazard, Feb. 3, 1788, *DHRC*, 7:1566.
139. King to Knox, Jan. 27, 1788, ibid., 1553 ("[H]e appears"); Henry Van Schaack to Peter Van Schaack, Feb. 4, 1788, ibid., 1575 ("industriously"); see also Maier, *Ratification*, 159, 193. On Hancock's "very precarious" health, which led the convention to appoint a vice president—the state's chief justice, William Cushing—to officiate in his absence, see Gore to Wadsworth, Jan. 9, 1788, *DHRC*, 3:603; see also Gore to Thatcher, Jan. 9, 1788, *DHRC*, 5:656. For another statement reporting the view that Hancock "has not declared his opinion upon the subject yet because he wishes first to know on what side the majority will be," see William Cranch to John Quincy Adams, Jan. 22, 27, 1788, *DHRC*, 7:1544. On Adams, see supra pp. 434–6. Adams's son died during the convention, which limited his participation in the debates. See Convention Journal, Jan. 18, *DHRC*, 6:1248; Introduction, ibid., 1108.

    For the preceding footnote, see King to Horatio Gates, Jan. 20, 1788, *DHRC*, 7:1538–9; see also King to George Thatcher, ibid., 1541.
140. King to Knox, Feb. 3, 1788, ibid., 1572 ("receive" and "that if"); Dalton to Stephen Hooper, Jan. 31, 1788, ibid., 1563 ("sacrifice[d]"); see also Knox to Robert R. Livingston, Feb. 10, 1788, ibid., 1586; From Tristram Dalton, Feb. 3, 1788, ibid., 1569; Introduction, ibid., 1118; Maier, *Ratification*, 194–5.
141. Hancock, Jan. 31, 1788, *DHRC*, 6:1379 (quotations); Proposed Amendments, ibid., 1381–2; see also Knox to Robert R. Livingston, Feb. 10, 1788, *DHRC*, 7:1586.
142. Adams, Jan. 31, *DHRC*, 6:1384.
143. Fisher Ames, Feb. 5, ibid., 1444 ("the fullest representation"); Charles Jarvis, Feb. 4, ibid., 1425–6 ("the influence" and "general"). For other Federalist statements supporting the proposed amendments, see James Bowdoin, Feb. 1, ibid., 1390; Increase Sumner, ibid., 1400; Caleb Strong and "several other gentlemen," Feb. 2, ibid., 1406. For Antifederalist denials of the convention's authority to propose amendments and of the likelihood that already ratifying states would approve them, see William Widgery, Feb. 1, ibid., 1401; Ebenezer Peirce, ibid., 1404; Thompson, Feb. 2, ibid., 1406.
144. Dalton to Michael Hodge, Jan. 30, 1788, *DHRC*, 7:1560 ("settle the matter"); Henry Van Schaack to Peter Van Schaack, Feb. 4, 1788, ibid., 1575 ("had an amazing" and "the opposition"); Gorham to Knox, Feb. 3, 1788, ibid., 1570; King to Madison, Jan. 30, 1788, ibid., 1561 ("our hopes," "character," and "disappoint"); see also King to Madison, Feb. 3, 1788, ibid., 1572. For additional optimistic assessments by Federalists after Hancock and Adams came out in favor of recommended amendments, see Isaac Backus to Susanna Backus, Feb. 1, 1788, ibid., 1564; Belknap to Ebenezer Hazard, Feb. 3, 1788, ibid., 1566; Gore to Thatcher, Feb. 3, 1788, ibid., 1569; King to Knox, Feb. 3, 1788, ibid., 1571; Lincoln to Washington, Feb. 3, 1788, ibid., 1572; see also James Sullivan to John Langdon, Feb. 3, 1788, ibid., 1574; Knox to Robert R. Livingston, Feb. 10, 1788, ibid.,

1586. Like King, Dalton expressed some doubts as to whether Hancock could be entirely relied upon (to Michael Hodge, supra).

145. Hancock, Feb. 6, *DHRC*, 6:1476 (quotation); Convention Journal, Feb. 2, ibid., 1405–6. For descriptions of the committee and the Federalist majority, see George Benson to Nicholas Brown, Feb. 3, 1788, ibid., 7:1568; Gorham to Knox, Feb. 3, 1788, ibid., 1570; and the sources cited in the preceding note; see also Jackson to Knox, Feb. 6, 1788, ibid., 1581; Introduction, ibid., 6:1121; Maier, *Ratification*, 199.

146. "The Republican Federalist" V, *Massachusetts Centinel*, Jan. 19, 1788, *DHRC*, 5:748 (quotation); Convention Journal, Feb. 5, *DHRC*, 6:1443 (adjournment motion); ibid., 1451 (vote on adjournment); see also George Benson to Nicholas Brown, Feb. 3, 1788, *DHRC*, 7:1567–8; Jackson to Knox, Feb. 6, 1788, ibid., 1581; Introduction, ibid., 6:1121–2; Maier, *Ratification*, 204; Rutland, *Ordeal of the Constitution*, 99, 103, 108. For an earlier suggestion that the convention adjourn, see William Thompson, Jan. 21, 1788, *DHRC*, 6:1291; see also Jackson to Knox, Jan. 23, 1788, *DHRC*, 7:1546. Even before the convention began, one Antifederalist essayist was appealing to convention delegates to support an adjournment ("The Republican Federalist" I, *Massachusetts Centinel*, Dec. 29, 1787, *DHRC*, 5:551).

147. Symmes, Feb. 6, *DHRC*, 6:1474 ("great defects," "a total rejection," "in the character," and "a ray of hope"); Charles Turner, ibid., 1471–2 ("been averse," "mind [was] reconciled," "respect," "catholic," and "universally accepted").

148. Convention Debates, Feb. 6, ibid., 1477 (quotations); ibid., 1487 (vote total).

149. Taylor, ibid., 1488 ("fairly beaten" and "his determination"); Widgery, ibid., 1487 ("by a majority" and "endeavor"); King to Madison, Feb. 6, 1788, *DHRC*, 7:1647 ("the minority," "magnanimity," and "ratification"); see also Abraham White and Josiah Whitney, Feb. 6, *DHRC*, 6:1487; Introduction, ibid., 1122–3; Lincoln to Washington, Feb. 6, 1788, *DHRC*, 7:1582; Jackson to Knox, Feb. 10, 1788, ibid., 1585; William Heath Diary, Feb. 7, 1788, ibid., 1525; Maier, *Ratification*, 209–10. Throughout the country, Federalists noted and applauded the magnanimous sentiments of the Massachusetts Antifederalists. See, e.g., New York *Daily Advertiser*, Feb. 18, 1788, *DHRC*, 20:771; John Howard to George Thatcher, Feb. 27, 1788, ibid., 818; Winchester *Virginia Gazette*, Mar. 19, 1788, *DHRC*, 7:1655; Extract of a Letter from Cambridge, Maryland (May 12), *Maryland Journal*, May 16, 1788, *DHRC*, 12:720; see also Governor John Hancock's Speech to the General Court, Feb. 27, 1788, *DHRC*, 7:1668.

150. Lee to George Thatcher, Mar. 20, 1788, ibid., 1726. For additional similar reports, see Providence *United States Chronicle*, Mar. 6, 1788, ibid., 1654; *Massachusetts Centinel*, Mar. 12, 1788, ibid.; John Avery, Jr., to George Thatcher, Mar. 10, 1788, ibid., 1675; Jackson to Knox, Feb. 24, 1788, ibid., 1707; see also Samuel Nasson to George Thatcher, Feb. 26, 1788, ibid., 1708; Jonathan Moore to Elijah Brigham, Mar. 17, 1788, ibid., 1725. The one prominent exception was General William Thompson, who continued to raise a ruckus against the Constitution after the convention ended. See, e.g., Thomas B. Wait to George Thatcher, Feb. 29, 1788, ibid., 1718–9.

151. Henry Van Schaack to Peter Van Schaack, June 21, 1788, quoted in Editors' Note, The State Elections, Apr. 7–May 29, 1788, ibid., 1732. For the other election results noted, see ibid., 1729–32. In his diary, John Quincy Adams noted the "revolution that has taken place in sentiments within one twelve month past. . . . The very men, who at the last election declared the Commonwealth would be ruined if Mr. Hancock was chosen, have now done every thing to get him in" (Apr. 7, 1788, quoted in ibid., 1731). For the notion of the spring elections as a referendum on the Constitution, see *Pennsylvania Gazette*, Apr. 30, 1788, ibid., 1680.

152. Knox to Washington, Feb. 10, 1788, ibid., 1587 ("now no secret" and "proceeded"); Jackson to Knox, Feb. 10, 1788, ibid., 1584 ("gained himself" and "a very active part"). Benjamin Lincoln also told Washington that "a very decided majority" had opposed ratification when the convention assembled (Feb. 9, 1788, ibid., 1688); see also Dalton to John Langdon, Feb. 6, 1788, ibid., 1579–80; Gillespie, "Massachusetts," 158, 161; McDonald, *We the People*, 183. For confirmation of the view that Hancock's support of ratification had proved critical, see Caleb Gibbs to Washington, Feb. 9, 1788, *DHRC*, 7:1687.

For the notion of Hancock's providing political cover to Antifederalist delegates, see William Widgery to George Thatcher, Feb. 9, 1788, ibid., 1690.

For the preceding footnote, see, on the Boston celebration, The Federal Procession, Feb. 8, 1788, ibid., 1615. For the sense that Baltimore was competing to outdo Boston's celebration, see Henry Hollingsworth to Levi Hollingsworth, May 6, 1788, *DHRC*, 12:719. For New Yorkers' bragging that their procession was the largest ever to take place in America, see Samuel Blachley Webb to Catherine Hogeboom, July 25, 1788, *DHRC*, 21:1619; Evert Bancker to Abraham Bancker, July 24, 1788, ibid., 1338.

153. Madison to Washington, Feb. 15, 1788, *DHRC*, 7:1701 (quotations); see also Maier, *Ratification*, 215. Knox, too, worried that "the example to the other states, particularly to this [New York], will not be so influential as if the majority had been larger" (to Washington, Feb. 14, 1788, *DHRC*, 7:1699). For an interesting effort to spin the narrow margin of victory in Massachusetts as advantageous to Federalists elsewhere, see John Avery, Jr., to George Thatcher, Feb. 13, 1788, ibid., 1693; see also Dalton to Langdon, Feb. 29, 1788, ibid., 1717.

154. Randolph to Madison, Feb. 29, 1788, *DHRC*, 8:436–7 (quotations). One New York Federalist, Abraham Bancker, shared Randolph's concern about the amendments proposed by the Massachusetts convention (to Evert Bancker, Feb. 15, 1788, *DHRC*, 20:782).

155. Washington to Madison, Mar. 2, 1788, *DHRC*, 8:452 ("a severe stroke"); Washington to King, Feb. 29, 1788, *PGW* (C.S.), 6:133 ("be productive"); Carrington to Knox, Mar. 13, 1788, *DHRC*, 8:491 ("perhaps the most"); Victor DuPont to Pierre Samuel DuPont de Nemours, Feb. 17, 1788, *DHRC*, 7:1703; see also Washington to Lincoln, Feb. 29, 1788, ibid., 1653; Washington to Jay, Mar. 3, 1788, *DHRC*, 8:455. For strong statements of the view that ratification by Massachusetts had, for all intents and purposes, settled the question for the entire nation, see Collin McGregor to Neil Jamieson, Feb. 18, 1788, *DHRC*, 20:786; Extract of a letter from a gentleman in one of the southern states (Mar. 1), Boston *Independent Chronicle*, Apr. 3, 1788, *DHRC*, 7:1729. For the view that ratification in Massachusetts had "silenced" many New York Antifederalists and "gained many more proselytes," see Extract of a letter from an American patriot and soldier (Apr. 4), *State Gazette of South Carolina*, May 8, 1788, *DHRC*, 20:1093; see also Ebenezer Hazard to Mathew Carey, Feb. 25, 1788, ibid., 809. For the view that Massachusetts's ratification had deflated Antifederalists in Pennsylvania, see Walter Stewart to William Irvine, Feb. 29, 1787, *DHRC*, 2:715; Thomas FitzSimons to William Irvine, Feb. 22, 1787, ibid., 716.

156. Langdon to Washington, Nov. 6, 1787, in *Documentary History of the Constitution of the United States* (Washington, D.C., 1905), 4:366 ("not heard"); Madison to Jefferson, Dec. 9, 1787, *PJM* (C.S.), 10:311 ("New Hampshire"); see also Madison to Jefferson, Oct. 24, 1787, ibid., 216; Yarbrough, "New Hampshire," 235.

157. Jere R. Daniell, "Ideology and Hardball: Ratification of the Federal Constitution in New Hampshire," in *New Hampshire: The State that Made Us a Nation* (William M. Gardner, Frank C. Mevers, and Richard F. Upton, eds., Portsmouth, NH, 1989), 8–9.

158. Caleb Gibbs to Washington, Feb. 9, 1788, *DHRC*, 7:1687 ("if Massachusetts adopted"); King to Madison, Feb. 6, 1788, ibid., 1647 ("New Hampshire will undoubtedly"); Madison to Washington, Feb. 15, 1788, ibid., 1701 ("be no question" and "seventh pillar"). For other statements, made after Massachusetts's ratification, confidently predicting New Hampshire's approval of the Constitution, see Joseph Barrell to Samuel Blachley Webb, Feb. 20, 1788, *DHRC*, 20:731; Dalton to Langdon, Feb. 6, 1788, *DHRC*, 7:1580; Jackson to Knox, Feb. 13, 1788, ibid., 1694; Jeremiah Hill to George Thatcher, Feb. 14, 1788, ibid., 1697; see also Editors' Note, New York and the Adjournment of the New Hampshire Convention, *DHRC*, 20:798. For a more modest appraisal of the likelihood that New Hampshire would ratify, see John Quincy Adams to William Cranch, Feb. 16, 1788, *DHRC*, 7:1702.

159. Sullivan to Knox, Feb. 11, 1788, quoted in Editors' Note, New York and the Adjournment of the New Hampshire Convention, *DHRC*, 20:799 ("not so favorable"); Langdon to Washington, Feb. 28, 1788, *PGW* (C.S.), 6:132 ("Contrary to the expectation"); see also Langdon to King, Feb. 23, 1788, *DHRC*, 16:183; Heideking, *The Constitution Before*

the *Judgment Seat*, 238–9; Rutland, *Ordeal of the Constitution*, 117; Boyd, *Politics of Opposition*, 63; Maier, *Ratification*, 218–9, 238; Yarbrough, "New Hampshire," 238–9; Daniell, "Ideology and Hardball," 9–10.

160. Langdon to King, Feb. 23, 1788, *DHRC*, 16:183 ("[A]fter spending"); Langdon to Washington, Feb. 28, 1788, *PGW* (C.S.), 6:132–3 ("an opportunity"); see also Madison to Randolph, Mar. 3, 1788, *PJM* (C.S.), 10:554; Jefferson to William Carmichael, June 3, 1788, *PTJ* (M.S.), 13:232; Jeremiah Hill to George Thatcher, Feb. 28, 1788, *DHRC*, 7:1716; Yarbrough, "New Hampshire," 239–49; Daniell, "Ideology and Hardball," 12–14; Rutland, *Ordeal of the Constitution*, 118.

161. Langdon to Washington, Feb. 28, 1788, *PGW* (C.S.), 6:133 (quotation); see also Langdon to King, Feb. 23, 1788, *DHRC*, 16:183; Madison to Randolph, Mar. 3, 1788, *PJM* (C.S.), 10:554–5; Daniell, "Ideology and Hardball," 10–12; Maier, *Ratification*, 219–20; *New Hampshire Provincial and State Papers* (Nathaniel Bouton, ed., Concord, NH, 1877), 10:13; Rutland, *Ordeal of the Constitution*, 119–20; Heideking, *The Constitution Before the Judgment Seat*, 299–300; editorial note, *DHRC*, 16:179–80.

162. Langdon to Washington, Feb. 28, 1788, *PGW* (C.S.), 6:132–3 (quotations); see also Langdon to King, May 6, 1788, *DHRC*, 16:183; Nicholas Gilman to Sullivan, Mar. 22, 1788, ibid., 461–2; editorial note, ibid., 180–1; Maier, *Ratification*, 221–2.

163. Madison to Randolph, Mar. 3, 1788, *DHRC*, 16:304 ("no small check," "take new spirits," "had almost extinguished," and "will probably be"); Gilman to Sullivan, Mar. 22, 1788, ibid., 461 ("pernicious effects" and "augmented their forces"); Antoine de la Forest to Comte de la Luzerne, Apr. 15, 1788, *DHRC*, 17:98 ("dangerous," "the most unfortunate," and "has taken"); Collin McGregor to Neil Jamieson, Mar. 4, 1788, *DHRC*, 20:843 (fall in price of federal securities); see also Rutland, *Ordeal of the Constitution*, 121–2. For other Federalist statements noting the damage that New Hampshire's adjournment had done to the cause of ratification, see Washington to Langdon, Apr. 2, 1788, *PGW* (C.S.), 6:187; Washington to Knox, Mar. 30, 1788, ibid., 183; Brown to James Breckinridge, Mar. 17, 1788, *DHRC*, 16:404; Knox to Sullivan, Apr. 9, 1788, *DHRC*, 17:40; Editors' Note, New York and the Adjournment of the New Hampshire Convention, *DHRC*, 20:799–800. For the point about New Hampshire's adjournment precluding the possibility of nine states having ratified by the time of the Virginia convention, see George Nicholas to Madison, Apr. 5, 1788, *DHRC*, 9:703; Cyrus Griffin to Thomas FitzSimons, Mar. 3, 1788, *DHRC*, 8:453; Editorial Note, *DHRC*, 16:182.

164. *United States Chronicle*, Mar. 6, 1788, *DHRC*, 24:129 (reporting House proceedings of Feb. 29); infra pp. 517–8; Maier, *Ratification*, 223–4; Rutland, *Ordeal of the Constitution*, 125–6.

165. Madison to Jefferson, Oct. 24, 1787, *PJM* (C.S.), 10:216 ("pretty good," "[t]he voice," and "as far as"); Dec. 9, 1787, ibid., 311 ("more formidable"); see also Daniel Carroll to Madison, Oct. 28, 1787, *DHRC*, 11:24. Washington also thought there would be very little opposition to ratification in Maryland (to Samuel Powel, Jan. 18, 1788, *PGW* (C.S.), 6:45). For predictions of somewhat greater opposition, see Lambert Cadwalader to George Mitchell, Oct. 8, 1787, *DHRC*, 3:138; Jefferson to William Carmichael, June 3, 1788, *PTJ* (M.S.), 13:232.

166. Luther Martin Addresses the House of Delegates, Nov. 29, 1787, *DHRC*, 11:88 (quotation); see also Luther Martin, Genuine Information II, Baltimore *Maryland Gazette*, Jan. 1, 1788, ibid., 135–6; Luther Martin to Daniel Carroll, May 20, 1788, *Farrand*, 3:322; Introduction, *DHRC*, 11:lii. On the opposition of Chase and Paca, see Grayson to William Short, Nov. 10, 1787, *DHRC*, 14:82; John Brown Cutting to Jefferson, July 11, 1788, *PTJ* (M.S.), 13:333. On the point about the speculation in confiscated Loyalist estates by Maryland's Antifederalist leaders, see Introduction, *DHRC*, 11:xxxix; "Steady," Baltimore *Maryland Gazette*, Sept. 28, 1787, ibid., 11–12; Extract of a letter from Baltimore (Apr. 24), *Pennsylvania Gazette*, Apr. 30, 1788, *DHRC*, 12:616; see also McDonald, *We the People*, 154. For the notion that Antifederalist legislators were behind the legislature's summons to the state's convention delegates to appear before it, see William Tilghman to Tench Coxe, Nov. 25, 1787, *DHRC*, 11:63; Richard Curson to Horatio Gates, Nov.

28, 1787, ibid., 64; Introduction, ibid., 68; Daniel Carroll to Benjamin Franklin, Dec. 2, 1787, ibid., 96.

167. Thomas Johnson to Washington, Dec. 11, 1787, *DHRC*, 14:404 (quotations); Onuf, "Maryland," 171–3, 190; Maier, *Ratification*, 246; Introduction, *DHRC*, 11:l.

168. William Tilghman to Tench Coxe, Apr. 20, 1788, *DHRC*, 12:613 (quotation); Nicholas to Madison, Apr. 5, 1788, *PJM* (C.S.), 11:8; see also Nicholas to David Stuart, Apr. 9, 1788, *DHRC*, 9:712; Madison to Nicholas, Apr. 8, 1788, *PJM* (C.S.), 11:12; Daniel Carroll to Madison, Feb. 10, 1788, ibid., 10:496; Extract of a letter from a gentleman in Richmond (Mar. 25), Baltimore *Maryland Gazette*, Apr. 4, 1788, *DHRC*, 9:702; Editorial Note, *DHRC*, 16:182–3. Washington believed that Maryland's ratification would "have a very considerable influence upon the decision in Virginia" (to Benjamin Lincoln, May 2, 1788, *DHRC*, 9:780).

169. Washington to Johnson, Apr. 20, 1788, *DHRC*, 9:743 ("be tantamount" and "would have the worst"); McHenry to Washington, Apr. 20, 1788, quoted in ibid., 764 n. 2 ("to push" and "do every thing"); see also Washington to McHenry, Apr. 27, 1788, ibid., 763; Editorial Note, George Washington and the Maryland convention, Apr. 20–27, 1788, *DHRC*, 12:520–2; Maier, *Ratification*, 241–3; Boyd, *Politics of Opposition*, 99, 101; Rutland, *Ordeal of the Constitution*, 151–3; Haw et al., *Stormy Patriot*, 148–9. Madison's letters to the Maryland Federalists have not survived, but that he wrote them is confirmed in Madison to Washington, Apr. 10, 1788, *PJM* (C.S.), 11:20.

170. On the rejection of the proposal for a property qualification for delegates of five hundred pounds, see House of Delegates proceedings, Nov. 26, 1787, *DHRC*, 11:75; see also McDonald, *We the People*, 149. On the election campaign for convention delegates in Maryland, see Heideking, *The Constitution Before the Judgment Seat*, 231–4. Newspapers reporting the list of convention delegates predicted a result very similar to the actual one. See The *New York Journal* and Maryland's Ratification of the Constitution, May 1–5, 1788, *DHRC*, 20:968–9; see also Alexander Contee Hanson to Tench Coxe, Apr. 11, 1788, *DHRC*, 12:609; Daniel of St. Thomas Jenifer to Washington, Apr. 15, 1788, ibid., 611; William Tilghman to Coxe, Apr. 20, 1788, ibid., 612–3.

171. Richard Butler to William Irvine, Apr. 27, 1788, *DHRC*, 12:628–9 (quotation); New York *Daily Advertiser*, Apr. 30, 1788, ibid., 627 (reporting rejection of Antifederalist motion to consider the Constitution by paragraphs); Maryland Convention Proceedings, Apr. 26, 1788, ibid., 647 (the vote); see also Boyd, *Politics of Opposition*, 31–2, 121–2; Heideking, *The Constitution Before the Judgment Seat*, 301–2; Bernard Steiner, "Maryland's Adoption of the Federal Constitution," *American Historical Review* (1899), 5:209–10; Introduction, *DHRC*, 12:543–4; Introduction, ibid., 618–20. On the decision to permit the Antifederalists to have their say, despite Federalists' enormous majority, see William Smith to Tench Coxe, Apr. 28, 1788, ibid., 542. From a similar wish not to "throw things into a ferment," in light of their huge majority, Federalists decided not to challenge the credentials of Antifederalist delegates who had been elected in counties other than those in which they resided—in violation of state law (Tilghman to Coxe, Apr. 20, 1788, ibid., 613).

172. Introduction, *DHRC*, 12:618–9; Extract of a letter from Annapolis (Apr. 28), *Pennsylvania Packet*, May 2, 1788, ibid., 649; Newspaper Report of Convention Proceedings, Apr. 29, 1788, ibid., 656; Address of the Antifederalist Minority of the Maryland Convention, May 1, 1788, ibid., 662–8; Draft of Federalist Address to the People of Maryland, in Alexander Contee Hanson to Madison, June 2, 1788, ibid., 675–80; see also Daniel Carroll to Madison, May 28, 1788, ibid., 740; Steiner, "Maryland's Adoption of the Federal Constitution," 213–7.

173. Amendments proposed by William Paca, *DHRC*, 12:650–2. On Marylanders' concerns that the federal courts would force the payment of prewar debts to British creditors, see William Tilghman to Tench Coxe, Nov. 25, 1787, *DHRC*, 11:63; see also Samuel Smith to Tench Coxe, Apr. 13, 1788, *DHRC*, 12:585; McDonald, *We the People*, 154–5. On the extent of Marylanders' indebtedness to British creditors, see Jensen, *New Nation*, 278.

174. Editorial note, *DHRC*, 12:660; "A Member of Convention: To the People of Maryland," Baltimore *Maryland Gazette*, May 13, 1788, ibid., 732; James McHenry to Washington,

May 18, 1788, ibid., 739. For an objection to the "despotic manner" in which Federalists abruptly adjourned the Maryland convention after "amusing" the Antifederalist minority by raising their hopes of suitable amendments, see "A Free Man," Philadelphia *Independent Gazetteer*, May 13, 1788, ibid., 733.

175. Introduction, *DHRC*, 12:618–9; Address of the Antifederalist Minority of the Maryland Convention, May 1, 1788, ibid., 660–9; Address to the Members of the New York and Virginia Conventions (probably written by John Francis Mercer), post–Apr. 30, 1788, *DHRC*, 17:257–8 (quotations); see also Samuel Chase to John Lamb, June 13, 1788, *DHRC*, 18:47–8; John Brown Cutting to Jefferson, July 11, 1788, *PTJ* (M.S.), 13:333–6; Boyd, *Politics of Opposition*, 122–3; Maier, *Ratification*, 245–6; Rutland, *Ordeal of the Constitution*, 158–9; Haw et al., *Stormy Patriot*, 154–5; Steiner, "Maryland's Adoption of the Federal Constitution," 220.

176. Jean-Baptiste Petry to le Marchal de Castries, Nov. 16, 1787, *DHRC*, 27:41 (quotations); see also Thomas Tudor Tucker to St. George Tucker, Nov. 21, 1787, ibid., 42.

177. Jean-Baptiste Petry to Comte de Montmorin, Jan. 12, 1788, ibid., 82 (quotations). David Ramsay, a leading proponent of ratification in South Carolina, explained that Federalists wanted the Constitution discussed in the legislature "for the sake of informing the country members" (to John Eliot, Jan. 19, 1788, ibid., 206); see also Ramsay to Benjamin Lincoln, Jan. 29, 1788, *DHRC*, 15:487.

178. Charles Cotesworth Pinckney in South Carolina House, Jan. 14, 1788, *DHRC*, 27:83; Rawlins Lowndes, ibid., 83–4; Pierce Butler, ibid., 84; Edward Rutledge, ibid.; The South Carolina General Assembly Calls a Convention, Jan. 8–29, 1788, ibid., 72–3; South Carolina House of Representatives Debates the Constitution, Jan. 16–18, 1788, ibid., 88; see also Penuel Bowen to Joseph Ward, Jan. 16, 1788, ibid., 195–6; Jean-Baptiste Petry to Comte de Montorin, Jan. 30, 1788, ibid., 199; Boyd, *Politics of Opposition*, 37. On Lowndes's speaking on behalf of the backcountry members, see supra p. 410.

179. South Carolina House Proceedings, Jan. 19, 1788, *DHRC*, 27:161 (unanimous vote to summon convention); ibid., 162–3 (vote on location); Boyd, *Politics of Opposition*, 38–9.

180. Archibald Maclaine to James Iredell, June 4, 1788, in Griffith J. McRee, *Life and Correspondence of James Iredell: One of the Associate Justices of the Supreme Court of the United States* (New York, 1858), 2:226 ("great pains"); Extract of a letter from Charleston (Jan. 22), Philadelphia *Freeman's Journal*, Feb. 13, 1788, *DHRC*, 27:209 ("heavy" and "entertain"); Arthur Bryan to George Bryan, Apr. 9, 1788, ibid., 251 ("[a]ccounts"). For another prediction of "great opposition . . . from the back country interest," see Extract of a letter from a gentleman in Charleston (Feb. 9), Philadelphia *Independent Gazetteer*, Apr. 22, 1788, ibid., 221. For a more confident Federalist view, see Butler to Gerry, Mar. 3, 1788, ibid., 229.

181. Extract of a letter from Charleston (May 1), *Massachusetts Centinel*, May 28, 1788, ibid., 262 (quotation); see also Weir, "South Carolina," 226. On the malapportionment, see supra p. 406.

182. Lowndes in South Carolina House, Jan. 17, 1788, *DHRC*, 27:125–8; Jan. 16, ibid., 107–10; Patrick Dollard at South Carolina convention, May 20, 1788, ibid., 378–80; see also Ramsay to Rush, Apr. 21, 1788, ibid., 261; Weir, "South Carolina," 220–2; Maier, *Ratification*, 247–8.

183. Charles Cotesworth Pinckney in South Carolina House, Jan. 17, 1788, *DHRC*, 27:122–4; Robert Barnwell, ibid., 132–3; Edward Rutledge, ibid., 135; Charles Pinckney at South Carolina convention, May 14, 1788, ibid., 335; "Caroliniensis," Charleston *City Gazette*, Jan. 3, 1788, ibid., 64; Pierce Butler to Weedon Butler, May 5, 1788, *DHRC*, 17:383–4; supra pp. 301–2, 337–9.

184. Aedanus Burke to John Lamb, June 23, 1788, *DHRC*, 18:56 (quotation); South Carolina convention, May 21, 1788, *DHRC*, 27:366 (vote on adjournment); South Carolina Receives News of Maryland Ratification, ibid., 285; Introduction, ibid., 304–5; Boyd, *Politics of Opposition*, 124; Weir, "South Carolina," 224; Maier, *Ratification*, 250–1; Rutland, *Ordeal of the Constitution*, 167.

185. Burke to John Lamb, June 23, 1788, *DHRC*, 18:56–7 (quotations); South Carolina convention, May 23, 1788, *DHRC*, 27:393–7 (vote on ratification); Introduction, ibid., 305–6; Weir, "South Carolina," 224–5; Maier, *Ratification*, 251–2.
186. Baldwin to Seaborn Jones, June 5, 1788, *DHRC*, 20:1129–30.
187. Madison to Washington, Mar. 3, 1788, *PJM* (C.S.), 10:555 (quotation); Yarbrough, "New Hampshire," 250; Daniell, "Ideology and Hardball," 14–15; Maier, *Ratification*, 314–5. For New Hampshire Antifederalists' complaints of Federalist domination of the press, see Joshua Atherton to John Lamb, June 11, 1788, *DHRC*, 18:46.
188. King to Hamilton, June 12, 1788, *DHRC*, 20:1127 (quotation). For other confident Federalist predictions of ratification by the reassembled New Hampshire convention, see e.g., William Bingham to Tench Coxe, May 25, 1788, ibid., 1110; Cyrus Griffin to Thomas FitzSimons, June 16, 1788, ibid., 1174; John Marshall at Virginia convention, June 10, 1788, *DHRC*, 9:1123; Hamilton to Madison, June 8, 1788, *PJM* (C.S.), 11:100; Jay to Washington, May 29, 1788, *PGW* (C.S.), 6:303; John Brown to Archibald Stuart, June 25, 1788, *DHRC*, 21:1226.
189. Yarbrough, "New Hampshire," 250–1; Heideking, *The Constitution Before the Judgment Seat*, 309–10; Maier, *Ratification*, 315–6.
190. Nicholas to Madison, Apr. 5, 1788, *PJM* (C.S.), 11:8 ("some of them"); Lee to Mason, May 7, 1788, *DHRC*, 9:784 ("depend much"); Maier, *Ratification*, 313; Banning, *Sacred Fire*, 234. On the importance of Virginia's ratification to the success of the union, see Comte de Moustier to Comte de Montmorin, June 25, 1788, *DHRC*, 21:1227; Tobias Lear to Washington, July 31, 1788, ibid., 1350–1; William Bingham to Tench Coxe, June 12, 1788, *DHRC*, 20:1150; Martin Oster to Comte de la Luzerne, Feb. 4, 1788, *DHRC*, 8:344; Carrington to Jefferson, May 14, 1788, *DHRC*, 9:795–6. Pennsylvania Federalist Tench Coxe told Madison that if Virginia rejected the Constitution, "it will be rendered extremely uncertain in New York, New Hampshire, and North Carolina" (May 19, 1788, ibid., 833). Collin McGregor, a New York merchant and bond speculator, wrote that "should Virginia reject the new Constitution final settlements and other continental debt will fall for a time; if she accedes they will appreciate immediately" (to Neil Jamieson, June 4, 1788, *DHRC*, 10:1575); see also editorial note, ibid., n. 2.
191. Washington to Madison, Oct. 10, 1787, *PGW* (C.S.), 5:367 ("any powerful opposition"); Randolph to Madison, c. Oct. 29, 1787, *DHRC*, 8:133 ("[t]he first raptures," "the tide," "daily stated," "the final event," "strong exertions," and "carry it"); Grayson to William Short, Nov. 10, 1787, *DHRC*, 14:82 ("very considerable" and "at a loss"); Jefferson to William Carmichael, Dec. 15, 1787, ibid., 481 ("the presumption"); see also Madison to Jefferson, Feb. 19, 1788, *PJM* (C.S.), 10:520; Dawson to Madison, Nov. 10, 1787, ibid., 248; Labunski, *James Madison*, 35–6; Banning, "Virginia," 277.
192. Washington to Knox, Mar. 30, 1788, *PGW* (C.S.), 6:183 ("The Kentucky district"); Nicholas to Madison, Apr. 5, 1788, *PJM* (C.S.), 11:10 ("[t]he only danger" and "from the Kentucky members"); see also Madison to Nicholas, Apr. 8, 1788, ibid., 12; John Brown to Jefferson, Aug. 10, 1788, *PTJ* (M.S.), 13:494; Nicholas Gilman to John Langdon, Apr. 19, 1788, *LDC*, 25:60; Banning, "Virginia," 280–2; Maier, *Ratification*, 238, 241; Watlington, *Partisan Spirit*, 150; Talbert, "Kentuckians in the Virginia Ratifying Convention," 188–9, 192; supra pp. 48–69.
193. Samuel McDowell et al., Circular Letter to Fayette County Court in Danville, Kentucky, Feb. 29, 1788, *DHRC*, 8:435 ("dragged by the power" and "never shall be able"); Washington to Knox, Mar. 30, 1788, *PGW* (C.S.), 6:183 ("becoming" and "has got hold"); see also John Brown to Jefferson, Aug. 10, 1788, *PTJ* (M.S.), 13:494; Harry Innes to John Brown, Feb. 20, 1788, *DHRC*, 8:386; Watlington, *Partisan Spirit*, 149. For the concern about Kentucky's not being able to impose import taxes to promote its own manufacturing, see Samuel McDowell to William Fleming, Dec. 20, 1787, *DHRC*, 8:255; Innes to Brown, supra.

Residents of Vermont voiced a similar concern about contested land titles, fearing that under the Constitution federal courts would favor claims made under New York law over those asserted under Vermont law. See Nathaniel Chipman to Hamilton, July 14, 1788, *PAH*, 5:161. (In 1777, Vermont had declared its independence from New York, written a constitution, and established its own legislature, even though the Confederation Congress refused to recognize it as an independent state.)

194. For objections to the Senate, see infra pp. 469–70. On the unpopularity of the slavery compromise, see Waldstreicher, *Slavery's Constitution*, 142; infra p. 470. Grayson, one of the state's leading Antifederalists, objected to equal state representation in the Senate and to the simple majority requirement for commercial legislation, which he said would "ruin the southern states" (to William Short, Nov. 10, 1787, *DHRC*, 14:82).

195. Dawson to Madison, Apr. 15, 1787, *PJM* (C.S.), 9:381 ("a large majority"); Randolph to Madison, c. Oct. 29, 1787, *DHRC*, 8:133 ("the most vulnerable" and "the danger"); Pierce to Knox, Oct. 26, 1787, ibid., 123 ("[t]he popular objection"); see also William Allason to John Likely, May 24, 1788, *DHRC*, 9:588. For discussion of the issue of the British debts at the Virginia ratifying convention, see infra pp. 470–1, 475. For discussion of the same issue in the Virginia legislature during and after the Revolutionary War, see Evans, "Private Indebtedness and the Revolution in Virginia," 352–67; see also Introduction, *DHRC*, 8:xxv–xxvii; Jensen, *New Nation*, 279–80; Madison to Jefferson, Jan. 9, 1785, *PJM* (C.S.), 8:229–30.

196. Madison to Randolph, Jan. 10, 1788, ibid., 10:355 ("would have been"); Carrington to Jefferson, Oct. 23, 1787, *DHRC*, 8:94 ("some difficulty" and "two of her"); see also Washington to Knox, Oct. 15, 1787, ibid., 57; Madison to Pendleton, Sept. 20, 1787, *PJM* (C.S.), 10:171.

197. Mason at Philadelphia convention, Aug. 31, *Farrand*, 2:479 ("chop off"); Sept. 15, ibid., 637–40 ("the shadow" at p. 638; "a monarchy" at p. 640). In a letter to Jefferson, Mason explained that he had intended to offer these objections "by way of protest, but was discouraged from doing so by the precipitate and intemperate, not to say indecent, manner in which the business was conducted during the last week of the convention, after the patrons of this new plan found they had a decided majority in their favor" (May 26, 1788, *DHRC*, 18:79). For Madison's perspective on Mason's principal grievances, see Madison to Jefferson, Oct. 24, 1787, *PJM* (C.S.), 10:215.

198. Madison to Jefferson, Oct. 24, 1787, *DHRC*, 8:106 ("in an exceeding," "A number," and "fixed disposition"); John Pierce to Henry Knox, Oct. 21, 1788, ibid., 88 ("the utmost"); Lear to Langdon, Dec. 3, 1788, ibid., 196–7 ("in manuscript"); George Mason's Objections to the Constitution of Government formed by the Convention, ibid., 43–6; editorial note, ibid., 40–3. Mason told Washington that "a little moderation and temper in the latter end of the convention might have removed" his objections to the Constitution (to Washington, Oct. 7, 1787, ibid., 43). An Antifederalist leader in New York reported that Mason, after the Philadelphia convention, had "been through the back counties of that state [Virginia], haranguing the inhabitants and pointing out the dangerous effects or consequences which would inevitably flow from the new Constitution. He is now, it is said, gone into North Carolina, on the same business and means to sound the alarm through the southern states" (Charles Tillinghast to Hugh Hughes, Oct. 12, 1787, ibid., 54).

199. Mason to Washington, Oct. 7, 1787, ibid., 43 ("most decidedly" and "should any attempt"); Nicholas to Madison, Apr. 5, 1788, *DHRC*, 9:703 ("immediately"); see also Washington to Madison, Oct. 10, 1787, *PJM* (C.S.), 10:190; Madison to Jefferson, Dec. 9, 1787, ibid., 312; Pierce to Knox, Oct. 26, 1787, *DHRC*, 8:123.

      For the preceding footnote, see Fairfax County Meeting, Oct. 2, 1787, *DHRC*, 8:23–4; The Election of Convention Delegates, *DHRC*, 9:561; see also Lear to John Langdon, Oct. 19, 1787, *DHRC*, 8:80.

200. Randolph at Philadelphia convention, Sept. 10, *Farrand*, 2:560–1 ("irreconcilably departed"); ibid., 563–4 ("end in tyranny" and "The only mode"); see also Aug. 31, ibid., 479; Sept. 15, ibid., 631.

201. Madison to Jefferson, Oct. 24, 1787, *DHRC*, 8:106 ("inveterate" and "unwillingness"); Carrington to Jefferson, Oct. 23, 1787, ibid., 94 ("has declared"); see also William Lewis to Thomas Lee Shippen, Oct. 11, 1787, *PTJ* (M.S.), 12:229. Randolph had written to Madison on Sept. 30, 1787 (*DHRC*, 8:25).

202. Supra pp. 250–1; Henry to Joseph Martin, Oct. 4, 1786, in Henry, *Patrick Henry*, 3:374 (quotations).

203. Madison to Jefferson, Oct. 24, 1787, *DHRC*, 8:107 ("[m]uch will depend" and "for granted"); Washington to Madison, Oct. 10, 1787, *PJM* (C.S.), 10:190 ("as the advocate"); Henry to Washington, Oct. 19, 1787, *PGW* (C.S.), 5:384 ("is really greater"); see also Lear to Langdon, Oct. 19, 1787, *DHRC*, 8:80; Henry to Thomas Madison, Oct. 21, 1787, ibid., 88. Henry had the good grace to add this qualification in his letter to Washington (who, of course, had presided over the convention that wrote the Constitution): "[P]erhaps more mature reflection may furnish me reasons to change my present sentiments into a conformity with the opinion of those personages for whom I have the highest reverence."

204. Turberville to Arthur Lee, Oct. 28, 1787, *DHRC*, 13:505–6 ("appear to be" and "The enthusiastic"); Arthur Lee to Edward Rutledge, Oct. 29, 1787, *DHRC*, 8:131 ("formidable" and "losing ground"). For Turberville's doubts about the Constitution, see also Turberville to Madison, Dec. 11, 1787, ibid., 231–4.

     Mason also perceived "great contrariety of opinion in Virginia" (to Elbridge Gerry, Oct. 20, 1787, ibid., 86). For slightly earlier predictions of considerable opposition to ratification in Virginia, see John Dawson to Madison, Sept. 25, 1787, ibid., 16; Arthur Lee to John Adams, Oct. 3, 1787, ibid., 34; Monroe to Madison, Oct. 13, 1787, ibid., 192. For the sense that opposition was increasing over time, see Joseph Jones to Madison, Oct. 29, 1787, ibid., 55; McClurg to Madison, Oct. 31, 1787, ibid., 137; see also Banning, *Sacred Fire*, 234–5.

205. Newspaper Reports of House Proceedings and Debates, Oct. 25, 1788, *DHRC*, 8:112–4; Monroe to Lambert Cadwalader, Oct. 15, 1787, ibid., 56; David Stuart to Washington, Oct. 16, 1787, ibid., 67; St. George Tucker to Frances Bland Tucker, Oct. 17, 1787, ibid., 68; John Dawson to Madison, Oct. 19, 1787, ibid., 78–9; Archibald Stuart to John Breckinridge, Oct. 21, 1787, ibid., 89; Stuart to Madison, Oct. 21, 1787, ibid., 90; Pierce to Knox, Oct. 21, 1787, ibid., 88–9; Nov. 12, 1787, ibid., 155; Washington to Madison, Nov. 5, 1787, *PGW* (C.S.), 6:409; see also The General Assembly Receives the Constitution, Oct. 15–16, 1787, *DHRC*, 8:57; The General Assembly Calls a Convention, Oct. 25–31, 1787, ibid., 110; Heideking, *The Constitution Before the Judgment Seat*, 42–3.

206. House Resolutions, Oct. 25, 1787, *DHRC*, 8:115–6 ("to a convention"); Washington to Bushrod Washington, Nov. 9, 1787, *PGW* (C.S.), 5:421 ("with the mark" and "to bias"); Madison to Pendleton, Oct. 28, 1787, *DHRC*, 8:126 ("a more prompt"); see also Pierce to Knox, Oct. 26, 1787, ibid., 123; The General Assembly Calls a Convention, ibid., 110; Boyd, *Politics of Opposition*, 27–8; Rutland, *Ordeal of the Constitution*, 182. The Federalist delegate Pierce thought that Federalists had "mistaken their point or were fearful of their force," or else they would have driven a harder bargain (to Knox, supra). Randolph was pleased with the resolution because he wanted the ratifying convention to propose amendments (to Madison, c. Oct. 29, 1787, ibid., 133). Madison thought the example afforded other states by the Virginia legislature would "have great weight, and the more so, as the disagreement of the deputation, will give it more the appearance of being the unbiased expression of the public mind" (to Pendleton, supra).

207. Washington to Madison, Nov. 5, 1787, ibid., 146 (quoting Stuart to Washington, Oct. 25) ("the variety"); Pierce to Knox, Oct. 26, 1787, ibid., 123 ("willing to delay"); Dawson to Madison, Nov. 10, 1787, ibid., 150; see also The General Assembly Calls a State Convention, ibid., 112; Boyd, *Politics of Opposition*, 28.

208. Monroe to Madison, Feb. 7, 1788, *DHRC*, 8:354–5 (quotations); see also Risjord, *Chesapeake Politics*, 300; Labunski, *James Madison*, 55–6. On the possibility of Virginia's using the delay in holding its convention to coordinate with other states on amendments, see infra pp. 459–60. On Monroe's initial reaction to the Constitution, which, on balance, was positive, see Monroe to Lambert Cadwalader, Oct. 15, 1787, *DHRC*, 8:56. On Monroe's opposition to ratification at the Virginia convention, see infra pp. 468–9 n. †, 476.

     Dawson stated a view similar to Monroe's, telling Madison that by holding a late convention, Virginia would be able "to act on the determinations of the other states and to determine ourselves as circumstances may point out" (Nov. 10, 1787, *DHRC*, 8:150).

209. Infra pp. 475–8.

When Washington learned of the late date set for the convention, he wrote: "[W]hether putting it off to so late a period will be favorable or otherwise, must be determined by circumstances, for if those states whose conventions are to meet sooner should adopt the plan, I think there is no doubt but they will be followed by this [Virginia], and if some of them should reject it, it is very probable that the opposers of it will exert themselves to add this state to the number" (to Langdon, Dec. 3, 1787, *DHRC*, 8:198).

Carrington told Jefferson that postponing the Virginia convention until a late date "was occasioned by unfriendly intentions towards it [the Constitution], but I apprehend the rapidity of the movements of the other states in the business will, by that time, have brought so many into the adoption that even its enemies will see the necessity of joining" (Nov. 10, 1787, ibid., 149).

210. Pierce to Knox, Nov. 12, 1787, ibid., 155 ("fires" and "to show"); Nov. 19, 1787, ibid., 168 ("attack"); see also Washington to Madison, Nov. 5, 1787, ibid., 146.

For the preceding footnote, see John Breckinridge to James Breckinridge, Jan. 25, 1788, ibid., 321.

211. House Proceedings, Nov. 30, 1787, ibid., 186–7 ("should such" and "deem it proper"); Archibald Stuart to Madison, Dec. 2, 1787, ibid., 196 ("southern" and "a door"); The General Assembly Adopts an Act for Paying the State Convention Delegates, Nov. 30– Dec. 27, 1787, ibid., 183–5; see also Washington to Madison, Dec. 7, 1787, ibid., 225; Monroe to Madison, Dec. 6, 1787, ibid., 207–8; Turberville to Madison, Dec. 11, 1787, ibid., 234.

212. Archibald Stuart to Madison, Dec. 2, 1787, ibid., 196 (quotations); see also Washington to Madison, Dec. 7, 1787, ibid., 225; Henry Lee to Madison, Dec. 7, 1787, ibid., 223.

213. An Act Concerning the State Convention (Dec. 12, 1787), ibid., 190–1 ("deem it necessary" and "the greatest unanimity"); see also Boyd, *Politics of Opposition*, 29; Rutland, *Ordeal of the Constitution*, 37; Heideking, *The Constitution Before the Judgment Seat*, 43.

214. King to Wadsworth, Dec. 23, 1787, *DHRC*, 8:258 ("[t]he nabobs"); Madison to Jefferson, Dec. 9, 1787, ibid., 226–7 (other quotations). Federalist delegate Pierce stated a concern very similar to Madison's. Noting that "the body of the people at large continue in favor" of the Constitution, Pierce worried that "[a] great majority of the members of the legislature are opposed to it . . . [and] when the representatives now here [in Richmond] return to their homes, . . . they will influence the people generally against it and it will fall" (to Henry Knox, Nov. 12, 1787, ibid., 155). For other statements of Madison's growing alarm at developments in Virginia, see Madison to Archibald Stuart, Dec. 14, 1787, ibid., 237– 8; Madison to Randolph, Jan. 10, 1788, ibid., 287–8; see also Madison to Washington, Nov. 18, 1787, ibid., 167. For a similar statement by someone else, see James Breckinridge to John Breckinridge, Dec. 14, 1787, ibid., 171.

215. Carrington to Madison, Jan. 18, 1788, ibid., 309 (quotations); see also Carrington to Knox, Mar. 13, 1788, ibid., 492.

216. Carrington to Madison, Feb. 10, 1788, ibid., 359–60; see also Carrington to Jefferson, Apr. 24, 1788, *DHRC*, 9:755.

217. Nicholas to Madison, Apr. 5, 1788, ibid., 703 ("almost avowedly," "real sentiments," and "friends"); Madison to Jefferson, Apr. 22, 1788, ibid., 745 ("to aim"); Madison to Randolph, Apr. 10, 1788, ibid., 731 ("desperate"). For other statements confirming and commenting on Henry's growing extremism, see Lear to Langdon, Dec. 3, 1787, *DHRC*, 8:197; Henry Lee to Madison, c. Dec. 20, 1787, ibid., 249; Randolph to Madison, Feb. 29, 1788, ibid., 346; John Blair Smith to Madison, June 12, 1788, *DHRC*, 9:607–8; Comte de Moustier to Comte de Montmorin, June 25, 1788, *DHRC*, 21:1227.

218. Stuart to Madison, Nov. 2, 1787, *DHRC*, 9:592 ("much anxiety," "coolly received," and "more confidence"); Randolph to Madison, c. Oct. 29, 1788, *DHRC*, 8:133 ("[t]he conjectures").

219. Meriwether Smith et al. to Randolph, Dec. 2, 1787, ibid., 194–5 (quotation); Randolph to Meriwether Smith et al., Dec. 10, 1787, ibid., 229; The Publication of Edmund Randolph's Reasons for Not Signing the Constitution, Dec. 27, 1787, ibid., 260–1; see also Maier, *Ratification*, 89–90.

220. Randolph to the Speaker of the House of Delegates (dated Oct. 10; published Dec. 27, 1787), *DHRC*, 8:262–70. Although Randolph dated the letter October 10, 1787, it certainly was not sent then, and possibly it was not written then.
221. Ibid., 270–2 (quotations at p. 272).
222. Ibid., 273.
223. Ibid., 274.
224. Madison to Washington, Jan. 25, 1788, ibid., 323 ("It is generally"); Turberville to Madison, Jan. 8, 1788, ibid., 285 ("has been of great service"); "A Plain Dealer" (possibly Spencer Roane), *Virginia Independent Chronicle*, Feb. 13, 1788, ibid., 363–6 ("of a free" and "either" at p. 364) ("either" is quoted from Lee to Randolph, Oct. 16, 1787, which was replying to Randolph to Lee, Sept. 17, 1787). For other statements indicating that the import of Randolph's letter was more favorable to Federalists than to their opponents, see Carrington to Madison, Jan. 18, 1788, ibid., 309; Lear to Langdon, Jan. 25, 1788, ibid., 322; Walter Rutherfurd to John Rutherfurd, Jan. 8, 15, 1788, *DHRC*, 20:578.
      Martin Oster, the French vice-consul in Richmond and Norfolk, reported that "[n]o one is pleased" with Randolph's arguments, which "are too confused and have something of sophistry." Oster thought there was "a duplicity there that no longer allows a doubt as to the active motives of the person. They consist principally of egoism, of the consuming desire to take the lead." He concluded that Randolph lacked "sound judgment" and was "of a character that bends according to how his interest varies, and in addition that always follows the strongest party" (to Comte de la Luzerne, Feb. 4, 1788, *DHRC*, 8:344).
225. Randolph to Madison, Feb. 29, 1788, ibid., 436; Madison to Randolph, Apr. 10, 1788, *DHRC*, 9:730 ("the only ground," "a coalition," and "[r]ecommendatory"); Randolph to Madison, Apr. 17, 1788, ibid., 741 ("the hope"). Other reports seem to confirm that Randolph was not the only Virginian whose opinion on ratification was being influenced by the procession of ratifications by other states. See, e.g., Lear to Langdon, Jan. 25, 1788, *DHRC*, 8:321–2; Lear to William Prescott, Jr., Mar. 4, 1788, ibid., 456; *Pennsylvania Herald*, Feb. 7, 1788, ibid., 357.
226. Washington to Randolph, Jan. 8, 1788, ibid., 286 ("would be productive"); Madison to Randolph, Apr. 10, 1788, *DHRC*, 9:731; Madison to Jefferson, Apr. 22, 1788, ibid., 744 ("so temperate"); see also Madison to Randolph, Jan. 10, 1788, *DHRC*, 8:289.
227. Nicholas to Madison, Apr. 5, 1788, *DHRC*, 9:703; see also Randolph to Madison, Apr. 17, 1788, ibid., 741.
228. Madison to Randolph, Apr. 10, 1788, ibid., 731 ("ripening fast"); Madison to Jefferson, Apr. 22, 1788, ibid., 745 ("Colonel Mason"); Hugh Williamson to John Gray Blount, June 3, 1788, *DHRC*, 10:1572 ("an assemblage," "knaves," "a parcel," "not a few," and "office hunters"); see also Cyrus Griffin to Thomas FitzSimons, Feb. 18, 1788, *DHRC*, 8:382; Lear to Langdon, Jan. 25, 1788, ibid., 322.
229. Washington to Madison, Oct. 10, 1787, ibid., 50 ("will be wanting"); Stuart to Madison, Nov. 2, 1787, *DHRC*, 9:596 ("it is generally" and "[F]or God's sake"); Lawrence Taliaferro to Madison, Dec. 16, 1787, ibid., 597 ("the federal system"). The elections for convention delegates took place from March 3 to March 27, depending on the first day of the court session in different localities. See Introduction, ibid., 561.
230. Madison to Ambrose Madison, Nov. 8, 1787, ibid., 597 ("the final decision" and "should proceed"); Madison to Washington, Feb. 20, 1788, ibid., 602 ("will involve," "public opposition," and "disagreeable"); see also Labunski, *James Madison*, 30.
231. Madison to Ambrose Madison, Nov. 8, 1787, *DHRC*, 9:597 ("many respectable," "to contribute," and "misconceptions"); Madison to Washington, Feb. 20, 1788, ibid., 602 ("to avoid," "a journey," and "informed"); Labunski, *James Madison*, 22–3, 30.
      For the preceding footnote, see Banning, *Sacred Fire*, 87, 433 n. 44.
232. Taliaferro to Madison, Dec. 16, 1787, *DHRC*, 9:597 ("You will be" and "from being"); Randolph to Madison, Jan. 3, 1788, *DHRC*, 8:284 ("must come" and "hazard it"); James Madison, Sr., to Madison, Jan. 30, 1788, *DHRC*, 9:599 ("generally opposed" and "suspend"). For other letters urging Madison to return home for the election, see Dawson to Madison, Feb. 18, 1788, ibid., 601; James Gordon, Jr., to Madison, Feb. 17, 1788, ibid., 600; William Moore to Madison, Jan. 31, 1788, ibid., 599–600; Andrew Shepherd to

Madison, Dec. 22, 1787, ibid., 598; Henry Lee to Madison, c. Dec. 20, 1787, *DHRC*, 8:249; Joseph Spencer to Madison, Feb. 28, 1788, ibid., 424–5; see also Labunski, *James Madison*, 44–6; Maier, *Ratification*, 216.

233. Madison to Eliza House Trist, Mar. 25, 1788, *DHRC*, 9:603 (quotations); see also Francis Taylor Diary, Mar. 24, 1788, ibid., 602; James Duncanson to James Maury, May 8, 1788, ibid., 604.

234. Madison to Eliza House Trist, Mar. 25, 1788, ibid., 603 (quotation); see also Francis Taylor Diary, Mar. 24, 1788, ibid., 602; Maier, *Ratification*, 236; Labunski, *James Madison*, 46–7. For other contemporary statements ascribing Madison's victory to his presence in the county, see John Vaughan to John Dickinson, c. Apr. 19, 1788, *DHRC*, 17:185–6; Cyrus Griffin to Madison, Apr. 7, 1788, *PJM* (C.S.), 11:11.

235. Madison to Jefferson, Apr. 22, 1788, *DHRC*, 9:745 (quotations). For similar assessments, see Washington to Knox, Mar. 30, 1788, *PGW* (C.S.), 6:183; Madison to John Brown, Apr. 9, 1788, *PJM* (C.S.), 11:16. For the Virginia election campaign generally, see Heideking, *The Constitution Before the Judgment Seat*, 211–20; Boyd, *Politics of Opposition*, 102–9; see also Risjord, *Chesapeake Politics*, 301.

236. Nicholas to Madison, Apr. 5, 1788, *DHRC*, 9:703 ("but that majority"); Mason to Jefferson, May 26, 1788, ibid., 883 ("so equally divided"); Randolph to Madison, Apr. 17, 1788, ibid., 741; see also King to Langdon, Apr. 16, 1788, *DHRC*, 17:130; Boyd, *Politics of Opposition*, 109. For calculations giving the Federalists a narrow—albeit uncertain—majority, see Charles Lee to Washington, Apr. 11, 1788, *DHRC*, 9:735; James Duncanson to James Maury, May 8, 1788, ibid., 604. Collin McGregor, a New York bond speculator, was confident enough in the Federalists' "small majority" that he bought more federal securities, expecting them to appreciate in value should Virginia ratify the Constitution (to Neil Jamieson, June 4, 1788, *DHRC*, 10:1575). Knox reported an assessment he had seen from Virginia giving the Federalists "a very decisive majority" of about twenty-two (to Wadsworth, Apr. 27, 1788, *DHRC*, 9:761–2; see also McDonald, *We the People*, 257–8). Mason observed that while some Federalists spoke of "a considerable majority," it was "notorious" that many of them "stick at no falsehood" (to John Francis Mercer, May 1, 1788, *DHRC*, 9:779). Washington told Jay that the elections left "little doubt" that Virginia would ratify the Constitution, unless a "mistake has been made with respect to the sentiments of the Kentucky members" (May 15, 1788, ibid., 803–4; see also Washington to Jay, June 8, 1788, *DHRC*, 10:1588).

237. Madison to John Brown, Apr. 9, 1788, *DHRC*, 9:711 ("[a] good deal"); Madison to Nicholas, May 17, 1788, ibid., 810 ("may come fettered"); Madison to Washington, Apr. 10, 1788, ibid., 732 ("several" and "with a view"); Washington to Knox, Mar. 30, 1788, *DHRC*, 8:521 ("have great weight"); see also Turberville to Madison, Apr. 16, 1788, ibid., 740. For the number of Kentucky delegates at the convention, see *DHRC*, 10:1694 n. 2.

238. Madison to Jefferson, Apr. 22, 1788, *DHRC*, 9:745 ("Kentucky"); Madison to Washington, June 4, 1788, *DHRC*, 10:1574 ("Kentucky has been"); Madison to King, June 13, 1788, ibid., 1619 ("the vote" and "generally under"); see also Madison to Washington, June 13, 1788, ibid.; Madison to John Brown, May 27, 1788, *DHRC*, 9:884; Nicholas to Madison, May 9, 1788, ibid., 793; Charles Lee to Washington, May 14, 1788, ibid., 797; Rutland, *Ordeal of the Constitution*, 197–8.

239. Hugh Williamson to John Gray Blount, June 3, 1788, *DHRC*, 10:1572 ("all eyes"); Jefferson to William Wirt, Aug. 4, 1805, in *Pennsylvania Magazine of History and Biography* (1910), 34:387 ("the greatest orator"); Maier, *Ratification*, 230, 232, 310; supra p. 409. On Henry's oratorical skills generally, see Spencer Roane to Philip Aylett, June 26, 1788, *DHRC*, 10:1713; Miller, *George Mason*, 288; Heideking, *The Constitution Before the Judgment Seat*, 280–2; Maier, *Ratification*, 230. On Henry's actions in the 1760s, see Richard R. Beeman, *Patrick Henry: A Biography* (New York, 1974), 11–22; Henry Mayer, *A Son of Thunder: Patrick Henry and the American Republic* (New York, 1986), 58–66; Labunski, *James Madison*, 28–9.

For the preceding footnote, see Short to Thomas Lee Shippen, May 31, 1788, *DHRC*, 9:895 ("a great weight" and "the powers"); James Breckinridge to John Breckinridge,

June 13, 1788, *DHRC*, 10:1621 ("eloquence"); Martin Oster to Comte de la Luzerne, June 28, 1788, ibid., 1690 ("displayed").

240. Labunski, *James Madison*, 72–4; Banning, *Sacred Fire*, 237. For examples of Henry's invoking his Revolutionary credentials, see June 5, *DHRC*, 9:960–4; June 9, ibid., 1063–4. For Federalist objections to Henry's unwillingness to be bound by the agreed-upon rules of debate, see, e.g., Randolph, June 5, ibid., 968; George Nicholas, June 6, ibid., 998–9; Randolph, June 10, ibid., 1092.

For the preceding footnote, see Sources for the Virginia Convention, ibid., 902–6; Maier, *Ratification*, 258; Hutson, "The Creation of the Constitution," 23–4.

241. Carrington to Knox, Mar. 13, 1788, *DHRC*, 8:493 ("a great proportion"); Henry Lee at Virginia convention, June 9, 1788, *DHRC*, 9:1072–3 ("solid argument" and "throwing"); see also Carrington to Madison, Feb. 10, 1788, *DHRC*, 8:360; Carrington to William Short, Apr. 25, 1788, *DHRC*, 9:758.

242. Jefferson to Alexander Donald, Feb. 7, 1788, *PTJ* (M.S.), 12:571 ("secure to us" and "refuse to accede"); Henry, June 12, *DHRC*, 10:1210 ("the counsel"); see also June 9, ibid., 1051–2; Jefferson to Madison, Feb. 6, 1788, *PTJ* (M.S.), 12:569; Maier, *Ratification*, 275–6; Labunski, *James Madison*, 98–9.

243. Pendleton, June 12, *DHRC*, 10:1201–2 ("a private individual" and "ought not"); Madison, ibid., 1223 ("own reason," "feelings," "would be for," and "the opinion"); Randolph, June 10, ibid., 9:1097 ("to prevent a schism"); see also Monroe to Jefferson, July 12, 1788, *PTJ* (M.S.), 13:352–3.

244. Henry, June 24, *DHRC*, 10:1476 (quotations); June 16, ibid., 1309–10; see also Mason, June 17, ibid., 1338; Maier, *Ratification*, 284, 294–5; Waldstreicher, *Slavery's Constitution*, 144.

For the preceding footnote, see Jefferson to Carrington, May 27, 1788, *PTJ* (M.S.), 13:208.

245. See, e.g., Henry, June 4, *DHRC*, 9:930; Mason, ibid., 936–40; Monroe, June 10, ibid., 1109–12; Mason, June 11, ibid., 1154–62; Grayson, June 12, ibid., 10:1185–7; Henry, ibid., 1212–3; Mason, June 19, ibid., 1401–3; see also Monroe to Jefferson, July 12, 1788, *PTJ* (M.S.), 13:352; Madison to King, June 13, 1788, *DHRC*, 10:1619; Banning, "Virginia," 278–80 & n. 62.

For the preceding footnote, see Monroe to Jefferson, July 12, 1788, *PTJ* (M.S.), 13:353 ("strong objections"); Monroe to Madison, Oct. 13, 1787, *DHRC*, 8:55 ("There are"); Madison to Jefferson, Apr. 22, 1788, *DHRC*, 9:744 ("Monroe"); Monroe to Jefferson, July 12, 1788, *DHRC*, 10:1705–6 ("loosely drawn"); James Monroe, Some Observations on the Constitution, c. May 25, 1788, *DHRC*, 9:846–76; see also Monroe to Lambert Cadwalader, Oct. 15, 1787, *DHRC*, 8:56; editorial note, *DHRC*, 9: 844–6.

246. Madison to King, June 13, 1788, *DHRC*, 10:1619 ("particularly"); Francis Corbin, June 13, ibid., 1256 ("very reprehensible"); Randolph, ibid., 1255 ("local interests" and "partial considerations"); see also George Nicholas, June 18, ibid., 1383; James Breckinridge to John Breckinridge, June 13, 1788, ibid., 1621; Labunski, *James Madison*, 94, 111–2; Banning, "Virginia," 278, 280–3.

247. Henry, June 7, *DHRC*, 9:1039 ("the loss"); June 12, ibid., 10:1220 ("the interest"); June 13, ibid., 1245 ("scuffling"). On Henry's correspondence with Kentucky political leaders, see John Blair Smith to Madison, June 12, 1788, *DHRC*, 9:608; Boyd, *Politics of Opposition*, 108. For additional references by Henry to the Mississippi issue, see June 9, *DHRC*, 9:1051; June 12, ibid., 10:1211–2; June 13, ibid., 1238; ibid., 1245–9.

248. Grayson, June 12, ibid., 1192 ("retain"); Monroe, June 13, ibid., 1235 ("the northern states"). For additional references to the Mississippi issue by Grayson, see ibid., 1235–8; ibid., 1242–5; June 14, ibid., 1259; June 18, ibid., 1282–3; June 19, ibid., 1387. See also Dawson, June 24, ibid., 1493–4.

249. Henry, June 12, ibid., 1218–9 ("[t]he two petty states"); Grayson, June 18, ibid., 1374–5.

250. June 24, ibid., 1496–8 (quotations); June 16, ibid., 1315–6; June 14, ibid., 1259; see also Banning, "Virginia," 279.

251. Henry, June 12, *DHRC*, 10:1222 ("subjects everything," "the most oppressive," and "unbounded power"); June 17, ibid., 1345–6; Mason, ibid., 1361 ("destruction and annihilation"); see also June 11, ibid., 9:1158–9.

252. Henry, June 20, ibid., 10:1422 ("venture to ruin" and "unjust and vexatious"); Grayson, June 21, ibid., 1447 ("procrastination"); see also Henry, June 23, ibid., 1466.

253. Mason, June 19, ibid., 1406–8 (quotations at p. 1406); see also Henry, ibid., 1422; Grayson, June 21, ibid., 1447; Madison to Washington, June 13, 1788, ibid., 1619; Madison to Hamilton, June 20, 1788, ibid., 1656–7.

254. Mason, June 17, ibid., 1344 ("from time to time"); Lee, ibid. ("trivial"); Madison, June 20, ibid., 1417 ("will do every," "virtue and intelligence," and "men of virtue"); Innes, June 25, ibid., 1520 ("[H]orrors"); Johnston, ibid., 1530.

255. Monroe to Jefferson, July 12, 1788, *PTJ* (M.S.), 13:352 ("the principal share"); Madison to Tench Coxe, June 11, 1788, *DHRC*, 10:1595 ("bilious attack," "extremely feeble," and "extreme heat"); see also Madison to Hamilton, June 9, 1788, ibid., 1589; Madison to King, June 13, 1788, ibid., 1618; William Nelson, Jr., to William Short, July 12, 1788, ibid., 1700; Labunski, *James Madison*, 2, 84, 89, 96–7; Maier, *Ratification*, 258, 282, 310. For occasions upon which the convention reporter had difficulty hearing Madison, see June 6, *DHRC*, 9:989; June 12, ibid., 10:1203; June 13, ibid., 1249; June 14, ibid., 1284. For contemporary praise of the role played by Madison at the convention, see Archibald Stuart to John Breckinridge, June 19, 1788, ibid., 1651; James Breckinridge to John Breckinridge, June 13, 1788, ibid., 1621; Martin Oster to Comte de la Luzerne, June 28, 1788, ibid., 1690; Extract of a letter from Richmond (June 18), *Pennsylvania Mercury*, June 26, 1788, ibid., 1688.

For the first of the two preceding footnotes, see Jefferson to William Carmichael, Dec. 15, 1787, *DHRC*, 14:481.

For the second of the two preceding footnotes, see Johnson, *Righteous Anger at the Wicked States*, 4–5; Maier, *Ratification*, 230. For their battles over payment of prewar debts to British creditors, see Evans, "Private Indebtedness and the Revolution in Virginia," 363–9.

256. Supra pp. 456, 461–3; Madison to John Brown, Apr. 9, 1788, *DHRC*, 9:711 (quotation); see also Bowen, *Miracle at Philadelphia*, 300–1; Moncure Daniel Conway, *Omitted Chapters of History Disclosed in the Life and Papers of Edmund Randolph* (New York, 2nd ed., 1889), 109.

257. Monroe to Jefferson, July 12, 1788, *PTJ* (M.S.), 13:352.

258. Randolph, June 4, *DHRC*, 9:932–3.

259. Ibid., 933 (all Randolph quotations); Madison to Washington, June 4, 1788, ibid., 10:1574 ("thrown himself"); see also Randolph, June 6, *DHRC*, 9:971–2; June 10, ibid., 1097; June 25, ibid., 10:1537; Labunski, *James Madison*, 77–80; Maier, *Ratification*, 260–1.

260. Henry, June 7, *DHRC*, 9:1036 ("very strange"); June 9, ibid., 1058; Randolph, ibid., 1081–2 ("with the least shadow"); see also Mason, June 11, ibid., 1162; John Brown Cutting to Jefferson, c. July 24, 1788, ibid., 10:1707; Gerry to James Warren, June 28, 1788, *DHRC*, 18:206; Labunski, *James Madison*, 80. For enthusiastic reactions by Federalists in New York City to news of Randolph's speech, see Cyrus Griffin to Thomas FitzSimons, June 16, 1788, *DHRC*, 20:1174; Nicholas Gilman to John Sullivan, June 12, 1788, *DHRC*, 10:1614; see also *DHRC*, 21:1197 n. 2. For similar reactions by Federalists elsewhere, see Washington to Jay, June 8, 1788, *DHRC*, 10:1587–8; John Vaughan to John Dickinson, June 11, 1788, ibid., 1597; Extract of a letter from Virginia (June 4), *Pennsylvania Gazette*, June 11, 1788, ibid., 1612; Extract of a letter from Richmond (June 18), *Pennsylvania Mercury*, June 26, 1788, ibid., 1688; see also Martin Oster to Comte de la Luzerne, June 28, 1788, ibid., 1690. For a strong defense of Randolph's position by a Virginia Federalist, see James Duncanson to James Maury, June 7, 13, 1788, ibid., 1582.

For the preceding footnote, see Grayson to Nathan Dane, June 4, 1788, ibid., 1573; see also James Duncanson to James Maury, June 7, 13, 1788, ibid., 1582.

261. Madison, June 24, ibid., 1503 ("struck with surprise," "usurpation," and "discourage"); June 17, ibid., 1343 ("great security" and "were greatly interested"); June 12, ibid., 1204 ("ought to satisfy").

262. Nicholas, June 16, ibid., 1313–4; Randolph, June 24, ibid., 1483 ("had the smallest suspicion"); Nicholas, June 17, ibid., 1341–2 ("opposed for being"); Innes, June 25, ibid., 1522–3; see also Waldstreicher, *Slavery's Constitution*, 142.

263. Madison, June 13, *DHRC*, 10:1248–9; ibid., 1240; June 12, ibid., 1225; Nicholas, June 13, ibid., 1250; Randolph, ibid., 1253–4. Madison had laid out the arguments made in this and the following paragraph in earlier correspondence (to Nicholas, May 17, 1788, *DHRC*, 9:805–10; to John Brown, Apr. 9, 1787, ibid., 711–2).

264. Madison, June 12, *DHRC*, 10:1208–9; June 13, ibid., 1241–2; John Marshall, June 10, ibid., 9:1116–7, 1123; Nicholas, ibid., 1129–31; Pendleton, June 12, ibid., 10:1200; Nicholas, June 13, ibid., 1249–52.

265. Innes, June 25, ibid., 1521 ("general spirit"); Madison, June 16, ibid., 1303 ("situation and circumstances"); Randolph, June 6, ibid., 9:977–8; Madison, June 11, ibid., 1145; June 24, ibid., 10:1502–3; see also Madison to George Thompson, Jan. 29, 1789, *PJM* (C.S.), 11:437.

266. Nicholas, June 6, *DHRC*, 9:1002–3 (quotations); Madison, June 13, ibid., 10:1241.

267. Randolph, June 17, ibid., 1360 ("ought to be paid" and "the honest convention"); Madison, June 23, ibid., 1469 ("get justice"); see also Randolph, June 21, ibid., 1455. In the mid-1780s, Madison had unsuccessfully pushed bills in the Virginia legislature to force the payment of prewar debts to British creditors, though by installments. See Madison to Monroe, Dec. 30, 1785, *PJM* (C.S.) 8:465–6; Banning, *Sacred Fire*, 56; Evans, "Private Indebtedness and the Revolution in Virginia," 363–5.

268. Madison, June 17, *DHRC*, 10:1356, 1362; Nicholas, ibid., 1358–9.

269. Mason to Jefferson, May 26, 1788, *DHRC*, 9:883 ("a great majority"); Madison to Hamilton, June 22, 1788, *DHRC*, 10:1665 ("the nice balance" and "to preface"); see also Theodorick Bland to Arthur Lee, June 13, 1788, ibid., 1617; James Breckinridge to John Breckinridge, June 13, 1788, ibid., 1621; Maier, *Ratification*, 292–3; Kaminski, "The Constitution Without a Bill of Rights," 35.

270. Henry, June 5, *DHRC*, 9:951 ("twelve states" and "with manly"); ibid., 966–7 ("egregiously misled," "hardly stand," "heart-burnings," and "[t]here were very respectable"); June 7, ibid., 1040 ("the greatest" and "propose[d] certain amendments"); June 9, ibid., 1057 ("be willing to indulge" and "aversion"); see also June 24, ibid., 10:1478; ibid., 1505–6.

271. Henry, June 7, *DHRC*, 9:1036–7 ("some small possibility"); June 9, ibid., 1072 ("I should be led"); June 24, ibid., 10:1477 ("Evils admitted"); see also June 7, ibid., 9:1015; June 9, ibid., 1070; June 25, ibid., 10:1535; Labunski, *James Madison*, 94–5, 110; Maier, *Ratification*, 294–5.

272. Monroe, June 25, *DHRC*, 10:1518–9.

273. Grayson, June 24, ibid., 1496–7 ("the idea of" and "carrying states"); June 11, ibid., 9:1168 ("by a hair"); Harrison, June 25, ibid., 10:1516–7 ("artifice"); see also Richard Henry Lee to Mason, May 7, 1788, *DHRC*, 9:784–5; Mason to Jefferson, May 26, 1788, ibid., 883; Maier, *Ratification*, 301–2.

274. Madison, June 24, *DHRC*, 10:1499–500 ("the demand," "mutual deference," "neither," "call on," and "for the preservation"); June 6, ibid., 9:993–4 ("heart-burnings" and "is increasing"); June 25, ibid., 10:1518; see also Madison to Jefferson, Apr. 22, 1788, ibid., 9:745.

275. Randolph, June 6, ibid., 973 ("to gratify"); June 10, ibid., 1092 ("a right to dictate"); June 24, ibid., 10:1481, 1487–8 ("there were peace" and "the union"); see also June 4, ibid., 9:933; Banning, "Virginia," 285–6.

276. Randolph, June 6, *DHRC*, 9:985 (quotation); ibid., 976–7, 979–80; June 9, ibid., 1084–6; see also Nicholas, June 10, ibid., 1132–3; George Wythe, June 24, ibid., 10:1473–4; Pendleton, June 12, ibid., 1201.

277. Corbin, June 6, *DHRC*, 9:1015 (quotation); Randolph, ibid., 979; Nicholas, ibid., 1001.

278. Madison to Washington, June 13, 1788, *DHRC*, 10:1619 ("The majority will"); Madison to King, June 13, 1788, ibid. ("more doubtful" and "the event"); Mason to Lamb, June 9, 1788, ibid., 9:818 ("so equally divided"); see also Madison to Hamilton, June 9, 1788, ibid., 10:1589; June 16, 1788, ibid., 1630; Henry to Lamb, June 9, 1788, ibid., 9:817;

Grayson to Lamb, June 9, 1788, ibid., 816; Theodorick Bland to Arthur Lee, June 13, 1788, ibid., 10:1617; Boyd, *Politics of Opposition*, 129. For the observation that each side seemed to believe that it had a majority on its side, or at least claimed to believe so, see James Duncanson to James Maury, June 7, 13, 1788, *DHRC*, 10:1583; Alexander White to Mary Wood, June 10–11, 1788, ibid., 1592; John Dawson to Larkin Stanard, June 12, 1788, ibid., 1613; Robert Morris to Horatio Gates, June 12, 1788, ibid.; Washington to Knox, June 17, 1788, ibid., 1633.

279. Madison to Hamilton, June 20, 1788, ibid., 1657 ("a very disagreeable uncertainty"); June 22, 1788, ibid., 1665 ("the smallness," "[A]nother circumstance," and "[it] unluckily happens"); see also Madison to Washington, June 18, 1788, ibid., 1637–8; Samuel Smith to Tench Coxe, June 22, 1788, ibid., 1666; Corbin to Benjamin Rush, June 23, 1788, ibid., 1668; Madison to Ambrose Madison, June 24, 1788, ibid., 1670. On the possibility of the Antifederalists' seeking an adjournment, which distressed the Federalists, see Madison to Hamilton, June 16, 1788, ibid., 1630; Henry Lee to Hamilton, June 16, 1788, ibid., 1631; Washington to Knox, June 17, 1788, ibid., 1633; Madison to King, June 18, 1788, ibid., 1618; Knox to King, June 19, 1788, ibid., 1652.

280. July 25, 1788, ibid., 1538–41; see also Editors' Note, The Ratification of the Constitution and the Recommendation of Amendments, June 25–27, 1788, ibid., 1512–5.

281. Ibid., 1542.

For the preceding footnote, see Carpenter, *The South as a Conscious Minority*, 212 n. 103 (reporting speech by Senator Louis T. Wigfall of Texas).

282. June 27, 1788, *DHRC*, 10:1551–3 ("certain natural rights" at p. 1551); see also Labunski, *James Madison*, 113–4; Maier, *Ratification*, 307–8.

283. June 27, 1787, *DHRC*, 10:1553–6; Heideking, *The Constitution Before the Judgment Seat*, 318–9.

284. Archibald Stuart to John Breckinridge, June 30, 1788, *DHRC*, 10:1696 ("The convention" and "in friendship"); Extract of a letter from a gentleman in Richmond (June 25), Philadelphia *Independent Gazetteer*, July 2, 1788, ibid., 1697–8 ("either wise"); see also Washington to Charles Cotesworth Pinckney, June 28, 1788, ibid., 1714. For an account of the "generous" reaction of the Antifederalists to their loss at the convention that is similar to Stuart's, see Extract of a letter from Richmond (June 25), *Pennsylvania Packet*, July 2, 1788, ibid., 1698.

285. Madison to Hamilton, June 27, 1788, ibid., 1688 ("highly objectionable," "fair professions," "he should submit," and "ill will"); Madison to Washington, June 27, 1788, ibid., 1688–9 ("to engage"); see also Maier, *Ratification*, 309.

286. Monroe to Jefferson, July 12, 1788, *PTJ* (M.S.), 13:352 ("carried"); Washington to Charles Carter, Dec. 14, 1787, *PGW* (C.S.), 5:492 ("that there is no alternative"); Jan. 12, 1788, ibid., 6:37 & n. 1; George Washington and the Constitution, *DHRC*, 5:788–9; see also Washington to Caleb Gibbs, Feb. 28, 1788, *DHRC*, 8:427; editorial note, *DHRC*, 7:1655; Grayson to Short, Nov. 10, 1787, *DHRC*, 14:82; Grayson at Virginia convention, June 24, 1788, *DHRC*, 10:1498; Hamilton, Conjectures, *PAH*, 4:275; Labunski, *James Madison*, 28, 117; Henry, *Patrick Henry*, 2:363–4; Boyd, *Politics of Opposition*, 130; Heideking, *The Constitution Before the Judgment Seat*, 319–20, 375–6; Jensen, *Making of the American Constitution*, 38–9.

Washington also promoted ratification through his voluminous correspondence. See Heideking, supra, 101–2. For the prevalent assumption that Washington would become the nation's first president (assuming that Virginia ratified the Constitution), see, e.g., "A Citizen of New-York," New York *Daily Advertiser*, Sept. 26, 1787, *DHRC*, 19:54; *Massachusetts Centinel*, Oct. 6, 1787, *DHRC*, 4:53; Alexander Donald to Jefferson, Nov. 12, 1787, *DHRC*, 8:155; William Ellery to Benjamin Huntington, Sept. 30, 1788, *DHRC*, 25:410. Two days into the Virginia ratifying convention, one newspaper reprinted Washington's circular to state executives of June 1783, which was one of his last public acts as commander-in-chief and had called for a strong federal government. See *Virginia Independent Chronicle*, June 4, 1788, *DHRC*, 10:1579 (and the editorial note).

287. Brown to Archibald Stuart, June 25, 1788, *DHRC*, 21:1225 ("We wait"); Thomas Tudor Tucker to St. George Tucker, July 22–28, 1788, ibid., 1334 ("certainly" and "would have followed"). For other predictions that if the Virginia convention rejected ratification, so would New York's, see Hamilton to Madison, May 19, 1788, *DHRC*, 20:1102–3; St. Jean de Crevecoeur to William Short, June 10, 1788, *DHRC*, 10:1592–3; Ebenezer Hazard to Washington, June 24, 1788, *DHRC*, 21:1222; William Duer to Madison, June 23, 1788, ibid., 1210; see also Philip Schuyler to Stephen Van Rensselaer, July 2, 1788, ibid., 1214.

288. "A Landholder" VIII, *Connecticut Courant*, Dec. 24, 1787, *DHRC*, 3:506; Hugh Ledlie to John Lamb, Jan. 15, 1788, *DHRC*, 20:610; Hugh Williamson to James Iredell, July 7, 1788, *DHRC*, 21:1295; Extract of a letter from a gentleman in New-York (May 24), Charleston *Columbian Herald*, June 19, 1788, ibid., 1204; An Extract of a Letter from John Williams (Jan. 29), Albany *Federal Herald*, Feb. 25, 1788, *DHRC*, 20:673; Timothy Pickering to John Pickering, Dec. 29, 1787, *DHRC*, 19:482; Kaminski, "New York," 52, 54; Maier, *Ratification*, 323–4; Eubanks, "New York," 305–6; Boyd, *Politics of Opposition*, 34; Rutland, *Ordeal of the Constitution*, 203.

289. Kaminski, "New York," 53; Maier, *Ratification*, 323; Eubanks, "New York," 305. For one Loyalist expressing confidence that the federal court system authorized by the Constitution would enhance his chances of recovering his confiscated property in Massachusetts, see William Vassall to John Lowell, Feb. 26, 1788, *DHRC*, 7:1709–10. New Yorkers were also unhappy with the Confederation Congress for not supporting New York's claims to the contested territory of Vermont and for failing to force the British to fulfill their treaty obligation to evacuate forts in upstate New York, a failure that was costing a great deal of money to New Yorkers involved in the fur trade. See Eubanks, supra, 305–7; McDonald, *We the People*, 290–1; supra p. 32.

  For the preceding footnote, see Antoine de La Forest to Comte de Montmorin, Dec. 15, 1787, *DHRC*, 19:424.

290. "A Columbian Patriot," *Observations*, *DHRC*, 16:287 ("that will undoubtedly lead"); Madison to Washington, Sept. 30, 1787, *PJM* (C.S.), 10:181 ("The general voice"); Grayson to William Short, Nov. 10, 1787, *DHRC*, 14:81 ("there is a great majority"); Kaminski, "New York," 65, 77. Overall, assessments of whether New York was likely to ratify were mixed. The majority view seems to have been that New York was unlikely to ratify. The minority view was that opinion in New York was evenly balanced, rendering predictions unreliable. For the former view, see, in addition to the sources cited above, James Freeman to Theophilus Lindsey, Mar. 29, 1788, *DHRC*, 16:504; Timothy Pickering to John Pickering, Dec. 29, 1787, *DHRC*, 19:482; Patrick Henry at Virginia convention, June 9, 1788, *DHRC*, 9:1056. For the view that opinion in New York was evenly divided and predictions were unreliable, see Gouverneur Morris to Washington, Oct. 30, 1787, *PGW* (C.S.), 5:399; Hamilton to Washington, Oct. 8–10, 1787, *DHRC*, 19:35; Don Diego de Gardoqui to Conde de Floridablanca, Dec. 6, 1787, ibid., 360–1; Knox to Washington, Mar. 10, 1788, *DHRC*, 20:852–3. Madison and Jay both predicted that New York's decision would be heavily influenced by that of neighboring states. Madison to Ambrose Madison, Nov. 8, 1787, *PJM* (C.S.), 10:244; Madison to Jefferson, Dec. 9, 1787, ibid., 311; Jay to Washington, Feb. 3, 1788, *DHRC*, 20:746.

291. Samuel Blachley Webb to Joseph Barrell, Jan. 13, 1788, *DHRC*, 15:362 ("astonishingly great"). For one statement of Clinton's extraordinary influence in New York, see Extract of a letter from a gentleman in New-York, Charleston *Columbian Herald*, *DHRC*, 21:1204–5. For background on Clinton's long-term governorship of the state and the policies he pursued, see Kaminski, "New York," 48–59; Kaminski, *George Clinton*, 59–111.

292. Don Diego de Gardoqui to Conde de Floridablanca, Dec. 6, 1787, *DHRC*, 19:360–1 ("violently opposed"); "Aristides," New York *Daily Advertiser*, Sept. 10, 1787, ibid., 21 ("secretly hostile"); Walter Rutherfurd to John Rutherfurd, Jan. 8, 15, 1788, *DHRC*, 20:578 ("had a hand"); Robert Yates and John Lansing, Jr., to Governor George Clinton, Dec. 21, 1787, *DHRC*, 19:456–9; Boyd, *Politics of Opposition*, 33; De Pauw, *Eleventh Pillar*, 73–4; Kaminski, *George Clinton*, 131–9; Alexander, *The Selling of the Constitutional Convention*, 127–9. Madison reported the prevalent view that Clinton was "a decided adversary" to

the Constitution (to William Short, Oct. 24, 1787, *DHRC*, 19:122), and Hamilton told Washington that "though the Governor has not publicly declared himself, his particular connections and confidential friends are loud against it" (Oct. 8–10, 1787, ibid., 35). See also John Stevens, Jr., to John Stevens, Sr., Oct. 1, 1787, ibid., 68; Collin McGregor to Neil Jamieson, Oct. 10, 1787, ibid., 78. For the view that Clinton was "laying by and not decisive, waiting to see how the wind will blow," see Elias Boudinot to William Bradford, Jr., Sept. 28, 1787, ibid., 61; see also Carrington to Jefferson, Oct. 23, 1787, ibid., 121. For background to the Federalists' decision to attack Clinton (including in a pseudonymous contribution by Hamilton), even before the Philadelphia convention had ended, for opposing the creation of a more powerful national government, see Kaminski, "New York," 67; Kaminski, *George Clinton*, 122–31; Alexander Hamilton Attacks Governor George Clinton, July 21–Oct. 31, 1787, *DHRC*, 19:9–11.

293. Richard Sill to Jeremiah Wadsworth, Jan. 12, 1788, *DHRC*, 20:602 ("best friends"); Egbert Benson to unidentified recipient, Feb. 1, 1788, ibid., 729 ("if the whole"). For the Antifederalists' resolution criticizing the Constitution, which they chose not to submit, see also Newspaper Report of Assembly Debates, Jan. 31, 1788, ibid., 712 (Benson). For doubts as to whether the New York legislature would call a convention, see Carrington to Madison, Feb. 10, 1788, *PJM* (C.S.), 10:494; Madison to Washington, Jan. 20, 1788, *DHRC*, 20:696–7; "Agrippa" III, *Massachusetts Gazette*, Nov. 30, 1787, *DHRC*, 4:343. For one New York Federalist's more confident view that the legislature would summon a convention, see Samuel Blachley Webb to Joseph Barrell, Jan. 13, 1788, *DHRC*, 20:608. For the legislature's deliberations over calling a convention, see generally Kaminski, "New York," 73–7; De Pauw, *Eleventh Pillar*, 87–90; Introduction, *DHRC*, 20:687–91.

294. Assembly Journal, Jan. 31, 1788, *DHRC*, 20:704 ("instead of" and "a new Constitution"); Newspaper Report of Assembly Debates, ibid., 709 (Benson) ("from the legislature," "throwing an odium," and "that they had gone"); ibid., 710 (Jones) ("was a simple detail"); ibid., 708 (Schoonmaker); Newspaper Reports of Senate Debates, Feb. 1, 1788, ibid., 719 (Duane) ("well informed," "not hoodwinked," and "whether the Convention"); ibid., 720 (Abraham Yates, Jr.); see also Egbert Benson to unidentified recipient, Feb. 1, 1788, ibid., 728; Introduction, ibid., 690; Kaminski, "New York," 74; Maier, *Ratification*, 327; Boyd, *Politics of Opposition*, 35–6; Heideking, *The Constitution Before the Judgment Seat*, 46–7.

295. Charles Tillinghast to Hugh Hughes, Jan. 27–28, 1788, *DHRC*, 20:669–70 (quotations); Introduction, ibid., 689; Boyd, *Politics of Opposition*, 35. Melancton Smith likewise concluded from the legislature's selection of "the warmest advocates for the [Constitution]" as congressional delegates that the Antifederalists did not have the legislative majority that some people had supposed they did (to Abraham Yates, Jr., Jan. 28, 1788, *DHRC*, 20:671).

Another favorable omen for Federalists at the legislative session was their defeat of a proposal in the senate for a new oath of allegiance for state officeholders. According to one Federalist's account, the oath proposed by the Antifederalists was "so framed as that they [state officeholders] should swear never to consent to any act or thing which had a tendency to destroy or alter the present constitution of the state." Antifederalists admitted that this proposal was an indirect attack on the federal Constitution. The senate rejected it by a margin of nine to six. See Philip Schuyler to Stephen Van Rensselaer, Jan. 27, 1788, ibid., 699; Introduction, ibid., 689. Conversely, the Federalists' effort to replace the state officeholders' oath swearing allegiance to New York "as a free and independent state" with one swearing allegiance "to the United States of America" was overwhelmingly defeated.

296. Newspaper Reports of Senate Debates, Feb. 1, 1788, *DHRC*, 20:717 (Duane) (quotations). For statements by Antifederalists emphasizing that they did not oppose calling a convention, see Newspaper Report of Senate Debates, Feb. 1, 1788, ibid., 716 (Lawrence); ibid., 718 (Williams); An Extract of a Letter from John Williams (Jan. 29), Albany *Federal Herald*, Feb. 25, 1788, ibid., 673; see also Newspaper Reports of Assembly Debates, Jan. 31, 1788, ibid., 710 (Harison); Boyd, *Politics of Opposition*, 36–7; Maier, *Ratification*, 326–7; Kaminski, "New York," 74–5. For Gouverneur Morris's speculations, which were similar to Duane's, as to why Antifederalist legislators who opposed

ratification were nonetheless willing to support calling a ratifying convention, see Morris to Washington, Oct. 30, 1787, *PGW* (C.S.), 5:399.

297. Newspaper Report of Assembly Debates, Jan. 31, 1788, *DHRC*, 20:713 (Jones) ("their free investigation"); ibid. (Benson) ("a reflection" and "had sent"); Assembly Proceedings, Jan. 31, 1788, ibid., 704–5 (the vote); see also Egbert Benson to unidentified recipient, Feb. 1, 1788, ibid., 728; Introduction, ibid., 690. For the Philadelphia convention's transmittal language, see Resolutions of the Convention Recommending the Procedures for Ratification and for the Establishment of Government Under the Constitution by the Confederation Congress, Sept. 17, 1787, *DHRC*, 1:318 ("for their assent"). Congress's endorsement of the Philadelphia convention's transmittal language is in Charles Thomson, Circular Letter to the Executives of the States, Sept. 28, 1787, ibid., 340.

298. Assembly Proceedings, Jan. 31, 1788, *DHRC*, 20:705–6; Introduction, ibid., 690; Maier, *Ratification*, 327–8. On the significant extent to which removing the property qualification for voting increased the size of the electorate choosing convention delegates, see Young, *Democratic Republicans of New York*, 85. On the puzzling suffrage expansion, see Kaminski, "New York," 76–7. On Poughkeepsie as a relatively neutral site, see Maier, supra, 345.

299. Joseph Barrell to Samuel Blachley Webb, Feb. 20, 1788, *DHRC*, 20:731 (quotations). Governor Clinton's nephew, De Witt Clinton, later observed that delaying the convention so long had been "a great error in policy," which he blamed on "a very cunning trick" by Federalist Assemblyman Egbert Benson (De Witt Clinton Journal, July 18, 1788, *DHRC*, 23:2232). Kaminski argues that both parties might have favored the delay. Federalists might have calculated that they needed time to change New Yorkers' views on the Constitution, and they hoped that nine states would have ratified by the time the New York convention assembled, which might influence the convention's proceedings. New York Antifederalists might have favored delay to enable them to coordinate opposition to ratification with allies in other states, and in the hope that another state, especially an influential one such as Virginia, might reject the Constitution before the New York convention met, thus removing some of the onus for defeating ratification from New York (Kaminski, "New York," 76).

300. Oothoudt to John McKesson, Apr. 3, 1788, *DHRC*, 21:1376 (quotation); Kaminski, *George Clinton*, 139–48; Kaminski, "New York," 72, 77–8, 92; De Pauw, *Eleventh Pillar*, 97, 101–2; Eubanks, "New York," 310; Maier, *Ratification*, 333; Heideking, *The Constitution Before the Judgment Seat*, 205–6.

301. Albany Federal Committee, *An Impartial Address* (c. Apr. 20, 1788), *DHRC*, 21:1398 (quotations); Editors' Note, New York and the Massachusetts Convention's Amendments to the Constitution, Feb. 6, 1788, *DHRC*, 20:751–2; New York City Celebrates Massachusetts Ratification of the Constitution, ibid., 766–9; Kaminski, "New York," 78.

302. A *Citizen of New-York* (Jay), *DHRC*, 20:936–8, 940–1 (quotation at p. 941). On the importance of Jay's pamphlet, which was widely circulated throughout the country, see Editorial Note, ibid., 924–7; see also Maier, *Ratification*, 336–8.

303. *Plebeian: To the Friends and Fellow Citizens of New York* (Apr. 17, 1788), *DHRC*, 20:944–5, 949–50 (all quotations at pp. 944–5) [hereinafter, *Plebeian*]; see also Albany Anti-Federal Committee Circular, Apr. 10, 1788, *DHRC*, 21:1383–4.

304. King to John Langdon, Apr. 16, 1788, *DHRC*, 17:130 ("[i]t is exquisitely problematical"); Knox to the Marquis de Lafayette, May 15, 1788, *DHRC*, 20:1096 ("it is probable"). For statements to similar effect, see Jay to Washington, Apr. 20, 1788, ibid., 963; Robert R. Livingston to Marquis de la Luzerne, May 7, 1788, ibid., 1087–8. For more optimistic Federalist assessments, see Samuel Blachley Webb to Joseph Barrell, Apr. 20, 1788, ibid., 964; Samuel A. Otis to Benjamin Lincoln, May 8, 1788, ibid., 1092. For detailed discussions of the election campaign in New York, see De Pauw, *Eleventh Pillar*, ch. 8; Heideking, *The Constitution Before the Judgment Seat*, 204–11; Kaminski, "New York," 80–99.

305. From the New York Federal Election Committee, June 6, 1788, *DHRC*, 20:1133–4; Kaminski, "New York," 79–80, 82, 86–7, 91, 94–5, 98–9; Maier, *Ratification*, 328, 341. For expressions of surprise at the lopsided outcome, see Abraham G. Lansing to Abraham Yates, Jr., June 1, 1788, *DHRC*, 20:1121; Hamilton to Madison, June 8, 1788, ibid., 1135.

Opinion in New York City was so overwhelmingly Federalist that even Governor Clinton could win only a relative handful of votes on the city ticket (however, he was elected as a delegate to the convention by his home county of Ulster). See Abraham Baldwin to Seaborn Jones, June 5, 1788, ibid., 1129.

306. Hamilton to Madison, June 8, 1788, ibid., 1135–6 (quotations); see also June 25, 1788, ibid., 21:1226; June 21, 1788, ibid., 23:2346. Henry Knox voiced a very similar opinion regarding the strategy of the Antifederalist leaders (to Otho Holland Williams, June 11, 1788, *DHRC*, 20:1139). See also Knox to Benjamin Lincoln, June 13, 1788, ibid., 1152; Richard Platt to Winthrop Sargent, June 14, 1788, ibid., 1169; William Duer to Madison, June 23, 1788, *DHRC*, 21:1209–10. Antifederalist leader Abraham Yates confirmed this Federalist understanding of Antifederalist strategy (to Abraham G. Lansing, June 1, 1788, *DHRC*, 20:1123).

For the preceding footnote, see John Brown Cutting to Jefferson, Aug. 30, 1788, *DHRC*, 21:1353; see also James R. Reid to Tench Coxe, Aug. 20, 1788, *DHFFE*, 1:94.

307. William Bingham to Tench Coxe, June 12, 1788, *DHRC*, 20:1150 ("so great" and "[t]he most sanguine"); *Massachusetts Centinel*, June 14, 1788, ibid., 1171 ("the ground" and "surrounded"); Duer to Madison, June 23, 1788, *DHRC*, 21:1209 ("cannot agree" and "may create"). For the view that an adjournment of the convention was the best New York Federalists could hope for, see Tench Coxe to Madison, June 11, 1788, *DHRC*, 20:1139; Carrington to Madison, June 17, 1788, *DHRC*, 21:1197. For the view that New York would eventually have to submit to the will of the nation once nine states had ratified, see New York *American Magazine*, June 3, 1788, *DHRC*, 20:1124; Jay to Jefferson, June 9, 1788, ibid., 1137–8. For one Federalist's more optimistic assessment of the chances for ratification in New York, see Cyrus Griffin to Thomas FitzSimons, June 16, 1788, ibid., 1174.

308. For the news of South Carolina's ratification reaching New York, see Editors' Note, New York City Newspapers Report South Carolina's Ratification of the Constitution, June 5–7, 1788, ibid., 1132–3. For the reports circulating among New York Federalists of a likely victory in Virginia, see Knox to Lincoln, June 13, 1788, ibid., 1152; Richard Platt to Winthrop Sargent, June 14, 1788, ibid., 1169.

309. John Lansing, Jr., to Abraham Yates, Jr., June 1, 1788, ibid., 1122–3 ("form a plan"); see also Abraham G. Lansing to Abraham Yates, Jr., ibid., 1121.

310. June 15, 1788, ibid., 1172 ("the opinion"); Abraham Yates, Jr., to Abraham G. Lansing, ibid., 1174 ("I don't," "from common conversation," "had some hopes," and "seem determined").

311. Robert Yates to Mason, June 21, 1788, *DHRC*, 22:1800 ("our fixed determination" and "neither sophistry"); James M. Hughes to John Lamb, June 18, 1788, *DHRC*, 21:1202 ("[u]nanimity," "to bend," and "shut[ting] out"). In Massachusetts, Elbridge Gerry was convinced that New York Antifederalists would hold out for conditional ratification (to James Warren, June 28, 1788, *DHRC*, 18:206). Massachusetts Antifederalist Nathan Dane reported from New York City that New York's Antifederalists were "more fixed" than those anywhere else in the nation and that even ratification by New Hampshire and Virginia might not lessen their determination to insist on antecedent amendments (to Samuel Holten, June 14, 1788, *DHRC*, 20:1168–9). Postmaster General Ebenezer Hazard told Washington that "better informed" observers "seem confident that they [New York Antifederalists] will make certain amendments the condition of their adopting it [the Constitution]" (June 24, 1788, ibid., 21:1222).

312. Jay to Washington, May 29, 1788, *DHRC*, 20:1119 ("principal leaders" and doubtful"); Duer to Madison, June 23, 1788, *DHRC*, 21:1209 ("hazard," "avowed themselves," "cannot agree," and "to create"). For another statement of the view that some of the Antifederalist rank and file were loyal to the union, even if most of their leaders were not, see Philip Schuyler to Stephen Van Rensselaer, July 2, 1788, ibid., 1214–5. Antifederalist leader Abraham Yates thought the Federalists "seem to be confident that the Anties will not agree among themselves" (to George Clinton, July 1, 1788, ibid., 1245). Hamilton, who was not above planting fabricated stories, told Gouverneur Morris, "It is reduced to a certainty that [George] Clinton has in several conversations declared the Union

unnecessary" (May 19, 1788, *DHRC*, 20:1104). For the view that Governor Clinton opposed ratification because it would threaten his hold on office, see Samuel A. Otis to Benjamin Lincoln, May 8, 1788, ibid., 1092. Federalist convention delegate Abraham Bancker believed that if Clinton had not so strenuously opposed ratification, the convention would have easily approved the Constitution (to Evert Bancker, June 28, 1788, *DHRC*, 21:1230; see also Kaminski, "New York," 114).

313. Hamilton to Madison, May 19, 1788, *DHRC*, 20:1102–3 (quotations); see also Hamilton to Gouverneur Morris, May 19, 1788, ibid., 1104. For other statements of the view that previous ratification by nine states would give the Federalists their best chance of success at the New York convention, see Henry Knox to the Marquis de Lafayette, May 15, 1788, ibid., 1096; William Bingham to Tench Coxe, May 25, 1788, ibid., 1110; James Kent to Robert Troup, June 20, 1788, *DHRC*, 22:1704. On the establishment of the express system, which Hamilton and Rufus King coordinated with John Sullivan and John Langdon in New Hampshire, and which Hamilton coordinated with Madison in Virginia, see The Federalist Express System between the New York, New Hampshire, and Virginia Conventions, June 24–26, 1788, *DHRC*, 10:1672–4; The Establishment of a Federalist Express System Between the New Hampshire and New York Conventions, June 4–16, 1788, *DHRC*, 20:1124–8; Hamilton to Sullivan, June 6, 1788, ibid., 1126; King to Langdon, June 10, 1788, ibid.; Hamilton to Madison, June 8, 1788, ibid., 1135–6; Maier, *Ratification*, 342.

314. Samuel Blachley Webb to Catherine Hogeboom, June 27, 1788, *DHRC*, 22:1976 ("elegant" and "one of the most"); De Witt Clinton to Charles Tillinghast, July 3, 1788, ibid., 2082 ("to ridicule"); Introduction, ibid., 1669, 1671; Maier, *Ratification*, 345–8; De Pauw, *Eleventh Pillar*, 196–200; see also Samuel Blachley Webb to Catherine Hogeboom, June 24–25, 1788, *DHRC*, 21:1222. For Smith's view that "[t]he principal labor of managing the controversy lies upon me," see Smith to Nathan Dane, June 28, 1788, *DHRC*, 22:2015. For another exaltation of Hamilton's talents, see Richard Platt to Winthrop Sargent, Aug. 8, 1788, *DHRC*, 21:1352. For one Antifederalist's concern that Jay's "manners and mode of address would probably do much mischief, were the [Antifederalist] members not as firm as they are," see Tillinghast to Lamb, June 21, 1788, *DHRC*, 22:1795. For the exchange in which Antifederalist leaders complained of what they (understandably) perceived as Robert R. Livingston's insulting condescension, see Robert R. Livingston, July 1, ibid., 2049–52; Gilbert Livingston, July 2, ibid., 2059–62; John Williams, ibid., 2063–4; Melancton Smith, ibid., 2064–6.

For the preceding footnote, see American National Biography Online; De Pauw, *Eleventh Pillar*, 199–200 ("a man" and "good and able").

315. Abraham G. Lansing to Abraham Yates, Jr., June 22, 1788, *DHRC*, 21:1207–8 ("eventually be injured," "Federalists would operate," "procrastinat[ing]," and "country friends"); Robert Yates to Mason, June 21, 1788, *DHRC*, 22:1799 ("to prevent"); Robert R. Livingston motion for clause-by-clause consideration of the Constitution, June 19, ibid., 1688; Editorial Note, ibid., 1672; see also Comte de Moustier to Comte de Montmorin, May 29, 1788, *DHRC*, 20:1120; John Lansing, Jr., to Abraham Yates, Jr., June 19, 1788, *DHRC*, 22:1702; Maier, *Ratification*, 349–50; Kaminski, "New York," 101–2, 114.

316. Convention Debates and Proceedings, June 26–July 2, 1788, *DHRC*, 22:1917–2069; see also Smith to Nathan Dane, June 28, 1788, ibid., 2015. On the "slow progress," see Abraham Bancker to Evert Bancker, July 5, 1788, ibid., 2106.

317. On the size of the House, see Convention Debates and Proceedings, June 20–23, 1788, ibid., 1715–828. On the Senate, see June 24–25, ibid., 1836–902. On Congress's power over congressional elections, see June 25–26, ibid., 1904–16. See also Hamilton to Madison, June 21, 1788, *PJM* (C.S.), 11:165; Hamilton to Madison, c. July 2, 1788, ibid., 185. For Federalists' emphasizing New York's vulnerability if the union dissolved, see Robert R. Livingston, June 19, *DHRC*, 22:1684–5; June 27, ibid., 1942; Hamilton, June 20, ibid., 1723–4.

318. Robert R. Livingston, June 25, ibid., 1899 ("the circumstances"); *Hudson Weekly Gazette*, June 24, 1788, *DHRC*, 21:1224 ("is materially"); News of New Hampshire and Virginia

Ratification Arrives in New York, June 24–July 2, 1788, ibid., 1210–1; Maier, *Ratification*, 361; De Pauw, *Eleventh Pillar*, 207–8. For additional Federalist newspaper statements observing that, since nine states had now ratified the Constitution, New York had no choice but to unconditionally ratify or else be left outside the union and facing a likely civil war, see *New York Packet*, July 15, 1788, *DHRC*, 22:2164; "Cato: To the People of the State of New-York," Poughkeepsie *Country Journal*, July 8, 1788, *DHRC*, 21:1302–3.

319. Smith, June 25, *DHRC*, 22:1902 ("solemn" and "it had not"); Lansing, ibid., 1903 ("it is still" and "to force us"). New Hampshire's ratification had more of an effect on Smith than he let on publicly. See infra pp. 494–5.

320. Clinton to John Lamb, June 28, 1788, *DHRC*, 23:2357 ("the least effect"); Clinton to Abraham Yates, Jr., ibid. ("are firm"); Abraham Yates, Jr., to Abraham G. Lansing, June 25, 1788, *DHRC*, 21:1228 ("the same" and "if all"). For additional Antifederalist statements to the effect that the news from New Hampshire had had no effect on Antifederalist convention delegates, see Abraham Yates, Jr., to George Clinton, July 1, 1788, ibid., 1245; Melancton Smith to Nathan Dane, June 28, 1788, *DHRC*, 22:2015; Henry Oothoudt to Abraham Yates, Jr., June 27, 1788, *DHRC*, 23:2354; Christopher P. Yates to Abraham Yates, Jr., ibid., 2355; see also Introduction, *DHRC*, 22:1672; Kaminski, "New York," 105.

321. Hamilton to Madison, June 27, 1788, *DHRC*, 21:1213 ("our only chance"); Hamilton to Madison, c. July 2, 1788, *PJM* (C.S.), 11:185 ("more and more" and "to be convinced"); Abraham G. Lansing to Abraham Yates, Jr., June 29, 1788, *DHRC*, 21:1235 ("more serious" and "the spirits"). For other Federalists' similarly observing that New Hampshire's ratification apparently had no effect on the Antifederalist delegates, see Abraham Bancker to Evert Bancker, June 28, 1788, ibid., 1230; Samuel Blachley Webb to Joseph Barrell, July 1–2, 1788, ibid., 1243.

322. Hamilton to Madison, June 8, 1788, *DHRC*, 20:1136 ("vast influence"); From Henry Izard, July 8, 1788, *DHRC*, 21:1297 ("Joy and hilarity"); see also Maier, *Ratification*, 370; De Pauw, *Eleventh Pillar*, 214–5; Kaminski, "New York," 106; Editors' Note: The Arrival in New York of the News of Virginia's Ratification of the Constitution, July 2, 1788, *DHRC*, 22:2084. For earlier Federalist predictions that Virginia's ratification would greatly influence the decision of the New York convention, see Peter Van Schaack to Henry Van Schaack, June 22, 1788, *DHRC*, 21:1208; Henry Knox to Jeremiah Wadsworth, June 8, 1788, in ibid., 1209 n. 2; William Duer to Madison, June 23, 1788, ibid., 1210; Ebenezer Hazard to Washington, June 24, 1788, ibid., 1222. On the Federalists' breaking out in cheers when the news from Virginia arrived in Poughkeepsie, see A Reminiscence of the Arrival in Poughkeepsie of the News of Virginia's Ratification of the Constitution, ibid., 1217–9. For another example of Federalist elation at the news from Virginia, see Philip Schuyler to Stephen Van Rensselaer, July 2, 1788, ibid., 1214.

323. Extract of a letter from New-York (July 6), *Massachusetts Centinel*, July 16, 1788, *DHRC*, 23:2371 ("took no more"); De Witt Clinton to Charles Tillinghast, July 3, 1788, *DHRC*, 22:2082 ("no impressions"); Schoonmaker to Peter Van Gaasbeek, July 2, 1788, ibid., 2083 ("I trust"); Lawrence to Lamb, July 3, 1788, *DHRC*, 21:1261 ("the information"); Lamb to Lawrence, July 6, 1788, ibid., 1292 ("stand firm" and "they will remain so").

324. Jay to Washington, July 4, 8, 1788, *DHRC*, 22:2114 ("disappointed" and "nevertheless"); John Swann to James Iredell, July 7, 1788, *DHRC*, 21:1294 ("astonishing," "determined," and "concurrence"); Extract of a letter from Poughkeepsie (July 3), New York *Daily Advertiser*, July 7, 1788, *DHRC*, 22:2093 ("fondly," "intent," and "destructive"). For additional statements by Federalists who reluctantly concluded that Virginia's ratification had not influenced New York Antifederalists, see Samuel Blachley Webb to Catherine Hogeboom, July 13, 1788, *DHRC*, 21:1314; Thomas Goadsby to Kirkman, Holmes & Co., July 3, 1788, ibid., 1260; see also David S. Bogart to Samuel Blachley Webb, July 8, 1788, ibid., 1296. For other Federalists' taking a more favorable view of the impact of the news from Virginia on Antifederalists' posture toward unconditional ratification, see New York *Daily Advertiser*, July 9, 1788, *DHRC*, 23:2366; Peleg Arnold to Welcome Arnold, July 11, 1788, ibid.; see also John Pintard to Elisha Boudinot, July 10, 1788, *DHRC*, 21:1308.

325. Nathaniel Lawrence to John Lamb, July 3, 1788, ibid., 1261; see also Introduction, *DHRC*, 22:1672; Editors' Note, The Arrival in New York of the News of Virginia's Ratification of the Constitution, July 2, 1788, ibid., 2086; Eubanks, "New York," 325; Maier, *Ratification*, 370; Heideking, *The Constitution Before the Judgment Seat*, 322; De Pauw, *Eleventh Pillar*, 202–3, 216. For similar reports of the Federalists' change in strategy after arrival of the news from Virginia, see *Albany Journal*, July 7, 1788, *DHRC*, 23:2364; Isaac Roosevelt to Richard Varick, July 5, 1788, ibid.; Abraham Bancker to Evert Bancker, July 5, 1788, *DHRC*, 22:2106. For the explanation of the Federalists' strategic shift noted in the text, see Kaminski, "New York," 107.

326. Convention Debates and Proceedings, July 4, 5, 7, *DHRC*, 22:2094–107; New York *Daily Advertiser*, July 8, 1788, *DHRC*, 22:2094; Kaminski, "New York," 107; Maier, *Ratification*, 370–1; De Pauw, *Eleventh Pillar*, 217–8.

327. Abraham Bancker to Evert Bancker, July 5, 1788, *DHRC*, 22:2106 (quotation); Yates at New York convention, July 8, ibid., 2117; Convention Debates and Proceedings, July 9, ibid., 2118; see also Hamilton to Madison, July 8, 1788, ibid., 2117; Jay to Washington, July 4, 8, 1788, ibid., 2115; Abraham Bancker to Evert Bancker, July 12, 1788, ibid., 2149; Jay to Corbin, July 4, 1788, *DHRC*, 23:2363–4; Kaminski, "New York," 107.

328. Hamilton to Madison, July 8, 1788, *DHRC*, 22:2117 ("We have good reason"); Jay to Washington, July 4, 8, 1788, ibid., 2114 ("the unanimity" and "their apparent determination"); see also Introduction, ibid., 1672; Kaminski, "New York," 107. Antifederalist delegate Cornelius Schoonmaker anticipated that Antifederalists would find agreeing on the form of the amendments a "difficult matter," especially as Federalists would "use every effort in their power to divide the opposition, who have hitherto been firmly united" (to William Smith, July 7, 1788, *DHRC*, 22:2115). Antifederalists had predicted all along that the Federalists hoped to exploit divisions among them. See Abraham Yates, Jr., to George Clinton, July 1, 1788, *DHRC*, 21:1245. For an Antifederalist's early report of the Federalist leaders' lobbying efforts, see Charles Tillinghast to John Lamb, June 21, 1788, *DHRC*, 22:1795; see also Introduction, ibid., 1670–1.

329. Most commentators agree that ratification by the New Hampshire and Virginia conventions tipped the balance in New York. See Editorial Note, *DHRC*, 21:1672; Kaminski, "New York," 106; Maier, *Ratification*, 382; Labunski, *James Madison*, 121; Boyd, *Politics of Opposition*, 130. For contemporary statements either predicting that the ratifications of New Hampshire and Virginia would influence the actions of the New York convention, or concluding that they had in fact done so, see Nicholas Gilman to John Langdon, July 8, 1788, *DHRC*, 21:1297; Comte de Moustier to Comte de Montmorin, July 2, 1788, ibid., 1248; Ezra L'Hommedieu to John Smith, July 20, 1788, ibid., 1329.

330. Abraham G. Lansing to Abraham Yates, Jr., July 9, 1788, ibid., 1307 ("received some"); Smith to Dane, June 28, 1788, *DHRC*, 22:2015 ("what is proper," "scarcely perceive," and "not be a sufficient degree"); Kaminski, "New York," 106. On the importance of Smith's conversion, see ibid., 115–6; see also infra pp. 503–6.

331. Dane to Smith, July 3, 1788, *DHRC*, 21:1254, 1258 ("there can be" and "to unite"); Smith to Dane, c. July 15, 1788, *DHRC*, 23:2369 ("do not accord," "arduous," "time and great industry," and "not without hopes"); Extract of a letter from New-York (July 6), *Massachusetts Centinel*, July 16, 1788, ibid., 2371 ("convinced"); see also Kaminski, "New York," 116; Maier, *Ratification*, 383–4. Another Federalist likewise noted that the Antifederalists had been "influenced by [Federalists'] arguments, but they are too proud to confess it" and would "persevere in their destructive scheme, at least for a time" (Extract of a letter from Poughkeepsie (July 11), *New York Morning Post*, July 14, 1788, *DHRC*, 23:2368).

332. New York *Daily Advertiser*, July 16, 1788, *DHRC*, 22:2113–4. On Antifederalists' having abandoned the notion of an outright rejection of the Constitution, see Jay to Washington, July 4, 8, 1788, ibid., 2115; see also Gilbert Livingston at New York convention, July 26, *DHRC*, 23:2322; Eubanks, "New York," 325–6.

333. Lansing at New York convention, July 10, *DHRC*, 22:2119–21 ("nothing" at p. 2120; "no power" at p. 2121); De Witt Clinton to Charles Tillinghast, July 12, 1788, ibid., 2150 ("some important").

334. Lansing at New York convention, July 10, ibid., 2121–7 ("in confidence" at p. 2126; "to exert" and "in the meantime" at pp. 2121–2).

335. Ibid., 2126–7; see also Maier, *Ratification*, 379–80; Kaminski, "New York," 108. For the point about why Antifederalists found this particular form of conditional amendment attractive, see De Witt Clinton to Charles Tillinghast, July 12, 1788, *DHRC*, 22:2150.

336. Ibid., 2150–1 (quotations); see also Kaminski, "New York," 108. Other Antifederalists likewise insisted that the party had gone to great lengths to compromise, and complained that the Federalists would concede nothing. See Smith at New York convention, July 11, *DHRC*, 22:2135; July 12, ibid., 2152, 2154; see also Matthew Adgate, July 24, *DHRC*, 23:2292.

337. Abraham Bancker to Evert Bancker, July 12, 1788, *DHRC*, 22:2149 ("gilded"); Hamilton to Madison, July 8, 1788, ibid., 2117 ("concur in" and "go as far"); Robert R. Livingston at New York convention, July 11, ibid., 2139 ("We will"); Jay, ibid., 2130; see also New York *Daily Advertiser*, July 16, 1788, ibid., 2148; Extract of a letter from Poughkeepsie (July 11), New York *Daily Advertiser*, July 15, ibid., 2147; Kaminski, "New York," 108. The Federalists saw themselves as compromising, just as the Antifederalists did. See, e.g., Hamilton at New York convention, July 25, *DHRC*, 23:2292.

338. New York *Daily Advertiser*, July 16, 1788, *DHRC*, 22:2164; ibid., 2114; ibid., 2148; Extract of a letter from Poughkeepsie, New York *Daily Advertiser*, July 15, 1788, ibid., 2127; Abraham Bancker to Evert Bancker, July 12, 1788, ibid., 2149. Jay insisted that he had entered the committee's deliberations prepared to compromise, only to discover that the Antifederalists were interested only in dictating the outcome (July 12, ibid., 2151).

339. Abraham Bancker to Evert Bancker, July 12, 1788, ibid., 2149 (quotations). For other predictions around this time that the convention would end soon, see *New York Journal*, July 10, 1788, ibid., 2105; John Jay to Sarah Jay, July 5, 1788, ibid., 2098; De Witt Clinton to Charles Tillinghast, July 12, 1788, ibid., 2150.

340. Hamilton at New York convention, July 12, ibid., 2160, 2161 ("to assent," "implies," and "no more" at p. 2160); Livingston, July 11, ibid., 2139; Richard Harison, July 14, *DHRC*, 23:2170. The New York legislature's resolution calling the convention is at *DHRC*, 20:705 ("in conformity"). The Philadelphia convention's resolution calling on state legislatures to summon ratifying conventions is at *DHRC*, 1:318 ("for their assent"). When, early in the New York convention, Abraham Yates learned that Federalist leaders intended to argue that the convention had power only to approve or reject the Constitution, he told Governor Clinton, "[T]he federal gentlemen had the most extraordinary talents of swallowing camels themselves and recommending others to stick at gnats" (July 1, 1788, *DHRC*, 21:1245).

341. New York *Daily Advertiser*, July 16, 1788, *DHRC*, 22:2164–5 ("utterly anti-constitutional" at p. 2165); Hamilton at New York convention, July 12, ibid., 2160, 2161–2; Jay, July 11, ibid., 2130–1, 2135–7; Robert R. Livingston, ibid., 2139–40; Harison, July 14, *DHRC*, 23:2170–1; Hamilton, ibid., 2172; Jay, July 15, ibid., 2179; Robert R. Livingston, ibid., 2181; see also Maier, *Ratification*, 380–1; Eubanks, "New York," 326. For New York's conditional ratification of the impost amendment in 1786, see supra p. 32.

342. Jay, July 11, *DHRC*, 22:2131–3 ("joint counsels" and "dictate" at p. 2132; "the best men" and "strong circumstantial" at p. 2133; "Are the other" at p. 2131); see also Robert R. Livingston, ibid., 2140; Harison, July 14, *DHRC*, 23:2170–1.

343. Hamilton, July 12, *DHRC*, 22:2161–2; Livingston, July 11, ibid., 2139–40; New York *Daily Advertiser*, July 16, 1788, ibid., 2165–6. On the idea of dismembering New York, in view of its insolence and vast territorial claims, see Oliver Wolcott, Sr., to Oliver Wolcott, Jr., July 23, 1788, *DHRC*, 21:1337.

344. Harison, July 14, *DHRC*, 23:2171–2 (quotation at p. 2172); Hamilton, July 12, *DHRC*, 22:2162; Jay, July 11, ibid., 2133–4; Livingston, ibid., 2138, 2140.

345. New York *Daily Advertiser*, July 16, 1788, ibid., 2148 ("under any restrictions"); Smith, July 12, ibid., 2154–5 ("opposed" and "satisfy"); Lansing, July 11, ibid., 2137.

346. Smith, ibid., 2135, 2136 (quotation at p. 2136); July 12, ibid., 2154; Lansing, ibid., 2156; John Williams, July 15, *DHRC*, 23:2183; see also De Witt Clinton to Tillinghast, July 12, 1788, *DHRC*, 22:2150. Governor Clinton argued strongly against an unconditional

ratification that would risk forfeiting the people's liberties forever, but he left to Smith and Lansing the task of responding to Federalist arguments that Congress would not accept the form of ratification in Lansing's proposal (George Clinton's Remarks Against Ratifying the Constitution, July 11, ibid., 2142–7).

347. Smith, July 12, ibid., 2152–3 (quotation at p. 2153); July 11, ibid., 2136; New York *Daily Advertiser*, July 16, 1788, ibid., 2148.

348. Lansing, July 12, ibid., 2155–6 ("imperfections" at p. 2155); Smith, ibid., 2153–4 ("affection" at p. 2154); July 11, ibid., 2135.

349. Jay, ibid., 2133 ("evil consequences"); New York *Daily Advertiser*, July 16, 1788, ibid., 2148 ("appealed to").

350. Jay, July 11, ibid., 2132–3 ("This government" at p. 2132); Livingston, ibid., 2139; Hamilton, July 12, ibid., 2161; Dane to Smith, July 3, 1788, *DHRC*, 21:1257 ("immediately" and "some of the most"); see also Kaminski, "New York," 116–7; Editors' Note, Confederation Congress Makes Provision to Put the New Government Under the Constitution Into Operation, July 2–Sept. 13, 1788, *DHRC*, 21:1250–1. Samuel Osgood made the same point in a letter to New York Antifederalist leaders Smith and Samuel Jones, observing that "the danger of not obtaining amendments such as we would wish for will in my opinion be greatly enhanced by the absence of New York" (July 11, 1788, ibid., 1309).

351. On Congress's awaiting New York's verdict on ratification before deciding upon the site where the new federal Congress would convene, see Nathan Dane to Caleb Strong, July 13, 1788, ibid., 1313; Ebenezer Hazard to Mathew Carey, July 15, 1788, ibid., 1317–8; Oliver Wolcott, Sr., to Oliver Wolcott, Jr., July 23, 1788, ibid., 1337; Madison to Washington, July 21, 1788, *PJM* (C.S.), 11:190–1; see also Bowling, *The Creation of Washington, D.C.*, 87–96. Writing from Poughkeepsie and expressing "great impatience," one New York Federalist urged that an act of the Confederation Congress putting the new government into motion would "add much energy to our arguments" and "change the nature of the ground" at the convention (Extract of a letter from Poughkeepsie (July 3), New York *Daily Advertiser*, July 7, 1788, *DHRC*, 22:2093).

352. Jay, July 11, ibid., 2133, 2134; Livingston, ibid., 2139–40, 2141. For other estimates of the economic value to a locality of housing the federal government, see Bowling, *The Creation of Washington, D.C.*, 3.

353. Samuel Osgood to Melancton Smith and Samuel Jones, July 11, 1788, *DHRC*, 21:1309 ("[t]he anxiety," "have all the blame," and "Philadelphia"); Samuel Blachley Webb to Catherine Hogeboom, July 13, 1788, ibid., 1314 ("not believe"). For another Federalist's warning of the outrage that would be directed at Antifederalists by New York City residents if their refusal to unconditionally ratify the Constitution cost the city the national capital, see Paine Wingate to John Pickering, July 17, 1788, *DHRC*, 23:2372 ("extraordinary pomp"). On New York City's grand procession celebrating the implementation of the Constitution, which was postponed more than once while awaiting the outcome of the New York convention, before finally taking place on July 23, when the convention was still in session, see Introduction, *DHRC*, 21: appendix I, 1584–8; see also De Pauw, *Eleventh Pillar*, 237–40.

354. Jay to Washington, May 29, 1788, *DHRC*, 20:1119 (quotation); see also Jay to Washington, July 4, 8, 1788, *DHRC*, 22:2114.

355. Livingston at New York convention, July 11, ibid., 2140, 2141 (quotation at p. 2140); Hamilton, July 17, *DHRC*, 23:2195. For other public statements of the likelihood that the southern counties would secede if New York remained outside the union, see New York *Daily Advertiser*, June 14, 1788, *DHRC*, 20:1170; "A Pennsylvanian to the New York Convention" (Tench Coxe), *Pennsylvania Gazette*, June 11, 1788, ibid., 1148–9; Extract of a letter from New-York (July 6), *Massachusetts Centinel*, July 16, 1788, *DHRC*, 23:2371; *Salem Mercury*, July 29, 1788, ibid., 2379. For similar statements in private correspondence, which confirm that the risk of secession was real, see Samuel Blachley Webb to Catherine Hogeboom, July 6, 1788, *DHRC*, 21:1293; Evert Bancker to Abraham Bancker, July 24, 1788, ibid., 1338; Nicholas Gilman to John Langdon, July 15, 1788, ibid., 1316; Jeremiah Wadsworth to Oliver Wolcott, Jr., July 15, 1788, ibid., 1320. For

foreign ministers and consuls predicting such secessions if New York failed to ratify, see Don Diego de Gardoqui to Conde de Floridablanca, July 25, 1788, ibid., 1342; Comte de Moustier to Comte de Montmorin, June 5, 1788, *DHRC*, 20:1131. See also De Pauw, *Eleventh Pillar*, 230–6; Eubanks, "New York," 327, 329.

356. Hamilton to Madison, c. July 2, 1788, *PJM* (C.S.), 11:185 ("arguments" and "to be convinced"); see also Kaminski, "New York," 115.

357. William Harper, July 14, *DHRC*, 23:2171; Lansing, July 16, ibid., 2190; New York *Daily Advertiser*, July 17, 1788, ibid., 2174; Wadsworth to Oliver Wolcott, Jr., July 15, 1788, *DHRC*, 21:1320 ("despair"); Knox to King, July 13, 1788, *DHRC*, 23:2368; see also David S. Bogart to Samuel Blachley Webb, July 14, 1788, ibid., 2175. For other predictions around this time of a Federalist defeat, see Nicholas Gilman to John Langdon, July 15, 1788, *DHRC*, 21:1316; Caleb S. Riggs to John Fitch, July 15, 1788, ibid., 1319; Madison to Randolph, July 16, 1788, ibid., 1321; Samuel A. Otis to George Thatcher, July 17, 1788, ibid., 1323; Robert Morris to Silas Talbot, July 19, 1788, ibid., 1326. For Federalist evaluations that were uncertain rather than pessimistic, see Ebenezer Hazard to Jeremy Belknap, July 17, 1788, ibid., 1323; John Jay to Sarah Jay, July 16, 1788, *DHRC*, 23:2370.

358. Abraham Bancker to Evert Bancker, July 18, 1788, ibid., 2226 ("the only means"); Hobart motion, July 16, ibid., 2185; Hamilton, July 17, ibid., 2193 ("things have changed," "consult[ing]," and "decent"); Pierse Long to Nicholas Gilman, July 22, 1788, *DHRC*, 21:1332 ("it would not be"); Extract of a letter from New-York (July 6), *Massachusetts Centinel*, July 16, 1788, *DHRC*, 23:2371; Robert R. Livingston, July 16, ibid., 2186–7, 2188; Jay, ibid., 2187, 2189; James Duane, ibid., 2187–8; see also De Witt Clinton to Charles Tillinghast, July 19, 1788, ibid., 2230; *New York Journal*, July 21, 1788, ibid., 2191. Many statements made outside of the convention around this time suggested that an adjournment was likely. See Extract of a letter from New-York (July 18), *Virginia Independent Chronicle*, July 30, 1788, ibid., 2380; *Massachusetts Centinel*, July 12, 1788, *DHRC*, 21:1312; Theodore Sedgwick to John Hancock, July 18, 1788, ibid., 1325; Kaminski, "New York," 110; Maier, *Ratification*, 386–7; Heideking, *The Constitution Before the Judgment Seat*, 323. More than two weeks earlier, Washington had expressed the view that, given the Antifederalists' majority, the "wisest" approach for the New York Federalists might be adjourning the convention to enable the people of New York to "consider the magnitude of the question and of the consequences involved in it, more coolly and deliberately" (to Charles Cotesworth Pinckney, June 28, 1788, *DHRC*, 21:1233).

359. Abraham Yates, Jr., to George Clinton, July 1, 1788, ibid., 1245 ("a farther opportunity"); Abraham Yates, Jr., to Abraham G. Lansing, June 29, 1788, ibid., 1240; Thomas Tredwell at New York convention, July 16, *DHRC*, 23:2189 ("the mind," "not accept," "without giving," "an affront," and "as the reasons"); Lansing, ibid., 2187; Convention Debates and Proceedings, July 17, ibid., 2199 (the vote); see also Kaminski, "New York," 107; De Pauw, *Eleventh Pillar*, 224. De Witt Clinton wrote that "the ostensible reason [for an adjournment] was that the members might go home and consult their constituents, but the real design was to spirit up the latter versus them" (Journal, July 16, 1788, *DHRC*, 23:2190–1).

For the preceding footnote, see Abraham G. Lansing to Abraham Yates, Jr., July 20, 1788, *DHRC*, 21:1330.

360. Convention Debates and Proceedings, July 17, *DHRC*, 23:2210 (the vote); editorial note, ibid., 2218 n. 18.

361. Smith, July 17, ibid., 2211, 2213.

362. Smith motion, ibid., 2214–5.

363. Smith motion, ibid., 2215 ("in the firmest") (emphasis added); ibid., 2212 ("not please" and "avoids"); see also Cornelius C. Schoonmaker to Peter Van Gaasbeek, July 18, 1788, ibid., 2229; De Witt Clinton to Charles Tillinghast, July 19, 1788, ibid., 2230; Jay to Washington, July 18, 1788, ibid., 2227; Kaminski, "New York," 109; De Pauw, *Eleventh Pillar*, 226. For Jay's statement putting the number of years at four, see July 24, *DHRC*, 23:2290. Smith had been contemplating a proposal such as this, which embraced a

"condition subsequent" rather than a "condition previous," since at least late June (to Nathan Dane, June 28, 1788, *DHRC*, 22:2015).

364. Abraham Bancker to Evert Bancker, July 18, 1788, *DHRC*, 23:2226 ("his mind," "every gleam," "a favorable omen," and "gained [him]"); Jay, July 18, ibid., 2232 ("less evil"); Schoonmaker to Peter Van Gaasbeek, July 18, 1788, ibid., 2229 ("as the most"); see also De Witt Clinton Journal, July 18, 1788, ibid., 2232–3; Jay to Washington, July 18, 1788, ibid., 2228; Hamilton, July 24, ibid., 2291; Kaminski, "New York," 109. Whether Congress would accept ratification on the terms of Smith's new proposal was another question. Rhode Island Federalist William Ellery disparaged Smith's proposal as "so childish, so repugnant to my notions of governmental federal compacts that I can hardly think that the majority could be serious in making that a condition of their acceding to the new Constitution. I am confident that no state would be admitted into the Union on such terms" (to Benjamin Huntington, July 28–29, 1788, *DHRC*, 25:366). Ezra L'Hommedieu, a New York state senator, thought that while Smith's plan was "much nearer an adoption than the others are, [it was] still subject to the objection of a condition, which I think will be fatal" (to John Smith, July 20, 1788, *DHRC*, 21:1328). By contrast, Federalist delegate Abraham Bancker was confident that, if amended, Smith's proposal would be acceptable to Congress (supra). Madison wrote a letter to the New York convention declaring that Smith's proposal was a conditional ratification that Congress would reject. See infra p. 507. For the view that it was simply unclear how Congress would receive ratification on these terms, see Thomas Tudor Tucker to St. George Tucker, July 22, 28, 1788, *DHRC*, 21:1334.

365. Extract of a letter from New-York (July 20), *Massachusetts Centinel*, July 26, 1788, *DHRC*, 23:2379 ("save their reputations"); De Witt Clinton Journal, July 18, 1788, ibid., 2232–3 ("[i]f it is not agreed to," "[s]ome of the violent," and "comes openly out"); see also Cornelius C. Schoonmaker to Peter Van Gaasbeek, July 18, 1788, ibid., 2229. For the pro-ratification sentiments that Jones was hearing from his constituents, see Ezra L'Hommedieu to John Smith, July 20, 1788, *DHRC*, 21:1328. Abraham Lansing noted that Jones was said to have been "intimidated by the threats of the Federalists" (to Abraham Yates, Jr., July 20, 1788, ibid., 1330; see also David S. Bogart to Samuel Blachley Webb, July 14, 1788, *DHRC*, 23:2176). De Witt Clinton also reported that two of the other Antifederalist delegates who supported Smith's proposal, Zephaniah Platt and Gilbert Livingston, had insisted that it would "be their ultimatum," from which they would not back down (Journal, July 19, 1788, ibid., 2253).

366. July 18, 1788, ibid., 2232–3 (quotations); see also July 16, 1788, ibid., 2191; Kaminski, "New York," 109. Abraham Lansing observed that if the "improper steps" charged against Smith were true, then "he has injured the cause of our country more than any Federalist" (to Abraham Yates, Jr., July 20, 1788, *DHRC*, 21:1330).

367. Cornelius C. Schoonmaker to Peter Van Gaasbeek, July 18, 1788, *DHRC*, 23:2229 ("very little" and "the lesser evil"); Jay to Washington, July 18, 1788, ibid., 2227–8 ("[a] long silence" and "seemed embarrassed"); see also Kaminski, "New York," 109; De Pauw, *Eleventh Pillar*, 226–7.

368. Hamilton to Madison, July 19, 1788, *DHRC*, 23:2374; Smith, July 19, ibid., 2242–3 (the vote); New York *Daily Advertiser*, July 21, 1788, ibid., 2253 (quotation); Abraham B. Bancker to Peter Van Gaasbeek, July 19, 1788, ibid., 2373; see also Kaminski, "New York," 109–10.

369. Convention Debates and Proceedings, July 19, *DHRC*, 23:2243–50; July 21, ibid., 2255–61 (specific examples at pp. 2258, 2259–60); July 22, ibid., 2264–74; Extract of a letter from Poughkeepsie (July 22), New York *Daily Advertiser*, July 25, 1788, ibid., 2262–4; see also Kaminski, "New York," 110; De Pauw, *Eleventh Pillar*, 227.

370. De Witt Clinton to Charles Tillinghast, July 19, 1788, *DHRC*, 23:2230 ("the political sky"); Madison to Randolph, July 22, 1788, *DHRC*, 21:1333 ("not yet"); Roosevelt to Richard Varick, July 22–23, 1788, *DHRC*, 23:2375 ("diversity"). For other statements of uncertainty around this time, see Poughkeepsie *Country Journal*, July 22, 1788, ibid., 2254; Hugh Williamson to James Iredell, July 26, 1788 (first letter), *DHRC*, 21:1347. For a more pessimistic Federalist prediction, see Evert Bancker to Abraham Bancker, July

24, 1788, ibid., 1338. For more optimistic assessments of the Federalists' chances, see Extract of a letter from New-York (July 18), *Virginia Independent Chronicle*, July 30, 1788, *DHRC*, 23:2380; Extract of a letter from Poughkeepsie (July 20), *Massachusetts Centinel*, July 30, 1788, ibid.; Webb to Hogeboom, July 20, 1788, *DHRC*, 21:1331.

371. Jones, July 23, *DHRC*, 23:2280; ibid., 2281 (the vote); Abraham B. Bancker to Peter Van Gaasbeek, July 23, 1788, ibid., 2285–6; see also Kaminski, "New York," 111; De Pauw, *Eleventh Pillar*, 241–2. On the regional split in Antifederalist ranks, see Extract of a letter from one of the convention delegates (July 23), New York *Independent Journal*, July 26, 1788, *DHRC*, 23:2282; see also Young, *Democratic Republicans of New York*, 116–7; McDonald, *We the People*, 288 & n. 125.

372. Copy of a letter from Poughkeepsie (July 25), New York *Independent Journal*, July 28, 1788 (Supplement Extraordinary), *DHRC*, 23:2283 (quotations); see also Smith, July 23, ibid., 2280.

373. Jay to Washington, July 23, 1788, ibid., 2286 ("mean to rally"); Lansing, July 24, ibid., 2290; ibid., 2294 ("some security" and "resist"); Clinton, ibid., 2295 ("heretofore"); Kaminski, "New York," 111. For statements that the Federalists' victory was all but assured after the vote on July 23, see Abraham B. Bancker to Peter Van Gaasbeek, July 23, 1788, *DHRC*, 23:2285–6; Extract of a letter from one of the convention delegates (July 23), New York *Independent Journal*, July 26, 1788, ibid., 2282.

374. Hamilton, July 24, ibid., 2291 ("the terms"); Extract of a letter from Poughkeepsie (July 25), New York *Independent Journal*, July 28, 1788 (Supplement Extraordinary), ibid., 2297–8 ("implied a distrust" and "would awaken") (describing Hamilton speech); see also Jay, July 24, ibid., 2290, 2292, 2296; Richard Morris, ibid., 2293; James Duane, ibid., 2296; De Pauw, *Eleventh Pillar*, 243.

375. Hamilton, July 24, *DHRC*, 23:2291; editorial note, ibid., 2297 n. 5; Lansing, ibid., 2291, 2293 ("an impression" at p. 2293); Madison to Hamilton, July 20, 1788, ibid., 2375; see also Kaminski, "New York," 112–3; De Pauw, *Eleventh Pillar*, 244; Maier, *Ratification*, 395–6; Eubanks, "New York," 327–8. Madison's reasoning is noted infra pp. 531–2.

376. Cornelius C. Schoonmaker to Peter Van Gaasbeek, July 25, 1788, *DHRC*, 23:2299 ("supposed to be," "most strenuously," and "convinced"); Smith, July 25, ibid., 2300 ("a middle ground"); Maier, *Ratification*, 396.

377. Convention Debates and Proceedings, July 25, *DHRC*, 23:2305–9. For Federalists' embrace of the circular letter, see Hamilton, July 24, ibid., 2291; Robert R. Livingston, ibid., 2293; see also Maier, *Ratification*, 396. On the propitiatory effect of the circular letter, see Cornelius C. Schoonmaker to Peter Van Gaasbeek, July 25, 1788, *DHRC*, 23:2299.

   For the preceding footnote, see Maier, *Ratification*, 400; Rutland, *Ordeal of the Constitution*, 298; Young, *Democratic Republicans of New York*, 124–5, 127.

378. Convention Debates and Proceedings, July 26, *DHRC*, 23:2325 ("earnestly requested"); Kaminski, "New York," 114; De Pauw, *Eleventh Pillar*, 245.

   For the preceding footnote, see Roll, "We, Some of the People," 21, 32–3.

379. Convention Debates and Proceedings, July 26, *DHRC*, 23:2325 (unanimous vote); Clinton, ibid. ("would not," "power," and "keep up"); New York Convention: Circular Letter to the Executives of the States, ibid., 2335–6 (all other quotations); see also Maier, *Ratification*, 398.

380. Dirck Wynkoop, July 25, *DHRC*, 23:2293 (quotation); Schoonmaker to Gaasbeek, July 25, 1788, ibid., 2298–9.

381. Isaac Roosevelt to Richard Varick, July 22–23, 1788, ibid., 2375 (quotations). On the impressiveness of the victory, see Richard Platt to Winthrop Sargent, Aug. 8, 1788, *DHRC*, 21:1352; Maier, *Ratification*, 399. On the point that it was the Federalists' patience that mattered, not their eloquence, see Kaminski, "New York," 114. As the New York convention entered its final stages, Madison, in a letter to Jefferson, offered a similar account of how circumstances were operating on the minds of the Antifederalist delegates (July 24–26, 1788, *DHRC*, 21:1338).

382. Schoonmaker to Gaasbeek, July 25, 1788, *DHRC*, 23:2298 (quotations).

383. Livingston, July 26, ibid., 2321–2 (quotations).

384. Madison to Washington, Aug. 24, 1788, *PJM* (C.S.), 11:240 (quotations); see also Sept. 14, 1788, ibid., 255; James Gordon, Jr., to Madison, Aug. 31, 1788, ibid., 245; Madison to Pendleton, Oct. 20, 1788, ibid., 306.

385. For the setting up of the new national government, see infra p. 798 n. 39.

386. Washington to Samuel Powel, Jan. 18, 1788, *PGW* (C.S.), 6:45 (quotation); see also Madison to Randolph, Jan. 10, 1788, *PJM* (C.S.), 10:358; Lear to Langdon, Jan. 25, 1788, *DHRC*, 8:322; Maier, *Ratification*, 404; Trenholme, *Ratification of the Federal Constitution in North Carolina*, 104, 135–6. Carrington reported to Madison a contrary view—that the postponement of the North Carolina convention "by no means indicates a disposition to follow the politics of Virginia" (Feb. 10, 1788, *PJM* (C.S.), 10:495). Trenholme argues that the North Carolina legislature set the date for the state's ratifying convention before it knew of the scheduled date for the Virginia convention, but this view seems mistaken (Trenholme, supra, 105, 127, 135–6).

387. Maier, *Ratification*, 404–6; Lienesch, "North Carolina," 345–8; McDonald, *We the People*, 316. On the "regulator" movement in North Carolina, see Marjoleine Cars, *Breaking Loose Together: The Regulator Rebellion in Pre-Revolutionary North Carolina* (Chapel Hill, NC, 2002).

388. Lienesch, "North Carolina," 348–9; Rutland, *Ordeal of the Constitution*, 273–4; Trenholme, *Ratification of the Federal Constitution in North Carolina*, 109, 151. For discussion of particular electoral contests in North Carolina, see Boyd, *Politics of Opposition*, 110–4. For contemporary statements noting strong opposition to ratification in North Carolina, see Patrick Henry to John Lamb, June 9, 1788, *DHRC*, 9:817; King to Langdon, Apr. 16, 1788, *DHRC*, 17:130; Gilman to Sullivan, Mar. 22, 1788, *DHRC*, 16:462; Washington to Richard Dobbs Spaight, May 25, 1788, *DHRC*, 9:843 (restating information Spaight reported to Washington on April 25).

389. Willie Jones at North Carolina convention, July 23, 1788, *Elliot*, 4:4; Iredell, ibid., 5 ("predetermined" and "information"); July 24, ibid., 14–5 ("may arrogate," "scarcely ever," and "trivial consideration"). On the North Carolina convention generally, see Trenholme, *Ratification of the Federal Constitution in North Carolina*, ch. 4. The expense involved in holding ratifying conventions was not trivial, and the North Carolina convention had well over 250 delegates, whose expenses would have to be paid by the state. See Heideking, *The Constitution Before the Judgment Seat*, 257.

390. Jones, July 23, *Elliot*, 4:7; July 24, ibid., 15 (vote in favor of clause-by-clause consideration); William Shepperd, ibid., 29 ("the friends"); William Maclaine, ibid., 30; William Davie, July 26, ibid., 102 ("suppressing," "highly improper," and "the precipitancy"); see also Maier, *Ratification*, 411; Lienesch, "North Carolina," 350; Edling, *Revolution in Favor of Government*, 19–20.

391. On the objections raised by North Carolina Antifederalists that were similar to those made by Antifederalists elsewhere, see, e.g., Joseph Taylor, July 24, *Elliot*, 4:24; James Galloway, ibid., 31; Samuel Spencer, July 25, ibid., 50–2; Timothy Bloodworth, ibid., 55; William Goudy, ibid., 56; Joseph M'Dowall, ibid., 57; Spencer, July 26, ibid., 75–7; M'Dowall, ibid., 87–8; July 28, ibid., 124; Spencer, ibid., 131–2; ibid., 136–9; July 29, ibid., 152–5; M'Dowall, ibid., 188; William Lenoir, July 30, ibid., 201–6; William Lancaster, ibid., 212–5.

392. M'Dowall, July 26, ibid., 88 ("extreme scarcity" and "[o]ur political existence"); Matthew Locke, July 29, ibid., 169–70 ("to save vast numbers," "public measures," and "insurrection"); Bloodworth, ibid., 185 ("ought to be particular"); M'Dowall, ibid., 188 ("the poor man").

393. North Carolina proposed amendment No. 25, Aug. 1, ibid., 247 ("directly"). For Antifederalists' expressing a concern about the retroactive effect of Article I, Section 10, see Bloodworth, July 29, ibid., 184–5; Galloway, ibid., 190–1; Lenoir, July 30, ibid., 205–6. For the Federalists' replies, see Stephen Cabarrus, July 29, ibid., 184; Iredell, ibid., 185; Davie, ibid., 191. On the ambiguity as to whether Article I, Section 10, would have retroactive application, which was a major issue in Rhode Island as well, see William Ellery to Benjamin Huntington, Sept. 30, 1788, *DHRC*, 25:409–10; Oct. 13, 1788, ibid., 412.

394. Spaight, July 30, *Elliot*, 4:208 ("whether the Constitution"); Iredell, July 24, ibid., 14 ("suppose [its] knowledge"); July 30, ibid., 217 ("no right" and "of an easy admission").

395. Ibid. ("the impossibility"); ibid., 222 ("have no share" and "probably be"); Davie, July 31, ibid., 237–8; Johnston, ibid., 224; Iredell, July 30, ibid., 219 ("perfectly safe" and "any [subsequent] amendments"); see also July 31, ibid., 233.

396. Griffith Rutherford, July 24, ibid., 15 ("as if no state"); Lenoir, July 30, ibid., 204 ("own judgments"); Jones, July 31, ibid., 226 ("dreadful consequences" and "run no risk"); ibid., 234–5; Bloodworth, ibid., 235; M'Dowall, July 25, ibid., 57.

397. Jones, July 30, ibid., 217 ("no person"); Bloodworth, July 28, ibid., 143 ("Many words"); Convention resolution, Aug. 1, ibid., 242 ("most ambiguous"); Aug. 2, ibid., 251 (the vote); see also Bloodworth, July 29, ibid., 185; North Carolina Convention Amendments, Aug. 2, 1788, *DHRC*, 18:312–3; Maier, *Ratification*, 422–3; Boyd, *Politics of Opposition*, 134.

398. Madison to Jefferson, Aug. 23, 1788, *PJM* (C.S.), 11:238 (quotations); see also Madison to James Madison, Sr., Sept. 6, 1788, ibid., 248. For other Federalist statements of shock and disappointment at the North Carolina result, see Benjamin Lincoln to Theodore Sedgwick, Sept. 7, 1788, *DHFFE*, 1:458–9; *Massachusetts Centinel*, Aug. 20, 1788, *DHRC*, 25:393. For Federalists' confident predictions, after ratification by Virginia, that North Carolina would follow suit, see Washington to Tobias Lear, June 29, 1788, *PGW* (C.S.), 6:364; Hugh Williamson to James Iredell, July 26, 1788 (second letter), *DHRC*, 21:1347; Lear to Washington, July 31, 1788, ibid., 1351; see also Comte de Moustier to Comte de Montmorin, July 2, 1788, ibid., 1248; Maier, *Ratification*, 403; Lienesch, "North Carolina," 343. Even North Carolina Antifederalist leader Timothy Bloodworth had predicted that if Virginia ratified, the event "will probably have a prevailing influence on our state" (to John Lamb, July 1, 1788, *DHRC*, 18:59).

399. "A Citizen and Soldier: To the People of the District of Edenton" (1788), in *A Plea for Federal Union* (North Carolina, 1788), 43–4 (quotation); Trenholme, *Ratification of the Federal Constitution in North Carolina*, 197–9, 202–8; Maier, *Ratification*, 457; Lienesch, "North Carolina," 363; Heideking, *The Constitution Before the Judgment Seat*, 330–1; McDonald, *We the People*, 312; Editors' Note, *DHRC*, 25:376.

400. Johnston and Iredell to Washington, May 10, 1788, quoted in *PGW* (P.S.), 3:48 note ("pleasing hope" and "as will remove"); Davie to Iredell, June 4, 1789, in McRee, *James Iredell*, 2:260 ("nothing ever gave me"); Davie to Madison, June 10, 1789, *PJM* (C.S.), 12:210–1 ("would never"); see also Trenholme, *Ratification of the Federal Constitution in North Carolina*, 211–2, 219, 227; Editors' Introduction, *DHRC*, 25:643.

401. *Providence Gazette*, Oct. 17, 1789 (reprinting report from *Wilmington Centinel*, Sept. 10), quoted in Editorial Introduction, *DHRC*, 25:644 ("undoubtedly satisfy"); Washington to Morris, Oct. 13, 1789, *PGW* (P.S.), 4:176–7.

402. Charles Johnson to Iredell, Nov. 23, 1789, reproduced in McRee, *James Iredell*, 2:273 ("amazing change"); William Dawson to Iredell, Nov. 22, 1789, in ibid., 272 ("acquiesce cheerfully," "their doubts," and "the approbation"); see also Trenholme, *Ratification of the Federal Constitution in North Carolina*, 213, 224–5, 233–43; Lienesch, "North Carolina," 364; Maier, *Ratification*, 457; Heideking, *The Constitution Before the Judgment Seat*, 331–2; Morrill, *Fiat Finance*, 51–2.

403. Supra pp. 122–3; Rhode Island General Assembly to the President of Congress, Sept. 15, 1787, *DHRC*, 24:19–20 (quotations); Philadelphia *Freeman's Journal*, Oct. 3, 1787, ibid., 29; see also Kaminski, "Paper Politics," 222–3.

404. John Francis to Nicholas Brown, Nov. 11, 1787, *DHRC*, 24:53 ("unhappy deluded state"); *Newport Herald*, Nov. 15, 1787, ibid., 56 ("to view"); Editorial Introduction, ibid., 42–3; Kaminski, "Paper Politics," 194–6, 205, 224, 235, 239; Polishook, *Rhode Island*, 154–5, 190; Introduction, *DHRC*, 24:xxxii–iv, xxxviii; Ellery to Huntington, Apr. 22, 1788, ibid., 255. Governor Arthur Fenner later admitted to President Washington that Rhode Island's refusal to ratify the Constitution for several years was "influenced by party considerations" (May 20, 1790, *DHRC*, 26:872).
    For the preceding footnote, see ibid., 874–5.

405. *Newport Herald*, Feb. 21, 1788, *DHRC*, 24:101 ("act wisely" and "persist"); Providence *United States Chronicle*, Mar. 6, 1788, ibid., 128 ("by the proposed Constitution" and "the

only mode"); Editorial Introduction, ibid., 121; see also *Maryland Journal*, Apr. 15, 1788, ibid., 227; Madison to George Nicholas, Apr. 8, 1788, *PJM* (C.S.), 11:14.

406. Providence *United States Chronicle*, Mar. 6, 1788, *DHRC*, 24:128–9 ("without precedent" and "ought to pay"); Mar. 13, 1788, ibid., 137 ("one afternoon" and "the merits"); "A Freeman," *Providence Gazette*, Mar. 15, 1788, ibid., 138 ("either leisure" and "all the light"); see also "A Freeman," *Newport Herald*, Mar. 20, 1788, ibid., 143; "A Rhode-Island Landholder," Providence *United States Chronicle*, Mar. 20, 1788, ibid., 149; Enos Hitchcock to Silas Talbot, Mar. 31, 1788, ibid., 219.

407. "A Rhode-Island Landholder," Providence *United States Chronicle*, Mar. 20, 1788, ibid., 148–51; Editorial Introduction, ibid., 151; Enos Hitchcock to Silas Talbot, Mar. 31, 1788, ibid., 219–20; *Massachusetts Centinel*, Apr. 2, 1788, ibid., 220; *Newport Herald*, Apr. 3, 1788, ibid., 225; *New York Packet*, Apr. 8, 1788, ibid., 226–7. On the vote tabulation, see Report of the Committee Counting Yeas and Nays Upon the New Constitution, Apr. 3, 1788, ibid., 233. For slightly different numbers, see *Newport Herald*, Apr. 10, 1788, ibid., 229; Kaminski, "Rhode Island," 379; Maier, *Ratification*, 223–4. Although the Federalist boycott distorted the vote totals, there is little doubt that a majority of Rhode Islanders at this point opposed ratification. See, e.g., Nicholas Brown and Brown & Francis to Richard Henry Lee, May 1, 1789, *DHRC*, 25:495.

408. The Governor of Rhode Island to the President of Congress, Apr. 5, 1788, *DHRC*, 24:235 (quotations); Editorial Introduction, ibid., 229.

409. William Ellery to Ebenezer Hazard, Mar. 10, 1788, ibid., 111 ("have a considerable effect"); *Newport Herald*, July 31, 1788, *DHRC*, 25:370 ("the last hopes" and "blasted"); Introduction, *DHRC*, 24:243. For predictions that the legislature would call a convention, see Little Compton Celebrates Ratification of the Constitution by Nine States, *Newport Herald*, July 10, 1788, *DHRC*, 25:345; July 31, 1788, ibid., 372. For demands that the legislature call a convention, see "A Rhode-Islander," July 10, 1788, ibid., 351; ibid., 352.
  For the preceding footnote, see Editorial Introduction, *DHRC*, 24:285–6.

410. "Phocion," Providence *United States Chronicle*, July 17, 1788, *DHRC*, 25:354–5 ("We shall then" and "the great entrepot"); "A Friend to the Union," *Providence Gazette*, Oct. 18, 1788, ibid., 415–6 ("chimerical"); "Rhodiensis," *Newport Herald*, Oct. 23, 1788, ibid., 418–22 ("a nest" at p. 419); see also "Solon, junior," *Providence Gazette*, Aug. 2, 1788, ibid., 377–8; "An Independent Elector," Providence *United States Chronicle*, Mar. 5, 1789, ibid., 466; "Address from the United States to Rhode-Island," Philadelphia *Federal Gazette*, Jan. 1, 1790, ibid., 656; "A Native American," *New York Packet*, June 6, 1789, ibid., 532–3; Polishook, *Rhode Island*, 195–6. On Rhode Island's long history of smuggling, which would have made it difficult for the United States to allow the state to remain independent, see Extract of a letter from the State of Rhode-Island, New York *Gazette of the United States*, Sept. 12, 1789, *DHRC*, 25:598; Antoine de la Forest to Comte de la Luzerne, June 1, 1790, *DHRC*, 26:1019; see also McDonald, *We the People*, 339.

411. The Antifederalist arguments are described in Ellery to Huntington, Aug. 31, 1788, *DHRC*, 25:405; *Massachusetts Centinel*, Aug. 27, 1788, ibid., 398 n. 2; Jabez Bowen to John Adams, Dec. 28, 1789, ibid., 652; Louis-Guillaume Otto to Comte de Montmorin, Mar. 13, 1790, *DHRC*, 26:762–3; see also Polishook, *Rhode Island*, 193–4.

412. "Rhodiensis," *Newport Herald*, Oct. 23, 1788, *DHRC*, 25:421 ("an obstinate opposition"); Editorial Introduction, ibid., 422; *Newport Herald*, Nov. 6, 1788, ibid., 423–5.

413. Introduction, ibid., 454–5; Kaminski, "Rhode Island," 379–82; William Ellery to Benjamin Huntington, June 15, 1789, *DHRC*, 25:541 (reporting views of Antifederalist leader Jonathan Hazard). In May, the country party passed a "curious" impost law that mirrored the duties to be enacted by Congress on foreign trade, with the proceeds designated to go into the state treasury. The party's leader, Hazard, explained that the object of the law was to signal to Congress that Rhode Island was disposed to pay its share of the national debt. See Ellery to Huntington, May 14, 1789, ibid., 505 ("curious" and reporting Hazard's statement). For the law, see *Newport Mercury*, May 11, 1789, ibid., 501–2. Federalist leader Jabez Bowen viewed the law more skeptically: "[M]ankind would suppose by this [the impost law] that Rhode Island was preparing to come into the union,

but there is no such idea at bottom; it rather seems calculated to lull Congress into a state of indifference respecting our affairs and that we shall come in by and by" (to John Adams, May 19, 1789, ibid., 508–9).

414. *Massachusetts Centinel*, July 23, 1788, ibid., 361 ("the virtuous"); Newport Town Meeting, Apr. 15, 1789, ibid., 483 ("wretched situation" and "oblige them"); Ellery to William Duer, May 21, 1789, ibid., 511 ("would be certain" and "the vengeance"); James Jackson, Speech in the US House of Representatives, June 8, 1789, ibid., 534 ("firm friends"); see also John Brown to Christopher Champlin, Feb. 16, 1789, ibid., 464; Providence Town Meeting: Instructions to Deputies, Mar. 10, 1789, ibid., 468–9; Nicholas Brown and Brown & Francis to Richard Henry Lee, May 1, 1789, ibid., 495; Bowen to John Adams, May 19, 1789, ibid., 509.

415. Ellery to Ebenezer Hazard, Mar. 10, 1788, *DHRC*, 24:111 ("stand out" and "nothing but"); Apr. 30, 1789, ibid., 25:491–2; May 14, 1789, ibid., 505; Benson to Sedgwick, June 27, 1789, ibid., 550 ("with contemptuous"); Extract of a Letter from a very respectable Member of Congress to his Friend in this State, *Providence Gazette*, June 20, 1789, ibid., 546; see also Bowen to Adams, Apr. 21, 1789, ibid., 487. For other statements by Ellery insisting that the Rhode Island Antifederalists would not capitulate until their interests were adversely affected, see Ellery to Huntington, Aug. 31, 1788, ibid., 404–5; June 15, 1789, ibid., 541. On June 5, 1789, Federalist congressman Egbert Benson of New York introduced a motion that Congress urge Rhode Island to summon a ratifying convention. But many representatives opposed the idea of Congress interfering with a state's decision whether to join the union, and Benson's motion was rejected. See US House of Representatives Considers Rhode Island, ibid., 527–31; see also James Manning to Nicholas Brown, May 21, 1789, ibid., 511; Fisher Ames to George Richards Minot, May 31, 1789, ibid., 524; James Sullivan to John Adams, June 10, 1789, ibid., 535; Gentlemen of Providence to George Washington, Mar. 27, 1789, ibid., 474–5.

416. John Swann to James Iredell, July 7, 1788, *DHRC*, 21:1294 ("veer about"). For similar predictions that the country party would change its tune on ratification once the state debt was redeemed, see Ellery to Huntington, Apr. 22, 1788, *DHRC*, 24:255; Ellery to Ebenezer Hazard, June 16, 1788, ibid., 277; Jan. 12, 1789, ibid., 25:460–1; *Newport Herald*, July 31, 1788, ibid., 372; see also Introduction, ibid., 24:238. On the August election results and predictions that the new legislature would call a convention, see Ellery to Huntington, Aug. 29, 1789, *DHRC*, 25:585; James Manning to James Madison, Aug. 29, 1789, ibid., 586; Henry Marchant to John Adams, Aug. 29, 1789, ibid., 588; Brown & Benson to Jenckes, Winsor & Co, Sept. 15, 1789, ibid., 599.

417. *Newport Herald*, Oct. 22, 1789, ibid., 617; Introduction, ibid., 455; see also Benjamin Bourne to Silas Talbot, Jan. 9, 1790, ibid., 662; Brown & Benson to Champion & Dickason, May 7, 1790, *DHRC*, 26:859. On the country party's tactical reasons for calling the legislature into special session, see Henry Marchant to John Adams, Dec. 19, 1789, *DHRC*, 25:649; see also Editorial Introduction, ibid., 599–600.

418. Rhode Island General Assembly to the President, the Senate, and the House of Representatives, Sept. 19, 1789, ibid., 605–6; Extract of a letter from Rhode-Island, Philadelphia *Federal Gazette*, Oct. 16, 1789, ibid., 619 ("gross insult"); see also Extract of a letter from a gentleman, *Massachusetts Centinel*, Oct. 7, 1789, ibid., 615; Polishook, *Rhode Island*, 187–8.

For the preceding footnote, see Introduction, *DHRC*, 25:455; Introduction, *DHRC*, 24:xxxiv–v; Polishook, supra, 162.

419. Act of Sept. 16, 1789, ch. 15, § 2, 1 Stat. 69; editorial note, *DHRC*, 25:631 n. 1; Maier, *Ratification*, 458; Kaminski, "Rhode Island," 382–3. Specifically, the law enacted by Congress on September 16 temporarily exempted Rhode Island ships from the Tonnage Act of July 20, which imposed duties of six cents per ton on US vessels, thirty cents per ton on vessels built in the United States but operated by foreigners, and fifty cents per ton on foreign vessels (editorial note, *DHRC*, 25:655 n. 5).

420. Ellery to Huntington, Dec. 12, 1789, ibid., 641 ("by the cords" and "despise"); John Adams to James Sullivan, June 18, 1789, ibid., 545 ("unanimously zealous"). For the interpretation of Congress's statute as an act of lenity, see Olney Winsor to Samuel

Winsor III, Oct. 6, 1789, ibid., 614. On Congress's predisposition toward leniency for Rhode Island, see James Manning to Nicholas Brown, May 21, 1789, ibid., 511; Ellery to Nathaniel Appleton, June 1, 1789, ibid., 525; Ellery to Huntington, Aug. 29, 1789, ibid., 584; see also Jefferson to Carrington, May 27, 1788, *PTJ* (M.S.), 13:209. For concern that Congress's assuming too dictatorial a tone with Rhode Island might backfire, see Providence *United States Chronicle*, Dec. 17, 1789, *DHRC*, 25:646–7. On the Rhode Island mercantile party's opposition to discriminatory trade measures that would affect their interests more immediately than those of inland farmers, see John Brown to John Adams, Aug. 24, 1789, ibid., 573; Providence Town Meetings, Aug. 25, 27, 1789, ibid., 576, 577–8; James Manning to James Madison, Aug. 29, 1789, ibid., 586; Henry Marchant to John Adams, Aug. 29, 1789, ibid., 588–9; Jabez Bowen to John Adams, Aug. 31, 1789, ibid., 591–2. For resistance in Congress to admitting Rhode Island (and Vermont) into the union because of the effect it would have on whether Congress remained in New York City, see Fisher Ames to George Richards Minot, July 9, 1789, ibid., 553; see also Richard Bassett to George Read, Mar. 1, 1790, *DHRC*, 26:749. In the summer of 1788, Alexander Hamilton had written to Jeremiah Olney, a Providence Federalist who had fought alongside Hamilton at the battle of Yorktown, to emphasize the importance of Rhode Island's immediately sending delegates to the Confederation Congress to influence the vote on whether Congress remained in New York City (Aug. 12, 1788, *DHRC*, 25:389). See also Nicholas Gilman to John Langdon, July 15, 1788, *DHRC*, 21:1316.

421. Adams to John Brown, Sept. 15, 1789, *DHRC*, 25:598–9 (quotations); see also Adams to Jabez Bowen, Sept. 18, 1789, ibid., 611.

422. Editorial Introduction, ibid., 620; ibid., 634; Providence *United States Chronicle*, Oct. 29, 1789, ibid., 633–4; *Newport Herald*, Nov. 5, 1789, ibid., 634; Henry Marchant to John Adams, Dec. 19, 1789, ibid., 649–50.

423. Washington to Jabez Bowen, Dec. 27, 1789, ibid., 651 ("entirely alone"); Bowen to Adams, Dec. 28, 1789, ibid., 652 ("our Antes" and "especially"); see also Providence *United States Chronicle*, Dec. 17, 1789, ibid., 646. For earlier predictions that North Carolina's ratification would influence Rhode Island, see Ellery to Huntington, June 15, 1789, ibid., 541; Dec. 12, 1789, ibid., 641. On the close coverage in the Rhode Island newspapers of developments related to ratification in North Carolina, see Editorial Introduction, ibid., 643–5. Federalist William Ellery observed that while "[t]he accession of North Carolina to the new government has given a considerable shock to our wicked majority, . . . nothing which doth not apply immediately and forcibly to their interest will ever induce them to embrace the union" (to Nathaniel Appleton, Jan. 2, 1790, ibid., 657; see also Jabez Bowen to George Washington, Dec. 15, 1789, ibid., 648). Federalist Henry Marchant thought that while North Carolina's ratification was a significant and joyful development, "[w]e have been often deceived in our hopes, and I do not wish to be sanguine" (to John Adams, Dec. 19, 1789, ibid., 649–50; see also Benjamin Bourne to Silas Talbot, Jan. 9, 1790, ibid., 662).

424. "Philanthropos," *Newport Herald*, Jan. 7, 1790, ibid., 660 (quotation); "A Federalist," *Newport Mercury*, Jan. 6, 1790, ibid., 658–9; Providence *United States Chronicle*, Dec. 31, 1789, ibid., 655. Private correspondence makes clear that the threats of secession were not idle. See, e.g., Bowen to Adams, Dec. 28, 1789, ibid., 652.

425. Providence *United States Chronicle*, Jan. 21, 1790, ibid., 673 (quotation); Editorial Introduction, ibid., 665–6; *Newport Herald*, Jan. 21, 1790, ibid., 669–71; Governor John Collins to President George Washington, Jan. 18, 1790, ibid., 677–8; see also Henry Marchant to John Adams, Jan. 18, 1790, ibid., 680–1; Kaminski, "Rhode Island," 383–5; Heideking, *The Constitution Before the Judgment Seat*, 334–6.

For the preceding footnote, see John Collins to George Washington, May 24, 1790, *DHRC*, 26:886–7; Editorial Introduction, ibid., 768. For the notion that Collins was a "sacrificial lamb," who enabled the country party to maintain its veneer of opposition to ratification while simultaneously setting in motion the events that led ultimately to Rhode Island's approval of the Constitution, see John P. Kaminski, "Political Sacrifice and Demise—John Collins and Jonathan J. Hazard, 1786–1790," *Rhode Island History* (Aug. 1976), 35:91–8 (quotation at p. 93).

426. Theodore Foster to Dwight Foster, Jan. 22, 1790, *DHRC*, 26:715 ("The Federal Temple"); Bowen to Washington, Jan. 17, 1790, *DHRC*, 25:678 ("finally adopted"); Marchant to Adams, Jan. 18, 1790, ibid., 681 ("not a reasonable doubt," "promised," "have a tendency," and "at least ten"); The North Carolina Act of Feb. 8, 1790, First Congress, Sess. II, Ch. 1, § 7; see also Jeremiah Olney to Henry Knox, Jan. 17, 1790, *DHRC*, 25:679; Extract of a letter from Providence, Philadelphia *Federal Gazette*, Jan. 30, 1790, ibid., 683; Feb. 1, 1790, *DHRC*, 26:716. For a more cautious appraisal of the prospects for ratification at the convention, see Ellery to Huntington, Feb. 2, 1790, ibid., 716.

427. Editorial Introduction, *DHRC*, 25:684; Brown & Benson to Hewes & Anthony, Feb. 4, 1790, ibid., 686; Jeremiah Olney to Alexander Hamilton, Feb. 12, 1790, ibid., 705–6; Bowen to John Adams, Feb. 15, 1790, ibid., 706–7; Henry Marchant to William Marchant, Feb. 15, 1790, ibid., 707; Brown & Francis to John Adams, Feb. 16, 1790, ibid.; William Peck to Henry Knox, Feb. 15, 1790, *DHRC*, 26:722; Richard Bassett to George Read, Mar. 1, 1790, ibid., 749; Brown & Benson to Thayer, Bartlett & Co., Mar. 6, 1790, ibid., 751.

428. Brown & Francis to Adams, Feb. 16, 1790, *DHRC*, 25:708 ("Congress will not"); Bowen to Adams, Feb. 15, 1790, ibid., 706–7; see also Jeremiah Olney to Hamilton, Feb. 12, 1790, ibid., 706.

   For the preceding footnote, see Adams to Bowen, Feb. 27, 1790, *DHRC*, 26:743; see also Adams to Brown & Francis, Feb. 28, 1790, ibid., 747–8; Adams to Ellery, Feb. 28, 1790, ibid., 748–9.

429. "A Friend to the State of Rhode-Island," *Newport Herald*, Feb. 18, 1790, ibid., 723–6 ("every reason," "consider the legislature," and "suffer a single"); "Solon, junior," *Providence Gazette*, Feb. 27, 1790, ibid., 745–6 ("various distresses"); see also "A Freeholder," *Newport Herald*, Feb. 18, 1790, ibid., 727–30; Providence *United States Chronicle*, Feb. 25, 1790, ibid., 740–2.

430. Rhode Island Act Calling a Convention to Consider the Constitution, Jan. 17, 1790, *DHRC*, 25:675 ("full and free") (emphasis added); Convention Debates, Mar. 6, 1790, *DHRC*, 26:959–60 (Benjamin Bourne); ibid., 961–2 (Henry Marchant); ibid., 962 (Governor William Bradford); ibid., 962–3 (General Nathan Miller); see also Marchant to Adams, Mar. 7, 1790, ibid., 981–3; Bowen to Adams, Mar. 9, 1790, ibid., 757; Introduction, ibid., 898–9. For the bill of rights and proposed amendments, see ibid., 976–81.

431. Convention Debates, Mar. 6, 1790, ibid., 960–1 (Hazard); ibid., 961 (E. Brown); ibid., 963 (vote on adjournment); *Newport Herald*, Mar. 11, 1790, ibid., 973.

432. Convention Debates, Mar. 6, 1790, ibid., 964 (Bourne) ("every man"); ibid. (G. Hazard) ("trifling"); ibid., 965 (General Miller); see also ibid., 966 (Colonel Barton); ibid. (Governor Bowen); see also Portsmouth Town Meeting, Feb. 27, 1790, *DHRC*, 25:701–2; Ellery to Huntington, Mar. 8, 1790, *DHRC*, 26:755–6.

433. Henry Sherburne to Knox, Mar. 7, 1790, ibid., 753 ("reason, duty"); Convention Debates, Mar. 6, 1790, ibid., 964 (General Stanton) ("the people"); ibid., 961 (Jonathan J. Hazard); ibid. (E. Brown); ibid., 963–8 (discussion of how long to adjourn for and votes on various motions); see also ibid., 967 (Williams); *Newport Herald*, Mar. 11, 1790, ibid., 973; Ellery to Adams, post–March 6, 1790, ibid., 752.

434. Henry Marchant to Adams, Mar. 7, 1790, ibid., 982 ("did not hesitate"); Henry Sherburne to Knox, Mar. 7, 1790, ibid., 753–4 ("cover"); see also Brown & Francis to Adams, Feb. 16, 1790, *DHRC*, 25:707; Ellery to Huntington, Mar. 28, 1790, *DHRC*, 26:800; Madison to Tench Coxe, Mar. 28, 1790, ibid., 801; Editorial Introduction, ibid., 768; ibid., 25:665; Kaminski, "Paper Politics," 247–8. To the extent the Antifederalists adjourned the convention for partisan purposes, their ploy was successful, as they won large majorities in both houses of the legislature in the April elections. See Ellery to Adams, May 13, 1790, *DHRC*, 26:866.

435. "A Friend to Justice and Freedom," Providence *United States Chronicle*, Feb. 4, 1790, *DHRC*, 25:688 ("pernicious" and "fix a grievous"); *Newport Herald*, Mar. 11, 1790, *DHRC*, 26:761 ("powerful reason" and "the expectation"); Bowen to Adams, Feb. 15,

1790, *DHRC*, 25:707 ("do so many"); see also Ellery to Adams, post–March 6, 1790, *DHRC*, 26:752. On Rhode Island Antifederalists' objections to the high salaries established by Congress, see *Newport Herald*, Nov. 5, 1789, *DHRC*, 25:635; Louis-Guillaume Otto to Comte de Montmorin, Dec. 5, 1789, ibid., 640; Bowen to Washington, Dec. 15, 1789, ibid., 648; "Z: To the Freemen of the State of Rhode-Island," *Newport Mercury*, Dec. 30, 1789, ibid., 653. For another strong statement of opposition to Hamilton's funding plan, see *Newport Herald*, Apr. 1, 1790, *DHRC*, 26:803.

436. Bowen to Adams, Mar. 9, 1790, ibid., 757 ("entirely"); Ellery to Huntington, Dec. 12, 1789, *DHRC*, 25:641 ("care not"); "A Friend to the State of Rhode-Island," *Newport Herald*, Feb. 18, 1790, *DHRC*, 26:725 ("glory"); see also Caleb Gannett to John Mellen, Jan. 12, 1790, *DHRC*, 25:664. For the Rhode Island Federalists' repeated warnings that the burden of trade restrictions would fall initially on the Federalist merchants, see Ellery to Huntington, supra; Ellery to Nathaniel Appleton, Jan. 2, 1790, ibid., 657; Marchant to Adams, Dec. 19, 1789, ibid., 650.

437. Caleb Strong to Theodore Foster, Feb. 28, 1790, *DHRC*, 26:749 ("which, after" and "justified even"); *Newport Herald*, Mar. 11, 1790, ibid., 761 ("upon the most"); US Senate Bill to Prohibit Commerce with Rhode Island, May 13, 1790, ibid., 845–7; see also Louis-Guillaume Otto to Comte de Montmorin, Mar. 13, 1790, ibid., 762–3; Adams to Marchant, Mar. 20, 1790, ibid., 791–2; Adams to Bowen, Mar. 28, 1790, ibid., 800. For Rhode Island Federalists' repeated assurances that their opponents would not ratify until they personally felt some pain, see Ellery to Huntington, May 3, 1790, ibid., 856; Apr. 5, 1790, ibid., 807–8; Mar. 8, 1790, ibid., 756; Dec. 12, 1789, *DHRC*, 25:641. On the Senate bill, see Editorial Introduction, *DHRC*, 26:837. On the disproportionately northern support for the coercion bill, see Louis-Guillaume Otto to Comte de Montmorin, June 1, 1790, ibid., 1020; Senate Journal, May 18, 1790, ibid., 843–4.

438. John Steele to Joseph Winston, May 22, 1790, ibid., 881–2 ("tyrannical"); Huntington to Ellery, May 8, 12, 1790, ibid., 860 ("many merciful men" and "agree to any"); Thomas Lloyd's Notes on House Debates, May 26, 1790, ibid., 849 ("sadly unbecoming"); *New York Daily Gazette*, May 27, 1790, ibid., 851 (Page) ("the indignation" and "would esteem"); New York *Gazette of the United States*, May 29, 1790, ibid., 852–3 (Page) ("malevolence resembling," "show a generous indulgence," and "she will come with"). For additional statements by members of Congress indicating opposition, at least at that time, to coercing Rhode Island, see William Maclay Journal, May 5, ibid., 839; May 10, ibid., 840; May 11, ibid., 841; May 18, ibid., 844–5; Thomas Lloyd's Notes on House Debates, May 26, 1790, ibid., 850 (reporting statement of Congressman James Jackson of Georgia); see also Louis-Guillaume Otto to Comte de Montmorin, June 1, 1790, ibid., 1020.

439. Fenner to Washington, May 20, 1790, ibid., 873, 875 (quotations).

440. Antoine de la Forest to Comte de la Luzerne, June 1, 1790, ibid., 1020 ("carefully managed delays"); Benson to Sedgwick, May 21, 1790, ibid., 880 ("made a very," "produced," and "the most sanguine"); see also Louis-Guillaume Otto to Comte de Montmorin, June 1, 1790, ibid., 1020–1. For the Rhode Island newspapers' publishing of the bill and of letters by congressmen calling attention to it, see Providence *United States Chronicle*, May 20, 1790, ibid., 845–7 & n. 1; ibid., 876–9; see also Extract of a letter from a Member of Congress, *Providence Gazette*, May 29, 1790, ibid., 896. Congressman Abraham Baldwin predicted that the House would pass the Senate bill if Rhode Island's convention failed to ratify the Constitution at its session in late May (to Joel Barlow, May 24, 1790, ibid., 886).

441. William Channing to Theodore Foster, May 18, 1790, ibid., 870 ("become desperate"); Providence: Instructions to Town's Delegates to the State Convention, May 24, 1790, ibid., 889–90; Ellery to Huntington, May 3, 1790, ibid., 856; Huntington to Ellery, May 8, 12, 1790, ibid., 859–60; Adams to Ellery, May 19, 1790, ibid., 871 ("If the inland"); see also Louis-Guillaume Otto to Comte de Montmorin, June 1, 1790, ibid., 1021.

442. Ellery to Huntington, May 11, 1790, ibid., 864 ("have talked" and "only to amuse"); Theodore Foster to William Channing, May 24, 1790, ibid., 887–8 ("strong hopes"); see also Ellery to Adams, May 13, 1790, ibid., 867.

443. Marchant to Adams, May 29, 1790, ibid., 1014 (quotations). The vote to select Newport as the venue at which the convention would reassemble in May is at Convention Debates, Mar. 6, 1790, ibid., 968.

444. Marchant to Adams, May 29, 1790, ibid., 1014 ("anxiety, labor"); Rhode Island Form of Ratification and Amendments, May 29, 1790, ibid., 996–1000 ("explanations," "confidence," and "an early and mature consideration" at p. 999); Introduction, ibid., 984–5; *New York Journal*, June 1, 1790, ibid., 1005. The unapproved amendment dealt with alterations in congressional pay. See infra pp. 579, 590. The legislature followed the convention's advice, ratifying, on June 11, 1790, eleven of the twelve amendments proposed by Congress. See editorial note, *DHRC*, 26:941 n. 14.

   For the preceding footnote, see Oliver Ellsworth to Abigail Ellsworth, June 7, 1790, ibid., 1040–1 (quotation); *Newport Herald*, June 3, 1790, ibid., 1028; *Providence Gazette*, June 5, 1790, ibid., 1029 n. 2.

445. Boston *Independent Chronicle*, June 3, 1790, ibid., 1031. On Washington's visit to Rhode Island, see Editorial Introduction, ibid., 1054–5.

446. Resolutions of the Convention Recommending the Procedures for Ratification, Sept. 17, 1787, *DHRC*, 1:318 ("their assent"); Randolph to the Speaker of the House of Delegates (dated Oct. 10; published Dec. 27, 1787), *DHRC*, 8:271 ("allowed universally"); supra p. 419.

447. Madison at Virginia convention, June 25, 1788, *DHRC*, 10:1518 (quotation); supra pp. 429, 438–41. For Federalists' initial denials that even merely recommended amendments were permissible, see Wilson at Pennsylvania convention, Dec. 4, 1787, *DHRC*, 2:470; McKean, Dec. 10, ibid., 533; Nov. 24, ibid., 337; see also Address of the Antifederalist Minority of the Maryland convention, May 1, 1788, *DHRC*, 12:662 (noting Federalist delegates' denying that the Maryland convention had authority to consider amendments); Maier, *Ratification*, 67–8, 105, 244–5; Labunski, *James Madison*, 50–1; Graham, "Pennsylvania," 64. Naturally, in Massachusetts, it was Antifederalists who denied that the convention had the power to recommend amendments (Taylor, Jan. 31, 1788, *DHRC*, 6:1385). For additional statements by Madison and his allies expressing horror at the idea of conditional ratification, see Madison to Nicholas, Apr. 8, 1788, *PJM* (C.S.), 11:12; Madison to Randolph, Apr. 10, 1788, ibid., 19; Madison to Jefferson, Apr. 22, 1788, ibid., 28; Nicholas to Madison, Apr. 5, 1788, ibid., 9; Madison to Jefferson, Dec. 9, 1787, ibid., 10:311.

448. Mason at Philadelphia convention, Sept. 15, 1787, *Farrand*, 2:632 ("know more" and "[i]t was improper"); Randolph, Sept. 17, ibid., 646 ("holding out"); see also Randolph motion, Sept. 15, ibid., 631; Randolph, Sept. 10, ibid., 564; Aug. 31, ibid., 479; Maier, *Ratification*, 45; Beeman, *Plain, Honest Men*, 340, 355–6; Labunski, *James Madison*, 10–11; Rutland, *Ordeal of the Constitution*, ch. 3.

449. Randolph to Madison, Aug. 13, 1788, *PJM* (C.S.), 11:231 ("the theory of the people," "equal respect," and "the theory of the convention"); Lee to Washington, Oct. 11, 1787, *PGW* (C.S.), 5:371 ("abounds," "fundamentally strong," and "the exercise"); Jefferson to Madison, Dec. 20, 1787, *PJM* (C.S.), 10:337 ("duly weighed" and "the parts"); New York Convention, Circular Letter to the Executives of the States, July 26, 1788, *DHRC*, 23:2336; see also Randolph to the Speaker of the House (dated Oct. 10; published Dec. 27, 1787), *DHRC*, 8:271–2; Richard Henry Lee to Randolph, Oct. 16, 1787, ibid., 61; Jay to Washington, Sept. 21, 1788, *PGW* (C.S.), 6:528; Maier, *Ratification*, 398, 426, 432; Labunski, *James Madison*, 53, 64, 66, 125, 129.

450. Pinckney at Philadelphia convention, Sept. 15, 1787, *Farrand*, 2:632 ("[n]othing but" and "[c]onventions"); Madison to Jefferson, Aug. 23, 1788, *PJM* (C.S.), 11:238 ("in every view"); Madison to Nicholas, Apr. 8, 1788, ibid., 13 ("contain men" and "on points"); see also Madison to Jefferson, Apr. 22, 1788, ibid., 28; Madison to Pendleton, Oct. 20, 1788, ibid., 307; Madison to Randolph, Apr. 10, 1788, ibid., 19; Jan. 10, 1788, ibid., 10:355; Washington to Randolph, Jan. 8, 1788, *PGW* (C.S.), 6:17–8; Maier, *Ratification*, 67–8, 425–6.

451. Innes at Virginia convention, June 25, 1788, *DHRC*, 10:1520.

452. Madison, June 24, ibid., 1500; Corbin, June 7, ibid., 9:1015 ("eternally revolving");
Madison to Hamilton, July 20, 1788, *PJM* (C.S.), 11:189 ("[t]he Constitution"); Iredell at
North Carolina convention, July 20, 1788, *Elliot*, 4:217; Robert R. Livingston at New York
convention, July 11, 1788, *DHRC*, 22:2139; see also Charles Jarvis at Massachusetts convention, Feb. 4, 1788, *DHRC*, 6:1425.

453. New York *Daily Advertiser*, May 6, 1789, in *The Documentary History of the First Federal
Congress of the United States, 1789–1791* (Charlene Bangs Bickford et al., eds., Baltimore,
1992), 10:445 (Madison); Labunski, *James Madison*, 191.

454. Madison to Jefferson, Apr. 22, 1788, *PJM* (C.S.), 11:28 ("that the states"); Madison to
Archibald Stuart, Dec. 14, 1787, ibid., 10:326 ("would find themselves"); Marshall at
Virginia convention, June 10, 1788, *DHRC*, 9:1117 ("enemies" and "amendments"); see
also Madison to Randolph, Apr. 10, 1788, *PJM* (C.S.), 11:19; Madison to Pendleton, Feb.
21, 1788, ibid., 10:533; Washington to John Armstrong, Sr., Apr. 25, 1788, *DHRC*, 9:759;
Albany Federal Committee, *An Impartial Address* (c. Apr. 20, 1788), *DHRC*, 21:1398;
Alexander White, "To the Citizens of Virginia," *Winchester Gazette* [Virginia], Feb. 29,
1788, *DHRC*, 8:444.

455. Washington to Charles Carter, Dec. 14, 1787, *PGW* (C.S.), 5:492 ("more discordant");
Madison to Jefferson, Apr. 22, 1788, *PJM* (C.S.), 11:28 ("if a second"); Madison to
Nicholas, Apr. 8, 1788, ibid., 12–13; *A Citizen of New-York* (Jay), *DHRC*, 20:936–8; see also
Charles Pinckney at Philadelphia convention, Sept. 15, 1787, *Farrand*, 2:632; Labunski,
James Madison, 52, 55; Maier, *Ratification*, 45, 337; Hendrickson, *Peace Pact*, 251–2.

456. *A Citizen of New-York* (Jay), *DHRC*, 20:938–9 ("daily" "to perfect," "discord," and
"encourage"); Madison to George Lee Turberville, Nov. 2, 1788, *PJM* (C.S.), 11:331–
2; Madison to George Eve, Jan. 2, 1789, ibid., 405; Madison to Nicholas, Apr. 8, 1788,
ibid., 12–13.

457. Lee to Mason, Oct. 1, 1787, *DHRC*, 8:29 (quotations); see also Richard Henry Lee to
Randolph, Oct. 16, 1787, ibid., 64; John Lansing, Jr., at New York convention, June 20,
1788, *DHRC*, 22:1705–6; Monroe at Virginia convention, June 10, 1788, *DHRC*, 9:1108;
Plebeian, *DHRC*, 20:947; Mercy Otis Warren to Catherine Macaulay Graham, Sept. 28,
1787, *DHRC*, 4:23; Silas Lee to George Thatcher, Feb. 14, 1788, *DHRC*, 7:1699; supra pp.
309–10.

458. Lee to Mason, May 7, 1788, *DHRC*, 9:785 ("the very arbitrary" and "every temperate");
Monroe at Virginia convention, June 25, 1788, *DHRC*, 10:1519 ("presumable"); Smith
at New York convention, June 25, 1788, *DHRC*, 22:1902 ("in such a manner"); see also
Lee to Mason, Oct. 1, 1787, *DHRC*, 8:28; Pennsylvania Minority Dissent, *DHRC*, 2:623;
William Symmes, Jr., to Peter Osgood, Jr., Nov. 15, 1787, *DHRC*, 4:244; "Candidus" I,
Boston *Independent Chronicle*, Dec. 6, 1787, ibid., 393; "An Old Whig" VII, Philadelphia
Independent Gazetteer, Nov. 28, 1787, *DHRC*, 2:300.

459. Henry at Virginia convention, June 24, 1788, *DHRC*, 10:1477 ("enter"); "A Columbian
Patriot," *Observations*, *DHRC*, 16:283 ("the precarious"); Atherton to John Lamb, June
11, 14, 1788, *DHRC*, 18:46 ("to ratify"); John Tyler at Virginia convention, June 25, 1788,
DHRC, 10:1525–6; Lansing at New York convention, July 11, 1788, *DHRC*, 22:2137–8;
see also *Plebeian*, *DHRC*, 20:944–5; Luther Martin, Address No. III, *Maryland Journal*,
Mar. 28, 1788, *DHRC*, 12:457–8, 460; Monroe at Virginia convention, June 25, 1788,
DHRC, 10:1518–9; Henry, June 24, ibid., 1477; June 7, ibid., 9:1042; Mason, June 11,
ibid., 1163; Banning, "Virginia," 284; Maier, *Ratification*, 294, 339, 380–1.

460. "A Columbian Patriot," *Observations*, *DHRC*, 16:282–4 ("very reprehensible," "before,"
and "the mad zeal"); Nathaniel Barrell at Massachusetts convention, Feb. 5, 1788,
DHRC, 6:1449 ("important transactions," "cool deliberation," and "hurried on"); Mason
to Gerry, Oct. 20, 1787, *DHRC*, 8:87 ("attempting"); *Plebeian*, *DHRC*, 20:947 ("be terrified" and "take time"); see also Benjamin Gale at Killingworth, Conn., Town Meeting,
Nov. 12, 1787, *DHRC*, 3:421; William Symmes, Jr., to Peter Osgood, Jr., Nov. 15, 1787,
DHRC, 4:244; Federal Farmer, *Letters to the Republican* (Nov. 8, 1787), Letter V, *DHRC*,
19:241; David Redick to William Irvine, Sept. 24, 1787, *DHRC*, 2:135; "Philadelphiensis"
I, Philadelphia *Freeman's Journal*, Nov. 7, 1787, ibid., 280–1; "A Federalist," *Boston*

Gazette, Nov. 26, 1787, *DHRC*, 4:321; "The Republican Federalist" V, *Massachusetts Centinel*, Jan. 19, 1788, *DHRC*, 5:748.

461. Pennsylvania Minority Dissent, *DHRC*, 2:620 ("were busily employed"); "Centinel" I, Philadelphia *Independent Gazetteer*, Oct. 5, 1787, *DHRC*, 2:166 ("our situation"); Monroe at Virginia convention, June 25, 1788, *DHRC*, 10:1518 ("a conditional ratification"); June 10, ibid., 9:1108 ("calmly and dispassionately"); see also Grayson, June 24, ibid., 10:1497; Atherton to Lamb, June 11, 14, 1788, *DHRC*, 18:46; Federal Farmer, *Letters to the Republican* (Nov. 8, 1787), Letter I, *DHRC*, 19:209–10; Maier, *Ratification*, 60–1, 76, 339; supra pp. 314–5.

462. Henry at Virginia convention, June 9, 1788, *DHRC*, 9:1050, 1054 ("precipitate," "to hurry," and "[u]nless there be"); June 4, ibid., 929, 931 ("a general peace," "calm and tranquil," and "wandering"); June 7, ibid., 1037 ("an imprudent," "in its defective," and "a schism"); see also June 5, ibid., 967.

463. Lee to Mason, Oct. 1, 1787, *DHRC*, 8:29 ("to push," "before," "business," and "the most rash"); Lee to Randolph, Oct. 16, 1787, ibid., 61 ("the most cool," "immense," and "neither prudent"); see also Lee to Washington, Oct. 11, 1787, ibid., 51; Lee to Mason, May 7, 1788, *DHRC*, 9:785; Lee to Samuel Adams, Apr. 28, 1788, ibid., 765–6.

464. Lee to Randolph, Oct. 16, 1787, *DHRC*, 8:61 ("[i]f with infinite" and "with equal"); Lowndes in South Carolina House, Jan. 17, 1788, *DHRC*, 27:128 ("the general sense"); "An Officer of the Late Continental Army," Philadelphia *Independent Gazetteer*, Nov. 6, 1787, *DHRC*, 2:215 ("the opinions," "secluded," and "the collective"); *Plebeian*, *DHRC*, 20:950–1 ("were kept," "material errors," and "the object"); see also Richard Henry Lee to Washington, Oct. 11, 1787, *DHRC*, 8:51; Tyler at Virginia convention, June 25, 1788, *DHRC*, 10:1527; Federal Farmer, *Letters to the Republican* (Nov. 8, 1787), Letter V, *DHRC*, 19:240; "Candidus" I, Boston *Independent Chronicle*, Dec. 6, 1787, *DHRC*, 4:395.

465. Madison to George Lee Turberville, Nov. 2, 1788, *PJM* (C.S.), 11:331 ("should tremble" and "the difficulties"); Madison to Randolph, Jan. 10, 1788, ibid., 10:355–6 ("would of course"); Apr. 10, 1788, ibid., 11:19 ("a second experiment"); see also Nicholas to Madison, Apr. 5, 1788, ibid., 9.

466. Supra pp. 246–54.

467. Pennsylvania Minority Dissent, *DHRC*, 2:622–3; see also "A Plain Citizen: To the Honorable the Convention of the State of Pennsylvania" (possibly James Wilson), Philadelphia *Independent Gazetteer*, Nov. 22, 1787, ibid., 291.

468. Virginia convention, June 27, 1788, *DHRC*, 10:1556–7 (voting by eighty-five to sixty-five against a motion to delete the amendment regarding the requisitioning of direct taxes); Labunski, *James Madison*, 115. Before voting to ratify unconditionally, the New York convention had taken a series of votes revealing that roughly two-thirds of the delegates preferred the Constitution with a variety of amendments, such as limiting Congress's power with regard to direct taxes and standing armies (New York convention, July 21, *DHRC*, 23:2256–61; July 22, ibid., 2265–72).

469. Shumer, "New Jersey," 82–7; Kaminski, "Paper Politics," 122–3; McCormick, *Experiment in Independence*, 276–7; McDonald, *We the People*, 123–4; but cf. Van Cleve, "Anti-Federalists' Toughest Challenge," 556.

For the preceding footnote, see Clay to John Pierce, Oct. 17, 1787, *DHRC*, 3:232 (quotation); see also Antoine de la Forest to Comte de Montmorin, Dec. 15, 1787, *DHRC*, 8:240.

470. Randolph to Madison, Mar. 27, 1787, *PJM* (C.S.), 9:335 ("detached from"); Madison to Jefferson, Dec. 9, 1787, ibid., 10:313 ("In Virginia" and "certainly surpasses"); "Publicola: An Address to the Freemen of North Carolina" (Archibald Maclaine), *State Gazette of North Carolina*, Mar. 20, 1788, *DHRC*, 16:438 ("[t]he greatest part"); see also Madison to Randolph, Jan. 10, 1788, *PJM* (C.S.), 10:355; Apr. 8, 1787, ibid., 9:369; *The Federalist No. 49* (Madison), at 315.

471. Aedanus Burke to John Lamb, June 23, 1788, *DHRC*, 18:55–6 ("despis[ing]"); see also "An Old Whig" VII, Philadelphia *Independent Gazetteer*, Nov. 28, 1787, *DHRC*, 2:300; Rakove, *Original Meanings*, 139; Edling, *Revolution in Favor of Government*, 24–5.

472. Morris at the Philadelphia convention, Aug. 31, 1787, *Farrand*, 2:478 ("with the sanction" and "[b]y degrees"); Martin, ibid. ("would not"); "Centinel" XII, Philadelphia

Independent Gazetteer, Jan. 23, 1788, *DHRC*, 15:448 ("allowing"); see also Lachlan McIntosh to John Wereat, Dec. 17, 1787, *DHRC*, 3:259; Gerry to James Warren, Oct. 18, 1787, *DHRC*, 13:407; Rutland, *Ordeal of the Constitution*, 19.

473. Boyd, *Politics of Opposition*, 8; Maier, *Ratification*, 125–6.

474. Supra p. 427; "Centinel" VIII, Philadelphia *Independent Gazetteer*, Jan. 2, 1788, *DHRC*, 15:233 (quotation); see also "Centinel" I, Oct. 5, 1787, ibid., 13:329; Pennsylvania Minority Dissent, *DHRC*, 2:622; Bouton, *Taming Democracy*, 180–1; Maier, *Ratification*, 59–61, 243–4.

475. Virginia Plan, resolution 13, May 29, *Farrand*, 1:22; Committee of Detail report, Art. XIX, Aug. 6, ibid., 2:188; Hamilton, Sept. 10, ibid., 558; ibid., 558–9 (agreeing, without dissent, that in addition to the convention route, Congress ought to be able to propose amendments, which would become part of the Constitution if agreed upon by three-fourths of the states). Despite the vote on September 10, the Committee of Style report, which was made two days later, actually did not provide for a constitutional convention at all: Congress could propose amendments either on its own initiative or on application of two-thirds of the state legislatures. On the penultimate day of the convention's deliberations, however, Mason objected that it was "exceptionable and dangerous" for both modes of amendment to run through Congress, and he predicted that "no amendments of the proper kind would ever be obtained by the people if the government should become oppressive." Gouverneur Morris and Gerry then moved to require Congress to call a constitutional convention upon application of two-thirds of the state legislatures, and the delegates agreed to that change without dissent. See Committee of Style report, Art. V, ibid., 602; Mason statement and Morris motion, seconded by Gerry, Sept. 15, ibid., 629; ibid., 629–30 (agreeing to the motion).

476. Madison to George Eve, Jan. 2, 1789, *PJM* (C.S.), 11:405 ("probably be"); Jefferson to Madison, Nov. 18, 1788, ibid., 354 ("not fear"); Labunski, *James Madison*, 129–30, 165; Maier, *Ratification*, 427, 441–2.

477. Rakove, *Original Meanings*, 116.

478. Benjamin Rush, Observations on the Fourth of July Procession in Philadelphia, *Pennsylvania Mercury*, July 15, 1788, *DHRC*, 18:266 ("[h]eaven," "the influence," and "as much"); Washington to the Marquis de Lafayette, May 28, 1788, *PGW* (C.S.), 6:299 ("so much beyond"). For a general analysis of such celebrations of ratification, which occurred in numerous cities, see Heideking, *The Constitution Before the Judgment Seat*, ch. 6.

479. Timothy Bloodworth at North Carolina convention, July 29, 1788, *Elliot*, 4:185.

480. Supra pp. 405–12.

481. Madison to Washington, Oct 28, 1787, *DHRC*, 8:127 ("a very strong," "tardy," and "either left"); Knox to the Marquis de Lafayette, May 15, 1788, *DHRC*, 20:1096 ("[w]ere the new"); see also William Ellery to Benjamin Huntington, July 28, 1788, *DHRC*, 21:1348–9.

482. Supra pp. 423, 438–42, 445–6.

483. De Witt Clinton Journal, July 18, 1788, *DHRC*, 23:2232 ("[i]t was a great"); *New York Packet*, July 15, 1788, *DHRC*, 22:2164 ("adopt" and "hazard"); Randolph at Virginia convention, June 4, 1788, *DHRC*, 9:933; see also New York *Daily Advertiser*, June 14, 1788, *DHRC*, 20:1170; Carrington to Madison, Feb. 10, 1788, *PJM* (C.S.), 10:494; Apr. 8, 1788, ibid., 11:15–6; Carrington to Jefferson, June 9, 1788, *DHRC*, 10:1590; Monroe to Jefferson, Apr. 10, 1788, *DHRC*, 9:733; Rakove, *Original Meanings*, 127; Maier, *Ratification*, 382; Edling, "A More Perfect Union," 402; supra pp. 475–9, 496–510.

484. Joshua Atherton to John Lamb, June 11, 14, 1788, *DHRC*, 18:47 ("not the least," "great majority," and "would immediately"); Henry at Virginia convention, June 12, 1788, *DHRC*, 10:1210–1; see also Archibald Stuart to Madison, Dec. 2, 1787, *PJM* (C.S.), 10:291; Reverend James Madison to Madison, Feb. 9, 1788, *DHRC*, 8:358; Boyd, *Politics of Opposition*, 127; supra pp. 472–3, 477–8, 481, 491–3, 508–10.

485. Albany Federal Committee, *An Impartial Address* (c. Apr. 20, 1788), *DHRC*, 21:1389.

486. Lamb to Richard Henry Lee, May 18, 1788, *DHRC*, 9:814 ("open" and "unite"); Lowndes to Lamb, June 21, 1788, *DHRC*, 18:51 ("Had your plan"); Lee to Lamb, June 27, 1788, *DHRC*, 9:826 ("would have produced"); see also An Attempt at Cooperation Between

Virginia and New York Antifederalists, May 8–Oct. 15, 1788, *DHRC*, 20:1090; The New York Federal Republican Committee Seeks Interstate Cooperation in Obtaining Amendments to the Constitution, May 18–Aug. 6, 1788, ibid., 1097–9; Boyd, *Politics of Opposition*, 126–35; Maier, *Ratification*, 279–81, 311–2; Rutland, *Ordeal of the Constitution*, 141, 209–10. The New York Federal Republican Committee wrote a follow-up letter once it had become clear that the Antifederalists had won an overwhelming victory in the election for delegates to the New York ratifying convention (From the New York Federal Republican Committee, June 6, 1788, *DHRC*, 9:815–6).

The Virginia Antifederalists were very receptive to the New Yorkers' proposal, appointing George Mason as the chair of their coordinating committee and directing him to send to New York a copy of the amendments they intended to propose at the Virginia convention. See Patrick Henry to Lamb, June 9, 1788, *DHRC*, 18:39–40; Mason to Lamb, ibid., 40–5; see also Lamb to George Clinton, June 17, 1788, *DHRC*, 22:1797–8; Clinton to Lamb, June 21, 1788, *DHRC*, 9:824; Robert Yates to Mason, June 21, 1788, ibid., 825. Atherton in New Hampshire and Bloodworth in North Carolina also responded favorably to Lamb's overtures. See Atherton to Lamb, June 11, 14, 1788, *DHRC*, 18:47; Bloodworth to Lamb, July 1, 1788, ibid., 58–9; June 23, 1788, ibid., 53–5. The New Yorkers' organizing efforts simply got started a month or two too late to be successful.

Much earlier in the ratifying process, George Mason and Richard Henry Lee had tried—without success—to coordinate the timing of the state ratifying conventions. Mason told Elbridge Gerry that if "the conventions in the different states could meet upon this important business about the same time," engage in "a regular and cordial communication of sentiments, confining themselves to a few necessary amendments," and "determin[e] to join heartily in the system so amended," then it might be possible, "without danger of public convulsion or confusion, [to] procure a general adoption of the new government" (Oct. 20, 1787, *DHRC*, 8:86; see also Boyd, *Politics of Opposition*, 19–23). For Lee's organizing efforts, see supra pp. 407–8 & n. 32.

For another individual's attempt to coordinate opposition to the Constitution around an alternative proposal, see "Candidus" II, Boston *Independent Chronicle*, Dec. 20, 1787, *DHRC*, 5:493.

For the first of the two preceding footnotes, see William Jackson to John Langdon, June 18, 1788, *DHRC*, 21:1203, 1204 n. 2.

For the second of the two preceding footnotes, see Governor George Clinton to Governor Edmund Randolph, May 8, 1788, *DHRC*, 20:1091 (quotations); An Attempt at Cooperation Between Virginia and New York Antifederalists, May 8–Oct. 15, 1788, ibid., 1089–90; Conway, *Life and Papers of Edmund Randolph*, 110–5; Henry, *Patrick Henry*, 2:363, 377; Rutland, supra, 242; supra pp. 459–60.

487. Richard Harison at New York convention, June 23, 1788, *DHRC*, 22:1802; John Dawson at Virginia convention, June 24, 1788, *DHRC*, 10:1489; Caleb Wallace to William Fleming, June 29, 1788, ibid., 1694–5; Joseph Jones to Madison, Oct. 29, 1787, *PJM* (C.S.), 10:228–9; Washington to Knox, Oct. 15, 1787, *DHRC*, 8:56; Hamilton, Conjectures, *PAH*, 4:275; Labunski, *James Madison*, 63–4; Beeman, *Plain, Honest Men*, 374–5; Boyd, *Politics of Opposition*, 15.

488. "Examiner," *Massachusetts Gazette*, Nov. 9, 1787, *DHRC*, 4:211 ("As objections"); Turner at Massachusetts convention, Feb. 6, 1788, *DHRC*, 6:1471 ("several" and "a constitution"); see also William Symmes, Jr., ibid., 1474; *The Federalist No. 38* (Madison), at 237–8; "Consideration," Boston *Independent Chronicle*, Nov. 15, 1787, *DHRC*, 4:247; "An American," Dec. 6, 1787, ibid., 399; Isaac Stearns to Samuel Adams, Dec. 31, 1787, *DHRC*, 5:558.

For the preceding footnote, see Smith at New York convention, June 20, 1788, *DHRC*, 22:1713; see also Albany Anti-Federal Committee Circular, Apr. 10, 1788, *DHRC*, 21:1382.

489. Joseph Barrell to Nathaniel Barrell, Dec. 20, 1787, *DHRC*, 5:491–2 ("mortification," "one consideration," and "viz: because"); Barrell at Massachusetts convention, Feb. 5, 1788, *DHRC*, 6:1450 ("with all," "excellent," "essentially," and "more difficult"); see also Wilson at Pennsylvania convention, Dec. 11, 1787, *DHRC*, 2:581; James Innes at Virginia convention, June 25, 1788, *DHRC*, 10:1524; "A Pennsylvanian to the New York

Convention," *Pennsylvania Gazette*, June 11, 1788, *DHRC*, 20:1142–3; Nathan Dane to Melancton Smith, July 3, 1788, *DHRC*, 21:1256.

490. Smith at New York convention, June 21, 1788, *DHRC*, 22:1754–5 ("into the contrary"); Dawson at Virginia convention, June 24, 1788, *DHRC*, 10:1491 ("been presented"); see also William Findley at Pennsylvania convention, Dec. 12, 1787, *DHRC*, 2:587; "Candidus" II, Boston *Independent Chronicle*, Dec. 20, 1787, *DHRC*, 5:493–5; Albany Anti-Federal Committee Circular, Apr. 10, 1788, *DHRC*, 21:1383; Lachlan McIntosh to John Wereat, Dec. 17, 1787, *DHRC*, 3:259; Cotton Tufts to Abigail Adams, Dec. 18, 1787, *DHRC*, 5:477–8; *Massachusetts Centinel*, Jan. 12, 1788, ibid., 704; Joseph Jones to Madison, Nov. 22, 1787, *DHRC*, 8:173–4; William Short to William Grayson, Jan. 31, 1788, ibid., 342.

For the preceding footnote, see McIntosh to Wereat, supra, 259–61. McIntosh was primarily concerned that Georgia might wish to continue importing slaves even after the twenty-year prohibition on Congress's banning the foreign slave trade had expired. For a similar proposal involving a sunset provision, see Extract of a letter from a young gentleman in New-York, Philadelphia *Independent Gazetteer*, May 15, 1788, *DHRC*, 20:1097.

Chapter 7

1. Jefferson to Madison, Dec. 20, 1787, *PJM* (C.S.), 10:337 ("[A] bill"); Adams to Jefferson, Nov. 10, 1787, *PTJ* (M.S.), 12:335 ("preceded"); see also Jefferson to Alexander Donald, Feb. 7, 1788, ibid., 571.
2. Ibid.; see also Jefferson to Madison, Feb. 6, 1788, ibid., 569.
3. Jefferson to Edward Carrington, May 27, 1788, ibid., 13:208 ("far preferable"); Jefferson to William Carmichael, June 3, 1788, ibid., 232 ("it is impossible" and "[i]t will be").
4. Madison to Jefferson, Oct. 17, 1788, *PJM* (C.S.), 11:297 (quotations); infra pp. 561–3.
5. Madison to Jefferson, Oct. 17, 1788, *PJM* (C.S.), 11:298–9; infra p. 562.
6. Jefferson to Madison, Mar. 15, 1789, *PJM* (C.S.), 12:13; supra pp. 159–61; see also Jefferson to Madison, Nov. 18, 1788, *PJM* (C.S.), 11:353–4; Rakove, *Original Meanings*, 306, 309, 323–4.
7. Aedanus Burke in the House of Representatives, Aug. 15, 1789, *Annals of Congress*, 1:774 (quotation); see also Labunski, *James Madison*, 212, 226; Banning, *Sacred Fire*, 280; Heideking, *The Constitution Before the Judgment Seat*, 408; Kenneth R. Bowling, "'A Tub to the Whale': The Founding Fathers and Adoption of the Federal Bill of Rights," *Journal of the Early Republic* (Autumn 1988), 8:224.
8. Mason at Philadelphia convention, Sept. 12, 1787, *Farrand*, 2:587 ("give great quiet"); Gerry's motion, seconded by Mason, ibid., 588; Charles Pinckney, Aug. 20, ibid., 341; motion by Pinckney and Gerry to protect liberty of the press, Sept. 14, ibid., 617; ibid., 618 (motion rejected by a vote of seven to four); U.S. Constitution, Art. I, § 9, cl. 2 ("cases" and "the public"); see also Labunski, *James Madison*, 8, 41–2; Maier, *Ratification*, 44. On Mason's drafting of the Virginia Declaration of Rights, see Rutland, *George Mason*, 49–61.
9. Sept. 12, *Farrand*, 2:588 (rejecting, by a vote of ten to zero, Gerry's motion to appoint a committee to prepare a bill of rights); Mason to Jefferson, May 26, 1788, *PTJ* (M.S.), 13:205 ("by the precipitate"); see also Madison to Jefferson, Oct. 24, 1787, *PJM* (C.S.), 10:215; Beeman, *Plain, Honest Men*, 341–2.
10. Mason to Jefferson, May 26, 1788, *PTJ* (M.S.), 13:204 (quotation); Mason, Objections, Sept. 15, *Farrand*, 2:637; Gerry, ibid., 633; Labunski, *James Madison*, 243; Holton, *Unruly Americans*, 253; Rakove, *Original Meanings*, 288; Beeman, *Plain, Honest Men*, 342; Bernard Schwartz, *The Great Rights of Mankind: A History of the American Bill of Rights* (New York, 1977), 113; Bowling, "'A Tub to the Whale,'" 225, 230; Kaminski, "The Constitution Without a Bill of Rights," 19, 23.
11. Wilson at Pennsylvania convention, Nov. 28, 1787, *DHRC*, 2:387 (quotation).
12. Pierce Butler to Weedon Butler, Oct. 8, 1787, *DHRC*, 27:8–9 ("injured"); Rutledge at Philadelphia convention, Aug. 18, 1787, *Farrand*, 2:328 ("the extreme"); Mason, Sept. 12, ibid., 588 ("be prepared"); see also Labunski, *James Madison*, 9; Beeman, *Plain, Honest Men*, 278, 287, 290, 343–4; Schwartz, *The Great Rights of Mankind*, 104; Warren

M. Billings, "'That All Men Are Born Equally Free and Independent': Virginians and the Origins of the Bill of Rights," in Conley and Kaminski, eds., *The Bill of Rights and the States*, 359.

13. Benjamin Rush at Pennsylvania convention, Nov. 30, 1787, *DHRC*, 2:434 (quotation); James Wilson's Speech in the State House Yard (Philadelphia), Oct. 6, 1787, ibid., 167–8.

14. Iredell at North Carolina convention, July 28, 1788, *Elliot*, 4:148–9 ("saying"); "A Landholder" VI, *Connecticut Courant*, Dec. 10, 1787, *DHRC*, 3:490 ("of burial" and "no power"); Wilson at Pennsylvania convention, Dec. 4, 1787, *DHRC*, 2:471; Dec. 1, 1787, ibid., 454–5; see also Nicholas at Virginia convention, June 16, 1788, *DHRC*, 10:1327–8; Charles Cotesworth Pinckney in South Carolina House, Jan. 18, 1788, *DHRC*, 27:158; Labunski, *James Madison*, 9, 104.

15. *The Federalist No. 84* (Hamilton), at 513–4 (quotations); see also Charles Cotesworth Pinckney in South Carolina House, Jan. 18, 1788, *DHRC*, 27:158.

16. James Wilson's Speech in the State House Yard (Philadelphia), Oct. 6, 1787, *DHRC*, 2:167–8; Joseph Bradley Varnum at Massachusetts convention, Jan. 23, 1788, *DHRC*, 6:1315; George Nicholas at Virginia convention, June 16, 1788, *DHRC*, 10:1333; Iredell at North Carolina convention, July 28, 1788, *Elliot*, 4:149.

17. Wilson at Pennsylvania convention, Nov. 28, 1787, *DHRC*, 2:388 (quotations); see also Randolph at Virginia convention, June 9, 1788, *DHRC*, 9:1085; Nicholas, June 16, ibid., 10:1332; *A Citizen of New-York*, *DHRC*, 20:933; *The Federalist No. 84* (Hamilton), at 510; James Jackson in the House of Representatives, June 8, 1789, *Annals of Congress*, 1:460; Labunski, *James Madison*, 199.

    For the preceding footnote, see "Brutus" IX, *New York Journal*, Jan. 17, 1788, *DHRC*, 15:394.

18. Mason at Virginia convention, June 16, 1788, *DHRC*, 10:1328 ("implication"); ibid., 1326; Patrick Henry, ibid., 1328, 1330–1; Grayson, ibid., 1332; Monroe, June 10, ibid., 9:1112; Samuel Spencer at North Carolina convention, July 29, 1788, *Elliot*, 4:152; John Smilie at Pennsylvania convention, Nov. 28, 1787, *DHRC*, 2:391–2; "An Old Whig" II, Philadelphia *Independent Gazetteer*, Oct. 17, 1787, *DHRC*, 8:402–3; "Brutus" II, *New York Journal*, Nov. 1, 1787, *DHRC*, 19:156–8.

19. Henry at Virginia convention, June 16, 1788, *DHRC*, 10:1331 ("if its necessity," "exclude," and "consume"); Grayson, ibid., 1332; Henry, June 17, ibid., 1345–6; Spencer at North Carolina convention, July 28, 1788, *Elliot*, 4:138 ("satisfy"); Robert Whitehill at Pennsylvania convention, Nov. 30, 1787, *DHRC*, 2:398; "Brutus" IX, *New York Journal*, Jan. 17, 1788, *DHRC*, 15:394; Richard Henry Lee to Samuel Adams, Oct. 27, 1787, *DHRC*, 8:485.

    For the preceding footnote, see Jasper Yeates at Pennsylvania convention, Nov. 30, 1787, *DHRC*, 2:435; Randolph at Virginia convention, June 17, 1788, *DHRC*, 10:1348–9.

20. Rush at Pennsylvania convention, Nov. 30, 1787, *DHRC*, 2:434 (quotation); Thomas Hartley, ibid., 430; Wilson, Nov. 28, ibid., 383; *The Federalist No. 84* (Hamilton), at 512–3; "A Landholder" VI, *Connecticut Courant*, Dec. 10, 1787, *DHRC*, 3:490; George Nicholas at Virginia convention, June 16, 1788, *DHRC*, 10:1333; Wood, *Creation of the American Republic*, 539; Rakove, *Original Meanings*, 326.

21. Mason at Virginia convention, June 16, 1788, *DHRC*, 10:1328 ("drawn from," "great," and "the people"); Henry, ibid., 1329 ("arm yourselves"); see also *Plebeian*, *DHRC*, 20:961; Labunski, *James Madison*, 105; Kaminski, "The Constitution Without a Bill of Rights," 33–4.

22. Sherman at Philadelphia convention, Sept. 12, 1787, *Farrand*, 2:588 ("[t]he state"); Mason, ibid.; see also Mason at Virginia convention, June 11, 1788, *DHRC*, 9:1158; "An American Citizen" IV, *On the Federal Government* (Oct. 21, 1787), *DHRC*, 13:434; "Brutus" II, *New York Journal*, Nov. 1, 1787, *DHRC*, 19:158–9; Maier, *Ratification*, 44.

23. Wilson at Pennsylvania convention, Nov. 28, 1787, *DHRC*, 2:391 ("[W]ho will be," "if the enumeration," and "everything not"); Iredell at North Carolina convention, July 28, 1788, *Elliot*, 4:149 ("might operate"); see also Samuel Johnston, ibid., 142; Charles Cotesworth Pinckney in South Carolina House, Jan. 18, 1788, *DHRC*, 27:158; Yeates at Pennsylvania convention, Nov. 30, 1787, *DHRC*, 2:434; Labunski, *James Madison*, 9; Maier, *Ratification*, 79.

24. Madison in the House of Representatives, June 8, 1789, *Annals of Congress*, 1:456 ("one of the most"); U.S. Constitution, amend. IX ("the enumeration").

25. Madison to Jefferson, Oct. 17, 1788, *PJM* (C.S.), 11:297, 299 (quotations); *The Federalist No. 51* (Madison), at 320–5; see also Alexander White, "To the Citizens of Virginia," *Winchester Gazette* [Virginia], Feb. 29, 1788, *DHRC*, 8:438; Wilson at Pennsylvania convention, Dec. 7, 1787, *DHRC*, 2:521; Richard Morris at New York convention, July 11, 1788, *DHRC*, 22:2135; Extract of a letter from William Pierce to St. George Tucker (Sept. 28, 1787), *Gazette of the State of Georgia*, Mar. 20, 1788, *DHRC*, 16:444; Labunski, *James Madison*, 160–1; Rakove, *Original Meanings*, 332.

26. "A Countryman" II (Sherman), *New Haven Gazette*, Nov. 22, 1787, *DHRC*, 3:472 ("parchment," "not worth," and "rulers"); *The Federalist No. 84* (Hamilton), at 514–5 ("the only solid," "public opinion," and "the general"); Rush at Pennsylvania Convention, Nov. 30, 1787, *DHRC*, 2:433–4 ("that this government"); see also Randolph at Virginia convention, June 17, 1788, *DHRC*, 10:1351–2; "America: To the Dissenting Members of the Late Convention of Pennsylvania" (Noah Webster), New York *Daily Advertiser*, Dec. 31, 1787, *DHRC*, 19:486; Rush to David Ramsay, Charleston *Columbian Herald*, Apr. 14, 1788, *DHRC*, 17:96. On the attainder example noted in the text, see George Nicholas at Virginia convention, June 16, 1788, *DHRC*, 10:1333; Randolph, June 6, ibid., 9:972. Antifederalists contested the accuracy of the Federalists' charge with regard to the attainder example. See Patrick Henry, June 7, ibid., 1038; Benjamin Harrison, June 10, ibid., 1127; see also editorial note, ibid., 1004 n. 5.

27. Jefferson to Madison, Mar. 15, 1789, *PJM* (C.S.), 12:14 ("[h]alf a loaf" and "absolutely"); Findley at Pennsylvania Convention, Nov. 30, 1787, *DHRC*, 2:439 ("because all").

28. Pinckney in South Carolina House, Jan. 18, 1788, *DHRC*, 27:158; Weir, "South Carolina," 222; see also Extract of a letter from William Pierce to St. George Tucker (Sept. 28, 1787), *Gazette of the State of Georgia*, Mar. 20, 1788, *DHRC*, 16:443.

29. Supra pp. 429, 530; Gillespie, "Massachusetts," 149.

30. Carrington to Madison, Feb. 10, 1788, *PJM* (C.S.), 10:494 ("even once"); Nicholas to Madison, Apr. 5, 1788, ibid., 11:9 ("industriously," "real sentiments," "only of," and "to particular"); Madison to Randolph, Jan. 10, 1788, ibid., 10:355 ("driving" and "not farther"); Apr. 10, 1788, ibid., 11:19 ("those who"); see also Madison to Jefferson, Apr. 22, 1788, ibid., 28.

31. Supra pp. 438–42.

32. Abraham Clark to Thomas Sinnickson, July 23, 1788, *DHRC*, 18:276 (quotation); see also Madison to Richard Peters, Aug. 19, 1789, *PJM* (C.S.), 12:347; Randolph to Madison, c. Oct. 29, 1787, *DHRC*, 8:133; Editors' Note, New York and the Massachusetts Convention's Amendments to the Constitution, Feb. 6, 1788, *DHRC*, 20:753; Maier, *Ratification*, 187, 192–3, 196–7, 251, 300, 398; Yarbrough, "New Hampshire," 237; Labunski, *James Madison*, 49–50, 103; supra pp. 452, 457–8, 479–80, 516, 529.

33. Supra pp. 475–8, 494–508, 513–4; Maier, *Ratification*, 193, 202, 294–305, 379–82, 385–93, 395–7, 421–3; Yarbrough, "New Hampshire," 251.

34. Maier, *Ratification*, 197, 307–9, 397; see also Proposed amendments, New York convention, July 26, 1788, *DHRC*, 23:2326–34; Proposed amendments, Virginia convention, June 27, 1788, *DHRC*, 10:1551–7.

35. Labunski, *James Madison*, 2; Rakove, *Original Meanings*, 330; Bowling, "'A Tub to the Whale,'" 224.

36. Henry at Virginia convention, June 25, 1788, *DHRC*, 10:1537 ("a peaceable" and "remove"); Spencer Roane to William Wirt, undated, quoted in Henry, *Patrick Henry*, 2:518 ("prejudice" and "astonished"); Burgess Ball to Madison, Dec. 8, 1788, *PJM* (C.S.), 11:385 ("disposed"); see also Madison to Hamilton, June 27, 1788, ibid., 182; William Nelson, Jr., to William Short, July 12, 1788, *DHRC*, 10:1701; Maier, *Ratification*, 304–5; Labunski, *James Madison*, 120, 123.

37. Madison to Jefferson, Dec. 8, 1788, *PJM* (C.S.), 11:384 ("omnipotent"); Washington to Madison, Nov. 17, 1788, ibid., 351 ("edicts" and "with less"); see also Henry Lee to Madison, Nov. 19, 1788, ibid., 357; James Duncanson to James Maury, Feb. 17, 1789, *DHFFE*, 2:404;

Tobias Lee to John Langdon, Jan. 31, 1789, ibid., 398. On the Antifederalists' legislative majority, see editorial note, ibid., 257.

38. Carrington to Madison, Oct. 19, 1788, *PJM* (C.S.), 11:305 ("anti-federalism" and "great circumspection"); Madison to Randolph, Nov. 2, 1788, ibid., 329 ("enmity," "the secret," and "certain"); see also Carrington to Madison, Oct. 24, 1788, ibid., 315; Labunski, *James Madison*, 120, 122.

39. Henry to Lee, Nov. 15, 1788, in Henry, *Patrick Henry*, 2:429–30 (quotations); see also Henry at Virginia convention, June 25, 1788, *DHRC*, 10:1535. The Confederation Congress had commenced deliberations on an ordinance setting up the new national government as soon as word that New Hampshire had become the ninth state to ratify the Constitution reached New York City in late June 1788. However, deep sectional disagreement over whether New York City should be the federal Congress's temporary residence prevented the Confederation Congress from agreeing until mid-September on the place where the new national government would convene early in 1789. For descriptions of these deliberations, see Madison to Washington, Sept. 14, 1788, *PJM* (C.S.), 11:254; Madison to Randolph, Sept. 14, 1788, ibid., 252–3; Madison to Jefferson, Aug. 10, 1788, ibid., 226; Richard Platt to Winthrop Sargent, Aug. 8, 1788, *DHRC*, 21:1351; *DHFFE*, 1:11–143; see also Bowling, *The Creation of Washington, D.C.*, 80, 87–96; Editors' Note, Confederation Congress Makes Provision to Put the New Government Under the Constitution into Operation, 2 July–13 Sept. 1788, *DHRC*, 21:1250–3; Maier, *Ratification*, 429–30.

40. Lee to Washington, Oct. 29, 1788, *PGW* (P.S.), 1:82 ("oppose," "as soon," and "a direct"); Turberville to Madison, Nov. 13, 1788, *PJM* (C.S.), 11:344 ("launched" and "brought"); see also Randolph to Madison, Oct. 23, 1788, ibid., 313; Carrington to Madison, Oct. 24, 1788, ibid., 315; James Duncanson to James Maury, Feb. 17, 1789, *DHFFE*, 2:405.

41. Carrington to Madison, Oct. 19, 1788, *PJM* (C.S.), 11:305–6 ("alarmed," "decided opinion," and "very well"); Henry Lee to Madison, Nov. 19, 1788, ibid., 356 ("exerted" and "strong"); Randolph to Madison, Oct. 23, 1788, ibid., 314; see also Joseph Jones to Madison, Oct. 20, 1788, ibid., 308; Banning, *Sacred Fire*, 269.

42. Patrick Henry to Richard Henry Lee, Nov. 15, 1788, in Henry, *Patrick Henry*, 2:429 ("to no purpose"); Charles Lee to Washington, Oct. 29, 1788, *PGW* (P.S.), 1:83 ("no person"); Henry Lee to Madison, Nov. 19, 1788, *PJM* (C.S.), 11:356–7 ("exclaimed against," "election," "an advocate," and "misunderstanding"); see also George Lee Turberville to Madison, Nov. 16, 1788, ibid., 346–7; Randolph to Madison, Nov. 10, 1788, ibid., 338–9; Madison to Jefferson, Dec. 8, 1788, ibid., 384; Labunski, *James Madison*, 136.

43. Henry Lee to Madison, Nov. 19, 1788, *PJM* (C.S.), 11:356 ("declarations"); Patrick Henry to Richard Henry Lee, Nov. 15, 1788, in Henry, *Patrick Henry*, 2:429 ("much displeased" and "urged"); Madison to Randolph, Nov. 23, 1788, *PJM* (C.S.), 11:362 ("present temper"); Washington to Benjamin Lincoln, Nov. 14, 1788, *PGW* (P.S.), 1:108 ("exceedingly mortified"); see also Randolph to Madison, Nov. 10, 1788, *PJM* (C.S.), 11:339.

44. Henry Lee to Madison, Nov. 19, 1788, ibid., 357 ("every measure"); Turberville to Madison, Nov. 10, 1788, ibid., 340 (other quotations); Virginia Legislature Application to Congress, Nov. 20, 1788, *DHRC*, 10:1765–6; Virginia Legislature to the State Executives, Nov. 20, 1788, ibid., 1767–8; see also Carrington to Madison, Nov. 9, 1788, *PJM* (C.S.), 11:336; James Duncanson to James Maury, Feb. 17, 1789, *DHFFE*, 2:405; editorial note, ibid., 273–4.

45. Madison to Randolph, Nov. 2, 1788, *PJM* (C.S.), 11:329 ("to afford" and "into quiet"); Nov. 23, 1788, ibid., 362 ("the real" and "be equally"); Oct. 17, 1788, ibid., 304–5 ("only be" and "the arrangements").

46. Turberville to Madison, Nov. 13, 1788, ibid., 343 ("to bend"); Carrington to Madison, Nov. 14, 1788, ibid., 345 ("the Antis").

47. Madison to Jefferson, Dec. 8, 1788, ibid., 384 ("pains" and "most devoted"); Mason to John Mason, Dec. 18, 1788, *PGM*, 3:1136; Burgess Ball to Madison, Dec. 8, 1788, *PJM* (C.S.), 11:385 ("extremely doubtful"); see also Randolph to Madison, Nov. 10, 1788, ibid., 339; Henry Lee to Madison, Nov. 19, 1788, ibid., 357; James Duncanson to James Maury, Feb. 17, 1789, *DHFFE*, 2:405; Labunski, *James Madison*, 139–40, 148–51.

48. Turberville to Madison, Nov. 13, 1788, *PJM* (C.S.), 11:344 ("with no" and "some favored"); Madison to Randolph, Nov. 23, 1788, ibid., 363 ("misinterpretation"); Carrington to Madison, Nov. 14, 1788, ibid., 345.

For the preceding footnote, see U.S. Constitution, Art. I, § 2, cl. 2; Carrington to Madison, Dec. 2, 1788, *PJM* (C.S.), 11:378–9; editorial note, ibid., 379 n. 2; Labunski, *James Madison*, 141.

49. Labunski, *James Madison*, 143–4, 152, 154. On Monroe's criticisms of the Constitution, see James Monroe, Some Observations on the Constitution, c. May 25, 1788, *DHRC*, 9:846–76; see also Monroe at Virginia convention, June 10, 1788, ibid., 1109–15; June 23, ibid., 10:1469; June 25, ibid., 1518–9.

50. Monroe to Jefferson, July 27, 1787, *PTJ* (M.S.), 11:631 (quotations); Labunski, *James Madison*, 153. On their joint land speculation, see Madison to Monroe, Mar. 14, 1786, *PJM* (C.S.), 8:497; Mar. 19, 1786, ibid., 505, 506 n. 2; see also Aug. 11, 1786, ibid., 9:90.

For the preceding footnote, see Monroe to Jefferson, July 27, 1787, *PTJ* (M.S.), 11:631.

51. Madison to Randolph, Nov. 23, 1788, *PJM* (C.S.), 11:363 (quotations); see also Madison to Jefferson, Dec. 8, 1788, ibid., 384. Bilder suggests that the project to which Madison referred may have been completing the revisions of his notes from the Philadelphia convention (*Madison's Hand*, 171).

52. Madison to Randolph, Mar. 1, 1789, *PJM* (C.S.), 11:453 ("pressing"); Nov. 23, 1788, ibid., 363 ("to counteract"); Ball to Madison, Dec. 8, 1788, ibid., 385 ("must take," "immediately," and "that *Great Man*") (emphasis in original); Carrington to Madison, Nov. 14, 1788, ibid., 346 ("come into"); see also Nov. 26, 1788, ibid., 369; Nicholas to Madison, Jan. 2, 1789, ibid., 406.

53. Madison to Jefferson, Oct. 17, 1788, ibid., 297 (quotations); infra pp. 572–5.

54. Madison to Jefferson, Oct. 17, 1788, *PJM* (C.S.), 11:297 (quotations); see also supra pp. 391–2.

55. Madison to Jefferson, Oct. 17, 1788, *PJM* (C.S.), 11:298; see also Rakove, *Original Meanings*, 313–4.

56. Madison to Jefferson, Oct. 17, 1788, *PJM* (C.S.), 11:297–8 ("experience," "Repeated," and "violated"); Madison at Virginia convention, June 12, 1788, *DHRC*, 10:1223 ("a bill of rights," "from that multiplicity," and "there is").

57. Madison to Jefferson, Oct. 17, 1788, *PJM* (C.S.), 11:297.

58. Ibid., 298–9. Madison was being disingenuous when he told Jefferson that he had always favored a bill of rights. At a minimum, Madison had voted against Mason's proposal for one at the Philadelphia convention, and at the Virginia ratifying convention, he had pronounced a declaration of rights both "unnecessary and dangerous" (June 24, 1788, *DHRC*, 10:1507; see Banning, *Sacred Fire*, 281).

59. Madison to Jefferson, Oct. 17, 1788, *PJM* (C.S.), 11:299.

60. Ibid., 297; Dec. 8, 1788, ibid., 382 (quotations).

61. Ibid., 382–3 (quotations); see also Dec. 12, 1788, ibid., 390; Madison to Pendleton, Oct. 20, 1788, ibid., 306.

62. Henry to Lee, Nov. 15, 1788, in Henry, *Patrick Henry*, 2:429–30.

63. Ball to Madison, Dec. 8, 1788, *PJM* (C.S.), 11:386 ("Baptist"); Jameson to Madison, Jan. 14, 1789, ibid., 419 (other quotations); see also Benjamin Johnson to Madison, Jan. 19, 1789, ibid., 423–4.

64. Nicholas to Madison, Jan. 2, 1789, ibid., 406–7 (quotations); see also Labunski, *James Madison*, 156–9.

65. Madison to Washington, Jan. 14, 1789, *PJM* (C.S.), 11:418 (quotations); see also Benjamin Johnson to Madison, Jan. 19, 1789, ibid., 423–4.

66. Madison to Washington, Jan. 14, 1789, ibid., 418 (quotation); see also Labunski, *James Madison*, 155–6, 163–72; Banning, *Sacred Fire*, 271–3; Maier, *Ratification*, 441–3; Bowling, "'A Tub to the Whale,'" 232–3. For the frostbite anecdote, see Observations by Mr. Madison (Montpelier, Virginia), Dec. 8, 1827, in Henry S. Randall, *The Life of Thomas Jefferson* (New York, 1858), 3:255 n. 2.

67. Madison to Thomas Mann Randolph, Jan. 13, 1789, *PJM* (C.S.), 11:415–6 (all quotations except "those serious"); Madison to George Eve, Jan. 2, 1789, ibid., 404 ("those serious").

For the preceding footnote, see Madison to Jefferson, Mar. 29, 1789, ibid., 12:37 ("between"); Observations by Mr. Madison (Montpelier, Virginia), Dec. 8, 1827, quoted in Randall, *Life of Thomas Jefferson*, 3:255 n. 2 ("there never" and "days").

68. Madison to a resident of Spotsylvania County, Jan. 27, 1789, *PJM* (C.S.), 11:428 ("as opening"); Madison to George Eve, Jan. 2, 1789, ibid., 404 ("if pursued"); Madison to Thomas Mann Randolph, Jan. 13, 1789, ibid., 416 ("by the strongest"); Madison to George Thompson, Jan. 29, 1789, ibid., 433–7. By repudiating the amendment requiring Congress to requisition states before levying direct taxes itself, Madison was violating the instruction from his state's ratifying convention that all of Virginia's congressional representatives "exert all their influence" to secure the enactment of all the amendments proposed by the convention (Proceedings of Virginia convention, June 27, 1788, *DHRC*, 10:1056).

69. Madison to Thomas Mann Randolph, Jan. 13, 1789, *PJM* (C.S.), 11:417 ("expeditious" and "certain"); Madison to George Eve, Jan. 2, 1789, ibid., 405 ("the safest," "probably be careful," and "meeting"); see also Madison to a resident of Spotsylvania County, Jan. 27, 1789, ibid., 429.

70. Madison to Eve, Jan. 2, 1789, ibid., 404–5.

71. Banning, *Sacred Fire*, 84–6, 90–7, 271–2; Labunski, *James Madison*, 159, 162–3. For an anonymous reminder to district voters during the congressional campaign of Madison's past service to the cause of religious liberty, see *Virginia Herald* (Fredericksburg), Jan. 15, 1789, *DHFFE*, 2:336–7; see also Benjamin Johnson to Madison, Jan. 19, 1789, *PJM* (C.S.), 11:424; From John Leland, c. Feb. 15, 1788, ibid., 442.

72. Carrington to Madison, Feb. 16, 1789, ibid., 445 ("personal attendance" and "an extensive"); Madison to Randolph, Mar. 1, 1789, ibid., 453 ("to repel"); Nicholas to Madison, Jan. 2, 1789, ibid., 407 ("an expression"); Maier, *Ratification*, 443; Labunski, *James Madison*, 174–5; Banning, *Sacred Fire*, 273. For Madison's own doubts during the campaign as to the likely outcome of the contest, see Madison to Washington, Jan. 14, 1789, *PJM* (C.S.), 11:418.

73. Thomas B. Wait to George Thatcher, Feb. 29, 1788, *DHRC*, 16:264.

74. Lear to Washington, June 22, 1788, *PGW* (C.S.), 6:350 ("were drawn"); Smith to Gilbert Livingston, Jan. 1, 1789, *DHRC*, 23:2497 ("The fair"); Monroe at Virginia convention, June 25, 1788, *DHRC*, 10:1518–9 ("Adopt it"); see also Nathan Dane to Samuel Adams, May 10, 1788, *DHRC*, 20:1093; Maier, *Ratification*, 309, 317; Yarbrough, "New Hampshire," 253; Kaminski, "The Constitution Without a Bill of Rights," 44. For a contrary prediction by a Massachusetts Antifederalist, see Samuel Osgood to Melancton Smith and Samuel Jones, July 11, 1788, *DHRC*, 21:1309.

75. Washington to McHenry, July 31, 1788, *PGW* (C.S.), 6:409–10 (quotations); see also Washington to Madison, Sept. 23, 1788, ibid., 534; Thomas Hartley to Tench Coxe, Oct. 6, 1788, *DHFFE*, 1:304.

    For the preceding footnote, see Hamilton to Washington, Sept. 1788, *PGW* (P.S.), 1:23 (quotation); see also Aug. 13, 1788, ibid. (C.S.), 6:444; Henry Lee to Washington, Sept. 13, 1788, ibid., 510–2; Benjamin Lincoln to Washington, Sept. 24, 1788, ibid. (P.S.), 1:6.

76. "Centinel" XX, Philadelphia *Independent Gazetteer*, Oct. 23, 1788, *DHFFE*, 1:320 ("last" and "to preserve"); "A Freeman to the Citizens of Pennsylvania," *Federal Gazette*, Oct. 6, 1788, ibid., 305 ("to creep," "clog," "in name," and "in practice"). On the importance of the Bill of Rights as a campaign issue in the first federal elections, see General Introduction, ibid., x; Introduction, ibid., 233; editorial note, ibid., 547. On the importance of state legislative elections in the fall of 1788 to putting the new national government into operation, see, e.g., Robert Smith to Tench Coxe, July 31, 1788, ibid., 2:109; Samuel Miles et al. to Timothy Pickering, Sept. 11, 1788, ibid., 1:270–1. For additional Antifederalist appeals to voters to support candidates who would work for amendments, see "Centinel" XIX, Philadelphia *Independent Gazetteer*, Oct. 7, 1788, ibid., 307; "Solon," Boston *Independent Chronicle*, Aug. 28, 1788, ibid., 454–5; "E on the Need for Amendments," *Boston Gazette*, Dec. 8, 1788, ibid., 548. On Federalist appeals to voters to elect Federalist candidates, who could be trusted to put the new system into operation and guard against improper amendments, see, e.g., "Federalism," Baltimore *Maryland Journal*, Sept. 26, 1788, ibid., 2:118–9; "A Marylander," Baltimore *Maryland Gazette*, Sept. 12, 1788, ibid.,

145; "An Inhabitant," Baltimore *Maryland Journal*, Dec. 26, 1788, ibid., 162–3; "Civis," Jan. 6, 1789, ibid., 186–7; "A Federal Centinel," *Pennsylvania Gazette*, Sept. 10, 1788, ibid., 1:269; "A Word to the Wise: To the Electors of Pennsylvania," *Pennsylvania Mercury*, Sept. 13, 1788, ibid., 273; "Cassius," *Federal Gazette*, Oct. 9, 1788, ibid., 311; James Wilson's Report of the Proceedings of the Lancaster Conference, Nov. 25, 1788, ibid., 326; "Steady," *Massachusetts Centinel*, Sept. 3, 1788, ibid., 457–8; "Constitution," Oct. 1, 1788, ibid., 464.

77. Boyd, *Politics of Opposition*, 88–9, 140–2, 144, 149–55; Heideking, *The Constitution Before the Judgment Seat*, 395–402; Veit et al., eds., *Bill of Rights*, xii; Maier, *Ratification*, 433. On the importance of at-large elections to the Federalists' success in the congressional races in Maryland (with six House seats), Pennsylvania (with eight), and New Hampshire (with three), see editorial note, *DHFFE*, 2:123; ibid., 158; "A.B.," Baltimore *Maryland Journal*, Feb. 13, 1789, ibid., 216; see also General Introduction, ibid., 1:x; Introduction, ibid., 770. New Jersey also used at-large elections for its congressional seats (ibid., 3:13 n. 1). In Pennsylvania, Federalists in control of the state legislature, fearful of losing their majority in state elections in October 1788, rushed through before the end of the legislative term a law providing for at-large election of congressmen. See Introduction, ibid., 1:231–2; Thomas FitzSimons to Samuel Meredith, Aug. 20, 1788, ibid., 253. For examples of Federalist candidates' supporting amendments, see William Tilghman to Tench Coxe, Jan. 2, 1789, ibid., 2:180; Francis Corbin to electors, *Virginia Independent Chronicle*, Jan. 21, 1789, ibid., 353–4; supra pp. 565–6; see also "Civis," *Pennsylvania Packet*, Sept. 19, 1788, *DHFFE*, 1:276. In Massachusetts, Federalists benefited from substantial malapportionment of the congressional districts. See Introduction, ibid., 438; editorial note, ibid., 476–7.

78. Madison to Randolph, Mar. 1, 1789, *PJM* (C.S.), 11:453 ("share in"); Madison to Jefferson, Mar. 29, 1789, ibid., 12:38 ("some conciliatory"); Lee to Leven Powell, Mar. 29, 1789, in Veit et al., eds., *Bill of Rights*, 225 ("little doubt"); Henry to Grayson, Mar. 31, 1789, ibid., 226 ("our highest toned").

79. Baldwin to Joel Barlow, Mar. 1, 1789, ibid., 217 ("[t]he advocates"); Wingate to Timothy Pickering, Mar. 25, 1789, ibid., 223 ("[p]ossibly," "that may quiet," and "rather inclined"). In the Massachusetts congressional election campaigns in the fall of 1788, some Federalists had run explicitly in opposition to amendments, at least until the new system had been given a fair trial. See, e.g., *Massachusetts Centinel*, Sept. 6, 1788, *DHFFE*, 1:458; supra pp. 567–8 & n. 76.

80. Madison to Pendleton, Apr. 8, 1789, in Veit et al., eds., *Bill of Rights*, 229 ("entirely" and "no great"); Madison to Randolph, Apr. 12, 1789, ibid., 230 ("the concurrence").

81. Coxe to George Thatcher, Mar. 12, 1789, ibid., 217–8 ("[i]f due attention" and "[s]ome declarations"); Coxe to Madison, June 18, 1789, ibid., 252 ("greatly tend," "who are not honest," and "stripped"); Lee to Leven Powell, Mar. 29, 1789, ibid., 225 ("conciliate" and "almost unanimous").

82. "A Citizen of New Haven" (Sherman), *New York Packet*, Mar. 24, 1789, ibid., 222 ("not be best") (hereinafter, "A Citizen of New Haven"); Ellery to Benjamin Huntington, Apr. 25, 1789, ibid., 232 ("perhaps it would"); Stiles to William Samuel Johnson, Apr. 3, 1789, ibid., 228 ("good" and "not until"); see also Richard Peters to Madison, July 5, 1789, ibid., 259.

83. Morris to Richard Peters, Aug. 24, 1789, ibid., 288 ("waste"); Izard to Jefferson, Apr. 3, 1789, ibid., 227 ("go to work" and "idle discussions"); Baldwin to Joel Barlow, June 14, 1789, ibid., 250 ("too busy").

84. "Pacificus" (Webster) to Madison (Aug. 14), New York *Daily Advertiser*, Aug. 17, 1789, ibid., 276 [hereinafter, "Pacificus"] ("disposed" and "revive"); Fenno to Joseph Ward, July 5, 1789, ibid., 259 ("[e]very movement"); Ellery to Huntington, Apr. 25, 1789, ibid., 232 ("some degree").

85. "A Citizen of New Haven" (Sherman), ibid., 222 ("the foundation" and detrimental"); Ellery to Huntington, Aug. 24, 1789, ibid., 287 ("expectations" and "unsettle"); Sedgwick to Pamela Sedgwick, Aug. 20, 1789, ibid., 283 ("a frivolity"). Indeed, Madison had made a similar argument against frequent constitutional change in *The Federalist* (*No. 49*, at 314–5).

86. Baldwin to Barlow, June 14, 1789, in Veit et al., eds., *Bill of Rights*, 250 ("[t]here is no"); Peters to Madison, July 5, 1789, ibid., 259 ("throw[ing]" and "afraid"); Wolcott to Oliver Ellsworth, June 27, 1789, ibid., 255 ("[t]o bind"); Belknap to Paine Wingate, May 29, 1789, ibid., 241 ("Should a man").
    For the preceding footnote, see Bowling, "'A Tub to the Whale,'" 223.
87. Ellery to Huntington, Apr. 25, 1789, in Veit et al., eds., *Bill of Rights*, 232.
88. Lee to Adams, Apr. 25, 1789, ibid., 233 ("deception" and "[d]eceit"); Burke to Richard Hampton, May 10, 1789, ibid., 238 ("high flying," "abound," and "[t]he wealthy"); see also Grayson to Patrick Henry, June 12, 1789, ibid., 248–9.
89. Washington to Madison, May 31, 1789, ibid., 242 ("not very essential"); Washington Inaugural Address, Apr. 30, 1789, *PJM* (C.S.), 12:123 ("the characteristic rights" and "endanger"); *Journal of the House of Representatives*, May 5, 1789, 1:27 ("receive"); Washington to Madison, May 5, 1789, *PJM* (C.S.), 12:131–2; Editorial Note, Address of the President to Congress, ibid., 120–1; Labunski, *James Madison*, 188–9; Maier, *Ratification*, 439–40; Banning, *Sacred Fire*, 274–5.
90. Madison to Jefferson, May 27, 1789, in Veit et al., *Bill of Rights*, 240 (quotation); see also ibid., 5.
91. Madison in the House, June 8, 1789, *Annals of Congress*, 1:448–9 (quotations); see also Alexander White, ibid., 445; Madison, Aug. 13, ibid., 733–4; Frederick A. Muhlenberg to Benjamin Rush, Aug. 18, 1789, in Veit et al., eds., *Bill of Rights*, 280.
92. Madison in the House, June 8, 1789, *Annals of Congress*, 1:449 (quotations); see also Elbridge Gerry, ibid., 463; Labunski, *James Madison*, 202, 210–2.
93. Dawson to Madison, June 28, 1789, *PJM* (C.S.), 12:264 ("which have," "materially affect," and "more secure"); Stuart to Madison, July 31, 1789, in Veit et al., eds., *Bill of Rights*, 270 ("party spirit").
94. Davie to Madison, June 10, 1789, *PJM* (C.S.), 12:210–1 (quotations); see also Davie to James Iredell, June 4, 1789, in McRee, *James Iredell*, 2:260.
95. Hawkins to Madison, June 1, 1789, in Veit et al., eds., *Bill of Rights*, 243 ("the friends," "possessed," and "motion"); July 3, 1789, ibid., 258 ("avail"). Rhode Island Federalist William Ellery believed that Congress's approval of amendments would provide Antifederalists in his state with a graceful means of abandoning their resistance to ratification (to Benjamin Huntington, Mar. 10, 1789, *DHRC*, 25:470–1; to William Duer, May 21, 1789, ibid., 510).
96. Madison in the House, June 8, 1789, *Annals of Congress*, 1:449–50.
97. Ibid., 455, 457 (quotations); see also Rakove, *Original Meanings*, 335; Rutland, *Bill of Rights*, 202; Banning, *Sacred Fire*, 493 n. 95.
98. Madison in the House, June 8, *Annals of Congress*, 1:455–6 (quotations); see also Madison, Aug. 15, ibid., 758.
99. Madison, June 8, ibid., 456, 459.
100. Page, ibid., 446 ("who dread"); Aug. 13, ibid., 734 ("in confidence" and "complain"); see also Gerry, June 8, ibid., 462; Labunski, *James Madison*, 205–7.
101. Maier, *Ratification*, 455–6; Heideking, *The Constitution Before the Judgment Seat*, 407–8; Boyd, *Politics of Opposition*, 134. On the demise of the movement for a second convention, see Heideking, supra, 392–3. On the state legislatures that had indicated no support for the New York circular letter supporting a second convention, see Jeremiah Wadsworth to Knox, Nov. 2, 1788, *DHFFE*, 2:27 (Connecticut); Thomas Mifflin to Wadsworth, Oct. 5, 1788, ibid., 1:295 (Pennsylvania).
102. Morris to Francis Hopkinson, Aug. 15, 1789, in Veit et al., eds., *Bill of Rights*, 278 ("poor Madison"); Fenno to Joseph Ward, July 5, 1789, ibid., 258–9 ("a very unpropitious," "universally acknowledged," and "a mixture"); Sedgwick to Benjamin Lincoln, July 19, 1789, ibid., 263–4 ("fair," "ardently wishes," "constantly haunted," and "that strength"); "Pacificus" (Webster), ibid., 276 ("amendments"); see also Robert Morris to Peters, Aug. 24, 1789, ibid., 288; Ellery to Huntington, Aug. 24, 1789, ibid., 287.
103. Jackson, June 8, *Annals of Congress*, 1:442–3 ("without revenue"); Vining, ibid., 447 ("quiet"); Sherman, ibid., 445 ("imprudent"); Burke, ibid., 443 ("immediately"); see also Smith, ibid., 441; Jackson, July 21, ibid., 687; Sedgwick, Aug. 13, ibid., 731; Smith,

ibid., 732; Thomas Hartley, ibid.; Gerry, ibid.; Frederick A. Muhlenberg to Rush, Aug. 18, 1789, in Veit et al., eds., *Bill of Rights*, 280; Maier, *Ratification*, 446; Labunski, *James Madison*, 194–6; Rutland, *Bill of Rights*, 200–1.

104. *Gazette of the United States*, June 10, 1789 (reporting Sherman speech of June 8), in Veit et al., eds., *Bill of Rights*, 65 ("the necessity"); Laurance, Aug. 13, *Annals of Congress*, 1:733 ("incur" and "more anxious"); Jackson, June 8, ibid., 442, 461 ("like to stand," "a vessel," and "she sails" at p. 442; "revolution" at p. 461); see also Vining, ibid., 447; Smith, ibid., 441; Labunski, *James Madison*, 194–5, 204.

105. *Gazette of the United States*, June 10, 1789 (reporting Sherman speech of June 8), in Veit et al., eds., *Bill of Rights*, 65 ("taking up"); Smith, June 8, *Annals of Congress*, 1:445–6 ("had done," "with ability," "was not to blame," and "important"); Grayson to Patrick Henry, June 12, 1789, in Veit et al., eds., *Bill of Rights*, 247 ("was so embarrassed" and "more owing"); see also Jackson, June 8, *Annals of Congress*, 1:462; Labunski, *James Madison*, 195, 210.

106. Madison to Samuel Johnston, June 21, 1789, in Veit et al., eds., *Bill of Rights*, 253; Benjamin Goodhue to Cotton Tufts, July 20, 1789, ibid., 264.

107. Madison, June 8, *Annals of Congress*, 1:444, 448 (quotations); see also Page, ibid., 446; Madison, Aug. 13, ibid., 731; Labunski, *James Madison*, 191–2, 207, 213–4.

108. See, e.g., Proposed amendments, Massachusetts convention, Feb. 6, 1788, *DHRC*, 6:1469–70; Proposed amendments, New York convention, July 26, 1788, *DHRC*, 23:2326–34; Proposed amendments, Virginia convention, June 27, 1788, *DHRC*, 10:1551–7; see also Veit et al., eds., *Bill of Rights*, 14–28. The structural proposals are canvassed in Heideking, *The Constitution Before the Judgment Seat*, 382–5; Bowling, "'A Tub to the Whale,'" 228–30.

109. Madison to Randolph, June 15, 1789, *PJM* (C.S.), 12:219 ("The structure" and "as little"); Chase to Richard Henry Lee, May 16, 1789, in Veit et al., eds., *Bill of Rights*, 240 ("one of" and "that no check"); Lee to Henry, May 28, 1789, *LRHL*, 2:487 ("not similar"); see also Labunski, *James Madison*, 209.

110. Clymer to Peters, June 8, 1789, in Veit et al., eds., *Bill of Rights*, 245 ("be so far" and "he means"); Clymer to Tench Coxe, June 28, 1789, ibid., 255 ("[l]ike a sensible," "bread pills," and "malades"); Ames to Thomas Dwight, June 11, 1789, ibid., 247 ("may do good").

111. Madison, June 8, *Annals of Congress*, 1:450 (all quotations but the last); Vining, ibid., 467 ("the principles"); see also Madison, Aug. 21, ibid., 800.

112. Randolph to Madison, Aug. 18, 1789, in Veit et al., eds., *Bill of Rights*, 281 ("great desideratum"); Washington to Jefferson, Aug. 31, 1788, *PGW* (C.S.), 6:493 ("that which goes" and "most strenuously"); see also Madison to Jefferson, Aug. 23, 1788, *PJM* (C.S.), 11:238; Miles King to Madison, Mar. 3, 1789, *DHFFE*, 2:407; Banning, *Sacred Fire*, 496 n. 122; Donald S. Lutz, "The States and the U.S. Bill of Rights," *Southern Illinois University Law Journal* (Winter 1992), 16:257–8.

113. Madison, Aug. 15, *Annals of Congress*, 1:775 ("a friend" and "those most"); Burke, ibid.; Madison, June 8, ibid., 450 ("some respectable" and "the great mass"); see also Madison, Aug. 21, ibid., 798; Madison to Randolph, June 15, 1789, in Veit et al., eds., *Bill of Rights*, 250–1; Labunski, *James Madison*, 226–7.

114. Burke's proposed amendment, Aug. 17, *Annals of Congress*, 1:780; Thomas Tudor Tucker, Aug. 15, ibid., 760; Madison, ibid., 766–7.

115. Madison's proposed amendment No. 8, June 8, *Annals of Congress*, 1:453 ("shall never"); Sherman, Aug. 18, ibid., 789 ("altogether"); Madison, ibid. ("the people").

116. Madison's proposed amendments Nos. 2, 3, and 6, June 8, *Annals of Congress*, 1:451; House Committee Report, amends. 2, 3, and 13, July 28, in Veit et al., eds., *Bill of Rights*, 29–32; House Resolution and Articles of Amendment, Aug. 24, Arts. 1, 2, and 11, ibid., 37–40; Madison, Aug. 14, *Annals of Congress*, 1:757 ("absolutely" and "it was desired"); Aug. 17, ibid., 784; see also Maier, *Ratification*, 447–50; Labunski, *James Madison*, 221–3. At the Philadelphia convention, Madison had favored doubling the size of the House (July 10, 1787, *Farrand*, 1:568).

117. Madison's proposed amendment No. 8, June 8, *Annals of Congress*, 1:453; Madison, ibid., 459 ("superfluous" and "no harm"); Aug. 18, ibid., 790 ("impossible"); Tucker's motion,

ibid.; Gerry's amendment, Aug. 21, ibid., 797; ibid. (Gerry's amendment defeated by a vote of thirty-two to seventeen); see also Labunski, *James Madison*, 230.

118. Ibid., 199–200. For a table listing all the provisions in the federal Bill of Rights and noting which state constitutions protected them, see Schwartz, *The Great Rights of Mankind*, 87–91; see also Lutz, "The States and the U.S. Bill of Rights," 259–60.

119. Madison's proposed amendment No. 4, June 8, *Annals of Congress*, 1:451; House Committee Report, amends. 4, 6, July 28, in Veit et al., eds., *Bill of Rights*, 30; Akhil Reed Amar, "The Bill of Rights as a Constitution," *Yale Law Journal* (Mar. 1991), 100:1157, 1165; see also Gerry, Aug. 17, *Annals of Congress*, 1:778; Huntington and Madison, Aug. 15, ibid., 757–8; but cf. District of Columbia v. Heller, 554 U.S. 570 (2008).

120. Amar, "Bill of Rights," 1133, 1182–3. On the rights that grew out of America's colonial experience and thus had no real precedent in British practice, see Slauter, "Rights," 449–50.

121. On juries, see Rakove, *Original Meanings*, 294, 303; Bouton, *Taming Democracy*, 20; Conley, "Rhode Island: Laboratory for the Internal 'Lively Experiment,'" 133–6. On the Establishment Clause, see Rakove, supra, 310–2. On criminal procedure rights as surrogate protections for religious and political dissidents, see William J. Stuntz, "The Substantive Origins of Criminal Procedure," *Yale Law Journal* (Nov. 1995), 105:393–447. On warrant requirements as constraints on the enforcement of revenue laws, see Address of the Antifederalist Minority of the Maryland convention, May 1, 1788, *DHRC*, 12:664–5; Chase, Objections, ibid., 638; Patrick Henry at Virginia convention, June 16, 1788, *DHRC*, 10:1331. For warnings that federal revenue officers might abuse women while searching their homes for evidence of tax violations, see "A Democratic Federalist," *Pennsylvania Herald*, Oct. 17, 1787, *DHRC*, 2:196; "A Son of Liberty," *New York Journal*, Nov. 8, 1787, *DHRC*, 19:135; Rutland, *Ordeal of the Constitution*, 201.

122. Madison's proposed amendment No. 5, June 8, *Annals of Congress*, 1:452; Madison, Aug. 17, ibid., 784 ("most valuable"); Labunski, *James Madison*, 202–3; supra pp. 154–8. The select committee later added freedom of speech to this amendment constraining state governments. See House Committee Report, amend. No. 12, July 28, in Veit et al., eds., *Bill of Rights*, 31.

123. Madison, June 8, *Annals of Congress*, 1:458; supra pp. 131–3.

124. Madison, June 8, *Annals of Congress*, 1:458; Tucker, Aug. 17, ibid., 783–4; see also Labunski, *James Madison*, 203, 228.

125. Madison, Aug. 13, *Annals of Congress*, 1:735; see also Madison to Alexander White, Aug. 24, 1789, in Veit et al., eds., *Bill of Rights*, 287–8.

126. Clymer, Aug. 13, *Annals of Congress*, 1:737 ("perfection"); Sherman, ibid., 734–5 ("ought not to," "destructive," "had the right," "act of the people," and "the acts of the state"); Stone, ibid., 737–8; Jackson, ibid., 741–2; Smith, ibid., 743; Gerry, ibid., 743–4; Aug. 19, ibid., 795 (Sherman's proposal to add amendments at the end of the document approved by two-thirds of the House); Madison to Alexander White, Aug. 24, 1789, in Veit et al., eds., *Bill of Rights*, 287 ("an unavoidable"); see also Sherman to Henry Gibbs, Aug. 4, 1789, ibid., 271; Ellery to Huntington, Aug. 24, 1789, ibid., 287.

127. Burke, Aug. 15, *Annals of Congress*, 1:774 ("already given" and "improper"); Benjamin Goodhue to Michael Hodge, July 30, 1789, in Veit et al., eds., *Bill of Rights*, 269 ("might quiet"); Gerry, Aug. 18, *Annals of Congress*, 1:786; Tucker, ibid., 790–2; Gerry, Aug. 15, ibid., 776; Tucker, Aug. 13, ibid., 736; Gerry, July 21, ibid., 687–8; Tucker, ibid., 689–90; Gerry, June 8, ibid., 463–4; Frederick A. Muhlenberg to Rush, Aug. 18, 1789, in Veit et al., eds., *Bill of Rights*, 280; Lambert Cadwalader to George Mitchell, July 22, 1789, ibid., 268; Labunski, *James Madison*, 229.

128. Burke, Aug. 15, *Annals of Congress*, 1:777 ("it would occasion" and "satisfactory"); Page, ibid. ("their freedom"); Tucker, Aug. 18, ibid., 786–7 ("might tend," "feel some," "naturally recur," "party spirit," "animosities," and "many of"); see also Labunski, *James Madison*, 230.

129. William Loughton Smith to Edward Rutledge, Aug. 15, 1789, in Veit et al., eds., *Bill of Rights*, 278 ("intensely hot" and "ill humor"); William Smith to Otho H. Williams, Aug. 17, 1789, ibid., 280 ("[t]he hot weather"); Aug. 22, 1789, ibid., 285 ("very high"); George

Leonard to Sylvanus Bourne, Aug. 16, 1789, ibid., 279 ("the political thermometer" and "high each day"); see also Muhlenberg to Rush, Aug. 18, 1789, ibid., 281; Hartley to Jasper Yeates, Aug. 16, 1789, ibid., 279.

For the preceding footnote, see Gerry to Samuel Gerry, June 30, 1790, quoted in Veit et al., eds., *Bill of Rights*, 278–9 n. 1; see also ibid., xv.

130. Gerry motion, Aug. 18, *Annals of Congress*, 1:786; ibid., 788 (defeating motion by a margin of thirty-four to sixteen); Aug. 22, ibid., 803–7 (debating and then rejecting by a margin of thirty-nine to nine Tucker's amendment to limit Congress's ability to levy direct taxes); Livermore, ibid., 804 (quotations).

131. Gerry, Aug. 15, ibid., 764–5 ("check against"); Hartley, ibid., 761 ("when the passions"); Clymer, ibid., 763 ("utterly destructive"); Tucker motion to add a right of instruction, ibid., 761; Burke, ibid., 774; Page, ibid., 772; Vining, ibid., 770; ibid., 776 (rejecting right of instruction by a margin of forty-one to ten); see also Labunski, *James Madison*, 224–7; supra p. 172.

132. Aug. 21, *Annals of Congress*, 1:797–802 (debating and then rejecting Burke's proposed amendment).

133. Burke, Aug. 15, ibid., 774, 775 ("very far," "sense," and "those solid"); Livermore, Aug. 22, ibid., 804, 805 ("would not value," "would be dissatisfied," and "[u]nless something"); see also Goodhue to Hodge, Aug. 20, 1789, in Veit et al., eds., *Bill of Rights*, 283; Cornell, *Other Founders*, 162.

134. Butler to Iredell, Aug. 11, 1789, in Veit et al., eds., *Bill of Rights*, 274 ("milk and water"); Henry to Lee, Aug. 28, 1789, ibid., 289–90 ("but a shadow," "tend to injure," "answer no purpose," and "who wish"); Grayson to Henry, Sept. 29, 1789, ibid., 300 ("good for nothing" and "do more harm"); see also June 12, 1789, ibid., 248–9; Richard Henry Lee to Henry, Sept. 14, 1789, ibid., 295; Richard Henry Lee to Charles Lee, Aug. 28, 1789, ibid., 290; Reverend James Madison to Madison, Aug. 15, 1789, ibid., 277; Labunski, *James Madison*, 210, 235, 242; Cornell, *Other Founders*, 159.

135. Hartley to Yeates, Aug. 16, 1789, in Veit et al., eds., *Bill of Rights*, 279 ("very curious" and "to force"); Brown to William Irvine, Aug. 17, 1789, ibid., 279 ("appear determined" and "not surprising"); William Smith to Otho H. Williams, ibid., 280 ("oppos[ing] their," "making every," and "go far"); Muhlenberg to Rush, Aug. 18, 1789, ibid., 281 ("their darling"); Madison to Randolph, Aug. 21, 1789, ibid., 284 ("exceedingly wearisome"); see also Goodhue to Hodge, Aug. 20, 1789, ibid., 283; William L. Smith to Edward Rutledge, Aug. 15, 1789, ibid., 278; Madison to Pendleton, Aug. 21, 1789, ibid., 284; Goodhue to the Salem Insurance Offices, Aug. 23, 1789, ibid., 285–6; Pendleton to Madison, Sept. 2, 1789, *PJM* (C.S.), 12:368–9.

136. Smith to Edward Rutledge, Aug. 9, 1789, in Veit et al., eds., *Bill of Rights*, 272–3 ("which will," "inoffensive," "do some good," and "North Carolina"); Ames to George R. Minot, Aug. 12, 1789, ibid., 275 ("of no consequence," "protested," and "reproached"); Goodhue to Hodge, Aug. 20, 1789, ibid., 283 ("quiet" and "weakening"); Ellery to Huntington, Aug. 24, 1789, ibid., 287 ("very innocent"); infra p. 594; Labunski, *James Madison*, 216–7, 235, 239; Banning, *Sacred Fire*, 289.

137. Goodhue to the Salem Insurance Offices, Aug. 23, 1789, in Veit et al., eds., *Bill of Rights*, 285; The Diary of William Maclay, Aug. 25, 1789, ibid., 289 ("contemptuously"); Lee to Henry, May 28, 1789, ibid., 241 ("when the plan"); Lee to Charles Lee, Aug. 28, 1789, ibid., 290 ("gain the whole"); see also Muhlenberg to Rush, Aug. 18, 1789, ibid., 280; Madison to Wilson Cary Nicholas, Aug. 2, 1789, ibid., 271.

138. Madison to Pendleton, Sept. 14, 1789, *PJM* (C.S.), 12:402 ("most salutary"); see also Paine Wingate to John Langdon, Sept. 17, 1789, in Veit et al., eds., *Bill of Rights*, 297; Labunski, *James Madison*, 237–8; Maier, *Ratification*, 453–4.

For the preceding footnote, see U.S. Constitution, Art. I, § 3, cl. 2.

139. Madison to Pendleton, Sept. 23, 1789, *PJM* (C.S.), 12:418–9 ("embarrassing," "too vague," and "too strict"); Goodhue to Samuel Phillips, Sept. 13, 1789, in Veit et al., eds., *Bill of Rights*, 294 ("the darling"); Grayson to Henry, Sept. 29, 1789, ibid., 300 ("so mutilated"); see also Richard Henry Lee to Francis Lightfoot Lee, Sept. 13, 1789, ibid., 294; Richard Henry Lee to Henry, Sept. 14, 1789, ibid., 295.

For the preceding footnote, see Articles of Amendment, as Agreed to by the Senate, Sept. 14, 1789, Art. 8, in Veit et al., eds., *Bill of Rights*, 48–9; Conference Committee Report, Sept. 24, 1789, ibid., 50; U.S. Constitution, amend. VI; Judiciary Act of 1789, ch. 20, § 2, 1 Stat. 73.

140. Grayson to Henry, Sept. 29, 1789, in Veit et al., eds., *Bill of Rights*, 300; Labunski, *James Madison*, 209, 236–7; see also Theodorick Bland Randolph to St. George Tucker, Sept. 9, 1789, in Veit et al., eds., *Bill of Rights*, 293; Henry to Richard Henry Lee, Jan. 29, 1790, in Henry, *Life of Patrick Henry*, 2:451.

141. Lee and Grayson to the Speaker of the Virginia House of Delegates, Sept. 28, 1789, in Veit et al., eds., *Bill of Rights*, 299 ("nothing"); Lee and Grayson to Governor Beverley Randolph of Virginia, Sept. 28, 1789, quoted in ibid., 300 n. 1 ("grief" and "inadequate"); Lee to Henry, Sept. 14, 1789, ibid., 295 (remaining quotations).

142. Lee to Francis Lightfoot Lee, Sept. 13, 1789, ibid., 294 ("What with design"); Lee to Henry, Sept. 14, 1789, ibid., 295; Sept. 27, 1789, ibid., 299 ("effectual" and "ought"); see also Cornell, *Other Founders*, 162–3; Maier, *Ratification*, 454–5; Labunski, *James Madison*, 242–3.

143. Mason to Samuel Griffin, Sept. 8, 1789, in Veit et al., eds., *Bill of Rights*, 292.

144. Labunski, *James Madison*, 245–6.

145. Lee and Grayson to the Speaker of the Virginia House of Delegates, Sept. 28, 1789, in Veit et al., eds., *Bill of Rights*, 299–300; Lee and Grayson to Governor Beverley Randolph of Virginia, Sept. 28, 1789, quoted in ibid., 300 n. 1; Madison to Washington, Dec. 5, 1789, *PJM* (C.S.), 12:458 (quotation); Henry to Richard Henry Lee, Aug. 28, 1789, in Veit et al., eds., *Bill of Rights*, 289–90; Labunski, *James Madison*, 246.

146. Carrington to Madison, Dec. 20, 1789, *PJM* (C.S.), 12:463 ("that the people" and "went away"); see also Madison to Washington, Nov. 20, 1789, ibid., 453; Randolph to Washington, Nov. 26, 1789, *PGW* (P.S.), 4:326; Nov. 22, 1789, ibid., 316.

147. Carrington to Madison, Dec. 20, 1789, *PJM* (C.S.), 12:464; *Journal of the Virginia House of Delegates of 1789*, Dec. 5, 1789, at 89 (reporting a division of sixty-two to sixty-two on the resolution); see also Labunski, *James Madison*, 250–1; Billings, "Virginians and the Origins of the Bill of Rights," 364–5.

148. Burnley to Madison, Nov. 28, 1789, *PJM* (C.S.), 12:456 (quotation); see also Carrington to Madison, Dec. 20, 1789, ibid., 464.

149. Madison to Washington, Dec. 5, 1789, *PJM* (C.S.), 12:459 (quotations); see also Labunski, *James Madison*, 249–50. By the time Madison wrote this letter, North Carolina's second convention had already ratified the Constitution, but he had yet to receive word of it.

150. Burnley to Madison, Nov. 28, 1789, *PJM* (C.S.), 12:456 (quotations); Carrington to Madison, Dec. 20, 1789, ibid., 464; Randolph to Washington, Nov. 26, 1789, *PGW* (P.S.), 4:326; Burnley to Madison, Dec. 5, 1789, ibid., 460; *Journal of the Virginia House of Delegates of 1789*, Nov. 30, 1789, at 79; George Lee Turberville to Madison, Jan. 20, 1790, *PJM* (C.S.), 12:471; Madison to Washington, Jan. 4, 1790, ibid., 467; Labunski, *James Madison*, 251–2; Billings, "Virginians and the Origins of the Bill of Rights," 364–5.

151. Labunski, *James Madison*, 252–6; Billings, "Virginians and the Origins of the Bill of Rights," 366.

152. Madison to Peters, Aug. 19, 1789, *PJM* (C.S.), 12:347 (quotations); supra pp. 547, 561–3; Labunski, *James Madison*, 232, 234.

For the preceding footnote, see Madison to Randolph, June 15, 1789, in Veit et al., eds., *Bill of Rights*, 251 (quotation); see also Labunski, *James Madison*, 222, 245. On the pay-alteration amendment, see Michael S. Paulsen, "A General Theory of Article V: The Constitutional Lessons of the Twenty-Seventh Amendment," *Yale Law Journal* (Dec. 1993), 103:678–83.

153. Madison to Peters, Aug. 19, 1789, *PJM* (C.S.), 12:347 (quotations). Madison apparently did not feel himself equally bound by the Virginia ratifying convention's instruction to the state's representatives in the new Congress to support all of the constitutional amendments the convention had endorsed.

154. Ibid., 347.

155. Ibid.

156. Peters to Madison, Aug. 28, 1789, in Veit et al., eds., *Bill of Rights*, 289.
157. Labunski, *James Madison*, 240; Veit et al., eds., *Bill of Rights*, xv–xvi.
158. Madison to Randolph, Apr. 10, 1788, *PJM* (C.S.), 11:18 (quotation); see also Banning, *Sacred Fire*, 280.
159. Madison to Jefferson, Oct. 17, 1788, *PJM* (C.S.), 11:297 ("so much divided" and "importance"); Randolph to Madison, Mar. 27, 1789, in Veit et al., eds., *Bill of Rights*, 223 ("Although I am"); Hamilton to Madison, July 19, 1788, *PAH*, 5:178 ("satisfy"); Grayson to Henry, June 12, 1789, in Veit et al., eds., *Bill of Rights*, 248–9 ("unquestionably" and "support amendments"); Muhlenberg to Rush, Aug. 18, 1789, ibid., 281; see also Abraham Baldwin to Joel Barlow, June 14, 1789, ibid., 250; ibid., xvi; Banning, *Sacred Fire*, 265–7, 280; Heideking, *The Constitution Before the Judgment Seat*, 403.
160. Davie to Iredell, June 4, 1789, in McRee, *James Iredell*, 2:260 ("remarking" and "confounded"); Carrington to Knox, Aug. 3, 1789, in Veit et al., eds., *Bill of Rights*, 271 ("well reconciled" and "becoming"); see also Carrington to Madison, Sept. 9, 1789, ibid., 292. For examples of Antifederalists' expressing certainty that Federalist promises of amendments made during the ratifying contest could be relied upon, see Extract of a letter from a gentleman of Massachusetts (Feb. 20), *Edenton Intelligencer* [North Carolina], Apr. 9, 1788, *DHRC*, 7:1656; William Symmes, Jr., at Massachusetts convention, Feb. 6, 1788, *DHRC*, 6:1475. Before the Massachusetts congressional elections, when it appeared that Federalists were backing off their earlier promises to support amendments in Congress, one Antifederalist issued a stern warning against "deceiving the people" in the first acts of the new government ("Honestus," Boston *Independent Chronicle*, Oct. 30, 1788, *DHFFE*, 1:473).
161. Pendleton to Madison, Sept. 2, 1789, *PJM* (C.S.), 12:368–9 ("a good effect" and "some degree"); Rhode Island Governor John Collins to the President and Congress, Sept. 26, 1789, in Veit et al., eds., *Bill of Rights*, 298 ("have already afforded" and "with clearness"); Madison to Washington, Nov. 20, 1789, *PJM* (C.S.), 12:453 ("One of the"); Jefferson to Lafayette, Apr. 2, 1790, *PTJ* (M.S.), 16:293 ("almost all").
162. Scholars disagree as to whether Madison ever did genuinely become enthusiastic about a bill of rights. For the more skeptical view, see Maier, *Ratification*, 443; Rakove, *Original Meanings*, 333; Ellis, *The Quartet*, 199, 205, 212–3; Bowling, "'A Tub to the Whale,'" 224. For the contrary view that Madison was ultimately converted into a genuine believer in the efficacy of a bill of rights, see Wood, *Creation of the American Republic*, 542–3; Banning, *Sacred Fire*, 280–1, 286–7; Labunski, *James Madison*, 62–3, 192, 194; Stuart Leibiger, "James Madison and Amendments to the Constitution, 1787–1789: 'Parchment Barriers,'" *Journal of Southern History* (Aug. 1993), 59:442–3.

      Prior to ratification, Federalists had tended to ask not whether a bill of rights would cause harm but rather whether it would do any good. After ratification, although most Federalists still doubted that a bill of rights would do much good, they proved willing to accept it because they did not believe it would cause any harm.
163. Sherman to Henry Gibbs, Aug. 4, 1789, in Veit et al., eds., *Bill of Rights*, 271 ("probably be"); Cadwalader to George Mitchell, July 22, 1789, ibid., 268 ("of little or no" and "calm the turbulence"); Hartley in the House, Aug. 15, 1789, *Annals of Congress*, 1:760 ("was disposed," "not incompatible," and "would tend"); see also Ellery to Huntington, Sept. 8, 1789, in Veit et al., eds., *Bill of Rights*, 291; Paine Wingate to Timothy Pickering, Mar. 25, 1789, ibid., 223; Benjamin Hawkins to Madison, June 1, 1789, ibid., 243.
164. Tucker to St. George Tucker, Oct. 2, 1789, in Veit et al., eds., *Bill of Rights*, 300 ("calculated"); Gerry to John Wendell, Sept. 14, 1789, ibid., 294 ("Constitution" and "to reconcile"); Lee to Henry, Sept. 27, 1789, ibid., 298–9 ("wonderfully scrupulous" and "right without"); see also Grayson to Henry, Sept. 29, 1789, ibid., 300; Cornell, *Other Founders*, 162; supra pp. 583–4.
165. "Pacificus" (Webster), in Veit et al., eds., *Bill of Rights*, 276 ("paper declarations"); Gideon v. Wainwright, 372 U.S. 335, 341 (1963) ("fundamental safeguards"); Hamilton, An Address to the Electors of the State of New York, Mar. 21, 1801, *PAH*, 25:356 ("scarcely any").

Chapter 8

1. Beeman, *Plain, Honest Men*, xi.
2. Supra pp. 102–22.
3. Charles Pinckney in the House, Feb. 14, 1820, *Annals of Congress*, 36:1313 (quotation); supra chs. 3, 6, and 7. For a nice statement of how unlikely ratification of the Constitution appeared to be, about halfway through the state ratifying contests of 1787–88, see Cyrus Griffin to Madison, Mar. 24, 1788, *DHRC*, 16:471.
4. Banning, *Sacred Fire*, 1; Bill Providing for Delegates to the Convention of 1787, Nov. 6, 1786, *PJM* (C.S.), 9:163–4; supra pp. 102–3, 109, 112–3.
5. Supra pp. 127–34.
6. Pierce, Character Sketches, *Farrand*, 3:94. On Madison's principal defeats at the convention, see supra pp. 254–5.
7. Supra pp. 453–81, 566–90.
8. King to Jonathan Jackson, June 11, 1786, *LDC*, 23:353 ("it is not possible"); Manning to Nathan Miller, June 12, 1786, ibid., 354 ("things are" and "without a"); Brown to James Breckinridge, Mar. 17, 1788, *DHRC*, 16:404 ("had already damned"); see also James White to Governor Samuel Johnston of North Carolina, Apr. 21, 1788, *LDC*, 25:68; supra ch. 1.
9. Madison to Randolph, Apr. 8, 1787, *PJM* (C.S.), 9:371 ("the partition"); John Dawson at Virginia ratifying convention, June 24, 1788, *DHRC*, 10:1493 ("diabolical"); John Marshall to Arthur Lee, Mar. 5, 1789, in *Life of Arthur Lee*, 2:321 ("he would rather") (quoting Henry); Charles Thomson's Notes of Debates, Aug. 18, 1786, *LDC*, 23:496 ("gentlemen") (quoting Henry Lee); King to John Adams, Nov. 2, 1785, *LCRK*, 1:113 ("a sub-confederation"); supra pp. 33–9, 48–69; see also Elbridge Gerry at Philadelphia convention, June 29, 1787, *Farrand*, 1:467; Charles Pinckney, July 2, ibid., 511; *A Citizen of New-York*, *DHRC*, 20:937; Hamilton to Madison, June 8, 1788, *PJM* (C.S.), 11:99–100; Letter from William Constable, Feb. 10, 1788, *DHRC*, 20:762; Martin Oster to Comte de la Luzerne, Feb. 4, 1788, *DHRC*, 8:344; Comte de Vergennes to Francois Barbé-Marbois, Dec. 14, 1784, in Bancroft, *History of the Formation of the Constitution*, 1:404; Hendrickson, *Peace Pact*, passim, esp. x, 3–4, 177, 204–5, 253–8; McCraw, *The Founders and Finance*, 49; Davis, *Sectionalism in American Politics*, 167; Banning, *Sacred Fire*, 67.
10. Autobiography of William Few, undated, *Farrand*, 3:423 ("without doing," "weeks of," "serious thoughts," and "the dissolution"); Hamilton, Conjectures, *PAH*, 4:276 ("it is probable"); Randolph at Virginia ratifying convention, June 24, 1788, *DHRC*, 10:1487–8 ("the union"); see also St. Jean de Crevecoeur to William Short, June 10, 1788, ibid., 1593; James Manning to Nathan Miller, June 12, 1786, *LDC*, 23:355; *A Citizen of New-York*, *DHRC*, 20:939; John Parkinson to Joel Lane, May 18, 1788, *DHRC*, 9:829.
11. Madison to Randolph, Feb. 25, 1787, *PJM* (C.S.), 9:299 ("many individuals"); Washington to Jay, Aug. 15, 1786, *PGW* (C.S.), 4:213 ("even respectable"); John Avery, Jr., to George Thatcher, Feb. 13, 1788, *DHRC*, 7:1693 ("dreaded," "no other," "anarchy," and "in the course"); see also Hamilton, Conjectures, *PAH*, 4:276; Madison to Philip Mazzei, Dec. 10, 1788, *PJM* (C.S.), 11:389; Isaac Stearns to Samuel Adams, Dec. 31, 1787, *DHRC*, 5:558–9; "Centinel" XV, Philadelphia *Independent Gazetteer*, Feb. 22, 1788, *DHRC*, 16:190; Davis, *Sectionalism in American Politics*, 161; supra ch. 2.
12. Robertson, *The Constitution and America's Destiny*, 21; Dahl, *How Democratic Is the American Constitution?*, 62–8, 74–7; Roche, "Founding Fathers," 810–1; see also Madison at Philadelphia convention, July 25, 1787, *Farrand*, 2:108; Grayson at Virginia ratifying convention, June 18, 1788, *DHRC*, 10:1373; supra pp. 165–6, 226–34.
13. *The Federalist No. 37* (Madison), at 230; Robertson, *The Constitution and America's Destiny*, 21; supra pp. 204–5.
14. *Federalist No. 37* (Madison), at 230 (quotations); Dahl, *How Democratic Is the American Constitution?*, 12–13; see also Madison to William Short, Oct. 24, 1787, *DHRC*, 8:109; Pierce Butler to Weedon Butler, Oct. 8, 1787, *DHRC*, 13:352.
15. Mason to George Mason, Jr., June 1, 1787, *PGM*, 3:892 ("America"); Franklin at Philadelphia convention, Sept. 17, 1787, *Farrand*, 2:642 ("all their"); see also Lachlan McIntosh to John Wereat, Dec. 17, 1787, *DHRC*, 3:259; Gouverneur Morris to James

LaCaze, Feb. 21, 1788, *DHRC*, 16:171; Beeman, *Plain, Honest Men*, x; Bouton, *Taming Democracy*, 9.

16. Mason to George Mason, Jr., June 1, 1787, *PGM*, 3:892 (quotation); Madison, Preface to Debates, *Farrand*, 3:551.

17. Hamilton to Madison, May 19, 1788, *PJM* (C.S.), 11:53–4 ("every species" and "count little"); Madison at Virginia ratifying convention, June 6, 1788, *DHRC*, 9:994 ("designing"); Washington to Bushrod Washington, Nov. 9, 1787, *PGW* (C.S.), 5:421 ("better calculated," "their local," and "not accord"); see also Washington to David Humphreys, Oct. 10, 1787, ibid., 365; Washington to Knox, Mar. 30, 1788, ibid., 6:183; Albany Federal Committee, *An Impartial Address* (c. Apr. 20, 1788), *DHRC*, 21:1389; Samuel Blachley Webb to Catherine Hogeboom, June 24–25, 1788, *DHRC*, 21:1222; Wood, "Interests and Disinterestedness," 83–93, 99–102; Wood, *Radicalism of the American Revolution*, 253–6; Cornell, *Other Founders*, 97–8. For a more charitable assessment by Madison, attributing the "diversity of opinions" on the Constitution to "the fallibility of human judgment" and "the imperfect progress yet made in the science of government," see Madison to Archibald Stuart, Oct. 30, 1787, *PJM* (C.S.), 10:232.

18. Supra ch. 1.

19. Williamson to Iredell, July 8, 1787, *Farrand*, 3:55 ("[t]he diverse"); Gerry at Philadelphia convention, June 29, 1787, ibid., 1:467 ("lamented"); Morris, July 5, ibid., 529 ("as a representative" twice, and "to truck"); see also Morris, July 10, ibid., 567; Franklin speech, read by Wilson, June 11, ibid., 197; Robertson, *The Constitution and America's Destiny*, 4.

20. Supra pp. 182–205, 265–77.
 For the preceding footnote, see George Read, July 9, *Farrand*, 1:561; convention proceedings, July 10, ibid., 566–8; Sept. 15, ibid., 2:623–4.

21. Madison, July 13, ibid., 1:601–2; Sept. 15, ibid., 2:624 (the vote).

22. Supra pp. 184, 192–3, 273–4, 279, 286.

23. Madison, Aug. 21, *Farrand*, 2:361 (quotation); supra pp. 281–2; see also Beeman, *Plain, Honest Men*, 330–1; McDonald, *Novus Ordo Seclorum*, 240.

24. Supra pp. 204–5, 223, 230–4.

25. Supra pp. 204–5, 282, 338–9, 474; see also Banning, *Sacred Fire*, 178–80.

26. Bedford (Yates's Notes), June 30, *Farrand*, 1:500.

27. Supra pp. 182–205.

28. Supra pp. 414–7.

29. *The Federalist No. 10* (Madison), at 77–84 ("refine" at p. 82); Madison, June 26, *Farrand*, 1:422 ("slid[ing]" and "sigh"); see also Madison, Observations on the Draft of a Constitution for Virginia, Oct. 15, 1788, *PJM* (C.S.), 11:288; Robertson, *The Constitution and America's Destiny*, 75; Rakove, *Original Meanings*, 314; Ellis, *The Quartet*, 123, 131.

30. Randolph to Madison, c. Oct. 29, 1787, *DHRC*, 8:133 (quotation). On the effect of the Jay imbroglio, see supra pp. 48–69, 335–6, 469. On the prewar debts, see supra pp. 454–5, 470–1. On the effect of New York's impost, see supra pp. 31–3, 151, 424.

31. Grayson to Monroe, May 29, 1787, *Farrand*, 3:30 ("for a very strong" and "wish"); Mason to George Mason, Jr., May 20, 1787, ibid., 23 ("extraordinary"); Gerry at the Philadelphia convention, June 5, 1787, ibid., 1:123 ("the wildest"); Hamilton, June 18, ibid., 289 ("the amazing"); supra pp. 88–92, 117. For some of the other many references to Shays's Rebellion at the convention, see Gerry, May 31, *Farrand*, 1:48; Randolph (Yates's Notes), June 16, ibid., 263; Charles Pinckney, Aug. 18, ibid., 2:332; King, Sept. 15, ibid., 626; supra pp. 149, 164.

32. Grayson to Madison, May 28, 1786, *PJM* (C.S.), 9:63 ("Congress"); Grayson at Virginia convention, June 11, 1788, *DHRC*, 9:1165 ("well aware"); William Symmes, Jr., at Massachusetts convention, Jan. 22, 1788, *DHRC*, 6:1308 ("many men"); see also Uriah Forrest to Thomas Jefferson, Dec. 11, 1787, *DHRC*, 11:111–2; Grayson to Patrick Henry, June 12, 1789, in *The Patrick Henry Papers* (Stanislaus V. Henkels, auction catalog, Philadelphia, 1910), 36; "Centinel" XVIII, Philadelphia *Independent Gazetteer*, Apr. 9, 1788, *DHRC*, 17:57; Davis, *Sectionalism in American Politics*, 107, 151–2, 159–61; Hall, *Politics Without Parties*, 256–7, 262. In the spring of 1786, Washington had similarly expressed doubt as to whether the "train of evils" had yet been sufficient for the people "to

retract from error" and support the necessary reforms to the Articles (to Jay, May 18, 1786, *PGW* (C.S.), 4:55; see also Washington to Lafayette, May 10, 1786, ibid., 42).

33. "The Landholder" XII, *Connecticut Courant*, Mar. 17, 1788, *DHRC*, 16:406 ("public injustice," "apostasy," and "silence[d]"); Smith at New York convention, June 27, 1788, *DHRC*, 22:1924 ("[A]s for"); "X.Y.," Philadelphia *Federal Gazette*, Apr. 22, 1788, *DHRC*, 24:256 ("amount," "the best," "[m]any worthy," and "with men"); see also Charles Thomson to William Ellery, May 26, 1788, ibid., 264; "A Landholder" V, *Connecticut Courant*, Dec. 3, 1787, *DHRC*, 3:484; Van Cleve, "Anti-Federalists' Toughest Challenge," 533, 543, 545, 552; Kaminski, "Paper Politics," 258; Polishook, *Rhode Island*, 165–72. Rhode Island also frequently served as a negative reference point for delegates to the Philadelphia convention. See, e.g., Gorham, July 18, *Farrand*, 2:42; Morris, ibid., 47.

34. James Freeman to Theophilus Lindsey, Mar. 29, 1788, *DHRC*, 16:504 ("less democratic" and "insurrection"); Breck to Knox, July 14, 1787, quoted in Van Cleve, "Anti-Federalists' Toughest Challenge," 549; see also Knox to Benjamin Lincoln, June 13, 1788, *DHRC*, 20:1152.

35. Supra pp. 83–6.

36. Supra pp. 74–83, 375–6, 385–7.

37. Supra pp. 161–4.

38. Supra pp. 159–60, 171–6, 208–11, 218–9.

39. Supra pp. 158–9, 175, 245.

40. Supra pp. 208, 210–1, 244–5, 371–2, 374–5, 537–8.

41. Wood, *Creation of the American Republic*, 562–4; Rakove, *Original Meanings*, 205.

42. Robert R. Livingston at New York convention, June 19, 1788, *DHRC*, 22:1683 ("of little"); Wilson at Pennsylvania convention, Dec. 1, 1787, *DHRC*, 2:448–9.

43. Supra pp. 312–3, 415–6.

44. *The Federalist No. 39* (Madison), at 241 ("directly"); Jefferson to "Henry Tompkinson" (Samuel Kercheval), July 12, 1816, *PTJ* (R.S.), 10:222 ("infancy," "we imagined," "to the mother," and "republican only"); see also Madison in the House, Aug. 15, 1789, *Annals of Congress*, 1:767; Hamilton at Philadelphia convention, June 18, 1787, *Farrand*, 1:290; Graham, "Pennsylvania," 64–5; Nelson, *Royalist Revolution*, 160–1, 188, 190, 207. Banning strongly resists the interpretation that Madison's professed commitment to popular sovereignty was more rhetorical than real (*Sacred Fire*, 100–1, 121, 127–30, 183–90, 251–2).

45. Madison (Yates's Notes), June 12, *Farrand*, 1:221 (quotation); supra pp. 99–101. Banning defends the notion that Madison was trying, by insulating the federal government from populist pressure, to save republican government from the threat posed by monarchy (*Sacred Fire*, 188–9).

46. Supra pp. 175, 360, 393–5.

47. Grayson to Monroe, May 29, 1787, *Papers of James Monroe*, 2:385 ("[t]he people" and "to pay"); Gerry at the Philadelphia convention, Aug. 23, *Farrand*, 2:388 ("a plan," "pushing," and "of a more democratic"); Holton, *Unruly Americans*, 238–9; supra p. 70.

48. Supra pp. 405–12, 540–3. For an outside observer's attributing the Federalists' victory, despite "great opposition" to the Constitution, to "the cleverness of the leaders," see Don Diego de Gardoqui to Conde de Floridablanca, July 25, 1788, *DHRC*, 21:1340.

49. Supra pp. 172–3, 207. For additional examples, see supra pp. 158, 166, 171, 175, 179, 241, 245.

50. Mason, Morris, and Hugh Williamson statements, July 26, *Farrand*, 2:127–8; Hamilton to Carrington, May 26, 1792, *PAH*, 11:428 ("multiplying obstacles"); Madison proposal to empower Congress to grant corporate charters, Aug. 18, *Farrand*, 2:325; Madison, Sept. 14, ibid., 615; King, ibid., 616; Bowling, *The Creation of Washington, D.C.*, 74–5; supra pp. 382–3.

51. Supra pp. 412–4, 540–3. On the important point that the states manifesting the greatest resistance to the Constitution tended to hold their conventions last, see Brown, *Charles Beard and the Constitution*, 143–4; see also McDonald, *We the People*, 113–5.

52. Randolph at Virginia convention, June 4, 1788, *DHRC*, 9:933–4 ("proved totally inadequate" and "political farce"); Madison, June 6, ibid., 991 ("Would the honorable"); supra pp. 533, 543–4.

53. Supra pp. 530–9, 545.

54. Fisher Ames at Massachusetts convention, Feb. 5, 1788, *DHRC*, 6:1444 (quotation). For inconsistent positions on the desirability of extended convention deliberations, see supra pp. 436, 449, 490, 511–2. For inconsistent positions on adjournments, see supra pp. 429, 441, 445–6, 447–9, 452, 502–3, 525–6. For inconsistent positions on whether conventions could propose amendments, see supra pp. 429, 440–1, 475–6.

55. Supra pp. 409, 427, 439–41, 501, 509, 520, 523, 528–9, 543 n. *.

56. Supra pp. 404–5, 559.

57. "A Landholder" II, *Connecticut Courant*, Nov. 12, 1787, *DHRC*, 3:402 ("[d]ebtors"); Charles Swift to Robert E. Griffiths, Oct. 18, 1787, *DHRC*, 2:198–9 ("a few interested"); Gore to George Thatcher, Feb. 3, 1788, *DHRC*, 7:1569 ("[i]ntegrity"); supra p. 403 & n. 19.

58. Gale at Killingworth, Conn., Town Meeting, Nov. 12, 1787, *DHRC*, 3:422 ("only a specious"); Albany Anti-Federal Committee Circular, Apr. 10, 1788, *DHRC*, 21:1382 ("the rich," "indefatigable," and "they and their"); supra p. 403 & n. 20. For statements of resentment at opponents' disparaging of motives, see Iredell at North Carolina convention, July 31, 1788, *Elliot*, 4:233–4; Samuel Johnston, ibid., 226–7; Willie Jones, ibid., 227; Hamilton at New York convention, June 28, 1788, *DHRC*, 22:1989; *A Citizen of New-York*, *DHRC*, 20:931–2; *Plebeian*, ibid., 943; Charles Tillinghast to Hugh Hughes, Jan. 27–28, 1788, ibid., 669; "Ocrico," *Massachusetts Gazette*, Dec. 21, 1787, *DHRC*, 5:504.

59. "Truth," *Massachusetts Centinel*, Nov. 24, 1787, *DHRC*, 4:234 (quotations). For appeals to farmers, see "A Landholder" I, Nov. 5, 1787, *Connecticut Courant*, Nov. 16, 1787, *DHRC*, 3:399; Wilson at Pennsylvania convention, Dec. 11, 1787, *DHRC*, 2:580; James Bowdoin at Massachusetts convention, Jan. 23, 1788, *DHRC*, 6:1319; Feb. 1, ibid., 1394; Albany Federal Committee, *An Impartial Address* (c. Apr. 20, 1788), *DHRC*, 21:1396; "An Independent Elector," Providence *United States Chronicle*, Mar. 5, 1789, *DHRC*, 25:466. For more appeals to urban laborers involved in the carrying trade, see "One of the Middle-Interest," *Massachusetts Centinel*, Dec. 5, 1787, *DHRC*, 4:386–7; "Z: To the Freemen of the State of Rhode-Island," *Newport Mercury*, Dec. 30, 1789, *DHRC*, 25:654–5; supra p. 337.

60. "The Landholder" X, *Connecticut Courant*, Mar. 3, 1788, *DHRC*, 16:305 ("nothing" and "force may"); Livingston at New York convention, June 27, 1788, *DHRC*, 22:1942; see also supra p. 491. For Federalist appeals to Kentuckians at the Virginia ratifying convention, see supra p. 474. For the Georgia land cession, see Rufus King to John Langdon, Apr. 16, 1788, *LCRK*, 1:326; Langdon to King, May 6, 1788, ibid., 328; James White to Governor Samuel Johnston of North Carolina, Apr. 21, 1788, *LDC*, 25:67–8.

61. Supra pp. 469–71; "Agrippa" VIII, *Massachusetts Gazette*, Dec. 25, 1787, *DHRC*, 5:516 (quotation). For an example of a raw appeal to the interests of Boston tradesmen to reject the Constitution, see "Truth," Nov. 14, 1787, *DHRC*, 4:233.

62. "A Farmer: To the Farmers of Connecticut," *New Haven Gazette*, Oct. 18, 1788, *DHRC*, 3:392–3; Thomas Dawes at Massachusetts convention, Jan. 21, 1788, *DHRC*, 6:1287–8; Madison at Virginia convention, June 12, 1788, *DHRC*, 10:1204 ("an insuperable"); Iredell at North Carolina convention, July 31, 1788, *Elliot*, 4:231; Holton, *Unruly Americans*, 239–43; supra pp. 329–30.

63. Gerry to James Warren, Oct. 18, 1787, *DHRC*, 13:407 ("the people will"); Patrick Henry at Virginia convention, June 7, 1788, *DHRC*, 9:1044 ("enormous"); Pennsylvania Minority Dissent, *DHRC*, 2:639 ("swarm"); Mason at Virginia convention, June 17, 1788, *DHRC*, 10:1355 ("taxed for centuries," "rapacious," "a few particular," and "a thousand"); Henry, June 12, ibid., 1216–7 ("collected"); June 17, ibid., 1346; Extract of a Letter from New-York (July 20), *Massachusetts Centinel*, July 26, 1788, *DHRC*, 23:2379 (reporting statement of Clinton); supra p. 325.

64. Supra pp. 388–91, 423–6; Banning, "Virginia," 287.

65. Supra pp. 429, 438–41, 475–8, 495–508, 513–4.

66. Supra pp. 530–4, 538–9.
67. Supra pp. 530–6.
68. Supra pp. 249–53, 536; *Plebeian, DHRC*, 20:951 ("previous to" and "it never was"); Randolph at Philadelphia convention, June 16, 1787, *Farrand*, 1:255 ("leave" and "[t]he present"). For sentiments similar to those voiced by "Plebeian," see "The Republican Federalist" II, *Massachusetts Centinel*, Jan. 2, 1788, *DHRC*, 5:591; Marinus Willett to John Tayler, Sept. 23, 1787, *DHRC*, 19:50.
69. Supra pp. 244, 247–50.
70. Madison to Randolph, Jan. 10, 1788, *PJM* (C.S.), 10:355 (quotation); supra pp. 536–8; see also Rakove, *Original Meanings*, 106–7.
71. "Solon," Boston *Independent Chronicle*, Oct. 18, 1787, *DHRC*, 4:103 (quoting the address to the people by the Massachusetts state convention of 1780); see also Gillespie, "Massachusetts," 153. On the tradition of localist, participatory decision-making in New England, see Polishook, *Rhode Island*, 32–6; Maier, *Ratification*, 139–41, 217; Holton, *Unruly Americans*, 165–6; Main, *Political Parties*, 16–7; Raphael, "The Democratic Moment," 121–35; Adams, *First American Constitutions*, 84–90, 175–6; Nelson, *Royalist Revolution*, 175; Daniell, "Ideology and Hardball," 2–4; Mevers, "New Hampshire Accepts the Bill of Rights," 166, 173; editorial note, *DHRC*, 26:948 n. 5.

    For the preceding footnote, see Randolph to Madison, Aug. 13, 1788, *PJM* (C.S.), 11:231.
72. Supra pp. 409–12, 441, 447, 530.
73. Supra pp. 408–9, 422–3, 427–30, 538. One Connecticut Antifederalist denounced "the malevolent, vindictive tempers of some of these harpies," directed against "anyone that dare either write, speak, or act or even think against their new Dagon Constitution" (Hugh Ledlie to John Lamb, Jan. 15, 1788, *DHRC*, 3:581; see also "Adelos," Northampton, Mass., *Hampshire Gazette*, Feb. 6, 1788, *DHRC*, 5:871).
74. Supra pp. 568–95.
75. Supra pp. 311–2; Maier, *Ratification*, 432–3, 456; De Pauw, *Eleventh Pillar*, 272; Robertson, *The Constitution and America's Destiny*, 238; see also Madison to Jefferson, Dec. 8, 1788, *PJM* (C.S.), 11:382.
76. Carrington to Madison, May 12, 1789, ibid., 12:156 (quotation); Madison to Jefferson, Mar. 29, 1789, ibid., 37; see also Madison to Washington, Nov. 20, 1789, ibid., 453; Labunski, *James Madison*, 176; Introduction, *DHFFE*, 2:254. On the earlier predictions that Antifederalists would do well in Virginia's first congressional elections, see George Mason to John Mason, Dec. 18, 1788, *PGM*, 3:1136; Washington to Benjamin Lincoln, Nov. 14, 1788, *PGW* (P.S.), 1:108.
77. Supra p. 568; Grayson to Henry, June 12, 1789, in Veit et al., eds., *Bill of Rights*, 248 (quotations); Boyd, *Politics of Opposition*, 153, 161.
78. Supra p. 516; Washington to Morris, Oct. 13, 1789, *PGW* (P.S.), 4:176 ("is either" and "to the satisfaction"); Jefferson to Lafayette, Apr. 2, 1790, *PTJ* (M.S.), 16:293 ("The opposition"); see also Maier, *Ratification*, 456.
79. Supra pp. 573–4, 593–4; Brown, *Redeeming the Republic*, 235.
80. Abraham Baldwin to Joel Barlow, Jan. 16, 1790, quoted in Brown, *Redeeming the Republic*, 236; Elkins and McKitrick, *The Age of Federalism*, 73; Edling, *Revolution in Favor of Government*, 132; McCraw, *The Founders and Finance*, 146; Einhorn, *American Taxation*, 184; Atack and Passell, *New Economic View*, 77.
81. Edling, *Revolution in Favor of Government*, 159, 207–9, 211; Brown, *Redeeming the Republic*, 235–6, 238; Holton, *Unruly Americans*, 267; Richards, *Shays's Rebellion*, 158–9; Edling and Kaplanoff, "Alexander Hamilton's Fiscal Reform," 729–39.
82. Boyd, *Politics of Opposition*, 161–4; Cornell, *Other Founders*, 12.
83. Randolph document found in the Mason Papers, undated, *Farrand*, 2:137.
84. Cornell, *Other Founders*, 12, 166–7, 172, 190–1, 195–7; Brown, *Redeeming the Republic*, 241; Rakove, *Original Meanings*, 201–2. On the rise of political parties generally, see Banning, *Sacred Fire*, ch. 11; Elkins and McKitrick, *The Age of Federalism*, ch. 7; Gordon S. Wood, *Empire of Liberty: A History of the Early Republic, 1789–1815* (New York, 2009), ch. 4.

    For the first of the two preceding footnotes, see Casto, *The Supreme Court in the Early Republic*, 129–63. While, in the 1790s, most federal judges (who, at this time, were all

Federalists) agreed with the Federalist position, the Supreme Court later ruled in favor of the Jeffersonian position (United States v. Hudson and Goodwin, 11 U.S. 32 (1812)).

For the second of the two preceding footnotes, see John C. Miller, *Crisis in Freedom: The Alien and Sedition Acts* (Boston, 1941); Elkins and McKitrick, *The Age of Federalism*, 590–3, 694–5, 700–6; Wood, supra, 247–50, 256–62.

85. Carpenter, *The South as a Conscious Minority*, 58; Cornell, *Other Founders*, 279–80. On the states' rights opposition to the Marshall Court's nationalizing decisions, see Newmyer, *John Marshall*, ch. 6.

86. Supra pp. 178–81; cf. Dahl, *How Democratic Is the American Constitution?*, 37–8. On the liberalization of access to suffrage and officeholding, see Fehrenbacher, *Constitutions and Constitutionalism*, 7–10; Keyssar, *The Right to Vote*, ch. 2.

87. Dahl, *How Democratic Is the American Constitution?*, 68, 82, 89; Tadahisa Kuroda, *The Origins of the Twelfth Amendment: The Electoral College in the Early Republic, 1787–1804* (Westport, CT, 1994), 74–7; but cf. Rufus King to C. King, Sept. 29, 1823, *Farrand*, 3:459–60.

88. Supra pp. 173, 341–2, 568 & n. 77; *Pennsylvania Mercury*, Sept. 16, 1788, *DHFFE*, 1:274 ("the characters"); *The Federalist No. 10* (Madison), at 82 ("to refine"); see also Cornell, *Other Founders*, 147–53; Holton, *Unruly Americans*, 254–6; Labunski, *James Madison*, 221.

89. Nathaniel W. Appleton to Noah Webster, Nov. 30, 1789, *DHFFE*, 1:506 (quotation); see also ibid., xxv–xxvi. For additional examples of Federalists' appealing for at-large elections along these lines, see "Numa: To the Inhabitants of States That Have Adopted the New Constitution," *Pennsylvania Gazette*, July 16, 1788, ibid., 246; *Maryland Journal*, Nov. 14, 1788, ibid., 2:125; Madison to Jefferson, Oct. 8, 1788, ibid., 1:303–4; "Honorius," *Herald of Freedom*, Nov. 3, 1788, ibid., 469–70. A few Federalists went so far as to argue that the districting of House elections violated the Constitution's requirement that members of the House be elected "by the People of the several states" (which, they said, implied that all of the voters in each state must have the opportunity to vote for all of the state's congressional representatives). See William Lewis in Pennsylvania Assembly Debates, Sept. 24, 1788, ibid., 283; Richard Peters, ibid., 284.

90. "Hampden" I (Roane), *Richmond Enquirer*, June 11, 1819, in Gerald Gunther, ed., *John Marshall's Defense of McCulloch v. Maryland* (Stanford, CA, 1969), 109 (quotation); see also Carpenter, *The South as a Conscious Minority*, 133–5. Marshall's broadest interpretations of Congress's powers were *Gibbons v. Ogden*, 22 U.S. (9 Wheat.) 1 (1824) and *McCulloch v. Maryland*, 17 U.S. (4 Wheat.) 316 (1819). Madison and Jefferson were also highly critical of Marshall's broad constructionism. See, e.g., Madison to Spencer Roane, Sept. 2, 1819, *PJM* (R.S.), 1:500–3; Jefferson to Spencer Roane, Sept. 6, 1819, *The Writings of Thomas Jefferson* (Paul Leicester Ford, ed., New York, 1899), 10:140–1; Mar. 9, 1821, ibid., 189; see also Newmyer, *John Marshall*, 299–300, 331–2.

91. Franklin D. Roosevelt, First Inaugural Address (Mar. 4, 1933). See generally Barry Cushman, *Rethinking the New Deal Court: The Structure of a Constitutional Revolution* (New York, 1998); William E. Leuchtenburg, *The Supreme Court Reborn: The Constitutional Revolution in the Age of Roosevelt* (New York, 1995).

92. On constitutional amendments generally, see Kyvig, *Explicit and Authentic Acts*.

93. Supra p. 277; see also Dahl, *How Democratic Is the American Constitution?*, 13, 15–6, 27–8, 53.

94. Kyvig, *Explicit and Authentic Acts*, 208–13; Levinson, *Our Undemocratic Constitution*, 161–2.
    For the preceding footnote, see Kyvig, supra, 150–1.

95. Dahl, *How Democratic Is the American Constitution?*, 79–80, 87–9; Levinson, *Our Undemocratic Constitution*, 82–3, 90, 96. In 1969, 81 percent of representatives in the House voted for a constitutional amendment providing that the president be selected by direct popular vote rather than through the electoral college system, only to see the measure filibustered to death in the Senate the following year (Kyvig, *Explicit and Authentic Acts*, 388–91).

96. Dahl, *How Democratic Is the Constitution?*, 48–54, 144–5; Levinson, *Our Undemocratic Constitution*, 50–62.

97. Dahl, *How Democratic Is the American Constitution?*, 50, 145.

98. Supra p. 168; Shugerman, *The People's Courts*, 276–7 app. A; Fehrenbacher, *Constitutions and Constitutionalism*, 91 n. 60; see also Jefferson to "Henry Tompkinson" (Samuel Kercheval), July 12, 1816, *PTJ* (R.S.), 10:223.

99. Dahl, *How Democratic Is the American Constitution?*, 18–9, 167; Levinson, *Our Undemocratic Constitution*, ch. 4. On the limited conception of judicial review that generally prevailed in the early republic, see Michael J. Klarman, "How Great Were the 'Great' Marshall Court Decisions?," *Virginia Law Review* (2001), 87:1113–7.

100. Dahl, *How Democratic Is the American Constitution?*, 160–1; Levinson, *Our Undemocratic Constitution*, ch. 6.

101. Gorham at Philadelphia convention, Aug. 8, 1787, *Farrand*, 2:221; see also Beeman, *Plain, Honest Men*, 282; but cf. Madison, June 29, *Farrand*, 1:464.

102. Mason, June 11, *Farrand*, 1:202–3 ("will certainly"); Gerry's Objections, *DHRC*, 13:549 ("the greatest"); "America: To the Dissenting Members of the Late Convention of Pennsylvania" (Webster), New York *Daily Advertiser*, Dec. 31, 1787, *DHRC*, 19:488 ("consummate," "all possible," "foresee," and "judge"); see also Gouverneur Morris to Robert Walsh, Feb. 5, 1811, *Farrand*, 3:418.

103. This flaw in the system was apparent to participants in the very first presidential election, as Federalists worried about a tie in the electoral college (which might cost Washington the presidency) if some Federalist electors did not "waste" their second votes on someone other than John Adams. See, e.g., William Tilghman to Tench Coxe, Jan. 2, 1789, *DHFFE*, 2:180; Benjamin Rush to Tench Coxe, Feb. 5, 1788, ibid., 1:401.

104. Kuroda, *Origins of the Twelfth Amendment*, 83–105; John Ferling, *Adams vs. Jefferson: The Tumultuous Election of 1800* (New York, 2004), 162–96; Bruce Ackerman, *The Failure of the Founding Fathers: Jefferson, Marshall, and the Rise of Presidential Democracy* (Cambridge, MA, 2005), 3–7, 30–5, 93–5; Dahl, *How Democratic Is the American Constitution?*, 78–9.

105. *The Federalist No. 51* (Madison), at 321–2; Daryl J. Levinson and Richard H. Pildes, "Separation of Parties, Not Powers," *Harvard Law Review* (2006), 119:2319–25.

106. Mason at the Philadelphia convention, Sept. 4, 1787, *Farrand*, 2:500 (quotation); supra p. 232; see also Kuroda, *Origins of the Twelfth Amendment*, 68–9; Beeman, *Plain, Honest Men*, 301–2.

107. Supra pp. 182–3, 191–2, 271–2.

108. Carpenter, *The South as a Conscious Minority*, 107–10; see also John C. Calhoun in the Senate, Mar. 4, 1850, *Congressional Globe*, 31st Cong., 1st Sess. 451.

109. On the date for Congress to assemble, see Ellsworth and others, Aug. 7, *Farrand*, 2:199–200. On the quorum requirement, see Mason, Aug. 10, ibid., 251–2. On recess appointments, see NLRB v. Noel Canning, 134 S. Ct. 2550, 2558 (2014) (Scalia, J., dissenting).

110. Rakove, *Original Meanings*, 162; Dahl, *How Democratic Is the American Constitution?*, 43–4.

111. Franklin, Sept. 17, *Farrand*, 2:642.

112. Dahl, *How Democratic Is the American Constitution?*, 122; see also Rakove, *Original Meanings*, 367.

113. Jefferson to "Henry Tompkinson" (Samuel Kercheval), July 12, 1816, *PTJ* (R.S.), 10:226–7.

BIBLIOGRAPHY

Books and Dissertations

Abbot, W. W., Philander D. Chase, and Dorothy Twohig, eds. *The Papers of George Washington.* 60 volumes in 5 series to date. Charlottesville: University Press of Virginia, 1983–.

Adams, Willi Paul. *The First American Constitutions: Republican Ideology and the Making of the State Constitutions in the Revolutionary Era.* Translated by Rita and Robert Kimber. Chapel Hill: Published for the Institute of Early American History and Culture, Williamsburg, VA, by the University of North Carolina Press, 1980.

Alexander, John K. *The Selling of the Constitutional Convention: A History of News Coverage.* Madison, WI: Madison House Publishers, 1990.

Atack, Jeremy, and Peter Passell. *A New Economic View of American History: From Colonial Times to 1940.* New York: Norton, 2nd ed., 1994.

Bailyn, Bernard. *The Ideological Origins of the American Revolution.* Enlarged ed. Cambridge, MA: Belknap Press of Harvard University Press, 1992.

Baker, Robert. *The Rescue of Joshua Glover: A Fugitive Slave, the Constitution, and the Coming of the Civil War.* Athens: Ohio University Press, 2006.

Bancroft, George. *History of the Formation of the Constitution of the United States of America.* 2 vols. New York: D. Appleton, 2nd ed., 1882.

Banning, Lance. *The Sacred Fire of Liberty: James Madison and the Founding of the Federal Republic.* Ithaca, NY: Cornell University Press, 1995.

Beard, Charles. *An Economic Interpretation of the Constitution of the United States.* New York: Macmillan, 2nd ed., 1935.

Beeman, Richard. *Plain, Honest Men: The Making of the American Constitution.* New York: Random House, 2009.

Beeman, Richard, Stephen Botein, and Edward C. Carter II, eds. *Beyond Confederation: Origins of the Constitution and American National Identity.* Chapel Hill: Published for the Institute of Early American History and Culture, Williamsburg, VA, by the University of North Carolina Press, 1987.

Berlin, Ira. *Generations of Captivity: A History of African-American Slaves.* Cambridge, MA: Harvard University Press, 2003.

———. *Many Thousands Gone: The First Two Centuries of Slavery in North America.* Cambridge, MA: Belknap Press of Harvard University Press, 1998.

Bilder, Mary Sarah. *Madison's Hand: Revising the Constitutional Convention.* Cambridge, MA: Harvard University Press, 2015.

Billias, George. *Elbridge Gerry: Founding Father and Republican Statesman.* New York: McGraw-Hill, 1976.

Bouton, Terry. *Taming Democracy: "The People," the Founders, and the Troubled Ending of the American Revolution.* New York: Oxford University Press, 2007.

Bowen, Catherine Drinker. *Miracle at Philadelphia: The Story of the Constitutional Convention, May to September, 1787.* Boston: Little, Brown, 2nd ed., 1986.

Bowling, Kenneth R. *The Creation of Washington, D.C.: The Idea and Location of the American Capital.* Fairfax, VA: George Mason University Press, 1991.

Boyd, Julian P., Charles T. Cullen, John Catanzariti, Barbara B. Oberg, and James P. McClure, eds. *The Papers of Thomas Jefferson.* 41 volumes to date. Princeton, NJ: Princeton University Press, 1950–.

Boyd, Steven R. *The Politics of Opposition: Antifederalists and the Acceptance of the Constitution.* Millwood, NY: KTO Press, 1979.

Brown, Robert E. *Charles Beard and the Constitution: A Critical Analysis of "An Economic Interpretation of the Constitution."* Princeton, NJ: Princeton University Press, 1956.

Brown, Roger H. *Redeeming the Republic: Federalists, Taxation, and the Origins of the Constitution.* Baltimore: Johns Hopkins University Press, 1993.

Burnett, Edmund Cody, ed. *Letters of Members of the Continental Congress.* 8 vols. Washington, DC: Carnegie Institution of Washington, 1921–36.

Carpenter, Jesse T. *The South as a Conscious Minority, 1789–1861: A Study in Political Thought.* New York: New York University Press, 1930.

Casto, William R. *The Supreme Court in the Early Republic: The Chief Justiceships of John Jay and Oliver Ellsworth.* Columbia: University of South Carolina Press, 1995.

Chernow, Ron. *Alexander Hamilton.* New York: Penguin Press, 2004.

Coleman, Kenneth. *The American Revolution in Georgia, 1763–1789.* Athens: University of Georgia Press, 1958.

Conley, Patrick T., and John P. Kaminski, eds. *The Bill of Rights and the States: The Colonial and Revolutionary Origins of American Liberties.* Madison, WI: Madison House, 1992.

Cornell, Saul. *The Other Founders: Anti-Federalism and the Dissenting Tradition in America, 1788–1828.* Chapel Hill: Published for the Omohundro Institute of Early American History and Culture, Williamsburg, VA, by the University of North Carolina Press, 1999.

Dahl, Robert. *How Democratic Is the American Constitution?* New Haven, CT: Yale University Press, 2nd ed., 2003.

Davis, Joseph L. *Sectionalism in American Politics, 1774–1787.* Madison: University of Wisconsin Press, 1977.

De Pauw, Linda Grant, *The Eleventh Pillar: New York State and the Federal Constitution.* Ithaca, NY: Published for the American Historical Association by Cornell University Press, 1966.

Edling, Max M. *A Revolution in Favor of Government: Origins of the U.S. Constitution and the Making of the American State.* New York: Oxford University Press, 2003.

Egerton, Douglas. *Death or Liberty: African Americans and Revolutionary America.* New York: Oxford University Press, 2009.

Einhorn, Robin L. *American Taxation, American Slavery.* Chicago: University of Chicago Press, 2006.

Elkins, Stanley, and Eric McKitrick. *The Age of Federalism: The Early American Republic, 1788–1800.* New York: Oxford University Press, 1993.

Elliot, Jonathan, ed. *The Debates in the Several State Conventions on the Adoption of the Federal Constitution.* 5 vols. Washington, DC, 1836–45.

Ellis, Joseph J. *The Quartet: Orchestrating the Second American Revolution, 1783–1789.* New York: Knopf, 2015.

Farrand, Max. *Records of the Federal Convention.* 4 vols. New Haven, CT: Yale University Press, 1966 reprint.

Fehrenbacher, Don E. *Constitutions and Constitutionalism in the Slaveholding South.* Athens: University of Georgia Press, 1989.

———. *The Dred Scott Case: Its Significance in American Law and Politics.* New York: Oxford University Press, 1978.

Ferguson, E. James. *The Power of the Purse: A History of American Public Finance, 1776–1790.* Chapel Hill: Published for the Institute of Early American History and Culture at Williamsburg, VA, by the University of North Carolina Press, 1961.

Ferguson, E. James, John Catanzariti, Elizabeth M. Nuxoll, and Mary A. Y. Gallagher, eds. *The Papers of Robert Morris.* 9 vols. Pittsburgh, University of Pittsburgh Press, 1973–99.

Finkelman, Paul. *An Imperfect Union: Slavery, Federalism, and Comity.* Chapel Hill: University of North Carolina Press, 1981.

Ford, Worthington Chauncey, Gaillard Hunt, John Clement Fitzpatrick, Roscoe R. Hill, Kenneth E. Harris, and Steven D. Tilley, eds. *Journals of the Continental Congress.* 34 vols. Washington, DC: US Government Printing Office, 1904–1937.

Freehling, William W. *The Road to Disunion.* Vol. 1, *Secessionists at Bay, 1776–1854.* New York: Oxford University Press, 1990.

Freehling, William W., and Craig M. Simpson. *Secession Debated: Georgia's Showdown in 1860.* New York: Oxford University Press, 1992.

Giesecke, Albert Anthony. *American Commercial Legislation Before 1789.* New York: D. Appleton, 1910.

Gillespie, Michael Allen, and Michael Lienesch, eds. *Ratifying the Constitution.* Lawrence: University Press of Kansas, 1989.

Gould, Eliga H. *Among the Powers of the Earth: The American Revolution and the Making of a New World Empire.* Cambridge, MA: Harvard University Press, 2012.

Graber, Mark A. *Dred Scott and the Problem of Constitutional Evil.* New York: Cambridge University Press, 2006.

Gray, Edward G., and Jane Kamensky, eds. *The Oxford Handbook of the American Revolution.* New York: Oxford University Press, 2013.

Hall, Van Beck. *Politics Without Parties: Massachusetts, 1780–1791.* Pittsburgh: University of Pittsburgh Press, 1972.

Haw, James, Francis F. Beirne, Rosamond R. Beirne, and R. Samuel Jett. *Stormy Patriot: The Life of Samuel Chase.* Baltimore: Maryland Historical Society, 1980.

Heideking, Jurgen. *The Constitution Before the Judgment Seat: The Prehistory and Ratification of the American Constitution, 1787–1791.* Edited by John P. Kaminski and Richard Leffler. Charlottesville: University of Virginia Press, 2012.

Henderson, H. James. *Party Politics in the Continental Congress.* New York: McGraw-Hill, 1974.

Hendrickson, David C. *Peace Pact: The Lost World of the American Founding.* Lawrence: University Press of Kansas, 2003.

Henry, William Wirt. *Patrick Henry: Life, Correspondence, and Speeches.* 3 vols. New York: Scribner's, 1891.

Holton, Woody. *Forced Founders: Indians, Debtors, Slaves, and the Making of the American Revolution in Virginia.* Chapel Hill: Published for the Omohundro Institute of Early American History and Culture at Williamsburg, VA, by the University of North Carolina Press, 1999.

———. *Unruly Americans and the Origins of the Constitution.* New York: Hill and Wang, 2007.

Hunt, Gaillard, ed. *The Writings of James Madison.* 9 vols. New York: Putnam's, 1910.

Hutchinson, William T., William M. E. Rachal, Robert Brugger, Robert A. Rutland, David B. Mattern et al., eds., *The Papers of James Madison.* 37 volumes in 4 series to date. Chicago: University of Chicago Press; Charlottesville: University of Virginia Press, 1962–.

Ireland, Owen S. *Religion, Ethnicity, and Politics: Ratifying the Constitution in Pennsylvania.* University Park: Pennsylvania State University Press, 1995.

Jefferson, Thomas. *Notes on the State of Virginia.* Edited by William Peden. Chapel Hill: Published for the Institute of Early American History and Culture at Williamsburg, VA, by the University of North Carolina Press, 1954.

Jensen, Merrill. *The Making of the American Constitution*. Princeton, NJ: Van Nostrand, 1964.

———. *The New Nation: A History of the United States During the Confederation, 1781–1789*. New York: Knopf, 1950.

Jensen, Merrill, Robert A. Becker, Gordon R. DenBoer, Lucy Trumbull Brown, Alfred Lindsay Skerpan, and Charles D. Hagerman, eds. *Documentary History of the First Federal Elections, 1788–1790*. 4 vols. Madison: University of Wisconsin Press, 1976–90.

Jillson, Calvin, and Rick K. Wilson. *Congressional Dynamics: Structure, Coordination, and Choice in the First American Congress, 1774–1789*. Stanford, CA: Stanford University Press, 1994.

Johnson, Calvin H. *Righteous Anger at the Wicked States: The Meaning of the Founders' Constitution*. New York: Cambridge University Press, 2005.

Johnston, Henry P., ed. *The Correspondence and Public Papers of John Jay*. 4 vols. New York: Putnam's, 1890–1893.

Kaminski, John P. *George Clinton: Yeoman Politician of the New Republic*. Madison, WI: Madison House, 1993.

———, ed. *A Necessary Evil? Slavery and the Debate over the Constitution*. Madison, WI: Madison House, 1995.

———. "Paper Politics: The Northern State Loan Offices During the Confederation, 1783–1790." PhD diss., University of Wisconsin, 1972.

Kaminski, John P., and Timothy D. Moore, eds. *An Assembly of Demigods: Word Portraits of the Delegates to the Constitutional Convention by Their Contemporaries*. Madison, WI: Parallel Press, 2012.

Kaminski, John P., Gaspare J. Saladino, Richard Leffler, Charles H. Schoenleber, and Margaret A. Hogan, eds. *The Documentary History of the Ratification of the Constitution*. 27 volumes to date. Madison: State Historical Society of Wisconsin, 1976–.

Keyssar, Alexander. *The Right to Vote: The Contested History of Democracy in the United States*. New York: Basic Books, 2000.

King, Charles R., ed. *The Life and Correspondence of Rufus King*. 6 vols. New York: Putnam's, 1894–1900.

Kohn, Richard H. *Eagle and Sword: The Federalists and the Creation of the Military Establishment in America, 1783–1802*. New York: Free Press, 1975.

Kramer, Larry D. *The People Themselves: Popular Constitutionalism and Judicial Review*. New York: Oxford University Press, 2004.

Kuroda, Tadahisa. *The Origins of the Twelfth Amendment: The Electoral College in the Early Republic, 1787–1804*. Westport, CT: Greenwood Press, 1994.

Kyvig, David E. *Explicit and Authentic Acts: Amending the U.S. Constitution, 1776–1995*. Lawrence: University Press of Kansas, 1996.

Labunski, Richard E. *James Madison and the Struggle for the Bill of Rights*. New York: Oxford University Press, 2006.

Levinson, Sanford. *Our Undemocratic Constitution: Where the Constitution Goes Wrong (And How We the People Can Correct It)*. New York: Oxford University Press, 2006.

Levy, Leonard W., and Dennis J. Mahoney, eds. *The Framing and Ratification of the Constitution*. New York: Macmillan, 1987.

Litwack, Leon F. *North of Slavery: The Negro in the Free States, 1790–1860*. Chicago: University of Chicago Press, 1961.

Lubet, Steven. *Fugitive Justice: Runaways, Rescuers, and Slavery on Trial*. Cambridge, MA: Belknap Press of Harvard University Press, 2010.

Maier, Pauline. *Ratification: The People Debate the Constitution, 1787–1788*. New York: Simon and Schuster, 2010.

Main, Jackson Turner. *The Antifederalists: Critics of the Constitution, 1781–1788*. Chapel Hill: Published for the Institute of Early American History and Culture at Williamsburg, VA, by the University of North Carolina Press, 1961.

———. *Political Parties Before the Constitution.* Chapel Hill: Published for the Institute of Early American History and Culture at Williamsburg, VA, by the University of North Carolina Press, 1973.

Marks, Frederick W., III. *Independence on Trial: Foreign Affairs and the Making of the Constitution.* Baton Rouge: Louisiana State University Press, 1973.

McCormick, Richard P. *Experiment in Independence: New Jersey in the Critical Period, 1781–1789.* New Brunswick, NJ: Rutgers University Press, 1950.

McCoy, Drew R. *The Elusive Republic: Political Economy in Jeffersonian America.* Chapel Hill: Published for the Institute of Early American History and Culture, Williamsburg, VA, by the University of North Carolina Press, 1980.

McCraw, Thomas K. *The Founders and Finance: How Hamilton, Gallatin, and Other Immigrants Forged a New Economy.* Cambridge, MA: Belknap Press of Harvard University Press, 2012.

McDonald, Forrest. *Novus Ordo Seclorum: The Intellectual Origins of the Constitution.* Lawrence: University Press of Kansas, 1985.

———. *We the People: The Economic Origins of the Constitution.* Chicago: University of Chicago Press, 1958.

McMillin, James A. *The Final Victims: Foreign Slave Trade to North America, 1783–1810.* Columbia: University of South Carolina Press, 2004.

McRee, Griffith J, ed. *Life and Correspondence of James Iredell, One of the Associate Justices of the Supreme Court of the United States.* 2 vols. New York: D. Appleton, 1857–58.

Miller, Helen Hill. *George Mason: Gentleman Revolutionary.* Chapel Hill: University of North Carolina Press, 1975.

Morgan, Edmund S. *American Slavery, American Freedom.* New York: Norton, 1975.

———. *Inventing the People: The Rise of Popular Sovereignty in England and America.* New York: Norton, 1988.

Morrill, James R. *The Practice and Politics of Fiat Finance: North Carolina in the Confederation, 1783–1789.* Chapel Hill: University of North Carolina Press, 1969.

Munroe, John A. *Federalist Delaware, 1775–1815.* New Brunswick, NJ: Rutgers University Press, 1954.

Nash, Gary B., and Jean R. Soderlund. *Freedom by Degrees: Emancipation in Pennsylvania and Its Aftermath.* New York: Oxford University Press, 1991.

Nelson, Eric. *The Royalist Revolution: Monarchy and the American Founding.* Cambridge, MA: Belknap Press of Harvard University Press, 2014.

Nettels, Curtis P. *The Emergence of a National Economy, 1775–1815.* Vol. 2, *The Economic History of the United States.* New York: Holt, Rinehart and Winston, 1962.

Nevins, Allan. *The American States During and After the Revolution, 1775–1789.* New York: Macmillan, 1924.

Newmyer, R. Kent. *John Marshall and the Heroic Age of the Supreme Court.* Baton Rouge: Louisiana State University Press, 2001.

Onuf, Peter S. *The Origins of the Federal Republic: Jurisdictional Controversies in the United States, 1775–1787.* Philadelphia: University of Pennsylvania Press, 1983.

Pasley, Jeffrey L. *"The Tyranny of Printers": Newspaper Politics in the Early American Republic.* Charlottesville: University Press of Virginia, 2001.

Perkins, Edwin J. *American Public Finance and Financial Services, 1700–1815.* Columbus: Ohio State University Press, 1994.

Polishook, Irwin H. *Rhode Island and the Union, 1774–1795.* Evanston, IL: Northwestern University Press, 1969.

Potter, David M. *The Impending Crisis, 1848–1861.* New York: Harper and Row, 1976.

Preston, Daniel, ed. *The Papers of James Monroe.* 5 volumes to date. Westport, CT: Greenwood Press, 2003–.

Quarles, Benjamin. *The Negro in the American Revolution.* Chapel Hill: Published for the Institute of Early American History and Culture, Williamsburg, VA, by University of North Carolina Press, 1961.

Rakove, Jack N. *The Beginnings of National Politics: An Interpretive History of the Continental Congress*. New York: Knopf, 1979.

———. *Original Meanings: Politics and Ideas in the Making of the Constitution*. New York: Knopf, 1996.

Read, William Thompson. *Life and Correspondence of George Read*. Philadelphia: J. B. Lippincott, 1870.

Richards, Leonard L. *Shays's Rebellion: The American Revolution's Final Battle*. Philadelphia: University of Pennsylvania Press, 2002.

Risjord, Norman K. *Chesapeake Politics, 1781–1800*. New York: Columbia University Press, 1978.

Robertson, David Brian. *The Constitution and America's Destiny*. New York: Cambridge University Press, 2005.

Robinson, Donald L. *Slavery in the Structure of American Politics, 1765–1820*. New York: Harcourt Brace Jovanovich, 1971.

Rossiter, Clinton, ed. *The Federalist Papers*. New York: Penguin Putnam, 1961.

———. *1787: The Grand Convention*. New York: Macmillan, 1966.

Rutland, Robert Allen. *The Birth of the Bill of Rights, 1776–1791*. Chapel Hill: Published for the Institute of Early American History and Culture, Williamsburg, VA, by the University of North Carolina Press, 1955.

———. *George Mason: Reluctant Statesman*. Baton Rouge: Louisiana State University Press, 1961.

———. *Ordeal of the Constitution: The Antifederalists and the Ratification Struggle of 1787–1788*. Norman: University of Oklahoma Press, 1966.

———, ed. *The Papers of George Mason*. 3 vols. Chapel Hill: University of North Carolina Press, 1970.

Sanders, Jennings B. *Evolution of Executive Departments of the Continental Congress, 1774–1789*. Chapel Hill: University of North Carolina Press, 1935.

Schwartz, Bernard. *The Great Rights of Mankind: A History of the American Bill of Rights*. New York: Oxford University Press, 1977.

Smith, Paul H. ed. *Letters of Delegates to Congress, 1774–1789*. 26 vols. Washington, DC: Library of Congress, 1976–2000.

Sparks, Jared, ed. *The Writings of George Washington*. 12 vols. Boston: Russell, Odiorne and Metcalf and Hillard, Gray, 1834–37.

Storing, Herbert, ed. *The Complete Anti-Federalist*. 7 vols. Chicago: University of Chicago Press, 1981.

Swift, Elaine K. *The Making of an American Senate: Reconstitutive Change in Congress, 1787–1841*. Ann Arbor: University of Michigan Press, 1996.

Syrett, Harold C., ed. *The Papers of Alexander Hamilton*. 27 vols. New York: Columbia University Press, 1961–87.

Szatmary, David P. *Shays' Rebellion: The Making of an Agrarian Insurrection*. Amherst: University of Massachusetts Press, 1980.

Trenholme, Louise Irby. *The Ratification of the Federal Constitution in North Carolina*. New York: Columbia University Press, 1932.

Van Cleve, George William. *A Slaveholders' Union: Slavery, Politics, and the Constitution in the Early American Republic*. Chicago: University of Chicago Press, 2010.

Veit, Helen E., Kenneth R. Bowling, and Charlene Bangs Bickford, eds. *Creating the Bill of Rights: The Documentary Record from the First Federal Congress*. Baltimore: Johns Hopkins University Press, 1991.

Waldstreicher, David. *Slavery's Constitution: From Revolution to Ratification*. New York: Hill and Wang, 2009.

Watlington, Patricia. *The Partisan Spirit: Kentucky Politics, 1779–1792*. New York: Atheneum, for the Institute of Early American History and Culture, 1972.

Whitaker, Arthur Preston. *The Spanish-American Frontier, 1783–1795*. Boston: Houghton Mifflin, 1927; reprinted, Gloucester, MA: Peter Smith, 1962.

Wood, Gordon S. *The Creation of the American Republic, 1776–1787*. Chapel Hill: Published for the Institute of Early American History and Culture at Williamsburg, VA, by the University of North Carolina Press, 1969.

———. *The Radicalism of the American Revolution*. New York: Knopf, 1992.

Young, Alfred F. *The Democratic Republicans of New York: The Origins, 1763–1797*. Chapel Hill, Published for the Institute of Early American History and Culture at Williamsburg, VA, by the University of North Carolina Press, 1967.

———. *Liberty Tree: Ordinary People and the American Revolution*. New York: New York University Press, 2006.

Zagarri, Rosemarie. *The Politics of Size: Representation in the United States, 1776–1850*. Ithaca, NY: Cornell University Press, 1987.

Articles and Book Chapters

Amar, Akhil Reed. "The Bill of Rights as a Constitution." *Yale Law Journal* (Mar. 1991), 100:1131–210.

———. "The Consent of the Governed: Constitutional Amendment Outside Article V." *Columbia Law Review* (1994), 94:457–508.

Banning, Lance. "The Constitutional Convention." In *The Framing and Ratification of the Constitution*, edited by Leonard W. Levy and Dennis J. Mahoney, 112–31.

———. "Virginia: Sectionalism and the General Good." In *Ratifying the Constitution*, edited by Michael Allen Gillespie and Michael Lienesch, 261–99.

Barry, James T., III. "The Council of Revision and the Limits of Judicial Power." *University of Chicago Law Review* (Winter 1989), 56:235–61.

Bates, Whitney K. "Northern Speculators and Southern State Debts: 1790." *William and Mary Quarterly* (Jan. 1962), 19:30–48.

Becker, Robert A. "Salus Populi Suprema Law: Public Peace and South Carolina Debtor Relief Laws, 1783–1788." *South Carolina Historical Review* (Jan. 1979), 80:65–75.

Best, Judith A. "The Presidency and the Executive Power." In *The Framing and Ratification of the Constitution*, edited by Leonard W. Levy and Dennis J. Mahoney, 209–21.

Billings, Warren M. "'That All Men Are Born Equally Free and Independent': Virginians and the Origins of the Bill of Rights." In *The Bill of Rights and the States: The Colonial and Revolutionary Origins of American Liberties*, edited by Patrick T. Conley and John P. Kaminski, 335–69.

Bouton, Terry. "The Trials of the Confederation." In *The Oxford Handbook of the American Revolution*, edited by Edward G. Gray and Jane Kamensky, 370–87.

Bowling, Kenneth R. "'A Tub to the Whale': The Founding Fathers and Adoption of the Federal Bill of Rights." *Journal of the Early Republic* (Autumn 1988), 8:223–51.

Boyd, Steven R. "The Contract Clause and the Evolution of American Federalism, 1789–1815." *William and Mary Quarterly* (July 1987), 44:529–48.

Brady, Patrick S. "The Slave Trade and Sectionalism in South Carolina, 1787–1808." *Journal of Southern History* (Nov. 1972), 38:601–20.

Brown, Christopher Leslie. "The Problems of Slavery." In *The Oxford Handbook of the American Revolution*, edited by Edward G. Gray and Jane Kamensky, 427–46.

Brown, Richard D. "Shays's Rebellion and the Ratification of the Federal Constitution in Massachusetts." In *Beyond Confederation*, edited by Richard Beeman, Stephen Botein, and Edward C. Carter II, 113–27.

Cashin, Edward J. "Georgia: Searching for Security." In *Ratifying the Constitution*, edited by Michael Allen Gillespie and Michael Lienesch, 93–116.

Conley, Patrick T. "Rhode Island: Laboratory for the Internal 'Lively Experiment.'" In *The Bill of Rights and the States: The Colonial and Revolutionary Origins of American Liberties*, edited by Patrick T. Conley and John P. Kaminski, 123–61.

Daniell, Jere R. "Ideology and Hardball: Ratification of the Federal Constitution in New Hampshire." In *New Hampshire: The State That Made Us a Nation*, edited by William M. Gardner, Frank C. Mevers, and Richard F. Upton (P. E. Randall, Portsmouth, NH, 1989), 1–17.

Denning, Brandon P. "Confederation-Era Discrimination Against Interstate Commerce and the Legitimacy of the Dormant Commerce Clause." *Kentucky Law Journal* (2005), 94:37–99.

Edling, Max M. "A More Perfect Union: The Framing and Ratification of the Constitution." In *The Oxford Handbook of the American Revolution*, edited by Edward G. Gray and Jane Kamensky, 388–406.

Edling, Max M., and Mark D. Kaplanoff, "Alexander Hamilton's Fiscal Reform: Transforming the Structure of Taxation in the Early Republic." *William and Mary Quarterly* (Oct. 2004), 61:713–44.

Elkins, Stanley, and Eric McKitrick. "The Founding Fathers: Young Men of the Revolution." *Political Science Quarterly* (June 1961), 76:181–216.

Ely, James W., Jr. "'The Good Old Cause': The Ratification of the Constitution and Bill of Rights in South Carolina." In *The South's Role in the Creation of the Bill of Rights*, edited by Robert J. Haws (Jackson, MS, 1991), 101–24.

Eubanks, Cecil L. "New York: Federalism and the Political Economy of Union." In *Ratifying the Constitution*, edited by Michael Allen Gillespie and Michael Lienesch, 300–40.

Evans, Emory G. "Private Indebtedness and the Revolution in Virginia, 1776 to 1796." *William and Mary Quarterly* (July 1971), 28:349–74.

Finkelman, Paul. "Slavery and the Constitutional Convention: Making a Covenant with Death." In *Beyond Confederation*, edited by Richard Beeman, Stephen Botein, and Edward C. Carter II, 188–225.

———. "Story Telling on the Supreme Court: *Prigg v. Pennsylvania* and Justice Joseph Story's Judicial Nationalism." *Supreme Court Review* (1994), 247–94.

Freehling, William W. "The Founding Fathers and Slavery." *American Historical Review* (Feb. 1972), 77:81–93.

Gillespie, Michael Allen. "Massachusetts: Creating Consensus." In *Ratifying the Constitution*, edited by Michael Allen Gillespie and Michael Lienesch, 138–67.

Gillespie, Michael Allen, and Michael Lienesch. "Introduction." In *Ratifying the Constitution*, edited by Michael Allen Gillespie and Michael Lienesch, 1–26.

Graham, George J., Jr. "Pennsylvania: Representation and the Meaning of Republicanism." In *Ratifying the Constitution*, edited by Michael Allen Gillespie and Michael Lienesch, 52–70.

Hobson, Charles F. "The Negative on State Laws: James Madison, the Constitution, and the Crisis of Republican Government." *William and Mary Quarterly* (Apr. 1979), 36:215–35.

Hutson, James H. "Country, Court, and Constitution: Antifederalism and the Historians." *William and Mary Quarterly* (July 1981), 38:337–68.

———. "The Creation of the Constitution: The Integrity of the Documentary Record." *Texas Law Review* (Nov. 1986), 65:1–39.

Kaminski, John P. "The Constitution Without a Bill of Rights." In *The Bill of Rights and the States: The Colonial and Revolutionary Origins of American Liberties*, edited by Patrick T. Conley and John P. Kaminski, 16–45.

———. "New York: The Reluctant Pillar." In *The Reluctant Pillar: New York and the Adoption of the Federal Constitution*, edited by Stephen L. Schechter (Troy, NY, 1985), 48–117.

———. "Political Sacrifice and Demise—John Collins and Jonathan J. Hazard, 1786–1790." *Rhode Island History* (Aug. 1976), 35:91–98.

———. "Rhode Island: Protecting State Interests." In *Ratifying the Constitution*, edited by Michael Allen Gillespie and Michael Lienesch, 368–90.

Kenyon, Cecelia M. "Men of Little Faith: The Anti-Federalists on the Nature of Representative Government." *William and Mary Quarterly* (Jan. 1955), 12:3–43.

Leibiger, Stuart, "James Madison and Amendments to the Constitution, 1787–1789: 'Parchment Barriers.'" *Journal of Southern History* (Aug. 1993), 59:441–68.

Libby, Orin Grant. "The Geographical Distribution of the Vote of the Thirteen States on the Federal Constitution, 1787–8." *Bulletin of the University of Wisconsin* (June 1894), 1:1–116.

Lienesch, Michael. "North Carolina: Preserving Rights." In *Ratifying the Constitution*, edited by Michael Allen Gillespie and Michael Lienesch, 343–67.

Lindert, Peter H., and Jeffrey G. Williamson. "American Incomes Before and After the Revolution." *Journal of Economic History* (Sept. 2013), 73:725–65.

Lutz, Donald S. "Connecticut: Achieving Consent and Assuring Control." In *Ratifying the Constitution*, edited by Michael Allen Gillespie and Michael Lienesch, 117–37.

———. "The States and the U.S. Bill of Rights." *Southern Illinois University Law Journal* (1992), 16:251–62.

Lynd, Staughton. "The Compromise of 1787." *Political Science Quarterly* (June 1966), 81:225–50.

McCormick, Richard P. "New Jersey Defies the Confederation: An Abraham Clark Letter." *Journal of the Rutgers University Library* (June 1950), 13:44–50.

McDonnell, Michael A. "The Struggle Within: Colonial Politics on the Eve of Independence." In *The Oxford Handbook of the American Revolution*, edited by Edward G. Gray and Jane Kamensky, 103–20.

Merritt, Eli. "Sectional Conflict and Secret Compromise: The Mississippi River Question and the United States Constitution." *American Journal of Legal History* (Apr. 1991), 35:117–71.

Mevers, Frank C. "New Hampshire Accepts the Bill of Rights." In *The Bill of Rights and the States: The Colonial and Revolutionary Origins of American Liberties*, edited by Patrick T. Conley and John P. Kaminski, 162–80.

Mihm, Stephen. "Funding the Revolution: Monetary and Fiscal Policy in Eighteenth-Century America." In *The Oxford Handbook of the American Revolution*, edited by Edward G. Gray and Jane Kamensky, 327–54.

Nash, Gary. "The African-Americans' Revolution." In *The Oxford Handbook of the American Revolution*, edited by Edward G. Gray and Jane Kamensky, 250–72.

Onuf, Peter S. "Maryland: The Small Republic in the New Nation." In *Ratifying the Constitution*, edited by Michael Allen Gillespie and Michael Lienesch, 171–200.

Opal, J. M. "The Republic in the World, 1783–1803." In *Oxford Handbook of the American Revolution*, edited by Edward G. Gray and Jane Kamensky, 595–611.

Polishook, Irwin H. "Trevett vs. Weeden and the Case of the Judges." *Newport History* (Apr. 1965), 38:45–69.

Pybus, Cassandra. "Jefferson's Faulty Math: The Question of Slave Defections in the American Revolution." *William and Mary Quarterly* (Apr. 2005), 62:243–64.

Rakove, Jack N. "The Madisonian Moment." *University of Chicago Law Review* (Winter 1988), 55:473–505.

Raphael, Ray. "The Democratic Moment: The Revolution and Popular Politics." In *Oxford Handbook of the American Revolution*, edited by Edward G. Gray and Jane Kamensky, 121–38.

Roche, John. "The Founding Fathers: A Reform Caucus in Action." *American Political Science Review* (Dec. 1961), 55:799–816.

Roll, Charles W., Jr. "We, Some of the People: Apportionment in the Thirteen State Conventions Ratifying the Constitution." *Journal of American History* (June 1969), 56:21–40.

Rossum, Ralph. "The Courts and the Judicial Power." In *The Framing and Ratification of the Constitution*, edited by Leonard W. Levy and Dennis J. Mahoney, 222–41.

Russel, Robert R. "Constitutional Doctrines with Regard to Slavery in Territories." *Journal of Southern History* (Nov. 1966), 32:466–86.

Saladino, Gaspare J. "Delaware: Independence and the Concept of a Commercial Republic." In *Ratifying the Constitution*, edited by Michael Allen Gillespie and Michael Lienesch, 29–51.

Shumer, Sara M. "New Jersey: Property and the Price of Republican Politics." In *Ratifying the Constitution*, edited by Michael Allen Gillespie and Michael Lienesch, 71–89.

Slauter, Eric. "Rights." In *Oxford Handbook of the American Revolution*, edited by Edward G. Gray and Jane Kamensky, 447–64.

Steiner, Bernard. "Maryland's Adoption of the Federal Constitution." *American Historical Review* (1899), 5:207–24.

Talbert, Charles Gano. "Kentuckians in the Virginia Convention of 1788." *Register of the Kentucky Historical Society* (July 1960), 58:187–93.

Van Cleve, George William. "The Anti-Federalists' Toughest Challenge: Paper Money, Debt Relief, and the Ratification of the Constitution." *Journal of the Early Republic* (Winter 2014), 34:529–60.

Weir, Robert M. "South Carolina: Slavery and the Structure of the Union." In *Ratifying the Constitution*, edited by Michael Allen Gillespie and Michael Lienesch, 201–34.

Wiecek, William M. "The Witch at the Christening: Slavery and the Constitution's Origins." In *The Framing and Ratification of the Constitution*, edited by Leonard W. Levy and Dennis J. Mahoney, 167–84.

Wood, Gordon S. "Interests and Disinterestedness in the Making of the Constitution." In *Beyond Confederation*, edited by Richard Beeman, Stephen Botein, and Edward C. Carter II, 69–109.

Yarbrough, Jean. "New Hampshire: Puritanism and the Moral Foundations of America." In *Ratifying the Constitution*, edited by Michael Allen Gillespie and Michael Lienesch, 235–58.

COMPLETE ILLUSTRATION INFORMATION

Figure 1.1   Robert Morris and Gouverneur Morris
Courtesy of the Pennsylvania Academy of the Fine Arts, Philadelphia. Bequest of Richard Ashhurst
Artist: Charles Willson Peale
Title: Gouverneur Morris and Robert Morris
Date: 1783
Medium: Oil on canvas
Size: 43 1/2 x 51 3/4 in. (110.5 x 131.4 cm)
Acc. No.: 1969.20.1

Figure 1.2   Rufus King
Courtesy of Independence National Historical Park
Charles Willson Peale, from life, 1818 (but painted to make him appear younger)

Figure 1.3   Don Diego de Gardoqui
Oil portrait of don Diego Maria Gardoqui, Spanish Minister to the United States, c. 1785? Courtesy of the Palace of the Governors Photo Archives (NMHM/DCA), negative number 191935; New Mexico History Museum collections number 11844/45

Figure 1.4   John Jay
John Jay, by Joseph Wright, 1786; oil on linen, 30 1/4 x 26 inches; negative #6066; object 1817.5, New-York Historical Society
Photography © New-York Historical Society

Figure 1.5   Henry Lee III ("Light-Horse Harry" Lee)
National Portrait Gallery, Smithsonian Institution / Art Resource, NY
Herring, James (1794–1867), after Gilbert Stuart's. Portrait of Henry Lee
("Lighthorse Harry"), revolutionary officer and statesman (1756–1818). Ca.
1834. Oil on canvas, 76 cm x 63.5 cm (29 15/16" x 25")

Figure 2.1   Governor James Bowdoin
Courtesy of Independence National Historical Park
Edgar Parker, 1870s (after Christian Gullager, c. 1791)

Figure 2.2   Benjamin Lincoln
Courtesy of Independence National Historical Park
Charles Willson Peale, from life, c. 1781–1783

Figure 2.3   Charles Pinckney
Library of Congress, Prints and Photographs Division
Charles Balthazar Julien Fevret de Saint-Mémin, 1770–1852, artist
1806 engraving
Library of Congress Reproduction Number: LC-USZ62-54941 (b&w film
copy neg.)

Figure 2.4   Henry Knox
Courtesy of Independence National Historical Park
Charles Willson Peale, from life, 1784

Figure 3.1   James Madison
Courtesy of Independence National Historical Park
James Sharples, Sr., from life, 1796–1797

Figure 3.2   Edmund Randolph
Library of Congress Prints and Photographs Division
Constantino Brumidi, 1805–1880, artist
Library of Congress Reproduction Number LC-DIG-det-4a26389 (digital file
from original)

Figure 3.3   Elbridge Gerry
Courtesy of Independence National Historical Park
James Bogle, 1861 (after John Vanderlyn, 1798 sketch)

Figure 3.4   John Dickinson
Courtesy of Independence National Historical Park
Charles Willson Peale, from life, 1782–83

Figure 3.5   Nathaniel Gorham
Museum of Fine Arts, Boston
Charles Willson Peale, American, 1741–1827
Nathaniel Gorham, about 1793
Oil on canvas mounted on Masonite
66.04 x 56.2 cm (26 x 22 1/8 in.)
Museum of Fine Arts, Boston
Gift of Edwin H. Abbot in memory of his brother, Philip Stanley Abbot
48.1356

Figure 3.6   William Paterson
Collection of the Supreme Court of the United States
Photographer Vic Boswell
1991-381-2
Photograph of Associate Justice William Paterson's official portrait
painted by C. Gregory Stapko

Figure 3.7   Benjamin Franklin
Courtesy National Gallery of Art, Washington
Jean-Francois Janinet and Joseph Siffred Duplessis
1789
color aquatint
plate: 41 x 31.5 cm (16 1/8 x 12 3/8 in.)
Gift of Mrs. W. Murray Crane
1955.4.19

Figure 3.8   Roger Sherman
Yale University Art Gallery
Artist: Ralph Earl, American, 1751–1801 Roger Sherman (1721–1793, M.A.
[Hon.] 1768)
ca. 1775 Oil on canvas
164.1 x 126 cm (64 5/8 x 49 5/8 in.)
Gift of Roger Sherman White, B.A. 1859, LL.B. 1862
1918.3

Figure 3.9   James Wilson
Collection of the Supreme Court of the United States
1973.2
Portrait – Associate Justice James Wilson
Portrait by Robert S. Susan

Figure 3.10 "Signing of the Constitution"
Architect of the Capitol
Howard Chandler Christy, "Signing of the Constitution"

Figure 3.11   John Lansing, Jr.
John Lansing, Jr. (1754–1829), 1888; etched by Albert Rosenthal, Phila.
(1863–1893), after unknown artist; from PR052 (Portrait File); neg#90928d,
New-York Historical Society
Photography © New-York Historical Society

Figure 4.1   Gouverneur Morris
Courtesy of Independence National Historical Park
Edward Dalton Marchant, 1873 (after Thomas Sully, 1808)

Figure 4.2   Charles Cotesworth Pinckney
National Portrait Gallery, Smithsonian Institution / Art Resource, NY
Henry Benbridge (1743–1812)
Portrait of Charles Cotesworth Pinckney (1746–1825), American Statesman
Ca. 1773
Oil on canvas
76.2 x 63.5 cm (30 x 25 in.)

Figure 4.3   Luther Martin
Courtesy of Independence National Historical Park
William Shaw Tiffany, 1875 (after Cephas Thompson c. 1804)

Figure 5.1   Alexander Hamilton
Courtesy National Gallery of Art, Washington
John Trumbull
c. 1792
oil on canvas
Gift of the Avalon Foundation
1952.1.1

Figure 5.2   Oliver Ellsworth
Collection of the Supreme Court of the United States
1991-343-2
Portrait - Chief Justice Oliver Ellsworth
Copy photography of Chief Justice Oliver Ellsworth's official portrait, painted
by William Wheeler

Figure 5.3   David Ramsay
Courtesy of Independence National Historical Park
Rembrandt Peale, 1796

Figure 6.1   Mercy Otis Warren
John Singleton Copley, American, 1738–1815
Mrs. James Warren (Mercy Otis), about 1763
Oil on canvas
126.05 x. 100.33 cm (49 5/8 x 39 1/2 in.)
Museum of Fine Arts, Boston
Bequest of Winslow Warren
31.212

Figure 6.2   William Findley
Courtesy of Independence National Historical Park
Rembrandt Peale, from life, 1805

Figure 6.3   Samuel Adams
John Singleton Copley, American, 1738–1815
Samuel Adams, about 1772
125.73 x 100.33 cm (49 1/2 x 39 1/2 in.)
Museum of Fine Arts, Boston
Deposited by the City of Boston
L-R 30.76c

Figure 6.4   John Hancock
John Singleton Copley, American, 1738–1815
John Hancock, 1765
Oil on canvas
124.8 x 100 cm (49 1/8 x 39 3/8 in.)
Museum of Fine Arts, Boston
Deposited by the City of Boston
L-R 30.76d

Figure 6.5   Massachusetts, The Sixth Pillar
Library of Congress Serial and Government Publications Division
Library of Congress Reproduction Number: LC-USZ62-45589 (b&w film copy neg. of Jan. 16, 1788)
woodcut, *Massachusetts Centinel*, 1788 January 16

Figure 6.6   Samuel Chase
Courtesy of Independence National Historical Park
Charles Willson Peale 1819, after his own 1773 portrait

Figure 6.7   Patrick Henry
Courtesy of Independence National Historical Park
unidentified artist, after Thomas Sully 1815 (copy of a miniature by Lawrence Sully)

Figure 6.8   George Clinton
Clinton, George, portrait by Ezra Ames, 1814; oil on canvas, 53 x 41 inches; negative #6108; object #1958.84, New-York Historical Society
Photography © New-York Historical Society

Figure 6.9   Robert R. Livingston
Chancellor Robert R. Livingston (1746–1813), by Gilbert Stuart, ca. 1794; oil on canvas, framed: 5/14 x 47 1/2 x 39 inches; negative #34794c; object #1960.89; New-York Historical Society
Photography © New-York Historical Society

Figure 6.10   William Davie
Courtesy of Independence National Historical Park
"Eliza M." miniature from life c. 1800

Figure 7.1   George Mason
Courtesy Independence National Historical Park
unidentified artist, possibly Herbert B. Welsh
after Boudet 1811, after a John Hesselins painting c. 1750

Figure 7.2   James Monroe
Library of Congress, Prints and Photographs Division
Library of Congress Reproduction Number: LC-USZ62-87925 (b&w film copy neg.) LC-DIG-pga-05286 (digital file from original item)

Figure 7.3   Theodore Sedgwick
Gilbert Stuart, American, 1755–1828
Theodore Sedgwick, about 1808
Oil on canvas
74.29 x 60.64 cm (29 1/4 x 23 7/8 in.)
Museum of Fine Arts, Boston
Bequest of Charles S. Rackemann
33.508

Figure 7.4   Richard Henry Lee
National Portrait Gallery, Smithsonian Institution / Art Resource, NY
Charles Willson Peale (1741–1827)
Richard Henry Lee (1732–1794). Revolutionary Statesman
1795–1805?
Oil on canvas, 76 x 63.5 cm (29 15/16" x 25")

INDEX